1869 — Francis Galton, Charles Darwin's cousin, publishes *Hereditary Genius*, in which he claims that intelligence is inherited. In **1876** he coins the expression "nature and nurture" to correspond with "heredity and environment."

1874 — Carl Wernicke, a German neurologist and psychiatrist, shows that damage to a specific area in the left temporal lobe (now called Wernicke's area) disrupts ability to comprehend or produce spoken or written language.

1878 — G. Stanley Hall receives from Harvard University's Department of Philosophy the first U.S. Ph.D. degree based on psychological research.

1879 — Wilhelm Wundt establishes at the University of Leipzig, Germany, the first psychology laboratory, which becomes a Mecca for psychology students from all over the world.

1883 — G. Stanley Hall, student of Wilhelm Wundt, establishes the first formal U.S. psychology laboratory at Johns Hopkins University.

1885 — Hermann Ebbinghaus publishes *On Memory*, summarizing his extensive research on learning and memory, including the "forgetting curve."

1886 — Joseph Jastrow receives from Johns Hopkins University the first Ph.D. degree in psychology awarded by a Department of Psychology in the United States.

1889 — Alfred Binet and Henri Beaunis establish the first psychology laboratory in France at the Sorbonne, and the first International Congress of Psychology meets in Paris.

1890 — William James, Harvard University philosopher and psychologist, publishes *The Principles of Psychology*, describing psychology as "the science of mental life."

1891 — James Mark Baldwin establishes the first psychology laboratory in the British Commonwealth at the University of Toronto.

1892 — G. Stanley Hall spearheads the founding of the American Psychological Association (APA) and becomes its first president.

1893 — Mary Whiton Calkins (pictured) and Christine Ladd-Franklin are the first women elected to membership in the APA.

1894 — Margaret Floy Washburn is the first woman to receive a Ph.D. degree in psychology (Cornell University).

Harvard University denies Mary Whiton Calkins admission to doctoral candidacy because of her gender, despite Hugo Münsterberg's claim that she was the best student he had ever had there.

1896 — John Dewey publishes "The Reflex Arc Concept in Psychology," helping to formalize the school of psychology called functionalism.

1898 — In "Animal Intelligence," Edward L. Thorndike, Columbia University, describes his learning experiments with cats in "puzzle boxes." In **1905**, he proposes the "law of effect."

1900 — Sigmund Freud publishes *The Interpretation of Dreams*, his major theoretical work on psychoanalysis.

1933 — Inez Beverly Prosser becomes the first African-American woman to receive a doctoral degree in psychology from a U.S. institution (Ph.D., University of Cincinnati).

1935 — Christiana Morgan and Henry Murray introduce the Thematic Apperception Test to elicit fantasies from people undergoing psychoanalysis.

1936 — Egas Moniz, Portuguese physician, publishes work on the first frontal lobotomies performed on humans.

1938 — B. F. Skinner publishes *The Behavior of Organisms*, which describes operant conditioning of animals.

In *Primary Mental Abilities*, Louis L. Thurstone proposes seven such abilities.

Ugo Cerletti and Lucino Bini use electroshock treatment with a human patient.

1939 — David Wechsler publishes the Wechsler-Bellevue intelligence test, forerunner of the Wechsler Intelligence Scale for Children (WISC) and the Wechsler Adult Intelligence Scale (WAIS).

Mamie Phipps Clark (pictured) receives a master's degree from Howard University. In collaboration with Kenneth B. Clark, she later extends her thesis, "The Development of Consciousness of Self in Negro Preschool Children," providing joint research cited in the U.S. Supreme Court's **1954** decision to end racial segregation in public schools.

Edward Alexander Bott helps found the Canadian Psychological Association. He becomes its first president in **1940**.

World War II provides many opportunities for psychologists to enhance the popularity and influence of psychology, especially in applied areas.

1943 — Psychologist Starke Hathaway and physician J. Charnley McKinley publish the Minnesota Multiphasic Personality Inventory (MMPI).

1945 — Karen Horney, who criticized Freud's theory of female sexual development, publishes *Our Inner Conflicts*.

1946 — Benjamin Spock's first edition of *The Commonsense Book of Baby and Child Care* appears; the book will influence child rearing in North America for several decades.

1948 — Alfred Kinsey and his colleagues publish *Sexual Behavior in the Human Male*, and they publish *Sexual Behavior in the Human Female* in **1953**.

B. F. Skinner's novel, *Walden Two*, describes a Utopian community based on positive reinforcement, which becomes a clarion call for applying psychological principles in everyday living, especially communal living.

Ernest R. Hilgard publishes *Theories of Learning*, which was required reading for several generations of psychology students in North America.

1949 — Raymond B. Cattell publishes the Sixteen Personality Factor Questionnaire (16PF).

Continued on inside back cover

Exploring
PSYCHOLOGY

Exploring
PSYCHOLOGY

NINTH EDITION

David G. Myers

Hope College
Holland, Michigan

Special Contributor
C. Nathan DeWall, University of Kentucky

WORTH PUBLISHERS

Senior Vice President, Editorial and Production:
Catherine Woods
Publisher: Kevin Feyen
Executive Marketing Manager: Katherine Nurre
Development Editors: Christine Brune, Nancy Fleming
Director of Print and Digital Development: Tracey Kuehn
Media Editor: Elizabeth Block
Supplements Editors: Betty Probert, Nadina Persaud
Photo Editor: Bianca Moscatelli
Photo Researcher: Donna Ranieri
Art Director: Babs Reingold
Cover Designers: Lyndall Culbertson and Babs Reingold
Interior and Chapter Opener Designer: Charles Yuen
Layout Designer: Lee Ann McKevitt
Cover Photo Illustrator: Lyndall Culbertson
Associate Managing Editor: Lisa Kinne
Project Editor: Jeanine Furino
Marketing Assistant: Julie Tompkins
Illustration Coordinators: Bill Page, Janice Donnola
Illustrations: TSI Graphics, Keith Kasnot, Todd Buck
Production Manager: Sarah Segal
Composition: TSI Graphics
Printing and Binding: RR Donnelley

Library of Congress Control Number: 2012948473

Hardcover:
ISBN-13: 978-1-4292-6679-6
ISBN-10: 1-4292-6679-1
Paperback:
ISBN-13: 978-1-4641-1172-3
ISBN-10: 1-4641-1172-3
Loose-Leaf:
ISBN-13: 978-1-4641-0840-2
ISBN-10: 1-4641-0840-4
PI edition:
ISBN-13: 978-1-4641-4705-0
ISBN-10: 1-4641-4705-1

Printed in the United States of America

All royalties from the sale of this book are assigned to the David and Carol Myers Foundation, which exists to receive and distribute funds to other charitable organizations.

Worth Publishers   Macmillan Higher Education
41 Madison Avenue   Houndmills, Basingstoke
New York, NY 10010   RG21 6XS, England
www.worthpublishers.com   www.macmillanhighered.com/
                          international

Photo Credits: **Cover:** *Profile of smiling woman*: JGI/Jamie Grill/Getty Images; *Man taking a photo*: Pedro Vidal/Shutterstock; *Mother with baby daughter*: Erik Isakson/age fotostock; *Circus juggler*: RubberBall/SuperStock; **Chapter 1: pp. viii, xlii–1, 31, 33:** *Spiral*: Charles Yuen; *Water*: Photodisc/Getty Images; *Rabbit*: Mike Kemp/Getty Images; *Magnifying glass*: Charles Yuen; *MRI*: Living Art Enterprises, LLC/Photo Researchers, Inc.; *Infant*: Lane Oatey/Getty Images; *Man holding boxes*: Erik Isakson/age fotostock; *Girl studying*: OJO Images Ltd/Alamy. **Chapter 2: pp. viii, 34–35 and 72, 75:** *Circuit boards*: Charles Yuen; *Female kicking*: Lev Olkha/Shutterstock; *Fox*: Eric Isselée/Shutterstock; *Brain scan*: Zephyr/Photo Researchers, Inc.; *Butterfly*: Dim154/Shutterstock. **Chapter 3: pp. ix, 76–77 and 113, 115:** *Butterflies*: Svetlana Larina/istockphoto; *Butterflies*: polarica/istockphoto; *Cup of coffee*: Vasca/Shutterstock; *Sleeping toddler*: swissmacky/Shutterstock; *Woman meditating*: INSADCO Photography/Alamy. **Chapter 4: pp. ix, 116–117 and 159, 161:** *Bucket in sand*: René/istockphoto; *Beach and palm tree*: Charles Yuen; *Beach ball*: WendellandCarolyn/istockphoto; *Mother helping daughter with homework*: Indeed/Getty Images; *Teens texting*: Allan Shoemake/Getty Images; *Bride and groom*: bluehand/Shutterstock; *Mother holding baby*: Erik Isakson/age fotostock; *Baby being fed with spoon*: Asia Images/Getty Images. **Chapter 5: pp. ix, 162–163 and 187, 189:** *Petri dish*: Samuel Ashfield/Photo Researchers, Inc.; *Chromosomes*: Pasieka/Photo Researchers, Inc.; *Swans*: The Boston Globe/John Tlumacki; *Dad and child*: MGP/Getty Images; *Teenagers of different heights*: Rob Lewine/Getty Images; *She-male*: vita khorzhevska/Shutterstock; *Teenage couple*: Petrenko Andriy/Shutterstock. **Chapter 6: pp. x, 190–191 and 232, 235:** *Herbs*: Ivonne Wierink/Shutterstock; *Herbs*: Margrit Hirsch/Shutterstock; *Citrus*: Lauren Burke/Jupiterimages; *Man with cello*: sbarabu/Shutterstock; *Child kissing mother's face*: Jose Luis Pelaez, Inc./Blend Images/Corbis; *Woman holding flower*: Asia Images Group/Superstock. **Chapter 7: pp. x, 236–237 and 267, 269:** *Nest with eggs*: Duncan Usher/Foto Natura/Getty Images; *Trees*: Yuriy Kulyk/Shutterstock, Tungphoto/Shutterstock, irin-k/Shutterstock, Perfect Picture Parts/Alamy; *Cat*: Eric Isselée/Shutterstock; *Pigeon*: Vitaly Titov & Maria SideInikova/Shutterstock; *Kids playing videogames*: Stanislav Sointsev/Getty Images; *Dog doing stunts*: Marina Jay/Shutterstock; *Girl on laptop*: Lauren Burke/Getty Images; *People with books on heads*: Image Source/SuperStock. **Chapter 8: pp. xi, 270–271 and 301, 303:** *Film strips*: Charles Yuen; *Mouse trap*: Darren Matthews/Alamy; *Cookie*: Jean Sandler/FeaturePics; *Girl studying*: Sigrid Olsson/PhotoAlto/Corbis; *Man taking photo*: Pedro Vidal/Shutterstock; *Hot air balloon*: D. Hurst/Alamy. **Chapter 9: pp. xi, 304–305 and 347, 349:** *Various balls*: Charles Yuen; *Woman running hurdles*: Ocean/Corbis; *Man doing crossword*: Ann Baldwin/Shutterstock; *Puzzle pieces*: Alexey Lebedev/Shutterstock; *Woman shooting basketball*: Blend Images/Jupiterimages; *Man playing saxophone*: Masterfile (Royalty-Free Division); *Elephant*: Johan Swanepoel/Alamy. **Chapter 10: pp. xii, 350–351 and 386:** *Vietnam landscape*: Charles Yuen; *Girl using cell phone*: Thomas Northcut/Jupiterimages; *Woman on treadmill*: PhotoObjects.net/Jupiterimages; *Teenage boys*: Photodisc/Jupiterimages; *Woman with arms raised*: Mark Andersen/agefotostock. **Chapter 11: pp. xii, 389–390 and 419, 421:** *Fruit and vegetables*: Charles Yuen; *Two women laughing*: Mark Andersen/Getty Images; *Man looking angry*: PhotoSpin, Inc./Alamy; *Man kissing dog*: Photos.com/Getty Images; *Man meditating*: Dean Mitchell/Shutterstock; *Woman touching ground*: IMAGEMORE/agefotostock: *Nun praying*: PhotosIndia.com LLC/Alamy; *Tissues, aspirin*: D. Hurst/Alamy. **Chapter 12: pp. xiii, 422–423 and 453, 455:** *Masks*: Charles Yuen, Bartosz Hadyniak/istockphoto, Perry Correll/Shutterstock, brytta/istockphoto, Hemera Technologies/Jupiterimages; *Happy dog*: Erik Lam/Shutterstock; *Centaur*: Liquidlibrary/Jupiterimages; *Girl*: Timothy Large/Shutterstock; *Circus juggler*: RubberBall/Superstock. **Chapter 13: pp. xiii, 456–457 and 501, 503:** *Aerial beach scene*: Brand X Pictures; *Football*: Todd Taulman/Shutterstock; *Blog links*: Lada Adamic and Natalie Glance; *Wrench*: Punchstock/Corbis; *Gaming console*: Microsoft Corporation; *Tattooed arm*: David Katzenstein/Photolibrary; *Dancing couple*: Photodisc/Jupiterimages. **Chapter 14: pp. xiii, 504–505 and 541:** *Upset woman*: Wavebreakmedia Ltd/Jupiterimages; *Eyes*: Blend Images/Alamy, Photodisc/Getty Images; *Tarantula*: Martin Harvey/Jupiterimages; *Snake*: Hemera Technologies/Jupiterimages; *Blindfolded woman leading man*: Erik Isakson/age footstock; *Depressed man*: Image Source/Getty Images. **Chapter 15: pp. xiv, 544–545 and 578, 580:** *Crocus flowers through snow*: Myotis/Shutterstock; *Couple on bicycle*: RubberBall/SuperStock; *Healthy woman*: RubberBall/Nicole Hill/Jupiterimages; *People in rainforest*: Randy Faris/Corbis.

For Sara Neevel
with gratitude for your meticulous
support, and for your friendship

ABOUT THE AUTHOR

DAVID MYERS received his psychology Ph.D. from the University of Iowa. He has spent his career at Hope College in Michigan, where he has taught dozens of introductory psychology sections. Hope College students have invited him to be their commencement speaker and voted him "outstanding professor."

His research and writings have been recognized by the Gordon Allport Intergroup Relations Prize, by a 2010 Honored Scientist award from the Federation of Associations in Behavioral & Brain Sciences, by a 2010 Award for Service on Behalf of Personality and Social Psychology, and by three honorary doctorates.

Myers' scientific articles have, with support from National Science Foundation grants, appeared in three dozen scientific periodicals, including *Science, American Scientist, Psychological Science,* and the *American Psychologist.* In addition to his scholarly writing and his textbooks for introductory and social psychology, he also digests psychological science for the general public. His writings have appeared in four dozen magazines, from *Today's Education* to *Scientific American.* He also has authored five general audience books, including *The Pursuit of Happiness* and *Intuition: Its Powers and Perils.*

David Myers has chaired his city's Human Relations Commission, helped found a thriving assistance center for families in poverty, and spoken to hundreds of college and community groups. Drawing on his experience, he also has written three dozen articles and a book *(A Quiet World)* about hearing loss, and he is advocating a transformation in American assistive listening technology (see www.hearingloop.org). For his leadership, he received an American Academy of Audiology Presidential Award in 2011, and the Hearing Loss Association of America Walter T. Ridder Award in 2012.

He bikes to work year-round and plays regular pick-up basketball. David and Carol Myers have raised two sons and a daughter, and have one granddaughter.

BRIEF CONTENTS

CONTENTS

Consciousness and the Two-Track Mind ... 77

CHAPTER 3

Developing Through the Life Span ... 117

CHAPTER 4

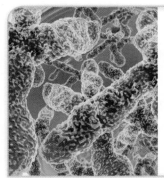

Gender and Sexuality ... 163

CHAPTER 5

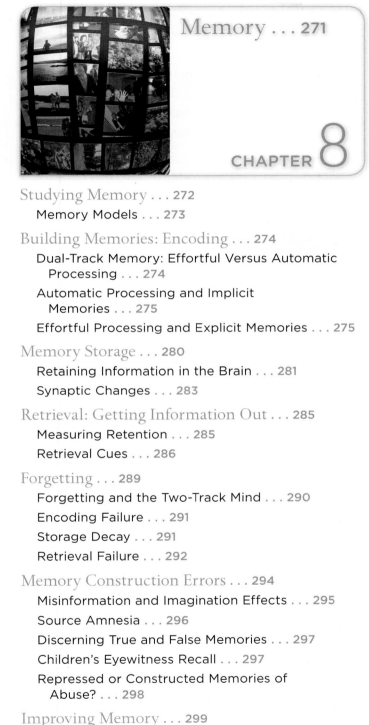

Memory . . . 271

CHAPTER 8

Thinking, Language, and Intelligence . . . 305

CHAPTER 9

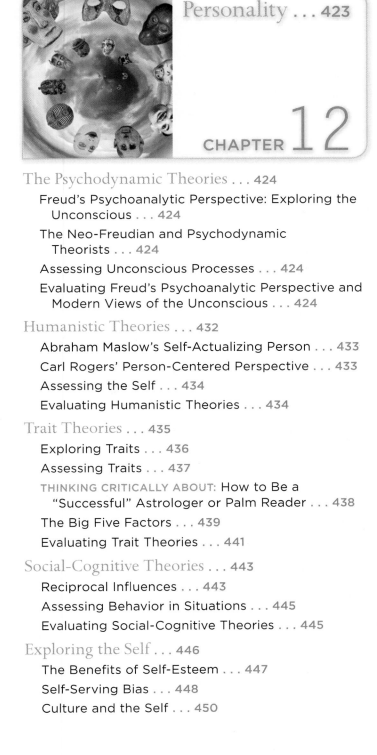

Personality . . . 423

CHAPTER 12

Social Psychology . . . 457

CHAPTER 13

Psychological Disorders . . . 505

CHAPTER 14

Therapy . . . 545

CHAPTER 15

Throughout its nine editions, my unwavering vision for *Exploring Psychology* has been *to merge rigorous science with a broad human perspective that engages both mind and heart*. I aim to offer a state-of-the-art introduction to psychological science that speaks to students' needs and interests. I aspire to help students understand and appreciate the wonders of their everyday lives. And I seek to convey the inquisitive spirit with which psychologists *do* psychology.

I am genuinely enthusiastic about psychology and its applicability to our lives. Psychological science has the potential to expand our minds and enlarge our hearts. By studying and applying its tools, ideas, and insights, we can supplement our intuition with critical thinking, restrain our judgmentalism with compassion, and replace our illusions with understanding. By the time students complete this guided tour of psychology, they will also, I hope, have a deeper understanding of our moods and memories, about the reach of our unconscious, about how we flourish and struggle, about how we perceive our physical and social worlds, and about how our biology and culture in turn shape us. (See **TABLES 1** and **2**, next page.)

Believing with Thoreau that "anything living is easily and naturally expressed in popular language," I seek to communicate psychology's scholarship with crisp narrative and vivid storytelling. "A writer's job," says my friend Mary Pipher, "is to tell stories that connect readers to all the people on Earth, to show these people as the complicated human beings they really are, with histories, families, emotions, and legitimate needs." Writing as a solo author, I hope to tell psychology's story in a way that is warmly personal as well as rigorously scientific. I love to reflect on connections between psychology and other realms, such as literature, philosophy, history, sports, religion, politics, and popular culture. And I love to provoke thought, to play with words, and to laugh. For his pioneering 1891 *Principles of Psychology,* William James sought "humor and pathos." And so do I.

I am grateful for the privilege of assisting with the teaching of this mind-expanding discipline to so many students, in so many countries, through so many different languages. To be entrusted with discerning and communicating psychology's insights is both an exciting honor and a great responsibility.

Creating this book is a team sport. Like so many human achievements, it is the product of a collective intelligence. Woodrow Wilson spoke for me: "I not only use all the brains I have, but all I can borrow." The thousands of instructors and millions of students across the globe who have taught or studied (or both!) with this book have contributed immensely to its development. Much of this contribution has occurred spontaneously, through correspondence and conversations. For this edition, we also formally involved 1061 researchers and teaching psychologists, and 251 students, in our efforts to gather accurate and up-to-date information about the field of psychology and the content, study aids, and supplements needs of instructors and students in the introductory course. We look forward to continuing feedback as we strive, over future editions, to create an ever better book and teaching package.

What's NEW?

This ninth edition is the most carefully reworked and extensively updated of all the revisions to date. This new edition features improvements to the organization and presentation, especially to our system of supporting student learning and remembering.

TABLE 1 Evolutionary Psychology and Behavior Genetics

TABLE 2 Neuroscience

NEW Study System Follows Best Practices From Learning and Memory Research

The new learning system harnesses the *testing effect,* which documents the benefits of actively retrieving information through self-testing (**FIGURE 1**). Thus, each chapter now offers 15 to 20 new *Retrieve It* questions interspersed throughout. Creating these *desirable difficulties* for students along the way optimizes the testing effect, as does *immediate feedback* (via inverted answers beneath each question).

In addition, each main section of text begins with numbered questions that establish *learning objectives* and direct student reading. The Chapter Review section repeats these questions as a further self-testing opportunity (with answers in the Complete Chapter Reviews appendix). The Chapter Review section also offers a page-referenced list of key terms and concepts, and new *Experience the Testing Effect* questions in multiple formats to promote optimal retention.

FIGURE 1
Testing effect For suggestions of how students may apply the testing effect to their own learning, watch this 5-minute YouTube animation: www.tinyurl.com/HowToRemember

Nearly 1000 New Research Citations

My ongoing scrutiny of dozens of scientific periodicals and science news sources, enhanced by commissioned reviews and countless e-mails from instructors and students, enables my integrating our field's most important, thought-provoking, and student-relevant new discoveries. Part of the pleasure that sustains this work is learning something new every day! (For a complete list of significant changes to the content, see www.worthpub.com/myers.)

Reorganized Chapters

In addition to the new study aids and updated coverage, I've introduced the following organizational changes:

- Chapter 1 concludes with a new section, "Improve Your Retention—And Your Grades." This guide will help students replace ineffective and inefficient old habits with new habits that increase retention and success.

- The contents of the previous edition's Nature, Nurture, and Human Diversity chapter are now integrated throughout the text, including in Chapters 2, 4, 5, 12, and 13. (See Table 4 on page xxi.)

- Chapter 4, Developing Through the Life Span, has been shortened by moving the Aging and Intelligence coverage to Chapter 9, Thinking, Language, and Intelligence.

- NEW Chapter 5, Gender and Sexuality, includes new and significantly reorganized discussions.

- Chapter 6, Sensation and Perception, now covers both topics in a more efficient and integrated fashion (rather than covering sensation first, then perception). Coverage of the deaf experience is now in Chapter 9, Thinking, Language, and Intelligence.

- Chapter 7, Learning, now has a separate Biology, Cognition, and Learning section that more fully explores the biological and cognitive constraints on learning.

- Chapter 8, Memory, follows a new format, and more clearly explains how different brain networks process and retain memories. I worked closely with Janie Wilson (Professor of Psychology at Georgia Southern University and Vice President for Programming of the Society for the Teaching of Psychology) in this chapter's revision.

- Chapter 10 now combines Motivation with Emotion.

- Chapter 11, Stress, Health, and Human Flourishing, now includes discussion of positive psychology, well-being, and personal control.

- Chapter 12, Personality, offers improved coverage of modern-day psychodynamic approaches, which are now more clearly distinguished from their historical Freudian roots.

- The Social Psychology chapter now follows the Personality chapter.

- Chapter 14, Psychological Disorders, now includes coverage of eating disorders, previously in the Motivation chapter.

Clinical Chapters Were Carefully Reviewed and Significantly Improved

With helpful guidance from clinical psychologist colleagues, I have strengthened the clinical perspective, which has improved the Personality, Psychological Disorders, and Therapy chapters, among others. For example, I cover problem-focused and emotion-focused coping strategies and the relationship of psychotherapy to cancer survival in the Stress, Health, and Human Flourishing chapter, and the Intelligence chapter describes how psychologists use intelligence tests in clinical settings. Material from today's positive psychology is also woven throughout (see **TABLE 3**).

In addition, the Personality and Therapy chapters now more clearly distinguish between historical psychoanalysis and modern-day psychodynamic theories.

TABLE 3   Examples of Positive Psychology

Coverage of **positive psychology** topics can be found in the following chapters:

Topic	Chapter
Altruism/Compassion	4, 9, 12, 13, 15
Coping	11
Courage	13
Creativity	8, 12, 13
Emotional intelligence	9, 13
Empathy	4, 7, 11, 13, 15
Flow	10
Gratitude	10, 11, 13
Happiness/Life Satisfaction	4, 10, 11
Humility	13
Humor	11, 13
Justice	13
Leadership	10, 12, 13, App B
Love	4, 5, 10, 11, 12, 13, 14, 15
Morality	4
Optimism	11, 12
Personal control	11
Resilience	4, 11, 13, 15
Self-discipline	4, 10, 12
Self-efficacy	11, 12
Self-esteem	10, 12
Spirituality	11, 13
Toughness (grit)	9, 10
Wisdom	3, 4, 9, 12, 13

New Time Management Section for Students

To help students maximize their reading, studying, and exam preparation efforts, a new student preface offers time management guidance.

Beautiful New Design and Contemporary New Photo Program

This new, more open and colorful design, chock full of new photos and illustrations, provides a modern visual context for the book's up-to-date coverage.

Dedicated Versions of Next-Generation Media

This ninth edition is accompanied by the dramatically enhanced **Psych-Portal,** which adds new features (**LearningCurve** formative assessment activities and **Launch Pad** carefully crafted prebuilt assignments) while incorporating the full range of Worth's psychology media products (Video Tool Kit, PsychInvestigator, PsychSim). (For details, see p. xxv.)

What Continues?

Eight Guiding Principles

Despite all the exciting changes, this new edition retains its predecessors' voice, as well as much of the content and organization. It also retains the goals—the guiding principles—that have animated the previous eight editions:

Facilitating the Learning Experience

1. **To teach critical thinking** By presenting research as intellectual detective work, I illustrate an inquiring, analytical mindset. Whether students are studying development, cognition, or social behavior, they will become involved in, and see the rewards of, critical reasoning. Moreover, they will discover how an empirical approach can help them evaluate competing ideas and claims for highly publicized phenomena—ranging from ESP and alternative therapies, to astrology and repressed and recovered memories.

2. **To integrate principles and applications** Throughout—by means of anecdotes, case histories, and the posing of hypothetical situations—I relate the findings of basic research to their applications and implications. Where psychology can illuminate pressing human issues—be they racism and sexism, health and happiness, or violence and war—I have not hesitated to shine its light.

3. **To reinforce learning at every step** Everyday examples and rhetorical questions encourage students to process the material actively. Concepts presented earlier are frequently applied, and reinforced, in later chapters. For instance, in Chapter 3, students learn that much of our information processing occurs *outside* of our conscious awareness. Ensuing chapters drive home this concept. Numbered Learning Objective Questions at the beginning of each main section, Retrieve It self-tests throughout each chapter, a marginal glossary, and Chapter Review key terms lists and self-tests help students learn and *retain* important concepts and terminology.

Demonstrating the Science of Psychology

4. **To exemplify the process of inquiry** I strive to show students not just the outcome of research, but how the research process works. Throughout, the book tries to excite the reader's curiosity. It invites readers to imagine themselves as participants in classic experiments. Several chapters introduce research stories as mysteries that progressively unravel as one clue after another falls into place.

5. **To be as up-to-date as possible** Few things dampen students' interest as quickly as the sense that they are reading stale news. While retaining psychology's classic studies and concepts, I also present the discipline's most important recent developments. More than 900 references in this edition are dated 2009–2012. Likewise, the new photos and everyday examples are drawn from today's world.

6. **To put facts in the service of concepts** My intention is not to fill students' intellectual file drawers with facts, but to reveal psychology's major concepts—to teach students how to think, and to offer psychological ideas worth thinking about. In each chapter, I place emphasis on those concepts I hope students will carry with them long after they complete the course. Always, I try to follow Albert Einstein's purported dictum that "everything should be made as simple as possible, but not simpler." Learning Objective Questions and Retrieve It questions throughout each chapter help students focus on the most important concepts.

Promoting Big Ideas and Broadened Horizons

7. **To enhance comprehension by providing continuity** Many chapters have a significant issue or theme that links subtopics, forming a thread that ties the chapter together. The Learning chapter conveys the idea that bold

thinkers can serve as intellectual pioneers. The Thinking, Language, and Intelligence chapter raises the issue of human rationality and irrationality. The Psychological Disorders chapter conveys empathy for, and understanding of, troubled lives. Other threads, such as cognitive neuroscience, dual processing, and cultural and gender diversity, weave throughout the whole book, and students hear a consistent voice.

8. **To convey respect for human unity and diversity** Throughout the book, readers will see evidence of our human kinship—our shared biological heritage, our common mechanisms of seeing and learning, hungering and feeling, loving and hating. They will also better understand the dimensions of our diversity—our *individual* diversity in development and aptitudes, temperament and personality, and disorder and health; and our *cultural* diversity in attitudes and expressive styles, child-rearing and care for the elderly, and life priorities.

Continually Improving Cultural and Gender Diversity Coverage

This edition presents an even more thoroughly cross-cultural perspective on psychology (**TABLE 4**)—reflected in research findings and text and photo examples. New Chapter 5, Gender and Sexuality, allows a separate-chapter focus on the psychology of women and men, though these topics are also thoroughly integrated throughout the text (see **TABLE 5**). In addition, I am working to offer a world-based psychology for our worldwide student readership. Thus, I continually search the world for research findings and text and photo examples, conscious that readers may be in Melbourne, Sheffield, Vancouver, or Nairobi. North American and European examples come easily, given that I reside in the United States, maintain contact with friends and colleagues in Canada, subscribe to several European periodicals, and live periodically in the U.K. This edition, for example, offers many dozens of Canadian, British, and Australian and New Zealand examples. We are all citizens of a shrinking world, thanks to increased migration and the growing global economy. Thus, American students, too, benefit from information and examples that internationalize their world-consciousness. And if psychology seeks to explain *human* behavior (not just American or Canadian or Australian behavior), the broader the scope of studies presented, the more accurate is our picture of this world's people. My aim is to expose all students to the world beyond their own culture, and I continue to welcome input and suggestions from all readers. Discussion of the relevance of cultural and gender diversity begins on the first page of the first chapter and continues throughout the text.

Strong Critical Thinking Coverage

I aim to introduce students to critical thinking throughout the book. Revised Learning Objective Questions at the beginning of each main section, and Retrieve It questions throughout each chapter, encourage critical reading to glean an understanding of important concepts. This ninth edition also includes the following opportunities for students to learn or practice their critical thinking skills.

- *Chapter 1, Thinking Critically With Psychological Science,* introduces students to psychology's research methods, emphasizing the fallacies of our everyday intuition and common sense and, thus, the need for psychological science. *Critical thinking* is introduced as a key term in this chapter (p. 15). Appendix A, Statistical Reasoning in Everyday Life, encourages students to "focus on thinking smarter by applying simple statistical principles to everyday reasoning."

TABLE 4 Culture and Multicultural Experience

TABLE 5 The Psychology of Men and Women

- *"Thinking Critically About . . ." boxes* are found throughout the book, modeling for students a critical approach to some key issues in psychology. For example, see the updated box "Thinking Critically About: The Fear Factor—Why We Fear the Wrong Things" (pages 310–311).

- *Detective-style stories* throughout the narrative get students thinking critically about psychology's key research questions. For example, in Chapter 14, I present the causes of schizophrenia piece by piece, showing students how researchers put the puzzle together.

- *"Apply this"* and *"Think about it"* style discussions keep students active in their study of each chapter. In Chapter 13, for example, students take the perspective of participants in a Solomon Asch conformity experiment, and later in one of Stanley Milgram's obedience experiments. I've also asked students to join the fun by taking part in activities they can try along the way. For example, in Chapter 6, they try out a quick sensory adaptation activity. In Chapter 10, they try matching expressions to faces and test the effects of different facial expressions on themselves.

- *Critical examinations of pop psychology* spark interest and provide important lessons in thinking critically about everyday topics. For example, Chapter 6 includes a close examination of ESP, and Chapter 8 addresses the controversial topic of repression of painful memories.

See **TABLE 6** for a complete list of this text's coverage of critical thinking topics and Thinking Critically About boxes.

TABLE 6 Critical Thinking and Research Emphasis

Critical thinking coverage, and in-depth stories of psychology's scientific research process, can be found on the following pages:

Thinking Critically About . . . boxes:
Addiction, p. 101
The Evolutionary Perspective on Human Sexuality, pp. 183–186
Can Subliminal Messages Control Our Behavior?, p. 195
ESP—Perception Without Sensation?, pp. 230–232
Does Viewing Media Violence Trigger Violent Behavior?, p. 265
The Fear Factor—Why We Fear the Wrong Things, pp. 310–311
Lie Detection, p. 379
How to Be a "Successful" Astrologer or Palm Reader, pp. 438–439
ADHD—Normal High Energy or Genuine Disorder?, p. 507
Insanity and Responsibility, p. 512

Critical Examinations of Pop Psychology:
The need for psychological science, p. 10
Perceiving order in random events, pp. 12–13
Do we use only 10 percent of our brains?, p. 56
Can hypnosis enhance recall? Coerce action? Be therapeutic? Alleviate pain?, pp. 97–98

Has the concept of "addiction" been stretched too far?, p. 101
Near-death experiences, p. 107
Critiquing the evolutionary perspective, pp. 185–186
How much credit or blame do parents deserve?, p. 147
Sensory restriction, pp. 97–100
Is there extrasensory perception?, pp. 230–232
Do other species exhibit language?, pp. 323–325
How valid is the Rorschach test?, pp. 429–430
Is repression a myth?, p. 431
Is Freud credible?, pp. 430–432
Is psychotherapy effective?, pp. 560–563
Evaluating alternative therapies, pp. 563–565
Do video games teach or release violence?, pp. 485–486

Thinking Critically With Psychological Science:
The limits of intuition and common sense, pp. 10–13
The scientific attitude, pp. 13–14

Critical thinking introduced as a key term, p. 15
The scientific method, pp. 15–17
Correlation and causation, pp. 21–22
Exploring cause and effect, pp. 22–23
Random assignment, pp. 22–23
Independent and dependent variables, pp. 23–24
Statistical reasoning, pp. A1–A4
Describing data, pp. A1–A4
Making inferences, pp. A7–A8

Scientific Detective Stories:
Is breast milk better than formula?, pp. 22–23
Our divided brains, pp. 59–61
Twin and adoption studies, pp. 63–66
Why do we sleep?, pp. 88–89
Why do we dream?, pp. 94–96
Is hypnosis an extension of normal consciousness or an altered state?, pp. 98–100
How a child's mind develops, pp. 124–129
What determines sexual orientation?, pp. 178–183

Parallel processing, pp. 205–206
How do we see in color?, pp. 206–208
How are memories constructed?, pp. 274–280
How do we store memories in our brains?, pp. 280–282
Do other species exhibit language?, pp. 323–325
Aging and intelligence, pp. 337–338
Why do we feel hunger?, pp. 357–359
Why—and in whom—does stress contribute to heart disease?, pp. 397–399
How and why is social support linked with health?, pp. 405–407
The pursuit of happiness: Who is happy, and why?, pp. 412–419
Self-esteem versus self-serving bias, pp. 448–450
Why do people fail to help in emergencies?, pp. 494–495
What causes mood disorders?, pp. 521–527
Do prenatal viral infections increase risk of schizophrenia?, pp. 531–532
Is psychotherapy effective?, pp. 560–561

APA Principles and New MCAT 2015 Guidelines

APA Principles for Quality Undergraduate Education and APA Learning Goals and Outcomes

In February 2011, the American Psychological Association (APA) approved the new *Principles for Quality Undergraduate Education in Psychology.* These broad-based principles and their associated recommendations were designed to "produce psychologically literate citizens who apply the principles of psychological science at work and at home." (See www.apa.org/education/undergrad/principles.aspx.)

APA's more specific 2002 Learning Goals and Outcomes (from their *Guidelines for the Undergraduate Psychology Major,* updated in 2006) were designed to gauge progress in students graduating with psychology majors. (See www.apa.org/ed/precollege/about/psymajor-guidelines.pdf) Many psychology departments have since used these goals and outcomes to help establish their own benchmarks for departmental assessment purposes. APA's 2009 Assessment CyberGuide for Learning Goals and Outcomes (www.apa.org/ed/governance/bea/assess.aspx) may assist your efforts.

Some instructors are eager to know whether a given text for the introductory course helps students get a good start at achieving these APA benchmarks. See www.worthpublishers.com/myers for detailed guides to how well *Exploring Psychology,* ninth edition, corresponds to both the 2011 APA Principles and the 2006 APA Learning Goals and Outcomes.

MCAT Will Include Psychology Starting in 2015

Beginning in 2015, the Medical College Admission Test (MCAT) is devoting 25 percent of its questions to the "Psychological, Social, and Biological Foundations of Behavior," with most of those questions coming from the psychological science taught in introductory psychology courses. From 1977 to 2014, the MCAT focused on biology, chemistry, and physics. Hereafter, reports the new *Preview Guide for MCAT 2015,* the exam will also recognize "the importance of socio-cultural and behavioral determinants of health and health outcomes." The exam's new psychology section covers the breadth of topics in this text. See, for example, **TABLE 7**, which outlines the precise correlation between the topics in this text's Sensation and Perception chapter and the corresponding portion of the MCAT exam. For a complete pairing of the new MCAT psychology topics with this book's contents, see www.worthpublishers.com/myers.

TABLE 7   Sample MCAT Correlation With *Exploring Psychology*, Ninth Edition

MCAT 2015: Categories in Sensation and Perception	Myers, *Exploring Psychology,* Ninth Edition, Correlations	
Content Category 6e: *Sensing the environment*	Section Title or Topic	Page Number
Sensory Processing	Sensation and Perception	191–235
Sensation	Sensation and Perception	193–195
Thresholds	Thresholds	193–195
Signal detection theory	Signal detection theory	193
Sensory adaptation	Sensory adaptation	196–197

Sample MCAT Correlation With *Exploring Psychology*, Ninth Edition, *continued*

MCAT 2015: Categories in Sensation and Perception	Myers, *Exploring Psychology*, Ninth Edition, Correlations	
Content Category 6e: *Sensing the environment*	Section Title or Topic	Page Number
Sensory receptors transduce stimulus energy and transmit signals to the central nervous system.	Transduction	192
Sensory pathways	Visual Information Processing	202–206
	The Ear	216–217
	Understanding Pain	221
	Taste	224–225
	Smell	225–226
	Body Position and Movement	227
Types of sensory receptors	The Eye	201–204
	The Ear	216–219
	Understanding Pain	221–222
	Taste	224–225
	Smell	225–226
	Body Position and Movement	227
The cerebral cortex controls voluntary movement and cognitive functions.	Functions of the Cortex	54–57
Information processing in the cerebral cortex	The Cerebral Cortex	53–57
Lateralization of cortical functions	The Cerebral Cortex	53–56
	Our Divided Brain	59–61
	Right-Left Differences in the Intact Brain	61–62
Vision	Vision	200–215
Structure and function of the eye	The Eye	200–202
Visual processing	Visual Information Processing	202–206
Visual pathways in the brain	Figure 6.16 Pathway from the eyes to the visual cortex	203
Parallel processing	Parallel processing	205–206
Feature detection	Feature detection	204–205
Hearing	Hearing	216–219
Auditory processing	Transduction of sound	216–217
Auditory pathways in the brain	Transduction of sound	216–217
Perceiving loudness and pitch	Perceiving Loudness	218
	Perceiving Pitch	219
Locating sounds	Locating Sounds	219
Sensory reception by hair cells	Photo of hair cells; detailed drawing of inner ear, including hair cells	216, 217
	The Ear	216
Other Senses	The Other Senses	220–227
Somatosensation		
Sensory systems in the skin	Sensory cortex	54–55
	Touch	220

Sample MCAT Correlation With *Exploring Psychology,* Ninth Edition, *continued*

MCAT 2015: Categories in Sensation and Perception	Myers, *Exploring Psychology,* Ninth Edition, Correlations	
Content Category 6e: *Sensing the environment*	Section Title or Topic	Page Number
Tactile pathways in the brain	Sensory cortex	54–55
	Figure 6.38 The pain circuit	221
Types of pain	Pain	221–222
Factors that influence pain	Biological Influences	221–222
	Psychological Influences	222
	Social-Cultural Influences	222–223
Taste	Taste	224–225
Taste buds/chemoreceptors that detect specific chemicals in the environment	Taste receptors and their functions	224–225
Gustatory pathways in the brain	Processing taste in the brain	226
Smell	Smell	225–227
Olfactory cells/chemoreceptors that detect specific chemicals in the environment	Olfactory receptor cells, and processing olfaction in the brain	225–226
Pheromones	Smell of sex-related hormones	181, 182
Olfactory pathways in the brain	Processing olfaction in the brain	225–226
Role of smell in perception of taste	Sensory Interaction	227–229
Perception	Sensation and Perception	191–235
Bottom-up/Top-down processing	Bottom-up and top-down processing	192, 221
Perceptual organization (i.e., depth, form, motion, constancy)	Visual Organization: Form Perception, Depth Perception (including Relative Motion), Perceptual Constancy	208–214
	Processing motion	205
Gestalt principles	Gestalt principles	208–209

Next-Generation Multimedia

Exploring Psychology, ninth edition, boasts impressive multimedia options. For more information about any of these choices, visit Worth Publishers' online catalog at www.worthpublishers.com.

PsychPortal With LearningCurve Quizzing

The ninth edition's dramatically enhanced **PsychPortal** adds new features (**LearningCurve** formative assessment activities and **Launch Pad** carefully crafted prebuilt assignments) while incorporating the full range of Worth's psychology media options (Video Tool Kit, PsychInvestigator, PsychSim).

Based on the latest findings from learning and memory research, LearningCurve combines adaptive question selection, personalized study plans, immediate and valuable feedback, and state-of-the-art question analysis reports. LearningCurve's game-like nature keeps students engaged while helping them learn and *remember* key concepts.

Launch Pad offers a set of prebuilt assignments, carefully crafted by a group of instructional designers and instructors with an abundance of teaching experience as well as deep familiarity with Worth content. Each Launch Pad unit contains videos, activities, and formative assessment pieces to build student understanding for each topic, culminating with a randomized summative quiz to hold students accountable for the unit. Assign units in just a few clicks, and find scores in your gradebook upon submission. Launch Pad appeals not only to instructors who have been interested in adding an online component to their course but haven't been able to invest the time, but also to experienced online instructors curious to see how other colleagues might scaffold a series of online activities. Customize units as you wish, adding and dropping content to fit your course. (See **FIGURE 2**.)

Faculty Support and Student Resources

- **New! Faculty Lounge**—http://psych.facultylounge.worthpublishers.com—(see **FIGURE 3**) is an online place to find and share favorite teaching ideas and materials, including videos, animations, images, PowerPoint® slides and lectures, news stories, articles, web links, and lecture activities. Includes publisher- as well as peer-provided resources—all faculty-reviewed for accuracy and quality.
- Instructor's Media Guide for Introductory Psychology
- Enhanced Course Management Solutions (including course cartridges)
- eBook in various available formats, with embedded Concepts in Action
- Book Companion Site

FIGURE 2
Launch Pad in PsychPortal

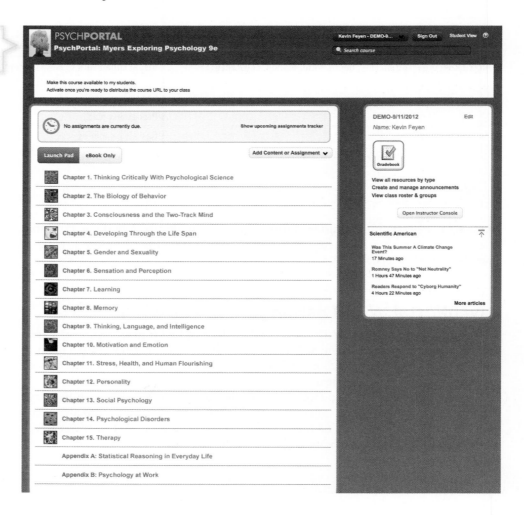

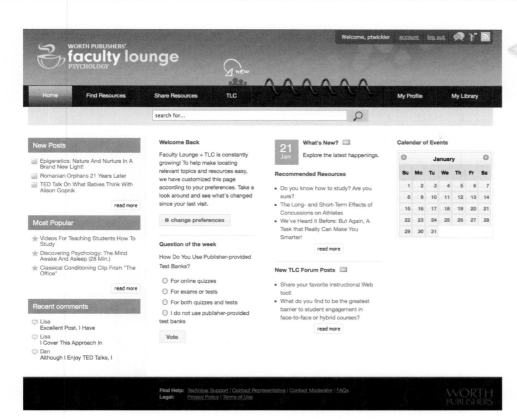

FIGURE 3
Sample from our Faculty
Lounge site
(psych.facultylounge.worthpublishers.com)

Video and Presentation

- **New! Worth Introductory Psychology Videos,** produced in conjunction with *Scientific American* and *Nature,* is a breakthrough collection of NEW modular, tutorial videos on core psychology topics. This set includes animations, interviews with top scientists, and carefully selected archival footage and is available on flash drive, or as part of the new Worth Video Anthology for Introductory Psychology.

- **New! The Worth Video Anthology for Introductory Psychology** is a complete collection, all in one place, of our video clips from the **Video Tool Kit,** the **Digital Media Archive,** and the third edition of the *Scientific American Frontiers Teaching Modules,* as well as from the new *Worth Introductory Psychology Videos* co-produced with *Scientific American* and *Nature.* Available on DVD or flash drive, the set is accompanied by its own Faculty Guide.

- **New! Interactive Presentation Slides for Introductory Psychology** is an extraordinary series of PowerPoint® lectures. This is a dynamic, yet easy-to-use new way to engage students during classroom presentations of core psychology topics. This collection provides opportunities for discussion and interaction, and includes an unprecedented number of embedded video clips and animations (including activities from our **ActivePsych** series).

Assessment

- **New! LearningCurve**
- Printed Test Banks
- Diploma Computerized Test Banks
- Online Quizzing
- i•clicker Radio Frequency Classroom Response System

Print

- Instructor's Resources
- Lecture Guides
- Study Guide
- *Pursuing Human Strengths: A Positive Psychology Guide*
- *Critical Thinking Companion,* Second Edition
- *Psychology and the Real World: Essays Illustrating Fundamental Contributions to Society.* This ©2011 project of the FABBS Foundation brought together a virtual "Who's Who" of contemporary psychological scientists to describe—in clear, captivating ways—the research they have passionately pursued and what it means to the "real world." Each contribution is an original essay written for this project.

From Scientific American

- Improving the Mind & Brain: A *Scientific American* Special Issue
- *Scientific American* Reader to Accompany Myers

In Appreciation

If it is true that "whoever walks with the wise becomes wise" then I am wiser for all the wisdom and advice received from my colleagues. Aided by thousands of consultants and reviewers over the last two decades, this has become a better, more accurate book than one author alone (this author, at least) could write. As my editors and I keep reminding ourselves, all of us together are smarter than any one of us.

My indebtedness continues to each of the teacher-scholars whose influence I acknowledged in the eight previous editions, to the innumerable researchers who have been so willing to share their time and talent to help me accurately report their research, and to the 1155 instructors and students who took the time to offer feedback over the phone, in a survey, or at one of our face-to-face focus groups. I also appreciated having detailed consultation on the Memory chapter from Janie Wilson (Georgia Southern University, and Vice President for Programming of the Society of the Teaching of Psychology).

Nathan DeWall (University of Kentucky) offered valuable input as a special contributor for this edition. He assisted with the revision of the Need to Belong section in Chapter 10, Motivation and Emotion; the Personal Control discussion in Chapter 11, Stress, Health, and Human Flourishing; and the Aggression discussion in Chapter 13, Social Psychology.

Amy Himsel (El Camino College), a gifted teacher with a keen ability to connect with students, guided creation of the self-test study aids found throughout this new edition.

My gratitude extends to the colleagues who contributed criticism, corrections, and creative ideas related to the content, pedagogy, and format of this new edition and its teaching package. For their expertise and encouragement, and the gifts of their time to the teaching of psychology, I thank the reviewers and consultants listed here.

Jennifer Adler,
Borough of Manhattan Community College, CUNY

David Alfano,
Community College of Rhode Island

Leslie Cramblet Alvarez,
Adams State College

Willow Aureala,
Hawaii Community College

Rosiana Azman,
Kapiolani Community College

Debra Bacon,
Bristol Community College— Fall River Campus

Robert Baker,
Sandhills Community College

Meeta Banerjee,
Michigan State University

Carol Batt,
Seattle Central Community College

Kiersten Baughman,
University of Oklahoma

Alexander Beaujean,
Baylor University

Karen Bekker,
Bergen Community College

Anjan Bhattacharyya,
New Jersey City University

Beth Bigler,
Pellissippi State Tech Community College

Melissa Birkett,
Northern Arizona University

Tim Boffeli,
Clarke University

Gregory Bolich,
Belmont Abbey College

Pamela Bradley,
Sandhills Community College

Jennifer Breneiser,
Valdosta State University

Gayle Brosnan-Watters,
Chandler Gilbert Community College

Cheryl Carmichael,
Brooklyn College, CUNY

Ana Carmona,
Austin Peay State University

Natalie Ceballos,
Texas State University—San Marcos

Kelly Charlton,
University of North Carolina at Pembroke

Barbara Chutroo,
Borough of Manhattan Community College, CUNY

Pamela Costa,
Tacoma Community College

Baine Craft,
Seattle Pacific University

Christy Cummings,
Community College of Denver

Drew Curtis,
Texas Woman's University

Robert Dale,
Butler University

Deborah Dalke,
Defiance College

Robert Daniel,
Bridgewater State College

Mary Fran Davis,
Austin Peay State University

Sarah D'Elia,
George Mason University

Meliksah Demir,
Northern Arizona University

Jean Desto,
Anna Maria College

Wendy Domjan,
University of Texas—Austin

Evelyn Doody,
College of Southern Nevada

Kathryn Dumper,
Bainbridge College

Robert Egbert,
Walla Walla University

Julie Ehrhardt,
Bristol Community College—New Bedford

Daniella Errett,
Penn Highlands Community College

Kim Felsenthal,
Berkeley College

Christopher Ferguson,
Texas A&M International University

Bill Flack,
Bucknell University

Jonathan Forbey,
Ball State University

Claire Ford,
Bridgewater State University

William Fry,
Youngstown State University

Crystal Gabert-Quillen,
Kent State University

Dennis Galvan,
Gallaudet University

Karen Gee-Atwood,
Foothill College

Inna Ghajoyan,
California State University—Northridge

Jennifer Gibson,
Tarleton State University

Amanda Gingerich,
Butler University

Wind Goodfriend,
Buena Vista University

Dan Grangaard,
Austin Community College

Melinda Green,
Cornell College

Kelly Hagan,
Bluegrass Community & Technical College

Diane Hall,
Bay Path College

Pamela Hall,
Barry University

Stephen Hampe,
Utica College

Rhiannon Hart,
Rochester Institute of Technology

Wendy Hart,
Arizona State University

Myra Harville,
Holmes Community College

Matthew Hayes,
Winthrop University

Carmon Hicks,
Ivy Tech Community College

Kathleen Hipp,
Daniel Webster College

Brian Hock,
Austin Peay State University

Lori Hokerson,
American River College

Mia Holland,
Bridgewater State College

Gary Homann,
Lincoln University of Missouri

Mildred Huffman,
Jefferson College of Health Sciences

Steven Isonio,
Golden West College

Lora Jacobi,
Stephen F. Austin State University

Jenny Jellison,
Waynesburg College

Barry Johnson,
Davidson County Community College

Peter Karl Jonason,
University of West Florida

Diana Joy,
Community College of Denver

Stephen Joy,
Albertus Magnus College

Tracy Juliao,
University of Michigan—Dearborn Campus

Deana Julka,
University of Portland

Bethany Jurs,
University of Wisconsin—Stout Campus

Diane Kappen,
Johnson County Community College

Katrina Kardiasmenos,
Bowie State University

Chithra KarunaKaran,
Borough of Manhattan Community College, CUNY

Brent King,
Adams State College

Teresa King,
Bridgewater State College

Annette Kluck,
Auburn University

Franz Klutschkowski,
North Central Texas College

Dana Kuehn,
Florida State College at Jacksonville

Carol LaLiberte,
Asnuntuck Community College

Donna Landon-Jimenez,
Caldwell College, Mount Saint Mary Academy

Cynthia Lausberg,
Pittsburg University

Melissa Lea,
Millsaps University

Fred Leavitt,
California State University—Hayward

Heather Lench,
Texas A&M University

Nicolette Lopez,
University of Texas at Arlington

Ken Luke,
Tyler Junior College

Melanie Maggard,
Mount San Jacinto College

Toby Marx,
Union County College

Jim Matiya,
Florida Gulf Coast University

Simone Matlock-Phillips,
Bay Path College

Elizabeth Matys-Rahbar,
Greenwich High School

Tammy McClain,
West Liberty University

Daniel McConnell,
University of Central Florida

Kyla McKay-Dewald,
*Bristol Community College—
Fall River Campus*

Thomas Meriweather,
Virginia Military Institute

Nadia Monosov,
California State University—Northridge

James Moore,
Marshall University

Robin Musselman,
Lehigh Carbon Community College

Michelle Mychajlowskyj,
Quinnipiac University

Robert Newby,
Tarleton State University

Arthur Olguin,
Santa Barbara City College

Don Osborn,
Bellarmine College

Neophytos Papaneophytou,
*Borough of Manhattan Community College,
CUNY*

Thomas Peterson,
Grand View University

Zehra Peynircioglu,
American University

Kellie Pierson,
Northern Kentucky University

Gary Popoli,
Stevenson University

Jack Powell,
University of Hartford

Patrick Progar,
Caldwell College

Michael Rader,
Johnson County Community College

Kimberly Renk,
University of Central Florida

Shannon Scott Rich,
Texas Woman's University

Cynthia Rickert,
Ivy Tech Community College

Hugh H. Riley,
Baylor University

Kristin Ritchey,
Ball State University

Clarence Rohrbaugh,
Fairmont State College

James Rollins,
Austin Peay State University

Jane Russell,
Austin Peay State University

Valerie Scott,
Indiana University Southeast

Neda Senehi,
California State University—Northridge

Tim Shearon,
The College of Idaho

LaTishia Smith,
Ivy Tech Community College

Rita Smith-Wade-El,
Millersville University

Kristin Sorensen,
Defiance College

Gary Springer,
Los Angeles College International

Jonathan D. Springer,
Kean University

Kimberly Stark-Wroblewski,
University of Central Missouri

Meri Stiles,
Lyndon State College

Deborah Stipp,
Ivy Tech Community College

Dawn Strongin,
California State University—Stanislaus

Donna Stuber-McEwen,
Friends University

Robert Tanner,
*Albuquerque Technical Vocational
Institute*

Yonca Toker,
Georgia Institute of Technology

Stephen Truhon,
Austin Peay State University

Lynda Vannice,
Umpqua Community College

Nancy Voorhees,
Ivy Tech Community College

Benjamin Wallace,
Cleveland State University

Thomas Westcott,
University of West Florida

Keilah Worth,
St. Catherine University

Frederic Wynn,
County College of Morris

At Worth Publishers a host of people played key roles in creating this ninth edition.

Although the information gathering is never ending, the formal planning began as the author-publisher team gathered for a two-day retreat in June 2010. This happy and creative gathering included John Brink, Thomas Ludwig, Richard Straub, and me from the author team, along with my assistants Kathryn Brownson and Sara Neevel. We were joined by Worth Publishers executives Tom Scotty, Elizabeth Widdicombe, Catherine Woods, Craig Bleyer, and Mark Resmer; editors Christine Brune, Kevin Feyen, Nancy Fleming, Tracey Kuehn, Betty Probert, and Trish Morgan; artistic director Babs Reingold; sales and marketing colleagues Tom Kling, Carlise Stembridge, John Britch, Lindsay Johnson, Cindi Weiss, Kari Ewalt, Mike Howard, and Matt Ours; and special guests Amy Himsel (El Camino Community College), Jennifer Peluso (Florida Atlantic University), Charlotte vanOyen Witvliet (Hope College), and Jennifer Zwolinski (University of San Diego). The input and brainstorming during this meeting of minds gave birth, among other things, to the study aids in this edition, the carefully revised clinical coverage, the separate gender and sexuality chapter, and the refreshing new design.

Christine Brune, chief editor for the last eight editions, is a wonder worker. She offers just the right mix of encouragement, gentle admonition, attention to detail, and passion for excellence. An author could not ask for more.

Development editor Nancy Fleming is one of those rare editors who is gifted both at "thinking big" about a chapter—and with a kindred spirit to my own—while also applying her sensitive, graceful, line-by-line touches.

Publisher Kevin Feyen is a valued team leader, thanks to his dedication, creativity, and sensitivity. Catherine Woods (Senior Vice President, Editorial and Production) helped construct and execute the plan for this text and its supplements. Catherine was also a trusted sounding board as we faced a seemingly unending series of discrete decisions along the way. Elizabeth Block and Nadina Persaud coordinated production of the huge media and print supplements package for this edition. Betty Probert efficiently edited and produced the print supplements and, in the process, also helped fine-tune the whole book. Nadina also provided invaluable support in commissioning and organizing the multitude of reviews, mailing information to professors, and handling numerous other daily tasks related to the book's development and production. Lee Ann McKevitt did a splendid job of laying out each page. Bianca Moscatelli and Donna Ranieri worked together to locate the myriad photos.

Tracey Kuehn, Director of Print and Digital Development, displayed tireless tenacity, commitment, and impressive organization in leading Worth's gifted artistic production team and coordinating editorial input throughout the production process. Production Manager Sarah Segal masterfully kept the book to its tight schedule, and Art Director Babs Reingold skillfully directed creation of the beautiful new design and art program. Production Manager Stacey Alexander, along with Supplements Production Editor Edgar Bonilla, did their usual excellent work of producing the many supplements.

To achieve our goal of supporting the teaching of psychology, this teaching package not only must be authored, reviewed, edited, and produced, but also made available to teachers of psychology. For their exceptional success in doing that, our author team is grateful to Worth Publishers' professional sales and marketing team. We are especially grateful to Executive Marketing Manager Kate Nurre, Marketing Manager Lindsay Johnson, and National Psychology and Economics Consultant Tom Kling both for their tireless efforts to inform our teaching colleagues of our efforts to assist their teaching, and for the joy of working with them.

At Hope College, the supporting team members for this edition included Kathryn Brownson, who researched countless bits of information and proofed hundreds of pages. Kathryn has become a knowledgeable and sensitive adviser on many matters, and Sara Neevel has become our high-tech manuscript developer, par excellence.

Again, I gratefully acknowledge the influence and editing assistance of my writing coach, poet Jack Ridl, whose influence resides in the voice you will be hearing in the pages that follow. He, more than anyone, cultivated my delight in dancing with the language, and taught me to approach writing as a craft that shades into art.

After hearing countless dozens of people say that this book's supplements have taken their teaching to a new level, I reflect on how fortunate I am to be a part of a team in which everyone has produced on-time work marked by the highest professional standards. For their remarkable talents, their long-term dedication, and their friendship, I thank John Brink, Thomas Ludwig, and Richard Straub, and I welcome Jennifer Peluso (Florida Atlantic University) to our teaching package team. I am grateful for Jenny's excellent work—building on the many years of creative effort contributed by the late Martin Bolt.

Finally, my gratitude extends to the many students and instructors who have written to offer suggestions, or just an encouraging word. It is for them, and those about to begin their study of psychology, that I have done my best to introduce the field I love.

The day this book went to press was the day I started gathering information and ideas for the tenth edition. Your input will again influence how this book continues to evolve. So, please, do share your thoughts.

David Myers

Hope College
Holland, Michigan 49422-9000 USA
davidmyers.org

www.tinyurl.com/MeetDavidMyers

TIME MANAGEMENT: OR, HOW TO BE A GREAT STUDENT AND STILL HAVE A LIFE

—Richard O. Straub University of Michigan, Dearborn

© Nick Parkas

Motivated students: This course at Bunker Hill Community College meets at the increasingly popular time of midnight to 2:00 A.M., allowing shift workers, busy parents, and others to make it to class.

We all face challenges in our schedules. Some of you may be taking midnight courses, others squeezing in an online course in between jobs or after putting children to bed at night. Some of you may be veterans using military benefits to jump-start a new life.

How can you balance all of your life's demands and be successful? Time management. Manage the time you have so that you can find the time you need.

In this section, I will outline a simple, four-step process for improving the way you make use of your time.

1. Keep a time-use diary to understand how you are using your time. You may be surprised at how much time you're wasting.

2. Design a new schedule for using your time more effectively.

3. Make the most of your study time so that your new schedule will work for you.

4. If necessary, refine your new schedule, based on what you've learned.

How Are You Using Your Time Now?

Although everyone gets 24 hours in the day and seven days in the week, we fill those hours and days with different obligations and interests. If you are like most people, you probably use your time wisely in some ways, and not so wisely in others. Answering the questions in **TABLE 1** can help you find trouble spots—and hopefully more time for the things that matter most to you.

The next thing you need to know is how you *actually* spend your time. To find out, record your activities in a *time-use diary* for one week. Be realistic. Take notes on how much time you spend attending class, studying, working, commuting, meeting personal and family needs, fixing and eating meals, socializing (don't forget texting, Facebooking, and gaming), exercising, and anything else that occupies your time, including life's small practical tasks, which can take up plenty of your 24/7. As you record your activities, take notes on how you are feeling at various times of the day. When does your energy slump, and when do you feel most energetic?

Design a Better Schedule

Take a good look at your time-use diary. Where do you think you may be wasting time? Do you spend a lot of time commuting, for example? If so, could you use that time more productively? If you take public transportation, commuting is a great time to read and test yourself for review.

Did you remember to include time for meals, personal care, work schedules, family commitments, and other fixed activities?

How much time do you sleep? In the battle to meet all of life's daily commitments and interests, we tend to treat sleep as optional. Do your best to manage your life so that you can get enough sleep to feel rested. You will feel better and be healthier, and you will also do better academically and in relationships with your family and friends. (You will read more about this in Chapter 3.)

Are you dedicating enough time for focused study? Take a last look at your notes to see if any other patterns pop out. Now it's time to create a new and more efficient schedule.

Plan the Term

Before you draw up your new schedule, think ahead. Buy a portable calendar that covers the entire school term, with a writing space for each day. Using the course outlines provided by your instructors, enter the dates of all exams, term-paper deadlines, and other important assignments. Also be sure to enter your own long-range personal plans (work and family commitments, etc.). Carry this calendar with you each day. Keep it up-to-date, refer to it often, and change it as needed. Through this process, you will develop a regular schedule that will help you achieve success.

Plan Your Week

To pass those exams, meet those deadlines, and keep up with your life outside of class, you will need to convert your long-term goals into a daily schedule. Be realistic—you will be living with this routine for the entire school term. Here are some more things to add to that portable calendar.

1. Enter your class times, work hours, and any other fixed obligations. Be thorough. Allow plenty of time for such things as commuting, meals, and laundry.

2. Set up a study schedule for each course. Remember what you learned about yourself in the study habits survey (Table 1) and your time-use diary. Close-Up: More Tips for Effective Scheduling (next page) offers some detailed guidance drawn from psychology's research.

3. After you have budgeted time for studying, fill in slots for other obligations, exercise, fun, and relaxation.

Table 1
Study Habits Survey

Answer the following questions, writing *Yes* or *No* for each line.

1. Do you usually set up a schedule to budget your time for studying, work, recreation, and other activities? _____

2. Do you often put off studying until time pressures force you to cram? _____

3. Do other students seem to study less than you do, but get better grades? _____

4. Do you usually spend hours at a time studying one subject, rather than dividing that time among several subjects? _____

5. Do you often have trouble remembering what you have just read in a textbook? _____

6. Before reading a chapter in a textbook, do you skim through it and read the section headings? _____

7. Do you try to predict test questions from your class notes and reading? _____

8. Do you usually try to summarize in your own words what you have just finished reading? _____

9. Do you find it difficult to concentrate for very long when you study? _____

10. Do you often feel that you studied the wrong material for a test? _____

Thousands of students have participated in similar surveys. Students who are fully realizing their academic potential usually respond as follows: (1) yes, (2) no, (3) no, (4) no, (5) no, (6) yes, (7) yes, (8) yes, (9) no, (10) no.

Do your responses fit that pattern? If not, you could benefit from improving your time management and study habits.

CLOSE UP

More Tips for Effective Scheduling

There are a few other things you will want to keep in mind when you set up your schedule.

Spaced study is more effective than massed study. If you need 3 hours to study one subject, for example, it's best to divide that into shorter periods spaced over several days.

Alternate subjects, but avoid interference. Alternating the subjects you study in any given session will keep you fresh and will, surprisingly, increase your ability to remember what you're learning in each different area. Studying similar topics back-to-back, however, such as two different foreign languages, could lead to interference in your learning. (You will hear more about this in Chapter 8.)

Determine the amount of study time you need to do well in each course. The time you need depends upon the difficulty of your courses and the effectiveness of your study methods. Ideally, you would spend at least 1 to 2 hours studying for each hour spent in class. Increase your study time slowly by setting weekly goals that will gradually bring you up to the desired level.

Create a schedule that makes sense. Tailor your schedule to meet the demands of each course. For the course that emphasizes lecture notes, plan a daily review of your notes soon after each class. If you are evaluated for class participation (for example, in a language course), allow time for a review just before the class meets. Schedule study time for your most difficult (or least motivating) courses during hours when you are the most alert and distractions are fewest.

Schedule open study time. Life can be unpredictable. Emergencies and new obligations can throw off your schedule. Or you may simply need some extra time for a project or for review in one of your courses. Try to allow for some flexibility in your schedule each week.

Following these guidelines will help you find a schedule that works for you!

Make Every Minute of Your Study Time Count

How do you study from a textbook? Many students simply read and reread in a passive manner. As a result, they remember the wrong things—the catchy stories but not the main points that show up later in test questions. To make things worse, many students take poor notes during class. Here are some tips that will help you get the most from your class and your text.

Take Useful Class Notes

Good notes will boost your understanding and retention. Are yours thorough? Do they form a sensible outline of each lecture? If not, you may need to make some changes.

Keep Each Course's Notes Separate and Organized

Keeping all your notes for a course in one location will allow you to flip back and forth easily to find answers to questions. Three options are (1) separate notebooks for each course, (2) clearly marked sections in a shared ring binder, or (3) carefully organized folders if you opt to take notes electronically. For the print options, removable pages will allow you to add new information and weed out past mistakes. Choosing notebook pages with lots of space, or using mark-up options in electronic files, will allow you to add comments when you review and revise your notes after class.

Use an Outline Format

Use roman numerals for major points, letters for supporting arguments, and so on. (See **FIGURE 1** for a sample.) In some courses, taking notes will be easy, but some instructors may be less organized, and you will have to work harder to form your outline.

Clean Up Your Notes After Class

Try to reorganize your notes soon after class. Expand or clarify your comments and clean up any hard-to-read scribbles while the material is fresh in your mind. Write important questions in the margin, or by using an electronic markup feature, next to notes that answer them. (For example: "What are the sleep stages?") This will help you when you review your notes before a test.

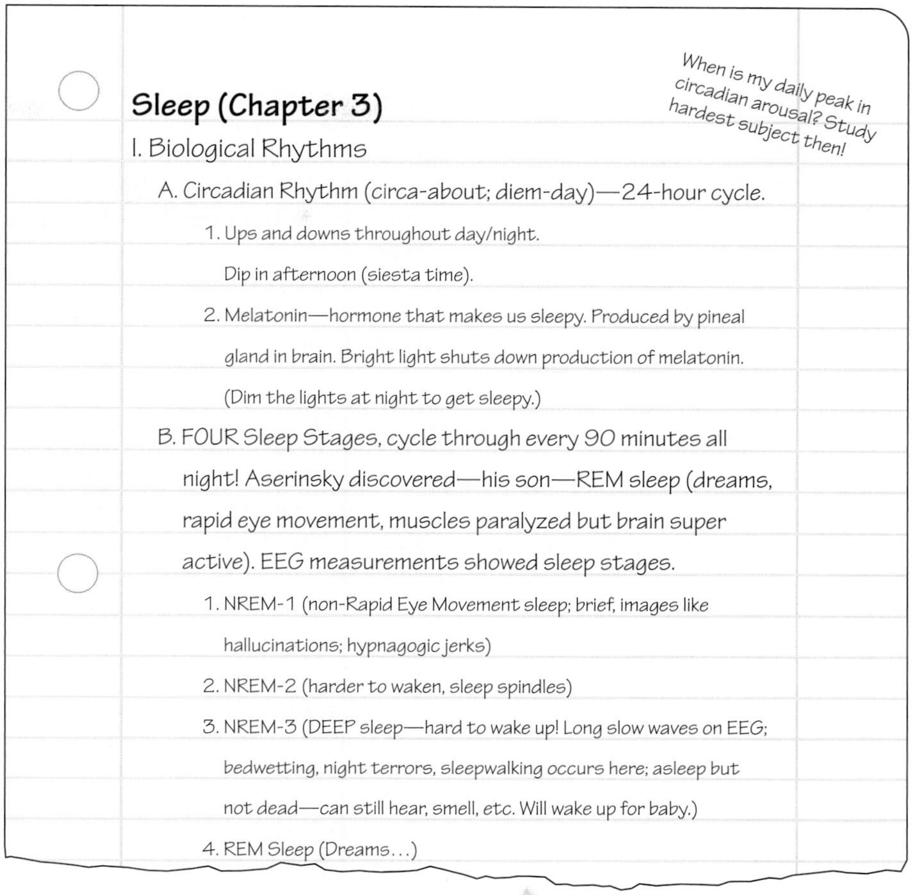

Create a Study Space That Helps You Learn

It's easier to study effectively if your work area is well designed.

Organize Your Space

Work at a desk or table, not in your bed or a comfy chair that will tempt you to nap.

Minimize Distractions

Turn the TV off, turn off your phone, and close Facebook and other distracting windows on your computer. If you must listen to music to mask outside noise, play soft instrumentals, not vocal selections that will draw your mind to the lyrics.

Ask Others to Honor Your Quiet Time

Tell roommates, family, and friends about your new schedule. Try to find a study place where you are least likely to be disturbed.

Set Specific, Realistic Daily Goals

The simple note "7–8 P.M.: Study Psychology" is too broad to be useful. Instead, break your studying into manageable tasks. For example, you will want to subdivide large reading assignments. If you aren't used to studying for long periods, start with relatively short periods of concentrated study, with breaks in between. In this text, for example, you might decide to read one major section before each break. Limit your breaks to 5 or 10 minutes to stretch or move around a bit.

Your attention span is a good indicator of whether you are pacing yourself successfully. At this early stage, it's important to remember that you're in training. If your attention begins to wander, get up immediately and take a short break. It is better to study effectively for 15 minutes and then take a break than to fritter away 45 minutes out of your study hour. As your endurance develops, you can increase the length of study periods.

Use SQ3R to Help You Master This Text

David Myers organized this text by using a system called SQ3R (Survey, Question, Read, Retrieve, Review). Using SQ3R can help you to understand what you read, and to retain that information longer.

When is my daily peak in circadian arousal? Study hardest subject then!

Sleep (Chapter 3)

I. Biological Rhythms

  A. Circadian Rhythm (circa-about; diem-day)—24-hour cycle.

    1. Ups and downs throughout day/night.

      Dip in afternoon (siesta time).

    2. Melatonin—hormone that makes us sleepy. Produced by pineal gland in brain. Bright light shuts down production of melatonin. (Dim the lights at night to get sleepy.)

  B. FOUR Sleep Stages, cycle through every 90 minutes all night! Aserinsky discovered—his son—REM sleep (dreams, rapid eye movement, muscles paralyzed but brain super active). EEG measurements showed sleep stages.

    1. NREM-1 (non-Rapid Eye Movement sleep; brief, images like hallucinations; hypnagogic jerks)

    2. NREM-2 (harder to waken, sleep spindles)

    3. NREM-3 (DEEP sleep—hard to wake up! Long slow waves on EEG; bedwetting, night terrors, sleepwalking occurs here; asleep but not dead—can still hear, smell, etc. Will wake up for baby.)

    4. REM Sleep (Dreams…)

FIGURE 1

Sample class notes in outline form Here is a sample from a student's notes taken in outline form from a lecture on sleep.

Applying SQ3R may feel at first as though it's taking more time and effort to "read" a chapter, but with practice, these steps will become automatic.

Survey

Before you read a chapter, survey its key parts. Scan the chapter outline. Note that main sections have numbered Learning Objective Questions to help you focus. Pay attention to headings, which indicate important subtopics, and to words set in bold type.

Surveying gives you the big picture of a chapter's content and organization. Understanding the chapter's logical sections will help you break your work into manageable pieces in your study sessions.

Question

As you survey, don't limit yourself to the numbered Learning Objective Questions that appear throughout the chapter. Jotting down additional questions of your own will cause you to look at the material in a new way. (You might, for example, scan this section's headings and ask "What does 'SQ3R' mean?") Information becomes easier to remember when you make it personally meaningful. Trying to answer your questions while reading will keep you in an active learning mode.

You will hear more about SQ3R in Chapter 1.

Read

As you read, keep your questions in mind and actively search for the answers. If you come to material that seems to answer an important question that you haven't jotted down, stop and write down that new question.

Be sure to read everything. Don't skip photo or art captions, graphs, boxes, tables, or quotes. An idea that seems vague when you read about it may become clear when you see it in a graph or table. Keep in mind that instructors sometimes base their test questions on figures and tables.

Retrieve

When you have found the answer to one of your questions, close your eyes and mentally recite the question and its answer. Then write the answer next to the question in your own words. Trying to explain something in your own words will help you figure out where there are gaps in your understanding. These kinds of opportunities to practice *retrieving* develop the skills you will need when you are taking exams. If you study without ever putting your book and notes aside, you may develop false confidence about what you know. With the material available, you may be able to recognize the correct answer to your questions. But will you be able to recall it later, when you take an exam without having your mental props in sight?

Test your understanding as often as you can. Testing yourself is part of successful learning, because the act of testing forces your brain to work at remembering, thus establishing the memory more permanently (so you can find it later for the exam!). Use the self-testing opportunities throughout each chapter, including the periodic Retrieve It items. Also take advantage of the self-testing that is available on the free book companion website (www.worthpublishers.com/myers).

Review

After working your way through the chapter, read over your questions and your written answers. Take an extra few minutes to create a brief written summary covering all of your questions and answers. At the end of the chapter, you should take advantage of three important opportunities for self-testing and review—a list of the chapter's Learning Objective Questions for you to try answering before checking

Appendix D (Complete Chapter Reviews), a list of the chapter's key terms for you to try to define before checking the referenced page, and a final self-test that covers all of the key chapter concepts (with answers in Appendix E).

Don't Forget About Rewards!

If you have trouble studying regularly, giving yourself a reward may help. What kind of reward works best? That depends on what you enjoy. You might start by making a list of 5 or 10 things that put a smile on your face. Spending time with a loved one, taking a walk or going for a bike ride, relaxing with a magazine or novel, or watching a favorite show can provide immediate rewards for achieving short-term study goals.

To motivate yourself when you're having trouble sticking to your schedule, allow yourself an immediate reward for completing a specific task. If running makes you smile, change your shoes, grab a friend, and head out the door! You deserve a reward for a job well done.

Do You Need to Revise Your New Schedule?

What if you've lived with your schedule for a few weeks, but you aren't making progress toward your academic and personal goals? What if your studying hasn't paid off in better grades? Don't despair and abandon your program, but do take a little time to figure out what's gone wrong.

Are You Doing Well in Some Courses But Not in Others?

Perhaps you need to shift your priorities a bit. You may need to allow more study time for Chemistry, for example, and less time for some other course.

Have You Received a Poor Grade on a Test?

Did your grade fail to reflect the effort you spent preparing for the test? This can happen to even the hardest-working student, often on a first test with a new instructor. This common experience can be upsetting. "What do I have to do to get an A?" "The test was unfair!" "I studied the wrong material!"

Try to figure out what went wrong. Analyze the questions you missed, dividing them into two categories: class-based questions and text-based questions. How many questions did you miss in each category? If you find far more errors in one category than in the other, you'll have some clues to help you revise your schedule. Depending on the pattern you've found, you can add extra study time to review of class notes, or to studying the text.

Are You Trying to Study Regularly for the First Time and Feeling Overwhelmed?

Perhaps you've set your initial goals too high. Remember, the point of time management is to identify a regular schedule that will help you achieve success. Like any skill, time management takes practice. Accept your limitations and revise your schedule to work slowly up to where you know you need to be—perhaps adding 15 minutes of study time per day.

★ ★ ★

I hope that these suggestions help make you more successful academically, and that they enhance the quality of your life in general. Having the necessary skills makes any job a lot easier and more pleasant. Let me repeat my warning not to attempt to make too drastic a change in your lifestyle immediately. Good habits require time and self-discipline to develop. Once established, they can last a lifetime.

REVIEW

Time Management: Or, How to Be a Great Student and Still Have a Life

1. How Are You Using Your Time Now?

- Identify your areas of weakness.
- Keep a time-use diary.
- Record the time you actually spend on activities.
- Record your energy levels to find your most productive times.

2. Design a Better Schedule

- Decide on your goals for the term and for each week.
- Enter class times, work times, social times (for family and friends), and time needed for other obligations and for practical activities.
- Tailor study times to avoid interference and to meet each course's needs.

3. Make Every Minute of Your Study Time Count

- Take careful class notes (in outline form) that will help you recall and rehearse material covered in lectures.
- Try to eliminate distractions to your study time, and ask friends and family to help you focus on your work.
- Set specific, realistic daily goals to help you focus on each day's tasks.
- Use the SQ3R system (survey, question, read, retrieve, review) to master material covered in your text.
- When you achieve your daily goals, reward yourself with something that you value.

4. Do You Need to Revise Your New Schedule?

- Allocate extra study time for courses that are more difficult, and a little less time for courses that are easy for you.
- Study your test results to help determine a more effective balance in your schedule.
- Make sure your schedule is not too ambitious. Gradually establish a schedule that will be effective for the long term.

Exploring
PSYCHOLOGY

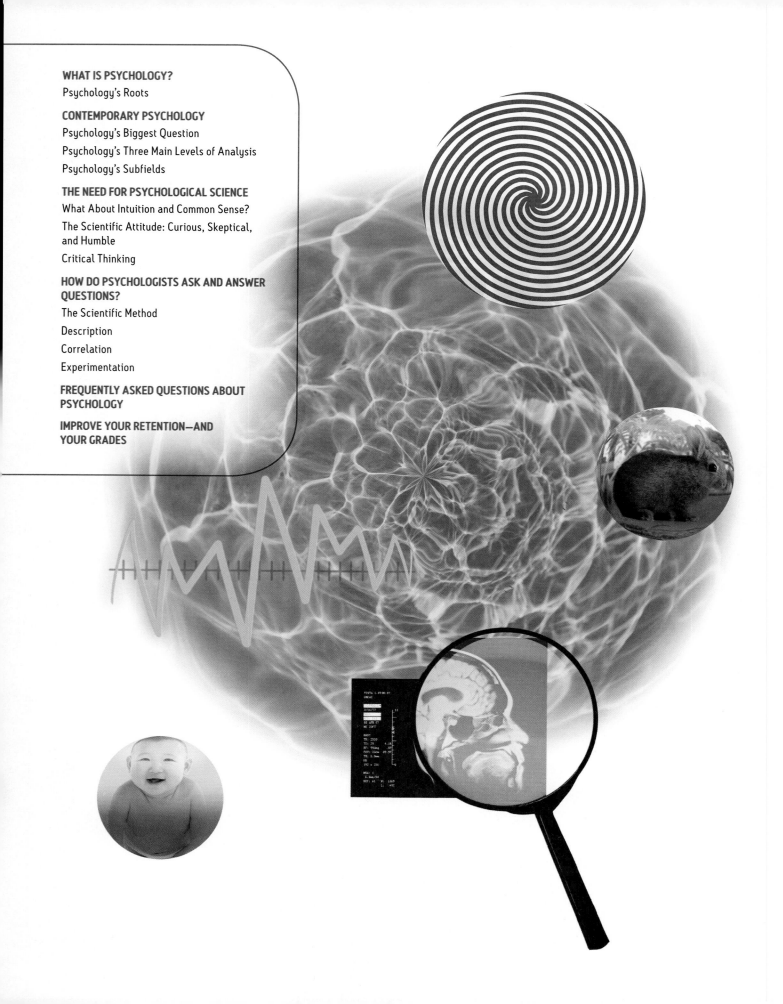

CHAPTER 1

Thinking Critically With Psychological Science

Hoping to satisfy their curiosity about people and to remedy their own woes, millions turn to "psychology." They listen to talk-radio counseling. They read articles on psychic powers. They attend stop-smoking hypnosis seminars. They immerse themselves in self-help websites and books on the meaning of dreams, the path to ecstatic love, and the roots of personal happiness.

Others, intrigued by claims of psychological truth, wonder: Do mothers and infants bond in the first hours after birth? How—and how much—does parenting shape children's personalities and abilities? What factors affect our drive to achieve? Does psychotherapy heal?

In working with such questions, how can we separate uninformed opinions from examined conclusions? *How can we best use psychology to understand why people think, feel, and act as they do?*

A smile is a smile the world around Throughout this book, you will see examples not only of our cultural and gender diversity but also of the similarities that define our shared human nature. People in different cultures vary in when and how often they smile, but a naturally happy smile *means* the same thing anywhere in the world.

What Is Psychology?

For people whose exposure to psychology comes from popular books, magazines, TV, and the Internet, psychologists seem to analyze personality, offer counseling, and dispense child-rearing advice. Do they? *Yes,* and much more. Consider some of psychology's questions, which perhaps have also been yours:

- Have you ever found yourself reacting to something as one of your biological parents would—perhaps in a way you vowed you never would—and then wondered how much of your personality you inherited? *To what extent do genes predispose our person-to-person personality differences? To what extent do home and community environments shape us?*

- Have you ever worried about how to act among people of a different culture, race, gender, or sexual orientation? *In what ways are we alike as members of the human family? How do we differ?*

- Have you ever awakened from a nightmare and, with a wave of relief, wondered why you had such a crazy dream? *How often, and why, do we dream?*

- Have you ever played peekaboo with a 6-month-old and wondered why the baby finds the game so delightful? The infant reacts as though, when you momentarily move behind a door, you actually disappear—only to reappear out of thin air. *What do babies actually perceive and think?*

- Have you ever wondered what fosters school and work success? *Are some people just born smarter? And does sheer intelligence explain why some people get richer, think more creatively, or relate more sensitively?*

- Have you ever wondered how the Internet, video games, and electronic social networks affect people? *How do today's electronic media influence how we think and how we relate?*

- Have you ever become depressed or anxious and wondered whether you'll ever feel "normal"? *What triggers our bad moods—and our good ones? What's the line between a normal mood swing and a psychological disorder for which someone should seek help?*

Psychology is a science that seeks to answer such questions.

Psychology's Roots

To assist your active learning of psychology, Learning Objectives, framed as questions, appear at the beginning of major sections. You can test your understanding by trying to answer the question before, and then again after, you read the section.

1-1: What are some important milestones in psychology's development?

To be human is to be curious about ourselves and the world around us. Before 300 B.C.E., the Greek naturalist and philosopher Aristotle theorized about learning and memory, motivation and emotion, perception and personality. Today we chuckle at some of his guesses, like his suggestion that the source of our personality is the heart. But credit Aristotle with asking the right questions.

Psychological Science Is Born

Information sources are cited in parentheses, with name and date. Every citation can be found in the end-of-book References, with complete documentation that follows American Psychological Association style.

Philosophers' thinking about thinking continued until the birth of psychology on a December day in 1879, in a small, third-floor room at Germany's University of Leipzig. There, two young men were helping an austere, middle-aged professor, Wilhelm Wundt, create an experimental apparatus. Their machine measured the time lag between people's hearing a ball hit a platform and their pressing a telegraph key (Hunt, 1993). Curiously, people responded in about one-tenth of a second when asked to press the key as soon as the sound occurred—and in about two-tenths of a second when asked to press the key as soon as they were consciously aware of perceiving the sound. (To be aware of one's awareness takes a little longer.) Wundt was seeking to measure "atoms of the mind"—the fastest and simplest mental processes. So began the first psychological laboratory, staffed by Wundt and by psychology's first graduate students.

Before long, this new science of psychology became organized into different branches, or schools of thought, each promoted by pioneering thinkers. Two early schools were **structuralism** and **functionalism.** As physicists and chemists discerned the structure of matter, so Wundt's student Edward Bradford Titchener aimed to discover the mind's structure. He engaged people in self-reflective *introspection* (looking inward), training them to report elements of their experience as they looked at a rose, listened to a metronome, smelled a scent, or tasted a substance. What were their immediate sensations, their images, their feelings? And how did these relate to one another? Alas, introspection proved somewhat unreliable. It required smart, verbal people, and its results varied from person to person and experience to experience. As introspection waned, so did structuralism.

Hoping to assemble the mind's structure from simple elements was rather like trying to understand a car by examining its disconnected parts. Philosopher-psychologist William James thought it would be more fruitful to consider the evolved *functions* of our thoughts and feelings. Smelling is what the nose does; thinking is what the brain does. But *why* do the nose and brain do these things? Under the influence of evolutionary theorist Charles Darwin, James assumed that thinking, like smelling, developed because it was *adaptive*—it contributed to our ancestors' survival. Consciousness serves a function. It enables us to consider our past, adjust to our present, and plan our future. As a *functionalist,* James encouraged explorations of down-to-earth emotions, memories, willpower, habits, and moment-to-moment streams of consciousness.

As these names illustrate, the early pioneers of most fields, including psychology, were predominantly men. In 1890, over the objections of Harvard's president, James admitted Mary Whiton Calkins into his graduate seminar (Scarborough & Furumoto, 1987). (In those years women lacked even the right to vote.) When Calkins joined, the other students (all men) dropped out. So James tutored her alone. Later, she finished all of Harvard's Ph.D. requirements, outscoring all the male students on the qualifying exams. Alas, Harvard denied her the degree she had earned, offering her instead a degree from Radcliffe College, its undergraduate "sister" school for women. Calkins resisted the unequal treatment and refused the degree. She nevertheless went on to become a distinguished memory researcher and the American Psychological Association's (APA's) first female president in 1905.

The honor of being the first female psychology Ph.D. later fell to Margaret Floy Washburn, who also wrote an influential book, *The Animal Mind,* and became the APA's second female president in 1921.

structuralism early school of thought promoted by Wundt and Titchener; used introspection to reveal the structure of the human mind.

functionalism early school of thought promoted by James and influenced by Darwin; explored how mental and behavioral processes function—how they enable the organism to adapt, survive, and flourish.

Throughout the text, important concepts are **boldfaced.** As you study, you can find these terms with their definitions in a nearby margin and in the Glossary at the end of the book.

Wilhelm Wundt Wundt established the first psychology laboratory at the University of Leipzig, Germany.
© Bettmann/Corbis

William James and Mary Whiton Calkins James was a legendary teacher-writer who authored an important 1890 psychology text. He mentored Calkins, who became a pioneering memory researcher and the first woman to be president of the American Psychological Association.
(left) Mary Evans Picture Library/Alamy; (right) Wellesley College Archives

Margaret Floy Washburn The first woman to receive a psychology Ph.D., Washburn synthesized animal behavior research in *The Animal Mind.*
Center for the History of Psychology Archives of the History of American Psychology, The University of Akron

Study Tip: Memory research reveals a *testing effect:* We retain information much better if we actively retrieve it by self-testing and rehearsing. To bolster your learning and memory, take advantage of the Retrieve It opportunities you'll find throughout this text.

RETRIEVE IT

• What event defined the start of scientific psychology?

ANSWER: Scientific psychology began in Germany in 1879 when Wilhelm Wundt opened the first psychology laboratory.

• Why did introspection fail as a method for understanding how the mind works?

ANSWER: People's self-reports varied, depending on the experience and the person's intelligence and verbal ability.

• _____ used introspection to define the mind's makeup; _____ focused on how mental processes enable us to adapt, survive, and flourish.

ANSWER: Structuralism; functionalism

Psychological Science Develops

In the field's early days, many psychologists shared with the English essayist C. S. Lewis the view that "there is one thing, and only one in the whole universe which we know more about than we could learn from external observation." That one thing, Lewis said, is ourselves: "We have, so to speak, inside information" (1960, pp. 18–19). Wundt and Titchener focused on inner sensations, images, and feelings. James engaged in introspective examination of the stream of consciousness and emotion. For these and other early pioneers, *psychology* was defined as "the science of mental life."

And so it continued until the 1920s, when the first of two provocative American psychologists appeared on the scene. John B. Watson, and later B. F. Skinner, dismissed introspection and redefined *psychology* as "the scientific study of observable *behavior*." You cannot observe a sensation, a feeling, or a thought, they said, but you *can* observe and record people's behavior as they respond to different situations. Many agreed, and the **behaviorists** became one of psychology's two major forces well into the 1960s.

The other major force was *Freudian psychology,* which emphasized the ways our unconscious thought processes and our emotional responses to childhood experiences affect our behavior. (In chapters to come, we'll look more closely at Sigmund Freud's ideas.)

As the behaviorists had rejected the early 1900s definition of psychology, two other groups rejected the behaviorist definition in the 1960s. The first, the **humanistic psychologists,** led by Carl Rogers and Abraham Maslow, found both Freudian psychology and behaviorism too limiting. Rather than focusing on the meaning of early childhood memories or on the learning of conditioned responses, the humanistic psychologists drew attention to ways that current environmental influences can nurture or limit our growth potential, and the importance of having our needs for love and acceptance satisfied. (More on this in Chapter 12.)

The second group of psychologists pioneered the 1960s *cognitive revolution,* leading the field back to its early interest in mental processes. *Cognitive psychology* scientifically explores how we perceive, process, and remember information, and even why we can get anxious or depressed. **Cognitive neuroscience,** an interdisciplinary study, has enriched our understanding of the brain activity underlying mental activity.

To encompass psychology's concern with observable behavior *and* with inner thoughts and feelings, today we define **psychology** as the *science of behavior and mental processes*. Let's unpack this definition. *Behavior* is anything an organism *does*—any action we can observe and record. Yelling, smiling, blinking, sweating, talking, and questionnaire marking are all observable behaviors. *Mental processes* are the internal, subjective experiences we infer from behavior—sensations, perceptions, dreams, thoughts, beliefs, and feelings.

John B. Watson and Rosalie Rayner Working with Rayner, Watson championed psychology as the science of behavior and demonstrated conditioned responses on a baby who became famous as "Little Albert." (More about Watson's controversial study in Chapter 7.)

(left) ©Underwood & Underwood/Corbis
(right) Center for the History of Psychology Archives of the History of American Psychology, The University of Akron

B. F. Skinner A leading behaviorist, Skinner rejected introspection and studied how consequences shape behavior.
Bachrach/Getty Images

Sigmund Freud The controversial ideas of this famed personality theorist and therapist have influenced humanity's self-understanding.
© Bettmann/Corbis

The key word in psychology's definition is *science*. Psychology is less a set of findings than a way of asking and answering questions. My aim, then, is not merely to report results but also to show you how psychologists play their game. You will see how researchers evaluate conflicting opinions and ideas. And you will learn how all of us, whether scientists or simply curious people, can think smarter when describing and explaining the events of our lives.

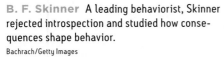

RETRIEVE IT

- How did the cognitive revolution affect the field of psychology?

ANSWER: It recaptured the field's early interest in mental processes and made them legitimate topics for scientific study.

Contemporary Psychology

This young science of psychology developed from the more established fields of philosophy and biology. Wundt was both a philosopher and a physiologist. Ivan Pavlov, who pioneered the study of learning (Chapter 7), was a Russian physiologist. Freud was an Austrian physician. Jean Piaget, the last century's most influential observer of children, (Chapter 4), was a Swiss biologist. James was an American philosopher. This list of pioneering psychologists—"Magellans of the mind," as Morton Hunt (1993) has called them—illustrates psychology's origins in many disciplines and countries.

Like the pioneers, today's psychologists are citizens of many lands. The International Union of Psychological Science has 71 member nations, from Albania to Zimbabwe. Psychology is *growing* and it is *globalizing*. The story of psychology is being written in many places, with interests ranging from nerve cell activity to international conflicts.

Psychology's Biggest Question

1-2: What is psychology's historic big issue?

Are our human traits present at birth, or do they develop through experience? The debate over this huge **nature–nurture issue** is ancient. The Greek philosopher Plato (428–348 B.C.E.) assumed that we inherit character and intelligence and that certain ideas are inborn. Aristotle (384–322 B.C.E.) countered that there is nothing in the mind that does not first come in from the external world through the senses.

behaviorism the view that psychology (1) should be an objective science that (2) studies behavior without reference to mental processes. Most research psychologists today agree with (1) but not with (2).

humanistic psychology historically significant perspective that emphasized the growth potential of healthy people.

cognitive neuroscience the interdisciplinary study of the brain activity linked with cognition (including perception, thinking, memory, and language).

psychology the science of behavior and mental processes.

nature–nurture issue the longstanding controversy over the relative contributions that genes and experience make to the development of psychological traits and behaviors. Today's psychological science sees traits and behaviors arising from the interaction of nature and nurture.

A nature-made nature–nurture experiment Because identical twins have the same genes, they are ideal participants in studies designed to shed light on hereditary and environmental influences on intelligence, personality, and other traits. Studies of identical and fraternal twins provide a rich array of findings—described in later chapters—that underscore the importance of both nature and nurture.

(left) © Hola Images/agefotostock; (right) WoodyStock /Alamy

More insight into nature's influence on behavior arose after a 22-year-old seafaring voyager, Charles Darwin, pondered the incredible species variation he encountered, including tortoises on one island that differed from those on nearby islands. His 1859 *On the Origin of Species* explained this diversity by proposing the evolutionary process of **natural selection:** From among chance variations, nature selects traits that best enable an organism to survive and reproduce in a particular environment. Darwin's principle of natural selection is still with us 150+ years later as biology's organizing principle, and now an important principle for twenty-first-century psychology. This would surely have pleased Darwin, for he believed his theory explained not only animal structures (such as a polar bear's white coat) but also animal behaviors (such as the emotional expressions associated with human lust and rage).

The nature–nurture issue recurs throughout this text as today's psychologists explore the relative contributions of biology and experience, asking, for example, how we humans are alike (because of our common biology and evolutionary history) and diverse (because of our differing environments). Are gender differences biologically predisposed or socially constructed? Is children's grammar mostly innate or formed by experience? How are intelligence and personality differences influenced by heredity, and by environment? Are sexual behaviors more "pushed" by inner biology or "pulled" by external incentives? Should we treat psychological disorders—depression, for example—as disorders of the brain, disorders of thought, or both?

Over and over again we will see that in contemporary science the nature–nurture tension dissolves: *Nurture works on what nature endows.* Our species is biologically endowed with an enormous capacity to learn and adapt. Moreover, every psychological event (every thought, every emotion) is simultaneously a biological event. Thus, depression can be both a brain disorder and a thought disorder.

RETRIEVE IT

• What is contemporary psychology's position on the nature–nurture debate?

ANSWER: Psychological events often stem from the interaction of nature and nurture, rather than from either of them acting alone.

Psychology's Three Main Levels of Analysis

1-3: What are psychology's levels of analysis and related perspectives?

natural selection the principle that, among the range of inherited trait variations, those contributing to reproduction and survival will most likely be passed on to succeeding generations.

levels of analysis the differing complementary views, from biological to psychological to social-cultural, for analyzing any given phenomenon.

biopsychosocial approach an integrated approach that incorporates biological, psychological, and social-cultural levels of analysis.

Each of us is a complex system that is part of a larger social system. But each of us is also composed of smaller systems, such as our nervous system and body organs, which are composed of still smaller systems—cells, molecules, and atoms.

These tiered systems suggest different **levels of analysis,** which offer complementary outlooks. It's like explaining why grizzly bears hibernate. Is it because hibernation helped their ancestors to survive and reproduce? Because their inner physiology drives them to do so? Because cold environments hinder food gathering during winter? Such perspectives are complementary because "everything is related to everything else" (Brewer, 1996). Together, different levels of analysis form a **biopsychosocial approach,** which integrates biological, psychological, and social-cultural factors (**FIGURE 1.1**).

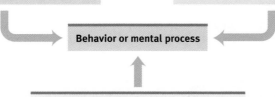

Biological influences:
- natural selection of adaptive traits
- genetic predispositions responding to environment
- brain mechanisms
- hormonal influences

Psychological influences:
- learned fears and other learned expectations
- emotional responses
- cognitive processing and perceptual interpretations

Behavior or mental process

Social-cultural influences:
- presence of others
- cultural, societal, and family expectations
- peer and other group influences
- compelling models (such as in the media)

FIGURE 1.1
Biopsychosocial approach This integrated viewpoint incorporates various levels of analysis and offers a more complete picture of any given behavior or mental process.

Each level provides a vantage point for viewing a behavior or mental process, yet each by itself is incomplete. Like different academic disciplines, psychology's varied perspectives ask different questions and have their own limits. The different perspectives described in **TABLE 1.1** complement one another. Consider, for example, how they shed light on anger:

- Someone working from a *neuroscience perspective* might study brain circuits that cause us to be "red in the face" and "hot under the collar."

- Someone working from the *evolutionary perspective* might analyze how anger facilitated the survival of our ancestors' genes.

- Someone working from the *behavior genetics perspective* might study how heredity and experience influence our individual differences in temperament.

- Someone working from the *psychodynamic perspective* might view an outburst as an outlet for unconscious hostility.

JUERGEN SCHWARZ/ AFP/Getty Images

Table 1.1

Psychology's Current Perspectives

Perspective	Focus	Sample Questions
Neuroscience	How the body and brain enable emotions, memories, and sensory experiences	How do pain messages travel from the hand to the brain? How is blood chemistry linked with moods and motives?
Evolutionary	How the natural selection of traits has promoted the survival of genes	How does evolution influence behavior tendencies?
Behavior genetics	How our genes and our environment influence our individual differences	To what extent are psychological traits such as intelligence, personality, sexual orientation, and vulnerability to depression products of our genes? Of our environment?
Psychodynamic	How behavior springs from unconscious drives and conflicts	How can someone's personality traits and disorders be explained by unfulfilled wishes and childhood traumas?
Behavioral	How we learn observable responses	How do we learn to fear particular objects or situations? What is the most effective way to alter our behavior, say, to lose weight or stop smoking?
Cognitive	How we encode, process, store, and retrieve information	How do we use information in remembering? Reasoning? Solving problems?
Social-cultural	How behavior and thinking vary across situations and cultures	How are we alike as members of one human family? How do we differ as products of our environment?

- Someone working from the *behavioral perspective* might attempt to determine which external stimuli trigger angry responses or aggressive acts.

- Someone working from the *cognitive perspective* might study how our interpretation of a situation affects our anger and how our anger affects our thinking.

- Someone working from the *social-cultural perspective* might explore how expressions of anger vary across cultural contexts.

The point to remember: Like two-dimensional views of a three-dimensional object, each of psychology's perspectives is helpful. But each by itself fails to reveal the whole picture.

> **RETRIEVE IT**
>
> - What advantage do we gain by using the biopsychosocial approach in studying psychological events?
>
> ANSWER: By incorporating different levels of analysis, the biopsychosocial approach can provide a more complete view than any one perspective could offer.

Psychology's Subfields

1-4: What are psychology's main subfields?

Picturing a chemist at work, you probably envision a white-coated scientist surrounded by glassware and high-tech equipment. Picture a psychologist at work and you would be right to envision

- a white-coated scientist probing a rat's brain.

- an intelligence researcher measuring how quickly an infant shows boredom by looking away from a familiar picture.

- an executive evaluating a new "healthy lifestyles" training program for employees.

- someone at a computer analyzing data on whether adopted teens' temperaments more closely resemble those of their adoptive parents or their biological parents.

- a therapist listening carefully to a client's depressed thoughts.

- a traveler visiting another culture and collecting data on variations in human values and behaviors.

- a teacher or writer sharing the joy of psychology with others.

"I'm a social scientist, Michael. That means I can't explain electricity or anything like that, but if you ever want to know about people I'm your man."

Psychology in court Forensic psychologists apply psychology's principles and methods in the criminal justice system. They may assess witness credibility, or testify in court on a defendant's state of mind and future risk.

Image Source/Punchstock

Ted Fitzgerald, Pool/AP Photo

The cluster of subfields we call psychology is a meeting ground for different disciplines. Thus, it's a perfect home for those with wide-ranging interests. In its diverse activities, from biological experimentation to cultural comparisons, psychology is united by a common quest: *describing and explaining behavior and the mind underlying it.*

Some psychologists conduct **basic research** that builds psychology's knowledge base. In the pages that follow we will meet a wide variety of such researchers, including *biological psychologists* exploring the links between brain and mind; *developmental psychologists* studying our changing abilities from womb to tomb; *cognitive psychologists* experimenting with how we perceive, think, and solve problems; *personality psychologists* investigating our persistent traits; and *social psychologists* exploring how we view and affect one another.

These and other psychologists also may conduct **applied research,** tackling practical problems. *Industrial-organizational psychologists,* for example, use psychology's concepts and methods in the workplace to help organizations and companies select and train employees, boost morale and productivity, design products, and implement systems.

Although most psychology textbooks focus on psychological science, psychology is also a helping profession devoted to such practical issues as how to have a happy marriage, how to overcome anxiety or depression, and how to raise thriving children. As a science, psychology at its best bases such interventions on *evidence of effectiveness.* **Counseling psychologists** help people to cope with challenges and crises (including academic, vocational, and marital issues) and to improve their personal and social functioning. **Clinical psychologists** assess and treat mental, emotional, and behavior disorders. Both counseling and clinical psychologists administer and interpret tests, provide counseling and therapy, and sometimes conduct basic and applied research. By contrast, **psychiatrists,** who also may provide psychotherapy, are medical doctors licensed to prescribe drugs and otherwise treat physical causes of psychological disorders.

To balance historic psychology's focus on human problems, Martin Seligman and others (2002, 2005, 2011) have called for more research on human strengths and human flourishing. Their **positive psychology** scientifically explores "positive emotions, positive character traits, and enabling institutions." What, they ask, can psychology contribute to a "good life" that engages one's skills, and to a "meaningful life" that points beyond oneself?

With perspectives ranging from the biological to the social, and with settings from the laboratory to the clinic, psychology relates to many fields. Psychologists teach not only in psychology departments, but also in medical schools, law schools, and theological seminaries, and they work in hospitals, factories, and corporate offices. They engage in interdisciplinary studies, such as psychohistory (the psychological analysis of historical characters), psycholinguistics (the study of language and thinking), and psychoceramics (the study of crackpots).[1]

---

[1] Confession: I wrote the last part of this sentence on April Fools' Day.

basic research pure science that aims to increase the scientific knowledge base.

applied research scientific study that aims to solve practical problems.

counseling psychology a branch of psychology that assists people with problems in living (often related to school, work, or relationships) and in achieving greater well-being.

clinical psychology a branch of psychology that studies, assesses, and treats people with psychological disorders.

psychiatry a branch of medicine dealing with psychological disorders; practiced by physicians who sometimes provide medical (for example, drug) treatments as well as psychological therapy.

positive psychology the scientific study of human functioning, with the goals of discovering and promoting strengths and virtues that help individuals and communities to thrive.

Want to learn more? See Appendix C, Subfields of Psychology, at the end of this book, and go to the regularly updated *Careers in Psychology* at www.yourpsychportal.com/myers to learn about the many interesting options available to those with bachelor's, master's, and doctoral degrees in psychology.

Psychology: A science and a profession Psychologists experiment with, observe, test, and treat behavior. Here we see psychologists testing a child, measuring emotion-related physiology, and doing face-to-face therapy.

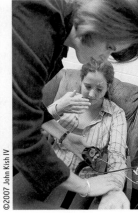

Psychology also influences culture. And psychology deepens our appreciation for how we humans perceive, think, feel, and act. By so doing it can indeed enrich our lives and enlarge our vision. Through this book I hope to help guide you toward that end. As educator Charles Eliot said a century ago: "Books are the quietest and most constant of friends, and the most patient of teachers."

RETRIEVE IT

- Match the specialty on the left with the description on the right.

  1. Clinical psychology
  2. Psychiatry
  3. Counseling psychology

  a. Helps people cope with educational and life challenges.
  b. Studies, assesses, and treats people with psychological disorders but usually does not provide medical therapy.
  c. Branch of medicine dealing with psychological disorders.

ANSWERS: 1. b, 2. c, 3. a

The Need for Psychological Science

Although in some ways we outsmart the smartest computers, our intuition often goes awry. To err is human. Enter psychological science. With its procedures for gathering and sifting evidence, science restrains error. As we familiarize ourselves with its strategies and incorporate its underlying principles into our daily thinking, we can think smarter. *Psychologists use the science of behavior and mental processes to better understand why people think, feel, and act as they do.*

What About Intuition and Common Sense?

1-5: How do hindsight bias, overconfidence, and the tendency to perceive order in random events illustrate why science-based answers are more valid than those based on intuition and common sense?

Some people suppose that psychology merely documents and dresses in jargon what people already know: "So what else is new—you get paid for using fancy methods to prove what my grandmother knew?" Others place their faith in human intuition. Former President George W. Bush described the feeling to journalist Bob Woodward (2002) in explaining his decision to launch the Iraq war: "I'm a gut player. I rely on my instincts." Today's psychological science does document a vast intuitive mind. As we will see, our thinking, memory, and attitudes operate on two levels—conscious and unconscious—with the larger part operating off-screen, automatically. Like jumbo jets, we fly mostly on autopilot.

So, are we smart to listen to the whispers of our inner wisdom, to simply trust "the force within"? Or should we more often be subjecting our intuitive hunches to skeptical scrutiny?

This much seems certain: We often underestimate intuition's perils. My geographical intuition tells me that Reno is east of Los Angeles, that Rome is south of New York, that Atlanta is east of Detroit. But I am wrong, wrong, and wrong. As novelist Madeleine L'Engle observed, "The naked intellect is an extraordinarily inaccurate instrument" (1973). Three phenomena—*hindsight bias, judgmental overconfidence,* and our *tendency to perceive patterns in random events*—illustrate why we cannot rely solely on intuition and common sense.

The limits of intuition Personnel interviewers tend to be overconfident of their gut feelings about job applicants. Their confidence stems partly from their recalling cases where their favorable impression proved right, and partly from their ignorance about rejected applicants who succeeded elsewhere.

"Those who trust in their own wits are fools."

Proverbs 28:26

Asia Images Group Pte Ltd / Alamy

Did We Know It All Along? Hindsight Bias

Consider how easy it is to draw the bull's eye *after* the arrow strikes. After the stock market drops, people say it was "due for a correction." After the football game, we credit the coach if a "gutsy play" wins the game, and fault the coach for the "stupid play" if it doesn't. After a war or an election, its outcome usually seems obvious. Although history may therefore seem like a series of inevitable events, the actual future is seldom foreseen. No one's diary recorded, "Today the Hundred Years War began."

This **hindsight bias** (also known as the *I-knew-it-all-along phenomenon*) is easy to demonstrate: Give half the members of a group some purported psychological finding, and give the other half an opposite result. Tell the first group, "Psychologists have found that separation weakens romantic attraction. As the saying goes, 'Out of sight, out of mind.'" Ask them to imagine why this might be true. Most people can, and nearly all will then view this true finding as unsurprising.

Tell the second group the opposite: "Psychologists have found that separation strengthens romantic attraction. As the saying goes, 'Absence makes the heart grow fonder.'" People given this untrue result can also easily imagine it, and most will also see it as unsurprising. When two opposite findings both seem like common sense, there is a problem.

Such errors in our recollections and explanations show why we need psychological research. Just asking people how and why they felt or acted as they did can sometimes be misleading—not because common sense is usually wrong, but because common sense more easily describes what *has* happened than what *will* happen.

Nevertheless, Grandma's intuition is often right. As Yogi Berra once said, "You can observe a lot by watching." (We have Berra to thank for other gems, such as "Nobody ever comes here—it's too crowded," and "If the people don't want to come out to the ballpark, nobody's gonna stop 'em.") Because we're all behavior watchers, it would be surprising if many of psychology's findings had *not* been foreseen. Many people believe that love breeds happiness, and they are right (we have what Chapter 10 calls a deep "need to belong"). Indeed, as Daniel Gilbert, Brett Pelham, and Douglas Krull (2003) have noted, "good ideas in psychology usually have an oddly familiar quality, and the moment we encounter them we feel certain that we once came close to thinking the same thing ourselves and simply failed to write it down." Good ideas are like good inventions; once created, they seem obvious. (Why did it take so long for someone to invent suitcases on wheels and Post-it Notes?)

hindsight bias the tendency to believe, after learning an outcome, that one would have foreseen it. (Also known as the *I-knew-it-all-along phenomenon.*)

"Life is lived forwards, but understood backwards."

Philosopher Søren Kierkegaard, 1813–1855

"Anything seems commonplace, once explained."

Dr. Watson to Sherlock Holmes

REUTERS/U.S. Coast Guard/Handout

Hindsight bias When drilling the Deepwater Horizon oil well in 2010, BP employees took some shortcuts and ignored some warning signs, without intending to put their company and the environment at serious risk. *After* the resulting Gulf oil spill, with the benefit of 20/20 hindsight, the foolishness of those judgments became obvious.

But sometimes Grandma's intuition, informed by countless casual observations, has it wrong. In later chapters we will see how research has overturned popular ideas—that familiarity breeds contempt, that dreams predict the future, and that most of us use only 10 percent of our brain. We will also see how research has surprised us with discoveries about how the brain's chemical messengers control our moods and memories, about other animals' abilities, and about the effects of stress on our capacity to fight disease.

Overconfidence

We humans tend to think we know more than we do. Asked how sure we are of our answers to factual questions *(Is Boston north or south of Paris?)*, we tend to be more confident than correct.[2] Or consider these three anagrams, which Richard Goranson (1978) asked people to unscramble:

WREAT → WATER
ETRYN → ENTRY
GRABE → BARGE

About how many seconds do you think it would have taken you to unscramble each of these? Knowing the answers tends to make us overconfident—surely the solution would take only 10 seconds or so? In reality, the average problem solver spends 3 minutes, as you also might, given a similar anagram without the solution: OCHSA.[3]

Are we any better at predicting social behavior? Ohio State University psychologist Philip Tetlock (1998, 2005) collected more than 27,000 expert predictions of world events, such as the future of South Africa or whether Quebec would separate from Canada. His repeated finding: These predictions, which experts made with 80 percent confidence on average, were right less than 40 percent of the time. Nevertheless, even those who erred maintained their confidence by noting they were "almost right." "The Québécois separatists *almost* won the secessionist referendum."

Overconfidence in history:

"We don't like their sound. Groups of guitars are on their way out."

Decca Records, in turning down a recording contract with the Beatles in 1962

"Computers in the future may weigh no more than 1.5 tons."

Popular Mechanics, 1949

"They couldn't hit an elephant at this distance."

General John Sedgwick, just before being killed during a U.S. Civil War battle, 1864

"The telephone may be appropriate for our American cousins, but not here, because we have an adequate supply of messenger boys."

British expert group, evaluating the invention of the telephone

---

RETRIEVE IT

• Why, after friends start dating, do we often feel that we *knew* they were meant to be together?

ANSWER: We often suffer from hindsight bias—after we've learned a situation's outcome, that outcome seems familiar and therefore obvious.

Perceiving Order in Random Events

In our natural eagerness to make sense of our world—what poet Wallace Stevens called our "rage for order"—we are prone to perceive patterns. People see a face on the moon, hear Satanic messages in music, or perceive the Virgin Mary's image on a grilled cheese sandwich. Even in random data we often find order, because—here's a curious fact of life—*random sequences often don't look random* (Falk et al., 2009; Nickerson, 2002, 2005). In actual random sequences, patterns and streaks (such as repeating digits) occur more often than people expect (Oskarsson et al., 2009). To demonstrate this phenomenon for myself, I flipped a coin 51 times, with these results:

1. H	11. T	21. T	31. T	41. H	51. T
2. T	12. H	22. T	32. T	42. H	
3. T	13. H	23. H	33. T	43. H	
4. T	14. T	24. T	34. T	44. H	
5. H	15. T	25. T	35. T	45. T	
6. H	16. H	26. T	36. H	46. H	
7. H	17. T	27. H	37. T	47. H	
8. T	18. T	28. T	38. T	48. T	
9. T	19. H	29. H	39. H	49. T	
10. T	20. H	30. T	40. T	50. T	

Maciej Oleksy /Shutterstock

---

[2] Boston is south of Paris.

[3] The anagram solution: CHAOS.

Looking over the sequence, patterns jump out: Tosses 10 to 22 provided an almost perfect pattern of pairs of tails followed by pairs of heads. On tosses 30 to 38 I had a "cold hand," with only one head in nine tosses. But my fortunes immediately reversed with a "hot hand"—seven heads out of the next nine tosses. Similar streaks happen—about as often as one would expect in random sequences—in basketball shooting, baseball hitting, and mutual fund stock pickers' selections (Gilovich et al., 1985; Malkiel, 2007; Myers, 2002). These sequences often don't look random and so are overinterpreted. ("When you're hot, you're hot!")

What explains these streaky patterns? Was I exercising some sort of paranormal control over my coin? Did I snap out of my tails funk and get in a heads groove? No such explanations are needed, for these are the sorts of streaks found in any random data. Comparing each toss to the next, 23 of the 50 comparisons yielded a changed result—just the sort of near 50-50 result we expect from coin tossing. Despite seeming patterns, the outcome of one toss gives no clue to the outcome of the next.

However, some happenings seem so extraordinary that we struggle to conceive an ordinary, chance-related explanation. In such cases, statisticians often are less mystified. When Evelyn Marie Adams won the New Jersey lottery *twice,* newspapers reported the odds of her feat as 1 in 17 trillion. Bizarre? Actually, 1 in 17 trillion are indeed the odds that a given person who buys a single ticket for each of two New Jersey lotteries will win both times. And given the millions of people who buy U.S. state lottery tickets, statisticians Stephen Samuels and George McCabe (1989) reported, it was "practically a sure thing" that someday, somewhere, someone would hit a state jackpot twice. Indeed, said fellow statisticians Persi Diaconis and Frederick Mosteller (1989), "with a large enough sample, any outrageous thing is likely to happen." An event that happens to but 1 in 1 billion people every day occurs about 7 times a day, over 2500 times a year.

The point to remember: Hindsight bias, overconfidence, and our tendency to perceive patterns in random events often lead us to overestimate our intuition. But scientific inquiry can help us sift reality from illusion.

Bizarre looking, perhaps. But actually no more unlikely than any other number sequence.

"The really unusual day would be one where nothing unusual happens."
Statistician Persi Diaconis (2002)

Given enough random events, some weird-seeming streaks will occur During the 2010 World Cup, a German octopus—Paul, "the oracle of Oberhausen"—was offered two boxes, each with mussels and with a national flag on one side. Paul selected the right box eight out of eight times in predicting the outcome of Germany's seven matches and Spain's triumph in the final.

The Scientific Attitude: Curious, Skeptical, and Humble

1-6: How do the scientific attitude's three main components relate to critical thinking?

Underlying all science is, first, a hard-headed *curiosity,* a passion to explore and understand without misleading or being misled. Some questions *(Is there life after death?)* are beyond science. Answering them in any way requires a leap of faith. With many other ideas *(Can some people demonstrate ESP?),* the proof is in the pudding. Let the facts speak for themselves.

The Amazing Randi The magician James Randi exemplifies skepticism. He has tested and debunked a variety of psychic phenomena.

AP Photo/Alan Diaz

Magician James Randi has used this *empirical approach* when testing those claiming to see auras around people's bodies:

RANDI: *Do you see an aura around my head?*

AURA SEER: *Yes, indeed.*

RANDI: *Can you still see the aura if I put this magazine in front of my face?*

AURA SEER: *Of course.*

RANDI: *Then if I were to step behind a wall barely taller than I am, you could determine my location from the aura visible above my head, right?*

Randi told me that no aura seer has agreed to take this simple test.

No matter how sensible-seeming or wild an idea, the smart thinker asks: *Does it work?* When put to the test, can its predictions be confirmed? Subjected to such scrutiny, crazy-sounding ideas sometimes find support. More often, science becomes society's garbage disposal, sending crazy-sounding ideas to the waste heap, atop previous claims of perpetual motion machines, miracle cancer cures, and out-of-body travels into centuries past. To sift reality from fantasy, sense from nonsense, therefore requires a scientific attitude: being skeptical but not cynical, open but not gullible.

"To believe with certainty," says a Polish proverb, "we must begin by doubting." As scientists, psychologists approach the world of behavior with a *curious skepticism,* persistently asking two questions: *What do you mean? How do you know?*

Putting a scientific attitude into practice requires not only curiosity and skepticism but also *humility*—an awareness of our own vulnerability to error and an openness to surprises and new perspectives. In the last analysis, what matters is not my opinion or yours, but the truths nature reveals in response to our questioning. If people or other animals don't behave as our ideas predict, then so much the worse for our ideas. This humble attitude was expressed in one of psychology's early mottos: "The rat is always right."

Historians of science tell us that these three attitudes—curiosity, skepticism, and humility—helped make modern science possible. Some deeply religious people today may view science, including psychological science, as a threat. Yet, many of the leaders of the scientific revolution, including Copernicus and Newton, were deeply religious people acting on the idea that "in order to love and honor God, it is necessary to fully appreciate the wonders of his handiwork" (Stark, 2003a,b).

Of course, scientists, like anyone else, can have big egos and may cling to their preconceptions. Nevertheless, the ideal of curious, skeptical, humble scrutiny of competing ideas unifies psychologists as a community as they check and recheck one another's findings and conclusions.

"I'm a skeptic not because I do not want to believe but because I want to *know*. I believe that the truth is out there. But how can we tell the difference between what we would like to be true and what is actually true? The answer is science."

Michael Shermer, "I Want to Believe," Scientific American, *2009*

"My deeply held belief is that if a god anything like the traditional sort exists, our curiosity and intelligence are provided by such a god. We would be unappreciative of those gifts . . . if we suppressed our passion to explore the universe and ourselves."

Carl Sagan, Broca's Brain, *1979*

Non Sequitur

Reprinted by permission of Universal Press Syndicate. © 1997 Wiley.

Critical Thinking

The scientific attitude prepares us to think smarter. Smart thinking, called **critical thinking,** examines assumptions, discerns hidden values, evaluates evidence, and assesses conclusions. Whether reading a news report or listening to a conversation, critical thinkers ask questions. Like scientists, they wonder, *How do they know that? What is this person's agenda? Is the conclusion based on anecdote and gut feelings, or on evidence? Does the evidence justify a cause-effect conclusion? What alternative explanations are possible?*

Has psychology's critical inquiry been open to surprising findings? The answer, as ensuing chapters illustrate, is plainly *Yes.* Believe it or not, massive losses of brain tissue early in life may have minimal long-term effects (see Chapter 2). Within days, newborns can recognize their mother's odor and voice (see Chapter 4). After brain damage, a person may be able to learn new skills yet be unaware of such learning (see Chapter 8). Diverse groups—men and women, old and young, rich and middle class, those with disabilities and without—report roughly comparable levels of personal happiness (see Chapter 11).

And has critical inquiry convincingly debunked popular presumptions? The answer, as ensuing chapters also illustrate, is again *Yes.* The evidence indicates that sleepwalkers are *not* acting out their dreams (see Chapter 3). Our past experiences are *not* all recorded verbatim in our brains; with brain stimulation or hypnosis, one *cannot* simply "hit the replay button" and relive long-buried or repressed memories (see Chapter 8). Most people do *not* suffer from unrealistically low self-esteem, and high self-esteem is not all good (see Chapter 12). Opposites do *not* generally attract (see Chapter 13). In each of these instances and more, what psychological science has learned is not what is widely believed.

> "The real purpose of the scientific method is to make sure Nature hasn't misled you into thinking you know something you don't actually know."
>
> *Robert M. Pirsig,* Zen and the Art of Motorcycle Maintenance, *1974*

RETRIEVE IT

• How does the scientific attitude contribute to critical thinking?

ANSWER: The scientific attitude combines (1) *curiosity* about the world around us, (2) *skepticism* toward various claims and ideas, and (3) *humility* about one's own understanding. Evaluating evidence, assessing conclusions, and examining our own assumptions are essential parts of critical thinking.

How Do Psychologists Ask and Answer Questions?

Psychologists arm their scientific attitude with the *scientific method*—a self-correcting process for evaluating ideas with observation and analysis. In its attempt to describe and explain human nature, psychological science welcomes hunches and plausible-sounding theories. And it puts them to the test. If a theory works—if the data support its predictions—so much the better for that theory. If the predictions fail, the theory will be revised or rejected.

The Scientific Method

1-7: How do theories advance psychological science?

In everyday conversation, we often use *theory* to mean "mere hunch." In science, a **theory** *explains* with principles that *organize* observations and *predict* behaviors or events. By organizing isolated facts, a theory simplifies. By linking facts with deeper principles, a theory offers a useful summary. As we connect the observed dots, a coherent picture emerges.

critical thinking thinking that does not blindly accept arguments and conclusions. Rather, it examines assumptions, discerns hidden values, evaluates evidence, and assesses conclusions.

theory an explanation using an integrated set of principles that organizes observations and predicts behaviors or events.

hypothesis a testable prediction, often implied by a theory.

operational definition a statement of the procedures (operations) used to define research variables. For example, *human intelligence* may be operationally defined as "what an intelligence test measures."

replication repeating the essence of a research study, usually with different participants in different situations, to see whether the basic finding extends to other participants and circumstances.

For more information about statistical methods that psychological scientists use in their work, see Appendix A, Statistical Reasoning in Everyday Life.

A good theory about sleep deprivation's effects on memory, for example, helps us organize countless sleep-related observations into a short list of principles. Imagine that we observe over and over that people with good sleep habits tend to answer questions accurately in class, and they do well at test time. We might therefore theorize that sleep improves memory. So far so good: Our sleep-retention principle neatly summarizes a list of facts about the effects of sleep loss.

Yet no matter how reasonable a theory may sound—and it does seem reasonable to suggest that sleep loss could affect memory—we must put it to the test. A good theory produces testable predictions, called **hypotheses.** By enabling us to test and to reject or revise our theory, such predictions direct research. They specify what results would support the theory and what results would disconfirm it. To test our theory about the effects of sleep on memory, we might assess people's retention of course materials after a good night's sleep, or a shortened night's sleep (**FIGURE 1.2**).

Our theories can bias our observations. Having theorized that better memory springs from more sleep, we may see what we expect: We may perceive sleepy people's comments as less insightful. The urge to see what we expect is ever-present, both inside and outside the laboratory, as when people's views of climate change influence their interpretation of local weather events.

As a check on their biases, psychologists report their research with precise **operational definitions** of procedures and concepts. *Hunger,* for example, might be defined as "hours without eating," *generosity* as "money contributed," *sleep loss* as "hours less" than one's natural sleep. Using these carefully worded statements, others can **replicate** (repeat) the original observations with different participants, materials, and circumstances. If they get similar results, confidence in the finding's reliability grows. The first study of hindsight bias aroused psychologists' curiosity. Now, after many successful replications with different people and questions, we feel sure of the phenomenon's power.

In the end, our theory will be useful if it (1) *organizes* a range of self-reports and observations, and (2) implies *predictions* that anyone can use to check the theory or to derive practical applications. (Does people's sleep predict their retention?) Eventually, our research may lead to a revised theory that better organizes and predicts what we know. Or, our research may be replicated and supported by similar findings. (This has been the case for sleep and memory studies, as you will see in Chapter 3.)

As we will see next, we can test our hypotheses and refine our theories using *descriptive* methods (which describe behaviors, often through case studies, naturalistic

FIGURE 1.2
The scientific method A self-correcting process for asking questions and observing nature's answers.

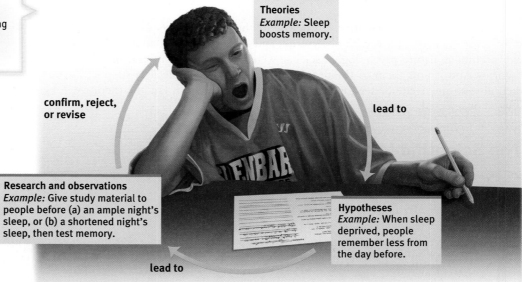

observations, or surveys), *correlational* methods (which associate different factors), and *experimental* methods (which manipulate factors to discover their effects). To think critically about popular psychology claims, we need to understand these methods and know what conclusions they allow.

case study an observation technique in which one person is studied in depth in the hope of revealing universal principles.

RETRIEVE IT

• What does a good theory do?

ANSWER: 1. It *organizes* observed facts. 2. It implies hypotheses that offer testable *predictions* and, sometimes, practical applications.

• Why is replication important?

ANSWER: Psychologists watch eagerly for new findings, but they also proceed with caution—by awaiting other investigators' repeating the research. Can the finding be confirmed (the result replicated)?

Description

1-8: How do psychologists use case studies, naturalistic observations, and surveys to observe and describe behavior, and why is random sampling important?

The starting point of any science is description. In everyday life, we all observe and describe people, often drawing conclusions about why they act as they do. Professional psychologists do much the same, though more objectively and systematically, through

- *case studies* (in-depth analyses of special individuals).
- *naturalistic observation* (watching and recording individuals' behavior in their natural setting).
- *surveys* and interviews (self-reports in which people answer questions about their behavior or attitudes).

The Case Study

Among the oldest research methods, the **case study** examines one individual in depth in the hope of revealing things true of us all. Some examples: Much of our early knowledge about the brain came from case studies of individuals who suffered a particular impairment after damage to a certain brain region. Jean Piaget taught us about children's thinking after carefully observing and questioning only a few children. Studies of only a few chimpanzees revealed their capacity for understanding and language. Intensive case studies are sometimes very revealing. They show us what *can* happen, and they often suggest directions for further study.

But individual cases may mislead us if the individual is atypical. Unrepresentative information can lead to mistaken conclusions. Indeed, anytime a researcher mentions a finding *("Smokers die younger: 95 percent of men over 85 are nonsmokers")* someone is sure to offer a contradictory anecdote *("Well, I have an uncle who smoked two packs a day and lived to be 89").* Dramatic stories and personal experiences (even psychological case examples) command our attention and are easily remembered. Journalists understand that, and so begin an article about bank foreclosures with the sad story of one family put out of their house, not with foreclosure statistics. Stories move us. But stories can mislead. Which of the following do you find more memorable? (1) "In one study of 1300 dream reports concerning a kidnapped child, only 5 percent correctly envisioned the child as dead" (Murray & Wheeler, 1937). (2) "I know a man who dreamed his sister was in a car accident, and two days later she died in a head-on collision!" Numbers can be numbing, but the plural of *anecdote* is not *evidence.* As psychologist Gordon Allport (1954, p. 9) said, "Given a thimbleful of [dramatic] facts we rush to make generalizations as large as a tub."

"'Well my dear,' said Miss Marple, 'human nature is very much the same everywhere, and of course, one has opportunities of observing it at closer quarters in a village.'"

Agatha Christie, The Tuesday Club Murders, *1933*

Freud and Little Hans Sigmund Freud's case study of 5-year-old Hans' extreme fear of horses led Freud to his theory of childhood sexuality. He conjectured that Hans felt unconscious desire for his mother, feared castration by his rival father, and then transferred this fear into his phobia about being bitten by a horse. As Chapter 12 will explain, today's psychological science discounts Freud's theory of childhood sexuality but acknowledges that much of the human mind operates outside our conscious awareness.

Skye Hohmann/Alamy

naturalistic observation observing and recording behavior in naturally occurring situations without trying to manipulate and control the situation.

survey a technique for ascertaining the self-reported attitudes or behaviors of a particular group, usually by questioning a representative, random sample of the group.

The point to remember: Individual cases can suggest fruitful ideas. What's true of all of us can be glimpsed in any one of us. But to discern the general truths that cover individual cases, we must answer questions with other research methods.

• Case studies do not enable us to learn about general principles that apply to all of us. Why not?

ANSWER: Case studies involve only one individual, so we can't know for sure whether the principles observed would apply to a larger population.

Naturalistic Observation

A second descriptive method records behavior in natural environments. These **naturalistic observations** range from watching chimpanzee societies in the jungle, to unobtrusively videotaping (and later systematically analyzing) parent-child interactions in different cultures, to recording racial differences in students' self-seating patterns in a school lunchroom.

Like the case study, naturalistic observation does not *explain* behavior. It *describes* it. Nevertheless, descriptions can be revealing. We once thought, for example, that only humans use tools. Then naturalistic observation revealed that chimpanzees sometimes insert a stick in a termite mound and withdraw it, eating the stick's load of termites. Such unobtrusive naturalistic observations paved the way for later studies of animal thinking, language, and emotion, which further expanded our understanding of our fellow animals. "Observations, made in the natural habitat, helped to show that the societies and behavior of animals are far more complex than previously supposed," chimpanzee observer Jane Goodall noted (1998). Thanks to researchers' observations, we know that chimpanzees and baboons use deception. Psychologists Andrew Whiten and Richard Byrne (1988) repeatedly saw one young baboon pretending to have been attacked by another as a tactic to get its mother to drive the other baboon away from its food. The more developed a primate species' brain, the more likely it is that the animals will display deceptive behaviors (Byrne & Corp, 2004).

A natural observer Chimpanzee researcher Frans de Waal (2005) reported, "I am a born observer. . . . When picking a seat in a restaurant I want to face as many tables as possible. I enjoy following the social dynamics—love, tension, boredom, antipathy—around me based on body language, which I consider more informative than the spoken word. Since keeping track of others is something I do automatically, becoming a fly on the wall of an ape colony came naturally to me."

Photo by Jack Kearse, Emory University for Yerkes National Primate Research Center

Naturalistic observations also illuminate human behavior. Here are three findings you might enjoy:

• *A funny finding.* We humans laugh 30 times more often in social situations than in solitary situations. (Have you noticed how seldom you laugh when alone?) As we laugh, 17 muscles contort our mouth and squeeze our eyes, and we emit a series of 75-millisecond vowel-like sounds, spaced about one-fifth of a second apart (Provine, 2001).

- *Sounding out students.* What, really, are introductory psychology students saying and doing during their everyday lives? To find out, Matthias Mehl and James Pennebaker (2003) equipped 52 such students from the University of Texas with belt-worn Electronically Activated Recorders (EARs). For up to four days, the EAR captured 30 seconds of the student's waking hours every 12.5 minutes, thus enabling the researchers to eavesdrop on more than 10,000 half-minute life slices by the end of the study. On what percentage of the slices do you suppose they found the students talking with someone? What percentage captured the students at a computer keyboard? The answers: 28 and 9 percent. (What percentage of *your* waking hours are spent in these activities?)

- *Culture, climate, and the pace of life.* Naturalistic observation also enabled Robert Levine and Ara Norenzayan (1999) to compare the pace of life in 31 countries. (Their operational definition of *pace of life* included walking speed, the speed with which postal clerks completed a simple request, and the accuracy of public clocks.) Their conclusion: Life is fastest paced in Japan and Western Europe and slower paced in economically less-developed countries. People in colder climates also tend to live at a faster pace (and are more prone to die from heart disease).

Naturalistic observation offers interesting snapshots of everyday life, but it does so without controlling for all the factors that may influence behavior. It's one thing to observe the pace of life in various places, but another to understand what makes some people walk faster than others.

Courtesy of Matthias Mehl

An EAR for naturalistic observation Psychologists Matthias Mehl and James Pennebaker have used Electronically Activated Recorders (EARs) to sample naturally occurring slices of daily life.

RETRIEVE IT

- What are the advantages and disadvantages of naturalistic observation, such as Mehl and Pennebaker used in their study?

ANSWER: Mehl and Pennebaker were able to carefully observe and record naturally occurring behaviors outside the artificiality of the lab. However, outside the lab they were not able to control for all the factors that may have influenced the everyday interactions they were recording.

The Survey

A **survey** looks at many cases in less depth. A survey asks people to report their behavior or opinions. Questions about everything from sexual practices to political opinions are put to the public. In recent surveys,

- half of all Americans reported experiencing more happiness and enjoyment than worry and stress on the previous day (Gallup, 2010).

- 1 in 5 people across 22 countries reported believing that alien beings have come to Earth and now walk among us disguised as humans (Ipsos, 2010b).

- 68 percent of all humans—some 4.6 billion people—say that religion is important in their daily lives (Diener et al., 2011).

But asking questions is tricky, and the answers often depend on question wording and respondent selection.

Wording Effects Even subtle changes in the order or wording of questions can have major effects. People are much more approving of "aid to the needy" than of "welfare," of "affirmative action" than of "preferential treatment," of "not allowing" televised cigarette ads and pornography than of "censoring" them, and of "revenue enhancers" than of "taxes." In 2009, three in four Americans in one national survey approved of giving people "a choice" of public (government-run) or private health insurance. Yet in another survey, most Americans were not in favor of "creating a public health care plan administered by the federal government that would compete directly with private health insurance companies" (Stein, 2009). Because wording is such a delicate matter, critical thinkers will reflect on how the phrasing of a question might affect people's expressed opinions.

This Modern World by Tom Tomorrow © 1991.

Random Sampling In everyday thinking, we tend to generalize from cases we observe, especially vivid cases. Given (a) a statistical summary of a professor's student evaluations and (b) the vivid comments of a biased sample—two irate students—an administrator's impression of the professor may be influenced as much by the two unhappy students as by the many favorable evaluations in the statistical summary. The temptation to ignore the *sampling bias* and to generalize from a few vivid but unrepresentative cases is nearly irresistible.

So how do you obtain a *representative sample*—say, of the students at your college or university? It's not always possible to survey the whole group you want to study and describe. How could you choose a group that would represent the total student **population?** Typically, you would seek a **random sample,** in which every person in the entire group has an equal chance of participating. You might number the names in the general student listing and then use a random number generator to pick your survey participants. (Sending each student a questionnaire wouldn't work because the conscientious people who returned it would not be a random sample.) Large representative samples are better than small ones, but a small representative sample of 100 is better than an unrepresentative sample of 500.

Political pollsters sample voters in national election surveys just this way. Using only 1500 randomly sampled people, drawn from all areas of a country, they can provide a remarkably accurate snapshot of the nation's opinions. Without random sampling, large samples—including call-in phone samples and TV or website polls—often merely give misleading results.

The point to remember: Before accepting survey findings, think critically: Consider the sample. The best basis for generalizing is from a representative sample. You cannot compensate for an unrepresentative sample by simply adding more people.

With very large samples, estimates become quite reliable. *E* is estimated to represent 12.7 percent of the letters in written English. *E,* in fact, is 12.3 percent of the 925,141 letters in Melville's *Moby Dick,* 12.4 percent of the 586,747 letters in Dickens' *A Tale of Two Cities,* and 12.1 percent of the 3,901,021 letters in 12 of Mark Twain's works (*Chance News,* 1997).

RETRIEVE IT

• What is an unrepresentative sample, and how do researchers avoid it?

ANSWER: An unrepresentative sample is a survey group that does not represent the population being studied. *Random sampling* helps researchers form a representative sample because each member of the population has an equal chance of being included.

Correlation

1-9: What are positive and negative correlations, and why do they enable prediction but not cause-effect explanation?

Describing behavior is a first step toward predicting it. Naturalistic observations and surveys often show us that one trait or behavior is related to another. In such cases, we say the two **correlate.** A statistical measure (the **correlation coefficient**) indicates how closely two things vary together, and thus how well either one *predicts* the other. Knowing how much aptitude test scores *correlate* with school success tells us how well the scores *predict* school success.

A *positive correlation* (between 0 and +1.00) indicates a *direct* relationship, meaning that two things increase together or decrease together.

A *negative correlation* (between 0 and −1.00) indicates an *inverse* relationship: As one thing increases, the other decreases. The weekly number of hours spent in TV watching and video gaming correlates negatively with grades. Negative correlations could go as low as −1.00, which means that, like people on the opposite ends of a teeter-totter, one set of scores goes down precisely as the other goes up.

Though informative, psychology's correlations usually leave most of the variation among individuals unpredicted. As we will see, there is a positive correlation between parents' abusiveness and their children's later abusiveness when they become parents. But

population all those in a group being studied, from which samples may be drawn. (*Note:* Except for national studies, this does *not* refer to a country's whole population.)

random sample a sample that fairly represents a population because each member has an equal chance of inclusion.

correlation a measure of the extent to which two factors vary together, and thus of how well either factor predicts the other.

correlation coefficient a statistical index of the relationship between two things (from −1 to +1).

this does not mean that most abused children become abusive. The correlation simply indicates a statistical relationship: Most abused children do not grow into abusers, but nonabused children are even less likely to become abusive. Correlations point us toward predictions, but usually imperfect ones.

The point to remember: A correlation coefficient helps us see the world more clearly by revealing the extent to which two things relate.

RETRIEVE IT

- Indicate whether each of the following statements describes a positive correlation or a negative correlation.

  1. The more children and youth use various media, the less happy they are with their lives (Kaiser, 2010). _____

  2. The more sexual content teens see on TV, the more likely they are to have sex (Collins et al., 2004). _____

  3. The longer children were breast-fed, the greater their later academic achievement (Horwood & Ferguson, 1998). _____

  4. The more income rose among a sample of poor families, the fewer psychiatric symptoms their children experienced (Costello et al., 2003). _____

ANSWERS: 1. negative, 2. positive, 3. positive, 4. negative

Correlation and Causation

Correlations help us predict. The *New York Times* reports that U.S. counties with high gun ownership rates tend to have high murder rates (Luo, 2011). Gun ownership predicts homicide. What might explain this guns-homicide correlation?

I can almost hear someone thinking, "Well, of course, guns kill people, often in moments of passion." If so, that could be an example of A (guns) causes B (murder). But I can hear other readers saying, "Not so fast. Maybe people in dangerous places buy more guns for self-protection—maybe B causes A." Or maybe some third factor C causes both A and B.

Another example: Self-esteem correlates negatively with (and therefore predicts) depression. (The lower people's self-esteem, the more they are at risk for depression.) So, does low self-esteem *cause* depression? If, based on the correlational evidence, you assume that it does, you have much company. A nearly irresistible thinking error is assuming that an association, sometimes presented as a correlation coefficient, proves causation. But no matter how strong the relationship, it does not.

RETRIEVE IT

- Length of marriage correlates with hair loss in men. Does this mean that marriage *causes* men to lose their hair (or that balding men make better husbands)?

ANSWER: In this case, as in many others, a third factor obviously explains the correlation: Golden anniversaries and baldness both accompany aging.

© Nancy Brown/Getty Images

As options 2 and 3 in **FIGURE 1.3** on the next page show, we'd get the same negative correlation between self-esteem and depression if depression caused people to be down on themselves, or if some third factor—such as heredity or distressing events—caused both low self-esteem and depression.

This point is so important—so basic to thinking smarter with psychology—that it merits one more example. A survey of over 12,000 adolescents found that the more teens feel loved by their parents, the less likely they are to behave in unhealthy ways—having early sex, smoking, abusing alcohol and drugs, exhibiting violence (Resnick et al., 1997). "Adults have a powerful effect on their children's

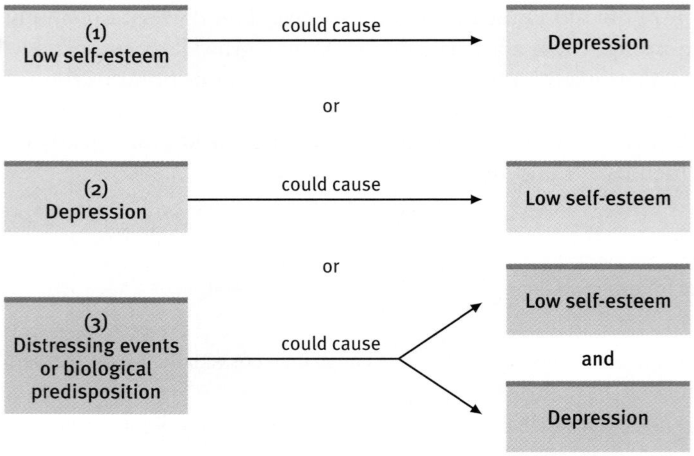

FIGURE 1.3

Three possible cause-effect relationships People low in self-esteem are more likely to report depression than are those high in self-esteem. One possible explanation of this negative correlation is that a bad self-image causes depressed feelings. But, as the diagram indicates, other cause-effect relationships are possible.

| (1) Low self-esteem | could cause → | Depression |

or

| (2) Depression | could cause → | Low self-esteem |

or

| (3) Distressing events or biological predisposition | could cause → | Low self-esteem **and** Depression |

A *New York Times* writer reported a massive survey showing that "adolescents whose parents smoked were 50 percent more likely than children of nonsmokers to report having had sex." He concluded (would you agree?) that the survey indicated a causal effect—that "to reduce the chances that their children will become sexually active at an early age" parents might "quit smoking" (O'Neil, 2002).

behavior right through the high school years," gushed an Associated Press (AP) story reporting the finding. But this correlation comes with no built-in cause-effect arrow. The AP could as well have reported, "Well-behaved teens feel their parents' love and approval; out-of-bounds teens more often think their parents are disapproving."

The point to remember (turn the volume up here): *Association does not prove causation.* Correlation indicates the *possibility* of a cause-effect relationship *but does not prove such.* Remember this principle and you will be wiser as you read and hear news of scientific studies.

Experimentation

1-10: What are the characteristics of experimentation that make it possible to isolate cause and effect?

Happy are they, remarked the Roman poet Virgil, "who have been able to perceive the causes of things." How might psychologists perceive causes in correlational studies, such as the correlation between breast feeding and intelligence?

Researchers have found that the intelligence scores of children who were breast-fed as infants are somewhat higher than the scores of children who were bottle-fed with cow's milk (Angelsen et al., 2001; Mortensen et al., 2002; Quinn et al., 2001). In Britain, breast-fed babies have also been more likely than their bottle-fed counterparts to eventually move into a higher social class (Martin et al., 2007). But the "breast is best" intelligence effect shrinks when researchers compare breast-fed and bottle-fed children from the same families (Der et al., 2006).

What do such findings mean? Do smarter mothers (who in modern countries more often breast feed) have smarter children? Or, as some researchers believe, do the nutrients of mother's milk contribute to brain development? To find answers to such questions—to isolate cause and effect—researchers can **experiment.** Experiments enable researchers to isolate the effects of one or more factors by (1) manipulating the factors of interest and (2) holding constant *(controlling)* other factors. To do so, they often create an **experimental group,** in which people receive the treatment, and a contrasting **control group** whose members do not receive the treatment. To minimize any preexisting differences between the two groups, researchers **randomly assign** people to the two conditions. If one-third of the volunteers for an experiment can wiggle their ears, then about one-third of the people in each group will be ear

Lane Oatey /Getty Images

experiment a research method in which an investigator manipulates one or more factors (independent variables) to observe the effect on some behavior or mental process (the dependent variable). By *random assignment* of participants, the experimenter aims to control other relevant factors.

experimental group in an experiment, the group exposed to the treatment, that is, to one version of the independent variable.

control group in an experiment, the group *not* exposed to the treatment; contrasts with the experimental group and serves as a comparison for evaluating the effect of the treatment.

random assignment assigning participants to experimental and control groups by chance, thus minimizing preexisting differences between the different groups.

wigglers. So, too, with ages, attitudes, and other characteristics, which will be similar in the experimental and control groups. Thus, if the groups differ at the experiment's end, we can surmise that the treatment had an effect.

To experiment with breast feeding, one research team randomly assigned some 17,000 Belarus newborns and their mothers either to a breast-feeding-promotion group or to a normal pediatric care program (Kramer et al., 2008). At three months of age, 43 percent of the experimental group infants were being exclusively breast-fed, as were 6 percent in the control group. At age 6, when nearly 14,000 of the children were restudied, those who had been in the breast-feeding-promotion group had intelligence test scores averaging six points higher than their control group counterparts.

No single experiment is conclusive, of course. But randomly assigning participants to one feeding group or the other effectively eliminated all factors except nutrition. This supported the conclusion that breast is indeed best for developing intelligence: If a behavior (such as test performance) changes when we vary an experimental factor (such as infant nutrition), then we infer that the factor is having an effect.

The point to remember: Unlike correlational studies, which uncover naturally occurring relationships, an experiment manipulates a factor to determine its effect.

Consider, then, how we might assess therapeutic interventions. Our tendency to seek new remedies when we are ill or emotionally down can produce misleading testimonies. If three days into a cold we start taking vitamin C tablets and find our cold symptoms lessening, we may credit the pills rather than the cold naturally subsiding. In the 1700s, bloodletting *seemed* effective. People sometimes improved after the treatment; when they didn't, the practitioner inferred the disease was too advanced to be reversed. So, whether or not a remedy is truly effective, enthusiastic users will probably endorse it. To determine its effect, we must control for other factors.

And that is precisely how investigators evaluate new drug treatments and new methods of psychological therapy (Chapter 15). They randomly assign participants either to the group receiving a treatment (such as a medication), or to a group receiving a pseudo-treatment—an inert *placebo* (perhaps a pill with no drug in it). The participants are often *blind* (uninformed) about what treatment, if any, they are receiving. If the study is using a **double-blind procedure,** neither the participants nor those who administer the drug or placebo and collect the data will know which group is receiving the treatment.

In such studies, researchers can check a treatment's actual effects apart from the participants' and the staff's belief in its healing powers. Just *thinking* you are getting a treatment can boost your spirits, relax your body, and relieve your symptoms. This **placebo effect** is well documented in reducing pain, depression, and anxiety (Kirsch, 2010). And the more expensive the placebo, the more "real" it seems to us—a fake pill that costs $2.50 works better than one costing 10 cents (Waber et al., 2008). To know how effective a therapy really is, researchers must control for a possible placebo effect.

double-blind procedure an experimental procedure in which both the research participants and the research staff are ignorant (blind) about whether the research participants have received the treatment or a placebo. Commonly used in drug-evaluation studies.

placebo [pluh-SEE-bo; Latin for "I shall please"] **effect** experimental results caused by expectations alone; any effect on behavior caused by the administration of an inert substance or condition, which the recipient assumes is an active agent.

"If I don't think it's going to work, will it still work?"

RETRIEVE IT

• What measure do researchers use to prevent the *placebo effect* from confusing their results?

ANSWER: Research designed to prevent the placebo effect randomly assigns participants to an experimental group (which receives the real treatment) or to a *control group* (which receives a placebo). A comparison of the results will demonstrate whether the real treatment produces better results than *belief* in that treatment.

Independent and Dependent Variables

Here is an even more potent example: The drug Viagra was approved for use after 21 clinical trials. One trial was an experiment in which researchers randomly assigned 329 men with erectile dysfunction to either an experimental group (Viagra takers) or a control group (placebo takers). It was a double-blind procedure—neither the men nor the person giving them the pills knew what they were receiving. The result: At peak doses, 69 percent of Viagra-assisted attempts at intercourse were successful, compared with 22 percent for men receiving the placebo (Goldstein et al., 1998). Viagra worked.

FIGURE 1.4

Experimentation To discern causation, psychologists may randomly assign some participants to an experimental group, others to a control group. Measuring the dependent variable (intelligence score in later childhood) will determine the effect of the independent variable (whether breast milk was promoted).

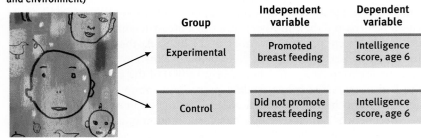

Random assignment (controlling for other variables such as parental intelligence and environment)

Group	Independent variable	Dependent variable
Experimental	Promoted breast feeding	Intelligence score, age 6
Control	Did not promote breast feeding	Intelligence score, age 6

This simple experiment manipulated just one factor: the drug dosage (none versus peak dose). We call this experimental factor the **independent variable** because we can vary it *independently* of other factors, such as the men's age, weight, and personality. These other factors, which could influence the experiment's results, are called **confounding variables.** Random assignment controls for possible confounding variables.

Experiments examine the effect of one or more independent variables on some measurable behavior, called the **dependent variable** because it can vary *depending* on what takes place during the experiment. Both variables are given precise *operational definitions,* which specify the procedures that manipulate the independent variable (in this study, the precise drug dosage and timing) or measure the dependent variable (the questions that assessed the men's responses). These definitions answer the "What do you mean?" question with a level of precision that enables others to repeat the study. (See **FIGURE 1.4** for the breast milk experiment's design.)

Let's pause to check your understanding using a simple psychology experiment: To test the effect of perceived ethnicity on the availability of rental housing, Adrian Carpusor and William Loges (2006) sent identically worded e-mail inquiries to 1115 Los Angeles–area landlords. The researchers varied the ethnic connotation of the sender's name and tracked the percentage of positive replies (invitations to view the apartment in person). "Patrick McDougall," "Said Al-Rahman," and "Tyrell Jackson" received, respectively, 89 percent, 66 percent, and 56 percent invitations.

RETRIEVE IT

• In the apartment rental experiment, what was the independent variable? The dependent variable?

ANSWER: The independent variable, which the researchers manipulated, was the ethnicity-related names. The dependent variable, which they measured, was the positive response rate.

Experiments can also help us evaluate social programs. Do early childhood education programs boost impoverished children's chances for success? What are the effects of different anti-smoking campaigns? Do school sex-education programs reduce teen pregnancies? To answer such questions, we can experiment: If an intervention is welcomed but resources are scarce, we could use a lottery to randomly assign some people (or regions) to experience the new program and others to a control condition. If later the two groups differ, the intervention's effect will be confirmed (Passell, 1993).

Let's recap. A *variable* is anything that can vary (infant nutrition, intelligence, TV exposure—anything within the bounds of what is feasible and ethical). Experiments aim to *manipulate* an *independent* variable, *measure* the *dependent* variable, and control *confounding* variables. An experiment has at least two different conditions: an *experimental condition* and a *comparison* or *control condition. Random assignment* works to minimize preexisting

independent variable the experimental factor that is manipulated; the variable whose effect is being studied.

confounding variable a factor other than the independent variable that might produce an effect in an experiment.

dependent variable the outcome factor; the variable that may change in response to manipulations of the independent variable.

Table 1.2
Comparing Research Methods

Research Method	Basic Purpose	How Conducted	What Is Manipulated	Weaknesses
Descriptive	To observe and record behavior	Do case studies, naturalistic observations, or surveys	Nothing	No control of variables; single cases may be misleading
Correlational	To detect naturally occurring relationships; to assess how well one variable predicts another	Collect data on two or more variables; no manipulation	Nothing	Does not specify cause and effect
Experimental	To explore cause and effect	Manipulate one or more factors; use random assignment	The independent variable(s)	Sometimes not feasible; results may not generalize to other contexts; not ethical to manipulate certain variables

differences between the groups before any treatment effects occur. In this way, an experiment tests the effect of at least one independent variable (what we manipulate) on at least one dependent variable (the outcome we measure). **TABLE 1.2** compares the features of psychology's research methods.

RETRIEVE IT

- Match the term on the left with the description on the right.

  1. double-blind procedure   a. helps researchers generalize from a small set of survey responses to a larger population

  2. random sampling   b. helps minimize preexisting differences between experimental and control groups

  3. random assignment   c. controls for the placebo effect; neither researchers nor participants know who receives the real treatment

  ANSWERS: 1. c, 2. a, 3. b

- Why, when testing a new drug to control blood pressure, would we learn more about its effectiveness from giving it to half the participants in a group of 1000 than to all 1000 participants?

  ANSWER: To determine the drug's effectiveness, we must compare its effect on those randomly assigned to receive it (the experimental group) with the other half of the participants (the control group), who receive a placebo. If we gave the drug to all 1000 participants, we would have no way of knowing whether the drug is serving as a placebo or is actually medically effective.

Frequently Asked Questions About Psychology

We have reflected on how a scientific approach can restrain biases. We have seen how case studies, naturalistic observations, and surveys help us describe behavior. We have also noted that correlational studies assess the association between two factors, which indicates how well one thing predicts another. We have examined the logic that underlies experiments, which use control conditions and random assignment of participants to isolate the effects of an independent variable on a dependent variable.

Yet, even knowing this much, you may still be approaching psychology with a mixture of curiosity and apprehension. So before we plunge in, let's entertain some frequently asked questions.

culture the enduring behaviors, ideas, attitudes, values, and traditions shared by a group of people and transmitted from one generation to the next.

1-11: Can laboratory experiments illuminate everyday life?

When you see or hear about psychological research, do you ever wonder whether people's behavior in the lab will predict their behavior in real life? For example, does detecting the blink of a faint red light in a dark room reveal anything useful about flying a plane at night? After viewing a violent, sexually explicit film, does an aroused man's increased willingness to push buttons that he thinks will electrically shock a woman really say anything about whether violent pornography makes a man more likely to abuse a woman?

Before you answer, consider: The experimenter *intends* the laboratory environment to be a simplified reality—one that simulates and controls important features of everyday life. Just as a wind tunnel lets airplane designers re-create airflow forces under controlled conditions, a laboratory experiment lets psychologists re-create psychological forces under controlled conditions.

An experiment's purpose is not to re-create the exact behaviors of everyday life but to test *theoretical principles* (Mook, 1983). In aggression studies, deciding whether to push a button that delivers a shock may not be the same as slapping someone in the face, but the principle is the same. *It is the resulting principles—not the specific findings—that help explain everyday behaviors.*

When psychologists apply laboratory research on aggression to actual violence, they are applying theoretical principles of aggressive behavior, principles refined through many experiments. Similarly, it is the principles of the visual system, developed from experiments in artificial settings (such as looking at red lights in the dark), that researchers apply to more complex behaviors such as night flying. And many investigations have demonstrated that principles derived in the laboratory do typically generalize to the everyday world (Anderson et al., 1999).

The point to remember: Psychological science focuses less on particular behaviors than on seeking general principles that help explain many behaviors.

1-12: Does behavior depend on one's culture and gender?

What can we learn about people in general from psychological studies done in one time and place—often with people from what Joseph Henrich, Steven Heine, and Ara Norenzayan (2010) call the WEIRD cultures (*W*estern, *E*ducated, *I*ndustrialized, *R*ich, and *D*emocratic cultures that contribute most study participants but are only 12 percent of humanity)? As we will see time and again, **culture**—shared ideas and behaviors that one generation passes on to the next—matters. Our culture shapes our standards of promptness and frankness, our attitudes toward premarital sex and varying body shapes, our tendency to be casual or formal, our willingness to make eye contact, our conversational distance, and much, much more. Being aware of such differences, we can restrain our assumptions that others will think and act as we do. Given the growing mixing and clashing of cultures, our need for such awareness is urgent.

It is also true, however, that our shared biological heritage unites us as a universal human family. The same underlying processes guide people everywhere:

- People diagnosed with dyslexia, a reading disorder, exhibit the same brain malfunction whether they are Italian, French, or British (Paulesu et al., 2001).

- Variation in languages may impede communication across cultures. Yet all languages share deep principles of grammar, and people from opposite hemispheres can communicate with a smile or a frown.

- People in different cultures vary in feelings of loneliness. But across cultures, loneliness is magnified by shyness, low self-esteem, and being unmarried (Jones et al., 1985; Rokach et al., 2002).

We are each in certain respects like all others, like some others, and like no other. Studying people of all races and cultures helps us discern our similarities and our differences, our human kinship and our diversity.

India is not Indiana Because culture shapes people's understanding of social behavior, actions that seem ordinary to us may seem quite odd to visitors from far away. Yet underlying these differences are powerful similarities. Supporters of newly elected leaders everywhere typically greet them with pleased deference, though not necessarily with bows and folded hands, as supporters of influential and popular Indian politician Sonia Gandhi did here.

Ami Vitale/Getty Images

You will see throughout this book that *gender* matters, too. Researchers report gender differences in what we dream, in how we express and detect emotions, and in our risk for alcohol dependence, depression, and eating disorders. Gender differences fascinate us, and studying them is potentially beneficial. For example, many researchers believe that women carry on conversations more readily to build relationships, while men talk more to give information and advice (Tannen, 2001). Knowing this difference can help us prevent conflicts and misunderstandings in everyday relationships.

But again, psychologically as well as biologically, women and men are overwhelmingly similar. Whether female or male, we learn to walk at about the same age. We experience the same sensations of light and sound. We feel the same pangs of hunger, desire, and fear. We exhibit similar overall intelligence and well-being.

The point to remember: Even when specific attitudes and behaviors vary by gender or across cultures, as they often do, the underlying processes are much the same.

1-13: Why do psychologists study animals, and what ethical guidelines safeguard human and animal research participants?

Many psychologists study animals because they find them fascinating. They want to understand how different species learn, think, and behave. Psychologists also study animals to learn about people. We humans are not *like* animals; we *are* animals, sharing a common biology. Animal experiments have therefore led to treatments for human diseases—insulin for diabetes, vaccines to prevent polio and rabies, transplants to replace defective organs.

Humans are more complex, but the same processes by which we learn are present in rats, monkeys, and even sea slugs. The simplicity of the sea slug's nervous system is precisely what makes it so revealing of the neural mechanisms of learning.

Sharing such similarities, should we respect rather than experiment on our animal relatives? The animal protection movement protests the use of animals in psychological, biological, and medical research.

Out of this heated debate, two issues emerge. The basic one is whether it is right to place the well-being of humans above that of animals. In experiments on stress and cancer, is it right that mice get tumors in the hope that people might not? Should some monkeys be exposed to an HIV-like virus in the search for an AIDS vaccine? Is our use and consumption of other animals as natural as the behavior of carnivorous hawks, cats, and whales? The answers to such questions vary by culture. In Gallup surveys in Canada and the United States, about 60 percent of adults have deemed medical testing on animals "morally acceptable." In Britain, only 37 percent have (Mason, 2003).

If we give human life first priority, what safeguards should protect the well-being of animals in research? In one survey of animal researchers, 98 percent supported government regulations protecting primates, dogs, and cats, and 74 percent supported regulations providing for the humane care of rats and mice (Plous & Herzog, 2000). Many professional associations and funding agencies already have such guidelines. British Psychological Society guidelines call for housing animals under reasonably natural living conditions, with companions for social animals (Lea, 2000). American Psychological Association (APA) guidelines state that researchers must ensure the "comfort, health, and humane treatment" of animals and minimize "infection, illness, and pain" (APA, 2002). The European Parliament now mandates standards for animal care and housing (Vogel, 2010).

Animals have themselves benefited from animal research. One Ohio team of research psychologists measured stress hormone levels in samples of millions of dogs brought each year to animal shelters. They devised handling and stroking methods to reduce stress and ease the dogs' transition to adoptive homes (Tuber et al., 1999). Other studies have helped improve care and management in animals' natural habitats. By revealing our behavioral kinship with animals and the remarkable intelligence of chimpanzees, gorillas, and other animals, experiments have also led to increased empathy and protection for them. At its best, a psychology concerned for humans and sensitive to animals serves the welfare of both.

"All people are the same; only their habits differ."

Confucius, 551–479 B.C.E

"Rats are very similar to humans except that they are not stupid enough to purchase lottery tickets."

Dave Barry, July 2, 2002

"Please do not forget those of us who suffer from incurable diseases or disabilities who hope for a cure through research that requires the use of animals."

Psychologist Dennis Feeney (1987)

"The greatness of a nation can be judged by the way its animals are treated."

Mahatma Gandhi, 1869-1948

Animal research benefiting animals
Thanks partly to research on the benefits of novelty, control, and stimulation, these gorillas have enjoyed an improved quality of life in New York's Bronx Zoo.

Ami Vitale/Getty Images

What about human participants? Does the image of white-coated scientists delivering electric shocks trouble you? If so, you'll be relieved to know that most psychological studies are free of such stress. With people, blinking lights, flashing words, and pleasant social interactions are more common. Moreover, psychology's experiments are mild compared with the stress and humiliation often inflicted by reality TV shows. In one episode of *The Bachelor,* a man dumped his new fiancée—on camera, at the producers' request—for the woman who earlier had finished second (Collins, 2009).

Occasionally, though, researchers do temporarily stress or deceive people, but only when they believe it is essential to a justifiable end, such as understanding and controlling violent behavior or studying mood swings. Some experiments won't work if participants know everything beforehand. (Wanting to be helpful, the participants might try to confirm the researcher's predictions.)

The APA ethics code urges researchers to (1) obtain human participants' **informed consent** before the experiment, (2) protect them from harm and discomfort, (3) keep information about individual participants confidential, and (4) fully **debrief** people (explain the research afterward). Moreover, university ethics committees screen research proposals and safeguard participants' well-being.

1-14: Is psychology free of value judgments?

Psychology is definitely not value free. Values affect what we study, how we study it, and how we interpret results. Researchers' values influence their choice of topics. Should we study worker productivity or worker morale? Sex discrimination or gender differences? Conformity or independence? Values can also color "the facts." As we noted earlier, our preconceptions can bias our observations and interpretations; sometimes we see what we want or expect to see (**FIGURE 1.5**).

Even the words we use to describe something can reflect our values. Are the sex acts we do not practice "perversions" or "sexual variations"? In psychology and in everyday speech, labels describe and labels evaluate: One person's *rigidity* is another's *consistency*. One person's *faith* is another's *fanaticism*. One country's *enhanced interrogation techniques,* such as cold-water immersion, become *torture* when practiced by its enemies. Our labeling someone as *firm* or *stubborn, careful* or *picky, discreet* or *secretive* reveals our own attitudes.

Popular applications of psychology also contain hidden values. If you defer to "professional" guidance about how to live—how to raise children, how to achieve self-fulfillment, what to do with sexual feelings, how to get ahead at work—you are accepting value-laden advice. A science of behavior and mental processes can help us reach our goals. But it cannot decide what those goals should be.

Knowledge transforms us. Learning about the solar system and the germ theory of disease alters the way people think and act. Learning about psychology's findings also changes people: They less often judge psychological disorders as moral failings, treatable by punishment and ostracism. They less often regard and treat women as men's mental inferiors. They less often view and rear children as ignorant, willful beasts in need of taming. "In each case," noted Morton Hunt (1990, p. 206), "knowledge has modified attitudes, and, through them, behavior." Once aware of psychology's well-researched ideas—about how body and mind connect, how a child's mind grows, how we construct our perceptions, how we remember (and misremember) our experiences, how people across the world differ (and are alike)—your mind may never again be quite the same.

But bear in mind psychology's limits. Don't expect it to answer the ultimate questions, such as those posed by Russian novelist Leo Tolstoy (1904): "Why should I live? Why should I do anything? Is there in life any purpose which the inevitable death that awaits me does not undo and destroy?"

Although many of life's significant questions are beyond psychology, some very important ones are illuminated by even a first psychology course. Through painstaking research, psychologists have gained insights into brain and mind, dreams and memories, depression and joy. Even the unanswered questions can renew our sense of mystery

Mike Kemp/Getty Images

© Roger Shepard

FIGURE 1.5

What do you see? Our expectations influence what we perceive. Did you see a duck or a rabbit? Show some friends this image with the rabbit photo above covered up and see if they are more likely to perceive a duck lying on its back instead. (From Shepard, 1990.)

about "things too wonderful" for us yet to understand. Moreover, your study of psychology can help teach you how to ask and answer important questions—how to think critically as you evaluate competing ideas and claims.

If some people see psychology as merely common sense, others have a different concern—that it is becoming dangerously powerful. Is it an accident that astronomy is the oldest science and psychology the youngest? To some, exploring the external universe seems far safer than exploring our own inner universe. Might psychology, they ask, be used to manipulate people?

Knowledge, like all power, can be used for good or evil. Nuclear power has been used to light up cities—and to demolish them. Persuasive power has been used to educate people—and to deceive them. Although psychology does indeed have the power to deceive, its purpose is to enlighten. Every day, psychologists are exploring ways to enhance learning, creativity, and compassion. Psychology speaks to many of our world's great problems—war, overpopulation, prejudice, family crises, crime—all of which involve attitudes and behaviors. Psychology also speaks to our deepest longings—for nourishment, for love, for happiness. Psychology cannot address all of life's great questions, but it speaks to some mighty important ones.

Psychology speaks In making its historic 1954 school desegregation decision, the U.S. Supreme Court cited the expert testimony and research of psychologists Kenneth Clark and Mamie Phipps Clark (1947). The Clarks had reported that, when given a choice between Black and White dolls, most African-American children chose the White doll, which seemingly indicated internalized anti-Black prejudice.

RETRIEVE IT

• How are human research participants protected?

ANSWER: Ethical principles developed by international psychological organizations urge researchers using human participants to obtain *informed consent*, to protect them from harm and discomfort, to treat their personal information confidentially, and to fully *debrief* all participants.

Improve Your Retention— and Your Grades

1-15: How can psychological principles help you learn and remember?

Do you, like most students, assume that the way to cement your new learning is to reread? What helps even more—and what this book therefore encourages—is repeated self-testing and rehearsal of previously studied material. Memory researchers Henry Roediger and Jeffrey Karpicke (2006) call this phenomenon the **testing effect.** (It is also sometimes called the *retrieval practice effect* or *test-enhanced learning.*) They note that "testing is a powerful means of improving learning, not just assessing it." In one of their studies, students recalled the meaning of 40 previously learned Swahili words much better if tested repeatedly than if they spent the same time restudying the words (Karpicke & Roediger, 2008).

As you will see in Chapter 8, to master information you must *actively process it.* Your mind is not like your stomach, something to be filled passively; it is more like a muscle that grows stronger with exercise. Countless experiments reveal that people learn and remember best when they put material in their own words, rehearse it, and then retrieve and review it again.

The **SQ3R** study method incorporates these principles (McDaniel et al., 2009; Robinson, 1970). SQ3R is an acronym for its five steps: *S*urvey, *Q*uestion, *R*ead, *R*etrieve[4], *R*eview.

To study a chapter, first *survey,* taking a bird's-eye view. Scan the headings, and notice how the chapter is organized.

Before you read each main section, try to answer its numbered Learning Objective *Question* (for this section: "How can psychological principles help you learn and

informed consent giving potential participants enough information about a study to enable them to decide whether they wish to participate.

debriefing the postexperimental explanation of a study, including its purpose and any deceptions, to its participants.

testing effect enhanced memory after retrieving, rather than simply rereading, information. Also sometimes referred to as a *retrieval practice effect* or *test-enhanced learning.*

SQ3R a study method incorporating five steps: *S*urvey, *Q*uestion, *R*ead, *R*etrieve, *R*eview.

---

[4] Also sometimes called "*Recite.*"

remember?"). Roediger and Bridgid Finn (2009) have found that "trying and failing to retrieve the answer is actually helpful to learning." Those who test their understanding *before* reading, and discover what they don't yet know, will learn and remember better.

Then *read,* actively searching for the answer to the question. At each sitting, read only as much of the chapter (usually a single main section) as you can absorb without tiring. Read actively and critically. Ask questions. Take notes. Make the ideas your own: How does what you've read relate to your own life? Does it support or challenge your assumptions? How convincing is the evidence?

Having read a section, *retrieve* its main ideas. *Test yourself.* This will help you figure out what you know. Moreover, the testing itself will help you learn and retain the information more effectively. Even better, test yourself repeatedly. To facilitate this, I offer periodic Retrieve It opportunities throughout each chapter (see, for example, the questions on pages 29 and 31). After trying to answer these questions yourself, you can check the inverted answers, and reread as needed.

Finally, *review:* Read over any notes you have taken, again with an eye on the chapter's organization, and quickly review the whole chapter. Write or say what a concept is before rereading to check your understanding.

Survey, question, read, retrieve, review. I have organized this book's chapters to facilitate your use of the SQ3R study system. Each chapter begins with a chapter outline that aids your *survey.* Headings and Learning Objective *Questions* suggest issues and concepts you should consider as you read. The material is organized into sections of readable length. The Retrieve It questions will challenge you to *retrieve* what you have learned, and thus better remember it. The end-of-chapter *Review* provides more opportunities for active processing and self-testing, focusing on the chapter's key terms and Learning Objective Questions. Complete Chapter Reviews can be found in Appendix D, at the end of this book.

Four additional study tips may further boost your learning:

Distribute your study time. One of psychology's oldest findings is that *spaced practice* promotes better retention than does *massed practice.* You'll remember material better if you space your practice time over several study periods—perhaps one hour a day, six days a week—rather than cram it into one long study blitz. For example, rather than trying to read an entire chapter in a single sitting, read just one main section and then turn to something else. *Interleaving* your study of psychology with your study of other subjects will boost your long-term retention and will protect against overconfidence (Kornell & Bjork, 2008; Taylor & Rohrer, 2010).

Spacing your study sessions requires a disciplined approach to managing your time. (Richard O. Straub explains time management in a helpful preface at the beginning of this text.)

Learn to think critically. Whether you are reading or in class, note people's assumptions and values. What perspective or bias underlies an argument? Evaluate evidence. Is it anecdotal? Or is it based on informative experiments? Assess conclusions. Are there alternative explanations?

Process class information actively. Listen for a lecture's main ideas and sub-ideas. *Write them down.* Ask questions during and after class. In class, as in your private study, process the information actively and you will understand and retain it better. As psychologist William James urged a century ago, *"No reception without reaction, no impression without . . . expression."* Make the information your own. Take notes in your own words. Relate what you read to what you already know. Tell someone else about it. (As any teacher will confirm, to teach is to remember.)

Overlearn. Psychology tells us that overlearning improves retention. We are prone to overestimating how much we know. You may understand a chapter as you read it, but that feeling of familiarity can be deceptively comforting. Using the Retrieve It opportunities, devote extra study time to testing your knowledge.

Memory experts Elizabeth Bjork and Robert Bjork (2011, p. 63) offer the bottom line for how to improve your retention and your grades:

OJO Images Ltd/Alamy

Spend less time on the input side and more time on the output side, such as summarizing what you have read from memory or getting together with friends and asking each other questions. Any activities that involve testing yourself—that is, activities that require you to retrieve or generate information, rather than just representing information to yourself—will make your learning both more durable and flexible.

RETRIEVE IT

• The _____ _____ describes the enhanced memory that results from repeated retrieval (as in self-testing) rather than from simple rereading of new information.

ANSWER: testing effect

• What does the acronym SQ3R stand for?

ANSWER: Survey, Question, Read, Retrieve, and Review

CHAPTER REVIEW

Thinking Critically With Psychological Science

LEARNING OBJECTIVES

Test Yourself by taking a moment to answer each of these Learning Objective Questions (repeated here from within the chapter). Then turn to Appendix D, Complete Chapter Reviews, to check your answers. Research suggests that trying to answer these questions on your own will improve your long-term memory of the concepts (McDaniel et al., 2009).

What is Psychology?

1-1: What are some important milestones in psychology's development?

Contemporary Psychology

1-2: What is psychology's historic big issue?

1-3: What are psychology's levels of analysis and related perspectives?

1-4: What are psychology's main subfields?

The Need for Psychological Science

1-5: How do hindsight bias, overconfidence, and the tendency to perceive order in random events illustrate why science-based answers are more valid than those based on intuition and common sense?

1-6: How do the scientific attitude's three main components relate to critical thinking?

How Do Psychologists Ask and Answer Questions?

1-7: How do theories advance psychological science?

1-8: How do psychologists use case studies, naturalistic observations, and surveys to observe and describe behavior, and why is random sampling important?

1-9: What are positive and negative correlations, and why do they enable prediction but not cause-effect explanation?

1-10: What are the characteristics of experimentation that make it possible to isolate cause and effect?

Frequently Asked Questions About Psychology

1-11: Can laboratory experiments illuminate everyday life?

1-12: Does behavior depend on one's culture and gender?

1-13: Why do psychologists study animals, and what ethical guidelines safeguard human and animal research participants?

1-14: Is psychology free of value judgments?

Improve Your Retention—and Your Grades

1-15: How can psychological principles help you learn and remember?

TERMS AND CONCEPTS TO REMEMBER

Test yourself on these terms by trying to write down the definition in your own words before flipping back to the referenced page to check your answer.

structuralism, p. 3
functionalism, p. 3
behaviorism, p. 4
humanistic psychology, p. 4
cognitive neuroscience, p. 4
psychology, p. 4
nature–nurture issue, p. 5
natural selection, p. 6
levels of analysis, p. 6
biopsychosocial approach, p. 6
basic research, p. 9
applied research, p. 9
counseling psychology, p. 9

clinical psychology, p. 9
psychiatry, p. 9
positive psychology, p. 9
hindsight bias, p. 11
critical thinking, p. 15
theory, p. 15
hypothesis, p. 16
operational definition, p. 16
replication, p. 16
case study, p. 17
naturalistic observation, p. 18
survey, p. 19
population, p. 20
random sample, p. 20
correlation, p. 20

correlation coefficient, p. 20
experiment, p. 22
experimental group, p. 22
control group, p. 22
random assignment, p. 22
double-blind procedure, p. 23
placebo effect, p. 23
independent variable, p. 24
confounding variable, p. 24
dependent variable, p. 24
culture, p. 26
informed consent, p. 28
debriefing, p. 28
testing effect, p. 29
SQ3R, p. 29

EXPERIENCE THE TESTING EFFECT

Test yourself repeatedly throughout your studies. This will not only help you figure out what you know and don't know; the testing itself will help you learn and remember the information more effectively thanks to the *testing effect.*

1. In 1879, in psychology's first experiment, _____ and his students measured the time lag between hearing a ball hit a platform and pressing a key.

2. William James would be considered a(n) _____. Wilhelm Wundt and Edward Titchener would be considered _____.
   a. functionalist; structuralists
   b. structuralist; functionalists
   c. evolutionary theorist; structuralists
   d. functionalist; evolutionary theorists

3. In the early twentieth century, _____ redefined psychology as "the science of observable behavior."
   a. John B. Watson
   b. Abraham Maslow
   c. William James
   d. Sigmund Freud

4. Nature is to nurture as
   a. personality is to intelligence.
   b. biology is to experience.
   c. intelligence is to biology.
   d. psychological traits are to behaviors.

5. "Nurture works on what nature endows." Describe what this means, using your own words.

6. A psychologist treating emotionally troubled adolescents at a local mental health agency is most likely to be a(n)
   a. research psychologist.
   b. psychiatrist.
   c. industrial-organizational psychologist.
   d. clinical psychologist.

7. A mental health professional with a medical degree who can prescribe medication is a _____.

8. A psychologist conducting basic research to expand psychology's knowledge base would be most likely to
   a. design a computer screen with limited glare and assess the effect on computer operators' eyes after a day's work.
   b. treat older people who are overcome by depression.
   c. observe 3- and 6-year-olds solving puzzles and analyze differences in their abilities.
   d. interview children with behavioral problems and suggest treatments.

9. _____ _____ refers to our tendency to perceive events as obvious or inevitable after the fact.

10. As scientists, psychologists
    a. approach research with a negative cynicism.
    b. assume that an article published in a reputable journal must be true.
    c. believe that every important human question can be studied scientifically.
    d. are willing to ask questions and to reject claims that cannot be verified by research.

11. How can you use your knowledge of the scientific attitude to help you evaluate claims in the media, even if you're not a scientific expert on the issue?

12. The predictions implied by a theory are called _____.

13. Which of the following is NOT one of the techniques psychologists use to observe and describe behavior?
    a. A case study
    b. Naturalistic observation
    c. Correlational research
    d. A phone survey

14. You wish to take an accurate poll in a certain country by questioning people who truly represent the country's adult population. Therefore, you need to ensure that you question a _____ sample of the population.

15. A study finds that the more childbirth training classes women attend, the less pain medication they require during childbirth. This finding can be stated as a _____ (positive/negative) correlation.

16. Knowing that two events are correlated provides
    a. a basis for prediction.
    b. an explanation of why the events are related.
    c. proof that as one increases, the other also increases.
    d. an indication that an underlying third factor is at work.

17. Here are some recently reported correlations, with interpretations drawn by journalists. Knowing just these correlations, can you come up with other possible explanations for each of these?
    a. Alcohol use is associated with violence. (One interpretation: Drinking triggers or unleashes aggressive behavior.)
    b. Educated people live longer, on average, than less-educated people. (One interpretation: Education lengthens life and enhances health.)
    c. Teens engaged in team sports are less likely to use drugs, smoke, have sex, carry weapons, and eat junk food than are teens who do not engage in team sports. (One interpretation: Team sports encourage healthy living.)
    d. Adolescents who frequently see smoking in movies are more likely to smoke. (One interpretation: Movie stars' behavior influences impressionable teens.)

18. To explain behaviors and clarify cause and effect, psychologists use _____.

19. To test the effect of a new drug on depression, we randomly assign people to control and experimental groups. Those in the control group take a pill that contains no medication. This is a _____.

20. In a double-blind procedure,
    a. only the participants know whether they are in the control group or the experimental group.
    b. experimental and control group members will be carefully matched for age, sex, income, and education level.
    c. neither the participants nor the researchers know who is in the experimental group or control group.
    d. someone separate from the researcher will ask people to volunteer for the experimental group or the control group.

21. A researcher wants to determine whether noise level affects workers' blood pressure. In one group, she varies the level of noise in the environment and records participants' blood pressure. In this experiment, the level of noise is the _____ _____.

22. The laboratory environment is designed to
    a. exactly re-create the events of everyday life.
    b. re-create psychological forces under controlled conditions.
    c. create opportunities for naturalistic observation.
    d. minimize the use of animals and humans in psychological research.

23. Which of the following is true regarding gender differences and similarities?
    a. Differences between the genders outweigh any similarities.
    b. Despite some gender differences, the underlying processes of human behavior are the same.
    c. Both similarities and differences between the genders depend more on biology than on environment.
    d. Gender differences are so numerous that it is difficult to make meaningful comparisons.

24. In defending their experimental research with animals, psychologists have noted that
    a. animals' physiology and behavior can tell us much about our own.
    b. animal experimentation sometimes helps animals as well as humans.
    c. advancing the well-being of humans justifies animal experimentation.
    d. All of these statements are correct.

Find answers to these questions in Appendix E, in the back of the book.

Experience more of the **TESTING** EFFECT

Multiple-format self-tests and more may be found at www.worthpublishers.com/myers.

CHAPTER 2

The Biology of Behavior

In 2000, a Virginia teacher began collecting sex magazines, visiting child pornography websites, and then making subtle advances on his young stepdaughter. When his wife called the police, he was arrested and later convicted of child molestation. Though put into a sexual addiction rehabilitation program, he still felt overwhelmed by his sexual urges. The day before being sentenced to prison, he went to his local emergency room complaining of a headache and thoughts of suicide. He was also distraught over his uncontrollable impulses, which led him to proposition nurses.

A brain scan located the problem—in his mind's biology. Behind his right temple there was an egg-sized brain tumor. After surgeons removed the tumor, his lewd impulses faded and he returned home to his wife and stepdaughter. Alas, a year later the tumor partially grew back, and with it the sexual urges. A second tumor removal again lessened the urges (Burns & Swerdlow, 2003).

This case illustrates what you likely believe: that you reside in your head. If surgeons transplanted all your organs below your neck, and even your skin and limbs, you would *(Yes?)* still be you. An acquaintance of mine received a new heart from a woman who, in a rare operation, had required a matched heart-lung transplant. When the two chanced to meet in their hospital ward, she introduced herself: "I think you have my heart." But only her heart. Her self, she assumed, still resided inside her skull. We rightly presume that our brain enables our mind.

Indeed, no principle is more central to today's psychology than this: *Everything psychological is simultaneously biological.*

biological psychology the scientific study of the links between biological (genetic, neural, hormonal) and psychological processes. (Some biological psychologists call themselves *behavioral neuroscientists, neuropsychologists, behavior geneticists, physiological psychologists,* or *biopsychologists.*)

neuron a nerve cell; the basic building block of the nervous system.

dendrites a neuron's bushy, branching extensions that receive messages and conduct impulses toward the cell body.

axon the neuron extension that passes messages through its branches to other neurons or to muscles or glands.

myelin [MY-uh-lin] **sheath** a fatty tissue layer segmentally encasing the axons of some neurons; enables vastly greater transmission speed as neural impulses hop from one node to the next.

glial cells (glia) cells in the nervous system that support, nourish, and protect neurons; they may also play a role in learning and thinking.

action potential a neural impulse; a brief electrical charge that travels down an axon.

threshold the level of stimulation required to trigger a neural impulse.

Biology and Behavior

2-1: Why are psychologists concerned with human biology?

Your every idea, every mood, every urge is a biological happening. You love, laugh, and cry with your body. Without your body—your genes, your brain, your appearance—you would, indeed, be nobody. Although we find it convenient to talk separately of biological and psychological influences on behavior, we need to remember: To think, feel, or act without a body would be like running without legs.

Biological psychologists study the links between our biology and behavior. In this chapter we start small and build from the bottom up—from nerve cells to the brain. We then consider how our genetic histories predispose our shared human nature, and, in combination with our environments, our individual differences.

Neural Communication

For scientists, it is a happy fact of nature that the information systems of humans and other animals operate similarly—so similarly that you could not distinguish between small samples of brain tissue from a human and a monkey. This similarity allows researchers to study relatively simple animals to discover how our neural systems operate. Cars differ, but all have engines, accelerators, steering wheels, and brakes. A Martian could study any one of them and grasp the operating principles. Likewise, animals differ, yet their nervous systems operate similarly. Though the human brain is more complex than a rat's, both follow the same principles.

Neurons

2-2: What are neurons, and how do they transmit information?

Our body's neural information system is complexity built from simplicity. Its building blocks are **neurons,** or nerve cells. To fathom our thoughts and actions, memories and moods, we must first understand how neurons work and communicate.

Neurons differ, but all are variations on the same theme (**FIGURE 2.1**). Each consists of a *cell body* and its branching fibers. The bushy **dendrite** fibers receive information and conduct it toward the cell body. From there, the cell's lengthy **axon** fiber passes the message through its terminal branches to other neurons or to muscles or glands. Dendrites listen. Axons speak.

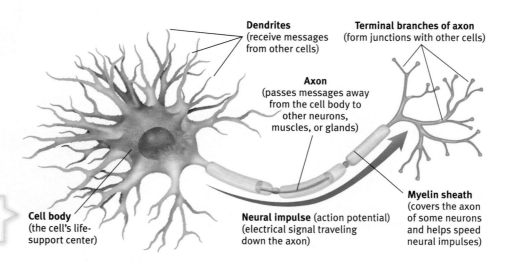

FIGURE 2.1
A motor neuron

Dendrites (receive messages from other cells)

Terminal branches of axon (form junctions with other cells)

Axon (passes messages away from the cell body to other neurons, muscles, or glands)

Cell body (the cell's life-support center)

Neural impulse (action potential) (electrical signal traveling down the axon)

Myelin sheath (covers the axon of some neurons and helps speed neural impulses)

Unlike the short dendrites, axons may be very long, projecting several feet through the body. A human neuron carrying orders to a leg muscle, for example, has a cell body and axon roughly on the scale of a basketball attached to a rope 4 miles long. Much as home electrical wire is insulated, some axons are encased in a **myelin sheath,** a layer of fatty tissue that insulates them and speeds their impulses. As myelin is laid down up to about age 25, neural efficiency, judgment, and self-control grows (Fields, 2008). If the myelin sheath degenerates, *multiple sclerosis* results: Communication to muscles slows, with eventual loss of muscle control.

Supporting our billions of nerve cells are nine times as many spidery **glial cells** ("glue cells"). Neurons are like queen bees; on their own they cannot feed or sheathe themselves. Glial cells are worker bees. They provide nutrients and insulating myelin, guide neural connections, and clean up after neurons send messages to one another. Glia may also play a role in learning and thinking. By "chatting" with neurons they may participate in information transmission and memory (Fields, 2009; Miller, 2005).

In more complex animal brains, the proportion of glia to neurons increases. A postmortem analysis of Einstein's brain did not find more or larger-than-usual neurons, but it did reveal a much greater concentration of glial cells than found in an average Albert's head (Fields, 2004).

Neuron **by sculptor Roxy Paine**

The Neural Impulse

Neurons transmit messages when stimulated by signals from our senses or when triggered by chemical signals from neighboring neurons. In response, a neuron fires an impulse, called the **action potential**—a brief electrical charge that travels down its axon.

Depending on the type of fiber, a neural impulse travels at speeds ranging from a sluggish 2 miles per hour to a breakneck 180 miles per hour. But even this top speed is 3 million times slower than that of electricity through a wire. We measure brain activity in milliseconds (thousandths of a second) and computer activity in nanoseconds (billionths of a second). Thus, unlike the nearly instantaneous reactions of a computer, your reaction to a sudden event, such as a child darting in front of your car, may take a quarter-second or more. Your brain is vastly more complex than a computer but slower at executing simple responses. And if you were an elephant—whose round-trip message travel time from a yank on the tail to the brain and back to the tail is 100 times longer than that of a tiny shrew—your reflexes would be slower yet (More et al., 2010).

Like batteries, neurons generate electricity from chemical events. In the neuron's chemistry-to-electricity process, *ions* (electrically charged atoms) are exchanged. The fluid outside an axon's membrane has mostly positively charged ions; a resting axon's fluid interior has mostly negatively charged ions. When a neuron fires, the first section of the axon opens its gates, rather like sewer covers flipping open, and positively charged sodium ions flood in through the cell membrane (**FIGURE 2.2** on the next page). This *depolarizes* that axon section, causing the next axon channel to open, and then the next, like a line of falling dominos, each tripping the next. During a resting pause, the neuron pumps the positively charged sodium ions back outside. Then it can fire again. The mind boggles when imagining this electrochemical process repeating up to 100 or even 1000 times a second. But this is just the first of many astonishments.

Each neuron is itself a miniature decision-making device performing complex calculations as it receives signals from hundreds, even thousands, of other neurons. Most signals are *excitatory,* somewhat like pushing a neuron's accelerator. Some are *inhibitory,* more like pushing its brake. If excitatory signals minus inhibitory signals exceed a minimum intensity, or **threshold,** the combined signals trigger an action potential. (Think of it this way: If the excitatory party animals outvote the inhibitory party poopers, the party's on.) The action potential then travels down the axon, which branches into junctions with hundreds or thousands of other neurons or with the body's muscles and glands.

"What one neuron tells another neuron is simply how much it is excited."

Francis Crick, The Astonishing Hypothesis, *1994*

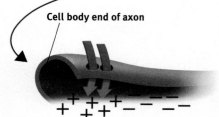

Cell body end of axon

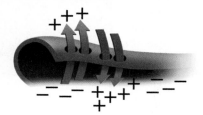

2. This depolarization produces another action potential a little farther along the axon. Gates in this neighboring area now open, and charged sodium atoms rush in. A pump in the cell membrane (the sodium/potassium pump) transports the sodium ions back out of the cell.

3. As the action potential continues speedily down the axon, the first section has now completely recharged.

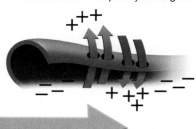

1. Neuron stimulation causes a brief change in electrical charge. If strong enough, this produces depolarization and an action potential.

Direction of action potential: toward axon terminals

FIGURE 2.2
Action potential

Increasing the level of stimulation above the threshold will not increase the neural impulse's intensity. The neuron's reaction is an *all-or-none response:* Like guns, neurons either fire or they don't. How, then, do we detect the intensity of a stimulus? How do we distinguish a gentle touch from a big hug? A strong stimulus can trigger *more* neurons to fire, and to fire more often. But it does not affect the action potential's strength or speed. Squeezing a trigger harder won't make a bullet go faster.

RETRIEVE IT

• When a neuron fires an action potential, the information travels through the axon, the dendrites, and the axon's terminal branches, but not in that order. Place these three structures in the correct order.

ANSWER: dendrites, axon, axon's terminal branches

• How does our nervous system allow us to experience the difference between a slap and a tap on the back?

ANSWER: Stronger stimuli (the slap) cause more neurons to fire and to fire more frequently than happens with weaker stimuli (the tap).

How Neurons Communicate

2-3: How do nerve cells communicate with other nerve cells?

Neurons interweave so intricately that even with a microscope you would have trouble seeing where one neuron ends and another begins. Scientists once believed that the axon of one cell fused with the dendrites of another in an uninterrupted fabric. Then British physiologist Sir Charles Sherrington (1857–1952) noticed that neural impulses were taking an unexpectedly long time to travel a neural pathway.

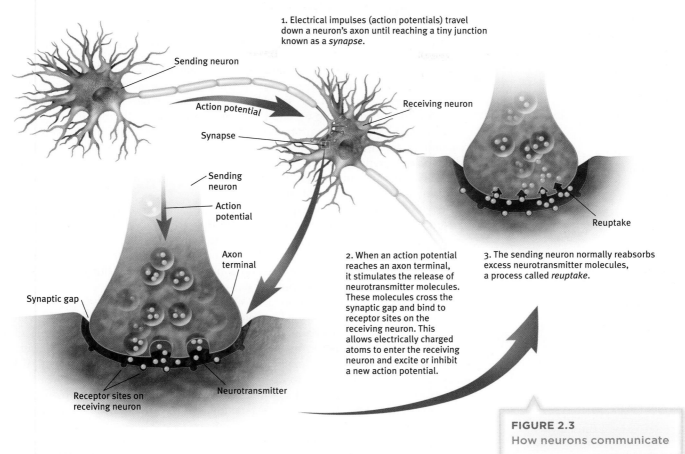

1. Electrical impulses (action potentials) travel down a neuron's axon until reaching a tiny junction known as a *synapse*.

Sending neuron

Action potential

Receiving neuron

Synapse

Sending neuron

Action potential

Axon terminal

Synaptic gap

Receptor sites on receiving neuron

Neurotransmitter

Reuptake

2. When an action potential reaches an axon terminal, it stimulates the release of neurotransmitter molecules. These molecules cross the synaptic gap and bind to receptor sites on the receiving neuron. This allows electrically charged atoms to enter the receiving neuron and excite or inhibit a new action potential.

3. The sending neuron normally reabsorbs excess neurotransmitter molecules, a process called *reuptake*.

FIGURE 2.3
How neurons communicate

Inferring that there must be a brief interruption in the transmission, Sherrington called the meeting point between neurons a **synapse.**

We now know that the axon terminal of one neuron is in fact separated from the receiving neuron by a *synaptic gap* (or *synaptic cleft*) less than a millionth of an inch wide. Spanish anatomist Santiago Ramón y Cajal (1852–1934) marveled at these near-unions of neurons, calling them "protoplasmic kisses." "Like elegant ladies air-kissing so as not to muss their makeup, dendrites and axons don't quite touch," noted poet Diane Ackerman (2004). How do the neurons execute this protoplasmic kiss, sending information across the tiny synaptic gap? The answer is one of the important scientific discoveries of our age.

When an action potential reaches the knob-like terminals at an axon's end, it triggers the release of chemical messengers, called **neurotransmitters** (**FIGURE 2.3**). Within 1/10,000th of a second, the neurotransmitter molecules cross the synaptic gap and bind to receptor sites on the receiving neuron—as precisely as a key fits a lock. For an instant, the neurotransmitter unlocks tiny channels at the receiving site, and electrically charged atoms flow in, exciting or inhibiting the receiving neuron's readiness to fire. Then, in a process called *reuptake,* the sending neuron reabsorbs the excess neurotransmitters from the synapse.

"All information processing in the brain involves neurons 'talking to' each other at synapses."

Neuroscientist Solomon H. Snyder (1984)

synapse [SIN-aps] the junction between the axon tip of the sending neuron and the dendrite or cell body of the receiving neuron. The tiny gap at this junction is called the *synaptic gap* or *synaptic cleft.*

neurotransmitters chemical messengers that cross the synaptic gaps between neurons. When released by the sending neuron, neurotransmitters travel across the synapse and bind to receptor sites on the receiving neuron, thereby influencing whether that neuron will generate a neural impulse.

RETRIEVE IT

• What happens in the *synaptic gap?*

ANSWER: Neurons send neurotransmitters (chemical messengers) across this tiny space between one neuron's terminal branch and the next neuron's dendrite or cell body.

How Neurotransmitters Influence Us

 2-4: How do neurotransmitters influence behavior?

"When it comes to the brain, if you want to see the action, follow the neurotransmitters."

Neuroscientist Floyd Bloom (1993)

In their quest to understand neural communication, researchers have discovered dozens of different neurotransmitters and almost as many new questions: Are certain neurotransmitters found only in specific places? How do they affect our moods, memories, and mental abilities? Can we boost or diminish these effects through drugs or diet?

Later chapters explore neurotransmitter influences on hunger and thinking, depression and euphoria, addictions and therapy. For now, let's glimpse how neurotransmitters influence our motions and emotions. A particular neurotransmitter may affect specific behaviors and emotions (**TABLE 2.1**), and a particular brain pathway may use only one or two neurotransmitters (**FIGURE 2.4**).

Acetylcholine (ACh), which plays a role in learning and memory, is one of the best-understood neurotransmitters. In addition, it is the messenger at every junction between motor neurons (which carry information from the brain and spinal cord to the body's tissues) and skeletal muscles. When ACh is released to our muscle cell receptors, the muscle contracts. If ACh transmission is blocked, as happens during some kinds of anesthesia, the muscles cannot contract and we are paralyzed.

Candace Pert and Solomon Snyder (1973) made an exciting discovery about neurotransmitters when they attached a radioactive tracer to morphine, showing where it was taken up in an animal's brain. The morphine, an opiate drug that elevates mood and eases pain, bound to receptors in areas linked with mood and pain sensations. But why would the brain have these "opiate receptors"? Why would it have a chemical lock, unless it also had a natural key to open it?

Physician Lewis Thomas, on the endorphins: "There it is, a biologically universal act of mercy. I cannot explain it, except to say that I would have put it in had I been around at the very beginning, sitting as a member of a planning committee."

The Youngest Science, 1983

Researchers soon confirmed that the brain does indeed produce its own naturally occurring opiates. Our body releases several types of neurotransmitter molecules similar to morphine in response to pain and vigorous exercise. These **endorphins** (short for *end*ogenous [produced within] m*orphine*) help explain good feelings such as the "runner's high," the painkilling effects of acupuncture, and the indifference to pain in some severely injured people.

Table 2.1
Some Neurotransmitters and Their Functions

Neurotransmitter	Function	Examples of Malfunctions
Acetylcholine (ACh)	Enables muscle action, learning, and memory.	With Alzheimer's disease, ACh-producing neurons deteriorate.
Dopamine	Influences movement, learning, attention, and emotion.	Oversupply linked to schizophrenia. Undersupply linked to tremors and decreased mobility in Parkinson's disease.
Serotonin	Affects mood, hunger, sleep, and arousal.	Undersupply linked to depression. Some antidepressant drugs raise serotonin levels.
Norepinephrine	Helps control alertness and arousal.	Undersupply can depress mood.
GABA (gamma-aminobutyric acid)	A major inhibitory neurotransmitter.	Undersupply linked to seizures, tremors, and insomnia.
Glutamate	A major excitatory neurotransmitter; involved in memory.	Oversupply can overstimulate brain, producing migraines or seizures (which is why some people avoid MSG, monosodium glutamate, in food).

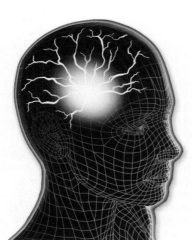

LiquidLibrary/Jupiterimages

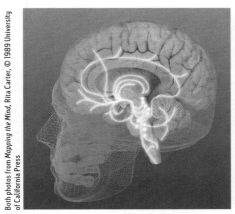
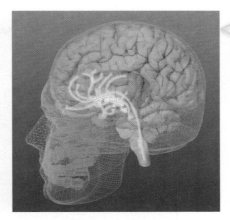

Both photos from *Mapping the Mind*, Rita Carter, © 1989 University of California Press

Serotonin pathways   Dopamine pathways

If indeed the endorphins lessen pain and boost mood, why not flood the brain with artificial opiates, thereby intensifying the brain's own "feel-good" chemistry? One problem is that when flooded with opiate drugs such as heroin and morphine, the brain may stop producing its own natural opiates. When the drug is withdrawn, the brain may then be deprived of any form of opiate, causing intense discomfort. For suppressing the body's own neurotransmitter production, nature charges a price.

RETRIEVE IT

• The endorphins, serotonin, and dopamine are all chemical messengers called _____.

ANSWER: neurotransmitters

The Nervous System

2-5: What are the functions of the nervous system's main divisions, and what are the three main types of neurons?

To live is to take in information from the world and the body's tissues, to make decisions, and to send back information and orders to the body's tissues. All this happens thanks to our body's **nervous system** (**FIGURE 2.5** on the next page). The brain and spinal cord form the **central nervous system (CNS)**, the body's decision maker. The **peripheral nervous system (PNS)** is responsible for gathering information and for transmitting CNS decisions to other body parts. **Nerves,** electrical cables formed of bundles of axons, link the CNS with the body's sensory receptors, muscles, and glands. The optic nerve, for example, bundles a million axons into a single cable carrying the messages each eye sends to the brain (Mason & Kandel, 1991).

Information travels in the nervous system through three types of neurons. **Sensory neurons** carry messages from the body's tissues and sensory receptors inward to the brain and spinal cord for processing. **Motor neurons** carry instructions from the central nervous system out to the body's muscles. Between the sensory input and motor output, information is processed via the brain's **interneurons.** Our complexity resides mostly in our interneuron systems. Our nervous system has a few million sensory neurons, a few million motor neurons, and billions and billions of interneurons.

endorphins [en-DOR-fins] "morphine within"—natural, opiate-like neurotransmitters linked to pain control and to pleasure.

nervous system the body's speedy, electrochemical communication network, consisting of all the nerve cells of the peripheral and central nervous systems.

central nervous system (CNS) the brain and spinal cord.

peripheral nervous system (PNS) the sensory and motor neurons that connect the central nervous system (CNS) to the rest of the body.

nerves bundled axons that form neural "cables" connecting the central nervous system with muscles, glands, and sense organs.

sensory (afferent) neurons neurons that carry incoming information from the sensory receptors to the brain and spinal cord.

motor (efferent) neurons neurons that carry outgoing information from the brain and spinal cord to the muscles and glands.

interneurons neurons within the brain and spinal cord that communicate internally and intervene between the sensory inputs and motor outputs.

FIGURE 2.5

The functional divisions of the human nervous system

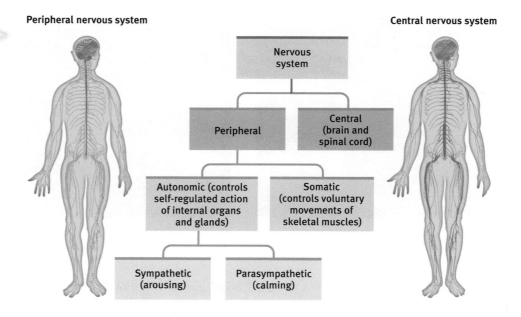

The Peripheral Nervous System

Our peripheral nervous system has two components—somatic and autonomic. Our **somatic nervous system** enables voluntary control of our skeletal muscles (and is also called the *skeletal nervous system*). As you reach the bottom of the next page, your somatic nervous system will report to your brain the current state of your skeletal muscles and carry instructions back, triggering your hand to turn the page.

Our **autonomic nervous system (ANS)** controls our glands and the muscles of our internal organs, influencing such functions as glandular activity, heartbeat, and digestion. (*Autonomic* means "self-regulating.") Like an automatic pilot, this system may be consciously overridden, but usually it operates on its own (autonomously).

The autonomic nervous system serves two important, basic functions (**FIGURE 2.6**). The **sympathetic nervous system** arouses and expends energy. If something alarms or challenges you (such as a longed-for job interview), your sympathetic nervous system will accelerate your heartbeat, raise your blood pressure, slow your digestion, raise your blood sugar, and cool you with perspiration, making you alert and ready for action. When the stress subsides (the interview is over), your **parasympathetic nervous system** will produce the opposite effects, conserving energy as it calms you by decreasing your heartbeat, lowering your blood sugar, and so forth. In everyday situations, the sympathetic and parasympathetic nervous systems work together to keep you in a steady internal state called *homeostasis* (more on this in Chapter 10).

I recently experienced my ANS in action. Before sending me into an MRI machine for a routine shoulder scan, the technician asked if I had issues with claustrophobia. "No, I'm fine," I assured her, with perhaps a hint of macho swagger. Moments later, as I found myself on my back, stuck deep inside a coffin-sized box and unable to move, my sympathetic nervous system had a different idea. As claustrophobia overtook me, my heart began pounding and I felt a desperate urge to escape. Just as I was about to cry out for release, I felt my calming parasympathetic nervous system kick in. My heart rate slowed and my body relaxed, though my arousal surged again before the 20-minute confinement ended. "You did well!" the technician said, unaware of my ANS roller-coaster ride.

somatic nervous system the division of the peripheral nervous system that controls the body's skeletal muscles. Also called the *skeletal nervous system.*

autonomic [aw-tuh-NAHM-ik] **nervous system (ANS)** the part of the peripheral nervous system that controls the glands and the muscles of the internal organs (such as the heart). Its sympathetic division arouses; its parasympathetic division calms.

sympathetic nervous system the division of the autonomic nervous system that arouses the body, mobilizing its energy in stressful situations.

parasympathetic nervous system the division of the autonomic nervous system that calms the body, conserving its energy.

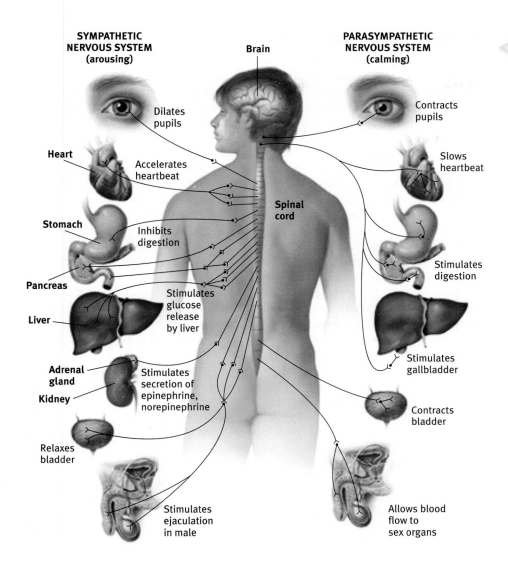

SYMPATHETIC
NERVOUS SYSTEM
(arousing)

Brain

PARASYMPATHETIC
NERVOUS SYSTEM
(calming)

Dilates
pupils

Contracts
pupils

Heart

Accelerates
heartbeat

Slows
heartbeat

Spinal
cord

Stomach

Inhibits
digestion

Stimulates
digestion

Pancreas

Liver

Stimulates
glucose
release
by liver

Stimulates
gallbladder

Adrenal
gland

Kidney

Stimulates
secretion of
epinephrine,
norepinephrine

Contracts
bladder

Relaxes
bladder

Stimulates
ejaculation
in male

Allows blood
flow to
sex organs

FIGURE 2.6
The dual functions of the autonomic nervous system The autonomic nervous system controls the more autonomous (or self-regulating) internal functions. Its sympathetic division arouses and expends energy. Its parasympathetic division calms and conserves energy, allowing routine maintenance activity. For example, sympathetic stimulation accelerates heartbeat, whereas parasympathetic stimulation slows it.

RETRIEVE IT

• Match the type of neuron to its description.

Type	Description
1. Motor neurons	a. carry incoming messages from sensory receptors to the CNS.
2. Sensory neurons	b. communicate within the CNS and intervene between incoming and outgoing messages.
3. Interneurons	c. carry outgoing messages from the CNS to muscles and glands.

ANSWERS: 1. c, 2. a, 3. b

• What bodily changes does your autonomic nervous system (ANS) direct before and after you give an important speech?

ANSWER: Responding to this challenge, your ANS' *sympathetic* division will arouse you. It accelerates your heartbeat, raises your blood pressure and blood sugar, slows your digestion, and cools you with perspiration. After you give the speech, your ANS' *parasympathetic* division will reverse these effects.

reflex a simple, automatic response to a sensory stimulus, such as the knee-jerk response.

endocrine [EN-duh-krin] **system** the body's "slow" chemical communication system; a set of glands that secrete hormones into the bloodstream.

hormones chemical messengers that are manufactured by the endocrine glands, travel through the bloodstream, and affect other tissues.

adrenal [ah-DREEN-el] **glands** a pair of endocrine glands that sit just above the kidneys and secrete hormones (epinephrine and norepinephrine) that help arouse the body in times of stress.

pituitary gland the endocrine system's most influential gland. Under the influence of the hypothalamus, the pituitary regulates growth and controls other endocrine glands.

"The body is made up of millions and millions of crumbs."

The Central Nervous System

From the simplicity of neurons "talking" to other neurons arises the complexity of the central nervous system's brain and spinal cord.

It is the brain that enables our humanity—our thinking, feeling, and acting. Tens of billions of neurons, each communicating with thousands of other neurons, yield an ever-changing wiring diagram. With some 40 billion neurons, each connecting with roughly 10,000 other neurons, we end up with perhaps 400 trillion synapses—places where neurons meet and greet their neighbors (de Courten-Myers, 2005).[1]

The brain's neurons cluster into work groups called *neural networks.* To understand why, Stephen Kosslyn and Olivier Koenig (1992, p. 12) have invited us to "think about why cities exist; why don't people distribute themselves more evenly across the countryside?" Like people networking with people, neurons network with nearby neurons with which they can have short, fast connections.

The other part of the CNS, the *spinal cord,* is a two-way information highway connecting the peripheral nervous system and the brain. Ascending neural fibers send up sensory information, and descending fibers send back motor-control information. The neural pathways governing our **reflexes**, our automatic responses to stimuli, illustrate the spinal cord's work. A simple spinal reflex pathway is composed of a single sensory neuron and a single motor neuron. These often communicate through an interneuron. The knee-jerk response, for example, involves one such simple pathway. A headless warm body could do it.

Another neural circuit enables the pain reflex (**FIGURE 2.7**). When your finger touches a flame, neural activity (excited by the heat) travels via sensory neurons to interneurons in your spinal cord. These interneurons respond by activating motor neurons leading to the muscles in your arm. Because the simple pain-reflex circuit runs through the spinal cord and right back out, your hand jerks away from the candle's flame *before* your brain receives and responds to the information that causes you to feel pain. That's why it feels as if your hand jerks away not by your choice, but on its own.

---

[1] Another research team, projecting from representative tissue samples, has estimated that the adult human male brain contains 86 billion neurons—give or take 8 billion (Azevedo et al., 2009). One moral: Distrust big round numbers, such as the familiar, undocumented claim that the human brain contains 100 billion neurons.

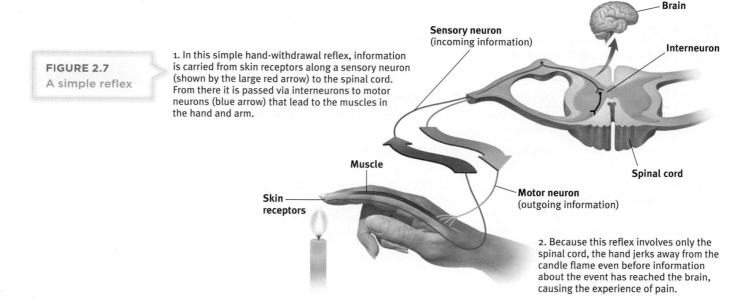

FIGURE 2.7
A simple reflex

1. In this simple hand-withdrawal reflex, information is carried from skin receptors along a sensory neuron (shown by the large red arrow) to the spinal cord. From there it is passed via interneurons to motor neurons (blue arrow) that lead to the muscles in the hand and arm.

Brain

Sensory neuron (incoming information)

Interneuron

Spinal cord

Motor neuron (outgoing information)

Muscle

Skin receptors

2. Because this reflex involves only the spinal cord, the hand jerks away from the candle flame even before information about the event has reached the brain, causing the experience of pain.

Information travels to and from the brain by way of the spinal cord. Were the top of your spinal cord severed, you would not feel pain from your body below. Nor would you feel pleasure. With your brain literally out of touch with your body, you would lose all sensation and voluntary movement in body regions with sensory and motor connections to the spinal cord below its point of injury. You would exhibit the knee jerk without feeling the tap. When the brain center keeping the brakes on erections is severed, men paralyzed below the waist may be capable of an erection (a simple reflex) if their genitals are stimulated (Goldstein, 2000). Women similarly paralyzed may respond with vaginal lubrication. But, depending on where and how completely the spinal cord is severed, they may be genitally unresponsive to erotic images and have no genital feeling (Kennedy & Over, 1990; Sipski & Alexander, 1999). To produce bodily pain or pleasure, the sensory information must reach the brain.

"If the nervous system be cut off between the brain and other parts, the experiences of those other parts are nonexistent for the mind. The eye is blind, the ear deaf, the hand insensible and motionless."

William James, Principles of Psychology, 1890

The Endocrine System

2-6: How does the endocrine system transmit information and interact with the nervous system?

So far, we have focused on the body's speedy electrochemical information system. Interconnected with your nervous system is a second communication system, the **endocrine system** (**FIGURE 2.8**). The endocrine system's glands secrete another form of chemical messengers, **hormones**, which travel through the bloodstream and affect other tissues, including the brain. When hormones act on the brain, they influence our interest in sex, food, and aggression.

Some hormones are chemically identical to neurotransmitters (the chemical messengers that diffuse across a synapse and excite or inhibit an adjacent neuron). The endocrine system and nervous system are therefore close relatives: Both produce molecules that act on receptors elsewhere. Like many relatives, they also differ. The speedy nervous system zips messages from eyes to brain to hand in a fraction of a second. Endocrine messages trudge along in the bloodstream, taking several seconds or more to travel from the gland to the target tissue. If the nervous system delivers information to a specific receptor site with the speed of a text message, the endocrine system is more like a snail-mail bulk mailing.

Endocrine messages tend to outlast the effects of neural messages. That helps explain why upset feelings may linger beyond our awareness of what upset us. When this happens, it takes time for us to "simmer down." In a moment of danger, for example, the ANS orders the **adrenal glands** on top of the kidneys to release *epinephrine* and *norepinephrine* (also called *adrenaline* and *noradrenaline*). These hormones increase heart rate, blood pressure, and blood sugar, providing a surge of energy. When the emergency passes, the hormones—and the feelings of excitement—linger a while.

The most influential endocrine gland is the **pituitary gland**, a pea-sized structure located in the core of the brain, where it is controlled by an adjacent brain area, the *hypothalamus* (more on that shortly). Among the hormones released by the pituitary is a growth hormone that stimulates physical development. Another is *oxytocin,* which enables contractions associated with birthing, milk flow during nursing, and orgasm. Oxytocin also promotes pair bonding, group cohesion, and social trust (De Dreu et al., 2010). During a laboratory game, those given a nasal squirt of oxytocin rather than a placebo were more likely to trust strangers with their money (Kosfeld et al., 2005).

FIGURE 2.8
The endocrine system

Hypothalamus
(brain region controlling the pituitary gland)

Pituitary gland
(secretes many different hormones, some of which affect other glands)

Parathyroids
(help regulate the level of calcium in the blood)

Thyroid gland
(affects metabolism)

Adrenal glands
(inner part helps trigger the "fight-or-flight" response)

Pancreas
(regulates the level of sugar in the blood)

Testis
(secretes male sex hormones)

Ovary
(secretes female sex hormones)

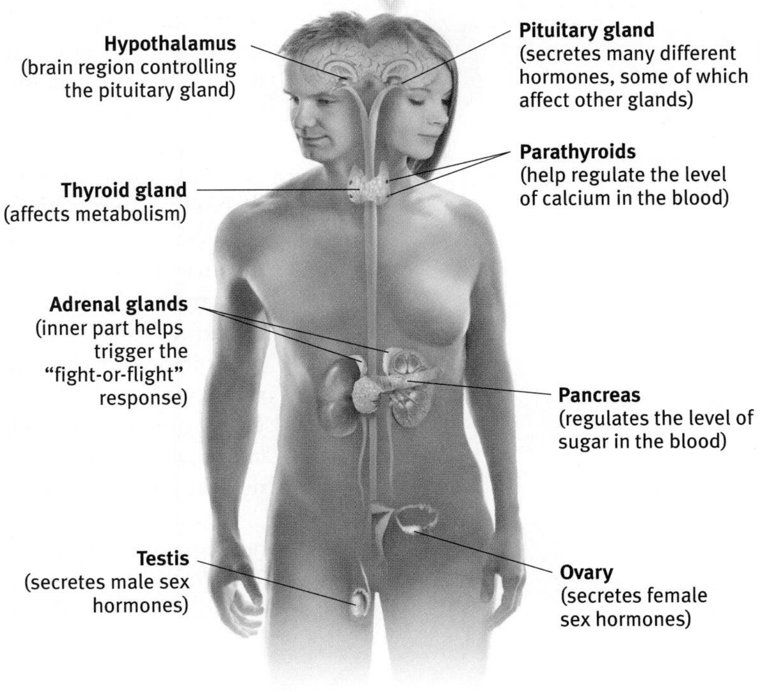

lesion [LEE-zhuhn] tissue destruction. A brain lesion is a naturally or experimentally caused destruction of brain tissue.

brainstem the oldest part and central core of the brain, beginning where the spinal cord swells as it enters the skull; the brainstem is responsible for automatic survival functions.

medulla [muh-DUL-uh] the base of the brainstem; controls heartbeat and breathing.

Pituitary secretions also influence the release of hormones by other endocrine glands. The pituitary, then, is a master gland (whose own master is the hypothalamus). For example, under the brain's influence, the pituitary triggers your sex glands to release sex hormones. These in turn influence your brain and behavior.

This feedback system (brain → pituitary → other glands → hormones → body and brain) reveals the intimate connection of the nervous and endocrine systems. The nervous system directs endocrine secretions, which then affect the nervous system. Conducting and coordinating this whole electrochemical orchestra is that maestro we call the brain.

RETRIEVE IT

• Why is the pituitary gland called the "master gland"?

ANSWER: Responding to signals from the hypothalamus, the pituitary releases hormones that trigger other endocrine glands to secrete hormones, which in turn influence our brain and our behavior.

• How are the nervous and endocrine systems alike, and how do they differ?

ANSWER: Both of these communication systems produce chemical molecules that act on the body's receptors to influence our behavior and emotions. The endocrine system, which secretes hormones into the bloodstream, delivers its messages much more slowly than the speedy nervous system, and the effects of the endocrine system's messages tend to linger much longer than those of the nervous system.

The Brain

2-7: How do neuroscientists study the brain's connections to behavior and mind?

The mind seeking to understand the brain—that is indeed among the ultimate scientific challenges. And so it will always be. To paraphrase cosmologist John Barrow, a brain simple enough to be understood is too simple to produce a mind able to understand it.

When you think *about* your brain, you're thinking *with* your brain—sending billions of neurotransmitter molecules across countless millions of synapses. Indeed, say neuroscientists, "the mind is what the brain does" (Minsky, 1986).

"I am a brain, Watson. The rest of me is a mere appendix."

Sherlock Holmes, in Arthur Conan Doyle's "The Adventure of the Mazarin Stone"

A century ago, scientists had no tools high powered yet gentle enough to reveal a living brain's activity. Clinical observations had unveiled some brain-mind connections. Physicians had noted that damage to one side of the brain often caused numbness or paralysis on the opposite side, suggesting that the body's right side is wired to the brain's left side, and vice versa. Others noticed that damage to the back of the brain disrupted vision, and that damage to the left-front part of the brain produced speech difficulties. Gradually, these early explorers were mapping the brain.

Now, within a lifetime, the whole brain-mapping process has changed. The known universe's most amazing organ is being probed and mapped by a new generation of neural mapmakers. Whether in the interests of science or medicine, they can selectively **lesion** (destroy) tiny clusters of normal or defective brain cells, leaving the surrounding tissue unharmed. Today's scientists can snoop on the messages of individual neurons, using modern microelectrodes with tips small enough to detect the electrical pulse in a single neuron. For example, they can now detect exactly where the information goes in a cat's brain when someone strokes its whisker. They can also stimulate various brain parts—electrically, chemically, or magnetically—and note the effects; eavesdrop on the chatter of billions of neurons; and see color representations of the brain's energy-consuming activity.

These techniques for peering into the thinking, feeling brain are doing for psychology what the microscope did for biology and the telescope did for astronomy. Close-Up: The Tools of Discovery on the next page looks at some techniques that enable neuroscientists to study the working brain.

Older Brain Structures

2-8: What structures make up the brainstem, and what are the functions of the brainstem, thalamus, and cerebellum?

American Images Inc/Getty Images

An animal's capacities come from its brain structures. In primitive animals, such as sharks, a not-so-complex brain primarily regulates basic survival functions: breathing, resting, and feeding. In lower mammals, such as rodents, a more complex brain enables emotion and greater memory. In advanced mammals, such as humans, a brain that processes more information enables increased foresight as well.

This increasing complexity arises from new brain systems built on top of the old, much as the Earth's landscape covers the old with the new. Digging down, one discovers the fossil remnants of the past—brainstem components performing for us much as they did for our distant ancestors. Let's start with the brain's basement and work up to the newer systems.

The Brainstem

The brain's oldest and innermost region is the **brainstem.** It begins where the spinal cord swells slightly after entering the skull. This slight swelling is the **medulla** (**FIGURE 2.9**). Here lie the controls for your heartbeat and breathing. As brain-damaged patients in a vegetative state illustrate, we need no higher brain or conscious mind to orchestrate our heart's pumping and lungs' breathing. The brainstem handles those tasks. Just above the medulla sits the *pons,* which helps coordinate movements.

If a cat's brainstem is severed from the rest of the brain above it, the animal will still breathe and live—and even run, climb, and groom (Klemm, 1990). But cut off from the brain's higher regions, it won't purposefully run or climb to get food.

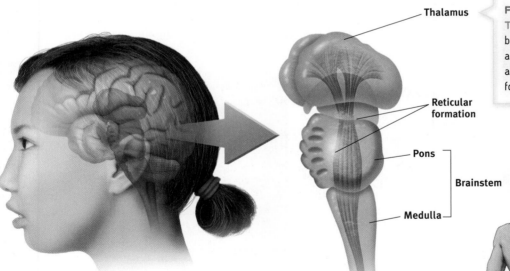
Thalamus
Reticular formation
Pons
Brainstem
Medulla

FIGURE 2.9
The brainstem and thalamus The brainstem, including the pons and medulla, is an extension of the spinal cord. The thalamus is attached to the top of the brainstem. The reticular formation passes through both structures.

The brainstem is a crossover point, where most nerves to and from each side of the brain connect with the body's opposite side (**FIGURE 2.10**). This peculiar cross-wiring is but one of the brain's many surprises.

RETRIEVE IT

• Nerves from the left side of the brain are mostly linked to the _____ side of the body, and vice versa.

ANSWER: right

FIGURE 2.10
The body's wiring

CLOSE UP:

The Tools of Discovery—Having Our Head Examined

Right now, your mental activity is emitting telltale electrical, metabolic, and magnetic signals that would enable neuroscientists to observe your brain at work. Electrical activity in your brain's billions of neurons sweeps in regular waves across its surface. An **electroencephalogram (EEG)** is an amplified readout of such waves (**FIGURE 2.11**). Researchers record the brain waves through a shower-cap-like hat that is filled with electrodes covered with a conductive gel.

"You must look into people, as well as at them," advised Lord Chesterfield in a 1746 letter to his son. Unlike EEGs, newer neuroimaging techniques give us that Superman-like ability to see inside the living brain. One such tool, the **PET (positron emission tomography) scan** (**FIGURE 2.12**), depicts brain activity by showing each brain area's consumption of its chemical fuel, the sugar glucose. Active neurons are glucose hogs, and after a person receives temporarily radioactive glucose, the PET scan can track the gamma rays released by this "food for thought" as the person performs a given task. Rather like weather radar showing rain activity, PET-scan "hot spots" show which brain areas are most active as the person does mathematical calculations, looks at images of faces, or daydreams.

In **MRI (magnetic resonance imaging)** brain scans, the person's head is put in a strong magnetic field, which aligns the spinning atoms of brain molecules. Then, a radio-wave pulse momentarily disorients the atoms. When the atoms return to their normal spin, they emit signals that provide a detailed picture of soft tissues, including the brain. MRI scans have revealed a larger-than-average neural area in the left hemisphere of musicians who display perfect pitch (Schlaug et al., 1995). They have also revealed enlarged *ventricles*—fluid-filled brain areas (marked by the red arrows in **FIGURE 2.13**)—in some patients who have schizophrenia, a disabling psychological disorder.

A special application of MRI—**fMRI (functional MRI)**—can reveal the brain's functioning as well as its structure. Where the brain is especially active, blood goes. By comparing MRI scans taken less than a second apart, researchers can watch the brain activate (with increased oxygen-laden bloodflow) as a person performs different mental functions. As the person looks at a scene, for example, the fMRI machine detects blood rushing to the back of the brain, which processes visual information (see Figure 2.21, in the discussion of cortex functions).

Such snapshots of the brain's changing activity are providing new insights into

© Philip Channing

Minding minds Neuroscientists Hanna Damasio and Antonio Damasio explore how the brain makes mind.

FIGURE 2.11
An electroencephalograph providing amplified tracings of waves of electrical activity in the brain

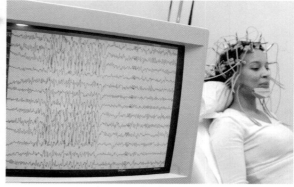

AJPhoto/Photo Researchers, Inc.

The Thalamus

thalamus [THAL-uh-muss] the brain's sensory router, located on top of the brainstem; it directs messages to the sensory receiving areas in the cortex and transmits replies to the cerebellum and medulla.

Sitting atop the brainstem is the **thalamus,** a pair of egg-shaped structures that act as the brain's sensory router (Figure 2.9). The thalamus receives information from all the senses except smell, and it routes that information to higher brain regions that deal with seeing, hearing, tasting, and touching. The thalamus also receives some of the higher brain's replies, which it then directs to the medulla and to the cerebellum (see the next page). Think of the thalamus as being to sensory information what London is to England's trains: a hub through which traffic passes en route to various destinations.

how the brain divides its labor. A mountain of recent fMRI studies suggests which brain areas are most active when people feel pain or rejection, listen to angry voices, think about scary things, feel happy, or become sexually excited. The technology enables a very crude sort of mind reading. After scanning 129 people's brains as they did eight different mental tasks (such as reading, gambling, or rhyming), neuroscientists were able, with 80 percent accuracy, to predict which of these mental activities people were doing (Poldrack et al., 2009).

To be learning about the neurosciences now is like studying world geography while Magellan was exploring the seas. This truly is the golden age of brain science.

• • • • •

electroencephalogram (EEG) an amplified recording of the waves of electrical activity sweeping across the brain's surface. These waves are measured by electrodes placed on the scalp.

PET (positron emission tomography) scan a visual display of brain activity that detects where a radioactive form of glucose goes while the brain performs a given task.

MRI (magnetic resonance imaging) a technique that uses magnetic fields and radio waves to produce computer-generated images of soft tissue. MRI scans show brain anatomy.

fMRI (functional MRI) a technique for revealing bloodflow and, therefore, brain activity by comparing successive MRI scans. fMRI scans show brain function.

FIGURE 2.12
The PET scan To obtain a PET scan, researchers inject volunteers with a low and harmless dose of a short-lived radioactive sugar. Detectors around the person's head pick up the release of gamma rays from the sugar, which has concentrated in active brain areas. A computer then processes and translates these signals into a map of the brain at work.

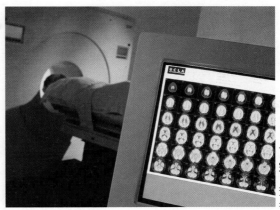
Mark Harmel/Getty Images

FIGURE 2.13
MRI scan of a healthy individual (left) and a person with schizophrenia (right) Note the enlarged ventricle, the fluid-filled brain region at the tip of the arrow in the image on the right.

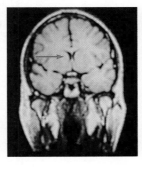 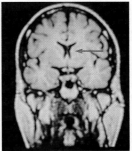
Both photos from Daniel Weinberger, M.D., CBDB, NIMH

RETRIEVE IT

• Match the scanning technique with the correct description.

Technique	Description
1. fMRI scan	a. tracks radioactive glucose to reveal brain activity.
2. PET scan	b. tracks successive images of brain tissue to show brain function.
3. MRI scan	c. uses magnetic fields and radio waves to show brain anatomy.

ANSWERS: 1. b, 2. a, 3. c

The Reticular Formation

Inside the brainstem, between your ears, lies the **reticular** ("net-like") **formation,** a finger-shaped network of neurons extending from the spinal cord right up through the thalamus. As the spinal cord's sensory input flows up to the thalamus, some of it travels through the reticular formation, which filters incoming stimuli, relays important information to other brain areas, and controls arousal.

In 1949, Giuseppe Moruzzi and Horace Magoun discovered that electrically stimulating a sleeping cat's reticular formation almost instantly produced an awake, alert

reticular formation a nerve network that travels through the brainstem and plays an important role in controlling arousal.

animal. When Magoun *severed* a cat's reticular formation without damaging nearby sensory pathways, the effect was equally dramatic: The cat lapsed into a coma from which it never awakened.

The Cerebellum

Extending from the rear of the brainstem is the baseball-sized **cerebellum,** meaning "little brain," which is what its two wrinkled halves resemble (**FIGURE 2.14**). As you will see in Chapter 8, the cerebellum enables nonverbal learning and memory. It also helps us judge time, modulate our emotions, and discriminate sounds and textures (Bower & Parsons, 2003). And it coordinates voluntary movement. When a soccer player executes a perfect bicycle kick, give his cerebellum some credit. Under alcohol's influence on the cerebellum, coordination suffers. And if you injured your cerebellum, you would have difficulty walking, keeping your balance, or shaking hands. Your movements would be jerky and exaggerated. Gone would be any dreams of being a dancer or guitarist.

★ ★ ★

Note: These older brain functions all occur without any conscious effort. This illustrates another of our recurring themes: *Our brain processes most information outside of our awareness.* We are aware of the *results* of our brain's labor (say, our current visual experience) but not of *how* we construct the visual image. Likewise, whether we are asleep or awake, our brainstem manages its life-sustaining functions, freeing our newer brain regions to think, talk, dream, or savor a memory.

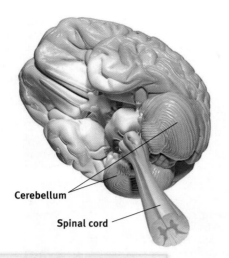

FIGURE 2.14

The brain's organ of agility Hanging at the back of the brain, the cerebellum coordinates our voluntary movements.

Ryan McVay/Getty Images

RETRIEVE IT

• In what brain region would damage be most likely to (1) disrupt your ability to skip rope? (2) disrupt your ability to hear and taste? (3) perhaps leave you in a coma? (4) cut off the very breath and heartbeat of life?

ANSWERS: 1. cerebellum, 2. thalamus, 3. reticular formation, 4. medulla

---

The Limbic System

2-9: What are the limbic system's structures and functions?

We've considered the brain's oldest parts, but we've not yet reached its newest and highest regions, the *cerebral hemispheres* (the two halves of the brain). Between the oldest and newest brain areas lies the **limbic system** (*limbus* means "border"). This system contains the *amygdala,* the *hypothalamus,* and the *hippocampus* (**FIGURE 2.15**). The hippocampus processes conscious memories. Animals or humans who lose their hippocampus to surgery or injury also lose their ability to form new memories of facts and events. Chapter 8 explains how our two-track mind processes our memories. For now, let's look at the limbic system's links to emotions such as fear and anger, and to basic motives such as those for food and sex.

The Amygdala Research has linked the **amygdala,** two lima-bean-sized neural clusters, to aggression and fear. In 1939, psychologist Heinrich Klüver and neurosurgeon Paul Bucy surgically removed a rhesus monkey's amygdala, turning the normally ill-tempered animal into the most mellow of creatures.

What then might happen if we electrically stimulated the amygdala of a normally placid domestic animal, such as a cat? Do so in one spot and the cat prepares to attack,

FIGURE 2.15

The limbic system This neural system sits between the brain's older parts and its cerebral hemispheres. The limbic system's hypothalamus controls the nearby pituitary gland.

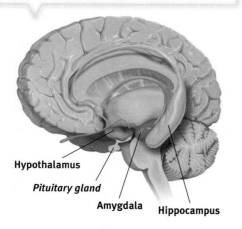

Hypothalamus

Pituitary gland

Amygdala   Hippocampus

hissing with its back arched, its pupils dilated, its hair on end. Move the electrode only slightly within the amygdala, cage the cat with a small mouse, and now it cowers in terror.

These and other experiments have confirmed the amygdala's role in rage and fear, including the perception of these emotions and the processing of emotional memories (Anderson & Phelps, 2000; Poremba & Gabriel, 2001). But we must be careful. The brain is not neatly organized into structures that correspond to our behavior categories. When we feel or act in aggressive or fearful ways, there is neural activity in many areas of our brain. Even within the limbic system, stimulating structures other than the amygdala can evoke aggression or fear. If you charge a car's dead battery, you can activate the engine. Yet the battery is merely one link in an integrated system.

Jane Burton/Dorling Kindersley/Getty Images

cerebellum [sehr-uh-BELL-um] the "little brain" at the rear of the brainstem; functions include processing sensory input, coordinating movement output and balance, and enabling nonverbal learning and memory.

limbic system neural system (including the *hippocampus, amygdala,* and *hypothalamus*) located below the cerebral hemispheres; associated with emotions and drives.

amygdala [uh-MIG-duh-la] two lima-bean-sized neural clusters in the limbic system; linked to emotion.

hypothalamus [hi-po-THAL-uh-muss] a neural structure lying below *(hypo)* the thalamus; it directs several maintenance activities (eating, drinking, body temperature), helps govern the endocrine system via the pituitary gland, and is linked to emotion and reward.

RETRIEVE IT

• Electrical stimulation of a cat's amygdala provokes angry reactions, suggesting the amygdala's role in aggression. Which ANS division is activated by such stimulation?

ANSWER: The sympathetic nervous system

The Hypothalamus Just below *(hypo)* the thalamus is the **hypothalamus** (**FIGURE 2.16**), an important link in the command chain governing bodily maintenance. Some neural clusters in the hypothalamus influence hunger; others regulate thirst, body temperature, and sexual behavior. Together, they help maintain a steady *(homeostatic)* internal state.

As the hypothalamus monitors the state of your body, it tunes into your blood chemistry and any incoming orders from other brain parts. For example, picking up signals from your brain's cerebral cortex that you are thinking about sex, your hypothalamus will secrete hormones. These hormones will in turn trigger the adjacent "master gland," your pituitary (see Figure 2.15), to influence your sex glands to release their hormones. These will intensify the thoughts of sex in your cerebral cortex. (Once again, we see the interplay between the nervous and endocrine systems: The brain influences the endocrine system, which in turn influences the brain.)

A remarkable discovery about the hypothalamus illustrates how progress in science often occurs—when curious, open-minded investigators make an unexpected observation. Two young McGill University neuropsychologists, James Olds and Peter Milner (1954), were trying to implant an electrode in a rat's reticular formation when they made a magnificent mistake: They placed the electrode incorrectly (Olds, 1975). Curiously, as if seeking more stimulation, the rat kept returning to the location where it had been stimulated by this misplaced electrode. On discovering that they had actually placed the device in a region of the hypothalamus, Olds and Milner realized they had stumbled upon a brain center that provides pleasurable rewards (Olds, 1975).

In a meticulous series of experiments, Olds (1958) went on to locate other "pleasure centers," as he called them. (What the rats actually experience only they know, and they aren't telling. Rather than attribute human feelings to rats, today's scientists refer to *reward centers,* not "pleasure centers.") When allowed to press pedals to trigger their own stimulation in these areas, rats would sometimes do so at a feverish pace—up to 7000 times per hour—until they dropped from exhaustion. Moreover, to get this stimulation, they would even cross an electrified floor that a starving rat would not cross to reach food (**FIGURE 2.17** on the next page).

Researchers later discovered other limbic system reward centers, such as the *nucleus accumbens* in front of the hypothalamus, in many other species, including dolphins and monkeys. In fact, animal research has revealed both a general dopamine-related reward system and specific centers associated with the pleasures of eating, drinking, and sex.

FIGURE 2.16

The hypothalamus This small but important structure, colored yellow/orange in this MRI-scan photograph, helps keep the body's internal environment in a steady state.

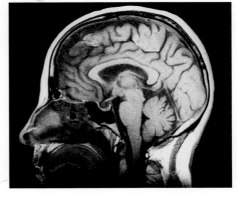

ISM/Phototake

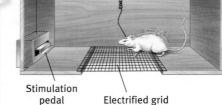

FIGURE 2.17
Rat with an implanted electrode
With an electrode implanted in a reward center of its hypothalamus, the rat readily crosses an electrified grid, accepting the painful shocks, to press a pedal that sends electrical impulses to that center.

Stimulation pedal   Electrified grid

"If you were designing a robot vehicle to walk into the future and survive, . . . you'd wire it up so that behavior that ensured the survival of the self or the species—like sex and eating—would be naturally reinforcing."

Candace Pert (1986)

Animals, it seems, come equipped with built-in systems that reward activities essential to survival.

Do humans have limbic centers for pleasure? Indeed we do. To calm violent patients, one neurosurgeon implanted electrodes in such areas. Stimulated patients reported mild pleasure; unlike Olds' rats, however, they were not driven to a frenzy (Deutsch, 1972; Hooper & Teresi, 1986).

Some researchers believe that addictive disorders, such as alcohol dependence, drug abuse, and binge eating, may stem from malfunctions in natural brain systems for pleasure and well-being. People genetically predisposed to this *reward deficiency syndrome* may crave whatever provides that missing pleasure or relieves negative feelings (Blum et al., 1996).

★ ★ ★

FIGURE 2.18 locates the brain areas we've discussed, as well as the *cerebral cortex,* our next topic.

FIGURE 2.18
Review: Brain structures and their functions

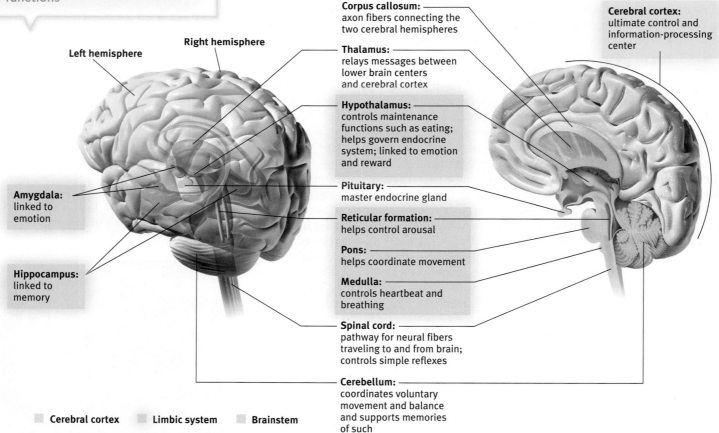

Left hemisphere

Right hemisphere

Corpus callosum: axon fibers connecting the two cerebral hemispheres

Cerebral cortex: ultimate control and information-processing center

Thalamus: relays messages between lower brain centers and cerebral cortex

Hypothalamus: controls maintenance functions such as eating; helps govern endocrine system; linked to emotion and reward

Amygdala: linked to emotion

Pituitary: master endocrine gland

Reticular formation: helps control arousal

Pons: helps coordinate movement

Hippocampus: linked to memory

Medulla: controls heartbeat and breathing

Spinal cord: pathway for neural fibers traveling to and from brain; controls simple reflexes

Cerebellum: coordinates voluntary movement and balance and supports memories of such

Cerebral cortex   Limbic system   Brainstem

• What are the three key structures of the limbic system, and what functions do they serve?

ANSWER: (1) The *amygdala* is involved in aggression and fear responses. (2) The *hypothalamus* is involved in bodily maintenance, pleasurable rewards, and control of the hormonal systems. (3) The *hippocampus* processes memory.

The Cerebral Cortex

2-10: What are the functions of the various cerebral cortex regions?

Older brain networks sustain basic life functions and enable memory, emotions, and basic drives. Newer neural networks within the *cerebrum*—the two cerebral hemispheres contributing 85 percent of the brain's weight—form specialized work teams that enable our perceiving, thinking, and speaking. Like other structures above the brainstem (including the thalamus, hippocampus, and amygdala), the cerebral hemispheres come as a pair. Covering those hemispheres, like bark on a tree, is the **cerebral cortex,** a thin surface layer of interconnected neural cells. It is your brain's thinking crown, your body's ultimate control and information-processing center.

As we move up the ladder of animal life, the cerebral cortex expands, tight genetic controls relax, and the organism's adaptability increases. Frogs and other small-cortex amphibians operate extensively on preprogrammed genetic instructions. The larger cortex of mammals offers increased capacities for learning and thinking, enabling them to be more adaptable. What makes us distinctively human mostly arises from the complex functions of our cerebral cortex.

• Which area of the human brain is most similar to that of less complex animals? Which part of the human brain distinguishes us most from less complex animals?

ANSWERS: The brainstem; the cerebral cortex

cerebral [seh-REE-bruhl] **cortex** the intricate fabric of interconnected neural cells covering the cerebral hemispheres; the body's ultimate control and information-processing center.

frontal lobes portion of the cerebral cortex lying just behind the forehead; involved in speaking and muscle movements and in making plans and judgments.

parietal [puh-RYE-uh-tuhl] **lobes** portion of the cerebral cortex lying at the top of the head and toward the rear; receives sensory input for touch and body position.

occipital [ahk-SIP-uh-tuhl] **lobes** portion of the cerebral cortex lying at the back of the head; includes areas that receive information from the visual fields.

temporal lobes portion of the cerebral cortex lying roughly above the ears; includes the auditory areas, each receiving information primarily from the opposite ear.

The people who first dissected and labeled the brain used the language of scholars—Latin and Greek. Their words are actually attempts at graphic description: For example, *cortex* means "bark," *cerebellum* is "little brain," and *thalamus* is "inner chamber."

Structure of the Cortex

If you opened a human skull, exposing the brain, you would see a wrinkled organ, shaped somewhat like the meat of an oversized walnut. Without these wrinkles, a flattened cerebral cortex would require triple the area—roughly that of a large pizza. The brain's ballooning left and right hemispheres are filled mainly with axons connecting the cortex to the brain's other regions. The cerebral cortex—that thin surface layer—contains some 20 to 23 billion nerve cells and 300 trillion synaptic connections (de Courten-Myers, 2005). Being human takes a lot of nerve.

Each hemisphere's cortex is subdivided into four *lobes,* separated by prominent *fissures,* or folds (**FIGURE 2.19**). Starting at the front of your brain and moving over the top, there are the **frontal lobes** (behind your forehead), the **parietal lobes** (at the top and to the rear), and the **occipital lobes** (at the back of your head). Reversing direction and moving forward, just above your ears, you find the **temporal lobes.** Each of the four lobes carries out many functions, and many functions require the interplay of several lobes.

FIGURE 2.19
The cortex and its basic subdivisions

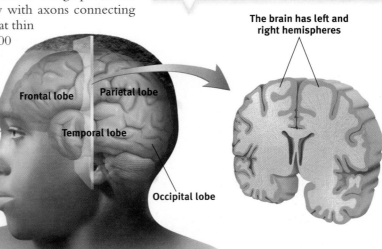

The brain has left and right hemispheres

Frontal lobe

Parietal lobe

Temporal lobe

Occipital lobe

Functions of the Cortex

More than a century ago, surgeons found damaged cortical areas during autopsies of people who had been partially paralyzed or speechless. This rather crude evidence did not prove that specific parts of the cortex control complex functions like movement or speech. After all, if the entire cortex controlled speech and movement, damage to almost any area might produce the same effect. A TV with its power cord cut would go dead, but we would be fooling ourselves if we thought we had "localized" the picture in the cord.

Motor Functions Scientists had better luck in localizing simpler brain functions. For example, in 1870, German physicians Gustav Fritsch and Eduard Hitzig made an important discovery: Mild electrical stimulation to parts of an animal's cortex made parts of its body move. The effects were selective: Stimulation caused movement only when applied to an arch-shaped region at the back of the frontal lobe, running roughly ear-to-ear across the top of the brain. Moreover, stimulating parts of this region in the left or right hemisphere caused movements of specific body parts on the *opposite* side of the body. Fritsch and Hitzig had discovered what is now called the **motor cortex.**

RETRIEVE IT

• Try moving your right hand in a circular motion, as if polishing a table. Then start your right foot doing the same motion, synchronized with your hand. Now reverse the right foot's motion, but not the hand's. Finally, try moving the *left* foot opposite to the right hand.

  1. Why is reversing the right foot's motion so hard?

  2. Why is it easier to move the left foot opposite to the right hand?

ANSWERS: 1. The right limbs' opposed activities interfere with each other because both are controlled by the same (left) side of your brain. 2. Opposite sides of your brain control your left and right limbs, so the reversed motion causes less interference.

MAPPING THE MOTOR CORTEX Lucky for brain surgeons and their patients, the brain has no sensory receptors. Knowing this, Otfrid Foerster and Wilder Penfield were able to map the motor cortex in hundreds of wide-awake patients by stimulating different cortical areas and observing the body's responses. They discovered that body areas requiring precise control, such as the fingers and mouth, occupy the greatest amount of cortical space (**FIGURE 2.20**).

In one of his many demonstrations of motor behavior mechanics, Spanish neuroscientist José Delgado stimulated a spot on a patient's left motor cortex, triggering the right hand to make a fist. Asked to keep the fingers open during the next stimulation, the patient, whose fingers closed despite his best efforts, remarked, "I guess, Doctor, that your electricity is stronger than my will" (Delgado, 1969, p. 114).

More recently, scientists were able to predict a monkey's arm motion a tenth of a second *before* it moved—by repeatedly measuring motor cortex activity preceding specific arm movements (Gibbs, 1996). Such findings have opened the door to research on brain-controlled computers.

What might happen, some researchers are asking, if we implanted a device to detect motor cortex activity? Could such devices help severely paralyzed people learn to command a cursor to write e-mail or work online? Clinical trials are now under way with people who have suffered paralysis or amputation (Andersen et al., 2010; Nurmikko et al., 2010). The first patient, a paralyzed 25-year-old man, was able to mentally control a TV, draw shapes on a computer screen, and play video games—all thanks to an aspirin-sized chip with 100 microelectrodes recording activity in his motor cortex (Hochberg et al., 2006).

Sensory Functions If the motor cortex sends messages out to the body, where does the cortex receive incoming messages? Penfield identified a cortical area—at the front of the parietal lobes, parallel to and just behind the motor cortex—that specializes in receiving information from the skin senses and from the movement of body parts. We

motor cortex an area at the rear of the frontal lobes that controls voluntary movements.

sensory cortex area at the front of the parietal lobes that registers and processes body touch and movement sensations.

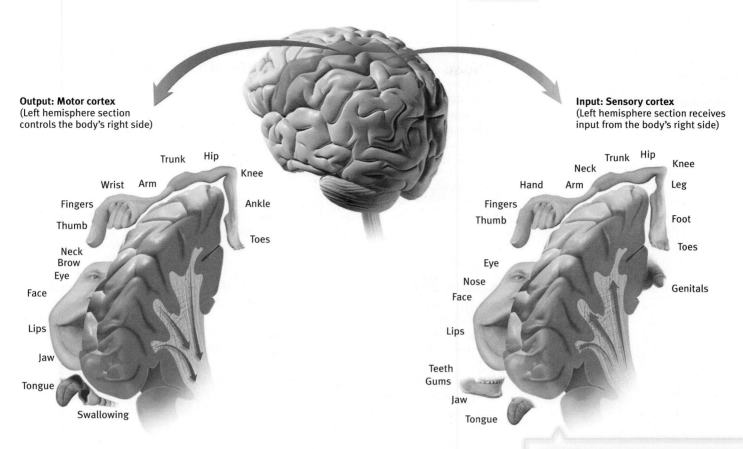

Output: Motor cortex
(Left hemisphere section controls the body's right side)

Trunk Hip Knee Ankle Toes
Wrist Arm
Fingers
Thumb
Neck
Brow
Eye
Face
Lips
Jaw
Tongue
Swallowing

Input: Sensory cortex
(Left hemisphere section receives input from the body's right side)

Neck Trunk Hip Knee Leg Foot Toes
Hand Arm
Fingers
Thumb
Eye
Nose
Face
Lips
Teeth
Gums
Jaw
Tongue
Genitals

now call this area the **sensory cortex** (Figure 2.20). Stimulate a point on the top of this band of tissue and a person may report being touched on the shoulder; stimulate some point on the side and the person may feel something on the face.

The more sensitive the body region, the larger the sensory cortex area devoted to it (Figure 2.20). Your supersensitive lips project to a larger brain area than do your toes, which is one reason we kiss with our lips rather than touch toes. Rats have a large area of the brain devoted to their whisker sensations, and owls to their hearing sensations.

Scientists have identified additional areas where the cortex receives input from senses other than touch. At this moment, you are receiving visual information in the visual cortex in your occipital lobes, at the back of your brain (**FIGURES 2.21** and **2.22**). Stimulated in the occipital lobes, you might see flashes of light or dashes of color. (In a sense, we *do* have eyes in the back of our head!) A friend of mine, having lost much of his right occipital lobe to a tumor removal, is now blind to the left half of his field of vision. Visual information travels from the occipital lobes to other areas that specialize in tasks such as identifying words, detecting emotions, and recognizing faces.

FIGURE 2.20
Left hemisphere tissue devoted to each body part in the motor cortex and the sensory cortex As you can see from this classic though inexact representation, the area devoted to a body part in the motor cortex (in the frontal lobes) or in the sensory cortex (in the parietal lobes) is not proportional to the body part's size. Rather, the brain devotes more tissue to sensitive areas and to areas requiring precise control. Thus, the fingers have a greater representation in the cortex than does the upper arm.

FIGURE 2.21
The brain in action This fMRI (functional MRI) scan shows the visual cortex in the occipital lobes activated (color representation of increased bloodflow) as a research participant looks at a photo. When the person stops looking, the region instantly calms down.

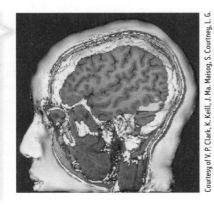

Courtesy of V. P. Clark, K. Keill, J. Ma. Maisog, S. Courtney, L. G. Ungerleider, and J. V. Haxby, National Institute of Mental Health

FIGURE 2.22
The visual cortex and auditory cortex The visual cortex in the occipital lobes at the rear of your brain receives input from your eyes. The auditory cortex, in your temporal lobes—above your ears—receives information from your ears.

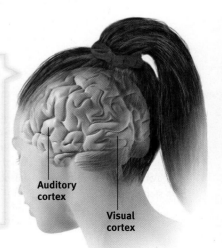

Auditory cortex

Visual cortex

association areas areas of the cerebral cortex that are not involved in primary motor or sensory functions; rather, they are involved in higher mental functions such as learning, remembering, thinking, and speaking.

Any sound you now hear is processed by your auditory cortex in your temporal lobes (just above your ears; see Figure 2.22). Most of this auditory information travels a circuitous route from one ear to the auditory receiving area above your opposite ear. If stimulated in your auditory cortex, you might hear a sound. MRI scans of people with schizophrenia have revealed active auditory areas in the temporal lobes during auditory hallucinations (Lennox et al., 1999). Even the phantom ringing sound experienced by people with hearing loss is—if heard in one ear—associated with activity in the temporal lobe on the brain's opposite side (Muhlnickel, 1998).

> **RETRIEVE IT**
>
> • Our brain's _____ cortex registers and processes body touch and movement sensations. The _____ cortex controls our voluntary movements.
>
> ANSWERS: sensory; motor

Association Areas So far, we have pointed out small cortical areas that either receive sensory input or direct muscular output. Together, these occupy about one-fourth of the human brain's thin, wrinkled cover. What, then, goes on in the remaining vast regions of the cortex? In these **association areas** (the peach-colored areas in **FIGURE 2.23**), neurons are busy with higher mental functions—many of the tasks that make us human.

Electrically probing an association area won't trigger any observable response. So, unlike the sensory and motor areas, association area functions cannot be neatly mapped. Their silence has led to what Donald McBurney (1996, p. 44) called "one of the hardiest weeds in the garden of psychology": the claim that we ordinarily use only 10 percent of our brain. (If true, wouldn't this imply a 90 percent chance that a bullet to your brain would land in an unused area?) Surgically lesioned animals and brain-damaged humans bear witness that association areas are not dormant. Rather, these areas interpret, integrate, and act on sensory information and link it with stored memories—a very important part of thinking.

Association areas are found in all four lobes. In the frontal lobes, they enable judgment, planning, and processing of new memories. People with damaged frontal lobes may have intact memories, high scores on intelligence tests, and great cake-baking skills. Yet they would not be able to plan ahead to *begin* baking a cake for a birthday party (Huey et al., 2006).

Frontal lobe damage also can alter personality and remove a person's inhibitions. Consider the classic case of railroad worker Phineas Gage. One afternoon in 1848, Gage, then 25 years old, was using a tamping iron to pack gunpowder into a rock. A spark ignited the gunpowder, shooting the rod up through his left cheek and out the top of his skull, leaving his frontal lobes massively damaged (**FIGURE 2.24**). To everyone's amazement, he was immediately able to sit up and speak, and after the wound healed he returned to work. But the affable, soft-spoken man was now irritable, profane, and dishonest. This person, said his friends, was "no longer Gage." His mental abilities and memories were intact, but his personality was not. (Although Gage lost his railroad job, he did, over time, adapt to his injury and find work as a stage coach driver [Macmillan & Lena, 2010].)

FIGURE 2.23
Areas of the cortex in four mammals More intelligent animals have increased "uncommitted" or association areas of the cortex. These vast areas of the brain are responsible for interpreting, integrating, and acting on sensory information and linking it with stored memories.

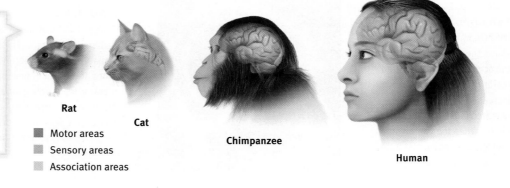

Rat

Cat

Chimpanzee

Human

■ Motor areas
■ Sensory areas
■ Association areas

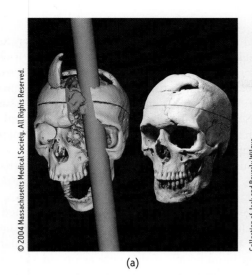

(a)

Collection of Jack and Beverly Wilgus

(b)

A blast from the past (a) Phineas Gage's skull was kept as a medical record. Using measurements and modern neuroimaging techniques, researchers have reconstructed the probable path of the rod through Gage's brain (Damasio et al., 1994). (b) This recently discovered photo shows Gage after his accident. The image has been reversed to show the features correctly. (Early photos, such as this one, were actually mirror images.)

More recent studies of people with damaged frontal lobes have revealed similar impairments. Not only may they become less inhibited (without the frontal lobe brakes on their impulses), but their moral judgments seem unrestrained by normal emotions. Would you advocate pushing one person in front of a runaway boxcar to save five others? Most people do not, but those with damage to a brain area behind the eyes often do (Koenigs et al., 2007). With their frontal lobes ruptured, people's moral compass seems to disconnect from their behavior.

Association areas also perform other mental functions. The parietal lobes, parts of which were large and unusually shaped in Einstein's normal-weight brain, enable mathematical and spatial reasoning (Witelson et al., 1999).

On the underside of the right temporal lobe, another association area enables us to recognize faces. If a stroke or head injury destroyed this area of your brain, you would still be able to describe facial features and to recognize someone's gender and approximate age, yet be strangely unable to identify the person as, say, Lady Gaga, or even your grandmother.

Nevertheless, complex mental functions don't reside in any one place. There is no one spot in a rat's small association cortex that, when damaged, will obliterate its ability to learn or remember a maze. And as we'll see in Chapter 9, distinct neural networks in the human brain coordinate to enable language. Memory, language, and attention result from the synchronized activity among distinct brain areas (Knight, 2007). Ditto for religious experience. More than 40 distinct brain regions become active in different religious states, such as prayer and meditation, indicating that there is no simple "God spot" (Fingelkurts & Fingelkurts, 2009). *The point to remember:* Our mental experiences arise from coordinated brain activity.

RETRIEVE IT

• Why are association areas important?

ANSWER: Association areas are involved in higher mental functions—interpreting, integrating, and acting on information processed in other areas.

The Brain's Plasticity

2-11: To what extent can a damaged brain reorganize itself, and what is neurogenesis?

Our brains are sculpted not only by our genes but also by our experiences. In Chapter 4, we'll focus more on how experience molds the brain. For now, let's turn to another aspect of the brain's **plasticity:** its ability to modify itself after damage.

plasticity the brain's ability to change, especially during childhood, by reorganizing after damage or by building new pathways based on experience.

neurogenesis the formation of new neurons.

Some brain-damage effects described earlier can be traced to two hard facts: (1) Severed brain and spinal cord neurons, unlike cut skin, usually do not regenerate. (If your spinal cord were severed, you would probably be permanently paralyzed.) And (2) some brain functions seem preassigned to specific areas. One newborn who suffered damage to temporal lobe facial recognition areas later remained unable to recognize faces (Farah et al., 2000). But there is good news: Some neural tissue can *reorganize* in response to damage. Under the surface of our awareness, the brain is constantly changing, building new pathways as it adjusts to little mishaps and new experiences.

Plasticity may also occur after serious damage, especially in young children (Kolb, 1989; see also **FIGURE 2.25**). The brain's plasticity is good news for those blind or deaf. Blindness or deafness makes unused brain areas available for other uses (Amedi et al., 2005). If a blind person uses one finger to read Braille, the brain area dedicated to that finger expands as the sense of touch invades the visual cortex that normally helps people see (Baringa, 1992a; Sadato et al., 1996). If magnetic stimulation temporarily "knocks out" the visual cortex, lifelong-blind people make more errors on a *language* task (Amedi et al., 2004). Plasticity also helps explain why some studies have found that deaf people have enhanced peripheral vision (Bosworth & Dobkins, 1999). In deaf people whose native language is sign, the temporal lobe area normally dedicated to hearing waits in vain for stimulation. Finally, it looks for other signals to process, such as those from the visual system.

Similar reassignment may occur when disease or damage frees up other brain areas normally dedicated to specific functions. If a slow-growing left hemisphere tumor disrupts language (which resides mostly in the left hemisphere), the right hemisphere may compensate (Thiel et al., 2006). If a finger is amputated, the sensory cortex that received its input will begin to receive input from the adjacent fingers, which then become more sensitive (Fox, 1984). So what do you suppose was the sexual intercourse experience of one patient whose lower leg had been amputated? "I actually experience my orgasm in my foot. [Note that in Figure 2.20, the toes region is adjacent to the genitals.] And there it's much bigger than it used to be because it's no longer just confined to my genitals" (Ramachandran & Blakeslee, 1998, p. 36).

Although the brain often attempts self-repair by reorganizing existing tissue, it sometimes attempts to mend itself by producing new brain cells. This process, known as **neurogenesis,** has been found in adult mice, birds, monkeys, and humans (Jessberger et al., 2008). These baby neurons originate deep in the brain and may then migrate elsewhere and form connections with neighboring neurons (Aimone et al., 2010; Gould, 2007).

Master stem cells that can develop into any type of brain cell have also been discovered in the human embryo. If mass-produced in a lab and injected into a damaged brain, might neural stem cells turn themselves into replacements for lost brain cells? Might surgeons someday be able to rebuild damaged brains, much as landscapers reseed damaged lawns? Might new drugs spur the production of new nerve cells? Stay tuned. Today's biotech companies are hard at work on such possibilities. In the meantime, we can all benefit from other natural promoters of neurogenesis, such as exercise, sleep, and nonstressful but stimulating environments (Iso et al., 2007; Pereira et al., 2007; Stranahan et al., 2006).

FIGURE 2.25

Brain plasticity This 6-year-old had surgery to end her life-threatening seizures. Although most of an entire hemisphere was removed (see MRI of hemispherectomy above), her remaining hemisphere compensated by putting other areas to work. One Johns Hopkins medical team reflected on the child hemispherectomies they had performed. Although use of the opposite arm was compromised, the team reported being "awed" by how well the children had retained their memory, personality, and humor (Vining et al., 1997). The younger the child, the greater the chance that the remaining hemisphere can take over the functions of the one that was surgically removed (Choi, 2008).

Joe McNally/Joe McNally Photography

Our Divided Brain

 2-12: What do split brains reveal about the functions of our two brain hemispheres?

We have seen that our brain's look-alike left and right hemispheres serve differing functions. This *lateralization* is apparent after brain damage. Research spanning more than a century has shown that left hemisphere accidents, strokes, and tumors can impair reading, writing, speaking, arithmetic reasoning, and understanding. Similar right hemisphere lesions seldom have such dramatic effects.

Does this mean that the right hemisphere is just along for the ride—a silent, "subordinate" or "minor" hemisphere? Many believed this was the case until 1960, when a fascinating chapter in psychology's history began to unfold: Researchers found that the "minor" right hemisphere was not so limited after all.

Splitting the Brain

In 1961, two Los Angeles neurosurgeons, Philip Vogel and Joseph Bogen, speculated that major epileptic seizures were caused by an amplification of abnormal brain activity bouncing back and forth between the two cerebral hemispheres. If so, they wondered, could they put an end to this biological tennis game by severing the **corpus callosum,** the wide band of axon fibers connecting the two hemispheres and carrying messages between them (**FIGURE 2.26**)? Vogel and Bogen knew that psychologists Roger Sperry, Ronald Myers, and Michael Gazzaniga had divided cats' and monkeys' brains in this manner, with no serious ill effects.

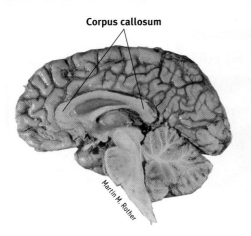

Corpus callosum

Martin M. Rother

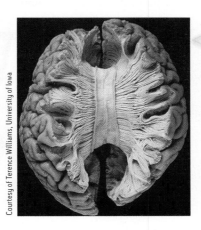

Courtesy of Terence Williams, University of Iowa

FIGURE 2.26

The corpus callosum This large band of neural fibers connects the two brain hemispheres. To photograph the half brain shown at left, a surgeon separated the hemispheres by cutting through the corpus callosum and lower brain regions. In the view on the right, brain tissue has been cut back to expose the corpus callosum and bundles of fibers coming out from it.

So the surgeons operated. The result? The seizures all but disappeared. The patients with these **split brains** were surprisingly normal, their personality and intellect hardly affected. Waking from surgery, one even joked that he had a "splitting headache" (Gazzaniga, 1967). By sharing their experiences, these patients have greatly expanded our understanding of interactions between the intact brain's two hemispheres.

To appreciate these findings, we need to focus for a minute on the peculiar nature of our visual wiring, illustrated in **FIGURE 2.27** on the next page. Note that each eye receives sensory information from both the right and left visual fields. In each eye, information from the left half of your field of vision goes to your right hemisphere, and information from the right half of your visual field goes to your left hemisphere, which usually controls speech. Data received by either hemisphere are quickly transmitted to the other across the corpus callosum. In a person with a severed corpus callosum, this information sharing does not take place.

corpus callosum [KOR-pus kah-LOW-sum] the large band of neural fibers connecting the two brain hemispheres and carrying messages between them.

split brain a condition resulting from surgery that isolates the brain's two hemispheres by cutting the fibers (mainly those of the corpus callosum) connecting them.

Knowing these facts, Sperry and Gazzaniga could send information to a patient's left or right hemisphere. As the person stared at a spot, they flashed a stimulus to its right or left. They could do this with you, too, but in your intact brain, the hemisphere receiving the information would instantly pass the news to the other side. Because the split-brain surgery had cut the communication lines between the hemispheres, the researchers could, with these patients, quiz each hemisphere separately.

In an early experiment, Gazzaniga (1967) asked these people to stare at a dot as he flashed HE·ART on a screen (**FIGURE 2.28**). Thus, HE appeared in their left visual field (which transmits to the right hemisphere) and ART in the right field (which transmits to the left hemisphere). When he then asked them to *say* what they had seen, the patients reported that they had seen ART. But when asked to *point* to the word they had seen, they were startled when their left hand (controlled by the right hemisphere) pointed to HE. Given an opportunity to express itself, each hemisphere indicated what it had seen. The right hemisphere (controlling the left hand) intuitively knew what it could not verbally report.

When a picture of a spoon was flashed to their right hemisphere, the patients could not *say* what they had viewed. But when asked to *identify* what they had viewed by feeling an assortment of hidden objects with their left hand, they readily selected the spoon. If the experimenter said, "Correct!" the patient might reply, "What? Correct? How could I possibly pick out the correct object when I don't know what I saw?" It is, of course, the left hemisphere doing the talking here, bewildered by what the nonverbal right hemisphere knows.

A few people who have had split-brain surgery have been for a time bothered by the unruly independence of their left hand, which might unbutton a shirt while the right hand buttoned it, or put grocery store items back on the shelf after the right hand put

---

FIGURE 2.27
The information highway from eye to brain

Left visual field / Right visual field

Optic nerves

Optic chiasm

Speech

Visual area of left hemisphere | Corpus callosum | Visual area of right hemisphere

"Do not let your left hand know what your right hand is doing."

Matthew 6:3

"Look at the dot."

(a)

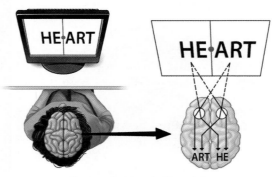

Two words separated by a dot are momentarily projected.

(b)

FIGURE 2.28

Testing the divided brain When an experimenter flashes the word HEART across the visual field, a woman with a split brain verbally reports seeing the portion of the word transmitted to her left hemisphere. However, if asked to indicate with her left hand what she saw, she points to the portion of the word transmitted to her right hemisphere. (From Gazzaniga, 1983.)

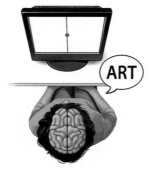

"What word did you see?"   or

"Point with your left hand to the word you saw."

(c)

them in the cart. It was as if each hemisphere was thinking "I've half a mind to wear my green (blue) shirt today." Indeed, said Sperry (1964), split-brain surgery leaves people "with two separate minds." With a split brain, both hemispheres can comprehend and follow an instruction to copy—*simultaneously*—different figures with the left and right hands (Franz et al., 2000; see also **FIGURE 2.29**). (Reading these reports, I fantasize a patient enjoying a solitary game of "rock, paper, scissors"—left versus right hand.)

When the "two minds" are at odds, the left hemisphere does mental gymnastics to rationalize reactions it does not understand. If a patient follows an order ("Walk") sent to the right hemisphere, a strange thing happens. The left hemisphere, unaware of the order, doesn't know why the patient begins walking. If asked why, the patient doesn't reply, "I don't know." Instead, the left hemisphere improvises—"I'm going into the house to get a Coke." Gazzaniga (1988), who considers these patients "the most fascinating people on earth," concluded that the conscious left hemisphere is an "interpreter" or press agent that instantly constructs theories to explain our behavior.

FIGURE 2.29

Try this! Joe, who has had split-brain surgery, can simultaneously draw two different shapes.

BBC

RETRIEVE IT

- (1) If we flash a red light to the right hemisphere of a person with a split brain, and flash a green light to the left hemisphere, will each observe its own color? (2) Will the person be aware that the colors differ? (3) What will the person verbally report seeing?

ANSWERS: 1. yes, 2. no, 3. green

Right-Left Differences in the Intact Brain

So, what about the 99.99+ percent of us with undivided brains? Does each of *our* hemispheres also perform distinct functions? Several different types of studies indicate they do. When a person performs a *perceptual* task, for example, brain waves, bloodflow, and glucose consumption reveal increased activity in the *right* hemisphere. When the person speaks or calculates, activity increases in the *left* hemisphere.

A dramatic demonstration of hemispheric specialization happens before some types of brain surgery. To locate the patient's language centers, the surgeon injects a sedative into the neck artery feeding blood to the left hemisphere, which usually controls speech. Before the injection, the patient is lying down, arms in the air, chatting with the doctor. Can you predict what probably happens when the drug puts the left hemisphere to sleep? Within seconds, the person's right arm falls limp. If the left hemisphere is controlling language, the patient will be speechless until the drug wears off. If the drug is injected into the artery to the right hemisphere, the *left* arm will fall limp, but the person will still be able to speak.

To the brain, language is language, whether spoken or signed. Just as hearing people usually use the left hemisphere to process spoken language, deaf people use the left hemisphere to process sign language (Corina et al., 1992; Hickok et al., 2001). Thus, a left hemisphere stroke disrupts a deaf person's signing, much as it would disrupt a hearing person's speaking. The same brain area is involved in both (Corina, 1998). (For more on how the brain enables language, see Chapter 9.)

Although the left hemisphere is adept at making quick, literal interpretations of language, the right hemisphere *helps us modulate our speech* to make meaning clear—as when we ask "What's that in the road ahead?" instead of "What's that in the road, a head?" (Heller, 1990). The right hemisphere also *helps orchestrate our self-awareness*. People who suffer partial paralysis will sometimes obstinately deny their impairment—strangely claiming they can move a paralyzed limb—if the damage is to the right hemisphere (Berti et al., 2005).

Simply looking at the two hemispheres, so alike to the naked eye, who would suppose they contribute uniquely to the harmony of the whole? Yet a variety of observations—of people with split brains, of people with normal brains, and even of other species' brains—converge beautifully, leaving little doubt that we have unified brains with specialized parts (Hopkins & Cantalupo 2008; MacNeilage et al., 2009).

Pop psychology's idea of hemispheric specialization
Alas, reality is more complex.

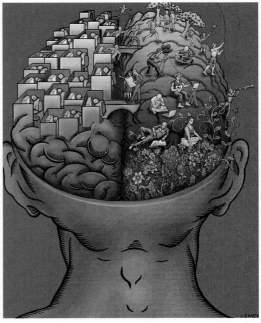

© Emek

How does the brain's intricate networking emerge? How does our heredity—the legacy of our ancestral history—conspire with our experiences to organize and "wire" the brain? To that we turn next.

Behavior Genetics: Predicting Individual Differences

2-13: What are genes, and how do behavior geneticists explain our individual differences?

Our shared brain architecture predisposes some common behavioral tendencies. Whether we live in the Arctic or the tropics, we sense the world, develop language, and feel hunger through identical mechanisms. We prefer sweet tastes to sour. We divide the color spectrum into similar colors. And we feel drawn to behaviors that produce and protect offspring.

Our human family shares not only a common biological heritage—cut us and we bleed—but also common social behaviors. Whether named Wong, Nkomo, Smith, or Gonzales, we start fearing strangers at about eight months, and as adults we prefer the company of those with attitudes and attributes similar to our own. As members of one species, we affiliate, conform, return favors, punish offenses, organize hierarchies of status, and grieve a child's death. A visitor from outer space could drop in anywhere and find humans dancing and feasting, singing and worshiping, playing sports and games, laughing and crying, living in families and forming groups. We are the leaves of one tree.

But in important ways, we also are each unique. We look different. We sound different. We have varying personalities, interests, and cultural and family backgrounds. What causes our striking diversity? How much of it is shaped by our differing genes, and how much by our **environment**—by every external influence, from maternal nutrition while in the womb to social support while nearing the tomb? How does our heredity interact with our experiences to create both our universal human nature and our individual and social diversity? Such questions intrigue **behavior geneticists.**

Genes: Our Codes for Life

Barely more than a century ago, few would have guessed that every cell nucleus in your body contains the genetic master code for your entire body. It's as if every room in Dubai's Burj Khalifa (the world's tallest building) contained a book detailing the architect's plans for the entire structure. The plans for your own book of life run to 46 chapters—23 donated by your mother's egg and 23 by your father's sperm. Each of these 46 chapters, called a **chromosome,** is composed of a coiled chain of the molecule **DNA** *(deoxyribonucleic acid)*. **Genes,** small segments of the giant DNA molecules, form the words of those chapters (**FIGURE 2.30**). All told, you have 20,000 to 25,000 gene words, which can be either active *(expressed)* or inactive. Environmental events "turn on" genes, rather like hot water enabling a tea bag to express its flavor. When turned on, genes provide the code for creating *protein molecules,* our body's building blocks.

Geneticists and psychologists are interested in the occasional variations found at particular gene sites in human DNA. Slight person-to-person variations from the common pattern give clues to our uniqueness—why one person has a disease that another does not, why one person is short and another tall, why one is outgoing and another shy.

Most of our traits are influenced by many genes. How tall you are, for example, reflects the size of your face, vertebrae, leg bones, and so forth—each of which may be influenced by different genes interacting with your specific environment. Complex traits such as intelligence, happiness, and aggressiveness are similarly influenced by groups of genes. Thus our genetic predispositions—our genetically influenced traits—help explain both our shared human nature and our human diversity.

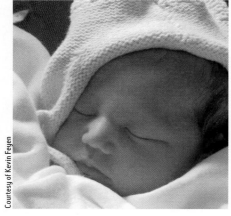

The nurture of nature Parents everywhere wonder: Will my baby grow up to be peaceful or aggressive? Homely or attractive? Successful or struggling at every step? What comes built in, and what is nurtured—and how? Research reveals that nature and nurture together shape our development—every step of the way.

"Your DNA and mine are 99.9 percent the same. . . . At the DNA level, we are clearly all part of one big worldwide family."

Francis Collins, Human Genome Project director, 2007

"We share half our genes with the banana."

Evolutionary biologist Robert May, president of Britain's Royal Society, 2001

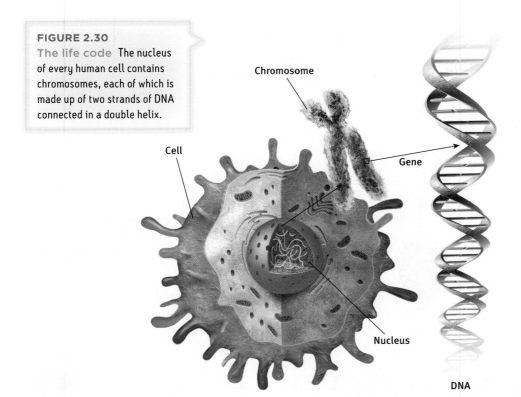

FIGURE 2.30

The life code The nucleus of every human cell contains chromosomes, each of which is made up of two strands of DNA connected in a double helix.

Chromosome

Cell

Gene

Nucleus

DNA

environment every nongenetic influence, from prenatal nutrition to the people and things around us.

behavior genetics the study of the relative power and limits of genetic and environmental influences on behavior.

chromosomes threadlike structures made of DNA molecules that contain the genes.

DNA *(deoxyribonucleic acid)* a complex molecule containing the genetic information that makes up the chromosomes.

genes the biochemical units of heredity that make up the chromosomes; segments of DNA capable of synthesizing proteins.

identical twins twins who develop from a single (monozygotic) fertilized egg that splits in two, creating two genetically identical organisms.

fraternal twins twins who develop from separate (dizygotic) fertilized eggs. They are genetically no closer than ordinary brothers and sisters, but they share a fetal environment.

RETRIEVE IT

• Put the following cell structures in order from *smallest to largest:* nucleus, gene, chromosome.

ANSWER: gene, chromosome, nucleus

• When the mother's egg and the father's sperm unite, each contributes 23 _____.

ANSWER: chromosomes

Twin and Adoption Studies

To scientifically tease apart the influences of environment and heredity, behavior geneticists would need to design two types of experiments. The first would control the home environment while varying heredity. The second would control heredity while varying the home environment. Such experiments with human infants would be unethical, but happily for our purposes, nature has done this work for us.

Identical Versus Fraternal Twins

Identical twins develop from a single *(monozygotic)* fertilized egg that splits in two. Thus they are *genetically* identical—nature's own human clones (**FIGURE 2.31** on the next page). Indeed, they are clones who share not only the same genes but the same conception and uterus, and usually the same birth date and cultural history.

Fraternal twins develop from separate *(dizygotic)* fertilized eggs. As womb-mates, they share a fetal environment, but they are genetically no more similar than ordinary brothers and sisters.

Shared genes can translate into shared experiences. A person whose identical twin has Alzheimer's disease, for example, has a 60 percent risk of getting the disease; if the affected twin is fraternal, the risk is 30 percent (Plomin et al., 1997). To study the effects of genes and

"Thanks for almost everything, Dad."

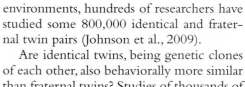

Identical twins

Fraternal twins

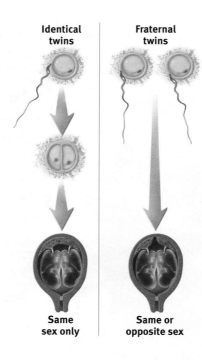

Same sex only

Same or opposite sex

Same fertilized egg, same genes; different eggs, different genes Identical twins develop from a single fertilized egg, fraternal twins from two.

environments, hundreds of researchers have studied some 800,000 identical and fraternal twin pairs (Johnson et al., 2009).

Are identical twins, being genetic clones of each other, also behaviorally more similar than fraternal twins? Studies of thousands of twin pairs in Sweden, Finland, and Australia have found that on the personality traits of extraversion (outgoingness) and neuroticism (emotional instability), identical twins are much more similar than fraternal twins.

Identical twins, more than fraternal twins, also report being treated alike. So, do their experiences rather than their genes account for their similarity? *No.* Studies have shown that identical twins whose parents treated them alike were not psychologically more alike than identical twins who were treated less similarly (Loehlin & Nichols, 1976). In explaining individual differences, genes matter.

Twins Curiously, twinning rates vary by race. The rate among Caucasians is roughly twice that of Asians and half that of Africans. In Africa and Asia, most twins are identical. In Western countries, most twins are fraternal, and fraternal twins have increased with the use of fertility drugs (Hall, 2003; Steinhauer, 1999).

Sweden has the world's largest national twin registry—140,000 living and dead twin pairs—which forms part of a massive registry of 600,000 twins currently being sampled in the world's largest twin study (Wheelwright, 2004; www.genomeutwin.org).

Twins Lorraine and Levinia Christmas, driving to deliver Christmas presents to each other near Flitcham, England, collided (Shepherd, 1997).

Separated Twins

Imagine the following science fiction experiment: A mad scientist decides to separate identical twins at birth, then rear them in differing environments. Better yet, consider a *true* story:

On a chilly February morning in 1979, some time after divorcing his first wife, Linda, Jim Lewis awoke in his modest home next to his second wife, Betty. Determined that this marriage would work, Jim made a habit of leaving love notes to Betty around the house. As he lay in bed he thought about others he had loved, including his son, James Alan, and his faithful dog, Toy.

Jim was looking forward to spending part of the day in his basement woodworking shop, where he had put in many happy hours building furniture, picture frames, and other items, including a white bench now circling a tree in his front yard. Jim also liked to spend free time driving his Chevy, watching stock-car racing, and drinking Miller Lite beer.

Jim was basically healthy, except for occasional half-day migraine headaches and blood pressure that was a little high, perhaps related to his chain-smoking habit. He had become overweight a while back but had shed some of the pounds. Having undergone a vasectomy, he was done having children.

What was extraordinary about Jim Lewis, however, was that at that same moment (I am not making this up) there existed another man—also named Jim—for whom all these things (right down to the dog's name) were also true.[2] This other Jim—Jim Springer—just happened, 38 years earlier, to have been his fetal partner. Thirty-seven days after their birth, these genetically identical twins were separated, adopted by blue-collar families, and reared with no contact or knowledge of each other's whereabouts until the day Jim Lewis received a call from his genetic clone (who, having been told he had a twin, set out to find him).

One month later, the brothers became the first twin pair tested by University of Minnesota psychologist Thomas Bouchard and his colleagues, beginning a study of separated twins that extends to the present (Holden, 1980a,b; Wright, 1998). Their voice intonations and inflections were so similar that, hearing a playback of an earlier interview, Jim Springer guessed "That's me." Wrong—it was his brother. Given tests measuring their personality, intelligence, heart rate, and brain waves, the Jim twins—despite 38 years of separation—were virtually as alike as the same person tested twice. Both married women named Dorothy Jane Scheckelburger. Okay, the last item is a joke. But as Judith Rich Harris (2006) has noted, it would hardly be weirder than some other reported similarities.

Aided by publicity in magazine and newspaper stories, Bouchard (2009) and his colleagues located and studied 74 pairs of identical twins reared apart. They continued to find similarities not only of tastes and physical attributes but also of personality (characteristic patterns of thinking, feeling, and acting), abilities, attitudes, interests, and even fears.

In Sweden, Nancy Pedersen and her co-workers (1988) identified 99 separated identical twin pairs and more than 200 separated fraternal twin pairs. Compared with equivalent samples of identical twins reared together, the separated identical twins had somewhat less identical personalities. Still, separated twins were more alike if genetically identical than if fraternal. And separation shortly after birth (rather than, say, at age 8) did not amplify their personality differences.

Stories of startling twin similarities have not impressed Bouchard's critics. "The plural of *anecdote* is not *data*," they have pointed out, noting that if any two strangers were to spend hours comparing their behaviors and life histories, they would probably discover many coincidental similarities. If researchers created a control group of biologically unrelated pairs of the same age, sex, and ethnicity, who had not grown up together but who were as similar to one another in economic and cultural background as are many of the separated twin pairs, wouldn't these pairs also exhibit striking similarities (Joseph, 2001)? Bouchard has replied that separated fraternal twins do not exhibit similarities comparable to those of separated identical twins.

Even the impressive data from personality assessments are clouded by the reunion of many of the separated twins some years before they were tested. Moreover, identical twins share an appearance, and the responses it evokes. Adoption agencies also tend to place separated twins in similar homes. Despite these criticisms, the striking twin-study results helped shift scientific thinking toward a greater appreciation of genetic influences.

If genetic influences help explain individual differences, do they also help explain group differences between men and women, or between people of different races? Not necessarily. Individual differences in height and weight, for example, are highly heritable; yet nutrition (an environmental factor) rather than genetic influences explains why, as a group, today's adults are taller and heavier than those of a century ago. The two groups differ, but not because human genes have changed in a mere century's eyeblink of time. Ditto aggressiveness, a genetically influenced trait. Today's peaceful Scandinavians differ from their more aggressive Viking ancestors, despite carrying many of the same genes.

©2006 Bob Sacha

Identical twins are people two Identical twins Jim Lewis and Jim Springer were separated shortly after birth and raised in different homes without awareness of each other. Research has shown remarkable similarities in the life choices of separated identical twins, lending support to the idea that genes influence personality.

"In some domains it looks as though our identical twins reared apart are . . . just as similar as identical twins reared together. Now that's an amazing finding and I can assure you none of us would have expected that degree of similarity."

Thomas Bouchard (1981)

Bouchard's famous twin research was, appropriately enough, conducted in Minneapolis, the "Twin City" (with St. Paul) and home to the Minnesota Twins baseball team.

Coincidences are not unique to twins. Patricia Kern of Colorado was born March 13, 1941, and named Patricia Ann Campbell. Patricia DiBiasi of Oregon also was born March 13, 1941, and named Patricia Ann Campbell. Both had fathers named Robert, worked as bookkeepers, and at the time of this comparison had children ages 21 and 19. Both studied cosmetology, enjoyed oil painting as a hobby, and married military men, within 11 days of each other. They are not genetically related. (From an AP report, May 2, 1983.)

---

[2] Actually, this description of the two Jims errs in one respect: Jim Lewis named his son James Alan. Jim Springer named his James Allan.

Biological Versus Adoptive Relatives

For behavior geneticists, nature's second real-life experiment—adoption—creates two groups: *genetic relatives* (biological parents and siblings) and *environmental relatives* (adoptive parents and siblings). For personality or any other given trait, we can therefore ask whether adopted children are more like their biological parents, who contributed their genes, or their adoptive parents, who contribute a home environment. While sharing that home environment, do adopted siblings also come to share traits?

The stunning finding from studies of hundreds of adoptive families is that people who grow up together, whether biologically related or not, do not much resemble one another in personality (McGue & Bouchard, 1998; Plomin, 2011; Rowe, 1990). In personality traits such as extraversion and agreeableness, adoptees are more similar to their biological parents than to their caregiving adoptive parents.

The finding is important enough to bear repeating: *The environment shared by a family's children has virtually no discernible impact on their personalities.* Two adopted children reared in the same home are no more likely to share personality traits with each other than with the child down the block. Heredity shapes other primates' personalities, too. Macaque monkeys raised by foster mothers exhibit social behaviors that resemble their biological, rather than foster, mothers (Maestripieri, 2003). Add all this to the similarity of identical twins, whether they grow up together or apart, and the effect of a shared rearing environment seems shockingly modest.

The genetic leash may limit the family environment's influence on personality, but this does not mean that adoptive parenting is a fruitless venture. Parents do influence their children's attitudes, values, manners, faith, and politics (Reifman & Cleveland, 2007). A pair of adopted children or identical twins *will,* especially during adolescence, have more similar religious beliefs if reared together (Koenig et al., 2005). Parenting matters!

Moreover, in adoptive homes, child neglect and abuse and even parental divorce are rare. (Adoptive parents are carefully screened; natural parents are not.) So it is not surprising that, despite a somewhat greater risk of psychological disorder, most adopted children thrive, especially when adopted as infants (Loehlin et al., 2007; van IJzendoorn & Juffer, 2006; Wierzbicki, 1993). Seven in eight report feeling strongly attached to one or both adoptive parents. As children of self-giving parents, they grow up to be more self-giving and altruistic than average (Sharma et al., 1998). Many score higher than their biological parents on intelligence tests, and most grow into happier and more stable adults. In one Swedish study, children adopted as infants grew up with fewer problems than were experienced by children whose biological mothers initially registered them for adoption but then decided to raise the children themselves (Bohman & Sigvardsson, 1990). Regardless of personality differences between adoptive family members, children benefit from adoption.

"We carry to our graves the essence of the zygote that was first us."

Mary Pipher, Seeking Peace: Chronicles of the Worst Buddhist in the World, *2009*

The greater uniformity of adoptive homes—mostly healthy, nurturing homes—helps explain the lack of striking differences when comparing child outcomes of different adoptive homes (Stoolmiller, 1999).

Nature or nurture or both? When talent runs in families, as with Wynton Marsalis, Branford Marsalis, and Delfeayo Marsalis, how do heredity and environment together do their work?

AP Photo/Charles Sykes

RETRIEVE IT

• How do researchers use twin and adoption studies to learn about psychological principles?

ANSWER: Researchers compare the traits and behaviors of identical twins (same genes) and fraternal twins (different genes, as in any two siblings). They also compare adopted children with their adoptive and biological parents. Some studies compare twins raised together or separately. These studies help us determine how much variation among individuals is due to genetic makeup and how much to environmental factors.

interaction the interplay that occurs when the effect of one factor (such as environment) depends on another factor (such as heredity).

epigenetics the study of environmental influences on gene expression that occur without a DNA change.

Gene-Environment Interaction

2-14: How do heredity and environment work together?

Among our similarities, the most important—the behavioral hallmark of our species—is our enormous adaptive capacity. Some human traits, such as having two eyes, develop the same in virtually every environment. But other traits are expressed only in particular environments. Go barefoot for a summer and you will develop toughened, callused feet—a biological adaptation to friction. Meanwhile, your shod neighbor will remain a tenderfoot. The difference between the two of you is, of course, an effect of environment. But it is also the product of a biological mechanism—adaptation.

Genes and environment—nature and nurture—work together, like two hands clapping. Genes are self-regulating. Rather than acting as blueprints that lead to the same result no matter the context, genes react. An African butterfly that is green in summer turns brown in fall, thanks to a temperature-controlled genetic switch. The genes that produce brown in one situation produce green in another.

To say that genes and experience are *both* important is true. But more precisely, they **interact.** Imagine two babies, one genetically predisposed to be attractive, sociable, and easygoing, the other less so. Assume further that the first baby attracts more affectionate and stimulating care and so develops into a warmer and more outgoing person. As the two children grow older, the more naturally outgoing child more often seeks activities and friends that encourage further social confidence.

What has caused their resulting personality differences? Neither heredity nor experience acts alone. Environments trigger gene activity. And our genetically influenced traits *evoke* significant responses in others. Thus, a child's impulsivity and aggression may evoke an angry response from a parent or teacher who reacts warmly to model children in the family or classroom. In such cases, the child's nature and the adult's nurture interact. Gene and scene dance together.

Evocative interactions may help explain why identical twins reared in different families recall their parents' warmth as remarkably similar—almost as similar as if they had had the same parents (Plomin et al., 1988, 1991, 1994). Fraternal twins have more differing recollections of their early family life—even if reared in the same family! "Children experience us as different parents, depending on their own qualities," noted Sandra Scarr (1990).

Recall that genes can be either active (expressed, as the hot water activates the tea bag) or inactive. A new field, **epigenetics** (meaning "in addition to" or "above and beyond" genetics), is studying the molecular mechanisms by which environments trigger genetic expression. Although genes have the potential to influence development, environmental triggers can switch them on or off, much as your computer's software switches your printer on and off. One such *epigenetic mark* is an organic methyl molecule attached to part of a DNA strand (**FIGURE 2.32**). It instructs the cell to ignore any gene present in that DNA stretch, thereby preventing the DNA from producing the proteins coded by that gene.

"Men's natures are alike; it is their habits that carry them far apart."

Confucius, Analects, *500 B.C.E.*

Dim154/Shutterstock

"Heredity deals the cards; environment plays the hand."

Psychologist Charles L. Brewer (1990)

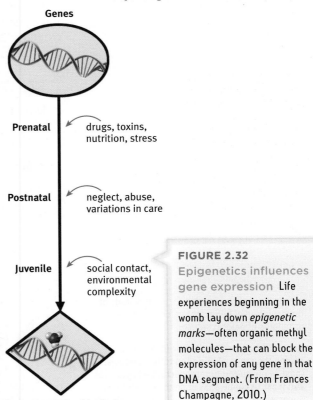

Genes

Prenatal — drugs, toxins, nutrition, stress

Postnatal — neglect, abuse, variations in care

Juvenile — social contact, environmental complexity

Gene expression blocked by epigenetic molecules

FIGURE 2.32
Epigenetics influences gene expression Life experiences beginning in the womb lay down *epigenetic marks*—often organic methyl molecules—that can block the expression of any gene in that DNA segment. (From Frances Champagne, 2010.)

Gene-environment interaction
Biological appearances have social consequences. People respond differently to a Channing Tatum (shown here in the movie *Dear John*), than to his fellow actor Mike Myers (shown here playing the character Austin Powers).

Environmental factors such as diet, drugs, toxins, and stress can affect the epigenetic molecules that regulate gene expression. In one experiment, infant rats deprived of their mothers' normal licking had more molecules that blocked access to the "on" switch for developing the brain's stress-hormone receptors. When stressed, the animals had above-average levels of free-floating stress hormones and were more stressed out (Champagne et al., 2003; Champagne & Mashoodh, 2009). Child abuse may similarly affect its victims. Suicide victims with a history of child abuse exhibit the epigenetic effect (McGowan et al., 2009). Researchers now wonder if epigenetics might help solve some scientific mysteries, such as why only one member of an identical twin pair may develop a genetically influenced mental disorder, and how experience leaves its fingerprints in our brains.

So, if Jaden Agassi, son of tennis stars Andre Agassi and Stefanie Graf, grows up to be a tennis star, should we attribute his superior talent to his Grand Slam genes? To his growing up in a tennis-rich environment? To high expectations? The best answer seems to be "All of the above." From conception onward, we are the product of a cascade of interactions between our genetic predispositions and our surrounding environments (McGue, 2010). Our genes affect how people react to and influence us. Forget nature *versus* nurture; think nature *via* nurture.

RETRIEVE IT

• Match the following terms to the correct explanation.

  1. Epigenetics   a. Study of the relative effects of our genes and our environment on our behavior.

  2. Behavior genetics   b. Study of environmental factors that affect how our genes are *expressed*.

ANSWERS: 1. b, 2. a

Evolutionary Psychology: Understanding Human Nature

evolutionary psychology the study of the evolution of behavior and the mind, using principles of natural selection.

natural selection the principle that, among the range of inherited trait variations, those contributing to reproduction and survival will most likely be passed on to succeeding generations.

2-15: How do evolutionary psychologists use natural selection to explain behavior tendencies?

Behavior geneticists explore the genetic and environmental roots of human differences. **Evolutionary psychologists** instead focus mostly on what makes us so much alike as humans. They use Charles Darwin's principle of **natural selection** to understand the roots of behavior and mental processes. Richard Dawkins (2007) calls natural selection "arguably the most momentous idea ever to occur to a human mind." The idea, simplified, is this:

- Organisms' varied offspring compete for survival.
- Certain biological and behavioral variations increase organisms' reproductive and survival chances in their particular environment.
- Offspring that survive are more likely to pass their genes to ensuing generations.
- Thus, over time, population characteristics may change.

To see these principles at work, let's consider a straightforward example in foxes.

mutation a random error in gene replication that leads to a change.

Natural Selection and Adaptation

A fox is a wild and wary animal. If you capture a fox and try to befriend it, be careful. Stick your hand in the cage and, if the timid fox cannot flee, it may snack on your fingers. Russian scientist Dmitry Belyaev wondered how our human ancestors had domesticated dogs from their equally wild wolf forebears. Might he, within a comparatively short stretch of time, accomplish a similar feat by transforming the fearful fox into a friendly fox?

Eric Isselée/Shutterstock

To find out, Belyaev set to work with 30 male and 100 female foxes. From their offspring he selected and mated the tamest 5 percent of males and 20 percent of females. (He measured tameness by the foxes' responses to attempts to feed, handle, and stroke them.) Over more than 30 generations of foxes, Belyaev and his successor, Lyudmila Trut, repeated that simple procedure. Forty years and 45,000 foxes later, they had a new breed of foxes that, in Trut's (1999) words, are "docile, eager to please, and unmistakably domesticated. . . . Before our eyes, 'the Beast' has turned into 'beauty,' as the aggressive behavior of our herd's wild [ancestors] entirely disappeared." So friendly and eager for human contact are they, so inclined to whimper to attract attention and to lick people like affectionate dogs, that the cash-strapped institute seized on a way to raise funds—marketing its foxes to people as house pets.

Over time, traits that confer a reproductive advantage on an individual or a species are *selected* and will prevail. Animal breeding experiments exploit genetic selection. Dog breeders have given us sheepdogs that herd, retrievers that retrieve, trackers that track, and pointers that point (Plomin et al., 1997). Psychologists, too, have bred animals to be serene or reactive, quick learners or slow ones.

Does the same process work with naturally occurring selection? Does natural selection explain our human tendencies? Nature has indeed selected advantageous variations from the new gene combinations produced at each human conception and the **mutations** (random errors in gene replication) that sometimes result. But the tight genetic leash that predisposes a dog's retrieving, a cat's pouncing, or an ant's nest building is looser on humans. The genes selected during our ancestral history endow us with a great capacity to learn and therefore to *adapt* to life in varied environments, from the tundra to the jungle. Genes and experience together wire the brain. Our adaptive flexibility in responding to different environments contributes to our *fitness*—our ability to survive and reproduce.

RETRIEVE IT

- How are Belyaev and Trut's breeding practices similar to, and how do they differ from, the way natural selection normally occurs?

ANSWER: Over multiple generations, Belyaev and Trut have been selecting and breeding foxes that exhibited a trait they desired: tameness. This process is similar to naturally occurring selection, but it differs in that natural selection normally favors traits (including those arising from mutations) that contribute to reproduction and survival.

Evolutionary Success Helps Explain Similarities

Our behavioral and biological similarities arise from our shared human *genome,* our common genetic profile. How did we develop our genetic kinship?

Our Genetic Legacy

At the dawn of human history, our ancestors faced certain questions: Who is my ally, who is my foe? With whom should I mate? What food should I eat? Some individuals answered those questions more successfully than others. For example, women who experienced nausea in the critical first three months of pregnancy were predisposed to avoid certain bitter, strongly flavored, and novel foods. Avoiding such foods has survival value, since they are the very foods most often toxic to prenatal development (Schmitt & Pilcher, 2004). Early humans disposed to eat nourishing rather than poisonous foods survived to contribute their genes to later generations. Those who deemed leopards "nice to pet" often did not.

Similarly successful were those whose mating helped them produce and nurture offspring. Over generations, the genes of individuals not so disposed tended to be lost from the human gene pool. As success-enhancing genes continued to be selected, behavioral tendencies and thinking and learning capacities emerged that prepared our Stone Age ancestors to survive, reproduce, and send their genes into the future, and into you.

As inheritors of this prehistoric genetic legacy, we are predisposed to behave in ways that promoted our ancestors' surviving and reproducing. But in some ways, we are biologically prepared for a world that no longer exists. We love the taste of sweets and fats, which prepared our ancestors to survive famines, and we heed their call from store shelves, fast-food outlets, and vending machines. With famine now rare in Western cultures, obesity is truly a growing problem. Our natural dispositions, rooted deep in history, are mismatched with today's junk-food environment and tomorrow's threats, such as climate change (Colarelli & Dettman, 2003).

Evolutionary Psychology Today

Darwin's theory of evolution has been an organizing principle for biology for a long time. As Jared Diamond (2001) has noted, "Virtually no contemporary scientists believe that Darwin was basically wrong." Today, Darwin's theory lives on in the *second Darwinian revolution:* the application of evolutionary principles to psychology. In concluding *On the Origin of Species,* Darwin (1859, p. 346) anticipated this, foreseeing "open fields for far more important researches. Psychology will be based on a new foundation."

In chapters to come, we'll address some questions that intrigue evolutionary psychologists: Why do infants start to fear strangers about the time they become mobile? Why are biological fathers so much less likely than unrelated boyfriends to abuse and murder the children with whom they share a home? Why do so many more people have phobias about spiders, snakes, and heights than about more dangerous threats, such as guns and electricity? And why do we fear air travel so much more than driving?

★ ★ ★

I know from my mail and from public opinion surveys that some readers feel troubled by the naturalism and evolutionism of contemporary science. Readers from other nations bear with me, but in the United States there is a wide gulf between scientific and lay thinking about evolution. "The idea that human minds are the product of evolution is . . . unassailable fact," declared a 2007 editorial in *Nature,* a leading science magazine. That sentiment concurs with a 2006 statement of "evidence-based facts" about evolution jointly issued by the national science academies of 66 nations (IAP, 2006). In *The Language of God,* Human Genome Project director Francis Collins (2006, pp. 141, 146), a self-described evangelical Christian, compiles the "utterly

Despite high infant mortality and rampant disease in past millennia, not one of your countless ancestors died childless.

compelling" evidence that leads him to conclude that Darwin's big idea is "unquestion-ably correct." Yet Gallup reports that half of U.S. adults do not believe in evolution's role in "how human beings came to exist on Earth" (Newport, 2007). Many of those who dispute the scientific story worry that a science of behavior (and evolutionary science in particular) will destroy our sense of the beauty, mystery, and spiritual significance of the human creature. For those concerned, I offer some reassuring thoughts.

When Isaac Newton explained the rainbow in terms of light of differing wavelengths, the poet Keats feared that Newton had destroyed the rainbow's mysterious beauty. Yet, as Richard Dawkins (1998) noted in *Unweaving the Rainbow,* Newton's analysis led to an even deeper mystery—Einstein's theory of special relativity. Moreover, nothing about Newton's optics need diminish our appreciation for the dramatic elegance of a rainbow arching across a brightening sky.

When Galileo assembled evidence that the Earth revolved around the Sun, not vice versa, he did not offer irrefutable proof for his theory. Rather, he offered a coherent explanation for a variety of observations, such as the changing shadows cast by the Moon's mountains. His explanation eventually won the day because it described and explained things in a way that made sense, that hung together. Darwin's theory of evolution likewise is a coherent view of natural history. It offers an organizing principle that unifies various observations.

Collins is not the only person of faith to find the scientific idea of human origins congenial with his spirituality. In the fifth century, St. Augustine (quoted by Wilford, 1999) wrote, "The universe was brought into being in a less than fully formed state, but was gifted with the capacity to transform itself from unformed matter into a truly marvelous array of structures and life forms." Some 1600 years later, Pope John Paul II in 1996 welcomed a science-religion dialogue, finding it noteworthy that evolutionary theory "has been progressively accepted by researchers, following a series of discoveries in various fields of knowledge."

Meanwhile, many people of science are awestruck at the emerging understanding of the universe and the human creature. It boggles the mind—the entire universe popping out of a point some 14 billion years ago, and instantly inflating to cosmologi-cal size. Had the energy of this Big Bang been the tiniest bit less, the universe would have collapsed back on itself. Had it been the tiniest bit more, the result would have been a soup too thin to support life. Astronomer Sir Martin Rees has described *Just Six Numbers* (1999), any one of which, if changed ever so slightly, would produce a cosmos in which life could not exist. Had gravity been a tad stronger or weaker, or had the weight of a carbon proton been a wee bit different, our universe just wouldn't have worked.

What caused this almost-too-good-to-be-true, finely tuned universe? Why is there something rather than nothing? How did it come to be, in the words of Harvard-Smithsonian astrophysicist Owen Gingerich (1999), "so extraordinarily right, that it seemed the universe had been expressly designed to produce intelligent, sentient beings"? Is there a benevolent superintelligence behind it all? Have there instead been an infinite number of universes born and we just happen to be the lucky inhabitants of one that, by chance, was exquisitely fine-tuned to give birth to us? Or does that idea violate *Occam's razor,* the principle that we should prefer the simplest of compet-ing explanations? On such matters, a humble, awed, scientific silence is appropriate, suggested philosopher Ludwig Wittgenstein: "Whereof one cannot speak, thereof one must be silent."

Rather than fearing science, we can welcome its enlarging our understanding and awakening our sense of awe. In *The Fragile Species,* Lewis Thomas (1992) described his utter amazement that the Earth in time gave rise to bacteria and eventually to Bach's *Mass in B Minor.* In a short 4 billion years, life on Earth has come from nothing to structures as complex as a 6-billion-unit strand of DNA and the incomprehensible intricacy of the human brain. Atoms no different from those in a rock somehow formed

Those who are troubled by an apparent conflict between scientific and religious accounts of human origins may find it helpful to recall (Chapter 1) that different perspectives of life can be complementary. For example, the scientific account attempts to tell us *when* and *how;* religious creation stories usually aim to tell about an ultimate *who* and *why.* As Galileo explained to the Grand Duchess Christina, "The Bible teaches how to go to heaven, not how the heavens go."

dynamic entities that became conscious. Nature, says cosmologist Paul Davies (2007), seems cunningly and ingeniously devised to produce extraordinary, self-replicating, information–processing systems—us. Although we appear to have been created from dust, over eons of time, the end result is a priceless creature, one rich with potential beyond our imagining.

RETRIEVE IT

- Behavior geneticists are most interested in exploring _____ (commonalities; differences) in our traits and behaviors, and evolutionary psychologists are most interested in exploring _____ (commonalities; differences).

ANSWERS: differences; commonalities

CHAPTER REVIEW

The Biology of Behavior

LEARNING OBJECTIVES

Test Yourself by taking a moment to answer each of these Learning Objective Questions (repeated here from within the chapter). Then turn to Appendix D, Complete Chapter Reviews, to check your answers. Research suggests that trying to answer these questions on your own will improve your long-term memory of the concepts (McDaniel et al., 2009).

Biology and Behavior

2-1: Why are psychologists concerned with human biology?

Neural Communication

2-2: What are neurons, and how do they transmit information?

2-3: How do nerve cells communicate with other nerve cells?

2-4: How do neurotransmitters influence behavior?

The Nervous System

2-5: What are the functions of the nervous system's main divisions, and what are the three main types of neurons?

The Endocrine System

2-6: How does the endocrine system transmit information and interact with the nervous system?

The Brain

2-7: How do neuroscientists study the brain's connections to behavior and mind?

2-8: What structures make up the brainstem, and what are the functions of the brainstem, thalamus, and cerebellum?

2-9: What are the limbic system's structures and functions?

2-10: What are the functions of the various cerebral cortex regions?

2-11: To what extent can a damaged brain reorganize itself, and what is neurogenesis?

2-12: What do split brains reveal about the functions of our two brain hemispheres?

Behavior Genetics: Predicting Individual Differences

2-13: What are genes, and how do behavior geneticists explain our individual differences?

2-14: How do heredity and environment work together?

Evolutionary Psychology: Understanding Human Nature

2-15: How do evolutionary psychologists use natural selection to explain behavior tendencies?

TERMS AND CONCEPTS TO REMEMBER

Test yourself on these terms by trying to write down the definition in your own words before flipping back to the referenced page to check your answer.

biological psychology, p. 36

neuron, p. 36

dendrites, p. 36

axon, p. 36

myelin [MY-uh-lin] sheath, p. 37

glial cells (glia), p. 37

action potential, p. 37

threshold, p. 37

synapse [SIN-aps], p. 39

neurotransmitters, p. 39

endorphins [en-DOR-fins], p. 40

nervous system, p. 41

central nervous system (CNS), p. 41

peripheral nervous system (PNS), p. 41

nerves, p. 41

sensory (afferent) neurons, p. 41

motor (efferent) neurons, p. 41

interneurons, p. 41

somatic nervous system, p. 42

autonomic [aw-tuh-NAHM-ik] nervous system (ANS), p. 42

sympathetic nervous system, p. 42

parasympathetic nervous system, p. 42

reflex, p. 44

endocrine [EN-duh-krin] system, p. 45

hormones, p. 45

adrenal [ah-DREEN-el] glands, p. 45

pituitary gland, p. 45

lesion [LEE-zhuhn], p. 46

brainstem, p. 47

medulla [muh-DUL-uh], p. 47

electroencephalogram (EEG), p. 48

PET (positron emission tomography) scan, p. 48

MRI (magnetic resonance imaging), p. 48

fMRI (functional MRI), p. 48

thalamus [THAL-uh-muss], p. 48

reticular formation, p. 49

cerebellum [sehr-uh-BELL-um], p. 50

limbic system, p. 50

amygdala [uh-MIG-duh-la], p. 50

hypothalamus [hi-po-THAL-uh-muss], p. 51

cerebral [seh-REE-bruhl] cortex, p. 53

frontal lobes, p. 53

parietal [puh-RYE-uh-tuhl] lobes, p. 53

occipital [ahk-SIP-uh-tuhl] lobes, p. 53

temporal lobes, p. 53

motor cortex, p. 54

sensory cortex, p. 55

association areas, p. 56

plasticity, p. 57

neurogenesis, p. 58

corpus callosum [KOR-pus kah-LOW-sum], p. 59

split brain, p. 59

environment, p. 62

behavior genetics, p. 62

chromosomes, p. 62

DNA *(deoxyribonucleic acid)*, p. 62

genes, p. 62

identical twins, p. 63

fraternal twins, p. 63

interaction, p. 67

epigenetics, p. 67

evolutionary psychology, p. 68

natural selection, p. 68

mutation, p. 69

EXPERIENCE THE TESTING EFFECT

Test yourself repeatedly throughout your studies. This will not only help you figure out what you know and don't know; the testing itself will help you learn and remember the information more effectively thanks to the *testing effect*.

1. The neuron fiber that passes messages through its branches to other neurons or to muscles and glands is the _____.

2. The tiny space between the axon of one neuron and the dendrite or cell body of another is called the

   a. axon terminal.

   b. branching fiber.

   c. synaptic gap.

   d. threshold.

3. Regarding a neuron's response to stimulation, the intensity of the stimulus determines

   a. whether or not an impulse is generated.

   b. how fast an impulse is transmitted.

   c. how intense an impulse will be.

   d. whether reuptake will occur.

4. In a sending neuron, when an action potential reaches an axon terminal, the impulse triggers the release of chemical messengers called _____.

5. Endorphins are released in the brain in response to
   a. morphine or heroin.
   b. pain or vigorous exercise.
   c. the all-or-none response.
   d. All these answers are correct.

6. The autonomic nervous system controls internal functions, such as heart rate and glandular activity. The word *autonomic* means
   a. calming.
   b. voluntary.
   c. self-regulating.
   d. arousing.

7. The sympathetic nervous system arouses us for action and the parasympathetic nervous system calms us down. Together, the two systems make up the _____ nervous system.

8. The neurons of the spinal cord are part of the _____ nervous system.

9. The most influential endocrine gland, known as the master gland, is the
   a. pituitary.
   b. hypothalamus.
   c. thyroid.
   d. pancreas.

10. The _____ _____ secrete(s) epinephrine and norepinephrine, helping to arouse the body during times of stress.

11. The part of the brainstem that controls heartbeat and breathing is the
    a. cerebellum.
    b. medulla.
    c. cortex.
    d. thalamus.

12. The thalamus functions like a(n)
    a. memory bank.
    b. balance center.
    c. breathing regulator.
    d. Internet router.

13. The lower brain structure that governs arousal is the
    a. spinal cord.
    b. cerebellum.
    c. reticular formation.
    d. medulla.

14. The part of the brain that coordinates voluntary movement and enables nonverbal learning and memory is the _____.

15. Two parts of the limbic system are the amygdala and the
    a. cerebral hemispheres.
    b. hippocampus.
    c. thalamus.
    d. pituitary.

16. A cat's ferocious response to electrical brain stimulation would lead you to suppose the electrode had touched the _____.

17. The neural structure that most directly regulates eating, drinking, and body temperature is the
    a. endocrine system.
    b. hypothalamus.
    c. hippocampus.
    d. amygdala.

18. The initial reward center discovered by Olds and Milner was located in the _____.

19. If a neurosurgeon stimulated your right motor cortex, you would most likely
    a. see light.
    b. hear a sound.
    c. feel a touch on the right arm.
    d. move your left leg.

20. How do different neural networks communicate with one another to let you respond when a friend greets you at a party?

21. Which of the following body regions has the greatest representation in the sensory cortex?
    a. Upper arm
    b. Toes
    c. Lips
    d. All regions are equally represented.

22. The "uncommitted" areas that make up about three-fourths of the cerebral cortex are called _____ _____.

23. Judging and planning are enabled by the _____ lobes.

24. What would it be like to talk on the phone if you didn't have temporal lobe association areas? What would you hear? What would you understand?

25. Plasticity is especially evident in the brains of
    a. split-brain patients.
    b. young adults.
    c. young children.
    d. right-handed people.

26. An experimenter flashes the word HERON across the visual field of a man whose corpus callosum has been sev-

ered. HER is transmitted to his right hemisphere and ON to his left hemisphere. When asked to indicate what he saw, the man says he saw _____ but points to _____.

27. Studies of people with split brains and brain scans of those with undivided brains indicate that the left hemisphere excels in
   a. processing language.
   b. visual perceptions.
   c. making inferences.
   d. neurogenesis.

28. Damage to the brain's right hemisphere is most likely to reduce a person's ability to
   a. recite the alphabet rapidly.
   b. make inferences.
   c. understand verbal instructions.
   d. solve arithmetic problems.

29. What do behavior geneticists study?

30. The threadlike structures made largely of DNA molecules are called _____.

31. A small segment of DNA that codes for particular proteins is referred to as a _____.

32. When the mother's egg and the father's sperm unite, each contributes
   a. one chromosome pair.
   b. 23 chromosomes.
   c. 23 chromosome pairs.
   d. 25,000 chromosomes.

33. Fraternal twins result when
   a. a single egg is fertilized by a single sperm and then splits.
   b. a single egg is fertilized by two sperm and then splits.
   c. two eggs are fertilized by two sperm.
   d. two eggs are fertilized by a single sperm.

34. _____ twins share the same DNA.

35. Adoption studies seek to understand genetic influences on personality. They do this mainly by
   a. comparing adopted children with nonadopted children.
   b. evaluating whether adopted children's personalities more closely resemble those of their adoptive parents or their biological parents.
   c. studying the effect of prior neglect on adopted children.
   d. studying the effect of children's age at adoption.

Find answers to these questions in Appendix E, in the back of the book.

Experience more of the TESTING EFFECT

Multiple-format self-tests and more may be found at www.worthpublishers.com/myers.

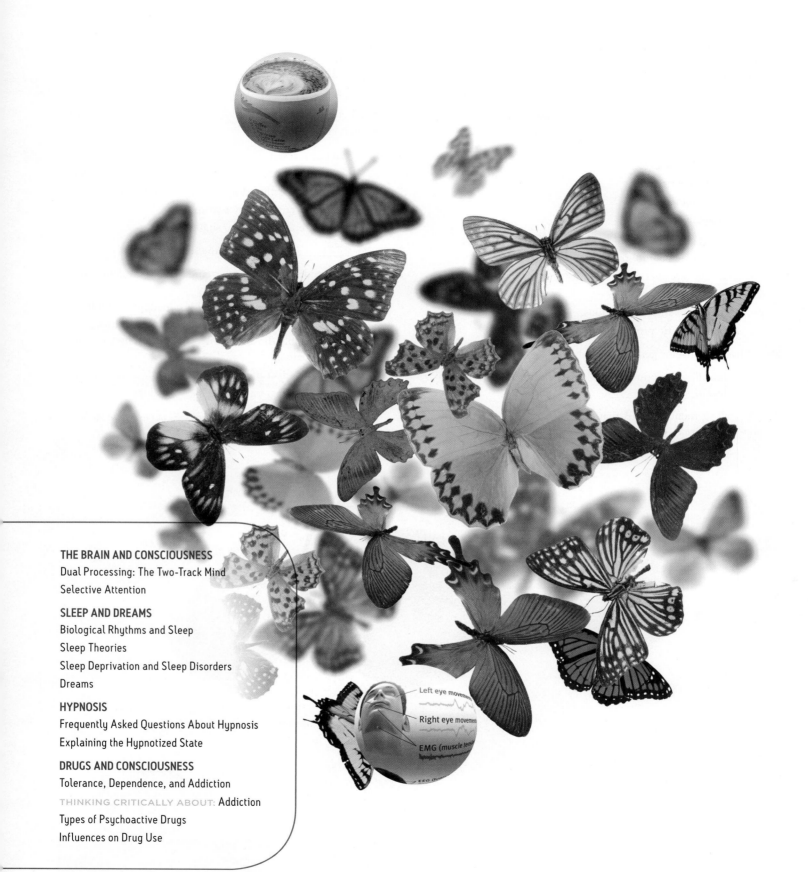

Left eye movement

Right eye movement

EMG (muscle tension

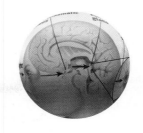

CHAPTER **3**

Consciousness and the Two-Track Mind

Consciousness can be a funny thing. It offers us weird experiences, as when entering sleep or leaving a dream, and sometimes it leaves us wondering who is really in control. After zoning me out with nitrous oxide, my dentist tells me to turn my head to the left. My conscious mind resists: *"No way,"* I silently say. *"You can't boss me around!"* Whereupon my robotic head, ignoring my conscious mind, turns obligingly under the dentist's control.

Then there are those times when consciousness seems to split. Reading *Green Eggs and Ham* to one of my preschoolers for the umpteenth time, my obliging mouth could say the words while my mind wandered elsewhere. And if someone were to drop by my office while I'm typing this sentence, it would not be a problem. My fingers could complete it as I strike up a conversation.

What do such experiences reveal? Was my drug-induced dental experience akin to people's experiences with other *psychoactive drugs* (mood- and perception-altering substances)? Was my automatic obedience to my dentist like people's responses to a hypnotist? Does a split in consciousness, as when our mind goes elsewhere while reading or typing, explain people's behavior while under hypnosis? And during sleep, when do those weird dream experiences occur, and why? Before considering these questions and more, let's ask a fundamental question: What is *consciousness?*

consciousness our awareness of ourselves and our environment.

cognitive neuroscience the interdisciplinary study of the brain activity linked with cognition (including perception, thinking, memory, and language).

"Psychology must discard all reference to consciousness."

Behaviorist John B. Watson (1913)

The Brain and Consciousness

3-1: What is the place of consciousness in psychology's history?

Every science has concepts so fundamental they are nearly impossible to define. Biologists agree on what is alive but not on precisely what life is. In physics, *matter* and *energy* elude simple definition. To psychologists, consciousness is similarly a fundamental yet slippery concept. At its beginning, *psychology* was "the description and explanation of states of consciousness" (Ladd, 1887). But during the first half of the twentieth century, the difficulty of scientifically studying consciousness led many psychologists—including those in the emerging school of *behaviorism* (Chapter 7)—to turn to direct observations of behavior. By the 1960s, psychology had nearly lost consciousness and was defining itself as "the science of behavior." Consciousness was likened to a car's speedometer: "It doesn't make the car go, it just reflects what's happening" (Seligman, 1991, p. 24).

After 1960, mental concepts reemerged. Neuroscience advances linked brain activity to sleeping, dreaming, and other mental states. Researchers began studying consciousness altered by hypnosis and drugs. Psychologists of all persuasions were affirming the importance of *cognition,* or mental processes. Psychology was regaining consciousness.

Most psychologists now define **consciousness** as our awareness of ourselves and our environment. This awareness allows us to assemble information from many sources as we reflect on our past and plan for our future. And it focuses our attention when we learn a complex concept or behavior. When learning to drive, we focus on the car and the traffic. With practice, driving becomes semi-automatic, freeing us to focus our attention on other things. Over time, we flit between various *states of consciousness,* including normal waking awareness and various altered states (**FIGURE 3.1**).

Today's science explores the biology of consciousness. Scientists now assume, in the words of neuroscientist Marvin Minsky (1986, p. 287), that "the mind is what the brain does."

Evolutionary psychologists speculate that consciousness offers a reproductive advantage (Barash, 2006). By considering consequences and helping us read others' intentions, consciousness helps us act in our long-term interests. Even so, that leaves us with the "hard problem": How do brain cells jabbering to one another create our awareness of the taste of a taco, the idea of infinity, the feeling of fright? Such questions are at the heart of **cognitive neuroscience**—the interdisciplinary study of the brain activity linked with our mental processes. Based on your cortical activation patterns, neuroscientists can now, in limited ways, read your mind (Bor, 2010). They could tell, for example, which of 10 similar objects (hammer, drill, and so forth) you were viewing (Shinkareva et al., 2008).

INSADCO Photography/Alamy

FIGURE 3.1

Altered states of consciousness
In addition to normal, waking awareness, consciousness comes to us in altered states, including daydreaming, sleeping, meditating, and drug-induced hallucinating.

Some states occur spontaneously	Daydreaming	Drowsiness	Dreaming
Some are physiologically induced	Hallucinations	Orgasm	Food or oxygen starvation
Some are psychologically induced	Sensory deprivation	Hypnosis	Meditation

Discovering which brain region becomes active with a particular conscious experience strikes many people as interesting but not mind blowing. (If everything psychological is simultaneously biological, then our ideas, emotions, and spirituality must all, somehow, be embodied.) What *is* mind blowing to many of us is the growing evidence that we have, so to speak, two minds, each supported by its own neural equipment.

> **dual processing** the principle that information is often simultaneously processed on separate conscious and unconscious tracks.

> **blindsight** a condition in which a person can respond to a visual stimulus without consciously experiencing it.

RETRIEVE IT

• Those working in the interdisciplinary field called _____ _____ study the brain activity associated with perception, thinking, memory, and language.

ANSWER: cognitive neuroscience

Dual Processing: The Two-Track Mind

3-2: What is the "dual-processing" being revealed by today's cognitive neuroscience?

At any moment, you and I are aware of little more than what's on the screen of our consciousness. But beneath the surface, unconscious information processing occurs simultaneously on many parallel tracks. When we look at a bird flying, we are consciously aware of the result of our cognitive processing ("It's a hummingbird!") but not of our subprocessing of the bird's color, form, movement, and distance. One of the grand ideas of recent cognitive neuroscience is that much of our brain work occurs off stage, out of sight. Perception, memory, thinking, language, and attitudes all operate on two levels—a conscious, deliberate "high road," and an unconscious, automatic "low road." Today's researchers call this **dual processing.** We know more than we know we know.

If you are a driver, consider how you move into a right lane. Drivers know this unconsciously, yet they cannot accurately explain it (Eagleman, 2011). Can you? Most say they would bank the steering wheel to the right, then straighten it out—a procedure that would actually steer them off the road. In reality, an experienced driver, after moving right, automatically reverses the wheel just as far to the left of center, and only then returns to the center position. The lesson: The human brain is a device for converting conscious into unconscious knowledge.

Or consider this story, which illustrates how science can be stranger than science fiction. During my sojourns at Scotland's University of St. Andrews, I came to know cognitive neuroscientists David Milner and Melvyn Goodale (2008). A local woman, whom they called D. F., had suffered brain damage when overcome by carbon monoxide, leaving her unable to recognize and discriminate objects visually. Consciously, D. F. could see nothing. Yet she exhibited **blindsight**—she acted *as though* she could see. Asked to slip a postcard into a vertical or horizontal mail slot, she could do so without error. Asked the width of a block in front of her, she was at a loss, but she could grasp it with just the right finger-thumb distance.

How could this be? Don't we have one visual system? Goodale and Milner knew from animal research that the eye sends information simultaneously to different brain areas, which support different tasks (Weiskrantz, 2009, 2010). Sure enough, a scan of D.F.'s brain activity revealed normal activity in the area concerned with reaching for, grasping, and navigating objects, but damage in the area concerned with consciously recognizing objects. (See another example in **FIGURE 3.2.**)

How strangely intricate is this thing we call vision, conclude Goodale and Milner in their aptly titled book, *Sight Unseen.* We may think of our vision as one system controlling our visually guided actions, but it is actually a dual-processing system. A *visual perception track* enables us "to think about the world"—to recognize things and to plan future actions. A *visual action track* guides our moment-to-moment movements.

FIGURE 3.2

When the blind can "see" In this compelling demonstration of blindsight and the two-track mind, researcher Lawrence Weiskrantz trailed a blindsight patient down a cluttered hallway. Although told the hallway was empty, the patient meandered around all the obstacles without any awareness of them.

selective attention the focusing of conscious awareness on a particular stimulus.

The dual-track mind can also be seen in a patient who lost all his left visual cortex, leaving him blind to objects presented on the right side of his field of vision. He is nevertheless able to sense the emotion expressed in faces, presented to his right, he does not consciously perceive (De Gelder, 2010). The same is true of normally sighted people whose visual cortex has been disabled with magnetic stimulation. Such findings suggest that brain areas below the cortex are processing emotion-related information.

People often have trouble accepting that much of our everyday thinking, feeling, and acting operates outside our conscious awareness (Bargh & Chartrand, 1999). We are understandably biased to believe that our intentions and deliberate choices rule our lives. But consciousness, though enabling us to exert voluntary control and to communicate our mental states to others, is but the tip of the information-processing iceberg. Being intensely focused on an activity (such as reading this chapter, I'd love to think) increases your total brain activity no more than 5 percent above its baseline rate. And even when you rest, "hubs of dark energy" are whirling inside your head (Raichle, 2010).

Unconscious *parallel processing* is faster than conscious *sequential processing,* but both are essential. Parallel processing enables your mind to take care of routine business. Sequential processing is skilled at solving new problems, which requires your focused attention. Try this: If you are right-handed, you can move your right foot in a smooth counterclockwise circle, and you can write the number 3 repeatedly with your right hand—but probably not at the same time. (If you are musically inclined, try something equally difficult: Tap a steady beat three times with your left hand while tapping four times with your right hand.) Both tasks require conscious attention, which can be in only one place at a time. If time is nature's way of keeping everything from happening at once, then consciousness is nature's way of keeping us from thinking and doing everything at once.

RETRIEVE IT

• What are the mind's two tracks, and what is "dual processing"?

ANSWER: Our mind has separate conscious and unconscious tracks that perform dual processing—organizing and interpreting information simultaneously.

Selective Attention

3-3: How much information do we consciously attend to at once?

Through **selective attention,** your awareness focuses, like a flashlight beam, on a minute aspect of all that you experience. By one estimate, your five senses take in 11,000,000 bits of information per second, of which you consciously process about 40 (Wilson, 2002). Yet your mind's unconscious track intuitively makes great use of the other 10,999,960 bits. Until reading this sentence, for example, you have been unaware that your shoes are pressing against your feet or that your nose is in your line of vision. Now, suddenly, your attentional spotlight shifts. Your feet feel encased, your nose stubbornly intrudes on the words before you. While focusing on these words, you've also been blocking other parts of your environment from awareness, though your peripheral vision would let you see them easily. You can change that. As you stare at the X below, notice what surrounds these sentences (the edges of the page, the desktop, the floor).

X

A classic example of selective attention is the *cocktail party effect*—your ability to attend to only one voice among many. Let another voice speak your name and your cognitive radar, operating on your mind's other track, will instantly bring that voice into consciousness. This effect might have prevented an embarrassing and dangerous situation in 2009, when two Northwest Airlines pilots "lost track of time." Focused on their laptops and conversation, they ignored alarmed air traffic controllers' attempts to reach them as they overflew their Minneapolis destination by 150 miles. If only the controllers had known and spoken the pilots' names.

"Has a generation of texters, surfers, and twitterers evolved the enviable ability to process multiple streams of novel information in parallel? Most cognitive psychologists doubt it."

Steven Pinker, "Not at All," 2010

Selective Attention and Accidents

Talk on the phone or attend to a music player or GPS while driving and your selective attention will shift back and forth between the road and its electronic competition. But when a demanding situation requires it, you'll probably give the road your full attention. You'll probably also blink less. When focused on a task, such as reading, people blink less than when their mind is wandering (Smilek et al., 2010). If you want to know whether your dinner companion is focused on what you're saying, watch for eyeblinks and hope there won't be too many.

We pay a toll for switching attentional gears, especially when we shift to complex tasks, like noticing and avoiding cars around us. The toll is a slight and sometimes fatal delay in coping (Rubenstein et al., 2001). About 28 percent of traffic accidents occur when people are chatting on cell phones or texting (National Safety Council, 2010). One study tracked long-haul truck drivers for 18 months. The video cameras mounted in their cabs showed they were at 23 times greater risk of a collision while texting (VTTI, 2009). Mindful of such findings, the United States in 2010 banned truckers and bus drivers from texting while driving (Halsey, 2010).

It's not just truck drivers who are at risk. One in four teen drivers with cell phones admit to texting while driving (Pew, 2009). Multitasking comes at a cost: fMRI scans offer a biological account of how multitasking distracts from brain resources allocated to driving. In areas vital to driving, brain activity decreases an average 37 percent when a driver is attending to conversation (Just et al., 2008).

Even hands-free cell-phone talking is more distracting than chatting with passengers, who can see the driving demands and pause the conversation. When University of Sydney researchers analyzed phone records for the moments before a car crash, they found that cell-phone users (even those with hands-free sets) were four times more at risk (McEvoy et al., 2005, 2007). Having a passenger increased risk only 1.6 times. This risk difference also appeared in an experiment that asked drivers to pull off at a freeway rest stop 8 miles ahead. Of drivers conversing with a passenger, 88 percent did so. Of those talking on a cell phone, 50 percent drove on by (Strayer & Drews, 2007).

"I wasn't texting. I was building this ship in a bottle."

Sally Forth

Driven to distraction In driving-simulation experiments, people whose attention is diverted by cell-phone conversation make more driving errors.

Selective Inattention

At the level of conscious awareness, we are "blind" to all but a tiny sliver of visual stimuli. Ulric Neisser (1979), Robert Becklen and Daniel Cervone (1983) demonstrated this **inattentional blindness** dramatically. They showed people a one-minute video in which images of three black-shirted men tossing a basketball were superimposed over the images of three white-shirted players. The viewers' supposed task was to press a key every time a black-shirted player passed the ball. Most focused their attention so completely on the game that they failed to notice a young woman carrying an umbrella saunter across the screen midway through the video. Seeing a replay of the video, viewers were astonished to see her (Mack & Rock, 2000). This inattentional blindness is a by-product of what we are really good at: focusing attention on some part of our environment.

inattentional blindness failing to see visible objects when our attention is directed elsewhere.

FIGURE 3.3

Gorilla in our midst When attending to one task (counting basketball passes by one of the three-person teams), about half the viewers displayed inattentional blindness by failing to notice a clearly visible gorilla passing through.

In a repeat of the experiment, smart-aleck researchers Daniel Simons and Christopher Chabris (1999) sent a gorilla-suited assistant through a swirl of players (**FIGURE 3.3**). During its 5- to 9-second cameo appearance, the gorilla paused to thump its chest. Still, half the conscientious pass-counting viewers failed to see it. In another follow-up experiment, only 1 in 4 students engrossed in a cell-phone conversation while crossing a campus square noticed a clown-suited unicyclist in their midst (Hyman et al., 2010). (Most of those not on the phone *did* notice.) Attention is powerfully selective. Your conscious mind is in one place at a time.

Given that most people miss someone in a gorilla suit while their attention is riveted elsewhere, imagine the fun that magicians can have by manipulating our selective attention. Misdirect people's attention and they will miss the hand slipping into the pocket. "Every time you perform a magic trick, you're engaging in experimental psychology," says magician Teller, a master of mind-messing methods (2009).

FIGURE 3.4

Change blindness While a man (white hair) provides directions to a construction worker, two experimenters rudely pass between them carrying a door. During this interruption, the original worker switches places with another person wearing different-colored clothing. Most people, focused on their direction giving, do not notice the switch. (From Simons & Levin, 1998.)

Magicians also exploit our **change blindness.** By selectively riveting our attention on their left hand's dramatic act, they entice us to overlook changes made with their other hand. Participants in laboratory experiments on change blindness have failed to notice that, after a brief visual interruption, a big Coke bottle had disappeared, a railing had risen, or clothing color had changed (Chabris & Simons, 2010; Resnick et al., 1997). Two-thirds of those who were focused on giving directions to a construction worker failed to notice when he was replaced by another worker during a staged interruption (**FIGURE 3.4**). Out of sight, out of mind.

Some stimuli, however, are so powerful, so strikingly distinct, that we experience *popout,* as with the only smiling face in **FIGURE 3.5.** We don't choose to attend to these stimuli; they draw our eye and demand our attention.

The dual-track mind is active even during sleep, as we see next.

FIGURE 3.5

The pop-out phenomenon

Sleep and Dreams

Sleep—the irresistible tempter to whom we inevitably succumb. Sleep—the equalizer of presidents and peasants. Sleep—sweet, renewing, mysterious sleep. While sleeping, you may feel "dead to the world," but you are not. Even when you are deeply asleep, your perceptual window is open a crack. You move around on your bed, but you manage not to fall out. The occasional roar of passing vehicles may leave your deep sleep undisturbed, but a cry from a baby's nursery quickly interrupts it. So does the sound of your name. EEG recordings confirm that the brain's auditory cortex responds to sound stimuli even during sleep (Kutas, 1990). And when you are asleep, as when you are awake, you process most information outside your conscious awareness.

Many of sleep's mysteries are now being solved as some people sleep, attached to recording devices, while others observe. By recording brain waves and muscle movements, and by observing and occasionally waking sleepers, researchers are glimpsing things that a thousand years of common sense never told us. Perhaps you can anticipate some of their discoveries. Are the following statements true or false?

1. When people dream of performing some activity, their limbs often move in concert with the dream.

2. Older adults sleep more than young adults.

3. Sleepwalkers are acting out their dreams.

4. Sleep experts recommend treating insomnia with an occasional sleeping pill.

5. Some people dream every night; others seldom dream.

All these statements (adapted from Palladino & Carducci, 1983) are *false*. To see why, read on.

Biological Rhythms and Sleep

Like the ocean, life has its rhythmic tides. Over varying time periods, our bodies fluctuate, and with them, our minds. Let's look more closely at two of those biological rhythms—our 24-hour biological clock and our 90-minute sleep cycle.

Circadian Rhythm

3-4: How do our biological rhythms influence our daily functioning?

The rhythm of the day parallels the rhythm of life—from our waking at a new day's birth to our nightly return to what Shakespeare called "death's counterfeit." Our bodies roughly synchronize with the 24-hour cycle of day and night by an internal biological clock called the **circadian rhythm** (from the Latin *circa,* "about," and *diem,* "day"). As morning approaches, body temperature rises, then peaks during the day, dips for a time in early afternoon (when many people take siestas), and begins to drop again in the evening. Thinking is sharpest and memory most accurate when we are at our daily peak in circadian arousal. Try pulling an all-nighter or working an occasional night shift. You'll feel groggiest in the middle of the night but may gain new energy when your normal wake-up time arrives.

Eric Isselée/Shutterstock

Age and experience can alter our circadian rhythm. Most 20-year-olds are evening-energized "owls," with performance improving across the day (May & Hasher, 1998).

change blindness failing to notice changes in the environment.

circadian [ser-KAY-dee-an] **rhythm** the biological clock; regular bodily rhythms (for example, of temperature and wakefulness) that occur on a 24-hour cycle.

"I love to sleep. Do you? Isn't it great? It really is the best of both worlds. You get to be alive and unconscious."

Comedian Rita Rudner, 1993

Dolphins, porpoises, and whales sleep with one side of their brain at a time (Miller et al., 2008).

REM sleep rapid eye movement sleep; a recurring sleep stage during which vivid dreams commonly occur. Also known as *paradoxical sleep,* because the muscles are relaxed (except for minor twitches) but other body systems are active.

alpha waves the relatively slow brain waves of a relaxed, awake state.

sleep periodic, natural loss of consciousness—as distinct from unconsciousness resulting from a coma, general anesthesia, or hibernation. (Adapted from Dement, 1999.)

hallucinations false sensory experiences, such as seeing something in the absence of an external visual stimulus.

delta waves the large, slow brain waves associated with deep sleep.

Most older adults are morning-loving "larks," with performance declining as the day wears on. By mid-evening, when the night has hardly begun for many young adults, retirement homes are typically quiet. After about age 20 (slightly earlier for women), we begin to shift from being owls to being larks (Roenneberg et al., 2004). Women become more morning oriented as they have children and also as they transition to menopause (Leonhard & Randler, 2009; Randler & Bausback, 2010). Morning types tend to do better in school, to take more initiative, and to be less vulnerable to depression (Randler, 2008, 2009; Randler & Frech, 2009).

Peter Chadwick/Photo Researchers, Inc.

Sleep Stages

3-5: What is the biological rhythm of our sleeping and dreaming stages?

Sooner or later, sleep overtakes us and consciousness fades as different parts of our brain's cortex stop communicating (Massimini et al., 2005). But rather than emitting a constant dial tone, the sleeping brain has its own biological rhythm.

About every 90 minutes, you cycle through four distinct sleep stages. This simple fact apparently was unknown until 8-year-old Armond Aserinsky went to bed one night in 1952. His father, Eugene, a University of Chicago graduate student, needed to test an electroencephalograph he had repaired that day (Aserinsky, 1988; Seligman & Yellen, 1987). Placing electrodes near Armond's eyes to record the rolling eye movements then believed to occur during sleep, Aserinsky watched the machine go wild, tracing deep zigzags on the graph paper. Could the machine still be broken? As the night proceeded and the activity recurred, Aserinsky realized that the periods of fast, jerky eye movements were accompanied by energetic brain activity. Awakened during one such episode, Armond reported having a dream. Aserinsky had discovered what we now know as **REM sleep** (rapid *e*ye *m*ovement sleep).

Similar procedures used with thousands of volunteers showed the cycles were a normal part of sleep (Kleitman, 1960). To appreciate these studies, imagine yourself as a participant. As the hour grows late, you feel sleepy and yawn in response to reduced brain metabolism. (Yawning, which can be socially contagious, stretches your neck muscles and increases your heart rate, which increases your alertness [Moorcroft, 2003].) When you are ready for bed, a researcher comes in and tapes electrodes to your scalp (to detect your brain waves), on your chin (to detect muscle tension), and just outside the corners of your eyes (to detect eye movements) (**FIGURE 3.6**). Other devices will record your heart rate, respiration rate, and genital arousal.

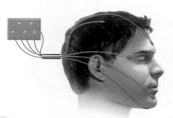
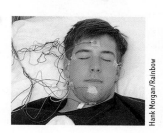
Hank Morgan/Rainbow

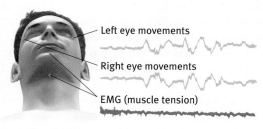
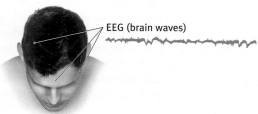

Left eye movements

Right eye movements

EMG (muscle tension)

EEG (brain waves)

FIGURE 3.6

Measuring sleep activity Sleep researchers measure brain-wave activity, eye movements, and muscle tension by electrodes that pick up weak electrical signals from the brain, eyes, and facial muscles. (From Dement, 1978.)

When you are in bed with your eyes closed, the researcher in the next room sees on the EEG the relatively slow **alpha waves** of your awake but relaxed state (**FIGURE 3.7**). As you adapt to all this equipment, you grow tired and, in an unremembered moment, slip into **sleep** (**FIGURE 3.8**). The transition is marked by the slowed breathing and the irregular brain waves of non-REM stage 1 sleep. Using the new American Academy of Sleep Medicine classification of sleep stages, this is called NREM-1 sleep (Silber et al., 2008).

In one of his 15,000 research participants, William Dement (1999) observed the moment the brain's perceptual window to the outside world slammed shut. Dement asked this sleep-deprived young man, lying on his back with eyelids taped open, to press a button every time a strobe light flashed in his eyes (about every 6 seconds). After a few minutes the young man missed one. Asked why, he said, "Because there was no flash." But there was a flash. He missed it because (as his brain activity revealed) he had fallen asleep for 2 seconds, missing not only the flash 6 inches from his nose but also the awareness of the abrupt moment of entry into sleep.

During this brief NREM-1 sleep you may experience fantastic images resembling **hallucinations**—sensory experiences that occur without a sensory stimulus. You may have a sensation of falling (at which moment your body may suddenly jerk) or of floating weightlessly. These *hypnagogic* sensations may later be incorporated into your memories. People who claim to have been abducted by aliens—often shortly after getting into bed—commonly recall being floated off (or pinned down on) their beds (Clancy, 2005).

You then relax more deeply and begin about 20 minutes of NREM-2 sleep, with its periodic *sleep spindles*—bursts of rapid, rhythmic brain-wave activity (see Figure 3.7). Although you could still be awakened without too much difficulty, you are now clearly asleep.

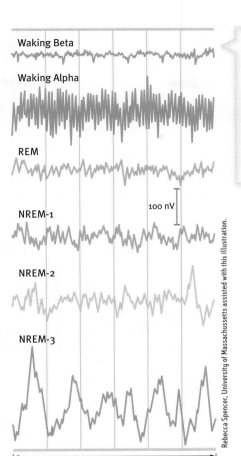

Rebecca Spencer, University of Massachussetts assisted with this illustration.

FIGURE 3.7

Brain waves and sleep stages The beta waves of an alert, waking state and the regular alpha waves of an awake, relaxed state differ from the slower, larger delta waves of deep NREM-3 sleep. Although the rapid REM sleep waves resemble the near-waking NREM-1 sleep waves, the body is more aroused during REM sleep than during NREM sleep.

To catch your own hypnagogic experiences, you might use your alarm's snooze function.

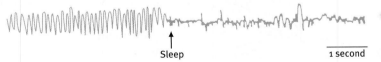

Sleep ↑   1 second

FIGURE 3.8

The moment of sleep We seem unaware of the moment we fall into sleep, but someone watching our brain waves could tell. (From Dement, 1999.)

Then you transition to the deep sleep of NREM-3. During this slow-wave sleep, which lasts for about 30 minutes, your brain emits large, slow **delta waves** and you are hard to awaken. (It is at the end of the deep, slow-wave NREM-3 sleep that children may wet the bed.)

REM Sleep

About an hour after you first fall asleep, a strange thing happens. Rather than continuing in deep slumber, you ascend from your initial sleep dive. Returning through NREM-2 (where you spend about half your night), you enter the most intriguing sleep phase—REM sleep (**FIGURE 3.9** on the next page). For about 10 minutes, your brain waves become rapid and saw-toothed, more like those of the nearly awake NREM-1 sleep. But unlike NREM-1, during REM sleep your heart rate rises, your

People rarely snore during dreams. When REM starts, snoring stops.

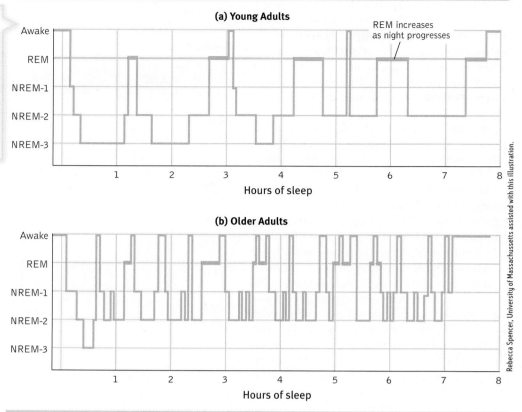

Rebecca Spencer, University of Massachussetts assisted with this illustration.

© 1994 by Sidney Harris.

*"Boy are my eyes tired!
I had REM sleep all night long."*

Horses, which spend 92 percent of
each day standing and can sleep
standing, must lie down for REM sleep
(Morrison, 2003).

breathing becomes rapid and irregular, and every
half-minute or so your eyes dart around in momentary bursts of activity behind closed lids. These eye
movements announce the beginning of a dream—
often emotional, usually story-like, and richly hallucinatory. Because anyone watching a sleeper's eyes
can notice these REM bursts, it is amazing that science was ignorant of REM sleep until 1952.

Except during very scary dreams, your genitals
become aroused during REM sleep. You have an
erection or increased vaginal lubrication and clito-
ral engorgement, regardless of whether the dream's
content is sexual (Karacan et al., 1966). Men's common "morning erection" stems from the night's last
REM period, often just before waking. In young
men, sleep-related erections outlast REM periods,
lasting 30 to 45 minutes on average (Karacan et al., 1983; Schiavi & Schreiner-Engel,
1988). A typical 25-year-old man therefore has an erection during nearly half his
night's sleep, a 65-year-old man for one-quarter. Many men troubled by *erectile dysfunction* (impotence) have sleep-related erections, suggesting the problem is not between
their legs.

Your brain's motor cortex is active during REM sleep, but your brainstem blocks
its messages. This leaves your muscles relaxed, so much so that, except for an occasional
finger, toe, or facial twitch, you are essentially paralyzed. Moreover, you cannot easily be
awakened. REM sleep is thus sometimes called *paradoxical* sleep: The body is internally
aroused, with waking-like brain activity, yet asleep and externally calm.

Uriel Sinai/Getty Images

Safety in numbers?

RETRIEVE IT

• Why would communal sleeping provide added protection for those whose safety depends upon vigilance, such as these soldiers?

ANSWER: With each soldier cycling through the sleep stages independently, it is very likely that at any given time at least one of them will be awake or easily wakened in the event of a threat.

The sleep cycle repeats itself about every 90 minutes for younger adults (somewhat more frequently for older adults). As the night wears on, deep NREM-3 sleep grows shorter and disappears. The REM and NREM-2 sleep periods get longer (see Figure 3.9). By morning, we have spent 20 to 25 percent of an average night's sleep—some 100 minutes—in REM sleep. Thirty-seven percent of people report rarely or never having dreams "that you can remember the next morning" (Moore, 2004). Yet even they will, more than 80 percent of the time, recall a dream after being awakened during REM sleep. We spend about 600 hours a year experiencing some 1500 dreams, or more than 100,000 dreams over a typical lifetime—dreams swallowed by the night but not acted out, thanks to REM's protective paralysis.

suprachiasmatic nucleus a pair of cell clusters in the hypothalamus that responds to light-sensitive retinal proteins; causes pineal gland to increase or decrease production of melatonin, thus modifying our feelings of sleepiness.

RETRIEVE IT

• What are the four sleep stages, and in what order do we normally travel through those stages?

• Can you match the cognitive experience with the sleep stage?

   1. NREM-1   a. story-like dreams
   2. NREM-3   b. fleeting images
   3. REM   c. minimal awareness

ANSWERS: 1. b, 2. c, 3. a

ANSWER: REM, NREM-1, NREM-2, NREM-3; normally we move through NREM-1, then NREM-2, then NREM-3, then back up through NREM-2 before we experience REM sleep.

What Affects Our Sleep Patterns?

3-6: How do biology and environment interact in our sleep patterns?

The idea that "everyone needs 8 hours of sleep" is untrue. Newborns sleep nearly two-thirds of their day, most adults no more than one-third. Still, there is more to our sleep differences than age. Some of us thrive with fewer than 6 hours per night; others regularly rack up 9 hours or more. Such sleep patterns are genetically influenced (Hor & Tafti, 2009). In studies of fraternal and identical twins, only the identical twins had strikingly similar sleep patterns and durations (Webb & Campbell, 1983). Today's researchers are discovering the genes that regulate sleep in humans and animals (Donlea et al., 2009; He et al., 2009).

In the United States and Canada, adults average 7 to 8 hours of sleep per night (Hurst, 2008; National Sleep Foundation, 2010; Robinson & Martin, 2009). North Americans are nevertheless sleeping less than their counterparts a century ago. Thanks to modern light bulbs, shift work, and social diversions, those who would have gone to bed at 9:00 P.M. are now up until 11:00 P.M. or later. With sleep, as with waking behavior, biology and environment interact.

Being bathed in light disrupts our 24-hour biological clock (Czeisler et al., 1999; Dement, 1999). Bright light affects our sleepiness by activating light-sensitive retinal proteins. This signals the brain's **suprachiasmatic nucleus** to decrease production of *melatonin,* a sleep-inducing hormone (**FIGURE 3.10**). Our ancestors' body clocks were

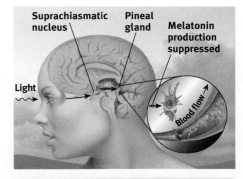

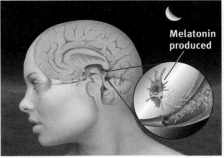

FIGURE 3.10

The biological clock Light striking the retina signals the suprachiasmatic nucleus (SCN) to suppress the pineal gland's production of the sleep hormone melatonin. At night, the SCN quiets down, allowing the pineal gland to release melatonin into the bloodstream.

A circadian disadvantage: One study of a decade's 24,121 Major League Baseball games found that teams who had crossed three time zones before playing a multiday series had nearly a 60 percent chance of losing their first game (Winter et al., 2009).

attuned to the rising and setting Sun of the 24-hour day. Many of today's young adults adopt something closer to a 25-hour day, by staying up too late to get 8 hours of sleep. Most animals, too, when placed under unnatural constant illumination will exceed a 24-hour day.

Sleep often eludes those who stay up late and sleep in on weekends, and then go to bed earlier on Sunday to prepare for the new week ahead (Oren & Terman, 1998). For North Americans who fly to Europe and need to be up when their circadian rhythm cries *"SLEEP,"* bright light (spending the next day outdoors) helps reset the biological clock (Czeisler et al., 1986, 1989; Eastman et al., 1995).

RETRIEVE IT

- The _____ nucleus helps monitor the brain's release of melatonin, which affects our _____ rhythm.

ANSWERS: suprachiasmatic nucleus; circadian

Sleep Theories

3-7: What are sleep's functions?

So, our sleep patterns differ from person to person and from culture to culture. But why do we have this need for sleep? Psychologists offer five possible reasons why sleep evolved.

"Sleep faster, we need the pillows."
Yiddish proverb

"Corduroy pillows make headlines."
Anonymous

1. ***Sleep protects.*** When darkness shut down the day's hunting, food gathering, and travel, our distant ancestors were better off asleep in a cave, out of harm's way. Those who didn't try to navigate around rocks and cliffs at night were more likely to leave descendants. This fits a broader principle: A species' sleep pattern tends to suit its ecological niche (Siegel, 2009). Animals with the greatest need to graze and the least ability to hide tend to sleep less. (For a sampling of animal sleep times, see **FIGURE 3.11**.)

2. ***Sleep helps us recuperate.*** It helps restore and repair brain tissue. Bats and other animals with high waking metabolism burn a lot of calories, producing a lot of *free radicals,* molecules that are toxic to neurons. Sleeping a lot gives resting neurons time to repair themselves, while pruning or weakening unused connections (Gilestro et al., 2009; Siegel, 2003; Vyazovskiy et al., 2008). Think of it this way: When consciousness leaves your house, brain construction workers come in for a makeover.

3. ***Sleep helps restore and rebuild our fading memories of the day's experiences.*** Sleep consolidates our memories—it strengthens and stabilizes neural memory traces (Racsmány et al., 2010; Rasch & Born, 2008). People trained to perform tasks therefore recall them better after a night's sleep, or even after a short nap, than after several hours awake (Stickgold & Ellenbogen, 2008). After sleeping well, older people remember more. And in both humans and rats, neural activity during slow-wave sleep re-enacts and promotes recall of prior novel experiences (Peigneux et al., 2004; Ribeiro et al., 2004). Sleep, it seems, strengthens memories in a way that being awake does not.

4. ***Sleep feeds creative thinking.*** On occasion, dreams have inspired noteworthy literary, artistic, and scientific achievements, such as the dream that clued chemist August Kekulé to the structure of benzene (Ross, 2006). More commonplace is the boost that a complete night's sleep gives to our thinking and learning. After working on a task, then sleeping on it, people solve problems more insightfully than do those who

FIGURE 3.11

Animal sleep times Would you rather be a brown bat and sleep 20 hours a day or a giraffe and sleep 2 hours (data from NIH, 2010)?

Kruglov_Orda/Shutterstock; Courtesy of Andrew D. Myers; © Anna63/Dreamstime.com; Steffen Foerster Photography/ Shutterstock; The Agency Collection/Punchstock; Eric Isselée/Shutterstock; pandapaw/Shutterstock

20 Hours   16 Hours   12 Hours   10 Hours   8 Hours   4 Hours   2 hours

stay awake (Wagner et al., 2004). They also are better at spotting connections among novel pieces of information (Ellenbogen et al., 2007). To think smart and see connections, it often pays to sleep on it.

5. ***Sleep supports growth.*** During deep sleep, the pituitary gland releases a growth hormone necessary for muscle development. A regular full night's sleep can also "*dramatically* improve your athletic ability," report James Maas and Rebecca Robbins (2010). Well-rested athletes have faster reaction times, more energy, and greater endurance. Teams that build 8 to 10 hours of daily sleep into their training show improved performance. As we age, we release less of this hormone and spend less time in deep sleep (Pekkanen, 1982).

Given all the benefits of sleep, it's no wonder that sleep loss hits us so hard.

RETRIEVE IT

• What five theories explain our need for sleep?

ANSWER: (1) Sleep has survival value. (2) Sleep helps restore and repair brain tissue. (3) During sleep we strengthen memory traces. (4) Sleep fuels creativity. (5) Sleep plays a role in the growth process.

Sleep Deprivation and Sleep Disorders

3-8: How does sleep loss affect us, and what are the major sleep disorders?

When our body yearns for sleep but does not get it, we begin to feel terrible. Trying to stay awake, we will eventually lose. In the tiredness battle, sleep always wins.

Effects of Sleep Loss

Today, more than ever, our sleep patterns leave us not only sleepy but drained of energy and feelings of well-being. After a succession of 5-hour nights, we accumulate a sleep debt that need not be entirely repaid but cannot be satisfied by one long sleep. "The brain keeps an accurate count of sleep debt for at least two weeks," reported sleep researcher William Dement (1999, p. 64).

Obviously, then, we need sleep. Sleep commands roughly one-third of our lives— some 25 years, on average. Allowed to sleep unhindered, most adults will sleep at least 9 hours a night (Coren, 1996). With that much sleep, we awake refreshed, sustain better moods, and perform more efficient and accurate work. The U.S. Navy and the National Institutes of Health have demonstrated the benefits of unrestricted sleep in experiments in which volunteers spent 14 hours daily in bed for at least a week. For the first few days, the volunteers averaged 12 hours of sleep a day or more, apparently paying off a sleep debt that averaged 25 to 30 hours. That accomplished, they then settled back to 7.5 to 9 hours nightly and felt energized and happier (Dement, 1999). In one Gallup survey (Mason, 2005), 63 percent of adults who reported getting the sleep they needed also reported being "very satisfied" with their personal life (as did only 36 percent of those needing more sleep).

College and university students are especially sleep deprived; 69 percent in one national survey reported "feeling tired" or "having little energy" on several or more days in the last two weeks (AP, 2009). In another survey, 28 percent of high school students acknowledged falling asleep in class at least once a week (Sleep Foundation, 2006). When the going gets boring, the students start snoring.

Sleep loss is a predictor of depression. Researchers who studied 15,500 young people, 12 to 18 years old, found that those who slept 5 or fewer hours a night had a 71 percent higher risk of depression than their peers who slept 8 hours or more (Gangwisch et al., 2010). This link does not appear to reflect sleep difficulties *caused* by depression.

In 1989, Michael Doucette was named America's Safest Driving Teen. In 1990, while driving home from college, he fell asleep at the wheel and collided with an oncoming car, killing both himself and the other driver. Michael's driving instructor later acknowledged never having mentioned sleep deprivation and drowsy driving (Dement, 1999).

"Maybe 'Bring Your Pillow To Work Day' wasn't such a good idea."

When children and youth are followed through time, sleep loss predicts depression rather than vice versa (Gregory et al., 2009). Moreover, REM sleep's processing of emotional experiences helps protect against depression (Walker & van der Helm, 2009). After a good night's sleep, we often do feel better the next day. And that may help to explain why parentally enforced bedtimes predict less depression, and why pushing back school start time leads to improved adolescent sleep, alertness, and mood (Gregory et al., 2009; Owens et al., 2010).

Sleep-deprived students often function below their peak. And they know it: Four in five teens and three in five 18- to 29-year-olds wish they could get more sleep on week-days (Mason, 2003, 2005). Yet that teen who staggers glumly out of bed in response to an unwelcome alarm, yawns through morning classes, and feels half-depressed much of the day may be energized at 11:00 P.M. and mindless of the next day's looming sleepiness (Carskadon, 2002). "Sleep deprivation has consequences—difficulty study-ing, diminished productivity, tendency to make mistakes, irritability, fatigue," noted Dement (1999, p. 231). A large sleep debt "makes you stupid."

It can also make you gain weight. Sleep deprivation increases *ghrelin,* a hunger-arousing hormone, and decreases its hunger-suppressing partner, *leptin* (more on these in Chapter 10). It also increases *cortisol*, a stress hormone that stimulates the body to make fat. Sure enough, children and adults who sleep less than normal are fatter than those who sleep more (Chen et al., 2008; Knutson et al., 2007; Schoenborn & Adams, 2008). And experimental sleep deprivation of adults increases appetite and eating (Nixon et al., 2008; Patel et al., 2006; Spiegel et al., 2004; Van Cauter et al., 2007). This may help explain the common weight gain among sleep-deprived students (although a review of 11 studies reveals that the mythical "freshman 15" is, on average, closer to a "first-year 4" [Hull et al., 2007]).

Sleep affects our immune system. When infections set in, we typically sleep more, boosting our immune cells. Sleep deprivation can suppress the immune cells that battle viral infections and cancer (Motivala & Irwin, 2007). In one experiment, when researchers exposed volunteers to a cold virus, those who had been averaging less than 7 hours sleep a night were three times more likely to develop the cold than were those sleeping 8 or more hours a night (Cohen et al., 2009). Sleep's protective effect may help explain why people who sleep 7 to 8 hours a night tend to outlive those who are chronically sleep deprived, and why older adults who have no difficulty falling or stay-ing asleep tend to live longer than their sleep-deprived agemates (Dement, 1999; Dew et al., 2003).

Sleep deprivation slows reactions and increases errors on visual attention tasks similar to those involved in screening airport baggage, performing surgery, and reading X-rays (Lim & Dinges, 2010). When sleepy frontal lobes confront an unexpected situation, mis-fortune often results. Consider the timing of the 1989 *Exxon Valdez* oil spill; Union Car-bide's 1984 Bhopal, India, disaster; and the 1979 Three Mile Island and 1986 Chernobyl nuclear accidents: All occurred after midnight, when operators in charge were likely to be drowsiest and unresponsive to signals requiring an alert response. Slow responses can also spell disaster for those operating equipment, piloting, or driving. Driver fatigue has contributed to an estimated 20 percent of American traffic accidents (Brody, 2002) and to some 30 percent of Australian highway deaths (Maas, 1999).

Stanley Coren capitalized on what is, for many North Americans, a semi-annual sleep-manipulation experiment—the "spring forward" to "daylight savings" time and "fall backward" to "standard" time. Searching millions of records, Coren found that in both Canada and the United States, accidents increased immediately after the time change that shortens sleep (**FIGURE 3.12**).

FIGURE 3.13 summarizes the effects of sleep deprivation. But there is good news! Psychologists have discovered a treatment that strengthens memory, increases concentra-tion, boosts mood, moderates hunger and obesity, fortifies the disease-fighting immune system, and lessens the risk of fatal accidents. Even better news: The treatment feels

"Remember to sleep because you have to sleep to remember."

James B. Maas and Rebecca S. Robbins, Sleep for Success, *2010*

insomnia recurring problems in falling or staying asleep.

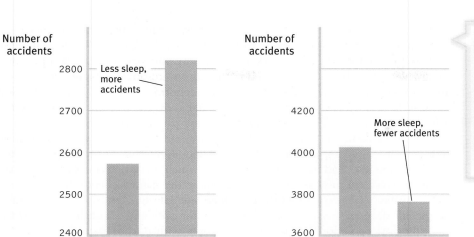

FIGURE 3.12
Canadian traffic accidents On the Monday after the spring time change, when people lose one hour of sleep, accidents increased, as compared with the Monday before. In the fall, traffic accidents normally increase because of greater snow, ice, and darkness, but they diminished after the time change. (Adapted from Coren, 1996.)

good, it can be self-administered, the supplies are limitless, and it's free! If you are a typical university-age student, often going to bed near 2:00 A.M. and dragged out of bed 6 hours later by the dreaded alarm, the treatment is simple: Each night just add an hour to your sleep.

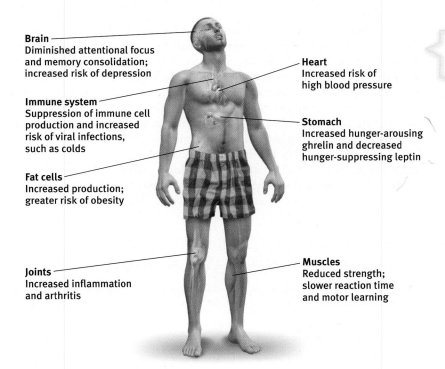

Brain
Diminished attentional focus and memory consolidation; increased risk of depression

Immune system
Suppression of immune cell production and increased risk of viral infections, such as colds

Fat cells
Increased production; greater risk of obesity

Joints
Increased inflammation and arthritis

Heart
Increased risk of high blood pressure

Stomach
Increased hunger-arousing ghrelin and decreased hunger-suppressing leptin

Muscles
Reduced strength; slower reaction time and motor learning

FIGURE 3.13
How sleep deprivation affects us

Major Sleep Disorders

No matter what their normal need for sleep, 1 in 10 adults, and 1 in 4 older adults, complain of **insomnia**—not an occasional inability to sleep when anxious or excited, but persistent problems in falling or staying asleep (Irwin et al., 2006).

Economic recession and stress can rob sleep A National Sleep Foundation (2009) survey found 27 percent of people reporting sleeplessness related to the economy, their personal finances, and employment, as seems evident in this man looking for work.

AP Photo/Paul Sakuma, File

"The lion and the lamb shall lie down together, but the lamb will not be very sleepy."

Woody Allen, in the movie
Love and Death, 1975

"Sleep is like love or happiness. If you pursue it too ardently it will elude you."

Wilse Webb,
Sleep: The Gentle Tyrant, 1992

Did Brahms need his own lullabies? Cranky, overweight, and nap-prone, classical composer Johannes Brahms exhibited common symptoms of sleep apnea (Margolis, 2000).

The Granger Collection, New York

From middle age on, awakening occasionally during the night becomes the norm, not something to fret over or treat with medication (Vitiello, 2009). Ironically, insomnia is worsened by fretting about one's insomnia. In laboratory studies, insomnia complainers do sleep less than others, but they typically overestimate—by about double—how long it takes them to fall asleep. They also underestimate by nearly half how long they actually have slept. Even if we have been awake only an hour or two, we may *think* we have had very little sleep because it's the waking part we remember.

The most common quick fixes for true insomnia—sleeping pills and alcohol—can aggravate the problem, reducing REM sleep and leaving the person with next-day blahs. Such aids can also lead to *tolerance*—a state in which increasing doses are needed to produce an effect. An ideal sleep aid would mimic the natural chemicals abundant during sleep, reliably producing sound sleep without side effects. Until scientists can supply this magic pill, sleep experts have offered some tips for getting better quality sleep (**TABLE 3.1**).

Falling asleep is not the problem for people with **narcolepsy** (from *narco,* "numbness," and *lepsy,* "seizure"), who have sudden attacks of overwhelming sleepiness, usually lasting less than 5 minutes. Narcolepsy attacks can occur at the most inopportune times, perhaps just after taking a terrific swing at a softball or when laughing loudly, shouting angrily, or having sex (Dement, 1978, 1999). In severe cases, the person collapses directly into a brief period of REM sleep, with loss of muscular tension. People with narcolepsy—1 in 2000 of us, estimated the Stanford University Center for Narcolepsy (2002)—must therefore live with extra caution. As a traffic menace, "snoozing is second only to boozing," says the American Sleep Disorders Association, and those with narcolepsy are especially at risk (Aldrich, 1989).

Although 1 in 20 of us have **sleep apnea,** it was unknown before modern sleep research. *Apnea* means "with no breath," and people with this condition intermittently stop breathing during sleep. After an airless minute or so, decreased blood oxygen arouses them and they wake up enough to snort in air for a few seconds, in a process that repeats hundreds of times each night, depriving them of slow-wave sleep. Apnea sufferers don't recall these episodes the next day. So, despite feeling fatigued and depressed—and hearing their mate's complaints about their loud "snoring"—many are unaware of their disorder (Peppard et al., 2006).

Sleep apnea is associated with obesity, and as the number of obese Americans has increased, so has sleep apnea, particularly among overweight men, including some football players (Keller, 2007). In addition to loud snoring, other warning signs are daytime sleepiness, irritability, and (possibly) high blood pressure, which increases the risk of a stroke or heart attack (Dement, 1999). If one doesn't mind looking a little goofy in the

Table 3.1
Some Natural Sleep Aids

- Exercise regularly but not in the late evening. (Late afternoon is best.)

- Avoid caffeine after early afternoon, and avoid food and drink near bedtime. The exception would be a glass of milk, which provides raw materials for the manufacture of serotonin, a neurotransmitter that facilitates sleep.

- Relax before bedtime, using dimmer light.

- Sleep on a regular schedule (rise at the same time even after a restless night) and avoid naps.

- Hide the clock face so you aren't tempted to check it repeatedly.

- Reassure yourself that temporary sleep loss causes no great harm.

- Realize that for any stressed organism, being vigilant is natural and adaptive. A personal conflict during the day often means a fitful sleep that night (Åkerstedt et al., 2007; Brissette & Cohen, 2002). Managing your stress levels will enable more restful sleeping. (See Chapter 11 for more on stress.)

- If all else fails, settle for less sleep, either going to bed later or getting up earlier.

dark, the treatment—a masklike device with an air pump that keeps the sleeper's airway open (imagine a snorkeler at a slumber party)—can effectively relieve apnea symptoms.

Unlike sleep apnea, **night terrors** target mostly children, who may sit up or walk around, talk incoherently, experience doubled heart and breathing rates, and appear terrified (Hartmann, 1981). They seldom wake up fully during an episode and recall little or nothing the next morning—at most, a fleeting, frightening image. Night terrors are not nightmares (which, like other dreams, typically occur during early morning REM sleep); night terrors usually occur during the first few hours of NREM-3.

Sleepwalking—another NREM-3 sleep disorder—and *sleeptalking* are usually childhood disorders and, like narcolepsy, they run in families. (Sleeptalking—usually garbled or nonsensical—can occur during any sleep stage [Mahowald & Ettinger, 1990].) Occasional childhood sleepwalking occurs for about one-third of those with a sleepwalking fraternal twin and half of those with a sleepwalking identical twin. The same is true for sleeptalking (Hublin et al., 1997, 1998). Sleepwalking is usually harmless. After returning to bed on their own or with the help of a family member, few sleepwalkers recall their trip the next morning. About 20 percent of 3- to 12-year-olds have at least one episode of sleepwalking, usually lasting 2 to 10 minutes; some 5 percent have repeated episodes (Giles et al., 1994). Young children, who have the deepest and lengthiest NREM-3 sleep, are the most likely to experience both night terrors and sleepwalking. As we grow older and deep NREM-3 sleep diminishes, so do night terrors and sleepwalking. After being sleep deprived, we sleep more deeply, which increases any tendency to sleepwalk (Zadra et al., 2008).

Dreams

Now playing at an inner theater near you: the premiere showing of a sleeping person's vivid dream. This never-before-seen mental movie features captivating characters wrapped in a plot so original and unlikely, yet so intricate and so seemingly real, that the viewer later marvels at its creativity.

Waking from a troubling dream, wrenched by its emotions, who among us has not wondered about this weird state of consciousness? How can our brain so creatively, colorfully, and completely construct this alternative world? In the shadowland between our dreaming and waking consciousness, we may even wonder for a moment which is real.

Discovering the link between REM sleep and dreaming opened a new era in dream research. Instead of relying on someone's hazy recall hours or days after having a dream, researchers could catch dreams as they happened. They could awaken people during or within 3 minutes after a REM sleep period and hear a vivid account.

What We Dream

3-9: What do we dream?

Daydreams tend to involve the familiar details of our life—perhaps picturing ourselves explaining to an instructor why a paper will be late, or replaying in our minds personal encounters we relish or regret. REM **dreams**—"hallucinations of the sleeping mind" (Loftus & Ketcham, 1994, p. 67)—are vivid, emotional, and bizarre—so vivid we may confuse them with reality. Awakening from a nightmare, a 4-year-old may be sure there is a bear in the house.

We spend 6 years of our life in dreams, many of which are anything but sweet. For both women and men, 8 in 10 dreams are marked by at least one negative event or emotion (Domhoff, 2007). Common themes are repeatedly failing in an attempt to do something; being attacked, pursued, or rejected; or experiencing misfortune (Hall et al., 1982). Dreams with sexual imagery occur less often than you might think. In one study, only 1 in 10 dreams among young men and 1 in 30 among young women had sexual content (Domhoff, 1996). More commonly, a dream's story line incorporates traces of previous days' nonsexual experiences and preoccupations (De Koninck, 2000):

narcolepsy a sleep disorder characterized by uncontrollable sleep attacks. The sufferer may lapse directly into REM sleep, often at inopportune times.

sleep apnea a sleep disorder characterized by temporary cessations of breathing during sleep and repeated momentary awakenings.

night terrors a sleep disorder characterized by high arousal and an appearance of being terrified; unlike nightmares, night terrors occur during NREM-3 sleep, within two or three hours of falling asleep, and are seldom remembered.

dream a sequence of images, emotions, and thoughts passing through a sleeping person's mind. Dreams are notable for their hallucinatory imagery, discontinuities, and incongruities, and for the dreamer's delusional acceptance of the content and later difficulties remembering it.

A dreamy take on dreamland The 2010 movie *Inception* creatively plays off our interest in finding meaning in our dreams and in understanding the layers of our consciousness. It further explores the idea of creating false memories through the power of suggestion—an idea we will explore in Chapter 8.

"I do not believe that I am now dreaming, but I cannot prove that I am not."

Philosopher Bertrand Russell (1872-1970)

Would you suppose that people dream if blind from birth? Studies in France, Hungary, Egypt, and the United States all found blind people dreaming of using their nonvisual senses—hearing, touching, smelling, tasting (Buquet, 1988; Taha, 1972; Vekassy, 1977).

MAXINE

> "For what one has dwelt on by day, these things are seen in visions of the night."
>
> *Menander of Athens (342–292 B.C.E.),*
> Fragments

A popular sleep myth: If you dream you are falling and hit the ground (or if you dream of dying), you die. (Unfortunately, those who could confirm these ideas are not around to do so. Some people, however, have had such dreams and are alive to report them.)

> "Follow your dreams, except for that one where you're naked at work."
>
> *Attributed to Henny Youngman*

- After suffering a trauma, people commonly report nightmares, which help extinguish daytime fears (Levin & Nielsen, 2007, 2009). One sample of Americans recording their dreams during September 2001 reported an increase in threatening dreams following the 9/11 attacks (Propper et al., 2007).

- After playing the computer game *Tetris* for 7 hours and then being awakened repeatedly during their first hour of sleep, 3 in 4 people reported experiencing images of the game's falling blocks (Stickgold et al., 2000).

- Compared with city dwellers, people in hunter-gatherer societies more often dream of animals (Mestel, 1997). Compared with nonmusicians, musicians report twice as many dreams of music (Uga et al., 2006).

Our two-track mind continues to monitor our environment while we sleep. Sensory stimuli—a particular odor or a phone's ringing—may be instantly and ingeniously woven into the dream story. In a classic experiment, researchers lightly sprayed cold water on dreamers' faces (Dement & Wolpert, 1958). Compared with sleepers who did not get the cold-water treatment, these people were more likely to dream about a waterfall, a leaky roof, or even about being sprayed by someone.

So, could we learn a foreign language by hearing it played while we sleep? If only it were so easy. While sleeping, we can learn to associate a sound with a mild electric shock (and to react to the sound accordingly). But we do not remember recorded information played while we are soundly asleep (Eich, 1990; Wyatt & Bootzin, 1994). In fact, anything that happens during the 5 minutes just before we fall asleep is typically lost from memory (Roth et al., 1988). This explains why sleep apnea patients, who repeatedly awaken with a gasp and then immediately fall back to sleep, do not recall the episodes. It also explains why dreams that momentarily awaken us are mostly forgotten by morning. To remember a dream, get up and stay awake for a few minutes.

Why We Dream

 3-10: What are the functions of dreams?

Dream theorists have proposed several explanations of why we dream, including these five:

To satisfy our own wishes. In 1900, in his landmark book *The Interpretation of Dreams,* Sigmund Freud offered what he thought was "the most valuable of all the discoveries it has been my good fortune to make." He proposed that dreams provide a psychic safety valve that discharges otherwise unacceptable feelings. He viewed a dream's **manifest**

content (the apparent and remembered story line) as a censored, symbolic version of its **latent content,** the unconscious drives and wishes that would be threatening if expressed directly. Although most dreams have no overt sexual imagery, Freud nevertheless believed that most adult dreams could be "traced back by analysis to erotic wishes." Thus, a gun might be a disguised representation of a penis.

Freud considered dreams the key to understanding our inner conflicts. However, his critics say it is time to wake up from Freud's dream theory, which is a scientific nightmare. Based on the accumulated science, "there is no reason to believe any of Freud's specific claims about dreams and their purposes," observed dream researcher William Domhoff (2003). Some contend that even if dreams are symbolic, they could be interpreted any way one wished. Others maintain that dreams hide nothing. A dream about a gun is a dream about a gun. Legend has it that even Freud, who loved to smoke cigars, acknowledged that "sometimes, a cigar is just a cigar." Freud's wish-fulfillment theory of dreams has in large part given way to other theories.

To file away memories. The *information-processing* perspective proposes that dreams may help sift, sort, and fix the day's experiences in our memory. Some studies support this view. When tested the day after learning a task, those who had been deprived of both slow-wave and REM sleep did not do as well as those who had slept undisturbed on their new learning (Stickgold et al., 2000, 2001). In other studies, people who heard unusual phrases or learned to find hidden visual images before bedtime remembered less the next morning if they had been awakened every time they began REM sleep than if awakened during other sleep stages (Empson & Clarke, 1970; Karni & Sagi, 1994).

Brain scans confirm the link between REM sleep and memory. The brain regions that buzzed as rats learned to navigate a maze, or as people learned to perform a visual-discrimination task, buzzed again during later REM sleep (Louie & Wilson, 2001; Maquet, 2001). So precise were these activity patterns that scientists could tell where in the maze the rat would be if awake. Some, however, are unpersuaded by these studies, noting that memory consolidation may also occur during non-REM sleep (Siegel, 2001; Vertes & Siegel, 2005). This much seems true: A night of solid sleep (and dreaming) has an important place in our lives. To sleep, perchance to remember.

This is important news for students, many of whom, observed researcher Robert Stickgold (2000), suffer from a kind of sleep bulimia—binge sleeping on the weekend. "If you don't get good sleep and enough sleep after you learn new stuff, you won't integrate it effectively into your memories," he warned. That helps explain why secondary students with high grades have averaged 25 minutes more sleep a night than their lower-achieving classmates (Wolfson & Carskadon, 1998).

To develop and preserve neural pathways. Perhaps dreams, or the brain activity associated with REM sleep, serve a *physiological* function, providing the sleeping brain with periodic stimulation. This theory makes developmental sense. As you will see in Chapter 4, stimulating experiences preserve and expand the brain's neural pathways.

To make sense of neural static. Other theories propose that dreams erupt from *neural activation* spreading upward from the brainstem (Antrobus, 1991; Hobson, 2003, 2004, 2009). According to one version, dreams are the brain's attempt to make sense of random neural activity. Much as a neurosurgeon can produce hallucinations by stimulating different parts of a patient's cortex, so can stimulation originating within the brain. These internal stimuli activate brain areas that process visual images, but not the visual cortex area, which receives raw input from the eyes. As Freud might have expected, PET scans of sleeping people also reveal increased activity in the emotion-related limbic system (in the amygdala) during REM sleep. In contrast, frontal lobe regions responsible for inhibition and logical thinking seem to idle, which may explain why our dreams are less inhibited than we are when awake (Maquet et al., 1996). Add the limbic system's emotional tone to the brain's visual bursts and—Voila!—we dream. Damage either the limbic system or the visual centers active during dreaming, and dreaming itself may be impaired (Domhoff, 2003).

manifest content according to Freud, the remembered story line of a dream (as distinct from its latent, or hidden, content).

latent content according to Freud, the underlying meaning of a dream (as distinct from its manifest content).

"When people interpret [a dream] as if it were meaningful and then sell those interpretations, it's quackery."

*Sleep researcher
J. Allan Hobson (1995)*

Rapid eye movements also stir the liquid behind the cornea; this delivers fresh oxygen to corneal cells, preventing their suffocation.

Question: Does eating spicy foods cause one to dream more?
Answer: Any food that causes you to awaken more increases your chance of recalling a dream (Moorcroft, 2003).

Table 3.2
Dream Theories

Theory	Explanation	Critical Considerations
Freud's wish-fulfillment	Dreams provide a "psychic safety valve"—expressing otherwise unacceptable feelings; contain manifest (remembered) content and a deeper layer of latent content (a hidden meaning).	Lacks any scientific support; dreams may be interpreted in many different ways.
Information-processing	Dreams help us sort out the day's events and consolidate our memories.	But why do we sometimes dream about things we have not experienced?
Physiological function	Regular brain stimulation from REM sleep may help develop and preserve neural pathways.	This does not explain why we experience *meaningful* dreams.
Neural activation	REM sleep triggers neural activity that evokes random visual memories, which our sleeping brain weaves into stories.	The individual's brain is weaving the stories, which still tells us something about the dreamer.
Cognitive development	Dream content reflects dreamers' cognitive development—their knowledge and understanding.	Does not address the neuroscience of dreams.

To reflect cognitive development. Some dream researchers dispute both the Freudian and neural activation theories, preferring instead to see dreams as part of brain maturation and cognitive development (Domhoff, 2010, 2011; Foulkes, 1999). For example, prior to age 9, children's dreams seem more like a slide show and less like an active story in which the dreamer is an actor. Dreams overlap with waking cognition and feature coherent speech. They simulate reality by drawing on our concepts and knowledge. They engage brain networks that also are active during daydreaming. Unlike the idea that dreams arise from bottom-up brain activation, the cognitive perspective emphasizes our mind's top-down control of our dream content (Nir & Tononi, 2010).

TABLE 3.2 compares these major dream theories. Although sleep researchers debate dreams' functions—and some are skeptical that dreams serve any function—there is one thing they agree on: We need REM sleep. Deprived of it by repeatedly being awakened, people return more and more quickly to the REM stage after falling back to sleep. When finally allowed to sleep undisturbed, they literally sleep like babies—with increased REM sleep, a phenomenon called **REM rebound.** Withdrawing REM-suppressing sleeping medications also increases REM sleep, but with accompanying nightmares.

Most other mammals also experience REM rebound, suggesting that the causes and functions of REM sleep are deeply biological. That REM sleep occurs in mammals—and not in animals such as fish, whose behavior is less influenced by learning—also fits the information-processing theory of dreams.

So does this mean that because dreams serve physiological functions and extend normal cognition, they are psychologically meaningless? Not necessarily. Every psychologically meaningful experience involves an active brain. We are once again reminded of a basic principle: *Biological and psychological explanations of behavior are partners, not competitors.*

Dreams are a fascinating altered state of consciousness. But they are not the only altered states. Hypnosis and drugs also alter conscious awareness.

RETRIEVE IT

• What five theories explain why we dream?

ANSWER: (1) Freud's wish-fulfillment (dreams as a psychic safety valve), (2) information-processing (dreams sort the day's events and form memories), (3) physiological function (dreams pave neural pathways), (4) neural activation (REM sleep triggers random neural activity that the mind weaves into stories), (5) cognitive development (dreams reflect the dreamer's developmental stage)

Hypnosis

> **3-11:** What is hypnosis, and what powers does a hypnotist have over a hypnotized subject?

Imagine you are about to be hypnotized. The hypnotist invites you to sit back, fix your gaze on a spot high on the wall, and relax. In a quiet voice the hypnotist suggests, "Your eyes are growing tired. . . . Your eyelids are becoming heavy . . . now heavier and heavier. . . . They are beginning to close. . . . You are becoming more deeply relaxed. . . . Your breathing is now deep and regular. . . . Your muscles are becoming more and more relaxed. Your whole body is beginning to feel like lead."

After a few minutes of this *hypnotic induction,* you may experience **hypnosis.** When the hypnotist suggests, "Your eyelids are shutting so tight that you cannot open them even if you try," it may indeed seem beyond your control to open your eyelids. Told to forget the number 6, you may be puzzled when you count 11 fingers on your hands. Invited to smell a sensuous perfume that is actually ammonia, you may linger delightedly over its pungent odor. Told that you cannot see a certain object, such as a chair, you may indeed report that it is not there, although you manage to avoid the chair when walking around (illustrating the *dual processing* talents of that mind of yours).

But is hypnosis really an *altered* state of consciousness? Let's start with some frequently asked questions.

Frequently Asked Questions About Hypnosis

Hypnotists have no magical mind-control power. Their power resides in the subjects' openness to suggestion and ability to focus (Bowers, 1984). But how open to suggestions are we?

- *Can anyone experience hypnosis?* To some extent, we are all open to suggestion. When people stand upright with their eyes closed and are told that they are swaying back and forth, most will indeed sway a little. In fact, *postural* sway is one of the items assessed on the Stanford Hypnotic Susceptibility Scale. People who respond to such suggestions without hypnosis are the same people who respond with hypnosis (Kirsch & Braffman, 2001).

  Highly hypnotizable people—say, the 20 percent who can carry out a suggestion not to smell or react to a bottle of ammonia held under their nose—typically become deeply absorbed in imaginative activities (Barnier & McConkey, 2004; Silva & Kirsch, 1992). Many researchers refer to this as hypnotic *ability*—the ability to focus attention totally on a task, to become imaginatively absorbed in it, to entertain fanciful possibilities.

- *Can hypnosis enhance recall of forgotten events?* Most people believe (wrongly, as Chapter 8 will explain) that our experiences are all "in there," recorded in our brain and available for recall if only we can break through our own defenses (Loftus, 1980). But 60 years of memory research disputes such beliefs. We do not encode everything that occurs around us. We permanently store only some of our experiences, and we may be unable to retrieve some memories we have stored.

  "Hypnotically refreshed" memories combine fact with fiction. Since 1980, thousands of people have reported being abducted by UFOs, but most such reports have come from people who are predisposed to believe in aliens, are highly hypnotizable, and have undergone hypnosis (Newman & Baumeister, 1996; Nickell, 1996). Without either person being aware of what is going on, a hypnotist's hints—"Did you hear loud noises?"—can plant ideas that become the subject's pseudomemory.

  So should testimony obtained under hypnosis be admissable in court? American, Australian, and British courts have agreed it should not. They generally ban testimony from witnesses who have been hypnotized (Druckman & Bjork, 1994; Gibson, 1995; McConkey, 1995).

REM rebound the tendency for REM sleep to increase following REM sleep deprivation (created by repeated awakenings during REM sleep).

hypnosis a social interaction in which one person (the hypnotist) suggests to another (the subject) that certain perceptions, feelings, thoughts, or behaviors will spontaneously occur.

"Hypnosis is not a psychological truth serum and to regard it as such has been a source of considerable mischief."

Researcher Kenneth Bowers (1987)

See Chapter 8 for a more detailed discussion of how people may construct false memories.

• ***Can hypnosis force people to act against their will?*** Researchers have induced hypnotized people to perform an apparently dangerous act: plunging one hand briefly into fuming "acid," then throwing the "acid" in a researcher's face (Orne & Evans, 1965). Interviewed a day later, these people emphatically denied their acts and said they would never follow such orders.

Had hypnosis given the hypnotist a special power to control others against their will? To find out, researchers Martin Orne and Frederich Evans unleashed that enemy of so many illusory beliefs—the control group. Orne asked other individuals to *pretend* they were hypnotized. Laboratory assistants, unaware that those in the experiment's control group had not been hypnotized, treated both groups the same. The result? All the *un*hypnotized participants (perhaps believing that the laboratory context assured safety) performed the same acts as those who were hypnotized.

> "It wasn't what I expected. But facts are facts, and if one is proved to be wrong, one must just be humble about it and start again."
>
> *Agatha Christie's Miss Marple*

• ***Can hypnosis help people heal or relieve their pain?*** *Hypnotherapists* try to help patients harness their own healing powers (Baker, 1987). **Posthypnotic suggestions** have helped alleviate headaches, asthma, and stress-related skin disorders.

In one statistical digest of 18 studies, the average client whose therapy was supplemented with hypnosis showed greater improvement than 70 percent of other therapy patients (Kirsch et al., 1995, 1996). Hypnosis seemed especially helpful for the treatment of obesity. However, drug, alcohol, and smoking addictions have not responded well to hypnosis (Nash, 2001). In controlled studies, hypnosis did speed the disappearance of warts, but so did the same positive suggestions given without hypnosis (Spanos, 1991, 1996).

Hypnosis *can* relieve pain (Druckman & Bjork, 1994; Jensen, 2008). When unhypnotized people put their arm in an ice bath, they felt intense pain within 25 seconds. When hypnotized people did the same after being given suggestions to feel no pain, they indeed reported feeling little pain. As some dentists know, light hypnosis can reduce fear, thus reducing hypersensitivity to pain.

Hypnosis inhibits pain-related brain activity. In surgical experiments, hypnotized patients have required less medication, recovered sooner, and left the hospital earlier than unhypnotized control patients (Askay & Patterson, 2007; Hammond, 2008; Spiegel, 2007). Nearly 10 percent of us can become so deeply hypnotized that even major surgery can be performed without anesthesia. Half of us can gain at least some pain relief from hypnosis. The surgical use of hypnosis has flourished in Europe, where one Belgian medical team has performed more than 5000 surgeries with a combination of hypnosis, local anesthesia, and a mild sedative (Song, 2006).

o44/ZUMA Press/Newscom

Stage hypnotist

RETRIEVE IT ⏎

• When is the use of hypnosis potentially harmful, and when can hypnosis be used to help?

ANSWER: Hypnosis can be harmful if used to "hypnotically refresh" memories, which may plant false memories. But posthypnotic suggestions have helped alleviate some ailments, and hypnosis can also help control pain.

Explaining the Hypnotized State

3-12: Is hypnosis an extension of normal consciousness or an altered state?

posthypnotic suggestion a suggestion, made during a hypnosis session, to be carried out after the subject is no longer hypnotized; used by some clinicians to help control undesired symptoms and behaviors.

We have seen that hypnosis involves heightened suggestibility. We have also seen that hypnotic procedures do not endow a person with special powers but can sometimes help people overcome stress-related ailments and cope with pain. So, just what is hypnosis? Psychologists have proposed two explanations.

Hypnosis as a Social Phenomenon

Our attentional spotlight and interpretations powerfully influence our ordinary perceptions. Might hypnotic phenomena reflect such workings of normal consciousness, as well as the power of social influence (Lynn et al., 1990; Spanos & Coe, 1992)? Advocates of the *social influence theory of hypnosis* believe they do.

Does this mean that subjects consciously fake hypnosis? No—like actors caught up in their roles, they begin to feel and behave in ways appropriate for "good hypnotic subjects." The more they like and trust the hypnotist, the more they allow that person to direct their attention and fantasies (Gfeller et al., 1987). "The hypnotist's ideas become the subject's thoughts," explained Theodore Barber (2000), "and the subject's thoughts produce the hypnotic experiences and behaviors." Told to scratch their ear later when they hear the word *psychology*, subjects will likely do so—but only if they think the experiment is still under way. If an experimenter eliminates their motivation for acting hypnotized—by stating that hypnosis reveals their "gullibility"—subjects become unresponsive. Such findings support the idea that hypnotic phenomena are an extension of normal social and cognitive processes.

These views illustrate a principle that Chapter 13 emphasizes: *An authoritative person in a legitimate context can induce people—hypnotized or not—to perform some unlikely acts.* Or as hypnosis researcher Nicholas Spanos (1982) put it, "The overt behaviors of hypnotic subjects are well within normal limits."

Hypnosis as Divided Consciousness

Other hypnosis researchers believe hypnosis is more than inducing someone to play the role of "good subject." How, they ask, can we explain why hypnotized subjects sometimes carry out suggested behaviors on cue, even when they believe no one is watching (Perugini et al., 1998)? And why does distinctive brain activity accompany hypnosis (Oakley & Halligan, 2009)? In one experiment, deeply hypnotized people were asked to imagine a color, and areas of their brain activated as if they were really seeing the color. To the hypnotized person's brain, mere imagination had become a compelling hallucination (Kosslyn et al., 2000).

These results would not have surprised famed researcher Ernest Hilgard (1986, 1992), who believed hypnosis involves not only social influence but also a special dual-processing state of **dissociation**—a split between different levels of consciousness. Hilgard viewed hypnotic dissociation as a vivid form of everyday mind splits—similar to doodling while listening to a lecture or typing the end of a sentence while starting a conversation. For example, Hilgard felt that when hypnotized people lower their arm into an ice bath, as in **FIGURE 3.14**, the hypnosis dissociates the sensation of the pain stimulus (of which the subjects are still aware) from the emotional suffering that defines their experience of pain. The ice water therefore feels cold—very cold—but not painful.

dissociation a split in consciousness, which allows some thoughts and behaviors to occur simultaneously with others.

> "The total possible consciousness may be split into parts which co-exist but mutually ignore each other."
>
> *William James,*
> Principles of Psychology, *1890*

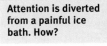

Attention is diverted from a painful ice bath. How?

Courtesy of News and Publications Service, Stanford University

Divided-consciousness theory:
Hypnosis has caused a split in awareness.

Social influence theory:
The subject is so caught up in the hypnotized role that she ignores the cold.

FIGURE 3.14
Dissociation or role-playing? This hypnotized woman tested by Ernest Hilgard exhibited no pain when her arm was placed in an ice bath. But asked to press a key if some part of her felt the pain, she did so. To Hilgard, this was evidence of dissociation, or divided consciousness. Proponents of social influence theory, however, maintain that people responding this way are caught up in playing the role of "good subject."

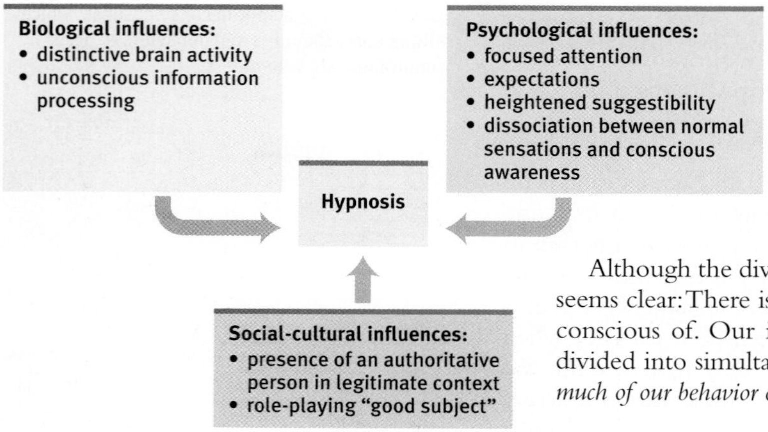

Biological influences:
- distinctive brain activity
- unconscious information processing

Psychological influences:
- focused attention
- expectations
- heightened suggestibility
- dissociation between normal sensations and conscious awareness

Hypnosis

Social-cultural influences:
- presence of an authoritative person in legitimate context
- role-playing "good subject"

FIGURE 3.15

Levels of analysis for hypnosis
Using a biopsychosocial approach, researchers explore hypnosis from complementary perspectives.

Another form of dual processing—*selective attention*—may also play a role in hypnotic pain relief. PET scans show that hypnosis reduces brain activity in a region that processes painful stimuli, but not in the sensory cortex, which receives the raw sensory input (Rainville et al., 1997). Hypnosis does not block sensory input, but it may block our attention to those stimuli. This helps explain why an injured athlete, caught up in the competition, may feel little or no pain until the game ends.

Although the divided-consciousness theory of hypnosis is controversial, this much seems clear: There is, without doubt, much more to thinking and acting than we are conscious of. Our information processing, which starts with selective attention, is divided into simultaneous conscious and nonconscious realms. In hypnosis as in life, *much of our behavior occurs on autopilot.* We have two-track minds (**FIGURE 3.15**).

★ ★ ★

There is controversy about whether hypnosis uniquely alters consciousness, but there is little dispute that some drugs do.

RETRIEVE IT

- Hilgard believed that hypnosis involves a state of divided consciousness called _____. His beliefs have been challenged by researchers who suggest _____ influence is involved.

ANSWERS: dissociation; social

Drugs and Consciousness

Let's imagine a day in the life of a legal-drug user. It begins with a wake-up latte. By midday, several cigarettes have calmed frazzled nerves before an appointment at the plastic surgeon's office for wrinkle-smoothing Botox injections. A diet pill before dinner helps stem the appetite, and its stimulating effects can later be partially offset with a glass of wine and two Tylenol PMs. And if performance needs enhancing, there are beta blockers for onstage performers, Viagra for middle-aged men, hormone-delivering "libido patches" for middle-aged women, and Adderall for students hoping to focus their concentration. Before drifting off into REM-depressed sleep, our hypothetical drug user is dismayed by news reports of pill-sharing, pill-popping college students.

Most of us manage to use some nonprescription drugs in moderation and without disrupting our lives. But some of us develop self-harming *substance-related disorders.* In such cases, the substances being used are **psychoactive drugs,** chemicals that change perceptions and moods. A drug's overall effect depends not only on its biological effects but also on the psychology of the user's expectations, which vary with social and cultural contexts (Ward, 1994). If one culture assumes that a particular drug produces euphoria (or aggression or sexual arousal) and another does not, each culture may find its expectations fulfilled. In the pages that follow, we'll take a closer look at these interacting forces in the use and potential abuse of particular psychoactive drugs. But first, let's see how our bodies react to the ongoing use of psychoactive drugs.

Tolerance, Dependence, and Addiction

3-13: What are tolerance, dependence, and addiction, and what are some common misconceptions about addiction?

psychoactive drug a chemical substance that alters perceptions and moods.

tolerance with repeated use, achieving the desired effect requires larger doses.

addiction compulsive drug craving and use, despite adverse consequences.

Why might a person who rarely drinks alcohol get buzzed on one can of beer while a long-term drinker shows few effects until the second six-pack? The answer is **tolerance.** With continued use of alcohol and some other drugs (marijuana is an exception), the user's brain chemistry adapts to offset the drug effect (a process called *neuroadaptation*). To experience the same effect, the user requires larger

THINKING CRITICALLY ABOUT:

Addiction

In recent pop psychology, the supposedly irresistible seduction of addiction has been extended to cover many behaviors formerly considered bad habits or even sins. Has the concept been stretched too far? Are addictions as irresistible as commonly believed? Let's consider three big questions.

1. **Do addictive drugs quickly corrupt?** For example, does morphine taken to control pain often lead to heroin abuse? Generally not. People given morphine for pain control rarely develop the cravings of the addict who uses morphine as a mood-altering drug (Melzack, 1990). Some—perhaps 10 percent—do indeed have a hard time using a psychoactive drug in moderation or stopping altogether. But controlled, occasional users of drugs such as alcohol and marijuana far outnumber those who become addicted to these substances (Gazzaniga, 1988; Siegel, 1990). "Even for a very addictive drug like cocaine, only 15 to 16 percent of people become addicted within 10 years of first use," observed Terry Robinson and Kent Berridge (2003).

2. **Does overcoming an addiction require therapy?** Addictions can be powerful, and some addicts do benefit from therapy or group support. Alcoholics Anonymous has supported many people in overcoming their alcohol dependence. But the recovery rates of treated and untreated groups differ less than one might suppose. Moreover, viewing addiction as an uncontrollable disease can undermine people's self-confidence and their belief that they can change. And that, critics say, would be unfortunate, for many people do voluntarily stop using addictive drugs, without any treatment. Most of America's 41 million ex-smokers kicked the habit on their own, usually after prior failed efforts or treatments.

3. **Can we extend the concept of addiction to cover not just drug dependencies, but a whole spectrum of repetitive, pleasure-seeking behaviors?** We can, and we have, but should we? The addiction-as-disease-needing-treatment idea has been suggested for a host of driven, excessive behaviors—eating, shopping, gambling, work, and sex. Used not as a metaphor ("I'm a science fiction addict") but as reality, "addiction" can become an all-purpose excuse. Moreover, labeling a behavior doesn't explain it. Attributing serial adultery, as in the case of Tiger Woods, to a "sex addiction" does not explain the sexual impulsiveness, say critics (Radford, 2010).

Sometimes, though, behaviors such as gambling, video gaming, or online surfing do become compulsive and dysfunctional, much like abusive drug taking (Gentile, 2009; Griffiths, 2001;

A social networking addiction?

Hoeft et al., 2008). Some Internet users, for example, do display an apparent inability to resist logging on, and staying on, even when this excessive use impairs their work and relationships (Ko et al., 2005). Are we justified in stretching the addiction concept to cover such social behaviors? Stay tuned. Debates over the addiction-as-disease model continue.

The odds of getting hooked after using various drugs:

Tobacco	32%
Heroin	23%
Alcohol	15%
Marijuana	9%

Source: National Academy of Science, Institute of Medicine (Brody, 2003).

and larger doses (**FIGURE 3.16**). In chronic alcohol abuse, for example, the person's brain, heart, and liver suffer damage from the excessive amounts of alcohol being "tolerated." Ever-increasing doses of most psychoactive drugs can pose a serious threat to health and may lead to **addiction:** The person craves and uses the substance despite its adverse consequences. (See Thinking Critically About: Addiction.) The World Health Organization (2008) has reported that, worldwide, 90 million people suffer from such problems related to alcohol and other drugs.

RETRIEVE IT

• What is the process that leads to drug tolerance?

ANSWER: With repeated exposure to a psychoactive drug, the drug's effect lessens. Thus, it takes bigger doses to get the desired effect.

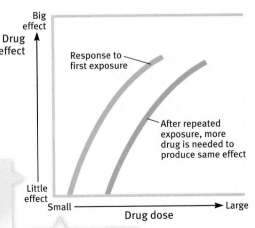

FIGURE 3.16
Drug tolerance

withdrawal the discomfort and distress that follow discontinuing the use of an addictive drug.

physical dependence a physiological need for a drug, marked by unpleasant withdrawal symptoms when the drug is discontinued.

psychological dependence a psychological need to use a drug, such as to relieve negative emotions.

depressants drugs (such as alcohol, barbiturates, and opiates) that reduce neural activity and slow body functions.

alcohol dependence (popularly known as alcoholism). Alcohol use marked by tolerance, withdrawal if suspended, and a drive to continue use.

Regular users often try to fight their addiction, but abruptly stopping the drug may lead to the undesirable side effects of **withdrawal.** As the body responds to the drug's absence, the user may feel physical pain and intense cravings, indicating **physical dependence.** People can also develop **psychological dependence,** particularly for stress-relieving drugs, such as alcohol. Although not always physically addictive, such drugs may nevertheless become an important part of the user's life, often as a way of relieving negative emotions. For someone who is either physically or psychologically dependent, obtaining and using the drug can become the day's focus.

Types of Psychoactive Drugs

The three major categories of psychoactive drugs are *depressants, stimulants,* and *hallucinogens.* All do their work at the brain's synapses, stimulating, inhibiting, or mimicking the activity of the brain's own chemical messengers, the neurotransmitters.

Depressants

3-14: What are depressants, and what are their effects?

Depressants are drugs such as alcohol, barbiturates (tranquilizers), and opiates that calm neural activity and slow body functions.

Alcohol True or false? In small amounts, alcohol is a stimulant. *False.* Low doses of alcohol may, indeed, enliven a drinker, but they do so by acting as a *disinhibitor*—they slow brain activity that controls judgment and inhibitions. Alcohol is an equal-opportunity drug: It increases (disinhibits) helpful tendencies, as when tipsy restaurant patrons leave extravagant tips (Lynn, 1988). And it increases harmful tendencies, as when sexually aroused men become more disposed to sexual aggression.

Alcohol + sex = the perfect storm. When drinking, both men and women are more disposed to casual sex (Cooper, 2006; Ebel-Lam et al., 2009). *The urges you would feel if sober are the ones you will more likely act upon when intoxicated.*

SLOWED NEURAL PROCESSING Low doses of alcohol relax the drinker by slowing sympathetic nervous system activity. Larger doses cause reactions to slow, speech to slur, and skilled performance to deteriorate. Paired with sleep deprivation, alcohol is a potent sedative. Add these physical effects to lowered inhibitions, and the result can be deadly. Worldwide, several hundred thousand lives are lost each year in alcohol-related accidents and violent crime. As blood-alcohol levels rise and judgment falters, people's qualms about drinking and driving lessen. In experiments, virtually all drinkers who had insisted when sober that they would not drive under the influence later decided to drive home from a bar, even when given a breathalyzer test and told they were intoxicated (Denton & Krebs, 1990; MacDonald et al., 1995). Alcohol can also be life threatening when heavy drinking follows an earlier period of moderate drinking, which depresses the vomiting response. People may poison themselves with an overdose that their bodies would normally throw up.

MEMORY DISRUPTION Alcohol can disrupt memory formation, and heavy drinking can have long-term effects on the brain and cognition. In rats, at a developmental period corresponding to human adolescence, binge drinking contributes to nerve cell death and reduces the birth of new nerve cells. It also impairs the growth of synaptic connections (Crews et al., 2006, 2007). In humans, heavy drinking may lead to blackouts, in which drinkers are unable to recall people they met the night before or what they said or did while intoxicated. These blackouts result partly from the way alcohol suppresses REM sleep, which helps fix the day's experiences into permanent memories.

The prolonged and excessive drinking that characterizes **alcohol dependence** can shrink the brain (**FIGURE 3.17**). Girls and young women (who have less of a stomach

"That is not one of the seven habits of highly effective people."

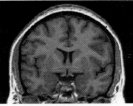

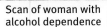

Scan of woman with
alcohol dependence

Scan of woman without
alcohol dependence

FIGURE 3.17
Alcohol dependence shrinks the brain
MRI scans show brain shrinkage in women with alcohol dependence (left) compared with women in a control group (right).

enzyme that digests alcohol) can become addicted to alcohol more quickly than boys and young men do, and they are at risk for lung, brain, and liver damage at lower consumption levels (CASA, 2003; Wuethrich, 2001).

REDUCED SELF-AWARENESS AND SELF-CONTROL In one experiment, those who consumed alcohol (rather than a placebo beverage) were doubly likely to be caught mind-wandering during a reading task, yet were *less* likely to notice that they zoned out (Sayette et al., 2009). Alcohol not only reduces self-awareness, it also produces a sort of "myopia" by focusing attention on an arousing situation (such as a provocation) and distracting attention from normal inhibitions and future consequences (Giancola et al., 2010; Hull et al., 1986; Steele & Josephs, 1990).

Reduced self-awareness may help explain why people who want to suppress their awareness of failures or shortcomings are more likely to drink than are those who feel good about themselves. Losing a business deal, a game, or a romantic partner sometimes elicits a drinking binge.

EXPECTANCY EFFECTS As with other drugs, expectations influence behavior. When people *believe* that alcohol affects social behavior in certain ways, and *believe,* rightly or wrongly, that they have been drinking alcohol, they will behave accordingly (Moss & Albery, 2009). In a classic experiment, researchers gave Rutgers University men (who had volunteered for a study on "alcohol and sexual stimulation") either an alcoholic or a nonalcoholic drink (Abrams & Wilson, 1983). (Both had strong tastes that masked any alcohol.) In each group, half the participants thought they were drinking alcohol and half thought they were not. After watching an erotic movie clip, the men who *thought* they had consumed alcohol were more likely to report having strong sexual fantasies and feeling guilt free. Being able to *attribute* their sexual responses to alcohol released their inhibitions—whether or not they had actually consumed any alcohol. Alcohol's effect lies partly in that powerful sex organ, the mind.

Barbiturates Like alcohol, the **barbiturate** drugs, or *tranquilizers,* depress nervous system activity. Barbiturates such as Nembutal, Seconal, and Amytal are sometimes prescribed to induce sleep or reduce anxiety. In larger doses, they can impair memory and judgment. If combined with alcohol—as sometimes happens when people take a sleeping pill after an evening of heavy drinking—the total depressive effect on body functions can be lethal.

Opiates The **opiates**—opium and its derivatives, morphine and heroin—also depress neural functioning. Pupils constrict, breathing slows, and lethargy sets in as blissful pleasure replaces pain and anxiety. For this short-term pleasure, opiate users may pay a long-term price: a gnawing craving for another fix, a need for progressively larger doses (as tolerance develops), and the extreme discomfort of withdrawal. When repeatedly flooded with an artificial opiate, the brain eventually stops producing *endorphins,* its own opiates. If the artificial opiate is then withdrawn, the brain lacks the normal level of these painkilling neurotransmitters. Those who cannot or choose not to tolerate this state may pay an ultimate price—death by overdose.

barbiturates drugs that depress central nervous system activity, reducing anxiety but impairing memory and judgment.

opiates opium and its derivatives, such as morphine and heroin; they depress neural activity, temporarily lessening pain and anxiety.

stimulants drugs (such as caffeine, nicotine, and the more powerful amphetamines, cocaine, Ecstasy, and methamphetamine) that excite neural activity and speed up body functions.

amphetamines drugs that stimulate neural activity, causing speeded-up body functions and associated energy and mood changes.

nicotine a stimulating and highly addictive psychoactive drug in tobacco.

Stimulants

> **3-15:** What are stimulants, and what are their effects?

A **stimulant** excites neural activity and speeds up body functions. Pupils dilate, heart and breathing rates increase, and blood sugar levels rise, causing a drop in appetite. Energy and self-confidence also rise.

Stimulants include caffeine, nicotine, the **amphetamines,** cocaine, methamphetamine ("speed"), and Ecstasy. People use stimulants to feel alert, lose weight, or boost mood or athletic performance. Unfortunately, stimulants can be addictive, as you may know if you are one of the many who use caffeine daily in your coffee, tea, soda, or energy drinks. Cut off from your usual dose, you may crash into fatigue, headaches, irritability, and depression (Silverman et al., 1992). A mild dose of caffeine typically lasts three or four hours, which—if taken in the evening—may be long enough to impair sleep.

Vasca/Shutterstock

Nicotine One of the most addictive stimulants is **nicotine,** found in cigarettes and other tobacco products. Imagine that cigarettes were harmless—except, once in every 25,000 packs, an occasional innocent-looking one is filled with dynamite instead of tobacco. Not such a bad risk of having your head blown off. But with 250 million packs a day consumed worldwide, we could expect more than 10,000 gruesome daily deaths (more than three times the 9/11 fatalities each and every day)—surely enough to have cigarettes banned everywhere.[1]

The lost lives from these dynamite-loaded cigarettes approximate those from today's actual cigarettes. A teen-to-the-grave smoker has a 50 percent chance of dying from the habit, and each year, tobacco kills nearly 5.4 million of its 1.3 billion customers worldwide. (Imagine the outrage if terrorists took down an equivalent of 25 loaded jumbo jets today, let alone tomorrow and every day thereafter.) By 2030, annual deaths are expected to increase to 8 million. That means that *1 billion* twenty-first-century people may be killed by tobacco (WHO, 2008). Eliminating smoking would increase life expectancy more than any other preventive measure.

Those addicted to nicotine find it very hard to quit because tobacco products are as powerfully and quickly addictive as heroin and cocaine. Attempts to quit even within the first weeks of smoking often fail (DiFranza, 2008). As with other addictions, smokers become *dependent,* and they develop *tolerance.* Quitting causes nicotine-withdrawal symptoms, including craving, insomnia, anxiety, irritability, and distractibility. Nicotine-deprived smokers trying to focus on a task experience a tripled rate of mind wandering (Sayette et al., 2010). When not craving a cigarette, they tend to underestimate the power of such cravings (Sayette et al., 2008).

All it takes to relieve this aversive state is a cigarette—a portable nicotine dispenser. Within 7 seconds, a rush of nicotine signals the central nervous system to release a flood of neurotransmitters (**FIGURE 3.18**). Epinephrine and norepinephrine diminish appetite and boost alertness and mental efficiency. Dopamine and opioids calm anxiety and reduce sensitivity to pain (Nowak, 1994; Scott et al., 2004).

Smoke a cigarette and nature will charge you 12 minutes—ironically, just about the length of time you spend smoking it (*Discover,* 1996).

Humorist Dave Barry (1995) recalling why he smoked his first cigarette the summer he turned 15: "Arguments against smoking: 'It's a repulsive addiction that slowly but surely turns you into a gasping, gray-skinned, tumor-ridden invalid, hacking up brownish gobs of toxic waste from your one remaining lung.' Arguments for smoking: 'Other teenagers are doing it.' Case closed! Let's light up!"

---

1 This analogy, adapted here with world-based numbers, was suggested by mathematician Sam Saunders, as reported by K. C. Cole (1998).

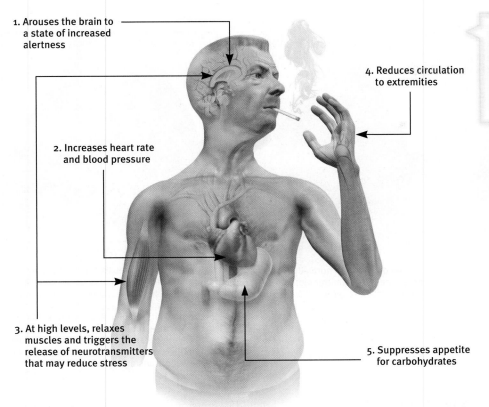

1. Arouses the brain to a state of increased alertness

4. Reduces circulation to extremities

2. Increases heart rate and blood pressure

3. At high levels, relaxes muscles and triggers the release of neurotransmitters that may reduce stress

5. Suppresses appetite for carbohydrates

FIGURE 3.18
Where there's smoke . . . : The physiological effects of nicotine
Nicotine reaches the brain within 7 seconds, twice as fast as intravenous heroin. Within minutes, the amount in the blood soars.

These rewards keep people smoking, even among the 8 in 10 smokers who wish they could stop (Jones, 2007). Each year, fewer than 1 in 7 smokers who want to quit will be able to resist. Even those who know they are committing slow-motion suicide may be unable to stop (Saad, 2002). Asked "If you had to do it all over again, would you start smoking?" more than 85 percent of adult smokers have answered *No* (Slovic et al., 2002).

Nevertheless, repeated attempts seem to pay off. Half of all Americans who have ever smoked have quit, sometimes aided by a nicotine replacement drug and with encouragement from a telephone counselor or a support group. Success is equally likely whether smokers quit abruptly or gradually (Fiore et al., 2008; Lichtenstein et al., 2010; Lindson et al., 2010). For those who endure, the acute craving and withdrawal symptoms gradually dissipate over the ensuing 6 months (Ward et al., 1997). After a year's abstinence, only 10 percent will relapse in the next year (Hughes et al., 2010). These nonsmokers may live not only healthier but also happier lives. Smoking correlates with higher rates of depression, chronic disabilities, and divorce (Doherty & Doherty, 1998; Vita et al., 1998). Healthy living seems to add both years to life and life to years.

RETRIEVE IT

• Why do tobacco companies try so hard to get customers hooked as teens?

ANSWER: Nicotine is powerfully addictive, expensive, and deadly. Those who start paving the neural pathways when young may find it very hard to stop using nicotine. As a result, tobacco companies may have lifelong customers.

Cocaine The recipe for Coca-Cola originally included an extract of the coca plant, creating a cocaine tonic for tired elderly people. Between 1896 and 1905, Coke was indeed "the real thing." But no longer. Cocaine is now snorted, injected, or smoked. It enters the bloodstream quickly, producing a rush of euphoria that depletes the brain's supply of the neurotransmitters dopamine, serotonin, and norepinephrine (**FIGURE**

"Cocaine makes you a new man. And the first thing that new man wants is more cocaine."

Comedian George Carlin (1937–2008)

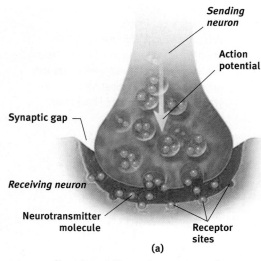

(a)

Neurotransmitters carry a message from a sending neuron across a synapse to receptor sites on a receiving neuron.

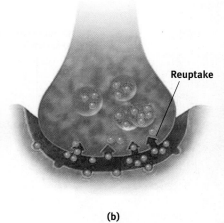

(b)

The sending neuron normally reabsorbs excess neurotransmitter molecules, a process called *reuptake*.

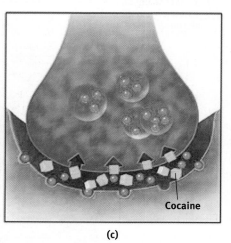

(c)

By binding to the sites that normally reabsorb neurotransmitter molecules, cocaine blocks reuptake of dopamine, norepinephrine, and serotonin (Ray & Ksir, 1990). The extra neurotransmitter molecules therefore remain in the synapse, intensifying their normal mood-altering effects and producing a euphoric rush. When the cocaine level drops, the absence of these neurotransmitters produces a crash.

FIGURE 3.19
Cocaine euphoria and crash

3.19). Within the hour, a crash of agitated depression follows as the drug's effect wears off. Many regular cocaine users chasing this high become addicted. In the lab, cocaine-addicted monkeys have pressed levers more than 12,000 times to gain one cocaine injection (Siegel, 1990).

In situations that trigger aggression, ingesting cocaine may heighten reactions. Caged rats fight when given foot shocks, and they fight even more when given cocaine *and* foot shocks. Likewise, humans ingesting high doses of cocaine in laboratory experiments impose higher shock levels on a presumed opponent than do those receiving a placebo (Licata et al., 1993). Cocaine use may also lead to emotional disturbances, suspiciousness, convulsions, cardiac arrest, or respiratory failure.

In national surveys, 3 percent of U.S. high school seniors and 6 percent of British 18- to 24-year-olds reported having tried cocaine during the past year (ACMD, 2009; Johnston et al., 2011). Nearly half had smoked *crack,* a faster-working crystallized form of cocaine that produces a briefer but more intense high, followed by a more intense crash. After several hours, the craving for more wanes, only to return several days later (Gawin, 1991).

Cocaine's psychological effects depend in part on the dosage and form consumed, but the situation and the user's expectations and personality also play a role. Given a placebo, cocaine users who *thought* they were taking cocaine often had a cocaine-like experience (Van Dyke & Byck, 1982).

Dramatic drug-induced decline This woman's methamphetamine addiction led to obvious physical changes. Her decline is evident in these two photos, taken at age 36 (left) and, after four years of addiction, at age 40 (right).

National Pictures/Topham/The Image Works

Methamphetamine **Methamphetamine** is chemically related to its parent drug, *amphetamine* (NIDA, 2002, 2005) but has even greater effects. Methamphetamine triggers the release of the neurotransmitter dopamine, which stimulates brain cells that enhance energy and mood, leading to eight hours or so of heightened energy and euphoria. Its aftereffects may include irritability, insomnia, hypertension, seizures, social isolation, depression, and occasional violent outbursts (Homer et al., 2008). Over time, methamphetamine may reduce baseline dopamine levels, leaving the user with depressed functioning.

Ecstasy Ecstasy, a street name for **MDMA** (methylenedioxymethamphetamine), is both a stimulant and a mild hallucinogen. As an amphetamine derivative, Ecstasy triggers dopamine release, but its major effect is releasing stored serotonin and blocking its reuptake, thus prolonging serotonin's feel-good flood (Braun, 2001). Users feel the effect about a half-hour after taking an Ecstasy pill. For three or four hours, they experience high energy, emotional elevation, and (given a social context) connectedness with those around them ("I love everyone").

During the 1990s, Ecstasy's popularity soared as a "club drug" taken at nightclubs and all-night raves (Landry, 2002). The drug's popularity crosses national borders, with an estimated 60 million tablets consumed annually in Britain (ACMD, 2009). There are, however, reasons not to be ecstatic about Ecstasy. One is its dehydrating effect, which—when combined with prolonged dancing—can lead to severe overheating, increased blood pressure, and death. Another is that long-term, repeated leaching of brain serotonin can damage serotonin-producing neurons, leading to decreased output and increased risk of permanently depressed mood (Croft et al., 2001; McCann et al., 2001; Roiser et al., 2005). Ecstasy also suppresses the disease-fighting immune system, impairs memory, slows thought, and disrupts sleep by interfering with serotonin's control of the circadian clock (Laws & Kokkalis, 2007; Pacifici et al., 2001; Schilt et al., 2007). Ecstasy delights for the night but dispirits the morrow.

The hug drug MDMA, known as Ecstasy, produces a euphoric high and feelings of intimacy. But repeated use can destroy serotonin-producing neurons and deflate mood and impair memory.

Hallucinogens

 **3-16:** What are hallucinogens, and what are their effects?

Hallucinogens distort perceptions and evoke sensory images in the absence of sensory input (which is why these drugs are also called *psychedelics,* meaning "mind-manifesting"). Some, such as LSD and MDMA (Ecstasy), are synthetic. Others, including the mild hallucinogen marijuana, are natural substances.

LSD Chemist Albert Hofmann created—and on one Friday afternoon in April 1943 accidentally ingested—**LSD** (lysergic acid diethylamide). The result—"an uninterrupted stream of fantastic pictures, extraordinary shapes with intense, kaleidoscopic play of colors"—reminded him of a childhood mystical experience that had left him longing for another glimpse of "a miraculous, powerful, unfathomable reality" (Siegel, 1984; Smith, 2006).

The emotions of an LSD trip vary from euphoria to detachment to panic. The user's current mood and expectations color the emotional experience, but the perceptual distortions and hallucinations have some commonalities. Whether provoked to hallucinate by drugs, loss of oxygen, or extreme sensory deprivation, the brain hallucinates in basically the same way (Siegel, 1982). The experience typically begins with simple geometric forms, such as a lattice, cobweb, or spiral. The next phase consists of more meaningful images; some may be superimposed on a tunnel or funnel, others may be replays of past emotional experiences. As the hallucination peaks, people frequently feel separated from their body and experience dreamlike scenes so real that they may become panic-stricken or harm themselves.

These sensations are strikingly similar to the **near-death experience,** an altered state of consciousness reported by about 15 percent of patients revived from cardiac arrest (Agrillo, 2011; Greyson, 2010). Many describe visions of tunnels (**FIGURE 3.20** on the next page), bright lights or beings of light, a replay of old memories, and out-of-body sensations (Siegel, 1980). Given that oxygen deprivation and other insults to the brain are known to produce hallucinations, it is difficult to resist wondering whether a brain under stress manufactures the near-death experience. Following temporal lobe seizures, patients have reported similarly profound mystical experiences. So have solitary sailors and polar explorers while enduring monotony, isolation, and cold (Suedfeld & Mocellin, 1987).

methamphetamine a powerfully addictive drug that stimulates the central nervous system, with speeded-up body functions and associated energy and mood changes; over time, appears to reduce baseline dopamine levels.

Ecstasy (MDMA) a synthetic stimulant and mild hallucinogen. Produces euphoria and social intimacy, but with short-term health risks and longer-term harm to serotonin-producing neurons and to mood and cognition.

hallucinogens psychedelic ("mind-manifesting") drugs, such as LSD, that distort perceptions and evoke sensory images in the absence of sensory input.

LSD a powerful hallucinogenic drug; also known as acid *(lysergic acid diethylamide).*

near-death experience an altered state of consciousness reported after a close brush with death (such as through cardiac arrest); often similar to drug-induced hallucinations.

FIGURE 3.20

Hallucination or near-death vision?
Psychologist Ronald Siegel (1977) reported that people under the influence of hallucinogenic drugs often see "a bright light in the center of the field of vision. . . . The location of this point of light create[s] a tunnel-like perspective." This is very similar to others' near-death experiences.

Marijuana For 5000 years, hemp has been cultivated for its fiber. The leaves and flowers of this plant, which are sold as marijuana, contain **THC** (delta-9-tetrahydrocannabinol). Whether smoked (getting to the brain in about 7 seconds) or eaten (causing its peak concentration to be reached at a slower, unpredictable rate), THC produces a mix of effects.

Marijuana is a difficult drug to classify. It is a mild hallucinogen, amplifying sensitivity to colors, sounds, tastes, and smells. But like alcohol, marijuana relaxes, disinhibits, and may produce a euphoric high. Both alcohol and marijuana impair the motor coordination, perceptual skills, and reaction time necessary for safely operating an automobile or other machine. "THC causes animals to misjudge events," reported Ronald Siegel (1990, p. 163). "Pigeons wait too long to respond to buzzers or lights that tell them food is available for brief periods; and rats turn the wrong way in mazes."

Marijuana and alcohol also differ. The body eliminates alcohol within hours. THC and its by-products linger in the body for a week or more, which means that regular users may achieve a high with smaller amounts of the drug than would be needed by occasional users. This is contrary to the usual path of tolerance, in which repeat users need to take larger doses to feel the same effect.

A user's experience can vary with the situation. If the person feels anxious or depressed, using marijuana may intensify these feelings. The more often the person uses marijuana, especially during adolescence, the greater the risk of anxiety or depression (Bambico et al., 2010; Hall, 2006; Murray et al., 2007). Daily use bodes a worse outcome than infrequent use.

Marijuana also disrupts memory formation and interferes with immediate recall of information learned only a few minutes before. Such cognitive effects outlast the period of smoking (Messinis et al., 2006). Heavy adult use for over 20 years is associated with a shrinkage of brain areas that process memories and emotions (Yücel et al., 2008). Prenatal exposure through maternal marijuana use impairs brain development (Berghuis et al., 2007; Huizink & Mulder, 2006).

Some states and countries have passed laws allowing marijuana to be used for medical purposes to relieve the pain and nausea associated with diseases such as AIDS and cancer (Munsey, 2010; Watson et al., 2000). In such cases, the Institute of Medicine recommends delivering the THC with medical inhalers. Marijuana smoke, like cigarette smoke, is toxic and can cause cancer, lung damage, and pregnancy complications.

★ ★ ★

Despite their differences, the psychoactive drugs summarized in **TABLE 3.3** share a common feature: They trigger negative aftereffects that offset their immediate positive effects and grow stronger with repetition. And that helps explain both tolerance and withdrawal. As the opposing, negative aftereffects grow stronger, it takes larger and larger doses to produce the desired high *(tolerance),* causing the aftereffects to worsen in the drug's absence *(withdrawal).* This in turn creates a need to switch off the withdrawal symptoms by taking yet more of the drug (which may lead to *addiction).*

THC the major active ingredient in marijuana; triggers a variety of effects, including mild hallucinations.

Table 3.3

A Guide to Selected Psychoactive Drugs

Drug	Type	Pleasurable Effects	Adverse Effects
Alcohol	Depressant	Initial high followed by relaxation and disinhibition	Depression, memory loss, organ damage, impaired reactions
Heroin	Depressant	Rush of euphoria, relief from pain	Depressed physiology, agonizing withdrawal
Caffeine	Stimulant	Increased alertness and wakefulness	Anxiety, restlessness, and insomnia in high doses; uncomfortable withdrawal
Methamphet-amine	Stimulant	Euphoria, alertness, energy	Irritability, insomnia, hypertension, seizures
Cocaine	Stimulant	Rush of euphoria, confidence, energy	Cardiovascular stress, suspiciousness, depressive crash
Nicotine	Stimulant	Arousal and relaxation, sense of well-being	Heart disease, cancer
Ecstasy (MDMA)	Stimulant; mild hallucinogen	Emotional elevation, disinhibition	Dehydration, overheating, depressed mood, impaired cognitive and immune functioning
Marijuana (THC)	Mild hallucinogen	Enhanced sensation, relief of pain, distortion of time, relaxation	Impaired learning and memory, increased risk of psychological disorders, lung damage from smoke

---

RETRIEVE IT

"How strange would appear to be this thing that men call pleasure! And how curiously it is related to what is thought to be its opposite, pain! . . . Wherever the one is found, the other follows up behind."

Plato, Phaedo, *fourth century B.C.E.*

• How does this pleasure-pain description apply to the repeated use of psychoactive drugs?

ANSWER: Psychoactive drugs create pleasure by altering brain chemistry. With repeated use of the drug, the brain develops tolerance and needs more of the drug to achieve the desired effect. (Marijuana is an exception.) As the user becomes dependent, discontinuing use of the substance produces painful or psychologically unpleasant withdrawal symptoms.

Influences on Drug Use

3-17: Why do some people become regular users of consciousness-altering drugs?

Drug use by North American youth increased during the 1970s. Then, with increased drug education and a more realistic and deglamorized media depiction of taking drugs, drug use declined sharply. After the early 1990s, the cultural antidrug voice softened, and drugs for a time were again glamorized in some music and films. Consider, for example, historical trends in the use of marijuana:

• In the University of Michigan's annual survey of 15,000 U.S. high school seniors, the proportion who said there is "great risk" in regular marijuana use rose from 35 percent in 1978 to 79 percent in 1991, then retreated to 47 percent in 2010 (Johnston et al., 2011).

• After peaking in 1978, marijuana use by U.S. high school seniors declined through 1992, then rose, but has recently been tapering off (see **FIGURE 3.21** on the next page). Among Canadian 15- to 24-year-olds, 23 percent report using marijuana monthly, weekly, or daily (Health Canada, 2012).

For some adolescents, occasional drug use represents thrill seeking. Why, though, do others become regular drug users? In search of answers, researchers have engaged biological, psychological, and social-cultural levels of analysis.

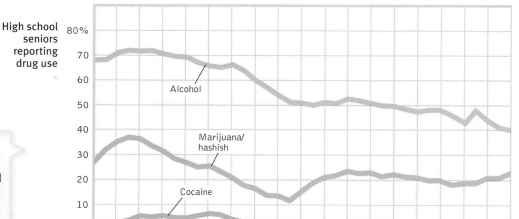

FIGURE 3.21

Trends in drug use The percentage of U.S. high school seniors who report having used alcohol, marijuana, or cocaine during the past 30 days declined from the late 1970s to 1992, when it partially rebounded for a few years. (From Johnston et al., 2012.)

Biological Influences

Some people may be biologically vulnerable to particular drugs. For example, heredity influences some aspects of substance abuse problems, especially those appearing by early adulthood (Crabbe, 2002):

- Having an identical rather than fraternal twin with alcohol dependence puts one at increased risk for alcohol problems. In marijuana use also, identical twins more closely resemble each other than do fraternal twins (Kendler et al., 2002).

- Boys who at age 6 are excitable, impulsive, and fearless (genetically influenced traits) are more likely as teens to smoke, drink, and use other drugs (Masse & Tremblay, 1997).

- Researchers have identified genes that are more common among people and animals predisposed to alcohol dependence, and they are seeking genes that contribute to tobacco addiction (NIH, 2006; Nurnberger & Bierut, 2007). These culprit genes seemingly produce deficiencies in the brain's natural dopamine reward system: While triggering temporary dopamine-produced pleasure, the addictive drugs disrupt normal dopamine balance. Studies of how drugs reprogram the brain's reward systems raise hopes for anti-addiction drugs that might block or blunt the effects of alcohol and other drugs (Miller, 2008; Wilson & Kuhn, 2005).

Psychological and Social-Cultural Influences

Throughout this text, you will see that biological, psychological, and social-cultural influences interact to produce behavior. So, too, with drug use (**FIGURE 3.22**). One psychological factor that has appeared in studies of youth and young adults is the feeling that life is meaningless and directionless (Newcomb & Harlow, 1986). This feeling is common among school dropouts who subsist without job skills, without privilege, and with little hope.

Sometimes the psychological influence is obvious. Many heavy users of alcohol, marijuana, and cocaine have experienced significant stress or failure and are depressed. Girls with a history of depression, eating disorders, or sexual or physical abuse are at risk for substance addiction. So are youth undergoing school or neighborhood transitions (CASA, 2003; Logan et al., 2002). Collegians who have not yet achieved a clear identity are also at greater risk (Bishop et al., 2005). By temporarily dulling the pain of self-awareness, psychoactive drugs may offer a way to avoid coping with depression, anger, anxiety, or insomnia. (As Chapter 7 explains, behavior is often controlled more by its immediate consequences than by its later ones.)

Nic-A-Teen Virtually nobody starts smoking past the vulnerable teen years. Eager to hook customers whose addiction will give them business for years to come, cigarette companies target teens. Portrayals of smoking by popular actors, such as Robert Pattinson in *Remember Me,* entice teens to imitate.

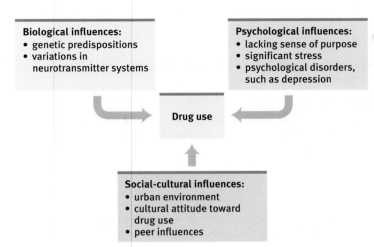

Biological influences:
• genetic predispositions
• variations in neurotransmitter systems

Psychological influences:
• lacking sense of purpose
• significant stress
• psychological disorders, such as depression

Drug use

Social-cultural influences:
• urban environment
• cultural attitude toward drug use
• peer influences

FIGURE 3.22
Levels of analysis for drug use The biopsychosocial approach enables researchers to investigate drug use from complementary perspectives.

Smoking usually begins during early adolescence. (If you are in college or university, and the cigarette manufacturers haven't yet made you their devoted customer, they almost surely never will.) Adolescents, self-conscious and often thinking the world is watching their every move, are vulnerable to smoking's allure. They may first light up to imitate glamorous celebrities, or to project a mature image, or to get the social reward of being accepted by other smokers (Cin et al., 2007; Tickle et al., 2006). Mindful of these tendencies, cigarette companies have effectively modeled smoking with themes that appeal to youths: sophistication, independence, adventure-seeking, social approval. Typically, teens who start smoking also have friends who smoke, who suggest its pleasures and offer them cigarettes (Rose et al., 1999). Among teens whose parents and best friends are nonsmokers, the smoking rate is close to zero (Moss et al., 1992; also see **FIGURE 3.23**). Most teen drinking is also done for social reasons, not as a way to cope with problems (Kuntsche et al., 2005).

Rates of drug use also vary across cultural and ethnic groups. One survey of 100,000 teens in 35 European countries found that marijuana use in the prior 30 days ranged from zero to 1 percent in Romania and Sweden, to 20 to 22 percent in Britain, Switzerland, and France (ESPAD, 2003). Independent U.S. government studies of drug use in households nationwide and among high schoolers in all regions reveal that African-American teens have sharply lower rates of drinking, smoking, and cocaine use (Johnston et al., 2007). Alcohol and other drug addiction rates have also been low among actively religious people, with extremely low rates among Orthodox Jews, Mormons, Mennonites, and the Amish (Trimble, 1994; Yeung et al., 2009). Relatively drug-free small towns and rural areas tend to constrain any genetic predisposition to drug use (Legrand et al., 2005). So does active parental monitoring (Lac & Crano, 2009). For those whose genetic predispositions nudge them toward substance use, cities offer more opportunities and less supervision.

Whether in cities or rural areas, peers influence attitudes about drugs. They also throw the parties and provide (or don't provide) the drugs. If an adolescent's friends use drugs, the odds are that he or she will, too. If the friends do not, the opportunity may not even arise. Teens who come from happy families, who do not begin drinking before age 15, and who do well in school tend not to use drugs, largely because they rarely associate with those who do (Bachman et al., 2007; Hingson et al., 2006; Odgers et al., 2008).

Peer influence is more than what friends do or say. Adolescents' expectations—what they *believe* friends are doing and favoring—influence their behavior (Vitória et al., 2009). One study surveyed sixth graders in 22 U.S. states. How many believed their friends had smoked marijuana? About 14 percent. How many of those friends acknowledged doing so? Only 4 percent

Culture and alcohol
Percentage drinking weekly or more:
United States   30%
Canada   40%
Britain   58%
(Gallup Poll, from Moore, 2006)

FIGURE 3.23
Peer influence Kids don't smoke if their friends don't (Philip Morris, 2003). A correlation-causation question: Does the close link between teen smoking and friends' smoking reflect peer influence? Teens seeking similar friends? Or both?

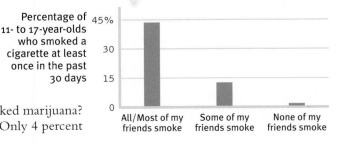

Percentage of 11- to 17-year-olds who smoked a cigarette at least once in the past 30 days

45%

30

15

0

All/Most of my friends smoke   Some of my friends smoke   None of my friends smoke

Table 3.4
Facts About "Higher" Education

College and university students drink more alcohol than their nonstudent peers and exhibit 2.5 times the general population's rate of substance abuse.
Fraternity and sorority members report nearly twice the binge-drinking rate of nonmembers.
Since 1993, campus smoking rates have declined, alcohol use has been steady, and abuse of prescription opioids, stimulants, tranquilizers, and sedatives has increased, as has marijuana use.

Source: NCASA, 2007.

SNAPSHOTS

Snapshots at jasonlove.com

(Wren, 1999). University students are not immune to such misperceptions: Drinking dominates social occasions partly because students overestimate their fellow students' enthusiasm for alcohol and underestimate their views of its risks (Prentice & Miller, 1993; Self, 1994) (**TABLE 3.4**). When students' overestimates of peer drinking are corrected, alcohol use often subsides (Moreira et al., 2009).

People whose beginning use of drugs was influenced by their peers are more likely to stop using when friends stop or the social network changes (Kandel & Raveis, 1989). One study that followed 12,000 adults over 32 years found that smokers tend to quit in clusters (Christakis & Fowler, 2008). Within a social network, the odds of a person's quitting increased when a spouse, friend, or co-worker stopped smoking. Similarly, most soldiers who became drug addicted while in Vietnam ceased their drug use after returning home (Robins et al., 1974).

As always with correlations, the traffic between friends' drug use and our own may be two-way: Our friends influence us. Social networks matter. But we also select as friends those who share our likes and dislikes.

What do the findings on drug use suggest for drug prevention and treatment programs? Three channels of influence seem possible:

- Educate young people about the long-term costs of a drug's temporary pleasures.

- Help young people find other ways to boost their self-esteem and purpose in life.

- Attempt to modify peer associations or to "inoculate" youths against peer pressures by training them in refusal skills.

People rarely abuse drugs if they understand the physical and psychological costs, feel good about themselves and the direction their lives are taking, and are in a peer group that disapproves of using drugs. These educational, psychological, and social-cultural factors may help explain why 26 percent of U.S. high school dropouts, but only 6 percent of those with a postgraduate education, report smoking (CDC, 2011).

RETRIEVE IT

- Studies have found that people who begin drinking in the early teens are much more likely to become alcohol dependent than are those who begin at age 21 or after. What possible explanations might there be for this correlation between early use and later abuse?

ANSWER: Possible explanations include (a) a biological predisposition to both early use and later abuse; (b) brain changes and taste preferences triggered by early use; and (c) enduring habits, attitudes, activities, or peer relationships that foster alcohol abuse.

CHAPTER REVIEW

Consciousness and the Two-Track Mind

LEARNING OBJECTIVES

Test Yourself by taking a moment to answer each of these Learning Objective Questions (repeated here from within the chapter). Then turn to Appendix D, Complete Chapter Reviews, to check your answers. Research suggests that trying to answer these questions on your own will improve your long-term memory of the concepts (McDaniel et al., 2009).

The Brain and Consciousness

3-1: What is the place of consciousness in psychology's history?

3-2: What is the "dual-processing" being revealed by today's cognitive neuroscience?

3-3: How much information do we consciously attend to at once?

Sleep and Dreams

3-4: How do our biological rhythms influence our daily functioning?

3-5: What is the biological rhythm of our sleeping and dreaming stages?

3-6: How do biology and environment interact in our sleep patterns?

3-7: What are sleep's functions?

3-8: How does sleep loss affect us, and what are the major sleep disorders?

3-9: What do we dream?

3-10: What are the functions of dreams?

Hypnosis

3-11: What is hypnosis, and what powers does a hypnotist have over a hypnotized subject?

3-12: Is hypnosis an extension of normal consciousness or an altered state?

Drugs and Consciousness

3-13: What are tolerance, dependence, and addiction, and what are some common misconceptions about addiction?

3-14: What are depressants, and what are their effects?

3-15: What are stimulants, and what are their effects?

3-16: What are hallucinogens, and what are their effects?

3-17: Why do some people become regular users of consciousness-altering drugs?

TERMS AND CONCEPTS TO REMEMBER

Test yourself on these terms by trying to write down the definition in your own words before flipping back to the referenced page to check your answer.

consciousness, p. 78

cognitive neuroscience, p. 78

dual processing, p. 79

blindsight, p. 79

selective attention, p. 80

inattentional blindness, p. 81

change blindness, p. 82

circadian [ser-KAY-dee-an] rhythm, p. 83

REM sleep, p. 84

alpha waves, p. 85

sleep, p. 85

hallucinations, p. 85

delta waves, p. 85

suprachiasmatic nucleus, p. 87

insomnia, p. 91

narcolepsy, p. 92

sleep apnea, p. 92

night terrors, p. 93

dream, p. 93

manifest content, p. 94

latent content, p. 95

EXPERIENCE THE TESTING EFFECT

Test yourself repeatedly throughout your studies. This will not only help you figure out what you know and don't know; the testing itself will help you learn and remember the information more effectively thanks to the *testing effect.*

1. Failure to see visible objects because our attention is occupied elsewhere is called _____ _____.

2. We register and react to stimuli outside of our awareness by means of _____ processing. When we devote deliberate attention to stimuli, we use _____ processing.

3. Our body temperature tends to rise and fall in sync with a biological clock, which is referred to as _____ _____.

4. During Stage NREM-1 sleep, a person is most likely to experience
   a. sleep spindles.
   b. hallucinations.
   c. night terrors or nightmares.
   d. rapid eye movements.

5. The brain emits large, slow delta waves during _____ sleep.

6. As the night progresses, what happens to the REM stage of sleep?

7. Which of the following is NOT one of the theories that have been proposed to explain why we need sleep?
   a. Sleep has survival value.
   b. Sleep helps us recuperate.
   c. Sleep rests the eyes.
   d. Sleep plays a role in the growth process.

8. What is the difference between narcolepsy and sleep apnea?

9. In interpreting dreams, Freud was most interested in their
   a. information-processing function.
   b. physiological function.
   c. manifest content, or story line.
   d. latent content, or hidden meaning.

10. What is the *neural activation* theory of dreaming?

11. "For what one has dwelt on by day, these things are seen in visions of the night" (Menander of Athens [342–292 B.C.E.], *Fragments*). How might the information-processing perspective on dreaming interpret this quote?

12. The tendency for REM sleep to increase following REM sleep deprivation is referred to as _____ _____.

13. People who are hypnotizable and will carry out a hypnotic suggestion typically
   a. are able to focus totally on a task.
   b. have low self-esteem.
   c. are subject to hallucinations.
   d. are faking their actions.

14. Most experts agree that hypnosis can be effectively used to
   a. elicit testimony about a "forgotten" event.
   b. re-create childhood experiences.
   c. relieve pain.
   d. block sensory input.

15. Hilgard believed that hypnosis involves a state of divided consciousness, or _____.

16. After continued use of a psychoactive drug, the drug user needs to take larger doses to get the desired effect. This is referred to as _____.

17. The depressants include alcohol, barbiturates,
   a. and opiates.
   b. cocaine, and morphine.
   c. caffeine, nicotine, and marijuana.
   d. and amphetamines.

18. Why might alcohol make a person more helpful *or* more aggressive?

19. Long-term use of Ecstasy can
    a. depress sympathetic nervous system activity.
    b. deplete the brain's supply of epinephrine.
    c. deplete the brain's supply of dopamine.
    d. damage serotonin-producing neurons.

20. Near-death experiences are strikingly similar to the hallucinations evoked by _____.

21. Use of marijuana
    a. impairs motor coordination, perception, reaction time, and memory.
    b. inhibits people's emotions.

    c. leads to dehydration and overheating.
    d. stimulates brain cell development.

22. An important psychological contributor to drug use is
    a. inflated self-esteem.
    b. the feeling that life is meaningless and directionless.
    c. genetic predispositions.
    d. overprotective parents.

Find answers to these questions in Appendix E, in the back of the book.

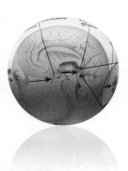

Experience more of the TESTING EFFECT

Multiple-format self-tests and more may be found at www.worthpublishers.com/myers.

CHAPTER 4

Developing Through the Life Span

Life is a journey, from womb to tomb. So it is for me, and so it will be for you. My story, and yours, began when a man and a woman contributed 20,000+ genes to an egg that became a unique person. Those genes coded the protein building blocks that, with astonishing precision, formed our bodies and predisposed our traits. My grandmother bequeathed to my mother a rare hearing-loss pattern, which she, in turn, gave to me (the least of her gifts). My father was an amiable extravert, and sometimes I forget to stop talking. As a child, my talking was impeded by painful stuttering, for which Seattle Public Schools gave me speech therapy.

Along with my parents' nature, I also received their nurture. Like you, I was born into a particular family and culture, with its own way of viewing the world. My values have been shaped by a family culture filled with talking and laughter, by a religious culture that speaks of love and justice, and by an academic culture that encourages critical thinking (asking, *What do you mean? How do you know?*).

We are formed by our genes, and by our contexts, so our stories will differ. But in many ways we are each like nearly everyone else on Earth. Being human, you and I have a need to belong. My mental video library, which began after age 4, is filled with scenes of social attachment. Over time, my attachments to parents loosened as peer friendships grew. After lacking confidence to date in high school, I fell in love with a college classmate and married at age 20. Natural selection disposes us to survive and perpetuate our genes. Sure enough, two years later a child entered our lives and I experienced a new form of love that surprised me with its intensity.

But life is marked by change. That child now lives 2000 miles away, and one of his two siblings has found her calling in South Africa. The tight rubber bands linking parent and child have loosened, as yours likely have as well.

Change also marks most vocational lives, which for me transitioned from a teen working in the family insurance agency, to a premed chemistry major and hospital aide, to (after discarding my half-completed medical school applications) a psychology professor and author. I predict that in 10 years you, too, will be doing things you do not currently anticipate.

Stability also marks our development. When I look in the mirror I do not see the person I once was, but I feel like the person I have always been. I am the same person who, as a late teen, played basketball and discovered love. A half-century later, I still play basketball and still love (with less passion but more security) the life partner with whom I have shared life's griefs and joys.

We experience a continuous self, but that self morphs through stages—growing up, raising children, enjoying a career, and, eventually, life's final stage, which will demand my presence. As I wend my way through this cycle of life and death, I am mindful that life's journey is a continuing process of development, seeded by nature and shaped by nurture, animated by love and focused by work, begun with wide-eyed curiosity and completed, for those blessed to live to a good old age, with peace and never-ending hope.

Across the life span we grow from newborn to toddler, from toddler to teenager, and from teen to mature adult. At each stage of life's journey there are physical, cognitive, and social milestones. Let's begin at the very beginning.

developmental psychology a branch of psychology that studies physical, cognitive, and social change throughout the life span.

zygote the fertilized egg; it enters a 2-week period of rapid cell division and develops into an embryo.

embryo the developing human organism from about 2 weeks after fertilization through the second month.

fetus the developing human organism from 9 weeks after conception to birth.

"Nature is all that a man brings with him into the world; nurture is every influence that affects him after his birth."

Francis Galton, English Men of Science, *1874*

Developmental Psychology's Major Issues

 4-1: What three issues have engaged developmental psychologists?

Developmental psychology examines our physical, cognitive, and social development across the life span, with a focus on three major issues:

1. ***Nature and nurture:*** How does our genetic inheritance *(our nature)* interact with our experiences *(our nurture)* to influence our development? How have your nature and your nurture influenced *your* life story?

2. ***Continuity and stages:*** What parts of development are gradual and continuous, like riding an escalator? What parts change abruptly in separate stages, like climbing rungs on a ladder?

3. ***Stability and change:*** Which of our traits persist through life? How do we change as we age?

We will reflect on these three developmental issues throughout this chapter.

Prenatal Development and the Newborn

4-2: What is the course of prenatal development, and how do teratogens affect that development?

Conception

Nothing is more natural than a species reproducing itself. And nothing is more wondrous. With humans, the process starts when a woman's ovary releases a mature egg—a cell roughly the size of the period at the end of this sentence. Like space voyagers approaching a huge planet, the 200 million or more deposited sperm begin their race upstream, approaching a cell 85,000 times their own size. The relatively few reaching the egg release digestive enzymes that eat away its protective coating (**FIGURE 4.1a**). As soon as one sperm penetrates that coating and is welcomed in (Figure 4.1b), the egg's surface blocks out the others. Before half a day elapses, the egg nucleus and the sperm nucleus fuse. The two have become one.

Consider it your most fortunate of moments. Among 200 million sperm, the one needed to make you, in combination with that one particular egg, won the race. And so it was for innumerable generations before us. If any one of our ancestors had been conceived with a different sperm or egg, or died before conceiving, or not chanced to meet the partner or . . . the mind boggles at the improbable, unbroken chain of events that produced you and me.

MICHAEL PHELPS

First known photo of Michael Phelps (If the playful cartoonist were to convey literal truth, a second arrow would also point to the egg that contributed the other half of Michael Phelps' genes.)

© Patrick Moberg/www.patrickmoberg.com

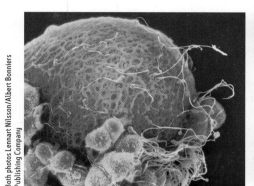
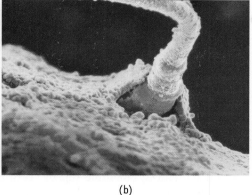

(a) (b)

Both photos Lennart Nilsson/Albert Bonniers Publishing Company

FIGURE 4.1
Life is sexually transmitted (a) Sperm cells surround an egg. (b) As one sperm penetrates the egg's jelly-like outer coating, a series of chemical events begins that will cause sperm and egg to fuse into a single cell. If all goes well, that cell will subdivide again and again to emerge 9 months later as a 100-trillion-cell human being.

Prenatal Development

Fewer than half of all fertilized eggs, called **zygotes,** survive beyond the first 2 weeks (Grobstein, 1979; Hall, 2004). But for you and me, good fortune prevailed. One cell became 2, then 4—each just like the first—until this cell division had produced some 100 identical cells within the first week. Then the cells began to differentiate—to specialize in structure and function. How identical cells do this—as if one decides "I'll become a brain, you become intestines!"—is a puzzle that scientists are just beginning to solve.

About 10 days after conception, the zygote attaches to the mother's uterine wall, beginning approximately 37 weeks of the closest human relationship. The zygote's inner cells become the **embryo** (**FIGURE 4.2a**). The outer cells become the *placenta,* the life-link that transfers nutrients and oxygen from mother to embryo. Over the next 6 weeks, the embryo's organs begin to form and function. The heart begins to beat.

By 9 weeks after conception, an embryo looks unmistakably human (Figure 4.2b). It is now a **fetus** (Latin for "offspring" or "young one"). During the sixth month, organs such as the stomach have developed enough to give the fetus a chance of survival if born prematurely.

At each prenatal stage, genetic and environmental factors affect our development. By the sixth month, microphone readings taken inside the uterus reveal that the fetus is responsive to sound and is exposed to the sound of its mother's muffled voice (Ecklund-Flores, 1992; Hepper, 2005). Immediately after birth, newborns prefer her voice to another woman's or to their father's (Busnel et al., 1992; DeCasper et al., 1984, 1986, 1994). They also prefer hearing their mother's language. If she spoke two languages during pregnancy, they display interest in both (Byers-Heinlein et al., 2010). And just after birth, the melodic ups and downs of newborns' cries bear the tuneful signature of their

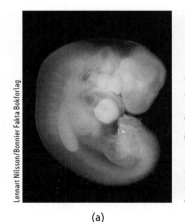
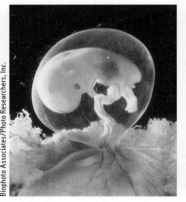
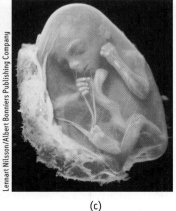

(a) (b) (c)

Lennart Nilsson/Bonnier Fakta Bokforlag

Biophoto Associates/Photo Researchers, Inc.

Lennart Nilsson/Albert Bonniers Publishing Company

FIGURE 4.2
Prenatal development (a) The embryo grows and develops rapidly. At 40 days, the spine is visible and the arms and legs are beginning to grow. (b) By the end of the second month, when the fetal period begins, facial features, hands, and feet have formed. (c) As the fetus enters the fourth month, its 3 ounces could fit in the palm of your hand.

teratogens (literally, "monster maker") agents, such as toxins, chemicals, and viruses, that can reach the embryo or fetus during prenatal development and cause harm.

fetal alcohol syndrome (FAS) physical and cognitive abnormalities in children caused by a pregnant woman's heavy drinking. In severe cases, symptoms include noticeable facial misproportions.

Prenatal development

zygote: conception to 2 weeks
embryo: 2 weeks through 8 weeks
fetus: 9 weeks to birth

"You shall conceive and bear a son. So then drink no wine or strong drink."

Judges 13:7

"I felt like a man trapped in a woman's body. Then I was born."

Comedian Chris Bliss

moodboard/JupiterImages

mother's native tongue (Mampe et al., 2009). Babies born to French-speaking mothers tend to cry with the rising intonation of French; babies born to German-speaking mothers cry with the falling tones of German. Would you have guessed? The learning of language begins in the womb.

In the two months before birth, fetuses demonstrate learning in other ways, as when they adapt to a vibrating, honking device placed on their mother's abdomen (Dirix et al., 2009). Like people who adapt to the sound of trains in their neighborhood, fetuses get used to the honking. Moreover, four weeks later, they recall the sound (as evidenced by their blasé response, compared with the reactions of those not previously exposed).

Sounds are not the only stimuli fetuses are exposed to in the womb. In addition to transferring nutrients and oxygen from mother to fetus, the placenta screens out many harmful substances, but some slip by. **Teratogens,** agents such as toxins, viruses, and drugs, can damage an embryo or fetus. This is one reason pregnant women are advised not to drink alcoholic beverages. A pregnant woman never drinks alone. As alcohol enters her bloodstream, and her fetus', it depresses activity in both their central nervous systems. Alcohol use during pregnancy may prime the woman's offspring to like alcohol and may put them at risk for heavy drinking and alcohol dependence during their teens. In experiments, when pregnant rats drank alcohol, their young offspring later displayed a liking for alcohol's taste and odor (Youngentob et al., 2007, 2009).

Even light drinking or occasional binge drinking can affect the fetal brain (Braun, 1996; Ikonomidou et al., 2000; Sayal et al., 2009). Persistent heavy drinking puts the fetus at risk for birth defects and for future behavior problems, hyperactivity, and lower intelligence. For 1 in about 800 infants, the effects are visible as **fetal alcohol syndrome (FAS),** marked by a small, misproportioned head and lifelong brain abnormalities (May & Gossage, 2001). The fetal damage may occur because alcohol has what Chapter 2 called an *epigenetic effect:* It leaves chemical marks on DNA that switch genes abnormally on or off (Liu et al., 2009).

RETRIEVE IT

• The first two weeks of prenatal development is the period of the _____. The period of the _____ lasts from 9 weeks after conception until birth. The time between those two prenatal periods is considered the period of the _____.

ANSWERS: zygote; fetus; embryo

The Competent Newborn

4-3: What are some newborn abilities, and how do researchers explore infants' mental abilities?

Babies come with software preloaded on their neural hard drives. Having survived prenatal hazards, we as newborns came equipped with automatic reflex responses ideally suited for our survival. We withdrew our limbs to escape pain. If a cloth over our face interfered with our breathing, we turned our head from side to side and swiped at it.

New parents are often in awe of the coordinated sequence of reflexes by which their baby gets food. When something touches their cheek, babies turn toward that touch, open their mouth, and vigorously *root* for a nipple. Finding one, they automatically close on it and begin *sucking*—which itself requires a coordinated sequence of reflexive *tonguing, swallowing,* and *breathing.* Failing to find satisfaction, the hungry baby may *cry*—a behavior parents find highly unpleasant and very rewarding to relieve.

The pioneering American psychologist William James presumed that newborns experience a "blooming, buzzing confusion," an assumption few people challenged until the 1960s. Then scientists discovered that babies can tell you a lot—if you know how to ask. To ask, you must capitalize on what babies can do—gaze, suck, turn their heads. So, equipped with eye-tracking machines and pacifiers wired to electronic gear, researchers set out to answer parents' age-old questions: What can my baby see, hear, smell, and think?

Consider how researchers exploit **habituation**—a decrease in responding with repeated stimulation. We saw this earlier when fetuses adapted to a vibrating, honking device placed on their mother's abdomen. The novel stimulus gets attention when first presented. With repetition, the response weakens. This seeming boredom with familiar stimuli gives us a way to ask infants what they see and remember.

Prepared to feed and eat Animals are predisposed to respond to their offsprings' cries for nourishment.

Indeed, even as newborns, we prefer sights and sounds that facilitate social responsiveness. We turn our heads in the direction of human voices. We gaze longer at a drawing of a face-like image (**FIGURE 4.3**). We prefer to look at objects 8 to 12 inches away, which—wonder of wonders—just happens to be the approximate distance between a nursing infant's eyes and its mother's (Maurer & Maurer, 1988).

Within days after birth, our brain's neural networks were stamped with the smell of our mother's body. Week-old nursing babies, placed between a gauze pad from their mother's bra and one from another nursing mother, have usually turned toward the smell of their own mother's pad (MacFarlane, 1978). What's more, that smell preference lasts. One experiment capitalized on the fact that some nursing mothers in a French maternity ward used a chamomile-scented balm to prevent nipple soreness (Delaunay-El Allam, 2010). Twenty-one months later, their toddlers preferred playing with chamomile-scented toys! Their peers who had not sniffed the scent while breast feeding showed no such preference. (This makes me wonder: Will adults, who as babies associated chamomile scent with their mother's breast, become devoted chamomile tea drinkers?)

FIGURE 4.3
Newborns' preference for faces When shown these two stimuli with the same elements, Italian newborns spent nearly twice as many seconds looking at the face-like image (Johnson & Morton, 1991). Canadian newborns—average age 53 minutes in one study—displayed the same apparently inborn preference to look toward faces (Mondloch et al., 1999).

Infancy and Childhood

As a flower unfolds in accord with its genetic instructions, so do we humans. **Maturation**—the orderly sequence of biological growth—decrees many of our commonalities. We stand before walking. We use nouns before adjectives. Severe deprivation or abuse can retard our development, but the genetic growth tendencies are inborn. Maturation (nature) sets the basic course of development; experience (nurture) adjusts it. Once again, we see genes and scenes interacting.

"It is a rare privilege to watch the birth, growth, and first feeble struggles of a living human mind."

Annie Sullivan, in Helen Keller's The Story of My Life, *1903*

Physical Development

4-4: During infancy and childhood, how do the brain and motor skills develop?

Brain Development

The formative nurture that conspired with nature began at conception, with the prenatal environment in the womb. Nurture continues outside the womb, where our early experiences foster brain development.

habituation decreasing responsiveness with repeated stimulation. As infants gain familiarity with repeated exposure to a visual stimulus, their interest wanes and they look away sooner.

maturation biological growth processes that enable orderly changes in behavior, relatively uninfluenced by experience.

At birth   3 months   15 months

FIGURE 4.4

Drawings of human cerebral cortex sections In humans, the brain is immature at birth. As the child matures, the neural networks grow increasingly complex.

Courtesy of C. Brune

Stringing the circuits young String musicians who started playing before age 12 have larger and more complex neural circuits controlling the note-making left-hand fingers than do string musicians whose training started later (Elbert et al., 1995).

In your mother's womb, your developing brain formed nerve cells at the explosive rate of nearly one-quarter million per minute. From infancy on, brain and mind—neural hardware and cognitive software—develop together. On the day you were born, you had most of the brain cells you would ever have. However, the wiring among these cells—your nervous system—was immature: After birth, these neural networks had a wild growth spurt branching and linking in patterns that would eventually enable you to walk, talk, and remember (**FIGURE 4.4**).

From ages 3 to 6, the most rapid brain growth was in your frontal lobes, which enable rational planning. During those years, your ability to control your attention and behavior developed rapidly (Garon et al., 2008; Thompson-Schill et al., 2009).

Frontal lobe development continues into adolescence and beyond. The last cortical areas to develop are the association areas—those linked with thinking, memory, and language. As they develop, mental abilities surge (Chugani & Phelps, 1986; Thatcher et al., 1987). The neural pathways supporting language and agility proliferate into puberty. Then, a use-it-or-lose-it *pruning process* shuts down unused links and strengthens others (Paus et al., 1999; Thompson et al., 2000).

Your genes dictated your overall brain architecture, rather like the lines of a coloring book, but experience fills in the details (Kenrick et al., 2009). So how do early experiences leave their "marks" in the brain? Mark Rosenzweig and David Krech opened a window on that process when they raised some young rats in solitary confinement in an impoverished environment, and others in a communal playground that simulated a natural environment. When the researchers later analyzed the rats' brains, those who died with the most toys had won. The rats living in the enriched environment had usually developed a heavier and thicker brain cortex (**FIGURE 4.5**).

Rosenzweig was so surprised by this discovery that he repeated the experiment several times before publishing his findings (Renner & Rosenzweig, 1987; Rosenzweig, 1984). So great are the effects that, shown brief video clips, you could tell from the rats' activity and curiosity whether their environment had been impoverished or enriched (Renner & Renner, 1993). After 60 days in the enriched environment, the rats' brain weights increased 7 to 10 percent and the number of synapses mushroomed by about 20 percent (Kolb & Whishaw, 1998).

Such results have motivated improvements in environments for laboratory, farm, and zoo animals—and for children in institutions. Stimulation by touch or massage also benefits infant rats and premature babies (Field et al., 2007). "Handled" infants of both species develop faster neurologically and gain weight more rapidly. By giving preemies massage therapy, neonatal intensive care units help them to go home sooner (Field et al., 2006).

Nature and nurture together sculpt our synapses. Brain maturation provides us with an abundance of neural connections. Experiences—sights and smells, touches and tugs—activate and strengthen some neural pathways while others weaken from disuse. Like forest pathways, popular tracks are broadened and less-traveled ones gradually disappear. The result by puberty is a massive loss of unemployed connections.

FIGURE 4.5

Experience affects brain development Mark Rosenzweig and David Krech raised rats either alone in an environment without playthings, or with other rats in an environment enriched with playthings changed daily. In 14 of 16 repetitions of this basic experiment, rats in the enriched environment developed significantly more cerebral cortex (relative to the rest of the brain's tissue) than did those in the impoverished environment.

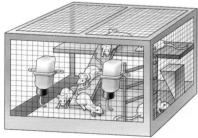
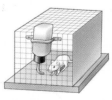

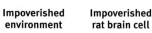

Impoverished environment   **Impoverished rat brain cell**   **Enriched environment**   **Enriched rat brain cell**

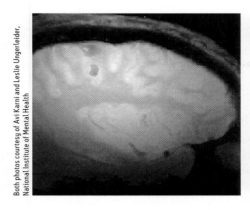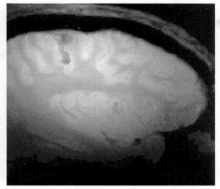

Both photos courtesy of Avi Karni and Leslie Ungerleider, National Institute of Mental Health

FIGURE 4.6
A trained brain A well-learned finger-tapping task activates more motor cortex neurons (orange area, right) than were active in the same brain before training (left). (From Karni et al., 1998.)

Here at the juncture of nurture and nature is the biological reality of early childhood learning. During early childhood—while excess connections are still on call—youngsters can most easily master such skills as the grammar and accent of another language. We seem to have a **critical period** for some skills. Lacking any exposure to spoken, written, or signed language before adolescence, a person will never master any language (see Chapter 9). Likewise, lacking visual experience during the early years, a person whose vision is restored by cataract removal will never achieve normal perceptions (more on this in Chapter 6). Without stimulation, the brain cells normally assigned to vision will die during the pruning process or be diverted to other uses. The maturing brain's rule: Use it or lose it.

Although normal stimulation during the early years is critical, the brain's development does not end with childhood. As we saw in Chapter 2's discussion of brain plasticity, our neural tissue is ever changing and new neurons are born. If a monkey pushes a lever with the same finger several thousand times a day, brain tissue controlling that finger changes to reflect the experience. Human brains work similarly (**FIGURE 4.6**). Whether learning to keyboard or skateboard, we perform with increasing skill as our brain incorporates the learning (Ambrose, 2010).

critical period an optimal period early in the life of an organism when exposure to certain stimuli or experiences produces normal development.

"Genes and experiences are just two ways of doing the same thing—wiring synapses."

Joseph LeDoux,
The Synaptic Self, *2002*

Motor Development

The developing brain enables physical coordination. As an infant's muscles and nervous system mature, skills emerge. With occasional exceptions, the sequence of physical (motor) development is universal. Babies roll over before they sit unsupported, and they usually crawl on all fours before they walk (**FIGURE 4.7**). These behaviors reflect not imitation but a maturing nervous system; blind children, too, crawl before they walk.

There are, however, individual differences in timing. In the United States, for example, 25 percent of all babies walk by 11 months of age, 50 percent within a week after their first birthday, and 90 percent by age 15 months (Frankenburg et al., 1992). The recommended infant *back-to-sleep position* (putting babies to sleep on their backs to reduce the risk of a smothering crib death) has been associated with somewhat later crawling but not with later walking (Davis et al., 1998; Lipsitt, 2003).

Genes guide motor development. Identical twins typically begin walking on nearly the same day (Wilson, 1979). Maturation—including the rapid development of the cerebellum at the back of the brain—creates our readiness to learn walking at about age 1. Experience before that time has a limited effect. The same is true for other physical skills, including bowel and bladder control. Before necessary muscular and neural maturation, neither pleading nor punishment will produce successful toilet training.

In the eight years following the 1994 launch of a U.S. Back to Sleep educational campaign, the number of infants sleeping on their stomach dropped from 70 to 11 percent—and SIDS (sudden infant death syndrome) deaths fell by half (Braiker, 2005).

FIGURE 4.7
Physical development Sit, crawl, walk, run—the sequence of these motor development milestones is the same the world around, though babies reach them at varying ages.

Juice Images/JupiterImages

Brain Maturation and Infant Memory

Can you recall your first day of preschool or your third birthday party? Our earliest memories seldom predate our third birthday. We see this *infantile amnesia* in the memories of some preschoolers who experienced an emergency fire evacuation caused by a burning popcorn maker. Seven years later, they were able to recall the alarm and what caused it—*if* they were 4 to 5 years old at the time. Those experiencing the event as 3-year-olds could not remember the cause and usually misrecalled being already outside when the alarm sounded (Pillemer, 1995). Other studies have confirmed that the average age of earliest conscious memory is 3.5 years (Bauer, 2002, 2007). As children mature, from 4 to 6 to 8 years, childhood amnesia is giving way, and they become increasingly capable of remembering experiences, even for a year or more (Bruce et al., 2000; Morris et al., 2010). The brain areas underlying memory, such as the hippocampus and frontal lobes, continue to mature into adolescence (Bauer, 2007).

Although we *consciously* recall little from before age 4, our brain was processing and storing information during those early years. In 1965, while finishing her doctoral work in psychology, Carolyn Rovee-Collier observed an infant memory. She was a new mom, whose colicky 2-month-old, Benjamin, could be calmed by moving a crib mobile. Weary of hitting the mobile, she strung a cloth ribbon connecting the mobile to Benjamin's foot. Soon, he was kicking his foot to move the mobile. Thinking about her unintended home experiment, Rovee-Collier realized that, contrary to popular opinion in the 1960s, babies are capable of learning. To know for sure that her son wasn't just a whiz kid, she repeated the experiment with other infants (Rovee-Collier, 1989, 1999). Sure enough, they, too, soon kicked more when hitched to a mobile, both on the day of the experiment and the day after. They had learned the link between moving legs and moving mobiles. If, however, she hitched them to a different mobile the next day, the infants showed no learning, indicating that they remembered the original mobile and recognized the difference. Moreover, when tethered to the familiar mobile a month later, they remembered the association and again began kicking (**FIGURE 4.8**).

Traces of forgotten childhood languages may also persist. One study tested English-speaking British adults who had no conscious memory of the Hindi or Zulu they had spoken as children. Yet, up to age 40, they could relearn subtle sound contrasts in these languages that other people could *not* learn (Bowers et al., 2009). What the conscious mind does not know and cannot express in words, the nervous system and our two-track mind somehow remembers.

Michael Newman/PhotoEdit

FIGURE 4.8

Infant at work Babies only 3 months old can learn that kicking moves a mobile, and they can retain that learning for a month. (From Rovee-Collier, 1989, 1997.)

Cognitive Development

4-5: From the perspectives of Piaget, Vygotsky, and today's researchers, how does a child's mind develop?

Cognition refers to all the mental activities associated with thinking, knowing, remembering, and communicating. Somewhere on your life journey, you became conscious. When was that, and how did your mind unfold from there? Developmental psychologist Jean Piaget [pee-ah-ZHAY] spent his life searching for the answers to such questions. His interest began in 1920, when he was in Paris developing questions for children's intelligence tests. While administering the tests, Piaget became intrigued by children's wrong answers, which were often strikingly similar among same-age children. Where others saw childish mistakes, Piaget saw intelligence at work.

cognition all the mental activities associated with thinking, knowing, remembering, and communicating.

schema a concept or framework that organizes and interprets information.

assimilation interpreting our new experiences in terms of our existing schemas.

accommodation adapting our current understandings (schemas) to incorporate new information.

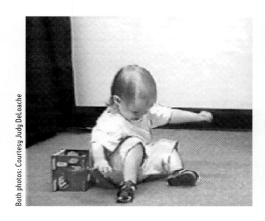

Both photos: Courtesy Judy DeLoache

FIGURE 4.9
Scale errors Psychologists Judy DeLoache, David Uttal, and Karl Rosengren (2004) have reported that 18- to 30-month-old children may fail to take the size of an object into account when trying to perform impossible actions with it. At left, a 21-month-old attempts to slide down a miniature slide. At right, a 24-month-old opens the door to a miniature car and tries to step inside.

A half-century spent with children convinced Piaget that a child's mind is not a miniature model of an adult's. Thanks partly to his work, we now understand that children reason *differently* than adults, in "wildly illogical ways about problems whose solutions are self-evident to adults" (Brainerd, 1996).

Piaget's studies led him to believe that a child's mind develops through a series of stages, in an upward march from the newborn's simple reflexes to the adult's abstract reasoning power. Thus, an 8-year-old can comprehend things a toddler cannot, such as the analogy that "getting an idea is like having a light turn on in your head," or that a miniature slide is too small for sliding, and a miniature car is much too small to get into (**FIGURE 4.9**).

Bill Anderson/Photo Researchers, Inc.

Jean Piaget (1896–1980) "If we examine the intellectual development of the individual or of the whole of humanity, we shall find that the human spirit goes through a certain number of stages, each different from the other" (1930).

Piaget's core idea is that the driving force behind our intellectual progression is an unceasing struggle to make sense of our experiences. To this end, the maturing brain builds **schemas,** concepts or mental molds into which we pour our experiences (**FIGURE 4.10**). By adulthood we have built countless schemas, ranging from *cats* and *dogs* to our concept of *love.*

To explain how we use and adjust our schemas, Piaget proposed two more concepts. First, we **assimilate** new experiences—we interpret them in terms of our current understandings (schemas). Having a simple schema for *dog,* for example, a toddler may call all four-legged animals *dogs.* But as we interact with the world, we also adjust, or **accommodate,** our schemas to incorporate information provided by new experiences. Thus, the child soon learns that the original *dog* schema is too broad and accommodates by refining the category.

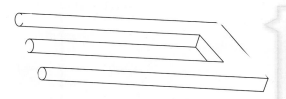

FIGURE 4.10
An impossible object Look carefully at this "devil's tuning fork." Now look away—no, better first study it some more—and then look away and draw it. . . . Not so easy, is it? Because this tuning fork is an impossible object, you have no schema for such an image.

Table 4.1
Piaget's Stages of Cognitive Development

Typical Age Range	Description of Stage	Developmental Phenomena
Birth to nearly 2 years	*Sensorimotor* Experiencing the world through senses and actions (looking, hearing, touching, mouthing, and grasping)	• Object permanence • Stranger anxiety
About 2 to about 6 or 7 years	*Preoperational* Representing things with words and images; using intuitive rather than logical reasoning	• Pretend play • Egocentrism
About 7 to 11 years	*Concrete operational* Thinking logically about concrete events; grasping concrete analogies and performing arithmetical operations	• Conservation • Mathematical transformations
About 12 through adulthood	*Formal operational* Abstract reasoning	• Abstract logic • Potential for mature moral reasoning

Image Source/Getty Images

Pretend play

sensorimotor stage in Piaget's theory, the stage (from birth to about 2 years of age) during which infants know the world mostly in terms of their sensory impressions and motor activities.

object permanence the awareness that things continue to exist even when not perceived.

Piaget's Theory and Current Thinking

Piaget believed that children construct their understanding of the world while interacting with it. Their minds experience spurts of change, followed by greater stability as they move from one cognitive plateau to the next, each with distinctive characteristics that permit specific kinds of thinking. **TABLE 4.1** summarizes the four stages in Piaget's theory.

Sensorimotor Stage In the **sensorimotor stage,** from birth to nearly age 2, babies take in the world through their senses and actions—through looking, hearing, touching, mouthing, and grasping. As their hands and limbs begin to move, they learn to make things happen.

Very young babies seem to live in the present: Out of sight is out of mind. In one test, Piaget showed an infant an appealing toy and then flopped his beret over it. Before the age of 6 months, the infant acted as if the toy ceased to exist. Young infants lack **object permanence**—the awareness that objects continue to exist when not perceived. By 8 months, infants begin exhibiting memory for things no longer seen. If you hide a toy, the infant will momentarily look for it (**FIGURE 4.11**). Within another month or two, the infant will look for it even after being restrained for several seconds.

So does object permanence in fact blossom at 8 months, much as tulips blossom in spring? Today's researchers think not. They believe object permanence unfolds gradually,

FIGURE 4.11

Object permanence Infants younger than 6 months seldom understand that things continue to exist when they are out of sight. But for this older infant, out of sight is definitely not out of mind.

Doug Goodman

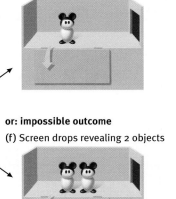

(a) Objects placed in case   **(b)** Screen comes up   **(c)** Empty hand enters   **(d)** One object removed

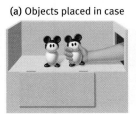 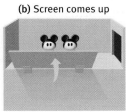 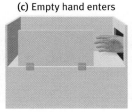 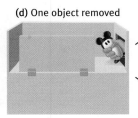

(e) Screen drops revealing 1 object

or: impossible outcome

(f) Screen drops revealing 2 objects

and they see development as more continuous than Piaget did. Even young infants will at least momentarily look for a toy where they saw it hidden a second before (Wang et al., 2004).

Researchers also believe Piaget and his followers underestimated young children's competence. Consider these simple experiments:

- *Baby physics:* Like adults staring in disbelief at a magic trick (the *"Whoa!"* look), infants look longer at an unexpected and unfamiliar scene of a car seeming to pass through a solid object, a ball stopping in midair, or an object violating object permanence by magically disappearing (Baillargeon, 1995, 2008; Wellman & Gelman, 1992).

- *Baby math:* Karen Wynn (1992, 2000) showed 5-month-olds one or two objects (**FIGURE 4.12a**). Then she hid the objects behind a screen, and visibly removed or added one (Figure 4.12d). When she lifted the screen, the infants sometimes did a double take, staring longer when shown a wrong number of objects (Figure 4.12f). But were they just responding to a greater or smaller *mass* of objects, rather than a change in *number* (Feigenson et al., 2002)? Later experiments showed that babies' number sense extends to larger numbers, to ratios, and to such things as drumbeats and motions (Libertus & Brannon, 2009; McCrink & Wynn, 2004; Spelke & Kinzler, 2007). If accustomed to a Daffy Duck puppet jumping three times on stage, they showed surprise if it jumped only twice.

Clearly, infants are smarter than Piaget appreciated. Even as babies, we had a lot on our minds.

Preoperational Stage Piaget believed that until about age 6 or 7, children are in a **preoperational stage**—too young to perform *mental operations* (such as imagining an action and mentally reversing it). For a 5-year-old, the milk that seems "too much" in a tall, narrow glass may become an acceptable amount if poured into a short, wide glass. Focusing only on the height dimension, this child cannot perform the operation of mentally pouring the milk back. Before about age 6, said Piaget, children lack the concept of **conservation**—the principle that quantity remains the same despite changes in shape (**FIGURE 4.13**).

FIGURE 4.12
Baby math Shown a numerically impossible outcome, 5-month-old infants stare longer. (From Wynn, 1992.)

preoperational stage in Piaget's theory, the stage (from about 2 to about 6 or 7 years of age) during which a child learns to use language but does not yet comprehend the mental operations of concrete logic.

conservation the principle (which Piaget believed to be a part of concrete operational reasoning) that properties such as mass, volume, and number remain the same despite changes in the forms of objects.

Bianca Moscatelli/Worth Publishers

FIGURE 4.13
Piaget's test of conservation This preoperational child does not yet understand the principle of conservation of substance. When the milk is poured into a tall, narrow glass, it suddenly seems like "more" than when it was in the shorter, wider glass. In another year or so, she will understand that the volume stays the same.

PRETEND PLAY A child who can perform mental operations can think in symbols and therefore begins to enjoy *pretend play*. Contemporary researchers have found that symbolic thinking appears at an earlier age than Piaget supposed. Judy DeLoache (1987) showed children a model of a room and hid a miniature stuffed dog behind its miniature couch. The 2½-year-olds easily remembered where to find the miniature toy, but they could not use the model to locate an actual stuffed dog behind a couch in a real room. Three-year-olds—only 6 months older—usually went right to the actual stuffed animal in the real room, showing they *could* think of the model as a symbol for the room. Piaget did not view the stage transitions as abrupt shifts. Even so, he probably would have been surprised to see symbolic thinking at such an early age.

EGOCENTRISM Piaget contended that preschool children are **egocentric:** They have difficulty perceiving things from another's point of view. Asked to "show Mommy your picture," 2-year-old Gabriella holds the picture up facing her own eyes. Three-year-old Gray makes himself "invisible" by putting his hands over his eyes, assuming that if he can't see his grandparents, they can't see him. Children's conversations also reveal their egocentrism, as one young boy demonstrated (Phillips, 1969, p. 61):

> "Do you have a brother?"
>
> "Yes."
>
> "What's his name?"
>
> "Jim."
>
> "Does Jim have a brother?"
>
> "No."

Like Gabriella, TV-watching preschoolers who block your view of the TV assume that you see what they see. They simply have not yet developed the ability to take another's viewpoint. Even we adults may overestimate the extent to which others share our opinions and perspectives, a trait known as the *curse of knowledge*. We assume that something will be clear to others if it is clear to us, or that e-mail recipients will "hear" our "just kidding" intent (Epley et al., 2004; Kruger et al., 2005). Children are even more susceptible to such egocentrism.

THEORY OF MIND When Little Red Riding Hood realized her "grandmother" was really a wolf, she swiftly revised her ideas about the creature's intentions and raced away. Preschoolers, although still egocentric, develop this ability to infer others' mental states when they begin forming a **theory of mind** (a term first coined by psychologists David Premack and Guy Woodruff [1978], to describe chimpanzees' seeming ability to read intentions).

As the ability to take another's perspective gradually develops, preschoolers come to understand what made a playmate angry, when a sibling will share, and what might make a parent buy a toy. And they begin to tease, empathize, and persuade. Between about 3½ and 4½, children worldwide come to realize that others may hold false beliefs (Callaghan et al., 2005; Sabbagh et al., 2006). Jennifer Jenkins and Janet Astington (1996) showed Toronto children a Band-Aids box and asked them what was inside. Expecting Band-Aids, the children were surprised to discover that the box actually contained pencils. Asked what a child who had never seen the box would think was inside, 3-year-olds typically answered "pencils." By age 4 to 5, the children's theory of mind had leapt forward, and they anticipated their friends' false belief that the box would hold Band-Aids. Children with *autism* (see Close-Up: Autism and "Mind Blindness," next page) have difficulty understanding that another's state of mind differs from their own.

Concrete Operational Stage By age 6 or 7, said Piaget, children enter the **concrete operational stage.** Given concrete (physical) materials, they begin to grasp conservation. Understanding that change in form does not mean change in quantity, they can mentally pour milk back and forth between glasses of different shapes. They also enjoy jokes that use this new understanding:

"It's too late, Roger—they've seen us."

Roger has not outgrown his early childhood egocentrism.

egocentrism in Piaget's theory, the preoperational child's difficulty taking another's point of view.

theory of mind people's ideas about their own and others' mental states—about their feelings, perceptions, and thoughts, and the behaviors these might predict.

concrete operational stage in Piaget's theory, the stage of cognitive development (from about 6 or 7 to 11 years of age) during which children gain the mental operations that enable them to think logically about concrete events.

formal operational stage in Piaget's theory, the stage of cognitive development (normally beginning about age 12) during which people begin to think logically about abstract concepts.

Mr. Jones went into a restaurant and ordered a whole pizza for his dinner. When the waiter asked if he wanted it cut into 6 or 8 pieces, Mr. Jones said, "Oh, you'd better make it 6, I could never eat 8 pieces!" (McGhee, 1976)

Piaget believed that during the concrete operational stage, children become able to comprehend mathematical transformations and conservation. When my daughter, Laura, was 6, I was astonished at her inability to reverse simple arithmetic. Asked, "What is 8 plus 4?" she required 5 seconds to compute "12," and another 5 seconds to then compute 12 minus 4. By age 8, she could answer a reversed question instantly.

Formal Operational Stage By about age 12, our reasoning expands from the purely concrete (involving actual experience) to encompass abstract thinking (involving imagined realities and symbols). As children approach adolescence, said Piaget, many become capable of thinking more like scientists. They can ponder hypothetical propositions and deduce consequences: *If* this, *then* that. Systematic reasoning, what Piaget called **formal operational** thinking, is now within their grasp.

Although full-blown logic and reasoning await adolescence, the rudiments of formal operational thinking begin earlier than Piaget realized. Consider this simple problem:

If John is in school, then Mary is in school. John is in school. What can you say about Mary?

Formal operational thinkers have no trouble answering correctly. But neither do most 7-year-olds (Suppes, 1982).

An Alternative Viewpoint: Lev Vygotsky and the Social Child

As Piaget was forming his theory of cognitive development, Russian psychologist Lev Vygotsky (1896–1934) was also studying how children think and learn. He noted that by age 7, they increasingly think in words and use words to solve problems. They do this, he said, by internalizing their culture's language and relying on inner speech (Fernyhough, 2008). Parents who say *"No, no!"* when pulling a child's hand away from a cake are giving the child a self-control tool. When the child later needs to resist temptation, he may likewise say *"No, no!"* Second-graders who muttered to themselves while doing math problems grasped third-grade math better the following year (Berk, 1994). Whether out loud or inaudibly, talking to themselves helps children control their behavior and emotions and master new skills.

Where Piaget emphasized how the child's mind grows through interaction with the physical environment, Vygotsky emphasized how the child's mind grows through interaction with the *social* environment. If Piaget's child was a young scientist, Vygotsky's was a young apprentice. By mentoring children and giving them new words, parents and others provide a temporary *scaffold* from which children can step to higher levels of thinking (Renninger & Granott, 2005). Language, an important ingredient of social mentoring, provides the building blocks for thinking, noted Vygotsky (who was born the same year as Piaget, but died prematurely of tuberculosis).

Lev Vygotsky (1896–1934) Vygotsky, a Russian developmental psychologist pictured here with his daughter, studied how a child's mind feeds on the language of social interaction.

Reflecting on Piaget's Theory

What remains of Piaget's ideas about the child's mind? Plenty—enough to merit his being singled out by *Time* magazine as one of the twentieth century's 20 most influential scientists and thinkers and rated in a survey of British psychologists as the last century's greatest psychologist (*Psychologist,* 2003). Piaget identified significant cognitive milestones and stimulated worldwide interest in how the mind develops. His emphasis was less on the ages at which children typically reach specific milestones than on their sequence. Studies around the globe, from aboriginal Australia to Algeria to North America, have confirmed that human cognition unfolds basically in the sequence Piaget described (Lourenco & Machado, 1996; Segall et al., 1990).

However, today's researchers see development as more continuous than did Piaget. By detecting the beginnings of each type of thinking at earlier ages, they have revealed conceptual abilities Piaget missed. Moreover, they view formal logic as a smaller part of cognition than he did. Piaget would not be surprised that today, as part of our own cognitive development, we are adapting his ideas to accommodate new findings.

"Assessing the impact of Piaget on developmental psychology is like assessing the impact of Shakespeare on English literature."

Developmental psychologist Harry Beilin (1992)

CLOSE UP:

Autism and "Mind-Blindness"

Diagnoses of **autism,** a disorder marked by social deficiencies, have been increasing. Once believed to affect 1 in 2500 children, autism or a related disorder now affects 1 in 110 American children and about 1 in 100 in Britain (CDC, 2009; Lilienfeld & Arkowitz, 2007; NAS, 2011). The increase in autism diagnoses has been offset by a decrease in the number of children considered "cognitively disabled" or "learning disabled," which suggests a relabeling of children's disorders (Gernsbacher et al., 2005; Grinker, 2007; Shattuck, 2006). A massive $6.7 billion National Children's Study now under way aims to enroll 100,000 pregnant women in 105 countries and to follow their babies until they turn 21. Researchers hope this study will help explain the rising rates of autism, as well as premature births, childhood obesity, and asthma (Belluck, 2010; Murphy, 2008).

The underlying source of autism's symptoms seems to be poor communication among brain regions that normally work together to let us take another's viewpoint. People with autism are therefore said to have an *impaired theory of mind* (Rajendran & Mitchell, 2007; Senju et al., 2009). They have difficulty inferring others' thoughts and feelings. They do not appreciate that playmates and parents might view things differently. Mind reading that most of us find intuitive *(Is that face conveying a smirk or a sneer?)* is difficult for those with autism. Most children learn that another child's pouting mouth signals sadness, and that twinkling eyes mean happiness or mischief. A child with autism fails to understand these signals (Frith & Frith, 2001). In hopes of a cure, desperate parents have sometimes subjected children to ineffective therapies (Shute, 2010).

Autism spectrum disorder is a term used to encompass a range of variations, one of which

· · · · ·
autism a disorder that appears in childhood and is marked by deficient communication, social interaction, and understanding of others' states of mind.

Autism This speech-language pathologist is helping a boy with autism learn to form sounds and words. Autism, which afflicts four boys for every girl, is marked by deficient social communication and difficulty grasping others' states of mind.

· ·

is *Asperger syndrome,* a high-functioning form of autism. Asperger syndrome is marked by normal intelligence, often accompanied by exceptional skill or talent in a specific area, but deficient social and communication skills and a tendency to become distracted by irrelevant stimuli (Remington et al., 2009).

Autism afflicts four boys for every girl. Children for whom amniotic fluid analyses indicated high prenatal testosterone develop more masculine and autistic traits (Auyeung et al., 2009). Psychologist Simon Baron-Cohen (2008, 2009) argues that autism represents an "extreme male brain." Girls are naturally predisposed to be "empathizers," he contends. They are better at reading facial expressions and gestures, though less so if given testosterone (van Honk et al., 2011). Reading faces is a challenging task for those with autism. Although the sexes overlap, boys are, Baron-Cohen believes, better "systemizers"—better at understanding things according to rules or laws, as in mathematical and mechanical systems.

"If two 'systemizers' have a child, this will increase the risk of the child having autism," Baron-Cohen theorizes. And because of *assortative mating*—people's tendency to seek spouses who share their interests—two

systemizers will indeed often mate. "I do not discount environmental factors," he notes. "I'm just saying, don't forget about biology."

Twin and sibling studies provide some evidence for biology's influence. If one identical twin is diagnosed with autism, the chances are 50 to 70 percent that the co-twin will also receive this diagnosis (Lichtenstein et al., 2010; Sebat et al., 2007). A younger sibling of a child with autism also is at a heightened risk (Sutcliffe, 2008). Random genetic mutations in sperm-producing cells may also play a role. As men age, these mutations become more frequent, which may help explain why an over-40 man has a much higher risk of fathering a child with autism than does a man under 30 (Reichenberg et al., 2007). Researchers are now sleuthing autism spectrum disorder's

Autism case number 1 In 1943, Donald Gray Triplett, an "odd" child with unusual gifts and social deficits, was the first person to receive the diagnosis of a previously unreported condition, which psychiatrist Leo Kanner termed *autism.* In 2010, at age 77, Triplett was still living in his native home and Mississippi town, where he often played golf (Donvan & Zucker, 2010).

Implications for Parents and Teachers Future parents and teachers, remember this: Young children are incapable of adult logic. Preschoolers who block one's view of the TV simply have not learned to take another's viewpoint. What seems simple and obvious to us—getting off a teeter-totter will cause a friend on the other end to crash—may be incomprehensible to a 3-year-old. Also remember that children are not

telltale signs in the brain's synaptic and gray matter (Crawley, 2007; Ecker et al., 2010; Garber, 2007).

Biology's role in autism also appears in brain-function studies. People without autism often yawn after seeing others yawn. And as they view and imitate another's smiling or frowning, they feel something of what the other is feeling. Not so among those with autism spectrum disorder, who are less imitative and show much less activity in brain areas involved in mirroring others' actions (Dapretto et al., 2006; Perra et al., 2008; Senju et al., 2007). When people with autism watch another person's hand movements, for example, their brain displays less-than-normal mirroring activity (Oberman & Ramachandran, 2007; Théoret et al., 2005). Scientists are continuing to explore and vigorously debate the idea that the brains of people with autism have "broken mirrors" (Gallese et al., 2011).

Seeking to "systemize empathy," Baron-Cohen and his Cambridge University colleagues (2007; Golan et al., 2010) collaborated with Britain's National Autistic Society and a film production company. Knowing that television shows with vehicles have been popular among kids with autism, they created animations with toy vehicle characters in a pretend boy's bedroom, grafting emotion-conveying faces onto toy trams, trains, and tractors (**FIGURE 4.14**). After the boy leaves for school, the characters come to life and have experiences that lead them to display various emotions (which I predict you would enjoy viewing at www.thetransporters.com). The children were surprisingly able to generalize what they had learned to a new, real context. By the intervention's end, their previously deficient ability to recognize emotions on real faces equaled that of children without autism.

RETRIEVE IT

• What does *theory of mind* have to do with autism?

ANSWER: Theory of mind focuses on our ability to understand our own and others' mental states. Those with autism struggle with this ability.

"The neighbor's dog has bitten people before. He is barking at Louise."

Point to the face that shows how Louise is feeling.

FIGURE 4.14

Transported into a world of emotion (a) A research team at Cambridge University's Autism Research Centre introduced children with autism to emotions experienced and displayed by toy vehicles. (b) After four weeks of viewing animations, the children displayed a markedly increased ability to recognize emotions not only in the toy faces but also in humans.

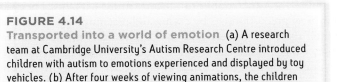

© Crown copyright MMVI, www.thetransporters.com, courtesy Changing Media Development

(a) Emotion-conveying faces were grafted onto toy trains.

Accuracy scores

After intervention, children with autism become better able to identify which facial emotion matches the context.

■ Typical control   ■ Faces intervention

(b) Children matched the correct face with the story. (The graph above shows data for two trials.)

passive receptacles waiting to be filled with knowledge. Better to build on what they already know, engaging them in concrete demonstrations and stimulating them to think for themselves. Finally, accept children's cognitive immaturity as adaptive. It is nature's strategy for keeping children close to protective adults and providing time for learning and socialization (Bjorklund & Green, 1992).

"Childhood has its own way of seeing, thinking, and feeling, and there is nothing more foolish than the attempt to put ours in its place."

Philosopher Jean-Jacques Rousseau, 1798

stranger anxiety the fear of strangers that infants commonly display, beginning by about 8 months of age.

attachment an emotional tie with another person; shown in young children by their seeking closeness to the caregiver and showing distress on separation.

imprinting the process by which certain animals form attachments during a critical period very early in life.

RETRIEVE IT

• Object permanence, pretend play, conservation, and abstract logic are developmental milestones for which of Piaget's stages, respectively?

ANSWER: Object permanence for the sensorimotor stage, pretend play for the preoperational stage, conservation for the concrete operational stage, and abstract logic for the formal operational stage.

• Match the developmental phenomena (1–6) to the correct cognitive developmental stage (a–d).

a. Sensorimotor   b. Preoperational   c. Concrete operational   d. Formal operational

  1. Thinking about abstract concepts, such as "freedom."

  2. Enjoying imaginary play (such as dress-up).

  3. Understanding that physical properties stay the same even when objects change form.

  4. Ability to reverse math operations.

  5. Understanding that something is not gone for good when it disappears from sight, as when Mom "disappears" behind the shower curtain.

  6. Difficulty taking another's point of view (as when blocking someone's view of the TV).

ANSWERS: 1. d, 2. b, 3. c, 4. c, 5. a, 6. b

Social Development

4-6: How do parent-infant attachment bonds form?

From birth, babies are social creatures, developing an intense bond with their caregivers. Infants come to prefer familiar faces and voices, then to coo and gurgle when given a parent's attention. After about 8 months, soon after object permanence emerges and children become mobile, a curious thing happens: They develop **stranger anxiety.** They may greet strangers by crying and reaching for familiar caregivers. "No! Don't leave me!" their distress seems to say. Children this age have schemas for familiar faces; when they cannot assimilate the new face into these remembered schemas, they become distressed (Kagan, 1984). Once again, we see an important principle: *The brain, mind, and social-emotional behavior develop together.*

Origins of Attachment

One-year-olds typically cling tightly to a parent when they are frightened or expect separation. Reunited after being apart, they shower the parent with smiles and hugs. No social behavior is more striking than the intense and mutual infant-parent bond. This **attachment** bond is a powerful survival impulse that keeps infants close to their caregivers. Infants become attached to those—typically their parents—who are comfortable and familiar. For many years, psychologists reasoned that infants became attached to those who satisfied their need for nourishment. It made sense. But an accidental finding overturned this explanation.

Body Contact During the 1950s, University of Wisconsin psychologists Harry Harlow and Margaret Harlow bred monkeys for their learning studies. To equalize experiences and to isolate any disease, they separated the infant monkeys from their mothers shortly after birth and raised them in sanitary individual cages, which included a cheese-cloth baby blanket (Harlow et al., 1971). Then came a surprise: When their blankets were taken to be laundered, the monkeys became distressed.

The Harlows recognized that this intense attachment to the blanket contradicted the idea that attachment derives from an association with nourishment. But how could they show this more convincingly? To pit the drawing power of a food source against the contact comfort of the blanket, they created two artificial mothers. One was a bare wire cylinder with a wooden head and an attached feeding bottle, the other a cylinder wrapped with terry cloth.

Stranger anxiety A newly emerging ability to evaluate people as unfamiliar and possibly threatening helps protect babies 8 months and older.

© Christina Kennedy/PhotoEdit

When raised with both, the monkeys overwhelmingly preferred the comfy cloth mother (**FIGURE 4.15**). Like other infants clinging to their live mothers, the monkey babies would cling to their cloth mothers when anxious. When exploring their environment, they used her as a *secure base,* as if attached to her by an invisible elastic band that stretched only so far before pulling them back. Researchers soon learned that other qualities—rocking, warmth, and feeding—made the cloth mother even more appealing.

Human infants, too, become attached to parents who are soft and warm and who rock, feed, and pat. Much parent-infant emotional communication occurs via touch (Hertenstein et al., 2006), which can be either soothing (snuggles) or arousing (tickles). Human attachment also consists of one person providing another with a secure base from which to explore and a safe haven when distressed. As we mature, our secure base and safe haven shift—from parents to peers and partners (Cassidy & Shaver, 1999). But at all ages we are social creatures. We gain strength when someone offers, by words and actions, a safe haven: "I will be here. I am interested in you. Come what may, I will support you" (Crowell & Waters, 1994).

Familiarity Contact is one key to attachment. Another is familiarity. In many animals, attachments based on familiarity form during a *critical period*—an optimal period when certain events must take place to facilitate proper development (Bornstein, 1989). As noted earlier, humans seem to have a critical period for language. Goslings, ducklings, and chicks have a critical period for attachment, called **imprinting**, which falls in the hours shortly after hatching, when the first moving object they see is normally their mother. From then on, the young fowl follow her, and her alone.

Konrad Lorenz (1937) explored this rigid attachment process. He wondered: What would ducklings do if he was the first moving creature they observed? What they did was follow him around: Everywhere that Konrad went, the ducks were sure to go. Although baby birds imprint best to their own species, they also will imprint on a variety of moving objects—an animal of another species, a box on wheels, a bouncing ball (Colombo, 1982; Johnson, 1992). Once formed, this attachment is difficult to reverse.

Children—unlike ducklings—do not imprint. However, they do become attached to what they've known. *Mere exposure* to people and things fosters fondness (see Chapter 13). Children like to reread the same books, rewatch the same movies, reenact family traditions. They prefer to eat familiar foods, live in the same familiar neighborhood, attend school with the same old friends. Familiarity is a safety signal. Familiarity breeds content.

Harlow Primate Laboratory, University of Wisconsin

FIGURE 4.15
The Harlows' mothers Psychologists Harry Harlow and Margaret Harlow raised monkeys with two artificial mothers—one a bare wire cylinder with a wooden head and an attached feeding bottle, the other a cylinder with no bottle but covered with foam rubber and wrapped with terry cloth. The Harlows' discovery surprised many psychologists: The infants much preferred contact with the comfortable cloth mother, even while feeding from the nourishing mother.

Mark Peterson/Redux

Imprinting Whooping cranes normally learn to migrate by following their parents. These cranes, hand-raised from eggs, imprinted on a crane-costumed ultralight pilot, who then guided them to winter nesting grounds (Mooallem, 2009).

temperament a person's characteristic emotional reactivity and intensity.

basic trust according to Erik Erikson, a sense that the world is predictable and trustworthy; said to be formed during infancy by appropriate experiences with responsive caregivers.

• What distinguishes imprinting from attachment?

ANSWER: Attachment is the normal process by which we form emotional ties with important others. Imprinting occurs only in certain animals that have a critical period very early in their development during which they must form their attachments, and they do so in an inflexible manner.

Attachment Differences

4-7: How have psychologists studied attachment differences, and what have they learned?

What accounts for children's attachment differences? To answer this question, Mary Ainsworth (1979) designed the *strange situation* experiment. She observed mother-infant pairs at home during their first six months. Later she observed the 1-year-old infants in a strange situation (usually a laboratory playroom). Such research has shown that about 60 percent of infants display *secure attachment*. In their mother's presence they play comfortably, happily exploring their new environment. When she leaves, they become distressed; when she returns, they seek contact with her.

Other infants avoid attachment or show *insecure attachment,* marked either by *anxiety* or *avoidance* of trusting relationships. They are less likely to explore their surroundings; they may even cling to their mother. When she leaves, they either cry loudly and remain upset or seem indifferent to her departure and return (Ainsworth, 1973, 1989; Kagan, 1995; van IJzendoorn & Kroonenberg, 1988).

Ainsworth and others found that sensitive, responsive mothers—those who noticed what their babies were doing and responded appropriately—had infants who exhibited secure attachment (De Wolff & van IJzendoorn, 1997). Insensitive, unresponsive mothers—mothers who attended to their babies when they felt like doing so but ignored them at other times—often had infants who were insecurely attached. The Harlows' monkey studies, with unresponsive artificial mothers, produced even more striking effects. When put in strange situations without their artificial mothers, the deprived infants were terrified (**FIGURE 4.16**).

But is attachment style the *result* of parenting? Or are other factors also at work?

FIGURE 4.16
Social deprivation and fear In the Harlows' experiments, monkeys raised with artificial mothers were terror-stricken when placed in strange situations without those mothers. (Today's climate of greater respect for animal welfare prevents such primate studies.)

Harlow Primate Laboratory, University of Wisconsin

Temperament and Attachment How does **temperament**—a person's characteristic emotional reactivity and intensity—affect attachment style? Temperament is genetically influenced. Shortly after birth, some babies are noticeably difficult—irritable, intense, and unpredictable. Others are easy—cheerful, relaxed, and feeding and sleeping on predictable schedules (Chess & Thomas, 1987).

The genetic effect appears in physiological differences. Anxious, inhibited infants have high and variable heart rates and a reactive nervous system. When facing new or strange situations, they become more physiologically aroused (Kagan & Snidman, 2004). One form of a gene that regulates the neurotransmitter serotonin predisposes a fearful temperament and, in combination with unsupportive caregiving, an inhibited child (Fox et al., 2007).

Temperament differences typically persist. Consider:

• The most emotionally reactive newborns have tended also to be the most reactive 9-month-olds (Wilson & Matheny, 1986; Worobey & Blajda, 1989).

• Exceptionally inhibited and fearful 2-year-olds often were still relatively shy as 8-year-olds; about half became introverted adolescents (Kagan et al., 1992, 1994).

• The most emotionally intense preschoolers have tended to be relatively intense young adults (Larsen & Diener, 1987). In one long-term study of more than 900 New Zealanders, emotionally reactive and impulsive 3-year-olds developed into somewhat more impulsive, aggressive, and conflict-prone 21-year-olds (Caspi, 2000).

Such evidence supports the conclusion that our biologically rooted temperament helps form our enduring personality (McCrae et al., 2000, 2007; Rothbart et al., 2000).

"Oh, he's cute, all right, but he's got the temperament of a car alarm."

Parenting studies that neglect such inborn differences, noted Judith Harris (1998), do the equivalent of "comparing foxhounds reared in kennels with poodles reared in apartments." To separate the effects of nature and nurture on attachment, we would need to vary parenting while controlling temperament. (Pause and think: If you were the researcher, how might you have done this?)

Dutch researcher Dymphna van den Boom's solution was to randomly assign 100 temperamentally difficult 6- to 9-month-olds to either an experimental group, in which mothers received personal training in sensitive responding, or to a control group, in which they did not. At 12 months of age, 68 percent of the experimental group infants were rated securely attached, as were only 28 percent of the control group infants. Other studies have confirmed that intervention programs can increase parental sensitivity and, to a lesser extent, infant attachment security (Bakermans-Kranenburg et al., 2003; Van Zeijl et al., 2006).

As many of these examples indicate, researchers have more often studied mother care than father care, but fathers are more than just mobile sperm banks. Despite the widespread attitude that "fathering a child" means impregnating, and "mothering" means nurturing, nearly 100 studies worldwide have shown that a father's love and acceptance are comparable to a mother's love in predicting an offspring's health and well-being (Rohner & Veneziano, 2001). In one mammoth British study following 7259 children from birth to adulthood, those whose fathers were most involved in parenting (through outings, reading to them, and taking an interest in their education) tended to achieve more in school, even after controlling for other factors such as parental education and family wealth (Flouri & Buchanan, 2004). Fathers matter.

Children's anxiety over separation from parents peaks at around 13 months, then gradually declines (**FIGURE 4.17**). This happens whether they live with one parent or two, are cared for at home or in a day-care center, live in North America, Guatemala, or the Kalahari Desert. Does this mean our need for and love of others also fades away? Hardly. Our capacity for love grows, and our pleasure in touching and holding those we love never ceases. The power of early attachment does nonetheless gradually relax, allowing us to move into a wider range of situations, communicate with strangers more freely, and stay emotionally attached to loved ones despite distance.

Attachment Styles and Later Relationships Developmental theorist Erik Erikson (1902–1994), working with his wife, Joan Erikson, believed that securely attached children approach life with a sense of **basic trust**—a sense that the world is predictable and reliable. He attributed basic trust not to environment or inborn temperament, but to early parenting. He theorized that infants blessed with sensitive, loving caregivers form a lifelong attitude of trust rather than fear.

Although debate continues, many researchers now believe that our early attachments form the foundation for our adult relationships (Birnbaum et al., 2006; Fraley, 2002). Our adult styles of romantic love tend to exhibit secure, trusting attachment; insecure-anxious attachment; or insecure-avoidant attachment (Feeney & Noller, 1990; Rholes & Simpson, 2004; Shaver & Mikulincer, 2007). Feeling insecurely attached to others during childhood, for example, may take two main forms in adulthood (Fraley et al., 2011). One is anxiety, in which people constantly crave acceptance but remain vigilant to signs of possible rejection. The other is avoidance, in which people experience discomfort getting close to others and use avoidant strategies to maintain distance from others.

Adult attachment styles can also affect relationships with one's own children. Avoidant people's discomfort with closeness makes parenting more stressful and unsatisfying (Rholes et al., 2006). But say this for those (nearly half of all humans) who exhibit insecure attachments: Anxious or avoidant tendencies have helped our groups detect or escape dangers (Ein-Dor et al., 2010).

d85/ZUMA Press/Newscom

Full-time dad Financial analyst Walter Cranford, shown here with his baby twins, is one of a growing number of stay-at-home dads. Cranford says the experience has made him appreciate how difficult the work can be: "Sometimes at work you can just unplug, but with this you've got to be going all the time."

"Out of the conflict between trust and mistrust, the infant develops hope, which is the earliest form of what gradually becomes faith in adults."

Erik Erikson (1983)

FIGURE 4.17
Infants' distress over separation from parents In an experiment, groups of infants were left by their mothers in an unfamiliar room. In both groups, the percentage who cried when their mother left peaked at about 13 months. Whether the infant had experienced day care made little difference. (From Kagan, 1976.)

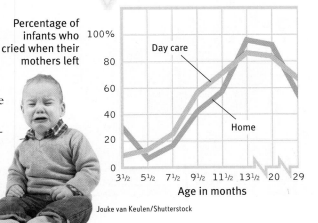

Jouke van Keulen/Shutterstock

Deprivation of Attachment

4-8: How does childhood neglect or abuse affect children's attachments?

"What is learned in the cradle, lasts to the grave."

French proverb

If secure attachment fosters social trust, what happens when circumstances prevent a child's forming attachments? In all of psychology, there is no sadder research literature. Babies locked away at home under conditions of abuse or extreme neglect are often withdrawn, frightened, even speechless. The same is true of those reared in institutions without the stimulation and attention of a regular caregiver, as was tragically illustrated during the 1970s and 1980s in Romania. Having decided that economic growth for his impoverished country required more human capital, Nicolae Ceauşescu, Romania's Communist dictator, outlawed contraception, forbade abortion, and taxed families with fewer than five children. The birthrate indeed skyrocketed. But unable to afford the children they had been coerced into having, many families abandoned them to government-run orphanages with untrained and overworked staff. Child-to-caregiver ratios often were 15 to 1, so the children were deprived of healthy attachments with at least one adult. When tested after Ceauşescu was assassinated in 1989, these children had lower intelligence scores and double the 20 percent rate of anxiety symptoms found in children assigned to quality foster care settings (Nelson et al., 2009). Dozens of other studies across 19 countries have confirmed that orphaned children tend to fare better on later intelligence tests if raised in family homes. This is especially so for those placed at an early age (van IJzendoorn et al., 2008).

Most children growing up under adversity (as did the surviving children of the Holocaust) are *resilient;* they become normal adults (Helmreich, 1992; Masten, 2001). So do most victims of childhood sexual abuse, notes Harvard researcher Susan Clancy (2010), while emphasizing that using children for sex is revolting and never the victim's fault.

But others, especially those who experience no sharp break from their abusive past, don't bounce back so readily. The Harlows' monkeys raised in total isolation, without even an artificial mother, bore lifelong scars. As adults, when placed with other monkeys their age, they either cowered in fright or lashed out in aggression. When they reached sexual maturity, most were incapable of mating. If artificially impregnated, females often were neglectful, abusive, even murderous toward their first-born. Another primate experiment confirmed the abuse-breeds-abuse phenomenon in rhesus monkeys: 9 of 16 females who had been abused by their mothers became abusive parents, as did *no* female raised by a nonabusive mother (Maestripieri, 2005).

In humans, too, the unloved may become the unloving. Most abusive parents—and many condemned murderers—have reported being neglected or battered as children (Kempe & Kempe, 1978; Lewis et al., 1988). Some 30 percent of people who have been abused later abuse their children—a rate lower than that found in the primate study, but four times the U.S. national rate of child abuse (Dumont et al., 2007; Kaufman & Zigler, 1987).

Although most abused children do *not* later become violent criminals or abusive parents, extreme early trauma may nevertheless leave footprints on the brain. Abused children exhibit hypersensitivity to angry faces (Pollak, 2008). As adults, they exhibit stronger startle responses (Jovanovic et al., 2009). If repeatedly threatened and attacked while young, normally placid golden hamsters grow up to be cowards when caged with same-sized hamsters, or bullies when caged with weaker ones (Ferris, 1996). Such animals show changes in the brain chemical serotonin, which calms aggressive impulses. A similarly sluggish serotonin response has been found in abused children who become aggressive teens and adults. "Stress can

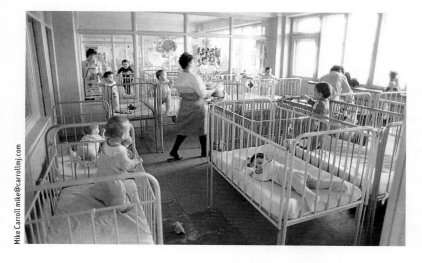

The deprivation of attachment In this Romanian orphanage, the 250 children between ages 1 and 5 outnumbered caregivers 10 to 1.

Mike Carroll mike@carrollmj.com

set off a ripple of hormonal changes that permanently wire a child's brain to cope with a malevolent world," concluded abuse researcher Martin Teicher (2002).

Such findings help explain why young children who have survived severe or prolonged physical abuse, childhood sexual abuse, or wartime atrocities are at increased risk for health problems, psychological disorders, substance abuse, and criminality (Freyd et al., 2005; Kendall-Tackett et al., 1993, 2004; Wegman & Stetler, 2009). Abuse victims are at considerable risk for depression *if* they carry a gene variation that spurs stress-hormone production (Bradley et al., 2008). As we will see again and again, behavior and emotion arise from a particular environment interacting with particular genes.

We adults also suffer when our attachment bonds are severed. Whether through death or separation, a break produces a predictable sequence. Agitated preoccupation with the lost partner is followed by deep sadness and, eventually, the beginnings of emotional detachment and a return to normal living (Hazan & Shaver, 1994). Newly separated couples who have long ago ceased feeling affection are sometimes surprised at their desire to be near the former partner. Deep and longstanding attachments seldom break quickly. Detaching is a process, not an event.

Day Care

4-9: How does day care affect children?

Developmental psychologists' research has uncovered no major impact of maternal employment on children's development, attachments, and achievements (Friedman & Boyle, 2008; Goldberg et al., 2008; Lucas-Thompson et al., 2010).

Contemporary research now focuses on the effects of differing quality of day care on different types and ages of children (Vandell et al., 2010). Sandra Scarr (1997) explained: Around the world, "high-quality child care consists of warm, supportive interactions with adults in a safe, healthy, and stimulating environment. . . . Poor care is boring and unresponsive to children's needs." Even well-run orphanages can produce healthy, thriving children. In Africa and Asia, where more and more children are losing parents to AIDS and other diseases, orphanages typically are unlike those in Ceauşescu's Romania, and the children living in quality orphanages fare about as well as those living in communities (Whetten et al., 2009).

Children thrive under varied types of responsive caregiving. Westernized attachment features one or two caregivers and their offspring, but multiple caregivers are the norm in other cultures, such as the Efe of Zaire (Field, 1996; Whaley et al., 2002). Even before an Efe mother holds her newborn, the baby is passed among several women. In the weeks to come, the infant will be constantly held (and fed) by other women and will form strong multiple attachments.

One ongoing study in 10 American cities has followed 1100 children since the age of 1 month. The researchers found that at ages 4½ to 6, children who had spent the most time in day care had slightly advanced thinking and language skills. They also had an increased rate of aggressiveness and defiance (NICHD, 2002, 2003, 2006). But the child's temperament, the parents' sensitivity, and the family's economic and educational level influenced aggression more than did the time spent in day care.

There is little disagreement that the children who merely exist for nine hours a day in understaffed centers deserve better. What all children need is a consistent, warm relationship with people they can learn to trust. The importance of such relationships extends beyond the preschool years, as Finnish psychologist Lea Pulkkinen (2006) observed in her career-long study of 285 individuals tracked from age 8 to 42. Her finding—that adult monitoring of children predicts favorable outcomes—led her to undertake, with support from Finland's parliament, a nationwide program of adult-supervised activities for all first and second graders (Pulkkinen, 2004; Rose, 2004).

An example of high-quality day care Research has shown that young children thrive socially and intellectually in safe, stimulating environments with a ratio of one caregiver for every three or four children.

AP Photo/Imperial Valley Press, Cuauhtemoc Beltran

Parenting Styles

4-10: What are three parenting styles, and how do children's traits relate to them?

Some parents spank, some reason. Some are strict, some are lax. Some show little affection, some liberally hug and kiss. Do such differences in parenting styles affect children?

The most heavily researched aspect of parenting has been how, and to what extent, parents seek to control their children. Investigators have identified three parenting styles:

1. *Authoritarian* parents impose rules and expect obedience: "Don't interrupt." "Keep your room clean." "Don't stay out late or you'll be grounded." "Why? Because I said so."

2. *Permissive* parents submit to their children's desires. They make few demands and use little punishment.

3. *Authoritative* parents are both demanding and responsive. They exert control by setting rules, but, especially with older children, they encourage open discussion and allow exceptions.

Too hard, too soft, and just right, these styles have been called. Research indicates that children with the highest self-esteem, self-reliance, and social competence usually have warm, concerned, *authoritative* parents (Baumrind, 1996; Buri et al., 1988; Coopersmith, 1967). Those with authoritarian parents tend to have less social skill and self-esteem, and those with permissive parents tend to be more aggressive and immature. The participants in most studies have been middle-class White families, and some critics suggest that effective parenting may vary by culture. Yet studies with families of other races and in more than 200 cultures worldwide have confirmed the social and academic correlates of loving and authoritative parenting (Rohner & Veneziano, 2001; Sorkhabi, 2005; Steinberg & Morris, 2001). For example, two studies of thousands of Germans found that those whose parents had maintained a curfew exhibited better adjustment and greater achievements in young adulthood than did those with permissive parents (Haase et al., 2008).

A word of caution: The association between certain parenting styles (being firm but open) and certain childhood outcomes (social competence) is correlational. *Correlation is not causation.* Perhaps you can imagine possible explanations for this parenting-competence link.

Parents who struggle with conflicting advice should also remember that *all advice reflects the advice giver's values.* For parents who prize unquestioning obedience or whose children live in dangerous environments, an authoritarian style may have the desired effect. For those who value children's sociability and self-reliance, authoritative firm-but-open parenting is advisable.

Cultures vary Parents everywhere care about their children, but raise and protect them differently depending on the surrounding culture. Parents raising children in New York City keep them close. In Scotland's Orkney Islands' town of Stromness, social trust has enabled parents to park their toddlers outside shops.

Culture and Child Rearing Child-rearing practices reflect not only individual values, but also cultural values, which vary across time and place. Should children be independent or comply? If you live in a Westernized culture, you likely prefer independence. "You are responsible for yourself," Western families and schools tell their children. "Follow your conscience. Be true to yourself. Discover your gifts. Think through your personal needs." A half-century ago and more, however, Western cultural values placed greater priority on obedience, respect, and sensitivity to others (Alwin, 1990; Remley, 1988). "Be true to your traditions," parents then taught their children. "Be loyal to your heritage and country. Show respect toward your parents and other superiors." Cultures can change.

Children across time and place have thrived under various child-rearing systems. Many Americans now give children their own bedrooms and entrust them to day care. Upper-class British parents tradition-ally handed off routine caregiving to nannies, then sent their 10-year-olds off to boarding school. These children generally grew up to be pillars of British society, as did their parents and their boarding-school peers.

Many Asian and African cultures place less value on independence and more on a strong sense of *family self*—a feeling that what shames the child shames the family, and what brings honor to the family brings honor to the self. These cultures also value emotional closeness, and infants and toddlers may sleep with their mothers and spend their days close to a family member (Morelli et al., 1992; Whiting & Edwards, 1988). In the African Gusii society, babies nurse freely but spend most of the day on their mother's back—with lots of body contact but little face-to-face and language interaction. When the mother becomes pregnant again, the toddler is weaned and handed over to someone else, often an older sibling. Westerners may wonder about the negative effects of this lack of verbal interaction, but then the African Gusii may in turn wonder about Western mothers pushing their babies around in strollers and leaving them in playpens (Small, 1997).

Such diversity in child rearing cautions us against presuming that our culture's way is the only way to rear children successfully. One thing is certain, however: Whatever our culture, the investment in raising a child buys many years not only of joy and love but of worry and irritation. Yet for most people who become parents, a child is one's biological and social legacy—one's personal investment in the human future. To para-phrase psychiatrist Carl Jung, we reach backward into our parents and forward into our children, and through their children into a future we will never see, but about which we must therefore care.

Parental involvement promotes development Parents in every culture facilitate their children's discovery of their world, but cultures differ in what they deem important. Asian cultures place more emphasis on school and hard work than do North American cultures. This may help explain why Japanese and Taiwanese children get higher scores on mathematics achievement tests.

"You are the bows from which your children as living arrows are sent forth."
Kahlil Gibran, The Prophet, *1923*

RETRIEVE IT

• The three parenting styles have been called "too hard, too soft, and just right." Which one is "too hard," which one "too soft," and which one "just right," and why?

ANSWER: The authoritarian style would be too hard, the permissive style too soft, and the authoritative style just right. Parents using the authoritative style tend to have children with high self-esteem, self-reliance, and social competence.

Reflections on Nature and Nurture

The unique gene combination created when our mother's egg engulfed our father's sperm helped form us, as individuals. Genes predispose both our shared humanity and our individual differences.

But it is also true that our experiences form us. In the womb, in our families, and in our peer social relationships, we learn ways of thinking and acting. Even differences initiated by our nature may be amplified by our nurture. We are not formed by either nature or nurture, but by the interaction between them. Biological, psychological, and social-cultural forces interact.

Mindful of how others differ from us, however, we often fail to notice the similari-ties stemming from our shared biology. Regardless of our culture, we humans share the same life cycle. We speak to our infants in similar ways and respond similarly to their coos and cries (Bornstein et al., 1992a,b). All over the world, the children of warm and supportive parents feel better about themselves and are less hostile than are the children of punishing and rejecting parents (Rohner, 1986; Scott et al., 1991). Although Hispanic, Asian, Black, and White Americans differ in school achievement and delinquency, the differences are "no more than skin deep." To the extent that family structure, peer influ-ences, and parental education predict behavior in one of these ethnic groups, they do so for the others as well. Compared with the person-to-person differences within groups, the differences between groups are small.

adolescence the transition period from childhood to adulthood, extending from puberty to independence.

puberty the period of sexual maturation, during which a person becomes capable of reproducing.

How will you look back on your life 10 years from now? Are you making choices that someday you will recollect with satisfaction?

At a five-year high school reunion, former best friends may be surprised at their divergence; a decade or more later, they may have trouble sustaining a conversation.

Erik Isakson/JupiterImages

Adolescence

4-11: How is adolescence defined, and how do physical changes affect developing teens?

Many psychologists once believed that childhood sets our traits. Today's developmental psychologists see development as lifelong. As this *life-span perspective* emerged, psychologists began to look at how maturation and experience shape us not only in infancy and childhood, but also in adolescence and beyond. **Adolescence**—the years spent morphing from child to adult—starts with the physical beginnings of sexual maturity and ends with the social achievement of independent adult status. In some cultures, where teens are self-supporting, this means that adolescence hardly exists.

G. Stanley Hall (1904), one of the first psychologists to describe adolescence, believed that the tension between biological maturity and social dependence creates a period of "storm and stress." Indeed, after age 30, many who grow up in independence-fostering Western cultures look back on their teenage years as a time they would not want to relive, a time when their peers' social approval was imperative, their sense of direction in life was in flux, and their feeling of alienation from their parents was deepest (Arnett, 1999; Macfarlane, 1964).

But for many, adolescence is a time of vitality without the cares of adulthood, a time of rewarding friendships, heightened idealism, and a growing sense of life's exciting possibilities.

Physical Development

Adolescence begins with **puberty,** the time when we mature sexually. Puberty follows a surge of hormones, which may intensify moods and which trigger a series of bodily changes outlined in Chapter 5, Gender and Sexuality.

Just as in the earlier life stages, the *sequence* of physical changes in puberty (for example, breast buds and visible pubic hair before *menarche*—the first menstrual period) is far more predictable than their *timing*. Some girls start their growth spurt at 9, some boys as late as age 16. Though such variations have little effect on height at maturity, they may have psychological consequences: It is not only when we mature that counts, but how people react to our physical development.

For boys, early maturation has mixed effects. Boys who are stronger and more athletic during their early teen years tend to be more popular, self-assured, and independent, though also more at risk for alcohol use, delinquency, and premature sexual activity (Conley & Rudolph, 2009; Copeland et al., 2010; Lynne et al., 2007). For girls, early maturation can be a challenge (Mendle et al., 2007). If a young girl's body and hormone-fed feelings are out of sync with her emotional maturity and her friends' physical development and experiences, she may begin associating with older adolescents or may suffer teasing or sexual harassment (Ge & Natsuaki, 2009).

An adolescent's brain is also a work in progress. Until puberty, brain cells increase their connections, like trees growing more roots and branches. Then, during adolescence, comes a selective pruning of unused neurons and connections (Blakemore, 2008). What we don't use, we lose.

As teens mature, their frontal lobes also continue to develop. The growth of *myelin,* the fatty tissue that forms around axons and speeds neurotransmission, enables better communication with other brain regions (Kuhn, 2006; Silveri et al., 2006). These developments bring improved judgment, impulse control, and long-term planning.

Maturation of the frontal lobes nevertheless lags behind that of the emotional limbic system. Puberty's hormonal surge and limbic system development help explain teens' occasional impulsiveness, risky behaviors, and emotional storms—slamming doors and turning up the music (Casey et al., 2008). No wonder younger teens (whose unfinished frontal lobes aren't yet fully equipped for making long-term plans and curbing impulses) so often succumb to the tobacco corporations, which most adult smokers could tell them they will later regret. Teens actually don't underestimate the risks of smoking—or fast driving or unprotected sex. They just, when reasoning from their gut, weigh the immediate benefits more heavily (Reyna & Farley, 2006; Steinberg, 2007, 2010). They seek thrills and rewards, but they can't yet locate the brake pedal controlling their impulses.

So, when Junior drives recklessly and academically self-destructs, should his parents reassure themselves that "he can't help it; his frontal cortex isn't yet fully grown"? They can at least take hope: The brain with which Junior begins his teens differs from the brain with which he will end his teens. Unless he slows his brain development with heavy drinking—leaving him prone to impulsivity and addiction—his frontal lobes will continue maturing until about age 25 (Beckman, 2004; Crews et al., 2007).

In 2004, the American Psychological Association joined seven other medical and mental health associations in filing U.S. Supreme Court briefs arguing against the death penalty for 16- and 17-year-olds. The briefs documented the teen brain's immaturity "in areas that bear upon adolescent decision making." Teens are "less guilty by reason of adolescence," suggested psychologist Laurence Steinberg and law professor Elizabeth Scott (2003; Steinberg et al., 2009). In 2005, by a 5-to-4 margin, the Court concurred, declaring juvenile death penalties unconstitutional.

Cognitive Development

4-12: How did Piaget, Kohlberg, and later researchers describe adolescent cognitive and moral development?

During the early teen years, reasoning is often self-focused. Adolescents may think their private experiences are unique, something parents just could not understand: "But, Mom, *you* don't really know how it feels to be in love" (Elkind, 1978). Capable of thinking about their own thinking, and about other people's thinking, they also begin imagining what others are thinking about *them*. (They might worry less if they understood their peers' similar self-absorption.) Gradually, though, most begin to reason more abstractly.

Developing Reasoning Power

When adolescents achieve the intellectual summit that Jean Piaget called *formal operations*, they apply their new abstract reasoning tools to the world around them. They may think about what is ideally possible and compare that with the imperfect reality of their society, their parents, and even themselves. They may debate human nature, good and evil, truth and justice. Their sense of what's fair changes from simple equality—to what's proportional to merit (Almas et al., 2010). Having left behind the concrete images of early childhood, they may now seek a deeper conception of God and existence (Elkind, 1970; Worthington, 1989). Reasoning hypothetically and deducing consequences also enables adolescents to detect inconsistencies and spot hypocrisy in others' reasoning, sometimes leading to heated debates with parents and silent vows never to lose sight of their own ideals (Peterson et al., 1986).

"Young man, go to your room and stay there until your cerebral cortex matures."

"If a gun is put in the control of the prefrontal cortex of a hurt and vengeful 15-year-old, and it is pointed at a human target, it will very likely go off."

National Institutes of Health brain scientist Daniel R. Weinberger, "A Brain Too Young for Good Judgment," 2001

"When the pilot told us to brace and grab our ankles, the first thing that went through my mind was that we must all look pretty stupid."

Jeremiah Rawlings, age 12, after a 1989 DC-10 crash in Sioux City, Iowa

"Ben is in his first year of high school, and he's questioning all the right things."

Demonstrating their reasoning ability Although on opposite sides of the immigration policy debate, these teens are all demonstrating their ability to think logically about abstract topics. According to Piaget, they are in the final cognitive stage, formal operations.

Moral reasoning Survivors of the 2010 Haiti earthquake were faced with a moral dilemma: Should they steal household necessities? Their reasoning likely reflected different levels of moral thinking, even if they behaved similarly.

Developing Morality

Two crucial tasks of childhood and adolescence are discerning right from wrong and developing character—the psychological muscles for controlling impulses. To be a moral person is to *think* morally and *act* accordingly. Jean Piaget and Lawrence Kohlberg proposed that moral reasoning guides moral actions. A more recent view builds on psychology's game-changing new recognition that much of our functioning occurs not on the "high road" of deliberate, conscious thinking but on the "low road" of unconscious, automatic thinking.

Moral Reasoning Piaget (1932) believed that children's moral judgments build on their cognitive development. Agreeing with Piaget, Lawrence Kohlberg (1981, 1984) sought to describe the development of *moral reasoning,* the thinking that occurs as we consider right and wrong. Kohlberg posed moral dilemmas (for example, whether a person should steal medicine to save a loved one's life) and asked children, adolescents, and adults whether the action was right or wrong. His analysis of their answers led him to propose three basic levels of moral thinking: preconventional, conventional, and postconventional (**TABLE 4.2**). Kohlberg claimed these levels form a moral ladder. As with all stage theories, the sequence is unvarying. We begin on the bottom rung and ascend to varying heights. Kohlberg's critics have noted that his postconventional stage is culturally limited, appearing mostly among people who prize individualism (Eckensberger, 1994; Miller & Bersoff, 1995).

Moral Intuition Psychologist Jonathan Haidt (2002, 2006, 2010) believes that much of our morality is rooted in *moral intuitions*—"quick gut feelings, or affectively laden intuitions." In this intuitionist view, the mind makes moral judgments as it makes aesthetic judgments—quickly and automatically. We *feel* disgust when seeing people engaged in degrading or subhuman acts. Even a disgusting taste in the mouth heightens people's disgust over various moral digressions (Eskine et al., 2011). We *feel* elevation—a tingly, warm, glowing feeling in the chest—when seeing people display exceptional generosity, compassion, or courage. Such feelings in turn trigger moral reasoning, says Haidt.

One woman recalled driving through her snowy neighborhood with three young men as they passed "an elderly woman with a shovel in her driveway. I did not think much of it, when one of the guys in the back asked the driver to let him off there. . . . When I saw him jump out of the back seat and approach the lady, my mouth dropped in shock as I realized that he was offering to shovel her walk for her." Witnessing this unexpected goodness triggered elevation: "I felt like jumping out of the car and hugging this guy. I felt like singing and running, or skipping and laughing. I felt like saying nice things about people" (Haidt, 2000).

"Could human morality really be run by the moral emotions," Haidt wonders, "while moral reasoning struts about pretending to be in control?" Consider the desire to punish. Laboratory games reveal that the desire to punish wrongdoings is mostly driven not

Table 4.2
Kohlberg's Levels of Moral Thinking

Level (approximate age)	Focus	Example
Preconventional morality (before age 9)	Self-interest; obey rules to avoid punishment or gain concrete rewards.	"If you save your dying wife, you'll be a hero."
Conventional morality (early adolescence)	Uphold laws and rules to gain social approval or maintain social order.	"If you steal the drug for her, everyone will think you're a criminal."
Postconventional morality (adolescence and beyond)	Actions reflect belief in basic rights and self-defined ethical principles.	"People have a right to live."

by reason (such as an objective calculation that punishment deters crime) but rather by emotional reactions, such as moral outrage (Darley, 2009). After the emotional fact, moral reasoning—our mind's press secretary—aims to convince us and others of the logic of what we have intuitively felt.

This intuitionist perspective on morality finds support in a study of moral paradoxes. Imagine seeing a runaway trolley headed for five people. All will certainly be killed unless you throw a switch that diverts the trolley onto another track, where it will kill one person. Should you throw the switch? Most say *Yes.* Kill one, save five.

Now imagine the same dilemma, except that your opportunity to save the five requires you to push a large stranger onto the tracks, where he will die as his body stops the trolley. Kill one, save five? The logic is the same, but most say *No.* Seeking to understand why, a Princeton research team led by Joshua Greene (2001) used brain imaging to spy on people's neural responses as they contemplated such dilemmas. Only when given the body-pushing type of moral dilemma did their brain's emotion areas activate. Despite the identical logic, the personal dilemma engaged emotions that altered moral judgment.

While the new research illustrates the many ways moral intuitions trump moral reasoning, other research reaffirms the importance of moral reasoning. The religious and moral reasoning of the Amish, for example, shapes their practices of forgiveness, communal life, and modesty (Narvaez, 2010). Joshua Greene (2010) likens our moral cognition to a camera. Usually, we rely on the automatic point-and-shoot mode. But sometimes we use reason to manually override the camera's automatic impulse.

"This might not be ethical. Is that a problem for anybody?"

"It is a delightful harmony when doing and saying go together."

Michel Eyquem de Montaigne (1533–1592)

Moral Action Our moral thinking and feeling surely affect our moral talk. But sometimes talk is cheap and emotions are fleeting. Morality involves *doing* the right thing, and what we do also depends on social influences. As political theorist Hannah Arendt (1963) observed, many Nazi concentration camp guards during World War II were ordinary "moral" people who were corrupted by a powerfully evil situation.

Today's character education programs tend to focus on the whole moral package—thinking, feeling, and *doing* the right thing. Research has demonstrated that as children's *thinking* matures, their *behavior* also becomes less selfish and more caring (Krebs & Van Hesteren, 1994; Miller et al., 1996). Programs now also teach children *empathy* for others' feelings, and the self-discipline needed to restrain one's own impulses—to delay small gratifications now to enable bigger rewards later. Those who have learned to *delay gratification* have become more socially responsible, academically successful, and productive (Funder & Block, 1989; Mischel et al., 1988, 1989). In service-learning programs, where teens have tutored, cleaned up their neighborhoods, and assisted older adults, their sense of competence and desire to serve has increased, and their school absenteeism and drop-out rates have diminished (Andersen, 1998; Piliavin, 2003). Moral action feeds moral attitudes.

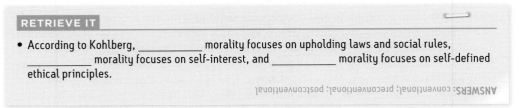

RETRIEVE IT

• According to Kohlberg, _____ morality focuses on upholding laws and social rules, _____ morality focuses on self-interest, and _____ morality focuses on self-defined ethical principles.

ANSWERS: conventional; preconventional; postconventional

Social Development

4-13: What are the social tasks and challenges of adolescence?

Theorist Erik Erikson (1963) contended that each stage of life has its own *psychosocial* task, a crisis that needs resolution. Young children wrestle with issues of *trust,* then *autonomy* (independence), then *initiative.* School-age children strive for *competence,* feeling able and productive. The adolescent's task is to synthesize past, present,

"Somewhere between the ages of 10 and 13 (depending on how hormone-enhanced their beef was), children entered adolescence, a.k.a. 'the de-cutening.'"

Jon Stewart et al., Earth (The Book), *2010*

Competence vs. inferiority

Intimacy vs. isolation

Table 4.3
Erikson's Stages of Psychosocial Development

Stage (approximate age)	Issue	Description of Task
Infancy (to 1 year)	Trust vs. mistrust	If needs are dependably met, infants develop a sense of basic trust.
Toddlerhood (1 to 3 years)	Autonomy vs. shame and doubt	Toddlers learn to exercise their will and do things for themselves, or they doubt their abilities.
Preschool (3 to 6 years)	Initiative vs. guilt	Preschoolers learn to initiate tasks and carry out plans, or they feel guilty about their efforts to be independent.
Elementary school (6 years to puberty)	Competence vs. inferiority	Children learn the pleasure of applying themselves to tasks, or they feel inferior.
Adolescence (teen years into 20s)	Identity vs. role confusion	Teenagers work at refining a sense of self by testing roles and then integrating them to form a single identity, or they become confused about who they are.
Young adulthood (20s to early 40s)	Intimacy vs. isolation	Young adults struggle to form close relationships and to gain the capacity for intimate love, or they feel socially isolated.
Middle adulthood (40s to 60s)	Generativity vs. stagnation	In middle age, people discover a sense of contributing to the world, usually through family and work, or they may feel a lack of purpose.
Late adulthood (late 60s and up)	Integrity vs. despair	Reflecting on his or her life, an older adult may feel a sense of satisfaction or failure.

and future possibilities into a clearer sense of self (**TABLE 4.3**). Adolescents wonder, "Who am I as an individual? What do I want to do with my life? What values should I live by? What do I believe in?" Erikson called this quest the adolescent's *search for identity.*

Forming an Identity

To refine their sense of identity, adolescents in individualistic cultures usually try out different "selves" in different situations. They may act out one self at home, another with friends, and still another at school or on Facebook. If two situations overlap—as when a teenager brings friends home—the discomfort can be considerable. The teen asks, "Which self should I be? Which is the real me?" The resolution is a self-definition that unifies the various selves into a consistent and comfortable sense of who one is—an **identity.**

For both adolescents and adults, group identities are often formed by how we differ from those around us. When living in Britain, I become conscious of my Americanness. When spending time with my daughter in Africa, I become conscious of my minority White race. When surrounded by women, I am mindful of my gender identity. For international students, for those of a minority ethnic group, for people with a disability, for those on a team, a **social identity** often forms around their distinctiveness.

Erikson noticed that some adolescents forge their identity early, simply by adopting their parents' values and expectations. (Traditional, less individualistic cultures teach adolescents who they are, rather than encouraging them to decide on their own.) Other adolescents may adopt the identity of a particular peer group—jocks, preps, geeks, goths.

Most young people do develop a sense of contentment with their lives. When American teens were asked whether a series of statements described them, 81 percent said *Yes* to "I would choose my life the way it is right now." The other 19 percent agreed that "I wish I were somebody else" (Lyons, 2004). Reflecting on their existence, 75 percent of American collegians say they "discuss religion/spirituality" with friends, "pray," and agree that "we are all spiritual beings" and "search for meaning/purpose in life" (Astin

> "Self-consciousness, the recognition of a creature by itself as a 'self,' [cannot] exist except in contrast with an 'other,' a something which is not the self."
>
> *C. S. Lewis, The Problem of Pain, 1940*

identity our sense of self; according to Erikson, the adolescent's task is to solidify a sense of self by testing and integrating various roles.

social identity the "we" aspect of our self-concept; the part of our answer to "Who am I?" that comes from our group memberships.

et al., 2004; Bryant & Astin, 2008). This would not surprise Stanford psychologist William Damon and his colleagues (2003), who have contended that a key task of adolescence is to achieve a purpose—a desire to accomplish something personally meaningful that makes a difference to the world beyond oneself.

Several nationwide studies indicate that young Americans' self-esteem falls during the early to mid-teen years, and, for girls, depression scores often increase. But then self-image rebounds during the late teens and twenties (Erol & Orth, 2011; Robins et al., 2002; Twenge & Nolen-Hoeksema, 2002). Late adolescence is also a time when agreeableness and emotional stability scores increase (Klimstra et al., 2009).

These are the years when many people in industrialized countries begin exploring new opportunities by attending college or working full time. Many college seniors have achieved a clearer identity and a more positive self-concept than they had as first-year students (Waterman, 1988). Collegians who have achieved a clear sense of identity are less prone to alcohol abuse (Bishop et al., 2005).

Erikson contended that adolescent identity formation (which continues into adulthood) is followed in young adulthood by a developing capacity for **intimacy,** the ability to form emotionally close relationships. Romantic relationships, which tend to be emotionally intense, are reported by some two in three North American 17-year-olds, but fewer among those in collectivist countries such as China (Collins et al., 2009; Li et al., 2010). Those who enjoy high-quality (intimate, supportive) relationships with family and friends tend also to enjoy similarly high-quality romantic relationships in adolescence, which set the stage for healthy adult relationships. Such relationships are, for most of us, a source of great pleasure.

Who shall I be today? By varying the way they look, adolescents try out different "selves." Although we eventually form a consistent and stable sense of identity, the self we present may change with the situation.

Parent and Peer Relationships

4-14: How do parents and peers influence adolescents?

As adolescents in Western cultures seek to form their own identities, they begin to pull away from their parents (Shanahan et al., 2007). The preschooler who can't be close enough to her mother, who loves to touch and cling to her, becomes the 14-year-old who wouldn't be caught dead holding hands with Mom. The transition occurs gradually (**FIGURE 4.18**), but this period is typically a time of diminishing parental influence and growing peer influence.

"She says she's someone from your past who gave birth to you, and raised you, and sacrificed everything so you could have whatever you wanted."

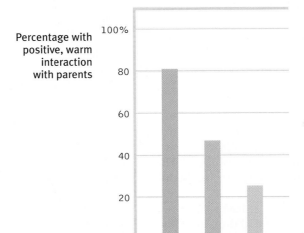

Percentage with positive, warm interaction with parents

Age of child in years

FIGURE 4.18
The changing parent-child relationship In a large, national study of Canadian families, interviews revealed that the typically close, warm relationships between parents and preschoolers loosened as children became older. (Data from Statistics Canada, 1999.)

intimacy in Erikson's theory, the ability to form close, loving relationships; a primary developmental task in late adolescence and early adulthood.

"Men resemble the times more than they resemble their fathers."

Ancient Arab proverb

"It's you who don't understand me—I've been fifteen, but you have never been forty-eight."

"I love u guys."

Emily Keyes' final text message to her parents before dying in a Colorado school shooting, 2006

Nine times out of ten, it's all about peer pressure.

As Aristotle long ago recognized, we humans are "the social animal." At all ages, but especially during childhood and adolescence, we seek to fit in with our groups and are influenced by them (Harris, 1998, 2000):

- Children who hear English spoken with one accent at home and another in the neighborhood and at school will invariably adopt the accent of their peers, not their parents. Accents (and slang) reflect culture, "and children get their culture from their peers," noted Judith Rich Harris (2007).

- Teens who start smoking typically have friends who model smoking, suggest its pleasures, and offer cigarettes (J. S. Rose et al., 1999; R. J. Rose et al., 2003). Part of this peer similarity may result from a *selection effect,* as kids seek out peers with similar attitudes and interests. Those who smoke (or don't) may select as friends those who also smoke (or don't).

- When Mihaly Csikszentmihalyi [chick-SENT-me-hi] and Jeremy Hunter (2003) used a beeper to sample the daily experiences of American teens, they found them unhappiest when alone and happiest when with friends.

By adolescence, parent-child arguments occur more often, usually over mundane things—household chores, bedtime, homework (Tesser et al., 1989). Conflict during the transition to adolescence tends to be greater with first-born than with second-born children, and greater with mothers than with fathers (Burk et al., 2009; Shanahan et al., 2007).

For a minority of parents and their adolescents, differences lead to real splits and great stress (Steinberg & Morris, 2001). But most disagreements are at the level of harmless bickering. And most adolescents—6000 of them in 10 countries, from Australia to Bangladesh to Turkey—have said they like their parents (Offer et al., 1988). "We usually get along but . . . ," adolescents often reported (Galambos, 1992; Steinberg, 1987).

Positive parent-teen relations and positive peer relations often go hand in hand. High school girls who had the most affectionate relationships with their mothers tended also to enjoy the most intimate friendships with girlfriends (Gold & Yanof, 1985). And teens who felt close to their parents have tended to be healthy and happy and to do well in school (Resnick et al., 1997). Of course, we can state this correlation the other way: Misbehaving teens are more likely to have tense relationships with parents and other adults.

Although heredity does much of the heavy lifting in forming individual temperament and personality differences, parents and peers influence teen's behaviors and attitudes (See Thinking Critically About: How Much Credit or Blame Do Parents Deserve?)

Most teens are herd animals, talking, dressing, and acting more like their peers than their parents. What their friends are, they often become, and what "everybody's doing," they often do. In teen calls to hotline counseling services, peer relationships have been the most discussed topic (Boehm et al., 1999). In 2008, according to a Nielsen study, the average American 13- to 17-year-old sent or received more than 1700 text messages a month (Steinhauer & Holson, 2008). Many adolescents become absorbed by social networking, sometimes with a compulsive use that produces "Facebook fatigue." Online communication stimulates intimate self-disclosure—both for better (support groups) and for worse (online predators and extremist groups) (Subrahmanyam & Greenfield, 2008; Valkenburg & Peter, 2009).

For those who feel excluded by their peers, the pain is acute. "The social atmosphere in most high schools is poisonously clique-driven and exclusionary," observed social psychologist Elliot Aronson (2001). Most excluded "students suffer in silence. . . . A small number act out in violent ways against their classmates." Those who withdraw are vulnerable to loneliness, low self-esteem, and depression (Steinberg & Morris, 2001). Peer approval matters.

Teens have tended to see their parents as having more influence in other areas—for example, in shaping their religious faith and in thinking about college and career choices (*Emerging Trends,* 1997). A Gallup Youth Survey revealed that most shared their parent's political views (Lyons, 2005).

How Much Credit or Blame Do Parents Deserve?

In procreation, a woman and a man shuffle their gene decks and deal a life-forming hand to their child-to-be, who is then subjected to countless influences beyond their control. Parents, nonetheless, feel enormous satisfaction in their children's successes, and feel guilt or shame over their failures. They beam over the child who wins an award. They wonder where they went wrong with the child who is repeatedly called into the principal's office. Freudian psychiatry and psychology encouraged such ideas, by blaming problems from asthma to schizophrenia on "bad mothering," and society has reinforced parent blaming. Believing that parents shape their offspring as a potter molds clay, people readily praise parents for their children's virtues and blame them for their children's vices. Popular culture endlessly proclaims the psychological harm toxic parents inflict on their fragile children. No wonder having and raising children can seem so risky.

But do parents really produce future adults with an inner wounded child by being (take your pick from the toxic-parenting lists) overbearing—or uninvolved? Pushy—or ineffectual? Overprotective—or distant? Are children really so easily wounded? If so, should we then blame our parents for our failings, and ourselves for our children's failings? Or does talk of wounding fragile children through normal parental mistakes trivialize the brutality of real abuse?

Parents do matter. The power of parenting is clearest at the extremes: the abused children who become abusive, the neglected who become neglectful, the loved but firmly handled who become self-confident and socially competent. The power of the family environment also appears in the remarkable academic and vocational successes of children of people who fled from Vietnam and Cambodia—successes attributed to close-knit, supportive, even demanding families (Caplan et al., 1992).

Yet in personality measures, shared environmental influences from the womb onward typically account for less than 10 percent of children's differences. In the words of behavior geneticists Robert Plomin and Denise Daniels (1987; Plomin, 2011), "Two children in the same family are [apart from their shared genes] as different from one another as are pairs of children selected randomly from the population."

"To be frank, officer, my parents never set boundaries."

"So I blame you for everything—whose fault is that?"

To developmental psychologist Sandra Scarr (1993), this implied that "parents should be given less credit for kids who turn out great and blamed less for kids who don't." Knowing children are not easily sculpted by parental nurture, perhaps parents can relax a bit more and love their children for who they are.

"If you want to blame your parents for your own adult problems, you are entitled to blame the genes they gave you, but you are not entitled—by any facts I know—to blame the way they treated you. . . . We are not prisoners of our past."

Martin Seligman, *What You Can Change and What You Can't*, 1994

Even among chimpanzees, when one infant is hurt by another, the victim's mother will often attack the offender's mother (Goodall, 1968).

Howard Gardner (1998) has concluded that parents and peers are complementary:

Parents are more important when it comes to education, discipline, responsibility, orderliness, charitableness, and ways of interacting with authority figures. Peers are more important for learning cooperation, for finding the road to popularity, for inventing styles of interaction among people of the same age. Youngsters may find their peers more interesting, but they will look to their parents when contemplating their own futures. Moreover, parents [often] choose the neighborhoods and schools that supply the peers.

Peer power As we develop, we play, mate, and partner with peers. No wonder children and youths are so sensitive and responsive to peer influences.

emerging adulthood for some people in modern cultures, a period from the late teens to mid-twenties, bridging the gap between adolescent dependence and full independence and responsible adulthood.

This power to select a child's neighborhood and schools gives parents an ability to influence the culture that shapes the child's peer group. And because neighborhood influences matter, parents may want to become involved in intervention programs that aim at a whole school or neighborhood. If the vapors of a toxic climate are seeping into a child's life, that climate—not just the child—needs reforming. Even so, peers are but one medium of cultural influence. As an African proverb declares, "It takes a village to raise a child."

> **RETRIEVE IT**
>
> • What is the *selection effect,* and how might it affect a teen's decision to join sports teams at school?
>
> **ANSWER:** Adolescents tend to *select* similar others and to sort themselves into like-minded groups. For an athletic teen, this could lead to finding other athletic teens and joining school athletic teams together.

Emerging Adulthood

4-15: What is emerging adulthood?

In the Western world, adolescence now roughly corresponds to the teen years. At earlier times, and in other parts of the world today, this slice of life has been much smaller (Baumeister & Tice, 1986). Shortly after sexual maturity, young people would assume adult responsibilities and status. The event might be celebrated with an elaborate initiation—a public rite of passage. The new adult would then work, marry, and have children.

When schooling became compulsory in many Western countries, independence was put on hold until after graduation. From Europe to Australia, adolescents are now taking more time to establish themselves as adults. In the United States, for example, the average age at first marriage has increased more than 4 years since 1960 (to 28 for men, 26 for women). In 1960, three in four women and two in three men had, by age 30, finished school, left home, become financially independent, married, and had a child. Today, fewer than half of 30-year-old women and one-third of men have achieved these five milestones (Henig, 2010).

Delayed independence has overlapped with an earlier onset of puberty. Together, later independence and earlier sexual maturity have widened the once-brief interlude between biological maturity and social independence (**FIGURE 4.19**). In prosperous communities, the time from 18 to the mid-twenties is an increasingly not-yet-settled

FIGURE 4.19

The transition to adulthood is being stretched from both ends In the 1890s, the average interval between a woman's first menstrual period and marriage, which typically marked a transition to adulthood, was about 7 years; in industrialized countries today it is about 12 years (Guttmacher, 1994, 2000). Although many adults are unmarried, later marriage combines with prolonged education and earlier menarche to help stretch out the transition to adulthood.

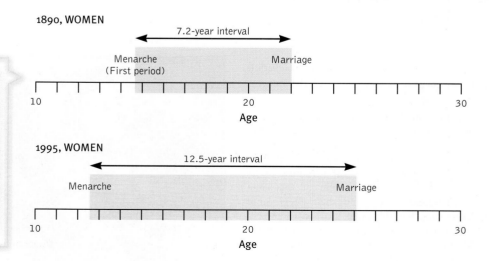

phase of life, which some now call **emerging adulthood** (Arnett, 2006, 2007; Reitzle, 2006). No longer adolescents, these emerging adults, having not yet assumed full adult responsibilities and independence, feel "in between." After high school, those who enter the job market or go to college may be managing their own time and priorities more than ever before. Yet they may be doing so from their parents' home—unable to afford their own place and perhaps still emotionally dependent as well. Recognizing today's more gradually emerging adulthood, the U.S. government now allows dependent children up to age 26 to remain on their parents' health insurance (Cohen, 2010).

"When I was your age, I was an adult."

RETRIEVE IT

- Match the psychosocial development stage below (1–8) with the issue that Erikson believed we wrestle with at that stage (a–h).

  1. Infancy
  2. Toddlerhood
  3. Preschool
  4. Elementary school
  5. Adolescence
  6. Young adulthood
  7. Middle adulthood
  8. Late adulthood

  a. Generativity vs. stagnation
  b. Integrity vs. despair
  c. Initiative vs. guilt
  d. Intimacy vs. isolation
  e. Identity vs. role confusion
  f. Competence vs. inferiority
  g. Trust vs. mistrust
  h. Autonomy vs. shame and doubt

  ANSWERS: 1. g, 2. h, 3. c, 4. f, 5. e, 6. d, 7. a, 8. b

Reflections on Continuity and Stages

Let's pause now to reflect on the second developmental issue introduced at the beginning of this chapter: *continuity* and *stages*. Do adults differ from infants as a giant redwood differs from its seedling—a difference created by gradual, cumulative growth? Or do they differ as a butterfly differs from a caterpillar—a difference of distinct stages?

Generally speaking, researchers who emphasize experience and learning see development as a slow, continuous shaping process. Those who emphasize biological maturation tend to see development as a sequence of genetically predisposed stages or steps: Although progress through the various stages may be quick or slow, everyone passes through the stages in the same order.

Are there clear-cut stages of psychological development, as there are physical stages such as walking before running? We have considered the stage theories of Jean Piaget on cognitive development, Lawrence Kohlberg on moral development, and Erik Erikson on psychosocial development (summarized in **FIGURE 4.20** on the next page). And we have seen their stage theories criticized: Young children have some abilities Piaget attributed to later stages. Kohlberg's work reflected an individualistic worldview and emphasized thinking over feeling and acting. And, as you will see in the next section, adult life does not progress through a fixed, predictable series of steps. Chance events can influence us in ways we would never have predicted.

Although research casts doubt on the idea that life proceeds through neatly defined, age-linked stages, the concept of *stage* remains useful. The human brain does experience growth spurts during childhood and puberty that correspond roughly to Piaget's stages (Thatcher et al., 1987). And stage theories contribute a developmental perspective on the whole life span, by suggesting how people of one age think and act differently when they arrive at a later age.

TOO MUCH COFFEE MAN BY SHANNON WHEELER

LIFE:

PLAY, SCHOOL, PLAY, SCHOOL, PLAY, SCHOOL, PLAY, SCHOOL, FIRST LOVE, BRIEF HAPPINESS, BREAK UP, REGRET, SCHOOL, SCHOOL, SCHOOL, SCHOOL, SCHOOL, SCHOOL, SCHOOL, SCHOOL, SCHOOL, SCHOOL, SCHOOL, SCHOOL, SCHOOL, SCHOOL, PLAY, WORK, PLAY, WORK, PLAY, WORK, PLAY, WORK, IDEALISM, EFFORT, REJECTION, FAILURE, WORK, EFFORT, FAILURE, COMPROMISE, WORK, WORK, WORK, WORK, WORK, WORK, PLAY, COMMITMENT, WORK, WORK, WORK, WORK, WORK, WORK, PLAY, WORK, WORK, WORK, WORK, WORK, WORK, WORK, WORK, PLAY, WORK, WORK, WORK, WORK, WORK, WORK, WORK, WORK, PLAY, WORK, WORK, WORK, WORK, WORK, WORK, WORK, WORK, PLAY, WORK, WORK, WORK, WORK, WORK, WORK, WORK, WORK, PLAY, WORK, WORK, WORK, WORK, WORK, WORK, WORK, WORK, PLAY, WORK, WORK, WORK, WORK, WORK, WORK, WORK, WORK, PLAY, WORK, WORK, WORK, WORK, WORK, WORK, WORK, WORK, PLAY, WORK, WORK, WORK, WORK, WORK, WORK, WORK, WORK, PLAY, WORK, WORK, WORK, WORK, WORK, WORK, WORK, WORK, PLAY, WORK, WORK, WORK, WORK, WORK, WORK, WORK, WORK, PLAY, WORK, WORK, WORK, WORK, WORK, WORK, WORK, WORK, PLAY, WORK, WORK, WORK, WORK, WORK, WORK, WORK, WORK, PLAY, WORK, WORK, WORK, WORK, WORK, WORK, WORK, WORK, PLAY, RETIRE, PLAY, DIE.

Stages of the life cycle

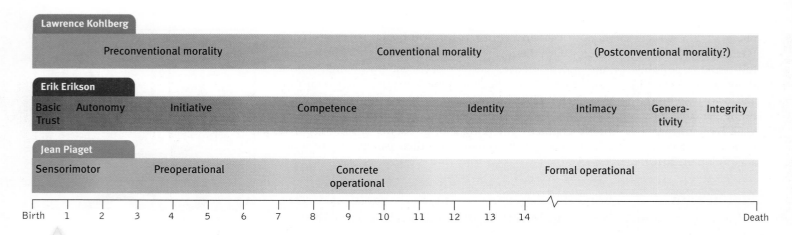

Lawrence Kohlberg		
Preconventional morality	Conventional morality	(Postconventional morality?)

Erik Erikson							
Basic Trust	Autonomy	Initiative	Competence	Identity	Intimacy	Genera-tivity	Integrity

Jean Piaget			
Sensorimotor	Preoperational	Concrete operational	Formal operational

Birth 1 2 3 4 5 6 7 8 9 10 11 12 13 14   Death

FIGURE 4.20
Comparing the stage theories
(With thanks to Dr. Sandra Gibbs, Muskegon Community College, for inspiring this illustration.)

RETRIEVE IT

• What findings in psychology support the stage theory of development? What findings challenge these ideas?

ANSWERS: Stage theory is supported by the work of Piaget (cognitive development), Kohlberg (moral development), and Erikson (psychosocial development), but it is challenged by findings that change is more gradual and less culturally universal than these theorists supposed.

Adulthood

The unfolding of people's adult lives continues across the life span. It is, however, more difficult to generalize about adulthood stages than about life's early years. If you know that James is a 1-year-old and Jamal is a 10-year-old, you could say a great deal about each child. Not so with adults who differ by a similar number of years. The boss may be 30 or 60; the marathon runner may be 20 or 50; the 19-year-old may be a parent who supports a child or a child who receives an allowance. Yet our life courses are in some ways similar. Physically, cognitively, and especially socially, we differ at age 50 from our 25-year-old selves. In the discussion that follows, we recognize these differences and use three terms: *early adulthood* (roughly twenties and thirties), *middle adulthood* (to age 65), and *late adulthood* (the years after 65). Within each of these stages, people will vary widely in physical, psychological, and social development.

"I just don't know what to do with myself in that long stretch after college but before social security."

Barbara Smaller/Funny Times

Physical Development

4-16: What physical changes occur during middle and late adulthood?

Like the declining daylight after the summer solstice, our physical abilities—muscular strength, reaction time, sensory keenness, and cardiac output—all begin an almost imperceptible decline in our mid-twenties. Athletes are often the first to notice. World-class sprinters and swimmers peak by their early twenties. Women—who mature earlier than men—also peak earlier. But most of us—especially those of us whose daily lives do not require top physical performance—hardly perceive the early signs of decline.

Physical Changes in Middle Adulthood

Post-40 athletes know all too well that physical decline gradually accelerates. During early and middle adulthood, physical vigor has less to do with age than with a person's health and exercise habits. Many of today's physically fit 50-year-olds run 4 miles with

menopause the time of natural cessation of menstruation; also refers to the biological changes a woman experiences as her ability to reproduce declines.

ease, while sedentary 25-year-olds find themselves huffing and puffing up two flights of stairs.

Aging also brings a gradual decline in fertility, especially for women. For a 35- to 39-year-old woman, the chances of getting pregnant after a single act of intercourse are only half those of a woman 19 to 26 (Dunson et al., 2002). Men experience a gradual decline in sperm count, testosterone level, and speed of erection and ejaculation. Women experience **menopause,** as menstrual cycles end, usually within a few years of age 50. Expectations and attitudes influence the emotional impact of this event. Is it a sign of lost femininity and growing old? Or is it liberation from menstrual periods and fears of pregnancy? For men, too, expectations can influence perceptions. Some experience distress related to a perception of declining virility and physical capacities, but most age without such problems.

With age, sexual activity lessens. Nevertheless, most men and women remain capable of satisfying sexual activity, and most express satisfaction with their sex life. This was true of 70 percent of Canadians surveyed (ages 40 to 64) and 75 percent of Finns (ages 65 to 74) (Kontula & Haavio-Mannila, 2009; Wright, 2006). In another survey, 75 percent of respondents reported being sexually active into their eighties (Schick et al., 2010). And in an American Association of Retired Persons sexuality survey, it was not until age 75 or older that most women and nearly half of men reported little sexual desire (DeLamater & Sill, 2005). Given good health and a willing partner, the flames of desire, though simmered down, live on. As Alex Comfort (1992, p. 240) jested, "The things that stop you having sex with age are exactly the same as those that stop you riding a bicycle (bad health, thinking it looks silly, no bicycle)."

Physical Changes in Later Life

Is old age "more to be feared than death" (Juvenal, *Satires*)? Or is life "most delightful when it is on the downward slope" (Seneca, *Epistulae ad Lucilium*)? What is it like to grow old?

Strength and Stamina Although physical decline begins in early adulthood, we are not usually acutely aware of it until later life, when the stairs get steeper, the print gets smaller, and other people seem to mumble more. Muscle strength, reaction time, and stamina diminish in late adulthood. As a lifelong basketball player, I find myself increasingly not racing for that loose ball. But even diminished vigor is sufficient for normal activities. Moreover, exercise slows aging. Active older adults tend to be mentally quick older adults. Physical exercise not only enhances muscles, bones, and energy and helps to prevent obesity and heart disease, it also stimulates brain cell development and neural connections, thanks perhaps to increased oxygen and nutrient flow (Erickson et al., 2010; Pereira et al., 2007).

Sensory Abilities With age, visual sharpness diminishes, and distance perception and adaptation to light-level changes are less acute. The eye's pupil shrinks and its lens becomes less transparent, reducing the amount of light reaching the retina: A 65-year-old retina receives only about one-third as much light as its 20-year-old counterpart (Kline & Schieber, 1985). Thus, to see as well as a 20-year-old when reading or driving, a 65-year-old needs three times as much light—a reason for buying cars with untinted windshields. This also explains why older people sometimes ask younger people, "Don't you need better light for reading?"

Adult abilities vary widely 97-year-olds: Don't try this. In 2002, George Blair became the world's oldest barefoot water skier, just days after reaching age 87. And he did it again in 2012, at age 97!

Rick Doyle/ Corbis

"*Happy fortieth. I'll take the muscle tone in your upper arms, the girlish timbre of your voice, your amazing tolerance for caffeine, and your ability to digest french fries. The rest of you can stay.*"

"For some reason, possibly to save ink, the restaurants had started printing their menus in letters the height of bacteria."

Dave Barry,
Dave Barry Turns Fifty, *1998*

Most stairway falls taken by older people occur on the top step, precisely where the person typically descends from a window-lit hallway into the darker stairwell (Fozard & Popkin, 1978). Our knowledge of aging could be used to design environments that would reduce such accidents (National Research Council, 1990).

cross-sectional study a study in which people of different ages are compared with one another.

longitudinal study research in which the same people are restudied and retested over a long period.

How old does a person have to be before you think of him or her as old? Depends on who you ask. For 18- to 29-year-olds, 67 was old. For those 60 and over, old was 76 (Yankelovich, 1995).

"I am still learning."

Michelangelo, 1560, at age 85

The senses of smell and hearing also diminish. In Wales, teens' loitering around a convenience store has been discouraged by a device that emits an aversive high-pitched sound almost no one over 30 can hear (Lyall, 2005). Some students have also used that pitch to their advantage with cell-phone ringtones their instructors cannot hear (Vitello, 2006).

Health For those growing older, there is both bad and good news about health. The bad news: The body's disease-fighting immune system weakens, making older adults more susceptible to life-threatening ailments, such as cancer and pneumonia. The good news: Thanks partly to a lifetime's accumulation of antibodies, people over 65 suffer fewer short-term ailments, such as common flu and cold viruses. One study found they were half as likely as 20-year-olds and one-fifth as likely as preschoolers to suffer upper respiratory flu each year (National Center for Health Statistics, 1990).

The Aging Brain Up to the teen years, we process information with greater and greater speed (Fry & Hale, 1996; Kail, 1991). But compared with teens and young adults, older people take a bit more time to react, to solve perceptual puzzles, even to remember names (Bashore et al., 1997; Verhaeghen & Salthouse, 1997). The neural processing lag is greatest on complex tasks (Cerella, 1985; Poon, 1987). At video games, most 70-year-olds are no match for a 20-year-old.

Slower neural processing combined with diminished sensory abilities can increase accident risks. As **FIGURE 4.21** indicates, fatal accident rates per mile driven increase sharply after age 75. By age 85, they exceed the 16-year-old level. Nevertheless, because older people drive less, they account for fewer than 10 percent of crashes (Coughlin et al., 2004).

Brain regions important to memory begin to atrophy during aging (Schacter, 1996). In young adulthood, a small, gradual net loss of brain cells begins, contributing by age 80 to a brain-weight reduction of 5 percent or so. Earlier, we noted that late-maturing frontal lobes help account for teen impulsivity. Late in life, atrophy of the inhibition-controlling frontal lobes seemingly explains older people's occasional blunt questions and comments ("Have you put on weight?") (von Hippel, 2007).

As noted earlier, exercise helps counteract some effects of brain aging. It aids memory by stimulating the development of neural connections and by promoting neurogenesis, the birth of new nerve cells, in the hippocampus. Sedentary older adults randomly assigned to aerobic exercise programs exhibit enhanced memory, sharpened judgment, and reduced risk of dementia (Colcombe et al., 2004; Liang et al., 2010; Nazimek, 2009).

Exercise also helps maintain the *telomeres,* which protect the ends of chromosomes (Cherkas et al., 2008; Erickson, 2009; Pereira et al., 2007). With age, telomeres wear down, much as the tip of a shoelace frays. This wear is accentuated by smoking, obesity, or stress. As telomeres shorten, aging cells may die without being replaced with perfect genetic replicas (Epel, 2009).

The message for seniors is clear: We are more likely to rust from disuse than to wear out from overuse.

FIGURE 4.21
Age and driver fatalities Slowing reactions contribute to increased accident risks among those 75 and older, and their greater fragility increases their risk of death when accidents happen (NHTSA, 2000). Would you favor driver exams based on performance, not age, to screen out those whose slow reactions or sensory impairments indicate accident risk?

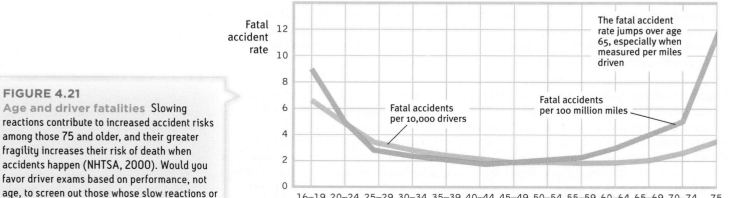

The fatal accident rate jumps over age 65, especially when measured per miles driven

Fatal accidents per 10,000 drivers

Fatal accidents per 100 million miles

Age in years

Cognitive Development

4-17: How does memory change with age?

Among the most intriguing developmental psychology questions is whether adult cognitive abilities, such as memory, intelligence, and creativity, parallel the gradually accelerating decline of physical abilities.

As we age, we remember some things well. Looking back in later life, people asked to recall the one or two most important events over the last half-century tend to name events from their teens or twenties (Conway et al., 2005; Rubin et al., 1998). Whatever people experience around this time of life—the events of 9/11, the civil rights movement, World War II—becomes pivotal (Pillemer, 1998; Schuman & Scott, 1989). Our teens and twenties are a time of so many memorable "firsts"—first date, first job, first day at college or university, first meeting of in-laws.

Early adulthood is indeed a peak time for some types of learning and remembering. In one test of recall, people (1205 of them) watched videotapes as 14 strangers said their names, using a common format: "Hi, I'm Larry" (Crook & West, 1990). Then those strangers reappeared and gave additional details. For example, saying "I'm from Philadelphia" provided visual *and* voice cues for remembering the person's name. As **FIGURE 4.22** shows, after a second and third replay of the introductions, everyone remembered more names, but younger adults consistently surpassed older adults.

Perhaps it is not surprising, then, that nearly two-thirds of people over age 40 say their memory is worse than it was 10 years ago (KRC, 2001). In fact, how well older people remember depends on the task. In another experiment (Schonfield & Robertson, 1966), when asked to *recognize* 24 words they had earlier tried to memorize, people showed only a minimal decline in memory. When asked to *recall* that information without clues, the decline was greater (**FIGURE 4.23**).

In our capacity to learn and remember, as in other areas of development, we differ. Younger adults vary in their abilities to learn and remember, but 70-year-olds vary much more. "Differences between the most and least able 70-year-olds become much greater than between the most and least able 50-year-olds," reports Oxford researcher Patrick Rabbitt (2006). Some 70-year-olds perform below nearly all 20-year-olds; other 70-year-olds match or outdo the average 20-year-old.

No matter how quick or slow we are, remembering seems also to depend on the type of information we are trying to retrieve. If the information is meaningless—nonsense syllables or unimportant events—then the older we are, the more errors we are likely to make. If the information is *meaningful,* older people's rich web of existing knowledge will help them to hold it. But they may take longer than younger adults to *produce* the words and things they know: Quick-thinking game show winners are usually young or middle-aged adults (Burke & Shafto, 2004). Older people's capacity to learn and remember *skills* declines less than their verbal recall (Graf, 1990; Labouvie-Vief & Schell, 1982; Perlmutter, 1983).

Chapter 9, Thinking, Language, and Intelligence, explores another dimension of cognitive development: intelligence. As we will see, **cross-sectional studies** (comparing people of different ages) and **longitudinal studies** (restudying people over time) have identified mental abilities that do and do not change as people age. Age is less a predictor of memory and intelligence than is proximity to death. Tell me whether someone is 8 months or 8 years from death and, regardless of age, you've given me a clue to that person's mental ability. Especially in the last three or four years of life, cognitive decline typically accelerates (Wilson et al., 2007). Researchers call this near-death drop *terminal decline* (Backman & MacDonald, 2006).

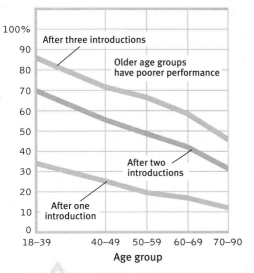

Percentage of names recalled

After three introductions

Older age groups have poorer performance

After two introductions

After one introduction

Age group

FIGURE 4.22

Tests of recall Recalling new names introduced once, twice, or three times is easier for younger adults than for older ones. (Data from Crook & West, 1990.)

If you are within 5 years of 20, what experiences from the past year will you likely never forget? (This is the time of your life you may best remember when you are 50.)

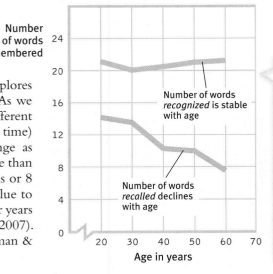

Number of words remembered

Number of words *recognized* is stable with age

Number of words *recalled* declines with age

Age in years

FIGURE 4.23

Recall and recognition in adulthood In this experiment, the ability to *recall* new information declined during early and middle adulthood, but the ability to *recognize* new information did not. (From Schonfield & Robertson, 1966.)

social clock the culturally preferred timing of social events such as marriage, parenthood, and retirement.

"Midway in the journey of our life I found myself in a dark wood, for the straight way was lost."

Dante, The Divine Comedy, *1314*

"The important events of a person's life are the products of chains of highly improbable occurrences."

Joseph Traub, "Traub's Law," 2003

Social Development

4-18: What themes and influences mark our social journey from early adulthood to death?

Many differences between younger and older adults are created by significant life events. A new job means new relationships, new expectations, and new demands. Marriage brings the joy of intimacy and the stress of merging two lives. The three years surrounding the birth of a child bring increased life satisfaction for most parents (Dyrdal & Lucas, 2011). The death of a loved one creates an irreplaceable loss. Do these adult life events shape a sequence of life changes?

Adulthood's Ages and Stages

As people enter their forties, they undergo a transition to middle adulthood, a time when they realize that life will soon be mostly behind instead of ahead of them. Some psychologists have argued that for many the *midlife transition* is a crisis, a time of great struggle, regret, or even feeling struck down by life. The popular image of the midlife crisis is an early-forties man who forsakes his family for a younger girlfriend and a hot sports car. But the fact—reported by large samples of people—is that unhappiness, job dissatisfaction, marital dissatisfaction, divorce, anxiety, and suicide do *not* surge during the early forties (Hunter & Sundel, 1989; Mroczek & Kolarz, 1998). Divorce, for example, is most common among those in their twenties, suicide among those in their seventies and eighties. One study of emotional instability in nearly 10,000 men and women found "not the slightest evidence" that distress peaks anywhere in the midlife age range (McCrae & Costa, 1990).

For the 1 in 4 adults who report experiencing a life crisis, the trigger is not age but a major event, such as illness, divorce, or job loss (Lachman, 2004). Some middle-aged adults describe themselves as a "sandwich generation," simultaneously supporting their aging parents and their emerging adult children or grandchildren (Riley & Bowen, 2005).

Life events trigger transitions to new life stages at varying ages. The **social clock**—the definition of "the right time" to leave home, get a job, marry, have children, or retire—varies from era to era and culture to culture. The once-rigid sequence for many Western women—of student to worker to wife to at-home mom to worker again—has loosened. Contemporary women occupy these roles in any order or all at once. The social clock still ticks, but people feel freer about being out of sync with it.

Even *chance events* can have lasting significance, by deflecting us down one road rather than another (Bandura, 1982). Albert Bandura (2005) recalls the ironic true story of a book editor who came to one of Bandura's lectures on the "Psychology of Chance Encounters and Life Paths"—and ended up marrying the woman who happened to sit next to him. The sequence that led to my authoring this book (which was not my idea) began with my being seated near, and getting to know, a distinguished colleague at an international conference. Chance events can change our lives.

Adulthood's Commitments

Two basic aspects of our lives dominate adulthood. Erik Erikson called them *intimacy* (forming close relationships) and *generativity* (being productive and supporting future generations). Researchers have chosen various terms—*affiliation* and *achievement, attachment* and *productivity, connectedness* and *competence.* Sigmund Freud (1935) put it most simply: The healthy adult, he said, is one who can *love* and *work.*

Love We typically flirt, fall in love, and commit—one person at a time. "Pair-bonding is a trademark of the human animal," observed anthropologist Helen Fisher (1993). From an evolutionary perspective, relatively monogamous pairing makes sense: Parents who cooperated to nurture their children to maturity were more likely to have their genes passed along to posterity than were parents who didn't.

Adult bonds of love are most satisfying and enduring when marked by a similarity of interests and values, a sharing of emotional and material support, and intimate self-disclosure (see Chapter 13). Couples who seal their love with commitment—via (in one Vermont study) marriage for heterosexual couples and civil unions for homosexual couples—more often endure (Balsam et al., 2008). Marriage bonds are especially likely to last when couples marry after age 20 and are well educated. Compared with their counterparts of 50 years ago, people in Western countries *are* better educated and marrying later. Yet, ironically, they are nearly twice as likely to divorce. (Both Canada and the United States now have about one divorce for every two marriages, and in Europe, divorce is only slightly less common.) The divorce rate partly reflects women's lessened economic dependence and men's and women's rising expectations. We now hope not only for an enduring bond, but also for a mate who is a wage earner, caregiver, intimate friend, and warm and responsive lover.

Might test driving life together in a "trial marriage" minimize divorce risk? In one Gallup survey of American twenty-somethings, 62 percent thought it would (Whitehead & Popenoe, 2001). In reality, in Europe, Canada, and the United States, those who cohabit before marriage have had *higher* rates of divorce and marital dysfunction than those who did not cohabit (Jose et al., 2009). The risk appears greatest for those cohabiting prior to engagement (Goodwin et al., 2010; Rhoades et al., 2009).

American children born to cohabiting parents are about five times more likely to experience their parents' separation than are children born to married parents (Osborne et al., 2007). Two factors contribute. First, cohabiters tend to be initially less committed to the ideal of enduring marriage. Second, they become even less marriage supporting while cohabiting.

Nonetheless, the institution of marriage endures. Worldwide, reports the United Nations, 9 in 10 heterosexual adults marry. And marriage is a predictor of happiness, sexual satisfaction, income, and physical and mental health (Scott et al., 2010). National Opinion Research Center surveys of nearly 50,000 Americans since 1972 reveal that 40 percent of married adults, though only 23 percent of unmarried adults, have reported being "very happy." Lesbian couples, too, report greater well-being than those who are alone (Peplau & Fingerhut, 2007; Wayment & Peplau, 1995). Moreover, neighborhoods with high marriage rates typically have low rates of social pathologies such as crime, delinquency, and emotional disorders among children (Myers & Scanzoni, 2005).

Marriages that last are not always devoid of conflict. Some couples fight but also shower each other with affection. Other couples never raise their voices yet also seldom praise each other or nuzzle. Both styles can last. After observing the interactions of 2000 couples, John Gottman (1994) reported one indicator of marital success: at least a five-to-one ratio of positive to negative interactions. Stable marriages provide five times more instances of smiling, touching, complimenting, and laughing than of sarcasm, criticism, and insults. So, if you want to predict which newlyweds will stay together, don't pay attention to how passionately they are in love. The couples who make it are more often those who refrain from putting down their partners. To prevent a cancerous negativity, successful couples learn to fight fair (to state feelings without insulting) and to steer conflict away from chaos with comments like "I know it's not your fault" or "I'll just be quiet for a moment and listen."

Often, love bears children. For most people, this most enduring of life changes is a happy event. "I feel an overwhelming love for my children unlike anything I feel for anyone else," said 93 percent of American mothers in a national survey (Erickson & Aird, 2005). Many fathers feel the same. A few weeks after the birth of my first child I was suddenly struck by a realization: "So *this* is how my parents felt about me?"

When children begin to absorb time, money, and emotional energy, satisfaction with the marriage itself may decline (Doss et al., 2009). This is especially likely among employed women who, more than they expected, carry the traditional burden of doing the chores at home. Putting effort into creating an equitable relationship can thus pay double dividends: a more satisfying marriage, which breeds better parent-child relations (Erel & Burman, 1995).

Lisa B./Corbis

Love Intimacy, attachment, commitment—love by whatever name—is central to healthy and happy adulthood.

What do you think? Does marriage correlate with happiness because marital support and intimacy breed happiness, because happy people more often marry and stay married, or both?

"Our love for children is so unlike any other human emotion. I fell in love with my babies so quickly and profoundly, almost completely independently of their particular qualities. And yet 20 years later I was (more or less) happy to see them go—I had to be happy to see them go. We are totally devoted to them when they are little and yet the most we can expect in return when they grow up is that they regard us with bemused and tolerant affection."

Developmental psychologist Alison Gopnik, "The Supreme Infant," 2010

bluehand/Shutterstock

Although love bears children, children eventually leave home. This departure is a significant and sometimes difficult event. For most people, however, an empty nest is a happy place (Adelmann et al., 1989; Gorchoff et al., 2008). Many parents experience a "postlaunch honeymoon," especially if they maintain close relationships with their children (White & Edwards, 1990). As Daniel Gilbert (2006) has said, "The only known symptom of 'empty nest syndrome' is increased smiling."

Work For many adults, the answer to "Who are you?" depends a great deal on the answer to "What do you do?" For women and men, choosing a career path is difficult, especially during bad economic times. Even in the best of times, few students in their first two years of college or university can predict their later careers.

In the end, happiness is about having work that fits your interests and provides you with a sense of competence and accomplishment. It is having a close, supportive companion who cheers your accomplishments (Gable et al., 2006). And for some, it includes having children who love you and whom you love and feel proud of.

> If you have left home, did your parents suffer the "empty nest syndrome"—a feeling of distress focusing on a loss of purpose and relationship? Did they mourn the lost joy of listening for you in the wee hours of Saturday morning? Or did they seem to discover a new freedom, relaxation, and (if together) renewed satisfaction with their own relationship?

RETRIEVE IT

• Freud defined the healthy adult as one who is able to _____ and to _____.

ANSWERS: love; work

Well-Being Across the Life Span

4-19: Do self-confidence and life satisfaction vary with life stages?

> "When you were born, you cried and the world rejoiced. Live your life in a manner so that when you die the world cries and you rejoice."
>
> *Native American proverb*

To live is to grow older. This moment marks the oldest you have ever been and the youngest you will henceforth be. That means we all can look back with satisfaction or regret, and forward with hope or dread. When asked what they would have done differently if they could relive their lives, people's most common answer has been "Taken my education more seriously and worked harder at it" (Kinnier & Metha, 1989; Roese & Summerville, 2005). Other regrets—"I should have told my father I loved him," "I regret that I never went to Europe"—have also focused less on mistakes made than on the things one *failed* to do (Gilovich & Medvec, 1995).

From the teens to midlife, people typically experience a strengthening sense of identity, confidence, and self-esteem (Huang, 2010; Robins & Trzesniewski, 2005). In later life, challenges arise: Income shrinks. Work is often taken away. The body deteriorates. Recall fades. Energy wanes. Family members and friends die or move away. The great enemy, death, looms ever closer. And for those in the terminal decline phase, life satisfaction does decline as death approaches (Gerstorf et al., 2008).

Small wonder that most presume that happiness declines in later life (Lacey et al., 2006). But worldwide, as Gallup researchers discovered, most find that the over-65 years are not notably unhappy (**FIGURE 4.24**). If anything, positive feelings, supported by enhanced emotional control, grow after midlife and negative feelings subside (Stone et al., 2010; Urry & Gross, 2010). Older adults increasingly use words that convey positive emotions (Pennebaker & Stone, 2003), and they attend less and less to negative information. Compared with younger adults, for example, they are slower to perceive negative faces and more attentive to positive news (Carstensen & Mikels, 2005; Scheibe & Carstensen, 2010). Older adults also have fewer problems in their social relationships (Fingerman & Charles, 2010), and they experience less intense anger, stress, and worry (Stone et al., 2010).

The aging brain may help nurture these positive feelings. Brain scans of older adults show that the amygdala, a neural processing center for emotions, responds less actively to negative events (but

FIGURE 4.24

Age and life satisfaction The Gallup Organization asked 142,682 people worldwide to rate their lives on a ladder, from 0 ("the worst possible life") to 10 ("the best possible life"). Age gave no clue to life satisfaction (Crabtree, 2010).

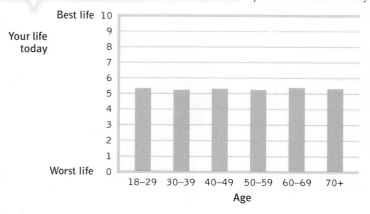

not to positive events), and it interacts less with the hippocampus, a brain memory-processing center (Mather et al., 2004; St. Jacques et al., 2009; Williams et al., 2006). Brain-wave reactions to negative images also diminish with age (Kisley et al., 2007).

Moreover, at all ages, the bad feelings we associate with negative events fade faster than do the good feelings we associate with positive events (Walker et al., 2003). This contributes to most older people's sense that life, on balance, has been mostly good. Given that growing older is an outcome of living (an outcome most prefer to early dying), the positivity of later life is comforting. Thanks to biological, psychological, and social-cultural influences, more and more people flourish into later life (**FIGURE 4.25**).

"At 20 we worry about what others think of us. At 40 we don't care what others think of us. At 60 we discover they haven't been thinking about us at all."

Anonymous

"The best thing about being 100 is *no peer pressure*."

Lewis W. Kuester, 2005, on turning 100

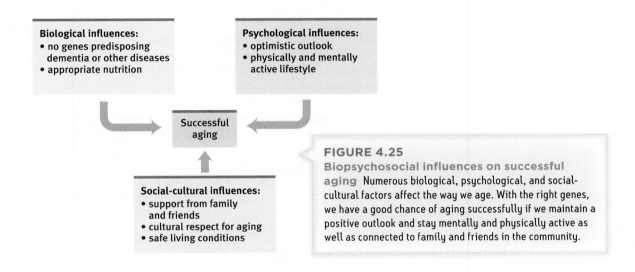

Biological influences:
• no genes predisposing dementia or other diseases
• appropriate nutrition

Psychological influences:
• optimistic outlook
• physically and mentally active lifestyle

Successful aging

Social-cultural influences:
• support from family and friends
• cultural respect for aging
• safe living conditions

FIGURE 4.25
Biopsychosocial influences on successful aging Numerous biological, psychological, and social-cultural factors affect the way we age. With the right genes, we have a good chance of aging successfully if we maintain a positive outlook and stay mentally and physically active as well as connected to family and friends in the community.

RETRIEVE IT

• What are some of the most significant challenges and rewards of growing old?

ANSWERS: Challenges: decline of muscular strength, reaction times, stamina, sensory keenness, cardiac output, and immune system functioning. Rewards: positive feelings tend to grow, negative emotions are less intense, and anger, stress, worry, and social-relationship problems decrease.

Death and Dying

4-20: A loved one's death triggers what range of reactions?

Warning: If you begin reading the next paragraph, you will die.

But of course, if you hadn't read this, you would still die in due time. Death is our inevitable end. Most of us will also suffer and cope with the deaths of relatives and friends. Usually, the most difficult separation is from a spouse—a loss suffered by five times more women than men. When, as usually happens, death comes at an expected late-life time, grieving may be relatively short-lived.

Grief is especially severe when a loved one's death comes suddenly and before its expected time on the social clock. The sudden illness or accident claiming a 45-year-old life partner or a child may trigger a year or more of memory-laden mourning that eventually subsides to a mild depression (Lehman et al., 1987).

For some, however, the loss is unbearable. One Danish long-term study of more than 1 million people found that about 17,000 of them had suffered the death of a child under 18. In the five years following that death, 3 percent of them had a first psychiatric hospitalization. This rate was 67 percent higher than the rate recorded for parents who had not lost a child (Li et al., 2005).

"Love—why, I'll tell you what love is: It's you at 75 and her at 71, each of you listening for the other's step in the next room, each afraid that a sudden silence, a sudden cry, could mean a lifetime's talk is over."

Brian Moore, The Luck of Ginger Coffey, 1960

Even so, reactions to a loved one's death range more widely than most suppose. Some cultures encourage public weeping and wailing; others hide grief. Within any culture, individuals differ. Given similar losses, some people grieve hard and long, others less so (Ott et al., 2007). Contrary to popular misconceptions, however,

- terminally ill and bereaved people do not go through identical predictable stages, such as denial before anger (Friedman & James, 2008; Nolen-Hoeksema & Larson, 1999). A Yale study following 233 bereaved individuals through time did, however, find that yearning for the loved one reached a high point four months after the loss, with anger peaking, on average, about a month later (Maciejewski et al., 2007).

- those who express the strongest grief immediately do not purge their grief more quickly (Bonanno & Kaltman, 1999; Wortman & Silver, 1989).

- bereavement therapy and self-help groups offer support, but there is similar healing power in the passing of time, the support of friends, and the act of giving support and help to others (Baddeley & Singer, 2009; Brown et al., 2008; Neimeyer & Carrier, 2009). Grieving spouses who talk often with others or receive grief counseling adjust about as well as those who grieve more privately (Bonanno, 2004; Stroebe et al., 2005).

We can be grateful for the waning of death-denying attitudes. Facing death with dignity and openness helps people complete the life cycle with a sense of life's meaningfulness and unity—the sense that their existence has been good and that life and death are parts of an ongoing cycle. Although death may be unwelcome, life itself can be affirmed even at death. This is especially so for people who review their lives not with despair but with what Erik Erikson called a sense of *integrity*—a feeling that one's life has been meaningful and worthwhile.

Reflections on Stability and Change

It's time to reflect on the third big developmental issue: As we follow lives through time, do we find more evidence for stability or change? If reunited with a long-lost grade-school friend, do we instantly realize that "it's the same old Andy"? Or do people we befriend during one period of life seem like strangers at a later period? (At least one acquaintance of mine would choose the second option. He failed to recognize a former classmate at his 40-year college reunion. The aghast classmate eventually pointed out that she was his long-ago first wife.)

Research reveals that we experience both stability and change. As we have seen, some of our characteristics, such as temperament, are very stable:

- One study followed 1000 New Zealanders through time, beginning at age 3. Those who had scored low in conscientiousness and self-control as preschoolers were more vulnerable to ill health, substance abuse, arrest, and single parenthood as 32-year-olds (Moffitt et al., 2011).

- Another research team interviewed adults who, 40 years earlier, had their talkativeness, impulsiveness, and humility rated by their elementary school teachers (Nave et al., 2010). To a striking extent, their traits persisted.

"As at 7, so at 70," says a Jewish proverb. The widest smilers in childhood and college photos are, years later, the ones most likely to enjoy enduring marriages (Hertenstein et al., 2009). While 1 in 4 of the weakest college smilers eventually divorced, only 1 in 20 of the widest smilers did so. As people grow older, personality gradually stabilizes (Ferguson, 2010; Hopwood et al., 2011; Kandler et al., 2010). The struggles of the present may be laying a foundation for a happier tomorrow.

We cannot, however, predict all of our eventual traits based on our early years of life (Kagan et al., 1978, 1998). Some traits, such as social attitudes, are much less stable than temperament (Moss & Susman, 1980). Older children and adolescents learn new ways of coping. Although delinquent children have elevated rates of later work problems, substance abuse, and crime, many confused and troubled children blossom into mature,

"Consider, friend, as you pass by, as you are now, so once was I. As I am now, you too shall be. Prepare, therefore, to follow me."

Scottish tombstone epitaph

"At 70, I would say the advantage is that you take life more calmly. You know that 'this, too, shall pass'!"

Eleanor Roosevelt, 1954

As adults grow older, there is continuity of self.

successful adults (Moffitt et al., 2002; Roberts et al., 2001; Thomas & Chess, 1986). Happily for them, life is a process of becoming.

In some ways, we *all* change with age. Most shy, fearful toddlers begin opening up by age 4, and most people become more conscientious, stable, agreeable, and self-confident in the years after adolescence (Lucas & Donnellan, 2009; Roberts et al., 2003, 2006, 2008; Shaw et al., 2010). Many irresponsible 18-year-olds have matured into 40-year-old business or cultural leaders. (If you are the former, you aren't done yet.) Such changes can occur without changing a person's position *relative to others* of the same age. The hard-driving young adult may mellow by later life, yet still be a relatively driven senior citizen.

Life requires *both* stability and change. Stability provides our identity. It enables us to depend on others and be concerned about the healthy development of the children in our lives. Our trust in our ability to change gives us our hope for a brighter future. It motivates our concerns about present influences and lets us adapt and grow with experience.

Smiles predict marital stability In one study of 306 college alums, 1 in 4 with yearbook expressions like the one on the left later divorced, as did only 1 in 20 with smiles like the one on the right (Hertenstein et al., 2009).

RETRIEVE IT

• What findings in psychology support the idea of stability in personality across the life span? What findings challenge these ideas?

ANSWER: Some traits, such as temperament, do exhibit remarkable stability across many years. But we do change in other ways, such as in our social attitudes, especially during life's early years.

CHAPTER REVIEW

Developing Through the Life Span

LEARNING OBJECTIVES

Test Yourself by taking a moment to answer each of these Learning Objective Questions (repeated here from within the chapter). Then turn to Appendix D, Complete Chapter Reviews, to check your answers. Research suggests that trying to answer these questions on your own will improve your long-term memory of the concepts (McDaniel et al., 2009).

Developmental Psychology's Major Issues

4-1: What three issues have engaged developmental psychologists?

Prenatal Development and the Newborn

4-2: What is the course of prenatal development, and how do teratogens affect that development?

4-3: What are some newborn abilities, and how do researchers explore infants' mental abilities?

Infancy and Childhood

4-4: During infancy and childhood, how do the brain and motor skills develop?

4-5: From the perspectives of Piaget, Vygotsky, and today's researchers, how does a child's mind develop?

4-6: How do parent-infant attachment bonds form?

4-7: How have psychologists studied attachment differences, and what have they learned?

4-8: How does childhood neglect or abuse affect children's attachments?

4-9: How does day care affect children?

4-10: What are three parenting styles, and how do children's traits relate to them?

Adolescence

4-11: How is adolescence defined, and how do physical changes affect developing teens?

4-12: How did Piaget, Kohlberg, and later researchers describe adolescent cognitive and moral development?

4-13: What are the social tasks and challenges of adolescence?

4-14: How do parents and peers influence adolescents?

4-15: What is emerging adulthood?

Adulthood

4-16: What physical changes occur during middle and late adulthood?

4-17: How does memory change with age?

4-18: What themes and influences mark our social journey from early adulthood to death?

4-19: Do self-confidence and life satisfaction vary with life stages?

4-20: A loved one's death triggers what range of reactions?

TERMS AND CONCEPTS TO REMEMBER

Test yourself on these terms by trying to write down the definition in your own words before flipping back to the referenced page to check your answer.

developmental psychology, p. 118

zygote, p. 119

embryo, p. 119

fetus, p. 119

teratogens, p. 120

fetal alcohol syndrome (FAS), p. 120

habituation, p. 121

maturation, p. 121

critical period, p. 123

cognition, p. 124

schema, p. 125

assimilation, p. 125

accommodation, p. 125

sensorimotor stage, p. 126

object permanence, p. 126

preoperational stage, p. 127

conservation, p. 127

egocentrism, p. 128

theory of mind, p. 128

concrete operational stage, p. 128

formal operational stage, p. 129

autism, p. 130

stranger anxiety, p. 132

attachment, p. 132

imprinting, p. 133

temperament, p. 134

basic trust, p. 135

adolescence, p. 140

puberty, p. 140

identity, p. 144

social identity, p. 144

intimacy, p. 145

emerging adulthood, p. 149

menopause, p. 151

cross-sectional study, p. 153

longitudinal study, p. 153

social clock, p. 154

EXPERIENCE THE TESTING EFFECT

Test yourself repeatedly throughout your studies. This will not only help you figure out what you know and don't know; the testing itself will help you learn and remember the information more effectively thanks to the *testing effect*.

1. The three major issues that interest developmental psychologists are nature/nurture, stability/change, and _____/_____.

2. Body organs first begin to form and function during the period of the _____; within 6 months, during the period of the _____, the organs are sufficiently functional to allow a chance of survival.
   a. zygote; embryo
   b. zygote; fetus
   c. embryo; fetus
   d. placenta; fetus

3. Chemicals that pass through the placenta's screen and may harm an embryo or fetus are called _____.

4. Stroke a newborn's cheek and the infant will root for a nipple. This illustrates
   a. a reflex.
   b. nurture.
   c. differentiation.
   d. continuity.

5. Between ages 3 and 6, the human brain experiences the greatest growth in the _____ lobes, which we use for rational planning, and which continue developing at least into adolescence.

6. Which of the following is true of motor-skill development?
   a. It is determined solely by genetic factors.
   b. The sequence, but not the timing, is universal.
   c. The timing, but not the sequence, is universal.
   d. It is determined solely by environmental factors.

7. Why can't we consciously recall how we learned to walk when we were infants?

8. Use Piaget's first three stages of cognitive development to explain why young children are not just miniature adults in the way they think.

9. Although Piaget's stage theory continues to inform our understanding of children's thinking, many researchers believe that
   a. Piaget's "stages" begin earlier and development is more continuous than he realized.
   b. children do not progress as rapidly as Piaget predicted.
   c. few children really progress to the concrete operational stage.
   d. there is no way of testing much of Piaget's theoretical work.

10. An 8-month-old infant who reacts to a new babysitter by crying and clinging to his father's shoulder is showing _____ _____.

11. In a series of experiments, the Harlows found that monkeys raised with artificial mothers tended, when afraid, to cling to their cloth mother, rather than to a wire mother holding the feeding bottle. Why was this finding important?

12. From the very first weeks of life, infants differ in their characteristic emotional reactions, with some infants being intense and anxious, while others are easygoing and relaxed. These differences are usually explained as differences in _____.

13. Adolescence is marked by the onset of
   a. an identity crisis.
   b. puberty.
   c. separation anxiety.
   d. parent-child conflict.

14. According to Piaget, a person who can think logically about abstractions is in the _____ _____ stage.

15. In Erikson's stages, the primary task during adolescence is
   a. attaining formal operations.
   b. forging an identity.
   c. developing a sense of intimacy with another person.
   d. living independent of parents.

16. Some developmental psychologists now refer to the period that occurs in some Western cultures from age 18 to the mid-twenties and beyond (up to the time of social independence) as _____ _____.

17. Developmental researchers who emphasize learning and experience are supporting _____; those who emphasize biological maturation are supporting _____.
   a. nature; nurture
   b. continuity; stages
   c. stability; change
   d. randomness; predictability

18. By age 65, a person would be most likely to experience a cognitive decline in the ability to
   a. recall and list all the important terms and concepts in a chapter.
   b. select the correct definition in a multiple-choice question.
   c. recall their own birth date.
   d. practice a well-learned skill, such as knitting.

19. How do cross-sectional and longitudinal studies differ?

20. Freud defined the healthy adult as one who is able to love and work. Erikson agreed, observing that the adult struggles to attain intimacy and _____.

21. Contrary to what many people assume,
   a. older people are much happier than adolescents.
   b. men in their forties express much greater dissatisfaction with life than do women of the same age.
   c. people of all ages report similar levels of happiness.
   d. those whose children have recently left home—the empty nesters—have the lowest level of happiness of all groups.

22. Although development is lifelong, there is stability of personality over time. For example,
   a. most personality traits emerge in infancy and persist throughout life.
   b. temperament tends to remain stable throughout life.
   c. few people change significantly after adolescence.
   d. people tend to undergo greater personality changes as they age.

Find answers to these questions in Appendix E, in the back of the book.

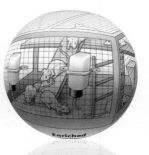

Experience more of the **TESTING** EFFECT

Multiple-format self-tests and more may be found at www.worthpublishers.com/myers.

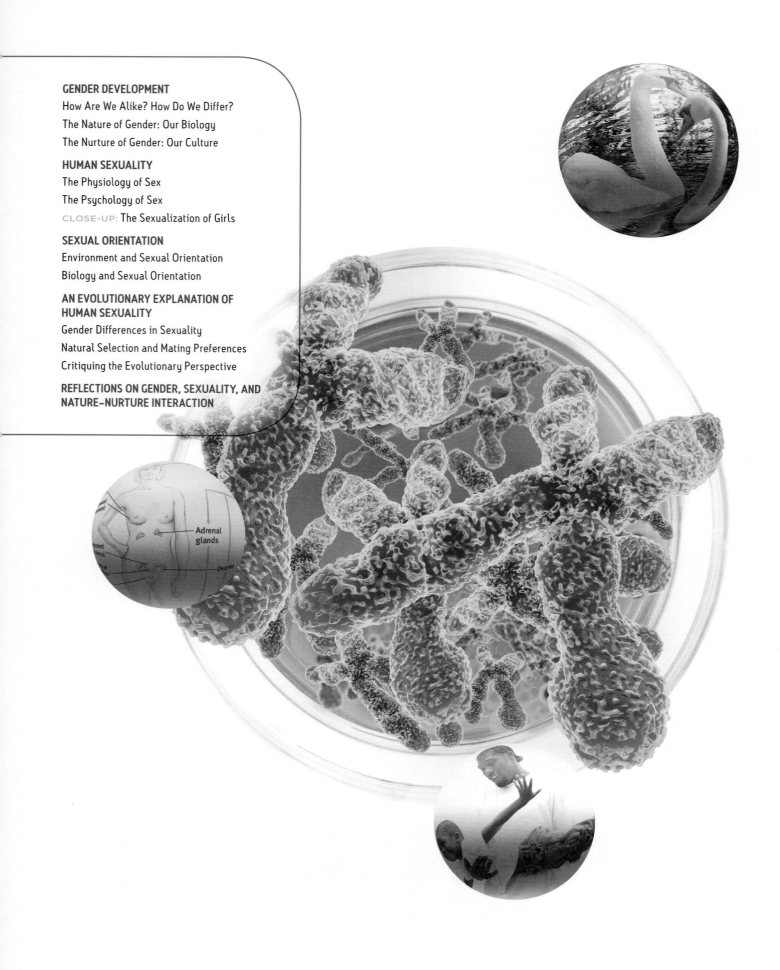

Adrenal
glands

Ovaries

Gender and Sexuality

In 1972, as the young chair of our psychology department, I was proud to make the announcement: We had concluded our search for a new colleague. We had found just who we were looking for—a bright, warm, enthusiastic woman about to receive her Ph.D. in developmental psychology. The vote was unanimous. Alas, our elderly chancellor rejected our recommendation. "As a mother of a preschooler," he said, "she should be home with her child, *not* working full time." No amount of pleading or arguing (for example, that it might be possible to parent a child while employed) could change his mind. So, with a heavy heart, I drove to her city to explain, face to face, my embarrassment in being able to offer her only a temporary position.

In this case, all's well that ends well. She accepted a temporary position and quickly became a beloved, tenured colleague who went on to found our college's women's studies program. But today, she and I marvel at the swift transformation in our culture's thinking about gender. In a thin slice of history, our ideas about the "proper" behavior for women and men have undergone an extreme makeover. Both women and men are now recognized as "fully capable of effectively carrying out organizational roles at all levels" (Wood & Eagly, 2002). Women's employment in formerly male occupations and men's employment in formerly female occupations have increased. And as this was happening, our views of what is "masculine" and what is "feminine" have also changed, as have our ideas about what we seek in a mate (Twenge, 1997).

In this chapter, we'll look at some of the ways nature and nurture interact to form us as males and females. We'll see what researchers tell us about how much males and females are alike, and how and why they differ. Along the way, we'll take a close look at human sexuality. As part of that close look, we'll see how evolutionary psychologists explain our sexuality.

Let's start by considering what gender is and how it develops.

Pink and blue baby outfits offer another example of how cultural norms vary and change. "The generally accepted rule is pink for the boy and blue for the girl," declared the publication *Earnshaw's Infants' Department* in June 1918 (Maglaty, 2011). "The reason is that pink being a more decided and stronger color is more suitable for the boy, while blue, which is more delicate and dainty, is prettier for the girls."

Gender Development

As we will see in Chapter 9, we humans share an irresistible urge to organize our worlds into simple categories. Among the ways we classify people—as tall or short, fat or slim, smart or dull—one stands out: Before or at your birth, everyone wanted to know, "Boy or girl?" From that time on, your sex (your biological status, defined by your chromosomes and anatomy) helped define your **gender**, the socially constructed roles and characteristics by which your culture defines *male* and *female*.

How Are We Alike? How Do We Differ?

5-1: What are some gender similarities and differences in aggression, social power, and social connectedness?

Having faced similar adaptive challenges, we are in most ways alike. Tell me whether you are male or female and you give me virtually no clues to your vocabulary, intelligence, and happiness, or to the mechanisms by which you see, hear, learn, and remember. Your "opposite" sex is, in reality, your very similar sex. At conception, you received 23 chromosomes from your mother and 23 from your father. Of those 46 chromosomes, 45 are unisex—the same for males and females. (Later in this chapter we'll return to that forty-sixth chromosome.)

But males and females do differ, and differences command attention—stimulating more than 18,000 studies (Ellis et al., 2008). Some much-talked-about gender differences are actually quite modest, as Janet Shibley Hyde (2005) illustrated by graphically representing male and female self-esteem scores across many studies (**FIGURE 5.1**). Other differences are more striking. Compared with the average man, the average woman enters puberty 2 years sooner, and her life span is 5 years longer. She carries 70 percent more fat, has 40 percent less muscle, and is 5 inches shorter. She expresses emotions more freely, can smell fainter odors, and is offered help more often. She can become sexually re-aroused soon after orgasm. She is also doubly vulnerable to depression and anxiety, and her risk of developing an eating disorder is 10 times greater than the average man's. Yet, he is some 4 times more likely to commit suicide or develop alcohol dependence. He is also more likely to be diagnosed with autism, color-blindness, attention-deficit hyperactivity disorder as a child, and antisocial personality disorder as an adult. Choose your gender and pick your vulnerability.

Gender differences appear throughout this book. For now, let's consider some gender differences in aggression, social power, and social connectedness.

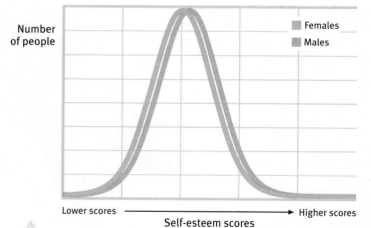

FIGURE 5.1

Much ado about a small difference in self-esteem These two normal distributions differ by the approximate magnitude of the gender difference in self-esteem, averaged over all available samples (Hyde, 2005). Moreover, such comparisons illustrate differences between the *average* woman and man. The variation among individual women greatly exceeds this difference, as it also does among individual men.

Gender and Aggression

In surveys, men admit to more **aggression** than women do. This aggression gender gap pertains to harmful physical aggression, rather than indirect or verbal relational aggression such as ostracism or spreading rumors. As John Archer (2004, 2006, 2009) has noted, based on statistical digests of dozen of studies, women may be slightly more likely to commit acts of relational aggression, such as passing along malicious gossip. The gap appears in everyday life at various ages and in various cultures, especially cultures with gender inequality (Archer, 2009).

Men's tendency to behave more aggressively can be seen in experiments where they deliver what they believe are more painful electric shocks (Card et al., 2008).

Violent crime rates illustrate the gender difference even more strikingly. The male-to-female arrest ratio for murder, for example, is 9 to 1 in the United States and 8 to 1 in Canada (FBI, 2009; Statistics Canada, 2010). Throughout the world, fighting, warring, and hunting are primarily men's activities (Wood & Eagly, 2002, 2007). Men also express more support for war. The Iraq war, for example, was consistently supported more by American men than by American women (Newport et al., 2007).

Deadly relational aggression
This documentary film (www.RatsAndBullies.com) tells the sad tale of 14-year-old Dawn-Marie Wesley, who committed suicide after suffering months of relational aggression by school bullies.

Gender and Social Power

Close your eyes and imagine two adults standing side by side. The one on the left is dominant, forceful, and independent. The one on the right is submissive, nurturing, and socially connected.

Did you see the person on the left as a man, and the one on the right as a woman? If so, you are not alone.

Around the world, from Nigeria to New Zealand, people perceive such power differences between men and women (Williams & Best, 1990). Indeed, in most societies men *do* place more importance on power and achievement and *are* socially dominant (Schwartz & Rubel-Lifschitz, 2009). When groups form, whether as juries or companies, leadership tends to go to males (Colarelli et al., 2006). When salaries are paid, those in traditionally male occupations receive more. And when political leaders are elected, they usually are men, who held 80 percent of the seats in the world's governing parliaments in 2011 (IPU, 2011). If perceived to be hungry for political power (thus violating gender norms), women more than men suffer voter backlash (Okimoto & Brescoll, 2010). Men's power hunger is more expected and accepted.

As leaders, men tend to be more *directive,* even autocratic. Women tend to be more *democratic,* more welcoming of subordinates' input in decision making (Eagly & Carli, 2007; van Engen & Willemsen, 2004). When people interact, men are more likely to utter opinions, women to express support (Aries, 1987; Wood, 1987). In everyday behavior, men tend to act as powerful people often do: They are more likely to talk assertively, interrupt, initiate touches, and stare. And they smile and apologize less (Leaper & Ayres, 2007; Major et al., 1990; Schumann & Ross, 2010). Such behaviors help sustain social power inequities.

Women's 2011 representation in national parliaments ranged from 11 percent in the Arab States to 42 percent in Scandinavia (IPU, 2011).

Gender and Social Connectedness

Females are more *interdependent* than males, and this difference surfaces early. In children's play, boys typically form large groups. Their games tend to be active and competitive, with little intimate discussion (Rose & Rudolph, 2006). Studies have found that girls usually play in smaller groups, often with one friend. Their play is less competitive and more imitative of social relationships (Maccoby, 1990; Roberts, 1991).

As adults, women take more pleasure in talking face to face, and they more often use conversation to explore relationships. Men enjoy doing activities side by side and tend to use conversation to communicate solutions (Tannen, 1990; Wright, 1989). The communication difference is apparent in student e-mails: In one New Zealand study, people could correctly guess the author's gender two-thirds of the time (Thomson & Murachver, 2001).

Gender differences also appear in phone-based communication. In the United States, the average teen girl sends and receives 80 texts daily; the average boy 30 (Lenhart, 2010). In France, women have made 63 percent of phone calls and, when talking to a woman, stayed connected longer (7.2 minutes) than have men when talking to other men (4.6 minutes) (Smoreda & Licoppe, 2000).

gender the socially constructed roles and characteristics by which a culture defines *male* and *female.*

aggression physical or verbal behavior intended to hurt someone.

Every man for himself, or tend and befriend? Gender differences in the way we interact with others begin to appear at a very young age.

Women worldwide have oriented their interests and vocations more to people and less to things (Eagly, 2009; Lippa, 2005, 2006, 2008). One analysis of more than a half-million people's responses to various interest inventories revealed that "men prefer working with things and women prefer working with people" (Su et al., 2009). On entering college, American men are seven times more likely than women to express interest in computer science, and they contribute 87 percent of Wikipedia articles (Cohen, 2011; Pryor et al., 2011). In the workplace, women have been less driven by money and status and more often opted for reduced work hours (Pinker, 2008). In the home, they have been five times more likely than men to claim primary responsibility for taking care of children (*Time,* 2009).

Women's emphasis on caring helps explain another interesting finding: Although 69 percent of people have said they have a close relationship with their father, 90 percent said they feel close to their mother (Hugick, 1989). When wanting understanding and someone with whom to share worries and hurts, both men and women usually turn to women, and both have reported their friendships with women to be more intimate, enjoyable, and nurturing (Rubin, 1985; Sapadin, 1988). And when coping with their own stress, women more than men turn to others for support—they *tend and befriend* (Tamres et al., 2002; Taylor, 2002).

Gender differences in social connectedness, power, and other traits peak in late adolescence and early adulthood—the very years most commonly studied (also the years of dating and mating). As teenagers, girls become progressively less assertive and more flirtatious; boys become more domineering and unexpressive. Following the birth of a first child, parents (women especially) become more traditional in their gender-related attitudes and behavior (Ferriman et al., 2009; Katz-Wise et al., 2010). But studies have shown that by age 50, parenthood-related gender differences subside. Men become more empathic and less domineering, and women—especially those working outside the home—become more assertive and self-confident (Kasen et al., 2006; Maccoby, 1998).

What explains our diversity? How much does biology bend the genders? To what extent are we shaped by our cultures? A biopsychosocial view suggests both are important, thanks to the interplay among our biological dispositions, our developmental experiences, and our current situations (Eagly, 2009).

"In the long years liker must they grow; The man be more of woman, she of man."

Alfred Lord Tennyson,
The Princess, *1847*

RETRIEVE IT

• _____ (Men/Women) are more likely to commit relational aggression, and _____ (men/women) are more likely to commit physical aggression.

ANSWERS: Women; men

• Worldwide, _____ (men/women) have tended to express more personal and professional interest in people and less interest in things.

ANSWER: women

The Nature of Gender: Our Biology

5-2: How is our biological sex determined, and how do sex hormones influence prenatal and adolescent development?

In domains where we face similar challenges—regulating heat with sweat, preferring foods that nourish, growing calluses where the skin meets friction—men and women are similar. Even when describing the ideal mate, both prize traits such as "kind," "honest," and "intelligent." But in mating-related domains, evolutionary psychologists contend, guys act like guys whether they are elephants or elephant seals, rural peasants or corporate presidents (Geary, 2010). Our biology may influence our gender differences in two ways: genetically, by our differing *sex chromosomes,* and physiologically, from our differing concentrations of *sex hormones.*

Prenatal Sexual Development

As noted earlier, males and females are variations on a single form—of the 46 chromosomes, 45 are unisex. So great is this similarity that until seven weeks after conception, you were anatomically indistinguishable from someone of the other sex. Then your genes activated your biological sex. Male or female, your sex was determined by your father's contribution to your twenty-third pair of chromosomes, the two sex chromosomes. You received an **X chromosome** from your mother. From your father, you received the one chromosome that is not unisex—either another X chromosome, making you a girl, or a **Y chromosome,** making you a boy.

The Y chromosome includes a single gene which, about seven weeks after conception, throws a master switch triggering the testes to develop and to produce the principal male hormone, **testosterone.** This hormone starts the development of external male sex organs. Females also have testosterone, but less of it.

Another key period for sexual differentiation falls during the fourth and fifth prenatal months. During this period, sex hormones bathe the fetal brain and influence its wiring. Different patterns for males and females develop under the influence of the male's greater testosterone and the female's ovarian hormones (Hines, 2004; Udry, 2000).

Adolescent Sexual Development

Pronounced physical differences emerge during adolescence, when boys and girls enter **puberty** and mature sexually. A surge of hormones triggers a two-year period of rapid physical development, usually beginning at about age 11 in girls and at about age 13 in boys. A year or two before that, however, boys and girls often feel the first stirrings of sexual attraction (McClintock & Herdt, 1996).

About the time of puberty, boys' growth propels them to greater height than their female counterparts (**FIGURE 5.2** on the next page). During this growth spurt, the **primary sex characteristics**—the reproductive organs and external genitalia—develop dramatically. So do **secondary sex characteristics,** the nonreproductive traits such as breasts and hips in girls, facial hair and deepened voice in boys, and pubic and underarm hair in both sexes (**FIGURE 5.3** on the next page).

In various countries, girls are developing breasts earlier (sometimes before age 10) and reaching puberty earlier than in the past. This phenomenon is variously attributed to increased body fat, increased hormone-mimicking chemicals, and increased stress related to family disruption (Biro et al., 2010).

Puberty's landmarks are the first ejaculation in boys *(spermarche),* usually by about age 14, and the first menstrual period in girls (**menarche**—meh-NAR-key), usually within a year of age 12½ (Anderson et al., 2003). Menarche appears to occur a few months earlier, on average, for girls who have experienced stresses related to father absence, sexual abuse, or insecure attachments (Belsky et al., 2010; Vigil et al., 2005; Zabin et al., 2005).

Courtesy of Nick Downes.

X chromosome the sex chromosome found in both men and women. Females have two X chromosomes; males have one. An X chromosome from each parent produces a female child.

Y chromosome the sex chromosome found only in males. When paired with an X chromosome from the mother, it produces a male child.

testosterone the most important of the male sex hormones. Both males and females have it, but the additional testosterone in males stimulates the growth of the male sex organs in the fetus and the development of the male sex characteristics during puberty.

puberty the period of sexual maturation, during which a person becomes capable of reproducing.

primary sex characteristics the body structures (ovaries, testes, and external genitalia) that make sexual reproduction possible.

secondary sex characteristics nonreproductive sexual traits, such as female breasts and hips, male voice quality, and body hair.

menarche [meh-NAR-key] the first menstrual period.

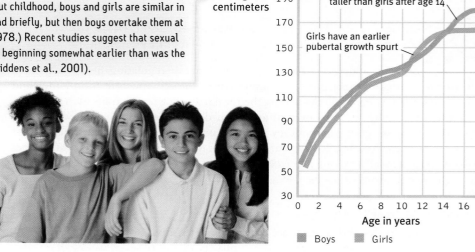

FIGURE 5.2

Height differences Throughout childhood, boys and girls are similar in height. At puberty, girls surge ahead briefly, but then boys overtake them at about age 14. (Data from Tanner, 1978.) Recent studies suggest that sexual development and growth spurts are beginning somewhat earlier than was the case a half-century ago (Herman-Giddens et al., 2001).

Boys keep growing and become taller than girls after age 14

Girls have an earlier pubertal growth spurt

Boys   Girls

Rob Lewine/Getty Images

Girls who have been prepared for menarche usually experience it as a positive life transition. Studies have shown that nearly all adult women recall their first menstrual period and remember experiencing a mixture of feelings—pride, excitement, embarrassment, and apprehension (Greif & Ulman, 1982; Woods et al., 1983). Most men have similarly recalled their first ejaculation, which usually occurs as a nocturnal emission (Fuller & Downs, 1990).

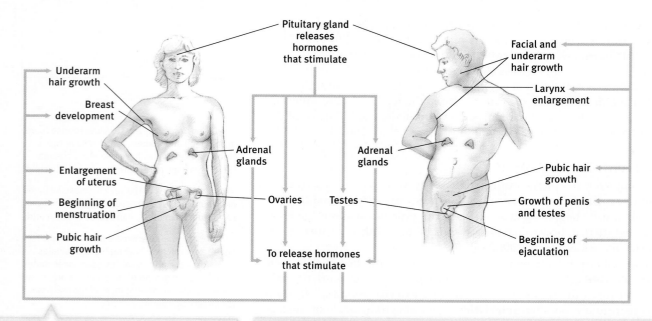

FIGURE 5.3

Body changes at puberty At about age 11 in girls and age 13 in boys, a surge of hormones triggers a variety of physical changes.

RETRIEVE IT

• Adolescence is marked by the onset of _____.

ANSWER: puberty

Variations on Sexual Development

Sometimes nature blurs the biological line between males and females. Atypical hormone exposure or sensitivity may cause atypical fetal development. *Intersex* individuals are born with intermediate or unusual combinations of male and female physical features. Genetic males, for example, may be born with normal male hormones and testes but without a penis or with a very small one.

Until recently, pediatricians and other medical experts often recommended surgery to create a female identity for these children. One study reviewed 14 cases of boys who had undergone early sex-reassignment surgery and had been raised as girls. Of those cases, 6 had later declared themselves as males, 5 were living as females, and 3 had an unclear gender identity (Reiner & Gearhart, 2004).

Although not born with an intersex condition, a little boy who lost his penis during a botched circumcision became a famous case illustrating the problems involved in sex-reassignment surgery. His parents followed a psychiatrist's advice to raise him as a girl rather than as a damaged boy. Alas, "Brenda" Reimer was not like most other girls. "She" didn't like dolls. She tore her dresses with rough-and-tumble play. At puberty she wanted no part of kissing boys. Finally, Brenda's parents explained what had happened, whereupon this young person immediately rejected the assigned female identity. He cut his hair and chose a male name, David. He eventually married a woman and became a stepfather. And, sadly, he later committed suicide (Colapinto, 2000).

The bottom line: "Sex matters," concluded the National Academy of Sciences (2001). In combination with the environment, sex-related genes and physiology "result in behavioral and cognitive differences between males and females." Nature and nurture work together.

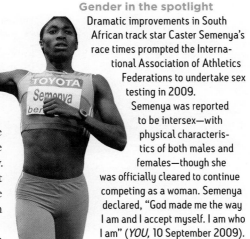

Gender in the spotlight
Dramatic improvements in South African track star Caster Semenya's race times prompted the International Association of Athletics Federations to undertake sex testing in 2009.
Semenya was reported to be intersex—with physical characteristics of both males and females—though she was officially cleared to continue competing as a woman. Semenya declared, "God made me the way I am and I accept myself. I am who I am" (*YOU*, 10 September 2009).

Reuters/Michael Dalder

The Nurture of Gender: Our Culture

5-3: How do gender roles and gender typing influence gender development?

For most people, their biological sex and their gender are tightly interwined. What biology initiates, culture accentuates.

Gender Roles

You may recall from Chapter 1 that *culture* is everything shared by a group and transmitted across generations. We can see culture's shaping power in **gender roles**—the social expectations that guide men's and women's behavior. (In psychology, as in the theater, a **role** refers to a cluster of prescribed actions, the behaviors we expect of those who occupy a particular social position.)

Gender roles vary over time and place. In North America, men were traditionally expected to initiate dates, drive the car, and pick up the check. Women were expected to decorate the home, buy and care for the children's clothes, and select the wedding gifts. Up through the 1990s, Mom (about 90 percent of the time in two-parent U.S. families) stayed home with a sick child, arranged for the babysitter, and called the doctor (Maccoby, 1995). Even in recent years, compared with employed women, employed men in the United States have spent about an hour and a half more on the job and about one hour less on daily household activities and caregiving (Amato et al., 2007; Bureau of Labor Statistics, 2004; Fisher et al., 2006). Ditto Australia, where, compared with men, women have devoted 54 percent more time to unpaid household work and 71 percent more time to child care (Trewin, 2001).

Other societies have different expectations. In nomadic societies of food-gathering people, there is little division of labor by sex. Boys and girls receive much the same upbringing. In agricultural societies, where women work in the nearby fields and men roam while herding livestock, children have typically been socialized into more distinct gender roles (Segall et al., 1990; Van Leeuwen, 1978).

Among industrialized countries, gender roles and attitudes vary widely. Australia and the Scandinavian countries offer the greatest gender equity, Middle Eastern and North African countries the least (Social Watch, 2006). And consider: Would you agree that "when jobs are scarce, men should have more rights to a job?" In the United States, Britain, and Spain, about one in eight adults agree. In Nigeria, Pakistan, and India, about four in five do (Pew, 2010). We are one species, but my how we differ.

"Sex brought us together, but gender drove us apart."

gender role a set of expected behaviors for males or for females.

role a set of expectations (norms) about a social position, defining how those in the position ought to behave.

The gendered tsunami In Sri Lanka, Indonesia, and India, the gendered division of labor helps explain the excess of female deaths from the 2004 tsunami. In some villages, 80 percent of those killed were women, who were mostly at home while the men were more likely to be at sea fishing or doing out-of-the-home chores (Oxfam, 2005).

To see how gender role attitudes vary over time, consider women's voting rights. At the opening of the twentieth century, only one country—New Zealand—granted women the right to vote (Briscoe, 1997). By the late 1960s and early 1970s, women had become a force in the voting booth and the workplace in many countries. Nearly 50 percent of employed Americans are now women, as are 54 percent of college graduates, up from 36 percent in just four decades (Fry & Cohn, 2010). In today's postindustrial economy, the jobs expected to grow the most in the years ahead are the ones women have gravitated toward—those that require not size and strength but social intelligence, open communication, and the ability to sit still and focus (Rosin, 2010). These are big gender changes in but a thin slice of history.

Gender roles can smooth social relations, avoiding irritating discussions about whose job it is to get the car fixed and who should buy the birthday presents. But these quick and easy assumptions come at a cost: If we deviate from conventions, we may feel anxious.

How Do We Learn to Be Male or Female?

Gender identity is a person's sense of being male or female. **Social learning theory** assumes that children acquire this identity by observing and imitating others' gender-linked behaviors and by being rewarded or punished for acting in certain ways themselves ("Nicole, you're such a good mommy to your dolls"; "Big boys don't cry, Alex."). Some critics have objected, saying that parental modeling and rewarding of male-female differences aren't enough to explain **gender typing,** the way some children seem more attuned than others to traditional male or female roles (Lytton & Romney, 1991). In fact, even in families that discourage traditional gender typing, children organize themselves into "boy worlds" and "girl worlds," each guided by rules for what boys and girls do.

Cognition (thinking) also matters. In your own childhood you formed *schemas,* or concepts that helped you make sense of your world. One of these was your *gender schema,* your framework for organizing boy-girl characteristics (Bem, 1987, 1993). This gender schema then became a lens through which you viewed your experiences.

Gender schemas form early in life, and social learning helps form them. Before age 1, you began to discriminate male and female voices and faces (Martin et al., 2002). After age 2, language forced you to begin organizing your world on the basis of gender. English, for example, uses the pronouns *he* and *she;* other languages classify objects as masculine ("*le* train") or feminine ("*la* table").

The social learning of gender Children observe and imitate parental models.

Young children are "gender detectives" (Martin & Ruble, 2004). Once they grasp that two sorts of people exist—and that they are of one sort—they search for clues about gender, and they find them in language, dress, toys, and songs. Girls, they may decide, are the ones with long hair. Having divided the human world in half, 3-year-olds will then like their own kind better and seek them out for play. And having compared themselves with their concept of gender, they will adjust their behavior accordingly. ("I am male—thus, masculine, strong, aggressive," or "I am female—therefore, feminine, sweet, and helpful.") These rigid boy-girl stereotypes peak at about age 5 or 6. If the new neighbor is a boy, a 6-year-old girl may assume he just cannot share her interests. For young children, gender looms large.

For some people, comparing themselves with their culture's concepts of gender produces feelings of confusion and discord. **Transgender** people's *gender identity* (their sense of being male or female) or *gender expression* (their communication of gender identity through behavior or appearance) differs from that typical of their birth sex (APA, 2010). A person may feel like a man in a woman's body, or a woman in a man's body. These include *transsexual* people, who live, or wish to live, as members of the gender opposite to their birth sex, often aided by medical treatment that supports gender reassignment. Note that gender identity is distinct from *sexual orientation* (the direction of one's sexual attraction). Transgender people may be heterosexual, homosexual, bisexual, or asexual.

Some transgender persons express their gender identity by dressing as a person of the other biological sex typically would. Most cross-dressers are biological males, the majority of whom feel an attraction to females (APA, 2010).

RETRIEVE IT

• What are gender roles, and what do their variations tell us about our human capacity for learning and adaptation?

ANSWER: *Gender roles* are sets of expected behaviors for females or for males. Gender roles vary widely in different cultures, which is proof that we are very capable of learning and adapting to the social demands of different environments.

Human Sexuality

As you've probably noticed, we can hardly talk about gender without talking about our sexuality. For all but the tiny fraction of us considered *asexual,* dating and mating become top priority from puberty on. Physiological and psychological influences affect our sexual feelings and behaviors.

The Physiology of Sex

Sex is not like hunger, because it is not an actual *need*. (Without it, we may feel like dying, but we will not.) Yet sex is part of life. Had this not been so for all your ancestors, you would not be reading this book. Sexual motivation is nature's clever way of making people procreate, thus enabling our species' survival. When two people feel an attraction, they hardly stop to think of themselves as guided by their genes. As the pleasure we take in eating is nature's method of getting our body nourishment, so the desires and pleasures of sex are our genes' way of preserving and spreading themselves. Life is sexually transmitted.

Hormones and Sexual Behavior

5-4: How do hormones influence human sexual motivation?

Among the forces driving sexual behavior are the *sex hormones*. The main male sex hormone, as we saw earlier, is *testosterone*. The main female sex hormones are the **estrogens,** such as estradiol. Sex hormones influence us at many points in the life span:

• During the prenatal period, they direct our development as males or females.

• During puberty, a sex hormone surge ushers us into adolescence.

• After puberty and well into the late adult years, sex hormones activate sexual behavior.

In most mammals, nature neatly synchronizes sex with fertility. Females become sexually receptive ("in heat") when their estrogens peak at ovulation. In experiments, researchers can cause female animals to become receptive by injecting them with estrogens. Male hormone levels are more constant, and hormone injection does not so easily manipulate the sexual behavior of male animals (Feder, 1984). Nevertheless, male rats that have had their testes (which manufacture testosterone) surgically removed will gradually lose much of their interest in receptive females. They gradually regain it if injected with testosterone.

"The more I was treated as a woman, the more woman I became."

Jan Morris, male-to-female transsexual

Kimberly A. C. Wilson/The Oregonian

The transgender mayor When Stu Rassmussen was elected Silverton, Oregon's mayor, he was a guy in pants. When reelected, he was openly transgender and wore a dress and makeup to his installation.

In a British survey of 18,876 people, 1 percent were seemingly asexual, having "never felt sexually attracted to anyone at all" (Bogaert, 2004, 2006b).

"It is a near-universal experience, the invisible clause on one's birth certificate stipulating that one will, upon reaching maturity, feel the urge to engage in activities often associated with the issuance of more birth certificates."

Science writer Natalie Angier, 2007

gender identity our sense of being male or female.

social learning theory the theory that we learn social behavior by observing and imitating and by being rewarded or punished.

gender typing the acquisition of a traditional masculine or feminine role.

transgender an umbrella term describing people whose gender identity or expression differs from that associated with their birth sex.

estrogens sex hormones, such as estradiol, secreted in greater amounts by females than by males and contributing to female sex characteristics. In nonhuman female mammals, estrogen levels peak during ovulation, promoting sexual receptivity.

Hormones do influence human sexual behavior, but in a looser way. Among women with mates, sexual desire rises slightly at ovulation (Pillsworth et al., 2004). One study invited partnered women not at risk for pregnancy to keep a diary of their sexual activity. (These women were either using intrauterine devices or had undergone surgery to prevent pregnancy.) On the days around ovulation, intercourse was 24 percent more frequent (Wilcox et al., 2004).

Other studies find that around ovulation, women fantasize more about sex with desirable partners, wear more sexually attractive clothing, and have slightly higher voice pitch (Bryant & Haselton, 2009; Pillsworth & Haselton, 2006; Sheldon et al., 2006). After sniffing a T-shirt worn by a woman, men display higher testosterone levels if she was ovulating rather than nonovulating (Miller & Maner, 2010, 2011). In a study of 5300 strip-club lap dancers, their hourly tips almost doubled on the days near ovulation, compared with days during menstruation (Miller et al., 2007).

Women more than other mammalian females are responsive to their testosterone level (van Anders & Dunn, 2009). You may recall that women have testosterone, though at lower levels than are found in men. If a woman's natural testosterone level drops, as happens with removal of the ovaries or adrenal glands, her sexual interest may wane. But as controlled experiments with hundreds of surgically or naturally menopausal women have demonstrated, testosterone-replacement therapy can often restore diminished sexual activity, arousal, and desire (Braunstein et al., 2005; Buster et al., 2005; Petersen & Hyde, 2011).

In human males with abnormally low testosterone levels, testosterone-replacement therapy often increases sexual desire and also energy and vitality (Yates, 2000). But normal fluctuations in testosterone levels, from man to man and hour to hour, have little effect on sexual drive (Byrne, 1982). Indeed, male hormones sometimes vary in *response* to sexual stimulation. In one study, Australian skateboarders' testosterone surged in the presence of an attractive female, contributing to riskier moves and more crash landings (Ronay & von Hippel, 2010). Thus, sexual arousal can be a *cause* as well as a consequence of increased testosterone levels. At the other end of the mating spectrum, studies in both North America and China have found that married fathers tend to have lower testosterone levels than do bachelors and married men without children (Gray et al., 2006).

Large hormonal surges or declines do affect men and women's desire. These shifts tend to occur at two predictable points in the life span, and sometimes at an unpredictable third point:

1. *As we have seen, a surge in sex hormones triggers the development of sex characteristics during puberty.* Interest in dating and sexual stimulation usually increases at this time. If the hormonal surge is precluded—as it was during the 1600s and 1700s for prepubertal boys who were castrated to preserve their soprano voices for Italian opera—sex characteristics and sexual desire do not develop normally (Peschel & Peschel, 1987).

2. *In later life, estrogen levels fall, and women experience menopause (Chapter 4).* As sex hormone levels decline, the frequency of sexual fantasies and intercourse declines as well (Leitenberg & Henning, 1995).

3. *For some, surgery or drugs may cause hormonal shifts.* When adult men were castrated, sex drive typically fell as testosterone levels declined sharply (Hucker & Bain, 1990). Male sex offenders who were taking Depo-Provera, a drug that reduces testosterone levels to that of a prepubertal boy, have similarly lost much of their sexual urge (Bilefsky, 2009; Money et al., 1983).

To summarize: We might compare human sex hormones, especially testosterone, to the fuel in a car. Without fuel, a car will not run. But if the fuel level is minimally adequate, adding more fuel to the gas tank won't change how the car runs. The analogy is imperfect, because hormones and sexual motivation interact. However, it correctly suggests that biology is a necessary but not sufficient explanation of human sexual behavior. The hormonal fuel is essential, but so are the psychological stimuli that turn on the engine, keep it running, and shift it into high gear.

"Fill'er up with testosterone."

The Sexual Response Cycle

5-5: What is the human sexual response cycle, and how do sexual dysfunctions and paraphilias differ?

In the 1960s, gynecologist-obstetrician William Masters and his collaborator Virginia Johnson (1966) made headlines by recording the physiological responses of volunteers who came to their lab to masturbate or have intercourse. With the help of 382 female and 312 male volunteers—a somewhat atypical sample, consisting only of people able and willing to display arousal and orgasm while scientists observed—Masters and Johnson monitored or filmed more than 10,000 sexual "cycles." Their description of the **sexual response cycle** identified four stages:

1. *Excitement:* The genital areas become engorged with blood, causing a woman's clitoris and a man's penis to swell. A woman's vagina expands and secretes lubricant; her breasts and nipples may enlarge.

2. *Plateau:* Excitement peaks as breathing, pulse, and blood pressure rates continue to increase. A man's penis becomes fully engorged and some fluid—frequently containing enough live sperm to enable conception—may appear at its tip. A woman's vaginal secretion continues to increase, and her clitoris retracts. Orgasm feels imminent.

3. *Orgasm:* Muscle contractions appear all over the body and are accompanied by further increases in breathing, pulse, and blood pressure rates. A woman's arousal and orgasm facilitate conception: They help propel semen from the penis, position the uterus to receive sperm, and draw the sperm further inward, increasing retention of deposited sperm (Furlow & Thornhill, 1996). The pleasurable feeling of sexual release apparently is much the same for both sexes. One panel of experts could not reliably distinguish between descriptions of orgasm written by men and those written by women (Vance & Wagner, 1976). In another study, PET scans showed that the same subcortical brain regions were active in men and women during orgasm (Holstege et al., 2003a,b). And when people passionately in love undergo fMRI scans while viewing photos of their beloved or of a stranger, men's and women's brain responses to their partner are pretty similar (Fisher et al., 2002).

4. *Resolution:* The body gradually returns to its unaroused state as the genital blood vessels release their accumulated blood. This happens relatively quickly if orgasm has occurred, relatively slowly otherwise. (It's like the nasal tickle that goes away rapidly if you have sneezed, slowly otherwise.) Men then enter a **refractory period** that lasts from a few minutes to a day or more, during which they are incapable of another orgasm. A woman's much shorter refractory period may enable her to have another orgasm if restimulated during or soon after resolution.

Sexual Dysfunctions and Paraphilias

Masters and Johnson sought not only to describe the human sexual response cycle but also to understand and treat the inability to complete it. **Sexual dysfunctions** are problems that consistently impair sexual arousal or functioning. Some involve sexual motivation, especially lack of sexual energy and arousability. For men, others include *erectile dysfunction* (inability to have or maintain an erection) and *premature ejaculation*. For women, the problem may be pain or *orgasmic dysfunction* (distress over infrequently or never experiencing orgasm). In separate surveys of some 3000 Boston women and 32,000 other American women, about 4 in 10 reported a sexual problem, such as

"I love the idea of there being two sexes, don't you?"

A nonsmoking 50-year-old male has about a 1-in-a-million chance of a heart attack during any hour. This increases to merely 2-in-a-million in the two hours during and following sex (with no increase for those who exercise regularly). Compared with risks associated with heavy exertion or anger (see Chapter 11), this risk seems not worth losing sleep (or sex) over (Jackson, 2009; Muller et al., 1996).

sexual response cycle the four stages of sexual responding described by Masters and Johnson—excitement, plateau, orgasm, and resolution.

refractory period a resting period after orgasm, during which a man cannot achieve another orgasm.

sexual dysfunction a problem that consistently impairs sexual arousal or functioning.

orgasmic dysfunction or low desire, but only about 1 in 8 reported that this caused personal distress (Lutfey et al., 2009; Shifren et al., 2008). Most women who have experienced sexual distress have related it to their emotional relationship with the partner during sex (Bancroft et al., 2003).

Therapy can help men and women with sexual dysfunction. In behaviorally oriented therapy, for example, men learn ways to control their urge to ejaculate, and women are trained to bring themselves to orgasm. Starting with the introduction of Viagra in 1998, erectile dysfunction has been routinely treated by taking a pill.

In the more troubling *paraphilias,* a person's sexual arousal is related to socially unacceptable behavior. The American Psychiatric Association classifies such behavior as disordered if a person's sexual urges, fantasies, or behaviors involve nonhuman objects; the suffering of self or others; and/or nonconsenting persons. Examples of paraphilias include *exhibitionism, fetishism,* and *pedophilia.*

Sexually Transmitted Infections

> **5-6:** How can sexually transmitted infections be prevented?

Rates of *sexually transmitted infections* (*STIs;* also called *STDs* for *sexually transmitted diseases*) are rising, and two-thirds of the new infections have occurred in people under 25 (CASA, 2004). Teenage girls, because of their not yet fully mature biological development and lower levels of protective antibodies, are especially vulnerable (Dehne & Riedner, 2005; Guttmacher, 1994). A Centers for Disease Control study of sexually experienced 14- to 19-year-old U.S. females found 39.5 percent had STIs (Forhan et al., 2008).

To comprehend the mathematics of infection transmission, imagine this scenario. Over the course of a year, Pat has sex with 9 people, each of whom over the same period has sex with 9 other people, who in turn have sex with 9 others. How many "phantom" sex partners (past partners of partners) will Pat have? The actual number—511—is more than five times the estimate given by the average student (Brannon & Brock, 1993).

Condoms offer only limited protection against certain skin-to-skin STIs, such as herpes, but they do reduce other risks (Medical Institute, 1994; NIH, 2001). The effects were clear when Thailand promoted 100 percent condom use by commercial sex workers. Over a four-year period, as condom use soared from 14 to 94 percent, the annual number of bacterial STIs plummeted from 410,406 to 27,362 (WHO, 2000).

Across the available studies, condoms also have been 80 percent effective in preventing transmission of *HIV* (*human immunodeficiency virus*—the virus that causes **AIDS**) from an infected partner (Weller & Davis-Beaty, 2002; WHO, 2003). Although AIDS can be transmitted by other means, such as needle sharing during drug use, its sexual transmission is most common. Women's AIDS rates are increasing fastest, partly because the virus is passed from man to woman much more often than from woman to man. A man's semen can carry more of the virus than can a woman's vaginal and cervical secretions. The HIV-infected semen can also linger for days in a woman's vagina and cervix, increasing the time of exposure (Allen & Setlow, 1991; WHO, 2004).

Most U.S. AIDS cases have been people in midlife and younger—ages 25 to 44 (U.S. Centers for Disease Control and Prevention, 2011). Given AIDS' long incubation period, this means that many of these young people were infected as teens. In 2009, the death of 1.8 million AIDS victims worldwide left behind countless grief-stricken partners and millions of orphaned children (UNAIDS, 2010). Sub-Saharan Africa is home to two-thirds of those infected with HIV, and medical treatment and care for the dying are sapping the region's social resources.

Many people assume that oral sex falls in the category of "safe sex," but recent studies show a significant link between oral sex and transmission of STIs, such as the *human papilloma virus (HPV).* Risks rise with the number of sexual partners (Gillison et al., 2012). Most HPVs can now be prevented with a vaccination administered before sexual contact.

AIDS (acquired immune deficiency syndrome) a life-threatening, sexually transmitted infection caused by the *human immunodeficiency virus* (HIV). AIDS depletes the immune system, leaving the person vulnerable to infections.

- The inability to complete the sexual response cycle may be considered a _____
  _____. Exhibitionism would be considered a _____.

ANSWERS: sexual dysfunction; paraphilia

- From a biological perspective, AIDS is passed more readily from women to men than from men to
  women. True or false?

ANSWER: False. AIDS is transmitted more easily and more often from men to women.

The Psychology of Sex

5-7: How do external and imagined stimuli contribute to sexual arousal?

Biological factors powerfully influence our sexual motivation and behavior. Yet the wide variations over time, across place, and among individuals document the great influence of psychological factors as well (**FIGURE 5.4**). Thus, despite the shared biology that underlies sexual motivation, the 281 expressed reasons for having sex (at last count) ranged widely—from "to get closer to God" to "to get my boyfriend to shut up" (Buss, 2008; Meston & Buss, 2007).

External Stimuli

Men and women become aroused when they see, hear, or read erotic material (Heiman, 1975; Stockton & Murnen, 1992). In 132 experiments, men's feelings of sexual arousal have much more closely mirrored their (more obvious) genital response than have women's (Chivers et al., 2010).

People may find sexual arousal either pleasing or disturbing. (Those who wish to control their arousal often limit their exposure to such materials, just as those wishing to control hunger limit their exposure to tempting cues.) With repeated exposure, the emotional response to any erotic stimulus often lessens, or *habituates*. During the 1920s, when Western women's rising hemlines first reached the knee, an exposed leg was a mildly erotic stimulus.

Can exposure to sexually explicit material have adverse effects? Research has indicated that it can. Depictions of women being sexually coerced—and liking it—have increased viewers' acceptance of the false idea that women enjoy rape, and have increased male viewers' willingness to hurt women (Malamuth & Check, 1981; Zillmann, 1989). Viewing images of sexually attractive women and men may also lead people to devalue their own partners and relationships. After male collegians viewed TV or magazine

© Anthony Singer

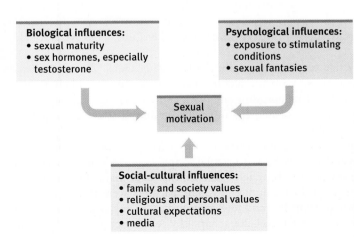

Biological influences:
- sexual maturity
- sex hormones, especially testosterone

Psychological influences:
- exposure to stimulating conditions
- sexual fantasies

Sexual motivation

Social-cultural influences:
- family and society values
- religious and personal values
- cultural expectations
- media

Petrenko Andriy/Shutterstock

FIGURE 5.4

Levels of analysis for sexual motivation Our sexual motivation is influenced by biological factors, but psychological and social-cultural factors play an even bigger role.

depictions of sexually attractive women, they often found an average woman, or their own girlfriend or wife, less attractive (Kenrick & Gutierres, 1980; Kenrick et al., 1989; Weaver et al., 1984). Viewing X-rated sex films has similarly tended to diminish people's satisfaction with their own sexual partner (Zillmann, 1989). Perhaps reading or watching erotica creates expectations that few men and women can fulfill.

Imagined Stimuli

The brain, it has been said, is our most significant sex organ. The stimuli inside our heads—our imagination—can influence sexual arousal and desire. People who, because of a spinal-cord injury, have no genital sensation can still feel sexual desire (Willmuth, 1987).

Wide-awake people become sexually aroused not only by memories of prior sexual activities but also by fantasies. About 95 percent of both men and women have said they have sexual fantasies. Men (whether gay or straight) fantasize about sex more often, more physically, and less romantically. They also prefer less personal and faster-paced sexual content in books and videos (Leitenberg & Henning, 1995). Fantasizing about sex does *not* indicate a sexual problem or dissatisfaction. If anything, sexually active people have more sexual fantasies.

RETRIEVE IT

• What factors influence our sexual motivation and behavior?

ANSWER: Influences include biological factors such as sexual maturity and sex hormones, psychological factors such as environmental stimuli and fantasies, and social-cultural factors such as the values and expectations absorbed from family and the surrounding culture.

Teen Pregnancy

5-8: What factors influence teenagers' sexual behaviors and use of contraceptives?

Compared with European teens, American teens have a higher rate of STIs and also of teen pregnancy (Call et al., 2002; Sullivan/Anderson, 2009). What environmental factors contribute to teen pregnancy?

Minimal communication about birth control Many teenagers are uncomfortable discussing contraception with their parents, partners, and peers. Teens who talk freely with parents, and who are in an exclusive relationship with a partner with whom they communicate openly, are more likely to use contraceptives (Aspy et al., 2007; Milan & Kilmann, 1987).

Guilt related to sexual activity In another survey, 72 percent of sexually active 12- to 17-year-old American girls said they regretted having had sex (Reuters, 2000). Sexual inhibitions or ambivalence can restrain sexual activity, but if passion overwhelms intentions they may also reduce attempts at birth control (Gerrard & Luus, 1995; MacDonald & Hynie, 2008).

Alcohol use Sexually active teens are typically alcohol-using teens (Zimmer-Gembeck & Helfand, 2008), and those who use alcohol prior to sex are less likely to use condoms (Kotchick et al., 2001). By depressing the brain centers that control judgment, inhibition, and self-awareness, alcohol disarms normal restraints, a phenomenon well known to sexually coercive males.

Mass media norms of unprotected promiscuity Media help write the "social scripts" that affect our perceptions and actions. So what sexual scripts do today's media write on our minds? An average hour of prime-time television on the three major U.S. networks has contained 15 sexual acts, words, and innuendos. The partners were usually unmarried, with no prior romantic relationship, and few communicated any concern for birth control or STIs (Brown et al., 2002; Kunkel, 2001; Sapolsky & Tabarlet, 1991). The more

"Condoms should be used on every conceivable occasion."

Anonymous

sexual content adolescents view (even when controlling for other predictors of early sexual activity), the more likely they are to perceive their peers as sexually active, to develop sexually permissive attitudes, and to experience early inter-course (Escobar-Chaves et al., 2005; Martino et al., 2005; Ward & Friedman, 2006). (See Close-Up: The Sexualization of Girls.)

The National Longitudinal Study of Adolescent Health among 12,000 teens found several factors that predicted several sexual restraint:

- *High intelligence* Teens with high rather than average intelligence test scores more often delayed sex, partly because they appreciated possible negative consequences and were more focused on future achievement than on here-and-now pleasures (Halpern et al., 2000).

- *Religious engagement* Actively religious teens have more often reserved sexual activity for adulthood (Lucero et al., 2008).

- *Father presence* In studies that followed hundreds of New Zealand and U.S. girls from age 5 to 18, a father's absence was linked to sexual activity before age 16 and to teen pregnancy (Ellis et al., 2003). These associations held even after adjusting for other adverse influences, such as poverty. Close family attachments—families that eat together and where parents know their teens' activities and friends—also predicted later sexual initiation (Coley et al., 2008).

- *Participation in service learning programs* Several experiments have found that teens volunteering as tutors or teachers' aides, or participating in community projects, had lower pregnancy rates than were found among comparable teens randomly assigned to control conditions (Kirby, 2002; O'Donnell et al., 2002). Researchers are unsure why. Does service learning promote a sense of personal competence, control, and responsibility? Does it encourage more future-oriented thinking? Or does it simply reduce opportunities for unprotected sex?

★ ★ ★

We have considered some of the research on the biological and psychological aspects of human sexuality. It's important to remember, though, that scientific research on human sexuality does not aim to define the personal meaning of sex in our own lives. We could know every available fact about sex—that the initial spasms of male and female orgasm

Keeping abreast of hypersexuality
An analysis of the 60 top-selling video games found 489 characters, 86 percent of whom were males (like most of the game players). The female characters were much more likely than the male characters to be "hyper-sexualized"—partially nude or revealingly clothed, with large breasts and tiny waists (Downs & Smith, 2010).

Eidos Scripps Howard Photo Service/Newscom

CLOSE UP:

The Sexualization of Girls

As you have surely noticed, TV, the Internet, music videos and lyrics, movies, magazines, sports media, and advertising often portray women and even girls as sexual objects. The frequent result, according to both an American Psychological Association (APA, 2007) task force and the Scottish Parliament (2010), is harm to their self-image, and unhealthy sexual development.

Sexualization occurs when girls

- are led to value themselves in terms of their sexual appeal.

- compare themselves to narrowly defined beauty standards.

- see themselves as sexual beings for others' use.

In experiments, the APA task force reported, being made self-conscious about one's body, such as by wearing a swimsuit, disrupts thinking when doing math computations or logical reasoning. Sexualization also contributes to eating disorders and depression, and to unrealistic expectations regarding sexuality.

Mindful of today's sexualizing media, the APA has some suggestions for countering these messages. Parents, teachers, and others can teach girls "to value themselves for who they are rather than how they look." They can teach boys "to value girls as friends, sisters, and girlfriends, rather than as sexual objects." And they can help girls and boys develop "media literacy skills" that enable them to recognize and resist the message that women are sexual objects and that a thin, sexy look is all that matters.

© T. Arroyo/JPegFoto/PictureGroup via AP Images

Sharing love For most adults, a sexual relationship fulfills not only a biological motive but also a social need for intimacy.

Image Source/Getty Images

come at 0.8-second intervals, that the female nipples expand 10 millimeters at the peak of sexual arousal, that systolic blood pressure rises some 60 points and respiration rate to 40 breaths per minute—but fail to understand the human significance of sexual intimacy.

Surely one significance of sexual intimacy is its expression of our profoundly social nature. One recent study asked 2035 married people when they started having sex (while controlling for education, religious engagement, and relationship length). Those whose relationship first developed to a deep commitment reported greater relationship satisfaction and stability—and better sex (Busby et al., 2010). Sex is a socially significant act. Men and women can achieve orgasm alone, yet most people find greater satisfaction—and experience a much greater surge in the *prolactin* hormone associated with sexual satisfaction and satiety—after intercourse and orgasm with their loved one (Brody & Tillmann, 2006). Sex at its human best is life uniting and love renewing.

In the remaining pages of this chapter, we'll consider two special topics: *sexual orientation* (the direction of our sexual interests), and evolutionary psychology's explanation of our sexual motivation.

RETRIEVE IT

• Which THREE of the following five factors contribute to unplanned teen pregnancies?

    a. Alcohol use   d. Mass media models

    b. Higher intelligence level   e. Increased communication about options

    c. Ignorance

ANSWERS: a, c, d

Sexual Orientation

> **5-9:** What has research taught us about sexual orientation?

We express the *direction* of our sexual interest in our **sexual orientation**—our enduring sexual attraction toward members of our own sex *(homosexual orientation),* the other sex *(heterosexual orientation),* or both sexes *(bisexual orientation).* As far as we know, all cultures in all times have been predominantly heterosexual (Bullough, 1990). Some cultures have condemned same-sex relations. (In Kenya and Nigeria, 98 percent have thought homosexuality is "never justified" [Pew, 2006].) Others have accepted same-sex unions. But in both cases, heterosexuality prevails and homosexuality endures.

How many people are exclusively homosexual? About 10 percent, as the popular press has often assumed? Nearly 25 percent, as average Americans estimated in a 2011 Gallup survey (Morales, 2011)? Not according to more than a dozen national surveys that have explored sexual orientation in Europe and the United States, using methods protecting the respondents' anonymity. The most accurate figure seems to be about 3 percent of men and 1 or 2 percent of women (Chandra et al., 2011; Herbenick et al., 2010a). Fewer than 1 percent of survey respondents—for example, only 12 people out of 7076 Dutch adults in one survey (Sandfort et al., 2001)—have reported being actively bisexual. A larger number of adults—13 percent of women and 5 percent of men in a U.S. National Center for Health Statistics survey—report some same-sex sexual contact during their lives (Chandra et al., 2011). And still more have had an occasional homosexual fantasy.

What does it feel like to be the "odd man (or woman) out" in a heterosexual culture? If you are heterosexual, one way to understand is to imagine how you would feel if you were socially isolated for openly admitting or displaying your feelings toward someone of the other sex. How would you react if you overheard people making crude jokes about heterosexual people, or if most movies, TV shows, and advertisements portrayed (or implied) homosexuality? And how would you answer if your family members were pleading with you to change your heterosexual lifestyle and to enter into a homosexual marriage?

sexual orientation an enduring sexual attraction toward members of either one's own sex (homosexual orientation), the other sex (heterosexual orientation), or both sexes (bisexual orientation).

Facing such reactions, homosexual people often struggle with their sexual orientation. They may at first try to ignore or deny their desires, hoping they will go away. But they don't. Some may try to change, through psychotherapy, willpower, or prayer. But the feelings typically persist, as do those of heterosexual people—who are similarly incapable of becoming homosexual (Haldeman, 1994, 2002; Myers & Scanzoni, 2005).

Most of today's psychologists therefore view sexual orientation as neither willfully chosen nor willfully changed. "Efforts to change sexual orientation are unlikely to be successful and involve some risk of harm," declared a 2009 American Psychological Association report. In 1973, the American Psychiatric Association dropped homosexuality from its list of "mental illnesses." In 1993, the World Health Organization did the same, as did Japan's and China's psychiatric associations in 1995 and 2001. Some have noted that rates of depression and attempted suicide are higher among gays and lesbians. Many psychologists believe, however, that these symptoms may result from experiences with bullying, harassment, and discrimination (Sandfort et al., 2001; Warner et al., 2004). "Homosexuality, in and of itself, is not associated with mental disorders or emotional or social problems," declared the American Psychological Association (2007).

Thus, sexual orientation in some ways is like handedness: Most people are one way, some the other. A very few are ambidextrous. Regardless, the way one is endures.

This conclusion is most strongly established for men. Compared with men's sexual orientation, women's tends to be less strongly felt and may be more variable (Chivers, 2005; Diamond, 2008; Peplau & Garnets, 2000). Men's lesser *erotic plasticity* (sexual variability) is apparent in many ways (Baumeister, 2000). Adult women's sexual drive and interests are more flexible and varying than are adult men's. Women, more than men, for example, prefer to alternate periods of high sexual activity with periods of almost none. They are also somewhat more likely than men to feel and act on bisexual attractions (Mosher et al., 2005).

Driven to suicide In 2010, Rutgers University student Tyler Clementi jumped off this bridge after his intimate encounter with another man reportedly became known. Reports then surfaced of other gay teens who had reacted in a similarly tragic fashion after being taunted.

Environment and Sexual Orientation

So, our sexual orientation is something we do not choose and (especially for males) seemingly cannot change. Where, then, do these preferences come from? Let's look first at possible environmental influences on sexual orientation. To see if you can anticipate the conclusions that have emerged from hundreds of studies, try answering *Yes* or *No* to these questions:

Note that the scientific question is not "What causes homosexuality?" (or "What causes heterosexuality?") but "What causes differing sexual orientations?" In pursuit of answers, psychological science compares the backgrounds and physiology of people whose sexual orientations *differ*.

1. Is homosexuality linked with problems in a child's relationships with parents, such as with a domineering mother and an ineffectual father, or a possessive mother and a hostile father?

2. Does homosexuality involve a fear or hatred of people of the other sex, leading individuals to direct their desires toward members of their own sex?

3. Is sexual orientation linked with levels of sex hormones currently in the blood?

4. As children, were most homosexuals molested, seduced, or otherwise sexually victimized by an adult homosexual?

The answer to all these questions has been *No* (Storms, 1983). In a search for possible environmental influences on sexual orientation, Kinsey Institute investigators interviewed nearly 1000 homosexuals and 500 heterosexuals. They assessed nearly every imaginable psychological cause of homosexuality—parental relationships, childhood sexual experiences, peer relationships, and dating experiences (Bell et al., 1981; Hammersmith, 1982). Their findings: Homosexuals were

Personal values affect sexual orientation less than they affect other forms of sexual behavior Compared with people who rarely attend religious services, for example, those who attend regularly are one-third as likely to have lived together before marriage, and they report having had many fewer sex partners. But (if male) they are just as likely to be homosexual (Smith, 1998).

no more likely than heterosexuals to have been smothered by maternal love or neglected by their father. And consider this: If "distant fathers" were more likely to produce homosexual sons, then shouldn't boys growing up in father-absent homes more often be gay? (They are not.) And shouldn't the rising number of such homes have led to a noticeable increase in the gay population? (It has not.) Most children raised by gay or lesbian parents grow up straight and well-adjusted (Gartrell & Bos, 2010).

A bottom line has emerged from a half-century's theory and research: If there are environmental factors that influence sexual orientation, we do not yet know what they are.

Biology and Sexual Orientation

The lack of evidence for environmental causes of homosexuality has motivated researchers to explore possible biological influences. They have considered

- evidence of homosexuality in other species,
- gay-straight brain differences,
- genetics, and
- prenatal hormones.

Juliet and Juliet Boston's beloved swan couple, "Romeo and Juliet," were discovered actually to be, as are many other animal partners, a same-sex pair.

Same-Sex Attraction in Other Species

In Boston's Public Gardens, caretakers have solved the mystery of why a much-loved swan couple's eggs never hatch. Both swans are female. In New York City's Central Park Zoo, penguins Silo and Roy spent several years as devoted same-sex partners. At least occasional same-sex relations have been observed in several hundred species (Bagemihl, 1999). Grizzlies, gorillas, monkeys, flamingos, and owls are all on the long list. Among rams, for example, some 7 to 10 percent (to sheep-breeding ranchers, the "duds") display same-sex attraction by shunning ewes and seeking to mount other males (Perkins & Fitzgerald, 1997). Some degree of homosexual behavior seems a natural part of the animal world.

Gay-Straight Brain Differences

Researcher Simon LeVay (1991) studied sections of the hypothalamus (a brain structure linked to emotion) taken from deceased heterosexual and homosexual people. As a gay man, LeVay wanted to do "something connected with my gay identity." To avoid biasing the results, he did a *blind study*, without knowing which donors were gay or straight. After nine months of peering through his microscope at a hypothalamus cell cluster that seemed to come in different sizes, he consulted the donor records. The cell cluster was reliably larger in heterosexual men than in women and homosexual men. "I was almost in a state of shock," LeVay said (1994). "I took a walk by myself on the cliffs over the ocean. I sat for half an hour just thinking what this might mean."

It should not surprise us that brains differ with sexual orientation. Remember, *everything psychological is simultaneously biological*. But when did the brain difference begin? At conception? During childhood or adolescence? Did experience produce the difference? Or was it genes or prenatal hormones (or genes via prenatal hormones)?

LeVay does not view this cell cluster as an "on-off button" for sexual orientation. Rather, he believes it is an important part of a brain pathway that is active during sexual behavior. He agrees that sexual behavior patterns could influence the brain's anatomy. (Neural pathways in our brain do grow stronger with use.) In fish, birds, rats, and humans, brain structures vary with experience—including sexual experience (Breedlove, 1997). But LeVay believes it more likely that brain anatomy influences sexual orientation. His hunch seems confirmed by the discovery of a similar difference found between the 7 to 10 percent of male sheep that display same-sex attraction and the 90+ percent attracted to females (Larkin et al., 2002; Roselli et al., 2002, 2004). Moreover, such differences seem to develop soon after birth, perhaps even before birth (Rahman & Wilson, 2003).

Since LeVay's discovery, other researchers have reported additional gay-straight brain activity differences. One is an area of the hypothalamus that governs sexual arousal (Savic et al., 2005). When straight women were given a whiff of a scent derived from men's sweat (which contains traces of male hormones), this area became active. Gay men's brains responded similarly to the men's scent. Straight men's brains did not. They showed the arousal response only to a female hormone sample. In a similar study, lesbians' responses differed from those of straight women (Kranz & Ishai, 2006; Martins et al., 2005).

> "Gay men simply don't have the brain cells to be attracted to women."
>
> *Simon LeVay,* The Sexual Brain, *1993*

Genetic Influences

Three lines of evidence suggest a genetic influence on sexual orientation.

Family Studies "Homosexuality does appear to run in families," noted Brian Mustanski and Michael Bailey (2003). Researchers have speculated about possible reasons why "gay genes" might persist in the human gene pool, given that same-sex couples cannot naturally reproduce. One possible answer is kin selection. Recall from Chapter 2 the evolutionary psychology reminder that many of our genes also reside in our biological relatives. Perhaps, then, gay people's genes live on through their supporting the survival and reproductive success of their nieces, nephews, and other relatives (who also carry many of the same genes). Gay men make generous uncles, suggests one study of Samoans (Vasey & VanderLaan, 2010).

An alternative "fertile females" theory suggests that maternal genetics may also be at work (Bocklandt et al., 2006). Homosexual men tend to have more homosexual relatives on their mother's side than on their father's (Camperio-Ciani et al., 2004, 2009; Zietsch et al., 2008). And the relatives on the mother's side also produce more offspring than do the maternal relatives of heterosexual men. Perhaps the genes that dispose women to be strongly attracted to men, and therefore to have more children, also dispose some men to be attracted to men (LeVay, 2011).

> "Studies indicate that male homosexuality is more likely to be transmitted from the mother's side of the family."
>
> *Robert Plomin, John DeFries, Gerald McClearn, and Michael Rutter,* Behavioral Genetics, *1997*

Twin Studies Twin studies indicate that genes influence sexual orientation. Identical twins (who have identical genes) are somewhat more likely than fraternal twins (whose genes are not identical) to share a homosexual orientation (Alanko et al., 2010; Lángström et al., 2008, 2010). However, because sexual orientation differs in many identical twin pairs (especially female twins), other factors must also play a role.

Fruit Fly Studies Laboratory experiments on fruit flies have altered a single gene and changed the flies' sexual orientation and behavior (Dickson, 2005). During courtship, females acted like males (pursuing other females) and males acted like females (Demir & Dickson, 2005). With humans, it's likely that multiple genes, possibly in interaction with other influences, shape sexual orientation. In search of such genetic markers, one study financed by the U.S. National Institutes of Health is analyzing the genes of more than 1000 gay brothers.

Prenatal Influences

Twins share not only genes, but also a prenatal environment. Two sets of findings indicate that the prenatal environment matters.

First, in humans, a critical period for brain development seems to fall between the middle of the second and fifth months after conception (Ellis & Ames, 1987; Gladue, 1990; Meyer-Bahlburg, 1995). Exposure to the hormone levels typically experienced by female fetuses during this period may predispose a person (female or male) to be attracted to males in later life. When pregnant sheep were injected with testosterone during a similar critical period, their female offspring later showed homosexual behavior (Money, 1987).

> "Modern scientific research indicates that sexual orientation is . . . partly determined by genetics, but more specifically by hormonal activity in the womb."
>
> *Glenn Wilson and Qazi Rahman,* Born Gay: The Psychobiology of Sex Orientation, *2005*

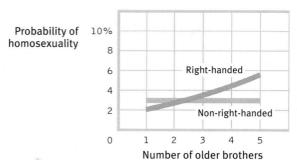

Probability of homosexuality

Right-handed

Non-right-handed

Number of older brothers

FIGURE 5.5

The fraternal birth-order effect

Researcher Ray Blanchard (2008) offered these approximate curves depicting a man's likelihood of homosexuality as a function of his number of older brothers. This correlation has been found in several studies, but only among right-handed men (as about 9 in 10 men are).

Second, the mother's immune system may play a role in the development of sexual orientation. Men who have older brothers are somewhat more likely to be gay—about one-third more likely for each additional older brother (Blanchard, 1997, 2008; Bogaert, 2003). If the odds of homosexuality are roughly 2 percent among first sons, they would rise to nearly 3 percent among second sons, 4 percent for third sons, and so on for each additional older brother (see **FIGURE 5.5**). The reason for this curious effect—called the *older-brother* or *fraternal birth-order effect*—is unclear. But the explanation does seem biological. The effect does not occur among adopted brothers (Bogaert, 2006). Researchers suspect the mother's immune system may have a defensive response to substances produced by male fetuses. After each pregnancy with a male fetus, the maternal antibodies may become stronger and may prevent the fetal brain from developing in a typical male pattern.

Gay-Straight Trait Differences

On several traits, gays and lesbians appear to fall midway between straight females and males (**TABLE 5.1**; see also LeVay, 2011; Rahman & Koerting, 2008). Gay men tend to be shorter and lighter than straight men—a difference that appears even at birth. Women in same-sex marriages were mostly heavier than average at birth (Bogaert, 2010; Frisch & Zdravkovic, 2010). Data from 20 studies have also revealed handedness differences: Homosexual participants were 39 percent more likely to not be right-handed (Blanchard, 2008; Lalumière et al., 2000).

Table 5.1
Biological Correlates of Sexual Orientation

Gay-straight trait differences

Sexual orientation is part of a package of traits. Studies—some in need of replication—indicate that homosexuals and heterosexuals differ in the following biological and behavioral traits:

- spatial abilities
- fingerprint ridge counts
- auditory system development
- handedness
- occupational preferences
- relative finger lengths
- gender nonconformity
- age of onset of puberty in males
- male body size
- sleep length
- physical aggression
- walking style

On average (the evidence is strongest for males), results for gays and lesbians fall between those of straight men and straight women. Three biological influences—brain, genetic, and prenatal—may contribute to these differences.

Brain differences

- One hypothalamic cell cluster is smaller in women and gay men than in straight men.
- Anterior commissure is larger in gay men than in straight men.
- Gay men's hypothalamus reacts as do straight women's to the smell of sex-related hormones.

Genetic influences

- Shared sexual orientation is higher among identical twins than among fraternal twins.
- Sexual attraction in fruit flies can be genetically manipulated.
- Male homosexuality often appears to be transmitted from the mother's side of the family.

Prenatal influences

- Altered prenatal hormone exposure may lead to homosexuality in humans and other animals.
- Men with several older biological brothers are more likely to be gay, possibly due to a maternal immune-system reaction.

Gay-straight spatial abilities also differ. On mental rotation tasks such as the one illustrated in **FIGURE 5.6**, straight men tend to outscore straight women but the scores of gays and lesbians fall between those of straight men and women (Rahman et al., 2003). But straight women and gays both outperform straight men at remembering objects' spatial locations in tasks like those found in memory games (Hassan & Rahman, 2007).

★ ★ ★

The consistency of the brain, genetic, and prenatal findings has swung the pendulum toward a biological explanation of sexual orientation (LeVay, 2011; Rahman & Koerting, 2008). Although "much remains to be discovered," concludes Simon LeVay (2011, p. xvii), "the same processes that are involved in the biological development of our bodies and brains as male or female are also involved in the development of sexual orientation."

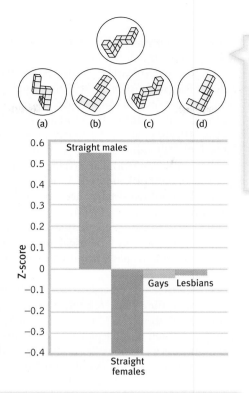

FIGURE 5.6
Spatial abilities and sexual orientation Which of the four figures can be rotated to match the target figure at the top? Straight males tend to find this an easier task than do straight females, with gays and lesbians intermediate. (From Rahman et al., 2003, with 60 people tested in each group.)

Answer: Figures a and d.

"There is no sound scientific evidence that sexual orientation can be changed."

UK Royal College of Psychiatrists, 2009

RETRIEVE IT

- Which THREE of the following five factors have researchers found to have an effect on sexual orientation?

    a. A domineering mother

    b. Size of certain cell clusters in the hypothalamus

    c. Prenatal hormone exposure

    d. A distant or ineffectual father

    e. For men, having multiple older biological brothers

ANSWERS: b, c, e

An Evolutionary Explanation of Human Sexuality

5-10: How might an evolutionary psychologist explain gender differences in sexuality and mating preferences?

Having faced many similar challenges throughout history, men and women have adapted in similar ways. Whether male or female, we eat the same foods, avoid the same predators, and perceive, learn, and remember similarly. It is only in those domains where we have faced differing adaptive challenges—most obviously in behaviors related to reproduction—that we differ, say evolutionary psychologists.

Gender Differences in Sexuality

And differ we do. Consider women's and men's sex drives. Who desires more frequent sex? Thinks more about sex? Masturbates more often? Sacrifices more to gain sex? Initiates more sex—worldwide? The answers—*Men, men, men, men,* and *men* (Baumeister et al., 2001). No surprise, then, that in one BBC survey of more than 200,000 people in 53

"Not tonight, hon, I have a concussion."

"It's not that gay men are oversexed; they are simply men whose male desires bounce off other male desires rather than off female desires."

Steven Pinker, How the Mind Works, *1997*

nations, men everywhere more strongly agreed that "I have a strong sex drive" and "It doesn't take much to get me sexually excited" (Lippa, 2008).

And there are other gender differences in sexuality (Hyde, 2005; Petersen & Hyde, 2010; Regan & Atkins, 2007). In a survey of 289,452 entering U.S. college students, 58 percent of men but only 34 percent of women agreed that "if two people really like each other, it's all right for them to have sex even if they've known each other for a very short time" (Pryor et al., 2005). "I can imagine myself being comfortable and enjoying 'casual' sex with different partners," agreed 48 percent of men and 12 percent of women in a survey of 4901 Australians (Bailey et al., 2000). Thus, university men in one study preferred casual hook-ups, while women preferred planned dating (Bradshaw et al., 2010). Casual, impulsive sex has been most frequent among males with traditional masculine attitudes (Pleck et al., 1993).

In surveys, gay men (like straight men) report more interest in uncommitted sex, more responsiveness to visual sexual stimuli, and more concern with their partner's physical attractiveness than do lesbian women (Bailey et al., 1994; Doyle, 2005; Schmitt, 2007).

In another survey of U.S. 18- to 59-year-olds, 48 percent of the women but only 25 percent of the men cited affection as a reason for first intercourse. And how often do they think about sex? "Every day" or "Several times a day," acknowledged 19 percent of the women and 54 percent of the men (Laumann et al., 1994). Ditto for the sexual thoughts of Canadians: "Several times a day," agreed 11 percent of women and 46 percent of men (Fischtein et al., 2007).

Natural Selection and Mating Preferences

Evolutionary psychologists use natural selection to explain why—worldwide—women's approach to sex is usually more *relational,* and men's more *recreational* (Schmitt, 2005, 2007). Our natural yearnings are our genes' way of reproducing themselves. "Humans are living fossils—collections of mechanisms produced by prior selection pressures," said evolutionary psychologist David Buss (1995).

The explanation goes like this: Most women incubate and nurse one infant at a time. Men, however, can spread their genes by mating with many females. In our ancestral history, men most often sent their genes into the future by pairing widely, women by pairing wisely. Thus, heterosexual women prefer stick-around dads over likely cads. They are attracted to men who seem mature, dominant, bold, and affluent, with a potential for long-term mating and investment in their joint offspring (Gangestad & Simpson, 2000; Singh, 1995). In one study of hundreds of Welsh pedestrians, men rated a woman as equally attractive whether pictured at the wheel of a humble Ford Fiesta or a swanky Bentley. Women, however, found the man more attractive if he was in the luxury car (Dunn & Searle, 2010). From an evolutionary perspective, such attributes connote a man's capacity to support and protect a family (Buss, 1996, 2009; Geary, 1998).

For heterosexual men, some desired traits, such as a woman's youthful appearance, cross place and time (Buss, 1994). Evolutionary psychologists say that men who were drawn to healthy, fertile-appearing women—women with smooth skin and a youthful shape suggesting many childbearing years to come—stood a better chance of sending their genes into the future. And sure enough, men feel most attracted to women whose waists (thanks to their genes or their surgeons) are roughly a third narrower than their hips—a sign of future fertility (Perilloux et al., 2010). Moreover, just as evolutionary psychology predicts, men are most attracted to women whose ages in the ancestral past (when ovulation began later than today) would have been associated with peak fertility (Kenrick et al., 2009). Thus, teen boys are most excited by a woman several years older than themselves, mid-twenties men prefer women around their own age, and older men prefer younger women. This pattern consistently appears across European singles ads, Indian marital ads, and marriage records from North and South America, Africa, and the Philippines (Singh, 1993; Singh & Randall, 2007).

There is a principle at work here, say evolutionary psychologists: Nature selects behaviors that increase the likelihood of sending one's genes into the future. As mobile gene machines, we are designed to prefer whatever worked for our ancestors in their environments. They were predisposed to act in ways that would leave grandchildren. Had they not been, we wouldn't be here. And as carriers of their genetic legacy, we are similarly predisposed.

The mating game Evolutionary psychologists are not surprised that older men, and not just Harrison Ford, 70 (pictured here with his wife, Calista Flockhart, 48), often prefer younger women whose features suggest fertility.

Valerie Hache/AFP/Getty Images

Critiquing the Evolutionary Perspective

5-11: What are the key criticisms of evolutionary explanations of human sexuality, and how do evolutionary psychologists respond?

Without disputing nature's selection of traits that enhance gene survival, critics see some problems with evolutionary psychology's explanation of our mating preferences. One is that evolutionary psychology starts with an effect (such as the gender sexuality difference) and works backwards to propose an explanation. They invite us to imagine a different result and reason backwards. If men were uniformly loyal to their mates, might we not reason that the children of these committed, supportive fathers would more often survive to pass on their father's genes? Might not this bond with one woman also increase their otherwise slim odds of conceiving a child, while also preventing her from mating with competing men? Might not a ritualized bond—a marriage—also spare women from chronic male harassment? Such suggestions are, in fact, evolutionary explanations for why humans tend to pair off monogamously (Gray & Anderson, 2010). One can hardly lose at hindsight explanation, which is, said paleontologist Stephen Jay Gould (1997), mere "speculation [and] guesswork in the cocktail party mode."

Some also worry about the social consequences of evolutionary psychology's approach. Does it suggest that genes are destiny? Does it mean that any effort to remake society is useless (Rose, 1999)? Does it undercut moral responsibility (Buller, 2005, 2009)? Could it be used to rationalize "high-status men marrying a series of young, fertile women" (Looy, 2001)?

Others argue that evolutionary explanations blur the line between genetic legacy and social-cultural tradition. Cultural expectations also shape socialization. If men are socialized to value lifelong commitment, they may sexually bond with one partner. If women are socialized to accept casual sex, they may willingly have sex with many partners.

Cultural expectations can bend the genders. Show Alice Eagly and Wendy Wood (1999; Eagly, 2009) a culture with gender inequality—where men are providers and women are homemakers—and they will show you a culture where men strongly desire youth and domestic skill in their potential mates, and where women seek status and earning potential in their mates. Show Eagly and Wood a culture with gender equality, and they will show you a culture with smaller gender differences in mate preferences.

Much of who we are is *not* hard-wired, agree evolutionary psychologists. "Evolution forcefully rejects a genetic determinism," insists one research team (Confer et al., 2010). Evolutionary psychologists remind us that men and women, having faced similar adaptive problems, are far more alike than different, and that humans have a great capacity for learning and social progress. Indeed, natural selection has prepared us to flexibly adjust and respond to varied environments, to adapt and survive, whether we live in igloos or tree houses.

Culture matters As this exhibit at San Diego's Museum of Man illustrates, children learn their culture. A baby's foot can step into any culture.

San Diego Museum of Man, photograph by Rose Tyson

Evolutionary psychologists acknowledge struggling to explain some traits and behaviors such as same-sex attraction and suicide (Confer et al., 2010). But they ask us to remember evolutionary psychology's testable predictions. Evolutionary psychologists predict, and have confirmed, that we tend to favor others to the extent that they share our genes or can later return our favors. They predict, and have confirmed, that human memory should be well-suited to retaining survival-relevant information (such as food locations, for which females exhibit superiority). They predict, and have confirmed, various other male and female mating strategies.

Evolutionary psychologists also remind us that the study of how we *came to be* need not dictate how we *ought to be*. Understanding our tendencies sometimes helps us overcome them.

RETRIEVE IT

- How do evolutionary psychologists explain gender differences in sexuality?

ANSWER: Evolutionary psychologists theorize that women have inherited their ancestors' tendencies to be more cautious sexually, because of the challenges associated with incubating and nurturing offspring. Men have inherited an inclination to be more casual about sex, because their act of fathering requires a smaller investment.

- What are the three main criticisms of the evolutionary explanation of human sexuality?

ANSWER: (1) It starts with an effect and works backwards to propose an explanation. (2) Unethical and immoral men could use such explanations to rationalize their behavior toward women. (3) This explanation may overlook the effects of cultural expectations and socialization.

Reflections on Gender, Sexuality, and Nature–Nurture Interaction

Our ancestral history helped form us as a species. Where there is variation, natural selection, and heredity, there will be evolution. Our genes form us. This is a great truth about human nature.

But our culture and experiences also form us. If their genes and hormones predispose males to be more physically aggressive than females, culture may magnify this gender difference by encouraging males to be macho and females to be the kinder, gentler sex. If men are encouraged toward roles that demand physical power, and women toward more nurturing roles, each may act accordingly. By exhibiting the actions expected of those who fill such roles, they will shape their own traits. Presidents in time become more presidential, servants more servile. Gender roles similarly shape us.

Today, in many cultures, gender roles are converging. Brute strength is becoming increasingly irrelevant to power and status (think Bill Gates and Hillary Clinton). From 1960 into the next century, women soared from 6 percent to 50 percent of U.S. medical students (AMA, 2010). In the mid-1960s, U.S. married women devoted *seven times* as many hours to housework as did their husbands; by 2003 this gap had shrunk to two times as many (Bianchi et al., 2000, 2006). Such swift changes signal that biology does not fix gender roles.

If nature and nurture jointly form us, are we "nothing but" the product of nature and nurture? Are we rigidly determined?

We *are* the product of nature and nurture, but we are also an open system. Genes are all pervasive but not all powerful; people may defy their genetic bent to reproduce by electing celibacy. Culture, too, is all pervasive but not all powerful; people may defy peer pressures and do the opposite of the expected. To excuse our failings by blaming our nature and nurture is what philosopher-novelist Jean-Paul Sartre called "bad faith"— attributing responsibility for one's fate to bad genes or bad influences.

In reality, we are both the creatures and the creators of our worlds. So many things about us—including our gender identity and mating behaviors—are the products of our genes and environments. Yet the future-shaping stream of causation runs through our present choices: Our decisions today design our environments tomorrow. Mind matters. The human environment is not like the weather—something that just happens. We are its architects. Our hopes, goals, and expectations influence our future. And that is what enables cultures to vary and to change.

CHAPTER REVIEW

Gender and Sexuality

LEARNING OBJECTIVES

Test Yourself by taking a moment to answer each of these Learning Objective Questions (repeated here from within the chapter). Then turn to Appendix D, Complete Chapter Reviews, to check your answers. Research suggests that trying to answer these questions on your own will improve your long-term memory of the concepts (McDaniel et al., 2009).

Gender Development

5-1: What are some gender similarities and differences in aggression, social power, and social connectedness?

5-2: How is our biological sex determined, and how do sex hormones influence prenatal and adolescent development?

5-3: How do gender roles and gender typing influence gender development?

Human Sexuality

5-4: How do hormones influence human sexual motivation?

5-5: What is the human sexual response cycle, and how do sexual dysfunctions and paraphilias differ?

5-6: How can sexually transmitted infections be prevented?

5-7: How do external and imagined stimuli contribute to sexual arousal?

5-8: What factors influence teenagers' sexual behaviors and use of contraceptives?

Sexual Orientation

5-9: What has research taught us about sexual orientation?

An Evolutionary Explanation of Human Sexuality

5-10: How might an evolutionary psychologist explain gender differences in sexuality and mating preferences?

5-11: What are the key criticisms of evolutionary explanations of human sexuality, and how do evolutionary psychologists respond?

Test yourself on these terms by trying to write down the definition in your own words before flipping back to the referenced page to check your answer.

gender, p. 164
aggression, p. 164
X chromosome, p. 167
Y chromosome, p. 167
testosterone, p. 167

puberty, p. 167
primary sex characteristics, p. 167
secondary sex characteristics, p. 167
menarche [meh-NAR-key], p. 167
gender role, p. 169
role, p. 169
gender identity, p. 170
social learning theory, p. 170
gender typing, p. 170

transgender, p. 170
estrogens, p. 171
sexual response cycle, p. 173
refractory period, p. 173
sexual dysfunction, p. 173
AIDS (acquired immune deficiency syndrome), p. 174
sexual orientation, p. 178

EXPERIENCE THE TESTING EFFECT

Test yourself repeatedly throughout your studies. This will not only help you figure out what you know and don't know; the testing itself will help you learn and remember the information more effectively thanks to the *testing effect*.

1. Females and males are very similar to each other. But one way they differ is that
   a. women are more physically aggressive than men.
   b. men are more democratic than women in their leadership roles.
   c. girls tend to play in small groups, while boys tend to play in large groups.
   d. women are more likely to commit suicide.

2. The fertilized egg will develop into a boy if it receives a _____ chromosome from its father.

3. Primary sex characteristics relate to _____; secondary sex characteristics refer to _____.
   a. ejaculation; menarche
   b. breasts and facial hair; ovaries and testes
   c. emotional maturity; hormone surges
   d. reproductive organs; nonreproductive traits

4. On average, girls begin puberty at about the age of _____, boys at about the age of _____.

5. Those born with sexual anatomy that differs from "standard" male or female babies may be considered _____.

6. *Gender role* refers to our
   a. sense of being male or female.
   b. expectations about the way males and females should behave.
   c. biological sex.
   d. unisex characteristics.

7. When children have developed a _____ _____, they have a sense of being male or female.

8. A striking effect of hormonal changes on human sexual behavior is the
   a. end of sexual desire in men over 60.
   b. sharp rise in sexual interest at puberty.
   c. decrease in women's sexual desire at the time of ovulation.
   d. increase in testosterone levels in castrated males.

9. In describing the sexual response cycle, Masters and Johnson noted that
   a. a plateau phase follows orgasm.
   b. men experience a refractory period during which they cannot experience orgasm.
   c. the feeling that accompanies orgasm is stronger in men than in women.
   d. testosterone is released equally in women and men.

10. What is the difference between sexual dysfunctions and paraphilias?

11. The use of condoms during sex _____ (does/doesn't) reduce the risk of getting HIV and _____ (does/doesn't) fully protect against skin-to-skin STIs.

12. An example of an external stimulus that might influence sexual behavior is
    a. blood level of testosterone.
    b. the onset of puberty.
    c. a sexually explicit film.
    d. an erotic fantasy or dream.

13. Factors contributing to unplanned teen pregnancies include
    a. low levels of testosterone during adolescence.
    b. higher intelligence level.
    c. too much communication.
    d. alcohol use.

14. Evolutionary psychologists are most likely to focus on
    a. how we differ from one another.
    b. the social consequences of sexual behaviors.
    c. natural selection of the fittest adaptations.
    d. cultural expectations about the "right" ways for men and women to behave.

15. Which factors have researchers thus far found to be *unrelated* to the development of our sexual orientation?

Find answers to these questions in Appendix E, in the back of the book.

Experience more of the
TESTING EFFECT

Multiple-format self-tests and more may be found at www.worthpublishers.com/myers.

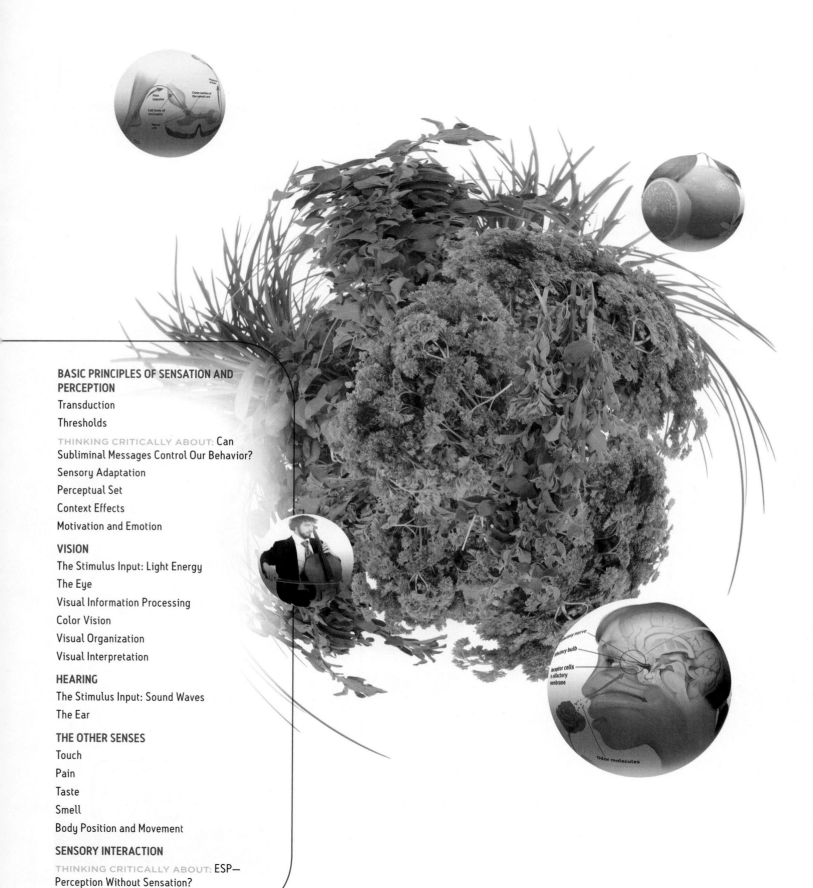

Sensation and Perception

I have perfect vision," explains my colleague, Heather Sellers, an acclaimed writer and teacher. Her vision may be fine, but there is a problem with her perception. In her memoir, *You Don't Look Like Anyone I Know,* Sellers (2010) tells of awkward moments resulting from her lifelong *prosopagnosia*—face blindness.

In college, on a date at the Spaghetti Station, I returned from the bathroom and plunked myself down in the wrong booth, facing the wrong man. I remained unaware he was not my date even as my date (a stranger to me) accosted Wrong Booth Guy, and then stormed out of the Station. . . . I do not recognize myself in photos or videos. I can't recognize my step-sons in the soccer pick-up line; I failed to determine which husband was mine at a party, in the mall, at the market.

Her inability to recognize faces means that people sometimes perceive her as snobby or aloof. "Why did you walk past me?" a neighbor might later ask. Similar to those of us with hearing loss who fake hearing during trite social conversation, Sellers sometimes fakes recognition. She often smiles at people she passes, in case she knows them. Or she pretends to know the person with whom she is talking. (To avoid the stress associated with such perception failures, people with serious hearing loss or with prosopagnosia often shy away from busy social situations.) But there is an upside: When encountering someone who previously irritated her, she typically won't feel ill will, because she doesn't recognize the person.

Unlike Sellers, most of us have a functioning area on the underside of our brain's right hemisphere that helps us recognize a familiar human face as soon as we detect it—in only one-seventh of a second (Jacques & Rossion, 2006). This ability illustrates a broader principle. *Nature's sensory gifts enable each animal to obtain essential information.* Some examples:

- Frogs, which feed on flying insects, have cells in their eyes that fire only in response to small, dark, moving objects. A frog could starve to death knee-deep in motionless flies. But let one zoom by and the frog's "bug detector" cells snap awake.

- Male silkworm moths' odor receptors can detect one-billionth of an ounce of sex attractant per second released by a female one mile away. That is why there continue to be silkworms.

- Human ears are most sensitive to sound frequencies that include human voices, especially a baby's cry.

In this chapter, we'll look more closely at what psychologists have learned about how we sense and perceive the world around us. We begin with some basic principles.

"Time's fun when you're having flies."
Kermit the Frog

FIGURE 6.1

What's going on here? Our sensory and perceptual processes work together to help us sort out the complex images, including the hidden couple in Sandro Del-Prete's drawing, *The Flowering of Love.*

Basic Principles of Sensation and Perception

6-1: What are *sensation* and *perception?* What do we mean by *bottom-up processing* and *top-down processing?*

Sellers' curious mix of "perfect vision" and face blindness illustrates the distinction between *sensation* and *perception.* When she looks at a friend, her **sensation** is normal: Her sensory receptors detect the same information yours would, and her nervous system transmits that information to her brain. And her **perception**—the processes by which her brain organizes and interprets sensory input—is *almost* normal. Thus, she may recognize people from their hair, gait, voice, or particular physique, just not their face. Her experience is much like the struggle you or I would have trying to recognize a specific penguin.

In our everyday experiences, sensation and perception blend into one continuous process. In this chapter, we slow down that process to study its parts. In real life, our sensory and perceptual processes work together to help us decipher the world around us.

- Our **bottom-up processing** starts at the sensory receptors and works up to higher levels of processing.
- Our **top-down processing** constructs perceptions from the sensory input by drawing on our experience and expectations.

As our brain absorbs the information in **FIGURE 6.1**, bottom-up processing enables our sensory systems to detect the lines, angles, and colors that form the flower and leaves. Using top-down processing we interpret what our senses detect.

But *how* do we do it? How do we create meaning from the blizzard of sensory stimuli bombarding our bodies 24 hours a day? Meanwhile, in a silent, cushioned, inner world, our brain floats in utter darkness. By itself, it sees nothing. It hears nothing. It feels nothing. *So, how does the world out there get in?* To phrase the question scientifically: How do we construct our representations of the external world? How do a campfire's flicker, crackle, and smoky scent activate neural connections? And how, from this living neurochemistry, do we create our conscious experience of the fire's motion and temperature, its aroma and beauty? In search of answers to such questions, let's look at some processes that cut across all our sensory systems.

Transduction

6-2: What three steps are basic to all our sensory systems?

Every second of every day, our sensory systems perform an amazing feat: They convert one form of energy into another. Vision processes light energy. Hearing processes sound waves. All our senses

- *receive* sensory stimulation, often using specialized receptor cells.
- *transform* that stimulation into neural impulses.
- *deliver* the neural information to our brain.

The process of converting one form of energy into another that your brain can use is called **transduction.** Later in this chapter, we'll focus on individual sensory systems. How do we see? Hear? Feel pain? Taste? Smell? Keep our balance? In each case, we'll consider these three steps—receiving, transforming, and delivering the information to the brain.

First, though, let's explore some strengths and weaknesses in our ability to detect and interpret stimuli in the vast sea of energy around us.

sensation the process by which our sensory receptors and nervous system receive and represent stimulus energies from our environment.

perception the process of organizing and interpreting sensory information, enabling us to recognize meaningful objects and events.

bottom-up processing analysis that begins with the sensory receptors and works up to the brain's integration of sensory information.

top-down processing information processing guided by higher-level mental processes, as when we construct perceptions drawing on our experience and expectations.

transduction conversion of one form of energy into another. In sensation, the transforming of stimulus energies, such as sights, sounds, and smells, into neural impulses our brain can interpret.

RETRIEVE IT

• What is the rough distinction between sensation and perception?

ANSWER: *Sensation* is the bottom-up process by which the physical sensory system receives and represents stimuli. *Perception* is the top-down mental process of organizing and interpreting sensory input.

absolute threshold the minimum stimulation needed to detect a particular stimulus 50 percent of the time.

signal detection theory a theory predicting how and when we detect the presence of a faint stimulus *(signal)* amid background stimulation *(noise)*. Assumes there is no single absolute threshold and that detection depends partly on a person's experience, expectations, motivation, and alertness.

Thresholds

6-3: What are the *absolute* and *difference thresholds,* and do stimuli below the absolute threshold have any influence on us?

At this moment, you and I are being struck by X-rays and radio waves, ultraviolet and infrared light, and sound waves of very high and very low frequencies. To all of these we are blind and deaf. Other animals with differing needs detect a world that lies beyond our experience. Migrating birds stay on course aided by an internal magnetic compass. Bats and dolphins locate prey using sonar, bouncing echoing sound off objects. Bees navigate on cloudy days by detecting invisible (to us) polarized light.

The shades on our own senses are open just a crack, allowing us a restricted awareness of this vast sea of energy. But for our needs, this is enough.

Absolute Thresholds

To some kinds of stimuli we are exquisitely sensitive. Standing atop a mountain on an utterly dark, clear night, most of us could see a candle flame atop another mountain 30 miles away. We could feel the wing of a bee falling on our cheek. We could smell a single drop of perfume in a three-room apartment (Galanter, 1962).

German scientist and philosopher Gustav Fechner (1801–1887) studied our awareness of these faint stimuli and called them our **absolute thresholds**—the minimum stimulation necessary to detect a particular light, sound, pressure, taste, or odor 50 percent of the time. To test your absolute threshold for sounds, a hearing specialist would expose each of your ears to varying sound levels (**FIGURE 6.2**). For each tone, the test would define where half the time you could detect the sound and half the time you could not. That 50-50 point would define your absolute threshold.

Detecting a weak stimulus, or signal, depends not only on the signal's strength (such as a hearing-test tone) but also on our psychological state—our experience, expectations, motivation, and alertness. **Signal detection theory** predicts when we will detect weak signals (measured as our ratio of "hits" to "false alarms"). Lonely, anxious people at speed-dating events tend to respond with a low threshold and thus can be unselective

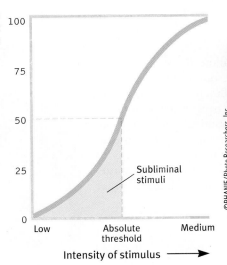

Percentage of correct detections

100

75

50

25

0

Low   Absolute threshold   Medium

Subliminal stimuli

Intensity of stimulus ⟶

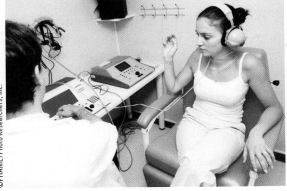

©PHANIE/Photo Researchers, Inc.

FIGURE 6.2
Absolute threshold
Can I detect this sound? An *absolute threshold* is the intensity at which a person can detect a stimulus half the time. Hearing tests locate these thresholds for various frequency levels.

© Inspirestock/Corbis

Signal detection

"The heart has its reasons which reason does not know."

Pascal, Pensées, *1670*

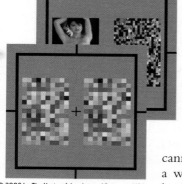

FIGURE 6.3

The hidden mind After an image of a nude man or woman was flashed to one side or another, then masked before being perceived, people's attention was unconsciously drawn to images in a way that reflected their sexual orientation (Jiang et al., 2006).

subliminal below one's absolute threshold for conscious awareness.

priming the activation, often unconsciously, of certain associations, thus predisposing one's perception, memory, or response.

difference threshold the minimum difference between two stimuli required for detection 50 percent of the time. We experience the difference threshold as a *just noticeable difference* (or *jnd*).

Weber's law the principle that, to be perceived as different, two stimuli must differ by a constant minimum percentage (rather than a constant amount).

in reaching out to potential dates (McClure et al., 2010). Signal detection theorists seek to understand why people respond differently to the same stimuli, and why the same person's reactions vary as circumstances change.

RETRIEVE IT

• What three factors will make it more likely that you detect the arrival of a text message?

ANSWER: (1) You are expecting a text. (2) It is important that you see the text and respond. (3) You are alert.

Stimuli you cannot detect 50 percent of the time are **subliminal**—below your absolute threshold (see Figure 6.2). Under certain conditions, you can be affected by stimuli so weak that you don't consciously notice them. An unnoticed image or word can reach your visual cortex and briefly **prime** your response to a later question. In a typical experiment, the image or word is quickly flashed, then replaced by a *masking stimulus* that interrupts the brain's processing before conscious perception (Van den Bussche et al., 2009). One such experiment illustrates the deep reality of sexual orientation. Researchers asked people to gaze at the center of a screen, and then flashed a photo of a nude person to one side and a scrambled version of the photo to the other side (Jiang et al., 2006). Because the images were immediately masked by a colored checkerboard, the volunteers saw nothing but flashes of color and were unable to guess where the nude had appeared. Then the researchers flashed a geometric figure to one side or the other, followed by the masking stimulus, and asked the volunteers to give the figure's angle (**FIGURE 6.3**). Straight men's answers were more accurate when the geometric figure appeared where a nude *woman* had appeared earlier. Gay men and straight women guessed more accurately when the geometric figure replaced a nude *man*. As other experiments confirm, we can evaluate a stimulus even when we are not consciously aware of it—and even when we are unaware of our evaluation (Ferguson & Zayas, 2009).

How do we feel or respond to what we do not know and cannot describe? An imperceptibly brief stimulus often triggers a weak response that *can* be detected by brain scanning (Blankenburg et al., 2003; Haynes & Rees, 2005, 2006). Only when a stimulus triggers synchronized activity in several brain areas does it reach consciousness (Dehaene, 2009). Once again we see the dual-track mind at work: *Much of our information processing occurs automatically, out of sight, off the radar screen of our conscious mind.*

So can we be controlled by subliminal messages? For more on that question, see Thinking Critically About: Can Subliminal Messages Control Our Behavior?

Difference Thresholds

To function effectively, we need absolute thresholds low enough to allow us to detect important sights, sounds, textures, tastes, and smells. We also need to detect small differences among stimuli. A musician must detect minute discrepancies when tuning an instrument. Parents must detect the sound of their own child's voice amid other children's voices. Even after living two years in Scotland, sheep *baa's* all sound alike to my ears. But not to those of ewes, which I have observed streaking, after shearing, directly to the *baa* of their lamb amid the chorus of other distressed lambs.

The **difference threshold** (or the *just noticeable difference [jnd]*) is the minimum difference a person can detect between any two stimuli half the time. That difference threshold

Eric Issele ©/Shutterstock

Can Subliminal Messages Control Our Behavior?

Hoping to penetrate our unconscious, entrepreneurs offer audio and video programs to help us lose weight, stop smoking, or improve our memories. Soothing ocean sounds may mask messages we cannot consciously hear: "I am thin"; "Smoke tastes bad"; or "I do well on tests—I have total recall of information." Such claims make two assumptions: (1) We can unconsciously sense subliminal (literally, "below threshold") stimuli. (2) Without our awareness, these stimuli have extraordinary suggestive powers. Can we? Do they?

As we have seen, subliminal *sensation* is a fact. Remember that an "absolute" threshold is merely the point at which we can detect a stimulus *half the time.* At or slightly below this threshold, we will still detect the stimulus some of the time.

But does this mean that claims of subliminal *persuasion* are also facts? The near-consensus among researchers is *No.* The laboratory research reveals a *subtle, fleeting* effect. Priming thirsty people with the subliminal word *thirst* might therefore, for a moment, make a thirst-quenching beverage ad more persuasive (Strahan et al., 2002). Likewise, priming thirsty people with Lipton Ice Tea may increase their choosing the primed brand (Karremans et al., 2006; Veltkamp et al., 2011; Verwijmeren et al., 2011a,b). But the subliminal-message hucksters claim something different: a *powerful, enduring* effect on behavior.

To test whether subliminal recordings have this enduring effect, Anthony Greenwald and his colleagues (1991, 1992) randomly assigned university students to listen daily for five weeks to commercial subliminal messages claiming to improve either self-esteem or memory. But the researchers played a practical joke and switched half the labels. Some students who thought they were receiving affirmations of self-esteem were actually hearing the memory-enhancement message. Others got the self-esteem message but thought their memory was being recharged.

Were the recordings effective? Students' test scores for self-esteem and memory, taken before and after the five weeks, revealed no effects. Yet the students *perceived* themselves receiving the benefits they *expected.* Those who *thought* they had heard a memory recording *believed* their memories had improved. Those who thought they had heard a self-esteem recording believed their self-esteem had grown. (Reading this research, one hears echoes of the testimonies that ooze from ads for such products. Some customers, having bought what is not supposed to be heard [and having indeed not heard it!] offer testimonials like, "I really know that your recordings were invaluable in reprogramming my mind.")

Over a decade, Greenwald conducted 16 double-blind experiments evaluating subliminal self-help recordings. His results were

Subliminal persuasion? Although subliminally presented stimuli *can* subtly influence people, experiments discount attempts at subliminal advertising and self-improvement. (The playful message here is not actually subliminal—because you can easily perceive it.)

uniform: Not one of the recordings helped more than a placebo (Greenwald, 1992). And placebos, you may remember, work only because we *believe* they will work.

---

increases with the size of the stimulus. Thus, if you add 1 ounce to a 10-ounce weight, you will detect the difference; add 1 ounce to a 100-ounce weight and you probably will not.

In the nineteenth century, Ernst Weber noted something so simple and so widely applicable that we still refer to it as **Weber's law.** This law states that for an average person to perceive a difference, two stimuli must differ by a constant *percentage* (not a constant *amount*). The exact percentage varies, depending on the stimulus. Two lights, for example, must differ in intensity by 8 percent. Two objects must differ in weight by 2 percent. And two tones must differ in frequency by only 0.3 percent (Teghtsoonian, 1971).

The LORD is my shepherd;
    I shall not want.
He maketh me to lie down
        in green pastures:
    he leadeth me
        beside the still waters.
He restoreth my soul:
    he leadeth me
        in the paths of righteousness
        for his name's sake.
Yea, though I walk through the valley
        of the shadow of death,
    I will fear no evil:
    for thou art with me;
        thy rod and thy staff
        they comfort me.
Thou preparest a table before me
        in the presence of mine enemies:
    thou anointest my head with oil,
        my cup runneth over.
Surely goodness and mercy
        shall follow me
        all the days of my life:
    and I will dwell
        in the house of the LORD
        for ever.

The difference threshold
In this computer-generated copy of the Twenty-third Psalm, each line of the typeface changes imperceptibly. How many lines are required for you to experience a just noticeable difference?

sensory adaptation diminished sensitivity as a consequence of constant stimulation.

perceptual set a mental predisposition to perceive one thing and not another.

"We need above all to know about changes; no one wants or needs to be reminded 16 hours a day that his shoes are on."

Neuroscientist David Hubel (1979)

FIGURE 6.4

The jumpy eye Our gaze jumps from one spot to another every third of a second or so, as eye-tracking equipment illustrated in this photograph of Edinburgh's Princes Street Gardens (Henderson, 2007). The circles represent visual fixations, and the numbers indicate the time of fixation in milliseconds (300 milliseconds = three-tenths of a second).

John M. Henderson

Sensory Adaptation

6-4: What is the function of sensory adaptation?

Entering your neighbors' living room, you smell a musty odor. You wonder how they can stand it, but within minutes you no longer notice it. **Sensory adaptation** has come to your rescue. When we are constantly exposed to a stimulus that does not change, we become less aware of it because our nerve cells fire less frequently. (To experience sensory adaptation, move your watch up your wrist an inch: You will feel it—but only for a few moments.)

Why, then, if we stare at an object without flinching, does it *not* vanish from sight? Because, unnoticed by us, our eyes are always moving (**FIGURE 6.4**). This continual flitting from one spot to another ensures that stimulation on the eyes' receptors continually changes.

What if we actually could stop our eyes from moving? Would sights seem to vanish, as odors do? To find out, psychologists have devised ingenious instruments that maintain a constant image on the eye's inner surface. Imagine that we have fitted a volunteer, Mary, with one of these instruments—a miniature projector mounted on a contact lens (**FIGURE 6.5a**). When Mary's eye moves, the image from the projector moves as well. So everywhere that Mary looks, the scene is sure to go.

If we project images through this instrument, what will Mary see? At first, she will see the complete image. But within a few seconds, as her sensory system begins to fatigue, things get weird. Bit by bit, the image vanishes, only to reappear and then disappear—often in fragments (Figure 6.5b).

Although sensory adaptation reduces our sensitivity to constant stimulation, it offers an important benefit: freedom to focus on *informative* changes in our environment without being distracted by background chatter. Stinky or heavily perfumed people don't notice their odor because, like you and me, they adapt to what's constant and detect only change. Our sensory receptors are alert to novelty; bore them with repetition and they free our attention for more important things. We will see this principle again and again: *We perceive the world not exactly as it is, but as it is useful for us to perceive it.*

Our sensitivity to changing stimulation helps explain television's attention-grabbing power. Cuts, edits, zooms, pans, sudden noises—all demand attention. The phenomenon is irresistible even to TV researchers. One noted that even during interesting conversations, "I cannot for the life of me stop from periodically glancing over to the screen" (Tannenbaum, 2002).

Sensory adaptation and sensory thresholds are important ingredients in our perceptions of the world around us. Much of what we perceive comes not just from what's "out there" but also from what's behind our eyes and between our ears.

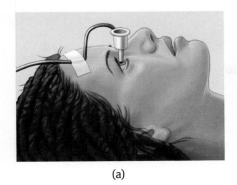
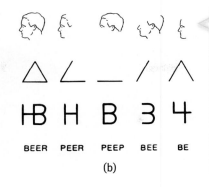

RETRIEVE IT

- Why is it that after wearing shoes for a while, you cease to notice them (until questions like this draw your attention back to them)?

ANSWER: The shoes provide constant stimulation. *Sensory adaptation* allows us to focus on changing stimuli.

Perceptual Set

6-5: How do our expectations, contexts, emotions, and motivation influence our perceptions?

As everyone knows, to see is to believe. As we less fully appreciate, to believe is to see. Through experience, we come to expect certain results. Those expectations may give us a **perceptual set,** a set of mental tendencies and assumptions that affects (top-down) what we hear, taste, feel, and see.

Consider: Is the middle image in **FIGURE 6.6** a man playing a saxophone or a woman's face? What we see in such a drawing can be influenced by first looking at either of the two unambiguous versions (Boring, 1930).

Everyday examples of perceptual set abound. In 1972, a British newspaper published unretouched photographs of a "monster" in Scotland's Loch Ness—"the most amazing pictures ever taken," stated the paper. If this information creates in you the same expectations it did in most of the paper's readers, you, too, will see the monster in the photo in **FIGURE 6.7** on the next page. But when a skeptical researcher approached the photos with different expectations, he saw a curved tree trunk—as had others the day the photo was shot (Campbell, 1986). With this different perceptual set, you may now notice that the object is floating motionless, with no ripples in the water around it—hardly what we would expect of a lively monster.

FIGURE 6.6
Perceptual set Show a friend either the left or right image. Then show the center image and ask, "What do you see?" Whether your friend reports seeing a saxophonist or a woman's face may depend on which of the other two drawings was viewed first. In each of those images, the meaning is clear, and it will establish perceptual expectations.

FIGURE 6.7
Believing is seeing What do you perceive? Is this Nessie, the Loch Ness monster, or a log?

Frank Searle, photo Adams/Corbis-Sygma

When shown the phrase
*Mary had a
a little lamb*
many people perceive what they expect, and miss the repeated word. Did you?

"We hear and apprehend only what we already half know."

Henry David Thoreau, Journal, 1860

Perceptual set can also affect what we hear. Consider the kindly airline pilot who, on a takeoff run, looked over at his depressed co-pilot and said, "Cheer up." Expecting to hear the usual "Gear up," the co-pilot promptly raised the wheels—before they left the ground (Reason & Mycielska, 1982).

Perceptual set similarly affects taste. One experiment invited bar patrons to sample free beer (Lee et al., 2006). When researchers added a few drops of vinegar to a brand-name beer, the tasters preferred it—unless they had been told they were drinking vinegar-laced beer. Then they expected, and usually experienced, a worse taste. In another experiment, preschool children, by a 6-to-1 margin, thought french fries tasted better when served in a McDonald's bag rather than a plain white bag (Robinson et al., 2007).

What determines our perceptual set? As Chapter 4 explained, through experience we form concepts, or *schemas,* that organize and interpret unfamiliar information. Our preexisting schemas for male saxophonists and women's faces, for monsters and tree trunks, all influence how we interpret ambiguous sensations with top-down processing.

In everyday life, stereotypes about gender (another instance of perceptual set) can color perception. Without the obvious cues of pink or blue, people will struggle over whether to call the new baby "he" or "she." But told an infant is "David," people (especially children) may perceive "him" as bigger and stronger than if the same infant is called "Diana" (Stern & Karraker, 1989). Some differences, it seems, exist merely in the eyes of their beholders.

Context Effects

A given stimulus may trigger radically different perceptions, partly because of our differing perceptual set, but also because of the immediate context. Some examples:

● Imagine hearing a noise interrupted by the words "eel is on the wagon." Likely, you would actually perceive the first word as *wheel*. Given "eel is on the orange," you

Culture and context effects What is above the woman's head? In one study, nearly all the East Africans who were questioned said the woman was balancing a metal box or can on her head and that the family was sitting under a tree. Westerners, for whom head-carrying is less common and corners and boxlike architecture are more common, were more likely to perceive the family as being indoors, with the woman sitting under a window. (Adapted from Gregory & Gombrich, 1973.)

would more likely hear *peel*. This curious phenomenon, discovered by Richard Warren, suggests that the brain can work backward in time to allow a later stimulus to determine how we perceive an earlier one. The context creates an expectation that, top-down, influences our perception (Grossberg, 1995).

- Does the pursuing monster in **FIGURE 6.8** look aggressive? Does the identical pursued one seem frightened? If so, you are experiencing a context effect.

- How tall is the shorter player in **FIGURE 6.9**? Here again, context creates expectations.

From Shepard (1990)

FIGURE 6.8
The interplay between context and emotional perception The context makes the pursuing monster look more aggressive than the pursued. It isn't.

Denis R. J. Geppert *Holland Sentinel.*

FIGURE 6.9
Big and "little" The "little guy" shown here is actually a 6'9" former Hope College basketball center who would tower over most of us. But he seemed like a short player when matched in a semi-pro game against the world's tallest basketball player at that time, 7'9" Sun Ming Ming from China.

Motivation and Emotion

Perceptions are also influenced, top-down, by our motivation and emotions.

Desired objects, such as a water bottle when thirsty, seem closer (Balcetis & Dunning, 2010). This perceptual bias energizes our going for it. Our motives also direct our perception of ambiguous images (**FIGURE 6.10**).

When angry, people more often perceive neutral objects as guns (Baumann & DeSteno, 2010). Dennis Proffitt (2006a,b; Schnall et al., 2008) and others have demonstrated the power of emotions with other clever experiments showing that

- walking destinations look farther away to those fatigued by prior exercise.

- a hill looks steeper to those who are wearing a heavy backpack or have just been exposed to sad, heavy classical music rather than light, bouncy music. As with so many of life's challenges, a hill also seems less steep to those with a friend beside them.

- a target seems farther away to those throwing a heavy rather than a light object at it.

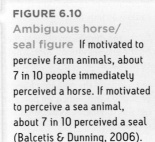

FIGURE 6.10
Ambiguous horse/ seal figure If motivated to perceive farm animals, about 7 in 10 people immediately perceived a horse. If motivated to perceive a sea animal, about 7 in 10 perceived a seal (Balcetis & Dunning, 2006).

"Ambiguity of form: Old and new" by G. H. Fisher, 1968, *Perception and Psychophysics*, 4, 189–192. Copyright 1968 by Psychonomic Society, Inc.

"When you're hitting the ball, it comes at you looking like a grapefruit. When you're not, it looks like a blackeyed pea."

Former Major League Baseball player George Scott

Even a softball appears bigger when you are hitting well, observed Jessica Witt and Proffitt (2005), after asking players to choose a circle the size of the ball they had just hit well or poorly.

Emotions can also color our social perceptions. Spouses who feel loved and appreciated perceive less threat in stressful marital events—"He's just having a bad day" (Murray et al., 2003). Professional referees, if told a soccer team has a history of aggressive behavior, will assign more penalty cards when watching videotaped fouls (Jones et al., 2002).

RETRIEVE IT

• In the context of sensation and perception, what does it mean to say that "believing is seeing"?

ANSWER: Because of *perceptual set*, our experiences, assumptions, and expectations sculpt our views of reality.

• Does *perceptual set* involve bottom-up or top-down processing? Why?

ANSWER: It involves top-down processing, drawing on our experiences, assumptions, and expectations.

Vision

Our eyes receive light energy and transduce (transform) it into neural messages that our brain then processes into what we consciously see. How does such a taken-for-granted yet remarkable thing happen?

The Stimulus Input: Light Energy

6-6: What is the energy that we see as visible light?

When you look at a bright red tulip, what strikes your eyes is not particles of the color red but pulses of electromagnetic energy that your visual system perceives as red. What we see as visible light is but a thin slice of the whole spectrum of electromagnetic energy, ranging from imperceptibly short gamma waves to the long waves of radio transmission (**FIGURE 6.11**). Other organisms are sensitive to differing portions of the spectrum. Bees, for instance, cannot see what we perceive as red but can see ultraviolet light.

Two physical characteristics of light help determine our sensory experience. Light's **wavelength**—the distance from one wave peak to the next (**FIGURE 6.12a**)—determines its **hue** (the color we experience, such as a tulip's red petals or green leaves). **Intensity,** the amount of energy in light waves (determined by a wave's *amplitude,* or height), influences brightness (Figure 6.12b). To understand *how* we transform physical energy into color and meaning, we first need to understand vision's window, the eye.

The Eye

6-7: How does the eye transform light energy into neural messages, and how do the eye and brain process that information?

Light enters the eye through the *cornea,* which protects the eye and bends light to provide focus (**FIGURE 6.13**). The light then passes through the *pupil,* a small adjustable opening surrounded by the *iris,* a colored muscle that controls the size of the pupil by dilating or constricting in response to light intensity and even to inner emotions. (When we're feeling amorous, our telltale dilated pupils and dark eyes subtly signal our interest.) Each iris is so distinctive that an iris-scanning machine can confirm our identity.

wavelength the distance from the peak of one light or sound wave to the peak of the next. Electromagnetic wavelengths vary from the short blips of cosmic rays to the long pulses of radio transmission.

hue the dimension of color that is determined by the wavelength of light; what we know as the color names *blue, green,* and so forth.

intensity the amount of energy in a light or sound wave, which we perceive as brightness or loudness, as determined by the wave's amplitude.

retina the light-sensitive inner surface of the eye, containing the receptor rods and cones plus layers of neurons that begin the processing of visual information.

accommodation the process by which the eye's lens changes shape to focus near or far objects on the retina.

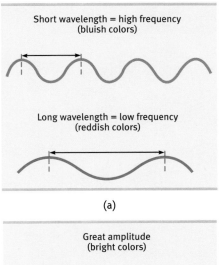

FIGURE 6.11

The wavelengths we see What we see as light is only a tiny slice of a wide spectrum of electromagnetic energy, which ranges from gamma rays as short as the diameter of an atom to radio waves over a mile long. The wavelengths visible to the human eye (shown enlarged) extend from the shorter waves of blue-violet light to the longer waves of red light.

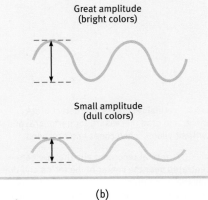

FIGURE 6.12

The physical properties of waves (a) Waves vary in wavelength (the distance between successive peaks). Frequency, the number of complete wavelengths that can pass a point in a given time, depends on the wavelength. The shorter the wavelength, the higher the frequency. (b) Waves also vary in amplitude (the height from peak to trough). Wave amplitude determines the intensity of colors.

Behind the pupil is a transparent *lens* that focuses incoming light rays into an image on the **retina,** a multilayered tissue on the eyeball's sensitive inner surface. The lens focuses the rays by changing its curvature and thickness, in a process called **accommodation.**

For centuries, scientists knew that when an image of a candle passes through a small opening, it casts an inverted mirror image on a dark wall behind. If the image passing through the pupil casts this sort of upside-down image on the retina, as in Figure 6.13, how can we see the world right side up? Eventually, the answer became clear: The retina doesn't "see" a whole image. Rather, its millions of receptor cells convert particles of light energy into neural impulses and forward those to the brain. *There,* the impulses are reassembled into a perceived, upright-seeming image.

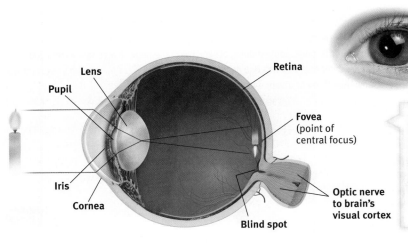

FIGURE 6.13

The eye Light rays reflected from a candle pass through the cornea, pupil, and lens. The curvature and thickness of the lens change to bring nearby or distant objects into focus on the retina. Rays from the top of the candle strike the bottom of the retina, and those from the left side of the candle strike the right side of the retina. The candle's image on the retina thus appears upside-down and reversed.

FIGURE 6.14
The retina's reaction to light

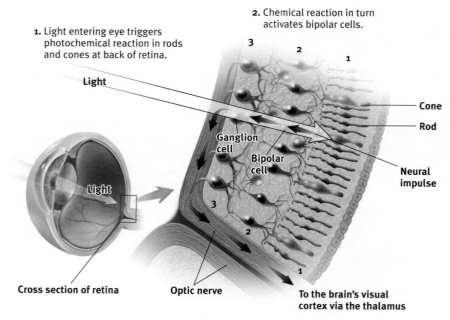

1. Light entering eye triggers photochemical reaction in rods and cones at back of retina.

2. Chemical reaction in turn activates bipolar cells.

Light

Cone

Rod

Ganglion cell

Bipolar cell

Neural impulse

Light

Cross section of retina

Optic nerve

To the brain's visual cortex via the thalamus

3. Bipolar cells then activate the ganglion cells, the axons of which converge to form the optic nerve. This nerve transmits information to the visual cortex (via the thalamus) in the brain.

rods retinal receptors that detect black, white, and gray; necessary for peripheral and twilight vision, when cones don't respond.

cones retinal receptor cells that are concentrated near the center of the retina and that function in daylight or in well-lit conditions. The cones detect fine detail and give rise to color sensations.

optic nerve the nerve that carries neural impulses from the eye to the brain.

blind spot the point at which the optic nerve leaves the eye, creating a "blind" spot because no receptor cells are located there.

fovea the central focal point in the retina, around which the eye's cones cluster.

Visual Information Processing

If you could follow a single light-energy particle to the back of your eye, you would first make your way through the retina's outer layer of cells to its buried receptor cells, the **rods** and **cones** (**FIGURE 6.14**). There, you would see the light energy trigger chemical changes that would spark neural signals, activating nearby *bipolar cells.* The bipolar cells in turn would activate the neighboring *ganglion cells,* whose axons twine together like the strands of a rope to form the **optic nerve.** That nerve will carry the information to your brain, where your thalamus stands ready to distribute the information. The optic nerve can send nearly 1 million messages at once through its nearly 1 million ganglion fibers. (The auditory nerve, which enables hearing, carries much less information through its mere 30,000 fibers.) We pay a small price for this eye-to-brain highway. Where the optic nerve leaves the eye, there are no receptor cells—creating a **blind spot** (**FIGURE 6.15**). Close one eye and you won't see a black hole, however. Without seeking your approval, your brain fills in the hole.

RETRIEVE IT

• There are no receptor cells where the optic nerve leaves the eye. This creates a blind spot in your vision. To demonstrate, first close your left eye, look at the spot, and move the page to a distance from your face at which one of the cars disappears (which one do you predict it will be?). Repeat with your right eye closed—and note that now the other car disappears. Can you explain why?

ANSWER: Your blind spot is on the nose side of each retina, which means that objects to your right may fall onto the right eye's blind spot. Objects to your left may fall on the left eye's blind spot. The blind spot does not normally impair your vision, because your eyes are moving and because one eye catches what the other misses.

FIGURE 6.15
The blind spot

Rods and cones differ in where they're found and in what they do (**TABLE 6.1**). *Cones* cluster in and around the **fovea,** the retina's area of central focus (see Figure 6.13). Many have their own hotline to the brain, which devotes a large area to input from the fovea. These direct connections preserve the cones' precise information, making them better able to detect fine detail.

Rods have no such hotline; they share bipolar cells with other rods, sending combined messages. To experience this rod–cone difference in sensitivity to details, pick a word in this sentence and stare directly at it, focusing its image on the cones in your fovea. Notice that words a few inches off to the side appear blurred? Their image strikes the outer regions of your retina, where rods predominate. Thus, when driving or biking, you can detect a car in your peripheral vision well before perceiving its details.

Cones also enable you to perceive color. In dim light they become ineffectual, so you see no colors. Rods, which enable black-and-white vision, remain sensitive in dim light. Several rods will funnel their faint energy output onto a single bipolar cell. Thus, cones and rods each provide a special sensitivity—cones to detail and color, and rods to faint light.

When you enter a darkened theater or turn off the light at night, your eyes adapt. Your pupils dilate to allow more light to reach your retina, but it typically takes 20 minutes or more before your eyes fully adapt. You can demonstrate dark adaptation by closing or covering one eye for up to 20 minutes. Then make the light in the room not quite bright enough to read this book with your open eye. Now open the dark-adapted eye and read (easily). This period of dark adaptation matches the average natural twilight transition between the Sun's setting and darkness. How wonderfully made we are.

Visual information percolates through progressively more abstract levels on its path through the thalamus and on to the visual cortex. At the entry level, the retina's neural layers don't just pass along electrical impulses; they also help to encode and analyze sensory information. The third neural layer in a frog's eye, for example, contains the "bug detector" cells that fire only in response to moving fly-like stimuli. Any given retinal area relays its information to a corresponding location in the visual cortex, in the occipital lobe at the back of your brain (**FIGURE 6.16**).

Table 6.1
Receptors in the Human Eye: Rod-Shaped Rods and Cone-Shaped Cones

	Cones	Rods
Number	6 million	120 million
Location in retina	Center	Periphery
Sensitivity in dim light	Low	High
Color sensitivity	High	Low
Detail sensitivity	High	Low

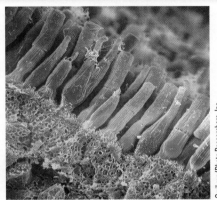

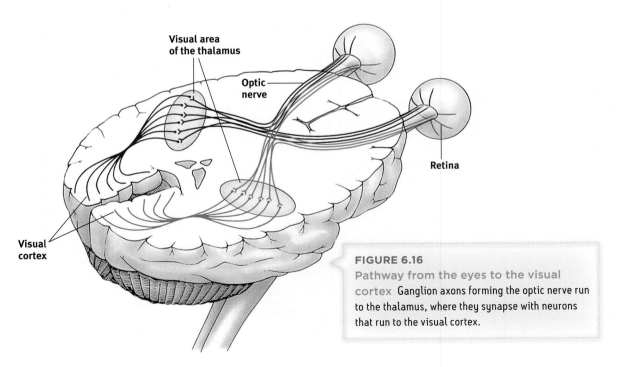

FIGURE 6.16
Pathway from the eyes to the visual cortex Ganglion axons forming the optic nerve run to the thalamus, where they synapse with neurons that run to the visual cortex.

feature detectors nerve cells in the brain that respond to specific features of the stimulus, such as shape, angle, or movement.

parallel processing the processing of many aspects of a problem simultaneously; the brain's natural mode of information processing for many functions, including vision. Contrasts with the step-by-step (serial) processing of most computers and of conscious problem solving.

The same sensitivity that enables retinal cells to fire messages can lead them to misfire, as you can demonstrate. Turn your eyes to the left, close them, and then gently rub the right side of your right eyelid with your fingertip. Note the patch of light to the left, moving as your finger moves. Why do you see light? Why at the left?

Your retinal cells are so responsive that even pressure triggers them. But your brain interprets their firing as light. Moreover, it interprets the light as coming from the left— the normal direction of light that activates the right side of the retina.

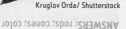

RETRIEVE IT

• Some nocturnal animals, such as toads, mice, rats, and bats, have impressive night vision thanks to having many more _____ (rods/cones) than _____ (rods/cones) in their retinas. These creatures probably have very poor _____ (color/black-and-white) vision.

Kruglov Orda/ Shutterstock

ANSWERS: rods; cones; color

• Cats are also able to open their _____ much wider than we can, which allows more light into their eyes so they can see better at night.

ANSWER: pupils

Feature Detection

David Hubel and Torsten Wiesel (1979) received a Nobel Prize for their work on **feature detectors.** These specialized neurons in the occipital lobe's visual cortex receive information from individual ganglion cells in the retina. Feature detector cells derive their name from their ability to respond to a scene's specific visual features—to particular edges, lines, angles, and movements. These cells pass this information to other cortical areas, where teams of cells *(supercell clusters)* respond to more complex patterns. As we noted earlier, one temporal lobe area by your right ear (**FIGURE 6.17**) enables you to perceive faces and, thanks to a specialized neural network, to recognize them from varied viewpoints (Connor, 2010). If this region were damaged, you might recognize other forms and objects, but, like Heather Sellers, not familiar faces. When researchers temporarily disrupt the brain's face-processing areas with magnetic pulses, people cannot recognize faces.

They will, however, be able to recognize houses, because the brain's face perception occurs separately from its object perception (McKone et al., 2007; Pitcher et al., 2007). Thus, functional MRI (fMRI) scans show different brain areas activating when people view varied objects (Downing et al., 2001). Brain activity is so specific (**FIGURE 6.18**) that, with the help of brain scans, "we can tell if a person is looking at a shoe, a chair, or a face, based on the pattern of their brain activity," noted one researcher (Haxby, 2001).

Research shows that for biologically important objects and events, monkey brains (and surely ours as well) have a "vast visual encyclopedia" distributed as specialized cells (Perrett et al., 1988, 1992, 1994). These cells respond to one type of stimulus, such as a specific gaze, head angle, posture, or body movement. Other supercell clusters integrate this information and fire only when the cues collectively indicate the direction of someone's attention and approach. This instant analysis, which aided our ancestors' survival, also helps a soccer goalkeeper anticipate the direction of an impending kick, and a driver anticipate a pedestrian's next movement.

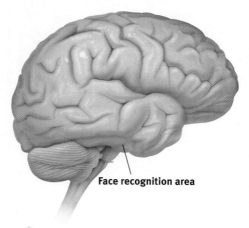

FIGURE 6.17

Face recognition processing In social animals such as humans, a dedicated brain system (shown here in a right-facing brain) assigns considerable neural bandwidth to the crucial task of face recognition.

Face recognition area

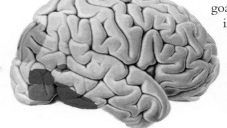

FIGURE 6.18

The telltale brain Looking at faces, houses, and chairs activates different brain areas in this right-facing brain.

■ Faces   ■ Chairs
■ Houses   ■ Houses and chairs

Reuters/Claro Cortes IV (China)

Well-developed supercells In this 2007 World Cup match, Brazil's Marta instantly processed visual information about the positions and movements of Australia's defenders and goalkeeper (Melissa Barbieri) and somehow managed to get the ball around them all and into the net.

Parallel Processing

Our brain achieves these and other remarkable feats by means of **parallel processing:** doing many things at once. To analyze a visual scene, the brain divides it into subdimensions—color, motion, form, depth—and works on each aspect simultaneously (Livingstone & Hubel, 1988). We then construct our perceptions by integrating the separate but parallel work of these different visual teams (**FIGURE 6.19**).

To recognize a face, your brain integrates information projected by your retinas to several visual cortex areas, compares it to stored information, and enables you to recognize the face: *Grandmother!* Scientists are debating whether this stored information is contained in a single cell or distributed over a network. Some supercells—"grandmother cells"—do appear to respond very selectively to 1 or 2 faces in 100 (Bowers, 2009). The whole face recognition process requires tremendous brain power—30 percent of the cortex (10 times the brain area devoted to hearing).

Destroy or disable a neural workstation for a visual subtask, and something peculiar results, as happened to "Mrs. M." (Hoffman, 1998). Since a stroke damaged areas near the rear of both sides of her brain, she has been unable to perceive movement. People in a room seem "suddenly here or there but I have not seen them moving." Pouring tea into a cup is a challenge because the fluid appears frozen—she cannot perceive it rising in the cup.

After stroke or surgery damage to the brain's visual cortex, others have experienced *blindsight* (a phenomenon we met in Chapter 3). Shown a series of sticks, they report seeing nothing. Yet when asked to guess whether the sticks are vertical or horizontal, their visual intuition typically offers the correct response. When told, "You got them all right," they are astounded. There is, it seems, a second "mind"—a parallel processing system—operating unseen. These separate visual systems for perception and action illustrate dual processing—the two-track mind.

Color   Motion   Form   Depth

FIGURE 6.19
Parallel processing Studies of patients with brain damage suggest that the brain delegates the work of processing color, motion, form, and depth to different areas. After taking a scene apart, the brain integrates these subdimensions into the perceived image. How does the brain do this? The answer to this question is the Holy Grail of vision research.

★ ★ ★

Think about the wonders of visual processing. As you look at that tiger in the zoo, information entering your eyes is transformed into millions of neural impulses sent up to your brain. Various brain areas focus on different aspects of the tiger's image. Finally, in some as yet mysterious way, these separate teams pool their work to produce a meaningful image. You compare this with previously stored images and recognize it—a crouching tiger (**FIGURE 6.20**).

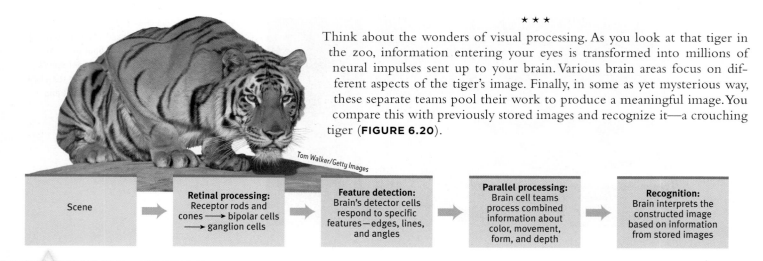

Tom Walker/Getty Images

| Scene | → | **Retinal processing:** Receptor rods and cones ⟶ bipolar cells ⟶ ganglion cells | → | **Feature detection:** Brain's detector cells respond to specific features—edges, lines, and angles | → | **Parallel processing:** Brain cell teams process combined information about color, movement, form, and depth | → | **Recognition:** Brain interprets the constructed image based on information from stored images |

FIGURE 6.20
A simplified summary of visual information processing

"I am . . . wonderfully made."

King David, Psalm 139:14

Think, too about what is happening as you read this page. The printed squiggles are transmitted by reflected light rays onto your retina, which triggers a process that sends formless nerve impulses to several areas of your brain, which integrates the information and decodes meaning, thus completing the transfer of information across time and space from my mind to your mind. That all of this happens instantly, effortlessly, and continuously is indeed awesome. As Roger Sperry (1985) observed, the "insights of science give added, not lessened, reasons for awe, respect, and reverence."

RETRIEVE IT

• What is the rapid sequence of events that occurs when you see and recognize a friend?

ANSWER: Light waves reflect off the person and travel into your eye, where the receptor cells in your retina convert the light waves' energy into neural impulses sent to your brain. Your brain processes the subdimensions of this visual input—including color, depth, movement, and form—separately but simultaneously. It interprets this information based on previously stored information and your expectations into a conscious perception of your friend.

Color Vision

6-8: What theories help us understand color vision?

We talk as though objects possess color: "A tomato is red." Perhaps you have pondered the old question, "If a tree falls in the forest and no one hears it, does it make a sound?" We can ask the same of color: If no one sees the tomato, is it red?

The answer is *No*. First, the tomato is everything *but* red, because it *rejects* (reflects) the long wavelengths of red. Second, the tomato's color is our mental construction. As Isaac Newton (1704) noted, "The [light] rays are not colored." Color, like all aspects of vision, resides not in the object but in the theater of our brains, as evidenced by our dreaming in color.

"Only mind has sight and hearing; all things else are deaf and blind."

Epicharmus, Fragments, 550 B.C.E.

One of vision's most basic and intriguing mysteries is how we see the world in color. How, from the light energy striking the retina, does the brain manufacture our experience of color—and of such a multitude of colors? Our difference threshold for colors is so low that we can discriminate more than 1 million different color variations (Neitz et al., 2001). At least most of us can. For about 1 person in 50, vision is color deficient—and that person is usually male, because the defect is genetically sex linked.

Modern detective work on the mystery of color vision began in the nineteenth century, when Hermann von Helmholtz built on the insights of an English physicist, Thomas Young. Knowing that any color can be created by combining the light waves of three primary colors—red, green, and blue—Young and von Helmholtz inferred that the eye must have three corresponding types of color receptors. Years later, researchers measured the response of various cones to different color stimuli and confirmed the **Young-Helmholtz trichromatic (three-color) theory,** which implies that the receptors do their color magic in teams of three. Indeed, the retina has three types of color receptors, each especially sensitive to one of three colors. And those colors are, in fact, red, green, and blue. When we stimulate combinations of these cones, we see other colors. For example, there are no receptors especially sensitive to yellow. We see yellow when mixing red and green light, which stimulates both red-sensitive and green-sensitive cones.

Most people with color-deficient vision are not actually "colorblind." They simply lack functioning red- or green-sensitive cones, or sometimes both. Their vision—perhaps unknown to them, because their lifelong vision *seems* normal—is monochromatic (one-color) or dichromatic (two-color) instead of trichromatic, making it impossible to distinguish the red and green in **FIGURE 6.21**. Dogs, too, lack receptors for the wavelengths of red, giving them only limited, dichromatic color vision (Neitz et al., 1989).

But how is it that people blind to red and green can often still see yellow? And why does yellow appear to be a pure color and not a mixture of red and green, the way purple is of red and blue? As Ewald Hering soon noted, trichromatic theory leaves some parts of the color vision mystery unsolved.

Hering, a physiologist, had found a clue in *afterimages.* Stare at a green square for a while and then look at a white sheet of paper, and you will see red, green's *opponent color.* Stare at a yellow square and its opponent color, blue, will appear on the white paper. (To experience this, try the flag demonstration in **FIGURE 6.22.**) Hering surmised that there must be two additional color processes, one responsible for red-versus-green perception, and one for blue-versus-yellow.

Indeed, a century later, researchers also confirmed Hering's **opponent-process theory.** Three sets of opponent retinal processes—*red-green, yellow-blue,* and *white-black*—enable color vision. In the retina and in the thalamus (where impulses from the retina are relayed en route to the visual cortex), some neurons are "turned on" by red but "turned off" by green. Others are turned on by green but off by red (DeValois & DeValois, 1975). Like red and green marbles sent down a narrow tube, "red" and "green" messages cannot both travel at once. Red and green are thus opponents, so we do not experience a reddish green. But red and blue travel in separate channels, so we *can* see a reddish-blue magenta.

James P. Gilman, C.R.A. / Phototake

FIGURE 6.21
Color-deficient vision The bottom photo shows how people with deficient red-green vision would perceive this scene.

Young-Helmholtz trichromatic (three-color) theory the theory that the retina contains three different color receptors—one most sensitive to red, one to green, one to blue—which, when stimulated in combination, can produce the perception of any color.

opponent-process theory the theory that opposing retinal processes (red-green, yellow-blue, white-black) enable color vision. For example, some cells are stimulated by green and inhibited by red; others are stimulated by red and inhibited by green.

FIGURE 6.22
Afterimage effect Stare at the center of the flag for a minute and then shift your eyes to the dot in the white space beside it. What do you see? (After tiring your neural response to black, green, and yellow, you should see their opponent colors.) Stare at a white wall and note how the size of the flag grows with the projection distance!

How then do we explain afterimages, such as in the flag demonstration? By staring at green, we tire our green response. When we then stare at white (which contains all colors, including red), only the red part of the green-red pairing will fire normally.

The present solution to the mystery of color vision is therefore roughly this: Color processing occurs in two stages. The retina's red, green, and blue cones respond in varying degrees to different color stimuli, as the Young-Helmholtz trichromatic theory suggested. Their responses are then processed by opponent-process cells, as Hering's theory proposed.

RETRIEVE IT

• What are two key theories of color vision? Are they contradictory or complementary? Explain.

ANSWER: The *Young-Helmholtz trichromatic theory* shows that the retina contains color receptors for red, green, and blue. The *opponent-process theory* shows that we have opponent-process cells in the retina and thalamus for red-green, yellow-blue, and white-black. These theories are complementary and outline the two stages of color vision: (1) The retina's receptors for red, green, and blue respond to different color stimuli. (2) The receptors' signals are then processed by the opponent-process cells on their way to the visual cortex in the brain.

Visual Organization

6-9: How did the Gestalt psychologists understand perceptual organization, and how do figure-ground and grouping principles contribute to our perceptions?

It's one thing to understand how we see shapes and colors. But how do we organize and interpret those sights (or sounds or tastes or smells) so that they become meaningful perceptions—a rose in bloom, a familiar face, a sunset?

FIGURE 6.23

A Necker cube What do you see: circles with white lines, or a cube? If you stare at the cube, you may notice that it reverses location, moving the tiny X in the center from the front edge to the back. At times, the cube may seem to float in front of the page, with circles behind it. At other times, the circles may become holes in the page through which the cube appears, as though it were floating behind the page. There is far more to perception than meets the eye. (From Bradley et al., 1976.)

Early in the twentieth century, a group of German psychologists noticed that when given a cluster of sensations, people tend to organize them into a **gestalt,** a German word meaning a "form" or a "whole." For example, look at **FIGURE 6.23**. Note that the individual elements of this figure, called a *Necker cube,* are really nothing but eight blue circles, each containing three converging white lines. When we view these elements all together, however, we see a cube that sometimes reverses direction. This phenomenon nicely illustrates a favorite saying of Gestalt psychologists: In perception, the whole may exceed the sum of its parts.

Over the years, the Gestalt psychologists demonstrated many principles we use to organize our sensations into perceptions. Underlying all of them is a fundamental truth: *Our brain does more than register information about the world.* Perception is not just opening a shutter and letting a picture print itself on the brain. We filter incoming information and construct perceptions. Mind matters.

Form Perception

Imagine designing a video-computer system that, like your eye-brain system, can recognize faces at a glance. What abilities would it need?

Figure and Ground To start with, the video-computer system would need to separate faces from their backgrounds. Likewise, in our eye-brain system, our first perceptual task is to perceive any object (the *figure*) as distinct from its surroundings (the *ground*).

gestalt an organized whole. Gestalt psychologists emphasized our tendency to integrate pieces of information into meaningful wholes.

figure-ground the organization of the visual field into objects (the *figures*) that stand out from their surroundings (the *ground*).

grouping the perceptual tendency to organize stimuli into coherent groups.

As you hear voices at a party, the one you attend to becomes the figure; all others are part of the ground. As you read, the words are the figure; the white paper is the ground. Sometimes the same stimulus can trigger more than one perception. In **FIGURE 6.24**, the **figure-ground** relationship continually reverses—but always we organize the stimulus into a figure seen against a ground.

Grouping Having discriminated figure from ground, we (and our video-computer system) must also organize the figure into a *meaningful* form. Some basic features of a scene—such as color, movement, and light-dark contrast—we process instantly and automatically (Treisman, 1987). Our minds bring order and form to stimuli by following certain rules for **grouping**. These rules, identified by the Gestalt psychologists and applied even by infants, illustrate how the perceived whole differs from the sum of its parts (Quinn et al., 2002; Rock & Palmer, 1990). Three examples:

FIGURE 6.24
Reversible figure and ground

Proximity We group nearby figures together. We see not six separate lines, but three sets of two lines.

Continuity We perceive smooth, continuous patterns rather than discontinuous ones. This pattern could be a series of alternating semicircles, but we perceive it as two continuous lines—one wavy, one straight.

Closure We fill in gaps to create a complete, whole object. Thus we assume that the circles on the left are complete but partially blocked by the (illusory) triangle. Add nothing more than little line segments to close off the circles and your brain stops constructing a triangle.

Proximity   Continuity   Closure

Such principles usually help us construct reality. Sometimes, however, they lead us astray, as when we look at the doghouse in **FIGURE 6.25.**

FIGURE 6.25
Grouping principles What's the secret to this impossible doghouse? You probably perceive this doghouse as a gestalt—a whole (though impossible) structure. Actually, your brain imposes this sense of wholeness on the picture. As Figure 6.29 shows, Gestalt grouping principles such as closure and continuity are at work here.

depth perception the ability to see objects in three dimensions although the images that strike the retina are two-dimensional; allows us to judge distance.

visual cliff a laboratory device for testing depth perception in infants and young animals.

binocular cues depth cues, such as retinal disparity, that depend on the use of two eyes.

retinal disparity a binocular cue for perceiving depth: By comparing images from the retinas in the two eyes, the brain computes distance—the greater the disparity (difference) between the two images, the closer the object.

monocular cues depth cues, such as interposition and linear perspective, available to either eye alone.

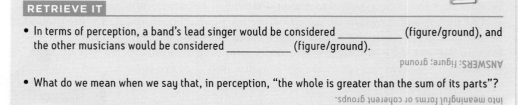

Depth Perception

6-10: How do we use binocular and monocular cues to perceive the world in three dimensions?

From the two-dimensional images falling on our retinas, we somehow organize three-dimensional perceptions. **Depth perception** enables us to estimate an object's distance from us. At a glance, we can estimate the distance of an oncoming car or the height of a house. Depth perception is partly innate, as Eleanor Gibson and Richard Walk (1960) discovered using a model of a cliff with a drop-off area (which was covered by sturdy glass). Gibson's inspiration for these **visual cliff** experiments occurred while she was picnicking on the rim of the Grand Canyon. She wondered: Would a toddler peering over the rim perceive the dangerous drop-off and draw back?

Back in their Cornell University laboratory, Gibson and Walk placed 6- to 14-month-old infants on the edge of a safe canyon and had the infants' mothers coax them to crawl out onto the glass (**FIGURE 6.26**). Most infants refused to do so, indicating that they could perceive depth.

Had they *learned* to perceive depth? Learning seems to be part of the answer because crawling, no matter when it begins, seems to increase infants' wariness of heights (Campos et al., 1992). Yet, the researchers observed, mobile newborn animals come prepared to perceive depth. Even those with virtually no visual experience—including young kittens, a day-old goat, and newly hatched chicks—will not venture across the visual cliff. Thus, it seems that biological maturation predisposes us to be wary of heights and experience amplifies that fear.

How do we do it? *How* do we transform two differing two-dimensional retinal images into a single three-dimensional perception?

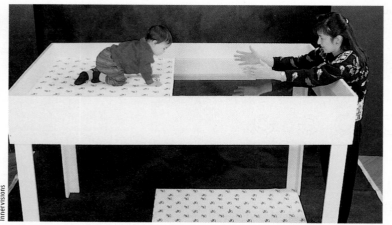

FIGURE 6.26

Visual cliff Eleanor Gibson and Richard Walk devised this miniature cliff with a glass-covered drop-off to determine whether crawling infants and newborn animals can perceive depth. Even when coaxed, infants are reluctant to venture onto the glass over the cliff.

Binocular Cues Try this: With both eyes open, hold two pens or pencils in front of you and touch their tips together. Now do so with one eye closed. With one eye, the task becomes noticeably more difficult, demonstrating the importance of **binocular cues** in judging the distance of nearby objects. Two eyes are better than one.

Because your eyes are about 2½ inches apart, your retinas receive slightly different images of the world. By comparing these two images, your brain can judge how close an object is to you. The greater the **retinal disparity,** or difference between the two images, the closer the object. Try it. Hold your two index fingers, with the tips about half an inch apart, directly in front of your nose, and your retinas will receive quite different views. If you close one eye and then the other, you can see the difference. (You may also create a finger sausage, as in **FIGURE 6.27.**) At a greater distance—say, when you hold your fingers at arm's length—the disparity is smaller.

We could easily build this feature into our video-computer system. Moviemakers can simulate or exaggerate retinal disparity by filming a scene with two cameras placed a few inches apart. Viewers then wear glasses that allow the left eye to see only the image from the left camera, and the right eye to see only the image from the right camera. The resulting 3-D effect, as 3-D movie fans know, mimics or exaggerates normal retinal disparity. Similarly, twin cameras in airplanes can take photos of terrain for integration into 3-D maps.

Monocular Cues How do we judge whether a person is 10 or 100 meters away? Retinal disparity won't help us here, because there won't be much difference between the images cast on our right and left retinas. At such distances, we depend on **monocular cues** (depth cues available to each eye separately). See **FIGURE 6.28** for some examples.

FIGURE 6.27
The floating finger sausage
Hold your two index fingers about 5 inches in front of your eyes, with their tips half an inch apart. Now look beyond them and note the weird result. Move your fingers out farther and the retinal disparity—and the finger sausage—will shrink.

Image courtesy Shaun P. Vecera, Ph.D., adapted from stimuli that appeared in Vecera et al., 2002

Relative height We perceive objects higher in our field of vision as farther away. Because we assume the lower part of a figure-ground illustration is closer, we perceive it as figure (Vecera et al., 2002). Invert this illustration and the black will become ground, like a night sky.

Relative motion As we move, objects that are actually stable may appear to move. If while riding on a bus you fix your gaze on some point—say, a house—the objects beyond the fixation point will appear to move with you. Objects in front of the point will appear to move backward. The farther an object is from the fixation point, the faster it will seem to move.

Direction of passenger's motion →

Relative size If we assume two objects are similar in size, *most* people perceive the one that casts the smaller retinal image as farther away.

Linear perspective Parallel lines appear to meet in the distance. The sharper the angle of convergence, the greater the perceived distance.

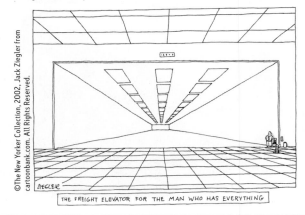

©The New Yorker Collection, 2002, Jack Ziegler from cartoonbank.com. All Rights Reserved.

Rene Magritte, *The Blank Signature*, oil on canvas, National Gallery of Art, Washington. Collection of Mr. and Mrs. Paul Mellon. Photo by Richard Carafelli.

Interposition (overlap) If one object partially blocks our view of another, we perceive it as closer. The depth cues provided by interposition make this an impossible scene.

Light and shadow Shading produces a sense of depth consistent with our assumption that light comes from above. If you invert this illustration, the hollow will become a hill.

From "Perceiving Shape From Shading" by Vilayanur S. Ramachandran. Copyright © 1988 by Scientific American, Inc. All Rights Reserved.

FIGURE 6.28
Monocular depth cues

Photo by Walter Wick. Reprinted from *GAMES* Magazine. © 1983 PCS Games Limited Partnership.

FIGURE 6.29

The solution Another view of the impossible doghouse in Figure 6.25 reveals the secrets of this illusion. From the photo angle in Figure 6.25, the grouping principle of closure leads us to perceive the boards as continuous.

"From there to here, from here to there, funny things are everywhere."

Dr. Seuss, One Fish, Two Fish, Red Fish, Blue Fish, *1960*

perceptual constancy perceiving objects as unchanging (having consistent color, brightness, shape, and size) even as illumination and retinal images change.

color constancy perceiving familiar objects as having consistent color, even if changing illumination alters the wavelengths reflected by the object.

RETRIEVE IT

• How do we normally perceive depth?

ANSWER: We are normally able to perceive depth thanks to the binocular cues that are based on our retinal disparity, and monocular cues including relative height, relative size, interposition, linear perspective, light and shadow, and relative motion.

Perceptual Constancy

6-11: How do perceptual constancies help us organize our sensations into meaningful perceptions?

So far, we have noted that our video-computer system must perceive objects as we do—as having a distinct form and location. Its next task is to recognize objects without being deceived by changes in their color, brightness, shape, or size—a top-down process called **perceptual constancy.** Regardless of the viewing angle, distance, and illumination, we can identify people and things in less time than it takes to draw a breath, a feat that challenges even advanced computers and has intrigued researchers for decades. This would be a monumental challenge for a video-computer system.

Color and Brightness Constancies Our experience of color depends on an object's *context*. If you view an isolated tomato through a paper tube, its color would seem to change as the light—and thus the wavelengths reflected from its surface—changed. But if you viewed that tomato as one item in a bowl of fresh vegetables, its color would remain roughly constant as the lighting shifts. This perception of consistent color is known as **color constancy.**

Though we take color constancy for granted, this ability is truly remarkable. A blue poker chip under indoor lighting reflects wavelengths that match those reflected by a sunlit gold chip (Jameson, 1985). Yet bring a bluebird indoors and it won't look like a goldfinch. The color is not in the bird's feathers. You and I see color thanks to our brain's computations of the light reflected by an object *relative to the objects surrounding it*. **FIGURE 6.30** dramatically illustrates the ability of a blue object to appear very different in three different contexts. Yet we have no trouble seeing these disks as blue.

Similarly, *brightness constancy* (also called *lightness constancy*) depends on context. We perceive an object as having a constant brightness even while its illumination varies. This perception of constancy depends on *relative luminance*—the amount of light an object reflects *relative to its surroundings* (**FIGURE 6.31**). White paper reflects 90 percent of the

FIGURE 6.30

Color depends on context Believe it or not, these three blue disks are identical in color (a). Remove the surrounding context and see what results (b).

R. Beau Lotto at University College, London

(a)

(b)

light falling on it; black paper, only 10 percent. Although a black paper viewed in sunlight may reflect 100 times more light than does a white paper viewed indoors, it will still look black (McBurney & Collings, 1984). But if you view sunlit black paper through a narrow tube so nothing else is visible, it may look gray, because in bright sunshine it reflects a fair amount of light. View it without the tube and it is again black, because it reflects much less light than the objects around it.

This principle—that we perceive objects not in isolation but in their environmental context—matters to artists, interior decorators, and clothing designers. Our perception of the color and brightness of a wall or of a streak of paint on a canvas is determined not just by the paint in the can but by the surrounding colors. The take-home lesson: *Comparisons govern our perceptions.*

FIGURE 6.31
Relative luminance Squares A and B are identical in color, believe it or not. (If you don't believe me, photocopy the illustration, cut out the squares, and compare.) But we perceive B as lighter, thanks to its surrounding context.

Shape and Size Constancies Sometimes an object whose actual shape cannot change *seems* to change shape with the angle of our view (**FIGURE 6.32**). More often, thanks to *shape constancy,* we perceive the form of familiar objects, such as the door in **FIGURE 6.33**, as constant even while our retinas receive changing images of them. Our brain manages this feat thanks to visual cortex neurons that rapidly learn to associate different views of an object (Li & DiCarlo, 2008).

Thanks to *size constancy,* we perceive objects as having a constant size, even while our distance from them varies. We assume a car is large enough to carry people, even when we see its tiny image from two blocks away. This assumption also illustrates the close connection between perceived *distance* and perceived *size.* Perceiving an object's distance gives us cues to its size. Likewise, knowing its general size—that the object is a car—provides us with cues to its distance.

Even in size-distance judgments, however, we consider an object's context. The monsters in Figure 6.8 cast identical images on our retinas. Using linear perspective as a cue (see Figure 6.28) our brain assumes that the pursuing monster is farther away. We therefore perceive it as larger. It isn't.

This interplay between perceived size and perceived distance helps explain several well-known illusions, including the *Moon illusion:* The Moon looks up to 50 percent larger when near the horizon than when high in the sky. Can you imagine why? For at least 22 centuries, scholars have debated this question (Hershenson, 1989). One reason is that cues to objects' distances make the horizon Moon—like the distant monster in Figure 6.8—appear farther away. If it's farther away, our brain assumes, it must be larger than the Moon high in the night sky (Kaufman & Kaufman, 2000). Take away the distance cue, by looking at the horizon Moon (or each monster) through a paper tube, and the object will immediately shrink.

Size-distance relationships also explain why in **FIGURE 6.34** on the next page the two same-age girls seem so different in size. As the diagram reveals, the girls are actually about the same size, but the room is distorted. Viewed with one eye through a peephole, the Ames room's trapezoidal walls produce the same images you would see in a normal

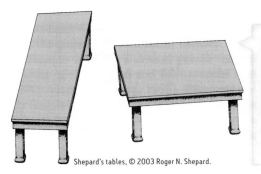

Shepard's tables, © 2003 Roger N. Shepard.

FIGURE 6.32
Perceiving shape Do the tops of these tables have different dimensions? They appear to. But—believe it or not—they are identical. (Measure and see.) With both tables, we adjust our perceptions relative to our viewing angle.

FIGURE 6.33
Shape constancy A door casts an increasingly trapezoidal image on our retinas as it opens, yet we still perceive it as rectangular.

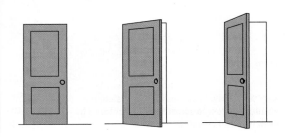

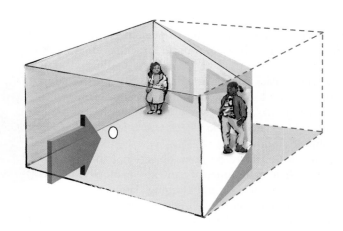

S. Schwartzenberg/The Exploratorium

FIGURE 6.34

The illusion of the shrinking and growing girls This distorted room, designed by Adelbert Ames, appears to have a normal rectangular shape when viewed through a peephole with one eye. The girl in the right corner appears disproportionately large because we judge her size based on the false assumption that she is the same distance away as the girl in the far corner.

rectangular room viewed with both eyes. Presented with the camera's one-eyed view, your brain makes the reasonable assumption that the room *is* normal and each girl is therefore the same distance from you. Given the different sizes of the girls' images on your retinas, your brain ends up calculating that the girls must be very different in size.

Perceptual illusions reinforce a fundamental lesson: Perception is not merely a projection of the world onto our brain. Rather, our sensations are disassembled into information bits that our brain then reassembles into its own functional model of the external world. During this reassembly process, our assumptions—such as the usual relationship between distance and size—can lead us astray. *Our brain constructs our perceptions.*

★ ★ ★

Form perception, depth perception, and perceptual constancies illuminate how we organize our visual experiences. Perceptual organization applies to our other senses, too. Listening to an unfamiliar language, we have trouble hearing where one word stops and the next one begins. Listening to our own language, we automatically hear distinct words. This, too, reflects perceptual organization. But it is more, for we even organize a string of letters—THEDOGATEMEAT—into words that make an intelligible phrase, more likely "The dog ate meat" than "The do gate me at" (McBurney & Collings, 1984). This process involves not only the organization we've been discussing, but also interpretation—discerning meaning in what we perceive.

Visual Interpretation

Philosophers have debated whether our perceptual abilities should be credited to our nature or our nurture. To what extent do we *learn* to perceive? German philosopher Immanuel Kant (1724–1804) maintained that knowledge comes from our *inborn* ways of organizing sensory experiences. Indeed, we come equipped to process sensory information. But British philosopher John Locke (1632–1704) argued that through our experiences we also *learn* to perceive the world. Indeed, we learn to link an object's distance with its size. So, just how important is experience? How radically does it shape our perceptual interpretations?

Experience and Visual Perception

"Let us then suppose the mind to be, as we say, white paper void of all characters, without any ideas: How comes it to be furnished? . . . To this I answer, in one word, from EXPERIENCE."

John Locke, An Essay Concerning Human Understanding, *1690*

6-12: What does research on restored vision, sensory restriction, and perceptual adaptation reveal about the effects of experience on perception?

perceptual adaptation in vision, the ability to adjust to an artificially displaced or even inverted visual field.

Restored Vision and Sensory Restriction Writing to John Locke, William Molyneux wondered whether "a man *born* blind, and now adult, taught by his *touch* to distinguish between a cube and a sphere" could, if made to see, visually distinguish the two. Locke's answer was *No,* because the man would never have *learned* to see the difference.

Molyneux's hypothetical case has since been put to the test with a few dozen adults who, though blind from birth, have gained sight (Gregory, 1978; von Senden, 1932). Most were born with cataracts—clouded lenses that allowed them to see only diffused light, rather as you might see a foggy image through a Ping-Pong ball sliced in half. After cataract surgery, the patients could distinguish figure from ground and could sense colors—suggesting that these aspects of perception are innate. But much as Locke supposed, they often could not visually recognize objects that were familiar by touch.

Seeking to gain more control than is provided by clinical cases, researchers have outfitted infant kittens and monkeys with goggles through which they could see only diffuse, unpatterned light (Wiesel, 1982). After infancy, when the goggles were removed, these animals exhibited perceptual limitations much like those of humans born with cataracts. They could distinguish color and brightness, but not the form of a circle from that of a square. Their eyes had not degenerated; their retinas still relayed signals to their visual cortex. But lacking stimulation, the cortical cells had not developed normal connections. Thus, the animals remained functionally blind to shape. Experience guides, sustains, and maintains the brain's neural organization that enables our perceptions.

In both humans and animals, similar sensory restrictions later in life do no permanent harm. When researchers cover the eye of an adult animal for several months, its vision will be unaffected after the eye patch is removed. When surgeons remove cataracts that develop during late adulthood, most people are thrilled at the return to normal vision.

The effect of sensory restriction on infant cats, monkeys, and humans suggests there is a *critical period* (Chapter 4) for normal sensory and perceptual development. Nurture sculpts what nature has endowed. In less dramatic ways, it continues to do so throughout our lives. Despite concerns about their social costs (more on this in Chapter 13), action video games sharpen spatial skills such as visual attention, eye-hand coordination and speed, and tracking multiple objects (Spence & Feng, 2010).

Perceptual Adaptation Given a new pair of glasses, we may feel slightly disoriented, even dizzy. Within a day or two, we adjust. Our **perceptual adaptation** to changed visual input makes the world seem normal again. But imagine a far more dramatic new pair of glasses—one that shifts the apparent location of objects 40 degrees to the left. When you first put them on and toss a ball to a friend, it sails off to the left. Walking forward to shake hands with the person, you veer to the left.

Could you adapt to this distorted world? Chicks cannot. When fitted with such lenses, they continue to peck where food grains *seem* to be (Hess, 1956; Rossi, 1968). But we humans adapt to distorting lenses quickly. Within a few minutes your throws would again be accurate, your stride on target. Remove the lenses and you would experience an aftereffect: At first your throws would err in the *opposite* direction, sailing off to the right; but again, within minutes you would readapt.

Indeed, given an even more radical pair of glasses—one that literally turns the world upside down—you could still adapt. Psychologist George Stratton (1896) experienced this when he invented, and for eight days wore, optical headgear that flipped left to right *and* up to down, making him the first person to experience a right-side-up retinal image while standing upright. The ground was up, the sky was down.

At first, when Stratton wanted to walk, he found himself searching for his feet, which were now "up." Eating was nearly impossible. He became nauseated and depressed. But he persisted, and by the eighth day he could comfortably reach for an object in the right direction and walk without bumping into things. When Stratton finally removed the headgear, he readapted quickly.

In later experiments, people wearing the optical gear have even been able to ride a motorcycle, ski the Alps, and fly an airplane (Dolezal, 1982; Kohler, 1962). The world around them still seemed above their heads or on the wrong side. But by actively moving about in these topsy-turvy worlds, they adapted to the context and learned to coordinate their movements.

AP Photo/Marcio Jose Sanchez

Learning to see At age 3, Mike May lost his vision in an explosion. Decades later, after a new cornea restored vision to his right eye, he got his first look at his wife and children. Alas, although signals were now reaching his visual cortex, it lacked the experience to interpret them. May could not recognize expressions, or faces, apart from features such as hair. Yet he can see an object in motion and has learned to navigate his world and to marvel at such things as dust floating in sunlight (Abrams, 2002).

Perceptual adaptation "Oops, missed," thought researcher Hubert Dolezal as he viewed the world through inverting goggles. Yet, believe it or not, kittens, monkeys, and humans can adapt to an inverted world.

Courtesy of Hubert Dolezal

audition the sense or act of hearing.

frequency the number of complete wavelengths that pass a point in a given time (for example, per second).

pitch a tone's experienced highness or lowness; depends on frequency.

middle ear the chamber between the eardrum and cochlea containing three tiny bones (hammer, anvil, and stirrup) that concentrate the vibrations of the eardrum on the cochlea's oval window.

cochlea [KOHK-lee-uh] a coiled, bony, fluid-filled tube in the inner ear; sound waves traveling through the cochlear fluid trigger nerve impulses.

The sounds of music A violin's short, fast waves create a high pitch, a cello's longer, slower waves a lower pitch. Differences in the waves' height, or amplitude, also create differing degrees of loudness.

Zdorov Kirill Vladimirovich/Shutterstock

sbarabu/Shutterstock

Hearing

6-13: What are the characteristics of air pressure waves that we hear as sound, and how does the ear transform sound energy into neural messages?

Like our other senses, our **audition,** or hearing, is highly adaptive. We hear a wide range of sounds, but the ones we hear best are those sounds with frequencies in a range corresponding to that of the human voice. Those with normal hearing are acutely sensitive to faint sounds, an obvious boon for our ancestors' survival when hunting or being hunted, or for detecting a child's whimper. (If our ears were much more sensitive, we would hear a constant hiss from the movement of air molecules.)

We are also remarkably attuned to variations in sounds. Among thousands of possible human voices, we easily recognize a friend on the phone, from the moment she says "Hi." A fraction of a second after such events stimulate the ear's receptors, millions of neurons have simultaneously coordinated in extracting the essential features, comparing them with past experience, and identifying the stimulus (Freeman, 1991). For hearing as for seeing, we wonder: How do we do it?

The Stimulus Input: Sound Waves

Draw a bow across a violin, and you will unleash the energy of sound waves. Jostling molecules of air, each bumping into the next, create waves of compressed and expanded air, like the ripples on a pond circling out from a tossed stone. As we swim in our ocean of moving air molecules, our ears detect these brief air pressure changes.

Like light waves, sound waves vary in shape. The *amplitude* of sound waves determines their *loudness.* Their length, or **frequency,** determines the **pitch** we experience. Long waves have low frequency—and low pitch. Short waves have high frequency—and high pitch. Sound waves produced by a violin are much shorter and faster than those produced by a cello or a bass guitar.

We measure sounds in *decibels,* with zero decibels representing the absolute threshold for hearing. Every 10 decibels correspond to a tenfold increase in sound intensity. Thus, normal conversation (60 decibels) is 10,000 times more intense than a 20-decibel whisper. And a temporarily tolerable 100-decibel passing subway train is 10 billion times more intense than the faintest detectable sound.

The Ear

The intricate process that transforms vibrating air into nerve impulses, which our brain decodes as sounds, begins when sound waves enter the *outer ear.* An intricate mechanical chain reaction begins as the visible outer ear channels the waves through the *auditory canal* to the *eardrum,* a tight membrane, causing it to vibrate (**FIGURE 6.35**). In the **middle ear,** a piston made of three tiny bones (the *hammer, anvil,* and *stirrup*) picks up the vibrations and transmits them to the **cochlea,** a snail-shaped tube in the **inner ear.** The incoming vibrations cause the cochlea's membrane (the *oval window*) to vibrate, jostling the fluid that fills the tube. This motion causes ripples in the *basilar membrane,* bending the *hair cells* lining its surface, not unlike the wind bending a wheat field. Hair cell movement triggers impulses in the adjacent nerve cells. Axons of those cells converge to form the *auditory nerve,* which sends neural messages (via the thalamus) to the *auditory cortex* in the brain's temporal lobe. From vibrating air to moving piston to fluid waves to electrical impulses to the brain: Voilà! We hear.

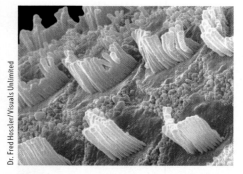
Dr. Fred Hossler/Visuals Unlimited

Be kind to your inner ear's hair cells When vibrating in response to sound, the hair cells shown here lining the cochlea produce an electrical signal.

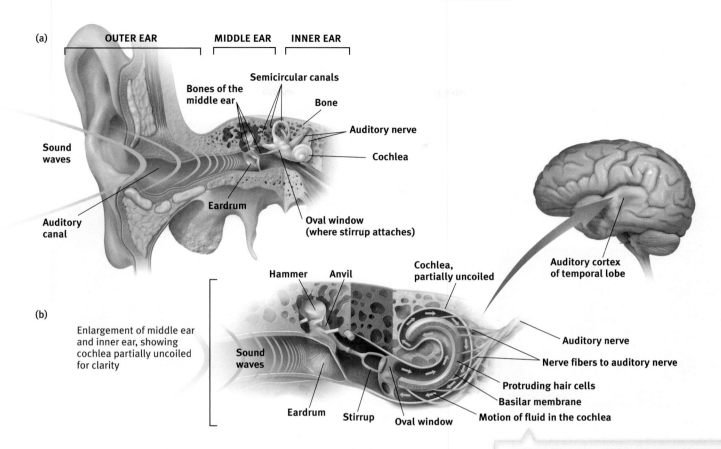

FIGURE 6.35

Hear here: How we transform sound waves into nerve impulses that our brain interprets (a) The outer ear funnels sound waves to the eardrum. The bones of the middle ear (hammer, anvil, and stirrup) amplify and relay the eardrum's vibrations through the oval window into the fluid-filled cochlea. (b) As shown in this detail of the middle and inner ear, the resulting pressure changes in the cochlear fluid cause the basilar membrane to ripple, bending the hair cells on its surface. Hair cell movements trigger impulses at the base of the nerve cells, whose fibers converge to form the auditory nerve. That nerve sends neural messages to the thalamus and on to the auditory cortex.

My vote for the most intriguing part of the hearing process is the hair cells—"quivering bundles that let us hear" thanks to their "extreme sensitivity and extreme speed" (Goldberg, 2007). A cochlea has 16,000 of them, which sounds like a lot until we compare that with an eye's 130 million or so photoreceptors. But consider their responsiveness. Deflect the tiny bundles of *cilia* on the tip of a hair cell by the width of an atom—the equivalent of displacing the top of the Eiffel Tower by half an inch—and the alert hair cell, thanks to a special protein at its tip, triggers a neural response (Corey et al., 2004).

Damage to the cochlea's hair cell receptors or their associated nerves can cause **sensorineural hearing loss** (or nerve deafness). (Less common is **conduction hearing loss,** caused by damage to the mechanical system that conducts sound waves to the cochlea.) Occasionally, disease causes sensorineural hearing loss, but more often the culprits are biological changes linked with heredity, aging, and prolonged exposure to ear-splitting noise or music.

Hair cells have been likened to carpet fibers. Walk around on them and they will spring back with a quick vacuuming. But leave a heavy piece of furniture on them and they may never rebound. As a general rule, if we cannot talk over a noise, it is potentially harmful, especially if prolonged and repeated (Roesser, 1998). Such experiences are common when sound exceeds 100 decibels, as happens in venues from frenzied sports arenas to bagpipe bands to iPods playing near maximum volume (**FIGURE 6.36** on the next page). Ringing of the ears after exposure to loud machinery or music indicates that we have been bad to our unhappy hair cells. As pain alerts us to possible bodily harm, ringing of the ears alerts us to possible hearing damage. It is hearing's equivalent of bleeding.

The rate of teen hearing loss, now 1 in 5, has risen by a third since the early 1990s (Shargorodsky et al., 2010). Teen boys more than teen girls or adults blast themselves with loud volumes for long periods (Zogby, 2006). Males' greater noise exposure may help explain why men's hearing tends to be less acute than women's. But male or female, those who spend many hours in a loud nightclub, behind a power mower, or above a jackhammer should wear earplugs. "Condoms or, safer yet, abstinence," say sex educators. "Earplugs or walk away," say hearing educators.

inner ear the innermost part of the ear, containing the cochlea, semicircular canals, and vestibular sacs.

sensorineural hearing loss hearing loss caused by damage to the cochlea's receptor cells or to the auditory nerves; also called *nerve deafness*.

conduction hearing loss hearing loss caused by damage to the mechanical system that conducts sound waves to the cochlea.

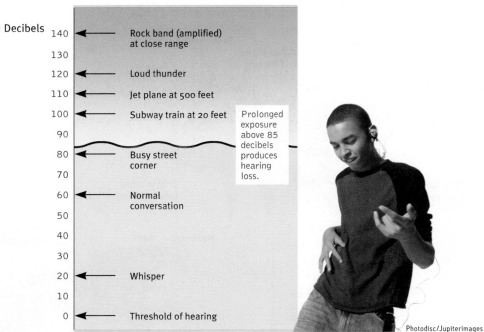

Gstottner, W. (2004). *American Scientist*, 92, 437.

> **FIGURE 6.36**
> The intensity of some
> common sounds

Decibels

- 140 ← Rock band (amplified) at close range
- 130
- 120 ← Loud thunder
- 110 ← Jet plane at 500 feet
- 100 ← Subway train at 20 feet
- 90
- 80 ← Busy street corner
- 70
- 60 ← Normal conversation
- 50
- 40
- 30
- 20 ← Whisper
- 10
- 0 ← Threshold of hearing

Prolonged exposure above 85 decibels produces hearing loss.

Photodisc/Jupiterimages

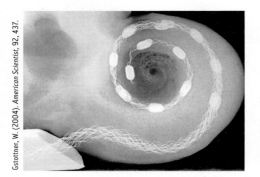

Hardware for hearing An X-ray image shows a cochlear implant's array of wires leading to 12 stimulation sites on the auditory nerve.

That Baylen may hear When Super Bowl-winning quarterback Drew Brees celebrated New Orleans' 2010 victory amid pandemonium, he used ear muffs to protect the vulnerable hair cells of his son, Baylen.

AP Photo/Mark J. Terrill

For now, the only way to restore hearing for people with nerve deafness is a sort of bionic ear—a **cochlear implant**, which, by 2009, had been given to 188,000 people worldwide (NIDCD, 2011). This electronic device translates sounds into electrical signals that, wired into the cochlea's nerves, convey information about sound to the brain. Cochlear implants given to deaf kittens and human infants have seemed to trigger an "awakening" of the pertinent brain area (Klinke et al., 1999; Sireteanu, 1999). They can help children become proficient in oral communication (especially if they receive them as preschoolers or even before age 1) (Dettman et al., 2007; Schorr et al., 2005).

The latest cochlear implants also can help restore hearing for most adults. However, the implants will not enable normal hearing in adults if their brain never learned to process sound during childhood. Similarly, cochlear implants did not enable hearing in deaf-from-birth cats that received them when fully grown, rather than as 8-week-old kittens (Ryugo et al., 2010).

RETRIEVE IT

- The amplitude of a sound wave determines our perception of _____ (loudness/pitch).

  ANSWER: loudness

- The longer the sound waves are, the _____ (lower/higher) their frequency is and the _____ (higher/lower) their pitch.

  ANSWERS: lower; lower

Perceiving Loudness

How do we detect loudness? It is not, as I would have guessed, from the intensity of a hair cell's response. Rather, a soft, pure tone activates only the few hair cells attuned to its frequency. Given louder sounds, neighboring hair cells also respond. Thus, the brain can interpret loudness from the *number* of activated hair cells.

If a hair cell loses sensitivity to soft sounds, it may still respond to loud sounds. This helps explain another surprise: Really loud sounds may seem loud to people with or without normal hearing. As a person with hearing loss, I used to wonder what really loud music must sound like to people with normal hearing. Now I realize it sounds much the same; where we differ is in our sensation of soft sounds.

Perceiving Pitch

6-14: What theories help us understand pitch perception?

How do we know whether a sound is the high-frequency, high-pitched chirp of a bird or the low-frequency, low-pitched roar of a truck? Current thinking on how we discriminate pitch, like current thinking on how we discriminate color, combines two theories.

- Hermann von Helmholtz's **place theory** presumes that we hear different pitches because different sound waves trigger activity at different places along the cochlea's basilar membrane. Thus, the brain determines a sound's pitch by recognizing the specific place (on the membrane) that is generating the neural signal. When Nobel laureate-to-be Georg von Békésy (1957) cut holes in the cochleas of guinea pigs and human cadavers and looked inside with a microscope, he discovered that the cochlea vibrated, rather like a shaken bedsheet, in response to sound. High frequencies produced large vibrations near the beginning of the cochlea's membrane, low frequencies near the end. But a problem remains: Place theory can explain how we hear high-pitched sounds but not low-pitched sounds. The neural signals generated by low-pitched sounds are not so neatly localized on the basilar membrane.

- **Frequency theory** suggests an alternative: The brain reads pitch by monitoring the frequency of neural impulses traveling up the auditory nerve. The whole basilar membrane vibrates with the incoming sound wave, triggering neural impulses to the brain at the same rate as the sound wave. If the sound wave has a frequency of 100 waves per second, then 100 pulses per second travel up the auditory nerve. But again, a problem remains: An individual neuron cannot fire faster than 1000 times per second. How, then, can we sense sounds with frequencies above 1000 waves per second (roughly the upper third of a piano keyboard)?

- Enter the *volley principle:* Like soldiers who alternate firing so that some can shoot while others reload, neural cells can alternate firing. By firing in rapid succession, they can achieve a *combined frequency* above 1000 waves per second. Thus, place theory best explains how we sense *high pitches,* frequency theory best explains how we sense *low pitches,* and some combination of place and frequency seems to handle the *pitches in the intermediate range.*

RETRIEVE IT

- Which theory of pitch perception would best explain a symphony audience's enjoyment of the high-pitched piccolo? How about the low-pitched cello?

ANSWERS: place theory; frequency theory

Locating Sounds

6-15: How do we locate sounds?

Why don't we have one big ear—perhaps above our one nose? "The better to hear you with," the wolf said to Red Riding Hood. As the placement of our eyes allows us to sense visual depth, so the placement of our two ears allows us to enjoy stereophonic ("three-dimensional") hearing.

Two ears are better than one for at least two reasons. If a car to the right honks, your right ear receives a more *intense* sound, and it receives sound slightly *sooner* than your left ear (**FIGURE 6.37**). Because sound travels 750 miles per hour and our ears are but 6 inches apart, the intensity difference and the time lag are extremely small. A just noticeable difference in the direction of two sound sources corresponds to a time difference of just 0.000027 second! Lucky for us, our supersensitive auditory system can detect such minute differences (Brown & Deffenbacher, 1979; Middlebrooks & Green, 1991).

cochlear implant a device for converting sounds into electrical signals and stimulating the auditory nerve through electrodes threaded into the cochlea.

place theory in hearing, the theory that links the pitch we hear with the place where the cochlea's membrane is stimulated.

frequency theory in hearing, the theory that the rate of nerve impulses traveling up the auditory nerve matches the frequency of a tone, thus enabling us to sense its pitch.

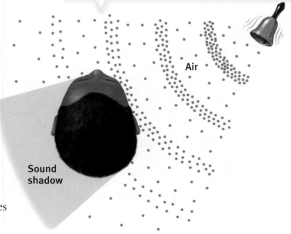

FIGURE 6.37

How we locate sounds Sound waves strike one ear sooner and more intensely than the other. From this information, our nimble brain computes the sound's location. As you might therefore expect, people who lose all hearing in one ear often have difficulty locating sounds.

Air

Sound shadow

© Jose Luis Pelaez, Inc./Blend Images/Corbis

The precious sense of touch As William James wrote in his *Principles of Psychology* (1890), "Touch is both the alpha and omega of affection."

The Other Senses

Although our brain gives seeing and hearing priority in the allocation of cortical tissue, extraordinary happenings occur within our four other senses—touch, taste, smell, and body position and movement. Sharks and dogs rely on their extraordinary sense of smell, aided by large brain areas devoted to smell. Without our own senses of touch, taste, smell, and body position and movement, we humans would also be seriously handicapped, and our capacities for enjoying the world would be devastatingly diminished.

Touch

6-16: How do we sense touch?

Although not the first sense to come to mind, touch is vital. Right from the start, touch is essential to our development. Infant rats deprived of their mother's grooming produce less growth hormone and have a lower metabolic rate—a good way to keep alive until the mother returns, but a reaction that stunts growth if prolonged. Infant monkeys allowed to see, hear, and smell—but not touch—their mother become desperately unhappy; those separated by a screen with holes that allow touching are much less miserable. As we noted in Chapter 4, premature human babies gain weight faster and go home sooner if they are stimulated by hand massage. As lovers, we yearn to touch—to kiss, to stroke, to snuggle. And even strangers, touching only the other's forearms and separated by a curtain, can communicate anger, fear, disgust, love, gratitude, and sympathy at levels well above chance (Hertenstein et al., 2006).

Humorist Dave Barry may be right to jest that your skin "keeps people from seeing the inside of your body, which is repulsive, and it prevents your organs from falling onto the ground." But skin does much more. Touching various spots on the skin with a soft hair, a warm or cool wire, and the point of a pin reveals that some spots are especially sensitive to pressure, others to warmth, others to cold, still others to pain. Our "sense of touch" is actually a mix of these four basic and distinct skin senses, and our other skin sensations are variations of pressure, warmth, cold, and pain:

- Stroking adjacent pressure spots creates a tickle.
- Repeated gentle stroking of a pain spot creates an itching sensation.
- Touching adjacent cold and pressure spots triggers a sense of wetness, which you can experience by touching dry, cold metal.

Touch sensations involve more than tactile stimulation, however. A self-administered tickle produces less somatosensory cortex activation than does the same tickle from something or someone else (Blakemore et al., 1998). (The brain is wise enough to be most sensitive to unexpected stimulation.)

Pain

6-17: How can we best understand and control pain?

Be thankful for occasional pain. Pain is your body's way of telling you something has gone wrong. Drawing your attention to a burn, a break, or a sprain, pain orders you to change your behavior—"Stay off that turned ankle!" The rare people born without the ability to feel pain may experience severe injury or even die before early adulthood. Without the discomfort that makes us occasionally shift position, their joints fail from excess strain, and without the warnings of pain, the effects of unchecked infections and injuries accumulate (Neese, 1991).

gate-control theory the theory that the spinal cord contains a neurological "gate" that blocks pain signals or allows them to pass on to the brain. The "gate" is opened by the activity of pain signals traveling up small nerve fibers and is closed by activity in larger fibers or by information coming from the brain.

More numerous are those who live with chronic pain, which is rather like an alarm that won't shut off. The suffering of such people, and of those with persistent or recurring backaches, arthritis, headaches, and cancer-related pain, prompts two questions: What is pain? How might we control it?

Understanding Pain

Our pain experiences vary widely. Women are more pain sensitive than men are (Wickelgren, 2009). Individual pain sensitivity varies, too, depending on genes, physiology, experience, attention, and surrounding culture (Gatchel et al., 2007; Reimann et al., 2010). Thus, our experience of pain reflects both bottom-up sensations and top-down cognition.

Biological Influences There is no one type of stimulus that triggers pain (as light triggers vision). Instead, there are different *nociceptors*—sensory receptors that detect hurtful temperatures, pressure, or chemicals (**FIGURE 6.38**).

Although no theory of pain explains all available findings, psychologist Ronald Melzack and biologist Patrick Wall's (1965, 1983) classic **gate-control theory** provides a useful model. The spinal cord contains small nerve fibers that conduct most pain signals, and larger fibers that conduct most other sensory signals. Melzack and Wall theorized that the spinal cord contains a neurological "gate." When tissue is injured, the small fibers activate and open the gate, and you feel pain. Large-fiber activity closes the gate, blocking pain signals and preventing them from reaching the brain. Thus, one way to treat chronic pain is to stimulate (by massage, electric stimulation, or acupuncture) "gate-closing" activity in the large neural fibers (Wall, 2000).

But pain is not merely a physical phenomenon of injured nerves sending impulses to a definable brain area—like pulling on a rope to ring a bell. Melzack and Wall noted that brain-to-spinal-cord messages can also close the gate, helping to explain some striking influences on pain. When we are distracted from pain (a psychological influence) and soothed by the release of our naturally painkilling *endorphins* (a biological influence), our experience of pain diminishes.

A pain-free, problematic life Ashlyn Blocker (right), shown here with her mother and sister, has a rare genetic disorder. She feels neither pain nor extreme hot and cold. She must frequently be checked for accidentally self-inflicted injuries that she herself cannot feel. "Some people would say [that feeling no pain is] a good thing," says her mother. "But no, it's not. Pain's there for a reason. It lets your body know something's wrong and it needs to be fixed. I'd give anything for her to feel pain" (quoted by Bynum, 2004).

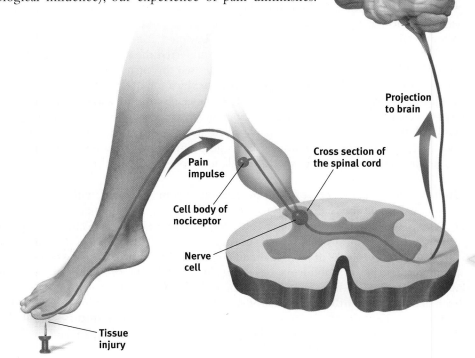

Projection to brain

Pain impulse

Cross section of the spinal cord

Cell body of nociceptor

Nerve cell

Tissue injury

FIGURE 6.38
The pain circuit Sensory receptors *(nociceptors)* respond to potentially damaging stimuli by sending an impulse to the spinal cord, which passes the message to the brain, which interprets the signal as pain.

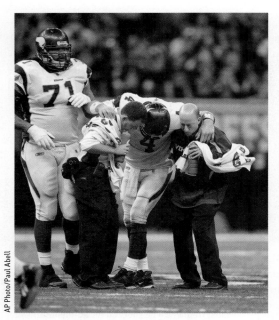

AP Photo/Paul Abell

Playing with pain In a 2010 Super Bowl playoff game, Vikings quarterback Brett Favre seriously injured his ankle and hamstring. He was taken out of the game briefly but came back and played through the pain, which reclaimed his attention after the game's end.

Sports injuries may go unnoticed until the after-game shower. People who carry a gene that boosts the availability of endorphins are less bothered by pain, and their brain is less responsive to pain (Zubieta et al., 2003). Others who carry a mutated gene that disrupts pain circuit neurotransmission experience little pain (Cox et al., 2006). Such discoveries may point the way toward new pain medications that mimic these genetic effects.

The brain can also create pain, as it does in people's experiences of *phantom limb sensations,* after a limb has been amputated. Their brain may misinterpret the spontaneous central nervous system activity that occurs in the absence of normal sensory input: As the dreamer may see with eyes closed, so 7 in 10 such people may feel pain or movement in nonexistent limbs (Melzack, 1992, 2005). (Some may also try to step off a bed onto a phantom limb or to lift a cup with a phantom hand.) Even those born without a limb sometimes perceive sensations from the absent arm or leg. The brain, Melzack (1998) has surmised, comes prepared to anticipate "that it will be getting information from a body that has limbs."

A similar phenomenon occurs with other senses. People with hearing loss often experience the sound of silence: phantom sounds—a ringing-in-the-ears sensation known as *tinnitus.* Those who lose vision to glaucoma, cataracts, diabetes, or macular degeneration may experience phantom sights—nonthreatening hallucinations (Ramachandran & Blakeslee, 1998). Some with nerve damage have had taste phantoms, such as ice water seeming sickeningly sweet (Goode, 1999). Others have experienced phantom smells, such as nonexistent rotten food. The point to remember: *We feel, see, hear, taste, and smell with our brain,* which can sense even without functioning senses.

Psychological Influences The psychological effects of distraction are clear in the stories of athletes who, focused on winning, play through the pain. We also seem to edit our *memories* of pain, which often differ from the pain we actually experienced. In experiments, and after medical procedures, people overlook a pain's duration. Their memory snapshots instead record two factors: their pain's *peak* moment (which can lead them to recall variable pain, with peaks, as worse [Stone et al., 2005]), and how much pain they felt at the *end.*

In one experiment, researchers asked people to immerse one hand in painfully cold water for 60 seconds, and then the other hand in the same painfully cold water for 60 seconds followed by a slightly less painful 30 seconds more (Kahneman et al., 1993). Which experience would you expect to recall as most painful? Curiously, when asked which trial they would prefer to repeat, most preferred the longer trial, with more net pain—but less pain at the end. Physicians have used this principle with patients undergoing colon exams—lengthening the discomfort by a minute, but lessening its intensity (Kahneman, 1999). Although the extended milder discomfort added to their net pain experience, patients experiencing this taper-down treatment later recalled the exam as less painful than did those whose pain ended abruptly. (If, at the end of a painful root canal, the oral surgeon asks if you'd like to go home or to have a few more minutes of milder discomfort, there's a case to be made for prolonging your hurt.)

Social-Cultural Influences Our perception of pain also varies with our social situation and our cultural traditions. We tend to perceive more pain when others also seem to be experiencing pain (Symbaluk et al., 1997). This may help explain other apparent social aspects of pain, as when pockets of Australian keyboard operators during the mid-1980s suffered outbreaks of severe pain during typing or other repetitive work—without any discernible physical abnormalities (Gawande, 1998). Sometimes the pain in sprain is mainly in the brain—literally. When feeling empathy for another's pain, a person's own brain activity may partly mirror that of the other's brain in pain (Singer et al, 2004).

Thus, our perception of pain is a biopsychosocial phenomenon (**FIGURE 6.39**). Viewing pain this way can help us better understand how to cope with pain and treat it.

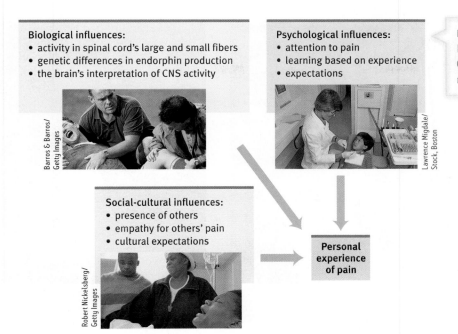

Biological influences:
• activity in spinal cord's large and small fibers
• genetic differences in endorphin production
• the brain's interpretation of CNS activity

Barros & Barros/ Getty Images

Psychological influences:
• attention to pain
• learning based on experience
• expectations

Lawrence Migdale/ Stock, Boston

Social-cultural influences:
• presence of others
• empathy for others' pain
• cultural expectations

Robert Nickelsberg/ Getty Images

Personal experience of pain

FIGURE 6.39
Biopsychosocial approach to pain
Our experience of pain is much more than neural messages sent to the brain.

Controlling Pain

If pain is where body meets mind—if it is both a physical and a psychological phenomenon—then it should be treatable both physically and psychologically. Depending on the patient's symptoms, pain control clinics select one or more therapies from a list that includes drugs, surgery, acupuncture, electrical stimulation, massage, exercise, hypnosis, relaxation training, and thought distraction.

Even an inert placebo can help, by dampening the central nervous system's attention and responses to painful experiences—mimicking analgesic drugs (Eippert et al., 2009; Wager, 2005). After being injected in the jaw with a stinging saltwater solution, men in one experiment received a placebo said to relieve pain, and they immediately felt better. Being given fake pain-killing chemicals caused the brain to dispense real ones, as indicated by activity in an area that releases natural pain-killing opiates (Scott et al., 2007; Zubieta et al., 2005). "Believing becomes reality," noted one commentator (Thernstrom, 2006), as "the mind unites with the body."

Distraction also works. Presenting pleasant images *("Think of a warm, comfortable environment")* or drawing attention away from painful stimulation *("Count backward by 3's")* are especially effective ways to activate pain-inhibiting circuits and increase pain tolerance (Edwards et al., 2009). A well-trained nurse may chat with needle-shy patients and ask them to look away when inserting the needle. For burn victims receiving excruciating wound care, an even more effective distraction comes from immersion in a computer-generated 3-D world, like the snow scene in **FIGURE 6.40** on the next page. Functional MRI (fMRI) scans reveal that playing in the virtual reality reduces the brain's pain-related activity (Hoffman, 2004). Because pain is in the brain, diverting the brain's attention may bring relief.

"Pain is increased by attending to it."
Charles Darwin, Expression of Emotions in Man and Animals, 1872

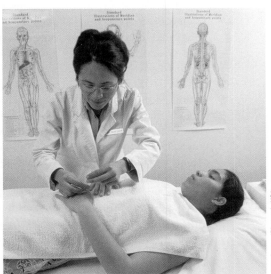

Acupuncture: A jab well done This acupuncturist is attempting to help this woman gain relief from back pain by using needles on points of the patient's hand.

Gary Conner/PhototakeUSA.com

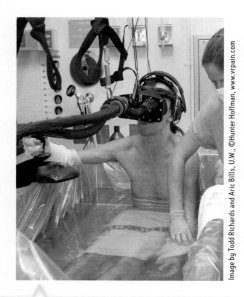

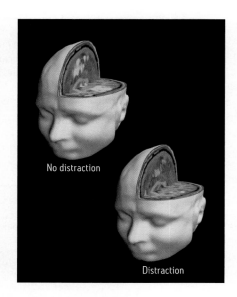

No distraction

Distraction

Image by Todd Richards and Aric Bills, U.W., ©Hunter Hoffman, www.vrpain.com

FIGURE 6.40

Virtual-reality pain control For burn victims undergoing painful skin repair, an escape into virtual reality can powerfully distract attention, thus reducing pain and the brain's response to painful stimulation. The fMRI scans on the right illustrate a lowered pain response when the patient is distracted.

Table 6.2
The Survival Functions of Basic Tastes

Taste	Indicates
Sweet	Energy source
Salty	Sodium essential to physiological processes
Sour	Potentially toxic acid
Bitter	Potential poisons
Umami	Proteins to grow and repair tissue

(Adapted from Cowart, 2005.)

> **RETRIEVE IT**
>
> • Which of the following options has NOT been proven to reduce pain?
>
> a. Distraction   b. Placebos   c. Phantom limb sensations   d. Endorphins
>
> ANSWER: c.

Taste

6-18: How do we experience taste and smell?

Like touch, our sense of taste involves several basic sensations. Taste's sensations were once thought to be sweet, sour, salty, and bitter, with all others stemming from mixtures of these four (McBurney & Gent, 1979). Then, as investigators searched for specialized nerve fibers for the four taste sensations, they encountered a receptor for what we now know is a fifth—the savory meaty taste of *umami,* best experienced as the flavor enhancer monosodium glutamate.

Tastes exist for more than our pleasure (see **TABLE 6.2**). Pleasureful tastes attracted our ancestors to energy- or protein-rich foods that enabled their survival. Aversive tastes deterred them from new foods that might be toxic. We see the inheritance of this biological wisdom in today's 2- to 6-year-olds, who are typically fussy eaters, especially when offered new meats or bitter-tasting vegetables, such as spinach and brussels sprouts (Cooke et al., 2003). Meat and plant toxins were both potentially dangerous sources of food poisoning for our ancestors, especially for children. Given repeated small tastes of disliked new foods, children will, however, typically begin to accept them (Wardle et al., 2003).

Taste is a chemical sense. Inside each little bump on the top and sides of your tongue are 200 or more taste buds, each containing a pore that catches food chemicals. Into each taste bud pore, 50 to 100 taste receptor cells project antenna-like hairs that sense food molecules. Some receptors respond mostly to sweet-tasting molecules, others to salty-, sour-, umami-, or bitter-tasting ones. It doesn't take much to trigger a response that alerts your brain's temporal lobe. If a stream of water is pumped across your tongue, the addition of a concentrated salty or sweet taste for but one-tenth of a second will get your attention (Kelling & Halpern, 1983). When a friend asks for "just a taste" of your soft drink, you can squeeze off the straw after a mere instant.

Taste receptors reproduce themselves every week or two, so if you burn your tongue with hot food it hardly matters. However, as you grow older, the number of taste buds decreases, as does taste sensitivity (Cowart, 1981). (No wonder adults enjoy strong-tasting foods that children resist.) Smoking and alcohol use accelerate these declines. Those who lose their sense of taste report that food tastes like "straw" and is hard to swallow (Cowart, 2005).

Essential as taste buds are, there's more to taste than meets the tongue. Expectations can influence taste. When told a sausage roll was "vegetarian," people in one experiment found it decidedly inferior to its identical partner labeled "meat" (Allen et al., 2008). In another experiment, being told that a wine cost $90 rather than its real $10 price made it taste better and triggered more activity in a brain area that responds to pleasant experiences (Plassmann et al., 2008).

Lauren Burke/Jupiterimages

Smell

Inhale, exhale. Inhale, exhale. Breaths come in pairs—beginning at birth and ending at death. Between those two moments, you will daily inhale and exhale nearly 20,000 breaths of life-sustaining air, bathing your nostrils in a stream of scent-laden molecules. The resulting experiences of smell *(olfaction)* are strikingly intimate: You inhale something of whatever or whoever it is you smell.

Like taste, smell is a chemical sense. We smell something when molecules of a substance carried in the air reach a tiny cluster of 5 million or more receptor cells at the top of each nasal cavity (**FIGURE 6.41**). These olfactory receptor cells, waving like sea anemones on a reef, respond selectively—to the aroma of a cake baking, to a wisp of smoke, to a friend's fragrance. Instantly, they alert the brain through their axon fibers.

Research has shown that even nursing infants and their mothers have a literal chemistry to their relationship: They quickly learn to recognize each other's scents (McCarthy, 1986). Aided by smell, a mother fur seal returning to a beach crowded with pups will find her own. Our human sense of smell is less acute than our senses

Impress your friends with your new word for the day: People unable to see are said to experience blindness. People unable to hear experience deafness. People unable to smell experience *anosmia.*

> **FIGURE 6.41**
>
> **The sense of smell** If you are to smell a flower, airborne molecules of its fragrance must reach receptors at the top of your nose. Sniffing swirls air up to the receptors, enhancing the aroma. The receptor cells send messages to the brain's olfactory bulb, and then onward to the temporal lobe's primary smell cortex and to the parts of the limbic system involved in memory and emotion.

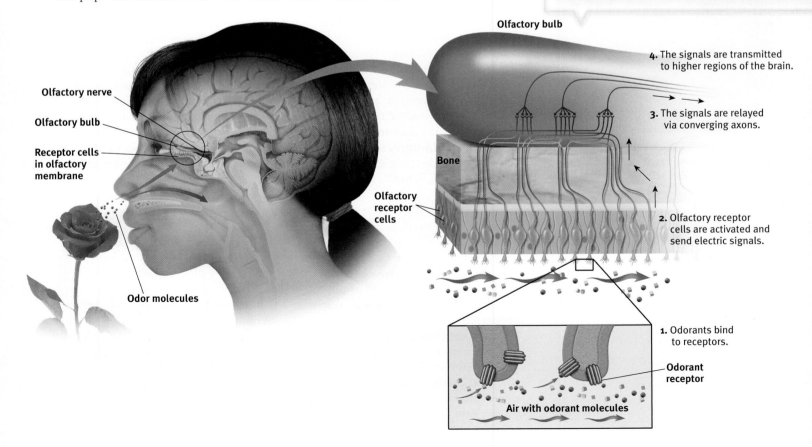

Olfactory bulb

4. The signals are transmitted to higher regions of the brain.

3. The signals are relayed via converging axons.

Olfactory nerve

Olfactory bulb

Receptor cells in olfactory membrane

Bone

Olfactory receptor cells

2. Olfactory receptor cells are activated and send electric signals.

Odor molecules

1. Odorants bind to receptors.

Odorant receptor

Air with odorant molecules

Tish1/Shutterstock

of seeing and hearing. Looking out across a garden, we see its forms and colors in exquisite detail and hear a variety of birds singing, yet we smell little of it without sticking our nose into the blossoms.

Odor molecules come in many shapes and sizes—so many, in fact, that it takes many different receptors to detect them. A large family of genes designs the 350 or so receptor proteins that recognize particular odor molecules (Miller, 2004). Linda Buck and Richard Axel (1991) discovered (in work for which they received a 2004 Nobel Prize) that these receptor proteins are embedded on the surface of nasal cavity neurons. As a key slips into a lock, so odor molecules slip into these receptors. Yet we don't seem to have a distinct receptor for each detectable odor. This suggests that some odors trigger a combination of receptors, in patterns that are interpreted by the olfactory cortex. As the English alphabet's 26 letters can combine to form many words, so odor molecules bind to different receptor arrays, producing the 10,000 odors we can detect (Malnic et al., 1999). It is the combinations of olfactory receptors, which activate different neuron patterns, that allow us to distinguish between the aromas of fresh-brewed and hours-old coffee (Zou et al., 2005).

For humans, the attractiveness of smells depends on learned associations (Herz, 2001). As babies nurse, their preference for the smell of their mother's breast builds. So, too, with other associations. As good experiences are linked with a particular scent, people come to like that scent, which helps explain why people in the United States tend to like the smell of wintergreen (which they associate with candy and gum) more than do those in Great Britain (where it often is associated with medicine). In another example of odors evoking unpleasant emotions, researchers frustrated Brown University students with a rigged computer game in a scented room (Herz et al., 2004). Later, if exposed to the same odor while working on a verbal task, the students' frustration was rekindled and they gave up sooner than others exposed to a different odor or no odor.

Though it's difficult to recall odors by name, we have a remarkable capacity to recognize long-forgotten odors and their associated memories (Engen, 1987; Schab, 1991). The smell of the sea, the scent of a perfume, or an aroma of a favorite relative's kitchen can bring to mind a happy time. It's a phenomenon the British travel agent chain Lunn Poly understood well. To evoke memories of lounging on sunny, warm beaches, the company once piped the aroma of coconut suntan oil into its shops (Fracassini, 2000).

Our brain's circuitry helps explain an odor's power to evoke feelings and memories (**FIGURE 6.42**). A hotline runs between the brain area receiving information from the nose and the brain's ancient limbic centers associated with memory and emotion. Thus, when put in a foul-smelling room, people expressed harsher judgments of immoral acts (such as lying or keeping a found wallet) and more negative attitudes toward gay men (Inbar et al., 2011; Schnall et al., 2008).

AP Photo/ The Charlotte Observer, Layne Bailey

The nose knows Humans have 10 to 20 million olfactory receptors. A bloodhound has some 200 million (Herz, 2001).

FIGURE 6.42

Taste, smell, and memory Information from the taste buds (yellow arrow) travels to an area between the frontal and temporal lobes of the brain. It registers in an area not far from where the brain receives information from our sense of smell, which interacts with taste. The brain's circuitry for smell (red circle) also connects with areas involved in memory storage, which helps explain why a smell can trigger a memory.

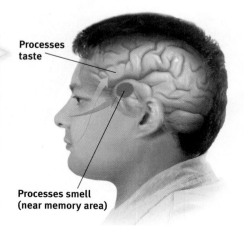

Processes taste

Processes smell (near memory area)

Body Position and Movement

6-19: How do we sense our body's position and movement?

Important sensors in your joints, tendons, and muscles enable your **kinesthesis**—your sense of the position and movement of your body parts. By closing your eyes or plugging your ears you can momentarily imagine being without sight or sound. But what would it be like to live without touch or kinesthesis—without, therefore, being able to sense the positions of your limbs when you wake during the night? Ian Waterman of Hampshire, England, knows. In 1972, at age 19, Waterman contracted a rare viral infection that destroyed the nerves enabling his sense of light touch and of body position and movement. People with this condition report feeling disembodied, as though their body is dead, not real, not theirs (Sacks, 1985). With prolonged practice, Waterman has learned to walk and eat—by visually focusing on his limbs and directing them accordingly. But if the lights go out, he crumples to the floor (Azar, 1998). Even for the rest of us, vision interacts with kinesthesis. Stand with your right heel in front of your left toes. Easy. Now close your eyes and you will probably wobble.

A companion **vestibular sense** monitors your head's (and thus your body's) position and movement. The biological gyroscopes for this sense of equilibrium are in your inner ear. The *semicircular canals,* which look like a three-dimensional pretzel (Figure 6.35a), and the *vestibular sacs,* which connect the canals with the cochlea, contain fluid that moves when your head rotates or tilts. This movement stimulates hairlike receptors, which send messages to the cerebellum at the back of the brain, thus enabling you to sense your body position and to maintain your balance.

If you twirl around and then come to an abrupt halt, neither the fluid in your semicircular canals nor your kinesthetic receptors will immediately return to their neutral state. The dizzy aftereffect fools your brain with the sensation that you're still spinning. This illustrates a principle that underlies perceptual illusions: Mechanisms that normally give us an accurate experience of the world can, under special conditions, fool us. Understanding how we get fooled provides clues to how our perceptual system works.

© Robert Kanavel

Bodies in space These high school competitive cheer team members can thank their inner ears for the information that enables their brains to monitor their bodies' position so expertly.

Sensory Interaction

6-20: How do our senses interact?

Our senses—seeing, hearing, touching, tasting, smelling—are not totally separate information channels. In interpreting the world, our brain blends their inputs. Consider what happens to your sense of taste if you hold your nose, close your eyes, and have someone feed you various foods. A slice of apple may be

kinesthesis [kin-ehs-THEE-sehs] the system for sensing the position and movement of individual body parts.

vestibular sense the sense of your head's (and thus your body's) movement and position, including the sense of balance.

sensory interaction the principle that one sense may influence another, as when the smell of food influences its taste.

indistinguishable from a chunk of raw potato. A piece of steak may taste like cardboard. Without their smells, a cup of cold coffee may be hard to distinguish from a glass of red wine. To savor a taste, we normally breathe the aroma through our nose—which is why eating is not much fun when you have a bad cold. Smell can also change our perception of taste: A drink's strawberry odor enhances our perception of its sweetness. Even touch can influence taste. Depending on its texture, a potato chip "tastes" fresh or stale (Smith, 2011). This is **sensory interaction** at work—the principle that one sense may influence another. Smell + texture + taste = flavor.

Vision and hearing may similarly interact. An almost imperceptible flicker of light is more easily visible when accompanied by a short burst of sound (Kayser, 2007). And a sound may be easier to hear with a visual cue. If I (as a person with hearing loss) watch a video with simultaneous captioning, I have no trouble hearing the words I am seeing (and may therefore think I don't need the captioning). If I then turn off the captioning, I suddenly realize I do need it. The eyes guide the ears (**FIGURE 6.43**).

But what do you suppose happens if the eyes and the ears disagree? What if we *see* a speaker saying one syllable while we *hear* another? Surprise: We may perceive a third syllable that blends both inputs. Seeing the mouth movements for *ga* while hearing *ba* we may perceive *da*. This phenomenon is known as the *McGurk effect,* after its discoverers, psychologist Harry McGurk and his assistant John MacDonald (1976).

Touch also interacts with our other senses. In detecting events, the brain can combine simultaneous touch and visual signals, thanks to neurons projecting from the somatosensory cortex back to the visual cortex (Macaluso et al., 2000). Touch even interacts with hearing. In one experiment, researchers blew a puff of air (such as our mouths produce when saying *pa* and *ta*) on the neck or hands as people heard either these sounds or the more airless sounds *ba* or *da*. To my surprise (and yours?), the people more often misheard *ba* or *da* as *pa* or *ta* when played with the faint puff (Gick & Derrick, 2009). Thanks to sensory interaction, they were hearing with their skin.

Our brain even blends our tactile and social judgments:

- After holding a warm drink rather than a cold one, people are more likely to rate someone more warmly, feel closer to them, and behave more generously (IJzerman & Semin, 2009; Williams & Bargh, 2008). Physical warmth promotes social warmth.

- After being given the cold shoulder by others in an experiment, people judge the room as colder than do those treated warmly (Zhong & Leonardelli, 2008). Social exclusion literally feels cold.

FIGURE 6.43

Sensory interaction When a hard-of-hearing listener sees an animated face forming the words being spoken at the other end of a phone line, the words become easier to understand (Knight, 2004).

Courtesy of RNID www.rnid.org.uk

- Holding a heavy rather than light clipboard makes job candidates seem more important. Holding rough objects makes social interactions seem more difficult (Ackerman et al., 2010).

- When leaning to the left—by sitting in a left- rather than right-leaning chair, or squeezing a hand-grip with their left hand, or using a mouse with their left hand—people lean more left in their expressed political attitudes (Oppenheimer & Trail, 2010).

These examples of **embodied cognition** illustrate how brain circuits processing our bodily sensations connect with brain circuits responsible for cognition.

So, the senses interact: As we attempt to decipher our world, our brain blends inputs from multiple channels. For many people, an odor, perhaps of mint or chocolate, can evoke a sensation of taste (Stevenson & Tomiczek, 2007). But in a few select individuals, the senses become joined in a phenomenon called *synaesthesia,* where one sort of sensation (such as hearing sound) produces another (such as seeing color). Thus, hearing music may activate color-sensitive cortex regions and trigger a sensation of color (Brang et al., 2008; Hubbard et al., 2005). Seeing the number 3 may evoke a taste sensation (Ward, 2003).

★ ★ ★

For a summary of our sensory systems, see **TABLE 6.3**. The river of perception is fed by sensation, cognition, and emotion. And that is why we need biological, psychological, and social-cultural levels of analysis.

If perception is the product of these three sources, what can we say about extrasensory perception, which claims that perception can occur apart from sensory input? For more on that question, see Thinking Critically About: ESP—Perception Without Sensation? on the next page.

★ ★ ★

To feel awe, mystery, and a deep reverence for life, we need look no further than our own perceptual system and its capacity for organizing formless nerve impulses into colorful sights, vivid sounds, and evocative smells. As Shakespeare's Hamlet recognized, "There are more things in Heaven and Earth, Horatio, than are dreamt of in your philosophy." Within our ordinary sensory and perceptual experiences lies much that is truly extraordinary—surely much more than has so far been dreamt of in our psychology.

embodied cognition the influence of bodily sensations, gestures, and other states on cognitive preferences and judgments.

Table 6.3
Summarizing the Senses

Sensory System	Source	Receptors
Vision	Light waves striking the eye	Rods and cones in the retina
Hearing	Sound waves striking the outer ear	Cochlear hair cells in the inner ear
Touch	Pressure, warmth, cold on the skin	Skin receptors detect pressure, warmth, cold, and pain
Taste	Chemical molecules in the mouth	Basic tongue receptors for sweet, sour, salty, bitter, and umami
Smell	Chemical molecules breathed in through the nose	Millions of receptors at top of nasal cavity
Position/movement of body parts—kinesthesis	Any change in position of a body part, interacting with vision	Kinesthetic sensors in joints, tendons, and muscles
Position/movement of head—vestibular sense	Movement of fluids in the inner ear caused by head/body movement	Hairlike receptors in the semi-circular canals and vestibular sacs

Sensory information travels to these areas of the brain's cerebral cortex:

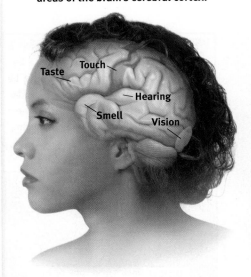

ESP—Perception Without Sensation?

6-21: What are the claims of ESP, and what have most research psychologists concluded after putting these claims to the test?

Without sensory input, are we capable of **extrasensory perception (ESP)**? Are there indeed people—any people—who can read minds, see through walls, or foretell the future? Nearly half of Americans believe there are (AP, 2007; Moore, 2005).

The most testable and, for this chapter, most relevant parapsychological concepts are claims of

- *telepathy:* mind-to-mind communication.
- *clairvoyance:* perceiving remote events, such as a house on fire in another state.
- *precognition:* perceiving future events, such as an unexpected death in the next month.

Closely linked is *psychokinesis,* or "mind over matter," such as levitating a table or influencing the roll of a die. (The claim is illustrated by the wry request, "Will all those who believe in psychokinesis please raise my hand?")

If ESP is real, we would need to overturn the scientific understanding that we are creatures whose minds are tied to our physical brains and whose perceptual experiences of the world are built of sensations. Sometimes new evidence does overturn our scientific preconceptions.

Science, as we will see throughout this book, offers us various surprises—about the extent of the unconscious mind, about the effects of emotions on health, about what heals and what doesn't, and much more.

Most research psychologists and scientists—including 96 percent of the scientists in the U.S. National Academy of Sciences—have been skeptical that paranormal phenomena exist (McConnell, 1991). But in reputable universities in many locations, including Great Britain, the Netherlands, and Australia, faculty researchers in **parapsychology** perform scientific experiments searching for possible ESP and other paranormal phenomena (Storm, 2010a,b; Turpin, 2005). Before seeing how they do research on ESP, let's consider some popular beliefs.

Premonitions or Pretensions?

Can psychics see into the future? Although one might wish for a psychic stock forecaster, the tallied forecasts of "leading psychics" reveal meager accuracy. During the 1990s, the tabloid psychics were all wrong in predicting surprising events. (Madonna did not become a gospel singer, the Statue of Liberty did not lose both its arms in a terrorist blast, Queen Elizabeth did not abdicate her throne to enter a convent.) And the psychics have missed recent big-news events. Where were the psychics on 9/10 when we needed them? Why, despite a $50 million reward offered, could none of them help locate Osama bin Laden after 9/11, or step forward to predict the impending stock crashes in 2008? In 30 years, unusual predictions have almost never come true, and psychics have virtually never anticipated any of the year's headline events (Emery, 2004, 2006). In 2010, when a mine collapse trapped 33 miners, the Chilean government reportedly consulted four psychics. Their verdict? "They're all dead" (Kraul, 2010). But 69 days later, all 33 were rescued.

Moreover, the hundreds of psychic visions offered to police departments have been no more accurate than guesses made by others (Nickell, 1994, 2005; Radford, 2010; Reiser, 1982). Their sheer volume does, however, increase the odds of an occasional correct guess, which psychics can then report to the media. Police departments are wise to all this. When researchers asked the police departments of America's 50 largest cities whether they ever had used psychics, 65 percent said *No* (Sweat & Durm, 1993). Of those that had, not one had found them helpful.

Psychics' vague predictions sometimes sound correct when later interpreted ("retrofitted") to match events that provide a perceptual set for "understanding" them. Nostradamus, a sixteenth-century French psychic, explained in an unguarded moment that his ambiguous prophecies "could not possibly be understood till they were interpreted after the event and by it."

Are the spontaneous "visions" of everyday people any more accurate? Do dreams, for example, foretell the future, as people from both Eastern and Western cultures tend to believe—making some people more reluctant to fly after dreaming of a plane crash (Morewedge & Norton, 2009)? Or do they only seem to do so when we recall or reconstruct them in light of what has already happened? Two Harvard psychologists tested the prophetic power of dreams after superhero aviator Charles Lindbergh's baby son was kidnapped and murdered in 1932, but before the body was discovered (Murray & Wheeler, 1937). When invited to report their dreams about the child, 1300 visionaries submitted dream reports. How many accurately envisioned the child

---

"To be sure of hitting the target, shoot first and call whatever you hit the target."

Writer-artist Ashleigh Brilliant, 1933–

"A person who talks a lot is sometimes right."

Spanish proverb

dead? Five percent. And how many also correctly anticipated the body's location—buried among trees? Only 4 of the 1300. Although this number was surely no better than chance, to those 4 dreamers the accuracy of their apparent precognitions must have seemed uncanny.

Given the billions of events in the world each day, and given enough days, some stunning coincidences are sure to occur. By one careful estimate, chance alone would predict that more than a thousand times a day someone on Earth will think of another person and then within the next five minutes will learn of that person's death (Charpak & Broch, 2004). Thus, when explaining an astonishing event, we should "give chance a chance" (Lilienfeld, 2009). With enough time and people, the improbable becomes inevitable.

Putting ESP to Experimental Test

When faced with claims of mind reading or out-of-body travel or communication with the dead, how can we separate bizarre ideas from those that sound bizarre but are true? At the heart of science is a simple answer: *Test them to see if they work.* If they do, so much the better for the ideas. If they don't, so much the better for our skepticism.

This scientific attitude has led both believers and skeptics to agree that what

"At the heart of science is an essential tension between two seemingly contradictory attitudes—an openness to new ideas, no matter how bizarre or counterintuitive they may be, and the most ruthless skeptical scrutiny of all ideas, old and new."

Carl Sagan (1987)

Magician Harry Houdini after fooling Sir Arthur Conan Doyle with a pseudo-psychic trick: "Now I beg of you, Sir Arthur, do not jump to the conclusion that certain things you see are necessarily 'supernatural,' or with the work of 'spirits,' just because you cannot explain them."

Quoted by William Kalush and Larry Sloman, *The Secret Life of Houdini*, 2007

Courtesy of Claire Cole

Testing psychic powers in the British population Hertfordshire University psychologist Richard Wiseman created a "mind machine" to see if people could influence or predict a coin toss. Using a touch-sensitive screen, visitors to festivals around the country were given four attempts to call heads or tails. Using a random-number generator, a computer then decided the outcome. When the experiment concluded in January 2000, nearly 28,000 people had predicted 110,972 tosses—with 49.8 percent correct.

parapsychology needs is a reproducible phenomenon and a theory to explain it. Parapsychologist Rhea White (1998) spoke for many in saying "The image of parapsychology that comes to my mind, based on nearly 44 years in the field, is that of a small airplane [that] has been perpetually taxiing down the runway of the Empirical Science Airport since 1882 . . . its movement punctuated occasionally by lifting a few feet off the ground only to bump back down on the tarmac once again. It has never taken off for any sustained flight."

How might we test ESP claims in a controlled, reproducible experiment? An experiment differs from a staged demonstration: In the laboratory, the experimenter controls what the "psychic" sees and hears; on stage, the psychic controls what the audience sees and hears.

Daryl Bem, a respected social psychologist, has been a skeptic of stage psychics;

he once quipped that "a psychic is an actor playing the role of a psychic" (1984). Yet he has reignited hopes for replicable evidence with nine experiments that seemed to show people anticipating future events (2011). In one, when an erotic scene was about to appear on a screen in one of two randomly selected positions, Cornell University participants guessed right 53.1 percent of the time (beating 50 percent by a small but statistically significant margin).

· · · · · ·

extrasensory perception (ESP) the controversial claim that perception can occur apart from sensory input; includes telepathy, clairvoyance, and precognition.

parapsychology the study of paranormal phenomena, including ESP and psychokinesis.

Continued on next page

In another, people viewed a set of words, took a recall test of those words, and then rehearsed a randomly selected subset of those words. People better remembered the rehearsed words—even though the rehearsal took place *after* the recall test. The upcoming rehearsal—a future event—apparently affected their ability to recall words.

Despite the published research having survived critical reviews by a top-tier journal, other critics found the methods "badly flawed" (Alcock, 2011) or the statistical analyses "biased" (Wagenmakers et al., 2011). "A result—especially one of this importance—must recur several times in tests by independent and skeptical researchers to gain scientific credibility," observed astronomer David Helfand (2011). "I have little doubt that Professor Bem's experiments will fail this test."

Anticipating such skepticism, Bem has made his computer materials available to anyone who wishes to replicate his studies, and replications are now under way (see Ritchie et al., 2012, for three attempts to replicate Bem's results). Regardless of the outcomes, science will have done its work. It will have been open to a finding that challenges its own worldview, and then, through follow-up research, it will have assessed its validity. And that is how science sifts crazy-sounding ideas, leaving most on the historical waste heap while occasionally surprising us.

One skeptic, magician James Randi, has a long-standing offer of $1 million to be given "to anyone who proves a genuine psychic power under proper observing conditions" (Randi, 1999; Thompson, 2010). French, Australian, and Indian groups have made similar offers of up to 200,000 euros (CFI, 2003). Large as these sums are, the scientific seal of approval would be worth far more. To refute those who say there is no ESP, one need only produce a single person who can demonstrate a single, reproducible ESP event. (To refute those who say pigs can't talk would take but one talking pig.) So far, no such person has emerged.

RETRIEVE IT

• What is the field of study that researches claims of extrasensory perception (ESP)?

ANSWER: parapsychology

CHAPTER REVIEW

Sensation and Perception

LEARNING OBJECTIVES

Test Yourself by taking a moment to answer each of these Learning Objective Questions (repeated here from within the chapter). Then turn to Appendix D, Complete Chapter Reviews, to check your answers. Research suggests that trying to answer these questions on your own will improve your long-term memory of the concepts (McDaniel et al., 2009).

Basic Principles of Sensation and Perception

6-1: What are *sensation* and *perception?* What do we mean by *bottom-up processing* and *top-down processing?*

6-2: What three steps are basic to all our sensory systems?

6-3: What are the absolute and difference thresholds, and do stimuli below the absolute threshold have any influence on us?

6-4: What is the function of sensory adaptation?

6-5: How do our expectations, contexts, emotions, and motivation influence our perceptions?

Vision

6-6: What is the energy that we see as visible light?

6-7: How does the eye transform light energy into neural messages, and how do the eye and brain process that information?

6-8: What theories help us understand color vision?

6-9: How did the Gestalt psychologists understand perceptual organization, and how do figure-ground and grouping principles contribute to our perceptions?

6-10: How do we use binocular and monocular cues to perceive the world in three dimensions?

6-11: How do perceptual constancies help us organize our sensations into meaningful perceptions?

6-12: What does research on restored vision, sensory restriction, and perceptual adaptation reveal about the effects of experience on perception?

Hearing

6-13: What are the characteristics of air pressure waves that we hear as sound, and how does the ear transform sound energy into neural messages?

6-14: What theories help us understand pitch perception?

6-15: How do we locate sounds?

The Other Senses

6-16: How do we sense touch?

6-17: How can we best understand and control pain?

6-18: How do we experience taste and smell?

6-19: How do we sense our body's position and movement?

Sensory Interaction

6-20: How do our senses interact?

6-21: What are the claims of ESP, and what have most research psychologists concluded after putting these claims to the test?

TERMS AND CONCEPTS TO REMEMBER

Test yourself on these terms by trying to write down the definition in your own words before flipping back to the referenced page to check your answer.

EXPERIENCE THE TESTING EFFECT

Test yourself repeatedly throughout your studies. This will not only help you figure out what you know and don't know; the testing itself will help you learn and remember the information more effectively thanks to the *testing effect*.

1. Sensation is to _____ as perception is to _____.
   a. absolute threshold; difference threshold
   b. bottom-up processing; top-down processing
   c. interpretation; detection
   d. grouping; priming

2. The process by which we organize and interpret sensory information is called _____.

3. Subliminal stimuli are
   a. too weak to be processed by the brain in any way.
   b. consciously perceived more than 50 percent of the time.
   c. always strong enough to affect our behavior.
   d. below our absolute threshold for conscious awareness.

4. Another term for difference threshold is the _____ _____ _____.

5. Weber's law states that for a difference to be perceived, two stimuli must differ by
   a. a fixed or constant energy amount.
   b. a constant minimum percentage.
   c. a constantly changing amount.
   d. more than 7 percent.

6. Sensory adaptation helps us focus on
   a. visual stimuli.
   b. auditory stimuli.
   c. constant features of the environment.
   d. important changes in the environment.

7. Our perceptual set influences what we perceive. This mental tendency reflects our
   a. experiences, assumptions, and expectations.
   b. perceptual adaptation.
   c. priming ability.
   d. difference thresholds.

8. The characteristic of light that determines the color we experience, such as blue or green, is _____.

9. The amplitude of a sound wave determines our perception of loudness. The amplitude of a light wave determines our perception of _____.
   a. brightness.
   b. color.
   c. meaning.
   d. distance.

10. The blind spot in your retina is located where
    a. there are rods but no cones.
    b. there are cones but no rods.
    c. the optic nerve leaves the eye.
    d. the bipolar cells meet the ganglion cells.

11. Cones are the eye's receptor cells that are especially sensitive to _____ light and are responsible for our _____ vision.
    a. bright; black-and-white
    b. dim; color
    c. bright; color
    d. dim; black-and-white

12. The cells in the visual cortex that respond to certain lines, edges, and angles are called _____ _____.

13. The brain's ability to process many aspects of an object or a problem simultaneously is called _____ _____.

14. Two theories together account for color vision. The Young-Helmholtz theory shows that the eye contains _____, and the Hering theory accounts for the nervous system's having _____.
    a. opposing retinal processes; three pairs of color receptors
    b. opponent-process cells; three types of color receptors
    c. three pairs of color receptors; opposing retinal processes
    d. three types of color receptors; opponent-process cells

15. What mental processes allow you to perceive a lemon as yellow?

16. Our tendencies to fill in the gaps and to perceive a pattern as continuous are two different examples of the organizing principle called
    a. the Ames illusion.
    b. depth perception.
    c. shape constancy.
    d. grouping.

17. In listening to a concert, you attend to the solo instrument and perceive the orchestra as accompaniment. This illustrates the organizing principle of
    a. figure-ground.
    b. shape constancy.
    c. grouping.
    d. depth perception.

18. The visual cliff experiments suggest that
    a. infants have not yet developed depth perception.
    b. crawling human infants and very young animals perceive depth.
    c. we have no way of knowing whether infants can perceive depth.
    d. unlike other species, humans are able to perceive depth in infancy.

19. Depth perception underlies our ability to
    a. group similar items in a gestalt.
    b. perceive objects as having a constant shape or form.
    c. judge distances.
    d. fill in the gaps in a figure.

20. Two examples of _____ depth cues are interposition and linear perspective.

21. Perceiving a tomato as consistently red, despite lighting shifts, is an example of
    a. shape constancy.
    b. perceptual constancy.
    c. a binocular cue.
    d. continuity.

22. After surgery to restore vision, patients who had been blind from birth had difficulty
    a. recognizing objects by touch.
    b. recognizing objects by sight.
    c. distinguishing figure from ground.
    d. distinguishing between bright and dim light.

23. In experiments, people have worn glasses that turned their visual fields upside down. After a period of adjustment, they learned to function quite well. This ability is called _____ _____.

24. The snail-shaped tube in the inner ear, where sound waves are converted into neural activity, is called the _____.

25. What are the basic steps in transforming sound waves into perceived sound?

26. _____ theory explains how we hear high-pitched sounds, and _____ theory explains how we hear low-pitched sounds.

27. The gate-control theory of pain proposes that
    a. special pain receptors send signals directly to the brain.
    b. pain is a property of the senses, not of the brain.
    c. small spinal cord nerve fibers conduct most pain signals, but large-fiber activity can close access to those pain signals.
    d. the stimuli that produce pain are unrelated to other sensations.

28. How does the biopsychosocial approach explain our experience of pain? Provide examples.

29. Why might it be helpful for people with chronic pain to meditate or exercise?

30. _____ is your sense of body position and movement. Your _____ _____ specifically monitors your head's movement, with sensors in the inner ear.

31. Why do you feel a little dizzy immediately after a roller coaster ride?

32. We have specialized nerve receptors for detecting which five tastes? How did this ability aid our ancestors?

33. A food's aroma can greatly enhance its taste. This is an example of
    a. sensory adaptation.
    b. chemical sensation.
    c. kinesthesis.
    d. sensory interaction.

34. Which of the following ESP phenomena is supported by solid, replicable scientific evidence?
    a. Telepathy
    b. Clairvoyance
    c. Precognition
    d. None of these answers

Find answers to these questions in Appendix E in the back of the book.

Experience more of the
TESTING EFFECT

Multiple-format self-tests and more may be found at www.worthpublishers.com/myers.

CHAPTER 7

Learning

When a chinook salmon first emerges from its egg in a stream's gravel bed, its genes provide most of the behavioral instructions it needs for life. It knows instinctively how and where to swim, what to eat, and how to avoid predators. Following a built-in plan, the young salmon soon begins its trek to the sea. After a few years in the ocean, the mature salmon somehow navigates hundreds of miles to return to its birthplace. At home in its ancestral spawning ground, the salmon seeks out the best gravel and water flow for breeding. It then mates and, its life mission accomplished, dies.

Unlike salmon, we are not born with a genetic plan for life. Much of what we do we learn from experience. Although we struggle to find the life direction a salmon is born with, our learning gives us more flexibility. We can learn how to build grass huts or snow shelters, submarines or space stations, and thereby adjust to almost any environment. Indeed, nature's most important gift to us may be our *adaptability*—our capacity to learn new behaviors that help us cope with changing circumstances.

Learning breeds hope. What is learnable we can potentially teach—a fact that encourages parents, educators, coaches, and animal trainers. What has been learned we can potentially change by new learning—an assumption that underlies counseling, psychotherapy, and rehabilitation programs. No matter how unhappy, unsuccessful, or unloving we are, that need not be the end of our story.

No topic is closer to the heart of psychology than *learning,* the process of acquiring new and relatively enduring information or behaviors. (Learning acquires information, and memory—our next chapter topic—retains it.) In earlier chapters we considered the learning of sleep patterns, of gender roles, and of visual perceptions. In later chapters we will see how learning shapes our thoughts, our emotions, our personalities, and our attitudes. This chapter examines some core processes of three types of learning: *classical conditioning, operant conditioning,* and *cognitive learning.*

learning the process of acquiring through experience new and relatively enduring information or behaviors.

associative learning learning that certain events occur together. The events may be two stimuli (as in classical conditioning) or a response and its consequences (as in operant conditioning).

stimulus any event or situation that evokes a response.

cognitive learning the acquisition of mental information, whether by observing events, by watching others, or through language.

classical conditioning a type of learning in which one learns to link two or more stimuli and anticipate events.

Most of us would be unable to name the order of the songs on our favorite album or playlist. Yet, hearing the end of one piece cues (by association) an anticipation of the next. Likewise, when singing your national anthem, you associate the end of each line with the beginning of the next. (Pick a line out of the middle and notice how much harder it is to recall the previous line.)

How Do We Learn?

7-1: What is learning, and what are some basic forms of learning?

One way we **learn** is by *association*. Our mind naturally connects events that occur in sequence. Suppose you see and smell freshly baked bread, eat some, and find it satisfying. The next time you see and smell fresh bread, you will expect that eating it will again be satisfying. So, too, with sounds. If you associate a sound with a frightening consequence, hearing the sound alone may trigger your fear. As one 4-year-old exclaimed after watching a TV character get mugged, "If I had heard that music, I wouldn't have gone around the corner!" (Wells, 1981).

Learned associations feed our habitual behaviors (Wood & Neal, 2007). As we repeat behaviors in a given context—sleeping in a certain posture in bed, walking certain routes on campus, eating popcorn in a movie theater—the behaviors become associated with the contexts. Our next experience of the context then evokes our habitual response. How long does it take to form such habits? To find out, one British research team asked 96 university students to choose some healthy behavior (such as running before dinner or eating fruit with lunch), to do it daily for 84 days, and to record whether the behavior felt automatic (something they did without thinking and would find it hard not to do). On average, behaviors became habitual after about 66 days (Lally et al., 2010). (Is there something you'd like to make a routine part of your life? Just do it every day for two months, or a bit longer for exercise, and you likely will find yourself with a new habit.)

Other animals also learn by association. Disturbed by a squirt of water, the sea slug *Aplysia* protectively withdraws its gill. If the squirts continue, as happens naturally in choppy water, the withdrawal response diminishes. But if the sea slug repeatedly receives an electric shock just after being squirted, its response to the squirt instead grows stronger. The animal has associated the squirt with the impending shock.

Complex animals can learn to associate their own behavior with its outcomes. An aquarium seal will repeat behaviors, such as slapping and barking, that prompt people to toss it a herring.

By linking two events that occur close together, both animals are exhibiting **associative learning.** The sea slug associates the squirt with an impending shock; the seal associates slapping and barking with a herring treat. Each animal has learned something important to its survival: predicting the immediate future.

This process of learning associations is *conditioning,* and it takes two main forms:

- In *classical conditioning,* we learn to associate two stimuli and thus to anticipate events. (A **stimulus** is any event or situation that evokes a response.) We learn that a flash of lightning signals an impending crack of thunder; when lightning flashes nearby, we start to brace ourselves (**FIGURE 7.1**).

Two related events:

Stimulus 1:
Lightning

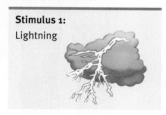

+

Stimulus 2:
Thunder

BOOM!

Response:
Startled reaction; wincing

Result after repetition:

Stimulus:
We see lightning

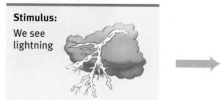

Response:
Anticipation of loud noise; wincing

FIGURE 7.1
Classical conditioning

FIGURE 7.2
Operant conditioning

(a) Response: Being polite   (b) Consequence: Getting a treat   (c) Behavior strengthened

- In *operant conditioning,* we learn to associate a response (our behavior) and its consequence. Thus we (and other animals) learn to repeat acts followed by good results (**FIGURE 7.2**) and avoid acts followed by bad results.

To simplify, we will explore these two types of associative learning separately. Often, though, they occur together, as on one Japanese cattle ranch, where the clever rancher outfitted his herd with electronic pagers, which he calls from his cell phone. After a week of training, the animals learn to associate two stimuli—the beep on their pager and the arrival of food (classical conditioning). But they also learn to associate their hustling to the food trough with the pleasure of eating (operant conditioning).

Conditioning is not the only form of learning. Through **cognitive learning** we acquire mental information that guides our behavior. *Observational learning,* one form of cognitive learning, lets us learn from others' experiences. Chimpanzees, for example, sometimes learn behaviors merely by watching others perform them. If one animal sees another solve a puzzle and gain a food reward, the observer may perform the trick more quickly. So, too, in humans: We look and we learn.

By learning, we humans adapt to our environments. We learn to expect and prepare for significant events such as food or pain *(classical conditioning).* We learn to repeat acts that bring rewards and to avoid acts that bring unwanted results *(operant conditioning).* We learn new behaviors by observing events and by watching others, and through language we learn things we have neither experienced nor observed *(cognitive learning).*

RETRIEVE IT

- Why are habits, such as having something sweet with that cup of coffee, so hard to break?

ANSWER: Habits form when we repeat behaviors in a given context and, as a result, learn associations—often without our awareness. For example, we may have eaten a sweet pastry with a cup of coffee often enough to associate the flavor of the coffee with the treat, so that the cup of coffee alone just doesn't seem right anymore!

Classical Conditioning

7-2: What are the basic components of classical conditioning, and what was behaviorism's view of learning?

For many people, the name Ivan Pavlov (1849–1936) rings a bell. His early twentieth-century experiments—now psychology's most famous research—are classics, and the phenomenon he explored we justly call **classical conditioning.**

Pavlov's work laid the foundation for many of psychologist John B. Watson's ideas. In searching for laws underlying learning, Watson (1913) urged his colleagues to discard reference to inner thoughts, feelings, and motives. The science of psychology should instead study how organisms respond to stimuli in their environments, said Watson: "Its theoretical goal is the prediction and control of behavior. Introspection forms no essential part of its methods." Simply said, psychology should be an objective science based on observable behavior.

Ivan Pavlov "Experimental investigation . . . should lay a solid foundation for a future true science of psychology" (1927).

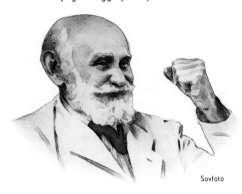

Sovfoto

This view, which influenced North American psychology during the first half of the twentieth century, Watson called **behaviorism.** Pavlov and Watson shared both a disdain for "mentalistic" concepts (such as consciousness) and a belief that the basic laws of learning were the same for all animals—whether dogs or humans. Few researchers today propose that psychology should ignore mental processes, but most now agree that classical conditioning is a basic form of learning by which all organisms adapt to their environment.

Pavlov's Experiments

Pavlov was driven by a lifelong passion for research. After setting aside his initial plan to follow his father into the Russian Orthodox priesthood, Pavlov received a medical degree at age 33 and spent the next two decades studying the digestive system. This work earned him Russia's first Nobel Prize in 1904. But his novel experiments on learning, which consumed the last three decades of his life, earned this feisty scientist his place in history.

PEANUTS

PEANUTS reprinted by permission of United Feature Syndicate, Inc.

Pavlov's new direction came when his creative mind seized on an incidental observation. Without fail, putting food in a dog's mouth caused the animal to salivate. Moreover, the dog began salivating not only to the taste of the food, but also to the mere sight of the food, or the food dish, or the person delivering the food, or even the sound of that person's approaching footsteps. At first, Pavlov considered these "psychic secretions" an annoyance—until he realized they pointed to a simple but important form of learning.

Pavlov and his assistants tried to imagine what the dog was thinking and feeling as it drooled in anticipation of the food. This only led them into fruitless debates. So, to explore the phenomenon more objectively, they experimented. To eliminate other possible influences, they isolated the dog in a small room, secured it in a harness, and attached a device to divert its saliva to a measuring instrument. From the next room, they presented food—first by sliding in a food bowl, later by blowing meat powder into the dog's mouth at a precise moment. They then paired various **neutral stimuli (NS)**—events the dog could see or hear but didn't associate with food—with food in the dog's mouth. If a sight or sound regularly signaled the arrival of food, would the dog learn the link? If so, would it begin salivating in anticipation of the food?

The answers proved to be *Yes* and *Yes.* Just before placing food in the dog's mouth to produce salivation, Pavlov sounded a tone. After several pairings of tone and food, the dog, now anticipating the meat powder, began salivating to the tone alone. In later experiments, a buzzer,[1] a light, a touch on the leg, even the sight of a circle set off the drooling. (This procedure works with people, too. When hungry young Londoners viewed abstract figures before smelling peanut butter or vanilla, their brain soon responded in anticipation to the abstract images alone [Gottfried et al., 2003].)

A dog doesn't learn to salivate in response to food in its mouth. Food in the mouth automatically, *unconditionally,* triggers a dog's salivary reflex (**FIGURE 7.3**). Thus, Pavlov called the drooling an **unconditioned response (UR).** And he called the food an **unconditioned stimulus (US).**

Salivation in response to the tone, however, is learned. Because it is *conditional* upon the dog's associating the tone and the food, we call this response the **conditioned response (CR).** The stimulus that used to be neutral (in this case, a previously meaningless tone that now triggers the salivation) is the **conditioned stimulus (CS).**

behaviorism the view that psychology (1) should be an objective science that (2) studies behavior without reference to mental processes. Most research psychologists today agree with (1) but not with (2).

neutral stimulus (NS) in classical conditioning, a stimulus that elicits no response before conditioning.

unconditioned response (UR) in classical conditioning, an unlearned, naturally occurring response (such as salivation) to an unconditioned stimulus (US) (such as food in the mouth).

unconditioned stimulus (US) in classical conditioning, a stimulus that unconditionally—naturally and automatically—triggers a response (UR).

conditioned response (CR) in classical conditioning, a learned response to a previously neutral (but now conditioned) stimulus (CS).

conditioned stimulus (CS) in classical conditioning, an originally irrelevant stimulus that, after association with an unconditioned stimulus (US), comes to trigger a conditioned response (CR).

---

[1] The "buzzer" (English translation) was perhaps Pavlov's supposed bell—a small electric bell (Tully, 2003).

BEFORE CONDITIONING

US (food in mouth) → UR (salivation)

NS (tone) → No salivation

An unconditioned stimulus (US) produces an unconditioned response (UR).

A neutral stimulus (NS) produces no salivation response.

DURING CONDITIONING

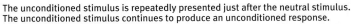

NS (tone) + US (food in mouth) → UR (salivation)

The unconditioned stimulus is repeatedly presented just after the neutral stimulus. The unconditioned stimulus continues to produce an unconditioned response.

AFTER CONDITIONING

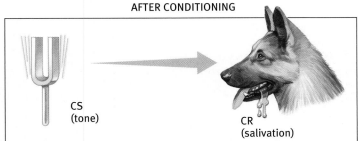

CS (tone) → CR (salivation)

The previously neutral stimulus alone now produces a conditioned response (CR), thereby becoming a conditioned stimulus (CS).

Distinguishing these two kinds of stimuli and responses is easy: Conditioned = learned; *unconditioned = unlearned.*

If Pavlov's demonstration of associative learning was so simple, what did he do for the next three decades? What discoveries did his research factory publish in his 532 papers on salivary conditioning (Windholz, 1997)? He and his associates explored five major conditioning processes: *acquisition, extinction, spontaneous recovery, generalization,* and *discrimination.*

> **FIGURE 7.3**
> **Pavlov's classic experiment** Pavlov presented a neutral stimulus (a tone) just before an unconditioned stimulus (food in mouth). The neutral stimulus then became a conditioned stimulus, producing a conditioned response.

RETRIEVE IT

- An experimenter sounds a tone just before delivering an air puff to your blinking eye. After several repetitions, you blink to the tone alone. What is the NS? The US? The UR? The CS? The CR?

ANSWERS: NS = tone before procedure; US = air puff; UR = blink to air puff; CS = tone after procedure; CR = blink to tone

Acquisition

7-3: In classical conditioning, what are the processes of acquisition, extinction, spontaneous recovery, generalization, and discrimination?

Acquisition is the initial learning of an association. How much time should elapse between presenting the NS (the tone, the light, the touch) and the US (the food), Pavlov and his associates wondered? In most cases, not much—half a second usually works well.

What do you suppose would happen if the food (US) appeared before the tone (NS) rather than after? Would conditioning occur? Not likely. With but a few exceptions, conditioning doesn't happen when the NS follows the US. *Remember, classical conditioning is biologically adaptive because it helps humans and other animals prepare for good or bad events.* To Pavlov's dogs, the originally neutral tone became a CS after signaling an important biological event—the arrival of food (US). To deer in the forest, the snapping of a twig (CS) may signal a predator's approach (US). If the good or bad event has already occurred, the tone or the sound won't help the animal prepare.

acquisition in classical conditioning, the initial stage, when one links a neutral stimulus and an unconditioned stimulus so that the neutral stimulus begins triggering the conditioned response. In operant conditioning, the strengthening of a reinforced response.

Eric Isselée/Shutterstock

More recent research on male Japanese quail shows how a CS can signal another important biological event (Domjan, 1992, 1994, 2005). Just before presenting a sexually approachable female quail, the researchers turned on a red light. Over time, as the red light continued to herald the female's arrival, the light caused the male quail to become excited. They developed a preference for their cage's red-light district, and when a female appeared, they mated with her more quickly and released more semen and sperm (Matthews et al., 2007). All in all, the quail's capacity for classical conditioning gives it a reproductive edge.

In humans, too, objects, smells, and sights associated with sexual pleasure—even a geometric figure in one experiment—can become conditioned stimuli for sexual arousal (Byrne, 1982). Onion breath does not usually produce sexual arousal. But when repeatedly paired with a passionate kiss, it can become a CS and do just that (**FIGURE 7.4**). The larger lesson: *Conditioning helps an animal survive and reproduce—by responding to cues that help it gain food, avoid dangers, locate mates, and produce offspring* (Hollis, 1997).

Remember:
NS = **N**eutral **S**timulus
US = **U**nconditioned **S**timulus
UR = **U**nconditioned **R**esponse
CS = **C**onditioned **S**timulus
CR = **C**onditioned **R**esponse

FIGURE 7.4

An unexpected CS Psychologist Michael Tirrell (1990) recalled: "My first girlfriend loved onions, so I came to associate onion breath with kissing. Before long, onion breath sent tingles up and down my spine. Oh what a feeling!"

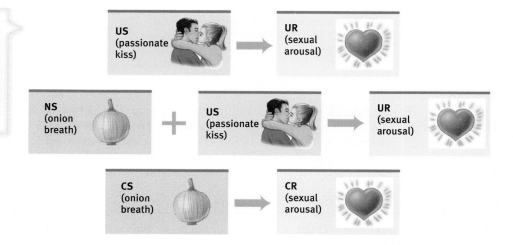

RETRIEVE IT

• In slasher movies, sexually arousing images of women are sometimes paired with violence against women. Based on classical conditioning principles, what might be an effect of this pairing?

ANSWER: If viewing an attractive nude or semi-nude woman (a US) elicits sexual arousal (a UR), then pairing the US with a new stimulus (violence) could turn the violence into a conditioned stimulus (CS) that also becomes sexually arousing, a conditioned response (CR).

Extinction and Spontaneous Recovery

What would happen, Pavlov wondered, if after conditioning, the CS occurred repeatedly without the US? If the tone sounded again and again, but no food appeared, would the tone still trigger salivation? The answer was mixed. The dogs salivated less and less, a reaction known as **extinction,** the diminished responding that occurs when the CS (tone) no longer signals an impending US (food). But a different picture emerged when Pavlov allowed several hours to elapse before sounding the tone again. After the delay, the dogs would again begin salivating to the tone (**FIGURE 7.5**). This **spontaneous recovery**—the reappearance of a (weakened) CR after a pause—suggested to Pavlov that extinction was suppressing the CR rather than eliminating it.

extinction the diminishing of a conditioned response; occurs in classical conditioning when an unconditioned stimulus does not follow a conditioned stimulus; occurs in operant conditioning when a response is no longer reinforced.

spontaneous recovery the reappearance, after a pause, of an extinguished conditioned response.

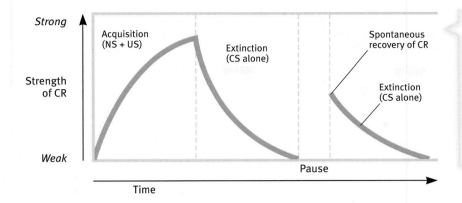

FIGURE 7.5
Idealized curve of acquisition, extinction, and spontaneous recovery The rising curve shows that the CR rapidly grows stronger as the NS becomes a CS as it is repeatedly paired with the US *(acquisition),* then weakens as the CS is presented alone *(extinction).* After a pause, the CR reappears *(spontaneous recovery).*

RETRIEVE IT

- The first step of classical conditioning, when an NS becomes a CS, is called _____. When a US no longer follows the CS, and the CR becomes weakened, this is _____.

ANSWERS: acquisition; extinction

Generalization

Pavlov and his students noticed that a dog conditioned to the sound of one tone also responded somewhat to the sound of a new and different tone. Likewise, a dog conditioned to salivate when rubbed would also drool a bit when scratched (Windholz, 1989) or when touched on a different body part (**FIGURE 7.6**). This tendency to respond likewise to stimuli similar to the CS is called **generalization.**

Generalization can be adaptive, as when toddlers taught to fear moving cars also become afraid of moving trucks and motorcycles. And generalized fears can linger. One Argentine writer who underwent torture still recoils with fear when he sees black shoes—his first glimpse of his torturers as they approached his cell. Generalized anxiety reactions have been demonstrated in laboratory studies comparing abused with nonabused children (**FIGURE 7.7**). When an angry face appeared on a computer screen, abused children's brain-wave responses were dramatically stronger and longer lasting (Pollak et al., 1998).

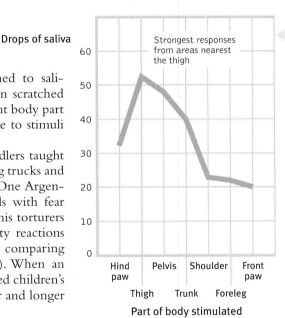

FIGURE 7.6
Generalization Pavlov demonstrated generalization by attaching miniature vibrators to various parts of a dog's body. After conditioning salivation to stimulation of the thigh, he stimulated other areas. The closer a stimulated spot was to the dog's thigh, the stronger the conditioned response. (From Pavlov, 1927.)

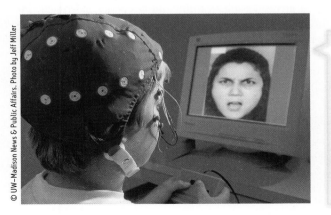

FIGURE 7.7
Child abuse leaves tracks in the brain Studies have shown that abused children's sensitized brains react more strongly to angry faces (Pollak et al., 1998). This generalized anxiety response may help explain their greater risk of psychological disorder.

generalization the tendency, once a response has been conditioned, for stimuli similar to the conditioned stimulus to elicit similar responses.

discrimination in classical conditioning, the learned ability to distinguish between a conditioned stimulus and stimuli that do not signal an unconditioned stimulus.

Stimuli similar to naturally disgusting objects will, by association, also evoke some disgust, as otherwise desirable fudge did when shaped to resemble dog feces (Rozin et al., 1986). Researchers have also found that we like unfamiliar people more if they look like someone we've learned to like rather than dislike (Verosky & Todorov, 2010). (They find this by subtly morphing the facial features of someone we've learned to like or dislike onto a novel face.) In these human examples, people's emotional reactions to one stimulus have generalized to similar stimuli.

Discrimination

Pavlov's dogs also learned to respond to the sound of a particular tone and *not* to other tones. This learned ability to *distinguish* between a conditioned stimulus (which predicts the US) and other irrelevant stimuli is called **discrimination.** Being able to recognize differences is adaptive. Slightly different stimuli can be followed by vastly different consequences. Confronted by a guard dog, your heart may race; confronted by a guide dog, it probably will not.

"I don't care if she's a tape dispenser. I love her."

> **RETRIEVE IT**
>
> • What conditioning principle is affecting the snail's affections?
>
> ANSWER: generalization

Pavlov's Legacy

7-4: Why does Pavlov's work remain so important, and what have been some applications of his work to human health and wellbeing?

What remains today of Pavlov's ideas? A great deal. Most psychologists now agree that classical conditioning is a basic form of learning. Judged by today's knowledge of the interplay of our biology, psychology, and social-cultural environment, Pavlov's ideas were incomplete. But if we see further than Pavlov did, it is because we stand on his shoulders.

Why does Pavlov's work remain so important? If he had merely taught us that old dogs can learn new tricks, his experiments would long ago have been forgotten. Why should we care that dogs can be conditioned to salivate at the sound of a tone? The importance lies first in this finding: *Many other responses to many other stimuli can be classically conditioned in many other organisms*—in fact, in every species tested, from earthworms to fish to dogs to monkeys to people (Schwartz, 1984). Thus, classical conditioning is one way that virtually all organisms learn to adapt to their environment.

Second, *Pavlov showed us how a process such as learning can be studied objectively.* He was proud that his methods involved virtually no subjective judgments or guesses about what went on in a dog's mind. The salivary response is a behavior measurable in cubic centimeters of saliva. Pavlov's success therefore suggested a scientific model for how the young discipline of psychology might proceed—by isolating the basic building blocks of complex behaviors and studying them with objective laboratory procedures.

> **RETRIEVE IT**
>
> • If the aroma of cake baking sets your mouth to watering, what is the US? The CS? The CR?
>
> ANSWERS: The cake (and its taste) are the US. The associated aroma is the CS. Salivation to the aroma is the CR.

Applications of Classical Conditioning

Other chapters in this text—on consciousness, motivation, emotion, health, psychological disorders, and therapy—show how Pavlov's principles can influence human health and well-being. Two examples:

* Former drug users often feel a craving when they are again in the drug-using context—with people or in places they associate with previous highs. Thus, drug counselors advise addicts to steer clear of people and settings that may trigger these cravings (Siegel, 2005).

* Classical conditioning even works on the body's disease-fighting immune system. When a particular taste accompanies a drug that influences immune responses, the taste by itself may come to produce an immune response (Ader & Cohen, 1985).

Pavlov's work also provided a basis for Watson's (1913) idea that human emotions and behaviors, though biologically influenced, are mainly a bundle of conditioned responses. Working with an 11-month-old, Watson and Rosalie Rayner (1920; Harris, 1979) showed how specific fears might be conditioned. Like most infants, "Little Albert" feared loud noises but not white rats. Watson and Rayner presented a white rat and, as Little Albert reached to touch it, struck a hammer against a steel bar just behind his head. After seven repeats of seeing the rat and hearing the frightening noise, Albert burst into tears at the mere sight of the rat. Five days later, he had generalized this startled fear reaction to the sight of a rabbit, a dog, and a sealskin coat, but not to dissimilar objects, such as toys.

For years, people wondered what became of Little Albert. Not until 2009 did some psychologist-sleuths identify him as Douglas Merritte, the son of a campus hospital wet nurse who received $1 for her tot's participation. Sadly, Albert died at age 6, apparently having suffered all his short life from congenital hydrocephalus, complicated later by meningitis. This brain damage must have influenced his behavior during Watson and Rayner's experiment (Beck et al., 2009, 2010; Fridlund et al., 2012a,b). People also wondered what became of Watson. After losing his Johns Hopkins professorship over an affair with Rayner (whom he later married), he joined the J. Walter Thompson Agency as their resident psychologist. There he used his knowledge of associative learning to conceive many successful advertising campaigns, including one for Maxwell House that helped make the "coffee break" an American custom (Hunt, 1993).

The treatment of Little Albert would be unacceptable by today's ethical standards. Also, some psychologists, noting that the infant's fear wasn't learned quickly, had difficulty repeating Watson and Rayner's findings with other children. Nevertheless, Little Albert's learned fears led many psychologists to wonder whether each of us might be a walking repository of conditioned emotions. If so, might extinction procedures or even new conditioning help us change our unwanted responses to emotion-arousing stimuli? One patient, who for 30 years had feared going into an elevator alone, did just that. Following his therapist's advice, he forced himself to enter 20 elevators a day. Within 10 days, his fear had nearly vanished (Ellis & Becker, 1982). In Chapters 14 and 15 we will see more examples of how psychologists use behavioral techniques to treat emotional disorders and promote personal growth.

John B. Watson Watson (1924) admitted to "going beyond my facts" when offering his famous boast: "Give me a dozen healthy infants, well-formed, and my own specified world to bring them up in and I'll guarantee to take any one at random and train him to become any type of specialist I might select—doctor, lawyer, artist, merchant-chief, and, yes, even beggar-man and thief, regardless of his talents, penchants, tendencies, abilities, vocations, and race of his ancestors."

Brown Brothers

Archives of the History of American Psychology, The University of Akron

RETRIEVE IT

* In Watson and Rayner's experiments, "Little Albert" learned to fear a white rat after repeatedly experiencing a loud noise as the rat was presented. In this experiment, what was the US? The UR? The NS? The CS? The CR?

ANSWERS: The US was the loud noise; the UR was the fear response; the NS was the rat before it was paired with the noise; the CS was the rat after pairing; the CR was fear.

operant conditioning a type of learning in which behavior is strengthened if followed by a reinforcer or diminished if followed by a punisher.

law of effect Thorndike's principle that behaviors followed by favorable consequences become more likely, and that behaviors followed by unfavorable consequences become less likely.

operant chamber in operant conditioning research, a chamber (also known as a *Skinner box*) containing a bar or key that an animal can manipulate to obtain a food or water reinforcer; attached devices record the animal's rate of bar pressing or key pecking.

reinforcement in operant conditioning, any event that *strengthens* the behavior it follows.

shaping an operant conditioning procedure in which reinforcers guide behavior toward closer and closer approximations of the desired behavior.

Eric Isselée/Shutterstock

FIGURE 7.8

Cat in a puzzle box Thorndike used a fish reward to entice cats to find their way out of a puzzle box (right) through a series of maneuvers. The cats' performance tended to improve with successive trials (left), illustrating Thorndike's *law of effect*. (Adapted from Thorndike, 1898.)

Operant Conditioning

 7-5: What is operant conditioning, and how is operant behavior reinforced and shaped?

It's one thing to classically condition a dog to salivate at the sound of a tone, or a child to fear moving cars. To teach an elephant to walk on its hind legs or a child to say *please,* we turn to operant conditioning.

Classical conditioning and operant conditioning are both forms of associative learning, yet their difference is straightforward:

- *Classical conditioning* forms associations between stimuli (a CS and the US it signals). It also involves *respondent behavior*—actions that are automatic responses to a stimulus (such as salivating in response to meat powder and later in response to a tone).

- In **operant conditioning,** organisms associate their own actions with consequences. Actions followed by reinforcers increase; those followed by punishers often decrease. Behavior that *operates* on the environment to *produce* rewarding or punishing stimuli is called *operant behavior.*

RETRIEVE IT

- With _____ conditioning, we learn associations between events we do not control.
  With _____ conditioning, we learn associations between our behavior and resulting events.

ANSWERS: classical; operant

Skinner's Experiments

B. F. Skinner (1904–1990) was a college English major and an aspiring writer who, seeking a new direction, studied psychology in graduate school. He went on to become modern behaviorism's most influential and controversial figure. Skinner's work elaborated on what psychologist Edward L. Thorndike (1874–1949) called the **law of effect:** Rewarded behavior is likely to recur (**FIGURE 7.8**). Using Thorndike's law of effect as a starting point, Skinner developed a behavioral technology that revealed principles of *behavior control.* These principles also enabled him to teach pigeons such unpigeon-like behaviors as walking in a figure 8, playing Ping-Pong, and keeping a missile on course by pecking at a screen target.

For his pioneering studies, Skinner designed an **operant chamber,** popularly known as a *Skinner box* (**FIGURE 7.9**). The box has a bar (a lever) that an animal presses (or a key [a disc] the animal pecks) to release a reward of food or water. It also has a device that records these responses. This design creates a stage on which rats and

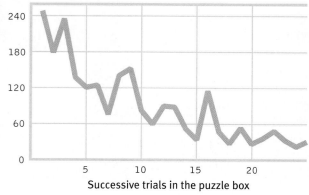

Time required to escape (seconds)

Successive trials in the puzzle box

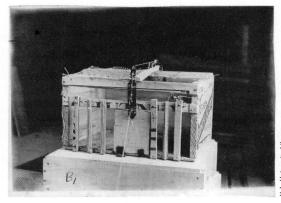

Yale University Library

others animals act out Skinner's concept of **reinforcement:** any event that strengthens (increases the frequency of) a preceding response. What is reinforcing depends on the animal and the conditions. For people, it may be praise, attention, or a paycheck. For hungry and thirsty rats, food and water work well. Skinner's experiments have done far more than teach us how to pull habits out of a rat. They have explored the precise conditions that foster efficient and enduring learning.

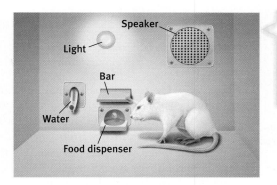

FIGURE 7.9
A Skinner box Inside the box, the rat presses a bar for a food reward. Outside, a measuring device (not shown here) records the animal's accumulated responses.

Shaping Behavior

Imagine that you wanted to condition a hungry rat to press a bar. Like Skinner, you could tease out this action with **shaping,** gradually guiding the rat's actions toward the desired behavior. First, you would watch how the animal naturally behaves, so that you could build on its existing behaviors. You might give the rat a bit of food each time it approaches the bar. Once the rat is approaching regularly, you would give the food only when it moves close to the bar, then closer still. Finally, you would require it to touch the bar to get food. With this method of *successive approximations,* you reward responses that are ever-closer to the final desired behavior, and you ignore all other responses. By making rewards contingent on desired behaviors, researchers and animal trainers gradually shape complex behaviors.

Shaping can also help us understand what nonverbal organisms perceive. Can a dog distinguish red and green? Can a baby hear the difference between lower- and higher-pitched tones? If we can shape them to respond to one stimulus and not to another, then we know they can perceive the difference. Such experiments have even shown that some animals can form concepts. When experimenters reinforced pigeons for pecking after seeing a human face, but not after seeing other images, the pigeons' behavior showed that they could recognize human faces (Herrnstein & Loveland, 1964). In this experiment, the human face was a *discriminative stimulus.* Like a green traffic light, discriminative stimuli signal that a response will be reinforced. After being trained to discriminate among classes of events or objects—flowers, people, cars, chairs—pigeons were usually able to identify the category in which a new pictured object belonged (Bhatt et al., 1988; Wasserman, 1993). They have even been trained to discriminate between the music of Bach and Stravinsky (Porter & Neuringer, 1984).

In everyday life, we continually reinforce and shape others' behavior, said Skinner, though we may not mean to do so. Billy's whining, for example, annoys his parents, but look how they typically respond:

BILLY: *Could you tie my shoes?*

FATHER: *(Continues reading paper.)*

BILLY: *Dad, I need my shoes tied.*

FATHER: *Uh, yeah, just a minute.*

BILLY: *DAAAAD! TIE MY SHOES!*

FATHER: *How many times have I told you not to whine? Now, which shoe do we do first?*

Billy's whining is reinforced, because he gets something desirable—his dad's attention. Dad's response is reinforced because it gets rid of something aversive—Billy's whining.

Or consider a teacher who pastes gold stars on a wall chart beside the names of children scoring 100 percent on spelling tests. As everyone can then see, some children consistently do perfect work. The others, who take the same test and may have worked harder than the academic all-stars, get no rewards. The teacher would be better advised to apply the principles of operant conditioning—to reinforce all spellers for gradual improvements (successive approximations toward perfect spelling of words they find challenging).

Reinforcers vary with circumstances What is reinforcing (a heat lamp) to one animal (a cold meerkat) may not be to another (an overheated child). What is reinforcing in one situation (a cold snap at the Taronga Zoo in Sydney) may not be in another (a sweltering summer day).

positive reinforcement increasing behaviors by presenting positive reinforcers. A positive reinforcer is any stimulus that, when *presented* after a response, strengthens the response.

negative reinforcement increasing behaviors by stopping or reducing negative stimuli. A negative reinforcer is any stimulus that, when *removed* after a response, strengthens the response. (*Note:* Negative reinforcement is not punishment.)

primary reinforcer an innately reinforcing stimulus, such as one that satisfies a biological need.

conditioned reinforcer a stimulus that gains its reinforcing power through its association with a primary reinforcer; also known as a *secondary reinforcer.*

Types of Reinforcers

7-6: How do positive and negative reinforcement differ, and what are the basic types of reinforcers?

Up to now, we've mainly been discussing **positive reinforcement,** which strengthens a response by *presenting* a typically pleasurable stimulus after a response. But, as we saw in the whining Billy story, there are *two* basic kinds of reinforcement (**TABLE 7.1**). **Negative reinforcement** *strengthens* a response by *reducing or removing* something negative. Billy's whining was *positively* reinforced, because Billy got something desirable—his father's attention. His dad's response to the whining (tying Billy's shoes) was negatively reinforced, because it ended an aversive event—Billy's whining. Similarly, taking aspirin may relieve your headache, and hitting *snooze* will silence your annoying alarm. These welcome results provide negative reinforcement and increase the odds that you will repeat these behaviors. For drug addicts, the negative reinforcement of ending withdrawal pangs can be a compelling reason to resume using (Baker et al., 2004). Note that *negative reinforcement is not punishment.* (Some friendly advice: Mentally repeat the last five words.) Rather, negative reinforcement *removes* a punishing (aversive) event.

Table 7.1
Ways to Increase Behavior

Operant Conditioning Term	Description	Examples
Positive reinforcement	Add a desirable stimulus	Pet a dog that comes when you call it; pay the person who paints your house.
Negative reinforcement	Remove an aversive stimulus	Take painkillers to end pain; fasten seat belt to end loud beeping.

Sometimes negative and positive reinforcement coincide. Imagine a worried student who, after goofing off and getting a bad exam grade, studies harder for the next exam. This increased effort may be *negatively* reinforced by reduced anxiety, and *positively* reinforced by a better grade. Whether it works by reducing something aversive, or by giving something desirable, *reinforcement is any consequence that strengthens behavior.*

RETRIEVE IT

• How is operant conditioning at work in this cartoon?

ANSWER: If the child follows her older friend's instructions, she will negatively reinforce her caregivers by ceasing her cries when they grant her wishes. Her caregivers will positively reinforce her whines with a treat.

REMEMBER, WHEN LIFE GIVES YOU LEMONS, WHINE AND POUT AND CRY UNTIL LIFE CAN'T TAKE IT ANYMORE AND GIVES YOU COOKIES JUST TO SHUT YOU UP.

Dave Coverly/Dist. by Creators Syndicate, Inc.

Primary and Conditioned Reinforcers Getting food when hungry or having a painful headache go away is innately satisfying. These **primary reinforcers** are unlearned. **Conditioned reinforcers,** also called *secondary reinforcers,* get their power through learned association with primary reinforcers. If a rat in a Skinner box learns that a light reliably signals a food delivery, the rat will work to turn on the light. The light has become a conditioned reinforcer. Our lives are filled with conditioned reinforcers—money, good grades, a pleasant tone of voice—each of which has been linked with more basic rewards.

Immediate and Delayed Reinforcers Let's return to the imaginary shaping experiment in which you were conditioning a rat to press a bar. Before performing this "wanted" behavior, the hungry rat will engage in a sequence of "unwanted" behaviors—scratching, sniffing, and moving around. If you present food immediately after any one of these behaviors, the rat will likely repeat that rewarded behavior. But what if the rat presses the bar while you are distracted, and you delay giving the reinforcer? If the delay lasts longer than about 30 seconds, the rat will not learn to press the bar. You will have reinforced other incidental behaviors—more sniffing and moving—that intervened between the bar press and the reinforcer.

Unlike rats, humans do respond to delayed reinforcers: the paycheck at the end of the week, the good grade at the end of the semester, the trophy at the end of the season. Indeed, to function effectively we must learn to delay gratification. In laboratory testing, some 4-year-olds showed this ability. In choosing a candy, they preferred having a big reward tomorrow to munching on a small one right away. Learning to control our impulses in order to achieve more valued rewards is a big step toward maturity (Logue, 1998a,b). No wonder children who make such choices have tended to become socially competent and high-achieving adults (Mischel et al., 1989).

To our detriment, small but immediate consequences (the enjoyment of watching late-night TV, for example) are sometimes more alluring than big but delayed consequences (feeling alert tomorrow). For many teens, the immediate gratification of risky, unprotected sex in passionate moments prevails over the delayed gratifications of safe sex or saved sex. And for many people, the immediate rewards of today's gas-guzzling vehicles, air travel, and air conditioning prevail over the bigger future consequences of global climate change, rising seas, and extreme weather.

"Oh, not bad. The light comes on, I press the bar, they write me a check. How about you?"

Reinforcement Schedules

7-7: How do different reinforcement schedules affect behavior?

In most of our examples, the desired response has been reinforced every time it occurs. This is **continuous reinforcement.** But **reinforcement schedules** vary. Continuous reinforcement is the best choice for mastering a behavior because learning occurs rapidly—but extinction also occurs rapidly. When reinforcement stops—when we stop delivering food after the rat presses the bar—the behavior soon stops. If a normally dependable candy machine fails to deliver a chocolate bar twice in a row, we stop putting money into it (although a week later we may exhibit spontaneous recovery by trying again).

Real life rarely provides continuous reinforcement. Salespeople do not make a sale with every pitch. But they persist because their efforts are occasionally rewarded. This persistence is typical with **partial (intermittent) reinforcement** schedules, in which responses are sometimes reinforced, sometimes not. Learning is slower to appear, but *resistance to extinction* is greater than with continuous reinforcement. Imagine a pigeon that has learned to peck a key to obtain food. If you gradually phase out the food delivery until it occurs only rarely, in no predictable pattern, the pigeon may peck 150,000 times without a reward (Skinner, 1953). Slot machines reward gamblers in much the same way—occasionally and unpredictably. And like pigeons, slot players keep trying, time and time again. With intermittent reinforcement, hope springs eternal.

Lesson for parents: Partial reinforcement also works with children. *Occasionally* giving in to children's tantrums for the sake of peace and quiet intermittently reinforces the tantrums. This is the very best procedure for making a behavior persist.

Skinner (1961) and his collaborators compared four schedules of partial reinforcement. Some are rigidly fixed, some unpredictably variable.

Fixed-ratio schedules reinforce behavior after a set number of responses. Coffee shops may reward us with a free drink after every 10 purchased. In the laboratory, rats may be reinforced on a fixed ratio of, say, one food pellet for every 30 responses. Once conditioned, animals will pause only briefly after a reinforcer before returning to a high rate of responding (**FIGURE 7.10** on the next page).

Variable-ratio schedules provide reinforcers after a seemingly unpredictable number of responses. This is what slot-machine players and fly-casting anglers

continuous reinforcement reinforcing the desired response every time it occurs.

reinforcement schedule a pattern that defines how often a desired response will be reinforced.

partial (intermittent) reinforcement reinforcing a response only part of the time; results in slower acquisition of a response but much greater resistance to extinction than does continuous reinforcement.

fixed-ratio schedule in operant conditioning, a reinforcement schedule that reinforces a response only after a specified number of responses.

variable-ratio schedule in operant conditioning, a reinforcement schedule that reinforces a response after an unpredictable number of responses.

Vitaly Titov & Maria Sidelnikova/Shutterstock

"The charm of fishing is that it is the
pursuit of what is elusive but attainable, a
perpetual series of occasions for hope."

Scottish author John Buchan (1875–1940)

experience—unpredictable reinforcement—and what makes
gambling and fly fishing so hard to extinguish even when both
are getting nothing for something. Because reinforcers increase
as the number of responses increases, variable-ratio schedules
produce high rates of responding.

Fixed-interval schedules reinforce the first response after
a fixed time period. Animals on this type of schedule tend to
respond more frequently as the anticipated time for reward draws
near. People check more frequently for the mail as the delivery time
approaches. A hungry child jiggles the Jell-O more often to see
if it has set. Pigeons peck keys more rapidly as the time for reinforcement draws nearer (see Figure 7.10).

Variable-interval schedules reinforce the first response after *varying* time periods.
Like the message that finally rewards persistence in rechecking for a Facebook or an e-
mail response, variable-interval schedules tend to produce slow, steady responding. This
makes sense, because there is no knowing when the waiting will be over (**TABLE 7.2**).

In general, response rates are higher when reinforcement is linked to the number of
responses (a ratio schedule) rather than to time (an interval schedule). But responding is
more consistent when reinforcement is unpredictable (a variable schedule) than when it
is predictable (a fixed schedule). Animal behaviors differ, yet Skinner (1956) contended
that the reinforcement principles of operant conditioning are universal. It matters little,
he said, what response, what reinforcer, or what species you use. The effect of a given
reinforcement schedule is pretty much the same: "Pigeon, rat, monkey, which is which?
It doesn't matter. . . . Behavior shows astonishingly similar properties."

fixed-interval schedule in operant
conditioning, a reinforcement schedule that
reinforces a response only after a specified time
has elapsed.

variable-interval schedule in operant
conditioning, a reinforcement schedule that
reinforces a response at unpredictable time
intervals.

Table 7.2
Schedules of Reinforcement

	Fixed	Variable
Ratio	*Every so many:* reinforcement after every *nth* behavior, such as buy 10 coffees, get 1 free, or pay per product unit produced	*After an unpredictable number:* reinforcement after a random number of behaviors, as when playing slot machines or fly casting
Interval	*Every so often:* reinforcement for behavior after a fixed time, such as Tuesday discount prices	*Unpredictably often:* reinforcement for behavior after a random amount of time, as in checking for a Facebook response

Punishment

7-8: How does punishment differ from negative reinforcement, and how does punishment affect behavior?

Reinforcement increases a behavior; **punishment** does the opposite. A *punisher* is any consequence that *decreases* the frequency of a preceding behavior (**TABLE 7.3**). Swift and sure punishers can powerfully restrain unwanted behavior. The rat that is shocked after touching a forbidden object and the child who is burned by touching a hot stove will learn not to repeat those behaviors. Some punishments, though unintentional, are nevertheless quite effective: A dog that has learned to come running at the sound of an electric can opener will stop coming if its owner runs the machine to attract the dog and banish it to the basement.

Criminal behavior, much of it impulsive, is also influenced more by swift and sure punishers than by the threat of severe sentences (Darley & Alter, 2011). Thus, when Arizona introduced an exceptionally harsh sentence for first-time drunk drivers, the drunk-driving rate changed very little. But when Kansas City police started patrolling a high crime area to increase the sureness and swiftness of punishment, that city's crime rate dropped dramatically.

How should we interpret the punishment studies in relation to parenting practices? Many psychologists and supporters of nonviolent parenting have noted four major drawbacks of physical punishment (Gershoff, 2002; Marshall, 2002):

1. *Punished behavior is suppressed, not forgotten. This temporary state may (negatively) reinforce parents' punishing behavior.* The child swears, the parent swats, the parent hears no more swearing and feels the punishment successfully stopped the behavior. No wonder spanking has been a hit with so many U.S. parents of 3- and 4-year-olds—more than 9 in 10 of whom acknowledged spanking their children (Kazdin & Benjet, 2003).

2. *Punishment teaches discrimination among situations.* In operant conditioning, *discrimination* occurs when an organism learns that certain responses, but not others, will be reinforced. Did the punishment effectively end the child's swearing? Or did the child simply learn that it's not okay to swear around the house, though okay elsewhere?

3. *Punishment can teach fear.* In operant conditioning, *generalization* occurs when an organism's response to similar stimuli is also reinforced. A punished child may associate fear not only with the undesirable behavior but also with the person who

Children see, children do? Children who often experience physical punishment tend to display more aggression.

David Strickler/The Image Works

Table 7.3
Ways to Decrease Behavior

Type of Punisher	Description	Examples
Positive punishment	Administer an aversive stimulus	Spray water on a barking dog; give a traffic ticket for speeding.
Negative punishment	Withdraw a rewarding stimulus	Take away a teen's driving privileges; revoke a library card for nonpayment of fines.

punishment an event that tends to *decrease* the behavior it follows.

delivered the punishment or the place it occurred. Thus, children may learn to fear a punishing teacher and try to avoid school, or may become more anxious (Gershoff et al., 2010). For such reasons, most European countries and most U.S. states now ban hitting children in schools and child-care institutions (www.stophitting.com). Twenty-nine countries further outlaw hitting by parents, providing children the same legal protection given to spouses.

4. *Physical punishment may increase aggression by modeling aggression as a way to cope with problems.* Studies find that spanked children are at increased risk for aggression (and depression and low self-esteem). We know, for example, that many aggressive delinquents and abusive parents come from abusive families (Straus & Gelles, 1980; Straus et al., 1997). Some researchers have noted a problem with this logic. Well, yes, they've said, physically punished children may be more aggressive, for the same reason that people who have undergone psychotherapy are more likely to suffer depression—because they had preexisting problems that triggered the treatments (Larzelere, 2000, 2004). Which is the chicken and which is the egg? Correlations don't hand us an answer.

If one adjusts for preexisting antisocial behavior, then an occasional single swat or two to misbehaving 2- to 6-year-olds looks more effective (Baumrind et al., 2002; Larzelere & Kuhn, 2005). That is especially so if two other conditions are met:

1. The swat is used only as a backup when milder disciplinary tactics, such as a time-out (removing them from reinforcing surroundings) fail.

2. The swat is combined with a generous dose of reasoning and reinforcing.

Other researchers remain unconvinced. After controlling for prior misbehavior, they report that more frequent spankings of young children predict future aggressiveness (Grogan-Kaylor, 2004; Taylor et al., 2010).

Parents of delinquent youths are often unaware of how to achieve desirable behaviors without screaming or hitting their children (Patterson et al., 1982). Training programs can help transform dire threats ("You clean up your room this minute or no dinner!") into positive incentives ("You're welcome at the dinner table after you get your room cleaned up"). Stop and think about it. Aren't many threats of punishment just as forceful, and perhaps more effective, when rephrased positively? Thus, "If you don't get your homework done, there'll be no car" would better be phrased as . . . .

In classrooms, too, teachers can give feedback on papers by saying, "No, but try this . . ." and "Yes, that's it!" Such responses reduce unwanted behavior while reinforcing more desirable alternatives. Remember: *Punishment tells you what* not *to do; reinforcement tells you* what *to do.*

What punishment often teaches, said Skinner, is how to avoid it. Most psychologists now favor an emphasis on reinforcement.

RETRIEVE IT

- Fill in the blanks below with one of the following terms: positive reinforcement (PR), negative reinforcement (NR), positive punishment (PP), and negative punishment (NP). I have provided the first answer (PR) for you.

Type of Stimulus	Give It	Take It Away
Desired (for example, a teen's use of the car):	1. PR	2.
Undesired/aversive (for example, an insult):	3.	4.

ANSWERS: 1. PR (positive reinforcement); 2. NP (negative punishment); 3. PP (positive punishment); 4. NR (negative reinforcement)

Skinner's Legacy

7-9: Why did Skinner's ideas provoke controversy, and how might his operant conditioning principles be applied at school, in sports, at work, and at home?

B. F. Skinner stirred a hornet's nest with his outspoken beliefs. He repeatedly insisted that external influences (not internal thoughts and feelings) shape behavior. And he urged people to use operant principles to influence others' behavior at school, work, and home. Knowing that behavior is shaped by its results, he said we should use rewards to evoke more desirable behavior.

Skinner's critics objected, saying that he dehumanized people by neglecting their personal freedom and by seeking to control their actions. Skinner's reply: External consequences already haphazardly control people's behavior. Why not administer those consequences toward human betterment? Wouldn't reinforcers be more humane than the punishments used in homes, schools, and prisons? And if it is humbling to think that our history has shaped us, doesn't this very idea also give us hope that we can shape our future?

B. F. Skinner "I am sometimes asked, 'Do you think of yourself as you think of the organisms you study?' The answer is yes. So far as I know, my behavior at any given moment has been nothing more than the product of my genetic endowment, my personal history, and the current setting" (1983).

Bachrach/Getty Images

Applications of Operant Conditioning

In later chapters we will see how psychologists apply operant conditioning principles to help people reduce high blood pressure or gain social skills. Reinforcement technologies have also been used in schools, sports, workplaces, and homes (Flora, 2004).

At School More than a generation ago, Skinner envisioned a day when teaching machines and textbooks would shape learning in small steps, immediately reinforcing correct responses. He believed such machines and texts would revolutionize education and free teachers to focus on each student's special needs.

Stand in Skinner's shoes for a moment and imagine two math teachers, each with a class of students ranging from whiz kids to slow learners. Teacher A gives the whole class the same lesson, knowing that the bright kids will breeze through the math concepts, and the slower ones will be frustrated and fail. Teacher B, faced with a similar class, paces the material according to each student's rate of learning and provides prompt feedback, with positive reinforcement, to both the slow and the fast learners. Thinking as Skinner did, how might you achieve the individualized instruction of Teacher B?

Computers were Skinner's final hope. "Good instruction demands two things," he said. "Students must be told immediately whether what they do is right or wrong and, when right, they must be directed to the step to be taken next." Thus, the computer could be Teacher B—pacing math drills to the student's rate of learning, quizzing the student to find gaps in understanding, giving immediate feedback, and keeping flawless records. To the end of his life, Skinner (1986, 1988, 1989) believed his ideal was achievable. The predicted education revolution has not occurred, partly because the early teaching machines often trained rote learning, not deep processing. Today's interactive student software, web-based learning, and online testing bring us closer to achieving Skinner's ideal.

Operant conditioning may also be effectively applied in behavior modification therapies (also known as applied behavior analysis). See Chapter 15 for more on this topic.

Computer-assisted learning Computers have helped realize Skinner's goal of individually paced instruction with immediate feedback.

Lauren Burke/Getty Images

In Sports The key to shaping behavior in athletic performance, as elsewhere, is first reinforcing small successes and then gradually increasing the challenge. Golf students can learn putting by starting with very short putts, and eventually, as they build mastery, stepping back farther and farther. Novice batters can begin with half swings at an oversized

respondent behavior behavior that occurs as an automatic response to some stimulus.

ball pitched from 10 feet away, giving them the immediate pleasure of smacking the ball. As the hitters' confidence builds with their success and they achieve mastery at each level, the pitcher gradually moves back—to 15, then 22, 30, and 40.5 feet—and eventually introduces a standard baseball and pitching distance. Compared with children taught by conventional methods, those trained by this behavioral method have shown faster skill improvement (Simek & O'Brien, 1981, 1988).

At Work Knowing that reinforcers influence productivity, many organizations have invited employees to share the risks and rewards of company ownership. Others have focused on reinforcing a job well done. Rewards are most likely to increase productivity if the desired performance is well defined and achievable. The message for managers? *Reward specific, achievable behaviors, not vaguely defined "merit."*

Operant conditioning also reminds us that reinforcement should be *immediate*. IBM legend Thomas Watson understood. When he observed an achievement, he wrote the employee a check on the spot (Peters & Waterman, 1982). But rewards need not be material, or lavish. An effective manager may simply walk the floor and sincerely affirm people for good work, or write notes of appreciation for a completed project. As Skinner said, "How much richer would the whole world be if the reinforcers in daily life were more effectively contingent on productive work?"

At Home Parent-training researchers have pointed out how much parents can learn from operant conditioning practices. By saying, "Get ready for bed" and then caving in to protests or defiance, parents reinforce such whining and arguing (Wierson & Forehand, 1994). Exasperated, they may then yell or gesture menacingly. When the child, now frightened, obeys, that reinforces the parents' angry behavior. Over time, a destructive parent-child relationship develops.

To disrupt this cycle, parents should remember that basic rule of shaping: *Notice people doing something right and affirm them for it.* Give children attention and other reinforcers when they are behaving *well*. Target a specific behavior, reward it, and watch it increase. When children misbehave or are defiant, don't yell at them or hit them. Simply explain the misbehavior and give them a time-out.

Finally, we can use operant conditioning in our own lives (see Close-Up: Training Our Partners). To reinforce your own desired behaviors (perhaps to exercise more often) and extinguish the undesired ones (to stop smoking, for example), psychologists suggest taking these steps:

1. *State your goal in measurable terms, and announce it.* You might, for example, aim to boost your study time by an hour a day and share that goal with some close friends.

2. *Monitor how often you engage in your desired behavior.* You might log your current study time, noting under what conditions you do and don't study. (When I began writing textbooks, I logged how I spent my time each day and was amazed to discover how much time I was wasting.)

3. *Reinforce the desired behavior.* To increase your study time, give yourself a reward (a snack or some activity you enjoy) only after you finish your extra hour of study. Agree with your friends that you will join them for weekend activities only if you have met your realistic weekly studying goal.

4. *Reduce the rewards gradually.* As your new behaviors become more habitual, give yourself a mental pat on the back instead of a cookie.

"I wrote another five hundred words. Can I have another cookie?"

Training Our Partners

By Amy Sutherland

For a book I was writing about a school for exotic animal trainers, I started commuting from Maine to California, where I spent my days watching students do the seemingly impossible: teaching hyenas to pirouette on command, cougars to offer their paws for a nail clipping, and baboons to skateboard.

I listened, rapt, as professional trainers explained how they taught dolphins to flip and elephants to paint. Eventually it hit me that the same techniques might work on that stubborn but lovable species, the American husband.

The central lesson I learned from exotic animal trainers is that I should reward behavior I like and ignore behavior I don't. After all, you don't get a sea lion to balance a ball on the end of its nose by nagging. The same goes for the American husband.

Back in Maine, I began thanking Scott if he threw one dirty shirt into the hamper. If he threw in two, I'd kiss him. Meanwhile, I would step over any soiled clothes on the floor without one sharp word, though I did sometimes kick them under the bed. But as he basked in my appreciation, the piles became smaller.

I was using what trainers call "approximations," rewarding the small steps toward learning a whole new behavior. . . . Once I started thinking this way, I couldn't stop. At the school in California, I'd be scribbling notes on how to walk an emu or have a wolf accept you as a pack member, but I'd be thinking, "I can't wait to try this on Scott. . . ."

After two years of exotic animal training, my marriage is far smoother, my husband much easier to love. I used to take his faults personally; his dirty clothes on the floor were an affront, a symbol of how he didn't care enough about me. But thinking of my husband as an exotic species gave me the distance I needed to consider our differences more objectively.

Excerpted with permission from Sutherland, A., (2006, June 25). What Shamu taught me about a happy marriage, *New York Times.*

RETRIEVE IT

• Ethan constantly misbehaves at preschool even though his teacher scolds him repeatedly. Why does Ethan's misbehavior continue, and what can his teacher do to stop it?

ANSWER: If Ethan is seeking attention, the teacher's scolding may be reinforcing rather than punishing. To change Ethan's behavior, his teacher could offer reinforcement (such as praise) each time he behaves well. The teacher might encourage Ethan toward increasingly appropriate behavior through shaping, or by rephrasing rules as rewards instead of punishments. ("You can have a snack if you play nicely with the other children" [reward] rather than "You will not get a snack if you misbehave!" [punishment].)

Contrasting Classical and Operant Conditioning

7-10: How does operant conditioning differ from classical conditioning?

Both classical and operant conditioning are forms of *associative learning.* Both involve *acquisition, extinction, spontaneous recovery, generalization,* and *discrimination.* But these two forms of learning also differ. Through classical (Pavlovian) conditioning, we associate different stimuli we do not control, and we respond automatically **(respondent behaviors)** (**TABLE 7.4**). Through operant conditioning, we associate our own

Table 7.4
Comparison of Classical and Operant Conditioning

	Classical Conditioning	Operant Conditioning
Basic idea	Organism associates events	Organism associates behavior and resulting events
Response	Involuntary, automatic	Voluntary, operates on environment
Acquisition	Associating events; NS is paired with US and becomes CS	Associating response with a consequence (reinforcer or punisher)
Extinction	CR decreases when CS is repeatedly presented alone	Responding decreases when reinforcement stops
Spontaneous recovery	The reappearance, after a rest period, of an extinguished CR	The reappearance, after a rest period, of an extinguished response
Generalization	The tendency to respond to stimuli similar to the CS	Organism's response to similar stimuli is also reinforced
Discrimination	The learned ability to distinguish between a CS and other stimuli that do not signal a US	Organism learns that certain responses, but not others, will be reinforced

operant behavior behavior that operates on the environment, producing consequences.

"O! This learning, what a thing it is."

William Shakespeare, The Taming of the Shrew, *1597*

behaviors that act on our environment to produce rewarding or punishing stimuli (**operant behaviors**) with their consequences.

As we shall next see, our biology and cognitive processes influence both classical and operant conditioning.

RETRIEVE IT

• Salivating in response to a tone paired with food is a(n) _____ behavior; pressing a bar to obtain food is a(n) _____ behavior.

ANSWERS: respondent; operant

Biology, Cognition, and Learning

From drooling dogs, running rats, and pecking pigeons we have learned much about the basic processes of learning. But conditioning principles don't tell us the whole story. Today's learning theorists recognize that learning is the product of the interaction of biological, psychological, and social-cultural influences (**FIGURE 7.11**).

Biological Constraints on Conditioning

7-11: How do biological constraints affect classical and operant conditioning?

Ever since Charles Darwin, scientists have assumed that all animals share a common evolutionary history and thus share commonalities in their makeup and functioning. Pavlov and Watson, for example, believed the basic laws of learning were essentially similar in all animals. So it should make little difference whether one studied pigeons or people. Moreover, it seemed that any natural response could be conditioned to any neutral stimulus.

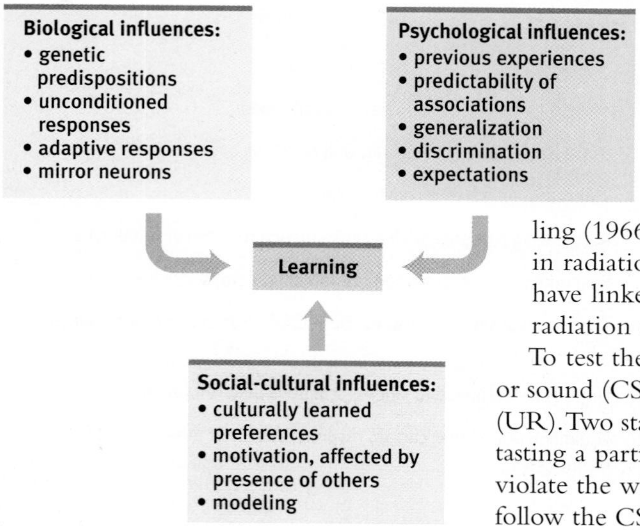

Limits on Classical Conditioning

In 1956, learning researcher Gregory Kimble proclaimed, "Just about any activity of which the organism is capable can be conditioned and . . . these responses can be conditioned to any stimulus that the organism can perceive" (p. 195). Twenty-five years later, he humbly acknowledged that "half a thousand" scientific reports had proven him wrong (Kimble, 1981). More than the early behaviorists realized, an animal's capacity for conditioning is constrained by its biology. Each species' predispositions prepare it to learn the associations that enhance its survival. Environments are not the whole story.

John Garcia was among those who challenged the prevailing idea that all associations can be learned equally well. While researching the effects of radiation on laboratory animals, Garcia and Robert Koelling (1966) noticed that rats began to avoid drinking water from the plastic bottles in radiation chambers. Could classical conditioning be the culprit? Might the rats have linked the plastic-tasting water (a CS) to the sickness (UR) triggered by the radiation (US)?

To test their hunch, Garcia and Koelling exposed the rats to a particular taste, sight, or sound (CS) and later also to radiation or drugs (US) that led to nausea and vomiting (UR). Two startling findings emerged: First, even if sickened as late as several hours after tasting a particular novel flavor, the rats thereafter avoided that flavor. This appeared to violate the widely held belief that for conditioning to occur, the US must immediately follow the CS.

FIGURE 7.11

Biopsychosocial influences on learning Our learning results not only from environmental experiences, but also from cognitive and biological influences.

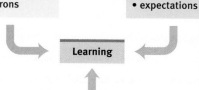

Biological influences:
• genetic predispositions
• unconditioned responses
• adaptive responses
• mirror neurons

Psychological influences:
• previous experiences
• predictability of associations
• generalization
• discrimination
• expectations

Learning

Social-cultural influences:
• culturally learned preferences
• motivation, affected by presence of others
• modeling

Second, the sickened rats developed aversions to tastes but not to sights or sounds. This contradicted the behaviorists' idea that any perceivable stimulus could serve as a CS. But it made adaptive sense. For rats, the easiest way to identify tainted food is to taste it; if sickened after sampling a new food, they thereafter avoid it. This response, called *taste aversion,* makes it difficult to eradicate a population of "bait-shy" rats by poisoning.

Humans, too, seem biologically prepared to learn some associations rather than others. If you become violently ill four hours after eating contaminated mussels, you will probably develop an aversion to the taste of mussels but usually not to the sight of the associated restaurant, its plates, the people you were with, or the music you heard there. (In contrast, birds, which hunt by sight, appear biologically primed to develop aversions to the *sight* of tainted food [Nicolaus et al., 1983].)

Garcia and Koelling's taste-aversion research is but one instance in which psychological experiments that began with the discomfort of some laboratory animals ended by enhancing the welfare of many others. In one conditioned taste-aversion study, coyotes and wolves were tempted into eating sheep carcasses laced with a sickening poison. Thereafter, they developed an aversion to sheep meat; two wolves later penned with a live sheep seemed actually to fear it (Gustavson et al., 1974, 1976). These studies not only saved the sheep from their predators, but also saved the sheep-shunning coyotes and wolves from angry ranchers and farmers who had wanted to destroy them. Similar applications have prevented baboons from raiding African gardens, raccoons from attacking chickens, ravens and crows from feeding on crane eggs, and Mexican wolves from preying on sheep. In all these cases, research helped preserve both the prey and their predators, who occupy an important ecological niche (Dingfelder, 2010; Garcia & Gustavson, 1997).

Such research supports Darwin's principle that natural selection favors traits that aid survival. Our ancestors who readily learned taste aversions were unlikely to eat the same toxic food again and were more likely to survive and leave descendants. Nausea, like anxiety, pain, and other bad feelings, serves a good purpose. Like a car's low-oil warning light, each alerts the body to a threat (Neese, 1991).

The tendency to learn behaviors favored by natural selection may help explain why we humans seem to be naturally disposed to learn associations between the color red and sexuality. Female primates display red when nearing ovulation. In human females, enhanced bloodflow produces the red blush of flirtation and sexual excitation. Does the frequent pairing of red and sex—with Valentine's hearts, red-light districts, and red lipstick—naturally enhance men's attraction to women? Experiments (**FIGURE 7.12**) have suggested that, without men's awareness, it does (Elliot & Niesta, 2008).

John Garcia As the laboring son of California farmworkers, Garcia attended school only in the off-season during his early childhood years. After entering junior college in his late twenties, and earning his Ph.D. in his late forties, he received the American Psychological Association's Distinguished Scientific Contribution Award "for his highly original, pioneering research in conditioning and learning." He was also elected to the National Academy of Sciences.

Courtesy of John Garcia

Taste aversion If you became violently ill after eating mussels, you probably would have a hard time eating them again. Their smell and taste would have become a CS for nausea. This learning occurs readily because our biology prepares us to learn taste aversions to toxic foods.

Antonio S./Shutterstock

Animal taste aversion As an alternative to killing wolves and coyotes that preyed on sheep, some ranchers have sickened the animals with lamb laced with a drug.

blickwinkel/Alamy

Courtesy of Kathryn Brownson, Hope College

FIGURE 7.12
Romantic red
In a series of experiments that controlled for other factors (such as the brightness of the image), men found women more attractive and sexually desirable when framed in red (Elliot & Niesta, 2008).

"All animals are on a voyage through time, navigating toward futures that promote their survival and away from futures that threaten it. Pleasure and pain are the stars by which they steer."

Psychologists Daniel T. Gilbert and Timothy D. Wilson, "Prospection: Experiencing the Future," 2007

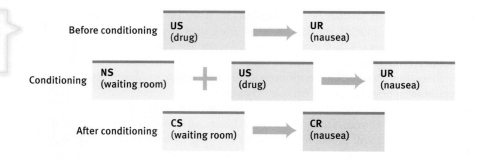

FIGURE 7.13
Nausea conditioning in cancer patients

A genetic predisposition to associate a CS with a US that follows predictably and immediately is adaptive: Causes often immediately precede effects. Often, but not always, as we saw in the taste-aversion findings. At such times, our predispositions can trick us. When chemotherapy triggers nausea and vomiting more than an hour following treatment, cancer patients may over time develop classically conditioned nausea (and sometimes anxiety) to the sights, sounds, and smells associated with the clinic (**FIGURE 7.13**) (Hall, 1997). Merely returning to the clinic's waiting room or seeing the nurses can provoke these conditioned feelings (Burish & Carey, 1986; Davey, 1992). Under normal circumstances, such revulsion to sickening stimuli would be adaptive.

> "Once bitten, twice shy."
>
> *G. F. Northall,* Folk-Phrases, *1894*

RETRIEVE IT

• How did Garcia and Koelling's taste-aversion studies help disprove Gregory Kimble's early claim that "just about any activity of which the organism is capable can be conditioned to any stimulus that the organism can perceive"? Explain.

ANSWER: Garcia and Koelling demonstrated that rats may learn an aversion to *tastes*, on which their survival depends, but not to sights or sounds.

Limits on Operant Conditioning

As with classical conditioning, nature sets limits on each species' capacity for operant conditioning. Mark Twain (1835–1910) said it well: "Never try to teach a pig to sing. It wastes your time and annoys the pig."

We most easily learn and retain behaviors that reflect our biological predispositions. Thus, using food as a reinforcer, you could easily condition a hamster to dig or to rear up, because these are among the animal's natural food-searching behaviors. But you won't be so successful if you use food as a reinforcer to shape face washing and other hamster behaviors that aren't normally associated with food or hunger (Shettleworth, 1973). Similarly, you could easily teach pigeons to flap their wings to avoid being shocked, and to peck to obtain food: Fleeing with their wings and eating with their beaks are natural pigeon behaviors. However, pigeons would have a hard time learning to peck to avoid a shock, or to flap their wings to obtain food (Foree & LoLordo, 1973). The principle: *Biological constraints predispose organisms to learn associations that are naturally adaptive.*

In the early 1940s, University of Minnesota graduate students Marian Breland and Keller Breland witnessed the power of operant conditioning while working with their mentor, B. F. Skinner (1961; Bailey & Gillaspy, 2005). Impressed with his results, they began training dogs, cats, chickens, parakeets, turkeys, pigs, ducks, and hamsters. The rest is history. The company they formed spent the next half-century training more than 15,000 animals from 140 species for movies, traveling shows, amusement parks, corporations, and the government. And along the way, the Brelands themselves mentored others, including Sea World's first director of training.

Natural athletes Animals can most easily learn and retain behaviors that draw on their biological predispositions, such as dogs' inborn tendency to rely on all four feet for mobility and balance.

Marina Jay/Shutterstock

In their early training days, the Brelands presumed that operant principles would work on almost any response an animal could make. But they, too, learned about biological constraints. In one act, pigs trained to pick up large wooden "dollars" and deposit them in a piggy bank began to drift back to their natural ways. They dropped the coin, pushed it with their snouts as pigs are prone to do, picked it up again, and then repeated the sequence—delaying their food reinforcer. This *instinctive drift* occurred as the animals reverted to their biologically predisposed patterns.

Cognition's Influence on Conditioning

7-12: How do cognitive processes affect classical and operant conditioning?

Cognition and Classical Conditioning

In their dismissal of "mentalistic" concepts such as consciousness, Pavlov and Watson underestimated the importance not only of biological constraints, but also the effects of cognitive processes (thoughts, perceptions, expectations). The early behaviorists believed that rats' and dogs' learned behaviors could be reduced to mindless mechanisms, so there was no need to consider cognition. But Robert Rescorla and Allan Wagner (1972) showed that an animal can learn the *predictability* of an event. If a shock always is preceded by a tone, and then may also be preceded by a light that accompanies the tone, a rat will react with fear to the tone but not to the light. Although the light is always followed by the shock, it adds no new information; the tone is a better predictor. The more predictable the association, the stronger the conditioned response. It's as if the animal learns an *expectancy,* an awareness of how likely it is that the US will occur.

Classical conditioning treatments that ignore cognition often have limited success. For example, people receiving therapy for alcohol dependence may be given alcohol spiked with a nauseating drug. Will they then associate alcohol with sickness? If classical conditioning were merely a matter of "stamping in" stimulus associations, we might hope so, and to some extent this does occur (as we will see in Chapter 15). However, one's awareness that the nausea is induced by the drug, not the alcohol, often weakens the association between drinking alcohol and feeling sick. So, even in classical conditioning, it is (especially with humans) not simply the CS-US association but also the thought that counts.

Cognition and Operant Conditioning

B. F. Skinner granted the biological underpinnings of behavior and the existence of private thought processes. Nevertheless, many psychologists criticized him for discounting cognition's importance.

A mere eight days before dying of leukemia in 1990, Skinner stood before the American Psychological Association convention. In this final address, he again resisted the growing belief that cognitive processes have a necessary place in the science of psychology and even in our understanding of conditioning. He viewed "cognitive science" as a throwback to early twentieth-century introspectionism. For Skinner, thoughts and emotions were behaviors that follow the same laws as other behaviors.

Nevertheless, the evidence of cognitive processes cannot be ignored. For example, animals on a fixed-interval reinforcement schedule respond more and more frequently as the time approaches when a response will produce a reinforcer. Although a strict behaviorist would object to talk of "expectations," the animals behave as if they expected that repeating the response would soon produce the reward.

Evidence of cognitive processes has also come from studying rats in mazes. Rats exploring a maze, given no obvious rewards, seem to develop a **cognitive map,** a mental

cognitive map a mental representation of the layout of one's environment. For example, after exploring a maze, rats act as if they have learned a cognitive map of it.

For more information on animal behavior, see books by (I am not making this up) Robin Fox and Lionel Tiger.

"All brains are, in essence, anticipation machines."

Daniel C. Dennett, Consciousness Explained, *1991*

"*Bathroom? Sure, it's just down the hall to the left, jog right, left, another left, straight past two more lefts, then right, and it's at the end of the third corridor on your right.*"

latent learning learning that occurs but is not apparent until there is an incentive to demonstrate it.

intrinsic motivation a desire to perform a behavior effectively for its own sake.

extrinsic motivation a desire to perform a behavior to receive promised rewards or avoid threatened punishment.

observational learning learning by observing others.

modeling the process of observing and imitating a specific behavior.

Latent learning Animals, like people, can learn from experience, with or without reinforcement. In a classic experiment, rats in one group repeatedly explored a maze, always with a food reward at the end. Rats in another group explored the maze with no food reward. But once given a food reward at the end, rats in the second group thereafter ran the maze as quickly as (and even faster than) the always-rewarded rats. (From Tolman & Honzik, 1930.)

representation of the maze. When an experimenter then places food in the maze's goal box, these rats run the maze as quickly and efficiently as other rats that were previously reinforced with food for this result. Like people sightseeing in a new town, the exploring rats seemingly experienced **latent learning** during their earlier tours. That learning became apparent only when there was some incentive to demonstrate it. Children, too, may learn from watching a parent but demonstrate the learning only much later, as needed. The point to remember: *There is more to learning than associating a response with a consequence; there is also cognition.* In Chapter 9 we will encounter more striking evidence of animals' cognitive abilities in solving problems and in using aspects of language.

The cognitive perspective has also shown us the limits of rewards: Promising people a reward for a task they already enjoy can backfire. Excessive rewards can destroy **intrinsic motivation**—the desire to perform a behavior effectively for its own sake. In experiments, children have been promised a payoff for playing with an interesting puzzle or toy. Later, they played with the toy *less* than other unpaid children did (Deci et al., 1999; Tang & Hall, 1995). Likewise, rewarding children with toys or candy for reading diminishes the time they spend reading (Marinak & Gambrell, 2008). It is as if they think, "If I have to be bribed into doing this, it must not be worth doing for its own sake."

To sense the difference between intrinsic motivation and **extrinsic motivation** (behaving in certain ways to gain external rewards or avoid threatened punishment), think about your experience in this course. Are you feeling pressured to finish this reading before a deadline? Worried about your grade? Eager for the credits that will count toward graduation? If *Yes,* then you are extrinsically motivated (as, to some extent, almost all students must be). Are you also finding the material interesting? Does learning it make you feel more competent? If there were no grade at stake, might you be curious enough to want to learn the material for its own sake? If *Yes,* intrinsic motivation also fuels your efforts.

Youth sports coaches who aim to promote enduring interest in an activity, not just to pressure players into winning, should focus on the intrinsic joy of playing and of reaching one's potential (Deci & Ryan, 1985, 2009). Giving people choices also enhances their intrinsic motivation (Patall et al., 2008). Nevertheless, rewards used to signal a job well done (rather than to bribe or control someone) can be effective (Boggiano et al., 1985). "Most improved player" awards, for example, can boost feelings of competence and increase enjoyment of a sport. Rightly administered, rewards can raise performance and spark creativity (Eisenberger & Aselage, 2009; Henderlong & Lepper, 2002). And extrinsic rewards (such as the admissions scholarships and jobs that often follow good grades) are here to stay. **TABLE 7.5** compares the biological and cognitive influences on classical and operant conditioning.

Table 7.5
Biological and Cognitive Influences on Conditioning

	Classical Conditioning	Operant Conditioning
Biological predispositions	Natural predispositions constrain what stimuli and responses can easily be associated.	Organisms best learn behaviors similar to their natural behaviors; unnatural behaviors instinctively drift back toward natural ones.
Cognitive processes	Organisms develop expectation that CS signals the arrival of US.	Organisms develop expectation that a response will be reinforced or punished; they also exhibit latent learning, without reinforcement.

RETRIEVE IT

• Instinctive drift and latent learning are examples of what important idea?

ANSWER: The success of operant conditioning is affected not just by environmental cues, but also by biological and cognitive factors.

Learning by Observation

7-13: What is observational learning, and how do some scientists believe it is enabled by mirror neurons?

Cognition is certainly a factor in **observational learning,** in which higher animals, especially humans, learn without direct experience, by watching and imitating others. A child who sees his sister burn her fingers on a hot stove learns not to touch it. We learn our native languages and various other specific behaviors by observing and imitating others, a process called **modeling.**

Albert Bandura was the pioneering researcher of observational learning. Picture this scene from one of his experiments (Bandura et al., 1961): A preschool child is working on a drawing, while an adult in another part of the room is building with Tinkertoys. As the child watches, the adult gets up and for nearly 10 minutes pounds, kicks, and throws around the room a large inflated Bobo doll, yelling, "Sock him in the nose. . . . Hit him down. . . . Kick him."

The child is then taken to another room filled with appealing toys. Soon the experimenter returns and tells the child she has decided to save these good toys "for the other children." She takes the now-frustrated child to a third room containing a few toys, including a Bobo doll. Left alone, what does the child do?

Compared with children not exposed to the adult model, those who viewed the model's actions were more likely to lash out at the doll. Observing the aggressive outburst apparently lowered their inhibitions. But *something more* was also at work, for the children imitated the very acts they had observed and used the very words they had heard (**FIGURE 7.14**).

That "something more," Bandura suggested, was this: By watching a model, we experience *vicarious reinforcement* or *vicarious punishment,* and we learn to anticipate a behavior's consequences in situations like those we are observing. We are especially likely to learn from people we perceive as similar to ourselves, or as successful, or as admirable. fMRI scans show that when people observe someone winning a reward (and especially when it's someone likable and similar to themselves) their own brain reward systems activate, much as if they themselves had won the reward (Mobbs et al., 2009). When we identify with someone, we experience their outcomes vicariously. Lord Chesterfield (1694–1773) had the idea: "We are, in truth, more than half what we are by imitation."

Albert Bandura "The Bobo doll follows me wherever I go. The photographs are published in every introductory psychology text and virtually every undergraduate takes introductory psychology. I recently checked into a Washington hotel. The clerk at the desk asked, 'Aren't you the psychologist who did the Bobo doll experiment?' I answered, 'I am afraid that will be my legacy.' He replied, 'That deserves an upgrade. I will put you in a suite in the quiet part of the hotel'" (2005).
Courtesy of Albert Bandura, Stanford University

FIGURE 7.14
The famous Bobo doll experiment
Notice how the children's actions directly imitate the adult's.

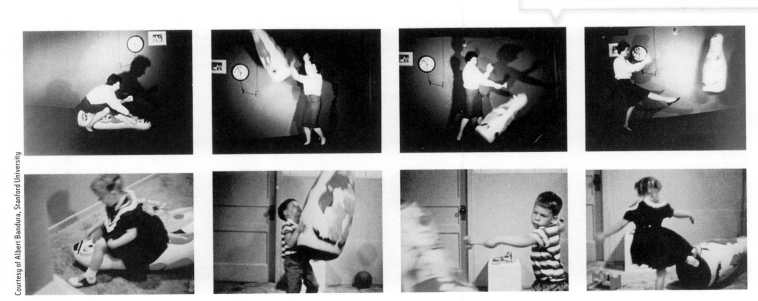

Courtesy of Albert Bandura, Stanford University

Mirror neurons at work?

David Sipress

SIPRESS

"Your back is killing me!"

"Children need models more than they need critics."

Joseph Joubert, Pensées, *1842*

Mirrors and Imitation in the Brain

On a 1991 hot summer day in Parma, Italy, a lab monkey awaited its researchers' return from lunch. The researchers had implanted wires next to its motor cortex, in a frontal lobe brain region that enabled the monkey to plan and enact movements. The monitoring device would alert the researchers to activity in that region of the monkey's brain. When the monkey moved a peanut into its mouth, for example, the device would buzz. That day, as one of the researchers reentered the lab, ice cream cone in hand, the monkey stared at him. As the researcher raised the cone to lick it, the monkey's monitor buzzed—as if the motionless monkey had itself moved (Blakeslee, 2006; Iacoboni, 2008, 2009).

The same buzzing had been heard earlier, when the monkey watched humans or other monkeys move peanuts to their mouths. The flabbergasted researchers, led by Giacomo Rizzolatti (2002, 2006), had, they believed, stumbled onto a previously unknown type of neuron. These presumed **mirror neurons** may provide a neural basis for everyday imitation and observational learning. When a monkey grasps, holds, or tears something, these neurons fire. And they likewise fire when the monkey observes another doing so. When one monkey sees, its neurons mirror what another monkey does.

In humans, imitation is pervasive. Our catchphrases, hem lengths, ceremonies, foods, traditions, vices, and fads all spread by one person copying another. Imitation shapes even very young humans' behavior (Bates & Byrne, 2010). Shortly after birth, a baby may imitate an adult who sticks out his tongue. By 8 to 16 months, infants imitate various novel gestures (Jones, 2007). By age 12 months (**FIGURE 7.15**), they look where an adult is looking (Meltzoff et al., 2009). And by age 14 months, children imitate acts modeled on TV (Meltzoff, 1988; Meltzoff & Moore, 1989, 1997). Even as 2½-year-olds, when many of their mental abilities are near those of adult chimpanzees, young humans surpass chimps at social tasks such as imitating another's solution to a problem (Herrmann et al., 2007). Children see, children do.

So strong is the human predisposition to learn from watching adults that 2- to 5-year-old children *overimitate*. Whether living in urban Australia or rural Africa, they copy even irrelevant adult actions. Before reaching for a toy in a plastic jar, they will first stroke the jar with a feather if that's what they have observed (Lyons et al., 2007). Or, imitating an adult, they will wave a stick over a box and then use the stick to push on a knob that opens the box—when all they needed to do to open the box was to push on the knob (Nielsen & Tomaselli, 2010).

Humans, like monkeys, have brains that support empathy and imitation. Researchers cannot insert experimental electrodes in human brains, but they can use fMRI scans to see brain activity associated with performing and with observing actions. So, is the human capacity to simulate another's action and to share in another's experience due to specialized mirror neurons? Or is it due to distributed brain networks? That issue is currently being debated (Gallese et al., 2011; Iacoboni, 2008, 2009; Mukamel et al., 2010). Regardless, children's brains enable their empathy and their ability to infer another's mental state, an ability known as *theory of mind*.

FIGURE 7.15

Imitation This 12-month-old infant sees an adult look left, and immediately follows her gaze. (From Meltzoff et al., 2009.)

Meltzoff, A. N., Kuhl, P. K., Movellan, J., & Sejnowski, T. J. (2009). Foundations for a new science of learning. *Science, 325,* 284–288

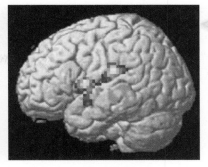

Pain   Empathy

Reprinted with permission from The American Association for the Advancement of Science. Subiaul et al. (2004). *Science*, 305, 407–410. AAAS.

The brain's response to observing others makes emotions contagious. Through its neurological echo, our brain simulates and vicariously experiences what we observe. So real are these mental instant replays that we may misremember an action we have observed as an action we have performed (Lindner et al., 2010). But through these reenactments, we grasp others' states of mind. Observing others' postures, faces, voices, and writing styles, we unconsciously synchronize our own to theirs—which helps us feel what they are feeling (Bernieri et al., 1994; Ireland & Pennebaker, 2010). We find ourselves yawning when they yawn, laughing when they laugh.

When observing movie characters smoking, smokers' brains spontaneously simulate smoking, which helps explain their cravings (Wagner et al., 2011). Seeing a loved one's pain, our faces mirror the other's emotion. But as **FIGURE 7.16** shows, so do our brains. In this fMRI scan, the pain imagined by an empathic romantic partner triggered some of the same brain activity experienced by the loved one who actually had the pain (Singer et al., 2004). Even fiction reading may trigger such activity, as we mentally simulate (and vicariously experience) the feelings and actions described (Mar & Oatley, 2008; Speer et al., 2009). The bottom line: *Brain activity underlies our intensely social nature.*

Applications of Observational Learning

So the big news from Bandura's studies and the mirror-neuron research is that we look, we mentally imitate, and we learn. Models—in our family, our neighborhood, or on TV—may have effects, good and bad.

Prosocial Effects

7-14: What is the impact of prosocial modeling and of antisocial modeling?

The good news is that **prosocial** (positive, helpful) models can have prosocial effects. Many business organizations effectively use *behavior modeling* to help new employees learn communication, sales, and customer service skills (Taylor et al., 2005). Trainees gain these skills faster when they are able to observe the skills being modeled effectively by experienced workers (or actors simulating them).

People who exemplify nonviolent, helpful behavior can also prompt similar behavior in others. India's Mahatma Gandhi and America's Martin Luther King, Jr., both drew on the power of modeling, making nonviolent action a powerful force for social change in both countries. Parents are also powerful models. European Christians who risked their lives to rescue Jews from the Nazis usually had a close relationship with at least one parent who modeled a strong moral or humanitarian concern; this was also true for U.S. civil rights activists in the 1960s (London, 1970; Oliner & Oliner, 1988). The observational learning of morality begins early. Socially responsive toddlers who readily

mirror neurons frontal lobe neurons that some scientists believe fire when performing certain actions or when observing another doing so. The brain's mirroring of another's action may enable imitation and empathy.

prosocial behavior positive, constructive, helpful behavior. The opposite of antisocial behavior.

Model of giving Children, such as this boy volunteering with his dad for a neighborhood revitalization project, learn positive behaviors and attitudes from the prosocial models in their lives. As the sixteenth-century proverb states, "Example is better than precept."

Jeff Greenberg/Photo Edit

imitated their parents tended to become preschoolers with a strong internalized conscience (Forman et al., 2004).

Models are most effective when their actions and words are consistent. Sometimes, however, models say one thing and do another. To encourage children to read, read to them and surround them with books and people who read. To increase the odds that your children will practice your religion, worship and attend religious activities with them. Many parents seem to operate according to the principle "Do as I *say,* not as I do." Experiments suggest that children learn to do both (Rice & Grusec, 1975; Rushton, 1975). Exposed to a hypocrite, they tend to imitate the hypocrisy—by doing what the model did and saying what the model said.

Antisocial Effects

The bad news is that observational learning may have *antisocial effects.* This helps us understand why abusive parents might have aggressive children, and why many men who beat their wives had wife-battering fathers (Stith et al., 2000). Critics note that being aggressive could be passed along by parents' genes. But with monkeys we know it can be environmental. In study after study, young monkeys separated from their mothers and subjected to high levels of aggression grew up to be aggressive themselves (Chamove, 1980). The lessons we learn as children are not easily replaced as adults, and they are sometimes visited on future generations.

TV is a powerful source of observational learning. While watching TV, children may "learn" that bullying is an effective way to control others, that free and easy sex brings pleasure without later misery or disease, or that men should be tough and women gentle. And they have ample time to learn such lessons. During their first 18 years, most children in developed countries spend more time watching TV than they spend in school. In the United States, where 9 in 10 teens watch TV daily, someone who lives to age 75 will have spent 9 years staring at the tube (Gallup, 2002; Kubey & Csikszentmihalyi, 2002). The average teen watches TV more than 4 hours a day, the average adult 3 hours (Robinson & Martin, 2009; Strasburger et al., 2010). With CNN reaching 212 countries, and MTV's networks broadcasting in 33 languages, television has created a global pop culture.

TV viewers are learning about life from a rather peculiar storyteller, one that reflects the culture's mythology but not its reality. During the late twentieth century, the average child viewed some 8000 TV murders and 100,000 other acts of violence before finishing elementary school (Huston et al., 1992). Between 1998 and 2006, prime-time violence reportedly increased another 75 percent (PTC, 2007). If we include cable programming and watching movies at home, the violence numbers escalate. An analysis of more than 3000 network and cable programs aired in the 1996–1997 season revealed that nearly 6 in 10 featured violence, that 74 percent of the violence went unpunished, that 58 percent did not show the victims' pain, that nearly half the incidents involved "justified" violence, and that nearly half involved an attractive perpetrator. These conditions define the recipe for the *violence-viewing effect* described in many studies (Donnerstein, 1998, 2011). To read more about this effect, see Thinking Critically About: Does Viewing Media Violence Trigger Violent Behavior?

"The problem with television is that the people must sit and keep their eyes glued to a screen: The average American family hasn't time for it. Therefore the showmen are convinced that . . . television will never be a serious competitor of [radio] broadcasting."

New York Times, *1939*

Does Viewing Media Violence Trigger Violent Behavior?

Was the judge who in 1993 tried two British 10-year-olds for their murder of a 2-year-old right to suspect that the pair had been influenced by "violent video films"? Were the American media right to think that the teen assassins who killed 13 of their Columbine High School classmates had been influenced by repeated exposure to *Natural Born Killers* and splatter games such as *Doom?* To understand whether violence viewing leads to violent behavior, researchers have done some 600 correlational and experimental studies (Anderson & Gentile, 2008; Comstock, 2008; Murray, 2008).

Correlational studies do support this link:

- In the United States and Canada, homicide rates doubled between 1957 and 1974, just when TV was introduced and spreading. Moreover, census regions with later dates for TV service also had homicide rates that jumped later.

- White South Africans were first introduced to TV in 1975. A similar near-doubling of the homicide rate began after 1975 (Centerwall, 1989).

- Elementary schoolchildren heavily exposed to media violence (via TV, videos, and video games) have also tended to get into more fights (**FIGURE 7.17**). As teens, such children are also at greater risk for violent behavior (Boxer et al., 2009).

But as we know from Chapter 1, correlation need not mean causation. So correlational studies like these do not prove that viewing violence *causes* aggression (Ferguson, 2009; Freedman, 1988; McGuire, 1986). Maybe aggressive children prefer violent programs. Maybe abused or neglected children are both more aggressive and more often left in front of the TV. Maybe violent programs reflect, rather than affect, violent trends.

To pin down causation, psychologists have experimented. They randomly assigned some viewers to observe violence and others to watch entertaining nonviolence. Does viewing cruelty prepare people, when irritated, to react more cruelly? To some extent, it does. This is especially so when an attractive person commits seemingly justified, realistic violence that goes unpunished and causes no visible pain or harm (Donnerstein, 1998, 2011).

The violence-viewing effect seems to stem from at least two factors. One is *imitation* (Geen & Thomas, 1986). Children as young as 14 months will imitate acts they observe on TV (Meltzoff & Moore, 1989, 1997). As they watch, their brains simulate the behavior, and after this inner rehearsal they become more likely to act it out. Thus, in one experiment, violent play increased sevenfold immediately after children viewed *Power Rangers* episodes (Boyatzis et al., 1995). As happened in the Bobo doll experiment, children often precisely imitated the models' violent acts—in this case, flying karate kicks.

Prolonged exposure to violence also *desensitizes* viewers. They become more indifferent to it when later viewing a brawl, whether on TV or in real life (Fanti et al., 2009; Rule & Ferguson, 1986). Adult males who spent three evenings watching sexually violent movies became progressively less bothered by the rapes and slashings. Compared with those in a control group, the film watchers later expressed less sympathy for domestic violence victims, and they rated the victims' injuries as less severe (Mullin & Linz, 1995). Likewise, moviegoers were less likely to help an injured woman pick up her crutches if they had just watched a violent rather than a nonviolent movie (Bushman & Anderson, 2009).

Drawing on such findings, the American Academy of Pediatrics (2009) has advised pediatricians that "media violence can contribute to aggressive behavior, desensitization to violence, nightmares, and fear of being harmed." Indeed, an evil psychologist could hardly imagine a better way to make people indifferent to brutality than to expose them to a graded series of scenes, from fights to killings to the mutilations in slasher movies (Donnerstein et al., 1987). Watching cruelty fosters indifference.

"Thirty seconds worth of glorification of a soap bar sells soap. Twenty-five minutes worth of glorification of violence sells violence."

U.S. Senator Paul Simon, Remarks to the Communitarian Network, 1993

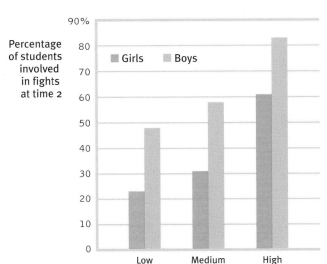

Stanislav Solntsev/Getty Images

FIGURE 7.17

Heavy exposure to media violence predicted future aggressive behavior Researchers studied more than 400 third- to fifth-graders. After controlling for existing differences in hostility and aggression, the researchers reported increased aggression in those heavily exposed to violent TV, videos, and video games (Gentile et al., 2004).

• Jason's parents and older friends all smoke, but they advise him not to. Juan's parents and friends don't smoke, but they say nothing to deter him from doing so. Will Jason or Juan be more likely to start smoking?

ANSWER: Jason may be more likely to smoke, because observational learning studies suggest that children tend to do as others do and say what they say.

★ ★ ★

TV's greatest effect may stem from what it displaces. Children and adults who spend four hours a day watching TV spend four fewer hours in active pursuits—talking, studying, playing, reading, or socializing with friends. What would you have done with your extra time if you had never watched TV, and how might you therefore be different?

Our knowledge of learning principles comes from the work of thousands of investigators. This chapter has focused on the ideas of a few pioneers—Ivan Pavlov, John Watson, B. F. Skinner, and Albert Bandura. They illustrate the impact that can result from single-minded devotion to a few well-defined problems and ideas. These researchers defined the issues and impressed on us the importance of learning. As their legacy demonstrates, intellectual history is often made by people who risk going to extremes in pushing ideas to their limits (Simonton, 2000).

• Match the examples (1–5) to the appropriate underlying learning principle (a–e):

  a. Classical conditioning   d. Observational learning
  b. Operant conditioning   e. Biological predispositions
  c. Latent learning

  1. Knowing the way from your bed to the bathroom in the dark
  2. Your little brothers getting in a fight after watching a violent action movie
  3. Salivating when you smell brownies in the oven
  4. Disliking the taste of chili after being violently sick a few hours after eating chili
  5. Your dog racing to greet you on your arrival home

ANSWERS: 1. c, 2. d, 3. a, 4. e, 5. b

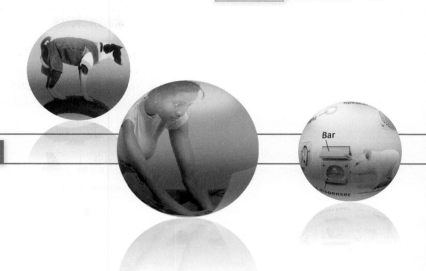

Learning

LEARNING OBJECTIVES

Test Yourself by taking a moment to answer each of these Learning Objective Questions (repeated here from within the chapter). Then turn to Appendix D, Complete Chapter Reviews, to check your answers. Research suggests that trying to answer these questions on your own will improve your long-term memory of the concepts (McDaniel et al., 2009).

How Do We Learn?

7-1: What is learning, and what are some basic forms of learning?

Classical Conditioning

7-2: What are the basic components of classical conditioning, and what was behaviorism's view of learning?

7-3: In classical conditioning, what are the processes of acquisition, extinction, spontaneous recovery, generalization, and discrimination?

7-4: Why does Pavlov's work remain so important, and what have been some applications of his work to human health and well-being?

Operant Conditioning

7-5: What is operant conditioning, and how is operant behavior reinforced and shaped?

7-6: How do positive and negative reinforcement differ, and what are the basic types of reinforcers?

7-7: How do different reinforcement schedules affect behavior?

7-8: How does punishment differ from negative reinforcement, and how does punishment affect behavior?

7-9: Why did Skinner's ideas provoke controversy, and how might his operant conditioning principles be applied at school, in sports, at work, and at home?

7-10: How does operant conditioning differ from classical conditioning?

Biology, Cognition, and Learning

7-11: How do biological constraints affect classical and operant conditioning?

7-12: How do cognitive processes affect classical and operant conditioning?

Learning by Observation

7-13: What is observational learning, and how do some scientists believe it is enabled by mirror neurons?

7-14: What is the impact of prosocial modeling and of antisocial modeling?

TERMS AND CONCEPTS TO REMEMBER

Test yourself on these terms by trying to write down the definition in your own words before flipping back to the referenced page to check your answer.

learning, p. 238
associative learning, p. 238
stimulus, p. 238
cognitive learning, p. 239

classical conditioning, p. 239
behaviorism, p. 240
neutral stimulus (NS), p. 240
unconditioned response (UR), p. 240
unconditioned stimulus (US), p. 240
conditioned response (CR), p. 240
conditioned stimulus (CS), p. 240
acquisition, p. 241

extinction, p. 242
spontaneous recovery, p. 242
generalization, p. 243
discrimination, p. 244
operant conditioning, p. 246
law of effect, p. 246
operant chamber, p. 246
reinforcement, p. 247

EXPERIENCE THE TESTING EFFECT

Test yourself repeatedly throughout your studies. This will not only help you figure out what you know and don't know; the testing itself will help you learn and remember the information more effectively thanks to the *testing effect*.

1. Learning is defined as "the process of acquiring through experience new and relatively enduring _____ or _____."

2. Two forms of associative learning are classical conditioning, in which the organism associates _____, and operant conditioning, in which the organism associates _____.

   a. two or more responses; a response and consequence

   b. two or more stimuli; two or more responses

   c. two or more stimuli; a response and consequence

   d. two or more responses; two or more stimuli

3. In Pavlov's experiments, the tone started as a neutral stimulus, and then became a(n) _____ stimulus.

4. Dogs have been taught to salivate to a circle but not to a square. This process is an example of _____.

5. After Watson and Rayner classically conditioned Little Albert to fear a white rat, the child later showed fear in response to a rabbit, a dog, and a sealskin coat. This illustrates

   a. extinction.

   b. generalization.

   c. spontaneous recovery.

   d. discrimination between two stimuli.

6. "Sex sells!" is a common saying in advertising. Using classical conditioning terms, explain how sexual images in advertisements can condition your response to a product.

7. Thorndike's law of effect was the basis for _____ work on operant conditioning and behavior control.

8. One way to change behavior is to reward natural behaviors in small steps, as they get closer and closer to a desired behavior. This process is called _____.

9. Your dog is barking so loudly that it's making your ears ring. You clap your hands, the dog stops barking, your ears stop ringing, and you think to yourself, "I'll have to do that when he barks again." The end of the barking was for you a

   a. positive reinforcer.

   b. negative reinforcer.

   c. positive punishment.

   d. negative punishment.

10. How could your psychology instructor use negative reinforcement to encourage your attentive behavior during class?

11. Reinforcing a desired response only some of the times it occurs is called _____ reinforcement.

12. A restaurant is running a special deal. After you buy four meals at full price, your fifth meal will be free. This is an example of a _____ schedule of reinforcement.

    a. fixed-ratio

    b. variable-ratio

    c. fixed-interval

    d. variable-interval

13. The partial reinforcement schedule that reinforces a response after unpredictable time periods is a _____-_____ schedule.

14. A medieval proverb notes that "a burnt child dreads the fire." In operant conditioning, the burning would be an example of a

    a. primary reinforcer.

    b. negative reinforcer.

    c. punisher.

    d. positive reinforcer.

15. Which research showed that conditioning can occur even when the unconditioned stimulus (US) does not immediately follow the neutral stimulus (NS)?

    a. The Little Albert experiment

    b. Pavlov's experiments with dogs

    c. Watson's behaviorism studies

    d. Garcia and Koelling's taste-aversion studies

16. Taste-aversion research has shown that some animals develop aversions to certain tastes but not to sights or sounds. This finding supports
    a. Pavlov's demonstration of generalization.
    b. Darwin's principle that natural selection favors traits that aid survival.
    c. Watson's belief that psychologists should study observable behavior, not mentalistic concepts.
    d. the early behaviorists' view that any organism can be conditioned to any stimulus.

17. Evidence that cognitive processes play an important role in learning comes in part from studies in which rats
    a. spontaneously recover previously learned behavior.
    b. develop cognitive maps.
    c. exhibit respondent behavior.
    d. generalize responses.

18. Rats that explored a maze without any reward were later able to run the maze as well as other rats that had received food rewards for running the maze. The rats that had learned without reinforcement demonstrated _____ _____.

19. Children learn many social behaviors by imitating parents and other models. This type of learning is called _____ _____.

20. According to Bandura, we learn by watching models because we experience _____ reinforcement or _____ punishment.

21. Parents are most effective in getting their children to imitate them if
    a. their words and actions are consistent.
    b. they have outgoing personalities.
    c. one parent works and the other stays home to care for the children.
    d. they carefully explain why a behavior is acceptable in adults but not in children.

22. Some scientists believe that the brain has _____ neurons that enable observation and imitation.

23. Most experts agree that repeated viewing of TV violence
    a. makes all viewers significantly more aggressive.
    b. has little effect on viewers.
    c. dulls viewers' sensitivity to violence.
    d. makes viewers angry and frustrated.

Find answers to these questions in Appendix E, in the back of the book.

Experience more of the
TESTING EFFECT

Multiple-format self-tests and more may be found at www.worthpublishers.com/myers.

 CHAPTER 8

Memory

This ninth edition Memory chapter is co-authored by Janie Wilson, Professor of Psychology at Georgia Southern University and Vice President for Programming of the Society for the Teaching of Psychology.

Be thankful for memory. We take it for granted, except when it malfunctions. But it is our memory that accounts for time and defines our life. It is our memory that enables us to recognize family, speak our language, find our way home, and locate food and water. It is our memory that enables us to enjoy an experience and then mentally replay and enjoy it again. And it is our memory that occasionally pits us against those whose offenses we cannot forget.

In large part, we are what we remember. Without memory—our storehouse of accumulated learning—there would be no savoring of past joys, no guilt or anger over painful recollections. We would instead live in an enduring present, each moment fresh. But each person would be a stranger, every language foreign, every task—dressing, cooking, biking—a new challenge. You would even be a stranger to yourself, lacking that continuous sense of self that extends from your distant past to your momentary present.

memory the persistence of learning over time through the storage and retrieval of information.

recall a measure of memory in which the person must retrieve information learned earlier, as on a fill-in-the-blank test.

recognition a measure of memory in which the person need only identify items previously learned, as on a multiple-choice test.

relearning a measure of memory that assesses the amount of time saved when learning material again.

Studying Memory

8-1: What is memory, and how is it measured?

Memory is learning that has persisted over time; it is information that has been acquired, stored, and can be retrieved. To a psychologist, evidence that learning persists includes these three *measures of retention,* which we will explore later in the chapter:

- **recall**—retrieving information that is not currently in your conscious awareness but that was learned at an earlier time. A fill-in-the-blank question tests your recall.

- **recognition**—identifying items previously learned. A multiple-choice question tests your recognition.

- **relearning**—learning something more quickly when you learn it a second or later time. When you study for a final exam or engage a language used in early childhood, you will relearn the material more easily than you did initially.

Research on memory's extremes has helped us understand how memory works. At age 92, my father suffered a small stroke that had but one peculiar effect. He was as mobile as before. His genial personality was intact. He knew us and enjoyed poring over family photo albums and reminiscing about his past. But he had lost most of his ability to lay down new memories of conversations and everyday episodes. He could not tell me what day of the week it was, or what he'd had for lunch. Told repeatedly of his brother-in-law's death, he was surprised and saddened each time he heard the news.

At the other extreme are people who would be gold medal winners in a memory Olympics. Russian journalist Shereshevskii, or S, had merely to listen while other reporters scribbled notes (Luria, 1968). You and I could parrot back a string of about 7—maybe even 9—digits. S could repeat up to 70, if they were read about 3 seconds apart in an otherwise silent room. Moreover, he could recall digits or words backward as easily as forward. His accuracy was unerring, even when recalling a list as much as 15 years later. "Yes, yes," he might recall. "This was a series you gave me once when we were in your apartment. . . . You were sitting at the table and I in the rocking chair. . . . You were wearing a gray suit. . . ."

Amazing? Yes, but consider your own impressive memory. You remember countless voices, sounds, and songs; tastes, smells, and textures; faces, places, and happenings. Imagine viewing more than 2500 slides of faces and places for 10 seconds each. Later, you see 280 of these slides, paired with others you've never seen. Actual participants in this experiment recognized 90 percent of the slides they had viewed in the first round (Haber, 1970). In a follow-up experiment, people exposed to 2800 images for only 3 seconds each spotted the repeats with 82 percent accuracy (Konkle et al., 2010).

Or imagine yourself looking at a picture fragment, such as the one in **FIGURE 8.1**. Also imagine that you had seen the complete picture for a couple of seconds 17 years earlier. This, too, was a real experiment, and participants who had previously seen the complete drawings were more likely to identify the objects than were members of a control group (Mitchell, 2006). Moreover, the picture memory reappeared even for those who did not consciously recall participating in the long-ago experiment!

How do we accomplish such memory feats? How does our brain pluck information out of the world around us and tuck that information away for later use? How can we remember things we have not thought about for years, yet forget the name of someone we met a minute ago? How are memories stored in our brains? Why will you be likely, later in this chapter, to misrecall this sentence: *"The angry rioter threw the rock at the window"*? In this chapter, we'll consider these fascinating questions and more, including tips on how we can improve our own memories.

FIGURE 8.1

What is this? People who had, 17 years earlier, seen the complete image (in Figure 8.4 when you turn the page) were more likely to recognize this fragment, even if they had forgotten the earlier experience (Mitchell, 2006).

Memory Models

8-2: How do psychologists describe the human memory system?

Architects make miniature house models to help clients imagine their future homes. Similarly, psychologists create memory models to help us think about how our brain forms and retrieves memories. *Information-processing models* are analogies that compare human memory to a computer's operations. Thus, to remember any event, we must

- *get information into our brain,* a process called **encoding.**
- *retain that information,* a process called **storage.**
- later *get the information back out,* a process called **retrieval.**

Like all analogies, computer models have their limits. Our memories are less literal and more fragile than a computer's. Moreover, most computers process information sequentially, even while alternating between tasks. Our dual-track brain processes many things simultaneously (some of them unconsciously) by means of *parallel processing.*

To focus on this complex, simultaneous processing, one information-processing model, *connectionism,* views memories as products of interconnected neural networks. Specific memories arise from particular activation patterns within these networks. Every time you learn something new, your brain's neural connections change, forming and strengthening pathways that allow you to interact with and learn from your constantly changing environment.

To explain our memory-forming process, Richard Atkinson and Richard Shiffrin (1968) proposed another model, with three stages:

1. We first record to-be-remembered information as a fleeting **sensory memory.**
2. From there, we process information into **short-term memory,** where we encode it through *rehearsal.*
3. Finally, information moves into **long-term memory** for later retrieval.

Other psychologists have updated this model (**FIGURE 8.2**) to include important newer concepts, including *working memory* and *automatic processing.*

encoding the processing of information into the memory system—for example, by extracting meaning.

storage the retention of encoded information over time.

retrieval the process of getting information out of memory storage.

sensory memory the immediate, very brief recording of sensory information in the memory system.

short-term memory activated memory that holds a few items briefly, such as seven digits of a phone number while dialing, before the information is stored or forgotten.

long-term memory the relatively permanent and limitless storehouse of the memory system. Includes knowledge, skills, and experiences.

working memory a newer understanding of short-term memory that focuses on conscious, active processing of incoming auditory and visual-spatial information, and of information retrieved from long-term memory.

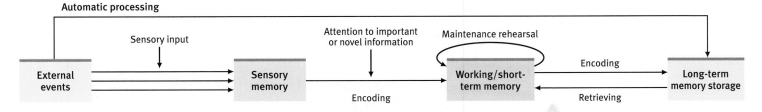

Working Memory

Alan Baddeley and others (Baddeley, 2001, 2002; Engle, 2002) challenged Atkinson and Shiffrin's view of short-term memory as a small, brief storage space for recent thoughts and experiences. Research shows that this stage is not just a temporary shelf for holding incoming information. It's an active desktop where your brain processes information, making sense of new input and linking it with long-term memories. Whether we hear *eye-screem* as "ice cream" or "I scream" will depend on how the context and our experience guide us in interpreting and encoding the sounds. To emphasize the active processing that takes place in this middle stage, psychologists use the term **working memory.** Right now, you are using your working memory to link the information you're reading with your previously stored information (Cowan, 2010; Kail & Hall, 2001).

FIGURE 8.2
A modified three-stage processing model of memory Atkinson and Shiffrin's classic three-step model helps us to think about how memories are processed, but today's researchers recognize other ways long-term memories form. For example, some information slips into long-term memory via a "back door," without our consciously attending to it *(automatic processing).* And so much active processing occurs in the short-term memory stage that many now prefer the term *working memory.*

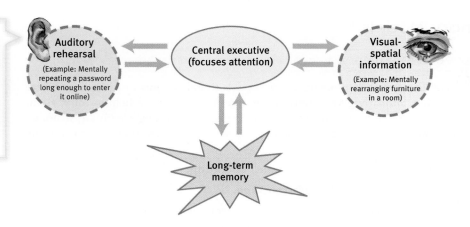

FIGURE 8.3

Working memory Alan Baddeley's (2002) model of working memory, simplified here, includes *visual* and *auditory rehearsal* of new information. A hypothetical *central executive* (manager) focuses attention and pulls information from long-term memory to help make sense of new information.

FIGURE 8.4

Now you know People who had seen this complete image were, 17 years later, more likely to recognize the fragment in Figure 8.1.

The pages you are reading may enter working memory through vision. You might also repeat the information using auditory rehearsal. As you integrate these memory inputs with your existing long-term memory, your attention is focused. Baddeley (2002) suggested a *central executive* handles this focused processing (**FIGURE 8.3**).

Without focused attention, information often fades. In one experiment, people read and typed new information they would later need, such as "An ostrich's eye is bigger than its brain." If they knew the information would be available online they invested less energy in remembering, and they remembered the trivia less well (Sparrow et al., 2011). Sometimes Google replaces rehearsal.

RETRIEVE IT

- What two new concepts update the classic Atkinson-Shiffrin three-stage information-processing model?

ANSWER: (1) We form some memories through *automatic processing*, without our awareness. The Atkinson-Shiffrin model focused only on conscious memories. (2) The newer concept of a *working memory* emphasizes the active processing that we now know takes place in Atkinson-Shiffrin's short-term memory stage.

- What are two basic functions of *working memory?*

ANSWER: (1) Active processing of incoming visual and auditory information, and (2) focusing our spotlight of attention.

Building Memories: Encoding

Dual-Track Memory: Effortful Versus Automatic Processing

 8-3: How do explicit and implicit memories differ?

As we have seen throughout this text, our mind operates on two tracks:

- Atkinson and Shiffrin's model focused on how we process our **explicit memories**—the facts and experiences we can consciously know and declare (thus, also called *declarative memories*). We encode explicit memories through conscious **effortful processing.**

- Behind the scenes, outside the Atkinson-Shiffrin stages, other information skips the conscious encoding track and barges directly into storage. This **automatic processing,** which happens without our awareness, produces **implicit memories** (also called *nondeclarative memories*).

explicit memory memory of facts and experiences that one can consciously know and "declare." (Also called *declarative memory.*)

effortful processing encoding that requires attention and conscious effort.

automatic processing unconscious encoding of incidental information, such as space, time, and frequency, and of well-learned information, such as word meanings.

implicit memory retention independent of conscious recollection. (Also called *nondeclarative memory.*)

Automatic Processing and Implicit Memories

8-4: What information do we automatically process?

Our implicit memories include *procedural* memory for automatic skills (such as how to ride a bike) and classically conditioned *associations* among stimuli. Visiting your dentist, you may, thanks to a conditioned association linking the dentist's office with the painful drill, find yourself with sweaty palms. You didn't plan to feel that way when you got to the dentist's office; it happened *automatically*.

Without conscious effort you also automatically process information about

- *space*. While studying, you often encode the place on a page where certain material appears; later, when you want to retrieve information about automatic processing, for example, you may visualize the location of that information on this page.

- *time*. While going about your day, you unintentionally note the sequence of its events. Later, realizing you've left your coat somewhere, the event sequence your brain automatically encoded will enable you to retrace your steps.

- *frequency*. You effortlessly keep track of how many times things happen, as when you suddenly realize, *This is the third time I've run into her today*.

Our two-track mind engages in impressively efficient information processing. As one track automatically tucks away many routine details, the other track is free to focus on conscious, effortful processing. This reinforces an important principle introduced in Chapter 6's description of parallel processing: Mental feats such as vision, thinking, and memory may seem to be single abilities, but they are not. Rather, we split information into different components for separate and simultaneous processing.

Effortful Processing and Explicit Memories

Automatic processing happens so effortlessly that it is difficult to shut off. When you see words in your native language, perhaps on the side of a delivery truck, you can't help but read them and register their meaning. *Learning* to read wasn't automatic. You may recall working hard to pick out letters and connect them to certain sounds. But with experience and practice, your reading became automatic. Imagine now learning to read reversed sentences like this:

.citamotua emoceb nac gnissecorp luftroffE

At first, this requires effort, but after enough practice, you would also perform this task much more automatically. We develop many skills in this way. We learn to drive, to text, to speak a new language with effort, but then these tasks become automatic.

Sensory Memory

8-5: How does sensory memory work?

Sensory memory (recall Figure 8.2) feeds our active working memory, recording momentary images of scenes or echoes of sounds. How much of this page could you sense and recall with less exposure than a lightning flash? In one experiment (Sperling, 1960), people viewed three rows of three letters each, for only one-twentieth of a second (**FIGURE 8.5**). After the nine letters disappeared, they could recall only about half of them.

Was it because they had insufficient time to glimpse them? *No*. The researcher, George Sperling, cleverly demonstrated that people actually *could* see and recall all the letters, but only momentarily. Rather than ask them to recall all nine letters at once, he sounded a high, medium, or low tone immediately *after* flashing the nine letters. This tone directed participants to report only the letters of the top, middle, or bottom row, respectively. Now they rarely missed a letter, showing that all nine letters were momentarily available for recall.

FIGURE 8.5
Momentary photographic memory When George Sperling flashed a group of letters similar to this for one-twentieth of a second, people could recall only about half the letters. But when signaled to recall a particular row immediately after the letters had disappeared, they could do so with near-perfect accuracy.

K	Z	R
Q	B	T
S	G	N

Sperling's experiment demonstrated **iconic memory,** a fleeting sensory memory of visual stimuli. For a few tenths of a second, our eyes register a photographic or picture-image memory of a scene, and we can recall any part of it in amazing detail. But if Sperling delayed the tone signal by more than half a second, the image faded and participants again recalled only about half the letters. Our visual screen clears quickly, as new images are superimposed over old ones.

We also have an impeccable, though fleeting, memory for auditory stimuli, called **echoic memory** (Cowan, 1988; Lu et al., 1992). Picture yourself in conversation, as your attention veers to the TV. If your mildly irked companion tests you by asking, "What did I just say?" you can recover the last few words from your mind's echo chamber. Auditory echoes tend to linger for 3 or 4 seconds.

Capacity of Short-Term and Working Memory

8-6: What is the capacity of our short-term and working memory?

George Miller (1956) proposed that short-term memory can retain about seven information bits (give or take two). Other researchers have confirmed that we can, if nothing distracts us, recall about seven digits, or about six letters or five words (Baddeley et al., 1975). How quickly do our short-term memories disappear? To find out, Lloyd Peterson and Margaret Peterson (1959) asked people to remember three-consonant groups, such as *CHJ*. To prevent rehearsal, the researchers asked them, for example, to start at 100 and count aloud backward by threes. After 3 seconds, people recalled the letters only about half the time; after 12 seconds, they seldom recalled them at all (**FIGURE 8.6**). Without the active processing that we now understand to be a part of our working memory, short-term memories have a limited life.

Working-memory capacity varies, depending on age and other factors. Compared with children and older adults, young adults have more working-memory capacity, so they can use their mental workspace more efficiently. This means their ability to multitask is relatively greater. But whatever our age, we do better and more efficient work when focused, without distractions, on one task at a time. *The bottom line:* It's probably a bad idea to try to watch TV, text your friends, and write a psychology paper all at the same time (Willingham, 2010)!

The Magical Number Seven has become psychology's contribution to an intriguing list of magic sevens—the seven wonders of the world, the seven seas, the seven deadly sins, the seven primary colors, the seven musical scale notes, the seven days of the week—seven magical sevens.

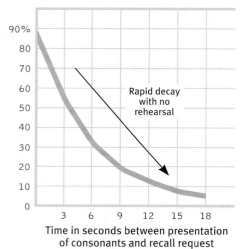

FIGURE 8.6
Short-term memory decay Unless rehearsed, verbal information may be quickly forgotten. (From Peterson & Peterson, 1959; see also Brown, 1958.)

Effortful Processing Strategies

8-7: What are some effortful processing strategies that can help us remember new information?

Research shows that several effortful processing strategies can boost our ability to form new memories. Later, when we try to retrieve a memory, these strategies can make the difference between success and failure.

Chunking Glance for a few seconds at row 1 of **FIGURE 8.7**, then look away and try to reproduce what you saw. Impossible, yes? But you can easily reproduce the second row, which is no less complex. Similarly, you will probably find row 4 much easier to remember than row 3, although both contain the same letters. And you could remember the sixth cluster more easily than the fifth, although both contain the same words. As these units demonstrate, **chunking** information—organizing items into familiar, manageable units—enables us to recall it more easily. Try remembering 43 individual numbers and letters. It would be impossible, unless chunked into, say, seven meaningful chunks, such as "Try remembering 43 individual numbers and letters."☺

1. ⊲⊃◘⊇⊗⊓⊏⊑
2. K L C I S N E

3. KLCISNE NVESE YNA NI CSTTIH TNDO
4. NICKELS SEVEN ANY IN STITCH DONT

5. NICKELS SEVEN ANY IN STITCH DONT
   SAVES AGO A SCORE TIME AND
   NINE WOODEN FOUR YEARS TAKE

6. DONT TAKE ANY WOODEN NICKELS
   FOUR SCORE AND SEVEN YEARS AGO
   A STITCH IN TIME SAVES NINE

FIGURE 8.7

Effects of chunking on memory When we organize information into meaningful units, such as letters, words, and phrases, we recall it more easily. (From Hintzman, 1978.)

Chunking usually occurs so naturally that we take it for granted. If you are a native English speaker, you can reproduce perfectly the 150 or so line segments that make up the words in the three phrases of item 6 in Figure 8.7. It would astonish someone unfamiliar with the language. I am similarly awed at a Chinese reader's ability to glance at **FIGURE 8.8** and then reproduce all the strokes; or of a varsity basketball player's recall of the positions of the players after a 4-second glance at a basketball play (Allard & Burnett, 1985). We all remember information best when we can organize it into personally meaningful arrangements.

Mnemonics To help them encode lengthy passages and speeches, ancient Greek scholars and orators also developed **mnemonics** (nih-MON-iks). Many of these memory aids use vivid imagery, because we are particularly good at remembering mental pictures. We more easily remember concrete, visualizable words than we do abstract words. (When I quiz you later, which three of these words—*bicycle, void, cigarette, inherent, fire, process*—will you most likely recall?) If you still recall the rock-throwing rioter sentence, it is probably not only because of the meaning you encoded but also because the sentence painted a mental image.

The *peg-word system* harnesses our superior visual-imagery skill. This mnemonic requires you to memorize a jingle: *"One is a bun; two is a shoe; three is a tree; four is a door; five is a hive; six is sticks; seven is heaven; eight is a gate; nine is swine; ten is a hen."* Without much effort, you will soon be able to count by peg words instead of numbers: *bun, shoe, tree* . . . and then to visually associate the peg words with to-be-remembered items. Now you are ready to challenge anyone to give you a grocery list to remember. Carrots? Stick them into the imaginary bun. Milk? Fill the shoe with it. Paper towels? Drape them over the tree branch. Think *bun, shoe, tree* and you see their associated images: carrots, milk, paper towels. With few errors, you will be able to recall the items in any order and to name any given item (Bugelski et al., 1968). Memory whizzes understand the power of such systems. A study of star performers in the World Memory Championships showed them not to have exceptional intelligence, but rather to be superior at using mnemonic strategies (Maguire et al., 2003).

Chunking and mnemonic techniques combined can be great memory aids for unfamiliar material. Want to remember the colors of the rainbow in order of wavelength? Think of the mnemonic ROY G. BIV (*r*ed, *o*range, *y*ellow, *g*reen, *b*lue, *i*ndigo, *v*iolet). Need to recall the names of North America's five Great Lakes? Just remember HOMES (*H*uron, *O*ntario, *M*ichigan, *E*rie, *S*uperior). In each case, we chunk information into a more familiar form by creating a word (called an *acronym*) from the first letters of the to-be-remembered items.

Hierarchies When people develop expertise in an area, they process information not only in chunks but also in *hierarchies* composed of a few broad concepts divided and subdivided into narrower concepts and facts. This section, for example, aims to help you organize memory concepts (**FIGURE 8.9** on the next page).

春夏秋冬

FIGURE 8.8

An example of chunking—for those who read Chinese After looking at these characters, can you reproduce them exactly? If so, you are literate in Chinese.

iconic memory a momentary sensory memory of visual stimuli; a photographic or picture-image memory lasting no more than a few tenths of a second.

echoic memory a momentary sensory memory of auditory stimuli; if attention is elsewhere, sounds and words can still be recalled within 3 or 4 seconds.

chunking organizing items into familiar, manageable units; often occurs automatically.

mnemonics [nih-MON-iks] memory aids, especially those techniques that use vivid imagery and organizational devices.

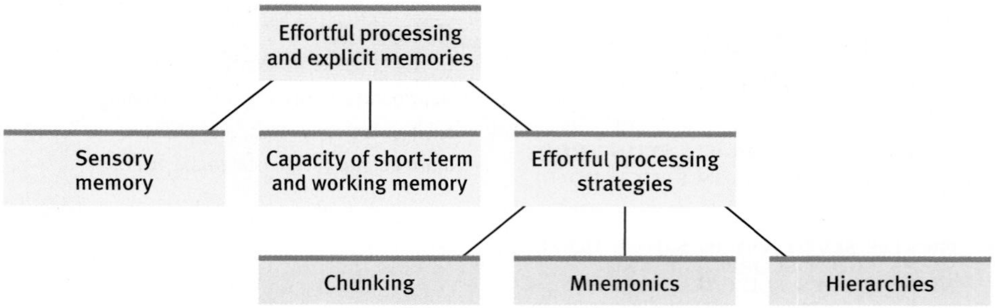

FIGURE 8.9

Hierarchies aid retrieval When we organize words or concepts into hierarchical groups, as illustrated here with some of the concepts from this section, we remember them better than when we see them presented randomly.

Effortful processing and explicit memories

Sensory memory

Capacity of short-term and working memory

Effortful processing strategies

Chunking

Mnemonics

Hierarchies

Organizing knowledge in hierarchies helps us retrieve information efficiently, as Gordon Bower and his colleagues (1969) demonstrated by presenting words either randomly or grouped into categories. When the words were organized into categories, recall was two to three times better. Such results show the benefits of organizing what you study—of giving special attention to the chapter outlines, headings, numbered Learning Objective questions, and Retrieve It and Testing Effect questions. Taking lecture and text notes in outline format—a type of hierarchical organization—may also prove helpful.

Distributed Practice

We retain information (such as classmates' names) better when our encoding is distributed over time. More than 300 experiments over the last century have consistently revealed the benefits of this **spacing effect** (Cepeda et al., 2006). *Massed practice* (cramming) can produce speedy short-term learning and feelings of confidence. But to paraphrase pioneer memory researcher Hermann Ebbinghaus (1885), those who learn quickly also forget quickly. *Distributed practice* produces better long-term recall. After you've studied long enough to master the material, further study becomes inefficient (Rohrer & Pashler, 2007). Better to spend that extra reviewing time later—a day later if you need to remember something 10 days hence, or a month later if you need to remember something 6 months hence (Cepeda et al., 2008).

Spreading your learning over several months, rather than over a shorter term, can help you retain information for a lifetime. In a 9-year experiment, Harry Bahrick and three of his family members (1993) practiced foreign language word translations for a given number of times, at intervals ranging from 14 to 56 days. Their consistent finding: The longer the space between practice sessions, the better their retention up to 5 years later.

One effective way to distribute practice is *repeated self-testing,* a phenomenon that researchers Henry Roediger and Jeffrey Karpicke (2006) have called the **testing effect.** In this text, for example, the Retrieve It and Testing Effect features offer such an opportunity. Better to practice retrieval (as any exam will demand) than merely to reread material (which may lull you into a false sense of mastery).

The point to remember: Spaced study and self-assessment beat cramming and rereading.

Levels of Processing

8-8: What are the levels of processing, and how do they affect encoding?

Memory researchers have discovered that we process verbal information at different levels, and that depth of processing affects our long-term retention. **Shallow processing** encodes on a very basic level, such as a word's letters or, at a more intermediate level, a word's sound. **Deep processing** encodes *semantically,* based on the meaning of the words. The deeper (more meaningful) the processing, the better our retention.

"The mind is slow in unlearning what it has been long in learning."

Roman philosopher Seneca (4 B.C.E.–65 C.E.)

spacing effect the tendency for distributed study or practice to yield better long-term retention than is achieved through massed study or practice.

testing effect enhanced memory after retrieving, rather than simply rereading, information. Also sometimes referred to as a *retrieval practice effect* or *test-enhanced learning.*

shallow processing encoding on a basic level based on the structure or appearance of words.

deep processing encoding semantically, based on the meaning of the words; tends to yield the best retention.

Making things memorable
For suggestions of how to apply the *testing effect* to your own learning, watch this 5-minute YouTube animation: youtu.be/rFIK5gutHKM

In one classic experiment, researchers Fergus Craik and Endel Tulving (1975) flashed words at people. Then they asked the viewers a question that would elicit different levels of processing. To experience the task yourself, rapidly answer the following sample questions:

Sample Questions to Elicit Processing	Word Flashed	Yes	No
1. Is the word in capital letters?	CHAIR	_____	_____
2. Does the word rhyme with train?	brain	_____	_____
3. Would the word fit in this sentence? The girl put the _____ on the table.	doll	_____	_____

Which type of processing would best prepare you to recognize the words at a later time? In Craik and Tulving's experiment, the deeper, semantic processing triggered by the third question yielded a much better memory than did the shallower processing elicited by the second question or the very shallow processing elicited by question 1 (which was especially ineffective).

Making Material Personally Meaningful

If new information is not meaningful or related to our experience, we have trouble processing it. Put yourself in the place of the students whom John Bransford and Marcia Johnson (1972) asked to remember the following recorded passage:

> The procedure is actually quite simple. First you arrange things into different groups. Of course, one pile may be sufficient depending on how much there is to do. . . . After the procedure is completed one arranges the materials into different groups again. Then they can be put into their appropriate places. Eventually they will be used once more and the whole cycle will then have to be repeated. However, that is part of life.

When the students heard the paragraph you have just read, without a meaningful context, they remembered little of it. When told the paragraph described washing clothes (something meaningful to them), they remembered much more of it—as you probably could now after rereading it.

Can you repeat the sentence about the rioter that I gave you at this chapter's beginning? ("The angry rioter threw . . .") Perhaps, like those in an experiment by William Brewer (1977), you recalled the sentence by the meaning you encoded when you read it (for example, "The angry rioter threw the rock *through* the window") and not as it was written ("The angry rioter threw the rock *at* the window"). Referring to such mental mismatches, Gordon Bower and Daniel Morrow (1990) have likened our minds to theater directors who, given a raw script, imagine the finished stage production. Asked later

Here is another sentence I will ask you about later: *"The fish attacked the swimmer."*

what we heard or read, we recall not the literal text but *what we encoded.* Thus, studying for an exam, you may remember your lecture notes rather than the lecture itself.

We can avoid some of these mismatches by rephrasing what we see and hear into meaningful terms. From his experiments on himself, German philosopher Hermann Ebbinghaus (1850–1909) estimated that, compared with learning nonsense material, learning meaningful material required one-tenth the effort. As memory researcher Wayne Wickelgren (1977, p. 346) noted, "The time you spend thinking about material you are reading and relating it to previously stored material is about the most useful thing you can do in learning any new subject matter."

Psychologist-actor team Helga Noice and Tony Noice (2006) have described how actors inject meaning into the daunting task of learning "all those lines." They do it by first coming to understand the flow of meaning: "One actor divided a half-page of dialogue into three [intentions]: 'to flatter,' 'to draw him out,' and 'to allay his fears.'" With this meaningful sequence in mind, the actor more easily remembered the lines.

We have especially good recall for information we can meaningfully relate to ourselves. Asked how well certain adjectives describe someone else, we often forget them; asked how well the adjectives describe us, we remember the words well. This tendency, called the *self-reference effect,* is especially strong in members of individualistic Western cultures (Symons & Johnson, 1997; Wagar & Cohen, 2003). Information deemed "relevant to me" is processed more deeply and remains more accessible. Knowing this, you can profit from taking time to find personal meaning in what you are studying.

The point to remember: The amount remembered depends both on the time spent learning and on your making it meaningful for deep processing.

RETRIEVE IT

• What is the difference between *automatic* and *effortful* processing, and what are some examples of each?

ANSWER: *Automatic* processing occurs unconsciously (automatically) for such things as the sequence and frequency of a day's events, and reading and comprehending words in our own language. *Effortful* processing requires attention and awareness and happens, for example, when we work hard to learn new material in class, or new lines for a play.

• At which of Atkinson-Shiffrin's three memory stages would *iconic* and *echoic* memory occur?

ANSWER: sensory memory

• Which strategies are better for long-term retention: cramming and rereading material, or spreading out learning over time and repeatedly testing yourself?

ANSWER: Although cramming may lead to short-term gains in knowledge, distributed practice and repeated self-testing will result in the greatest long-term retention.

• If you try to make the material you are learning personally meaningful, are you processing at a shallow or a deep level? Which level leads to greater retention?

ANSWER: Making material personally meaningful involves processing at a deep level, because you are processing *semantically*—based on the meaning of the words. Deep processing leads to greater retention.

Memory Storage

8-9: What are the capacity and location of our long-term memories?

In Arthur Conan Doyle's *A Study in Scarlet,* Sherlock Holmes offers a popular theory of memory capacity:

> I consider that a man's brain originally is like a little empty attic, and you have to stock it with such furniture as you choose. . . . It is a mistake to think that that little room has elastic walls and can distend to any extent. Depend upon it, there comes a time when for every addition of knowledge you forget something that you knew before.

hippocampus a neural center located in the limbic system; helps process explicit memories for storage.

Contrary to Holmes' "memory model," our capacity for storing long-term memories is essentially limitless. Our brains are *not* like attics, which once filled can store more items only if we discard old ones.

Retaining Information in the Brain

I marveled at my aging mother-in-law, a retired pianist and organist. At age 88, her blind eyes could no longer read music. But let her sit at a keyboard and she would flawlessly play any of hundreds of hymns, including ones she had not thought of for 20 years. Where did her brain store those thousands of sequenced notes?

For a time, some surgeons and memory researchers marveled at patients' seeming vivid memories triggered by brain stimulation during surgery. Did this prove that our whole past, not just well-practiced music, is "in there," in complete detail, just waiting to be relived? On closer analysis, the seeming flashbacks appeared to have been invented, not relived (Loftus & Loftus, 1980). In a further demonstration that memories do not reside in single, specific spots, psychologist Karl Lashley (1950) trained rats to find their way out of a maze, then surgically removed pieces of their brain's cortex and retested their memory. No matter which small brain section he removed, the rats retained at least a partial memory of how to navigate the maze.

The point to remember: Despite the brain's vast storage capacity, we do not store information as libraries store their books, in discrete, precise locations. Instead, many parts of the brain interact as we encode, store, and retrieve the information that forms our memories.

Explicit-Memory System: The Frontal Lobes and Hippocampus

8-10: What roles do the frontal lobes and hippocampus play in memory storage?

As with perception, language, emotion, and much more, memory requires brain networks. The network that processes and stores your explicit memories for facts and episodes includes your frontal lobes and hippocampus. When you summon up a mental encore of a past experience, many brain regions send input to your frontal lobes for working memory processing (Fink et al., 1996; Gabrieli et al., 1996; Markowitsch, 1995). The left and right frontal lobes process different types of memories. Recalling a password and holding it in working memory, for example, would activate the left frontal lobe. Calling up a visual party scene would more likely activate the right frontal lobe.

Cognitive neuroscientists have found that the **hippocampus,** a temporal-lobe neural center located in the limbic system, is the brain's equivalent of a "save" button for explicit memories (**FIGURE 8.10;** Anderson et al., 2007). Brain scans, such as PET scans of people recalling words, and autopsies of people who had *amnesia* (memory loss), have revealed that new explicit memories of names, images, and events are laid down via the hippocampus (Squire, 1992).

Damage to this structure therefore disrupts recall of explicit memories. Chickadees and other birds can store food in hundreds of places and return to these unmarked caches months later—but not if their hippocampus has been removed (Kamil & Cheng, 2001; Sherry & Vaccarino, 1989). With left-hippocampus damage, people have trouble remembering verbal information, but they have no trouble recalling visual designs and locations. With right-hippocampus damage, the problem is reversed (Schacter, 1996).

Subregions of the hippocampus also serve different functions. One part is active as people learn to associate names with faces (Zeineh et al., 2003). Another part is active as memory champions engage in spatial mnemonics (Maguire et al., 2003b). The rear area, which processes spatial memory, grows bigger the longer a London cabbie has navigated the maze of streets (Maguire et al., 2003a).

Memories are not permanently stored in the hippocampus. Instead, this structure seems to act as a loading dock where the brain registers and temporarily holds the elements of a remembered episode—its smell, feel, sound, and location. Then, like older files shifted to a basement storeroom, memories migrate for storage elsewhere.

> "Our memories are flexible and superimposable, a panoramic blackboard with an endless supply of chalk and erasers."
>
> *Elizabeth Loftus and Katherine Ketcham, The Myth of Repressed Memory, 1994*

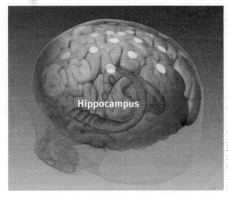

FIGURE 8.10

The hippocampus Explicit memories for facts and episodes are processed in the hippocampus and fed to other brain regions for storage.

Hippocampus hero Among animals, one contender for champion memorist would be a mere birdbrain—the Clark's Nutcracker—which during winter and spring can locate up to 6000 caches of pine seed it had previously buried (Shettleworth, 1993).

© Tim Zurowski/All Canada Photos/Corbis

Sleep supports memory consolidation. During deep sleep, the hippocampus processes memories for later retrieval. After a training experience, the greater the hippocampus activity during sleep, the better the next day's memory will be (Peigneux et al., 2004). Researchers have watched the hippocampus and brain cortex displaying simultaneous activity rhythms during sleep, as if they were having a dialogue (Euston et al., 2007; Mehta, 2007). They suspect that the brain is replaying the day's experiences as it transfers them to the cortex for long-term storage. Cortex areas surrounding the hippocampus support the processing and storing of explicit memories (Squire & Zola-Morgan, 1991).

Implicit-Memory System: The Cerebellum and Basal Ganglia

8-11: What roles do the cerebellum and basal ganglia play in our memory processing?

Your hippocampus and frontal lobes are processing sites for your *explicit* memories. But you could lose those areas and still, thanks to automatic processing, lay down *implicit* memories for skills and conditioned associations. Joseph LeDoux (1996) recounted the story of a brain-damaged patient whose amnesia left her unable to recognize her physician as, each day, he shook her hand and introduced himself. One day, she yanked her hand back, for the physician had pricked her with a tack in his palm. The next time he returned to introduce himself she refused to shake his hand but couldn't explain why. Having been *classically conditioned,* she just wouldn't do it.

The *cerebellum* plays a key role in forming and storing the implicit memories created by classical conditioning. With a damaged cerebellum, people cannot develop certain conditioned reflexes, such as associating a tone with an impending puff of air—and thus do not blink in anticipation of the puff (Daum & Schugens, 1996; Green & Woodruff-Pak, 2000). When researchers surgically disrupted the function of different pathways in the cerebellum of rabbits, the rabbits became unable to learn a conditioned eyeblink response (Krupa et al., 1993; Steinmetz, 1999). Implicit memory formation needs the cerebellum **(FIGURE 8.11)**.

The *basal ganglia,* deep brain structures involved in motor movement, facilitate formation of our procedural memories for skills (Mishkin, 1982; Mishkin et al., 1997). The basal ganglia receive input from the cortex but do not return the favor of sending information back to the cortex for conscious awareness of procedural learning. If you have learned how to ride a bike, thank your basal ganglia.

Our implicit memory system, enabled partly by the cerebellum and basal ganglia, helps explain why the reactions and skills we learned during infancy reach far into our future. Yet as adults, our *conscious* memory of our first three years is blank, an experience called *infantile amnesia.* In one study, events children experienced and discussed with their mothers at age 3 were 60 percent remembered at age 7 but only 34 percent remembered at age 9 (Bauer et al., 2007). Two influences contribute to infantile amnesia: First, we index much of our explicit memory using words that nonspeaking children have not learned. Second, the hippocampus is one of the last brain structures to mature.

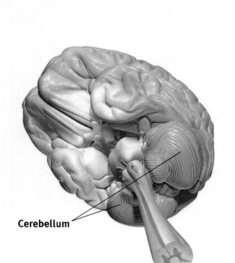

Cerebellum

FIGURE 8.11

Cerebellum The cerebellum plays an important part in our forming and storing of implicit memories.

flashbulb memory a clear memory of an emotionally significant moment or event.

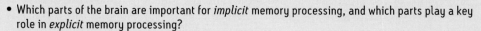

RETRIEVE IT

• Which parts of the brain are important for *implicit* memory processing, and which parts play a key role in *explicit* memory processing?

ANSWER: The frontal lobes and hippocampus are important for *explicit* memory formation, and the cerebellum and basal ganglia are key to *implicit* memory processing.

• Your friend has experienced brain damage in an accident. He can remember how to tie his shoes but has a hard time remembering anything told him during a conversation. What's going on here?

ANSWER: Our *explicit* memories (facts and episodes) differ from our *implicit* memories of skills and procedures. Our implicit memories are processed by more ancient brain areas, which apparently escaped damage during the accident.

The Amygdala, Emotions, and Memory

8-12: How do emotions affect our memory processing?

Our emotions trigger stress hormones that influence memory formation. When we are excited or stressed, these hormones make more glucose energy available to fuel brain activity, signaling the brain that something important has happened. Moreover, stress hormones provoke the *amygdala* (two limbic system, emotion-processing clusters) to initiate a memory trace in the frontal lobes and basal ganglia and to boost activity in the brain's memory-forming areas (Buchanan, 2007; Kensinger, 2007) (**FIGURE 8.12**). The result? Emotional arousal can sear certain events into the brain, while disrupting memory for neutral events around the same time (Birnbaum et al., 2004; Brewin et al., 2007).

Emotions often persist without our conscious awareness of what caused them. In one ingenious experiment, patients with hippocampal damage (which left them unable to form new explicit memories) watched a sad film and later a happy film. After the viewing, they did not consciously recall the films, but the sad or happy emotion persisted (Feinstein et al., 2010).

Significantly stressful events can form almost indelible memories. After traumatic experiences—a wartime ambush, a house fire, a rape—vivid recollections of the horrific event may intrude again and again. It is as if they were burned in: "Stronger emotional experiences make for stronger, more reliable memories," noted James McGaugh (1994, 2003). This makes adaptive sense. Memory serves to predict the future and to alert us to potential dangers. Conversely, weaker emotions mean weaker memories. People given a drug that blocked the effects of stress hormones later had more trouble remembering the details of an upsetting story (Cahill, 1994).

Emotion-triggered hormonal changes help explain why we long remember exciting or shocking events, such as our first kiss or our whereabouts when learning of a loved one's death. In a 2006 Pew survey, 95 percent of American adults said they could recall exactly where they were or what they were doing when they first heard the news of the 9/11 attack. This perceived clarity of memories of surprising, significant events leads some psychologists to call them **flashbulb memories.** It's as if the brain commands, "Capture this!"

The people who experienced a 1989 San Francisco earthquake did just that. A year and a half later, they had perfect recall of where they had been and what they were doing (verified by their recorded thoughts within a day or two of the quake). Others' memories for the circumstances under which they merely *heard* about the quake were more prone to errors (Neisser et al., 1991; Palmer et al., 1991).

Our flashbulb memories are noteworthy for their vividness and the confidence with which we recall them. But as we relive, rehearse, and discuss them, these memories may come to err, as misinformation seeps in (Conway et al., 2009; Talarico et al., 2003; Talarico & Rubin, 2007).

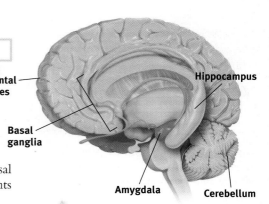

FIGURE 8.12
Review key memory structures in the brain
Frontal lobes and *hippocampus:* explicit memory formation
Cerebellum and *basal ganglia:* implicit memory formation
Amygdala: emotion-related memory formation

Labels: Frontal lobes, Hippocampus, Basal ganglia, Amygdala, Cerebellum

Which is more important—your experiences or your memories of them?

Synaptic Changes

8-13: How do changes at the synapse level affect our memory processing?

As you read this chapter and think and learn about memory characteristics and processes, your brain is changing. Given increased activity in particular pathways, neural interconnections are forming and strengthening (see Chapter 4).

The quest to understand the physical basis of memory—how information becomes embedded in brain matter—has sparked study of the synaptic meeting places where neurons communicate with one another via their neurotransmitter messengers. Eric Kandel and James Schwartz (1982) observed synaptic changes during learning in the sending neurons of the California sea slug, *Aplysia,* a simple animal with a mere 20,000

"The biology of the mind will be as scientifically important to this [new] century as the biology of the gene [was] to the twentieth century."

Eric Kandel, acceptance remarks for the 2000 Nobel Prize

Aplysia   The California sea slug, which neuroscientist Eric Kandel studied for 45 years, has increased our understanding of the neural basis of learning.

Marty Snyderman/Visuals Unlimited, Inc.

or so unusually large and accessible nerve cells. Chapter 7 noted how the sea slug can be classically conditioned (with electric shock) to reflexively withdraw its gills when squirted with water, much as a shell-shocked soldier jumps at the sound of a snapping twig. By observing the slug's neural connections before and after conditioning, Kandel and Schwartz pinpointed changes. When learning occurs, the slug releases more of the neurotransmitter *serotonin* onto certain neurons. These cells then become more efficient at transmitting signals.

In experiments with people, rapidly stimulating certain memory-circuit connections has increased their sensitivity for hours or even weeks to come. The sending neuron now needs less prompting to release its neurotransmitter, and more connections exist between neurons (**FIGURE 8.13**). This increased efficiency of potential neural firing, called **long-term potentiation (LTP),** provides a neural basis for learning and remembering associations (Lynch, 2002; Whitlock et al., 2006). Several lines of evidence confirm that LTP is a physical basis for memory:

- Drugs that block LTP interfere with learning (Lynch & Staubli, 1991).
- Mutant mice engineered to lack an enzyme needed for LTP couldn't learn their way out of a maze (Silva et al., 1992).
- Rats given a drug that enhanced LTP learned a maze with half the usual number of mistakes (Service, 1994).
- Injecting rats with a chemical that blocked the preservation of LTP erased recent learning (Pastalkova et al., 2006).

After long-term potentiation has occurred, passing an electric current through the brain won't disrupt old memories. But the current will wipe out very recent memories. Such is the experience both of laboratory animals and of severely depressed people given *electroconvulsive therapy* (see Chapter 15). A blow to the head can do the same. Football players and boxers momentarily knocked unconscious typically have no memory of events just before the knockout (Yarnell & Lynch, 1970). Their working memory had no time to consolidate the information into long-term memory before the lights went out.

Some memory-biology explorers have helped found companies that are competing to develop memory-altering drugs. The target market for memory-boosting drugs includes millions of people with Alzheimer's disease, millions more with *mild cognitive impairment* that often becomes Alzheimer's, and countless millions who would love to turn back the clock on age-related memory decline. From expanding memories perhaps will come bulging profits.

In your lifetime, will you have access to safe and legal drugs that boost your fading memory without nasty side effects and without cluttering your mind with trivia best forgotten? That question has yet to be answered. But in the meantime, one safe and free memory enhancer is already available on your college campus: effective study

FIGURE 8.13

Doubled receptor sites   Electron microscope image (a) shows just one receptor site (gray) reaching toward a sending neuron before long-term potentiation. Image (b) shows that, after LTP, the receptor sites have doubled. This means that the receiving neuron has increased sensitivity for detecting the presence of the neurotransmitter molecules that may be released by the sending neuron. (From Toni et al., 1999.)

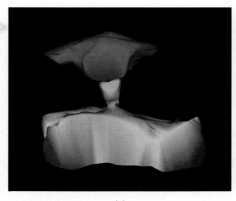

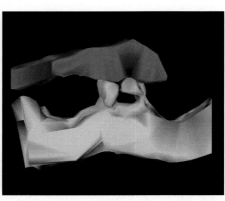

Both photos: From N. Toni et al., *Nature, 402,* Nov. 25, 1999. Courtesy of Dominique Muller

(a)   (b)

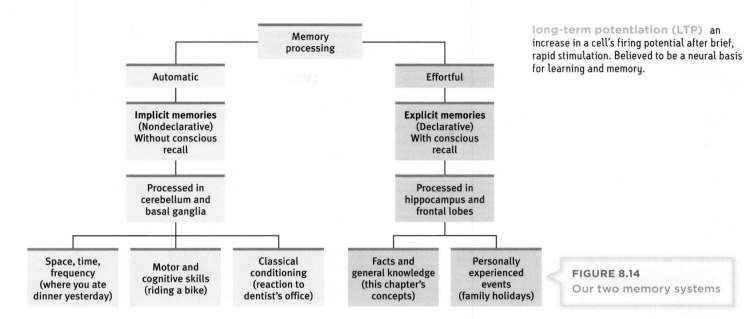

long-term potentiation (LTP) an increase in a cell's firing potential after brief, rapid stimulation. Believed to be a neural basis for learning and memory.

FIGURE 8.14
Our two memory systems

techniques followed by adequate *sleep!* (You'll find study tips in Chapter 1 and at the end of this chapter, and sleep coverage in Chapter 3.)

FIGURE 8.14 summarizes the brain's two-track memory processing and storage system for implicit (automatic) and explicit (effortful) memories.

RETRIEVE IT

• Which brain area responds to stress hormones by helping to create stronger memories?

ANSWER: the amygdala

• This neural basis for learning and memory, found at the synapses in memory-circuit connections, results from brief, rapid stimulation. It is called _____-_____ _____.

ANSWER: long-term potentiation

Retrieval: Getting Information Out

8-14: How do external cues, internal emotions, and order of appearance influence memory retrieval?

After the magic of brain encoding and storage, we still have the daunting task of retrieving the information. What triggers retrieval? How do psychologists study this phenomenon?

Remembering things past Even if Oprah Winfrey and Brad Pitt had not become famous, their high school classmates would most likely still recognize their yearbook photos.

Measuring Retention

To measure retention of memories, psychologists may test for *recall*, *recognition*, or *relearning* speed. Long after you cannot recall most of the people in your high school graduating class, you may still be able to recognize their yearbook pictures from a photographic lineup and pick their names from a list of names. In one experiment, people who had graduated 25 years earlier could not recall many of their old classmates, but they could recognize 90 percent of their pictures and names (Bahrick et al., 1975). If you are like most students, you, too, could probably recognize more names of Snow White's Seven Dwarfs than you could recall (Miserandino, 1991).

Both Photos Spanky's Yearbook Archive

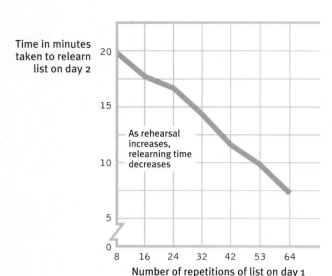

Time in minutes taken to relearn list on day 2

As rehearsal increases, relearning time decreases

Number of repetitions of list on day 1

FIGURE 8.15

Ebbinghaus' retention curve
Ebbinghaus found that the more times he practiced a list of nonsense syllables on day 1, the fewer repetitions he required to relearn it on day 2. Speed of relearning is one measure of memory retention. (From Baddeley, 1982.)

Our recognition memory is impressively quick and vast. "Is your friend wearing a new or old outfit?" "Old." "Is this 5-second movie clip from a film you've ever seen?" "Yes." "Have you ever seen this person before—this minor variation on the same old human features (two eyes, one nose, and so on)?" "No." Before the mouth can form our answer to any of millions of such questions, the mind knows, and knows that it knows.

Our speed at *relearning* also reveals memory. Hermann Ebbinghaus showed this more than a century ago, in his learning experiments, using nonsense syllables. He randomly selected a sample of syllables, practiced them, and tested himself. To get a feel for his experiments, rapidly read aloud, eight times over, the following list (from Baddeley, 1982), then look away and try to recall the items:

> JIH, BAZ, FUB, YOX, SUJ, XIR, DAX, LEQ, VUM, PID, KEL, WAV, TUV, ZOF, GEK, HIW.

The day after learning such a list, Ebbinghaus could recall few of the syllables. But they weren't entirely forgotten. As **FIGURE 8.15** portrays, the more frequently he repeated the list aloud on day 1, the fewer repetitions he required to *relearn* the list on day 2. Additional rehearsal *(overlearning)* of verbal information increases retention, especially when practice is distributed over time.

The point to remember: Tests of recognition and of time spent relearning demonstrate that *we remember more than we can recall.*

RETRIEVE IT

• Multiple-choice questions test our

  a. recall.   c. relearning.

  b. recognition.   d. sensory memory.

ANSWER: b

• Fill-in-the blank questions test our _____.

ANSWER: recall

• If you want to be sure to remember what you're learning for an upcoming test, would it be better to use *recall* or *recognition* to check your memory? Why?

ANSWER: It would be better to test your memory with *recall* (such as with short-answer or fill-in-the-blank self-test questions) rather than *recognition* (such as with multiple-choice questions). Recalling information is harder than recognizing it, so if you can recall it that means your retention of the material is better than if you could only recognize it, and your chances of test success are therefore greater.

Retrieval Cues

Imagine a spider suspended in the middle of her web, held up by the many strands extending outward from her in all directions to different points. If you were to trace a pathway to the spider, you would first need to create a path from one of these anchor points and then follow the strand down into the web.

The process of retrieving a memory follows a similar principle, because memories are held in storage by a web of associations, each piece of information interconnected with others. When you encode into memory a target piece of information, such as the name of the person sitting next to you in class, you associate with it other bits of information about your surroundings, mood, seating position, and so on. These bits can serve as *retrieval cues* that you can later use to access the information. The more retrieval cues you have, the better your chances of finding a route to the suspended memory.

Priming

The best retrieval cues come from associations we form at the time we encode a memory—smells, tastes, and sights that can evoke our memory of the associated person or event. To call up visual cues when trying to recall something, we may mentally place

"Memory is not like a container that gradually fills up; it is more like a tree growing hooks onto which memories are hung."

Peter Russell, The Brain Book, *1979*

priming the activation, often unconsciously, of particular associations in memory.

ourselves in the original context. After losing his sight, John Hull (1990, p. 174) described his difficulty recalling such details:

> I knew I had been somewhere, and had done particular things with certain people, but where? I could not put the conversations ... into a context. There was no background, no features against which to identify the place. Normally, the memories of people you have spoken to during the day are stored in frames which include the background.

Often our associations are activated without our awareness. Philosopher-psychologist William James referred to this process, which we call **priming,** as the "wakening of associations." Seeing or hearing the word *rabbit* primes associations with *hare,* even though we may not recall having seen or heard *rabbit* (**FIGURE 8.16**).

Priming is often "memoryless memory"—invisible memory, without your conscious awareness. If, walking down a hallway, you see a poster of a missing child, you may then unconsciously be primed to interpret an ambiguous adult-child interaction as a possible kidnapping (James, 1986). Although you no longer have the poster in mind, it predisposes your interpretation.

Priming can influence behaviors as well. In one study, participants primed with money-related words were less likely to help another person when asked (Vohs, 2006). In such cases, money may prime our materialism and self-interest rather than the social norms that encourage us to help (Ariely, 2009).

Context-Dependent Memory

Putting yourself back in the context where you experienced something can prime your memory retrieval. As **FIGURE 8.17** illustrates, when scuba divers listened to a word list in two different settings (either 10 feet underwater or sitting on the beach), they recalled more words if retested in the same place (Godden & Baddeley, 1975).

You may have experienced similar context effects. Consider this scenario: While taking notes from this book, you realize you need to sharpen your pencil. You get up and walk into another room, but then you cannot remember why. After returning to your desk it hits you: "I wanted to sharpen this pencil!" What happens to create this frustrating experience? In one context (desk, reading psychology), you realize your pencil needs sharpening. When you go to the other room and are in a different context, you have few cues to lead you back to that thought. When you are once again at your desk, you are back in the context in which you encoded the thought *("This pencil is dull").*

In several experiments, Carolyn Rovee-Collier (1993) found that a familiar context could activate memories even in 3-month-olds. After infants learned that kicking a crib mobile would make it move (via a connecting ribbon from the ankle), the infants kicked more when tested again in the same crib with the same bumper than when in a different context.

Seeing or hearing the word *rabbit*

Activates concept

Primes spelling the spoken word *hair/hare* as *h-a-r-e*

FIGURE 8.16
Priming—awakening associations
After seeing or hearing *rabbit,* we are later more likely to spell the spoken word as *h-a-r-e.* The spreading of associations unconsciously activates related associations. This phenomenon is called priming. (Adapted from Bower, 1986.)

Ask a friend two rapid-fire questions: (a) How do you pronounce the word spelled by the letters *s-h-o-p?* (b) What do you do when you come to a green light? If your friend answers "stop" to the second question, you have demonstrated priming.

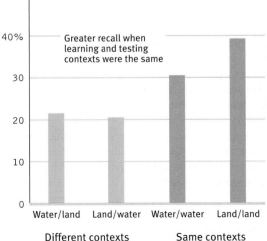

Percentage of words recalled

40%

Greater recall when learning and testing contexts were the same

30

20

10

0

Water/land   Land/water   Water/water   Land/land

Different contexts for hearing and recall

Same contexts for hearing and recall

Fred McConnaughey/Photo Researchers

FIGURE 8.17
The effects of context on memory
In this experiment, words heard underwater were best recalled underwater. Words heard on land were best recalled on land. (Adapted from Godden & Baddeley, 1975.)

"I can't remember what we're arguing about, either. Let's keep yelling, and maybe it will come back to us."

"When a feeling was there, they felt as if it would never go; when it was gone, they felt as if it had never been; when it returned, they felt as if it had never gone."

George MacDonald,
What's Mine's Mine, *1886*

mood-congruent memory the tendency to recall experiences that are consistent with one's current good or bad mood.

serial position effect our tendency to recall best the last (a *recency effect*) and first items (a *primacy effect*) in a list.

State-Dependent Memory

Closely related to context-dependent memory is *state-dependent memory*. What we learn in one state—be it drunk or sober—may be more easily recalled when we are again in that state. What people learn when drunk they don't recall well in *any* state (alcohol disrupts storage). But they recall it slightly better when again drunk. Someone who hides money when drunk may forget the location until drunk again.

Our mood states provide an example of memory's state dependence. Emotions that accompany good or bad events become retrieval cues (Fiedler et al., 2001). Thus, our memories are somewhat **mood congruent.** If you've had a bad evening—your date never showed, your Toledo Mud Hens hat disappeared, your TV went out 10 minutes before the end of a show—your gloomy mood may facilitate recalling other bad times. Being depressed sours memories by priming negative associations, which we then use to explain our current mood. In many experiments, people put in a buoyant mood—whether under hypnosis or just by the day's events (a World Cup soccer victory for the German participants in one study)—have recalled the world through rose-colored glasses (DeSteno et al., 2000; Forgas et al., 1984; Schwarz et al., 1987). They judged themselves competent and effective, other people benevolent, happy events more likely.

Knowing this mood-memory connection, we should not be surprised that in some studies *currently* depressed people have recalled their parents as rejecting, punitive, and guilt promoting, whereas *formerly* depressed people's recollections more closely resembled the more positive descriptions given by those who never suffered depression (Lewinsohn & Rosenbaum, 1987; Lewis, 1992). Similarly, adolescents' ratings of parental warmth in one week gave little clue to how they would rate their parents six weeks later (Bornstein et al., 1991). When teens were down, their parents seemed inhuman; as their mood brightened, their parents morphed from devils into angels. You and I may nod our heads knowingly. Yet, in a good or bad mood, we persist in attributing to reality our own changing judgments, memories, and interpretations. In a bad mood, we may read someone's look as a glare and feel even worse. In a good mood, we may encode the same look as interest and feel even better. Passions exaggerate.

This retrieval effect helps explain why our moods persist. When happy, we recall happy events and therefore see the world as a happy place, which helps prolong our good mood. When depressed, we recall sad events, which darkens our interpretations of current events. For those of us with a predisposition to depression, this process can help maintain a vicious, dark cycle.

Serial Position Effect

Another memory-retrieval quirk, the **serial position effect,** can leave us wondering why we have large holes in our memory of a list of recent events. Imagine it's your first day in a new job, and your manager is introducing co-workers. As you meet each person, you silently repeat everyone's name, starting from the beginning. As the last person smiles and turns away, you feel confident you'll be able to greet your new co-workers by name the next day.

Don't count on it. Because you have spent more time rehearsing the earlier names than the later ones, those are the names you'll probably recall more easily the next day. In experiments, when people view a list of items (words, names, dates, even odors) and immediately try to recall them in any order, they fall prey to the serial position effect (Reed, 2000). They briefly recall the last items especially quickly and well (a *recency effect*), perhaps because those last items are still in working memory. But after a delay, when they have shifted their attention away from the last items, their recall is best for the first items (a *primacy effect;* see **FIGURE 8.18**).

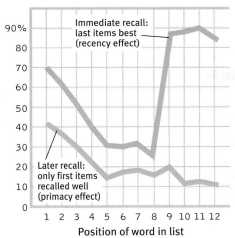

Percentage of words recalled

90%
80
70
60
50
40
30
20
10
0

Immediate recall: last items best (recency effect)

Later recall: only first items recalled well (primacy effect)

1 2 3 4 5 6 7 8 9 10 11 12

Position of word in list

Ian West-WPA Pool/Getty Images

FIGURE 8.18

The serial position effect Immediately after newlyweds Prince William and Kate Middleton made their way through the receiving line of special guests, they would probably have recalled the names of the last few people best. But later they may have been able to recall the first few people best.

RETRIEVE IT

- What is priming?

ANSWER: *Priming* is the activation (often without our awareness) of associations.

- When we are tested immediately after viewing a list of words, we tend to recall the first and last items best, which is known as the _____ _____ effect.

ANSWER: serial position

Forgetting

8-15: Why do we forget?

Amid all the applause for memory—all the efforts to understand it, all the books on how to improve it—have any voices been heard in praise of forgetting? William James (1890, p. 680) was such a voice: "If we remembered everything, we should on most occasions be as ill off as if we remembered nothing." To discard the clutter of useless or out-of-date information—where we parked the car yesterday, a friend's old phone number, restaurant orders already cooked and served—is surely a blessing. The Russian memory whiz S, whom we met at the beginning of this chapter, was haunted by his junk heap of memories. They dominated his consciousness. He had difficulty thinking abstractly—generalizing, organizing, evaluating. After reading a story, he could recite it but would struggle to summarize its gist.

A more recent case of a life overtaken by memory is "A. J.," whose experience has been studied and verified by a University of California at Irvine research team (Parker et al., 2006). A. J., who has identified herself as Jill Price, compares her memory to "a running movie that never stops. It's like a split screen. I'll be talking to someone and seeing something else. . . . Whenever I see a date flash on the television (or anywhere for that matter) I automatically go back to that day and remember where I was, what I was doing, what day it fell on, and on and on and on and on. It is nonstop, uncontrollable, and totally exhausting." A good memory is helpful, but so is the ability to forget. If a memory-enhancing pill becomes available, it had better not be *too* effective.

More often, however, our unpredictable memory dismays and frustrates us. Memories are quirky. My own memory can easily call up such episodes as that wonderful first kiss with the woman I love, or trivial facts like the air mileage from London to Detroit. Then it abandons me when I discover I have failed to encode, store, or retrieve a student's name, or where I left my sunglasses.

"Amnesia seeps into the crevices of our brains, and amnesia heals."

Joyce Carol Oates, "Words Fail, Memory Blurs, Life Wins," 2001

Robert Hanashiro, *USA Today*

The woman who can't forget "A. J." in real life is Jill Price, who, with writer Bart Davis, told her story in a 2008 published memoir. Price remembers every day of her life since age 14 with detailed clarity, including both the joys and the unforgotten hurts.

Cellist Yo-Yo Ma forgot his 266-year-old, $2.5 million cello in a New York taxi. (He later recovered it.)

"Waiter, I'd like to order, unless I've eaten, in which case bring me the check."

Studying a famous brain Jacopo Annese and other scientists at the University of California, San Diego's Brain Observatory are preserving Henry Molaison's brain for the benefit of future generations. Their careful work will result in a freely available online brain atlas.

Forgetting and the Two-Track Mind

English novelist and critic C. S. Lewis described the forgetting that plagues us all. We are

> bombarded every second by sensations, emotions, thoughts . . . nine-tenths of which [we] must simply ignore. The past [is] a roaring cataract of billions upon billions of such moments: Any one of them too complex to grasp in its entirety, and the aggregate beyond all imagination. . . . At every tick of the clock, in every inhabited part of the world, an unimaginable richness and variety of 'history' falls off the world into total oblivion.

For some, memory loss is severe and permanent. Consider Henry Molaison (known as "H. M.," 1926–2008). For 55 years after having brain surgery to stop severe seizures, Molaison was unable to form new conscious memories. He was, as before his surgery, intelligent and did daily crossword puzzles. Yet, reported neuroscientist Suzanne Corkin (2005), "I've known H. M. since 1962, and he still doesn't know who I am." For about 20 seconds during a conversation he could keep something in mind. When distracted, he would lose what was just said or what had just occurred. Thus, he never figured out how to use a TV remote (Dittrich, 2010).

Molaison suffered from **anterograde amnesia**—he could recall his past, but he could not form new memories. (Those who cannot recall their past—the old information stored in long-term memory—suffer from **retrograde amnesia.**)

Neurologist Oliver Sacks (1985, pp. 26–27) described another patient, Jimmie, who had anterograde amnesia resulting from brain damage. Jimmie had no memories—thus, no sense of elapsed time—beyond his injury in 1945.

When Jimmie gave his age as 19, Sacks set a mirror before him: "Look in the mirror and tell me what you see. Is that a 19-year-old looking out from the mirror?"

Jimmie turned ashen, gripped the chair, cursed, then became frantic: "What's going on? What's happened to me? Is this a nightmare? Am I crazy? Is this a joke?" When his attention was diverted to some children playing baseball, his panic ended, the dreadful mirror forgotten.

Sacks showed Jimmie a photo from *National Geographic*. "What is this?" he asked.

"It's the Moon," Jimmie replied.

"No, it's not," Sacks answered. "It's a picture of the Earth taken from the Moon."

"Doc, you're kidding? Someone would've had to get a camera up there!"

"Naturally."

"Hell! You're joking—how the hell would you do that?" Jimmie's wonder was that of a bright young man from nearly 70 years ago reacting with amazement to his travel back to the future.

Careful testing of these unique people reveals something even stranger: Although incapable of recalling new facts or anything they have done recently, Molaison, Jimmie, and others with similar conditions can learn nonverbal tasks. Shown hard-to-find figures in pictures (in the *Where's Waldo?* series), they can quickly spot them again later. They can find their way to the bathroom, though without being able to tell you where it is. They can learn to read mirror-image writing or do a jigsaw puzzle, and they have even been taught complicated job skills (Schacter, 1992, 1996; Xu & Corkin, 2001). They can be classically conditioned. However, *they do all these things with no awareness of having learned them.*

Molaison and Jimmie lost their ability to form new explicit memories, but their automatic processing ability remained intact. Like Alzheimer's patients, whose *explicit* memories for new people and events are lost, they can form new *implicit* memories (Lustig & Buckner, 2004). They can learn *how* to do something, but they will have no conscious recall of learning their new skill. Such sad cases confirm that we have two distinct memory systems, controlled by different parts of the brain.

For most of us, forgetting is a less drastic process. Let's consider some of the reasons we forget.

Encoding Failure

Much of what we sense we never notice, and what we fail to encode, we will never remember (**FIGURE 8.19**). Age can affect encoding efficiency. The brain areas that jump into action when young adults encode new information are less responsive in older adults. This slower encoding helps explain age-related memory decline (Grady et al., 1995).

anterograde amnesia an inability to form new memories.

retrograde amnesia an inability to retrieve information from one's past.

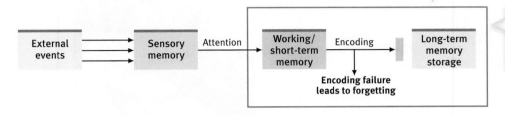

FIGURE 8.19
Forgetting as encoding failure We cannot remember what we have not encoded.

But no matter how young we are, we selectively attend to few of the myriad sights and sounds continually bombarding us. When texting during class, students may fail to encode lecture details that their more attentive classmates are encoding for next week's test. Without effort, many potential memories never form.

Storage Decay

Even after encoding something well, we sometimes later forget it. To study the durability of stored memories, Ebbinghaus (1885) learned more lists of nonsense syllables and measured how much he retained when relearning each list, from 20 minutes to 30 days later. The result, confirmed by later experiments, was his famous forgetting curve: *The course of forgetting is initially rapid, then levels off with time* (**FIGURE 8.20;** Wixted & Ebbesen, 1991). Harry Bahrick (1984) found a similar forgetting curve for Spanish vocabulary learned in school. Compared with those just completing a high school or college Spanish course, people 3 years out of school had forgotten much of what they had learned (**FIGURE 8.21** on the next page). However, what people remembered then, they still remembered 25 and more years later. Their forgetting had leveled off.

One explanation for these forgetting curves is a gradual fading of the physical memory trace. Cognitive neuroscientists are getting closer to solving the mystery of the physical

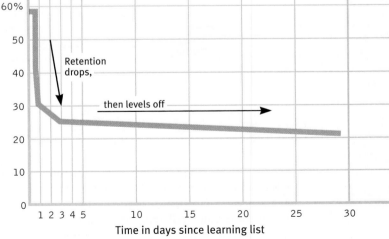

Hermann Ebbinghaus
Bettmann/Corbis

FIGURE 8.20
Ebbinghaus' forgetting curve After learning lists of nonsense syllables, such as YOX and JIH, Ebbinghaus studied how much he retained up to 30 days later. He found that memory for novel information fades quickly, then levels out. (Adapted from Ebbinghaus, 1885.)

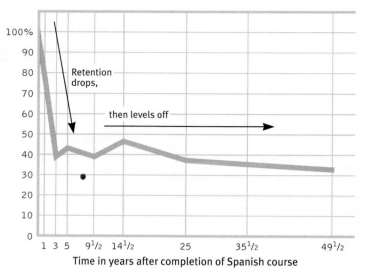

Bill Aron/Photo Edit

FIGURE 8.21

FIGURE 8.21

The forgetting curve for Spanish learned in school Compared with people just completing a Spanish course, those 3 years out of the course remembered much less. Compared with the 3-year group, however, those who studied Spanish even longer ago did not forget much more. (Adapted from Bahrick, 1984.)

Deaf persons fluent in sign language experience a parallel "tip of the fingers" phenomenon (Thompson et al., 2005).

storage of memory and are increasing our understanding of how memory storage could decay. Like books you can't find in your campus library, memories may be inaccessible for many reasons. Some were never acquired (not encoded). Others were discarded (stored memories decay). And others are out of reach because we can't retrieve them.

Retrieval Failure

Often, forgetting is not memories faded but memories unretrieved. We store in long-term memory what's important to us or what we've rehearsed. But sometimes important events defy our attempts to access them (**FIGURE 8.22**). How frustrating when a name lies poised on the tip of our tongue, just beyond reach. Given retrieval cues *("It begins with an M")*, we may easily retrieve the elusive memory. Retrieval problems contribute to the occasional memory failures of older adults, who more frequently are frustrated by tip-of-the-tongue forgetting (Abrams, 2008).

Do you recall the gist of the second sentence I asked you to remember? If not, does the word *shark* serve as a retrieval cue? Experiments show that *shark* (likely what you visualized) more readily retrieves the image you stored than does the sentence's actual word, *fish* (Anderson et al., 1976). (The sentence was *"The fish attacked the swimmer."*)

But retrieval problems occasionally stem from interference and, perhaps, from motivated forgetting.

FIGURE 8.22
Retrieval failure
Sometimes even stored information cannot be accessed, which leads to forgetting.

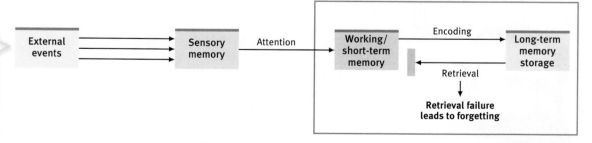

Interference

As you collect more and more information, your mental attic never fills, but it surely gets cluttered. Sometimes the clutter interferes, as new learning and old collide. **Proactive** *(forward-acting)* **interference** occurs when prior learning disrupts your recall of new information. Your well-rehearsed Facebook password may interfere with your retrieval of your newly learned copy machine code.

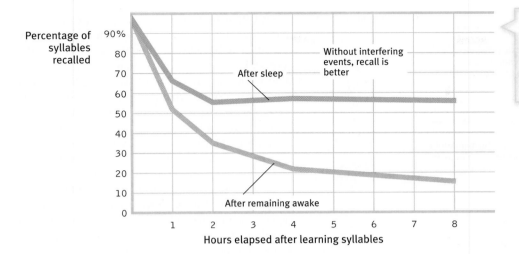

Percentage of syllables recalled

Hours elapsed after learning syllables

Without interfering events, recall is better

After sleep

After remaining awake

FIGURE 8.23
Retroactive interference More forgetting occurred when a person stayed awake and experienced other new material. (From Jenkins & Dallenbach, 1924.)

Retroactive *(backward-acting)* **interference** occurs when new learning disrupts recall of old information. If someone sings new lyrics to the tune of an old song, you may have trouble remembering the original words. It is rather like a second stone tossed in a pond, disrupting the waves rippling out from the first.

Information presented in the hour before sleep is protected from retroactive interference because the opportunity for interfering events is minimized (Diekelmann & Born, 2010; Nesca & Koulack, 1994). Researchers John Jenkins and Karl Dallenbach (1924) first discovered this in a now-classic experiment. Day after day, two people each learned some nonsense syllables, then tried to recall them after up to eight hours of being awake or asleep at night. As **FIGURE 8.23** shows, forgetting occurred more rapidly after being awake and involved with other activities. The investigators surmised that "forgetting is not so much a matter of the decay of old impressions and associations as it is a matter of interference, inhibition, or obliteration of the old by the new" (1924, p. 612).

The hour before sleep is a good time to commit information to memory (Scullin & McDaniel, 2010), though information presented in the *seconds* just before sleep is seldom remembered (Wyatt & Bootzin, 1994). If you're considering learning *while* sleeping, forget it. We have little memory for information played aloud in the room during sleep, although the ears do register it (Wood et al., 1992).

Old and new learning do not always compete with each other, of course. Previously learned information (Latin) often facilitates our learning of new information (French). This phenomenon is called *positive transfer*.

Motivated Forgetting

To remember our past is often to revise it. Years ago, the huge cookie jar in our kitchen was jammed with freshly baked chocolate chip cookies. Still more were cooling across racks on the counter. Twenty-four hours later, not a crumb was left. Who had taken them? During that time, my wife, three children, and I were the only people in the house. So while memories were still fresh, I conducted a little memory test. Andy admitted wolfing down as many as 20. Peter thought he had eaten 15. Laura guessed she had stuffed her then-6-year-old body with 15 cookies. My wife, Carol, recalled eating 6, and I remembered consuming 15 and taking 18 more to the office. We sheepishly accepted responsibility for 89 cookies. Still, we had not come close; there had been 160.

Why do our memories fail us? This happens in part because, as Carol Tavris and Elliot Aronson have pointed out, memory is an "unreliable, self-serving historian" (2007, p. 6). Consider one study, in which researchers told some participants about the benefits of frequent toothbrushing. Those individuals then recalled (more than others did) having frequently brushed their teeth in the preceding two weeks (Ross et al., 1981).

proactive interference the disruptive effect of prior learning on the recall of new information.

retroactive interference the disruptive effect of new learning on the recall of old information.

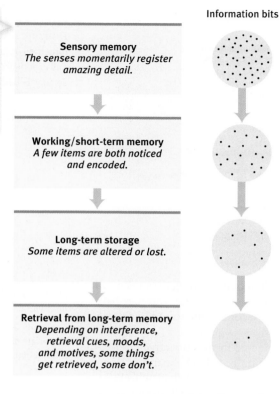

Information bits

Sensory memory
The senses momentarily register amazing detail.

Working/short-term memory
A few items are both noticed and encoded.

Long-term storage
Some items are altered or lost.

Retrieval from long-term memory
Depending on interference, retrieval cues, moods, and motives, some things get retrieved, some don't.

FIGURE 8.24 reminds us that as we process information we filter, alter, or lose much of it. So why were my family and I so far off in our estimates of the cookies we had eaten? Was it an *encoding* problem? (Did we just not notice what we had eaten?) Was it a storage problem? (Might our memories of cookies, like Ebbinghaus' memory of nonsense syllables, have melted away almost as fast as the cookies themselves?) Or was the information still intact but not *retrievable* because it would be embarrassing to remember?[1]

Sigmund Freud might have argued that our memory systems self-censored this information. He proposed that we **repress** painful or unacceptable memories to protect our self-concept and to minimize anxiety. But the repressed memory lingers, he believed, and can be retrieved by some later cue or during therapy. Repression was central to Freud's psychoanalytic theory (more on that in Chapter 12) and was a popular idea in mid-twentieth-century psychology and beyond. In one study, 9 in 10 university students agreed that "memories for painful experiences are sometimes pushed into unconsciousness" (Brown et al., 1996). Therapists often assume it. Today, however, increasing numbers of memory researchers think repression rarely, if ever, occurs. People's efforts to intentionally forget neutral material often succeed, but not when the to-be-forgotten material is emotional (Payne & Corrigan, 2007). Thus, we may have intrusive memories of the very traumatic experiences we would most like to forget.

RETRIEVE IT

• What are three ways we forget, and how does each of these happen?

ANSWER: (1) *Encoding failure:* Unattended information never entered our memory system. (2) *Storage decay:* Information fades from our memory. (3) *Retrieval failure:* We cannot access stored information accurately, sometimes due to interference or motivated forgetting.

Memory Construction Errors

8-16: How do misinformation, imagination, and source amnesia influence our memory construction? How do we decide whether a memory is real or false?

Memory is not precise. Like scientists who infer a dinosaur's appearance from its remains, we infer our past from stored information plus what we later imagined, expected, saw, and heard. We don't just retrieve memories, we reweave them, noted Daniel Gilbert (2006, p. 79): "Information acquired after an event alters memory of the event." We often construct our memories as we encode them, and every time we "replay" a memory, we replace the original with a slightly modified version (Hardt et al., 2010). (Memory researchers call this *reconsolidation.*) So, in a sense, said Joseph LeDoux (2009), "your memory is only as good as your last memory. The fewer times you use it, the more pristine it is." This means that, to some degree, "all memory is false" (Bernstein & Loftus, 2009). Let's examine some of the ways we rewrite our past.

© Sipress, 1988

---

[1] One of my cookie-scarfing sons, on reading this in his father's textbook years later, confessed he had fibbed "a little."

Misinformation and Imagination Effects

In more than 200 experiments, involving more than 20,000 people, Elizabeth Loftus has shown how eyewitnesses reconstruct their memories after a crime or an accident. In one experiment, two groups of people watched a film of a traffic accident and then answered questions about what they had seen (Loftus & Palmer, 1974). Those asked, "How fast were the cars going when they *smashed* into each other?" gave higher speed estimates than those asked, "How fast were the cars going when they *hit* each other?" A week later, when asked whether they recalled seeing any broken glass, people who had heard *smashed* were more than twice as likely to report seeing glass fragments (**FIGURE 8.25**). In fact, the film showed no broken glass.

repression in psychoanalytic theory, the basic defense mechanism that banishes from consciousness anxiety-arousing thoughts, feelings, and memories.

misinformation effect incorporating misleading information into one's memory of an event.

Leading question:
"About how fast were the cars going when they smashed into each other?"

Depiction of actual accident   Memory construction

FIGURE 8.25
Memory construction In this experiment, people viewed a film of a car accident (left). Those who later were asked a leading question recalled a more serious accident than they had witnessed. (From Loftus & Palmer, 1974.)

In many follow-up experiments around the world, others have witnessed an event, received or not received misleading information about it, and then taken a memory test. The repeated result is a **misinformation effect:** Exposed to misleading information, we tend to misremember. A yield sign becomes a stop sign, hammers become screwdrivers, Coke cans become peanut cans, breakfast cereal becomes eggs, and a clean-shaven man morphs into a man with a mustache (Loftus et al., 1992). So powerful is the misinformation effect that it can influence later attitudes and behaviors (Bernstein & Loftus, 2009).

Just hearing a vivid retelling of an event can implant false memories. One experiment falsely suggested to some Dutch university students that, as children, they became ill after eating spoiled egg salad (Geraerts et al., 2008). After absorbing that suggestion, a significant minority were less likely to eat egg-salad sandwiches, both immediately and four months later.

Even repeatedly *imagining* nonexistent actions and events can create false memories. American and British university students were asked to imagine certain childhood events, such as breaking a window with their hand or having a skin sample removed from a finger. One in four of them later recalled the imagined event as something that had really happened (Garry et al., 1996; Mazzoni & Memon, 2003).

Digitally altered photos have also produced this *imagination inflation.* In experiments, researchers have altered photos from a family album to show some family members taking a hot-air balloon ride. After viewing these photos (rather than photos showing just the balloon), children reported more false memories and indicated high confidence in those memories. When interviewed several days later, they reported even richer details of their false memories (Strange et al., 2007; Wade et al., 2002).

In British and Canadian university surveys, nearly one-fourth of students have reported autobiographical memories that they later realized were not accurate (Mazzoni et al., 2010). I empathize. For decades, my cherished earliest memory was of my parents getting off the bus and walking to our house, bringing my baby brother home from the hospital. When, in middle age, I shared that memory with my father, he assured me they did *not* bring their newborn home on the Seattle Transit System. The human mind, it seems, comes with built-in Photoshopping software.

"Memory is insubstantial. Things keep replacing it. Your batch of snapshots will both fix and ruin your memory. . . . You can't remember anything from your trip except the wretched collection of snapshots."

Annie Dillard, "To Fashion a Text," 1988

© D. Hurst/Alamy

"It isn't so astonishing, the number of things I can remember, as the number of things I can remember that aren't so."

Mark Twain (1835–1910)

DOONESBURY

By Garry Trudeau DOONESBURY © 1994 G. B. Trudeau. Reprinted with permission of UNIVERSAL PRESS SYNDICATE.

In the discussion of mnemonics, I gave you six words and told you I would quiz you about them later. How many of these words can you now recall? Of these, how many are high-imagery words? How many are low-imagery? (You can check your list against the six inverted words below.)

ssəɔoɹd
Bicycle, void, cigarette, inherent, fire, process

"Do you ever get that strange feeling of vujà dé? Not déjà vu; vujà dé. It's the distinct sense that, somehow, something just happened that has never happened before. Nothing seems familiar. And then suddenly the feeling is gone. Vujà dé."

George Carlin (1937–2008), in Funny Times, *December 2001*

Source Amnesia

Among the frailest parts of a memory is its source. We may recognize someone but have no idea where we have seen the person. We may dream an event and later be unsure whether it really happened. We may misrecall how we learned about something (Henkel et al., 2000). Psychologists are not immune to the process. Famed child psychologist Jean Piaget was startled as an adult to learn that a vivid, detailed memory from his childhood—a nursemaid's thwarting his kidnapping—was utterly false. He apparently constructed the memory from repeatedly hearing the story (which his nursemaid, after undergoing a religious conversion, later confessed had never happened). In attributing his "memory" to his own experiences, rather than to his nursemaid's stories, Piaget exhibited **source amnesia** (also called *source misattribution*). Misattribution is at the heart of many false memories. Authors and songwriters sometimes suffer from it. They think an idea came from their own creative imagination, when in fact they are unintentionally plagiarizing something they earlier read or heard.

Debra Poole and Stephen Lindsay (1995, 2001, 2002) demonstrated source amnesia among preschoolers. They had the children interact with "Mr. Science," who engaged them in activities such as blowing up a balloon with baking soda and vinegar. Three months later, on three successive days, their parents read them a story describing some things the children had experienced with Mr. Science and some they had not. When a new interviewer asked what Mr. Science had done with them—"Did Mr. Science have a machine with ropes to pull?"—4 in 10 children spontaneously recalled him doing things that had happened only in the story.

Source amnesia also helps explain **déjà vu** (French for "already seen"). Two-thirds of us have experienced this fleeting, eerie sense that "I've been in this exact situation before." It happens most commonly to well-educated, imaginative young adults, especially when tired or stressed (Brown, 2003, 2004; McAneny, 1996). Some wonder, "How could I recognize a situation I'm experiencing for the first time?" Others may think of reincarnation ("I must have experienced this in a previous life") or precognition ("I viewed this scene in my mind before experiencing it").

The key to déjà vu seems to be familiarity with a stimulus without a clear idea of where we encountered it before (Cleary, 2008). Normally, we experience a feeling of *familiarity* (thanks to temporal lobe processing) before we consciously remember details (thanks to hippocampus and frontal lobe processing). When these functions (and brain regions) are out of sync, we may experience a feeling of familiarity without conscious recall. Our amazing brains try to make sense of such an improbable situation, and we get an eerie feeling that we're reliving some earlier part of our life. After all, the situation is familiar, even though we have no idea why. Our source amnesia forces us to do our best to make sense of an odd moment.

Discerning True and False Memories

Because the misinformation effect and source amnesia happen outside our awareness, it is nearly impossible to sift suggested ideas out of the larger pool of real memories (Schooler et al., 1986). Perhaps you can recall describing a childhood experience to a friend and filling in memory gaps with reasonable guesses and assumptions. We all do it, and after more retellings, those guessed details—now absorbed into our memories—may feel as real as if we had actually experienced them (Roediger et al., 1993). Much as perceptual illusions may seem like real perceptions, unreal memories *feel* like real memories.

False memories can be very persistent. Imagine that I were to read aloud a list of words such as *candy, sugar, honey,* and *taste.* Later, I ask you to recognize the presented words from a larger list. If you are at all like the people tested by Henry Roediger and Kathleen McDermott (1995), you would err three out of four times—by falsely remembering a nonpresented similar word, such as *sweet.* We more easily remember the gist than the words themselves.

Memory construction helps explain why 79 percent of 200 convicts exonerated by later DNA testing had been misjudged based on faulty eyewitness identification (Garrett, 2008). It explains why "hypnotically refreshed" memories of crimes so easily incorporate errors, some of which originate with the hypnotist's leading questions *("Did you hear loud noises?")*. It explains why dating partners who fell in love have *over*estimated their first impressions of one another *("It was love at first sight")*, while those who broke up *under*estimated their earlier liking *("We never really clicked")* (McFarland & Ross, 1987). How people feel today tends to be how they recall they have always felt (Mazzoni & Vannucci, 2007; and recall from Chapter 1 our tendency to *hindsight bias*). As George Vaillant (1977, p. 197) noted after following adult lives through time, "It is all too common for caterpillars to become butterflies and then to maintain that in their youth they had been little butterflies. Maturation makes liars of us all."

Children's Eyewitness Recall

8-17: How reliable are young children's eyewitness descriptions, and why are reports of repressed and recovered memories so hotly debated?

If memories can be sincere, yet sincerely wrong, might children's recollections of sexual abuse be prone to error? "It would be truly awful to ever lose sight of the enormity of child abuse," observed Stephen Ceci (1993). Yet Ceci and Maggie Bruck's (1993, 1995) studies of children's memories have made them aware of how easily children's memories can be molded. For example, they asked 3-year-olds to show on anatomically correct dolls where a pediatrician had touched them. Of the children who had not received genital examinations, 55 percent pointed to either genital or anal areas.

In other experiments, the researchers studied the effect of suggestive interviewing techniques (Bruck & Ceci, 1999, 2004). In one study, children chose a card from a deck of possible happenings, and an adult then read the card to them. For example, "Think real hard, and tell me if this ever happened to you. Can you remember going to the hospital with a mousetrap on your finger?" In interviews, the same adult repeatedly asked children to think about several real and fictitious events. After 10 weeks of this, a new adult asked the same question. The stunning result: 58 percent of preschoolers produced false (often vivid) stories regarding one or more events they had never experienced (Ceci et al., 1994). Here's one of those stories:

source amnesia attributing to the wrong source an event we have experienced, heard about, read about, or imagined. (Also called *source misattribution.*) Source amnesia, along with the misinformation effect, is at the heart of many false memories.

déjà vu that eerie sense that "I've experienced this before." Cues from the current situation may subconsciously trigger retrieval of an earlier experience.

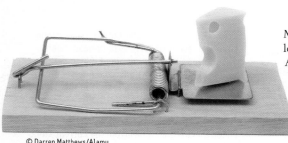

© Darren Matthews/Alamy

My brother Colin was trying to get Blowtorch [an action figure] from me, and I wouldn't let him take it from me, so he pushed me into the wood pile where the mousetrap was. And then my finger got caught in it. And then we went to the hospital, and my mommy, daddy, and Colin drove me there, to the hospital in our van, because it was far away. And the doctor put a bandage on this finger.

Given such detailed stories, professional psychologists who specialize in interviewing children could not reliably separate the real memories from the false ones. Nor could the children themselves. The above child, reminded that his parents had told him several times that the mousetrap incident never happened—that he had imagined it—protested, "But it really did happen. I remember it!" In another experiment, preschoolers merely overheard an erroneous remark that a magician's missing rabbit had gotten loose in their classroom. Later, when the children were suggestively questioned, 78 percent of them recalled actually seeing the rabbit (Principe et al., 2006). "[The] research leads me to worry about the possibility of false allegations. It is not a tribute to one's scientific integrity to walk down the middle of the road if the data are more to one side," said Ceci (1993).

Does this mean that children can never be accurate eyewitnesses? *No.* When questioned about their experiences in neutral words they understood, children often accurately recalled what happened and who did it (Goodman, 2006; Howe, 1997; Pipe, 1996). And when interviewers used less suggestive, more effective techniques, even 4- to 5-year-old children produced more accurate recall (Holliday & Albon, 2004; Pipe et al., 2004). Children were especially accurate when they had not talked with involved adults prior to the interview and when their disclosure was made in a first interview with a neutral person who asked nonleading questions.

Repressed or Constructed Memories of Abuse?

The research on source amnesia and the misinformation effect raises concerns about therapist-guided "recovered" memories. There are two tragedies related to adult recollections of child abuse. One happens when people don't believe abuse survivors who tell their secret. The other happens when innocent people are falsely accused.

Some well-intentioned therapists have reasoned with patients that "people who've been abused often have your symptoms, so you probably were abused. Let's see if, aided by hypnosis or drugs, or helped to dig back and visualize your trauma, you can recover it." Patients exposed to such techniques may then form an image of a threatening person. With further visualization, the image grows more vivid. The patient ends up stunned, angry, and ready to confront or sue the remembered abuser. The equally stunned and devastated parent or relative vigorously denies the accusation.

Critics are not questioning most therapists' professionalism. Nor are they questioning the accusers' sincerity; even if false, their memories are heartfelt. Critics' charges are specifically directed against clinicians who use "memory work" techniques, such as "guided imagery," hypnosis, and dream analysis to recover memories. "Thousands of families were cruelly ripped apart," with "previously loving adult daughters" suddenly accusing fathers (Gardner, 2006). Irate clinicians have countered that those who argue that recovered memories of abuse never happen are adding to abused people's trauma and playing into the hands of child molesters.

In an effort to find a sensible common ground that might resolve psychology's "memory war," professional organizations (the American Medical, American Psychological, and American Psychiatric Associations; the Australian Psychological Society; the British Psychological Society; and the Canadian Psychiatric Association) have convened study panels and issued public statements. Those committed to protecting abused children and those committed to protecting wrongly accused adults have agreed on the following:

- **Sexual abuse happens.** And it happens more often than we once supposed. Although sexual abuse can leave its victims at risk for problems ranging from sexual dysfunction to depression (Freyd et al., 2007), there is no characteristic "survivor syndrome"—no group of symptoms that lets us spot victims of sexual abuse (Kendall-Tackett et al., 1993).

- *Injustice happens.* Some innocent people have been falsely convicted. And some guilty people have evaded responsibility by casting doubt on their truth-telling accusers.

- *Forgetting happens.* Many of those actually abused were either very young when abused or may not have understood the meaning of their experience—circumstances under which forgetting is common. Forgetting isolated past events, both negative and positive, is an ordinary part of everyday life.

- *Recovered memories are commonplace.* Cued by a remark or an experience, we all recover memories of long-forgotten events, both pleasant and unpleasant. What many psychologists debate is twofold: Does the unconscious mind sometimes *forcibly repress* painful experiences? If so, can these experiences be retrieved by certain therapist-aided techniques? (Memories that surface naturally are more likely to be verified [Geraerts et al., 2007].)

- *Memories of things happening before age 3 are unreliable.* We cannot reliably recall happenings from our first three years. As noted earlier, this infantile amnesia happens because our brain pathways have not yet developed enough to form the kinds of memories we will form later in life. Most psychologists—including most clinical and counseling psychologists—therefore doubt "recovered" memories of abuse during infancy (Gore-Felton et al., 2000; Knapp & VandeCreek, 2000). The older a child was when suffering sexual abuse, and the more severe the abuse, the more likely it is to be remembered (Goodman et al., 2003).

- *Memories "recovered" under hypnosis or the influence of drugs are especially unreliable.* Under hypnosis, people will incorporate all kinds of suggestions into their memories, even memories of "past lives."

- *Memories, whether real or false, can be emotionally upsetting.* Both the accuser and the accused may suffer when what was born of mere suggestion becomes, like an actual trauma, a stinging memory that drives bodily stress (McNally, 2003, 2007). Some people knocked unconscious in unremembered accidents know this all too well. They have later developed stress disorders after being haunted by memories they constructed from photos, news reports, and friends' accounts (Bryant, 2001).

So, does *repression* of threatening memories ever occur? Or is this concept—the cornerstone of Freud's theory and of so much popular psychology—misleading? In Chapter 12, we will return to this hotly debated issue. For now, this much appears certain: The most common response to a traumatic experience (witnessing a loved one's murder, being terrorized by a hijacker or a rapist, losing everything in a natural disaster) is not banishment of the experience into the unconscious. Rather, such experiences are typically etched on the mind as vivid, persistent, haunting memories (Porter & Peace, 2007). As Robert Kraft (2002) said of the experience of those trapped in the Nazi death camps, "Horror sears memory, leaving . . . the consuming memories of atrocity."

> "When memories are 'recovered' after long periods of amnesia, particularly when extraordinary means were used to secure the recovery of memory, there is a high probability that the memories are false."
>
> *Royal College of Psychiatrists Working Group on Reported Recovered Memories of Child Sexual Abuse (Brandon et al., 1998)*

RETRIEVE IT

- What—given the commonality of source amnesia—might life be like if we remembered all our waking experiences and all our dreams?

ANSWER: Real experiences would be confused with those we dreamed. When meeting someone, we might therefore be unsure whether we were reacting to something they previously did or to something we dreamed they did.

Improving Memory

8-18: How can you use memory research findings to do better in this and other courses?

Biology's findings benefit medicine. Botany's findings benefit agriculture. So, too, can psychology's research on memory benefit education. Here, for easy reference, is a summary of some research-based suggestions that could help you

© Sigrid Olsson/PhotoAlto/Corbis

Thinking and memory Actively thinking as we read, by rehearsing and relating ideas, and by making the material personally meaningful, yields the best retention.

remember information when you need it. The SQ3R—*Survey, Question, Read, Retrieve, Review*—study technique introduced in Chapter 1 incorporates several of these strategies:

Rehearse repeatedly. To master material, use distributed (spaced) practice. To learn a concept, give yourself many separate study sessions. Take advantage of life's little intervals—riding a bus, walking across campus, waiting for class to start. New memories are weak; exercise them and they will strengthen. To memorize specific facts or figures, Thomas Landauer (2001) has advised, "rehearse the name or number you are trying to memorize, wait a few seconds, rehearse again, wait a little longer, rehearse again, then wait longer still and rehearse yet again. The waits should be as long as possible without losing the information." Reading complex material with minimal rehearsal yields little retention. Rehearsal and critical reflection help more. It pays to study actively.

Make the material meaningful. You can build a network of retrieval cues by taking text and class notes in your own words. Apply the concepts to your own life. Form images. Understand and organize information. Relate the material to what you already know or have experienced. As William James (1890) suggested, "Knit each new thing on to some acquisition already there." Restate concepts in your own words. Mindlessly repeating someone else's words won't supply many retrieval cues. On an exam, you may find yourself stuck when a question uses phrasing different from the words you memorized.

Activate retrieval cues. Mentally re-create the situation and the mood in which your original learning occurred. Jog your memory by allowing one thought to cue the next.

Use mnemonic devices. Associate items with peg words. Make up a story that incorporates vivid images of the items. Chunk information into acronyms. Create rhythmic rhymes *("i before* e, *except after* c*")*.

Minimize interference. Study before sleep. Do not schedule back-to-back study times for topics that are likely to interfere with each other, such as Spanish and French.

Sleep more. During sleep, the brain reorganizes and consolidates information for long-term memory. Sleep deprivation disrupts this process.

Test your own knowledge, both to rehearse it and to find out what you don't yet know. Don't be lulled into overconfidence by your ability to recognize information. Test your recall using the Retrieve It items found throughout each chapter, and the numbered Learning Objective and Testing Effect Questions in the Review sections at the end of each chapter. Outline sections on a blank page. Define the terms and concepts listed at each chapter's end before turning back to their definitions. Take practice tests; the websites and study guides that accompany many texts, including this one, are a good source for such tests.

RETRIEVE IT

• What are the recommended memory strategies you just read about?

ANSWER: Study repeatedly to boost long-term recall. Schedule spaced (not crammed) study times. Spend more time rehearsing or actively thinking about the material. Make the material personally meaningful, with well-organized and vivid associations. Refresh your memory by returning to contexts and moods to activate retrieval cues. Use mnemonic devices. Minimize interference. Plan for a complete night's sleep. Test yourself repeatedly—retrieval practice is a proven retention strategy.

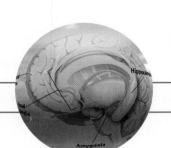

CHAPTER REVIEW

Memory

Test Yourself by taking a moment to answer each of these Learning Objective Questions (repeated here from within the chapter). Then turn to Appendix D, Complete Chapter Reviews, to check your answers. Research suggests that trying to answer these questions on your own will improve your long-term memory of the concepts (McDaniel et al., 2009).

Studying Memory

8-1: What is memory, and how is it measured?

8-2: How do psychologists describe the human memory system?

Building Memories: Encoding

8-3: How do explicit and implicit memories differ?

8-4: What information do we automatically process?

8-5: How does sensory memory work?

8-6: What is the capacity of our short-term and working memory?

8-7: What are some effortful processing strategies that can help us remember new information?

8-8: What are the levels of processing, and how do they affect encoding?

Memory Storage

8-9: What are the capacity and location of our long-term memories?

8-10: What roles do the frontal lobes and hippocampus play in memory storage?

8-11: What roles do the cerebellum and basal ganglia play in our memory processing?

8-12: How do emotions affect our memory processing?

8-13: How do changes at the synapse level affect our memory processing?

Retrieval: Getting Information Out

8-14: How do external cues, internal emotions, and order of appearance influence memory retrieval?

Forgetting

8-15: Why do we forget?

Memory Construction Errors

8-16: How do misinformation, imagination, and source amnesia influence our memory construction? How do we decide whether a memory is real or false?

8-17: How reliable are young children's eyewitness descriptions, and why are reports of repressed and recovered memories so hotly debated?

Improving Memory

8-18: How can you use memory research findings to do better in this and other courses?

Test yourself on these terms by trying to write down the definition in your own words before flipping back to the referenced page to check your answer.

memory, p. 272

recall, p. 272

recognition, p. 272

relearning, p. 272

encoding, p. 273

storage, p. 273

retrieval, p. 273

sensory memory, p. 273

short-term memory, p. 273

long-term memory, p. 273

working memory, p. 273

explicit memory, p. 274

effortful processing, p. 274

automatic processing, p. 274

implicit memory, p. 274

iconic memory, p. 276

echoic memory, p. 276

EXPERIENCE THE TESTING EFFECT

Test yourself repeatedly throughout your studies. This will not only help you figure out what you know and don't know; the testing itself will help you learn and remember the information more effectively thanks to the *testing effect.*

1. A psychologist who asks you to write down as many objects as you can remember having seen a few minutes earlier is testing your _____.

2. The psychological terms for taking in information, retaining it, and later getting it back out are _____, _____, and _____.

3. The concept of working memory
   a. clarifies the idea of short-term memory by focusing on the active processing that occurs in this stage.
   b. splits short-term memory into two substages—sensory memory and working memory.
   c. splits short-term memory into two areas—working (retrievable) memory and inaccessible memory.
   d. clarifies the idea of short-term memory by focusing on space, time, and frequency.

4. Sensory memory may be visual (_____ memory) or auditory (_____ memory).

5. Our short-term memory for new information is limited to about _____ items.

6. Memory aids that use visual imagery (such as peg words) or other organizational devices (such as acronyms) are called _____.

7. The hippocampus seems to function as a
   a. temporary processing site for explicit memories.
   b. temporary processing site for implicit memories.
   c. permanent storage area for emotion-based memories.
   d. permanent storage area for iconic and echoic memories.

8. Amnesia following hippocampus damage typically leaves people unable to learn new facts or recall recent events. However, they may be able to learn new skills, such as riding a bicycle, which is an _____ (explicit/implicit) memory.

9. Long-term potentiation (LTP) refers to
   a. emotion-triggered hormonal changes.
   b. the role of the hippocampus in processing explicit memories.
   c. an increase in a cell's firing potential after brief, rapid stimulation.
   d. aging people's potential for learning.

10. Specific odors, visual images, emotions, or other associations that help us access a memory are examples of
    a. relearning.
    b. déjà vu.
    c. declarative memories.
    d. retrieval cues.

11. When you feel sad, why might it help to look at pictures that reawaken some of your best memories?

12. When tested immediately after viewing a list of words, people tend to recall the first and last items more readily than those in the middle. When retested after a delay, they are most likely to recall
    a. the first items on the list.
    b. the first and last items on the list.
    c. a few items at random.
    d. the last items on the list.

13. When forgetting is due to encoding failure, meaningless information has not been transferred from
    a. the environment into sensory memory.
    b. sensory memory into long-term memory.
    c. long-term memory into short-term memory.
    d. short-term memory into long-term memory.

14. Ebbinghaus' "forgetting curve" shows that after an initial decline, memory for novel information tends to
    a. increase slightly.
    b. decrease noticeably.
    c. decrease greatly.
    d. level out.

15. The hour before sleep is a good time to memorize information, because going to sleep after learning new material minimizes _____ interference.

16. Freud proposed that painful or unacceptable memories are blocked from consciousness through a mechanism called _____.

17. One reason false memories form is our tendency to fill in memory gaps with our reasonable guesses and assumptions, sometimes based on misinformation. This tendency is an example of
    a. proactive interference.
    b. the misinformation effect.
    c. retroactive interference.
    d. the forgetting curve.

18. Eliza's family loves to tell the story of how she "stole the show" as a 2-year-old, dancing at her aunt's wedding reception. Even though she was so young, Eliza can recall the event clearly. How is this possible?

19. We may recognize a face at a social gathering but be unable to remember how we know that person. This is an example of _____ _____.

20. When a situation triggers the feeling that "I've been here before," you are experiencing _____ _____.

21. Children can be accurate eyewitnesses if
    a. interviewers give the children hints about what really happened.
    b. a neutral person asks nonleading questions soon after the event, in words the children can understand.
    c. the children have a chance to talk with involved adults before the interview.
    d. interviewers use precise technical and medical terms.

22. Psychologists involved in the study of memories of abuse tend to DISAGREE about which of the following statements?
    a. Memories of events that happened before age 3 are not reliable.
    b. We tend to repress extremely upsetting memories.
    c. Memories can be emotionally upsetting.
    d. Sexual abuse happens.

Find answers to these questions in Appendix E, in the back of the book.

Experience more of the **TESTING** EFFECT

Multiple-format self-tests and more may be found at www.worthpublishers.com/myers.

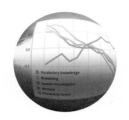

CHAPTER 9

Thinking, Language, and Intelligence

Throughout history, we humans have both bemoaned our foolishness and celebrated our wisdom. The poet T. S. Eliot was struck by "the hollow men . . . Headpiece filled with straw." But Shakespeare's Hamlet extolled the human species as "noble in reason! . . . infinite in faculties! . . . in apprehension how like a god!" In the preceding chapters, we have likewise marveled at both our abilities and our errors.

We have studied the human brain—three pounds of wet tissue the size of a small cabbage, yet containing staggeringly complex circuitry. We have appreciated the amazing abilities of newborns. We have marveled at our sensory system's translating visual stimuli into nerve impulses, distributing them for parallel processing, and reassembling them into colorful perceptions. We have pondered our memory's enormous capacity, and the ease with which our two-track mind processes information, with and without our awareness. Little wonder that our species has had the collective genius to invent the camera, the car, and the computer; to unlock the atom and crack the genetic code; to travel out to space and into our brain's depths.

Yet we have also seen that our species is kin to the other animals, influenced by the same principles that produce learning in rats and pigeons. We have noted that we not-so-wise humans are easily deceived by perceptual illusions, pseudopsychic claims, and false memories.

In this chapter, we encounter further instances of these two images of the human condition—the rational and the irrational. We will consider how we use—and misuse—the information we receive, perceive, store, and retrieve. We will look at our gifts for language and intelligence. And we will reflect on how deserving we are of our species name, *Homo sapiens*—wise human.

Thinking

Concepts

9-1: What is cognition, and what are the functions of concepts?

Psychologists who study **cognition** focus on the mental activities associated with thinking, knowing, remembering, and communicating information. One of these activities is forming **concepts**—mental groupings of similar objects, events, ideas, and people. The concept *chair* includes many items—a baby's high chair, a reclining chair, a dentist's chair.

Concepts simplify our thinking. Imagine life without them. We would need a different name for every person, event, object, and idea. We could not ask a child to "throw the ball" because there would be no concept of *throw* or *ball*. Instead of saying, "They were angry," we would have to describe expressions, intensities, and words. Concepts such as *ball* and *anger* give us much information with little cognitive effort.

We often form our concepts by developing a **prototype**—a mental image or best example of a category (Rosch, 1978). People more quickly agree that "a robin is a bird" than that "a penguin is a bird." For most of us, the robin is the birdier bird; it more closely resembles our *bird* prototype. And the more closely something matches our prototype of a concept—*bird* or *car*—the more readily we recognize it as an example of the concept.

Once we place an item in a category, our memory of it later shifts toward the category prototype, as it did for Belgian students who viewed ethnically blended faces. For example, when viewing a blended face in which 70 percent of the features were Caucasian and 30 percent were Asian, the students categorized the face as Caucasian (**FIGURE 9.1**). Later, as their memory shifted toward the Caucasian prototype, they were more likely to remember an 80 percent Caucasian face than the 70 percent Caucasian they had actually seen (Corneille et al., 2004). Likewise, if shown a 70 percent Asian face, they later remembered a more prototypically Asian face. So, too, with gender: People who viewed 70 percent male faces categorized them as male (no surprise there) and then later misremembered them as even more prototypically male (Huart et al., 2005).

Move away from our prototypes, and category boundaries may blur. Is a tomato a fruit? Is a 17-year-old female a girl or a woman? Is a whale a fish or a mammal? Because a whale fails to match our *mammal* prototype, we are slower to recognize it as a mammal. Similarly, when symptoms don't fit one of our disease prototypes, we are slow to perceive an illness (Bishop, 1991). People whose heart attack symptoms (shortness of breath, exhaustion, a dull weight in the chest) don't match their *heart attack* prototype (sharp chest pain) may not seek help. And when behaviors don't fit our *discrimination* prototypes—of White against Black, male against female, young against old—we often fail to notice prejudice. People more easily detect male prejudice against females than female against males or female against females (Inman & Baron, 1996; Marti et al., 2000). Concepts speed and guide our thinking. But they don't always make us wise.

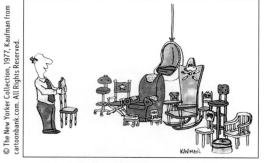

"Attention, everyone! I'd like to introduce the newest member of our family."

Toying with our prototypes It takes a bit longer to conceptualize a Smart Car as an actual car, because it looks more like a toy than our mental prototype for *car*.

© Oleksiy Maksymenko/agefotostock

FIGURE 9.1

Categorizing faces influences recollection Shown a face that was 70 percent Caucasian, people tended to classify the person as Caucasian and to recollect the face as more Caucasian than it was. (From Corneille et al., 2004.)

| 90% CA | 80% CA | 70% CA | 60% CA | 50%/50% | 60% AS | 70% AS | 80% AS | 90% AS |

Courtesy of Olivier Corneille

Problem Solving: Strategies and Obstacles

9-2: What cognitive strategies assist our problem solving, and what obstacles hinder it?

One tribute to our rationality is our problem-solving skill. What's the best route around this traffic jam? How shall we handle a friend's criticism? How can we get in the house without our keys?

Some problems we solve through *trial and error.* Thomas Edison tried thousands of light bulb filaments before stumbling upon one that worked. For other problems, we use **algorithms,** step-by-step procedures that guarantee a solution. But step-by-step algorithms can be laborious and exasperating. To find a word using the 10 letters in *SPLOYOCHYG,* for example, you could try each letter in each of the 10 positions—907,200 permutations in all. Rather than give you a computing brain the size of a beach ball, nature resorts to **heuristics,** simpler thinking strategies. Thus, you might reduce the number of options in the *SPLOYOCHYG* example by grouping letters that often appear together (*CH* and *GY*) and excluding rare letter combinations (such as two Y's together). By using heuristics and then applying trial and error, you may hit on the answer. Have you guessed it?[1]

Sometimes we puzzle over a problem and the pieces suddenly fall together in a flash of **insight**—an abrupt, true-seeming, and often satisfying solution (Topolinski & Reber, 2010). Ten-year-old Johnny Appleton's insight solved a problem that had stumped construction workers: how to rescue a young robin from a narrow 30-inch-deep hole in a cement-block wall. Johnny's solution: Slowly pour in sand, giving the bird enough time to keep its feet on top of the constantly rising pile (Ruchlis, 1990).

Teams of researchers have identified brain activity associated with sudden flashes of insight (Kounios & Beeman, 2009; Sandkühler & Bhattacharya, 2008). They gave people a problem: Think of a word that will form a compound word or phrase with each of three other words in a set (such as *pine, crab,* and *sauce*), and press a button to sound a bell when you know the answer. (If you need a hint: The word is a fruit.[2]) EEGs or fMRIs (functional MRIs) revealed the problem solvers' brain activity. In the first experiment, about half the solutions were by a sudden Aha! insight. Before the Aha! moment, the problem solvers' frontal lobes (which are involved in focusing attention) were active, and there was a burst of activity in the right temporal lobe, just above the ear (**FIGURE 9.2** on the next page).

Insight strikes suddenly, with no prior sense of "getting warmer" or feeling close to a solution (Knoblich & Oellinger, 2006; Metcalfe, 1986). When the answer pops into mind *(apple!),* we feel a happy sense of satisfaction. The joy of a joke may similarly lie in our sudden comprehension of an unexpected ending or a double meaning: "You don't need a parachute to skydive. You only need a parachute to skydive twice."

Insightful as we are, other cognitive tendencies may lead us astray. For example, we more eagerly seek out and favor evidence that supports our ideas than evidence that refutes them (Klayman & Ha, 1987; Skov & Sherman, 1986). In a classic experiment, Peter Wason (1960) demonstrated this tendency, known as **confirmation bias,** by giving British university students the three-number sequence *2-4-6* and asking them to guess the rule he had used to devise the series. (The rule was simple: any three ascending numbers.) Before submitting answers, students generated their own three-number sets and Wason told them whether their sets conformed to his rule. Once *certain* they had the rule, they could announce it. The result? Seldom right but never in doubt. Most students formed a wrong idea *("Maybe it's counting by twos")* and then searched only for confirming evidence (by testing *6-8-10, 100-102-104,* and so forth).

"Ordinary people," said Wason (1981), "evade facts, become inconsistent, or systematically defend themselves against the threat of new information relevant to the

---

[1] Answer to SPLOYOCHYG anagram: PSYCHOLOGY.

[2] The word is *apple:* pineapple, crabapple, applesauce.

cognition the mental activities associated with thinking, knowing, remembering, and communicating.

concept a mental grouping of similar objects, events, ideas, and people.

prototype a mental image or best example of a category. Matching new items to a prototype provides a quick and easy method for sorting items into categories (as when comparing feathered creatures to a prototypical bird, such as a robin).

algorithm a methodical, logical rule or procedure that guarantees solving a particular problem. Contrasts with the usually speedier—but also more error-prone—use of *heuristics.*

heuristic a simple thinking strategy that often allows us to make judgments and solve problems efficiently; usually speedier but also more error prone than *algorithms.*

insight a sudden realization of a problem's solution; contrasts with strategy-based solutions.

confirmation bias a tendency to search for information that supports our preconceptions and to ignore or distort contradictory evidence.

Heuristic searching To search for guava juice, you could search every supermarket aisle (an algorithm), or check the bottled beverage, natural foods, and produce sections (heuristics). The heuristics approach is often speedier, but an algorithmic search guarantees you will find it eventually.

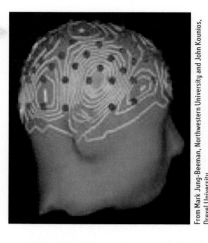

FIGURE 9.2

The Aha! moment A burst of right temporal lobe EEG activity accompanied insight solutions to word problems (Jung-Beeman et al., 2004). The red dots designate EEG electrodes. The white lines show the distribution of high-frequency activity accompanying insight. The insight-related activity is centered in the right temporal lobe (yellow area).

"The human understanding, when any proposition has been once laid down . . . forces everything else to add fresh support and confirmation."

Francis Bacon, Novum Organum, *1620*

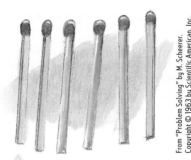

FIGURE 9.3

The matchstick problem How would you arrange six matches to form four equilateral triangles?

"The problem is I can't tell the difference between a deeply wise, intuitive nudge from the Universe and one of my own bone-headed ideas!"

issue." Thus, once people form a belief—that vaccines cause autism, that President Barack Obama is a Kenyan-born Muslim, that gun control does (or does not) save lives—they prefer belief-confirming information. The results can be momentous. The U.S. war against Iraq was launched on the belief that Saddam Hussein possessed weapons of mass destruction (WMD) that posed an immediate threat. When that assumption turned out to be false, the bipartisan U.S. Senate Select Committee on Intelligence (2004) identified confirmation bias as partly to blame: Administration analysts "had a tendency to accept information which supported [their presumptions] . . . more readily than information which contradicted" them. Sources denying such weapons were deemed "either lying or not knowledgeable about Iraq's problems," while those sources who reported ongoing WMD activities were seen as "having provided valuable information."

Once we incorrectly represent a problem, it's hard to restructure how we approach it. If the solution to the matchstick problem in **FIGURE 9.3** eludes you, you may be experiencing *fixation*—an inability to see a problem from a fresh perspective. (For the solution, turn the page to see **FIGURE 9.6**.)

A prime example of fixation is **mental set,** our tendency to approach a problem with the mind-set of what has worked for us previously. Indeed, solutions that worked in the past often do work on new problems. Consider:

Given the sequence *O-T-T-F-?-?-?,* what are the final three letters?

Most people have difficulty recognizing that the three final letters are *F*(ive), *S*(ix), and *S*(even). But solving this problem may make the next one easier:

Given the sequence *J-F-M-A-?-?-?,* what are the final three letters? (If you don't get this one, ask yourself what month it is.)

As a *perceptual set* predisposes what we perceive, a mental set predisposes how we think; sometimes this can be an obstacle to problem solving, as when our mental set from our past experiences with matchsticks predisposes us to arrange them in two dimensions.

Forming Good and Bad Decisions and Judgments

9-3: What is intuition, and how can the availability heuristic, overconfidence, belief perseverance, and framing influence our decisions and judgments?

When making each day's hundreds of judgments and decisions (*Is it worth the bother to take an umbrella? Can I trust this person? Should I shoot the basketball or pass to the player who's hot?*), we seldom take the time and effort to reason systematically. We just follow our **intuition,** our fast, automatic, unreasoned feelings and thoughts. After interviewing policy makers in government, business, and education, social psychologist Irving Janis (1986) concluded that they "often do not use a reflective problem-solving approach. How do they usually arrive at their decisions? If you ask, they are likely to tell you . . . they do it mostly by *the seat of their pants*."

The Availability Heuristic

When we need to act quickly, the mental shortcuts we call *heuristics* enable snap judgments. Thanks to our mind's automatic information processing, intuitive judgments are instantaneous and usually effective. However, research by cognitive psychologists Amos Tversky and Daniel Kahneman (1974) showed how these generally helpful shortcuts

"In creating these problems, we didn't set out to fool people. All our problems fooled us, too."
Amos Tversky (1985)

"Intuitive thinking [is] fine most of the time. . . . But sometimes that habit of mind gets us in trouble."
Daniel Kahneman (2005)

mental set a tendency to approach a problem in one particular way, often a way that has been successful in the past.

intuition an effortless, immediate, automatic feeling or thought, as contrasted with explicit, conscious reasoning.

availability heuristic estimating the likelihood of events based on their availability in memory; if instances come readily to mind (perhaps because of their vividness), we presume such events are common.

can lead even the smartest people into dumb decisions.[3] The **availability heuristic** operates when we estimate the likelihood of events based on how mentally available they are. Casinos entice us to gamble by signaling even small wins with bells and lights—making them vividly memorable—while keeping big losses soundlessly invisible.

The availability heuristic can distort our judgments of other people, too. Anything that makes information "pop" into mind—its vividness, recency, or distinctiveness—can make it seem commonplace. If someone from a particular ethnic group commits a terrorist act, as happened on September 11, 2001, our readily available memory of the dramatic event may shape our impression of the whole group.

Even during that horrific year, terrorist acts claimed comparatively few lives. Yet when the statistical reality of greater dangers (see **FIGURE 9.4**) was pitted against a single vivid case, the memorable case won: Emotion-laden images of terror exacerbated our fears (Sunstein, 2007).

We often fear the wrong things. We fear flying because we play old films of air disasters in our head. We fear letting our sons and daughters walk to school because we

"Kahneman and his colleagues and students have changed the way we think about the way people think."
American Psychological Association president, Sharon Brehm, 2007

[3] Tversky and Kahneman's joint work on decision making received the 2002 Nobel Prize; sadly, only Kahneman was alive to receive the honor.

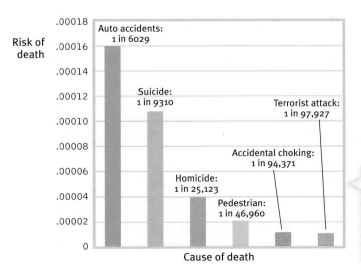

FIGURE 9.4
Risk of death from various causes in the United States, 2001 (Data assembled from various government sources by Randall Marshall et al., 2007.)

The Fear Factor—Why We Fear the Wrong Things

After 9/11, many people feared flying more than driving. In a 2006 Gallup survey, only 40 percent of Americans reported being "not afraid at all" to fly. Yet from 2005 to 2007 Americans were—mile for mile—170 times more likely to die in an automobile or pickup truck crash than on a scheduled flight (National Safety Council, 2010). In 2009 alone, 33,808 Americans were killed in motor vehicle accidents—that's 650 dead people *each week*. Meanwhile, in 2009 (as in 2007 and 2008), *zero* died from accidents on scheduled airline flights.

In a late 2001 essay, I calculated that if—because of 9/11—we flew 20 percent less and instead drove half those unflown miles, about 800 more people would die in the year after 9/11 (Myers, 2001). German psychologist Gerd Gigerenzer (2004, 2006) later checked this estimate against actual accident data. (Why didn't I think of that?) U.S. traffic deaths did indeed increase significantly in the last three months of 2001 (**FIGURE 9.5**). By the end of 2002, Gigerenzer estimated, 1600

Americans had "lost their lives on the road by trying to avoid the risk of flying." Despite our greater fear of flying, flying's greatest danger is, for most people, the drive to the airport.

Why do we fear the wrong things? Why do we judge terrorism to be a greater risk than accidents? Psychologists have identified four influences that feed fear and cause us to ignore higher risks:

1. *We fear what our ancestral history has prepared us to fear.* Human emotions were

Lars Christensen/Shutterstock

© Transtock/Corbis

FIGURE 9.5

Scared onto deadly highways Images of 9/11 etched a sharper image in American minds than did the millions of fatality-free flights on U.S. airlines during 2002 and after. Dramatic events are readily available to memory, and they shape our perceptions of risk. In the three months after 9/11, those faulty perceptions led more Americans to travel, and some to die, by car. (Adapted from Gigerenzer, 2004.)

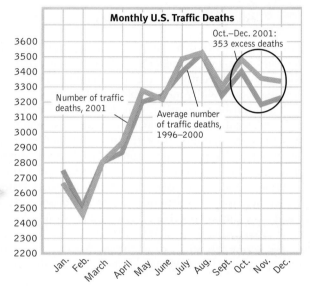

see mental snapshots of abducted and brutalized children. We fear swimming in ocean waters because we replay *Jaws* with ourselves as victims. Even passing by a person who sneezes and coughs can heighten our perceptions of various health risks (Lee et al., 2010). And so, thanks to such readily available images, we come to fear extremely rare events. Dramatic outcomes make us gasp; probabilities we hardly grasp. (See Thinking Critically About: The Fear Factor.)

Meanwhile, the lack of comparably available images of global climate change—which some scientists regard as a future "Armageddon in slow motion"—has left most people little concerned (Pew, 2007). The vividness of a recent local cold day reduces their concern about long-term global warming and overwhelms less memorable scientific data (Li et al., 2011).

As of 2012, some 40 nations have sought to harness the positive power of vivid, memorable images by putting eye-catching warnings and graphic photos on cigarette packages (Wilson, 2011). This campaign may work, where others have failed. As psychologist Paul Slovic (2007) points out, we reason emotionally and neglect probabilities. We overfeel and underthink. In one experiment, donations to a starving 7-year-old were greater when her image was *not* accompanied by statistical information about the

"Don't believe everything you think"

Bumper sticker

overconfidence the tendency to be more confident than correct—to overestimate the accuracy of our beliefs and judgments.

road tested in the Stone Age. Our old brain prepares us to fear yesterday's risks: snakes, lizards, and spiders (which combined now kill a tiny fraction of the number killed by modern-day threats, such as cars and cigarettes). Yesterday's risks also prepare us to fear confinement and heights, and therefore flying.

2. *We fear what we cannot control.* Driving we control; flying we do not.

3. *We fear what is immediate.* The dangers of flying are mostly telescoped into the moments of takeoff and landing. The dangers of driving are diffused across many moments to come, each trivially dangerous.

4. *Thanks to the availability heuristic, we fear what is most readily available in memory.* Powerful, vivid images, like that of United Flight 175 slicing into the World Trade Center, feed our judgments of risk. Thousands of safe car trips have extinguished our anxieties about driving. Similarly, we remember (and fear) widespread disasters (hurricanes, tornadoes, earthquakes) that kill people dramatically, in bunches. But we fear too little the less dramatic threats that claim lives quietly, one by one, continuing into the distant future. Bill Gates has noted that each year a half-million

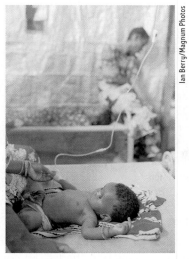

Dramatic deaths in bunches breed concern and fear The memorable 2010 Haitian earthquake that killed some 250,000 people stirred an outpouring of justified concern. Meanwhile, according to the World Health Organization, a silent earthquake of poverty-related malaria was killing about that many people, mostly in Africa, *every four months.*

children worldwide die from rotavirus. This is the equivalent of four 747s full of children every day, and we hear nothing of it (Glass, 2004).

The news, and our own memorable experiences, can make us disproportionately fearful of infinitesimal risks. As one risk analyst explained, "If it's in the news, don't worry about it. The very definition of *news* is 'something that hardly ever happens'" (Schneier, 2007). Despite people's fear of dying in a terrorist attack on an airplane, the last decade produced one terrorist attempt for every 10.4 million flights—less than one-twentieth the chance of any one of us being struck by lightning (Silver, 2009).

The point to remember: It is perfectly normal to fear purposeful violence from those who hate us. When terrorists strike again, we will all recoil in horror. But smart thinkers will check their fears against the facts and resist those who aim to create a culture of fear. By so doing, we take away the terrorists' most omnipresent weapon: exaggerated fear.

"Fearful people are more dependent, more easily manipulated and controlled, more susceptible to deceptively simple, strong, tough measures and hard-line postures."

Media researcher George Gerbner to U.S. Congressional Subcommittee on Communications, 1981

millions of needy African children like her (Small et al., 2007). "If I look at the mass I will never act," Mother Teresa reportedly said. "If I look at the one, I will." "The more who die, the less we care," noted Slovic (2010).

Overconfidence

Sometimes our judgments and decisions go awry simply because we are more confident than correct. Across various tasks, people overestimate their performance (Metcalfe, 1998). If 60 percent of people correctly answer a factual question, such as "Is absinthe a liqueur or a precious stone?," they will typically average 75 percent confidence (Fischhoff et al., 1977). (It's a licorice-flavored liqueur.) This tendency to overestimate the accuracy of our knowledge and judgments is **overconfidence.**

It was an overconfident BP that, before its exploded drilling platform spewed oil into the Gulf of Mexico, downplayed safety concerns, and then downplayed the spill's magnitude (Mohr et al., 2010; Urbina, 2010). It is overconfidence that drives stockbrokers and investment managers to market their ability to outperform stock market averages, despite overwhelming evidence to the contrary (Malkiel, 2004). A purchase of stock X, recommended by a broker who judges this to be the time to buy, is usually balanced

FIGURE 9.6
Solution to the matchstick problem To solve this problem, you must view it from a new perspective, breaking the fixation of limiting solutions to two dimensions.

Predict your own behavior When will you finish reading this chapter?

"When you know a thing, to hold that you know it; and when you do not know a thing, to allow that you do not know it; this is knowledge."

Confucius (551–479 B.C.E.), Analects

by a sale of stock X by someone who judges this to be the time to sell. Despite their confidence, buyer and seller cannot both be right.

Classrooms are full of overconfident students who expect to finish assignments and write papers ahead of schedule (Buehler et al., 1994). In fact, the projects generally take about twice the number of days predicted.

We also overestimate our future leisure time (Zauberman & Lynch, 2005). Anticipating how much more we will accomplish next month, we happily accept invitations and assignments, only to discover we're still just as busy when the day rolls around. And believing we will have more money next year, we take out loans or buy on credit. Despite our past overconfident predictions, we remain overly confident of our next prediction.

Overconfidence can have adaptive value. People who err on the side of overconfidence live more happily, make tough decisions more easily, and seem more credible than others (Baumeister, 1989; Taylor, 1989). Moreover, given prompt and clear feedback, as weather forecasters receive after each day's predictions, we can learn to be more realistic about the accuracy of our judgments (Fischhoff, 1982). The wisdom to know when we know a thing and when we do not is born of experience.

Belief Perseverance

Our overconfidence in our judgments is startling; equally startling is our tendency to cling to our beliefs in the face of contrary evidence. **Belief perseverance** often fuels social conflict, as it did in a classic study of people with opposing views of capital punishment (Lord et al., 1979). Each side studied two supposedly new research findings, one supporting and the other refuting the claim that the death penalty deters crime. Each side was more impressed by the study supporting its own beliefs, and each readily disputed the other study. Thus, showing the pro- and anti-capital-punishment groups the *same* mixed evidence actually *increased* their disagreement.

If you want to rein in belief perseverance, a simple remedy exists: *Consider the opposite.* When the same researchers repeated the capital-punishment study, they asked some participants to be "as *objective* and *unbiased* as possible" (Lord et al., 1984). The plea did nothing to reduce biased evaluations of evidence. They asked another group to consider "whether you would have made the same high or low evaluations had exactly the same study produced results on the *other* side of the issue." Having imagined and pondered *opposite* findings, these people became much less biased.

The more we come to appreciate why our beliefs might be true, the more tightly we cling to them. Once we have explained to ourselves why we believe a child is "gifted" or has a "learning disability," or why candidate X or Y will be a better commander-in-chief, or why company Z is a stock worth owning, we tend to ignore evidence undermining our belief. Prejudice persists. Once beliefs form and get justified, it takes more compelling evidence to change them than it did to create them.

The Effects of Framing

Framing, the way we present an issue, sways our decisions and judgments and can be a powerful persuasion tool. Carefully posed options can nudge people toward decisions that could benefit them or society as a whole (Thaler & Sunstein, 2008):

- *Life and death.* Imagine two surgeons explaining a surgery risk. One tells patients that 10 percent of people die during this surgery. The other tells patients that 90 percent will survive. The information is the same. The effect is not. In surveys, both patients and physicians perceive greater risk when they hear that 10 percent will *die* (Marteau, 1989; McNeil et al., 1988; Rothman & Salovey, 1997).

- *Why choosing to be an organ donor depends on where you live.* In many European countries as well as the United States, those renewing their driver's license can decide whether they want to be organ donors. In some countries, the default option is *Yes,*

"I'm happy to say that my final judgment of a case is almost always consistent with my prejudgment of the case."

but people can opt out. Nearly 100 percent of the people in opt-out countries have agreed to be donors. In the United States, Britain, and Germany, the default option is *No*, but people can "opt in." In these countries, only about 25 percent have agreed to be donors (Johnson & Goldstein, 2003).

- *How to help employees decide to save for their retirement.* A 2006 U.S. pension law recognized the framing effect. Before that law, employees who wanted to contribute to a 401(k) retirement plan typically had to choose a lower take-home pay, which few people will do. Companies can now automatically enroll their employees in the plan but allow them to opt out (which would raise the employees' take-home pay). In both plans, the decision to contribute is the employee's. But under the new "opt-out" arrangement, enrollments in one analysis of 3.4 million workers soared from 59 to 86 percent (Rosenberg, 2010).

The point to remember: Framing influences decisions.

The Perils and Powers of Intuition

9-4: How do smart thinkers use intuition?

The perils of intuition—irrational fears, clouded judgment, illogical reasoning—can feed gut fears and prejudices. Irrational thinking can persist even when people are offered extra pay for thinking smart, even when they are asked to justify their answers, and even when they are expert physicians or clinicians (Shafir & LeBoeuf, 2002). So, are our heads indeed filled with straw?

Throughout this book you will see examples of smart intuition. In brief,

- *Intuition is analysis "frozen into habit" (Simon, 2001).* It is implicit knowledge—what we've learned but can't fully explain, such as the tacit expertise chess masters display in "blitz chess," where after barely more than a glance they intuitively know the right move (Burns, 2004). We see this expertise in seasoned nurses, firefighters, art critics, car mechanics, and hockey players. And in you, too, for anything in which you have developed a special expertise. In each case, what feels like instant intuition is an acquired ability to size up a situation in an eyeblink.

- *Intuition is usually adaptive, enabling quick reactions.* Our fast and frugal heuristics let us intuitively assume that fuzzy looking objects are far away—which they usually are, except on foggy mornings. Our learned associations surface as gut feelings, right or wrong: Seeing a stranger who looks like someone who has harmed or threatened us in the past, we may automatically react warily.

- *Intuition is huge.* Today's cognitive science offers many examples of unconscious automatic influences on our judgments (Custers & Aarts, 2010). Consider: Most people guess that the more complex the choice, the smarter it is to make decisions rationally rather than intuitively (Inbar et al., 2010). Actually, Dutch psychologists have shown that in making complex decisions, we benefit by letting our brain work on a problem without thinking about it (Strick et al., 2010). In one series of experiments, they showed three groups of people complex information (about apartments or roommates or art posters or soccer matches). They invited one group to state their preference immediately after reading information about each of four options. A second group, given several minutes to analyze the information, made slightly smarter decisions. But wisest of all, in study after study, was the third group, whose attention was distracted for a time, enabling their minds to engage in automatic, unconscious processing of the complex information. Critics of this research remind us that deliberate, conscious thought also is part of smart thinking (Gonzáles-Vallejo et al., 2008; Lassiter et al., 2009; Newell et al., 2008; Payne et al., 2008). Nevertheless,

belief perseverance clinging to one's initial conceptions after the basis on which they were formed has been discredited.

framing the way an issue is posed; how an issue is framed can significantly affect decisions and judgments.

Analysis frozen into habit In 1998, World Checkers Champion Ron "Suki" King of Barbados set a new record by simultaneously playing 385 players in 3 hours and 44 minutes. Thus, while his opponents often had hours to plot their game moves, King could only devote about 35 seconds to each game. Yet he still managed to win all 385 games!

Courtesy of Cameras on Wheels

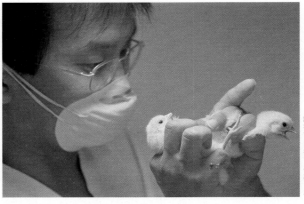

Chick sexing When acquired expertise becomes an automatic habit, as it is for experienced chicken sexers, it feels like intuition. At a glance, they just know, yet cannot easily tell you how they know.

Jean-Philippe Ksiazek/AFP

letting a problem "incubate" while we attend to other things can pay dividends (Sio & Ormerod, 2009). Facing a difficult decision involving lots of facts, we're wise to gather all the information we can, and then say, "Give me some time *not* to think about this." By taking time to sleep on it, we let our unconscious mental machinery work on, and await, the intuitive result of this automatic processing.

The bottom line: Our two-track mind makes sweet harmony as smart, critical thinking listens to the creative whispers of our vast unseen mind and then evaluates evidence, tests conclusions, and plans for the future.

Thinking Creatively

9-5: What is creativity, and what fosters it?

Creativity is the ability to produce ideas that are both novel and valuable (Hennessey & Amabile, 2010). Consider Princeton mathematician Andrew Wiles' incredible, creative moment. Pierre de Fermat, a seventeenth-century mischievous genius, had challenged mathematicians of his day to match his solutions to various number theory problems. His most famous challenge—*Fermat's last theorem*—baffled the greatest mathematical minds, even after a $2 million prize (in today's dollars) was offered in 1908 to whoever first created a proof.

Wiles had pondered Fermat's theorem for more than 30 years and had come to the brink of a solution. One morning, out of the blue, the final "incredible revelation" struck him. "It was so indescribably beautiful; it was so simple and so elegant. I couldn't understand how I'd missed it. . . . It was the most important moment of my working life" (Singh, 1997, p. 25).

Creativity like Wiles' is supported by a certain level of *aptitude* (ability to learn). Those who score exceptionally high in quantitative aptitude as 13-year-olds, for example, are more likely to obtain graduate science and math degrees and create published or patented work (Park et al., 2008; Robertson et al., 2010). But creativity is more than school smarts, and it requires a different kind of thinking:

- Aptitude tests, such as the SAT, demand a single correct answer. They require **convergent thinking.**

- Creativity tests *(How many uses can you think of for a brick?)* require expansive, **divergent thinking.**

Robert Sternberg and his colleagues believe creativity has five components (Sternberg, 1988, 2003; Sternberg & Lubart, 1991, 1992):

1. ***Expertise***—a well-developed base of knowledge—furnishes the ideas, images, and phrases we use as mental building blocks. "Chance favors only the prepared mind,"

creativity the ability to produce novel and valuable ideas.

convergent thinking narrows the available problem solutions to determine the single best solution.

divergent thinking expands the number of possible problem solutions (creative thinking that diverges in different directions).

observed Louis Pasteur. The more blocks we have, the more chances we have to combine them in novel ways. Wiles' well-developed base of knowledge put the needed theorems and methods at his disposal.

2. **Imaginative thinking skills** provide the ability to see things in novel ways, to recognize patterns, and to make connections. Having mastered a problem's basic elements, we redefine or explore it in a new way. Copernicus first developed expertise regarding the solar system and its planets, and then creatively defined the system as revolving around the Sun, not the Earth. Wiles' imaginative solution combined two partial solutions.

3. **A venturesome personality** seeks new experiences, tolerates ambiguity and risk, and perseveres in overcoming obstacles. Wiles said he labored in near-isolation from the mathematics community partly to stay focused and avoid distraction. Such determination is an enduring trait. As girls, notably creative women were typically "intelligent, hard working, imaginative, and strong willed," noted Sally Reis (2001).

4. **Intrinsic motivation** is being driven more by interest, satisfaction, and challenge than by external pressures (Amabile & Hennessey, 1992). Creative people focus less on extrinsic motivators—meeting deadlines, impressing people, or making money—than on the pleasure and stimulation of the work itself. Asked how he solved such difficult scientific problems, Isaac Newton reportedly answered, "By thinking about them all the time." Wiles concurred: "I was so obsessed by this problem that . . . I was thinking about it all the time—[from] when I woke up in the morning to when I went to sleep at night" (Singh & Riber, 1997).

5. **A creative environment** sparks, supports, and refines creative ideas. Wiles stood on the shoulders of others and collaborated with a former student. After studying the careers of 2026 prominent scientists and inventors, Dean Keith Simonton (1992) noted that the most eminent were mentored, challenged, and supported by their colleagues. Creativity-fostering environments support innovation, team building, and communication (Hülsheger et al., 2009). They also support contemplation. After Jonas Salk solved a problem that led to the polio vaccine while in a monastery, he designed the Salk Institute to provide contemplative spaces where scientists could work without interruption (Sternberg, 2006).

For those seeking to boost the creative process, see Close-Up: Fostering Your Own Creativity.

CLOSE UP:

Fostering Your Own Creativity

Creative achievement springs from creativity-spawning persons and situations. To grow your own creativity,

- *develop your expertise.* Ask yourself what you care about and most enjoy. Follow your passion and become an expert at something.

- *allow time for incubation.* Given sufficient knowledge available for novel connections, a period of inattention to a problem ("sleeping on it") allows for unconscious processing to form associations (Zhong et al., 2008). So think hard on a problem, then set it aside and come back to it later.

- *set aside time for the mind to roam freely.* Take time away from attention-absorbing television, social networking, and video gaming. Jog, go for a long walk, or meditate.

- *experience other cultures and ways of thinking.* Living abroad sets the creative juices flowing. Even after controlling for other variables, students who have spent time abroad are more adept at working out creative solutions to problems (Leung et al., 2008; Maddux et al., 2009, 2010). Multicultural experiences expose us to multiple perspectives and facilitate flexible thinking.

A creative environment.

Imaginative thinking Cartoonists often display creativity as they see things in new ways or make unusual connections.

"For the love of God, is there a doctor in the house?"

Everyone held up their crackers as David threw the cheese log into the ceiling fan.

RETRIEVE IT

- Match the process or strategy listed below (1–10) with the descriptions.

1. Algorithm
2. Intuition
3. Insight
4. Heuristics

5. Fixation
6. Confirmation bias
7. Overconfidence

8. Framing
9. Belief perseverance
10. Creativity

a. Inability to view problems from a new angle; focuses thinking but hinders creative problem solving.

b. Methodical rule or procedure that guarantees the solution but requires time and effort.

c. Fast, automatic, effortless feelings and thoughts based on our experience; huge and adaptive but can lead us to overfeel and underthink.

d. Simple thinking shortcuts that allow us to act quickly and efficiently but put us at risk for errors.

e. Sudden Aha! reaction that provides instant realization of the solution.

f. Tendency to search for support for our own views and ignore contradictory evidence.

g. Ignoring evidence that proves our beliefs are wrong; closes our mind to new ideas.

h. Overestimating the accuracy of our beliefs and judgments; allows us to be happy and to make decisions easily, but puts us at risk for errors.

i. Wording a question or statement so that it evokes a desired response; can influence others' decisions and produce a misleading result.

j. The ability to produce novel and valuable ideas.

ANSWERS: 1.b, 2.c, 3.e, 4.d, 5.a, 6.f, 7.h, 8.i, 9.g, 10.j.

Do Other Species Share Our Cognitive Skills?

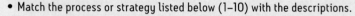

9-6: What do we know about animal thinking?

Animals are smarter than we often realize. As the pioneering psychologist Margaret Floy Washburn explained in her 1908 book, *The Animal Mind,* animal consciousness and intelligence can be inferred from their behavior.

Using Concepts and Numbers Even pigeons—mere birdbrains—can sort objects (pictures of cars, cats, chairs, flowers) into categories, or concepts. Shown a picture of a never-before-seen chair, the pigeon will reliably peck a key that represents *chairs*

(Wasserman, 1995). The great apes also form concepts, such as *cat* and *dog*. After monkeys have learned these concepts, certain frontal lobe neurons in their brain fire in response to new "catlike" images, others to new "doglike" images (Freedman et al., 2001).

Until his death in 2007, Alex, an African Grey parrot, categorized and named objects (Pepperberg, 2006, 2009). Among his jaw-dropping numerical skills was the ability to comprehend numbers up to 6. He could speak the number of objects. He could add two small clusters of objects and announce the sum. He could indicate which of two numbers was greater. And he gave correct answers when shown various groups of objects. Asked, for example, "What color four?" (meaning "What's the color of the objects of which there are four?"), he could speak the answer.

Life on white/Alamy

Displaying Insight Psychologist Wolfgang Köhler (1925) showed that we are not the only creatures to display insight. He placed a piece of fruit and a long stick outside the cage of a chimpanzee named Sultan, beyond his reach. Inside the cage, he placed a short stick, which Sultan grabbed, using it to try to reach the fruit. After several failed attempts, he dropped the stick and seemed to survey the situation. Then suddenly, as if thinking "Aha!" Sultan jumped up and seized the short stick again. This time, he used it to pull in the longer stick—which he then used to reach the fruit. Apes have even exhibited foresight by storing a tool they could use to retrieve food the next day (Mulcahy & Call, 2006).

Using Tools and Transmitting Culture Like humans, many other species invent behaviors and transmit cultural patterns to their peers and offspring (Boesch-Achermann & Boesch, 1993). Forest-dwelling chimpanzees select different tools for different purposes—a heavy stick for making holes, a light, flexible stick for fishing for termites (Sanz et al., 2004). They break off the reed or stick, strip off any leaves, carry it to a termite mound, twist it just so, and carefully remove it. Termites for lunch! (This is very reinforcing for a chimpanzee.) One anthropologist, trying to mimic the animal's deft fishing moves, failed miserably.

Researchers have found at least 39 local customs related to chimpanzee tool use, grooming, and courtship (Whiten & Boesch, 2001). One group may slurp termites directly from a stick, another group may pluck them off individually. One group may break nuts with a stone hammer, another with a wooden hammer. These group differences, along with differing communication and hunting styles, are the chimpanzee version of cultural diversity.

Other animals have also shown surprising cognitive talents (**FIGURE 9.7** on the next page). In tests, elephants have demonstrated self-awareness and displayed their abilities to learn, remember, discriminate smells, empathize, cooperate, teach, and spontaneously use tools (Byrne et al., 2009). As social creatures, chimpanzees have shown altruism, cooperation, and group aggression. Like humans, they will kill their neighbor to gain land, and they grieve over dead relatives (Anderson et al., 2010; Biro et al., 2010; Mitani et al., 2010).

There is no question that other species display many remarkable cognitive skills. But one big question remains: Do they, like humans, exhibit language? First, let's consider what language is, and how it develops.

Johan Swanepoel/Alamy

FIGURE 9.7

Tool-using animals (a) New Caledonian crows studied by Christopher Bird and Nathan Emery (2009) quickly learned to raise the water level in a tube and nab a floating worm by dropping stones into the water. Other crows have used twigs to probe for insects, and bent strips of metal to reach food. (b) One male chimpanzee in Sweden's Furuvik Zoo was observed every morning collecting stones into a neat little pile, which later in the day he used as ammunition to pelt visitors (Osvath, 2009). (c) Dolphins form coalitions, cooperatively hunt, and learn tool use from one another (Bearzi & Stanford, 2010). This bottlenose dolphin in Shark Bay, Western Australia, belongs to a small group that uses marine sponges as protective nose guards when probing the sea floor for fish (Krützen et al., 2005).

Chris Bird & Nathan Emery

(a)

Mathias Osvath

(b)

Copyright Amanda K. Coakes

(c)

Language

Imagine an alien species that could pass thoughts from one head to another merely by pulsating air molecules in the space between them. Perhaps these weird creatures could inhabit a future Spielberg movie?

Actually, we are those creatures. When we speak, our brain and voice apparatus conjure up air-pressure waves that we send banging against another's eardrum—enabling us to transfer thoughts from our brain into theirs. As cognitive scientist Steven Pinker (1998) has noted, we sometimes sit for hours "listening to other people make noise as they exhale, because those hisses and squeaks contain *information*." And thanks to all those funny sounds created in our heads from the air-pressure waves we send out, we get people's attention, we get them to do things, and we maintain relationships (Guerin, 2003). Depending on how you vibrate the air after opening your mouth, you may get slapped or kissed.

But **language** is more than vibrating air. As I create this paragraph, my fingers on a keyboard generate electronic binary numbers that are translated into the squiggles in front of you. When transmitted by reflected light rays into your retina, those squiggles trigger formless nerve impulses that project to several areas of your brain, which integrate the information, compare it to stored information, and decode meaning. Thanks to language, information is moving from my mind to yours. Monkeys mostly know what they see. Thanks to language (spoken, written, or signed), we comprehend much that we've never seen and that our distant ancestors never knew.

If you were able to retain only one cognitive ability, make it language, suggests researcher Lera Boroditsky (2009). Without sight or hearing, you could still have friends, family, and a job. But without language, could you have these things? "Language is so fundamental to our experience, so deeply a part of being human, that it's hard to imagine life without it."

Language Structure

language our spoken, written, or signed words and the ways we combine them to communicate meaning.

phoneme in a language, the smallest distinctive sound unit.

morpheme in a language, the smallest unit that carries meaning; may be a word or a part of a word (such as a prefix).

grammar in a language, a system of rules that enables us to communicate with and understand others. In a given language, *semantics* is the set of rules for deriving meaning from sounds, and *syntax* is the set of rules for combining words into grammatically sensible sentences.

9-7: What are the structural components of a language?

Consider how we might go about inventing a language. For a spoken language, we would need three building blocks:

- **Phonemes** are the smallest distinctive sound units in a language. To say *bat,* English speakers utter the phonemes *b, a,* and *t.* (Phonemes aren't the same as letters. *Chat* also has three phonemes—*ch, a,* and *t.*) Linguists surveying nearly 500 languages have identified 869 different phonemes in human speech, but no language uses all of them (Holt, 2002; Maddieson, 1984). English uses about 40; other languages use anywhere from half to more than twice that many. As a general rule, consonant phonemes carry more information than do vowel phonemes. *The treth ef thes stetement shed be evedent frem thes bref demenstretien.*

- **Morphemes** are the smallest units that carry meaning in a given language. In English, a few morphemes are also phonemes—the personal pronoun *I* and the article *a,* for instance. But most morphemes combine two or more phonemes. Some, like *bat,* are words. Others—like the prefix *pre-* in *preview* or the suffix *-ed* in *adapted*—are parts of words.

- **Grammar** is the system of rules that enables us to communicate with one another. Grammatical rules guide us in deriving meaning from sounds *(semantics)* and in ordering words into sentences *(syntax).*

Like life constructed from the genetic code's simple alphabet, language is complexity built of simplicity. In English, for example, 40 or so phonemes can be combined to form more than 100,000 morphemes, which alone or in combination produce the 616,500 word forms in the *Oxford English Dictionary.* Using those words, we can then create an infinite number of sentences, most of which (like this one) are original.

"Let me get this straight now. Is what you want to build a jean factory or a gene factory?"

From *The Wall Street Journal*—permission Cartoon Features Syndicate.

RETRIEVE IT

- How many morphemes are in the word *cats?* How many phonemes?

ANSWERS: Two morphemes—*cat* and *s,* and four phonemes—*c, a, t,* and *s*

Language Development

9-8: What are the milestones in language development, and how do we acquire language?

Make a quick guess: How many words did you learn during the years between your first birthday and your high school graduation? Although you use only 150 words for about half of what you say, you probably learned about 60,000 words in your native language during those years (Bloom, 2000; McMurray, 2007). That averages (after age 2) to nearly 3500 words each year, or nearly 10 each day! How you did it—how those 3500 words could so far outnumber the roughly 200 words your schoolteachers consciously taught you each year—is one of the great human wonders.

Could you even state all your language's rules of syntax (the correct way to string words together to form sentences)? Most of us cannot. Yet, before you were able to add 2 + 2, you were creating your own original and grammatically appropriate sentences. As a preschooler, you comprehended and spoke with a facility that puts to shame college students struggling to learn a foreign language.

We humans have an astonishing facility for language. With remarkable efficiency, we sample tens of thousands of words in our memory, effortlessly assemble them with near-perfect syntax, and spew them out, three words a second (Vigliocco & Hartsuiker, 2002). Seldom do we form sentences in our minds before speaking them. Rather we organize them on the fly as we speak. And while doing all this, we also adapt our utterances to our social and cultural context. Given how many ways there are to mess up, it's amazing that we can master this social dance. So when and how does it happen?

Jaimie Duplass/Shutterstock

When Do We Learn Language?

Receptive Language Children's language development moves from simplicity to complexity. Infants start without language (*in fantis* means "not speaking"). Yet by 4 months of age, babies can recognize differences in speech sounds (Stager & Werker, 1997). They can also read lips: They prefer to look at a face that matches a sound, so we know they can recognize that *ah* comes from wide-open lips and *ee* from a mouth with corners pulled back (Kuhl & Meltzoff, 1982). This marks the beginning of the development of babies' *receptive language,* their ability to understand what is said to and about them. At 7 months and beyond, babies grow in their power to do what you and I find difficult when listening to an unfamiliar language: to segment spoken sounds into individual words.

Productive Language Babies' *productive language,* their ability to produce words, matures after their receptive language. Before nurture molds their speech, nature enables a wide range of possible sounds in the **babbling stage,** beginning around 4 months of age. Many of these spontaneously uttered sounds are consonant-vowel pairs formed by simply bunching the tongue in the front of the mouth (*da-da, na-na, ta-ta*) or by opening and closing the lips *(ma-ma),* both of which babies do naturally for feeding (MacNeilage & Davis, 2000). Babbling is not an imitation of adult speech—it includes sounds from various languages, including those not spoken in the household. From this early babbling, a listener could not identify an infant as being, say, French, Korean, or Ethiopian. Deaf infants who observe their deaf parents signing begin to babble more with their hands (Petitto & Marentette, 1991).

By the time infants are about 10 months old, their babbling has changed so that a trained ear can identify the household language (de Boysson-Bardies et al., 1989). Without exposure to other languages, babies lose their ability to hear and produce sounds and tones found outside their native language (Meltzoff et al., 2009; Pallier et al., 2001). Thus, by adulthood, those who speak only English cannot discriminate certain sounds in Japanese speech. Nor can Japanese adults with no training in English hear the difference between the English *r* and *l.* For a Japanese-speaking adult, *la-la-ra-ra* may sound like the same syllable repeated.

Around their first birthday, most enter the **one-word stage.** They have already learned that sounds carry meanings, and if repeatedly trained to associate, say, *fish* with a picture of a fish, 1-year-olds will look at a fish when a researcher says, "Fish, fish! Look at the fish!" (Schafer, 2005). They now begin to use sounds—usually only one barely recognizable syllable, such as *ma* or *da*—to communicate meaning. But family members quickly learn to understand, and gradually the infant's language conforms more to the family's language. Across the world, baby's first words are often nouns that label objects or people (Tardif et al., 2008). At this one-word stage, a single inflected word *("Doggy!")* may equal a sentence. *("Look at the dog out there!")*

At about 18 months, children's word learning explodes from about a word per week to a word per day. By their second birthday, most have entered the **two-word stage** (**TABLE 9.1**). They start uttering two-word sentences in **telegraphic speech.**

"Got idea. Talk better. Combine words. Make sentences."

© 1994 by Sidney Harris.

babbling stage beginning at about 4 months, the stage of speech development in which the infant spontaneously utters various sounds at first unrelated to the household language.

one-word stage the stage in speech development, from about age 1 to 2, during which a child speaks mostly in single words.

two-word stage beginning about age 2, the stage in speech development during which a child speaks mostly in two-word statements.

telegraphic speech early speech stage in which a child speaks like a telegram—"go car"—using mostly nouns and verbs.

Table 9.1
Summary of Language Development

Month (approximate)	Stage
4	Babbles many speech sounds ("Ah-goo").
10	Babbling resembles household language ("Ma-ma").
12	One-word stage ("Kitty!").
24	Two-word, telegraphic speech ("Get ball.").
24+	Language develops rapidly into complete sentences.

Like today's texts or yesterday's telegrams that charged by the word (TERMS ACCEPTED. SEND MONEY), a 2-year-old's speech contains mostly nouns and verbs *("Want juice")*. (Children recognize noun-verb differences—as shown by their responses to a misplaced noun or verb—earlier than they utter sentences with nouns and verbs [Bernal et al., 2010].) Also like telegrams, a 2-year-old's speech follows rules of syntax, arranging words in a sensible order. English-speaking children typically place adjectives before nouns— *white house* rather than *house white*. Spanish reverses this order, as in *casa blanca*.

Moving out of the two-word stage, children quickly begin uttering longer phrases (Fromkin & Rodman, 1983). If they get a late start on learning a particular language, such as after receiving a cochlear implant or being adopted by a family in another country, their language development still proceeds through the same sequence, although usually at a faster pace (Ertmer et al., 2007; Snedeker et al., 2007). By early elementary school, children understand complex sentences and begin to enjoy the humor conveyed by double meanings: "You never starve in the desert because of all the sand-which-is there."

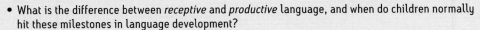

RETRIEVE IT

- What is the difference between *receptive* and *productive* language, and when do children normally hit these milestones in language development?

ANSWER: Infants normally start developing *receptive language* skills (ability to understand what is said to and about them) around 4 months of age. Then, starting with babbling at 4 months and beyond, infants normally start building *productive language* skills (ability to produce sounds and eventually words).

Explaining Language Development

The world's 7000 or so languages are structurally very diverse (Evans & Levinson, 2009). Behaviorist B. F. Skinner (1957) believed we can explain this diversity with familiar learning principles, such as *association* (of the sights of things with the sounds of words); *imitation* (of the words and syntax modeled by others); and *reinforcement* (with smiles and hugs when the child says something right). Linguist Noam Chomsky has argued that all languages nonetheless share some basic elements, which he calls *universal grammar*. All human languages, for example, have nouns, verbs, and adjectives as grammatical building blocks. Moreover, said Chomsky, we humans are born with a built-in predisposition to learn grammar rules, which helps explain why preschoolers pick up language so readily and use grammar so well. It happens so naturally—as naturally as birds learn to fly—that training hardly helps.

We are not, however, born with a built-in *specific* language. Europeans and Native Australia–New Zealand populations, though geographically separated for 50,000 years, can readily learn each others' languages (Chater et al., 2009). And whatever language we experience as children, whether spoken or signed, we all readily learn its specific grammar and vocabulary (Bavelier et al., 2003). But no matter what language we learn, we start speaking it mostly in nouns *(kitty, da-da)* rather than in verbs and adjectives (Bornstein et al., 2004). Biology and experience work together.

Critical Periods Childhood seems to represent a *critical* (or "sensitive") *period* for mastering certain aspects of language before the language-learning window closes (Hernandez & Li, 2007). People who learn a second language as adults usually speak it with the accent of their native language, and they also have difficulty mastering the new grammar. In one experiment, Korean and Chinese immigrants considered 276 English sentences *("Yesterday the hunter shoots a deer")* and decided whether they were grammatically correct or incorrect (Johnson & Newport, 1991). All had been in the United States for approximately 10 years: Some had arrived in early childhood, others as adults. As **FIGURE 9.8** on the next page reveals, those who learned their second language early learned it best. The older one is when moving to a new country, the harder it will be to learn its language and to absorb its culture (Cheung et al., 2011; Hakuta et al., 2003).

Creating a language Brought together as if on a desert island (actually a school), Nicaragua's young deaf children over time drew upon sign gestures from home to create their own Nicaraguan Sign Language, complete with words and intricate grammar. Our biological predisposition for language does not create language in a vacuum. But activated by a social context, nature and nurture work creatively together (Osborne, 1999; Sandler et al., 2005; Senghas & Coppola, 2001).

Susan Meiselas/Magnum Photos

"Childhood is the time for language, no doubt about it. Young children, the younger the better, are good at it; it is child's play. It is a onetime gift to the species."

Lewis Thomas, The Fragile Species, *1992*

FIGURE 9.8

Our ability to learn a new language diminishes with age Ten years after coming to the United States, Asian immigrants took an English grammar test. Although there is no sharply defined critical period for second language learning, those who arrived before age 8 understood American English grammar as well as native speakers did. Those who arrived later did not. (From Johnson & Newport, 1991.)

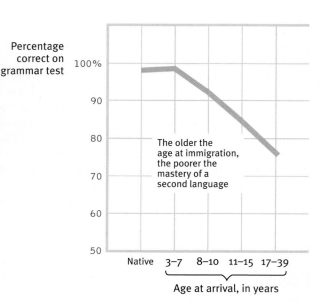

The older the age at immigration, the poorer the mastery of a second language

Percentage correct on grammar test

Age at arrival, in years

George Ancona

"Don't" means *"don't"*—no matter how you say it! Deaf children of deaf-signing parents and hearing children of hearing parents have much in common. They develop language skills at about the same rate, and they are equally effective at opposing parental wishes and demanding their way.

aphasia impairment of language, usually caused by left-hemisphere damage either to Broca's area (impairing speaking) or to Wernicke's area (impairing understanding).

Broca's area controls language expression—an area of the frontal lobe, usually in the left hemisphere, that directs the muscle movements involved in speech.

Wernicke's area controls language reception—a brain area involved in language comprehension and expression; usually in the left temporal lobe.

The window on language learning closes gradually in early childhood. Later-than-usual exposure to language (at age 2 or 3) unleashes the idle language capacity of a child's brain, producing a rush of language. But by about age 7, those who have not been exposed to either a spoken or a signed language gradually lose their ability to master *any* language.

The impact of early experiences is evident in language learning in the 90+ percent of prelingually deaf children born to hearing-nonsigning parents. These children typically do not experience language during their early years. Natively deaf children who learn sign language after age 9 never learn it as well as those who lose their hearing at age 9 after learning a spoken language such as English. They also never learn English as well as other natively deaf children who learned sign in infancy (Mayberry et al., 2002). Those who learn to sign as teens or adults are like immigrants who learn English after childhood: They can master basic words and learn to order them, but they never become as fluent as native signers in producing and comprehending subtle grammatical differences (Newport, 1990). As a flower's growth will be stunted without nourishment, so, too, children will typically become linguistically stunted if isolated from language during the critical period for its acquisition.

RETRIEVE IT

• What was the basic disagreement in B. F. Skinner's and Noam Chomsky's explanations of language development?

ANSWER: Skinner believed humans learn language as we learn other behaviors—through association, imitation, and reinforcement. Chomsky maintained that all languages share a universal grammar, and humans are biologically predisposed to learn the grammar rules of language.

• Why is it so difficult to learn a new language in adulthood?

ANSWER: Our brain's *critical period* for language learning is in childhood, when we can absorb language structure almost effortlessly. As we move past that stage in our brain's development, our ability to learn a new language diminishes dramatically.

The Brain and Language

9-9: What brain areas are involved in language processing and speech?

We think of speaking and reading, or writing and reading, or singing and speaking as merely different examples of the same general ability—language. But consider this curious finding: **Aphasia,** an impairment of language, can result from damage to any of several cortical areas. Even more curious, some people with aphasia can speak fluently but cannot read (despite good vision), while others can comprehend what they read but cannot speak. Still others can write but not read, read but not write, read numbers but not letters, or sing but not speak. These cases suggest that language is complex, and that different brain areas must serve different language functions.

Indeed, in 1865, French physician Paul Broca reported that after damage to an area of the left frontal lobe (later called **Broca's area**) a person would struggle to *speak* words while still being able to sing familiar songs and comprehend speech.

In 1874, German investigator Carl Wernicke discovered that after damage to an area of the left temporal lobe (**Wernicke's area**) people could speak only meaningless words. Asked to describe a picture that showed two boys stealing cookies behind a woman's back, one patient responded: "Mother is away her working her work to get her better, but when she's looking the two boys looking the other part. She's working another time" (Geschwind, 1979). Damage to Wernicke's area also disrupts understanding.

Today's neuroscience has confirmed brain activity in Broca's and Wernicke's areas during language processing (**FIGURE 9.9**). But language functions are distributed across other brain areas as well. Functional MRI scans show that what you experience as a continuous, indivisible stream of experience—language—is actually but the visible tip of a subdivided information-processing iceberg. Different neural networks are activated by nouns and verbs (or objects and actions); by different vowels; and by reading stories of visual versus motor experiences (Shapiro et al., 2006; Speer et al., 2009). If you are bilingual, the neural networks that enable your native language differ from those that enable your second language (Perani & Abutalebi, 2005).

The big point to remember: In processing language, as in other forms of information processing, *the brain operates by dividing its mental functions—speaking, perceiving, thinking, remembering—into subfunctions.* Your conscious experience of reading this page *seems* indivisible, but you are engaging many different neural networks in your brain to compute each word's form, sound, and meaning (Posner & Carr, 1992). We saw this also in Chapter 6, in the discussion of vision, as the brain engaged in specialized visual subtasks (discerning color, depth, movement, and form).

(a)
Hearing words
(auditory cortex and Wernicke's area)

(b)
Speaking words
(Broca's area and the motor cortex)

FIGURE 9.9
Brain activity when hearing and speaking words

"It is the way systems interact and have a dynamic interdependence that is—unless one has lost all sense of wonder—quite awe-inspiring."

Simon Conway Morris,
"The Boyle Lecture," 2005

RETRIEVE IT

• _____ _____ is the part of the brain that, if damaged, might impair your ability to *speak* words. If you damage _____ _____, you might impair your ability to understand language.

ANSWERS: Broca's area; Wernicke's area

Do Other Species Have Language?

9-10: Do other animals share our capacity for language?

Humans have long and proudly proclaimed that language sets us above all other animals. "When we study human language," asserted Chomsky (1972), "we are approaching what some might call the 'human essence,' the qualities of mind that are, so far as we know, unique [to humans]."

If in our use of language we humans are, as the psalmist long ago rhapsodized, "little lower than God," where, then, do other animals fit in the scheme of things? Are they "little lower than humans"?

Animals display impressive comprehension and communication. Vervet monkeys sound different alarm cries for different predators: a barking call for a leopard, a cough for an eagle, and a chuttering for a snake. Hearing the leopard alarm, other vervets climb the nearest tree. Hearing the eagle alarm, they rush into the bushes. Hearing the snake chutter, they stand up and scan the ground (Byrne, 1991). To indicate such things as a type of threat—an eagle, leopard, falling tree, or neighboring group—monkeys will combine 6 different calls into a 25-call sequence (Balter, 2010). But is this language? This question has launched many studies with chimpanzees.

In the late 1960s, psychologists Allen Gardner and Beatrix Gardner (1969) aroused enormous scientific and public interest when they built on chimpanzees' natural tendencies for gestured communication and taught sign language to a chimpanzee named Washoe (c. 1965–2007). After four years, Washoe could use 132 signs; by her life's end, she was using 245 signs (Metzler et al., 2010; Sanz et al., 1998).

During the 1970s, as more and more reports came in, it seemed apes might indeed be "little lower than human" (**FIGURE 9.10**). One *New York Times* reporter, having learned sign language from his deaf parents, visited Washoe and exclaimed, "Suddenly I realized I was conversing with a member of another species in my native tongue." Some chimpanzees strung signs together to form sentences. Washoe, for example, signed "You me go out, please." Some word combinations seemed very creative— saying *water bird* for "swan" or *apple-which-is-orange* for "orange" (Patterson, 1978; Rumbaugh, 1977).

By the late 1970s, some psychologists were growing skeptical. Were the chimps language champs or were the researchers chumps? Consider, said the skeptics:

- Ape vocabularies and sentences are simple, rather like those of a 2-year-old child. And unlike speaking or signing children, who easily soak up dozens of new words a week (and 60,000 by adulthood), apes gain their limited vocabularies only with great difficulty (Wynne, 2004, 2008). Saying that apes can learn language because they can sign words is like saying humans can fly because they can jump.

- Chimpanzees can make signs or push buttons in sequence to get a reward. But pigeons, too, can peck a sequence of keys to get grain (Straub et al., 1979). The apes' signing might be nothing more than aping their trainers' signs and learning that certain arm movements produce rewards (Terrace, 1979).

- Studies of perceptual set (Chapter 6) show that when information is unclear, we tend to see what we want or expect to see. Interpreting chimpanzee signs as language may be little more than the trainers' wishful thinking (Terrace, 1979). When Washoe signed *water bird,* she may have been separately naming *water* and *bird*.

- "Give orange me give eat orange me eat orange . . ." is a far cry from the exquisite syntax of a 3-year-old (Anderson, 2004; Pinker, 1995). To the child, "You tickle" and "Tickle you" communicate different ideas. A chimpanzee, lacking human syntax, might use the same sequence of signs for both phrases.

Controversy can stimulate progress, and in this case, it triggered more evidence of chimpanzees' abilities to think and communicate. One surprising finding was that Washoe trained her adopted son Loulis to use the signs she had learned. After her second infant died, Washoe became withdrawn when told, "Baby dead, baby gone, baby finished." Two weeks later, researcher caretaker Roger Fouts (1992, 1997) signed

FIGURE 9.10

Talking hands Chimpanzees' use of sign language builds upon their natural gestured words (such as a hand extended for "I want some"). Among wild chimpanzees, researchers have identified 66 distinct gestures (Hobaiter & Byrne, 2011). Human language appears to have evolved from such gestured communications (Corballis, 2002, 2003; Pollick & de Waal, 2007). Even today, gestures are naturally associated with spontaneous speech, especially speech that has spatial content. Both gesture and speech communicate, and when they convey the same rather than different information (as they do in baseball's sign language), we humans understand faster and more accurately (Hostetter, 2011; Kelly et al., 2010). Outfielder William Hoy, the first deaf player to join the major leagues (1892), invented hand signals for "Strike!" "Safe!" (shown here) and "Yerr Out!" (Pollard, 1992). Referees in all sports now use invented signs, and fans are fluent in sports sign language.

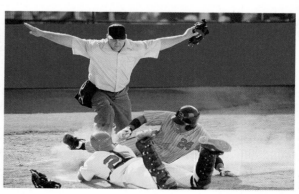

Jim Cummins/Getty Images

better news: "I have baby for you." Washoe reacted with instant excitement. Hair on end, she swaggered and panted while signing over and again, "Baby, my baby." It took several hours for the foster mom and infant to warm to each other, but then Washoe broke the ice by signing, "Come baby" and cuddling Loulis. In the months that followed, Loulis, without human assistance, picked up 68 signs, simply by observing Washoe and three other language-trained chimps signing together.

Even more stunning was a report that Kanzi, a bonobo with a reported 384-word vocabulary, could understand syntax in spoken English (Savage-Rumbaugh et al., 1993, 2009). Kanzi has responded appropriately when asked, "Can you show me the light?" and "Can you bring me the [flash]light?" and "Can you turn the light on?" Given stuffed animals and asked—for the first time—to "make the dog bite the snake," he put the snake to the dog's mouth.

So, how should we interpret these studies? Are humans the only language-using species? If by *language* we mean verbal or signed expression of complex grammar, most psychologists would now agree that humans alone possess language. If we mean, more simply, an ability to communicate through a meaningful sequence of symbols, then apes are indeed capable of language.

Comprehending canine Border collie Rico has a 200 human-word vocabulary. If asked to retrieve a toy with a name he has never heard, Rico will pick out a new toy from a group of familiar items (Kaminski et al., 2004). Hearing that name for the second time four weeks later, Rico more often than not retrieves the same toy. Another border collie, Chaser, has set an animal record by learning 1022 object names (Pilley & Reid, 2011). Like a 3-year-old child, she can also categorize them by function and shape. She can "fetch a ball" or "fetch a doll."

One thing is certain: Studies of animal language and thinking have moved psychologists toward a greater appreciation of other species, not only for the traits we share with them but also for their own remarkable abilities. In the past, many psychologists doubted that other species could plan, form concepts, count, use tools, show compassion, or use language (Thorpe, 1974). Today, thanks to animal researchers, we know better. It's true that humans alone are capable of complex sentences.

But is this language? Chimpanzees' ability to express themselves in American Sign Language (ASL) raises questions about the very nature of language. Here, the trainer is asking, "What is this?" The sign in response is "Baby." Does the response constitute language?

Moreover, 2½-year-old children display some cognitive abilities, such as following an actor's gaze to a target, that are unmatched even by chimpanzees (Herrmann et al., 2010). Nevertheless, other species do exhibit insight, show family loyalty, communicate with one another, care for one another, and transmit cultural patterns across generations. Working out what this means for the moral rights of other animals is an unfinished task.

★ ★ ★

Returning to our debate about how deserving we humans are of our name *Homo sapiens*, let's pause to issue an interim report card. On decision making and risk assessment, our error-prone species might rate a C+. On problem solving, where humans are inventive yet vulnerable to foibles such as fixation, we would probably receive a better mark, perhaps a B. On cognitive efficiency and creativity, our fallible but quick heuristics and divergent thinking earn us an A. And when it comes to learning and using language, the awestruck experts would surely award the human species an A+.

RETRIEVE IT

• If your dog barks at a stranger at the front door, does this qualify as language? What if the dog yips in a telltale way to let you know she needs to go out?

ANSWER: These are definitely communications. But if language consists of words and the grammatical rules we use to combine them to communicate meaning, few scientists would label a dog's barking and yipping as language.

linguistic determinism Whorf's hypothesis that language determines the way we think.

Thinking and Language

> **9-11:** What is the relationship between thinking and language, and what is the value of thinking in images?

Thinking and language intricately intertwine. Asking which comes first is one of psychology's chicken-and-egg questions. Do our ideas come first and we wait for words to name them? Or are our thoughts conceived in words and therefore unthinkable without them?

Language Influences Thinking

Linguist Benjamin Lee Whorf (1956) contended that language *determines* the way we think: "Language itself shapes a [person's] basic ideas." The Hopi, who have no past tense for their verbs, could not readily *think* about the past, said Whorf.

Whorf's **linguistic determinism** hypothesis is too extreme. We all think about things for which we have no words. (Can you think of a shade of blue you cannot name?) And we routinely have *unsymbolized* (wordless, imageless) thoughts, as when someone, while watching two men carry a load of bricks, wondered whether the men would drop them (Heavey & Hurlburt, 2008; Hurlburt & Akhter, 2008).

Nevertheless, to many who speak two dissimilar languages, such as English and Japanese, it seems obvious that a person may think differently in different languages (Brown, 1986). Unlike English, which has a rich vocabulary for self-focused emotions such as anger, Japanese has more words for interpersonal emotions such as sympathy (Markus & Kitayama, 1991). Many bilingual individuals report that they have different senses of self, depending on which language they are using (Matsumoto, 1994). In one series of studies with bilingual Israeli Arabs (who speak both Arabic and Hebrew), participants thought differently about their social world, with differing automatic associations with Arabs and Jews, depending on which language the testing session used (Danziger & Ward, 2010).

Bilingual individuals have even revealed different personality profiles when taking the same test in their two languages, as happened when China-born, bilingual University of Waterloo students were asked to describe themselves in English or Chinese (Dinges & Hull, 1992; Ross et al., 2002). The students' English-language self-descriptions fit typical Canadian profiles: They expressed mostly positive self-statements and moods. Responding in Chinese, the same students gave typically Chinese self-descriptions: They reported more agreement with Chinese values and roughly equal positive and negative self-statements and moods. Similar personality changes have been shown when bicultural, bilingual Americans and Mexicans shifted between the cultural frames associated with English and Spanish (Ramírez-Esparza et al., 2006). "Learn a new language and get a new soul," says a Czech proverb.

Our words may not *determine* what we think, but they do *influence* our thinking (Boroditsky, 2011). We use our language in forming categories. In Brazil, the isolated Piraha people have words for the numbers 1 and 2, but numbers above that are simply "many." Thus, if shown 7 nuts in a row, they find it very difficult to lay out the same number from their own pile (Gordon, 2004).

Words also influence our thinking about colors. Whether we live in New Mexico, New South Wales, or New Guinea, we *see* colors much the same, but we use our native language to *classify* and *remember* colors (Davidoff, 2004; Roberson et al., 2004, 2005). Imagine participating in a study in which you view three colors. Two are what Americans call "yellow" and one is "blue." If you speak the language of Papua New Guinea's Berinmo tribe, who have words for two different shades of yellow, you would more speedily perceive and better recall the variations between the two yellows. But if your language is Russian, which

Culture and color In Papua New Guinea, Berinmo children have words for different shades of "yellow," which might enable them to spot and recall yellow variations more quickly. Here and everywhere, "the languages we speak profoundly shape the way we think, the way we see the world, the way we live our lives," notes psychologist Lera Boroditsky (2009).

Prisma Bildagentur AG/Alamy

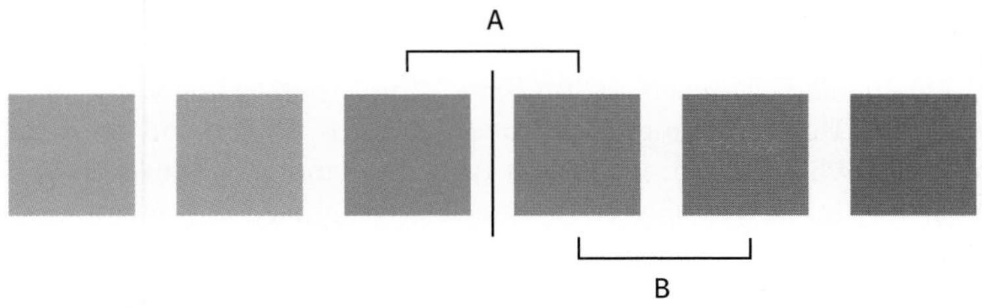

FIGURE 9.11

Language and perception When people view blocks of equally different colors, they perceive those with different names as more different. Thus the "green" and "blue" in contrast A may appear to differ more than the two similarly different "blues" in contrast B (Özgen, 2004).

has distinct names for various shades of blue, such as *goluboy* and *sinly,* you might later recall the yellows as more similar and remember the blue better. Words matter.

Perceived differences grow when we assign different names to colors. On the color spectrum, blue blends into green—until we draw a dividing line between the portions we call "blue" and "green." Although equally different on the color spectrum, two different items that share the same color name (as the two "blues" do in **FIGURE 9.11**, contrast B) are harder to distinguish than two items with different names ("blue" and "green," as in Figure 9.11, contrast A) (Özgen, 2004).

Given words' subtle influence on thinking, we do well to choose our words carefully. Does it make any difference whether I write, "A child learns language as *he* interacts with *his* caregivers" or "Children learn language as *they* interact with *their* caregivers"? Many studies have found that it does. When hearing the generic *he* (as in "the artist and his work") people are more likely to picture a male (Henley, 1989; Ng, 1990). If *he* and *his* were truly gender free, we shouldn't skip a beat when hearing that "man, like other mammals, nurses his young."

To expand language is to expand the ability to think. Young children's thinking develops hand in hand with their language (Gopnik & Meltzoff, 1986). Indeed, it is very difficult to think about or conceptualize certain abstract ideas (*commitment, freedom,* or *rhyming*) without language! And what is true for preschoolers is true for everyone: *It pays to increase your word power.* That's why most textbooks, including this one, introduce new words—to teach new ideas and new ways of thinking.

Increased word power helps explain what McGill University researcher Wallace Lambert (1992; Lambert et al., 1993) calls the *bilingual advantage.* Although their vocabulary in each language is somewhat smaller than that of people speaking a single language, bilingual people are skilled at inhibiting one language while using the other. And thanks to their well-practiced "executive control" over language, they also are better at inhibiting their attention to irrelevant information (Bialystock & Craik, 2010).

Lambert helped devise a Canadian program that immerses English-speaking children in French. (The number of enrolled non-Quebec children rose from 65,000 in 1981 to 300,000 in 2007 [Statistics Canada, 2010].) For most of their first three years in school, the English-speaking children are taught entirely in French, and thereafter they gradually shift to classes mostly in English. Not surprisingly, the children attain a natural French fluency unrivaled by other methods of language teaching. Moreover, compared with similarly capable children in control groups, they do so without detriment to their English fluency, and with increased aptitude scores, creativity, and appreciation for French-Canadian culture (Genesee & Gándara, 1999; Lazaruk, 2007).

Whether we are in the linguistic minority or majority, language links us to one another. Language also connects us to the past and the future. "To destroy a people, destroy their language," observed poet Joy Harjo.

Perceived distances between cities also grow when two cities are in different rather than in the same countries or states (Burris & Branscombe, 2005; Mishra & Mishra, 2010).

"All words are pegs to hang ideas on."

Henry Ward Beecher, Proverbs from Plymouth Pulpit, *1887*

RETRIEVE IT

• Benjamin Lee Whorf's controversial hypothesis, called _____ _____, suggested that we cannot think about things unless we have words for those concepts or ideas.

ANSWER: linguistic determinism

"When we see a person walking down the street talking to himself, we generally assume that he is mentally ill. But we all talk to ourselves continuously—we just have the good sense of keeping our mouths shut. . . . It's as though we are having a conversation with an imaginary friend possessed of infinite patience. Who are we talking to?"

Sam Harris, "We Are Lost in Thought," 2011

Thinking in Images

When you are alone, do you talk to yourself? Is "thinking" simply conversing with yourself? Words do convey ideas. But sometimes ideas precede words. To turn on the cold water in your bathroom, in which direction do you turn the handle? To answer, you probably thought not in words but with *implicit* (nondeclarative, procedural) memory— a mental picture of how you do it (see Chapter 8).

Indeed, we often think in images. Artists think in images. So do composers, poets, mathematicians, athletes, and scientists. Albert Einstein reported that he achieved some of his greatest insights through visual images and later put them into words. Pianist Liu Chi Kung showed the value of thinking in images. One year after placing second in the 1958 Tchaikovsky piano competition, Liu was imprisoned during China's cultural revolution. Soon after his release, after seven years without touching a piano, he was back on tour, the critics judging his musicianship better than ever. How did he continue to develop without practice? "I did practice," said Liu, "every day. I rehearsed every piece I had ever played, note by note, in my mind" (Garfield, 1986).

For someone who has learned a skill, such as ballet dancing, even *watching* the activity will activate the brain's internal simulation of it, reported one British research team after taking fMRIs as people watched videos (Calvo-Merino et al., 2004). So, too, will *imagining* a physical experience, which activates some of the same neural networks that are active during the actual experience (Grèzes & Decety, 2001). Small wonder, then, that mental practice has become a standard part of training for Olympic athletes (Suinn, 1997).

One experiment on mental practice and basketball foul shooting tracked the University of Tennessee women's team over 35 games (Savoy & Beitel, 1996). During that time, the team's free-throw shooting increased from approximately 52 percent in games following standard physical practice to some 65 percent after mental practice. Players had repeatedly imagined making foul shots under various conditions, including being "trash-talked" by their opposition. In a dramatic conclusion, Tennessee won the national championship game in overtime, thanks in part to their foul shooting.

Mental rehearsal can also help you achieve an academic goal, as researchers demonstrated with two groups of introductory psychology students facing a midterm exam one week later (Taylor et al., 1998). (Scores of other students, not engaging in any mental simulation, formed a control group.) The first group spent five minutes each day visualizing themselves scanning the posted grade list, seeing their A, beaming with joy, and feeling proud. This *outcome simulation* had little effect, adding only 2 points to their exam-score average. Another group spent five minutes each day visualizing themselves effectively studying—reading the chapters, going over notes, eliminating distractions, declining an offer to go out. This *process simulation* paid off: This second group began studying sooner, spent more time at it, and beat the others' average by 8 points.

The point to remember: It's better to spend your fantasy time planning *how* to get somewhere than to dwell on the imagined destination.

★ ★ ★

What, then, should we say about the relationship between thinking and language? As we have seen, language influences our thinking. But if thinking did not also affect language, there would never be any new words. And new words and new combinations of old words express new ideas. The basketball term *slam dunk* was coined after the act itself had become fairly common. So, let us say that *thinking affects our language, which then affects our thought* (**FIGURE 9.12**).

Psychological research on thinking and language suggests that the human mind is simultaneously capable of striking intellectual failures and of striking intellectual power. Misjudgments are common and can have disastrous consequences. So we do well to appreciate our capacity for error. Yet our efficient heuristics often serve us well. Moreover, our ingenuity at problem solving and our extraordinary power of language mark humankind as almost "infinite in faculties."

Blend Images/Jupiterimages

Thinking

EPA/XU JIAN/Newscom

Language

FIGURE 9.12
The interplay of thought and language The traffic runs both ways between thinking and language. Thinking affects our language, which affects our thought.

intelligence mental quality consisting of the ability to learn from experience, solve problems, and use knowledge to adapt to new situations.

RETRIEVE IT

• What is "mental practice," and how can it help you to prepare for an upcoming event?

ANSWER: Mental practice uses visual imagery to mentally rehearse future behaviors, activating some of the same brain areas used during the actual behaviors. Visualizing the details of the process is more effective than visualizing only your end goal.

Intelligence

So far, we have considered how humans as a species think and communicate. But we humans also differ from one another in these abilities. School boards, courts, and scientists debate the use and fairness of tests that assess people's mental abilities and assign them a score. In psychology, no controversy has been more heated than the question of whether there exists in each person a general intellectual capacity that can be measured and quantified as a number.

In this section, we consider some findings from a century of research, as psychologists have searched for answers to these questions and more:

• What is intelligence? Is it one general ability or many different abilities?

• How can we best assess intelligence?

• How do heredity and experience together weave the fabric of intelligence?

What Is Intelligence?

9-12: How do psychologists define *intelligence,* and what are the arguments for *g?*

In many research studies, *intelligence* has been defined as whatever intelligence tests measure, which has tended to be school smarts. Intelligence is not a quality like height or weight, which has the same meaning in all generations, all around the globe. *Intelligence* is a concept, a term people apply to the qualities that enable success in their own time and in their own culture (Sternberg & Kaufman, 1998). In the Amazon rain forest, intelligence may be understanding the medicinal qualities of local plants. In a North American high school, it may be mastering difficult concepts in tough courses. In both locations, **intelligence** is the ability to learn from experience, solve problems, and use knowledge to adapt to new situations.

You probably know some people with talents in science, others who excel at the humanities, and still others gifted in athletics, art, music, or dance. You may also know a

Hands-on healing The socially constructed concept of intelligence varies from culture to culture. This folk healer in Peru displays his intelligence in his knowledge about his medicinal plants and understanding of the needs of the people he is helping.

© Maya Goded/Magnum Photos

"g is one of the most reliable and valid measures in the behavioral domain . . . and it predicts important social outcomes such as educational and occupational levels far better than any other trait."

Behavior geneticist Robert Plomin (1999)

© Ocean/Corbis

talented artist who is stumped by the simplest math problem, or a brilliant math student with little aptitude for literary discussion. Are all these people intelligent? Could you rate their intelligence on a single scale? Or would you need several different scales? Simply put, is intelligence a single overall ability or several specific abilities?

Spearman's General Intelligence Factor

Charles Spearman (1863–1945) believed we have one **general intelligence** (often shortened to *g*) that is at the heart of all of our intelligent behavior, from navigating the sea to excelling in school. He granted that people often have special, outstanding abilities. But he noted that those who score high in one area, such as verbal intelligence, typically score higher than average in other areas, such as spatial or reasoning ability. Spearman's belief stemmed in part from his work with *factor analysis,* a statistical procedure that identifies clusters of related items.

In this view, mental abilities are much like physical abilities: The ability to run fast is distinct from the eye-hand coordination required to throw a ball on target. Yet there remains some tendency for good things to come packaged together—for running speed and throwing accuracy to correlate. In both athleticism and intelligence, several distinct abilities tend to cluster together and to correlate enough to define a general underlying factor.

Theories of Multiple Intelligences

9-13: How do Gardner's and Sternberg's theories of multiple intelligences differ?

Other psychologists, particularly since the mid-1980s, have sought to extend the definition of *intelligence* beyond the idea of academic smarts.

Gardner's Eight Intelligences Howard Gardner (1983, 2006) views intelligence as multiple abilities that come in different packages. He asks us to consider studies of people with brain damage, who may lose one ability while others remain intact. Or consider people with **savant syndrome.** Despite their island of brilliance, these people often score low on intelligence tests and may have limited or no language ability (Treffert & Wallace, 2002). Some can render incredible works of art or musical performance. Others can compute numbers as quickly and accurately as an electronic calculator, or identify almost instantly the day of the week that matches any given date in history (Miller, 1999).

Islands of genius: Savant syndrome
Matt Savage, a 19-year-old, award-winning jazz musician, has released nine albums and is studying at Berklee College of Music. His success has been hard-won given his early childhood diagnosis of autism, which came with struggles to communicate and an initial inability to tolerate sounds of any kind.

Joanne Rathe/The Boston Globe via Getty Images

Four in five people with savant syndrome are males. Many also have *autism,* a developmental disorder (see Chapter 4). The late memory whiz Kim Peek (who did not have autism) was the inspiration for the movie *Rain Man.* In 8 to 10 seconds, he could read and remember a page. During his lifetime, he memorized 9000 books, including Shakespeare's plays and the Bible, by heart. He learned maps from the front of phone books and could provide MapQuest-like travel directions within any major U.S. city. Yet he could not button his clothes, and he had little capacity for abstract concepts. Asked by his father at a restaurant to "lower your voice," he slid lower in his chair to lower his voice box. Asked for Lincoln's Gettysburg Address, he responded, "227 North West Front Street. But he only stayed there one night—he gave the speech the next day" (Treffert & Christensen, 2005).

Gardner has identified a total of eight *relatively independent intelligences,* including the verbal and mathematical aptitudes assessed by standard tests (**FIGURE 9.13**). Thus, the computer programmer, the poet, the street-smart adolescent who becomes a crafty executive, and the basketball team's play-making point guard exhibit different kinds of intelligence (Gardner, 1998). To Gardner, a numerical score representing general intelligence is like the overall rating of a city—which tells you something but doesn't give much specific information about its schools, streets, or nightlife.

Sternberg's Three Intelligences Robert Sternberg (1985, 1999, 2003) agrees with Gardner that there is more to success than traditional intelligence and that we have multiple intelligences. But his *triarchic theory* proposes three, not eight, intelligences:

- *Analytical intelligence* (school smarts; traditional academic problem solving)
- *Creative intelligence* (the ability to react adaptively to new situations and generate novel ideas)

general intelligence (*g*) a general intelligence factor that, according to Spearman and others, underlies specific mental abilities and is therefore measured by every task on an intelligence test.

savant syndrome a condition in which a person otherwise limited in mental ability has an exceptional specific skill, such as in computation or drawing.

"You have to be careful, if you're good at something, to make sure you don't think you're good at other things that you aren't necessarily so good at. . . . Because I've been very successful at [software development] people come in and expect that I have wisdom about topics that I don't."

Bill Gates (1998)

FIGURE 9.13
Gardner's eight intelligences

- *Practical intelligence* (street smarts; skill at handling everyday tasks, which may be ill defined, with multiple solutions)

Street smarts This child selling candy on the streets of Manaus, Brazil, is developing practical intelligence at a very young age.

David R. Frazier Photolibrary, Inc./Alamy

Sternberg (2006, 2007, 2010) and a team of collaborators have developed new measures of creativity (such as thinking up a caption for an untitled cartoon) and practical thinking (such as figuring out how to move a large bed up a winding staircase). Initial results indicate that these more comprehensive assessments improve prediction of American students' first-year college grades, and they do so with reduced ethnic-group differences.

Gardner and Sternberg differ in some areas, but they agree on two important points: Multiple abilities can contribute to life success, and differing varieties of giftedness add spice to life and challenges for education. Under their influence, many teachers have been trained to appreciate such variety and to apply multiple intelligence theories in their classrooms.

Criticisms of Multiple Intelligence Theories Wouldn't it be wonderful if the world were so just that a weakness in one area would be compensated by genius in some other area? Alas, say critics, the world is not just (Ferguson, 2009; Scarr, 1989). Recent research, using factor analysis, has confirmed that there *is* a general intelligence factor (Johnson et al., 2008): *g* matters. It predicts performance on various complex tasks and in various jobs (Gottfredson, 2002a,b, 2003a,b). In one study, youths' intelligence test scores correlated with their later income (**FIGURE 9.14**). Much as jumping ability is not a predictor of jumping performance when the bar is set a foot off the ground—but becomes a predictor when the bar is set higher—so extremely high cognitive ability scores predict exceptional attainments, such as doctoral degrees and publications (Kuncel & Hezlett, 2010).

Bees, birds, chimpanzees, and other species also require time and experience to acquire peak expertise in skills such as foraging (Helton, 2008). As with humans, performance tends to peak near midlife.

Even so, "success" is not a one-ingredient recipe. High intelligence may help you get into a profession (via the schools and training programs that take you there), but it won't make you successful once there. The recipe for success combines talent with *grit:* Those who become highly successful tend also to be conscientious, well connected, and doggedly energetic. Researchers report a *10-year rule:* A common ingredient of expert performance in chess, dancing, sports, computer programming, music, and medicine is "about 10 years of intense, daily practice" (Ericsson, 2002, 2007; Simon & Chase, 1973). (For more on how self-disciplined grit feeds achievement, see Appendix B.)

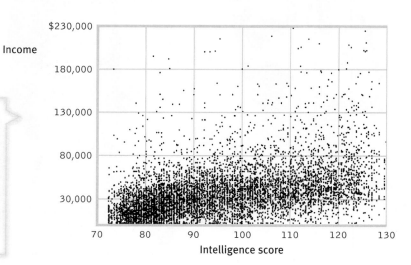

FIGURE 9.14

Smart and rich? Jay Zagorsky (2007) tracked 7403 participants in the U.S. National Longitudinal Survey of Youth across 25 years. As shown in this graph, their intelligence scores showed a small but significant correlation (.30) with their later income. Each dot indicates a given youth's intelligence score and later adult income.

"You're wise, but you lack tree smarts."

RETRIEVE IT

• How does the existence of savant syndrome support Gardner's theory of multiple intelligences?

ANSWER: People with savant syndrome have limited mental ability overall but possess one or more exceptional skills. According to Howard Gardner, this suggests that our abilities come in separate packages rather than being fully expressed by one general intelligence that encompasses all our talents.

Emotional Intelligence

9-14: What are the four components of emotional intelligence?

Is being in tune with yourself and others also a sign of intelligence, distinct from academic intelligence? Some researchers say *Yes*. They define *social intelligence* as the know-how involved in social situations and managing yourself successfully (Cantor & Kihlstrom, 1987). People with high social intelligence can read social situations the way a skilled football player reads the defense or a seafarer reads the weather. The concept was first proposed in 1920 by psychologist Edward Thorndike, who noted, "The best mechanic in a factory may fail as a foreman for lack of social intelligence" (Goleman, 2006, p. 83).

One line of research has explored a specific aspect of social intelligence called **emotional intelligence,** consisting of four abilities (Mayer et al., 2002, 2008):

• *Perceiving* emotions (recognizing them in faces, music, and stories)

• *Understanding* emotions (predicting them and how they may change and blend)

• *Managing* emotions (knowing how to express them in varied situations)

• *Using* emotions to enable adaptive or creative thinking

Emotionally intelligent people are both socially aware and self-aware. Those who score high on managing emotions enjoy higher-quality interactions with friends (Lopes et al., 2004). They avoid being hijacked by overwhelming depression, anxiety, or anger. They can read others' emotional cues and know what to say to soothe a grieving friend, encourage a workmate, and manage a conflict.

These emotional intelligence high scorers also perform modestly better on the job (Joseph & Newman, 2010; Van Rooy & Viswesvaran, 2004; Zeidner et al., 2008). On and off the job, they can delay gratification in pursuit of long-range rewards, rather than being overtaken by immediate impulses. Simply said, they are emotionally smart. Thus, they often succeed in career, marriage, and parenting situations where academically smarter (but emotionally less intelligent) people fail (Cherniss, 2001a,b; Ciarrochi et al., 2006).

Some scholars, however, are concerned that emotional intelligence stretches the concept of intelligence too far (Visser et al., 2006). Howard Gardner (1999) includes interpersonal and intrapersonal intelligences as two of his eight forms of multiple intelligences. But let us also, he acknowledges, respect emotional sensitivity, creativity, and motivation as important but different. Stretch *intelligence* to include everything we prize and the word will lose its meaning.

★ ★ ★

For a summary of Spearman's, Gardner's, and Sternberg's theories, see **TABLE 9.2** on the next page.

Assessing Intelligence

An **intelligence test** assesses people's mental abilities and compares them with others, using numerical scores. How do we design such tests, and what makes them credible? Consider why psychologists created tests of mental abilities and how they have used them.

"I worry about [intelligence] definitions that collapse assessments of our cognitive powers with statements about the kind of human beings we favor."

Howard Gardner, "Rethinking the Concept of Intelligence," 2000

emotional intelligence the ability to perceive, understand, manage, and use emotions.

intelligence test a method for assessing an individual's mental aptitudes and comparing them with those of others, using numerical scores.

Table 9.2
Comparing Theories of Intelligence

Theory	Summary	Strengths	Other Considerations
Spearman's general intelligence (g)	A basic intelligence predicts our abilities in varied academic areas.	Different abilities, such as verbal and spatial, do have some tendency to correlate.	Human abilities are too diverse to be encapsulated by a single general intelligence factor.
Gardner's multiple intelligences	Our abilities are best classified into eight independent intelligences, which include a broad range of skills beyond traditional school smarts.	Intelligence is more than just verbal and mathematical skills. Other abilities are equally important to our human adaptability.	Should all of our abilities be considered *intelligences*? Shouldn't some be called less vital *talents*?
Sternberg's triarchic theory	Our intelligence is best classified into three areas that predict real-world success: analytical, creative, and practical.	These three domains can be reliably measured.	1. These three domains may be less independent than Sternberg thought and may actually share an underlying *g* factor. 2. Additional testing is needed to determine whether these domains can reliably predict success.

What Do Intelligence Tests Test?

9-15: When and why were intelligence tests created, and how do today's tests differ from early intelligence tests?

Barely a century ago, psychologists began designing tests to assess people's abilities. Some measured **aptitude** (ability to learn). Others assessed **achievement** (what people have already learned).

Alfred Binet: Predicting School Achievement Modern intelligence testing traces its birth to early twentieth-century France, where a new law required all children to attend school. French officials knew that some children, including many newcomers to Paris, would need special classes. But how could the schools make fair judgments about children's learning potential? Teachers might assess children who had little prior education as slow learners. Or they might sort children into classes on the basis of their social backgrounds. To minimize such bias, France's minister of public education in 1904 gave Alfred Binet (1857–1911) and others, including Théodore Simon, the task of studying this problem.

Binet and Simon began by assuming that all children follow the same course of intellectual development but that some develop more rapidly. A "dull" child should therefore score much like a typical younger child, and a "bright" child like a typical older child. Binet and Simon now had a clear goal: They would measure each child's **mental age,** the level of performance typically associated with a certain chronological age. The average 8-year-old, for example, has a mental age of 8. An 8-year-old with a below-average mental age (perhaps performing at the level of a typical 6-year-old) would struggle with schoolwork considered normal for 8-year-olds.

Binet and Simon tested a variety of reasoning and problem-solving questions on Binet's two daughters, and then on "bright" and "backward" Parisian schoolchildren. The items they developed eventually predicted how well French children would handle their schoolwork. Binet hoped his test would be used to improve children's education, but he also feared it would be used to label children and limit their opportunities (Gould, 1981) .

Alfred Binet "Some recent philosophers have given their moral approval to the deplorable verdict that an individual's intelligence is a fixed quantity, one which cannot be augmented. We must protest and act against this brutal pessimism" (Binet, 1909, p. 141).
National Library of Medicine

"The IQ test was invented to predict academic performance, nothing else. If we wanted something that would predict life success, we'd have to invent another test completely."

Social psychologist Robert Zajonc (1984b)

RETRIEVE IT

• What did Binet hope to achieve by establishing a child's *mental age?*

ANSWER: Binet hoped that the child's *mental age* (the age that typically corresponds to the child's level of performance) would help identify appropriate school placements with children of similar abilities.

Lewis Terman: The Innate IQ Soon after Binet's death in 1911, others adapted his tests for wider use. One of them was a Stanford University professor, Lewis Terman (1877–1956). Terman found that the Paris-developed questions and age norms worked poorly with California schoolchildren. He adapted some items, added others, and established new standards for various ages. He also extended the upper end of the test's range from teenagers to "superior adults" and gave his revision the name it retains today—the **Stanford-Binet.**

German psychologist William Stern's contribution to intelligence testing was the famous **intelligence quotient,** or **IQ.** The IQ was simply a person's mental age divided by *chronological age* (age in years) and multiplied by 100 to get rid of the decimal point.

Thus, an average child, whose mental age (8) and chronological age (8) are the same has an IQ of 100. But an 8-year-old who answers questions at the level of a typical 10-year-old has an IQ of 125:

$$IQ = \frac{\text{mental age of 10}}{\text{chronological age of 8}} \times 100 = 125$$

The original IQ formula worked fairly well for children but not for adults. (Should a 40-year-old who does as well on the test as an average 20-year-old be assigned an IQ of only 50?) Most current intelligence tests, including the Stanford-Binet, no longer compute an IQ (though the term *IQ* still lingers in everyday vocabulary as shorthand for "intelligence test score"). Instead, they represent the test-taker's performance *relative to the average performance of others the same age.* This average performance is arbitrarily assigned a score of 100, and about two-thirds of all test-takers fall between 85 and 115.

aptitude test a test designed to predict a person's future performance; *aptitude* is the capacity to learn.

achievement test a test designed to assess what a person has learned.

mental age a measure of intelligence test performance devised by Binet; the chronological age that most typically corresponds to a given level of performance. Thus, a child who does as well as an average 8-year-old is said to have a mental age of 8.

Stanford-Binet the widely used American revision (by Terman at Stanford University) of Binet's original intelligence test.

intelligence quotient (IQ) defined originally as the ratio of mental age *(ma)* to chronological age *(ca)* multiplied by 100 (thus, IQ = *ma/ca* × 100). On contemporary intelligence tests, the average performance for a given age is assigned a score of 100.

Wechsler Adult Intelligence Scale (WAIS) the WAIS is the most widely used intelligence test; contains verbal and performance (nonverbal) subtests.

RETRIEVE IT

- An employer with a pool of applicants for a single available position is interested in testing each applicant's potential as a part of her selection process. She should use an _____ (achievement/aptitude) test. That same employer wishing to test the effectiveness of a new, on-the-job training program would be wise to use an _____ (achievement/aptitude) test.

  ANSWERS: aptitude; achievement

- What is the IQ of a 4-year-old with a mental age of 5?

  ANSWER: 125 (5 ÷ 4 × 100 = 125)

David Wechsler: Separate Scores for Separate Skills Psychologist David Wechsler created what is now the most widely used intelligence test, the **Wechsler Adult Intelligence Scale (WAIS).** There is a version for school-age children (the *Wechsler Intelligence Scale for Children [WISC]*), and another for preschool children. The WAIS (2008) edition consists of 15 subtests, broken into verbal and performance areas, including these:

- *Similarities*—Considering the commonality of two objects or concepts, such as "In what way are wool and cotton alike?"

- *Vocabulary*—Naming pictured objects, or defining words ("What is a guitar?")

- *Block design*—Visual abstract processing, such as "Using the four blocks, make one just like this."

- *Letter-number sequencing*—On hearing a series of numbers and letters, repeat the numbers in ascending order, and then the letters in alphabetical order: *"R-2-C-1-M-3."*

The WAIS yields both an overall intelligence score and separate scores for verbal comprehension, perceptual organization, working memory, and processing speed. Striking differences among these scores can provide clues to cognitive strengths or weaknesses.

Matching patterns Block design puzzles test visual abstract processing ability. Wechsler's individually administered intelligence test comes in forms suited for adults and children.

Lew Merrim/Photo Researchers, Inc.

standardization defining uniform testing procedures and meaningful scores by comparison with the performance of a pretested group.

normal curve the bell-shaped curve that describes the distribution of many physical and psychological attributes. Most scores fall near the average, and fewer and fewer scores lie near the extremes.

reliability the extent to which a test yields consistent results, as assessed by the consistency of scores on two halves of the test, or on retesting.

For example, a low verbal comprehension score combined with high scores on other subtests could indicate a reading or language disability. Other comparisons can help a therapist establish a rehabilitation plan for a stroke patient. In such ways, tests help realize Binet's aim: to identify opportunities for improvement and strengths that teachers and others can build upon.

Three Tests of a "Good" Test

 9-16: What is a normal curve, and what does it mean to say that a test has been standardized and is reliable and valid?

To be widely accepted, a psychological test must be *standardized, reliable,* and *valid.* The Stanford-Binet and Wechsler tests meet these requirements.

Was the Test Standardized? The number of questions you answer correctly on an intelligence test would tell you almost nothing. To know how well you performed, you would need some basis for comparison. That's why test-makers give new tests to a representative sample of people. The scores from this pretested group become the basis for future comparisons. If you later take the test following the same procedures, your score will be meaningful when compared with others. This process is called **standardization.**

If we construct a graph of test-takers' scores, they typically form a bell-shaped pattern called the **normal curve.** No matter what attributes we measure—height, weight, or mental aptitude—people's scores tend to form a "bell curve." The highest point is the midpoint, or the average score. On an intelligence test, we give this average score a value of 100 (**FIGURE 9.15**). Moving out from the average, toward either extreme, we find fewer and fewer people. For the Stanford-Binet and Wechsler tests, a person's score indicates whether that person's performance fell above or below the average. A performance higher than all but 2 percent of all scores earns an intelligence score of 130. A performance lower than 98 percent of all scores earns an intelligence score of 70.

Recall from Chapter 1 that the lowest correlation, –1.0, represents perfect disagreement between two sets of scores—as one score goes up, the other score goes down. A correlation of 0.0 represents no association. The highest correlation, +1.0, represents perfect agreement—as the first score goes up, the other score goes up.

Is the Test Reliable? Knowing your score in comparison to the standardization group scores still won't tell you much unless the test has **reliability.** A reliable test gives consistent scores, no matter who takes the test or when they take it. To check a test's reliability, researchers test people many times. They may retest people using the same test, or they may split the test in half and see whether odd-question scores and even-question scores agree. If the two sets of scores generally agree, or *correlate,* the test is reliable. The higher the correlation, the higher the test's reliability. The tests we have considered so far—the Stanford-Binet, the WAIS, and the WISC—are very reliable: about +.9. When retested, people's scores generally match their first score closely.

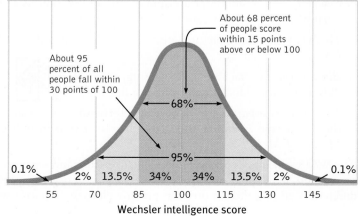

FIGURE 9.15

The normal curve Scores on aptitude tests tend to form a normal, or bell-shaped, curve around an average score. For the Wechsler scale, for example, the average score is 100.

Is The Test Valid? High reliability does not ensure a test's **validity**—the extent to which the test actually measures or predicts what it promises. Imagine using a miscalibrated tape measure to measure people's heights. Your results would be very reliable. No matter how many times you measured, people's heights would be the same. But your results would not be valid—you would not be giving the information you promised—real height.

Tests that tap the pertinent behavior, or *criterion,* have **content validity.** The road test for a driver's license has content validity because it samples the tasks a driver routinely faces. Course exams have content validity if they assess your mastery of relevant course material. But we expect intelligence tests to have **predictive validity:** They should predict future performance, and to some extent they do. (See Close-Up: Extremes of Intelligence on the next page.)

The predictive power of aptitude tests is fairly strong in the early school years, but later it weakens. Past grades, which reflect both aptitude and motivation, are better predictors of future achievements.

validity the extent to which a test measures or predicts what it is supposed to. (See also *content validity* and *predictive validity.*)

content validity the extent to which a test samples the behavior that is of interest.

predictive validity the success with which a test predicts the behavior it is designed to predict; it is assessed by computing the correlation between test scores and the criterion behavior. (Also called *criterion-related validity.*)

crystallized intelligence our accumulated knowledge and verbal skills; tends to increase with age.

fluid intelligence our ability to reason speedily and abstractly; tends to decrease during late adulthood.

RETRIEVE IT

- What three criteria must a psychological test meet in order to be widely accepted? Explain.

ANSWER: A psychological test must be *standardized* (pretested on a similar group of people), *reliable* (yielding consistent results), and *valid* (measuring what it is supposed to measure).

Aging and Intelligence

9-18: How does aging affect crystallized and fluid intelligence?

Does intelligence increase, decrease, or remain constant as we age? The answer depends on the type of intellectual performance we measure:

- **Crystallized intelligence**—our accumulated knowledge as reflected in vocabulary and analogies tests—*increases* up to old age.

- **Fluid intelligence**—our ability to reason speedily and abstractly, as when solving novel logic problems—*decreases* beginning in the twenties and thirties, slowly up to age 75 or so, then more rapidly, especially after age 85 (Cattell, 1963; Horn, 1982; Salthouse, 2009).

How do we know? Developmental psychologists use longitudinal studies (restudying the same group at different times across their life span) and cross-sectional studies (comparing members of different age groups at the same time) to study the way intelligence and other traits change with age. (See Appendix A for more information.) With age we lose and we win. We lose recall memory and processing speed, but we gain vocabulary and knowledge (**FIGURE 9.16**). Fluid intelligence may decline, but

Ann Baldwin/Shutterstock

"Knowledge is knowing a tomato is a fruit; wisdom is not putting it in a fruit salad."

Anonymous

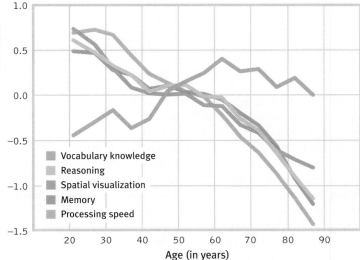

FIGURE 9.16
With age, we lose and we win. Data from studies by Timothy Salthouse (2010b) reveal that word power grows with age, while fluid intelligence dimensions decline.

CLOSE UP:

Extremes of Intelligence

9-17: What are the traits of those at the low and high intelligence extremes?

One way to glimpse the validity and significance of any test is to compare people who score at the two extremes of the normal curve. The two groups should differ noticeably, and they do.

The Low Extreme

At one extreme of the intelligence test normal curve are those with unusually low scores. The American Association on Intellectual and Developmental Disabilities guidelines list two criteria for a diagnosis of **intellectual disability** (formerly referred to as *mental retardation*):

1. A test score indicating performance below 98 percent of test-takers (Schalock et al., 2010). For an intelligence test with a midpoint of 100, that is a score of approximately 70 or below.

2. Difficulty adapting to the normal demands of independent living, as expressed in three areas:

- *conceptual skills* (such as language, literacy, and concepts of money, time, and number).

- *social skills* (such as interpersonal skills, social responsibility, and the ability to follow basic rules and laws and avoid being victimized).

- *practical skills* (such as daily personal care, occupational skill, and travel and health care).

Intellectual disability is a developmental condition that is apparent before age 18, sometimes with a known physical cause. **Down syndrome,** for example, is a disorder of varying intellectual and physical severity caused by an extra copy of chromosome 21.

Consider one reason why people diagnosed with a mild intellectual disability—those just below the 70 score—might be better able to live independently today than many decades ago, when they were institutionalized. The tests have been periodically restandardized. As that happened, individuals who scored near 70 on earlier tests have suddenly lost about 6 test-score points. Two people with the same ability level could thus be classified differently, depending on when they were tested (Kanaya et al., 2003; Reynolds et al., 2010). As the intellectual-disability boundary has shifted, more people have become eligible for special education and for Social Security payments. And in the United States (one of only a few industrialized countries with the death penalty), fewer people are now eligible for execution: The U.S. Supreme Court ruled in 2002 that the execution of people with an intellectual disability is "cruel and unusual

Mainstreaming in Chile Most Chilean children with Down syndrome attend separate schools for children with special needs. However, this boy is a student at the Altamira School, where children with differing abilities share the classroom.

punishment." For people near that score of 70, intelligence testing can be a high-stakes competition. And so it was for Teresa Lewis, a "dependant personality" with limited intellect, who was executed by the state of Virginia in 2010. Lewis, whose reported test score was 72, reportedly agreed to a plot in which two men killed her husband and stepson in exchange for a split of a life insurance payout (Eckholm, 2010). If only she had scored 69.

older adults' social reasoning skills increase, as shown by an ability to take multiple perspectives, to appreciate knowledge limits, and to offer helpful wisdom in times of social conflict (Grossman et al., 2010). Decisions also become less distorted by negative emotions such as anxiety, depression, and anger (Blanchard-Fields, 2007; Carstensen & Mikels, 2005).

Age-related cognitive differences help explain why older adults are less likely to embrace new technologies (Charness & Boot, 2009). In 2010, only 31 percent of Americans ages 65 and older had broadband Internet at home, compared with 80 percent of adults under 30 (Pew, 2010). These cognitive differences also help explain why mathematicians and scientists produce much of their most creative work during their late twenties or early thirties, when fluid intelligence is at its peak. In contrast, people working in literature, history, and philosophy tend to produce their best work in their forties, fifties, and beyond—after accumulating more knowledge (Simonton, 1988, 1990). Poets, for example, who depend on fluid intelligence, reach their peak output earlier than prose authors, who need the deeper knowledge reservoir that accumulates with age. This finding holds in every major literary tradition, for both living and dead languages.

"In youth we learn, in age we understand."

Marie Von Ebner-Eschenbach,
Aphorisms, *1883*

AP Photo/Damian Dovarganes

The extremes of intelligence Ten-year-old Moshe Kai Cavallin, who hopes to become an astrophysicist, was carrying an A+ average as a sophomore at East Los Angeles College when shown in this statistics class.

The High Extreme

In one famous project begun in 1921, Lewis Terman studied more than 1500 California schoolchildren with IQ scores over 135. Terman's high-scoring children (the "Termites") were healthy, well-adjusted, and unusually successful academically (Koenen et al., 2009; Lubinski, 2009a; Stanley, 1997). When restudied over the next seven decades, most had attained high levels of education (Austin et al., 2002; Holahan & Sears, 1995). Many were doctors, lawyers, professors, scientists, and writers, but no Nobel Prize winners. (The two future physics Nobel laureates Terman tested failed to score above his gifted-sample cutoff [Hulbert, 2005].)

A more recent study of precocious youths who aced the math SAT at age 13—by scoring in the top quarter of 1 percent of their age group—were at age 33 twice as likely to have patents as were those in the bottom quarter of the top 1 percent (Wai et al., 2005). Compared with the math aces, 13-year-olds scoring high on verbal aptitude were more likely to have become humanities professors or written a novel (Park et al., 2007). About 1 percent of Americans earn doctorates. But among those scoring in the top 1 in 10,000 on the SAT at age 12 or 13, more than half have done so (Lubinski, 2009b).

These whiz kids remind me of Jean Piaget, who by age 15 was publishing scientific articles

intellectual disability a condition of limited mental ability, indicated by an intelligence test score of 70 or below and difficulty in adapting to the demands of life. (Formerly referred to as *mental retardation*.)

Down syndrome a condition of mild to severe intellectual disability and associated physical disorders caused by an extra copy of chromosome 21.

on mollusks and who went on to become the twentieth century's most famous developmental psychologist (Hunt, 1993). Children with extraordinary academic gifts are sometimes more isolated, introverted, and in their own worlds (Winner, 2000). But most thrive.

"Joining Mensa means that you are a genius. . . . I worried about the arbitrary 132 cutoff point, until I met someone with an IQ of 131 and, honestly, he was a bit slow on the uptake."

Comedian Steve Martin, 1997

> **RETRIEVE IT**
>
> • Why do psychologists NOT diagnose an intellectual disability based solely on the person's intelligence test score?
>
> ANSWER: An intelligence test score is only one measure of a person's ability to function. Other important factors to consider in an overall assessment include conceptual skills, social skills, and practical skills.

Genetic and Environmental Influences on Intelligence

9-19: What evidence points to a genetic influence on intelligence, and what is heritability?

Intelligence runs in families. But why? Are our intellectual abilities mostly inherited? Or are they molded by our environment? Few issues in psychology arouse so much passion. Let's examine some of the evidence.

Twin and Adoption Studies

Does sharing the same genes also mean sharing the same mental abilities? As you can see from **FIGURE 9.17** on the next page, which summarizes many studies, the answer is clearly *Yes*.

Identical twins who grow up together have intelligence test scores nearly as similar as those of the same person taking the same test twice (Haworth et al., 2009; Lykken, 1999). (Fraternal twins, who typically share only half their genes, differ more.) Even when

"I told my parents that if grades were so important they should have paid for a smarter egg donor."

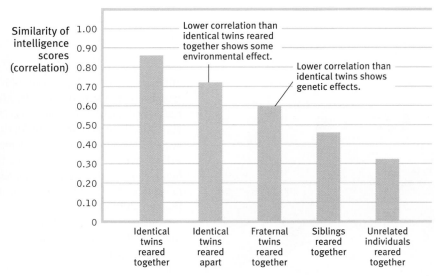

Similarity of intelligence scores (correlation)

Lower correlation than identical twins reared together shows some environmental effect.

Lower correlation than identical twins shows genetic effects.

Identical twins reared together · Identical twins reared apart · Fraternal twins reared together · Siblings reared together · Unrelated individuals reared together

FIGURE 9.17

Intelligence: Nature and nurture The most genetically similar people have the most similar intelligence scores. Remember: 1.0 indicates a perfect correlation; zero indicates no correlation at all. (Data from McGue et al., 1993.)

identical twins are adopted by two different families, their scores are very similar. Estimates of the **heritability** of intelligence—the extent to which intelligence test score variation can be attributed to genetic variation—range from 50 to 80 percent (Johnson et al., 2009; Neisser et al., 1996; Plomin, 2003). Identical twins also exhibit substantial similarity (and heritability) in specific talents, such as music, math, and sports (Vinkhuyzen et al., 2009).

Scans of identical twins' brains reveal that gray- and white-matter volume is similar, and areas associated with verbal and spatial intelligence are virtually the same (Deary et al., 2009; Thompson et al., 2001). Their brains also show similar activity while doing mental tasks (Koten et al., 2009).

Although genes matter, there is no known "genius" gene. Intelligence appears to be *polygenetic,* involving many genes, each accounting for much less than 1 percent of our differences (Butcher et al., 2008). Intelligence is thus like height, suggests Wendy Johnson (2010): Research shows that 54 specific gene variations together account for 5 percent of our individual differences in height, leaving the rest yet to be explained.

Other evidence points to an additional effect of environment. Where environments vary widely, as they do among children of less-educated parents, environmental differences are more predictive of intelligence scores (Rowe et al., 1999; Tucker-Drob et al., 2011; Turkheimer et al., 2003). And fraternal twins, who are genetically no more alike than any other siblings—but who are treated more alike because they are the same age—tend to score more alike than other siblings. Other studies also show that adoption of mistreated or neglected children enhances their intelligence scores (van IJzendoorn & Juffer, 2005, 2006).

So should we expect biologically unrelated children adopted into the same family to share similar aptitudes? Seeking to untangle genes and environment, researchers have compared the intelligence test scores of adopted children with those of their family members. These include their *biological parents* (the providers of their genes), their *adoptive parents* (the providers of their home environment), and their *adoptive siblings* (who share that home environment). During childhood, adoptive siblings' test scores correlate modestly. What do you think happens as the years go by and adopted children settle in with their adoptive families? Would you expect the family-environment effect to grow stronger and the genetic-legacy effect to shrink?

If you said *Yes,* behavior geneticists have a stunning surprise for you. Mental similarities between adopted children and their adoptive families *lessen* with age, dropping to roughly zero by adulthood (McGue et al., 1993). Genetic influences—not environmental ones—become more apparent as we accumulate life experience. Identical twins' similarities, for example, continue or increase into their eighties (Deary et al., 2009). In one massive study of 11,000 twin pairs in four countries, the heritability of *g* increased from 41 percent in middle childhood, to 55 percent in adolescence, to 66 percent in young adulthood (Haworth et al., 2010). Similarly, adopted children's verbal ability scores over time become more like those of their biological parents (**FIGURE 9.18**). Who would have guessed?

heritability the proportion of variation among individuals that we can attribute to genes. The heritability of a trait may vary, depending on the range of populations and environments studied.

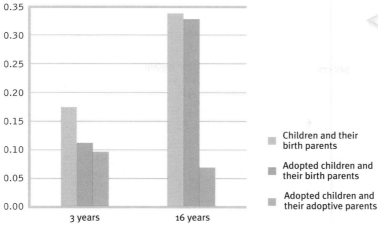

Child-parent correlation in verbal ability scores

(bar chart with y-axis from 0.00 to 0.35, x-axis showing "3 years" and "16 years")

Legend:
- Children and their birth parents
- Adopted children and their birth parents
- Adopted children and their adoptive parents

> **FIGURE 9.18**
> **In verbal ability, adopted children resemble their birth parents.** As the years went by in their adoptive families, children's verbal ability scores became modestly more like their *biological* parents' scores. (Adapted from Plomin & DeFries, 1998.)

"Selective breeding has given me an aptitude for the law, but I still love fetching a dead duck out of freezing water."

RETRIEVE IT

- A check on your understanding of heritability: If environments become more equal, the heritability of intelligence would

  a. increase.　　　　b. decrease.　　　　c. be unchanged.

ANSWER: a. (Heritability—variation explained by genetic influences—will increase as environmental variation decreases.)

Environmental Influences

9-20: What does evidence reveal about environmental influences on intelligence?

We have seen that biology and experience intertwine. Nowhere is this more apparent than in the most hopeless human environments. Severe deprivation leaves footprints on the brain, as J. McVicker Hunt (1982) observed in a destitute Iranian orphanage. The typical child Hunt observed there could not sit up unassisted at age 2 or walk at age 4. The little care the infants received was not in response to their crying, cooing, or other behaviors, so the children developed little sense of personal control over their environment. They were instead becoming passive "glum lumps." Extreme deprivation was crushing native intelligence—a finding confirmed by other studies of orphanage-reared children in Romania and elsewhere (Nelson et al., 2009; van IJzendoorn et al., 2008).

Mindful of the effect of early experiences and early intervention, Hunt began a training program for caregivers, teaching them to play language-fostering games with 11 infants. They learned to imitate the babies' babbling. They engaged them in vocal follow-the-leader. And, finally, they taught the infants sounds from the Persian language. The results were dramatic. By 22 months of age, the infants could name more than 50 objects and body parts. They so charmed visitors that most were adopted—an unprecedented success for the orphanage.

So, extreme conditions—malnutrition, sensory deprivation, and social isolation—can retard normal brain development. Is the reverse also true? Will an "enriched" environment give normal children a superior intellect? Most experts are doubtful (Bruer, 1999), but some parents disagree. After exposing their 12- to 18-month-olds to educational DVDs such as from the *Baby Einstein* series, they believe they have observed their baby's vocabulary growing. To see whether such cognitive growth is a result of the DVD exposure, or simply of infants' natural language explosion, two research teams assigned babies to DVD exposure or a control group (DeLoache et al., 2010; Reichert et al., 2010). Their common finding: The two groups' word learning did not differ.

Devastating neglect Some Romanian orphans, such as this child in the Lagunul Pentro Copii orphanage in 1990, had minimal interaction with caregivers, and suffered delayed development.

All babies should have normal exposure to sights, sounds, and speech. Beyond that, Sandra Scarr's (1984) verdict still is widely shared: "Parents who are very concerned about providing special educational lessons for their babies are wasting their time." There is no environmental recipe for fast-forwarding a normal infant into a genius.

Later in life, however, schooling does pay intelligence score dividends. Schooling and intelligence interact, and both enhance later income (Ceci & Williams, 1997, 2009). But what we accomplish with our genes and experiences depends also on our own beliefs and motivation. One analysis of 72,431 collegians found that study motivation and study skills rivaled aptitude and previous grades as predictors of academic achievement (Credé & Kuncel, 2008). Motivation can even affect intelligence test performance. Four dozen studies show that, when promised money for doing well, adolescents score higher on such tests (Duckworth et al., 2011).

Group Differences in Intelligence Test Scores

If there were no group differences in aptitude scores, psychologists could politely debate hereditary and environmental influences in their ivory towers. But there are group differences. What are they? And what shall we make of them?

Gender Similarities and Differences

9-21: How and why do the genders differ in mental ability scores?

In science, as in everyday life, differences, not similarities, excite interest. Compared with the anatomical and physiological similarities between men and women, our differences are minor. In one 1932 study that tested Scottish 11-year-olds, for example, the girls' average intelligence score was 100.6 and the boys' was 100.5 (Deary et al., 2003). So far as *g* is concerned, boys and girls, men and women, are the same species.

Yet, most people find differences more newsworthy. Girls outpace boys in spelling, verbal fluency, locating objects, detecting emotions, and sensitivity to touch, taste, and color (Halpern et al., 2007). Boys outperform girls in tests of spatial ability and complex math problems, though in math computation and overall math performance, boys and girls hardly differ (Else-Quest et al., 2010; Hyde & Mertz, 2009; Lindberg et al., 2010). Males' mental ability scores also vary more than females'. Thus, boys worldwide outnumber girls at both the low extreme and the high extreme (Machin & Pekkarinen, 2008; Strand et al., 2006; also see **FIGURE 9.19**). Boys, for example, are more often found in special education classes. And among 12- to 14-year-olds scoring extremely high (700 or higher) on SAT math, boys outnumber girls 4 to 1 (Wai et al., 2010).

The most reliable male edge appears in spatial ability tests like the one shown in **FIGURE 9.20**. The solution requires speedily rotating three-dimensional objects in one's mind (Collins & Kimura, 1997; Halpern, 2000). Today, such skills help when fitting suitcases into a car trunk, playing chess, or doing certain types of geometry problems. From an evolutionary perspective, those same skills would have helped our ancestral fathers track prey and make their way home (Geary, 1995, 1996; Halpern et al., 2007). The survival of our ancestral mothers may have benefited more from a keen memory for the location of edible plants—a legacy that lives today in women's superior memory for objects and their location.

But experience matters. One experiment found that playing action video games boosts spatial abilities (Feng et al., 2007). And you probably won't be surprised to know that among entering American

"A high IQ and a subway token will only get you into town."

Psychologist Richard Nisbett (quoted by Michael Balter), 2011

"It is our choices . . . that show what we truly are, far more than our abilities."

Professor Dumbledore to Harry Potter in J. K. Rowling's Harry Potter and the Chamber of Secrets, *1999*

FIGURE 9.19

Gender and variability In a 1932 intelligence testing of nearly 90,000 Scottish 11-year-olds, the average IQ score for girls and boys was essentially identical. But as other studies have found, boys were overrepresented at the low and high extremes. (Adapted from Johnson et al., 2008.)

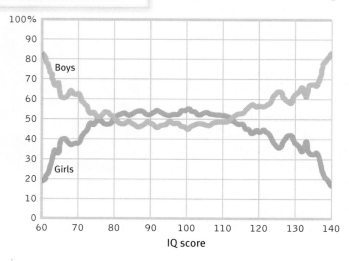

Percentage of boys vs. girls at each score level

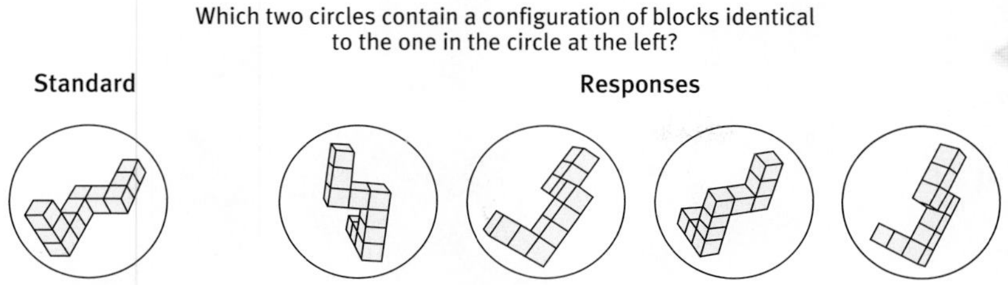

Which two circles contain a configuration of blocks identical
to the one in the circle at the left?

Standard

Responses

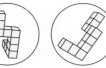

FIGURE 9.20

The mental rotation test This is a
test of spatial abilities. (From Vandenberg
& Kuse, 1978.) See inverted answer below.

ANSWER: The first and fourth alternatives.

collegians, six times as many men (23 percent) as women (4 percent) report playing
video or computer games six or more hours a week (Pryor et al., 2010).

Social expectations and opportunities also matter. Gender-equal cultures, such as
Sweden and Iceland, exhibit little of the gender math gap found in gender-unequal
cultures, such as Turkey and Korea (Guiso et al., 2008).

Racial and Ethnic Similarities and Differences

9-22: How and why do racial and ethnic groups differ in mental
ability scores?

Fueling the group-differences debate are two other disturbing but agreed-
upon facts:

- Racial and ethnic groups differ in their average intelligence test scores.
- High-scoring people (and groups) are more likely to attain high levels of education
  and income.

There are many group differences in average intelligence test scores. New Zealanders
of European descent outscore native Maori New Zealanders. Israeli Jews outscore Israeli
Arabs. Most Japanese outscore most Burakumin, a stigmatized Japanese minority. Those
who can hear outscore those born deaf (Braden, 1994; Steele, 1990; Zeidner, 1990). And
White Americans have outscored Black Americans. This Black–White difference has
diminished somewhat in recent years, especially among children (Dickens & Flynn, 2006;
Nisbett, 2009). Such *group* differences provide little basis for judging individuals. Worldwide, women outlive men by four years, but knowing only that you are male or female
won't tell us much about how long you will live.

We have seen that heredity contributes to *individual* differences in intelligence. But
group differences in a heritable trait may be entirely environmental. Consider one of
nature's experiments: Allow some children to grow up hearing their culture's dominant
language, while others, born deaf, do not. Then give both groups an intelligence test
rooted in the dominant language, and (no surprise) those with expertise in that language
will score highest. Although individual performance differences may be substantially
genetic, the group difference is not (**FIGURE 9.21**).

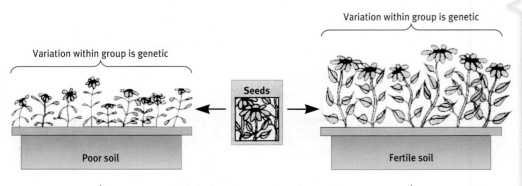

Variation within group is genetic

Variation within group is genetic

Seeds

Poor soil

Fertile soil

Variation between groups is environmental

FIGURE 9.21

Group differences and
environmental impact Even if the
variation between members within a group
reflects genetic differences, the average
difference between groups may be wholly due
to the environment. Imagine that seeds from
the same mixture are sown in different soils.
Although height differences *within* each window
box will be genetic, the height difference
between the two groups will be environmental.
(From Lewontin, 1976.)

© Larry Williams/CORBIS

Nature's own morphing Nature draws no sharp boundaries between races, which blend gradually one into the next around the Earth. Thanks to the human urge to classify, however, people socially define themselves in racial categories, which become catchall labels for physical features, social identity, and nationality.
© Paul Almasy/Corbis; © Rob Howard/ Corbis;
© Barbara Bannister; Gallo Images/ Corbis;
© David Turnley/Corbis; © Dave Bartruff/Corbis;
© Haruyoshi Yamaguchi/Corbis;
© Richard T. Nowitz/Corbis; © Owen Franken/Corbis;
© Paul Almasy/Corbis; © John-Francis Bourke/zefa/Corbis

"Do not obtain your slaves from Britain, because they are so stupid and so utterly incapable of being taught."

Cicero, 106–43 B.C.E.

Might the racial gap be similarly environmental? Consider:

Genetics research reveals that under the skin, the races are remarkably alike. The average genetic difference between two Icelandic villagers or between two Kenyans greatly exceeds the group difference between Icelanders and Kenyans (Cavalli-Sforza et al., 1994; Rosenberg et al., 2002). Moreover, looks can deceive. Light-skinned Europeans and dark-skinned Africans are genetically closer than are dark-skinned Africans and dark-skinned Aboriginal Australians.

Race is not a neatly defined biological category. Many social scientists see race primarily as a social construction without well-defined physical boundaries, as each race blends seamlessly into the race of its geographical neighbors (Helms et al., 2005; Smedley & Smedley, 2005). People with varying ancestry may categorize themselves in the same race. Moreover, with increasingly mixed ancestries, more and more people defy neat racial categorization and self-identify as multiracial (Pauker et al., 2009).

The intelligence test performance of today's better-fed, better-educated, and more test-prepared population exceeds that of the 1930s population—by a greater margin than the intelligence test score of the average White today exceeds that of the average Black. One research review noted that the average intelligence test performance of today's sub-Saharan Africans is the same as British adults in 1948, with the possibility of similar gains to come, given improved nutrition, economic development, and education (Wicherts et al., 2010). No one attributes generational group differences to genetics.

When Blacks and Whites have or receive the same pertinent knowledge, they exhibit similar information-processing skill. "The data support the view that cultural differences in the provision of information may account for racial differences in [intelligence test performance]," reported researchers Joseph Fagan and Cynthia Holland (2007).

Schools and culture matter. Countries whose economies create a large wealth gap between rich and poor tend also to have a large rich-versus-poor intelligence test score gap (Nisbett, 2009). Moreover, educational policies such as kindergarten attendance, school discipline, and instructional time per year predict national differences in intelligence and knowledge tests (Rindermann & Ceci, 2009). Math achievement and aptitude test differences may reflect conscientiousness more than competence. Asian students, who have outperformed North American students on such tests, have also spent 30 percent more time in school and much more time in and out of school studying math (Geary et al., 1996; Larson & Verma, 1999; Stevenson, 1992).

In different eras, different ethnic groups have experienced golden ages—periods of remarkable achievement. Twenty-five-hundred years ago, it was the Greeks and the Egyptians, then the Romans. In the eighth and ninth centuries, genius seemed to reside in the Arab world. Five hundred years ago, the Aztec Indians and the peoples of Northern Europe were the superachievers. Today, people marvel at Asians' technological genius and Jews' cultural success. Cultures rise and fall over centuries; genes do not. That fact makes it difficult to attribute a natural superiority to any race.

RETRIEVE IT

• The heritability of intelligence scores will be greater in a society marked by equal opportunity than in a society of peasants and aristocrats. Why?

ANSWER: Perfect environmental equality would create 100 percent heritability, because genes alone would account for any remaining human differences.

The Question of Bias

9-23: Are intelligence tests inappropriately biased?

If one assumes that *race* is a meaningful concept, the debate over race differences in intelligence divides into three camps (Hunt & Carlson, 2007):

- There are genetically disposed racial differences in intelligence.
- There are socially influenced racial differences in intelligence.
- There are racial differences in test scores, but the tests are inappropriate or biased.

We have considered group differences from the first and second perspectives. Let's turn now to the third: Are intelligence tests biased? The answer depends on the definition of *bias* we use, and on our understanding of stereotypes.

Two Meanings of Bias The *scientific* meaning of *bias* hinges on a test's validity—on whether it predicts future behavior only for some groups of test-takers. For example, if the SAT accurately predicted the college achievement of women but not that of men, then the test would be biased. In this statistical meaning of the term, the near-consensus among psychologists (as summarized by the U.S. National Research Council's Committee on Ability Testing and the American Psychological Association's Task Force on Intelligence) has been that the major U.S. aptitude tests are *not* biased (Hunt & Carlson, 2007; Neisser et al., 1996; Wigdor & Garner, 1982). The tests' predictive validity is roughly the same for women and men, for various races, and for rich and poor. If an intelligence test score of 95 predicts slightly below-average grades, that rough prediction usually applies equally to all.

But we can also consider a test biased if it makes predictions based not only on innate differences in intelligence but also on past cultural experiences. This in fact happened to Eastern European immigrants in the early 1900s. Lacking the experience to answer questions about their new culture, many were classified as feeble-minded. In this popular sense, intelligence tests are biased. They measure your developed abilities, which reflect, in part, your education and experiences.

You may have read examples of intelligence test items that make middle-class assumptions (for example, that a cup goes with a saucer). Such items can bias the test against those who do not use saucers. Could such questions explain cultural differences in test performance? In such cases, tests can be a vehicle for discrimination, consigning potentially capable children (some of whom may have a different native language) to dead-end classes and jobs. For such reasons, some intelligence researchers recommend creating culture-neutral questions—such as assessing people's ability to learn novel words, sayings, and analogies—to enable culture-fair aptitude tests (Fagan & Holland, 2007, 2009).

So, test-makers' expectations can introduce bias in an intelligence test. This is consistent with an observation you have seen throughout this text: Our expectations and attitudes can influence our perceptions and behaviors. This is also true for the person taking the test.

What time is it now? When I asked you (in the section on overconfidence) to estimate how quickly you would finish this chapter, did you underestimate or overestimate?

Jason Goltz

The culture of scholarship The children of Indochinese refugee families have excelled in school (Caplan et al., 1992). On weekday nights after dinner, the family clears the table and begins homework. Family cooperation is valued, and older siblings help younger ones.

RETRIEVE IT

- What is the difference between a test that is biased culturally and a test that is biased in terms of its validity?

ANSWER: A test may be *culturally* biased if higher scores are achieved by those with certain cultural experiences. That same test may not be biased in terms of *validity* if it predicts what it is supposed to predict. For example, the SAT may be culturally biased in favor of those with experience in the U.S. school system, but it does still accurately predict U.S. college success.

Stereotype Threat If, when taking an intelligence test or an exam, you are worried that your group or "type" often doesn't do well, your self-doubts and self-monitoring may hijack your working memory and impair your performance (Schmader, 2010). This self-confirming concern that you will be evaluated based on a negative viewpoint

stereotype threat a self-confirming concern that one will be evaluated based on a negative stereotype.

"Math class is tough!"

"Teen talk" talking Barbie doll (introduced February 1992, recalled October 1992)

"Almost all the joyful things of life are outside the measure of IQ tests."

Madeleine L'Engle, A Circle of Quiet, 1972

"[Einstein] showed that genius equals brains plus tenacity squared."

Walter Isaacson, "Einstein's Final Quest," 2009

is called **stereotype threat,** and it may impair your attention and learning (Inzlicht & Kang, 2010; Rydell, 2010).

When Steven Spencer and his colleagues (1997) gave a difficult math test to equally capable men and women, women did not do as well—except when they had been led to expect that women usually do as well as men on the test. Otherwise, the women apparently felt apprehensive, which affected their performance. And with Claude Steele and Joshua Aronson, Spencer (2002) again observed stereotype threat when Black students were reminded of their race just before taking verbal aptitude tests and performed worse. Follow-up experiments have confirmed that negatively stereotyped minorities and women may have unrealized academic potential (Nguyen & Ryan, 2008; Walton & Spencer, 2009).

Critics note that stereotype threat does not fully account for Black-White aptitude score differences (Sackett et al., 2004, 2008). But it does help explain why Blacks have scored higher when tested by Blacks than when tested by Whites (Danso & Esses, 2001; Inzlicht & Ben-Zeev, 2000). It gives us insight into why women have scored higher on math tests with no male test-takers present, and why women's chess play drops sharply when they *think* they are playing a male opponent (Maass et al., 2008). It also explains "the Obama effect"—the finding that African-American adults performed better if they took a verbal aptitude test immediately after watching then-candidate Barack Obama's stereotype-defying nomination-acceptance speech, or just after his 2008 presidential victory (Marx et al., 2009).

Steele (1995, 2010) concludes that telling students they probably won't succeed (as is sometimes implied by remedial "minority support" programs) functions as a stereotype that can erode performance. Minority students in university programs that have challenged them to believe in their potential, or to focus on the idea that intelligence is malleable and not fixed, have produced markedly higher grades and had lower dropout rates (Wilson, 2006).

These observations lend support to other research by psychologist Carol Dweck (2006, 2007, 2008). She reports that the belief that intelligence is changeable can foster a *growth mind-set,* which focuses on learning and growing. Collegians with a growth mind-set tend to flourish happily (Howell, 2009). To foster this mind-set, Dweck has developed interventions to teach early teens that the brain is like a muscle that grows stronger with use as neuron connections grow. Indeed, as noted earlier, superior achievements in fields from sports to science to music arise from disciplined effort and sustained practice (Ericsson et al., 2007). Believing in our ability to learn, and applying ourselves with sustained effort, we are likely to fulfill our potential.

★ ★ ★

Perhaps, then, our goals for tests of mental abilities should be threefold.

- We should realize the benefits Alfred Binet foresaw—to enable schools to recognize who might profit most from early intervention.

- We must remain alert to Binet's fear that intelligence test scores may be misinterpreted as literal measures of a person's worth and potential.

- We must remember that the competence that general intelligence tests sample is important; without such tests, those who decide on jobs and admissions would rely more on other considerations, such as personal opinion. But these tests reflect only one aspect of personal competence. Our practical intelligence and emotional intelligence matter, too, as do other forms of creativity, talent, and character.

The point to remember: There are many ways of being successful: Our differences are variations of human adaptability. Life's great achievements result not only from "can do" abilities but also from "will do" motivation. Competence + Diligence → Accomplishment.

CHAPTER REVIEW

Thinking, Language, and Intelligence

LEARNING OBJECTIVES

Test Yourself by taking a moment to answer each of these Learning Objective Questions (repeated here from within the chapter). Then turn to Appendix D, Complete Chapter Reviews, to check your answers. Research suggests that trying to answer these questions on your own will improve your long-term memory of the concepts (McDaniel et al., 2009).

Thinking

9-1: What is cognition, and what are the functions of concepts?

9-2: What cognitive strategies assist our problem solving, and what obstacles hinder it?

9-3: What is intuition, and how can the availability heuristic, overconfidence, belief perseverance, and framing influence our decisions and judgments?

9-4: How do smart thinkers use intuition?

9-5: What is creativity, and what fosters it?

9-6: What do we know about animal thinking?

Language

9-7: What are the structural components of a language?

9-8: What are the milestones in language development, and how do we acquire language?

9-9: What brain areas are involved in language processing and speech?

9-10: Do other animals share our capacity for language?

Thinking and Language

9-11: What is the relationship between thinking and language, and what is the value of thinking in images?

Intelligence

9-12: How do psychologists define *intelligence,* and what are the arguments for *g*?

9-13: How do Gardner's and Sternberg's theories of multiple intelligences differ?

9-14: What are the four components of emotional intelligence?

9-15: When and why were intelligence tests created, and how do today's tests differ from early intelligence tests?

9-16: What is a normal curve, and what does it mean to say that a test has been standardized and is reliable and valid?

9-17: What are the traits of those at the low and high intelligence extremes?

9-18: How does aging affect crystallized and fluid intelligence?

9-19: What evidence points to a genetic influence on intelligence, and what is heritability?

9-20: What does evidence reveal about environmental influences on intelligence?

9-21: How and why do the genders differ in mental ability scores?

9-22: How and why do racial and ethnic groups differ in mental ability scores?

9-23: Are intelligence tests inappropriately biased?

TERMS AND CONCEPTS TO REMEMBER

Test yourself on these terms by trying to write down the definition in your own words before flipping back to the referenced page to check your answer.

cognition, p. 306

concept, p. 306

prototype, p. 306

algorithm, p. 307

heuristic, p. 307

insight, p. 307

confirmation bias, p. 307

mental set, p. 308

intuition, p. 308

availability heuristic, p. 309

overconfidence, p. 311

belief perseverance, p. 312

framing, p. 312

creativity, p. 314

convergent thinking, p. 314

divergent thinking, p. 314

language, p. 318

phoneme, p. 319

morpheme, p. 319

grammar, p. 319

babbling stage, p. 320

one-word stage, p. 320

two-word stage, p. 320

telegraphic speech, p. 320

aphasia, p. 322

Broca's area, p. 323

Wernicke's area, p. 323

linguistic determinism, p. 326

intelligence, p. 329

general intelligence (g), p. 330

savant syndrome, p. 330

emotional intelligence, p. 333

intelligence test, p. 333

aptitude test, p. 334

achievement test, p. 334

mental age, p. 334

Stanford-Binet, p. 334

intelligence quotient (IQ), p. 334

Wechsler Adult Intelligence Scale (WAIS), p. 334

standardization, p. 336

normal curve, p. 336

reliability, p. 336

validity, p. 337

content validity, p. 337

predictive validity, p. 337

crystallized intelligence, p. 337

fluid intelligence, p. 337

intellectual disability, p. 338

Down syndrome, p. 338

heritability, p. 340

stereotype threat, p. 346

EXPERIENCE THE TESTING EFFECT

Test yourself repeatedly throughout your studies. This will not only help you figure out what you know and don't know; the testing itself will help you learn and remember the information more effectively thanks to the *testing effect.*

1. A mental grouping of similar things is called a _____.

2. The most systematic procedure for solving a problem is a(n) _____.

3. Oscar describes his political beliefs as "strongly liberal," but he has decided to explore opposing viewpoints. How might he be affected by *confirmation bias* and *belief perseverance* in this effort?

4. A major obstacle to problem solving is fixation, which is a(n)
   a. tendency to base our judgments on vivid memories.
   b. tendency to wait for insight to occur.
   c. inability to view a problem from a new perspective.
   d. rule of thumb for judging the likelihood of an event in terms of our mental image of it.

5. After the 9/11 attacks by foreign-born terrorists, some observers initially assumed that the 2003 U. S. East Coast blackout was probably also the work of foreign-born terrorists. This assumption illustrates the _____ heuristic.

6. When consumers respond more positively to ground beef described as "75 percent lean" than to the same product labeled "25 percent fat," they have been influenced by _____.

7. Which of the following is NOT a characteristic of a creative person?
   a. Expertise
   b. Extrinsic motivation
   c. A venturesome personality
   d. Imaginative thinking skills

8. Children reach the one-word stage of speech development at about
   a. 4 months.
   b. 6 months.
   c. 1 year.
   d. 2 years.

9. The three basic building blocks of language are _____, _____, and _____.

10. When young children speak in short phrases using mostly verbs and nouns, this is referred to as _____ _____.

11. According to Chomsky, all languages share a(n) _____ _____.

12. Most researchers agree that apes can
    a. communicate through symbols.
    b. reproduce most human speech sounds.
    c. master language in adulthood.
    d. surpass a human 3-year-old in language skills.

13. Charles Spearman suggested we have one _____ _____ underlying success across a variety of intellectual abilities.

14. The existence of savant syndrome seems to support
    a. Sternberg's distinction among three types of intelligence.
    b. criticism of multiple intelligence theories.
    c. Gardner's theory of multiple intelligences.
    d. Thorndike's view of social intelligence.

15. Sternberg's three types of intelligence are _____, _____, and _____.

16. Emotionally intelligent people tend to
    a. seek immediate gratification.
    b. understand their own emotions but not those of others.
    c. understand others' emotions but not their own.
    d. succeed in their careers.

17. The IQ of a 6-year-old with a measured mental age of 9 would be
    a. 67.
    b. 133.
    c. 86.
    d. 150.

18. The Wechsler Adult Intelligence Scale (WAIS) is best able to tell us
    a. what part of an individual's intelligence is determined by genetic inheritance.
    b. whether the test-taker will succeed in a job.
    c. how the test-taker compares with other adults in vocabulary and arithmetic reasoning.
    d. whether the test-taker has specific skills for music and the performing arts.

19. The Stanford-Binet, the Wechsler Adult Intelligence Scale, and the Wechsler Intelligence Scale for Children yield consistent results, for example on retesting. In other words, these tests have high _____.

20. The strongest support for heredity's influence on intelligence is the finding that
    a. identical twins, but not other siblings, have nearly identical intelligence test scores.
    b. the correlation between intelligence test scores of fraternal twins is higher than that for other siblings.
    c. mental similarities between adopted siblings increase with age.
    d. children in impoverished families have similar intelligence scores.

21. To say that the heritability of intelligence is about 50 percent means that 50 percent of
    a. an individual's intelligence is due to genetic factors.
    b. the similarities between two groups of people are attributable to genes.
    c. the variation in intelligence within a group of people is attributable to genetic factors.
    d. intelligence is due to the mother's genes and the rest is due to the father's genes.

22. The environmental influence that has the clearest, most profound effect on intellectual development is
    a. exposing normal infants to educational DVDs before age 1.
    b. growing up in an economically disadvantaged home or neighborhood.
    c. being raised in conditions of extreme deprivation.
    d. being an identical twin.

23. In prosperous country X everyone eats all they want. In country Y the rich are well fed, but the semistarved poor are often thin. In which country will the heritability of body weight be greater?

24. _____ _____ can lead to poor performance on tests by undermining test-takers' belief that they can do well on the test.

Find answers to these questions in Appendix E, in the back of the book.

Experience more of the **TESTING** EFFECT

Multiple-format self-tests and more may be found at www.worthpublishers.com/myers.

CHAPTER 10

Motivation and Emotion

After an ill-fated spring Saturday in 2003, experienced mountaineer Aron Ralston understood how motivation can energize and direct behavior. Having bagged nearly all of Colorado's tallest peaks, Ralston ventured some solo canyon hiking that seemed so risk free he didn't bother to tell anyone where he was going. In Utah's narrow Bluejohn Canyon, just 150 yards above his final rappel, he was climbing over an 800-pound rock when disaster struck: The rock shifted and pinned his right wrist and arm. He was, as the title of his book says, caught *Between a Rock and a Hard Place.*

Realizing no one would be rescuing him, Ralston tried with all his might to dislodge the rock. Then, with a dull pocketknife, he tried chipping away at it. When that, too, failed, he rigged up ropes to lift the rock. Alas, nothing worked. Hour after hour, then cold night after cold night, he was stuck.

By Tuesday, he had run out of food and water. On Wednesday, as thirst and hunger gnawed, he began saving and sipping his own urine. Using his video recorder, he said good-bye to family and friends, for whom he now felt intense love: "So again love to everyone. Bring love and peace and happiness and beautiful lives into the world in my honor. Thank you. Love you."

On Thursday, surprised to find himself still alive, Ralston had a seemingly divine insight into his reproductive future, a vision of a preschool boy being scooped up by a one-armed man. With this inspiration, he summoned his remaining strength and his enormous will to live and, over the next hour, willfully broke his arm bones and then proceeded to use that dull knife to cut off his arm. He put on a tourniquet, chopped through the last piece of skin, and, after 127 hours, broke free. He then rappelled with his bleeding half-arm down a 65-foot cliff and hiked 5 miles before finding someone. He was, in his own words, "just reeling with this euphoria . . . having been dead and standing in my grave, leaving my last will and testament, etching 'Rest in peace' on the wall, all of that, gone and then replaced with having my life again. It was undoubtedly the sweetest moment that I will ever experience" (Ralston, 2004). Aron Ralston's thirst and hunger, his sense of belonging to others, and his brute will to live highlight the force of *motivation:* a need or desire that energizes behavior and directs it toward a goal. His intense emotional experiences of love and joy demonstrate the close ties between our feelings, or *emotions,* and our motivated behaviors. In this chapter, we explore both of these human forces.

"What do you think . . . should we get started on that motivation research or not?"

Motivational Concepts

10-1: How do psychologists define *motivation?* From what perspectives do they view motivated behavior?

Psychologists today define **motivation** as a need or desire that energizes and directs behavior. Our motivations arise from the interplay between nature (the bodily "push") and nurture (the "pulls" from our thought processes and culture).

In their attempts to understand motivated behavior, psychologists have viewed it from four perspectives:

- *Instinct theory* (now replaced by the *evolutionary perspective*) focuses on genetically predisposed behaviors.

- *Drive-reduction theory* focuses on how we respond to our inner pushes.

- *Arousal theory* focuses on finding the right level of stimulation.

- Abraham Maslow's *hierarchy of needs* focuses on the priority of some needs over others.

Instincts and Evolutionary Psychology

Early in the twentieth century, as the influence of Charles Darwin's evolutionary theory grew, it became fashionable to classify all sorts of behaviors as instincts. If people criticized themselves, it was because of their "self-abasement instinct." If they boasted, it reflected their "self-assertion instinct." After scanning 500 books, one sociologist compiled a list of 5759 supposed human instincts! Before long, this instinct-naming fad collapsed under its own weight. Rather than *explaining* human behaviors, the early instinct theorists were simply *naming* them. It was like "explaining" a bright child's low grades by labeling the child an "underachiever." To name a behavior is *not* to explain it.

To qualify as an **instinct,** a complex behavior must have a fixed pattern throughout a species and be unlearned (Tinbergen, 1951). Such behaviors are common in other species (recall imprinting in birds in Chapter 4 and the return of salmon to their birthplace in Chapter 7). Some human behaviors, such as infants' innate reflexes for rooting

Same motive, different wiring The more complex the nervous system, the more adaptable the organism. Both humans and weaverbirds satisfy their need for shelter in ways that reflect their inherited capacities. Human behavior is flexible; we can learn whatever skills we need to build a house. The bird's behavior pattern is fixed; it can build only this kind of nest.

Annika Erickson/Getty Images

Tony Brandenburg/Bruce Coleman, Inc.

and sucking, also exhibit unlearned fixed patterns, but many more are directed by both physiological needs and psychological wants.

Instinct theory failed to explain most human motives, but its underlying assumption continues in evolutionary psychology: Genes do predispose some species-typical behavior. We saw this in Chapter 7's discussion of the limits that biological predispositions place on conditioning, and in Chapter 9's discussion of human language. Later in this chapter, we'll see how our taste preferences aid our survival. And we will see this in discussions of how evolution might influence our helping behaviors and our romantic attractions (Chapter 13), and our phobias (Chapter 14).

Drives and Incentives

When the original instinct theory of motivation collapsed, it was replaced by **drive-reduction theory**—the idea that a physiological need (food, water) creates an aroused, motivated state (a *drive,* such as hunger or thirst) that pushes the organism to reduce the need by, say, eating or drinking (**FIGURE 10.1**). With few exceptions, when a physiological need increases, so does a psychological drive.

The physiological aim of drive reduction is **homeostasis**—the maintenance of a steady internal state. An example of homeostasis (literally "staying the same") is the body's temperature-regulation system, which works like a room's thermostat. Both systems operate through feedback loops: Sensors feed room temperature to a control device. If the room's temperature cools, the control device switches on the furnace. Likewise, if our body's temperature cools, our blood vessels constrict (to conserve warmth) and we feel driven to put on more clothes or seek a warmer environment.

Not only are we *pushed* by our need to reduce drives, we also are *pulled* by **incentives**—positive or negative environmental stimuli that lure or repel us. This is one way our individual learning histories influence our motives. Depending on our learning, the aroma of good food, whether fresh roasted peanuts or toasted ants, can motivate our behavior. So can the sight of those we find attractive or threatening.

When there is both a need and an incentive, we feel strongly driven. The food-deprived person who smells baking bread feels a strong hunger drive. In the presence of that drive, the baking bread becomes a compelling incentive. For each motive, we can therefore ask, "How is it pushed by our inborn physiological needs and pulled by incentives in the environment?"

Optimum Arousal

We are much more than homeostatic systems, however. Some motivated behaviors actually *increase* arousal. Well-fed animals will leave their shelter to explore and gain information, seemingly in the absence of any need-based drive. Curiosity drives monkeys to monkey around trying to figure out how to unlock a latch that opens nothing or how to open a window that allows them to see outside their room (Butler, 1954). It drives the 9-month-old infant to investigate every accessible corner of the house. It drives the scientists whose work this text discusses. And it drives explorers and adventurers such as Aron Ralston and George Mallory. Asked why he wanted to climb Mount Everest, Mallory answered, "Because it is there." Those who, like Mallory and Ralston, enjoy high arousal are most likely to seek out intense music, novel foods, and risky behaviors (Zuckerman, 1979, 2009). They are "sensation-seekers."

motivation a need or desire that energizes and directs behavior.

instinct a complex behavior that is rigidly patterned throughout a species and is unlearned.

drive-reduction theory the idea that a physiological need creates an aroused tension state (a drive) that motivates an organism to satisfy the need.

homeostasis a tendency to maintain a balanced or constant internal state; the regulation of any aspect of body chemistry, such as blood glucose, around a particular level.

incentive a positive or negative environmental stimulus that motivates behavior.

FIGURE 10.1

Drive-reduction theory Drive-reduction motivation arises from *homeostasis*—an organism's natural tendency to maintain a steady internal state. Thus, if we are water deprived, our thirst drives us to drink and to restore the body's normal state.

Driven by curiosity Baby monkeys and young children are fascinated by things they've never experienced before. Their drive to explore the relatively unfamiliar is one of several motives that do not fill any immediate physiological need.

So, human motivation aims not to eliminate arousal but to seek optimum levels of arousal. Having all our biological needs satisfied, we feel driven to experience stimulation and we hunger for information. We are "infovores," said neuroscientists Irving Biederman and Edward Vessel (2006), after identifying brain mechanisms that reward us for acquiring information. Lacking stimulation, we feel bored and look for a way to increase arousal to some optimum level. However, with too much stimulation comes stress, and we then look for a way to decrease arousal.

Two early-twentieth-century psychologists studied the relationship of arousal to performance and identified what we now call the **Yerkes–Dodson law,** suggesting that moderate arousal would lead to optimal performance (Yerkes & Dodson, 1908). When taking an exam, for example, it pays to be moderately aroused—alert but not trembling with nervousness. We have since learned that optimal arousal levels depend upon the task as well, with more difficult tasks requiring lower arousal for best performance (Hembree, 1988) (**FIGURE 10.2**).

FIGURE 10.2
Arousal and performance

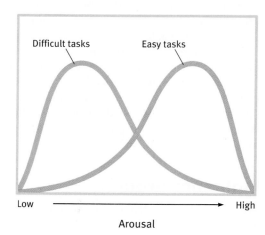

RETRIEVE IT

- Performance peaks at lower levels of arousal for difficult tasks, and at higher levels for easy or well-learned tasks. (1) How might this phenomenon affect runners? (2) How might this phenomenon affect anxious test-takers facing a difficult exam? (3) How might the performance of anxious students be affected by relaxation training?

Yerkes–Dodson law the principle that performance increases with arousal only up to a point, beyond which performance decreases.

ANSWERS: (1) Runners tend to excel when aroused by competition. (2) High anxiety in test-takers may disrupt their performance. (3) Teaching anxious students how to relax before an exam can enable them to perform better (Hembree, 1988).

A Hierarchy of Motives

Some needs take priority over others. At this moment, with your needs for air and water hopefully satisfied, other motives—such as your desire to achieve—are energizing and directing your behavior. Let your need for water go unsatisfied and your thirst will pre-occupy you. Just ask Aron Ralston. Deprived of air, your thirst would disappear.

Abraham Maslow (1970) described these priorities as a **hierarchy of needs** (**FIGURE 10.3**). At the base of this pyramid are our physiological needs, such as those for food and water. Only if these needs are met are we prompted to meet our need for safety, and then to satisfy the uniquely human needs to give and receive love and to enjoy self-esteem. Beyond this, said Maslow (1971), lies the need for *self-actualization,* to realize one's full potential. (More on self-esteem and self-actualization in Chapter 12.)

Near the end of his life, Maslow proposed that some of us also reach a level of self-transcendence. At the self-actualization level, we seek to realize our *own* potential. At the *self-transcendence* level, we strive for meaning, purpose, and communion that are transpersonal, beyond the self (Koltko-Rivera, 2006).

Maslow's hierarchy is somewhat arbitrary: The order of such needs is not universally fixed. People have starved themselves to make a political statement. Culture also matters: Self-esteem matters most in individualist nations, whose citizens tend to focus more on personal achievements than on family and community identity (Oishi et al., 1999). And, while agreeing with Maslow's basic levels of need, today's evolutionary psychologists note that gaining and retaining mates and parenting offspring are also universal human motives (Kenrick et al., 2010).

Nevertheless, the simple idea that some motives are more compelling than others provides a framework for thinking about motivation. Worldwide life-satisfaction surveys support this basic idea (Oishi et al., 1999; Tay & Diener, 2011). In poorer nations that lack easy access to money and the food and shelter it buys, financial satisfaction more strongly predicts feelings of well-being. In wealthy nations, where most are able to meet basic needs, home-life satisfaction is a better predictor.

Let's take a closer look now at three specific motives, beginning at the basic level with *hunger* and working up to higher-level needs: the *need to belong* and the *need to achieve.* As you read about these motives, watch for ways that incentives (the psychological "pull") interact with physiological needs (the biological "push").

hierarchy of needs Maslow's pyramid of human needs, beginning at the base with physiological needs that must first be satisfied before higher-level safety needs and then psychological needs become active.

"Hunger is the most urgent form of poverty."

Alliance to End Hunger, 2002

Self-transcendence needs
Need to find meaning and identity beyond the self

Self-actualization needs
Need to live up to our fullest and unique potential

Esteem needs
Need for self-esteem, achievement, competence, and independence; need for recognition and respect from others

Belongingness and love needs
Need to love and be loved, to belong and be accepted; need to avoid loneliness and separation

Safety needs
Need to feel that the world is organized and predictable; need to feel safe

Physiological needs
Need to satisfy hunger and thirst

FIGURE 10.3

Maslow's hierarchy of needs Once our lower-level needs are met, we are prompted to satisfy our higher-level needs. (From Maslow, 1970.) For survivors of the disastrous tornadoes that swept across the Midwest and Southeastern United States in 2011, satisfying very basic needs for water, food, and safety became top priority. Higher-level needs on Maslow's hierarchy, such as respect, self-actualization, and meaning, become far less important during such times.

©REUTERS/Tami Chappell

- How do instinct theory, drive-reduction theory, and arousal theory contribute to our understanding of motivated behavior?

ANSWER: Instincts and evolutionary psychology help explain the genetic basis for our unlearned, species-typical behaviors. From drive-reduction theory we know that our physiological needs (such as hunger) create an aroused state that drives us to reduce the need (for example by eating). Arousal theory suggests we need to maintain an optimal level of arousal, which helps explain our motivation toward behaviors that meet no physiological need.

- After hours of driving alone in an unfamiliar city, you finally see a diner. Although it looks deserted and a little creepy, you stop because you are *really* hungry. How would Maslow's hierarchy of needs explain your behavior?

ANSWER: According to Maslow, our drives to meet the physiological needs of hunger and thirst take priority over safety needs, prompting us to take risks at times in order to eat.

Hunger

The power of physiological needs was vividly demonstrated when Ancel Keys (the creator of Army K rations) and his research team (1950) conducted a now-classic study of semistarvation. They first fed 36 male volunteers (all wartime conscientious objectors) just enough to maintain their initial weight. Then, for six months, they cut this food level in half. The effects soon became visible. Without thinking about it, the men began conserving energy. They appeared sluggish and dull. After dropping rapidly, their body weights stabilized at about 25 percent below their starting point.

As Maslow might have guessed, the men became food obsessed. They talked food. They daydreamed food. They collected recipes, read cookbooks, and feasted their eyes on delectable forbidden food. Preoccupied with their unmet basic need, they lost interest in sex and social activities. As one man reported, "If we see a show, the most interesting part of it is contained in scenes where people are eating. I couldn't laugh at the funniest picture in the world, and love scenes are completely dull."

The semistarved men's preoccupations illustrate how activated motives can hijack our consciousness. As journalist Dorothy Dix (1861–1951) observed, "Nobody wants to kiss when they are hungry." When we're hungry, thirsty, fatigued, or sexually aroused, little else seems to matter. When we're not, food, water, sleep, or sex just doesn't seem like that big a thing in life, now or ever.

In studies, people in a motivational "hot" state (from fatigue, hunger, or sexual arousal) have easily recalled such feelings in their own past and have perceived them as driving forces in others' behavior (Nordgren et al., 2006, 2007). (You may recall from Chapter 8 a parallel effect of our current good or bad mood on our memories.) Grocery shop with an empty stomach and you are more likely to see those jelly-filled doughnuts as just what you've always loved and will be wanting tomorrow. *Motives matter mightily.*

"Nature often equips life's essentials—sex, eating, nursing—with built-in gratification."

Frans de Waal, "Morals Without God?" 2010

"The full person does not understand the needs of the hungry."

Irish proverb

"Never hunt when you're hungry."

The Physiology of Hunger

10-2: What physiological factors produce hunger?

Deprived of a normal food supply, Keys' semistarved volunteers were clearly hungry. But what precisely triggers hunger? Are the pangs of an empty stomach the source of hunger? So it seemed to A. L. Washburn. Working with Walter Cannon (Cannon & Washburn, 1912), Washburn agreed to swallow a balloon attached to a recording device (**FIGURE 10.4**). When inflated to fill his stomach, the balloon transmitted his stomach contractions. Washburn supplied information about his *feelings* of hunger by pressing a key each time he felt a hunger pang. The discovery: Washburn was indeed having stomach contractions whenever he felt hungry.

Can hunger exist without stomach pangs? To answer that question, researchers removed some rats' stomachs and created a direct path to their small intestines (Tsang, 1938). Did the rats continue to eat? Indeed they did. Some hunger persists similarly in humans whose stomachs have been removed as a treatment for ulcers or cancer. So the pangs of an empty stomach are not the *only* source of hunger. What else might trigger hunger?

glucose the form of sugar that circulates in the blood and provides the major source of energy for body tissues. When its level is low, we feel hunger.

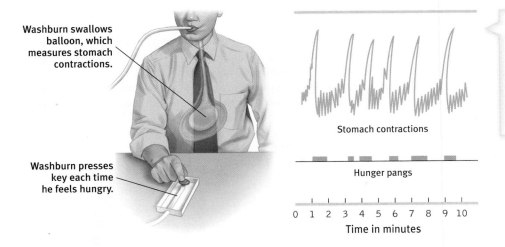

Washburn swallows balloon, which measures stomach contractions.

Washburn presses key each time he feels hungry.

Stomach contractions

Hunger pangs

0 1 2 3 4 5 6 7 8 9 10
Time in minutes

FIGURE 10.4
Monitoring stomach contractions Using this procedure, Washburn showed that stomach contractions (transmitted by the stomach balloon) accompany feelings of hunger (indicated by a key press). (From Cannon, 1929.)

Body Chemistry and the Brain

Somehow, somewhere, your body is keeping tabs on the energy it takes in and the energy it uses. If this weren't true, you would be unable to maintain a stable body weight. A major resource of energy in your body is the blood sugar **glucose.** If your blood glucose level drops, you won't consciously feel this change, but your stomach, intestines, and liver will signal your brain to motivate eating. Your brain, which is automatically monitoring your blood chemistry and your body's internal state, will then trigger hunger.

How does the brain integrate these messages and sound the alarm? The work is done by several neural areas, some housed deep in the brain within the hypothalamus (**FIGURE 10.5**). This neural traffic intersection includes areas that influence eating. For example, one neural arc (called the *arcuate nucleus*) has a center that secretes appetite-stimulating hormones, and another center that secretes appetite-suppressing hormones. Explorations of this neural area and others reveal that when an appetite-enhancing center is stimulated electrically, well-fed animals begin to eat. If the area is destroyed, even starving animals have no interest in food. The opposite occurs when an appetite-suppressing area is stimulated: Animals will stop eating. Destroy this area and animals become extremely fat (Duggan & Booth, 1986; Hoebel & Teitelbaum, 1966) (**FIGURE 10.6** on the next page).

FIGURE 10.5
The hypothalamus As we saw in Chapter 2, the hypothalamus (colored red) performs various body maintenance functions, including control of hunger.

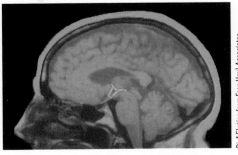

Pix* Elation from Fran Heyl Associates

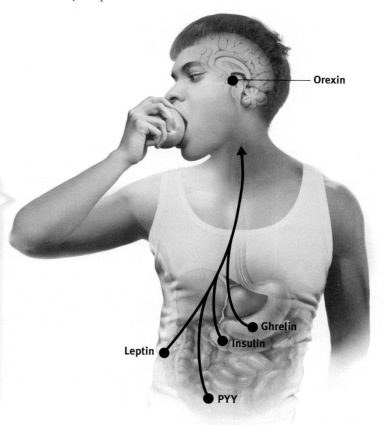

Richard Howard

FIGURE 10.6

Evidence for the brain's control of eating Destroying an appetite-suppressing area of the hypothalamus caused this rat's weight to triple.

Blood vessels supply the hypothalamus, enabling it to respond to our current blood chemistry as well as to incoming neural information about the body's state. One of its tasks is monitoring levels of appetite hormones, such as *ghrelin,* a hunger-arousing hormone secreted by an empty stomach. During bypass surgery for severe obesity, surgeons seal off part of the stomach. The remaining stomach then produces much less ghrelin, and the person's appetite lessens (Lemonick, 2002). Other appetite hormones include *insulin, leptin, orexin,* and *PYY;* **FIGURE 10.7** describes how they influence your feelings of hunger.

The interaction of appetite hormones and brain activity suggests that the body has some sort of "weight thermostat." When semistarved rats fall below their normal weight, this system signals the body to restore the lost weight. The rats' hunger increases and their energy output decreases. If body weight rises—as happens when rats are force fed—hunger decreases and energy expenditure increases. In this way, rats (and humans) tend to hover around a stable weight, or **set point,** influenced in part by heredity (Keesey & Corbett, 1983).

We humans (and other species, too) vary in our **basal metabolic rate,** a measure of how much energy we use to maintain basic body functions when our body is at rest. But we share a common response to decreased food intake: Our basal metabolic rate drops, as it did for participants in Keys' experiment. After 24 weeks of semistarvation, they stabilized at three-quarters of their normal weight, although they were taking in only *half* their previous calories. How did their bodies achieve this dieter's nightmare? They reduced their energy expenditure, partly by being less active, but partly by dropping their basal metabolic rate by 29 percent.

Over the next 40 years you will eat about 20 tons of food. If, during those years, you increase your daily intake by just .01 ounce more than required for your energy needs, you will gain an estimated 24 pounds (Martin et al., 1991).

"Never get a tattoo when you're drunk and hungry."

FIGURE 10.7

The appetite hormones

- *Insulin:* Hormone secreted by pancreas; controls blood glucose.
- *Ghrelin:* Hormone secreted by empty stomach; sends "I'm hungry" signals to the brain.
- *Leptin:* Protein hormone secreted by fat cells; when abundant, causes brain to increase metabolism and decrease hunger.
- *Orexin:* Hunger-triggering hormone secreted by hypothalamus.
- *PYY:* Digestive tract hormone; sends "I'm not hungry" signals to the brain.

Orexin

Ghrelin

Insulin

Leptin

PYY

Some researchers have suggested that the idea of a biologically *fixed* set point is too rigid to explain some things. One thing it doesn't address is that slow, sustained changes in body weight can alter a person's set point (Assanand et al., 1998). Another is that when we have unlimited access to a wide variety of tasty foods, we tend to overeat and gain weight (Raynor & Epstein, 2001). And set points don't explain why psychological factors influence hunger. For all these reasons, some prefer the looser term *settling point* to indicate the level at which a person's weight settles in response to caloric intake and energy use. As we will see next, these factors are influenced by environment as well as biology.

set point the point at which your "weight thermostat" is supposedly set. When your body falls below this weight, increased hunger and a lowered metabolic rate may combine to restore the lost weight.

basal metabolic rate the body's resting rate of energy expenditure.

RETRIEVE IT

• Hunger occurs in response to _____ (low/high) blood glucose and _____ (low/high) levels of ghrelin.

ANSWERS: low; high

The Psychology of Hunger

10-3: What cultural and situational factors influence hunger?

We have seen that our eagerness to eat is pushed by our body chemistry and brain activity. Yet there is more to hunger than meets the stomach. This was strikingly apparent when trickster researchers tested two patients who had no memory for events occurring more than a minute ago (Rozin et al., 1998). If offered a second lunch 20 minutes after eating a normal lunch, both patients readily consumed it . . . and usually a third meal offered 20 minutes after they finished the second. This suggests that one part of our decision to eat is our memory of the time of our last meal. As time passes, we think about eating again, and those thoughts trigger feelings of hunger.

Taste Preferences: Biology and Culture

Body chemistry and environmental factors together influence not only the when of hunger, but also the what—our taste preferences. When feeling tense or depressed, do you crave starchy, carbohydrate-laden foods? Carbohydrates such as pasta, chips, and sweets help boost levels of the neurotransmitter serotonin, which has calming effects. When stressed, even rats find it extra rewarding to scarf Oreos (Artiga et al., 2007; Boggiano et al., 2005).

Our preferences for sweet and salty tastes are genetic and universal, but conditioning can intensify or alter those preferences. People given highly salted foods may develop a liking for excess salt (Beauchamp, 1987). People sickened by a food may develop an aversion to it. (The frequency of children's illnesses provides many chances for them to learn to avoid certain foods.)

Our culture teaches us that some foods are acceptable but others are not. Bedouins enjoy eating the eye of a camel, which most North Americans would find repulsive. North Americans and Europeans also shun horse, dog, and rat meat, all of which are prized elsewhere.

But there is biological wisdom to many of our taste preferences. Environments can influence the human genetics that affect diet and taste. In places where agriculture has produced milk, for example, survival patterns have favored people with lactose tolerance (Arjamaa & Vuorisalo, 2010). And in hot climates (where foods spoil more quickly) recipes often include spices that inhibit the growth of bacteria (**FIGURE 10.8** on the next page). India averages nearly 10 spices per meat recipe; Finland, 2 spices. Pregnancy's food dislikes— and the nausea associated with them—peak about the tenth week, when the developing embryo is most vulnerable to toxins.

An acquired taste People everywhere learn to enjoy the fatty, bitter, or spicy foods common in their culture. For Yupik Alaska Natives (left), but not for most other North Americans, *akutaq* (sometimes called "Eskimo ice cream"), traditionally made with reindeer fat, seal oil, and wild berries, is a tasty treat. For Peruvians, roasted guinea pig (right) is similarly delicious.

AP Photo/Al Grillo

Jeffrey Jackson/Alamy

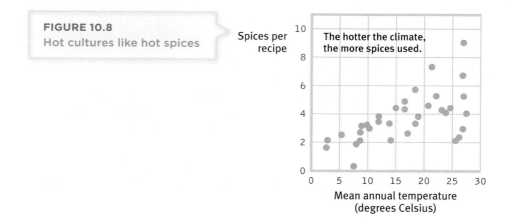

FIGURE 10.8
Hot cultures like hot spices

Spices per recipe

The hotter the climate, the more spices used.

Mean annual temperature (degrees Celsius)

Rats tend to avoid unfamiliar foods (Sclafani, 1995). So do we, especially those that are animal based. This *neophobia* (dislike of things unfamiliar) surely was adaptive for our ancestors by protecting them from potentially toxic substances. In time, though, most people who repeatedly sample an initially novel fruit drink or ethnic food come to appreciate the new taste (Pliner, 1982, Pliner et al., 1993).

Situational Influences on Eating

To a surprising extent, situations also control our eating—a phenomenon psychologists have called the *ecology of eating*. Here are three situations you may have noticed but underestimated:

- Do you eat more when eating with others? Most of us do (Herman et al., 2003; Hetherington et al., 2006). After a party, you may realize you've overeaten. This happens because the presence of others tends to amplify our natural behavior tendencies. (You'll hear more about *social facilitation* in Chapter 13.)

- *Unit bias* occurs with similar mindlessness. Working with researchers at France's National Center for Scientific Research, Andrew Geier and his colleagues (2006) explored a possible explanation of why French waistlines are smaller than American waistlines. From soda drinks to yogurt sizes, the French offer foods in smaller portion sizes. Does it matter? (One could as well order two small sandwiches as one large one.) To find out, the investigators offered people varieties of free snacks. For example, in the lobby of an apartment house, they laid out either full or half pretzels, big or little Tootsie Rolls, or a big bowl of M&M's with either a small or large serving scoop. Their consistent result: Offered a supersized standard portion, people put away more calories. In other studies (Wansink, 2006, 2007), even nutrition experts helped themselves to 31 percent more ice cream when given a big bowl rather than a small one, and 15 percent more when scooping with a big rather than a small scoop. Portion size matters.

- *Food variety* also stimulates eating. Offered a dessert buffet, we eat more than we do when asked to choose a portion from one favorite dessert. For our early ancestors, these behaviors were adaptive. When foods were abundant and varied, eating more provided a wide range of vitamins and minerals and produced fat that protected them during winter cold or famine. When a bounty of varied foods was unavailable, eating less extended the food supply until winter or famine ended (Polivy et al., 2008; Remick et al., 2009).

RETRIEVE IT

- After an eight-hour hike without food, your long-awaited favorite dish is placed in front of you, and your mouth waters in anticipation. Why?

ANSWER: You have learned to respond to the sight and aroma that signal the food about to enter your mouth. Both *physiological* cues (low blood sugar) and *psychological* cues (anticipation of the tasty meal) heighten your experienced hunger.

Obesity and Weight Control

10-4: What factors predispose some people to become and remain obese?

Obesity can be socially toxic, by affecting both how you are treated and how you feel about yourself. Obesity has been associated with lower psychological well-being, especially among women, and increased risk of depression (de Wit et al., 2010; Luppino et al., 2010; Mendes, 2010). Obese 6- to 9-year-olds are 60 percent more likely to suffer bullying (Lumeng et al., 2010). And, as we will see, obesity has physical health risks as well. Yet few overweight people win the battle of the bulge. Why? And why do some people gain weight while others eat the same amount and seldom add a pound?

The Physiology of Obesity

Our bodies store fat for good reasons. Fat is an ideal form of stored energy—a high-calorie fuel reserve to carry the body through periods when food is scarce—a common occurrence in our prehistoric ancestors' world. No wonder that in many developing societies today (as in Europe in earlier centuries) people find heavier bodies attractive: Obesity signals affluence and social status (Furnham & Baguma, 1994; Swami et al., 2011).

In parts of the world where food and sweets are now abundantly available, the rule that once served our hungry distant ancestors—*When you find energy-rich fat or sugar, eat it!*—has become dysfunctional. Pretty much everywhere this book is being read, people have a growing problem. The World Health Organization (WHO) (2007) has estimated that more than 1 billion people worldwide are overweight, and 300 million of them are clinically *obese,* defined by the WHO as a *body mass index* (BMI) of 30 or more. (See cdc.gov/healthyweight/assessing/bmi to calculate your BMI.) In the United States, the adult obesity rate has more than doubled in the last 40 years, reaching 34 percent, and child-teen obesity has quadrupled (Flegal et al., 2010).

Significant obesity increases the risk of diabetes, high blood pressure, heart disease, gallstones, arthritis, and certain types of cancer, thus increasing health care costs and shortening life expectancy (de Gonzales et al., 2010; Jarrett et al., 2010; Sun, 2009). Recent research also has linked women's obesity to their risk of late-life cognitive decline, including Alzheimer's disease and brain tissue loss (Bruce-Keller et al., 2009; Whitmer et al., 2008). One experiment found improved memory performance 12 weeks after severely obese people had weight-loss surgery and lost significant weight. Those not having the surgery showed some further cognitive decline (Gunstad et al., 2011).

Research on the physiology of obesity challenges the stereotype of severely overweight people being weak-willed gluttons.

Set Point and Metabolism Once we become fat, we require less food to maintain our weight than we did to attain it. Fat has a lower metabolic rate than does muscle—it takes less food energy to maintain. When an overweight person's body drops below its previous set (or settling) point, the person's hunger increases and metabolism decreases. Thus, the body adapts to starvation by burning off fewer calories.

Lean people also seem naturally disposed to move about. They burn more calories than do energy-conserving overweight people who tend to sit still longer (Levine et al., 2005). These individual differences in resting metabolism help explain why two people of the same height, age, and activity level can maintain the same weight, even if one of them eats much less than the other does.

The Genetic Factor Do our genes predispose us to fidget or sit still? Studies do reveal a genetic influence on body weight. Consider two examples:

- Despite shared family meals, adoptive siblings' body weights are uncorrelated with one another or with those of their adoptive parents. Rather, people's weights resemble those of their biological parents (Grilo & Pogue-Geile, 1991).

"Americans, on average, report that they weigh 177 pounds, but would like to weigh 161."

Elizabeth Mendes, www.gallup.com, 2010

• Identical twins have closely similar weights, even when reared apart (Hjelmborg et al., 2008; Plomin et al., 1997). Across studies, their weight correlates +.74. The much lower +.32 correlation among fraternal twins suggests that genes explain two-thirds of our varying body mass (Maes et al., 1997).

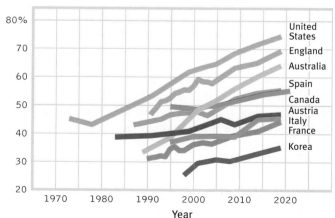

PhotoObjects.net/Jupiterimages

The Food and Activity Factors Genes tell an important part of the obesity story. But environmental factors are mighty important, too.

Studies in Europe, Japan, and the United States show that children and adults who suffer from *sleep loss* are more vulnerable to obesity (Keith et al., 2006; Nedeltcheva et al., 2010; Taheri, 2004a,b). With sleep deprivation, the levels of leptin (which reports body fat to the brain) fall, and ghrelin (the appetite-stimulating stomach hormone) rise.

Social influence is another factor. One 32-year study of 12,067 people found them most likely to become obese when a friend became obese (Christakis & Fowler, 2007). If the obese friend was a close one, the odds of likewise becoming obese almost tripled. Moreover, the correlation among friends' weights was not simply a matter of seeking out similar people as friends. Friends matter.

The strongest evidence that environment influences weight comes from *our fattening world* (**FIGURE 10.9**). What explains this growing problem? Changing *food consumption* and *activity levels* are at work. We are eating more and moving less, with lifestyles approaching those of animal feedlots (where farmers fatten inactive animals). In the United States, jobs requiring moderate physical activity declined from about 50 percent in 1960 to 20 percent in 2011 (Church et al., 2011).

The "bottom" line: New stadiums, theaters, and subway cars—but not airlines—are widening seats to accommodate the girth growth (Hampson, 2000; Kim & Tong, 2010). Washington State Ferries abandoned a 50-year-old standard: "Eighteen-inch butts are a thing of the past" (Shepherd, 1999). New York City, facing a large problem with Big Apple bottoms, has mostly replaced 17.5-inch bucket-style subway seats with bucketless seats (Hampson, 2000). In the end, today's people need more room.

Note how these findings reinforce a familiar lesson from Chapter 9's study of intelligence: There can be high levels of heritability (genetic influence on individual differences) without heredity explaining group differences. Genes mostly determine why one person today is heavier than another. Environment mostly determines why people today

"We put fast food on every corner, we put junk food in our schools, we got rid of [physical education classes], we put candy and soda at the checkout stand of every retail outlet you can think of. The results are in. It worked."

Harold Goldstein, Executive Director of the California Center for Public Health Advocacy, 2009, when imagining a vast U.S. national experiment to encourage weight gain

FIGURE 10.9

Past and projected overweight rates, by the Organisation for Economic Co-operation and Development

CLOSE UP:

Waist Management

Perhaps you are shaking your head: "Slim chance I have of becoming and staying thin." People struggling with obesity are well advised to seek medical evaluation and guidance. For others who wish to take off a few pounds, researchers have offered these tips.

Begin only if you feel motivated and self-disciplined. For most people, permanent weight loss requires making a career of staying thin—a lifelong change in eating habits combined with increased exercise.

Exercise and get enough sleep. Inactive people are often overweight (**FIGURE 10.10**). Especially when supported by 7 to 8 hours of sleep a night, exercise empties fat cells, builds muscle, speeds up metabolism, and helps lower your settling point (Bennett, 1995; Kolata, 1987; Thompson et al., 1982).

Minimize exposure to tempting food cues. Food shop only on a full stomach. Keep tempting foods out of the house, and store other appealing foods out of sight.

Limit variety and eat healthy foods. Given more variety, people consume more; eat simple meals with whole grains, fruits, and vegetables. Healthy fats, such as those found in olive oil and fish, help regulate appetite and artery-clogging cholesterol (Taubes, 2001, 2002). Better crispy greens than Krispy Kremes.

Reduce portion sizes. Serve food with smaller bowls, plates, and utensils.

Don't starve all day and eat one big meal at night. This eating pattern, common among overweight people, slows metabolism. Moreover, those who eat a balanced breakfast are, by late morning, more alert and less fatigued (Spring et al., 1992).

Beware of the binge. Especially for men, eating slowly can lead to eating less (Martin et al., 2007). Among people who do consciously restrain their eating, drinking alcohol or feeling anxious or depressed can unleash the urge to eat (Herman & Polivy, 1980).

Before eating with others, decide how much you want to eat. Eating with friends can distract us from monitoring our own eating (Ward & Mann, 2000).

Remember, most people occasionally lapse. A lapse need not become a full collapse.

Connect to a support group. Join with others, either face-to-face or online, with whom you can share your goals and progress (Freedman, 2011).

FIGURE 10.10

American idle: Couch potatoes beware—TV watching correlates with obesity As lifestyles have become more sedentary and TV watching has increased, so has the percentage of overweight people in Britain, Canada, and the United States (Pagani et al., 2010). When California children were placed in a TV-reduction educational program, they watched less—and lost weight (Robinson, 1999). Don't watch TV? Then watch out for other screen time that keeps your motor idling.

Tony Freeman/PhotoEdit

Skinfold fat measure (mm)

Hours of television watched per day in 1990s study

■ Boys ■ Girls

are heavier than their counterparts 50 years ago. Our eating behavior also demonstrates the now-familiar interaction among biological, psychological, and social-cultural factors. For tips on shedding unwanted pounds, see Close-Up: Waist Management.

RETRIEVE IT

• Which THREE of the following five strategies help prevent unwanted weight gain?

a. Proper sleep

b. Regular exercise

c. Eating the heaviest meal in the evening

d. Eating with friends

e. Joining a support group

ANSWERS: a, b, e.

The Need to Belong

10-5: What evidence points to our human need to belong?

The social stigma attached to obesity may bother an overweight person as much as, or more than, the health concerns. Why? We are what Greek philosopher Aristotle called *the social animal.* Cut off from friends or family—alone in prison or at a new school or in a foreign land—most people feel keenly their lost connections with important others. This deep *need to belong* seems to be a basic human motivation (Baumeister & Leary, 1995). We have a need to affiliate with others, even to become strongly attached to certain others in enduring, close relationships. Human beings, contended personality theorist Alfred Adler, have an "urge to community" (Ferguson, 1989, 2001, 2010). Our psychological needs drive our adaptive behaviors and, when satisfied, enhance our psychological well-being (Sheldon, 2011).

The Benefits of Belonging

Social bonds boosted our early ancestors' chances of survival. Adults who formed attachments were more likely to reproduce and to co-nurture their offspring to maturity. Attachment bonds helped keep those children close to their caregivers, protecting them from many threats. Indeed, to be "wretched" literally means, in its Middle English origin *(wrecche),* to be without kin nearby.

Cooperation also enhanced survival. In solo combat, our ancestors were not the toughest predators. But as hunters, they learned that six hands were better than two. As food gatherers, they gained protection from two-footed and four-footed enemies by traveling in groups. Those who felt a need to belong survived and reproduced most successfully, and their genes now predominate. We are innately social creatures. People in every society on Earth belong to groups and (as Chapter 13 explains) prefer and favor "us" over "them."

Do you have close friends—people with whom you freely disclose your ups and downs? Having someone who rejoices with us over good news helps us feel even better about the good news, as well as about the friendship (Reis et al., 2010). The need to belong runs deeper, it seems, than any need to be rich. One study found that *very* happy university students were distinguished not by their money but by their "rich and satisfying close relationships" (Diener & Seligman, 2002).

The need to belong colors our thoughts and emotions. We spend a great deal of time thinking about actual and hoped-for relationships. When relationships form, we often feel joy. Falling in mutual love, people have been known to feel their cheeks ache from their irrepressible grins. Asked, "What is necessary for your happiness?" or "What is it that makes your life meaningful?" most people have mentioned—before anything else—close, satisfying relationships with family, friends, or romantic partners (Berscheid, 1985). Happiness hits close to home.

Consider: What was your most satisfying moment in the past week? Researchers asked that question of American and South Korean collegians, then asked them to rate how much that moment had satisfied various needs (Sheldon et al., 2001). In both countries, the peak moment had contributed most to satisfaction of self-esteem and relatedness-belonging needs. When our need for relatedness is satisfied in balance with two other basic psychological needs—*autonomy* (a sense of personal control) and *competence*—we experience a deep sense of well-being, and our self-esteem rides high (Deci & Ryan, 2002, 2009; Milyavskaya et al., 2009; Sheldon & Niemiec, 2006). Indeed, *self-esteem* is a gauge of how valued and accepted we feel (Leary et al., 1998).

Is it surprising, then, that so much of our social behavior aims to increase our feelings of belonging? To gain acceptance, we generally conform to group standards. We monitor our behavior, hoping to make a good impression. We spend billions on clothes, cosmetics, and diet and fitness aids—all motivated by our search for love and acceptance.

"We must love one another or die."

W. H. Auden "September 1, 1939"

Photodisc

By drawing a sharp circle around "us," the need to belong feeds both deep attachments and menacing threats. Out of our need to define a "we" come loving families, faithful friendships, and team spirit, but also teen gangs, ethnic rivalries, and fanatic nationalism.

For good or for bad, we work hard to build and maintain our relationships. Familiarity breeds liking, not contempt. Thrown together in groups at school, at work, in a tornado shelter, we behave like magnets, moving closer, forming bonds. Parting, we feel distress. We promise to call, to write, to come back for reunions.

This happens in part because feelings of love activate brain reward and safety systems. In one experiment involving exposure to heat, deeply-in-love university students felt markedly less pain when looking at their beloved's picture (rather than viewing someone else's photo or being distracted by a word task) (Younger et al., 2010). Pictures of our loved ones also activate a brain region associated with safety—the prefrontal cortex—that dampens feelings of physical pain (Eisenberger et al., 2011). Love is a natural painkiller.

AP/Wide World Photos

The need to connect Six days a week, women from the Philippines work as "domestic helpers" in 154,000 Hong Kong households. On Sundays, they throng to the central business district to picnic, dance, sing, talk, and laugh. "Humanity could stage no greater display of happiness," reported one observer (*Economist,* 2001).

Even when bad relationships break, people suffer. In one 16-nation survey, and in repeated U.S. surveys, separated and divorced people have been half as likely as married people to say they were "very happy" (Inglehart, 1990; NORC, 2010). After such separations, loneliness and anger—and sometimes even a strange desire to be near the former partner—linger. For those in abusive relationships, the fear of being alone sometimes seems worse than the certainty of emotional or physical pain.

Children who move through a series of foster homes or through repeated family relocations know the fear of being alone. After repeated disruption of budding attachments, they may have difficulty forming deep attachments (Oishi & Schimmack, 2011). The evidence is clearest at the extremes—the children who grow up in institutions without a sense of belonging to anyone, or who are locked away at home and severely neglected. Too many become withdrawn, frightened, speechless. Feeling insecurely attached to others during childhood can persist into adulthood, in two main forms (Fraley et al., 2011). Some display *insecure anxious attachment,* constantly craving acceptance but remaining vigilant to signs of possible rejection. Others are trapped in *insecure avoidant attachment,* feeling such discomfort over getting close to others that they employ avoidant strategies to maintain their distance.

No matter how secure our early years were, we all experience anxiety, loneliness, jealousy, or guilt when something threatens or dissolves our social ties. Much as life's best moments occur when close relationships begin—making a new friend, falling in love, having a baby—life's worst moments happen when close relationships end (Jaremka et al., 2011). Bereaved, we may feel life is empty, pointless. Even the first weeks living on a college campus away from home can be distressing.

For immigrants and refugees moving alone to new places, the stress and loneliness can be depressing. After years of placing individual families in isolated communities, U.S. immigration policies began to encourage *chain migration* (Pipher, 2002). The second refugee Sudanese family settling in a town generally has an easier adjustment than the first.

Social isolation can put us at risk for mental decline and ill health (Cacioppo & Hawkley, 2009). But if feelings of acceptance and connection increase, so will self-esteem, positive feelings, and the desire to help rather than hurt others (Blackhart et al., 2009; Buckley & Leary, 2001).

The Pain of Being Shut Out

Can you recall feeling excluded or ignored or shunned? Perhaps you received the silent treatment. Perhaps people avoided you or averted their eyes in your presence or even mocked you behind your back. If you are like others, even being in a group speaking a different language may have left you feeling excluded, a linguistic outsider (Dotan-Eliaz,

The Granger Collection, New York

Enduring the pain of ostracism
Caucasian cadets at the United States Military Academy at West Point ostracized Henry Flipper for years, hoping he would drop out. He somehow resisted their cruelty and in 1877 became the first African-American West Point graduate.

Note: The researchers later *debriefed* and reassured the participants.

2009). In one mock-interview study, women felt more excluded if interviewers used gender-exclusive language *(he, his, him)* rather than inclusive *(his or her)* or neutral *(their)* language (Stout & Dasgupta, 2011).

All these experiences are instances of *ostracism*—of social exclusion (Williams et al., 2007, 2009). Worldwide, humans use many forms of ostracism—exile, imprisonment, solitary confinement—to punish, and therefore control, social behavior. For children, even a brief time-out in isolation can be punishing. Asked to describe personal episodes that made them feel especially *bad* about themselves, people will—about four times in five—describe a relationship difficulty (Pillemer et al., 2007). Feelings of loneliness can also spread from person to person like a disease, through one's social network (Cacioppo et al., 2009).

Being shunned—given the cold shoulder or the silent treatment, with others' eyes avoiding yours—threatens one's need to belong (Williams & Zadro, 2001). "It's the meanest thing you can do to someone, especially if you know they can't fight back. I never should have been born," said Lea, a lifelong victim of the silent treatment by her mother and grandmother. Like Lea, people often respond to ostracism with depressed moods, initial efforts to restore their acceptance, and then withdrawal. After two years of silent treatment by his employer, Richard reported, "I came home every night and cried. I lost 25 pounds, had no self-esteem and felt that I wasn't worthy."

To experience ostracism is to experience real pain, as social psychologists Kipling Williams and his colleagues were surprised to discover in their studies of *cyber-ostracism* (Gonsalkorale & Williams, 2006). (Perhaps you can recall the feeling of being unfriended or having few followers on a social networking site, being ignored in a chat room, or having a text message or e-mail go unanswered.) Such ostracism, they discovered, takes a toll: It elicits increased activity in brain areas, such as the *anterior cingulate cortex,* that also activate in response to physical pain (Kross et al., 2011; Lieberman & Eisenberger, 2009). That helps explain another surprising finding: The pain-reliever acetaminophen (as in Tylenol and Anacin) lessens *social* as well as physical pain (DeWall et al., 2010). Across cultures, people use the same words (for example, *hurt, crushed*) for social pain and physical pain (MacDonald & Leary, 2005). Psychologically, we seem to experience social pain with the same emotional unpleasantness that marks physical pain.

Pain, whatever its source, focuses our attention and motivates corrective action. Rejected and unable to remedy the situation, people may seek new friends or relieve stress in a strengthened religious faith (Aydin et al., 2010). Or they may turn nasty. In a series of experiments, researchers (Baumeister et al., 2002; Twenge et al., 2001, 2002, 2007) told some students (who had taken a personality test) that they were "the type likely to end up alone later in life," or that people they had met didn't want them in a group that was forming. They told other students that they would have "rewarding relationships throughout life," or that "everyone chose you as someone they'd like to work with." Those excluded became much more likely to engage in self-defeating behaviors and to underperform on aptitude tests. The rejection also interfered with their empathy

CBS/Getty Images

Social acceptance and rejection Successful participants on the reality TV show *Survivor* form alliances and gain acceptance among their peers. The rest receive the ultimate social punishment as they are "voted off the island."

for others and made them more likely to act in disparaging or aggressive ways against those who had excluded them (blasting them with noise, for example). "If intelligent, well-adjusted, successful . . . students can turn aggressive in response to a small laboratory experience of social exclusion," noted the research team, "it is disturbing to imagine the aggressive tendencies that might arise from . . . chronic exclusion from desired groups in actual social life." Indeed, as Williams (2007) has observed, ostracism "weaves through case after case of school violence."

RETRIEVE IT

- How have students reacted in studies where they were made to feel rejected and unwanted? What helps explain these results?

ANSWER: These students' basic *need to belong* seems to have been disrupted. They engaged in more self-defeating behaviors, underperformed on aptitude tests, and displayed less empathy and more aggression.

Connecting and Social Networking

10-6: How does social networking influence us?

As social creatures, we live for connection. Asked what he had learned from studying 238 Harvard University men from the 1930s to the end of their lives, researcher George Vaillant (2009) replied, "The only thing that really matters in life are your relationships to other people." A South African Zulu saying captures the idea: *Umuntu ngumuntu ngabantu*—"a person is a person through other persons."

Mobile Networks and Social Media

Look around and see humans connecting: talking, texting, posting, chatting, social gaming, e-mailing. The changes in how we connect have been fast and vast:

- Cell phones have been history's most rapidly adopted technology. At the end of 2010, the world had 6.9 billion people and 5.3 billion mobile cell-phone subscriptions (ITU, 2010). Asia and Europe lead the way. In India, 618 million people have mobile phone access—reportedly almost double the 366 million with access to a toilet (*Harper's*, 2010). But American youth are keeping up with the world: 85 percent of 15- to 18-year-olds are cell-phone users (Kaiser, 2010).

- Texting and e-mailing have been displacing phone talking, which now accounts for less than half of U.S. mobile network traffic (Wortham, 2010). Now, in Canada and elsewhere, e-mailing is itself declining, displaced by texting, Facebook, and other messaging technology (IPSOS, 2010a). Speedy texting is not really writing, observes John McWhorter (2012), but rather a new form of conversation— "fingered speech."

- Ninety percent of U.S. teens text, up from 50 percent in 2006. Half (mostly females) send 50 or more texts daily; one-third send 200 (Lenhart, 2010). For many, it's as though friends, for better or worse, are always present.

- How many of us are using social networking sites, such as Facebook? Among 2010's entering American collegians, 94 percent were (Pryor et al., 2011). With a "critical mass" of your friends on a social network, its lure becomes hard to resist. Such is our need to belong. Check in or miss out.

The Social Effects of Social Networking

By connecting like-minded people, the Internet serves as a social amplifier. It also functions as an online dating matchmaker (more on those topics in Chapter 13). As electronic communication becomes part of the "new normal," researchers are exploring how these changes affect our relationships.

"There's no question in my mind about what stands at the heart of the communication revolution—the human desire to connect."

Skype President Josh Silverman, 2009

Thomas Northcut/Jupiterimages

Are Social Networking Sites Making Us More, or Less, Socially Isolated? In the Internet's early years, when online communication in chat rooms and during social games was mostly between strangers, the adolescents and adults who spent more time online spent less time with friends (Kraut et al., 1998; Mesch, 2001; Nie, 2001). As a result, their offline relationships suffered. Even today, lonely people tend to spend greater-than-average time online (Bonetti et al., 2010; Stepanikova et al., 2010). Social networkers are less likely to know their real-world neighbors and are "64 percent less likely than non-Internet users to rely on neighbors for help in caring for themselves or a family member" (Pew, 2009).

Despite the decrease in neighborliness, the Internet is diversifying our social networks. (I am now connected to other hearing-technology advocates across the world.) Social networking is also mostly strengthening our connections with people we already know (DiSalvo, 2010; Valkenburg & Peter, 2010). If your Facebook page helps you connect with friends, stay in touch with extended family, or find support in facing challenges, then you are not alone (Rainie et al., 2011). For many, though, being alone is not the problem. If you are like other students, two days of Facebook deprivation would be followed by a glut of Facebook use, much as you would eat voraciously after a two-day food fast (Sheldon et al., 2011). Social networks connect us, but they can also become a gigantic time- and attention-sucking diversion. For some research-based strategies, see Close-Up: Managing Your Social Networking.

© 2009 Isabella Bannerman. King Features Syndicate

Does Electronic Communication Stimulate Healthy Self-Disclosure? As we will see in Chapter 11, confiding in others can be a healthy way of coping with day-to-day challenges. When communicating electronically rather than face to face, we often are less focused on others' reactions, less self-conscious, and thus less inhibited. We become more willing to share joys, worries, and vulnerabilities. Sometimes this is taken to an extreme, as when "sexting" teens send nude photos of themselves, or "cyber-bullies" hound a victim, or hate groups post messages promoting bigotry or crimes. More often, however, the increased self-disclosure serves to deepen friendships (Valkenburg & Peter, 2010).

Although electronic networking pays dividends, nature has designed us for face-to-face communication, which appears to be the better predictor of life satisfaction (Killingsworth & Gilbert, 2010; Lee et al., 2011). Texting and e-mailing are rewarding, but eye-to-eye conversation with family and friends is even more so.

Do Social Networking Profiles and Posts Reflect People's Actual Personalities? We've all heard stories of Internet predators hiding behind false personalities, values, and motives. Generally, however, social networks reveal people's real personalities. In one study, participants completed a personality test twice. In one test, they described their "actual personality"; in the other, they described their "ideal self." Volunteers then used the participants' Facebook profiles to create an independent set of personality ratings. The ratings based on Facebook profiles were much closer to the participants' actual personalities than to their ideal personalities (Back et al., 2010). In another study, people who seemed most likable on their Facebook page also seemed most likable in face-to-face meetings (Weisbuch et al., 2009). Your Facebook profile may indeed reflect the real you!

ICP-UK/Alamy

Managing Your Social Networking

In today's world, each of us is challenged to find a healthy balance between our real-world time with people and our online sharing. In both Taiwan and the United States, excessive online socializing and gaming have been associated with lower grades (Chen & Fu, 2008; Kaiser Foundation, 2010). In one U.S. survey, 47 percent of the heaviest users of the Internet and other media were receiving mostly *C* grades or lower, as were 23 percent of the lightest users (Kaiser Foundation, 2010). Except when sleeping, the heaviest users may be almost constantly connected.

If you're trying to maintain a healthy balance between online connecting and real-world responsibilities, experts offer these practical suggestions:

- *Monitor your time.* Keep a log of how you use your time. Then ask yourself, "Does my time use reflect my priorities? Am I spending more time online than I intended? Is my time online interfering with school or work performance? Have family or friends commented on this?"

- *Monitor your feelings.* Again, ask yourself, "Am I emotionally distracted by online preoccupations? When I disconnect and move on to another activity, how do I feel?"

- *"Hide" your more distracting online friends.* And in your own postings, practice the golden rule. Before you post, ask yourself, "Is this something I'd care about reading if someone else posted it?"

- *Try turning off your handheld devices or leaving them elsewhere.* Selective attention—the flashlight of your mind—can be in only one place at a time. "One of the most stubborn, persistent phenomena of the mind," notes cognitive psychologist Daniel Willingham (2010), "is that when you do two things at once, you don't do either one as well as when you do them one at a time." When you want to study or work productively, squelch the temptation to check for messages, posts, or e-mails. And disable sound alerts and pop-ups.

These distractions can interrupt your work and hijack your attention just when you've managed to get focused.

- *Try a Facebook fast (give it up for an hour, a day, or a week) or a time-controlled social media diet (check in only after homework is done, or only during a lunch break).* Take notes on what you're losing and gaining on your new "diet."

- *Replenish your focus with a nature walk.* University of Michigan researchers have reported that a walk in the woods, unlike walking on a busy street, replenishes people's capacity for focused attention (Berman et al., 2008). People learn better after a peaceful walk that restores their fatigued attention.

"The solution is not to bemoan technology but to develop strategies of self-control, as we do with every other temptation in life."

Psychologist Steven Pinker, "Mind Over Mass Media," 2010

DOONESBURY   BY GARRY TRUDEAU

Does Social Networking Promote Narcissism? *Narcissism* is self-esteem gone awry. Narcissistic people are self-important, self-focused, and self-promoting. Some personality tests assess narcissism with items such as "I like to be the center of attention." Given our constant social comparison—our measuring ourselves against others—many Facebook users can't resist comparing numbers of friends. (The average is about 125—near the 150 people with whom evolutionary psychologist Robin Dunbar [1992, 2010] estimates we can have meaningful, supportive relationships [also a typical size of tribal villages].)

© Campbell Sandilands

Calum's road: What grit can accomplish Having spent his life on the Scottish island of Raasay, farming a small patch of land, tending its lighthouse, and fishing, Malcolm ("Calum") MacLeod (1911–1988) felt anguished. His local government repeatedly refused to build a road that would enable vehicles to reach his north end of the island. With the once-flourishing population there having dwindled to two— MacLeod and his wife—he responded with heroic determination. One spring morning in 1964, MacLeod, then in his fifties, gathered an ax, a chopper, a shovel, and a wheelbarrow. By hand, he began to transform the existing footpath into a 1.75-mile road (Miers, 2009).

"With a road," a former neighbor explained, "he hoped new generations of people would return to the north end of Raasay," restoring its culture (Hutchinson, 2006). Day after day he worked through rough hillsides, along hazardous cliff faces, and over peat bogs. Finally, 10 years later, he completed his supreme achievement. The road, which the government has since surfaced, remains a visible example of what vision plus determined grit can accomplish. It bids us each to ponder: What "roads"—what achievements—might we, with sustained effort, build in the years before us?

"Genius is 1% inspiration and 99% perspiration."

Thomas Edison, 1847–1931

Those who score high on narcissism are especially active on social networking sites. They collect more superficial "friends." They offer more staged, glamorous photos. And, not surprisingly, they *seem* more narcissistic to strangers viewing their pages (Buffardi & Campbell, 2008).

For narcissists, social networking sites are more than a gathering place; they are a feeding trough. In one study, college students were randomly assigned either to edit and explain their MySpace page for 15 minutes, or to use that time to study and explain a Google Maps routing (Freeman & Twenge, 2010). After completing their tasks, all were tested. Who then scored higher on a narcissism measure? Those who had spent the time focused on themselves.

RETRIEVE IT

• Social networking tends to _____ (strengthen/weaken) your relationships with people you already know, _____ (increase/decrease) your self-disclosure, and _____ (reveal/hide) your true personality.

ANSWERS: strengthen; increase; reveal

Achievement Motivation

10-7: What is achievement motivation?

The biological perspective on motivation—the idea that physiological needs drive us to satisfy those needs—provides only a partial explanation of what energizes and directs our behavior. Hunger and the need to belong have social as well as biological components. Moreover, there are motives that seem to have little obvious survival value. Billionaires may be motivated to make ever more money, movie stars to become ever more famous, politicians to achieve ever more power, daredevils to seek ever greater thrills. Such motives seem not to diminish when they are fed. The more we achieve, the more we may need to achieve.

Think of someone you know who strives to succeed by excelling at any task where evaluation is possible. Now think of someone who is less driven. Psychologist Henry Murray (1938) defined the first person's **achievement motivation** as a desire for significant accomplishment, for mastering skills or ideas, for control, and for rapidly attaining a high standard.

As you might expect from their persistence and eagerness for realistic challenges, people with high achievement motivation do achieve more. One study followed the lives of 1528 California children whose intelligence test scores were in the top 1 percent. Forty years later, when researchers compared those who were most and least successful professionally, they found a motivational difference. Those most successful were more ambitious, energetic, and persistent. As children, they had more active hobbies. As adults, they participated in more groups and favored being sports participants to being spectators (Goleman, 1980). Gifted children are able learners. Accomplished adults are tenacious doers. Most of us are energetic doers when starting and finishing a project. It's easiest—have you noticed?—to "get stuck in the middle," which is when high achievers keep going (Bonezzi et al., 2011).

In other studies of both secondary school and university students, self-discipline has been a better predictor of school performance, attendance, and graduation honors than intelligence scores have been. When combined with a positive enthusiasm, sustained, gritty effort predicts success for teachers, too—with their students making good academic progress (Duckworth et al., 2009). "Discipline outdoes talent," concluded researchers Angela Duckworth and Martin Seligman (2005, 2006).

Discipline also refines talent. By their early twenties, top violinists have accumulated some 10,000 lifetime practice hours—double the practice time of other violin students aiming to be teachers (Ericsson 2001, 2006, 2007). From his studies, Herbert Simon (1998), a psychologist who won a Nobel Prize in Economics, formed what Chapter 9 called the *10-year rule:* World-class experts in a field typically have invested "at least 10 years of hard work—say, 40 hours a week for 50 weeks a year." A study of outstanding scholars, athletes, and artists found that all were highly motivated and self-disciplined, willing to dedicate hours every day to the pursuit of their goals (Bloom, 1985). These superstar achievers were distinguished not so much by their extraordinary natural talent as by their extraordinary daily discipline.

What distinguishes extremely successful individuals from their equally talented peers, note Duckworth and Seligman, is *grit*—passionate dedication to an ambitious, long-term goal. Although intelligence is distributed like a bell curve, achievements are not. That tells us that achievement involves much more than raw ability. That is why organizational psychologists seek ways to engage and motivate ordinary people doing ordinary jobs (see Appendix B: Psychology at Work). And that is why training students in "hardiness"—resilience under stress—leads to better grades (Maddi et al., 2009).

achievement motivation a desire for significant accomplishment, for mastery of skills or ideas, for control, and for rapidly attaining a high standard.

Emotion: Arousal, Behavior, and Cognition

10-8: How do arousal, cognition, and expressive behavior interact in emotion?

Motivated behavior is often connected to powerful emotions. My own need to belong was unforgettably challenged one day. I went to a huge store to drop off film and brought along Peter, my toddler first-born child. As I set Peter down on his feet and prepared to complete the paperwork, a passerby warned, "You'd better be careful or you'll lose that boy!" Not more than a few breaths later, after dropping the film in the slot, I turned and found no Peter beside me.

With mild anxiety, I peered around one end of the counter. No Peter in sight. With slightly more anxiety, I peered around the other end. No Peter there, either. Now, with my heart accelerating, I circled the neighboring counters. Still no Peter anywhere. As anxiety turned to panic, I began racing up and down the store aisles. He was nowhere to be found. Apprised of my alarm, the store manager used the public-address system to ask customers to assist in looking for a missing child. Soon after, I passed the customer who had warned me. "I told you that you were going to lose him!" he now scorned. With visions of kidnapping (strangers routinely adored that beautiful child), I braced for the possibility that my negligence had caused me to lose what I loved above all else, and that I might have to return home and face my wife without our only child.

But then, as I passed the customer service counter yet again, there he was, having been found and returned by some obliging customer. In an instant, the arousal of terror spilled into ecstasy. Clutching my son, with tears suddenly flowing, I found myself unable to speak my thanks and stumbled out of the store awash in grateful joy.

Where do such emotions come from? Why do we have them? What are they made of? Emotions don't exist just to give us interesting experiences. They are our body's adaptive response, increasing our chances of survival. When we face challenges, emotions focus our attention and energize our actions (Cyders & Smith, 2008). Our heart races. Our pace quickens. All our senses go on high alert. Receiving unexpected good news, we may find our eyes tearing up. We raise our hands triumphantly. We feel exuberance and a newfound confidence.

Courtesy of David G. Myers

Not only emotion, but most psychological phenomena (vision, sleep, memory, sex, and so forth) can be approached these three ways—physiologically, behaviorally, and cognitively.

As my panicked search for Peter illustrates, **emotions** are a mix of:

- *bodily arousal* (heart pounding).
- *expressive behaviors* (quickened pace).
- *conscious experience,* including thoughts *("Is this a kidnapping?")* and feelings (panic, fear, joy).

The puzzle for psychologists is figuring out how these three pieces fit together. To do that, we need answers to two big questions:

1. A chicken-and-egg debate: Does your bodily arousal come *before* or *after* your emotional feelings? (Did I first notice my racing heart and faster step, and then feel terror about losing Peter? Or did my sense of fear come first, stirring my heart and legs to respond?)

2. How do *thinking* (cognition) and *feeling* interact? Does cognition always come before emotion? (Did I think about a kidnapping threat before I reacted emotionally?)

Historical emotion theories, as well as current research, have sought to answer these questions.

Historical Emotion Theories

James-Lange Theory: Arousal Comes Before Emotion

Common sense tells most of us that we cry because we are sad, lash out because we are angry, tremble because we are afraid. First comes conscious awareness, then the feeling. But to pioneering psychologist William James, this commonsense view of emotion had things backward. Rather, "We feel sorry because we cry, angry because we strike, afraid because we tremble" (1890, p. 1066). James' idea was also proposed by Danish physiologist Carl Lange, and so is called the **James–Lange theory.** James and Lange might have guessed that I noticed my racing heart and then, shaking with fright, felt the whoosh of emotion—that my feeling of fear *followed* my body's response.

Cannon-Bard Theory: Arousal and Emotion Occur Simultaneously

Physiologist Walter Cannon (1871–1945) disagreed with James and Lange. Does a racing heart signal fear or anger or love? The body's responses—heart rate, perspiration, and body temperature—are too similar, and they change too slowly, to *cause* the different emotions, said Cannon. He, and later another physiologist, Philip Bard, concluded that our bodily arousal and emotional experience occur simultaneously. So, according to the **Cannon–Bard theory,** my heart began pounding *as* I experienced fear. The emotion-triggering stimulus traveled to my sympathetic nervous system, causing my body's arousal. *At the same time,* it traveled to my brain's cortex, causing my awareness of my emotion. My pounding heart did not cause my feeling of fear, nor did my feeling of fear cause my pounding heart. Bodily responses and experienced emotions are separate.

The Cannon-Bard theory has been challenged by studies of people with severed spinal cords, including a survey of 25 soldiers who suffered such injuries in World War II (Hohmann, 1966). Those with *lower-spine injuries,* who had lost sensation only in their legs, reported little change in their emotions' intensity. Those with *high spinal cord injuries,* who could feel nothing below the neck, did report changes. Some reactions were much less intense than before the injuries. Anger, one man confessed, "just doesn't have the heat to it that it used to. It's a mental kind of anger." Other emotions, those expressed mostly in body areas above the neck, were felt *more* intensely. These men reported increases in weeping, lumps in the throat, and getting choked up when saying good-bye, worshiping, or watching a touching movie. Such evidence has led some researchers to view feelings as "mostly shadows" of our bodily responses and behaviors (Damasio, 2003).

But most researchers now agree that our emotions also involve cognition (Averill, 1993; Barrett, 2006). Whether we fear the man behind us on the dark street depends entirely on whether we interpret his actions as threatening or friendly.

Joy expressed According to the James-Lange theory, we don't just smile because we share our teammates' joy. We also share the joy because we are smiling with them.

REUTERS/Matt Sullivan

• According to the Cannon-Bard theory, (a) our *physiological response* to a stimulus (for example, a pounding heart), and (b) the *emotion* we experience (for example, fear) occur _____ (simultaneously/sequentially). According to the James-Lange theory, (a) and (b) occur _____ (simultaneously/sequentially).

ANSWERS: simultaneously; sequentially (first the physiological response, and then the experienced emotion)

Schachter-Singer Two-Factor Theory: Arousal + Label = Emotion

Stanley Schachter and Jerome Singer (1962) proposed a third theory: Our physical reactions and our thoughts (perceptions, memories, and interpretations) together create emotion. In their **two-factor theory,** emotions therefore have two ingredients: physical arousal and cognitive appraisal. In their view, an emotional experience requires a conscious interpretation of arousal.

Consider how arousal spills over from one event to the next. Imagine arriving home after an invigorating run and finding a message that you got a longed-for job. With arousal lingering from the run, would you feel more elated than if you received this news after awakening from a nap?

To explore this *spillover effect*, Schachter and Singer injected college men with the hormone epinephrine, which triggers feelings of arousal. Picture yourself as a participant: After receiving the injection, you go to a waiting room, where you find yourself with another person (actually an accomplice of the experimenters) who is acting either euphoric or irritated. As you observe this person, you begin to feel your heart race, your body flush, and your breathing become more rapid. If you had been told to expect these effects from the injection, what would you feel? The actual volunteers felt little emotion—because they attributed their arousal to the drug. But if you had been told the injection would produce no effects, what would you feel? Perhaps you would react as another group of participants did. They "caught" the apparent emotion of the other person in the waiting room. They became happy if the accomplice was acting euphoric, and testy if the accomplice was acting irritated.

This discovery—that a stirred-up state can be experienced as one emotion or another, depending on how we interpret and label it—has been replicated in dozens of experiments (Reisenzein, 1983; Sinclair et al., 1994; Zillmann, 1986). As Daniel Gilbert (2006) noted, "Feelings that one interprets as fear in the presence of a sheer drop may be interpreted as lust in the presence of a sheer blouse."

The point to remember: Arousal fuels emotion; cognition channels it.

emotion a response of the whole organism, involving (1) physiological arousal, (2) expressive behaviors, and (3) conscious experience.

James-Lange theory the theory that our experience of emotion is our awareness of our physiological responses to emotion-arousing stimuli.

Cannon-Bard theory the theory that an emotion-arousing stimulus simultaneously triggers (1) physiological responses and (2) the subjective experience of emotion.

two-factor theory the Schachter-Singer theory that to experience emotion one must (1) be physically aroused and (2) cognitively label the arousal.

The spillover effect Arousal from a soccer match can fuel anger, which can descend into rioting or other violent confrontations.

Reuters/Corbis

• According to Schachter and Singer, two factors lead to our experience of an emotion: (1) physiological arousal and (2) _____ appraisal.

ANSWER: cognitive

Zajonc, LeDoux, and Lazarus: Does Cognition Always Precede Emotion?

But is the heart always subject to the mind? Must we *always* interpret our arousal before we can experience an emotion? Robert Zajonc (pronounced ZI-yence; 1980, 1984a) contended that we actually have many emotional reactions apart from, or even before, our interpretation of a situation. Perhaps you can recall liking something or someone immediately, without knowing why.

In earlier chapters, we noted that when people repeatedly view stimuli flashed too briefly for them to interpret, they come to prefer those stimuli. Unaware of having previously seen them, they nevertheless rather like them. We have an acutely sensitive automatic radar for emotionally significant information, such that even a subliminally flashed stimulus can prime us to feel better or worse about a follow-up stimulus (Murphy et al., 1995; Zeelenberg et al., 2006). In experiments, thirsty people were given a fruit-flavored drink after viewing a subliminally flashed (thus unperceived) face. Those exposed to a happy face drank about 50 percent more than those exposed to a neutral face (Berridge & Winkielman, 2003). Those flashed an angry face drank substantially less.

Neuroscientists are charting the neural pathways of both "bottom-up" and "top-down" emotions (Ochsner et al., 2009). Our emotional responses can follow two different brain pathways. Some emotions (especially more complex feelings like hatred and love) travel a "high road." A stimulus following this path would travel (by way of the thalamus) to the brain's cortex (**FIGURE 10.11a**). There, it would be analyzed and labeled before the command is sent out, via the amygdala (an emotion-control center), to respond.

But sometimes our emotions (especially simple likes, dislikes, and fears) take what Joseph LeDoux (2002) has called the "low road," a neural shortcut that bypasses the cortex. Following the low-road pathway, a fear-provoking stimulus would travel from the eye or ear (again via the thalamus) directly to the amygdala (Figure 10.11b). This shortcut, bypassing the cortex, enables our greased-lightning emotional response before our intellect intervenes.

FIGURE 10.11

The brain's pathways for emotions In the two-track brain, sensory input may be routed (a) to the cortex (via the thalamus) for analysis and then transmission to the amygdala; or (b) directly to the amygdala (via the thalamus) for an instant emotional reaction.

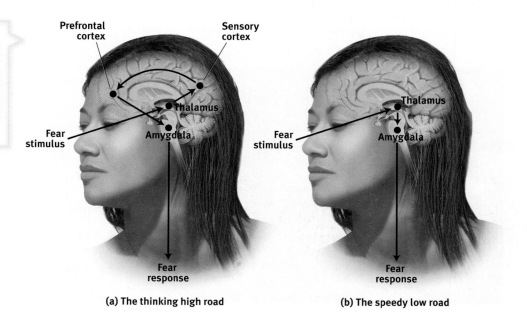

(a) The thinking high road

(b) The speedy low road

Like speedy reflexes that also operate apart from the brain's thinking cortex, the amygdala reactions are so fast that we may be unaware of what's transpired (Dimberg et al., 2000).

The amygdala sends more neural projections up to the cortex than it receives back, which makes it easier for our feelings to hijack our thinking than for our thinking to rule our feelings (LeDoux & Armony, 1999). Thus, in the forest, we can jump at the sound of rustling bushes nearby and leave it to our cortex to decide later whether the sound was made by a snake or by the wind. Such experiences support Zajonc's belief that *some* of our emotional reactions involve no deliberate thinking.

Emotion researcher Richard Lazarus (1991, 1998) conceded that our brains process vast amounts of information without our conscious awareness, and that some emotional responses do not require *conscious* thinking. Much of our emotional life operates via the automatic, speedy low road. But, he asked, how would we *know* what we are reacting to if we did not in some way appraise the situation? The appraisal may be effortless and we may not be conscious of it, but it is still a mental function. To know whether a stimulus is good or bad, the brain must have some idea of what it is (Storbeck et al., 2006). Thus, said Lazarus, emotions arise when we *appraise* an event as harmless or dangerous, whether we truly *know* it is or not. We appraise the sound of the rustling bushes as the presence of a threat. Later, we realize that it was "just the wind."

So, as Zajonc and LeDoux have demonstrated, some emotional responses—especially simple likes, dislikes, and fears—involve no conscious thinking (**FIGURE 10.12**). We may fear a big spider, even if we "know" it is harmless. Such responses are difficult to alter by changing our thinking. We may automatically like one person more than another. This instant appeal can even influence our political decisions if we vote (as many people do) for a candidate we *like* over the candidate expressing positions closer to our own (Westen, 2007).

But our feelings about politics are also subject to our memories, expectations, and interpretations, as Lazarus, Schachter, and Singer might have predicted. Moreover, highly emotional people are intense partly *because* of their interpretations. They may *personalize* events as being somehow directed at them, and they may *generalize* their experiences by blowing single incidents out of proportion (Larsen et al., 1987). Thus, learning to *think* more positively can help people *feel* better. Although the emotional low road functions automatically, the thinking high road allows us to retake some control over our emotional life. Together, automatic emotion and conscious thinking weave the fabric of our emotional lives. (**TABLE 10.1** summarizes these emotion theories.)

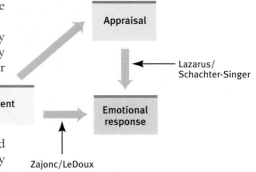

FIGURE 10.12

Two pathways for emotions Zajonc and LeDoux have emphasized that some emotional responses are immediate, before any conscious appraisal. Lazarus, Schachter, and Singer emphasized that our appraisal and labeling of events also determine our emotional responses.

Table 10.1
Summary of Emotion Theories

Theory	Explanation of Emotions	Example
James-Lange	Emotions arise from our awareness of our specific bodily responses to emotion-arousing stimuli.	We observe our heart racing after a threat and then feel afraid.
Cannon-Bard	Emotion-arousing stimuli trigger our bodily responses and simultaneous subjective experience.	Our heart races at the same time that we feel afraid.
Schachter-Singer	Our experience of emotion depends on two factors: general arousal and a conscious cognitive label.	We may interpret our arousal as fear or excitement, depending on the context.
Zajonc; LeDoux	Some embodied responses happen instantly, without conscious appraisal.	We automatically feel startled by a sound in the forest before labeling it as a threat.
Lazarus	Cognitive appraisal ("Is it dangerous or not?")—sometimes without our awareness—defines emotion.	The sound is "just the wind."

Embodied Emotion

Whether you are falling in love or grieving a death, you need little convincing that emotions involve the body. Feeling without a body is like breathing without lungs. Some physical responses are easy to notice. Other emotional responses we experience without awareness. Before examining our physical responses to specific emotions, consider another big question: How many distinct emotions are there?

The Basic Emotions

10-9: What are some of the basic emotions?

"Fear lends wings to his feet."

Virgil, Aeneid, *19 B.C.E.*

Carroll Izard (1977) isolated 10 basic emotions (joy, interest-excitement, surprise, sadness, anger, disgust, contempt, fear, shame, and guilt), most present in infancy (**FIGURE 10.13**). Others (Tracey & Robins, 2004) believe that pride is also a distinct emotion, signaled by a small smile, head slightly tilted back, and an open posture. Love, too, may be a basic emotion (Shaver et al., 1996). Izard has argued that other emotions are combinations of these 10, with love, for example, being a mixture of joy and interest-excitement. But are these emotions biologically distinct?

FIGURE 10.13
Infants' naturally occurring emotions To identify the emotions present from birth, Carroll Izard analyzed the facial expressions of infants.

(a) Joy (mouth forming smile, cheeks lifted, twinkle in eye)

(b) Anger (brows drawn together and downward, eyes fixed, mouth squarish)

(c) Interest (brows raised or knitted, mouth softly rounded, lips may be pursed)

(d) Disgust (nose wrinkled, upper lip raised, tongue pushed outward)

(e) Surprise (brows raised, eyes widened, mouth rounded in oval shape)

(f) Sadness (brows' inner corners raised, mouth corners drawn down)

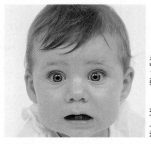

(g) Fear (brows level, drawn in and up, eyelids lifted, mouth corners retracted)

Emotions and the Autonomic Nervous System

10-10: What is the link between emotional arousal and the autonomic nervous system?

As we saw in Chapter 2, in a crisis, the *sympathetic division* of your *autonomic nervous system (ANS)* mobilizes your body for action (**FIGURE 10.14**). It triggers your adrenal glands to release the stress hormones epinephrine (adrenaline) and norepinephrine (noradrenaline). To provide energy, your liver pours extra sugar into your bloodstream. To help burn the sugar, your respiration increases to supply needed oxygen. Your heart rate and blood pressure increase. Your digestion slows, diverting blood from your internal organs to your muscles. With blood sugar driven into the large muscles, running becomes easier. Your pupils dilate, letting in more light. To cool your stirred-up body, you perspire. If wounded, your blood would clot more quickly.

When the crisis passes, the *parasympathetic division* of your ANS gradually calms your body, as stress hormones slowly leave your bloodstream. After your next crisis, think of this: Without any conscious effort, your body's response to danger is wonderfully coordinated and adaptive—preparing you to *fight or flee*. So, do the different emotions have distinct arousal fingerprints?

The Physiology of Emotions

10-11: Do different emotions activate different physiological and brain-pattern responses?

Imagine conducting an experiment measuring the physiological responses of emotion. In each of four rooms, you have someone watching a movie: In the first, the person is viewing a horror show; in the second, an anger-provoking film; in the third, a sexually arousing film; in the fourth, a boring film. From the control center you monitor each person's perspiration, breathing, and heart rate. Could you tell who is frightened? Who is angry? Who is sexually aroused? Who is bored?

With training, you could probably pick out the bored viewer. But discerning physiological differences among fear, anger, and sexual arousal would be much more difficult (Barrett, 2006). Different emotions do not have sharply distinct biological signatures.

FIGURE 10.14
Emotional arousal Like a crisis control center, the autonomic nervous system arouses the body in a crisis and calms it when danger passes.

Autonomic Nervous System Controls Physiological Arousal

Sympathetic division (arousing)		Parasympathetic division (calming)
Pupils dilate	EYES	Pupils contract
Decreases	SALIVATION	Increases
Perspires	SKIN	Dries
Increases	RESPIRATION	Decreases
Accelerates	HEART	Slows
Inhibits	DIGESTION	Activates
Secrete stress hormones	ADRENAL GLANDS	Decrease secretion of stress hormones
Reduced	IMMUNE SYSTEM FUNCTIONING	Enhanced

Nor do they engage sharply distinct brain regions. Consider the broad emotional portfolio of the *insula,* a neural center deep inside the brain. The insula is activated when we experience various social emotions, such as lust, pride, and disgust. In brain scans, it becomes active when people bite into some disgusting food, smell the same disgusting food, think about biting into a disgusting cockroach, or feel moral disgust over a sleazy business exploiting a saintly widow (Sapolsky, 2010).

Nevertheless, despite their similarities, fear, anger, and sexual arousal *feel* different to you and me, and they often *look* different to others. We may appear "paralyzed with fear" or "ready to explode." Research has pinpointed some real, though subtle, physiological distinctions among the emotions. For example, the finger temperatures and hormone secretions that accompany fear and rage do sometimes differ (Ax, 1953; Levenson, 1992). Fear and joy, although they prompt similar increased heart rate, stimulate different facial muscles. During fear, your brow muscles tense. During joy, muscles in your cheeks and under your eyes pull into a smile (Witvliet & Vrana, 1995).

> "No one ever told me that grief felt so much like fear. I am not afraid, but the sensation is like being afraid. The same fluttering in the stomach, the same restlessness, the yawning. I keep on swallowing."
>
> C. S. Lewis, A Grief Observed, *1961*

Emotional arousal Elated excitement and panicky fear involve similar physiological arousal. That allows us to flip rapidly between the two emotions.

FotoStor.co.uk/Alamy

Some emotions also differ in their brain circuits (Panksepp, 2007). Observers watching (and subtly mimicking) fearful faces showed more activity in their amygdala, an emotional control center, than did other observers who watched angry faces (Whalen et al., 2001). Brain scans and EEG recordings show that emotions also activate different areas of the brain's cortex. When you experience negative emotions such as disgust, your right prefrontal cortex tends to be more active than the left. Depression-prone people, and those with generally negative personalities, also show more right frontal lobe activity (Harmon-Jones et al., 2002).

Positive moods tend to trigger more left frontal lobe activity. People with positive personalities—exuberant infants and alert, enthusiastic, energized, and persistently goal-directed adults—also show more activity in the left frontal lobe than in the right (Davidson, 2000, 2003; Urry et al., 2004).

To sum up, we can't easily see differences in emotions from tracking heart rate, breathing, and perspiration. But facial expressions and brain activity can vary from one emotion to another. So, do we, like Pinocchio, give off telltale signs when we lie? For more on that question, see Thinking Critically About: Lie Detection.

RETRIEVE IT

• How do the two divisions of the autonomic nervous system affect our emotional responses?

ANSWER: The *sympathetic division* of the ANS arouses us for more intense experiences of emotion, pumping out stress hormones to prepare our body for fight or flight. The *parasympathetic division of the ANS* takes over when a crisis passes, restoring our body to a calm physiological and emotional state.

Expressed and Experienced Emotion

> "Your face, my thane, is a book where men may read strange matters."
>
> Lady Macbeth to her husband, in William Shakespeare's Macbeth

Expressive behavior implies emotion. Dolphins, with smiles seemingly plastered on their faces, appear happy. To decipher people's emotions we read their bodies, listen to their voice tones, and study their faces. Does nonverbal language vary with culture—or is it universal? And do our expressions influence our experienced emotions?

THINKING CRITICALLY ABOUT:

Lie Detection

10-12: How effective are polygraphs in using body states to detect lies?

Can a *lie detector*—a **polygraph**— reveal lies? Polygraphs don't literally detect lies. Instead, they measure emotion-linked changes in breathing, cardiovascular activity, and perspiration. If you were taking this test, an examiner would monitor these responses as you answered questions. She might ask, "In the last 20 years, have you ever taken something that didn't belong to you?" This item is a control question, aimed at making everyone a little nervous. If you lied and said *"No!"* (as many people do) the polygraph would detect arousal. This response will establish a baseline, a useful comparison for your responses to *critical questions ("Did you ever steal anything from your previous employer?")*. If your responses to critical questions are weaker than to control questions, the examiner will infer you are telling the truth.

Critics point out two problems: First, our physiological arousal is much the same from one emotion to another. Anxiety, irritation, and guilt all prompt similar physiological reactivity. Second, many innocent people do respond with heightened tension to the accusations implied by the critical questions (**FIGURE 10.15**). Many rape victims, for example, have "failed" these tests when reacting emotionally but truthfully (Lykken, 1991).

A 2002 U.S. National Academy of Sciences report noted that "no spy has ever been caught [by] using the polygraph." It is not for lack of trying. The FBI, CIA, and Departments of Defense and Energy in the United States have tested tens of thousands of employees, and polygraph use in Europe has also increased (Meijer & Verschuere, 2010). But Aldrich Ames, a Russian spy within the CIA, went undetected. Ames took many "polygraph tests and passed them all," noted Robert Park (1999). "Nobody thought to investigate the source of his sudden wealth—after all, he was passing the lie detector tests."

A more effective approach to lie detection uses a *guilty knowledge test,* which assesses a suspect's physiological responses to crime-scene details known only to the police and the guilty person (Ben-Shakhar & Elaad, 2003). If a camera and computer had been stolen, for example, only a guilty person should react strongly to the brand names of the stolen items. Given enough such specific probes, an innocent person will seldom be wrongly accused.

FIGURE 10.15

How often do lie detection tests lie? In one study, polygraph experts interpreted the polygraph data of 100 people who had been suspects in theft crimes (Kleinmuntz & Szucko, 1984). Half the suspects were guilty and had confessed; the other half had been proven innocent. Had the polygraph experts been the judges, more than one-third of the innocent would have been declared guilty, and one-fourth of the guilty would have been declared innocent.

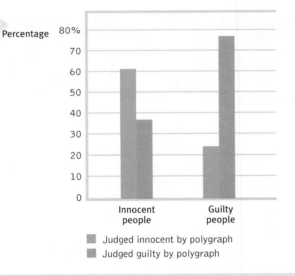

Percentage

- Judged innocent by polygraph
- Judged guilty by polygraph

polygraph a machine, commonly used in attempts to detect lies, that measures several of the physiological responses (such as perspiration and cardiovascular and breathing changes) accompanying emotion.

Detecting Emotion in Others

10-13: How do we communicate nonverbally?

To Westerners, a firm handshake conveys an outgoing, expressive personality (Chaplin et al., 2000). A gaze, an averted glance, or a stare communicates intimacy, submission, or dominance (Kleinke, 1986). When two people are passionately in love, they typically spend time—quite a bit of time—gazing into each other's eyes (Rubin, 1970). Would such gazes stir these feelings between strangers? To find out, researchers have asked unacquainted male-female pairs to gaze intently for 2 minutes either at each other's hands or into each other's eyes. After separating, the eye gazers reported feeling a tingle of attraction and affection (Kellerman et al., 1989).

A silent language of emotion Hindu classic dance uses the face and body to effectively convey 10 different emotions (Hejmadi et al., 2000).

Most of us read nonverbal cues well. Shown 10 seconds of video from the end of a speed-dating interaction, people can often detect whether one person is attracted to another (Place et al., 2009). We are especially good at detecting nonverbal threats. In a series of subliminally flashed words, we more often sense the presence of negative ones, such as *snake* or *bomb* (Dijksterhuis & Aarts, 2003). In a crowd of faces, a single angry face "pops out" faster than a single happy one (Hansen & Hansen, 1988; Pinkham et al., 2010). And even when hearing another language, most of us readily detect anger (Scherer et al., 2001).

Experience can sensitize us to particular emotions, as shown by experiments using a series of faces (like those in **FIGURE 10.16**) that morph from anger to fear (or sadness). Viewing such faces, physically abused children are much quicker than other children to spot the signals of anger. Shown a face that is 60 percent fear and 40 percent anger, they are as likely to perceive anger as fear. Their perceptions become sensitively attuned to glimmers of danger that nonabused children miss.

Hard-to-control facial muscles reveal signs of emotions you may be trying to conceal. Lifting just the inner part of your eyebrows, which few people do consciously, reveals distress or worry. Eyebrows raised and pulled together signal fear. Activated muscles under the eyes and raised cheeks suggest a natural smile. A feigned smile, such as one we make for a photographer, often continues for more than 4 or 5 seconds. Most authentic expressions have faded by that time. Feigned smiles are also switched on and off more abruptly than is a genuine happy smile (Bugental, 1986).

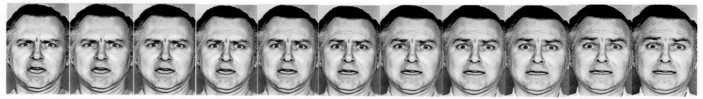

Used by permission of S. D. Pollack, D. J. Kistler, and the National Academy of Sciences

FIGURE 10.16
Experience influences how we perceive emotions Viewing the morphed middle face, evenly mixing fear with anger, physically abused children were more likely than nonabused children to perceive the face as angry (Pollak & Kistler, 2002; Pollak & Tolley-Schell, 2003).

Our brains are rather amazing detectors of subtle expressions. Just *how* amazing was clear when researchers filmed teachers talking to unseen schoolchildren (Babad et al., 1991). A mere 10-second clip of the teacher's voice or face provided enough clues for both young and old viewers to determine whether the teacher liked and admired a child. In other experiments, even glimpsing a face for one-tenth of a second enabled people to judge people's attractiveness or trustworthiness or to rate politicians' competence and predict their voter support (Willis & Todorov, 2006). "First impressions . . . occur with astonishing speed," note Christopher Olivola and Alexander Todorov (2010).

Despite our brain's emotion-detecting skill, we find it difficult to detect deceiving expressions (Porter & ten Brinke, 2008). In one digest of 206 studies of discerning truth from lies, people were just 54 percent accurate—barely better than a coin toss (Bond & DePaulo, 2006). Moreover, contrary to claims that some experts can spot lies, the available research indicates that virtually no one—save perhaps police professionals in high-stakes situations—beats chance by much (Bond & DePaulo, 2008; O'Sullivan et al., 2009). The behavioral differences between liars and truth tellers are too minute for most people to detect (Hartwig & Bond, 2011).

Some of us are, however, more sensitive than others to physical cues. In one study, hundreds of people were asked to

Dr. Paul Ekman, University of California at San Francisco

Which of researcher Paul Ekman's smiles is feigned, which natural? The smile on the right engages the facial muscles of a natural smile.

name the emotion in brief film clips they watched. The clips showed portions of a person's emotionally expressive face or body, sometimes accompanied by a garbled voice (Rosenthal et al., 1979). For example, after a 2-second scene revealing only the face of an upset woman, the researchers would ask whether the woman was criticizing someone for being late or was talking about her divorce. Given such "thin slices," some people were much better emotion detectors than others. Introverts tend to excel at reading others' emotions, while extraverts are generally easier to read (Ambady et al., 1995).

Gestures, facial expressions, and voice tones, which are absent in written communication, convey important information. The difference was clear in one study. In one group, participants heard 30-second recordings of people describing their marital separations. In the other group, participants read a script of the recording. Those who heard the recording were better able to predict a separated person's current and future adjustment (Mason et al., 2010). The absence of expressive emotion can make for ambiguous emotion in electronic communications. To partly remedy that, we sometimes embed visual cues to emotion (ROFL!) in our texts, e-mails, and online posts. Without the vocal nuances that signal whether a statement is serious, kidding, or sarcastic, we are in danger of what Piaget called *egocentrism,* by failing to perceive how others interpret our "just kidding" message (Kruger et al., 2005).

Obvious emotions Graphic novel authors use facial expressions and other design elements to express emotion, reducing the need to explain how the characters are feeling.

Gender and Emotion

10-14: How do women and men differ in their emotional expressions and experiences?

Is women's intuition, as so many believe, superior to men's? After analyzing 125 studies of sensitivity to nonverbal cues, Judith Hall (1984, 1987) concluded that women generally do surpass men at reading people's emotional cues when given thin slices of behavior. Women have also surpassed men in other assessments of emotional cues, such as deciding whether a male-female couple is a genuine romantic couple or a posed phony couple, and in discerning which of two people in a photo is the other's supervisor (Barnes & Sternberg, 1989).

Women's nonverbal sensitivity helps explain their greater emotional literacy. Invited to describe how they would feel in certain situations, men described simpler emotional reactions (Barrett et al., 2000). You might like to try this yourself: Ask some people how they might feel when saying good-bye to friends after graduation. Research suggests men are more likely to say, simply, "I'll feel bad," and women to express more complex emotions: "It will be bittersweet; I'll feel both happy and sad."

Women's skill at decoding others' emotions may also contribute to their greater emotional responsiveness (Vigil, 2009). In studies of 23,000 people from 26 cultures, women more than men reported themselves open to feelings (Costa et al., 2001). That helps explain the extremely strong perception that emotionality is "more true of women"—a perception expressed by nearly 100 percent of 18- to 29-year-old Americans (Newport, 2001).

One exception: Quickly—imagine an angry face. What gender is the person? If you're like 3 in 4 Arizona State University students, you imagined a male (Becker et al., 2007). The researchers also found that when a gender-neutral face was made to look angry, most people perceived it as male. If the face was smiling, they were more likely to perceive it as female (**FIGURE 10.17** on the next page). Anger strikes most people as a more masculine emotion.

The perception of women's emotionality feeds—and is fed by—people's attributing women's emotionality to their disposition and men's to their circumstances: "She's emotional. He's having a bad day" (Barrett & Bliss-Moreau, 2009). Nevertheless, there are some gender differences in descriptions of emotional experiences. When surveyed, women are far more likely than men to describe themselves as empathic. If you have

FIGURE 10.17

Male or female? Researchers manipulated a gender-neutral face. People were more likely to see it as a male when it wore an angry expression, and as a female when it wore a smile (Becker et al., 2007).

empathy, you identify with others and imagine what it must be like to walk in their shoes. You rejoice with those who rejoice and weep with those who weep.

Physiological measures of empathy, such as one's heart rate while seeing another's distress, confirm a gender gap, though a smaller one than is indicated in survey self-reports (Eisenberg & Lennon, 1983; Rueckert et al., 2010). Females are also more likely to *express* empathy—to cry and to report distress when observing someone in distress. As **FIGURE 10.18** shows, this gender difference was clear in videotapes of male and female students watching film clips that were sad (children with a dying parent), happy (slapstick comedy), or frightening (a man nearly falling off the ledge of a tall building) (Kring & Gordon, 1998). Women also tend to experience emotional events, such as viewing pictures of mutilation, more deeply, displaying more activation in emotion-sensitive brain areas. And they better remember the scenes three weeks later (Canli et al., 2002).

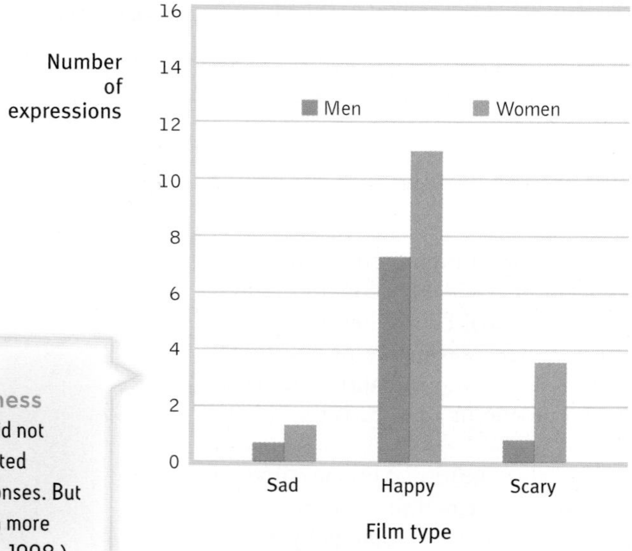

FIGURE 10.18

Gender and expressiveness
Male and female film viewers did not differ dramatically in self-reported emotions or physiological responses. But the women's faces *showed* much more emotion. (From Kring & Gordon, 1998.)

Number of expressions

[Bar chart with y-axis labeled 0 to 16, x-axis labeled "Film type" with categories Sad, Happy, Scary; legend shows Men and Women]

RETRIEVE IT

- _____ (Women/Men) report experiencing emotions more deeply, and they tend to be more adept at reading nonverbal behavior.

ANSWER: Women

Culture and Emotion

10-15: Do gestures and facial expressions mean the same thing in all cultures?

The meaning of *gestures* varies from culture to culture. U.S. President Richard Nixon learned this after making the North American "A-OK" sign before a welcoming crowd of Brazilians, not realizing it was a crude insult in that country. In 1968, the cultural variability of gestures was again demonstrated when North Korea publicized photos of supposedly happy officers from a captured U.S. Navy spy ship. In the photo, three men had raised their middle finger, telling their captors it was a "Hawaiian good luck sign" (Fleming & Scott, 1991).

Do *facial expressions* also have different meanings in different cultures? To find out, two investigative teams showed photographs of various facial expressions to people in different parts of the world and asked them to guess the emotion (Ekman et al., 1975, 1987, 1994; Izard, 1977, 1994). You can try this matching task yourself by pairing the six emotions with the six faces of **FIGURE 10.19**.

Regardless of your cultural background, you probably did pretty well. A smile's a smile the world around. Ditto for anger, and to a lesser extent the other basic expressions (Elfenbein & Ambady, 1999). (There is no culture where people frown when they are happy.)

Facial expressions do convey some nonverbal accents that provide clues to one's culture (Marsh et al., 2003). Thus, data from 182 studies show that our judgments are slightly more accurate when we are interpreting emotional expressions from our own culture (Elfenbein & Ambady, 2002, 2003a,b). Still, the telltale signs of emotion generally cross cultures. The world over, children cry when distressed, shake their heads when defiant, and smile when they are happy. So, too, with blind children who have never seen a face (Eibl-Eibesfeldt, 1971). People blind from birth spontaneously exhibit the common facial expressions associated with such emotions as joy, sadness, fear, and anger (Galati et al., 1997).

Musical expressions of emotion also cross cultures. Happy and sad music feels happy and sad around the world. Whether you live in an African village or a European city, fast-paced music seems happy, and slow-paced music seems sadder (Fritz et al., 2009).

Do these shared emotional categories reflect shared *cultural* experiences, such as movies and TV broadcasts seen around the world? Apparently not. Paul Ekman and his team asked isolated people in New Guinea to respond to such statements as, "Pretend your child has died." When North American collegians viewed the taped responses, they easily read the New Guineans' facial reactions.

So we can say that facial muscles speak a universal language. This discovery would not have surprised Charles Darwin (1809–1882) who argued that in prehistoric times, before our ancestors communicated in words, they communicated threats, greetings, and submission with facial expressions. Their shared expressions helped them survive (Hess & Thibault, 2009). In confrontations, for example, a human sneer retains elements of an animal baring its teeth in a snarl. Emotional expressions may enhance our survival in other ways, too. Surprise raises the eyebrows and widens the eyes, enabling us to take in more information. Disgust wrinkles the nose, closing it from foul odors.

Smiles are social as well as emotional events. Bowlers seldom smile when they score a strike; they smile when they turn to face their companions (Jones et al., 1991; Kraut & Johnston, 1979). Euphoric Olympic gold-medal winners typically don't smile when they are awaiting their ceremony. But they wear broad grins when interacting with officials and facing the crowd and cameras (Fernández-Dols & Ruiz-Belda, 1995).

Although we share a universal facial language, it has been adaptive for us to interpret faces in particular contexts (**FIGURE 10.20** on the next page). People judge an angry face set in a frightening situation as afraid. They judge a fearful face set in a painful situation as pained (Carroll & Russell, 1996). Movie directors harness this phenomenon by creating contexts and soundtracks that amplify our perceptions of particular emotions.

Although cultures share a universal facial language for basic emotions, they differ in how *much* emotion they express. Those that encourage individuality, as in Western Europe, Australia, New Zealand, and North America, display mostly visible emotions (van Hemert et al., 2007). Those that encourage people to adjust to others, as in China, tend to have less visible displays of personal emotions (Matsumoto et al., 2009b; Tsai et al., 2007). In Japan, people infer emotion more from the surrounding context. Moreover, the mouth, which is so expressive in North Americans, conveys less emotion than do the telltale eyes (Masuda et al., 2008; Yuki et al., 2007).

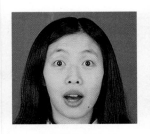

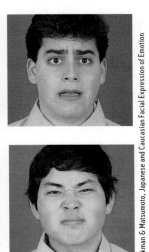
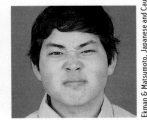

Ekman & Matsumoto, Japanese and Caucasian Facial Expression of Emotion

FIGURE 10.19

Culture-specific or culturally universal expressions? As people of differing cultures, do our faces speak differing languages? Which face expresses disgust? Anger? Fear? Happiness? Sadness? Surprise? (From Matsumoto & Ekman, 1989.) See inverted answers below.

From left to right, top to bottom: happiness, surprise, fear, sadness, anger, disgust.

"For news of the heart, ask the face."

Guinean proverb

While weightless, astronauts' internal bodily fluids move toward their upper body and their faces become puffy. This has made nonverbal communication more difficult, especially among multinational crews (Gelman, 1989).

Angry, Disgusted, or Afraid? Studies on the Malleability of Emotion Perception, Hillel Aviezer, Ran R. Hassin, Jennifer Ryan, Cheryl Grady, Josh Susskind, Adam Anderson, Morris Moscovitch, Shlomo Bentin

FIGURE 10.20

We read faces in context Tears on a face (above) make its expression seem sadder (Provine et al., 2009). Whether we perceive the man on the right as disgusted or angry depends on which body his face appears on (Aviezer et al., 2008).

Cultural differences also exist *within* nations. The Irish and their Irish-American descendants tend to be more expressive than the Scandinavians and their Scandinavian-American descendants (Tsai & Chentsova-Dutton, 2003). And that reminds us of a familiar lesson: Like most psychological events, emotion is best understood not only as a biological and cognitive phenomenon, but also as a social-cultural phenomenon.

> **RETRIEVE IT**
>
> • Are people in different cultures more likely to differ in their interpretations of facial expressions, or of gestures?
>
> ANSWER: gestures

The Effects of Facial Expressions

10-16: How do our facial expressions influence our feelings?

As William James (1890) struggled with feelings of depression and grief, he came to believe that we can control emotions by going "through the outward movements" of any emotion we want to experience. "To feel cheerful," he advised, "sit up cheerfully, look around cheerfully, and act as if cheerfulness were already there."

Studies of emotional effects of facial expressions reveal precisely what James might have predicted. Expressions not only communicate emotion, they also amplify and regulate it. In *The Expression of the Emotions in Man and Animals,* Charles Darwin (1872) contended that "the free expression by outward signs of an emotion intensifies it.... He who gives way to violent gestures will increase his rage."

Want to test Darwin's hypothesis? Try this: Fake a big grin. Now scowl. Can you feel the "smile therapy" difference? Participants in dozens of experiments have felt a difference. James Laird and his colleagues (1974, 1984, 1989) subtly induced students to make a frowning expression by asking them to "contract these muscles" and "pull your brows together" (supposedly to help the researchers attach facial electrodes). The results? The students reported feeling a little angry. So, too, for other basic emotions. For example, people reported feeling more fear than anger, disgust, or sadness when made to construct a fearful expression: "Raise your eyebrows. And open your eyes wide. Move your whole head back, so that your chin is tucked in a little bit, and let your mouth relax and hang open a little" (Duclos et al., 1989).

This **facial feedback effect** has been repeated many times, in many places, for many basic emotions (**FIGURE 10.21**). Just activating one of the smiling muscles by holding a pen in the teeth (rather than with the lips, which activates a frowning muscle) is enough to make cartoons seem more amusing (Strack et al., 1988). A heartier smile—made not just with the mouth but with raised cheeks that crinkle the eyes—enhances positive feelings even more when you are reacting to something pleasant or funny (Soussignan,

"Whenever I feel afraid
I hold my head erect
And whistle a happy tune."

Richard Rodgers and Oscar Hammerstein, The King and I, *1958*

facial feedback effect the tendency of facial muscle states to trigger corresponding feelings, such as fear, anger, or happiness.

2001). Smile warmly on the outside and you feel better on the inside. When smiling, you will even more quickly understand sentences that describe pleasant events (Havas et al., 2007). Scowl and the whole world seems to scowl back.

A request from your author: Smile often as you read this book.

RETRIEVE IT

• (1) Based on the *facial feedback effect,* how might students in this experiment report feeling when the rubberbands raise their cheeks as though in a smile? (2) How might they report feeling when the rubberbands pull their cheeks downward?

ANSWERS: (1) Most report feeling more happy than sad when their cheeks are raised upward. (2) Most report feeling more sad than happy when their cheeks are pulled downward.

So your face is more than a billboard that displays your feelings; it also feeds your feelings. No wonder depressed patients reportedly feel better after between-the-eyebrows Botox injections that paralyze the frowning muscles (Finzi & Wasserman, 2006). Two months after the treatment, 9 of the 10 nonfrowning patients given this treatment were no longer depressed. Follow-up studies have found that Botox paralysis of the frowning muscles slows people's reading of sadness or anger-related sentences, and it slows activity in emotion-related brain circuits (Havas et al., 2010; Hennenlotter et al., 2008). In such ways, Botox smooths life's emotional wrinkles.

With studies of bodily posture and vocal expressions, researchers have observed a broader *behavior feedback effect* (Flack, 2006; Snodgrass et al., 1986). You can duplicate the participants' experience: Walk for a few minutes with short, shuffling steps, keeping your eyes downcast. Now walk around taking long strides, with your arms swinging and your eyes looking straight ahead. Can you feel your mood shift? Going through the motions awakens the emotions.

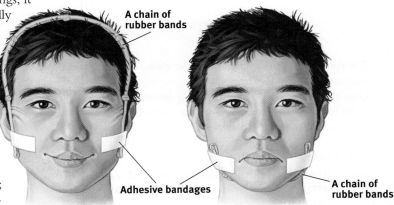

FIGURE 10.21

How to make people smile without telling them to smile Do as Kazuo Mori and Hideko Mori (2009) did with students in Japan: Attach rubberbands to the sides of the face with adhesive bandages, and then run them either over the head or under the chin.

Likewise, people perceive ambiguous behaviors differently depending on which finger they move up and down while reading a story. (This was said to be a study of the effect of using finger muscles "located near the reading muscles on the motor cortex".) If participants read the story while moving an extended middle finger, the story behaviors seemed more hostile. If read with a thumb up, they seemed more positive. Hostile gestures prime hostile perceptions (Chandler & Schwarz, 2009; Goldin-Meadow & Beilock, 2010).

You can use your understanding of feedback effects to become more empathic: Let your own face mimic another person's expression. Acting as another acts helps us feel what another feels (Vaughn & Lanzetta, 1981). Our natural mimicry of others' emotions helps explain why emotions are contagious (Dimberg et al., 2000; Neumann & Strack, 2000). Indeed, losing this ability can leave us struggling to make emotional connections, as one social worker with Moebius syndrome, a rare facial paralysis disorder, discovered while working with Hurricane Katrina refugees: When people made a sad expression, "I wasn't able to return it. I tried to do so with words and tone of voice, but it was no use. Stripped of the facial expression, the emotion just dies there, unshared" (Carey, 2010).

★ ★ ★

We have seen how our motivated behaviors, triggered by the forces of nature and nurture, often go hand in hand with significant emotional responses. Our often-adaptive psychological emotions likewise come equipped with physical reactions. Nervous about an important encounter, we feel stomach butterflies. Anxious over public speaking, we frequent the bathroom. Smoldering over a family conflict, we get a splitting headache. Negative emotions and the prolonged high arousal that may accompany them can tax the body and harm our health. You'll hear more about this in Chapter 11.

CHAPTER REVIEW

Motivation and Emotion

LEARNING OBJECTIVES

Test Yourself by taking a moment to answer each of these Learning Objective Questions (repeated here from within the chapter). Then turn to Appendix D, Complete Chapter Reviews, to check your answers. Research suggests that trying to answer these questions on your own will improve your long-term memory of the concepts (McDaniel et al., 2009).

Motivational Concepts

10-1: How do psychologists define *motivation?* From what perspectives do they view motivated behavior?

Hunger

10-2: What physiological factors produce hunger?

10-3: What cultural and situational factors influence hunger?

10-4: What factors predispose some people to become and remain obese?

The Need to Belong

10-5: What evidence points to our human need to belong?

10-6: How does social networking influence us?

Achievement Motivation

10-7: What is achievement motivation?

Emotion: Arousal, Behavior, and Cognition

10-8: How do arousal, cognition, and expressive behavior interact in emotion?

Embodied Emotion

10-9: What are some of the basic emotions?

10-10: What is the link between emotional arousal and the autonomic nervous system?

10-11: Do different emotions activate different physiological and brain-pattern responses?

10-12: How effective are polygraphs in using body states to detect lies?

Expressed and Experienced Emotion

10-13: How do we communicate nonverbally?

10-14: How do women and men differ in their emotional expressions and experiences?

10-15: Do gestures and facial expressions mean the same thing in all cultures?

10-16: How do our facial expressions influence our feelings?

TERMS AND CONCEPTS TO REMEMBER

Test yourself on these terms by trying to write down the definition in your own words before flipping back to the referenced page to check your answer.

motivation, p. 352

instinct, p. 352

drive-reduction theory, p. 353

homeostasis, p. 353

incentive, p. 353

Yerkes-Dodson law, p. 354

hierarchy of needs, p. 355

glucose, p. 357

set point, p. 358

basal metabolic rate, p. 358

achievement motivation, p. 370

emotion, p. 372

James-Lange theory, p. 372

Cannon-Bard theory, p. 372

two-factor theory, p. 373

polygraph, p. 379

facial feedback effect, p. 384

EXPERIENCE THE TESTING EFFECT

Test yourself repeatedly throughout your studies. This will not only help you figure out what you know and don't know; the testing itself will help you learn and remember the information more effectively thanks to the *testing effect*.

1. Today's evolutionary psychology shares an idea that was an underlying assumption of instinct theory. That idea is that
   a. physiological needs arouse psychological states.
   b. genes predispose species-typical behavior.
   c. physiological needs increase arousal.
   d. external needs energize and direct behavior.

2. An example of a physiological need is _____.
   An example of a psychological drive is _____.
   a. hunger; a "push" to find food
   b. a "push" to find food; hunger
   c. curiosity; a "push" to reduce arousal
   d. a "push" to reduce arousal; curiosity

3. Jan walks into a friend's kitchen, smells bread baking, and begins to feel very hungry. The smell of baking bread is a(n) _____ (incentive/drive).

4. _____ theory attempts to explain behaviors that do NOT reduce physiological needs.

5. With a challenging task, such as taking a difficult exam, performance is likely to peak when arousal is
   a. very high.   c. very low.
   b. moderate.   d. absent.

6. According to Maslow's hierarchy of needs, our most basic needs are physiological, including the need for food and water; just above these are _____ needs.
   a. safety   c. belongingness
   b. self-esteem   d. self-transcendence

7. Journalist Dorothy Dix (1861-1951) once remarked, "Nobody wants to kiss when they are hungry." Which motivation theory best supports her statement?

8. According to the concept of set point, our body maintains itself at a particular weight level. This "weight thermostat" is an example of _____.

9. Which of the following is a genetically predisposed response to food?
   a. An aversion to eating cats and dogs
   b. An interest in novel foods
   c. A preference for sweet and salty foods
   d. An aversion to carbohydrates

10. The blood sugar _____ provides the body with energy. When it is _____ (low/high), we feel hungry.

11. The rate at which your body expends energy while at rest is referred to as the _____ _____ rate.

12. Obese people find it very difficult to lose weight permanently. This is due to several factors, including the fact that
    a. dieting triggers neophobia.
    b. the set point of obese people is lower than average.
    c. with dieting, metabolism increases.
    d. there is a genetic influence on body weight.

13. Sanjay recently adopted the typical college diet high in fat and sugar. He knows he may gain weight, but he figures it's no big deal because he can lose the extra pounds in the future. How would you evaluate Sanjay's plan?

14. Which of the following is NOT part of the evidence presented to support the view that humans are strongly motivated by a need to belong?
    a. Students who rated themselves as "very happy" also tended to have satisfying close relationships.
    b. Social exclusion—such as exile or solitary confinement—is considered a severe form of punishment.
    c. As adults, adopted children tend to resemble their biological parents and to yearn for an affiliation with them.
    d. Children who are extremely neglected become withdrawn, frightened, and speechless.

15. What are some ways to manage our social networking time successfully?

16. The _____-_____ theory of emotion maintains that a physiological response happens BEFORE we know what we are feeling.

17. Assume that after spending an hour on a treadmill, you receive a letter saying that your scholarship request has been approved. The two-factor theory of emotion would predict that your physical arousal will
    a. weaken your happiness.
    b. intensify your happiness.
    c. transform your happiness into relief.
    d. have no particular effect on your happiness.

18. Zajonc and LeDoux maintain that some emotional reactions occur before we have had the chance to label or interpret them. Lazarus disagreed. These psychologists differ about whether emotional responses occur in the absence of
    a. physical arousal.
    b. the hormone epinephrine.
    c. cognitive processing.
    d. learning.

19. What does a polygraph measure and why are its results questionable?

20. When people are induced to assume fearful expressions, they often report feeling a little fear. This result is know as the _____ _____ effect.

Find answers to these questions in Appendix E, in the back of the book.

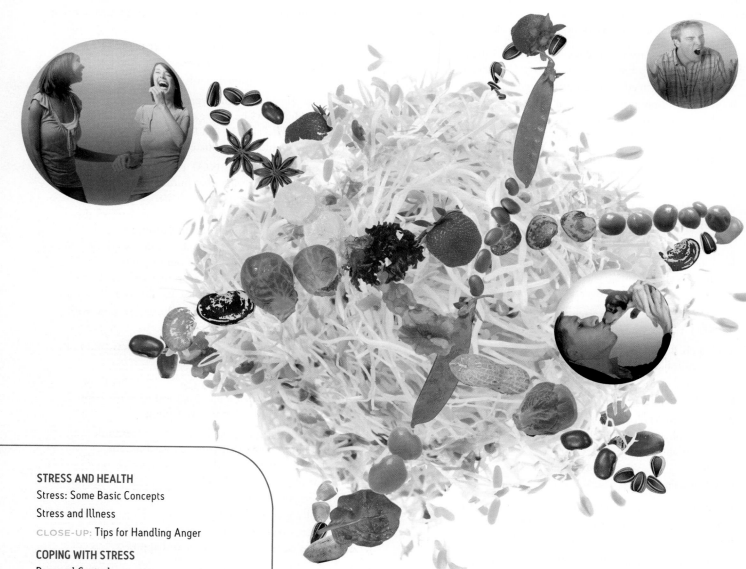

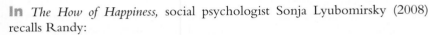

CHAPTER **11**

Stress, Health, and Human Flourishing

In *The How of Happiness,* social psychologist Sonja Lyubomirsky (2008) recalls Randy:

> [He] endured a lot as a child. He lost two people close to him to suicide, at age twelve his father and at age seventeen his best friend. When he was in fifth grade, his mother left his father and moved the family out of state and away from everyone he knew in order that she could live with her boyfriend, Roy. Although Randy's bond with his mother was, and still is, strong, Roy belittled Randy, and their relationship was strained. [Randy married] too soon and too young. His marriage was fraught with difficulty and finally ended when he discovered the extent of his wife's infidelities. Still, he was devastated initially by the breakup and felt that he had more than his share of loss and death.
>
> Today Randy is one of those happy people who make everyone around them smile and laugh. He picked himself up after his divorce, moved to another city, found work as a safety engineer, and eventually remarried. He is now forty-three, remarried for three years, and stepfather to three boys. How did he do it? Randy is an eternal optimist and claims that seeing the "silver lining in the cloud" has always been his key to survival. For example, although some of his coworkers find their jobs frustrating and stressful, he says that his allows him "to think outside the box." Moreover, while a friend of his struggles with stepchildren, Randy is overjoyed by "the opportunity to be a dad." (pp. 29–30)

Randy's life embodies what this chapter explores: the challenges of stress, the ways we interpret events and cope, and the possibilities for a happy, flourishing life.

Stress and Health

How often do you experience stress in your daily life? Never? Rarely? Sometimes? Or frequently? When pollsters put a similar question to other collegians, some 85 percent recalled experiencing stress during the last three months—and most said it had disrupted their school work at least once (AP, 2009). On entering college or university, 18 percent of men and 39 percent of women reported having been "frequently over-whelmed" by all they had to do during the past year (Pryor et al., 2011).

Stress often strikes without warning. Imagine being 21-year-old Ben Carpenter on the world's wildest and fastest wheelchair ride. As he crossed an intersection on a sunny summer afternoon in 2007, the light changed. A large truck, whose driver didn't see him, started moving into the inter-section. As they bumped, the wheelchair turned to face forward, and its handles got stuck in the truck's grille. Off they went, the driver unable to hear Ben's cries for help. As they sped down the highway about an hour from my home, passing motorists caught the bizarre sight of a truck pushing a wheelchair at 50 miles per hour and started calling 911. (The first caller: "You are not going to believe this. There is a semi truck pushing a guy in a wheelchair on Red Arrow highway!") Lucky for Ben, one passerby was an undercover police officer. Pulling a quick U-turn, he followed the truck to its destination a couple of miles from where the wild ride had started, and informed the disbelieving driver that he had a passenger hooked in his grille. "It was very scary," said Ben, who has muscular dystrophy.

AP Photo/Michigan State Police

Extreme stress Ben Carpenter experienced the wildest of rides after his wheelchair got stuck in a truck's grille.

In this chapter, we take a close look at stress and how it affects our health and well-being. Let's begin with some basic terms.

Stress: Some Basic Concepts

11-1: What events provoke stress responses, and how do we respond and adapt to stress?

Stress is a slippery concept. We sometimes use the word informally to describe threats or challenges ("Ben was under a lot of stress"), and at other times our responses ("Ben experienced acute stress"). To a psychologist, the dangerous truck ride was a *stressor*. Ben's physical and emotional responses were a *stress reaction*. And the process by which he related to the threat was *stress*. Thus, **stress** is the process of appraising and responding to a threatening or challenging event (**FIGURE 11.1**). Stress arises less from events themselves than from how we appraise them (Lazarus, 1998). One person, alone in a house, ignores its creaking sounds and experiences no stress; someone else suspects an intruder and becomes alarmed. One person regards a new job as a welcome challenge; someone else appraises it as risking failure.

FIGURE 11.1

Stress appraisal The events of our lives flow through a psychological filter. How we appraise an event influences how much stress we experience and how effectively we respond.

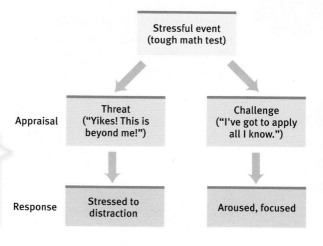

Image 100/Corbis

Stressful event
(tough math test)

Appraisal

Threat
("Yikes! This is beyond me!")

Challenge
("I've got to apply all I know.")

Response

Stressed to distraction

Aroused, focused

When short-lived, or when perceived as challenges, stressors can have positive effects. A momentary stress can mobilize the immune system for fending off infections and healing wounds (Segerstrom, 2007). Stress also arouses and motivates us to conquer problems. Championship athletes, successful entertainers, and great teachers and leaders all thrive and excel when aroused by a challenge (Blascovich et al., 2004). Having conquered cancer or rebounded from a lost job, some people emerge with stronger self-esteem and a deepened spirituality and sense of purpose. Indeed, some stress early in life is conducive to later emotional resilience (Landauer & Whiting, 1979). Adversity can beget growth.

Extreme or prolonged stress can harm us. Children who suffer severe or prolonged abuse are later at risk of chronic disease (Repetti et al., 2002). Troops who had post-traumatic stress reactions to heavy combat in the Vietnam war later suffered greatly elevated rates of circulatory, digestive, respiratory, and infectious diseases (Boscarino, 1997). People who lose their jobs, especially later in their working life, are at increased risk of heart problems and death (Gallo et al., 2006; Sullivan & von Wachter, 2009).

So there is an interplay between our heads and our health. This isn't surprising. Psychological states are physiological events that influence other parts of our physiological system. Just pausing to *think* about biting into an orange section—the sweet, tangy juice from the pulpy fruit flooding across your tongue—can trigger salivation. We'll explore that interplay shortly, but first, let's look more closely at stressors and stress reactions.

stress the process by which we perceive and respond to certain events, called *stressors,* that we appraise as threatening or challenging.

Stressors—Things That Push Our Buttons

Stressors fall into three main types: catastrophes, significant life changes, and daily hassles. All can be toxic.

Catastrophes Catastrophes are unpredictable large-scale events, such as wars, earthquakes, and famines. After such events, damage to emotional and physical health can be significant. In surveys taken in the three weeks after the 9/11 terrorist attacks, two-thirds of Americans said they were having some trouble concentrating and sleeping (Wahlberg, 2001). In the New York area, people were especially likely to report such symptoms, and sleeping pill prescriptions rose by a reported 28 percent (HMHL, 2002). In the four months after Hurricane Katrina, New Orleans' suicide rate reportedly tripled (Saulny, 2006).

For those who respond to catastrophes by relocating to another country, the stress is twofold. The trauma of uprooting and family separation combine with the challenges of adjusting to the new culture's language, ethnicity, climate, and social norms (Pipher, 2002; Williams & Berry, 1991). In the first half-year, before their morale begins to rebound, newcomers often experience culture shock and deteriorating well-being (Markovizky & Samid, 2008). Such relocations may become increasingly common due to climate change in years to come.

Daniel Morel/AFP/Getty/Newscom

Toxic stress: Unpredictable large-scale events, such as the severe earthquake that devastated Haiti in 2010, trigger significant levels of stress-related ills. When an earthquake struck Los Angeles in 1994, sudden-death heart attacks increased fivefold. Most occurred in the first two hours after the quake and near its center and were unrelated to physical exertion (Muller & Verier, 1996).

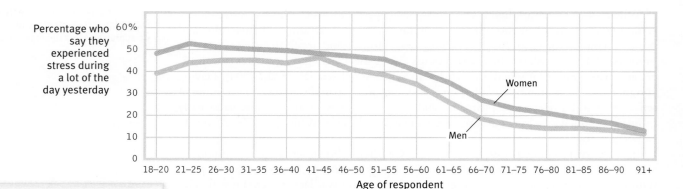

FIGURE 11.2

Age and stress A Gallup-Healthways survey of more than 650,000 Americans during 2008 and 2009 found daily stress highest among younger adults (Newport & Pelham, 2009).

Significant Life Changes Life transitions—leaving home, becoming divorced, losing a job, having a loved one die—are often keenly felt. Even happy events, such as getting married, can be stressful. Many of these transitions happen during young adulthood. One survey, in which 15,000 Canadian adults were asked whether "You are trying to take on too many things at once," found the highest stress levels among young adults. Young adult stress appeared again when 650,000 Americans were asked if they had experienced a lot of stress "yesterday" (**FIGURE 11.2**).

Some psychologists study the health effects of life changes by following people over time. Others compare the life changes recalled by those who have or have not suffered a specific health problem, such as a heart attack. In such studies, those recently widowed, fired, or divorced have been more vulnerable to disease (Dohrenwend et al., 1982; Strully, 2009). One Finnish study of 96,000 widowed people found that the survivor's risk of death doubled in the week following a partner's death (Kaprio et al., 1987). A cluster of crises—losing a job, home, and partner—puts one even more at risk.

Daily Hassles Events don't have to remake our lives to cause stress. Stress also comes from *daily hassles*—rush-hour traffic, aggravating housemates, long lines at the store, too many things to do, family frustrations, and friends who won't pick up their phone (Kohn & Macdonald, 1992; Repetti et al., 2009; Ruffin, 1993). Some people can simply shrug off such hassles. For others, the everyday annoyances add up and take a toll on health and well-being.

Many people face more significant daily hassles. As the Great Recession of 2008–2009 bottomed out, Americans' most oft-cited stressors related to money (76 percent), work (70 percent), and the economy (65 percent) (APA, 2010). In impoverished areas—where many people routinely face inadequate income, unemployment, solo parenting, and overcrowding—such stressors are part of daily life.

Daily economic pressures may be compounded by anti-gay prejudice or racism, which—like other stressors—can have both psychological and physical consequences (Pascoe & Richman, 2009; Rostosky et al., 2010; Swim et al., 2009). Thinking that some of the people you encounter each day will dislike you, distrust you, or doubt your abilities makes daily life stressful. When prolonged, such stress takes a toll on our health, especially our cardiovascular system. For many African-Americans, stress helps drive up blood pressure levels (Mays et al., 2007; Ong et al., 2009).

The Stress Response System

Medical interest in stress dates back to Hippocrates (460–377 B.C.E.). In the 1920s, Walter Cannon (1929) confirmed that the stress response is part of a unified mind-body system. He observed that extreme cold, lack of oxygen, and emotion-arousing events all trigger an outpouring of the stress hormones epinephrine and norepinephrine from the core of the adrenal glands. When alerted by any of a number of brain pathways, the sympathetic nervous system arouses us, preparing the body for the wonderfully adaptive response

"You've got to know when to hold' em; know when to fold' em. Know when to walk away, and know when to run."

Kenny Rogers, "The Gambler," 1978

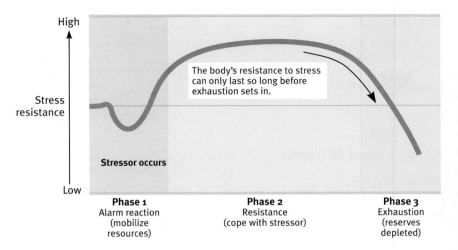

The body's resistance to stress can only last so long before exhaustion sets in.

High

Stress resistance

Stressor occurs

Low

Phase 1
Alarm reaction
(mobilize resources)

Phase 2
Resistance
(cope with stressor)

Phase 3
Exhaustion
(reserves depleted)

FIGURE 11.3
Selye's general adaptation syndrome
When a gold and copper mine in Chile collapsed in 2010, family and friends rushed to the scene, fearing the worst. Many of those holding vigil outside the mine were nearly exhausted with the stress of waiting and worrying when, after 18 days, they received news that all 33 of the miners inside were alive and well.

that Cannon called *fight or flight.* It increases heart rate and respiration, diverts blood from digestion to the skeletal muscles, dulls feelings of pain, and releases sugar and fat from the body's stores (see Figure 10.14).

Canadian scientist Hans Selye's (1936, 1976) 40 years of research on stress extended Cannon's findings. His studies of animals' reactions to various stressors, such as electric shock and surgery, helped make stress a major concept in both psychology and medicine. Selye proposed that the body's adaptive response to stress is so general that, like a single burglar alarm, it sounds, no matter what intrudes. He named this response the **general adaptation syndrome (GAS),** and he saw it as a three-phase process (**FIGURE 11.3**). Let's say you suffer a physical or an emotional trauma. In Phase 1, you have an *alarm reaction,* as your sympathetic nervous system is suddenly activated. Your heart rate zooms. Blood is diverted to your skeletal muscles. You feel the faintness of shock.

With your resources mobilized, you are now ready to fight back. During Phase 2, *resistance,* your temperature, blood pressure, and respiration remain high. Your adrenal glands pump hormones into your bloodstream. You are fully engaged, summoning all your resources to meet the challenge.

As time passes, with no relief from stress, your body's reserves dwindle. You have reached Phase 3, *exhaustion.* With exhaustion, you become more vulnerable to illness or even, in extreme cases, collapse and death.

Selye's basic point: Although the human body copes well with temporary stress, prolonged stress can damage it. Even fearful, stressed rats have been found to die sooner (after about 600 days) than their more confident siblings, which average 700-day life spans (Cavigelli & McClintock, 2003).

There are other options for dealing with stress. One is a common response to a loved one's death: Withdraw. Pull back. Conserve energy. Faced with an extreme disaster, such as a ship sinking, some people become paralyzed by fear. Another **tend-and-befriend** stress response, found especially among women, is to seek and give support (Taylor et al., 2000, 2006).

Facing stress, men more often than women tend to withdraw socially, turn to alcohol, or become aggressive. Women more often respond to stress by nurturing and banding together. This may in part be due to *oxytocin,* a stress-moderating hormone associated with pair-bonding in animals and released by cuddling, massage, and breast-feeding in humans (Campbell, 2010; Taylor, 2006).

It often pays to spend our resources in fighting or fleeing an external threat. But we do so at a cost. When stress is momentary, the cost is small. When stress persists, we may pay a much higher price, with lowered resistance to infections and other threats to mental and physical well-being.

"You may be suffering from what's known as full-nest syndrome."

general adaptation syndrome (GAS) Selye's concept of the body's adaptive response to stress in three phases—alarm, resistance, exhaustion.

tend and befriend under stress, people (especially women) often provide support to others (tend) and bond with and seek support from others (befriend).

health psychology a subfield of psychology that provides psychology's contribution to behavioral medicine.

psychoneuroimmunology the study of how psychological, neural, and endocrine processes together affect the immune system and resulting health.

Stress and Illness

11-2: How does stress make us more vulnerable to disease?

To study how stress and healthy and unhealthy behaviors influence health and illness, psychologists and physicians have created the interdisciplinary field of *behavioral medicine,* integrating behavioral and medical knowledge. One subfield, **health psychology,** provides psychology's contribution to behavioral medicine. Another subfield, **psychoneuroimmunology,** focuses on mind-body interactions (Kiecolt-Glaser, 2009). This awkward name makes sense when said slowly: Your thoughts and feelings *(psycho)* influence your brain *(neuro),* which influences the endocrine hormones that affect your disease-fighting immune system. And this subfield is the study of *(ology)* those interactions.

If you've ever had a stress headache, or felt your blood pressure rise with anger, you don't need to be convinced that our psychological states have physiological effects. Stress can even leave you less able to fight off disease because your nervous and endocrine systems influence your immune system (Sternberg, 2009). You can think of your immune system as a complex surveillance system. When it functions properly, it keeps you healthy by isolating and destroying bacteria, viruses, and other invaders. Four types of cells are active in these search-and-destroy missions (**FIGURE 11.4**):

• *B lymphocytes* (white blood cells) mature in the *b*one marrow and release antibodies that fight bacterial infections.

• *T lymphocytes* (white blood cells) mature in the *t*hymus and other lymphatic tissue and attack cancer cells, viruses, and foreign substances.

• *Macrophages* ("big eaters") identify, pursue, and ingest harmful invaders and worn-out cells.

• *Natural killer cells* (NK cells) pursue diseased cells (such as those infected by viruses or cancer).

Your age, nutrition, genetics, body temperature, and stress all influence your immune system's activity. If it doesn't function properly, your immune system can err in two directions:

1. Responding too strongly, the immune system may attack the body's own tissues, causing an allergic reaction or a self-attacking disease such as lupus, multiple sclerosis, or some forms of arthritis. Women, who are immunologically stronger than men, are more susceptible to self-attacking diseases (Morell, 1995; Pido-Lopez et al., 2001).

2. Underreacting, the immune system may allow a bacterial infection to flare, a dormant virus to erupt, or cancer cells to multiply. To protect transplanted organs, which the recipient's immune system would view as a foreign substance, surgeons may deliberately suppress the patient's immune system.

Stress can also trigger immune suppression by reducing the release of disease-fighting lymphocytes. This has been observed when animals were stressed by physical restraints, unavoidable electric shocks, noise, crowding, cold water, social defeat, or separation from their mothers (Maier et al., 1994). One six-month study monitored immune responses in 43 monkeys (Cohen et al., 1992). Half were left in stable groups. The others (21) were

"In the eyes of God or biology or what have you, it is just very important to have women."

Immunologist Norman Talal (1995)

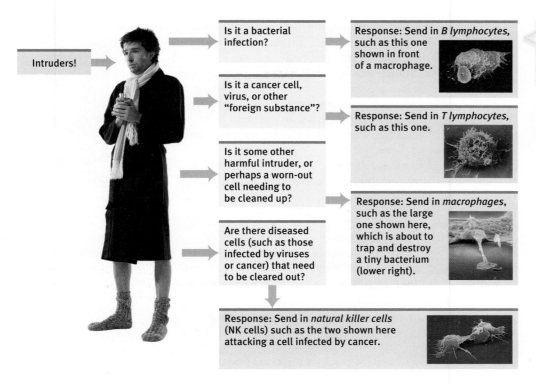

FIGURE 11.4
A simplified view of immune responses

Man at far left: Fuse/Getty Images
Right-hand photos:
Top: CNRI/Photo Researchers, Inc.
Second: NIBSC/Photo Researchers, Inc.
Third: Eye of Science/Photo Researchers, Inc.
Fourth (bottom): Lennart Nilsson/Boehringer Ingelheim International GmbH

stressed by being housed with new roommates—3 or 4 new monkeys each month. By the end of the experiment, the socially disrupted monkeys had weaker immune systems. Human immune systems react similarly. Two examples:

- *Surgical wounds heal more slowly in stressed people.* In one experiment, dental students received punch wounds (precise small holes punched in the skin). Compared with wounds placed during summer vacation, those placed three days before a major exam healed 40 percent more slowly (Kiecolt-Glaser et al., 1998). In other studies, marriage conflict has also slowed punch-wound healing (Kiecolt-Glaser et al., 2005).

- *Stressed people are more vulnerable to colds.* Major life stress increases the risk of a respiratory infection (Pedersen et al., 2010). When researchers dropped a cold virus into the noses of stressed and relatively unstressed people, 47 percent of those living stress-filled lives developed colds (**FIGURE 11.5**). Among those living relatively free of stress, only 27 percent did. In follow-up research, the happiest and most relaxed people were likewise markedly less vulnerable to an experimentally delivered cold virus (Cohen et al., 2003, 2006).

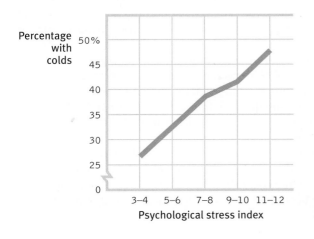

FIGURE 11.5
Stress and colds In an experiment by Sheldon Cohen and colleagues (1991), people with the highest life stress scores were also most vulnerable when exposed to an experimentally delivered cold virus.

The stress effect on immunity makes physiological sense. It takes energy to track down invaders, produce swelling, and maintain fevers. Thus, when diseased, your body reduces its muscular energy output by decreasing activity and increasing sleep. Stress does the opposite. It creates a competing energy need. During an aroused fight-or-flight reaction, your stress responses divert energy from your disease-fighting immune system and send it to your muscles and brain (see Figure 10.14). This increases your vulnerability to illness.

The point to remember: Stress does not make us sick, but it does alter our immune functioning, which leaves us less able to resist infection.

D. Hurst/Alamy

RETRIEVE IT

• _____ _____ provides psychology's contribution to behavioral medicine. _____ focuses on mind-body interactions, including the effects of psychological, neural, and endocrine functioning on the immune system and overall health.

ANSWERS: Health psychology; Psychoneuroimmunology

• What general effect does stress have on our overall health?

ANSWER: Stress tends to reduce our immune system's ability to function properly, so that higher stress generally leads to a greater incidence of physical illness.

Stress and AIDS

We know that stress suppresses immune functioning. What does this mean for people with AIDS *(acquired immune deficiency syndrome)*? As its name tells us, AIDS is an immune disorder, caused by the *human immunodeficiency virus (HIV)*. AIDS has become the world's fourth-leading cause of death and Africa's number-one killer.

Ironically, if a disease is spread by human contact (as AIDS is, through the exchange of bodily fluids, primarily semen and blood), and if it kills slowly (as AIDS does), it can be lethal to more people. Those who acquire HIV often spread it in the highly contagious first few weeks before they know they are infected. Worldwide, some 2.7 million people—slightly more than half of them women—became infected with HIV in 2010, often without their awareness (UNAIDS, 2011). Years after the initial infection, when AIDS appears, people have difficulty fighting off other diseases, such as pneumonia. More than 25 million people worldwide have died of AIDS (UNAIDS, 2010).

Stress cannot give people AIDS. But could stress and negative emotions speed the transition from HIV infection to AIDS in someone already infected? Might stress predict a faster decline in those with AIDS? The answer to both questions seems to be *Yes* (Bower et al., 1998; Kiecolt-Glaser & Glaser, 1995; Leserman et al., 1999). HIV-infected men who experience stressful events, such as the loss of a partner, exhibit somewhat greater immune suppression and travel a faster disease course.

Would efforts to reduce stress help control the disease? Again, the answer appears to be *Yes*. Educational initiatives, bereavement support groups, cognitive therapy, relaxation training, and exercise programs that reduce distress have all had positive consequences for HIV-positive people (Baum & Posluszny, 1999; McCain et al., 2008; Schneiderman, 1999). But the benefits are small, compared with available drug treatments.

Although AIDS is now more treatable than ever before, preventing HIV infection is a far better option. This is the focus of many educational programs, such as the comprehensive ABC (*A*bstinence, *B*e faithful, use *C*ondoms) program that has been used with seeming success in Uganda (Altman, 2004; UNAIDS, 2005).

In North America and Western Europe, 74 percent of people with AIDS are men. In sub-Saharan Africa, 60 percent of people with AIDS are women (UNAIDS, 2010).

Africa is ground zero for AIDS In Lesotho, Uganda, and elsewhere, prevention efforts have included the "ABC" Campaign—*A*bstinence, *B*e faithful, and use *C*ondoms.

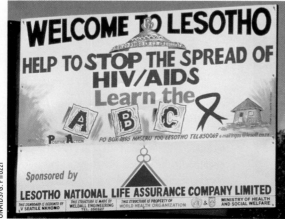

UNAIDS/G. Pirozzi

Stress and Cancer

Stress does not create cancer cells. But in a healthy, functioning immune system, lymphocytes, macrophages, and NK cells search out and destroy cancer cells and cancer-damaged cells. If stress weakens the immune system, might this weaken a person's ability to fight off cancer? To explore a possible connection between stress and cancer, experimenters have implanted tumor cells in rodents or given them *carcinogens* (cancer-producing substances). They then exposed some rodents to uncontrollable stress, such as inescapable shocks, which weakened their immune systems. Those rodents were indeed more prone to developing cancer (Sklar & Anisman, 1981). Their tumors developed sooner and grew larger than in nonstressed rodents.

Does this stress-cancer link also hold with humans? The results are mixed. Some studies find that people are at increased risk for cancer within a year after experiencing depression, helplessness, or bereavement (Chida et al., 2008; Steptoe et al., 2010). In one large Swedish study, the risk of colon cancer was 5.5 times greater among people with a history of workplace stress than among those who reported no such problems. This difference was not attributable to group differences in age, smoking, drinking, or physical characteristics (Courtney et al., 1993). Other studies, however, have found no link between stress and human cancer (Coyne et al., 2010; Petticrew et al., 1999, 2002). Concentration camp survivors and former prisoners of war, for example, do not have elevated cancer rates.

One danger in hyping reports on emotions and cancer is that some patients may then blame themselves for their illness: "If only I had been more expressive, relaxed, and hopeful." A corollary danger is a "wellness macho" among the healthy, who take credit for their "healthy character" and lay a guilt trip on the ill: "She has cancer? That's what you get for holding your feelings in and being so nice." Dying thus becomes the ultimate failure.

It's important enough to repeat: *Stress does not create cancer cells.* At worst, it may affect their growth by weakening the body's natural defenses against multiplying malignant cells (Antoni & Lutgendorf, 2007). Although a relaxed, hopeful state may enhance these defenses, we should be aware of the thin line that divides science from wishful thinking. The powerful biological processes at work in advanced cancer or AIDS are not likely to be completely derailed by avoiding stress or maintaining a relaxed but determined spirit (Anderson, 2002; Kessler et al., 1991). And that explains why research consistently indicates that psychotherapy does not extend cancer patients' survival (Coyne et al., 2007, 2009; Coyne & Tennen, 2010).

coronary heart disease the clogging of the vessels that nourish the heart muscle; the leading cause of death in many developed countries.

"I didn't give myself cancer."
Mayor Barbara Boggs Sigmund (1939–1990), Princeton, New Jersey

When organic causes of illness are unknown, it is tempting to invent psychological explanations. Before the germ that causes tuberculosis was discovered, personality explanations of TB were popular (Sontag, 1978).

Stress and Heart Disease

11-3: Why are some of us more prone than others to coronary heart disease?

Stress is much more closely linked to North America's leading cause of death. In **coronary heart disease,** the blood vessels that nourish the heart muscle gradually close. *Hypertension* (high blood pressure) and a family history of the disease increase the risk of coronary heart disease. So do many behavioral factors (smoking, obesity, a high-fat diet, physical inactivity), physiological factors (an elevated cholesterol level), and psychological factors (stress responses and personality traits).

In a classic study, Meyer Friedman, Ray Rosenman, and their colleagues tested the idea that stress increases heart disease risk by measuring the blood cholesterol level and clotting speed of 40 U.S. male tax accountants at different times of year (Friedman & Ulmer, 1984). From January through March, the test results were completely normal. Then, as the accountants began scrambling to finish their clients' tax returns before the April 15 filing deadline, their cholesterol and clotting measures rose to dangerous levels. In May and June, with the deadline past, the measures

Photo Spin, Inc./Alamy

returned to normal. Stress predicted heart attack risk for these men. The researchers' hunch had paid off, launching a nine-year study of more than 3000 healthy men, aged 35 to 59.

At the start of the study, the researchers interviewed each man for 15 minutes, noting his work and eating habits, manner of talking, and other behavior patterns. Those who seemed the most reactive, competitive, hard driving, impatient, time conscious, super-motivated, verbally aggressive, and easily angered they called **Type A.** The roughly equal number who were more easygoing they called **Type B.** Which group do you suppose turned out to be the most prone to coronary heart disease?

Nine years later, 257 men had suffered heart attacks, and 69 percent of them were Type A. Moreover, not one of the "pure" Type Bs—the most mellow and laid back of their group—had suffered a heart attack.

As often happens in science, this exciting discovery provoked enormous public interest. But after that initial honeymoon period, researchers wanted to know more. Was the finding reliable? If so, what was the toxic component of the Type A profile: Time consciousness? Competitiveness? Anger?

More than 700 studies have now explored possible psychological correlates or predictors of cardiovascular health (Chida & Hamer, 2008; Chida & Steptoe, 2009). These reveal that Type A's toxic core is negative emotions—especially the anger associated with an aggressively reactive temperament. When we are harassed or challenged, our active sympathetic nervous system redistributes bloodflow to our muscles, pulling it away from our internal organs. One of those organs, the liver, which normally removes cholesterol

In both India and America, Type A bus drivers are literally hard-driving: They brake, pass, and honk their horns more often than their more easygoing Type B colleagues (Evans et al., 1987).

"The fire you kindle for your enemy often burns you more than him."

Chinese proverb

CLOSE UP:

Tips for Handling Anger

11-4: What are some healthful ways to cope with feelings of anger?

Behavioral medicine research provides a reminder of one of contemporary psychology's overriding themes: *Mind and body interact; everything psychological is simultaneously physiological.* When we face a threat or challenge, fear triggers flight but anger triggers fight—each at times an adaptive behavior. Yet chronic hostility, as in the Type A personality, is linked to heart disease. How, then, can we rid ourselves of our anger?

Individualistic cultures encourage people to vent their rage. Such advice is seldom heard in cultures where people's identity is centered more on the group. People who keenly sense their *inter*dependence see anger as a threat to group harmony (Markus & Kitayama, 1991). In Tahiti, for instance, people learn to be considerate and gentle. In Japan, from infancy on, angry expressions are less common than in Western cultures, where in recent politics, anger seems all the rage.

The Western vent-your-anger advice presumes that we can achieve emotional release, or **catharsis,** through aggressive action or fantasy.

Anger can indeed be *temporarily* calming if it does not leave us feeling guilty or anxious (Geen & Quanty, 1977; Hokanson & Edelman, 1966).

However, catharsis usually fails to cleanse one's rage. More often, expressing anger breeds more anger. For one thing, it may provoke further retaliation, thus escalating a minor conflict into a major confrontation. For another, expressing anger can magnify anger. (Recall the behavior feedback research from Chapter 10: *Acting* angry can make us *feel* angrier.)

In one study, people who had been provoked were asked to wallop a punching bag while ruminating about the person who had angered them. Later, when given a chance for revenge, they became even more aggressive (Bushman, 2002). Angry outbursts that temporarily calm us are dangerous in another way: They may be reinforcing and therefore habit forming. If stressed managers find they can drain off some of their tension by berating an employee, then the next time they feel irritated and tense they may be more likely to explode again. Think about it: The next time you are angry you are

likely to repeat whatever relieved your anger in the past.

What, then, is the best way to handle our anger? Experts offer two suggestions. First, wait. You can bring down the level of physiological arousal of anger by waiting. "It is true of the body as of arrows," noted Carol Tavris (1982), "what goes up must come down. Any emotional arousal will simmer down if you just wait long enough." Second, deal with anger in a way that involves neither being chronically angry over every little annoyance, nor sulking and rehearsing your grievances. Ruminating inwardly about the causes of your anger serves only to increase it (Rusting & Nolen-Hoeksema, 1998). Calm yourself by exercising, playing an instrument, or talking it through with a friend.

Anger is not always wrong. Used wisely, it can communicate strength and competence (Tiedens, 2001). It can benefit a relationship when it expresses a grievance in ways that promote reconciliation rather than retaliation. Controlled expressions of anger are more adaptive than either hostile outbursts or pent-up angry feelings. Civility means not only keeping silent about trivial irritations but also communicating important ones clearly

and fat from the blood, can't do its job. Type A individuals are more often "combat ready." Thus, excess cholesterol and fat may continue to circulate in their blood and later get deposited around the heart. Further stress—sometimes conflicts brought on by their own abrasiveness—may trigger altered heart rhythms. In people with weakened hearts, this altered pattern can cause sudden death (Kamarck & Jennings, 1991). Hostility also correlates with other risk factors, such as smoking, drinking, and obesity (Bunde & Suls, 2006). In important ways, people's minds and hearts interact.

Hundreds of other studies of young and middle-aged men and women have confirmed the finding that people who react with anger over little things are most prone to heart disease. As researchers have noted, rage "seems to lash back and strike us in the heart muscle" (Spielberger & London, 1982). (See Close-Up: Tips for Handling Anger.)

Pessimism seems to be similarly toxic. Laura Kubzansky and her colleagues (2001) studied 1306 initially healthy men who a decade earlier had scored as optimists, pessimists, or neither. Even after other risk factors such as smoking had been ruled out, pessimists were more than twice as likely as optimists to develop coronary heart disease (**FIGURE 11.6** on the next page). (More on optimism and pessimism in the next section, Coping With Stress.)

Depression, too, can be lethal. Happy people tend to be healthier and to outlive their unhappy peers (Diener & Chan, 2011; Siahpush et al., 2008). Even a big, happy smile predicts longevity, as researchers discovered when they examined the photographs of 150 Major League Baseball players who had

Type A Friedman and Rosenman's term for competitive, hard-driving, impatient, verbally aggressive, and anger-prone people.

Type B Friedman and Rosenman's term for easygoing, relaxed people.

catharsis in psychology, the idea that "releasing" aggressive energy (through action or fantasy) relieves aggressive urges.

© Sean Locke/istockphoto

Mike Hutchings/Reuters/Newscom

Blowing off steam My daughter, now a resident of South Africa, experienced a temporary catharsis while cheering on her new country in a World Cup soccer match. "Every time I got angry at Uruguay, blowing that vuvuzela and joining the chorus of dissent released something in me."

and assertively. A nonaccusing statement of feeling—perhaps letting one's housemate know that "I get irritated when the dirty dishes are left for me to clean up"—can help resolve the conflicts that cause anger.

What if someone's behavior really hurts you, and you cannot resolve the conflict? Research commends the age-old response of forgiveness. Without letting the offender off the hook or inviting further harm, forgiveness

releases anger and calms the body. To explore the bodily effects of forgiveness, Charlotte Witvliet and her co-researchers (2001) invited college students to recall an incident where someone had hurt them. As the students mentally rehearsed forgiveness, their negative feelings—and their perspiration, blood pressure, heart rate, and facial tension—all were lower than when they rehearsed their grudges.

"Venting to reduce anger is like using gasoline to put out a fire."

Researcher Brad Bushman (2002)

"Anger will never disappear so long as thoughts of resentment are cherished in the mind."

The Buddha 500 B.C.E.

RETRIEVE IT

• Which one of the following IS an effective strategy for reducing angry feelings?

    a. Retaliate verbally or physically.

    b. Wait or "simmer down."

    c. Express anger in action or fantasy.

    d. Review the grievance silently.

ANSWER: b.

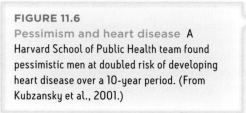

FIGURE 11.6

Pessimism and heart disease A Harvard School of Public Health team found pessimistic men at doubled risk of developing heart disease over a 10-year period. (From Kubzansky et al., 2001.)

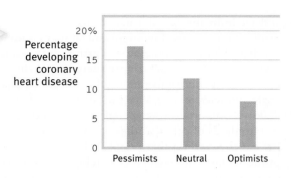

"A cheerful heart is a good medicine, but a downcast spirit dries up the bones."

Proverbs 17:22

appeared in the 1952 *Baseball Register* and had died by 2009 (Abel & Kruger, 2010). On average, the nonsmilers had died at 73, compared with an average 80 years for those with a broad, genuine smile.

The accumulated evidence from 57 studies suggests that "depression substantially increases the risk of death, especially death by unnatural causes and cardiovascular disease" (Wulsin et al., 1999). After following 63,469 women over a dozen years, researchers found more than a doubled rate of heart attack death among those who initially scored as depressed (Whang et al., 2009). In the years following a heart attack, people with high depression scores were four times more likely than their low-scoring counterparts to develop further heart problems (Frasure-Smith & Lesperance, 2005). Depression is disheartening.

Depressed people tend to smoke more and exercise less (Whooley et al., 2008), but stress itself is also disheartening:

- When following 17,415 middle-aged American women, researchers found an 88 percent increased risk of heart attacks among those facing significant work stress (Slopen et al., 2010).

- In Denmark, a study of 12,116 female nurses found that those reporting "much too high" work pressures had a 40 percent increased risk of heart disease (Allesøe et al., 2010).

- In the United States, a 10-year study of middle-aged workers found that involuntary job loss more than doubled their risk of a heart attack (Gallo et al., 2006). A 14-year study of 1059 women found that those with five or more trauma-related stress symptoms had three times the normal risk of heart disease (Kubzansky et al., 2009).

Heart disease and depression may both result when stress triggers persistent inflammation (Matthews, 2005; Miller & Blackwell, 2006). As the body focuses its energies on fleeing or fighting a threat, stress hormones boost the production of proteins that contribute to inflammation. Persistent inflammation can lead to asthma or clogged arteries and can worsen depression.

★ ★ ★

We can view the stress effect on our disease resistance as a price we pay for the benefits of stress. Stress invigorates our lives by arousing and motivating us. An unstressed life would hardly be challenging or productive. But as we have seen, stress can also harm us (**FIGURE 11.7**). Knowing that, we can work to promote and maintain our health.

Traditionally, people have thought about their health only when something goes wrong—visiting a physician for diagnosis and treatment. That, say health psychologists, is like ignoring a car's maintenance and going to a mechanic only when the car breaks down. Health maintenance begins with implementing strategies that prevent illness by alleviating stress and enhancing well-being.

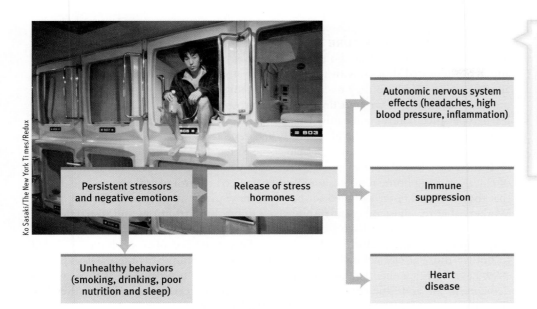

Ko Sasaki/The New York Times/Redux

Persistent stressors and negative emotions → Release of stress hormones

Autonomic nervous system effects (headaches, high blood pressure, inflammation)

Immune suppression

Unhealthy behaviors (smoking, drinking, poor nutrition and sleep)

Heart disease

FIGURE 11.7

Stress can have a variety of health-related consequences This is especially so when stress is experienced by angry, depressed, or anxious people. Job and income loss caused by the recent economic recession has created stress for many people, such as this jobless Japanese man living in a Tokyo "capsule hotel."

Coping With Stress

11-5: In what two ways do people try to alleviate stress?

Stressors are unavoidable. This fact, coupled with the fact that persistent stress correlates with heart disease, depression, and lowered immunity, gives us a clear message: We need to learn to **cope** with the stress in our lives, alleviating it with emotional, cognitive, or behavioral methods.

Some stressors we address directly, with **problem-focused coping.** If our impatience leads to a family fight, we may go directly to that family member to work things out. We tend to use problem-focused strategies when we feel a sense of control over a situation and think we can change the circumstances, or at least change ourselves to deal with the circumstances more capably.

We turn to **emotion-focused coping** when we cannot—or *believe* we cannot—change a situation. If, despite our best efforts, we cannot get along with that family member, we may search for stress relief by reaching out to friends for support and comfort. Emotion-focused strategies can move us toward better long-term health, as when we exercise or keep busy with hobbies to avoid thinking about an old addiction. Emotion-focused strategies can be maladaptive, however, as when students worried about not keeping up with the reading in class go out to party to get it off their mind. Sometimes a problem-focused strategy (catching up with the reading) more effectively reduces stress and promotes long-term health and satisfaction.

When challenged, some of us tend to respond with cool problem-focused coping, others with emotion-focused coping (Connor-Smith & Flachsbart, 2007). Our feelings of personal control, our explanatory style, and our supportive connections all influence our ability to cope successfully.

Personal Control

11-6: How does a perceived lack of control affect health?

Picture the scene: Two rats receive simultaneous shocks. One can turn a wheel to stop the shocks. The helpless rat, but not the wheel turner, becomes more susceptible to ulcers and lowered immunity to disease (Laudenslager & Reite, 1984). In humans, too, uncontrollable threats trigger the strongest stress responses (Dickerson & Kemeny, 2004).

coping alleviating stress using emotional, cognitive, or behavioral methods.

problem-focused coping attempting to alleviate stress directly—by changing the stressor or the way we interact with that stressor.

emotion-focused coping attempting to alleviate stress by avoiding or ignoring a stressor and attending to emotional needs related to one's stress reaction.

learned helplessness the hopelessness and passive resignation an animal or human learns when unable to avoid repeated aversive events.

Feeling helpless and oppressed may lead to a state of passive resignation called **learned helplessness** (**FIGURE 11.8**). Experimenter Martin Seligman (1975, 1991) discovered this in some long-ago experiments in which dogs were strapped in a harness and given repeated shocks, with no opportunity to avoid them. Later, when placed in another situation where they *could* escape the punishment by simply leaping a hurdle, the dogs cowered as if without hope. In contrast, animals able to escape the first shocks learned personal control and easily escaped the shocks in the new situation.

Humans can also learn helplessness. When repeatedly faced with traumatic events over which they have no control, people come to feel helpless, hopeless, and depressed.

Perceiving a loss of control, we become more vulnerable to ill health. A famous study of elderly nursing home residents with little perceived control over their activities found that they declined faster and died sooner than those given more control (Rodin, 1986). Workers able to adjust office furnishings and control interruptions and distractions in their work environment have experienced less stress (O'Neill, 1993). Such findings may help explain why British civil service workers at the executive grades have tended to outlive those at clerical or laboring grades, and why Finnish workers with low job stress have been less than half as likely to die of strokes or heart disease as those with a demanding job and little control. The more control workers have, the longer they live (Bosma et al., 1997, 1998; Kivimaki et al., 2002; Marmot et al., 1997).

Increasing self-control—allowing prisoners to move chairs and control room lights and the TV, having workers participate in decision making, offering nursing home patients choices about their environment—noticeably improves health and morale (Humphrey et al., 2007; Wang et al., 2010). In the case of the nursing home patients, 93 percent of those encouraged to exert more control became more alert, active, and happy (Rodin, 1986). As researcher Ellen Langer (1983, p. 291) concluded, "Perceived control is basic to human functioning."

Control may also help explain a well-established link between economic status and longevity (Jokela et al., 2009). In one study of 843 grave markers in an old graveyard in Glasgow, Scotland, those with the costliest, highest pillars (indicating the most affluence) tended to have lived the longest (Carroll et al., 1994). Likewise, those living in Scottish regions with the least overcrowding and unemployment have the greatest longevity. There and elsewhere, high economic status predicts a lower risk of heart and respiratory diseases (Sapolsky, 2005). Wealthy predicts healthy among children, too (Chen, 2004). With higher economic status come reduced risks of low birth weight, infant mortality, smoking, and violence. Even among other primates, individuals at the bottom of the social pecking order have been more likely than their higher-status companions to become sick when exposed to a cold-like virus (Cohen et al., 1997). But high status also entails stress: High-status baboons and monkeys who frequently have to physically defend their dominant position show high stress levels (Sapolsky, 2005).

Why does perceived loss of control predict health problems? Because losing control provokes an outpouring of stress hormones. When rats cannot control shock or when primates or humans feel unable to control their environment, stress hormone levels rise, blood pressure increases, and immune responses drop (Rodin, 1986; Sapolsky, 2005).

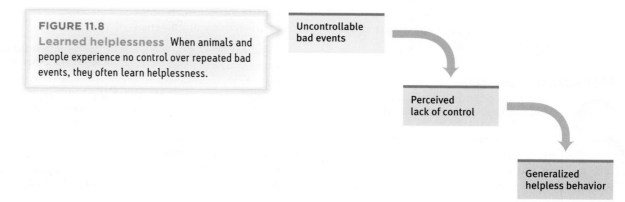

FIGURE 11.8

Learned helplessness When animals and people experience no control over repeated bad events, they often learn helplessness.

Uncontrollable bad events

Perceived lack of control

Generalized helpless behavior

Captive animals therefore experience more stress and are more vulnerable to disease than are wild animals (Roberts, 1988). Human studies have confirmed that crowding in high-density neighborhoods, prisons, and college and university dorms is another source of diminished feelings of control—and of elevated levels of stress hormones and blood pressure (Fleming et al., 1987; Ostfeld et al., 1987).

RETRIEVE IT

- To cope with stress, we tend to use _____-focused (emotion/problem) strategies when we feel in control of our world, and _____-focused (emotion/problem) strategies when we believe we cannot change a situation.

ANSWERS: problem; emotion

Internal Versus External Locus of Control

If experiencing a loss of control can be stressful and unhealthy, do people who generally feel in control of their lives enjoy better health? Consider your own feelings of control. Do you believe that your life is beyond your control? That getting a good job depends mainly on being in the right place at the right time? Or do you more strongly believe that what happens to you is your own doing? That being a success is a matter of hard work? Did your parents influence your feelings of control? Did your culture?

Hundreds of studies have compared people who differ in their perceptions of control. On one side are those who have what psychologist Julian Rotter called an **external locus of control**—the perception that chance or outside forces determine their fate. On the other are those who perceive an **internal locus of control,** who believe that they control their own destiny. In study after study, "internals" have achieved more in school and work, acted more independently, enjoyed better health, and felt less depressed than did "externals" (Lefcourt, 1982; Ng et al., 2006). Moreover, they were better at delaying gratification and coping with various stressors, including marital problems (Miller & Monge, 1986). One study followed 7551 British people for two decades. Those who expressed a more internal locus of control at age 10 exhibited less obesity, hypertension, and distress at age 30 (Gale et al., 2008). Other studies have found that people who believe in free will, or that willpower is controllable, learn better, perform better at work, and are more helpful (Job et al., 2010; Stillman et al., 2010).

Compared with their parents' generation, more Americans now endorse an external locus of control (Twenge et al., 2004). This shift may help explain an associated increase in rates of depression and other psychological disorders in the new generation (Twenge et al., 2010).

Depleting and Strengthening Self-Control

Self-control is the ability to control impulses and delay short-term gratification for longer-term rewards. In studies, this ability has predicted good adjustment, better grades, and social success (Tangney et al., 2004). Students who planned their day's activities and then lived out their day as planned were also at low risk for depression (Nezlek, 2001).

Self-control often fluctuates. Like a muscle, self-control temporarily weakens after an exertion, replenishes with rest, and becomes stronger with exercise (Baumeister & Exline, 2000; Hagger et al., 2010; Vohs & Baumeister, 2011). Exercising willpower temporarily depletes the mental energy needed for self-control on other tasks (Gailliott & Baumeister, 2007). In one experiment, hungry people who had resisted the temptation to eat chocolate chip cookies abandoned a tedious task sooner than those who had not resisted the cookies. And after expending willpower on laboratory tasks, such as stifling prejudice or saying the color of words (for example, "red" even if the red-colored word was *green*), people were less restrained in their aggressive responses to provocation and in their sexuality (DeWall et al., 2007; Gaillot & Baumeister, 2007).

external locus of control the perception that chance or outside forces beyond our personal control determine our fate.

internal locus of control the perception that you control your own fate.

self-control the ability to control impulses and delay short-term gratification for greater long-term rewards.

Extreme self-control Our ability to exert self-control increases with practice, and some of us have practiced more than others! Magician David Blaine (left) endured standing in a block of ice (in which a small space had been carved out for him) for nearly 62 hours for a stunt in New York's Times Square. A number of performing artists make their living as very convincing human statues, as does this actress (right) performing on The Royal Mile in Edinburgh, Scotland.

Researchers have found that exercising willpower depletes the blood sugar and neural activity associated with mental focus (Inzlicht & Gutsell, 2007). What, then, might be the effect of deliberately boosting their blood sugar when self-control is depleted? Giving energy-boosting sugar (in a naturally rather than an artificially sweetened lemonade) had a sweet effect: It strengthened people's effortful thinking and reduced their financial impulsiveness (Masicampo & Baumeister, 2008; Wang & Dvorak, 2010). Even dogs can experience self-control depletion and rejuvenation with sugar (Miller et al., 2010).

In the long run, self-control requires attention and energy. With physical exercise and time-managed study programs, people have strengthened their self-control, as seen in both their performance on laboratory tasks and their improved self-management of eating, drinking, smoking, and household chores (Oaten & Cheng, 2006a,b). *The bottom line:* We can grow our willpower muscles—our capacity for self-regulation. But doing so requires some (dare I say it?) willpower.

Optimism Versus Pessimism

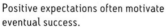

11-7: What are the links among basic outlook on life, social support, stress, and health?

We have seen that our outlook—what we expect from the world—influences our risk of heart disease. Our outlook also affects our ability to cope with stress and our overall health. *Pessimists* attribute their poor performance to a basic lack of ability ("I can't do this") or to situations enduringly beyond their control ("There is nothing I can do about it"). *Optimists* expect to have more control, to cope better with stressful events, and to enjoy better health (Aspinwall & Tedeschi, 2010; Carver et al., 2010; Rasmussen et al., 2010). During a semester's last month, students previously identified as optimistic reported less fatigue and fewer coughs, aches, and pains. And during the stressful first few weeks of law school, those who were optimistic ("It's unlikely that I will fail") enjoyed better moods and stronger immune systems (Segerstrom et al., 1998). Optimists also respond to stress with smaller increases in blood pressure, and they recover more quickly from heart bypass surgery.

Optimistic students have also tended to get better grades because they often respond to setbacks with the hopeful attitude that effort, good study habits, and self-discipline make a difference (Noel et al., 1987; Peterson & Barrett, 1987). When dating couples wrestle with conflicts, optimists and their partners see each other as engaging constructively, and they then tend to feel more supported and satisfied with the resolution and with their relationship (Srivastava et al., 2006). Optimism also relates to well-being and success in China and Japan (Qin & Piao, 2011). Realistic positive expectations fuel motivation and success (Oettingen & Mayer, 2002).

Consider the consistency and startling magnitude of the optimism and positive emotions factor in several other studies:

- One research team followed 941 Dutch people, ages 65 to 85, for nearly a decade (Giltay et al., 2004, 2007). Among those in the lowest optimism quartile, 57 percent died, as did only 30 percent of the top optimism quartile.

Positive expectations often motivate eventual success.

"We just haven't been flapping them hard enough."

The oldest Holocaust survivor explaining her 107 years:
"In a word: optimism. I look at the good. When you are relaxed, your body is always relaxed."

Alice Herz-Sommer, 2010

- When Finnish researchers followed 2428 men for up to a decade, the number of deaths among those with a bleak, hopeless outlook was more than double that found among their optimistic counterparts (Everson et al., 1996). American researchers found the same when following 4256 Vietnam-era veterans (Phillips et al., 2009).

- A now-famous study followed up on 180 Catholic nuns who had written brief autobiographies at about 22 years of age and had thereafter lived similar lifestyles. Those who had expressed happiness, love, and other positive feelings in their autobiographies lived an average 7 years longer than their more dour counterparts (Danner et al., 2001). By age 80, some 54 percent of those expressing few positive emotions had died, as had only 24 percent of the most positive spirited.

Optimism runs in families, so some people truly are predisposed to have a sunny, hopeful outlook. In identical twins, if one is optimistic, the other will often independently show signs of optimism as well (Mosing et al., 2009). One genetic marker of optimism is a receptor gene for the social-bonding hormone *oxytocin* (Saphire-Bernstein et al., 2011).

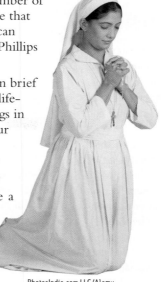

PhotosIndia.com LLC/Alamy

Social Support

Social support—feeling liked and encouraged by intimate friends and family—promotes both health and happiness. In massive investigations, some following thousands of people for several years, close relationships have predicted health. People are less likely to die early if supported by close relationships (Uchino, 2009). When Brigham Young University researchers combined data from 148 studies totaling more than 300,000 people worldwide, they confirmed a striking effect of social support (Holt-Lunstad et al., 2010). Those with ample social connections had survival rates about 50 percent greater than those with meager connections. The meager-connections health handicap appeared roughly equal to the effect of smoking 15 cigarettes a day or of being alcohol dependent, and it was double the effect of not exercising or being obese.

People need people. Some fill this need by connecting with friends, family, co-workers, members of a faith community, or other support groups. Others connect in positive, happy, supportive marriages. People in low-conflict marriages live longer, healthier lives than the unmarried (De Vogli et al., 2007; Kaplan & Kronick, 2006; Sbarra, 2009). This correlation holds regardless of age, sex, race, and income (National Center for Health Statistics, 2004). One seven-decades-long study found that at age 50, healthy aging is better predicted by a good marriage than by a low cholesterol level (Vaillant, 2002). But the married versus never-married health gap has shrunk (Liu, 2009).

What explains the link between social support and health? Are middle-aged and older adults who live with little social engagement more likely to smoke, be obese, and have high cholesterol—and therefore to have a doubled risk of heart attacks (Nielsen et al., 2006)? Or are healthy people simply more sociable? Research suggests that social support itself creates health benefits.

Social support calms us and reduces blood pressure and stress hormones. More than 50 studies support this finding (Graham et al., 2006; Uchino et al., 1996, 1999). To see if social support might calm people's response to threats, one research team subjected happily married women, while lying in an fMRI machine, to the threat of electric shock to an ankle (Coan et al., 2006). During the experiment, some women held their husband's hand. Others held the hand of an unknown person or no hand at all. While awaiting the occasional shocks, women holding their husband's hand showed less activity in threat-responsive areas. This soothing benefit was greatest for those reporting the highest-quality marriages. Supportive family and friends—human and nonhuman—help buffer threats. After stressful events, Medicare patients who have a dog or other companionable pet are less likely to visit their doctor (Siegel, 1990). (See Close-Up: Pets Are Friends, Too on the next page.)

Laughter among friends is good medicine Laughter arouses us, massages muscles, and then leaves us feeling relaxed (Robinson, 1983). Humor (though not hostile sarcasm) may defuse stress, ease pain, and strengthen immune activity (Ayan, 2009; Berk et al., 2001; Kimata, 2001). People who laugh a lot also tend to have lower rates of heart disease (Clark et al., 2001).

Getty Images/Rubberball

CLOSE UP:

Pets Are Friends, Too

Have you ever wished for a friend who would love you just as you are? One who would never judge you? Who would be there for you, no matter your mood? For many tens of millions of people that friend exists, and it is a loyal dog or a friendly cat.

Many people describe their pet as a cherished family member who helps them feel calm, happy, and valued. Can pets also help people handle stress? If so, might pets have healing power? The evidence is, as yet, mixed and meager (Herzog, 2010). But Karen Allen (2003), Deborah Wells (2009), and Allen McConnell and colleagues (2011) have reported that pets have sometimes been found to provide social support, to increase the odds of survival after a heart attack, to relieve depression among AIDS patients, and to lower the level of blood pressure and blood lipids that contribute to cardiovascular risk. As nursing pioneer Florence

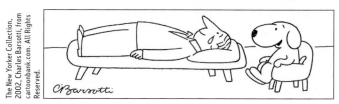

"Well, I think you're wonderful"

Nightingale (1860) foresaw, "A small pet animal is often an excellent companion for the sick." In one study, women's blood pressure rose as they struggled with challenging math problems in the presence of a best friend or even a spouse, but much less so when accompanied by their dog (Allen, 2003).

So, would pets be good medicine for people who do not have pets? To find out, Karen Allen experimented. The participants were a group of stockbrokers who lived alone, described their work as stressful, and had high blood

pressure. She randomly selected half to adopt an animal shelter cat or dog. When later facing stress, all participants experienced higher blood pressure. But among the new pet owners, the increase was less than half as high as the increase in the no-pet group. The effect was greatest for pet owners with few social contacts or friends. Allen's conclusion: For lowering blood pressure, pets are no substitute for effective drugs and exercise. But for people who enjoy animals, and especially for those who live alone, pets are a healthy pleasure.

Social support fosters stronger immune functioning. Volunteers in studies of resistance to cold viruses showed this benefit (Cohen et al., 1997, 2004). Healthy volunteers inhaled nasal drops laden with a cold virus and were quarantined and observed for five days. (In these experiments, more than 600 volunteers received $800 each to endure this experience.) Age, race, sex, smoking, and other health habits being equal, those with the most social ties were least likely to catch a cold. If they did catch one, they produced less mucus. More sociability meant less susceptibility. The cold fact is that the effect of social ties is nothing to sneeze at!

Close relationships give us an opportunity for "open heart therapy," a chance to confide painful feelings (Frattaroli, 2006). Talking about a stressful event can temporarily arouse us, but in the long run it calms us, by calming limbic system activity (Lieberman et al., 2007; Mendolia & Kleck, 1993). In one study, 33 Holocaust survivors spent two hours recalling their experiences, many in intimate detail never before disclosed (Pennebaker et al., 1989). In the weeks following, most watched a tape of their recollections and showed it to family and friends. Those who were most self-disclosing had the most improved health 14 months later. Confiding is good for the body and the soul. In another study of surviving spouses of people who had committed suicide or died in car accidents, those who bore their grief alone had more health problems than those who could express it openly (Pennebaker & O'Heeron, 1984).

"Woe to one who is alone and falls and does not have another to help."

Ecclesiastes 4:10

Suppressing emotions can be detrimental to physical health. When health psychologist James Pennebaker (1985) surveyed more than 700 undergraduate women, about 1 in 12 reported a traumatic childhood sexual experience. The sexually abused women—especially those who had kept their secret to themselves—reported more headaches and stomach ailments than did other women who had experienced nonsexual traumas, such as parental death or divorce. Another study, of 437 Australian ambulance drivers, confirmed the ill effects of suppressing one's emotions after witnessing traumas (Wastell, 2002).

Even writing about personal traumas in a diary can help (Burton & King, 2008; Hemenover, 2003; Lyubomirsky et al., 2006). In one experiment, volunteers who did so had fewer health problems during the ensuing four to six months (Pennebaker, 1990). As one participant explained, "Although I have not talked with anyone about what I wrote, I was finally able to deal with it, work through the pain instead of trying to block it out. Now it doesn't hurt to think about it."

If we are aiming to exercise more, drink less, quit smoking, or attain a healthy weight, our social ties can tug us away from or toward our goal. Studies of networks of thousands of people followed over years suggest that clusters of friends may "infect" one another with either bad health practices or good behaviors (Christakis & Fowler, 2009). Obesity, for example, spreads within networks in ways that seem not merely to reflect people's seeking out similar others.

RETRIEVE IT

• Some research finds that people with companionable pets are less likely than those without pets to visit their doctors after stressful events (Siegel, 1990). How can the health benefits from social support shed light on this finding?

ANSWER: Feeling social support—even from a pet—might calm people and lead to lower levels of stress hormones and blood pressure.

Photos.com/Getty Images

Reducing Stress

Having a sense of control, developing more optimistic thinking, and building social support can help us *experience* less stress and thus improve our health. Moreover, these factors interrelate: People who are upbeat about themselves and their future tend also to enjoy health-promoting social ties (Stinson et al., 2008). But sometimes we cannot alleviate stress and simply need to *manage* our stress. Aerobic exercise, relaxation, meditation, and active spiritual engagement may help us gather inner strength and lessen stress effects.

Aerobic Exercise

11-8: How effective is aerobic exercise as a way to manage stress and improve well-being?

Aerobic exercise is sustained, oxygen-consuming exercise—such as jogging, swimming, or biking—that increases heart and lung fitness. It's hard to find bad things to say about exercise. By one estimate, moderate exercise adds not only quantity of life—two additional years, on average—but also quality of life, with more energy and better mood (Seligman, 1994).

Exercise helps fight heart disease by strengthening the heart, increasing bloodflow, keeping blood vessels open, and lowering both blood pressure and the blood pressure reaction to stress (Ford, 2002; Manson, 2002). Inactivity can be toxic. People who exercise suffer half as many heart attacks as do others who are inactive (Powell et al., 1987; Visich & Fletcher, 2009). Exercise makes your muscles hungry for the fats that, if not used by muscles, can contribute to clogged arteries (Barinaga, 1997). In one 20-year study of adult Finnish twins, daily conditioning exercise (other things being equal) reduced death risk by 43 percent (Kujala et al., 1998). Regular exercise in later life also

aerobic exercise sustained exercise that increases heart and lung fitness; may also alleviate depression and anxiety.

Kathryn Brownson

The mood boost When energy or spirits are sagging, few things reboot the day better than exercising (as I can confirm from my daily noontime basketball). Aerobic exercise appears to counteract depression partly by increasing arousal (replacing depression's low-arousal state) and by doing naturally what Prozac does—increasing the brain's serotonin activity.

predicts better cognitive functioning and reduced risk of dementia and Alzheimer's disease (Kramer & Erickson, 2007).

Does exercise also boost the spirit? Many studies reveal that aerobic exercise can reduce stress, depression, and anxiety. Americans, Canadians, and Britons who have at least three weekly aerobic exercise sessions manage stress better, exhibit more self-confidence, and feel more vigor and less depression and fatigue than do their inactive peers (McMurray, 2004; Mead et al., 2010; Puetz et al., 2006). And in a 21-country survey of university students, physical exercise was a "strong" and consistent predictor of life satisfaction (Grant et al., 2009).

But we could state this observation another way: Stressed and depressed people exercise less. These findings are correlations, and cause and effect are unclear. To sort out cause and effect, researchers experiment. They randomly assign stressed, depressed, or anxious people either to an aerobic exercise group or to a control group. One classic experiment randomly assigned mildly depressed female collegians to three groups. One-third participated in a program of aerobic exercise. Another third took part in a program of relaxation exercises. The remaining third (the control group) formed a no-treatment group (McCann & Holmes, 1984). As **FIGURE 11.9** shows, 10 weeks later, the women in the aerobic exercise program reported the greatest decrease in depression. Many had, quite literally, run away from their troubles.

Dozens of other experiments confirm that exercise prevents or reduces depression and anxiety (Conn, 2010; Rethorst et al., 2009; Windle et al., 2010). Vigorous exercise provides a substantial and immediate mood boost (Watson, 2000). Even a 10-minute walk stimulates 2 hours of increased well-being by raising energy levels and lowering tension (Thayer, 1987, 1993).

Some studies have indicated that not only is exercise as effective as drugs, it better prevents symptom recurrence (Babyak et al., 2000; Salmon, 2001). *Why?* Because exercise in some ways works like an antidepressant drug. It increases arousal, thus counteracting depression's low arousal state. It often leads to muscle relaxation and sounder sleep. It also orders up mood-boosting chemicals from our body's internal pharmacy—neurotransmitters such as norepinephrine, serotonin, and the endorphins (Jacobs, 1994; Salmon, 2001). Exercise may even foster *neurogenesis.* In mice, exercise causes the brain to produce a molecule that stimulates the production of new, stress-resistant neurons (Hunsberger et al., 2007; Reynolds, 2009; van Praag, 2009).

FIGURE 11.9

Aerobic exercise and depression Mildly depressed college women who participated in an aerobic exercise program showed markedly reduced depression, compared with those who did relaxation exercises or received no treatment. (From McCann & Holmes, 1984.)

Paik Photography/Alamy

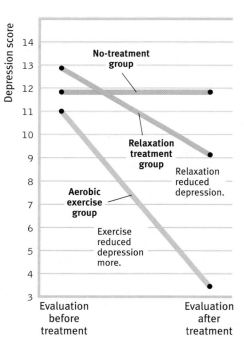

On a simpler level, the sense of accomplishment and improved physique and body image that often accompany a successful exercise routine may enhance one's self-image, leading to a better emotional state. Exercising at least a half-hour on 5 or more days each week is like taking a drug that prevents and treats disease, increases energy, calms anxiety, and boosts mood—a drug we would all take, if available. Yet few people (only 1 in 4 in the United States) take advantage of it (Mendes, 2010).

Relaxation and Meditation

11-9: In what ways might relaxation and meditation influence stress and health?

Knowing the damaging effects of stress, could we learn to counteract our stress responses by altering our thinking and lifestyle? In the late 1960s, some respected psychologists, including Neal Miller, began experimenting with *biofeedback,* a system of recording, amplifying, and feeding back information about subtle physiological responses, many controlled by the autonomic nervous system. Biofeedback instruments mirror the results of a person's own efforts, enabling the person to learn which techniques do (or do not) control a particular physiological response. After a decade of study, however, the initial claims for biofeedback seemed overblown and oversold (Miller, 1985). In 1995, a National Institutes of Health panel declared that biofeedback works best on tension headaches.

Simple methods of relaxation, which require no expensive equipment, produce many of the results biofeedback once promised. Figure 11.9 pointed out that aerobic exercise reduces depression. But did you notice in that figure that depression also decreased among women in the relaxation treatment group? More than 60 studies have found that relaxation procedures can also help alleviate headaches, hypertension, anxiety, and insomnia (Nestoriuc et al., 2008; Stetter & Kupper, 2002).

Such findings would not surprise Meyer Friedman and his colleagues. They tested relaxation in a program designed to help Type A heart attack survivors reduce their risk of future attacks. They randomly assigned hundreds of middle-aged men to one of two groups. The first group received standard advice from cardiologists about medications, diet, and exercise habits. The second group received similar advice, but they also were taught ways of modifying their lifestyles. They learned to slow down and relax by walking, talking, and eating more slowly. They learned to smile at others and laugh at themselves. They learned to admit their mistakes, to take time to enjoy life, and to renew their religious faith. The training paid off (**FIGURE 11.10**). During the next three years, the lifestyle modification group had half as many repeat heart attacks as did the first group. This, wrote the exuberant Friedman, was an unprecedented, spectacular reduction in heart-attack recurrence. A

FIGURE 11.10

Recurrent heart attacks and lifestyle modification The San Francisco Recurrent Coronary Prevention Project offered counseling from a cardiologist to survivors of heart attacks. Those who were also guided in modifying their Type A lifestyle suffered fewer repeat heart attacks. (From Friedman & Ulmer, 1984.)

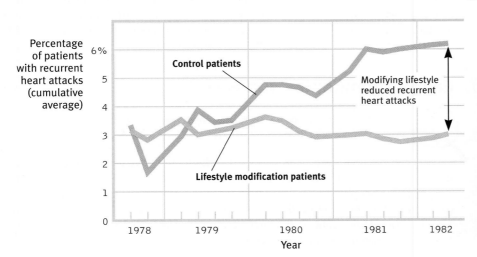

smaller-scale British study similarly divided heart-attack–prone people into control and lifestyle modification groups (Eysenck & Grossarth-Maticek, 1991). During the next 13 years, people trained to alter their thinking and lifestyle showed a 50 percent reduction in death rate. After suffering a heart attack at age 55, Friedman started taking his own behavioral medicine—and lived to age 90 (Wargo, 2007).

Cardiologist Herbert Benson (1996) became intrigued with reports that experienced meditators could lower their blood pressure, heart rate, and oxygen consumption and raise their fingertip temperature. His research led to what he has called the *relaxation response,* a state of calm marked by relaxed muscles, slowed breathing and heart rate, and decreased blood pressure. According to Benson, relaxation practiced once or twice daily has lasting stress-reducing benefits.

To experience the relaxation response, the Benson-Henry Institute for Mind Body Medicine recommends these steps: Sit quietly in a comfortable position. Close your eyes. Relax your muscles, starting with your feet, then your calves, and upward through your thighs, shoulders, neck, and head. Breathe slowly. As you exhale each breath, repeat a focus word, phrase, or prayer—something drawn from your own belief system. When other thoughts intrude, don't worry. Just return to your repetition and continue for 10 to 20 minutes. When finished, sit quietly for another minute or two, then open your eyes and sit for a few more moments.

Tibetan Buddhists deep in meditation and Franciscan nuns deep in centering prayer report a diminished sense of self, space, and time. Brain scans reveal the neural footprints of such spiritual feelings during these mystical experiences: A part of the parietal lobe that tracks our location in space is less active than usual, and a frontal lobe area involved in focused attention is more active (Cahn & Polich, 2006; Newberg & D'Aquili, 2001). Another difference appears in the brain's left frontal lobe. In Buddhist monks experienced in meditation, this area displays elevated levels of activity usually associated with positive emotions.

Was this high rate of activity a *result* of meditation, or simply a correlation unrelated to cause and effect? To find out, the researchers experimented, comparing "before" and "after" brain scans of volunteers who were not experienced meditators (Davidson et al., 2003). First, they took baseline scans of volunteers' normal levels of brain activity. They then randomly assigned them either to a control group or to an eight-week course in *mindfulness meditation,* which has been shown to lessen anxiety and depression (Hofmann et al., 2010). Compared with both the control group and their own baseline, the meditation participants showed noticeably more left-hemisphere activity after the training, and they also had improved immune functioning. Such effects may help explain the results of another study, which found that hypertension patients assigned to meditation training had (compared with other treatment groups) a 30 percent lower cardiovascular death rate over the ensuing 19 years (Schneider et al., 2005). This benefit may have resulted from the lessened anxiety and improved mood that accompanies meditation (Hofmann et al., 2010).

Exercise and meditation are not the only routes to relaxation. As we noted in earlier chapters, massage has proven therapeutic for both premature infants and those suffering pain. A meta-analysis of 17 clinical experiments revealed another benefit: Massage therapy relaxes muscles and helps alleviate depression (Hou et al., 2010).

Faith Communities and Health

11-10: What is the faith factor, and what are some possible explanations for the link between faith and health?

A wealth of studies—some 1800 of them in the twenty-first century's first decade alone—has revealed another curious correlation: the *faith factor* (Koenig et al., 2011). Religiously active people tend to live longer than those who are not religiously active. One such study compared the death rates for 3900 people living in two Israeli communities. The first community contained 11 religiously orthodox collective settlements; the second contained 11 matched, nonreligious collective settlements (Kark et al., 1996). Over a 16-year

Meditation is a modern phenomenon with a long history: "Sit down alone and in silence. Lower your head, shut your eyes, breathe out gently, and imagine yourself looking into your own heart.... As you breathe out, say 'Lord Jesus Christ, have mercy on me.' ... Try to put all other thoughts aside. Be calm, be patient, and repeat the process very frequently" (Gregory of Sinai, died 1346).

And then there are the mystics who seek to use the mind's power to enable novocaine-free cavity repair. Their aim: transcend dental medication.

Dean Mitchell/Shutterstock

period, "belonging to a religious collective was associated with a strong protective effect" not explained by age or economic differences. In every age group, religious community members were about half as likely to have died as were their nonreligious counterparts. This difference is roughly comparable to the gender difference in mortality.

How should we interpret such findings? Correlations are not cause-effect statements, and they leave many factors uncontrolled (Sloan et al., 1999, 2000, 2002, 2005). Here is another possible interpretation: Women are more religiously active than men, and women outlive men. Might religious involvement merely reflect this gender-longevity link? Apparently not. One 8-year National Institutes of Health study followed 92,395 women (ages 50 to 79). After controlling for many factors, researchers found that women attending religious services weekly (or more) experienced an approximately 20 percent reduced risk of death during the study period (Schnall et al., 2010). Moreover, the association between religious involvement and life expectancy is also found among men (Benjamins et al., 2010; McCullough et al., 2000, 2005, 2009). A 28-year study that followed 5286 Californians found that, after controlling for age, gender, ethnicity, and education, frequent religious attendees were 36 percent less likely to have died in any year (**FIGURE 11.11**). In another 8-year controlled study of more than 20,000 people (Hummer et al., 1999), this effect translated into a life expectancy at age 20 of 83 years for frequent attendees at religious services and 75 years for infrequent attendees.

These correlational findings do not indicate that people who have not been religiously active can suddenly add 8 years to their lives if they start attending services and change nothing else. But the findings do indicate that religious involvement, like nonsmoking and exercise, is a *predictor* of health and longevity.

Recall that when Friedman and Rosenman's studies showed that Type A people were more prone to heart attacks, other researchers wanted to know more. What was the toxic ingredient? Similarly, researchers have wanted to know *why* religious involvement predicts health and longevity. Can you imagine what intervening variables might account for the correlation? Research points to three possible sets of influences (**FIGURE 11.12** on the next page):

- *Healthy behaviors:* Religion promotes self-control (McCullough & Willoughby, 2009), and religiously active people tend to smoke and drink much less and to have healthier lifestyles (Koenig & Vaillant, 2009; Park, 2007; Strawbridge et al., 2001). In one Gallup survey of 550,000 Americans, 15 percent of the very religious were smokers, as were 28 percent of those nonreligious (Newport et al., 2010). But such lifestyle differences are not great enough to explain the dramatically reduced mortality in the Israeli religious settlements. In American studies, too, about 75 percent of the longevity difference remained when researchers controlled for unhealthy behaviors, such as inactivity and smoking (Musick et al., 1999).

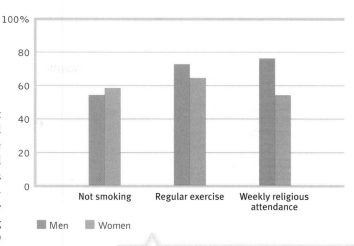

Risk of dying relative to others

■ Men   ■ Women

FIGURE 11.11

Predictors of longer life: Not smoking, frequent exercise, and regular religious attendance

Epidemiologist William Strawbridge and his co-workers (1997, 1999; Oman et al., 2002) followed 5286 Alameda, California, adults over 28 years. After adjusting for age and education, the researchers found that not smoking, regular exercise, and religious attendance all predicted a lowered risk of death in any given year. Women attending weekly religious services, for example, were only 54 percent as likely to die in a typical study year as were nonattendees.

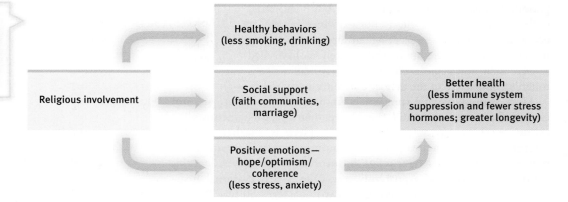

FIGURE 11.12
Possible explanations for the correlation between religious involvement and health/longevity

- *Social support:* Could social support explain the faith factor (Ai et al., 2007; George et al., 2002)? In Judaic, Christian, and Islamic religions, faith is a communal experience. To belong to one of these faith communities is to have access to a support network. Religiously active people are there for one another when misfortune strikes. Moreover, religion encourages marriage, another predictor of health and longevity. In the Israeli religious settlements, for example, divorce has been almost nonexistent.

- *Positive emotions:* Even after controlling for gender, unhealthy behaviors, preexisting health problems, and social support, the mortality studies still find that religiously engaged people tend to live longer (Chida et al., 2009). Researchers therefore speculate that religiously active people may benefit from a stable, coherent worldview, a sense of hope for the long-term future, feelings of ultimate acceptance, and the relaxed meditation of prayer or Sabbath observance. These intervening variables may also help to explain why the religiously active seem to have healthier immune functioning, fewer hospital admissions, and, for AIDS patients, fewer stress hormones and longer survival (Ironson et al., 2002; Koenig & Larson, 1998; Lutgendorf et al., 2004).

RETRIEVE IT

- What are some of the tactics we can use to manage the stress we cannot avoid?

ANSWERS: Aerobic exercise, relaxation procedures, meditation, and religious engagement

---

Happiness

11-11: What are the main effects of being happy?

People aspire to, and wish one another, health and happiness. And for good reason. Our state of happiness or unhappiness colors everything. Happy people perceive the world as safer and feel more confident. They are more decisive, cooperative, and tolerant. They rate job applicants more favorably, savor their positive past experiences without dwelling on the negative, and are more socially connected. They live healthier and more energized and satisfied lives (Briñol et al., 2007; Liberman et al., 2009; Mauss et al., 2011).

When your mood is gloomy, life as a whole seems depressing and meaningless—and you think more skeptically and attend more critically to your surroundings. Let your mood brighten, and your thinking broadens and becomes more playful and creative (Baas et al., 2008; Forgas, 2008b; Fredrickson, 2006). Relationships, self-image, and hopes for the future also seem more promising. One study that surveyed thousands of U.S. college students in 1976 and restudied them at age 37 found that happy students had gone on to earn significantly more money than their less-happy-than-average peers (Diener et al., 2002).

Moreover—and this is one of psychology's most consistent findings—happiness doesn't just feel good, it does good. In study after study, a mood-boosting experience (finding money, succeeding on a challenging task, recalling a happy event) has made people more likely to give money, pick up someone's dropped papers, volunteer time, and do other good deeds. Psychologists call it the **feel-good, do-good phenomenon** (Salovey, 1990). (The reverse is also true: Doing good also promotes good feeling, a phenomenon some happiness coaches harness when they have clients perform a daily "random act of kindness" and keep records of the results.)

Positive Psychology

11-12: What is subjective well-being, and what topics do positive psychology researchers explore? What are the three "pillars" of the movement?

William James was writing about the importance of happiness ("the secret motive for all [we] do") as early as 1902. By the 1960s, the *humanistic psychologists* were interested in advancing human fulfillment. In the twenty-first century, under the leadership of American Psychological Association past-president Martin Seligman, **positive psychology** is using scientific methods to study human flourishing. This young subfield includes studies of **subjective well-being**—our feelings of happiness (sometimes defined as a high ratio of positive to negative feelings) or sense of satisfaction with life. For example, researchers are exploring:

Martin E. P. Seligman "The main purpose of a positive psychology is to measure, understand, and then build the human strengths and the civic virtues."

- *positive emotions* by assessing exercises and interventions aimed at increasing happiness (Schueller, 2010; Sin & Lyubomirsky, 2009).

- *positive health* by studying how positive emotions enhance and sustain physical well-being (Seligman, 2008; Seligman et al., 2011).

- *positive neuroscience* by examining the biological foundations of positive emotions, resilience, and social behavior.

- *positive education* by evaluating educational efforts to increase students' engagement, resilience, character strengths, optimism, and sense of meaning (Seligman et al., 2009).

Taken together, satisfaction with the past, happiness with the present, and optimism about the future define the movement's first pillar: *positive well-being*. Seligman views happiness as a by-product of a pleasant, engaged, and meaningful life.

Positive psychology is about building not just a pleasant life, says Seligman, but also a good life that engages one's skills, and a meaningful life that points beyond oneself. Thus, the second pillar, *positive character,* focuses on exploring and enhancing creativity, courage, compassion, integrity, self-control, leadership, wisdom, and spirituality.

The third pillar, *positive groups, communities,* and *cultures,* seeks to foster a positive social ecology. This includes healthy families, communal neighborhoods, effective schools, socially responsible media, and civil dialogue.

"Positive psychology," say Seligman and colleagues (2005), "is an umbrella term for the study of positive emotions, positive character traits, and enabling institutions." Its focus differs from psychology's traditional interests during its first century, when attention was directed toward understanding and alleviating negative states—abuse and anxiety, depression and disease, prejudice and poverty. Indeed, articles on selected negative emotions since 1887 have outnumbered those on positive emotions by 17 to 1.

feel-good, do-good phenomenon people's tendency to be helpful when already in a good mood.

positive psychology the scientific study of optimal human functioning; aims to discover and promote strengths and virtues that enable individuals and communities to flourish.

subjective well-being self-perceived happiness or satisfaction with life. Used along with measures of objective well-being (for example, physical and economic indicators) to evaluate people's quality of life.

In ages past, times of relative peace and prosperity have enabled cultures to turn their attention from repairing weakness and damage to promoting what Seligman (2002) has called "the highest qualities of life." Prosperous fifth-century Athens nurtured philosophy and democracy. Flourishing fifteenth-century Florence nurtured great art. Victorian England, flush with the bounty of the British Empire, nurtured honor, discipline, and duty. In this millennium, Seligman believes, thriving Western cultures have a parallel opportunity to create, as a "humane, scientific monument," a more positive psychology, concerned not only with weakness and damage but also with strength and virtue. Thanks to his leadership, the movement has gained strength, with supporters in 77 countries from Croatia to China (IPPA, 2009, 2010; Seligman, 2004, 2011). Their research on human flourishing has given us insights into many aspects of our well-being, including studies of the predictors of happiness, as we'll see in the following pages.

What Affects Our Well-Being?

11-13: How do time, wealth, adaptation, and comparison affect our happiness levels?

The Short Life of Emotional Ups and Downs

Are some days of the week happier than others? In what is surely psychology's biggest-ever data sample, social psychologist Adam Kramer (at my request and in cooperation with Facebook) did a naturalistic observation of emotion words in "billions" of status updates. After eliminating exceptional days, such as holidays, he tracked the frequency of positive and negative emotion words by day of the week. The most positive moods days? Friday and Saturday (**FIGURE 11.13**). A similar analysis of emotion-related words in 59 million Twitter messages found Friday to Sunday the week's happiest days (Golder & Macy, 2011). For you, too?

Over the long run, our emotional ups and downs tend to balance out. This is true even over the course of the day. Positive emotion rises over the early to middle part of most days and then drops off (Kahneman et al., 2004; Watson, 2000). A stressful event—an argument, a sick child, a car problem—can trigger a bad mood. No surprise there. But by the next day, the gloom nearly always lifts (Affleck et al., 1994; Bolger et al., 1989; Stone & Neale, 1984). If anything, people tend to rebound from bad days to a *better-than-usual* good mood the following day.

Even when negative events drag us down for longer periods, our bad mood usually ends. Romantic breakups feel devastating, but eventually the wound heals. Faculty members up for tenure expect their lives would be deflated by a negative decision. Actually, 5 to 10 years later, their happiness level is about the same as for those who received tenure (Gilbert et al., 1998).

Grief over the loss of a loved one or anxiety after a severe trauma (such as child abuse, rape, or the terrors of war) can linger. But usually, even tragedy is not permanently depressing. People who become blind or paralyzed usually recover near-normal levels of day-to-day happiness. So do those who must go on kidney dialysis or have permanent colostomies (Gerhart et al., 1994; Riis et al., 2005; Smith et al., 2009). And in European studies, 8- to 12-year-olds with cerebral palsy experienced normal psychological well-being (Dickinson et al., 2007).

People mostly cope well with a permanent disability, although they may not rebound all the way back to their former emotions (Diener et al., 2006; Smith et al., 2009). A major disability leaves people somewhat less happy than average, yet much happier than able-bodied people with depression (Kübler et al., 2005; Lucas, 2007a,b; Oswald & Powdthavee, 2006; Schwartz & Estrin, 2004). "If you are a paraplegic," explained Daniel

FIGURE 11.13

Using web science to track happy days Adam Kramer (personal correspondence, 2010) tracked positive and negative emotion words in many "billions" (the exact number is proprietary information) of status updates of U.S. users of Facebook between September 7, 2007, and November 17, 2010.

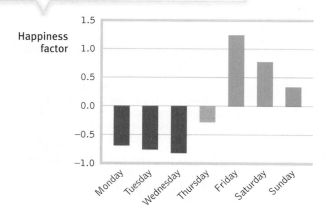

Kahneman (2005), "you will gradually start thinking of other things, and the more time you spend thinking of other things the less miserable you are going to be." Contrary to what many people believe, most patients "locked in" a motionless body do not say they want to die (Bruno et al., 2008, 2011; Smith & Delargy, 2005).

The surprising reality: *We overestimate the duration of our emotions and underestimate our resiliency.*

"Weeping may tarry for the night, but joy comes with the morning."

Psalm 30:5

Wealth and Well-Being

"Do you think you would be happier if you made more money?" *Yes,* replied 73 percent of Americans in a 2006 Gallup poll. How important is "being very well off financially"? *Very important,* say 80 percent of entering U.S. collegians (**FIGURE 11.14**).

Indeed, having enough money to buy your way out of hunger and hopelessness does buy some happiness (Diener & Biswas-Diener, 2009; Howell & Howell, 2008; Lucas & Schimmack, 2009). As Robert Cummins (2006) confirmed with Australian data, the power of more money to increase happiness is significant at low incomes and diminishes as income rises. A $1000 annual wage increase does a lot more for the average person in Malawi than for the average person in Switzerland. This implies, he adds, that raising low incomes will do more to increase happiness than raising high incomes.

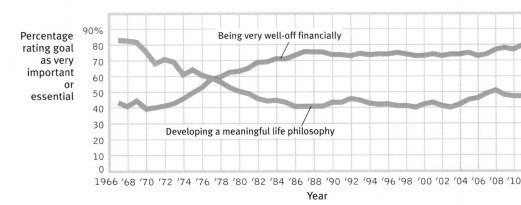

FIGURE 11.14

The changing materialism of entering collegians Surveys of more than 200,000 entering U.S. collegians per year have revealed an increasing desire for wealth after 1970. (From *The American Freshman* surveys, UCLA, 1966 to 2011.)

Once one has enough money for comfort and security, piling up more and more matters less and less. Experiencing luxury diminishes our savoring of life's simpler pleasures (Quoidbach et al., 2010). If you've skied the Alps, your neighborhood sledding hill pales.

And consider this: During the last half-century, the average U.S. citizen's buying power almost tripled. Did this greater wealth—enabling twice as many cars per person, not to mention laptops, smartphones, and HDTVs—also buy more happiness? As **FIGURE 11.15** on the next page shows, the average American, though certainly richer, is not a bit happier. In 1957, some 35 percent said they were "very happy," as did slightly fewer—29 percent—in 2010. Much the same has been true of Europe, Australia, and Japan, where increasing real incomes have *not* produced increasing happiness (Australian Unity, 2008; Diener & Biswas-Diener, 2002, 2009; Di Tella & MacCulloch, 2010). Ditto China, where living standards have risen but satisfaction has not (Brockmann et al., 2009). These findings lob a bombshell at modern materialism: *Economic growth in affluent countries has provided no apparent boost to morale or social well-being.*

Ironically, in every culture, those who strive hardest for wealth have tended to live with lower well-being (Ryan, 1999), especially when those hard-driving people were seeking money to prove themselves, gain power, or show off rather than support their families (Niemiec et al., 2009; Srivastava et al., 2001). Those who instead strive for intimacy, personal growth, and contribution to the community experience a higher quality of life (Kasser, 2002, 2011).

© H. L. Schwadron

"*But on the positive side, money can't buy happiness—so who cares?*"

"Australians are three times richer than their parents and grandparents were in the 1950s, but they are not happier."

A Manifesto for Well-Being, *2005*

FIGURE 11.15

Does money buy happiness? It surely helps us to avoid certain types of pain. Yet, though buying power has almost tripled since the 1950s, the average American's reported happiness has remained almost unchanged. (Happiness data from National Opinion Research Center surveys; income data from *Historical Statistics of the United States* and *Economic Indicators*.)

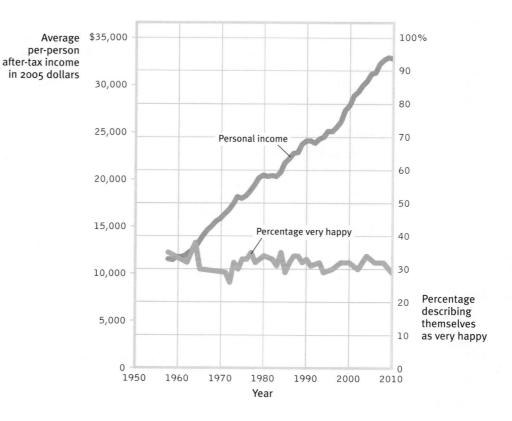

Happiness Is Relative: Adaptation and Comparison

Two psychological principles explain why, for those who are not poor, more money buys little more than a temporary surge of happiness and why our emotions seem attached to elastic bands that pull us back from highs or lows. In its own way, each principle suggests that happiness is relative.

Happiness Is Relative to Our Own Experience The **adaptation-level phenomenon** describes our tendency to judge various stimuli in comparison with our past experiences. As psychologist Harry Helson (1898–1977) explained, we adjust our *neutral* levels—the points at which sounds seem neither loud nor soft, temperatures neither hot nor cold, events neither pleasant nor unpleasant—based on our experience. We then notice and react to variations up or down from these levels. Thus, after an initial surge of pleasure, improvements become our "new normal," and we require something even better to give us a happiness boost.

So, could we ever create a permanent social paradise? Probably not (Campbell, 1975; Di Tella & MacCulloch, 2010). People who have experienced a recent windfall—from a lottery, an inheritance, or a surging economy—typically feel some elation (Diener & Oishi, 2000; Gardner & Oswald, 2007). So would you, if you woke up tomorrow to your utopia—perhaps a world with no bills, no ills, perfect scores, someone who loves you unreservedly. But after a time, you would gradually recalibrate your adaptation level, and you would adjust your new neutral level to include these new experiences. Before long, you would again sometimes feel gratified (when events exceed your expectations) and sometimes feel deprived (when they fall below), and sometimes feel neutral. *The point to remember:* Feelings of satisfaction and dissatisfaction, success and failure are judgments we make based on our prior experience. Satisfaction, as Richard Ryan (1999) said, "has a short half life." Ditto disappointment, which means that you may bounce back from a setback sooner than you expect.

"No happiness lasts for long."

Seneca, Agamemnon, *C.E. 60*

"Continued pleasures wear off. . . . Pleasure is always contingent upon change and disappears with continuous satisfaction."

Dutch psychologist Nico Frijda (1988)

"I have a 'fortune cookie maxim' that I'm very proud of: Nothing in life is quite as important as you think it is while you are thinking about it. So, nothing will ever make you as happy as you think it will."

Nobel laureate psychologist Daniel Kahneman, Gallup interview, "What Were They Thinking?" 2005

Happiness Is Relative to Others' Success We are always comparing ourselves with others. And whether we feel good or bad depends on who those others are (Lyubomirsky, 2001). We are slow-witted or clumsy only when others are smarter or more agile. This sense that we are worse off than others with whom we compare ourselves is called **relative deprivation.**

When expectations soar above attainments, the result is disappointment. Thus, the middle- and upper-income people in a given country, who can compare themselves with the relatively poor, tend to be more satisfied with life than are their less-fortunate compatriots. Nevertheless, once people reach a moderate income level, further increases buy little more happiness. Why? Because as people climb the ladder of success they mostly compare themselves with local peers who are at or above their current level (Gruder, 1977; Suls & Tesch, 1978; Zell & Alicke, 2010). "Beggars do not envy millionaires, though of course they will envy other beggars who are more successful," noted British philosopher Bertrand Russell (1930, p. 90). Thus, "Napoleon envied Caesar, Caesar envied Alexander, and Alexander, I daresay, envied Hercules, who never existed. You cannot, therefore, get away from envy by means of success alone, for there will always be in history or legend some person even more successful than you are" (pp. 68–69).

Just as comparing ourselves with those who are better off creates envy, so counting our blessings as we compare ourselves with those worse off boosts our contentment. In one study, University of Wisconsin-Milwaukee women considered others' deprivation and suffering (Dermer et al., 1979). They viewed vivid depictions of how grim life was in Milwaukee in 1900. They imagined and then wrote about various personal tragedies, such as being burned and disfigured. Later, the women expressed greater satisfaction with their own lives. Similarly, when mildly depressed people have read about someone who was even more depressed, they felt somewhat better (Gibbons, 1986). "I cried because I had no shoes," states a Persian saying, "until I met a man who had no feet."

What Predicts Our Happiness Levels?

11-14: What are some predictors of happiness, and how can we be happier?

Happy people share many characteristics (**TABLE 11.1**). But why are some people normally so joyful and others so somber? Here, as in so many other areas, the answer is found in the interplay between nature and nurture.

Happiness is genetically influenced. In one study of 254 identical and fraternal twins, about 50 percent of the difference among people's happiness ratings was

adaptation-level phenomenon our tendency to form judgments (of sounds, of lights, of income) relative to a neutral level defined by our prior experience.

relative deprivation the perception that one is worse off relative to those with whom one compares oneself.

The effect of comparison with others helps explain why students of a given level of academic ability tend to have a higher academic self-concept if they attend a school where most other students are not exceptionally able (Marsh & Parker, 1984). If you were near the top of your graduating class, you might feel inferior upon entering a college or university where all students were near the top of their class.

"Researchers say I'm not happier for being richer, but do you know how much researchers make?"

Table 11.1
Happiness Is . . .

Researchers Have Found That Happy People Tend to	However, Happiness Seems Not Much Related to Other Factors, Such As
Have high self-esteem (in individualistic countries).	Age.
Be optimistic, outgoing, and agreeable.	Gender (women are more often depressed, but also more often joyful).
Have close friendships or a satisfying marriage.	Parenthood (having children or not).
Have work and leisure that engage their skills.	Physical attractiveness.
Have an active religious faith.	
Sleep well and exercise.	

Sources: Summarized from DeNeve & Cooper (1998); Diener et al. (2003); Headey et al. (2010); Lucas et al. (2004); Myers (1993, 2000); Myers & Diener (1995, 1996); and Steel et al. (2008). Veenhoven (2009) offers a database of more than 11,000 correlates of happiness at worlddatabaseofhappiness.eur.nl.

Studies of chimpanzees in zoos reveal that happiness in chimpanzees, as rated by 200 employees, is also genetically influenced (Weiss et al., 2000, 2002).

"I could cry when I think of the years I wasted accumulating money, only to learn that my cheerful disposition is genetic."

heritable—attributable to genes (Lykken & Tellegen, 1996). Other twin studies report similar or slightly less heritability (Bartels & Boomsma, 2009; Lucas, 2008; Nes et al., 2010). Identical twins raised apart are often similarly happy.

But our personal history and our culture matter, too. On the personal level, as we have seen, our emotions tend to balance around a level defined by our experience. On the cultural level, groups vary in the traits they value. Self-esteem and achievement matter more to Westerners, who value individualism. Social acceptance and harmony matter more to those in communal cultures such as Japan that stress family and community (Diener et al., 2003; Uchida & Kitayama, 2009).

Depending on our genes, our outlook, and our recent experiences, our happiness seems to fluctuate around our "happiness set point," which disposes some people to be ever upbeat and others more negative. Even so, after following thousands of lives over two decades, researchers have determined that our satisfaction with life is not fixed (Lucas & Donnellan, 2007). Happiness rises and falls, and it can be influenced by factors that are under our control. A striking example: In a long-term German study, married partners were as similarly satisfied with their lives as were identical twins (Schimmack & Lucas, 2007). Genes matter. But as this study hints, relationship quality matters, too. (For research-based hints on enhancing your own happiness, see Close-Up: Want to Be Happier?)

If we can enhance our happiness on an *individual* level, could we use happiness research to refocus our *national* priorities more on advancing psychological well-being? Many

CLOSE UP:

Want to Be Happier?

Your happiness, like your cholesterol level, is genetically influenced. Yet as cholesterol is also influenced by diet and exercise, so happiness is partly under your control (Nes, 2010; Sin & Lyubomirsky, 2009). Here are some research-based suggestions for improving your mood and increasing your satisfaction with life.

Realize that enduring happiness may not come from financial success. We adapt to change by adjusting our expectations. Neither wealth, nor any other circumstance we long for, will guarantee happiness.

Take control of your time. Happy people feel in control of their lives. To master your use of time, set goals and break them into daily aims. This may be frustrating at first because we all tend to overestimate how much we will accomplish in any given day. The good news is that we generally *underestimate* how much we can accomplish in a year, given just a little progress every day.

Act happy. As you saw in Chapter 10, people who were manipulated into a smiling expression felt better. So put on a happy face. Talk as *if* you feel positive self-esteem, are optimistic, and are outgoing. We can often act our way into a happier state of mind.

Seek work and leisure that engage your skills. Happy people often are in a zone called

flow—absorbed in tasks that challenge but don't overwhelm them. The most expensive forms of leisure (sitting on a yacht) often provide less flow experience than simpler forms, such as gardening, socializing, or craft work. Money also buys more happiness when spent on experiences you can look forward to, enjoy, and remember than when spent on material stuff (Carter & Gilovich, 2010). As pundit Art Buchwald said, "The best things in life aren't things."

Join the "movement" movement. Aerobic exercise can relieve mild depression and anxiety as it promotes health and energy. Sound minds reside in sound bodies. Off your duffs, couch potatoes!

Give your body the sleep it wants. Happy people live active lives yet reserve time for renewing sleep and solitude. Many people suffer from sleep debt, with resulting fatigue, diminished alertness, and gloomy moods.

Give priority to close relationships. Intimate friendships can help you weather difficult times. Confiding is good for soul and body. Compared with unhappy people, happy people engage in less superficial small talk and more meaningful conversations (Mehl et al., 2010).

So resolve to nurture your closest relationships by *not* taking your loved ones for granted. This means displaying to them the sort of kindness you display to others, affirming them, playing together, and sharing together.

Focus beyond self. Reach out to those in need. Happiness increases helpfulness (those who feel good do good). But doing good also makes one feel good.

Count your blessings and record your gratitude. Keeping a gratitude journal heightens well-being (Emmons, 2007; Seligman et al., 2005). Try pausing each day to savor good moments and to record when and why positive events occurred. Express your gratitude to others.

Nurture your spiritual self. For many people, faith provides a support community, a reason to focus beyond self, and a sense of purpose and hope. That helps explain why people active in faith communities report greater-than-average happiness, and why they often cope well in crises.

Digested from David G. Myers, *The Pursuit of Happiness* (Harper).

psychologists believe we could. Ed Diener (2006, 2009), supported by 52 colleagues, has proposed ways in which nations might measure national well-being. Happiness research offers new ways to assess the impacts of various public policies, argue Diener and his colleagues. Happy societies are not only prosperous but are also places where people trust one another, feel free, and enjoy close relationships (Oishi & Schimmack, 2010). Thus, when debating such issues as economic inequality, tax rates, divorce laws, and health care, people's psychological well-being should be a prime consideration—a point now affirmed by the Canadian, French, German, and British governments. Each has added well-being measures to their national agendas (Cohen, 2011; Gertner, 2010; Stiglitz, 2009). Such measures may help guide nations toward policies that decrease stress and foster human flourishing.

RETRIEVE IT

• Which of the following factors do NOT predict self-reported happiness? Which factors are better predictors?

a. Age

b. Personality traits

c. Close relationships

d. Gender

e. Engaging work and leisure

f. Active religious faith

ANSWERS: Age and gender (a. and d.) do NOT effectively predict happiness levels. Better predictors are personality traits, close relationships, "flow" in work and leisure, and religious faith (b., c., e., and f.).

CHAPTER REVIEW

Stress, Health, and Human Flourishing

LEARNING OBJECTIVES

Test Yourself by taking a moment to answer each of these Learning Objective Questions (repeated here from within the chapter). Then turn to Appendix D, Complete Chapter Reviews, to check your answers. Research suggests that trying to answer these questions on your own will improve your long-term memory of the concepts (McDaniel et al., 2009).

Stress and Health

11-1: What events provoke stress responses, and how do we respond and adapt to stress?

11-2: How does stress make us more vulnerable to disease?

11-3: Why are some of us more prone than others to coronary heart disease?

11-4: What are some healthful ways to cope with feelings of anger?

Coping With Stress

11-5: In what two ways do people try to alleviate stress?

11-6: How does a perceived lack of control affect health?

11-7: What are the links among basic outlook on life, social support, stress, and health?

Reducing Stress

11-8: How effective is aerobic exercise as a way to manage stress and improve well-being?

11-9: In what ways might relaxation and meditation influence stress and health?

11-10: What is the faith factor, and what are some possible explanations for the link between faith and health?

Happiness

11-11: What are the main effects of being happy?

11-12: What is subjective well-being, and what topics do positive psychology researchers explore? What are the three "pillars" of the movement?

11-13: How do time, wealth, adaptation, and comparison affect our happiness levels?

11-14: What are some predictors of happiness, and how can we be happier?

TERMS AND CONCEPTS TO REMEMBER

Test yourself on these terms by trying to write down the definition in your own words before flipping back to the referenced page to check your answer.

stress, p. 390

general adaptation syndrome (GAS), p. 393

tend and befriend, p. 393

health psychology, p. 394

psychoneuroimmunology, p. 394

coronary heart disease, p. 397

Type A, p. 398

Type B, p. 398

catharsis, p. 398

coping, p. 401

problem-focused coping, p. 401

emotion-focused coping, p. 401

learned helplessness, p. 402

external locus of control, p. 403

internal locus of control, p. 403

self-control, p. 403

aerobic exercise, p. 407

feel-good, do-good phenomenon, p. 413

positive psychology, p. 413

subjective well-being, p. 413

adaptation-level phenomenon, p. 416

relative deprivation, p. 417

EXPERIENCE THE TESTING EFFECT

Test yourself repeatedly throughout your studies. This will not only help you figure out what you know and don't know; the testing itself will help you learn and remember the information more effectively thanks to the *testing effect*.

1. Selye's general adaptation syndrome (GAS) consists of an alarm reaction followed by _____, then _____.

2. When faced with stress, women are more likely than men to experience the _____-and-_____ response.

3. The number of short-term illnesses and stress-related psychological disorders was higher than usual in the months following an earthquake. Such findings suggest that
   a. daily hassles have adverse health consequences.
   b. experiencing a very stressful event increases a person's vulnerability to illness.
   c. the amount of stress a person feels is directly related to the number of stressors experienced.
   d. small, bad events don't cause stress, but large ones can be toxic.

4. Which of the following is NOT one of the three main types of stressors?
   a. Catastrophes
   b. Significant life changes
   c. Daily hassles
   d. Threatening events that we hear about

5. Stress hormones released in response to a signal from the brain suppress _____, the immune cells that ordinarily attack bacteria, viruses, cancer cells, and other foreign substances.

6. Research has shown that people are at increased risk for cancer a year or so after experiencing depression, helplessness, or bereavement. In describing this link, researchers are quick to point out that
   a. accumulated stress causes cancer.
   b. anger is the negative emotion most closely linked to cancer.
   c. stress does not create cancer cells, but it weakens the body's natural defenses against them.
   d. feeling optimistic about chances of survival ensures that a cancer patient will get well.

7. A Chinese proverb warns, "The fire you kindle for your enemy often burns you more than him." How is this true of Type A individuals?

8. The components of the Type A personality that have been linked most closely to coronary heart disease are anger and other _____ feelings.

9. When faced with a situation over which you feel you have no sense of control, it is most effective to use _____ (emotion/problem)-focused coping.

10. Seligman's research showed that a dog will respond with learned helplessness if it has received repeated shocks and has had

    a. the opportunity to escape.

    b. no control over the shocks.

    c. pain or discomfort.

    d. no food or water prior to the shocks.

11. When elderly patients take an active part in managing their own care and surroundings, their morale and health tend to improve. Such findings indicate that people do better when they experience an _____ (internal/external) locus of control.

12. People who have close relationships are less likely to die prematurely than those who do not, supporting the idea that

    a. social ties can be a source of stress.

    b. gender influences longevity.

    c. Type A behavior is responsible for many premature deaths.

    d. social support has a beneficial effect on health.

13. Because it triggers the release of mood-boosting neurotransmitters such as norepinephrine, serotonin, and the endorphins, _____ exercise raises energy levels and helps alleviate depression and anxiety.

14. Research on the faith factor has found that

    a. pessimists tend to be healthier than optimists.

    b. our expectations influence our feelings of stress.

    c. religiously active people tend to outlive those who are not religiously active.

    d. religious engagement promotes isolation, repression, and ill health.

15. One of the most consistent findings of psychological research is that happy people are also

    a. more likely to express anger.

    b. generally luckier than others.

    c. concentrated in the wealthier nations.

    d. more likely to help others.

16. _____ psychology is a scientific field of study focused on how humans thrive and flourish.

17. After moving to a new apartment, you find the street noise irritatingly loud, but after a while, it no longer bothers you. This reaction illustrates the

    a. relative deprivation principle.

    b. adaptation-level phenomenon.

    c. feel-good, do-good phenomenon.

    d. catharsis principle.

18. A philosopher observed that we cannot escape envy, because there will always be someone more successful, more accomplished, or richer with whom to compare ourselves. In psychology, this observation is embodied in the _____ _____ principle.

Find answers to these questions in Appendix E, in the back of the book.

CHAPTER 12

Personality

Lord of the Rings hobbit-hero Frodo Baggins knew that throughout his difficult journey there was one who would never fail him—his loyal and ever-cheerful companion, Sam Gamgee. Even before they left their beloved homes in the Shire, Frodo warned Sam that the journey would not be easy.

> "It is going to be very dangerous, Sam. It is already dangerous.
>   Most likely neither of us will come back."
>   "If you don't come back, sir, then I shan't, that's certain," said Sam. "[The Elves told me] 'Don't you leave him!' Leave him! I said. I never mean to. I am going with him, if he climbs to the Moon; and if any of those Black Riders try to stop him, they'll have Sam Gamgee to reckon with." (J.R.R. Tolkien, *The Fellowship of the Ring*, p. 96)

And so they did! Later in the story, when it becomes clear that Frodo's path will lead him into the dreaded land of Mordor, it is Sam who insists he will be at Frodo's side, come what may. It is Sam who lifts Frodo's spirits with songs and stories from their boyhood. And it is Sam whom Frodo leans upon when he can barely take another step. When Frodo is overcome by the evil of the ring he carries, it is Sam who saves him. In the end, it is Sam who helps Frodo successfully reach the end of his journey. Sam Gamgee—cheerful, optimistic, emotionally stable—never falters in his faithfulness or his belief that they will overcome the threatening darkness.

As he appears and reappears throughout the series, Tolkien's Sam Gamgee exhibits the distinctive and enduring behaviors that define **personality**—a person's characteristic pattern of thinking, feeling, and acting. Earlier chapters have focused on our similar ways of developing, perceiving, learning, remembering, thinking, and feeling. This chapter focuses on what makes us each unique.

Much of this book deals with personality. We have considered biological influences on personality, personality development across the life span, and personality-related aspects of learning, motivation, emotion, and health. In later chapters we will study social influences on personality and disorders of personality.

Two historically significant theories have become part of our cultural legacy. Sigmund Freud's *psychoanalytic* theory proposed that childhood sexuality and unconscious motivations influence personality. The *humanistic* approach focused on our inner capacities for growth and self-fulfillment. These sweeping perspectives on human nature laid the foundation for later personality theorists and are complemented by what this chapter goes on to explore: newer scientific research on specific aspects of personality. Today's personality researchers study the basic dimensions of personality, the biological roots of these dimensions, and the interaction of persons and environments. They also study self-esteem, self-serving bias, and cultural influences on one's sense of self. And they study the unconscious mind—with findings that probably would have surprised Freud himself.

personality an individual's characteristic pattern of thinking, feeling, and acting.

Sigmund Freud, 1856–1939 "I was the only worker in a new field."
© Bettman/Corbis

"The female . . . acknowledges the fact of her castration, and with it, too, the superiority of the male and her own inferiority; but she rebels against this unwelcome state of affairs."

Sigmund Freud, Female Sexuality, 1931

psychodynamic theories view personality with a focus on the unconscious and the importance of childhood experiences.

psychoanalysis Freud's theory of personality that attributes thoughts and actions to unconscious motives and conflicts; the techniques used in treating psychological disorders by seeking to expose and interpret unconscious tensions.

unconscious according to Freud, a reservoir of mostly unacceptable thoughts, wishes, feelings, and memories. According to contemporary psychologists, information processing of which we are unaware.

free association in psychoanalysis, a method of exploring the unconscious in which the person relaxes and says whatever comes to mind, no matter how trivial or embarrassing.

Psychodynamic Theories

Psychodynamic theories of personality view human behavior as a dynamic interaction between the conscious and unconscious mind, including associated motives and conflicts. These theories are descended from Freud's **psychoanalysis,** Freud's theory of personality and the associated techniques for treating psychological disorders. Freud's work was the first to focus clinical attention on our unconscious mind.

Freud's Psychoanalytic Perspective: Exploring the Unconscious

12-1: How did Sigmund Freud's treatment of psychological disorders lead to his view of the unconscious mind?

Ask 100 people on the street to name a notable deceased psychologist, suggested Keith Stanovich (1996, p. 1), and "Freud would be the winner hands down." In the popular mind, he is to psychology's history what Elvis Presley is to rock music's history. Freud's influence lingers in psychiatry and clinical psychology, but also in literary and film interpretation. Almost 9 in 10 American college courses that reference psychoanalysis are outside of psychology departments (Cohen, 2007). Today's psychological science is, as we will see, skeptical about many of Freud's ideas and methods. Yet his early twentieth-century concepts penetrate our twenty-first-century language. Without realizing their source, we may speak of *ego, repression, projection, sibling rivalry, Freudian slips,* and *fixation.* So, who was Freud, and what did he teach?

Like all of us, Sigmund Freud was a product of his times. His Victorian era was a time of tremendous discovery and scientific advancement, but it is also known today as a time of sexual repression and male dominance. Men's and women's roles were clearly defined, with male superiority assumed and only male sexuality generally acknowledged (discreetly).

Long before entering the University of Vienna in 1873, young Freud showed signs of independence and brilliance. He so loved reading plays, poetry, and philosophy that he once ran up a bookstore debt beyond his means. As a teen he often took his evening meal in his tiny bedroom in order to lose no time from his studies. After medical school he set up a private practice specializing in nervous disorders. Before long, however, he faced patients whose disorders made no neurological sense. For example, a patient might have lost all feeling in a hand—yet there is no sensory nerve that, if damaged, would numb the entire hand and nothing else. Freud's search for a cause for such disorders set his mind running in a direction destined to change human self-understanding.

Might some neurological disorders have psychological causes? Observing patients led Freud to his belief that beneath our awareness is a larger **unconscious** mind, a dwelling place of largely unacceptable thoughts, wishes, feelings, and memories. He speculated that lost feeling in one's hand might be caused by a fear of touching one's genitals; that unexplained blindness or deafness might be caused by not wanting to see or hear something that aroused intense anxiety. How might such disorders be treated? After some early unsuccessful trials with hypnosis, Freud turned to **free association,** in which he told the patient to relax and say whatever came to mind, no matter how embarrassing or trivial. He assumed that a line of mental dominoes had fallen from his patients' distant past to their troubled present, and that the chain of thought revealed by free association would allow him to retrace that line into a patient's unconscious. Painful memories, often from childhood, could then be retrieved from the unconscious and brought into conscious awareness.

Basic to Freud's theory was his belief that the mind is mostly hidden (**FIGURE 12.1**). Our *conscious* awareness is like the part of an iceberg that floats above the surface. Beneath our awareness is the larger *unconscious* mind, with its thoughts, wishes, feelings, and memories. Some of these thoughts we store temporarily in a *preconscious* area, from which we can retrieve them into conscious awareness. Of greater interest to Freud was the mass of unacceptable passions and thoughts that he believed we *repress,* or forcibly block from our

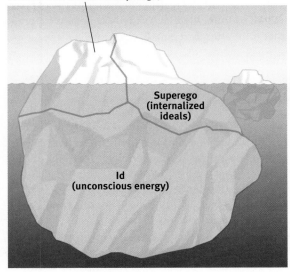

Ego
(mostly conscious; makes peace between the id and the superego)

Conscious mind

Preconscious (outside awareness but accessible)

Superego
(internalized ideals)

Id
(unconscious energy)

Unconscious mind

FIGURE 12.1

Freud's idea of the mind's structure

Psychologists have used an iceberg image to illustrate Freud's idea that the mind is mostly hidden beneath the conscious surface. Note that the id is totally unconscious, but the ego and superego operate both consciously and unconsciously. Unlike the parts of an iceberg, however, the id, ego, and superego interact.

consciousness because they would be too unsettling to acknowledge. Freud believed that without our awareness, these troublesome feelings and ideas powerfully influence us. Such feelings, he said, sometimes surface in disguised forms—the work we choose, the beliefs we hold, our daily habits, our troubling symptoms.

Personality Structure

"Fifty is plenty."   "Hundred and fifty."

The ego struggles to reconcile the demands of superego and id, said Freud.

12-2: What was Freud's view of personality?

In Freud's view, human personality—including its emotions and strivings—arises from a conflict between impulse and restraint—between our aggressive, pleasure-seeking biological urges and our internalized social controls over these urges. Freud believed personality arises from our efforts to resolve this basic conflict—to express these impulses in ways that bring satisfaction without also bringing guilt or punishment. To understand the mind's dynamics during this conflict, Freud proposed three interacting systems: the *id*, *ego*, and *superego* (Figure 12.1).

The **id's** unconscious psychic energy constantly strives to satisfy basic drives to survive, reproduce, and aggress. The id operates on the *pleasure principle:* It seeks immediate gratification. To envision an id-dominated person, think of a newborn infant crying out for satisfaction, caring nothing for the outside world's conditions and demands. Or think of people with a present rather than future time perspective—those who heavily use tobacco, alcohol, and other drugs, and would sooner party now than sacrifice today's pleasure for future success and happiness (Keough et al., 1999).

As the **ego** develops, the young child responds to the real world. The ego, operating on the *reality principle*, seeks to gratify the id's impulses in realistic ways that will bring long-term pleasure. (Imagine what would happen if, lacking an ego, we expressed all our unrestrained sexual or aggressive impulses.) The ego contains our partly conscious perceptions, thoughts, judgments, and memories.

Around age 4 or 5, Freud theorized, a child's ego recognizes the demands of the newly emerging **superego,** the voice of our moral compass (conscience) that forces the ego to consider not only the real but the *ideal*. The superego focuses on how we *ought* to behave. It strives for perfection, judging actions and producing positive feelings of pride or negative feelings of guilt. Someone with an exceptionally strong superego may be virtuous yet guilt ridden; another with a weak superego may be wantonly self-indulgent and remorseless.

id a reservoir of unconscious psychic energy that, according to Freud, strives to satisfy basic sexual and aggressive drives. The id operates on the *pleasure principle,* demanding immediate gratification.

ego the largely conscious, "executive" part of personality that, according to Freud, mediates among the demands of the id, superego, and reality. The ego operates on the *reality principle,* satisfying the id's desires in ways that will realistically bring pleasure rather than pain.

superego the part of personality that, according to Freud, represents internalized ideals and provides standards for judgment (the conscience) and for future aspirations.

Because the superego's demands often oppose the id's, the ego struggles to reconcile the two. It is the personality "executive," mediating among the impulsive demands of the id, the restraining demands of the superego, and the real-life demands of the external world. If chaste Jane feels sexually attracted to John, she may satisfy both id and superego by joining a volunteer organization that John attends regularly.

Personality Development

12-3: What developmental stages did Freud propose?

Analysis of his patients' histories convinced Freud that personality forms during life's first few years. He concluded that children pass through a series of **psychosexual stages,** during which the id's pleasure-seeking energies focus on distinct pleasure-sensitive areas of the body called *erogenous zones* (**TABLE 12.1**). Each stage offers its own challenges, which Freud saw as conflicting tendencies.

Freud believed that during the *phallic stage,* for example, boys seek genital stimulation, and they develop both unconscious sexual desires for their mother and jealousy and hatred for their father, whom they consider a rival. Given these feelings, he thought, boys also experience guilt and a lurking fear of punishment, perhaps by castration, from their father. Freud called this collection of feelings the **Oedipus complex** after the Greek legend of Oedipus, who unknowingly killed his father and married his mother. Some psychoanalysts in Freud's era believed that girls experienced a parallel *Electra complex*.

Children eventually cope with the threatening feelings, said Freud, by repressing them and by trying to become like the rival parent. It's as though something inside the child decides, "If you can't beat 'em [the same-sex parent], join 'em." Through this **identification** process, children's superegos gain strength as they incorporate many of their parents' values. Freud believed that identification with the same-sex parent provides what psychologists now call our *gender identity*—our sense of being male or female. Freud presumed that our early childhood relations—especially with our parents and caregivers—influence our developing identity, personality, and frailties.

In Freud's view, conflicts unresolved during earlier psychosexual stages could surface as maladaptive behavior in the adult years. At any point in the oral, anal, or phallic stages, strong conflict could lock, or **fixate,** the person's pleasure-seeking energies in that stage. A person who had been either orally overindulged or deprived (perhaps by abrupt, early weaning) might fixate at the oral stage. This orally fixated adult could exhibit either passive dependence (like that of a nursing infant) or an exaggerated denial of this dependence (by acting tough or uttering biting sarcasm). Or the person might continue to seek oral gratification by smoking or excessive eating. In such ways, Freud suggested, the twig of personality is bent at an early age.

"I heard that as soon as we become aware of our sexual impulses, whatever they are, we'll have to hide them."

"Oh, for goodness' sake! Smoke!"

psychosexual stages the childhood stages of development (oral, anal, phallic, latency, genital) during which, according to Freud, the id's pleasure-seeking energies focus on distinct erogenous zones.

Oedipus [ED-uh-puss] **complex** according to Freud, a boy's sexual desires toward his mother and feelings of jealousy and hatred for the rival father.

identification the process by which, according to Freud, children incorporate their parents' values into their developing superegos.

fixation according to Freud, a lingering focus of pleasure-seeking energies at an earlier psychosexual stage, in which conflicts were unresolved.

Table 12.1
Freud's Psychosexual Stages

Stage	Focus
Oral (0–18 months)	Pleasure centers on the mouth—sucking, biting, chewing
Anal (18–36 months)	Pleasure focuses on bowel and bladder elimination; coping with demands for control
Phallic (3–6 years)	Pleasure zone is the genitals; coping with incestuous sexual feelings
Latency (6 to puberty)	A phase of dormant sexual feelings
Genital (puberty on)	Maturation of sexual interests

Freud's ideas of sexuality were controversial in his own time. "Freud was called a dirty-minded pansexualist and Viennese libertine," noted Morton Hunt, historian of psychology (2007, p. 211). Today Freud's ideas of Oedipal conflict and castration anxiety are disputed even by psychodynamic theorists and therapists (Shedler, 2010b). Yet we still teach them as part of the history of Western ideas.

Defense Mechanisms

12-4: How did Freud think people defended themselves against anxiety?

Anxiety, said Freud, is the price we pay for civilization. As members of social groups, we must control our sexual and aggressive impulses, not act them out. But sometimes the ego fears losing control of this inner id-superego war. The presumed result is a dark cloud of unfocused anxiety that leaves us feeling unsettled but unsure why.

Freud proposed that the ego protects itself with **defense mechanisms**—tactics that reduce or redirect anxiety by distorting reality. *All defense mechanisms function indirectly and unconsciously.* Just as the body unconsciously defends itself against disease, so also does the ego unconsciously defend itself against anxiety. For example, **repression** banishes anxiety-arousing wishes and feelings from consciousness. According to Freud, *repression underlies all the other defense mechanisms.* However, because repression is often incomplete, repressed urges may appear as symbols in dreams or as slips of the tongue in casual conversation.

Freud believed he could glimpse the unconscious seeping through when a financially stressed patient, not wanting any large pills, said, "Please do not give me any bills, because I cannot swallow them." Similarly, he viewed jokes as expressions of repressed sexual and aggressive tendencies, and dreams as the "royal road to the unconscious." The remembered content of dreams (their *manifest content*) he believed to be a censored expression of the dreamer's unconscious wishes (the dream's *latent content*). In his dream analyses, Freud searched for patients' inner conflicts.

TABLE 12.2 describes a sampling of six other well-known defense mechanisms.

defense mechanisms in psychoanalytic theory, the ego's protective methods of reducing anxiety by unconsciously distorting reality.

repression in psychoanalytic theory, the basic defense mechanism that banishes from consciousness anxiety-arousing thoughts, feelings, and memories.

"Good morning, beheaded—uh, I mean beloved."

Table 12.2
Six Defense Mechanisms

Freud believed that *repression,* the basic mechanism that banishes anxiety-arousing impulses, enables other defense mechanisms, six of which are listed here.

Defense Mechanism	Unconscious Process Employed to Avoid Anxiety-Arousing Thoughts or Feelings	Example
Regression	Retreating to a more infantile psychosexual stage, where some psychic energy remains fixated.	A little boy reverts to the oral comfort of thumb sucking in the car on the way to his first day of school.
Reaction formation	Switching unacceptable impulses into their opposites.	Repressing angry feelings, a person displays exaggerated friendliness.
Projection	Disguising one's own threatening impulses by attributing them to others.	"The thief thinks everyone else is a thief" (an El Salvadoran saying).
Rationalization	Offering self-justifying explanations in place of the real, more threatening unconscious reasons for one's actions.	A habitual drinker says she drinks with her friends "just to be sociable."
Displacement	Shifting sexual or aggressive impulses toward a more acceptable or less threatening object or person.	A little girl kicks the family dog after her mother sends her to her room.
Denial	Refusing to believe or even perceive painful realities.	A partner denies evidence of his loved one's affair.

Regression Faced with a mild stressor, children and young orangutans seek protection and comfort from their caregivers. Freud might have interpreted these behaviors as regression, a retreat to an earlier developmental stage.

VStock/Alamy

Barbara Von Hoffmann/Animals Animals

The Neo-Freudian and Later Psychodynamic Theorists

12-5: Which of Freud's ideas did his followers accept or reject?

Freud's writings were controversial, but they soon attracted followers, mostly young, ambitious physicians who formed an inner circle around their strong-minded leader. These pioneering psychoanalysts, whom we often call *neo-Freudians,* accepted Freud's basic ideas: the personality structures of id, ego, and superego; the importance of the unconscious; the shaping of personality in childhood; and the dynamics of anxiety and the defense mechanisms. But they broke away from Freud in two important ways. First, they placed more emphasis on the conscious mind's role in interpreting experience and in coping with the environment. And second, they doubted that sex and aggression were all-consuming motivations. Instead, they tended to emphasize loftier motives and social interactions.

Alfred Adler and Karen Horney [HORN-eye], for example, agreed with Freud that childhood is important. But they believed that childhood *social,* not sexual, tensions are crucial for personality formation (Ferguson, 2003). Adler (who had proposed the still-popular idea of the *inferiority complex*) himself struggled to overcome childhood illnesses and accidents, and he believed that much of our behavior is driven by efforts to conquer childhood inferiority feelings that trigger our strivings for superiority and power. Horney said childhood anxiety triggers our desire for love and security. She also countered Freud's assumptions, arising as they did in his conservative culture, that women have weak superegos and suffer "penis envy," and she attempted to balance the bias she detected in his masculine view of psychology.

Carl Jung—Freud's disciple-turned-dissenter—placed less emphasis on social factors and agreed with Freud that the unconscious exerts a powerful influence. But to Jung [Yoong], the unconscious contains more than our repressed thoughts and feelings. He believed we also have a **collective unconscious,** a common reservoir of images, or *archetypes,* derived from our species' universal experiences. Jung said that the collective unconscious explains why, for many people, spiritual concerns are deeply rooted and why people in different cultures share certain myths and images, such as mother as a symbol of nurturance. (Most of today's psychodynamic psychologists discount the idea of inherited experiences. But many psychodynamic and other psychological theorists do believe that our shared evolutionary history shaped some universal dispositions.)

Freud died in 1939. Since then, some of his ideas have been incorporated into the diversity of perspectives that make up psychodynamic theory. "Most contemporary [psychodynamic] theorists and therapists are not wedded to the idea that sex is the basis of personality," noted Drew Westen (1996). They "do not talk about ids and egos, and do not go around classifying their patients as oral, anal, or phallic characters." What they

collective unconscious Carl Jung's concept of a shared, inherited reservoir of memory traces from our species' history.

projective test a personality test, such as the Rorschach, that provides ambiguous stimuli designed to trigger projection of one's inner dynamics.

Rorschach inkblot test the most widely used projective test, a set of 10 inkblots, designed by Hermann Rorschach; seeks to identify people's inner feelings by analyzing their interpretations of the blots.

Alfred Adler "The individual feels at home in life and feels his existence to be worthwhile just so far as he is useful to others and is overcoming feelings of inferiority" (*Problems of Neurosis*, 1964).
National Library of Medicine

Karen Horney "The view that women are infantile and emotional creatures, and as such, incapable of responsibility and independence is the work of the masculine tendency to lower women's self-respect" (*Feminine Psychology*, 1932).
The Bettmann Archive/Corbis

Carl Jung "From the living fountain of instinct flows everything that is creative; hence the unconscious is the very source of the creative impulse" (*The Structure and Dynamics of the Psyche*, 1960).
Archive of the History of American Psychology/ University of Akron

do assume, with Freud and with much support from today's psychological science, is that much of our mental life is unconscious. With Freud, they also assume that we often struggle with inner conflicts among our wishes, fears, and values, and that childhood shapes our personality and ways of becoming attached to others.

Assessing Unconscious Processes

12-6: What are projective tests, how are they used, and what are some criticisms of them?

Personality assessment tools are useful to those who study personality or provide therapy. Such tools differ because they are tailored to specific theories. How might psychodynamic clinicians attempt to assess personality characteristics?

The first requirement would be some sort of a road into the unconscious, to unearth the residue of early childhood experiences, to move beneath surface pretensions and reveal hidden conflicts and impulses. Objective assessment tools, such as agree-disagree or true-false questionnaires, would be inadequate because they would merely tap the conscious surface.

Projective tests aim to provide this "psychological X-ray," by asking test-takers to describe an ambiguous stimulus or tell a story about it. The clinician may presume that any hopes, desires, and fears that people see in the ambiguous image are projections of their own inner feelings or conflicts.

The most widely used projective test left some blots on the name of Swiss psychiatrist Hermann Rorschach [ROAR-shock; 1884–1922]. He based his famous **Rorschach inkblot test,** in which people describe what they see in a series of inkblots (**FIGURE 12.2**), on a childhood game. He and his friends would drip ink on a paper, fold it, and then say what they saw in the resulting blot (Sdorow, 2005). Do you see predatory animals or weapons? Perhaps you have aggressive tendencies. But is this a reasonable assumption? The answer varies.

"The forward thrust of the antlers shows a determined personality, yet the small sun indicates a lack of self-confidence. . . ."

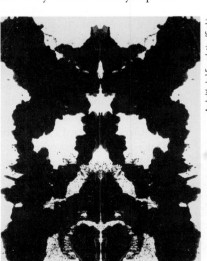

FIGURE 12.2
The Rorschach test In this projective test, people tell what they see in a series of symmetrical inkblots. Some who use this test are confident that the interpretation of ambiguous stimuli will reveal unconscious aspects of the test-taker's personality.

"We don't see things as they are; we see things as we are."

The Talmud

"The Rorschach Inkblot Test has been resoundingly discredited. I call it the Dracula of psychological tests, because no one has been able to drive a stake through the cursed thing's heart."

Carol Tavris, "Mind Games: Psychological Warfare Between Therapists and Scientists," 2003

"Many aspects of Freudian theory are indeed out of date, and they should be: Freud died in 1939, and he has been slow to undertake further revisions."

Psychologist Drew Westen (1998)

ScienceCartoonsPlus.com

Some clinicians cherish the Rorschach, even offering Rorschach-based assessments of criminals' violence potential to judges. Others view it as a helpful source of suggestive leads, or an icebreaker, or a revealing interview technique.

Critics of the Rorschach insist the test is no emotional MRI. They argue that only a few of the many Rorschach-derived scores, such as ones for hostility and anxiety, have demonstrated reliability and validity (Wood, 2006). Inkblot assessments diagnose many normal adults as pathological (Wood et al., 2003, 2006, 2010). Alternative projective assessment techniques fare little better. "Even seasoned professionals can be fooled by their intuitions and their faith in tools that lack strong evidence of effectiveness," warned Scott Lilienfeld, James Wood, and Howard Garb (2001). "When a substantial body of research demonstrates that old intuitions are wrong, it is time to adopt new ways of thinking."

The Society for Personality Assessment (2005) has commended the "responsible use" (which would *not* include inferring past childhood sexual abuse) of the Rorschach. And—in response to criticisms of test scoring and interpretation (Sechrest et al., 1998)—a research-based, computer-aided tool was designed to improve agreement among raters and enhance the test's validity (Erdberg, 1990; Exner, 2003).

Evaluating Freud's Psychoanalytic Perspective and Modern Views of the Unconscious

12-7: How do today's psychologists view Freud's psychoanalysis?

Modern Research Contradicts Many of Freud's Ideas

We critique Freud from an early twenty-first-century perspective, a perspective that itself will be subject to revision. Freud did not have access to neurotransmitter or DNA studies, or to all that we have since learned about human development, thinking, and emotion. To criticize his theory by comparing it with today's thinking, some say, is like criticizing Henry Ford's Model T by comparing it with today's hybrid cars. (How tempting it always is to judge people in the past from our perspective in the present.)

But both Freud's admirers and his critics agree that recent research contradicts many of his specific ideas. Today's developmental psychologists see our development as lifelong, not fixed in childhood. They doubt that infants' neural networks are mature enough to sustain as much emotional trauma as Freud assumed. Some think Freud overestimated parental influence and underestimated peer influence. They also doubt that conscience and gender identity form as the child resolves the Oedipus complex at age 5 or 6. We gain our gender identity earlier and become strongly masculine or feminine even without a same-sex parent present. And they note that Freud's ideas about childhood sexuality arose from his skepticism of stories of childhood sexual abuse told by his female patients—stories that some scholars believe he attributed to their own childhood sexual wishes and conflicts (Esterson, 2001; Powell & Boer, 1994). Today, we understand how Freud's questioning might have created false memories of abuse, and we also know that childhood sexual abuse does happen.

As we saw in Chapter 3, new ideas about why we dream dispute Freud's belief that dreams disguise and fulfill wishes. And slips of the tongue can be explained as competition between similar verbal choices in our memory network. Someone who says "I don't want to do that—it's a lot of brothel" may simply be blending *bother* and *trouble* (Foss & Hakes, 1978). Researchers find little support for Freud's idea that defense mechanisms disguise sexual and aggressive impulses (though our cognitive gymnastics do indeed work to protect our self-esteem). History also has failed to support another of Freud's ideas—that suppressed sexuality causes psychological disorders. From Freud's time to ours, sexual inhibition has diminished; psychological disorders have not.

Psychologists also criticize Freud's theory for its scientific shortcomings. Recall from Chapter 1 that good scientific theories explain observations and offer testable hypotheses. Freud's theory rests on few objective observations, and parts of it offer few testable hypotheses. (For Freud, his own recollections and interpretations of patients' free associations, dreams, and slips were evidence enough.)

What is the most serious problem with Freud's theory? It offers after-the-fact explanations of any characteristic (of one person's smoking, another's fear of horses, another's sexual orientation) yet fails to *predict* such behaviors and traits. If you feel angry at your mother's death, you illustrate his theory because "your unresolved childhood dependency needs are threatened." If you do not feel angry, you again illustrate his theory because "you are repressing your anger." That, said Calvin Hall and Gardner Lindzey (1978, p. 68), "is like betting on a horse after the race has been run." A good theory makes testable predictions.

So, should psychology post an "Allow Natural Death" order on this old theory? Freud's supporters object. To criticize Freudian theory for not making testable predictions is, they say, like criticizing baseball for not being an aerobic exercise, something it was never intended to be. Freud never claimed that psychoanalysis was predictive science. He merely claimed that, looking back, psychoanalysts could find meaning in our state of mind (Rieff, 1979).

Supporters also note that some of Freud's ideas *are* enduring. It was Freud who drew our attention to the unconscious and the irrational, to our self-protective defenses, to the importance of human sexuality, and to the tension between our biological impulses and our social well-being. It was Freud who challenged our self-righteousness, punctured our pretensions, and reminded us of our potential for evil.

Modern Research Challenges the Idea of Repression

Psychoanalytic theory rests on the assumption that the human mind often *represses* offending wishes, banishing them into the unconscious until they resurface, like long-lost books in a dusty attic. Recover and resolve childhood's conflicted wishes, and emotional healing should follow. Repression became a widely accepted concept, used to explain hypnotic phenomena and psychological disorders. Some of Freud's psychodynamic followers extended repression to explain apparently lost and recovered memories of childhood traumas (Boag, 2006; Cheit, 1998; Erdelyi, 2006). In one survey, 88 percent of university students believed that painful experiences commonly get pushed out of awareness and into the unconscious (Garry et al., 1994).

Today's researchers agree that we sometimes spare our egos by neglecting threatening information (Green et al., 2008). Yet, many contend that repression, if it ever occurs, is a rare mental response to terrible trauma. Even those who witnessed a parent's murder or survived Nazi death camps have retained their unrepressed memories of the horror (Helmreich, 1992, 1994; Malmquist, 1986; Pennebaker, 1990). "Dozens of formal studies have yielded not a single convincing case of repression in the entire literature on trauma," concluded personality researcher John Kihlstrom (2006).

Some researchers do believe that extreme, prolonged stress, such as the stress some severely abused children experience, might disrupt memory by damaging the hippocampus, which is important for processing conscious memories (Schacter, 1996). But the far more common reality is that high stress and associated stress hormones *enhance* memory (see Chapter 8). Indeed, rape, torture, and other traumatic events haunt survivors, who experience unwanted flashbacks. They are seared onto the soul. "You see the babies," said Holocaust survivor Sally H. (1979). "You see the screaming mothers. You see hanging people. You sit and you see that face there. It's something you don't forget."

The Modern Unconscious Mind

12-8: How has modern research developed our understanding of the unconscious?

Freud was right about a big idea that underlies today's psychodynamic thinking: We indeed have limited access to all that goes on in our minds (Erdelyi, 1985, 1988, 2006; Norman, 2010). Our two-track mind has a vast out-of-sight realm.

Nevertheless, many of today's research psychologists now think of the unconscious not as seething passions and repressive censoring but as cooler information

"We are arguing like a man who should say, 'If there were an invisible cat in that chair, the chair would look empty; but the chair does look empty; therefore there is an invisible cat in it.'"

C. S. Lewis, Four Loves, *1958*

"During the Holocaust, many children . . . were forced to endure the unendurable. For those who continue to suffer [the] pain is still present, many years later, as real as it was on the day it occurred."

Eric Zillmer, Molly Harrower, Barry Ritzler, and Robert Archer, The Quest for the Nazi Personality, *1995*

processing that occurs without our awareness. To these researchers, the unconscious also involves:

- the schemas that automatically control our perceptions and interpretations (Chapter 6).

- the priming by stimuli to which we have not consciously attended (Chapters 6 and 8).

- the right-hemisphere activity that enables the split-brain patient's left hand to carry out an instruction the patient cannot verbalize (Chapter 2).

- the implicit memories that operate without conscious recall, even among those with amnesia (Chapter 8).

- the emotions that activate instantly, before conscious analysis (Chapter 10).

- the stereotypes that automatically and unconsciously influence how we process information about others (Chapter 13).

More than we realize, we fly on autopilot. Our lives are guided by off-screen, out-of-sight, unconscious information processing. The unconscious mind is huge. This understanding of unconscious information processing is more like the pre-Freudian view of an underground, unattended stream of thought from which spontaneous behavior and creative ideas surface (Bargh & Morsella, 2008).

Recent research has also supported Freud's idea of our unconscious defense mechanisms. For example, Roy Baumeister and his colleagues (1998) found that people tend to see their foibles and attitudes in others, a phenomenon that Freud called *projection* and that today's researchers call the *false consensus effect*, the tendency to overestimate the extent to which others share our beliefs and behaviors. People who cheat on their taxes or break speed limits tend to think many others do likewise. People who see others as happy, kind, and trustworthy tend to be so themselves (Wood et al., 2010).

Evidence also confirms the unconscious mechanisms that defend self-esteem, such as reaction formation. Defense mechanisms, Baumeister concluded, are motivated less by the sexual and aggressive undercurrents that Freud presumed than by our need to protect our self-image.

RETRIEVE IT

- What are three values that Freud's work in psychoanalytic theory has contributed? What are three ways in which Freud's work has been criticized?

ANSWER: Freud first drew attention to (1) the importance of childhood experiences, (2) the existence of the unconscious mind, and (3) our self-protective defense mechanisms. Freud's work has been criticized as (1) not scientifically testable—drawing on after-the-fact explanations, (2) focusing too much on sexual conflicts in childhood, and (3) based upon the idea of repression, which has not been supported by modern research.

- Which elements of traditional psychoanalysis do modern-day *psychodynamic* theorists and therapists retain, and which elements have they mostly left behind?

ANSWER: Today's psychodynamic theories still rely on the interviewing techniques that Freud used, and they still tend to focus on childhood experiences and attachments, unresolved conflicts, and unconscious influences. However, they are not likely to dwell on fixation at any psychosexual stage, or the idea that resolution of sexual issues is the basis of our personality.

---

humanistic theories view personality with a focus on the potential for healthy personal growth.

self-actualization according to Maslow, one of the ultimate psychological needs that arises after basic physical and psychological needs are met and self-esteem is achieved; the motivation to fulfill one's potential.

unconditional positive regard according to Rogers, an attitude of total acceptance toward another person.

Humanistic Theories

12-9: How did humanistic psychologists view personality, and what was their goal in studying personality?

By the 1960s, some personality psychologists had become discontented with the sometimes bleak focus on drives and conflicts in psychodynamic theory and the mechanistic psychology of B. F. Skinner's behaviorism (see Chapter 7). In contrast to Freud's study of the base motives of "sick" people, these **humanistic theorists** focused on the ways "healthy" people strive for self-determination and self-realization. In contrast to behaviorism's scientific objectivity, they studied people through their own self-reported experiences and feelings.

Two pioneering theorists—Abraham Maslow (1908–1970) and Carl Rogers (1902–1987)—offered a *third-force perspective* that emphasized human potential.

Abraham Maslow's Self-Actualizing Person

Maslow proposed that we are motivated by a *hierarchy of needs* (Chapter 10). If our physiological needs are met, we become concerned with personal safety; if we achieve a sense of security, we then seek to love, to be loved, and to love ourselves; with our love needs satisfied, we seek self-esteem. Having achieved self-esteem, we ultimately seek **self-actualization** (the process of fulfilling our potential) and *self-transcendence* (meaning, purpose, and communion beyond the self).

Maslow (1970) developed his ideas by studying healthy, creative people rather than troubled clinical cases. He based his description of self-actualization on a study of those, such as Abraham Lincoln, who seemed notable for their rich and productive lives. Maslow reported that such people shared certain characteristics: They were self-aware and self-accepting, open and spontaneous, loving and caring, and not paralyzed by others' opinions. Secure in their sense of who they were, their interests were problem-centered rather than self-centered. They focused their energies on a particular task, one they often regarded as their mission in life. Most enjoyed a few deep relationships rather than many superficial ones. Many had been moved by spiritual or personal *peak experiences* that surpassed ordinary consciousness.

These, said Maslow, are mature adult qualities, ones found in those who have learned enough about life to be compassionate, to have outgrown their mixed feelings toward their parents, to have found their calling, to have "acquired enough courage to be unpopular, to be unashamed about being openly virtuous, etc." Maslow's work with college students led him to speculate that those likely to become self-actualizing adults were likeable, caring, "privately affectionate to those of their elders who deserve it," and "secretly uneasy about the cruelty, meanness, and mob spirit so often found in young people."

Abraham Maslow "Any theory of motivation that is worthy of attention must deal with the highest capacities of the healthy and strong person as well as with the defensive maneuvers of crippled spirits" (*Motivation and Personality*, 1970, p. 33).
© Bettmann/Corbis

Carl Rogers' Person-Centered Perspective

Fellow humanistic psychologist Carl Rogers agreed with much of Maslow's thinking. Rogers believed that people are basically good and are, as Maslow said, endowed with self-actualizing tendencies. Unless thwarted by a growth-inhibiting environment, each of us is like an acorn, primed for growth and fulfillment. Rogers (1980) believed that a growth-promoting climate required three conditions:

- ● ***Genuineness:*** When people are *genuine,* they are open with their own feelings, drop their facades, and are transparent and self-disclosing.

- ● ***Acceptance:*** When people are *accepting,* they offer **unconditional positive regard,** an attitude of grace that values us even knowing our failings. It is a profound relief to drop our pretenses, confess our worst feelings, and discover that we are still accepted. In a good marriage, a close family, or an intimate friendship, we are free to be spontaneous without fearing the loss of others' esteem.

- ● ***Empathy:*** When people are *empathic,* they share and mirror other's feelings and reflect their meanings. "Rarely do we listen with real understanding, true empathy," said Rogers. "Yet listening, of this very special kind, is one of the most potent forces for change that I know."

Genuineness, acceptance, and empathy are, Rogers believed, the water, sun, and nutrients that enable people to grow like vigorous oak trees. For "as persons are accepted and prized, they tend to develop a more caring attitude toward themselves" (Rogers, 1980, p. 116). As persons are empathically heard, "it becomes possible for them to listen more accurately to the flow of inner experiencings."

The picture of empathy Being open and sharing confidences is easier when the listener shows real understanding. Within such relationships people can relax and fully express their true selves.
Dylan Martinez/Reuters

A father *not* offering unconditional positive regard:

P. BYRNES.

"Just remember, son, it doesn't matter whether you win or lose—unless you want Daddy's love."

Writer Calvin Trillin (2006) recalled an example of parental genuineness and acceptance at a camp for children with severe disorders, where his wife, Alice, worked. L., a "magical child," had genetic diseases that meant she had to be tube-fed and could walk only with difficulty. Alice recalled,

> One day, when we were playing duck-duck-goose, I was sitting behind her and she asked me to hold her mail for her while she took her turn to be chased around the circle. It took her a while to make the circuit, and I had time to see that on top of the pile [of mail] was a note from her mom. Then I did something truly awful. . . . I simply had to know what this child's parents could have done to make her so spectacular, to make her the most optimistic, most enthusiastic, most hopeful human being I had ever encountered. I snuck a quick look at the note, and my eyes fell on this sentence: "If God had given us all of the children in the world to choose from, L., we would only have chosen you." Before L. got back to her place in the circle, I showed the note to Bud, who was sitting next to me. "Quick. Read this," I whispered. "It's the secret of life."

Maslow and Rogers would have smiled knowingly. For them a central feature of personality is one's **self-concept**—all the thoughts and feelings we have in response to the question, "Who am I?" If our self-concept is positive, we tend to act and perceive the world positively. If it is negative—if in our own eyes we fall far short of our *ideal self*—said Rogers, we feel dissatisfied and unhappy. A worthwhile goal for therapists, parents, teachers, and friends is therefore, he said, to help others know, accept, and be true to themselves.

Assessing the Self

12-10: How did humanistic psychologists assess a person's sense of self?

Humanistic psychologists sometimes assessed personality by asking people to fill out questionnaires that would evaluate their self-concept. One questionnaire, inspired by Carl Rogers, asked people to describe themselves both as they would *ideally* like to be and as they *actually* are. When the ideal and the actual self are nearly alike, said Rogers, the self-concept is positive. Assessing his clients' personal growth during therapy, he looked for successively closer ratings of actual and ideal selves.

Some humanistic psychologists believed that any standardized assessment of personality, even a questionnaire, is depersonalizing. Rather than forcing the person to respond to narrow categories, these humanistic psychologists presumed that interviews and intimate conversation would provide a better understanding of each person's unique experiences.

Evaluating Humanistic Theories

12-11: How have humanistic theories influenced psychology? What criticisms have they faced?

One thing said of Freud can also be said of the humanistic psychologists: Their impact has been pervasive. Maslow's and Rogers' ideas have influenced counseling, education, child rearing, and management. And they laid the groundwork for today's scientific positive psychology (Chapter 11).

They have also influenced—sometimes in ways they did not intend—much of today's popular psychology. Is a positive self-concept the key to happiness and success? Do acceptance and empathy nurture positive feelings about oneself? Are people basically good and capable of self-improvement? Many people answer *Yes, Yes,* and *Yes.* Responding to a 1992 *Newsweek* Gallup poll, 9 in 10 people rated self-esteem as very important for "motivating a person to work hard and succeed." Given a choice, today's North American collegians say they'd rather get a self-esteem boost, such as a compliment or good grade on a paper, than enjoy a favorite food or sexual activity (Bushman et al., 2011). Humanistic psychology's message has been heard.

self-concept all our thoughts and feelings about ourselves, in answer to the question, "Who am I?"

The prominence of the humanistic perspective set off a backlash of criticism. First, said the critics, its concepts are vague and *subjective*. Consider Maslow's description of self-actualizing people as open, spontaneous, loving, self-accepting, and productive. Is this a scientific description? Isn't it merely a description of the theorist's own values and ideals? Maslow, noted M. Brewster Smith (1978), offered impressions of his own personal heroes. Imagine another theorist who began with a different set of heroes—perhaps Napoleon, John D. Rockefeller, Sr., and Donald Trump. This theorist would likely describe self-actualizing people as "undeterred by others' needs and opinions," "motivated to achieve," and "comfortable with power."

Critics also objected to the idea that, as Rogers put it, "The only question which matters is, 'Am I living in a way which is deeply satisfying to me, and which truly expresses me?'" (quoted by Wallach & Wallach, 1985). This emphasis on *individualism*—trusting and acting on one's feelings, being true to oneself, fulfilling oneself—could lead to self-indulgence, selfishness, and an erosion of moral restraints (Campbell & Specht, 1985; Wallach & Wallach, 1983). Indeed, it is those who focus beyond themselves who are most likely to experience social support, to enjoy life, and to cope effectively with stress (Crandall, 1984).

Humanistic psychologists have countered by saying that a secure, nondefensive self-acceptance is actually the first step toward loving others. Indeed, people who feel intrinsically liked and accepted—for who they are, not just for their achievements—exhibit less-defensive attitudes (Schimel et al., 2001).

A final critique has been that humanistic psychology is *naive,* that it fails to appreciate the reality of our human capacity for evil (May, 1982). Faced with climate change, overpopulation, terrorism, and the spread of nuclear weapons, we may become apathetic from either of two rationalizations. One is a starry-eyed optimism that denies the threat ("People are basically good; everything will work out"). The other is a dark despair ("It's hopeless; why try?"). Action requires enough realism to fuel concern and enough optimism to provide hope.

"We do pretty well when you stop to think that people are basically good."

RETRIEVE IT

• How did humanistic psychology provide a fresh perspective?

ANSWER: This movement sought to turn psychology's attention away from drives and conflicts and toward our growth potential, with a focus on the way healthy people strive for self-determination and self-realization, which was in contrast to Freudian theory and strict behaviorism.

• What does it mean to be *empathic?* How about *self-actualized?* Which humanistic psychologists used these terms?

ANSWERS: To be *empathic* is to share and mirror another person's feelings. Carl Rogers believed that people nurture growth in others by being empathic. Abraham Maslow proposed that *self-actualization,* the motivation to fulfill one's potential, is one of the ultimate psychological needs (the other is self-transcendence).

Trait Theories

12-12: How do psychologists use traits to describe personality?

Rather than focusing on unconscious forces and thwarted growth opportunities, some researchers attempt to define personality in terms of stable and enduring behavior patterns, such as Sam Gamgee's loyalty and optimism. This perspective can be traced in part to a remarkable meeting in 1919, when Gordon Allport, a curious 22-year-old psychology student, interviewed Sigmund Freud in Vienna. Allport soon discovered just how preoccupied the founder of psychoanalysis was with finding hidden motives, even in Allport's own behavior during the interview. That experience ultimately led Allport to do what Freud did not do—to describe personality in terms of fundamental **traits**—people's characteristic behaviors and conscious

trait a characteristic pattern of behavior or a disposition to feel and act, as assessed by self-report inventories and peer reports.

Stephen Colbert: The extravert Trait labels such as *extraversion* can describe our temperament and typical behaviors.

motives (such as the curiosity that actually motivated Allport to see Freud). Meeting Freud, said Allport, "taught me that [psychoanalysis], for all its merits, may plunge too deep, and that psychologists would do well to give full recognition to manifest motives before probing the unconscious." Allport came to define personality in terms of identifiable behavior patterns. He was concerned less with *explaining* individual traits than with *describing* them.

Exploring Traits

Classifying people as one or another distinct personality type fails to capture their full individuality. We are each a unique complex of multiple traits. So how else could we describe our personalities? We might describe an apple by placing it along several trait dimensions—relatively large or small, red or green, sweet or sour. By placing people on several trait dimensions simultaneously, psychologists can describe countless individual personality variations. (Remember from Chapter 6 that variations on just three color dimensions—hue, saturation, and brightness—create many thousands of colors.)

What trait dimensions describe personality? If you had an upcoming blind date, what personality traits might give you an accurate sense of the person? Allport and his associate H. S. Odbert (1936) counted all the words in an unabridged dictionary with which one could describe people. There were almost 18,000! How, then, could psychologists condense the list to a manageable number of basic traits?

Factor Analysis

One technique is *factor analysis,* the statistical procedure used to identify clusters (factors) of test items that tap basic components of a trait (such as, for intelligence, spatial ability or verbal skill). Imagine that people who describe themselves as outgoing also tend to say that they like excitement and practical jokes and dislike quiet reading. Such a statistically correlated cluster of behaviors reflects a basic factor, or trait—in this case, *extraversion*.

British psychologists Hans Eysenck and Sybil Eysenck [EYE-zink] believed that we can reduce many of our normal individual variations to two or three dimensions, including *extraversion–introversion* and *emotional stability–instability* (**FIGURE 12.3**). People in 35 countries around the world, from China to Uganda to Russia, have taken the *Eysenck Personality Questionnaire*. When their answers were analyzed, the extraversion and emotionality factors inevitably emerged as basic personality dimensions (Eysenck, 1990, 1992). The Eysencks believed that these factors are genetically influenced, and research supports this belief.

FIGURE 12.3

Two personality dimensions Map makers can tell us a lot by using two axes (north–south and east–west). Two primary personality factors (extraversion–introversion and stability–instability) are similarly useful as axes for describing personality variation. Varying combinations define other, more specific traits. (From Eysenck & Eysenck, 1963.) Those who are naturally introverted, such as primatologist Jane Goodall, may be particularly gifted in field studies. Successful politicians, including former U.S. President Bill Clinton, are often natural extraverts.

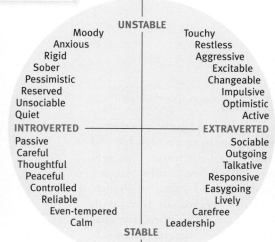

UNSTABLE

Moody   Touchy
Anxious   Restless
Rigid   Aggressive
Sober   Excitable
Pessimistic   Changeable
Reserved   Impulsive
Unsociable   Optimistic
Quiet   Active

INTROVERTED ——————— EXTRAVERTED

Passive   Sociable
Careful   Outgoing
Thoughtful   Talkative
Peaceful   Responsive
Controlled   Easygoing
Reliable   Lively
Even-tempered Carefree
Calm   Leadership

STABLE

Biology and Personality

Brain-activity scans of extraverts add to the growing list of traits and mental states that have been explored with brain-imaging procedures. Such studies indicate that extraverts seek stimulation because their normal *brain arousal* is relatively low. For example, PET scans have shown that a frontal lobe area involved in behavior inhibition is less active in extraverts than in introverts (Johnson et al., 1999). Dopamine and dopamine-related neural activity tend to be higher in extraverts (Wacker et al., 2006).

Our biology influences our personality in other ways as well. As you may recall from the twin and adoption studies in Chapter 2, our genes have much to say about the temperament and behavioral style that help define our personality. Children's shyness and inhibition may differ as an aspect of autonomic nervous system reactivity: Those with a reactive autonomic nervous system respond to stress with greater anxiety and inhibition (Kagan, 2010). The fearless, curious child may become the rock-climbing or fast-driving adult.

Personality differences among dogs (in energy, affection, reactivity, and curious intelligence) are as evident, and as consistently judged, as personality differences among humans (Gosling et al., 2003; Jones & Gosling, 2005). Monkeys, chimpanzees, orangutans, and even birds also have stable personalities (Weiss et al., 2006). Among the Great Tit (a European relative of the American chickadee), bold birds more quickly inspect new objects and explore trees (Groothuis & Carere, 2005; Verbeek et al., 1994). By selective breeding, researchers can produce bold or shy birds. Both have their place in natural history. In lean years, bold birds are more likely to find food; in abundant years, shy birds feed with less risk.

Erik Lam/Shutterstock

RETRIEVE IT

• Which two primary dimensions did Hans and Sybil Eysenck propose for describing personality variation?

ANSWER: introversion–extraversion and emotional stability–instability

---

Assessing Traits

12-13: What are personality inventories, and what are their strengths and weaknesses as trait-assessment tools?

If stable and enduring traits guide our actions, can we devise valid and reliable tests of them? Several trait assessment techniques exist—some more valid than others (see Thinking Critically About: How to Be a "Successful" Astrologer or Palm Reader on the next page). Some provide quick assessments of a single trait, such as extraversion, anxiety, or self-esteem. **Personality inventories**—longer questionnaires covering a wide range of feelings and behaviors—assess several traits at once.

The classic personality inventory is the **Minnesota Multiphasic Personality Inventory (MMPI).** Although it assesses "abnormal" personality tendencies rather than normal personality traits, the MMPI illustrates a good way of developing a personality inventory. One of its creators, Starke Hathaway (1960), compared his effort to that of Alfred Binet. Binet, as you may recall from Chapter 9, developed the first intelligence test by selecting items that identified children who would probably have trouble progressing normally in French schools. Like Binet's items, the MMPI items were **empirically derived:** From a large pool of items, Hathaway and his colleagues selected those on which particular diagnostic groups differed. They then grouped the questions into 10 clinical scales, including scales that assess depressive tendencies, masculinity–femininity, and introversion–extraversion.

personality inventory a questionnaire (often with *true-false* or *agree-disagree* items) on which people respond to items designed to gauge a wide range of feelings and behaviors; used to assess selected personality traits.

Minnesota Multiphasic Personality Inventory (MMPI) the most widely researched and clinically used of all personality tests. Originally developed to identify emotional disorders (still considered its most appropriate use), this test is now used for many other screening purposes.

empirically derived test a test (such as the MMPI) developed by testing a pool of items and then selecting those that discriminate between groups.

How to Be a "Successful" Astrologer or Palm Reader

Can we discern people's traits from the alignment of the stars and planets at the time of their birth? From their handwriting? From lines on their palms?

Astronomers scoff at the naiveté of astrology—the constellations have shifted in the millennia since astrologers formulated their predictions (Kelly, 1997, 1998). Humorists mock it: "No offense," wrote Dave Barry, "but if you take the horoscope seriously your frontal lobes are the size of Raisinets." Psychologists instead ask questions: Does it work? Can astrologers surpass chance when given someone's birth date and asked to identify the person from a short lineup of different personality descriptions? Can people pick out their own horoscopes from a lineup of horoscopes? Do people's astrological signs correlate with predicted traits?

The consistent answers have been *No, No, No,* and *No* (British Psychological Society, 1993; Carlson, 1985; Kelly, 1997, Reichardt, 2010). After examining census data from 20 million married people in England and Wales, one researcher found that "astrological sign has no impact on the probability of

marrying—and staying married to—someone of any other sign" (Voas, 2008).

Results have similarly been no better than chance when graphologists have tried to predict people's occupations from examining several

pages of their handwriting (Beyerstein & Beyerstein, 1992; Dean et al., 1992). Nevertheless, graphologists—and introductory psychology students—will often *perceive* correlations between personality and handwriting even where there are none (King & Koehler, 2000).

If all these perceived correlations evaporate under close scrutiny, how do astrologers, palm readers, and crystal-ball gazers persuade millions of people worldwide to buy their services? Ray Hyman (1981), palm reader turned research psychologist, has revealed some of their suckering methods.

The first technique, the "stock spiel," builds on the observation that each of us is in some

People have had fun spoofing the MMPI with their own mock items: "Weeping brings tears to my eyes," "Frantic screams make me nervous," and "I stay in the bathtub until I look like a raisin" (Frankel et al., 1983).

Hathaway and others initially gave hundreds of true-false statements ("No one seems to understand me"; "I get all the sympathy I should"; "I like poetry") to groups of psychologically disordered patients and to "normal" people. They retained any statement—no matter how silly it sounded—on which the patient group's answer differed from that of the normal group. "Nothing in the newspaper interests me except the comics" may seem senseless, but it just so happened that depressed people were more likely to answer *True*. Today's MMPI-2 has additional scales, assessing work attitudes, family problems, and anger.

Unlike subjective projective tests, personality inventories are scored objectively—so objectively that a computer can administer and score them. (The computer can also provide descriptions of people who previously responded similarly.) Objectivity does not, however, guarantee validity. Individuals taking the MMPI for employment purposes can give socially desirable answers to create a good impression. But in so doing they may

ways like no one else and in other ways just like everyone else. That some things are true of us all enables the "seer" to offer statements that seem impressively accurate: "I sense that you worry about things more than you let on, even to your best friends." A number of such generally true statements can be combined into a personality description. Imagine that you take a personality test and then receive the following character sketch:

> You have a strong need for other people to like and to admire you. You have a tendency to be critical of yourself. . . . You pride yourself on being an independent thinker and do not accept other opinions without satisfactory proof. You have found it unwise to be too frank in revealing yourself to others. At times you are extraverted, affable, sociable; at other times you are introverted, wary, and reserved. Some of your aspirations tend to be pretty unrealistic (Davies, 1997; Forer, 1949).

In experiments, college students have received stock assessments like this one, drawn from statements in a newsstand astrology book. When they thought the bogus, generic feedback was prepared just for them and when it was favorable, they nearly always rated the description as either "good" or "excellent" (Davies, 1997). Even skeptics, given a flattering description attributed to an astrologer, have thought that "maybe there's something to this astrology stuff after all" (Glick et al., 1989). This acceptance of stock, positive descriptions is called the *Barnum effect,* named in honor of master showman P. T. Barnum's dictum, "We've got something for everyone."

"Perhaps you'd like a second opinion?"

An astrologer, it has been said, is someone "prepared to tell you what you think of yourself" (Jones, 2000). Another way of doing that is to "read" your clothing, physical features, gestures, and reactions. An expensive wedding ring and black dress might, for example, suggest a wealthy woman who was recently widowed.

You, too, could read such clues, says Hyman. If people seek you out for a reading, start with some safe sympathy: "I sense you're having some problems lately. You seem unsure what to do. I get the feeling another person is involved." Then tell them what they want to hear. Memorize some Barnum statements from astrology and fortune-telling manuals and use them liberally. Tell people it is their responsibility to cooperate by relating your message to their specific experiences. Later they will recall that you predicted those specific details. Phrase statements as questions, and when you detect a positive response assert the statement strongly. Finally, be a good listener, and later, in different words, reveal to people what they earlier revealed to you. If you dupe them, they will come.

Better yet, beware of others who exploit people with these techniques. They are fortune takers rather than fortune tellers.

> "A petite fortune teller who escapes from prison is a small medium at large."
>
> Anonymous

also score high on a *lie scale* that assesses faking (as when people respond *False* to a universally true statement, such as "I get angry sometimes"). The objectivity of the MMPI has contributed to its popularity and to its translation into more than 100 languages.

The Big Five Factors

12-14: Which traits seem to provide the most useful information about personality variation?

Today's trait researchers believe that simple trait factors, such as the Eysencks' introverted–extraverted and stability–instability dimensions, are important, but they do not tell the whole story. A slightly expanded set of factors—dubbed the *Big Five*—does a better job (Costa & McCrae, 2009). If a test specifies where you are on the five

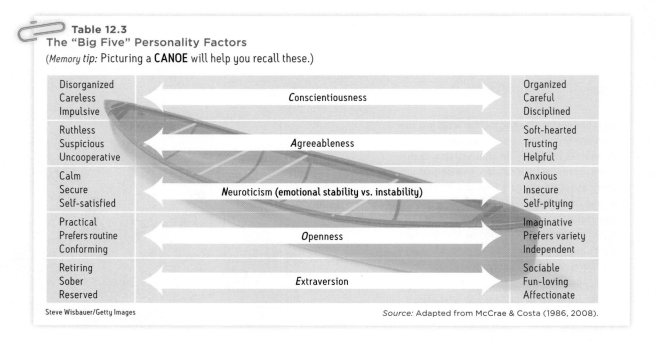

Table 12.3
The "Big Five" Personality Factors
(*Memory tip:* Picturing a **CANOE** will help you recall these.)

Disorganized Careless Impulsive	*Conscientiousness*	Organized Careful Disciplined
Ruthless Suspicious Uncooperative	*Agreeableness*	Soft-hearted Trusting Helpful
Calm Secure Self-satisfied	*Neuroticism (emotional stability vs. instability)*	Anxious Insecure Self-pitying
Practical Prefers routine Conforming	*Openness*	Imaginative Prefers variety Independent
Retiring Sober Reserved	*Extraversion*	Sociable Fun-loving Affectionate

Steve Wisbauer/Getty Images

Source: Adapted from McCrae & Costa (1986, 2008).

dimensions (conscientiousness, agreeableness, neuroticism, openness, and extraversion; see **TABLE 12.3**), it has said much of what there is to say about your personality. Around the world—across 56 nations and 29 languages in one study (Schmitt et al., 2007)—people describe others in terms roughly consistent with this list. The Big Five may not be the last word: Some researchers (Block, 2010; De Raad et al., 2010) report that basic personality dimensions can be described by only two or three factors (such as conscientiousness, agreeableness, and extraversion). But for now at least, five is the winning number in the personality lottery (Heine & Buchtel, 2009; McCrae, 2009). The Big Five is currently our best approximation of the basic trait dimensions. This "common currency for personality psychology" (Funder, 2001) has been the most active personality research topic since the early 1990s, as researchers have explored these questions and more:

- *How stable are the Big Five traits?* In adulthood, these traits are quite stable, with some tendencies (emotional instability, extraversion, and openness) waning a bit during early and middle adulthood, and others (agreeableness and conscientiousness) rising (McCrae, 2011; Vaidya et al., 2002). Conscientiousness increases the most during our twenties, as we mature and learn to manage our jobs and relationships. Agreeableness increases the most during our thirties and continues to increase through our sixties (Srivastava et al., 2003).

- *How heritable are these traits?* Heritability (the extent to which individual differences are attributable to genes) varies with the diversity of people studied. It generally runs 50 percent or a tad more for each dimension, and genetic influences are similar in different nations (Loehlin et al., 1998; Yamagata et al., 2006). Many genes, each having small effects, combine to influence our traits (McCrae et al., 2010). Researchers have also identified brain areas associated with the various Big Five traits, such as a frontal lobe area that is sensitive to reward and is larger in extraverts (DeYoung et al., 2010).

- *Do the Big Five traits predict our actual behaviors?* Yes. If people report being outgoing, conscientious, and agreeable, "they probably are telling the truth," reports Big Five researcher Robert McCrae (2011). For example, our traits appear in our language patterns. In text messaging, extraversion predicts use of personal pronouns. Agreeableness predicts positive-emotion words. Neuroticism (emotional instability) predicts negative-emotion words (Holtgraves, 2011).

By exploring such questions, Big Five research has sustained trait psychology and renewed appreciation for the importance of personality. Traits matter.

Hemera Technologies/Jupiterimages

Evaluating Trait Theories

12-15: Does research support the consistency of personality traits over time and across situations?

Are our personality traits stable and enduring? Or does our behavior depend on where and with whom we find ourselves? J.R.R. Tolkien created characters, like the loyal Sam Gamgee, whose personality traits were consistent across various times and places. The Italian playwright Luigi Pirandello had a different view. For him, personality was ever-changing, tailored to the particular role or situation. In one of Pirandello's plays, Lamberto Laudisi describes himself: "I am really what you take me to be; though, my dear madam, that does not prevent me from also being really what your husband, my sister, my niece, and Signora Cini take me to be—because they also are absolutely right!" To which Signora Sirelli responds, "In other words you are a different person for each of us."

"There is as much difference between us and ourselves, as between us and others."

Michel de Montaigne, Essays, 1588

The Person-Situation Controversy

Who, then, typifies human personality, Tolkien's consistent Sam Gamgee or Pirandello's inconsistent Laudisi? Both. Our behavior is influenced by the interaction of our inner disposition with our environment. Still, the question lingers: Which is more important? Are we *more* as Tolkien or as Pirandello imagined us to be?

When we explore this *person-situation controversy,* we look for genuine personality traits that persist over time *and* across situations. Are some people dependably conscientious and others unreliable? Some cheerful and others dour? Some friendly and outgoing and others shy? If we are to consider friendliness a trait, friendly people must act friendly at different times and places. Do they?

In considering research that has followed lives through time, some scholars (especially those who study infants) are impressed with personality change; others are struck by personality stability during adulthood. As **FIGURE 12.4** illustrates, data from 152 long-term studies reveal that personality trait scores are positively correlated with scores obtained seven years later, and that as people grow older their personality stabilizes. Interests may change—the avid tropical-fish collector may become an avid gardener. Careers may change—the determined salesperson may become a determined social worker. Relationships may change—the hostile spouse may start over with a new partner. But most people recognize their traits as their own, as Robert McCrae and Paul Costa noted (1994), "and it is well that they do. A person's recognition of the inevitability of his or her one and only personality is . . . the culminating wisdom of a lifetime."

"*I'm going to France—I'm a different person in France.*"

Change and consistency can co-exist. If all people were to become somewhat less shy with age, there would be personality change, but there would also be relative stability and predictability.

FIGURE 12.4
Personality stability With age, personality traits become more stable, as reflected in the stronger correlation of trait scores with follow-up scores seven years later. (Data from Roberts & DelVecchio, 2000.)

Trait score correlations over seven years

Children	Collegians	30-year-olds	50- to 70-year-olds
0.31	0.54	0.64	0.74

*"Mr. Coughlin over there was the founder of one of
the first motorcycle gangs."*

So most people—including most psychologists—would probably side with Tolkien's assumption of stability of personality traits. Moreover, our traits are socially significant. They influence our health, our thinking, and our job performance (Deary & Matthews, 1993; Hogan, 1998). Studies that follow lives through time show that personality traits rival socioeconomic status and cognitive ability as predictors of mortality, divorce, and occupational attainment (Roberts et al., 2007).

Although our personality *traits* may be both stable and potent, the consistency of our specific *behaviors* from one situation to the next is another matter. As Walter Mischel (1968, 2009) has pointed out, people do not act with predictable consistency. Mischel's studies of college students' conscientiousness revealed but a modest relationship between a student's being conscientious on one occasion (say, showing up for class on time) and being similarly conscientious on another occasion (say, turning in assignments on time). Pirandello would not have been surprised. If you've noticed how outgoing you are in some situations and how reserved you are in others, perhaps you're not surprised either (though for certain traits, Mischel reports, you may accurately assess yourself as more consistent).

This inconsistency in behaviors also makes personality test scores weak predictors of behaviors. People's scores on an extraversion test, for example, do not neatly predict how sociable they actually will be on any given occasion. If we remember such results, says Mischel, we will be more cautious about labeling and pigeonholing individuals. Years in advance, science can tell us the phase of the Moon for any given date. A day in advance, meteorologists can often predict the weather. But we are much further from being able to predict how *you* will feel and act tomorrow.

However, people's *average* outgoingness, happiness, or carelessness over many situations is predictable (Epstein, 1983a,b). People who know a person well do generally agree when rating that individual's shyness or agreeableness (Kenrick & Funder, 1988). The predictability of average behavior across many situations was again confirmed when researchers collected snippets of people's daily experience via body-worn recording devices: Extraverts really do talk more (Mehl et al., 2006). (I have repeatedly vowed to cut back on my jabbering and joking during my noontime pickup basketball games with friends. Alas, moments later, the irrepressible chatterbox inevitably reoccupies my body.) As our best friends can verify, we do have genetically influenced personality traits. And those traits even lurk, report Samuel Gosling and his colleagues in a series of studies, in our

- *music preferences.* Classical, jazz, blues, and folk music lovers tend to be open to experience and verbally intelligent; country, pop, and religious music lovers tend to be cheerful, outgoing, and conscientious (Rentfrow & Gosling, 2003, 2006). On first meeting, students often disclose their music preferences to each other; in doing so, they are swapping information about their personalities.

- *dorm rooms and offices.* Our personal spaces display our identity and leave a behavioral residue (in our scattered laundry or neat desktop). That helps explain why just a few minutes' inspection of our living and working spaces can enable someone to assess with reasonable accuracy our conscientiousness, our openness to new experiences, and even our emotional stability (Gosling et al., 2002, 2008).

- *personal websites.* Is a personal website or a Facebook profile also a canvas for self-expression? Or is it an opportunity for people to present themselves in false or misleading ways? It's more the former (Back et al., 2010; Gosling et al., 2007; Marcus et al., 2006). Visitors quickly gain important clues to the creator's extraversion, conscientiousness, and openness to experience.

- *electronic communications.* If you have ever felt you could detect others' personality from their writing voice, you are right!! (What a cool, exciting finding!!!) People's ratings of personality based solely on their e-mails or blogs correlate with actual personality scores on measures such as extraversion and neuroticism (Gill et al., 2006; Oberlander & Gill, 2006; Yarkoni, 2010). Extraverts, for example, use more adjectives.

In unfamiliar, formal situations—perhaps as a guest in the home of a person from another culture—our traits remain hidden as we carefully attend to social cues. In familiar, informal situations—just hanging out with friends—we feel less constrained, allowing our traits to emerge (Buss, 1989). In these informal situations, our expressive styles—our animation, manner of speaking, and gestures—are impressively consistent. That's why those very thin slices of someone's behavior—even just three 2-second clips of a teacher—have been so revealing (Ambady & Rosenthal, 1992, 1993).

To sum up, we can say that at any moment the immediate situation powerfully influences a person's behavior. Social psychologists have assumed, albeit without much evidence, that this is especially so when a "strong situation" makes clear demands (Cooper & Withey, 2009). We can better predict drivers' behavior at traffic lights from knowing the color of the lights than from knowing the drivers' personalities. Averaging our behavior across many occasions does, however, reveal distinct personality traits. Traits exist. We differ. And our differences matter.

Room with a cue Even at "zero acquaintance," people can discern something of others' personality from glimpsing their website, dorm room, or office. So, what is your read on University of Texas researcher Samuel Gosling?

John Langford Photography

RETRIEVE IT

• How well do personality test scores predict our behavior? Explain.

ANSWER: Our scores on personality tests predict our *average* behavior across many situations much better than they predict our specific behavior in any given situation.

Social-Cognitive Theories

12-16: How do social-cognitive theorists view personality development, and how do they explore behavior?

Today's psychological science views individuals as biopsychosocial organisms. The **social-cognitive perspective** on personality proposed by Albert Bandura (1986, 2006, 2008) emphasizes the interaction of our traits with our situations. Much as nature and nurture always work together, so do individuals and their situations.

Social-cognitive theorists believe we learn many of our behaviors either through conditioning or by observing and imitating others. (That's the "social" part.) They also emphasize the importance of mental processes: What we *think* about a situation affects our behavior in that situation. (That's the "cognitive" part.) Instead of focusing solely on how our environment *controls* us (behaviorism), social-cognitive theorists focus on how we and our environment *interact:* How do we interpret and respond to external events? How do our schemas, our memories, and our expectations influence our behavior patterns?

Reciprocal Influences

Bandura (1986, 2006) views the person-environment interaction as **reciprocal determinism.** "Behavior, internal personal factors, and environmental influences," he said, "all operate as interlocking determinants of each other" (**FIGURE 12.5** on the next page). For example, children's TV-viewing habits (past behavior) influence their viewing preferences (internal factor), which influence how television (environmental factor) affects their current behavior. The influences are mutual.

social-cognitive perspective views behavior as influenced by the interaction between people's traits (including their thinking) and their social context.

reciprocal determinism the interacting influences of behavior, internal cognition, and environment.

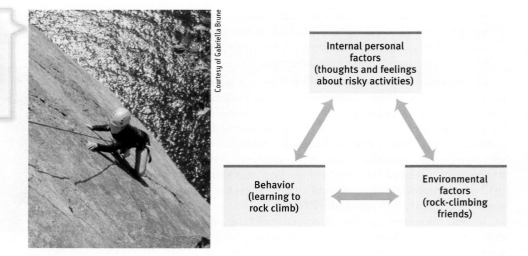

FIGURE 12.5

Reciprocal determinism The social-cognitive perspective proposes that our personalities are shaped by the interaction of our personal traits (including our thoughts and feelings), our environment, and our behaviors.

Consider three specific ways in which individuals and environments interact:

1. ***Different people choose different environments.*** The school you attend, the reading you do, the TV programs you watch, the music you listen to, the friends you associate with—all are part of an environment you have chosen, based partly on your dispositions (Funder, 2009; Ickes et al., 1997). You choose your environment and it then shapes you.

2. ***Our personalities shape how we interpret and react to events.*** Anxious people, for example, are attuned to potentially threatening events (Eysenck et al., 1987). Thus, they perceive the world as threatening, and they react accordingly.

3. ***Our personalities help create situations to which we react.*** How we view and treat people influences how they in turn treat us. If we expect someone to be angry with us, we may give the person a cold shoulder, touching off the very anger we expect. If we have an easygoing, positive disposition, we will likely enjoy close, supportive friendships (Donnellan et al., 2005; Kendler, 1997).

In such ways, we are both the products and the architects of our environments.

If all this has a familiar ring, it may be because it parallels and reinforces a pervasive theme in psychology and in this book: *Behavior emerges from the interplay of external and internal influences.* Boiling water turns an egg hard and a potato soft. A threatening environment turns one person into a hero, another into a scoundrel. Extraverts enjoy greater well-being in an extraverted culture than in an introverted one (Fulmer et al., 2010). *At every moment,* our behavior is influenced by our biology, our social and cultural experiences, and our cognition and dispositions (**FIGURE 12.6**).

FIGURE 12.6

The biopsychosocial approach to the study of personality As with other psychological phenomena, personality is fruitfully studied at multiple levels.

Biological influences:
• genetically determined temperament
• autonomic nervous system reactivity
• brain activity

Psychological influences:
• learned responses
• unconscious thought processes
• expectations and interpretations

Personality

Social-cultural influences:
• childhood experiences
• influence of the situation
• cultural expectations
• social support

Assessing Behavior in Situations

Social-cognitive psychologists explore how people interact with situations. To predict behavior, they often observe behavior in realistic situations.

One ambitious example was the U.S. Army's World War II strategy for assessing candidates for spy missions. Rather than using paper-and-pencil tests, Army psychologists subjected the candidates to simulated undercover conditions. They tested their ability to handle stress, solve problems, maintain leadership, and withstand intense interrogation without blowing their cover. Although time-consuming and expensive, this assessment of behavior in a realistic situation helped predict later success on actual spy missions (OSS Assessment Staff, 1948).

Military and educational organizations and many Fortune 500 companies are adopting assessment center strategies (Bray & Byham, 1991, 1997; Eurich et al., 2009). AT&T has observed prospective managers doing simulated managerial work. Many colleges assess students' potential via internships and student teaching and assess potential faculty members' teaching abilities by observing them teach. Armies assess their soldiers by observing them during military exercises. Most American cities with populations of 50,000 or more have used assessment centers in evaluating police and fire officers (Lowry, 1997).

Assessment center exercises have some limitations. They are more revealing of visible dimensions, such as communication ability, than of others, such as inner achievement drive (Bowler & Woehr, 2006). Nevertheless, these procedures exploit a valid principle: The best means of predicting future behavior is neither a personality test nor an interviewer's intuition; rather, it is *the person's past behavior patterns in similar situations* (Mischel, 1981; Ouellette & Wood, 1998; Schmidt & Hunter, 1998). As long as the situation and the person remain much the same, the best predictor of future job performance is past job performance; the best predictor of future grades is past grades; the best predictor of future aggressiveness is past aggressiveness; the best predictor of young-adult drug use is high-school drug use. If you can't check the person's past behavior, the next-best thing is to create an assessment situation that simulates the task so you can see how the person handles it (Lievens et al., 2009; Meriac et al., 2008).

AP Photo/Jennifer Szymaszek

Assessing behavior in situations
Reality TV shows, such as Donald Trump's *The Apprentice*, may take "show me" job interviews to the extreme, but they do illustrate a valid point. Seeing how a potential employee behaves in a job-relevant situation helps predict job performance.

A *New York Times* analysis of 100 rampage murders over the last half-century revealed that 55 of the killers had regularly exploded in anger and 63 had threatened violence (Goodstein & Glaberson, 2000). Most didn't, out of the blue, "just snap."

Evaluating Social-Cognitive Theories

12-17: What criticisms have social-cognitive theorists faced?

Social-cognitive theories of personality sensitize researchers to how situations affect, and are affected by, individuals. More than other personality theories (see **TABLE 12.4** on the next page), they build from psychological research on learning and cognition.

Critics charge that social-cognitive theories focus so much on the situation that they fail to appreciate the person's inner traits. Where is the person in this view of personality, ask the dissenters, and where are human emotions? True, the situation does guide our behavior. But, say the critics, in many instances our unconscious motives, our emotions, and our pervasive traits shine through. Personality traits have been shown to predict behavior at work, love, and play. Our biologically influenced traits really do matter. Consider Percy Ray Pridgen and Charles Gill. Each faced the same situation: They had jointly won a $90 million lottery jackpot (Harriston, 1993). When Pridgen learned of

Table 12.4
Comparing the Major Personality Theories

Personality Theory	Key Proponents	Assumptions	View of Personality	Personality Assessment Methods
Psychoanalytic	Freud	Emotional disorders spring from unconscious dynamics, such as unresolved sexual and other childhood conflicts, and fixation at various developmental stages. Defense mechanisms fend off anxiety.	Personality consists of pleasure-seeking impulses (the id), a reality-oriented executive (the ego), and an internalized set of ideals (the superego).	Free association, projective tests, dream analysis
Psychodynamic	Jung, Adler, Horney	The unconscious and conscious minds interact. Childhood experiences and defense mechanisms are important.	The dynamic interplay of conscious and unconscious motives and conflicts shape our personality.	Projective tests, therapy sessions
Humanistic	Rogers, Maslow	Rather than examining the struggles of sick people, it's better to focus on the ways healthy people strive for self-realization.	If our basic human needs are met, we will strive toward self-actualization. In a climate of unconditional positive regard, we can develop self-awareness and a more realistic and positive self-concept.	Questionnaires, therapy sessions
Trait	Allport, Eysenck, McCrae, Costa	We have certain stable and enduring characteristics, influenced by genetic predispositions.	Scientific study of traits has isolated important dimensions of personality, such as the Big Five traits (stability, extraversion, openness, agreeableness, and conscientiousness).	Personality inventories
Social-Cognitive	Bandura	Our traits and the social context interact to produce our behaviors.	Conditioning and observational learning interact with cognition to create behavior patterns.	Our behavior in one situation is best predicted by considering our past behavior in similar situations.

the winning numbers, he began trembling uncontrollably, huddled with a friend behind a bathroom door while confirming the win, then sobbed. When Gill heard the news, he told his wife and then went to sleep.

RETRIEVE IT

• According to the social-cognitive perspective, what is the best way to predict a person's future behavior?

ANSWER: Examine the person's past behavior patterns in similar situations.

Exploring the Self

12-18: Why has psychology generated so much research on the self? How important is self-esteem to psychology and to our well-being?

self in contemporary psychology, assumed to be the center of personality, the organizer of our thoughts, feelings, and actions.

spotlight effect overestimating others' noticing and evaluating our appearance, performance, and blunders (as if we presume a spotlight shines on us).

self-esteem one's feelings of high or low self-worth.

self-efficacy one's sense of competence and effectiveness.

Psychology's concern with people's sense of self dates back at least to William James, who devoted more than 100 pages of his 1890 *Principles of Psychology* to the topic. By 1943, Gordon Allport lamented that the self had become "lost to view." Although humanistic psychology's later emphasis on the self did not instigate much scientific research, it did help renew the concept of self and keep it alive. Now, more than a century after James, the self is one of Western psychology's most vigorously researched topics. Every year, new studies galore appear on self-esteem, self-disclosure, self-awareness, self-schemas, self-monitoring, and so forth. Even neuroscientists have searched for self, by identifying a central frontal lobe region that activates when people respond to self-reflective questions about their traits and dispositions (Damasio, 2010; Mitchell, 2009). Underlying all this research is an assumption that the **self,** as organizer of our thoughts, feelings, and actions, is the center of personality.

One example of thinking about self is the concept of *possible selves* put forth by Hazel Markus and her colleagues (Cross & Markus, 1991; Markus & Nurius, 1986). Your possible selves include your visions of the self you dream of becoming—the rich self, the successful self, the loved and admired self. They also include the self you fear becoming—the unemployed self, the lonely self, the academically failed self. Such possible selves motivate us by laying out specific goals and calling forth the energy to work toward them. University of Michigan students in a combined undergraduate/ medical school program earn higher grades if they undergo the program with a clear vision of themselves as successful doctors. Dreams do often give birth to achievements.

Our self-focused perspective may motivate us, but it can also lead us to presume too readily that others are noticing and evaluating us. Thomas Gilovich (1996) demonstrated this **spotlight effect** by having individual Cornell University students don Barry Manilow T-shirts before entering a room with other students. Feeling self-conscious, the T-shirt wearers guessed that nearly half their peers would take note of the shirt as they walked in. In reality, only 23 percent did. This absence of attention applies not only to our dorky clothes and bad hair but also to our nervousness, irritation, or attraction: Fewer people notice than we presume (Gilovich & Savitsky, 1999). Others are also less aware than we suppose of the variability—the ups and downs—of our appearance and performance (Gilovich et al., 2002). Even after a blunder (setting off a library alarm, showing up in the wrong clothes), we stick out like a sore thumb less than we imagine (Savitsky et al., 2001). Knowing about the spotlight effect can be empowering. Help public speakers to understand that their natural nervousness is not so apparent to their audience and their speaking performance improves (Savitsky & Gilovich, 2003).

> "The first step to better times is to imagine them."
>
> *Chinese fortune cookie*

Trinity Mirror/Mirrorpix/Alamy/Timothy Large/Shutterstock

The Benefits of Self-Esteem

Our **self-esteem**—our feelings of high or low self-worth—is also important. So also is **self-efficacy,** our sense of competence on a task. A person with high self-esteem will strongly agree with self-affirming questionnaire statements such as, "I am fun to be with," or "I have good ideas." A low–self-esteem person responds to these statements with qualifying adjectives, such as *somewhat* or *sometimes.*

High self-esteem pays dividends. People who feel good about themselves have fewer sleepless nights. They are less likely to give in to pressures to conform. They are more persistent at difficult tasks; they are less shy, anxious, and lonely. They try harder to shake their bad moods because they think they deserve better (Wood et al., 2009). And they are just plain happier (Greenberg, 2008; Orth et al., 2008, 2009).

But is high self-esteem the horse or the cart? Is it really "the armor that protects kids" from life's problems (McKay, 2000)? Some psychologists have had their doubts (Baumeister, 2006; Dawes, 1994; Leary, 1999; Seligman, 1994, 2002). Children's academic self-efficacy— their confidence that they can do well in a subject—predicts school achievement, but their general self-image does not (Marsh & Craven, 2006; Swann et al., 2007; Trautwein et al., 2006). Maybe self-esteem simply reflects reality. Maybe feeling good *follows* doing well. Maybe it's a side effect of meeting challenges and surmounting difficulties. Maybe self-esteem is a gauge that reads out the state of our relationships with others. If so, isn't pushing the gauge artificially higher ("You are special") akin to forcing a car's low fuel gauge to display "full"? And if problems and failures cause low self-esteem, won't the best boost therefore come not from our repeatedly telling children how wonderful they are but from their own effective coping and hard-won achievements?

> "When kids increase in self-control, their grades go up later. But when kids increase their self-esteem, there is no effect on their grades."
>
> *Angela Duckworth,* In Character *interview, 2009*

However, experiments have revealed an *effect* of low self-esteem. When researchers temporarily deflated people's self-image (by telling them they did poorly on an aptitude test or by disparaging their personality), they were more likely to disparage others or to express heightened racial prejudice (Ybarra, 1999). In other studies, people who were negative about themselves also tended to be oversensitive and judgmental (Baumgardner et al., 1989; Pelham, 1993). And people made to feel insecure often became excessively critical, as if to impress others with their own brilliance (Amabile, 1983). Such findings are consistent with Maslow's and Rogers' presumptions that a healthy self-image pays dividends. Accept yourself and you'll find it easier to accept others. Disparage yourself and you will be prone to the floccinaucinihilipilification[1] of others. Said more simply, people who are down on themselves tend to be down on others. Some people "love their neighbors as themselves"; others loathe their neighbors as themselves.

Self-Serving Bias

12-19: What evidence reveals self-serving bias, and how do defensive and secure self-esteem differ?

Carl Rogers (1958) once objected to the religious doctrine that humanity's problems arise from excessive self-love, or pride. He noted that most people he had known "despise themselves, regard themselves as worthless and unlovable." Mark Twain had a similar idea: "No man, deep down in the privacy of his heart, has any considerable respect for himself."

Actually, most of us have a good reputation with ourselves. In studies of self-esteem, even those who score low respond in the midrange of possible scores. Moreover, one of psychology's most provocative and firmly established recent conclusions concerns our potent **self-serving bias**—our readiness to perceive ourselves favorably (Mezulis et al., 2004; Myers, 2013). Consider:

People accept more responsibility for good deeds than for bad, and for successes than for failures. Athletes often privately credit their victories to their own prowess, and their losses to bad breaks, lousy officiating, or the other team's exceptional performance. Most students who receive poor grades on an exam criticize the test, not themselves. Drivers filling out insurance forms explain their accidents in such words as: "An invisible car came out of nowhere, struck my car, and vanished." "As I reached an intersection, a hedge sprang up, obscuring my vision, and I did not see the other car." "A pedestrian hit me and went under my car." The question "What have I done to deserve this?" is one we usually ask of our troubles, not our successes—those, we assume we deserve.

Most people see themselves as better than average. This is true for nearly any commonplace behavior that is subjectively assessed and socially desirable (Myers, 2013):

- In national surveys, most business executives say they are more ethical than their average counterpart.

- In several studies, 90 percent of business managers and more than 90 percent of college professors rated their performance as superior to that of their average peer.

- In the National Survey of Families and Households, 49 percent of men said they provided half or more of the child care, though only 31 percent of their wives or partners saw things that way (Galinsky et al., 2008).

- In Australia, 86 percent of people rate their job performance as above average, and only 1 percent as below average.

---

self-serving bias a readiness to perceive oneself favorably.

[1] I couldn't resist throwing that in. But don't worry, you won't be tested on floccinaucinihilipilification, which is the act of estimating something as worthless (and was the longest nontechnical word in the first edition of the *Oxford English Dictionary*).

The self-serving bias reflects our overestimation of ourselves rather than an underestimation of others (Epley & Dunning, 2000). This phenomenon is less striking in Asia, where people value modesty (Falk et al., 2009; Heine & Hamamura, 2007). Yet self-serving biases have been observed worldwide: among Dutch, Australian, and Chinese students; Japanese drivers; Indian Hindus; and French people of most walks of life. In every one of 53 countries surveyed, people expressed self-esteem above the midpoint of the most widely used scale (Schmitt & Allik, 2005).

PEANUTS

Ironically, people even see themselves as more immune than others to self-serving bias (Pronin, 2007). The world, it seems, is Garrison Keillor's Lake Wobegon writ large—a place where "all the women are strong, all the men are good-looking, and all the children are above average." And so are the pets. Three in four owners believe their pet is smarter than average (Nier, 2004).

Threatened egotism, more than low self-esteem, it seems, predisposes aggression. This is true even in childhood, when the recipe for frequent fighting mixes high self-esteem with social rejection. The most aggressive children tend to have high self-regard that gets punctured by other kids' dislike (van Boxtel et al., 2004).

An adolescent or adult whose swelled head is deflated by insults is potentially dangerous. Finding their self-esteem threatened, people with large egos may react violently. "Aryan pride" fueled Nazi atrocities. "These biases have the effect of making wars more likely to begin and more difficult to end," noted Daniel Kahneman and Jonathan Renshon (2007).

Brad Bushman and Roy Baumeister (1998; Bushman et al., 2009) experimented with what they call the "dark side of high self-esteem." They had 540 undergraduate volunteers write a paragraph, in response to which another supposed student gave them either praise ("Great essay!") or stinging criticism ("One of the worst essays I have read!"). Then the essay writers played a reaction-time game against the other student. After wins, they could assault their opponent with noise of any intensity for any duration.

Can you anticipate the result? After criticism, those with inflated high self-esteem were "exceptionally aggressive." They delivered three times the auditory torture of those with normal self-esteem. "Encouraging people to feel good about themselves when they haven't earned it" poses problems, Baumeister (2001) concluded. "Conceited, self-important individuals turn nasty toward those who puncture their bubbles of self-love."

Are self-serving perceptions on the rise in North America? Some researchers believe they are. From 1980 to 2007, popular song lyrics became more self-focused (DeWall et al., 2011). From 1988 to 2008, self-esteem scores increased among American collegians, high schoolers, and especially middle school students (Gentile et al., 2010). On one prominent self-esteem inventory on which 40 is the highest possible self-esteem score, 51 percent of 2008 collegians scored 35 or more.

Narcissism—excessive self-love and self-absorption—is also rising, reports psychologist Jean Twenge (2006; Twenge & Foster, 2010). After tracking self-importance across the last several decades, Twenge found that what she calls *Generation Me* (born in the 80s and 90s) is expressing more narcissism by agreeing more often with statements such as, "If I ruled the world, it would be a better place," or "I think I am a special person." Agreement with such narcissistic statements correlates with materialism, the desire to be famous, inflated expectations, more hookups with fewer committed relationships, more gambling, and more cheating, all of which have been increasing as narcissism has increased.

Some critics of the concept of self-serving bias claim that it overlooks those who feel worthless and unlovable: If self-serving bias prevails, why do so many people disparage themselves? For four reasons:

"If you are like most people, then like most people, you don't know you're like most people. Science has given us a lot of facts about the average person, and one of the most reliable of these facts is the average person doesn't see herself as average."

Daniel Gilbert, Stumbling on Happiness, *2006*

"The enthusiastic claims of the self-esteem movement mostly range from fantasy to hogwash. The effects of self-esteem are small, limited, and not all good."

Roy Baumeister (1996)

narcissism excessive self-love and self-absorption.

• Self-directed put-downs can be *subtly strategic:* They elicit reassuring strokes. Saying "No one likes me" may at least elicit "But not everyone has met you!"

• Before an important event, such as a game or an exam, self-disparaging comments *prepare us for possible failure.* The coach who extols the superior strength of the upcoming opponent makes a loss understandable, a victory noteworthy.

• A self-disparaging "How could I have been so stupid!" can help us *learn from our mistakes.*

• Self-disparagement frequently *pertains to one's old self.* Asked to remember their really bad behaviors, people recall things from long ago; good behaviors more easily come to mind from their recent past (Escobedo & Adolphs, 2010). People are much more critical of their distant past selves than of their current selves—even when they have not changed (Wilson & Ross, 2001). "At 18, I was a jerk; today I'm more sensitive." In their own eyes, chumps yesterday, champs today.

Even so, it's true: All of us some of the time, and some of us much of the time, do feel inferior—especially when we compare ourselves with those who are a step or two higher on the ladder of status, looks, income, or ability. The deeper and more frequently we have such feelings, the more unhappy, even depressed, we are. But for most people, thinking has a naturally positive bias.

While recognizing the dark side of self-serving bias and self-esteem, some researchers prefer isolating the effects of two types of self-esteem—defensive and secure (Kernis, 2003; Lambird & Mann, 2006; Ryan & Deci, 2004). *Defensive self-esteem* is fragile. It focuses on sustaining itself, which makes failures and criticism feel threatening. Such egotism exposes one to perceived threats, which feed anger and disorder (Crocker & Park, 2004).

Secure self-esteem is less fragile, because it is less contingent on external evaluations. Feeling accepted for who we are, and not for our looks, wealth, or acclaim, relieves pressures to succeed and enables us to focus beyond ourselves. By losing ourselves in relationships and purposes larger than self, we may achieve a more secure self-esteem and greater quality of life (Crocker & Park, 2004). Authentic pride, rooted in actual achievement, supports self-confidence and leadership (Tracy et al., 2009; Williams & DeSteno, 2009).

> "If you compare yourself with others, you may become vain and bitter; for always there will be greater and lesser persons than yourself."
>
> *Max Ehrmann, "Desiderata," 1927*

RETRIEVE IT

• The tendency to accept responsibility for success and blame circumstances or bad luck for failures is called _____-_____ _____. The tendency to overestimate others' attention to and evaluation of our appearance, performance, and blunders is called the _____ _____.

ANSWERS: self-serving bias; spotlight effect

• _____ (Secure/Defensive) self-esteem correlates with aggressive and antisocial behavior. _____ (Secure/Defensive) self-esteem is a healthier self-image that allows us to focus beyond ourselves and enjoy a higher quality of life.

ANSWERS: Defensive; Secure

Culture and the Self

12-20: How do individualist and collectivist cultures influence people?

Our consideration of personality—of people's characteristic ways of thinking, feeling, and acting—concludes with a look at cultural variations in how people think, feel, and act. Imagine that someone were to rip away your social connections, making you a solitary refugee in a foreign land. How much of your identity would remain intact?

individualism giving priority to one's own goals over group goals and defining one's identity in terms of personal attributes rather than group identifications.

collectivism giving priority to the goals of one's group (often one's extended family or work group) and defining one's identity accordingly.

If as our solitary traveler you pride yourself on your **individualism,** a great deal of your identity would remain intact—the very core of your being, the sense of "me," the awareness of your personal convictions and values. Individualists (often people from North America, Western Europe, Australia, or New Zealand) give relatively greater priority to personal goals and define their identity mostly in terms of personal attributes (Schimmack et al., 2005). They strive for personal control and individual achievement. In American culture, with its relatively big *I* and small *we,* 85 percent of people have agreed that it is possible "to pretty much be who you want to be" (Sampson, 2000).

Individualists share the human need to belong. They join groups. But they are less focused on group harmony and doing their duty to the group (Brewer & Chen, 2007). And being more self-contained, they more easily move in and out of social groups. They feel relatively free to switch places of worship, switch jobs, or even leave their extended families and migrate to a new place. Marriage is often for as long as they both shall love.

If set adrift in a foreign land as a **collectivist,** you might experience a greater loss of identity. Cut off from family, groups, and loyal friends, you would lose the connections that have defined who you are. In a collectivist culture, group identifications provide a sense of belonging, a set of values, a network of caring individuals, an assurance of security. In return, collectivists have deeper, more stable attachments to their groups— their family, clan, or company. In South Korea, for example, people place less value on expressing a consistent, unique self-concept, and more on tradition and shared practices (Choi & Choi, 2002).

Valuing communal solidarity means placing a premium on preserving group spirit and ensuring that others never lose face. What people say reflects not only what they feel (their inner attitudes) but what they presume others feel (Kashima et al., 1992). Avoiding direct confrontation, blunt honesty, and uncomfortable topics, collectivists often defer to others' wishes and display a polite, self-effacing humility (Markus & Kitayama, 1991). Elders and superiors receive respect, and duty to family may trump personal career and mate preferences (Zhang & Kline, 2009). In new groups, people may be shy and more easily embarrassed than their individualist counterparts (Singelis et al., 1995, 1999). Compared with Westerners, people in Japanese and Chinese cultures, for example, exhibit greater shyness toward strangers and greater concern for social harmony and loyalty (Bond, 1988; Cheek & Melchior, 1990; Triandis, 1994). When the priority is "we," not "me," that individualized latte— "decaf, single shot, skinny, extra hot"—that feels so good to a North American might sound more like a selfish demand in Seoul (Kim & Markus, 1999).

A collectivist culture Although the United States is largely individualist, many cultural subgroups remain collectivist. This is true for Alaska Natives, who demonstrate respect for tribal elders, and whose identity springs largely from their group affiliations.

Considerate collectivists Japan's collectivist values, including duty to others and social harmony, were on display after the devastating 2011 earthquake and tsunami. Virtually no looting was reported, and residents remained calm and orderly, as shown here while waiting for drinking water.

Table 12.5
Value Contrasts Between Individualism and Collectivism

Concept	Individualism	Collectivism
Self	Independent (identity from individual traits)	Interdependent (identity from belonging)
Life task	Discover and express one's uniqueness	Maintain connections, fit in, perform role
What matters	Me—personal achievement and fulfillment; rights and liberties; self-esteem	Us—group goals and solidarity; social responsibilities and relationships; family duty
Coping method	Change reality	Accommodate to reality
Morality	Defined by individuals (self-based)	Defined by social networks (duty-based)
Relationships	Many, often temporary or casual; confrontation acceptable	Few, close and enduring; harmony valued
Attributing behavior	Behavior reflects one's personality and attitudes	Behavior reflects social norms and roles

Sources: Adapted from Thomas Schoeneman (1994) and Harry Triandis (1994).

"One needs to cultivate the spirit of sacrificing the *little me* to achieve the benefits of the *big me.*"

Chinese saying

FIGURE 12.7

A child like no other Americans' individualist tendencies are reflected in their choice of names for their babies. In recent years, the percentage of American babies receiving one of that year's 10 most common names has plunged. (Adapted from Twenge et al., 2010.)

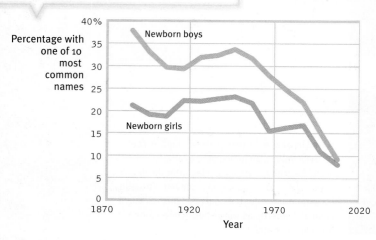

To be sure, there is diversity within cultures. Even in the most individualistic countries, some people manifest collectivist values. Within many countries, there are also distinct cultures related to one's religion, economic status, and region (Cohen, 2009). And in collectivist Japan, a spirit of individualism marks the "northern frontier" island of Hokkaido (Kitayama et al., 2006). But in general, people (especially men) in competitive, individualist cultures have more personal freedom, are less geographically bound to their families, enjoy more privacy, and take more pride in personal achievements (**TABLE 12.5**).

They even prefer unusual names, as psychologist Jean Twenge noticed while seeking a name for her first child. Over time, the most common American names listed by year on the U.S. Social Security baby names website were becoming less desirable. An analysis of the first names of 325 million American babies born between 1880 and 2007 confirmed this trend (Twenge et al., 2010). As **FIGURE 12.7** illustrates, the percentage of boys and girls given one of the 10 most common names for their birth year has plunged, especially in recent years. (No wonder my parents, who bore me in a less individualistic age, gave me such a common first name.)

The individualist-collectivist divide appeared in reactions to medals received during the 2000 and 2002 Olympic games. U.S. gold medal winners and the U.S. media covering them attributed the achievements mostly to the athletes themselves (Markus et al., 2006). "I think I just stayed focused," explained swimming gold medalist Misty Hyman. "It was time to show the world what I could do. I am just glad I was able to do it." Japan's gold medalist in the women's marathon, Naoko Takahashi, had a different explanation: "Here is the best coach in the world, the best manager in the world, and all of the people who support me—all of these things were getting together and became a gold medal." Even when describing friends, Westerners tend to use trait-describing adjectives *("she is helpful")*, whereas East Asians more often use verbs that describe behaviors in context *("she helps her friends")* (Maass et al., 2006).

Individualism's benefits can come at the cost of more loneliness, higher divorce and homicide rates, and more stress-related disease (Popenoe, 1993; Triandis et al., 1988). Demands for more romance and personal fulfillment in marriage can subject relationships to more pressure (Dion & Dion, 1993). In one survey, "keeping romance alive" was rated as important to a good marriage by 78 percent of U.S. women but only 29 percent of Japanese women (*American Enterprise,* 1992). In China, love songs often express enduring commitment and friendship (Rothbaum & Tsang, 1998): "We will be together from now on . . . I will never change from now to forever."

★ ★ ★

Roughly speaking, enduring, inner influences on behavior are the focus of personality psychology, and the temporary, external influences on behavior are the focus of social psychology—the area we turn to next. In actuality, behavior always depends on the interaction of persons with situations.

RETRIEVE IT

- How do individualist and collectivist cultures differ?

ANSWER: Individualists give priority to personal goals over group goals and tend to define their identity in terms of their own personal attributes. Collectivists give priority to group goals over individual goals and tend to define their identity in terms of group identifications.

CHAPTER REVIEW

Personality

LEARNING OBJECTIVES

Test Yourself by taking a moment to answer each of these Learning Objective Questions (repeated here from within the chapter). Then turn to Appendix D, Complete Chapter Reviews, to check your answers. Research suggests that trying to answer these questions on your own will improve your long-term memory of the concepts (McDaniel et al., 2009).

Psychodynamic Theories

12-1: How did Sigmund Freud's treatment of psychological disorders lead to his view of the unconscious mind?

12-2: What was Freud's view of personality?

12-3: What developmental stages did Freud propose?

12-4: How did Freud think people defended themselves against anxiety?

12-5: Which of Freud's ideas did his followers accept or reject?

12-6: What are projective tests, how are they used, and what are some criticisms of them?

12-7: How do today's psychologists view Freud's psychoanalysis?

12-8: How has modern research developed our understanding of the unconscious?

Humanistic Theories

12-9: How did humanistic psychologists view personality, and what was their goal in studying personality?

12-10: How did humanistic psychologists assess a person's sense of self?

12-11: How have humanistic theories influenced psychology? What criticisms have they faced?

Trait Theories

12-12: How do psychologists use traits to describe personality?

12-13: What are personality inventories, and what are their strengths and weaknesses as trait-assessment tools?

12-14: Which traits seem to provide the most useful information about personality variation?

12-15: Does research support the consistency of personality traits over time and across situations?

Social-Cognitive Theories

12-16: How do social-cognitive theorists view personality development, and how do they explore behavior?

12-17: What criticisms have social-cognitive theorists faced?

Exploring the Self

12-18: Why has psychology generated so much research on the self? How important is self-esteem to psychology and to our well-being?

12-19: What evidence reveals self-serving bias, and how do defensive and secure self-esteem differ?

12-20: How do individualist and collectivist cultures influence people?

TERMS AND CONCEPTS TO REMEMBER

Test yourself on these terms by trying to write down the definition in your own words before flipping back to the referenced page to check your answer.

personality, p. 423
psychodynamic theories, p. 424
psychoanalysis, p. 424
unconscious, p. 424
free association, p. 424
id, p. 425
ego, p. 425
superego, p. 425
psychosexual stages, p. 426
Oedipus [ED-uh-puss] complex, p. 426

identification, p. 426
fixation, p. 426
defense mechanisms, p. 427
repression, p. 427
collective unconscious, p. 428
projective test, p. 429
Rorschach inkblot test, p. 429
humanistic theories, p. 432
self-actualization, p. 433
unconditional positive regard, p. 433
self-concept, p. 434
trait, p. 435
personality inventory, p. 437

Minnesota Multiphasic Personality Inventory (MMPI), p. 437
empirically derived test, p. 437
social-cognitive perspective, p. 443
reciprocal determinism, p. 443
self, p. 447
spotlight effect, p. 447
self-esteem, p. 447
self-efficacy, p. 447
self-serving bias, p. 448
narcissism, p. 449
individualism, p. 451
collectivism, p. 451

EXPERIENCE THE TESTING EFFECT

Test yourself repeatedly throughout your studies. This will not only help you figure out what you know and don't know; the testing itself will help you learn and remember the information more effectively thanks to the *testing effect.*

1. Freud believed that we may block painful or unacceptable thoughts, wishes, feelings, or memories from consciousness through an unconscious process called _____.

2. According to Freud's view of personality structure, the "executive" system, the _____, seeks to gratify the impulses of the _____ in more acceptable ways.
   a. id; ego
   b. ego; superego
   c. ego; id
   d. id; superego

3. Freud proposed that the development of the "voice of conscience" is related to the _____, which internalizes ideals and provides standards for judgments.

4. According to the psychoanalytic view of development, we all pass through a series of psychosexual stages, including the oral, anal, and phallic stages. Conflicts unresolved at any of these stages may lead to
   a. dormant sexual feelings.
   b. fixation at that stage.
   c. preconscious blocking of impulses.
   d. a distorted gender identity.

5. Freud believed that defense mechanisms are unconscious attempts to distort or disguise reality, all in an effort to reduce our _____.

6. _____ tests ask test-takers to respond to an ambiguous stimulus, for example, by describing it or telling a story about it.

7. In general, neo-Freudians such as Adler and Horney accepted many of Freud's views but placed more emphasis than he did on
   a. development throughout the life span.
   b. the collective unconscious.
   c. the role of the id.
   d. social interactions.

8. Modern day psychodynamic theorists and therapists agree with Freud about
   a. the existence of unconscious mental processes.
   b. the Oedipus complex.
   c. the predictive value of Freudian theory.
   d. the superego's role as the executive part of personality.

9. Which of the following is NOT part of the contemporary view of the unconscious?
   a. Repressed memories of anxiety-provoking events
   b. Schemas that influence our perceptions and interpretations
   c. Parallel processing that occurs without our conscious knowledge
   d. Instantly activated emotions and implicit memories of learned skills

10. Maslow's hierarchy of needs proposes that we must satisfy basic physiological and safety needs before we seek ultimate psychological needs, such as self-actualization. Maslow based his ideas on
    a. Freudian theory.
    b. his experiences with patients.
    c. a series of laboratory experiments.
    d. his study of healthy, creative people.

11. How might Freud and Rogers differ in their explanations of how the environment influences the development of a criminal?

12. The total acceptance Rogers advocated as part of a growth-promoting environment is called _____ _____ _____.

13. The _____ theory of personality focuses on describing characteristic behavior patterns, such as agreeableness or extraversion.

14. One famous personality inventory is the
    a. Extraversion–Introversion Scale.
    b. Person–Situation Inventory.
    c. MMPI.
    d. Rorschach.

15. Which of the following is NOT one of the Big Five personality factors?
    a. Conscientiousness
    b. Anxiety
    c. Extraversion
    d. Agreeableness

16. Our scores on personality tests best predict
    a. our behavior on a specific occasion.
    b. our average behavior across many situations.
    c. behavior involving a single trait, such as conscientiousness.
    d. behavior that depends on the situation or context.

17. The social-cognitive perspective proposes our personality is shaped by a process called reciprocal determinism, as personal factors, environmental factors, and behaviors interact. An example of an environmental factor is
    a. the presence of books in a home.
    b. a preference for outdoor play.
    c. the ability to read at a fourth-grade level.
    d. the fear of violent action on television.

18. Critics say that _____ – _____ personality theory is very sensitive to an individual's interactions with particular situations, but that it gives too little attention to the person's enduring traits.

19. Researchers have found that low self-esteem tends to be linked with life problems. How should this link be interpreted?
    a. Life problems cause low self-esteem.
    b. The answer isn't clear because the link is correlational and does not indicate cause and effect.
    c. Low self-esteem leads to life problems.
    d. Because of the self-serving bias, we must assume that external factors cause low self-esteem.

20. A fortune cookie advises, "Love yourself and happiness will follow." Is this good advice?

21. Individualist cultures tend to value _____; collectivist cultures tend to value _____.
    a. interdependence; independence
    b. independence; interdependence
    c. group solidarity; uniqueness
    d. duty to family; personal fulfillment

Find answers to these questions in Appendix E, in the back of the book.

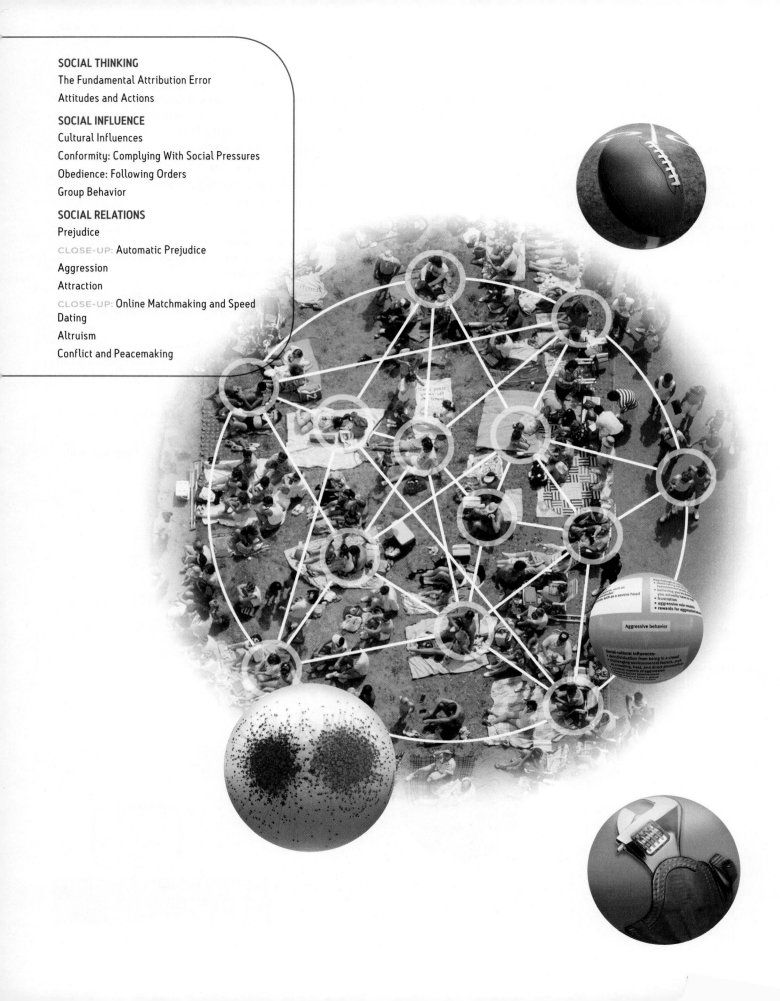

Social Psychology

Dirk Willems faced a moment of decision in 1569. Threatened with torture and death as a member of a persecuted religious minority, he escaped from his Asperen, Holland, prison and fled across an ice-covered pond. His stronger and heavier jailer pursued him but fell through the ice and, unable to climb out, pled for help.

With his freedom in front of him, Willems acted with ultimate selflessness. He turned back and rescued his pursuer, who, under orders, took him back to captivity. A few weeks later Willems was condemned to be "executed with fire, until death ensues." For his martyrdom, present-day Asperen has named a street in honor of its folk hero (Toews, 2004).

What drives people to feel contempt for minority-group members, such as Dirk Willems, and to act so spitefully? And what motivated the selflessness of Willems' response, and of so many who have died trying to save others? Indeed, what motivates any of us when we volunteer kindness and generosity toward others?

As such examples demonstrate, we are social animals. We may assume the best or the worst in others. We may approach them with closed fists or open arms. Yet as the novelist Herman Melville remarked, "We cannot live for ourselves alone. Our lives are connected by a thousand invisible threads." *Social psychologists* explore these connections by scientifically studying how we *think about, influence,* and *relate to* one another.

Unlike sociology, which studies societies and social groupings, social psychologists focus more on how *individuals* view and affect one another.

Social Thinking

> **13-1:** What do social psychologists study? How do we tend to explain others' behavior and our own?

Personality psychologists (Chapter 12) focus on the person. They study the personal traits and dynamics that explain why *different people* may act differently *in a given situation,* such as the one Willems faced. (Would you have helped the jailer out of the icy water?) **Social psychologists** focus on the situation. They study the social influences that explain why *the same person* will act differently in *different situations.* Might the jailer have acted differently—opting not to march Willems back to jail—under differing circumstances?

The Fundamental Attribution Error

Our social behavior arises from our social thinking. Especially when the unexpected occurs, we want to understand and explain why people act as they do. After studying how people explain others' behavior, Fritz Heider (1958) proposed an **attribution theory:** We can attribute the behavior to the person's stable, enduring traits (a *dispositional attribution*). Or we can attribute it to the situation (a *situational attribution*).

For example, in class, we notice that Juliette seldom talks. Over coffee, Jack talks nonstop. That must be the sort of people they are, we decide. Juliette must be shy and Jack outgoing. Such attributions—to their dispositions—can be valid, because people do have enduring personality traits. But sometimes we fall prey to the **fundamental attribution error** (Ross, 1977): We overestimate the influence of personality and underestimate the influence of situations. In class, Jack may be as quiet as Juliette. Catch Juliette at a party and you may hardly recognize your quiet classmate.

David Napolitan and George Goethals (1979) demonstrated the fundamental attribution error in an experiment with Williams College students. They had students talk, one at a time, with a young woman who acted either cold and critical or warm and friendly. Before the talks, the researchers told half the students that the woman's behavior would be spontaneous. They told the other half the truth—that they had instructed her to *act* friendly (or unfriendly).

Did hearing the truth affect students' impressions of the woman? Not at all! If the woman acted friendly, both groups decided she really was a warm person. If she acted unfriendly, both decided she really was a cold person. They attributed her behavior to her personal disposition *even when told that her behavior was situational*—that she was merely acting that way for the purposes of the experiment.

What Factors Affect Our Attributions?

The fundamental attribution error appears more often in some cultures than in others. Individualist Westerners more often attribute behavior to people's personal traits. People in East Asian cultures are somewhat more sensitive to the power of the situation (Heine & Ruby, 2010; Kitayama et al., 2009). This difference has appeared in experiments that asked people to view scenes, such as a big fish swimming. Americans focused more on the individual fish, and Japanese people more on the whole scene (Chua et al., 2005; Nisbett, 2003).

We all commit the fundamental attribution error. Consider: Is your psychology instructor shy or outgoing?

If you answer "outgoing," remember that you know your instructor from one situation—the classroom, which demands outgoing behavior. Your instructor (who observes his or her own behavior not only in the classroom, but also with family, in meetings, when traveling)

An etching of Dirk Willems by Dutch artist Jan Luyken (from *The Martyrs Mirror,* 1685)

social psychology the scientific study of how we think about, influence, and relate to one another.

attribution theory the theory that we explain someone's behavior by crediting either the situation or the person's disposition.

fundamental attribution error the tendency for observers, when analyzing another's behavior, to underestimate the impact of the situation and to overestimate the impact of personal disposition.

might say, "Me, outgoing? It all depends on the situation. In class or with good friends, yes, I'm outgoing. But at professional meetings I'm really rather shy." Outside their assigned roles, professors seem less professorial, presidents less presidential, lawyers less legalistic.

When we explain *our own* behavior, we are sensitive to how behavior changes with the situation (Idson & Mischel, 2001). (Chapter 12 discussed an important exception: We more often attribute our intentional and admirable actions not to situations but to our own good reasons [Malle, 2006; Malle et al., 2007].) We also are sensitive to the power of the situation when we explain the behavior of people we know well and have seen in different contexts. We more often commit the fundamental attribution error when a stranger acts badly. Having only seen that red-faced fan screaming at the referee in the heat of competition, we may assume he is a bad person. But outside the stadium, he may be a good neighbor and a great parent.

Could we broaden our thinking by taking the other's view? To test this idea, researchers have reversed the perspectives of *actor* and *observer*. They filmed some interactions and then had participants view a replay—filmed from the other person's perspective. This reversed their attributions of the behaviors (Lassiter & Irvine, 1986; Storms, 1973). Seeing the world from the actor's perspective, the observers better appreciated the situation. (As we interact, our eyes look outward; we see others' faces, not our own.) Taking the observer's point of view, the actors became more aware of their own personal style.

What Are the Consequences of Our Attributions?

The way we explain others' actions, attributing them to the person or the situation, can have important real-life effects (Fincham & Bradbury, 1993; Fletcher et al., 1990). A person must decide whether to attribute another's friendliness to romantic or sexual interest. A jury must decide whether a shooting was malicious or in self-defense. A voter must decide whether a candidate's promises will be kept or forgotten. A partner must decide whether a loved one's tart-tongued remark reflects a bad day or a mean disposition.

Finally, consider the social and economic effects of attribution. How do we explain poverty or unemployment? In Britain, India, Australia, and the United States (Furnham, 1982; Pandey et al., 1982; Wagstaff, 1982; Zucker & Weiner, 1993), political conservatives tend to place the blame on the personal dispositions of the poor and unemployed: "People generally get what they deserve. Those who don't work are freeloaders. Those who take initiative can still get ahead." Political liberals (and social scientists) are more likely to blame past and present situations: "If you or I had to live with the same poor education, lack of opportunity, and discrimination, would we be any better off? Or might a medical condition make normal day-to-day life a challenge?" To understand and prevent terrorism, they say, consider the situations that breed terrorists. Better to drain the swamps than swat the mosquitoes.

The point to remember: Our attributions—to a person's disposition or to the situation—have real consequences.

Some 7 in 10 college women report having experienced a man misattributing her friendliness as a sexual come-on (Jacques-Tiura et al., 2007).

"Otis, shout at that man to pull himself together."

An attribution question
Whether we attribute poverty and homelessness to social circumstances or to personal dispositions affects and reflects our political views.

attitude feelings, often influenced by our beliefs, that predispose us to respond in a particular way to objects, people, and events.

peripheral route persuasion occurs when people are influenced by incidental cues, such as a speaker's attractiveness.

central route persuasion occurs when interested people focus on the arguments and respond with favorable thoughts.

Attitudes and Actions

13-2: How do attitudes and actions interact?

Attitudes are feelings, often influenced by our beliefs, that predispose our reactions to objects, people, and events. If we *believe* someone is threatening us, we may *feel* fear and anger toward the person and *act* defensively. The traffic between our attitudes and our actions is two-way. Our attitudes affect our actions. And our actions affect our attitudes.

Attitudes Affect Actions

Consider the climate-change debate. On one side are climate-change activists: "Almost all climate scientists are of one mind about the threat of global warming," reports *Science* magazine (Kerr, 2009). "It's real, it's dangerous, and the world needs to take action immediately." On the other side are climate-change skeptics: The number of Americans who told Gallup pollsters that global warming is "generally exaggerated" increased from 30 percent in 2006 to 48 percent in 2010 (Newport, 2010).

Knowing that public attitudes affect public policies, activists on both sides are aiming to persuade. Persuasion efforts generally take two forms:

- **Peripheral route persuasion** doesn't engage systematic thinking, but does produce fast results as people respond to uninformative cues (such as celebrity endorsements), and make snap judgments. A perfume ad may lure us with images of beautiful people in love.

- **Central route persuasion** offers evidence and arguments that aim to trigger favorable thoughts. It occurs mostly when people are naturally analytical or involved in the issue. Environmental advocates may show us evidence of rising temperatures, melting glaciers, rising seas, and northward shifts in vegetation and animal life. Because it is more thoughtful and less superficial, it is more durable.

Those who attempt to persuade us by any means are trying to influence our behavior by changing our attitudes. But other factors, including the situation, also influence behavior. Strong social pressures, for example, can weaken the attitude-behavior connection (Wallace et al., 2005). In roll-call votes, politicians will sometimes vote what their supporters demand, despite privately disagreeing with those demands (Nagourney, 2002). In such cases, external pressure overrides the attitude-behavior link.

Attitudes are especially likely to affect behavior when external influences are minimal, and when the attitude is stable, specific to the behavior, and easily recalled (Glasman & Albarracín, 2006). One experiment used vivid, easily recalled information to persuade people that sustained tanning put them at risk for future skin cancer. One month later, 72 percent of the participants, and only 16 percent of those in a waitlist control group, had lighter skin (McClendon & Prentice-Dunn, 2001). Persuasion changed attitudes (concerning skin cancer risk) which changed behavior (less tanning).

Actions Affect Attitudes

Now consider a more surprising principle: Not only will people stand up for what they believe, they also will believe more strongly in what they have stood up for. Many streams of evidence confirm that *attitudes follow behavior* (**FIGURE 13.1**).

The Foot-in-the-Door Phenomenon How do you think you would react if someone induced you to act against your beliefs? In many cases, people adjust their attitudes. During the Korean war, many U.S. prisoners of war were held in war camps run by Chinese communists. Without using brutality, the captors secured the prisoners' collaboration in various activities. Some prisoners merely ran errands or accepted favors. Others made radio appeals and false confessions. Still others informed on fellow prisoners and divulged military information. When the war ended,

FIGURE 13.1

Attitudes follow behavior Cooperative actions, such as those performed by people on sports teams, feed mutual liking. Such attitudes, in turn, promote positive behavior.

Actions

Attitudes

Vasily Fedosenko/Reuters

21 prisoners chose to stay with the communists. Some of the others returned home "brainwashed"—convinced that communism was a good thing for Asia.

How did the Chinese captors achieve these amazing results? A key ingredient was their effective use of the **foot-in-the-door phenomenon:** They knew that people who agreed to a small request would find it easier to comply later with a larger one. The Chinese began with harmless requests, such as copying a trivial statement, but gradually escalated their demands (Schein, 1956). The next statement to be copied might list flaws of capitalism. Then, to gain privileges, the prisoners participated in group discussions, wrote self-criticisms, or uttered public confessions. After doing so, they often adjusted their beliefs to be more consistent with their public acts. The point is simple: To get people to agree to something big, start small and build (Cialdini, 1993). A trivial act makes the next act easier. Succumb to a temptation and you will find the next temptation harder to resist.

In dozens of experiments, researchers have coaxed people into acting against their attitudes or violating their moral standards, with the same result: Doing becomes believing. After giving in to a request to harm an innocent victim—by making nasty comments or delivering electric shocks—people begin to disparage their victim. After speaking or writing on behalf of a position they have qualms about, they begin to believe their own words.

Fortunately, the attitudes-follow-behavior principle works with good deeds as well. The foot-in-the-door tactic has helped boost charitable contributions and blood donations, as well as product sales. In one classic experiment, researchers posing as safe-driving volunteers asked Californians to permit the installation of a large, poorly lettered "Drive Carefully" sign in their front yards. Only 17 percent consented. They approached other home owners with a small request first: Would they display a 3-inch-high "Be a Safe Driver" sign? Nearly all readily agreed. When reapproached two weeks later to allow the large, ugly sign in their front yards, 76 percent consented (Freedman & Fraser, 1966). To secure a big commitment, it often pays to put your foot in the door: Start small and build.

Racial attitudes likewise follow behavior. In the years immediately following the introduction of school desegregation in the United States and the passage of the Civil Rights Act of 1964, White Americans expressed diminishing racial prejudice. And as Americans in different regions came to act more alike—thanks to more uniform national standards against discrimination—they began to think more alike. Experiments confirm the observation. Moral action strengthens moral convictions.

Role Playing Affects Attitudes When you adopt a new **role**—when you become a college student, marry, or begin a new job—you are mindful of the social prescriptions. At first, your behaviors in the new role may feel phony, because you are *acting* a role. Soldiers may at first feel they are playing war games. Newlyweds may feel they are "playing house." Before long, however, what began as play acting in the theater of life becomes *you*. Researchers have confirmed this effect by assessing people's attitudes before and after they adopt a new role, sometimes in laboratory situations, sometimes in everyday situations, such as before and after taking a job.

Role playing morphed into real life in one famous study in which male college students volunteered to spend time in a simulated prison (Zimbardo, 1972). Psychologist Philip Zimbardo randomly assigned some volunteers to be guards. He gave them uniforms, clubs, and whistles and instructed them to enforce certain rules. Others became prisoners, locked in barren cells and forced to wear humiliating outfits. For a day or two, the volunteers self-consciously "played" their roles. Then the simulation became real—too real. Most guards developed disparaging attitudes, and some devised cruel and degrading routines. One by one, the prisoners broke down, rebelled, or became passively resigned. After only six days, Zimbardo called off the study.

Role playing can train torturers (Staub, 1989). In the early 1970s, the Greek military government eased men into their roles. First, a trainee stood guard outside an interrogation cell. After this "foot in the door" step, he stood guard inside. Only then was he ready to become actively involved in the questioning and torture. What we do, we gradually become.

"If the King destroys a man, that's proof to the King it must have been a bad man."
Thomas Cromwell, in Robert Bolt's A Man for All Seasons, *1960*

"Fake it until you make it."
Alcoholics Anonymous saying

foot-in-the-door phenomenon the tendency for people who have first agreed to a small request to comply later with a larger request.

role a set of expectations (norms) about a social position, defining how those in the position ought to behave.

The power of the situation In his 1972 Stanford Prison simulation, Philip Zimbardo created a toxic situation (left). Those assigned to the guard role soon degraded the prisoners. In real life in 2004, some U.S. military guards tormented Iraqi prisoners at the U.S.-run Abu Ghraib prison (right). To Zimbardo (2004, 2007), it was a bad barrel rather than a few bad apples that led to the Abu Ghraib atrocities: "When ordinary people are put in a novel, evil place, such as most prisons, Situations Win, People Lose."

Philip G. Zimbardo, Inc.

Associated Press

Yet people differ. In Zimbardo's Stanford Prison simulation and in other atrocity-producing situations, some people have succumbed to the situation and others have not (Carnahan & McFarland, 2007; Haslam & Reicher, 2007; Mastroianni & Reed, 2006; Zimbardo, 2007). Person and situation interact. Much as water dissolves salt but not sand, so rotten situations turn some people into bad apples while others resist (Johnson, 2007).

Cognitive Dissonance: Relief From Tension So far we have seen that actions can affect attitudes, sometimes turning prisoners into collaborators, doubters into believers, and compliant guards into abusers. But why? One explanation is that when we become aware that our attitudes and actions don't coincide, we experience tension, or *cognitive dissonance*. To relieve such tension, according to Leon Festinger's (1957) **cognitive dissonance theory,** we often bring our attitudes into line with our actions.

Dozens of experiments have explored this cognitive dissonance phenomenon. Many have made people feel responsible for behavior that clashed with their attitudes and had foreseeable consequences. In one of these experiments, you might agree for a measly $2 to help a researcher by writing an essay that supports something you don't believe in (perhaps a tuition increase). Feeling responsible for the statements (which are inconsistent with your attitudes), you would probably feel dissonance, especially if you thought an administrator would be reading your essay. To reduce the uncomfortable tension you might start believing your phony words. At such times, it's as if we rationalize, "If I chose to do it (or say it), I must believe in it." The less coerced and more responsible we feel for a troubling act, the more dissonance we feel. The more dissonance we feel, the more motivated we are to find consistency, such as changing our attitudes to help justify the act.

The pressure to reduce dissonance helped explain the evolution of American attitudes toward the U.S. invasion of Iraq. When the war began, the stated reason for the invasion was the presumed threat of Saddam Hussein's weapons of mass destruction (WMD). Would the war be justified if Iraq did not have WMD? Only 38 percent of Americans surveyed said it would be (Gallup, 2003). Nearly 80 percent believed such weapons would be found (Duffy, 2003; Newport et al., 2003). When no WMD were found, many Americans felt dissonance, which was heightened by their awareness of the war's financial and human costs, by scenes of chaos in Iraq, and by inflamed anti-American and pro-terrorist sentiments in some parts of the world.

To reduce dissonance, some people revised their memories of the war's rationale. The invasion then became a movement to liberate an oppressed people and promote democracy in the Middle East. Before long, 58 percent of Americans—a majority—said they supported the war even if no WMD were found (Gallup, 2003).

The attitudes-follow-behavior principle has a heartening implication: We cannot directly control all our feelings, but we can

"Look, I have my misgivings, too, but what choice do we have except stay the course?"

influence them by altering our behavior. (Recall from Chapter 10 the emotional effects of facial expressions and of body postures.) If we are down in the dumps, we can do as cognitive-behavioral therapists advise and talk in more positive, self-accepting ways with fewer self–put-downs. If we are unloving, we can become more loving by behaving as if we were so—by doing thoughtful things, expressing affection, giving affirmation. That helps explain why teens' doing volunteer work promotes a compassionate identity. "Assume a virtue, if you have it not," says Hamlet to his mother. "For use can almost change the stamp of nature." Pretense can become reality. Conduct sculpts character. What we do we become.

The point to remember: Cruel acts shape the self. But so do acts of good will. Act as though you like someone, and you soon may. Changing our behavior can change how we think about others and how we feel about ourselves.

> "Sit all day in a moping posture, sigh, and reply to everything with a dismal voice, and your melancholy lingers. . . . If we wish to conquer undesirable emotional tendencies in ourselves, we must . . . go through the outward movements of those contrary dispositions which we prefer to cultivate."
>
> *William James,* Principles of Psychology, *1890*

RETRIEVE IT

- Driving to school one snowy day, Marco narrowly misses a car that slides through a red light. "Slow down! What a terrible driver," he thinks to himself. Moments later, Marco himself slips through an intersection and yelps, "Wow! These roads are awful. The city plows need to get out here." What social psychology principle has Marco just demonstrated? Explain.

  ANSWER: By attributing the other person's behavior to the person ("what a terrible driver") and his own to the situation ("these roads are awful"), Marco has exhibited the *fundamental attribution error.*

- How do our attitudes and our actions affect each other?

  ANSWER: Our attitudes often influence our actions as we behave in ways consistent with our beliefs. However, our attitudes also follow our actions; we come to believe in what we have done.

- When people act in a way that is not in keeping with their attitudes, and then change their attitudes to match those actions, _____ _____ theory attempts to explain why.

  ANSWER: cognitive dissonance

Social Influence

Social psychology's great lesson is the enormous power of social influence. This influence can be seen in our conformity, our obedience to authority, and our group behavior. Suicides, bomb threats, airplane hijackings, and UFO sightings all have a curious tendency to come in clusters. On campus, jeans are the dress code; on New York's Wall Street or London's Bond Street, dress suits are the norm. When we know how to act, how to groom, how to talk, life functions smoothly. Armed with social influence principles, advertisers, fundraisers, and campaign workers aim to sway our decisions to buy, to donate, to vote. Isolated with others who share their grievances, dissenters may gradually become rebels, and rebels may become terrorists. We'll start by considering the nature of our cultural influences. Then we will examine the pull of our social strings. How strong are they? How do they operate? When do we break them?

> "Have you ever noticed how one example—good or bad—can prompt others to follow? How one illegally parked car can give permission for others to do likewise? How one racial joke can fuel another?"
>
> *Marian Wright Edelman,* The Measure of Our Success, *1992*

Cultural Influences

13-3: How do cultural norms affect our behavior?

Compared with the narrow path taken by flies, fish, and foxes, the road along which environment drives us is wider. The mark of our species—nature's great gift to us—is our ability to learn and adapt. We come equipped with a huge cerebral hard drive ready to receive cultural software.

Culture is the behaviors, ideas, attitudes, values, and traditions shared by a group of people and transmitted from one generation to the next (Brislin, 1988; Cohen, 2009). Human nature, notes Roy Baumeister (2005), seems designed for culture. We are social animals, but more. Wolves are social animals; they live and hunt in packs. Ants

cognitive dissonance theory the theory that we act to reduce the discomfort (dissonance) we feel when two of our thoughts (cognitions) are inconsistent. For example, when we become aware that our attitudes and our actions clash, we can reduce the resulting dissonance by changing our attitudes.

culture the enduring behaviors, ideas, attitudes, values, and traditions shared by a group of people and transmitted from one generation to the next.

are incessantly social, never alone. But "culture is a better way of being social," notes Baumeister. Wolves function pretty much as they did 10,000 years ago. You and I enjoy things unknown to most of our century-ago ancestors, including electricity, indoor plumbing, antibiotics, and the Internet.

We can thank our mastery of language for this *preservation of innovation*. Moreover, culture enables an efficient *division of labor*. Although one lucky person gets his name on this book's cover, the product actually results from the coordination and commitment of a team of people, no one of whom could produce it alone.

Across cultures, we differ in our language, our monetary systems, our sports, which fork—if any—we eat with, even which side of the road we drive on. But beneath these differences is our great similarity—our capacity for culture. Culture transmits the customs and beliefs that enable us to communicate, to exchange money for things, to play, to eat, and to drive with agreed-upon rules and without crashing into one another.

Variation Across Cultures

We see our adaptability in cultural variations among our beliefs and our values, in how we raise our children and bury our dead, and in what we wear (or whether we wear anything at all). I am ever mindful that the readers of this book are culturally diverse. You and your ancestors reach from Australia to Africa and from Singapore to Sweden.

Riding along with a unified culture is like biking with the wind: As it carries us along, we hardly notice it is there. When we try riding *against* the wind we feel its force. Face to face with a different culture, we become aware of the cultural winds. Stationed in Iraq, Afghanistan, and Kuwait, American and European soldiers were reminded how liberal their home cultures were. Each cultural group evolves its own **norms**—rules for accepted and expected behavior. The British have a norm for orderly waiting in line. Many South Asians use only the right hand's fingers for eating. Sometimes social expectations seem oppressive: "Why should it matter what I wear?" Yet, norms grease the social machinery and can free us from self-preoccupation.

When cultures collide, their differing norms often befuddle. Should we greet people by shaking hands or kissing each cheek? The answer depends on the surrounding culture. Learning when to clap or bow, how to order at a new restaurant, and what sorts of gestures and compliments are appropriate helps us avoid accidental insults and embarrassment.

Variation Over Time

Like biological creatures, cultures vary and compete for resources, and thus evolve over time (Mesoudi, 2009). Consider how rapidly cultures may change. English poet Geoffrey Chaucer (1342–1400) is separated from a modern Briton by only 20 generations, but the two would converse with great difficulty. In the thin slice of history since 1960, most Western cultures have changed with remarkable speed. Middle-class people today fly to places they once only read about. They enjoy the convenience of air-conditioned housing, online shopping, anywhere-anytime electronic communication, and—enriched by doubled per-person real income—eating out more than twice as often as did their grandparents back in the culture of 1960. Most minority groups are enjoying expanded human rights. And, with greater economic independence, today's women more often marry for love and less often endure abusive relationships (Circle of Prevention, 2002).

But some changes seem not so wonderfully positive. Had you fallen asleep in the United States in 1960 and awakened today, you would open your eyes to a culture with more divorce and depression. You would also find North Americans—like their counterparts in Britain, Australia, and New Zealand—spending more hours at work, fewer hours with friends and family, and fewer hours asleep (BLS, 2011; Putnam, 2000).

Whether we love or loathe these changes, we cannot fail to be impressed by their breathtaking speed. And we cannot explain them by changes in the human gene pool, which evolves far too slowly to account for high-speed cultural transformations. Cultures vary. Cultures change. And cultures shape our lives.

norm an understood rule for accepted and expected behavior. Norms prescribe "proper" behavior.

Conformity: Complying With Social Pressures

13-4: What is automatic mimicry, and how do conformity experiments reveal the power of social influence?

Automatic Mimicry

Fish swim in schools. Birds fly in flocks. And humans, too, tend to go with their group, to think what it thinks and do what it does. Behavior is contagious. Chimpanzees are more likely to yawn after observing another chimpanzee yawn (Anderson et al., 2004). Ditto for humans. If one of us yawns, laughs, coughs, stares at the sky, or checks a cell phone, others in our group will soon do the same. Like the chameleon lizards that take on the color of their surroundings, we humans take on the emotional tones of those around us. Just hearing someone reading a neutral text in either a happy- or sad-sounding voice creates "mood contagion" in listeners (Neumann & Strack, 2000). We are natural mimics, unconsciously imitating others' expressions, postures, and voice tones.

Tanya Chartrand and John Bargh captured this mimicry, which they call the *chameleon effect* (Chartrand & Bargh, 1999). They had students work in a room alongside another person, who was actually a confederate working for the experimenters. Sometimes the confederates rubbed their own face. Sometimes they shook their foot. Sure enough, the students tended to rub their face when with the face-rubbing person and shake their foot when with the foot-shaking person.

Automatic mimicry helps us to *empathize*—to feel what others are feeling. This helps explain why we feel happier around happy people than around depressed people. It also helps explain why studies of groups of British nurses and accountants have revealed *mood linkage*—sharing up and down moods (Totterdell et al., 1998). Empathic people yawn more after seeing others yawn (Morrison, 2007). And empathic mimicking fosters fondness (van Baaren et al., 2003, 2004). Perhaps you've noticed that when someone nods their head as you do and echoes your words, you feel a certain rapport and liking?

Suggestibility and mimicry sometimes lead to tragedy. In the eight days following the 1999 shooting rampage at Colorado's Columbine High School, every U.S. state except Vermont experienced threats of copycat violence. Pennsylvania alone recorded 60 such threats (Cooper, 1999). Sociologist David Phillips and his colleagues (1985, 1989) found

Conforming to nonconformity Are these students asserting their individuality or identifying themselves with others of the same microculture?

When I see synchrony and mimicry—whether it concerns yawning, laughing, dancing, or aping—I see social connection and bonding."

Primatologist Frans de Waal "The Empathy Instinct," 2009

NON SEQUITUR by WILEY

BANKING on the YOUTH MARKET...

TATTOO & PIERCING

BE LIKE ALL YOUR FRIENDS AND EXPRESS YOUR INDIVIDUALITY

OPEN

NON SEQUITUR © 2000 Wiley. Dist. by Universal Press Syndicate. Reprinted with permission.

conformity adjusting our behavior or thinking to coincide with a group standard.

normative social influence influence resulting from a person's desire to gain approval or avoid disapproval.

informational social influence influence resulting from one's willingness to accept others' opinions about reality.

that suicides, too, sometimes increase following a highly publicized suicide. In the wake of screen idol Marilyn Monroe's suicide on August 6, 1962, for example, the number of suicides in the United States exceeded the usual August count by 200.

What causes behavior clusters? Do people act similarly because of their influence on one another? Or because they are simultaneously exposed to the same events and conditions? Seeking answers to such questions, social psychologists have conducted experiments on group pressure and conformity.

Conformity and Social Norms

Suggestibility and mimicry are subtle types of **conformity**—adjusting our behavior or thinking toward some group standard. To study conformity, Solomon Asch (1955) devised a simple test. As a participant in what you believe is a study of visual perception, you arrive in time to take a seat at a table with five other people. The experimenter asks the group to state, one by one, which of three comparison lines is identical to a standard line. You see clearly that the answer is Line 2, and you await your turn to say so. Your boredom begins to show when the next set of lines proves equally easy.

Now comes the third trial, and the correct answer seems just as clear-cut (**FIGURE 13.2**). But the first person gives what strikes you as a wrong answer: "Line 3." When the second person and then the third and fourth give the same wrong answer, you sit up straight and squint. When the fifth person agrees with the first four, you feel your heart begin to pound. The experimenter then looks to you for your answer. Torn between the unanimity voiced by the five others and the evidence of your own eyes, you feel tense and suddenly unsure. You hesitate before answering, wondering whether you should suffer the discomfort of being the oddball. What answer do you give?

In Asch's experiments, college students, answering questions alone, erred less than 1 percent of the time. But what about when several others—confederates working for the experimenter—answered incorrectly? Although most people told the truth even when others did not, Asch was disturbed by his result: More than one-third of the time, these "intelligent and well-meaning" college students were then "willing to call white black" by going along with the group.

Later investigations have not always found as much conformity as Asch found, but they have revealed that we are more likely to conform when we

- are made to feel incompetent or insecure.
- are in a group with at least three people.
- are in a group in which everyone else agrees. (If just one other person disagrees, the odds of our disagreeing greatly increase.)
- admire the group's status and attractiveness.
- have not made a prior commitment to any response.
- know that others in the group will observe our behavior.
- are from a culture that strongly encourages respect for social standards.

FIGURE 13.2

Asch's conformity experiments Which of the three comparison lines is equal to the standard line? What do you suppose most people would say after hearing five others say, "Line 3"? In this photo from one of Asch's experiments, the student in the center shows the severe discomfort that comes from disagreeing with the responses of other group members (in this case, accomplices of the experimenter).

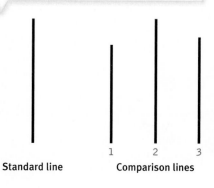

Standard line   Comparison lines
                 1   2   3

William Vendivert/*Scientific American*

Why do we so often think what others think and do what they do? Why in college residence halls do students' attitudes become more similar to those living near them (Cullum & Harton, 2007)? Why in classrooms are hand-raised answers to controversial questions less diverse than anonymous electronic clicker responses (Stowell et al., 2010)? Why do we clap when others clap, eat as others eat, believe what others believe, say what others say, even see what others see?

Frequently, we conform to avoid rejection or to gain social approval. In such cases, we are responding to **normative social influence.** We are sensitive to social norms because the price we pay for being different can be severe. We need to belong.

At other times, we conform because we want to be accurate. Groups provide information, and only an uncommonly stubborn person will never listen to others. "Those who never retract their opinions love themselves more than they love truth," observed Joseph Joubert, an eighteenth-century French essayist. When we accept others' opinions about reality, we are responding to **informational social influence.** As Rebecca Denton demonstrated in 2004, sometimes it pays to assume others are right and to follow their lead. Denton set a record for the furthest distance driven on the wrong side of a British divided highway—30 miles, with only one minor sideswipe, before the motorway ran out and police were able to puncture her tires. Denton later explained that she thought the hundreds of other drivers coming at her were all on the wrong side of the road (Woolcock, 2004).

Is conformity good or bad? The answer depends partly on our culturally influenced values. Western Europeans and people in most English-speaking countries tend to prize *individualism* (cultural focus on an independent self). People in many Asian, African, and Latin American countries place a higher value on honoring group standards. In social influence experiments across 17 countries, conformity rates have been lower in individualist cultures (Bond & Smith, 1996).

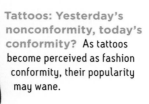

Tattoos: Yesterday's nonconformity, today's conformity? As tattoos become perceived as fashion conformity, their popularity may wane.

David Katzenstein/Photolibrary

"I love the little ways you're identical to everyone else."

© The New Yorker Collection, 2006, Mike Twohy from cartoonbank.com. All Rights Reserved.

RETRIEVE IT

• Which of the following strengthens conformity to a group?

   a. Finding the group attractive   c. Coming from an individualist culture

   b. Feeling secure   d. Having made a prior commitment

ANSWER: a

Obedience: Following Orders

13-5: What did Milgram's obedience experiments teach us about the power of social influence?

Social psychologist Stanley Milgram (1963, 1974), a student of Solomon Asch, knew that people often give in to social pressures. But how would they respond to outright commands? To find out, he undertook what became social psychology's most famous and controversial experiments (Benjamin & Simpson, 2009).

Imagine yourself as one of the nearly 1000 people who took part in Milgram's 20 experiments. You respond to an advertisement for participants in a Yale University psychology study of the effect of punishment on learning. Professor Milgram's assistant asks you and another person to draw slips from a hat to see who will be the "teacher" and who will be the "learner." Because both slips say "teacher," you draw a "teacher" slip and are asked to sit down in front of a machine, which has a series of labeled switches. The supposed learner, a mild and submissive-seeming man, is led to an adjoining room and

Stanley Milgram (1933–1984) This social psychologist's obedience experiments "belong to the self-understanding of literate people in our age" (Sabini, 1986).

Courtesy of CUNY Graduate School and University Center

strapped into a chair. From the chair, wires run through the wall to "your" machine. You are given your task: Teach and then test the learner on a list of word pairs. If the learner gives a wrong answer, you are to flip a switch to deliver a brief electric shock. For the first wrong answer, you will flip the switch labeled "15 Volts—Slight Shock." With each succeeding error, you will move to the next higher voltage. With each flip of a switch, lights flash and relay switches buzz.

The experiment begins, and you deliver the shocks after the first and second wrong answers. If you continue, you hear the learner grunt when you flick the third, fourth, and fifth switches. After you activate the eighth switch ("120 Volts—Moderate Shock"), the learner cries out that the shocks are painful. After the tenth switch ("150 Volts—Strong Shock"), he begins shouting. "Get me out of here! I won't be in the experiment anymore! I refuse to go on!" You draw back, but the stern experimenter prods you: "Please continue—the experiment requires that you continue." You resist, but the experimenter insists, "It is absolutely essential that you continue," or "You have no other choice, you *must* go on."

If you obey, you hear the learner shriek in apparent agony as you continue to raise the shock level after each new error. After the 330-volt level, the learner refuses to answer and falls silent. Still, the experimenter pushes you toward the final, 450-volt switch. Ask the question, he says, and if no correct answer is given, administer the next shock level.

Would you follow the experimenter's commands to shock someone? At what level would you refuse to obey? Milgram asked that question in a survey before he started his experiments. Most people were sure they would stop playing such a sadistic-seeming role soon after the learner first indicated pain, certainly before he shrieked in agony. Forty psychiatrists agreed with that prediction when Milgram asked them. Were the predictions accurate? Not even close. When Milgram conducted the experiment with men aged 20 to 50, he was astonished. More than 60 percent complied fully—right up to the last switch. Even when Milgram ran a new study, with 40 new "teachers," and the learner complained of a "slight heart condition," the results were similar. A full 65 percent of the new teachers obeyed every one of the experimenter's commands, right up to 450 volts (**FIGURE 13.3**). In 10 later studies, women obeyed at rates similar to men's (Blass, 1999).

Cultures change over time. Are people today less likely to obey an order to hurt someone? To find out, Jerry Burger (2009) replicated Milgram's basic experiment. Seventy percent of the participants obeyed up to the 150-volt point, a slight reduction from Milgram's result. And in a French reality TV show replication, 80 percent of people, egged on by a cheering audience, obeyed and tortured a screaming victim (de Moraes, 2010).

FIGURE 13.3

Milgram's follow-up obedience experiment In a repeat of the earlier experiment, 65 percent of the adult male "teachers" fully obeyed the experimenter's commands to continue. They did so despite the "learner's" earlier mention of a heart condition and despite hearing cries of protest after they administered what they thought were 150 volts and agonized protests after 330 volts. (Data from Milgram, 1974.)

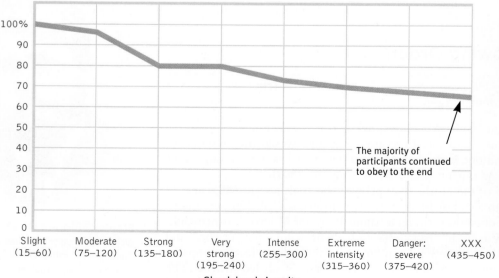

Percentage of participants who obeyed experimenter

The majority of participants continued to obey to the end

Shock levels in volts

Slight (15–60) Moderate (75–120) Strong (135–180) Very strong (195–240) Intense (255–300) Extreme intensity (315–360) Danger: severe (375–420) XXX (435–450)

Did the teachers figure out the hoax—that no real shock was being delivered and the learner was in fact a confederate who was pretending to feel pain? Did they realize the experiment was really testing their willingness to comply with commands to inflict punishment? *No.* The teachers typically displayed genuine distress: They perspired, trembled, laughed nervously, and bit their lips.

Milgram's use of deception and stress triggered a debate over his research ethics. In his own defense, Milgram pointed out that, after the participants learned of the deception and actual research purposes, virtually none regretted taking part (though perhaps by then the participants had reduced their cognitive dissonance). When 40 of the teachers who had agonized most were later interviewed by a psychiatrist, none appeared to be suffering emotional aftereffects. All in all, said Milgram, the experiments provoked less enduring stress than university students experience when facing and failing big exams (Blass, 1996).

In later experiments, Milgram discovered some things that influence people's behavior. When he varied the situation, full obedience ranged from 0 to 93 percent. Obedience was highest when

"Drive off the cliff, James, I want to commit suicide."

- *the person giving the orders was close at hand and was perceived to be a legitimate authority figure.* (Such was the case in 2005 when Temple University's basketball coach sent a 250-pound bench player, Nehemiah Ingram, into a game with instructions to commit "hard fouls." Following orders, Ingram fouled out in four minutes after breaking an opposing player's right arm.)

- *the authority figure was supported by a prestigious institution.* Compliance was somewhat lower when Milgram dissociated his experiments from Yale University.

- *the victim was depersonalized or at a distance, even in another room.* (Similarly, many soldiers in combat either have not fired their rifles at an enemy they can see, or have not aimed them properly. Such refusals to kill have been rare among soldiers who were operating long-distance artillery or aircraft weapons [Padgett, 1989]. In modern warfare, those who kill from a distance—by operating remotely piloted aircraft ["drones"]—have suffered much less post-traumatic stress disorder than have Afghanistan and Iraq war veterans [Miller, 2012].)

- *there were no role models for defiance.* (Teachers did not see any other participant disobey the experimenter.)

The power of legitimate, close-at-hand authorities was apparent among those who followed orders to carry out the Holocaust atrocities. Obedience alone does not explain the Holocaust. Anti-Semitic ideology also contributed (Mastroianni, 2002). But obedience was a factor. In the summer of 1942, nearly 500 middle-aged German reserve police officers were dispatched to German-occupied Jozefow, Poland. On July 13, the group's visibly upset commander informed his recruits, mostly family men, of their orders. They were to round up the village's Jews, who were said to be aiding the enemy. Able-bodied men would be sent to work camps, and all the rest would be shot on the spot.

The commander gave the recruits a chance to refuse to participate in the executions. Only about a dozen immediately refused. Within 17 hours, the remaining 485 officers killed 1500 helpless women, children, and elderly, shooting them in the back of the head as they lay face down. Hearing the victims' pleas, and seeing the gruesome results, some 20 percent of the officers did eventually dissent, managing either to miss their victims or to wander away and hide until the slaughter was over (Browning, 1992). In real life, as in Milgram's experiments, those who resisted were the minority.

Another story played out in the French village of Le Chambon. There, French Jews destined for deportation to Germany were sheltered by villagers who openly defied orders to cooperate with

Standing up for democracy Some individuals—roughly one in three in Milgram's experiments—resist social coercion, as did this unarmed man in Beijing, by single-handedly challenging an advancing line of tanks the day after the 1989 Tiananmen Square student uprising was suppressed.

the "New Order." The villagers' ancestors had themselves been persecuted, and their pastors taught them to "resist whenever our adversaries will demand of us obedience contrary to the orders of the Gospel" (Rochat, 1993). Ordered by police to give a list of sheltered Jews, the head pastor modeled defiance: "I don't know of Jews, I only know of human beings." Without realizing how long and terrible the war would be, or how much punishment and poverty they would suffer, the resisters made an initial commitment to resist. Supported by their beliefs, their role models, their interactions with one another, and their own initial acts, they remained defiant to the war's end.

Lessons From the Conformity and Obedience Studies

What do the Asch and Milgram experiments teach us about ourselves? How does judging the length of a line or flicking a shock switch relate to everyday social behavior? Recall from Chapter 1 that psychological experiments aim not to re-create the literal behaviors of everyday life but to capture and explore the underlying processes that shape those behaviors. Participants in the Asch and Milgram experiments confronted a dilemma we all face frequently: Do I adhere to my own standards, or do I respond to others?

In Milgram's experiments and their modern replications, participants were torn. Should they respond to the pleas of the victim or the orders of the experimenter? Their moral sense warned them not to harm another, yet it also prompted them to obey the experimenter and to be a good research participant. With kindness and obedience on a collision course, obedience usually won.

These experiments demonstrated that strong social influences can make people conform to falsehoods or capitulate to cruelty. Milgram saw this as the fundamental lesson of this work: "Ordinary people, simply doing their jobs, and without any particular hostility on their part, can become agents in a terrible destructive process" (1974, p. 6).

Focusing on the end point—450 volts, or someone's real life reprehensible deceit or violence—we can hardly comprehend the inhumanity. But we ignore how they get there, in tiny increments. Milgram did not entrap his teachers by asking them first to zap learners with enough electricity to make their hair stand on end. Rather, he exploited the foot-in-the-door effect, beginning with a little tickle of electricity and escalating step by step. In the minds of those throwing the switches, the small action became justified, making the next act tolerable. In Le Chambon, as in Milgram's experiments, those who resisted usually did so early. After the first acts of compliance or resistance, attitudes began to follow and justify behavior.

So it happens when people succumb, gradually, to evil. In any society, great evils sometimes grow out of people's compliance with lesser evils. The Nazi leaders suspected that most German civil servants would resist shooting or gassing Jews directly, but they found them surprisingly willing to handle the paperwork of the Holocaust (Silver & Geller, 1978). Milgram found a similar reaction in his experiments. When he asked 40 men to administer the learning test while someone else did the shocking, 93 percent complied. Cruelty does not require devilish villains. All it takes is ordinary people corrupted by an evil situation. Ordinary students may follow orders to haze initiates into their group. Ordinary employees may follow orders to produce and market harmful products. Ordinary soldiers may follow orders to punish and then torture prisoners (Lankford, 2009).

> ""I was only following orders."
>
> *Adolf Eichmann, Director of Nazi deportation of Jews to concentration camps*

> "The normal reaction to an abnormal situation is abnormal behavior."
>
> *James Waller,* Becoming Evil: How Ordinary People Commit Genocide and Mass Killing, *2007*

RETRIEVE IT

- Psychology's most famous obedience experiments, in which most participants obeyed an authority figure's demands to inflict presumed life-threatening shocks on an innocent other, were conducted by social psychologist _____ _____.

ANSWER: Stanley Milgram

- What situations have researchers found to be most likely to encourage obedience in participants?

ANSWER: The Milgram studies showed that people were most likely to follow orders when the experimenter was nearby and was a legitimate authority figure, the victim was not nearby, and there were no models for defiance.

Group Behavior

13-6: How is our behavior affected by the presence of others?

Imagine yourself standing in a room, holding a fishing pole. Your task is to wind the reel as fast as you can. On some occasions you wind in the presence of another participant who is also winding as fast as possible. Will the other's presence affect your own performance?

In one of the social psychology's first experiments, Norman Triplett (1898) reported that adolescents would wind a fishing reel faster in the presence of someone doing the same thing. Although a modern reanalysis revealed that the difference was modest (Stroebe, 2012), he helped inspire later social psychologists to study how others' presence affects our behavior. Group influences operate in such simple groups—one person in the presence of another—and in more complex groups.

Social Facilitation

Triplett's claim—of strengthened performance in others' presence—is called **social facilitation.** But on tougher tasks (learning nonsense syllables or solving complex multiplication problems), people perform worse when observers or others working on the same task are present. Further studies revealed that the presence of others sometimes helps and sometimes hinders performance (Guerin, 1986; Zajonc, 1965). Why? Because when others observe us, we become aroused, and this arousal amplifies our other reactions. It strengthens our most *likely* response—the correct one on an easy task, an incorrect one on a difficult task. Thus, expert pool players who made 71 percent of their shots when alone made 80 percent when four people came to watch them (Michaels et al., 1982). Poor shooters, who made 36 percent of their shots when alone, made only 25 percent when watched.

The energizing effect of an enthusiastic audience probably contributes to the home advantage that has shown up in studies of more than a quarter million college and professional athletic events in various countries (Jamieson, 2010). Home teams win about 6 in 10 games (somewhat fewer for baseball, cricket, and football, somewhat more for basketball, rugby, and soccer—see **TABLE 13.1**).

Social facilitation also helps explain a funny effect of crowding. Comedians and actors know that a "good house" is a full one. Crowding triggers arousal, which, as we have seen, strengthens other reactions, too. Comedy routines that are mildly amusing to people in an uncrowded room seem funnier in a densely packed room (Aiello et al., 1983; Freedman & Perlick, 1979). And in experiments, when participants have been seated close to one another, they liked a friendly person even more, an unfriendly person even less (Schiffenbauer & Schiavo, 1976; Storms & Thomas, 1977). So, for an energetic class or event, choose a room or set up seating that will just barely accommodate everyone.

The point to remember: What you do well, you are likely to do even better in front of an audience, especially a friendly audience. What you normally find difficult may seem all but impossible when you are being watched.

Todd Taulman/Shutterstock

Social Loafing

Social facilitation experiments test the effect of others' presence on performance on an individual task, such as shooting pool. But what happens to performance when people perform the task as a group? In a team tug-of-war, for example, do you suppose your

social facilitation improved performance on simple or well-learned tasks in the presence of others.

Social facilitation Skilled athletes often find they are "on" before an audience. What they do well, they do even better when people are watching.

© James Lumb/Demotix/Corbis

Table 13.1
Home Advantage in Team Sports

Sport	Games Studied	Home Team Winning Percentage
Baseball	120,576	55.6%
Cricket	513	57.0
American football	11,708	57.3
Ice hockey	50,739	59.5
Basketball	30,174	62.9
Rugby	2,653	63.7
Soccer	40,380	67.4

Source: From Jeremy Jamieson (2010).

Working hard, or hardly working? In group projects, social loafing often occurs, as individuals free-ride on the efforts of others.

effort would be more than, less than, or the same as the effort you would exert in a one-on-one tug-of-war? To find out, a University of Massachusetts research team asked blindfolded students "to pull as hard as you can" on a rope. When they fooled the students into believing three others were also pulling behind them, they exerted only 82 percent as much effort as when they knew they were pulling alone (Ingham et al., 1974). And consider what happened when blindfolded people seated in a group clapped or shouted as loud as they could while hearing (through headphones) other people clapping or shouting loudly (Latané, 1981). When they thought they were part of a group effort, the participants produced about one-third less noise than when clapping or shouting "alone."

Bibb Latané and his colleagues (1981; Jackson & Williams, 1988) described this diminished effort as **social loafing.** Experiments in the United States, India, Thailand, Japan, China, and Taiwan have recorded social loafing on various tasks, though it was especially common among men in individualist cultures (Karau & Williams, 1993). What causes social loafing? Three things:

- People acting as part of a group feel less accountable, and therefore worry less about what others think.

- Group members may view their individual contributions as dispensable (Harkins & Szymanski, 1989; Kerr & Bruun, 1983).

- When group members share equally in the benefits, regardless of how much they contribute, some may slack off (as you perhaps have observed on group assignments). Unless highly motivated and strongly identified with the group, people may *free-ride* on others' efforts.

Deindividuation

We've seen that the presence of others can arouse people (social facilitation), or it can diminish their feelings of responsibility (social loafing). But sometimes the presence of others does both. The uninhibited behavior that results can range from a food fight to vandalism or rioting. This process of losing self-awareness and self-restraint, called **deindividuation,** often occurs when group participation makes people both *aroused* and *anonymous*. In one experiment, New York University women dressed in depersonalizing Ku Klux Klan-style hoods. Compared with identifiable women in a control group, the hooded women delivered twice as much electric shock to a victim (Zimbardo, 1970). (As in all such experiments, the "victim" did not actually receive the shocks.)

Deindividuation During England's 2011 riots and looting, rioters were disinhibited by social arousal and by the anonymity provided by darkness and their hoods and masks. Later, some of those arrested expressed bewilderment over their own behavior.

Deindividuation thrives, for better or for worse, in many different settings. Tribal warriors who depersonalize themselves with face paints or masks are more likely than those with exposed faces to kill, torture, or mutilate captured enemies (Watson, 1973). Online, Internet trollers and bullies, who would never say "You're a fraud" to someone's face, will hide behind anonymity. When we shed self-awareness and self-restraint—whether in a mob, at a rock concert, at a ballgame, or at worship—we become more responsive to the group experience—bad or good.

★ ★ ★

We have examined the conditions under which being in the *presence* of others can motivate people to exert themselves or tempt them to free-ride on the efforts of others, make easy tasks easier and difficult tasks harder, and enhance humor or fuel mob violence. Research also shows that *interacting* with others can similarly have both bad and good effects.

Group Polarization

13-7: What are group polarization and groupthink, and how much power do we have as individuals?

Over time, initial differences between groups of college students tend to grow. If the first-year students at College X tend to be artistic, and those at College Y tend to be business-savvy, those differences will probably be even greater by the time they graduate. Similarly, gender differences tend to widen over time, as Eleanor Maccoby (2002) noted from her decades of observing gender development. Girls talk more intimately than boys do and play and fantasize less aggressively; these differences will be amplified as boys and girls interact mostly with their own gender.

In each case, the beliefs and attitudes we bring to a group grow stronger as we discuss them with like-minded others. This process, called **group polarization,** can have beneficial results, as when it amplifies a sought-after spiritual awareness or reinforces the resolve of those in a self-help group. But it can also have dire consequences. George Bishop and I discovered that when high-prejudice students discussed racial issues, they became *more* prejudiced (**FIGURE 13.4**). (Low-prejudice students became even more accepting.) Thus ideological separation + deliberation = polarization between groups.

This polarizing effect can also feed suicide terrorism. Analyses of terrorist organizations around the world reveals that the terrorist mentality does not erupt suddenly, on a whim (McCauley, 2002; McCauley & Segal, 1987; Merari, 2002). It usually begins slowly, among people who share a grievance. As they interact in isolation (sometimes with other "brothers" and "sisters" in camps) their views grow more and more extreme. Increasingly, they categorize the world as "us" against "them" (Moghaddam, 2005; Qirko, 2004). The like-minded echo chamber will continue to polarize people, speculated a 2006 U.S. National Intelligence estimate: "We assess that the operational threat from self-radicalized cells will grow."

Although I cut my eye teeth in social psychology with experiments on group polarization, I never imagined the potential dangers, or the creative possibilities, of polarization in *virtual* groups. Electronic communication and social networking have created virtual town halls where people can isolate themselves from those whose perspective differs. People read blogs that reinforce their views, and those blogs link to kindred blogs (**FIGURE 13.5** on the next page). As the Internet connects the like-minded and pools their ideas, climate-change skeptics, UFO abductees, and conspiracy theorists find support for their shared ideas and suspicions. White supremacists may become more racist. And militia members may become more terror prone.

But the Internet-as-social-amplifier can also work for good. Social networking sites, such as Facebook, connect friends and family members sharing common interests or coping with similar challenges. Peacemakers, cancer survivors, and bereaved parents can find strength and solace from kindred spirits. By amplifying shared concerns and ideas, Internet-enhanced communication can also foster social ventures. (I know this personally from social networking with others with hearing loss in an effort to transform American assistive listening technology.)

The point to remember: By linking and magnifying the inclinations of like-minded people, the Internet can be very, very bad, but also very, very good.

social loafing the tendency for people in a group to exert less effort when pooling their efforts toward attaining a common goal than when individually accountable.

deindividuation the loss of self-awareness and self-restraint occurring in group situations that foster arousal and anonymity.

group polarization the enhancement of a group's prevailing inclinations through discussion within the group.

"What explains the rise of facism in the 1930s? The emergence of student radicalism in the 1960s? The growth of Islamic terrorism in the 1990s? . . . The unifying theme is simple: *When people find themselves in groups of like-minded types, they are especially likely to move to extremes.* [This] is the phenomenon of *group polarization.*"

Cass Sunstein, Going to Extremes, *2009*

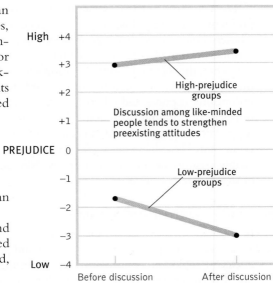

FIGURE 13.4

Group polarization If a group is like-minded, discussion strengthens its prevailing opinions. Talking over racial issues increased prejudice in a high-prejudice group of high school students and decreased it in a low-prejudice group (Myers & Bishop, 1970).

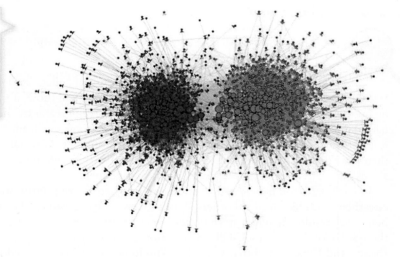

Groupthink

So, group interaction can influence our personal decisions. Does it ever distort important national decisions? Consider the "Bay of Pigs fiasco." In 1961, President John F. Kennedy and his advisers decided to invade Cuba with 1400 CIA-trained Cuban exiles. When the invaders were easily captured and soon linked to the U.S. government, Kennedy wondered in hindsight, "How could we have been so stupid?"

Social psychologist Irving Janis (1982) studied the decision-making procedures leading to the ill-fated invasion. He discovered that the soaring morale of the recently elected president and his advisers fostered undue confidence. To preserve the good feeling, group members suppressed or self-censored their dissenting views, especially after President Kennedy voiced his enthusiasm for the scheme. Since no one spoke strongly against the idea, everyone assumed the support was unanimous. To describe this harmonious but unrealistic group thinking, Janis coined the term **groupthink.**

Later studies showed that groupthink—fed by overconfidence, conformity, self-justification, and group polarization—contributed to other fiascos as well. Among them were the failure to anticipate the 1941 Japanese attack on Pearl Harbor; the escalation of the Vietnam war; the U.S. Watergate cover-up; the Chernobyl nuclear reactor accident (Reason, 1987); the U.S. space shuttle *Challenger* explosion (Esser & Lindoerfer, 1989); and the Iraq war, launched on the false idea that Iraq had weapons of mass destruction (U.S. Senate Intelligence Committee, 2004).

Despite the dangers of groupthink, two heads are better than one in solving many problems. Knowing this, Janis also studied instances in which U.S. presidents and their advisers collectively made good decisions, such as when the Truman administration formulated the Marshall Plan, which offered assistance to Europe after World War II, and when the Kennedy administration successfully prevented the Soviets from installing missiles in Cuba. In such instances—and in the business world, too, Janis believed—groupthink is prevented when a leader welcomes various opinions, invites experts' critiques of developing plans, and assigns people to identify possible problems. Just as the suppression of dissent bends a group toward bad decisions, so open debate often shapes good ones. This is especially so with diverse groups, whose varied perspectives often enable creative or superior outcomes (Nemeth & Ormiston, 2007; Page, 2007). None of us is as smart as all of us.

The Power of Individuals

In affirming the power of social influence, we must not overlook the power of individuals. *Social control* (the power of the situation) and *personal control* (the power of the individual) interact. People aren't billiard balls. When feeling coerced, we may react by doing the opposite of what is expected, thereby reasserting our sense of freedom (Brehm & Brehm, 1981).

"One of the dangers in the White House, based on my reading of history, is that you get wrapped up in groupthink and everybody agrees with everything, and there's no discussion and there are no dissenting views."

Barack Obama, December 1, 2008, press conference

"Truth springs from argument among friends."

Philosopher David Hume, 1711-1776

"If you have an apple and I have an apple and we exchange apples then you and I will still each have one apple. But if you have an idea and I have an idea and we exchange these ideas, then each of us will have two ideas."

Attributed to dramatist George Bernard Shaw, 1856-1950

CHAPTER 13 > SOCIAL PSYCHOLOGY   **475**

Committed individuals can sway the majority and make social history. Were this not so, communism would have remained an obscure theory, Christianity would be a small Middle Eastern sect, and Rosa Parks' refusal to sit at the back of the bus would not have ignited the U.S. civil rights movement. Technological history, too, is often made by innovative minorities who overcome the majority's resistance to change. To many, the railroad was a nonsensical idea; some farmers even feared that train noise would prevent hens from laying eggs. People derided Robert Fulton's steamboat as "Fulton's Folly." As Fulton later said, "Never did a single encouraging remark, a bright hope, a warm wish, cross my path." Much the same reaction greeted the printing press, the telegraph, the incandescent lamp, and the typewriter (Cantril & Bumstead, 1960).

The power of one or two individuals to sway majorities is *minority influence* (Moscovici, 1985). In studies of groups in which one or two individuals consistently express a controversial attitude or an unusual perceptual judgment, one finding repeatedly stands out: When you are the minority, you are far more likely to sway the majority if you hold firmly to your position and don't waffle. This tactic won't make you popular, but it may make you influential, especially if your self-confidence stimulates others to consider *why* you react as you do. Even when a minority's influence is not yet visible, people may privately develop sympathy for the minority position and rethink their views (Wood et al., 1994). The powers of social influence are enormous, but so are the powers of the committed individual.

Gandhi As the life of Hindu nationalist and spiritual leader Mahatma Gandhi powerfully testifies, a consistent and persistent minority voice can sometimes sway the majority. Gandhi's nonviolent appeals and fasts were instrumental in winning India's independence from Britain in 1947.

RETRIEVE IT

• What is social facilitation, and under what circumstances is it most likely to occur?

ANSWER: This improved performance in the presence of others is most likely to occur with a well-learned task, because the added arousal caused by an audience tends to strengthen the most likely response.

• People tend to exert less effort when working with a group than they would alone, which is called _____ _____.

ANSWER: social loafing

• You are organizing a meeting of fiercely competitive political candidates. To add to the fun, friends have suggested handing out masks of the candidates' faces for supporters to wear. What phenomenon might these masks engage?

ANSWER: The anonymity provided by the masks, combined with the arousal of the contentious setting, might create *deindividuation* (lessened self-awareness and self-restraint.).

• When like-minded groups discuss a topic, and the result is the strengthening of the prevailing opinion, this is called _____ _____.

ANSWER: group polarization

• When a group's desire for harmony overrides its realistic analysis of other options, _____ has occurred.

ANSWER: groupthink

Social Relations

We have sampled how we *think* about and *influence* one another. Now we come to social psychology's third focus—how we *relate* to one another. What causes us to harm or to help or to fall in love? How can we move a destructive conflict toward a just peace? We will ponder the bad and the good: from prejudice and aggression to attraction, altruism, and peacemaking.

groupthink the mode of thinking that occurs when the desire for harmony in a decision-making group overrides a realistic appraisal of alternatives.

prejudice an unjustifiable and usually negative attitude toward a group and its members. Prejudice generally involves stereotyped beliefs, negative feelings, and a predisposition to discriminatory action.

stereotype a generalized (sometimes accurate but often overgeneralized) belief about a group of people.

discrimination unjustifiable negative behavior toward a group and its members.

Prejudice

13-8: What is prejudice? What are its social and emotional roots?

Prejudice means "prejudgment." It is an unjustifiable and usually negative attitude toward a group—often a different cultural, ethnic, or gender group. Like all attitudes, prejudice is a three-part mixture of

- *beliefs* (in this case, called **stereotypes**).
- *emotions* (for example, hostility or fear).
- predispositions to *action* (to discriminate).

To *believe* that obese people are gluttonous, to feel *dislike* for an obese person, and to be hesitant to hire or date an obese person is to be prejudiced. Prejudice is a negative *attitude*. **Discrimination** is a negative *behavior*.

How Prejudiced Are People?

To assess prejudice, we can observe what people say and what they do. Americans' expressed gender and racial attitudes have changed dramatically in the last 70 years. The one-third of Americans who in 1937 told Gallup pollsters that they would vote for a qualified woman whom their party nominated for president soared to 89 percent in 2007 (Gallup Brain, 2008; Jones & Moore, 2003). Nearly everyone now agrees that women and men should receive the same pay for the same job, and that children of all races should attend the same schools.

Support for all forms of racial contact, including interracial dating, has also dramatically increased. Among 18- to 29-year-old Americans, 9 in 10 now say they would be fine with a family member marrying someone of a different race (Pew, 2010).

Yet as *overt* prejudice wanes, *subtle* prejudice lingers. Despite increased verbal support for interracial marriage, many people admit that in socially intimate settings (dating, dancing, marrying) they would feel uncomfortable with someone of another race. And many people who *say* they would feel upset with someone making racist slurs actually, when hearing such racism, respond indifferently (Kawakami et al., 2009). In Western Europe, where many "guest workers" and refugees settled at the end of the twentieth century, "modern prejudice"—rejecting immigrant minorities as job applicants for supposedly nonracial reasons—has been replacing blatant prejudice (Jackson et al., 2001; Lester, 2004; Pettigrew, 1998, 2006). A slew of recent experiments illustrates that prejudice can be not only subtle but also automatic and unconscious (see Close-Up: Automatic Prejudice).

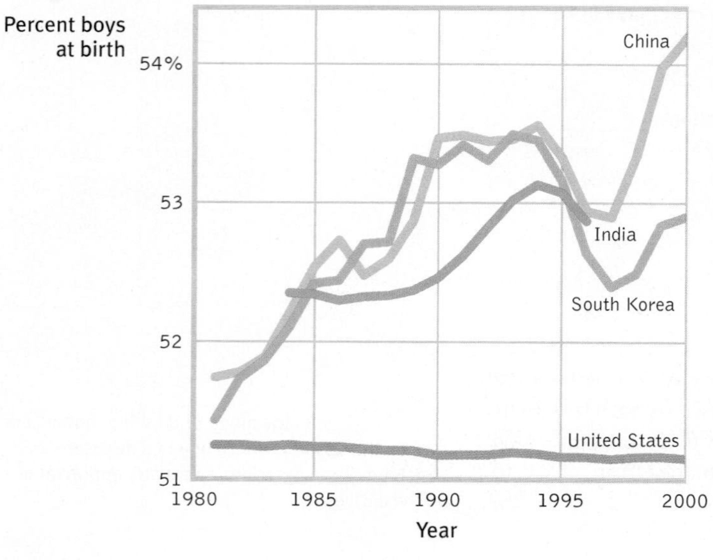

In most places in the world, gays and lesbians cannot comfortably acknowledge who they are and whom they love. Gender prejudice and discrimination persist, too. Despite gender equality in intelligence scores, people have tended to perceive their fathers as more intelligent than their mothers (Furnham & Wu, 2008). In Saudi Arabia, women are still not allowed to drive. In Western countries, we still pay more to those (usually men) who care for our streets than to those (usually women) who care for our children. Worldwide, women have been more likely to live in poverty (Lipps, 1999), and they represent two-thirds of illiterate adults (CIA, 2010).

Female infants are no longer left out on a hillside to die of exposure, as was the practice in ancient Greece. Yet natural female mortality and the normal male-to-female newborn ratio (105-to-100) hardly explain the world's estimated 163 million (say that number slowly) "missing women" (Hvistendahl, 2011). In many places, sons are valued more than daughters. With testing that enables sex-selective abortions, several South Asian countries have experienced a shortfall in female births (**FIGURE 13.6**). Although

FIGURE 13.6
Missing girls In several Asian countries, especially in China, which has mandated one-child families, boy babies have been overrepresented (Abrevaya, 2009). China had this overrepresentation still occurring in 2009, with 54.5 percent of babies being boys, and only 45.5 percent being girls (Hvistendahl, 2010).

Automatic Prejudice

As we have seen throughout this book, the human mind processes thoughts, memories, and attitudes on two different tracks. Sometimes that processing is explicit—on the radar screen of our awareness. To an even greater extent, it is implicit—below the radar, leaving us unaware of how our attitudes are influencing our behavior. Modern studies indicate that prejudice is often implicit, an automatic attitude that is an unthinking knee-jerk response. Consider these findings:

Implicit racial associations Using Implicit Association Tests, researchers have demonstrated that even people who deny harboring racial prejudice may carry negative associations (Greenwald et al., 1998, 2009). (By 2011, nearly 5 million people had taken the Implicit Association Test, as you can at implicit.harvard.edu.) For example, 9 in 10 White respondents took longer to identify pleasant words (such as peace and paradise) as "good" when presented with Black-sounding names (such as Latisha and Darnell) rather than with White-sounding names (such as Katie and Ian). Moreover, people who more quickly associate good things with White names or faces also are the quickest to perceive anger and apparent threat in Black faces (Hugenberg & Bodenhausen, 2003).

Although the test is useful for studying automatic prejudice, critics caution against using it to assess or label individuals (Blanton et al., 2006, 2007, 2009). Defenders counter that implicit biases predict behaviors that range from simple acts of friendliness to the evaluation of work quality (Greenwald et al., 2009). In the 2008 U.S. presidential election, implicit as well as explicit prejudice predicted voters' response to candidate Barack Obama, whose election in turn served to reduce implicit prejudice (Bernstein et al., 2010; Payne et al., 2010).

Unconscious patronization When White university women evaluated a flawed essay said to be written by a Black fellow student, they gave markedly higher ratings and never expressed the harsh criticisms they assigned to flawed essays supposedly written by White students (Harber, 1998). Did the evaluators calibrate their evaluations to their racial stereotypes, leading to less exacting standards and a patronizing attitude? In real-world evaluations, such low expectations and the resulting "inflated praise and insufficient criticism" could hinder minority student achievement, the researcher noted. (To preclude such bias, many teachers read essays while "blind" to their authors.)

Race-influenced perceptions Our expectations influence our perceptions. In 1999, Amadou Diallo was accosted as he approached his apartment house doorway by police officers looking for a rapist. When he pulled out his wallet, the officers, perceiving a gun, riddled his body with 19 bullets from 41 shots. Curious about this tragic killing of an unarmed, innocent man, two research teams reenacted the situation (Correll et al., 2002, 2007; Greenwald et al., 2003). They asked viewers to press buttons quickly to "shoot" or not shoot men who suddenly appeared on screen. Some of the on-screen men held a gun. Others held a harmless object, such as a flashlight or bottle. People (both Blacks and Whites, in one study) more often shot Black men than White men who were holding the harmless objects. Priming people with a flashed Black rather than White face also makes them more likely then to misperceive a flashed tool as a gun (**FIGURE 13.7**).

Reflexive bodily responses Even people who consciously express little prejudice may give off telltale signals as their body responds selectively to another's race. Neuroscientists can detect these signals when people look at White and Black faces. The viewers' implicit prejudice may show up in facial-muscle responses and in the activation of their emotion-processing amygdala (Cunningham et al., 2004; Eberhardt, 2005; Stanley et al., 2008).

If your own gut check reveals you sometimes have feelings you would rather not have about other people, remember this: It is what we do with our feelings that matters. By monitoring our feelings and actions, and by replacing old habits with new ones based on new friendships, we can work to free ourselves from prejudice.

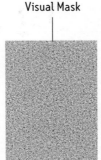

Visual Mask

Punchstock/Corbis

FIGURE 13.7
Race primes perceptions In experiments by Keith Payne (2006), people viewed a White or Black face, immediately followed by a gun or hand tool, which was then followed by a visual mask. Participants were more likely to misperceive a tool as a gun when it was preceded by a Black rather than White face.

China has declared that sex-selective abortions—gender genocide—are now a criminal offense, the country's newborn sex ratio is still 118 boys for every 100 girls (Hvistendahl, 2009, 2010, 2011), and 95 percent of the children in Chinese orphanages are girls (Webley, 2009). With under-age-20 males exceeding females by 32 million, many Chinese bachelors will be unable to find mates (Zhu et al., 2009).

THERE IS NO JUSTICE IN THE WORLD.

THERE IS SOME JUSTICE IN THE WORLD.

THE WORLD IS JUST.

Social Roots of Prejudice

Why does prejudice arise? Social inequalities and divisions are partly responsible.

Social Inequalities When some people have money, power, and prestige and others do not, the "haves" usually develop attitudes that justify things as they are. The **just-world phenomenon** reflects an idea we commonly teach our children—that good is rewarded and evil is punished. From this it is but a short leap to assume that those who succeed must be good and those who suffer must be bad. Such reasoning enables the rich to see both their own wealth and the poor's misfortune as justly deserved.

Are women naturally unassertive but sensitive? This common perception suggests that women are well-suited for the caretaking tasks they have traditionally performed (Hoffman & Hurst, 1990). In an extreme case, slave "owners" perceived slaves as innately lazy, ignorant, and irresponsible—as having the very traits that justified enslaving them. Stereotypes rationalize inequalities.

Victims of discrimination may react with either self-blame or anger (Allport, 1954). Either reaction can feed prejudice through the classic *blame-the-victim* dynamic. Do the circumstances of poverty breed a higher crime rate? If so, that higher crime rate can be used to justify discrimination against those who live in poverty.

Us and Them: Ingroup and Outgroup We have inherited our Stone Age ancestors' need to belong, to live and love in groups. There was safety in solidarity (those who didn't band together left fewer descendants). Whether hunting, defending, or attacking, 10 hands were better than 2. Dividing the world into "us" and "them" entails prejudice and war, but it also provides the benefits of communal solidarity. Thus, we cheer for our groups, kill for them, die for them. Indeed, we define who we are partly in terms of our groups. Through our *social identities* we associate ourselves with certain groups and contrast ourselves with others (Hogg, 1996, 2006; Turner, 1987, 2007). When Ian identifies himself as a man, an Aussie, a Labourite, a University of Sydney student, a Catholic, and a MacGregor, he knows who he is, and so do we.

Evolution prepared us, when encountering strangers, to make instant judgments: friend or foe? Those from our group, those who look like us, and also those who *sound* like us—with accents like our own—we instantly tend to like, from childhood onward (Gluszek & Dovidio, 2010; Kinzler et al., 2009). Mentally drawing a circle defines "us," the **ingroup.** But the social definition of who you are also states who you are not. People outside that circle are "them," the **outgroup.** An **ingroup bias**—a favoring of our own group—soon follows. Even arbitrarily creating us-them groups by tossing a coin creates this bias. In experiments, people have favored their own group when dividing any rewards (Tajfel, 1982; Wilder, 1981).

The ingroup Scotland's famed "Tartan Army" soccer fans, shown here during a match against archrival England, share a social identity that defines "us" (the Scottish ingroup) and "them" (the English outgroup).

The urge to distinguish enemies from friends predisposes prejudice against strangers (Whitley, 1999). To Greeks of the classical era, all non-Greeks were "barbarians." In our own era, most children believe their school is better than all other schools in town. Many high school students form cliques—goths/emos, theater people, athletes (sorted by sport), gangsters, preps, nerds—and disparage those outside their own group. Even chimpanzees have been seen to wipe clean the spot where they were touched by a chimpanzee from another group (Goodall, 1986). They also display ingroup empathy, by yawning more after seeing ingroup (rather than outgroup) members yawn (Campbell & de Waal, 2011).

Ingroup bias explains the cognitive power of political partisanship (Cooper, 2010; Douthat, 2010). In the United States in the late 1980s, most Democrats believed inflation had risen under Republican president Ronald Reagan (it had dropped). In 2010, most Republicans believed that taxes had increased under Democrat president Barack Obama (for most, they had decreased).

Emotional Roots of Prejudice

Prejudice springs not only from the divisions of society but also from the passions of the heart. **Scapegoat theory** notes that when things go wrong, finding someone to blame can provide a target for anger. Following the 9/11 attacks, some outraged people lashed out at innocent Arab-Americans. Others called for eliminating Saddam Hussein, the Iraqi leader whom Americans had been grudgingly tolerating. "Fear and anger create aggression, and aggression against citizens of different ethnicity or race creates racism and, in turn, new forms of terrorism," noted Philip Zimbardo (2001). A decade after 9/11, anti-Muslim animosities still flared in the United States, with mosque burnings and efforts to block construction of an Islamic community center near Ground Zero in New York City.

Evidence for the scapegoat theory of prejudice comes from high prejudice among economically frustrated people, and from experiments in which a temporary frustration intensifies prejudice. Students who experienced failure or were made to feel insecure often restored their self-esteem by disparaging a rival school or another person (Cialdini & Richardson, 1980; Crocker et al., 1987). To boost our own sense of status when we're down, it helps to have others to denigrate. That is why a rival's misfortune sometimes provides a twinge of pleasure. By contrast, those made to feel loved and supported have become more open to and accepting of others who differ (Mikulincer & Shaver, 2001).

Negative emotions nourish prejudice. When facing death, fearing threats, or experiencing frustration, people cling more tightly to their ingroup and their friends. As the terror of death heightens patriotism, it also produces loathing and aggression toward "them"—those who threaten our world (Pyszczynski et al., 2002, 2008). The few individuals who lack fear and its associated amygdala activity—such as children with the genetic disorder, Williams syndrome—also display a notable lack of racial stereotypes and prejudice (Santos et al., 2010).

Cognitive Roots of Prejudice

13-9: What are the cognitive roots of prejudice?

Prejudice springs from a culture's divisions, the heart's passions, and also from the mind's natural workings. Stereotyped beliefs are a by-product of how we cognitively simplify the world.

Forming Categories One way we simplify our world is to categorize. A chemist categorizes molecules as organic and inorganic. Therapists categorize psychological disorders. All of us categorize people by race, with mixed-race people often assigned to their minority identity. Despite his mixed-race background and his rearing by a White mother and White grandparents, President Obama is perceived by White Americans as Black. Researchers believe this happens because, after learning the features of a familiar

"For if [people were] to choose out of all the customs in the world [they would] end by preferring their own."
Greek historian Herodotus, 440 B.C.E.

"The misfortunes of others are the taste of honey."
Japanese saying

"If the Tiber reaches the walls, if the Nile does not rise to the fields, if the sky doesn't move or the Earth does, if there is famine, if there is plague, the cry is at once: 'The Christians to the lion!'"
Tertullian, Apologeticus, C.E. 197

just-world phenomenon the tendency for people to believe the world is just and that people therefore get what they deserve and deserve what they get.

ingroup "Us"—people with whom we share a common identity.

outgroup "Them"—those perceived as different or apart from our ingroup.

ingroup bias the tendency to favor our own group.

scapegoat theory the theory that prejudice offers an outlet for anger by providing someone to blame.

| 100% Chinese | 80% Chinese 20% Caucasian | 60% Chinese 40% Caucasian | 40% Chinese 60% Caucasian | 20% Chinese 80% Caucasian | 100% Caucasian |

Dr. Jamin Halberstadt

FIGURE 13.8

Categorizing mixed race people When New Zealanders quickly classified 104 photos by race, those of European descent more often than those of Chinese descent classified the ambiguous middle two as Chinese (Halberstadt et al., 2011).

racial group, the observer's selective attention is drawn to the distinctive features of the less-familiar minority. Jamin Halberstadt and his colleagues (2011) illustrated this learned-association effect by showing New Zealanders blended Chinese-Caucasian faces. Compared with Chinese participants, the Caucasian New Zealanders more readily classified ambiguous faces as Chinese (see **FIGURE 13.8**).

In categorizing people into groups, we often stereotype them. We recognize how greatly *we* differ from other individuals in *our* groups. But we overestimate the homogeneity of other groups. "They"—the members of some other group—seem to look and act alike, while "we" are more diverse (Bothwell et al., 1989). To those in one ethnic group, members of another often seem more alike than they really are in attitudes, personality, and appearance. Our greater recognition for individual own-race faces—called the **other-race effect** (also called the *cross-race* effect or *own-race bias*)—emerges during infancy, between 3 and 9 months of age (Gross, 2009; Kelly et al., 2007).

With effort and with experience, people get better at recognizing individual faces from another group (Hugenberg et al., 2010). People of European descent, for example, more accurately identify individual African faces if they have watched a great deal of basketball on television, exposing them to many African-heritage faces (Li et al., 1996). And the longer Chinese people have resided in a Western country, the less they exhibit the other-race effect (Hancock & Rhodes, 2008).

© Dave Coverly

Remembering Vivid Cases As we saw in Chapter 9, we often judge the frequency of events by instances that readily come to mind. In a classic experiment, researchers showed two groups of University of Oregon students lists containing information about 50 men (Rothbart et al., 1978). The first group's list included 10 men arrested for *nonviolent* crimes, such as forgery. The second group's list included 10 men arrested for *violent* crimes, such as assault. Later, both groups were asked how many men on their list had committed *any* sort of crime. The second group overestimated the number. Vivid (violent) cases are more readily available to our memory and feed our stereotypes (**FIGURE 13.9**).

Believing the World Is Just As we noted earlier, people often justify their prejudices by blaming victims. If the world is just, "people must get what they deserve." As one German civilian is said to have remarked when visiting the Bergen-Belsen concentration camp shortly after World War II, "What terrible criminals these prisoners must have been to receive such treatment."

FIGURE 13.9

Vivid cases feed stereotypes The 9/11 Muslim terrorists created, in many minds, an exaggerated stereotype of Muslims as terror prone. Actually, reported a U.S. National Research Council panel on terrorism, when offering this inexact illustration, most terrorists are not Muslim and "the vast majority of Islamic people have no connection with and do not sympathize with terrorism" (Smelser & Mitchell, 2002).

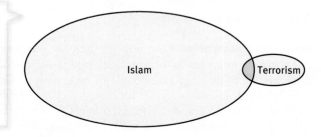

Hindsight bias is also at work here (Carli & Leonard, 1989). Have you ever heard people say that rape victims, abused spouses, or people with AIDS got what they deserved? In some countries, such as Pakistan, women who have been raped have sometimes been sentenced to severe punishment for having violated a law against adultery (Mydans, 2002). In one experiment illustrating the blame-the-victim phenomenon, people were given a detailed account of a date that ended with the woman being raped (Janoff-Bulman et al., 1985). They perceived the woman's behavior as at least partly to blame, and in hindsight, they thought, "She should have known better." (Blaming the victim also serves to reassure people that it couldn't happen to them.) Others, given the same account with the rape ending deleted, did not perceive the woman's behavior as inviting rape.

People also have a basic tendency to justify their culture's social systems (Jost et al., 2009; Kay et al., 2009). We're inclined to see the way things are as the way they ought to be. This natural conservatism makes it difficult to legislate major social changes, such as health care or climate-change policies. Once such policies are in place, our "system justification" tends to preserve them.

other-race effect the tendency to recall faces of one's own race more accurately than faces of other races. Also called the *cross-race effect* and the *own-race bias*.

aggression any physical or verbal behavior intended to hurt or destroy.

RETRIEVE IT

- When prejudiced judgment causes us to find an undeserving person to blame for a problem, that person is called a _____.

ANSWER: scapegoat

Aggression

13-10: How does psychology's definition of *aggression* differ from everyday usage? What biological factors make us more prone to hurt one another?

Prejudice hurts, but aggression often hurts more. In psychology, **aggression** is any behavior intended to harm someone, whether done out of hostility or as a calculated means to an end. The assertive, persistent salesperson is not aggressive. Nor is the dentist who makes you wince with pain. But the person who passes along a vicious rumor about you, someone who bullies you in person or online, and the attacker who mugs you for your money are aggressive. People behave aggressively toward both strangers and close relationship partners. Indeed, one out of every six married or cohabiting American couples has acknowledged experiencing at least one physically aggressive act in their relationship over the past year (Schafer et al., 1998).

Aggressive behavior emerges from the interaction of biology and experience. For a gun to fire, the trigger must be pulled; with some people, as with hair-trigger guns, it doesn't take much to trip an explosion. Let's look first at some biological factors that influence our thresholds for aggressive behavior, then at the psychological factors that pull the trigger.

The Biology of Aggression

Aggression varies too widely from culture to culture, era to era, and person to person to be considered an unlearned instinct. But biology does *influence* aggression. We can look for biological influences at three levels—genetic, biochemical, and neural.

Genetic Influences Genes influence aggression. We know this because animals have been bred for aggressiveness—sometimes for sport, sometimes for research. The effect of genes also appears in human twin studies (Miles & Carey, 1997; Rowe et al., 1999). If one identical twin admits to "having a violent temper," the other twin will often independently admit the same. Fraternal twins are much less likely to respond similarly. Researchers

In the last 40 years in the United States, well over 1 million people—more than all deaths in all wars in American history—have been killed by firearms in nonwar settings. Compared with people of the same sex, race, age, and neighborhood, those who keep a gun in the home (ironically, often for protection) are almost three times more likely to be murdered in the home—nearly always by a family member or close acquaintance. For every self-defense use of a gun in the home, there have been 4 unintentional shootings, 7 criminal assaults or homicides, and 11 attempted or completed suicides (Kellermann et al., 1993, 1997, 1998; see also Branas et al., 2009).

A lean, mean fighting machine—the testosterone-laden female hyena The hyena's unusual embryology pumps testosterone into female fetuses. The result is revved-up young female hyenas who seem born to fight.

"We could avoid two-thirds of all crime simply by putting all able-bodied young men in cryogenic sleep from the age of 12 through 28."

David T. Lykken, The Antisocial Personalities, *1995*

continue to search for genetic markers in those who commit the most violence. One is already well known and is carried by half the human race: the Y chromosome. Another such marker is the *monoamine oxidase A (MAOA) gene,* which helps break down neurotransmitters such as dopamine and serotonin, and is sometimes called the "warrior gene." People who have low MAOA gene expression tend to behave aggressively when provoked. In one experiment, low (compared to high) MAOA gene carriers gave more unpleasant hot sauce to someone who provoked them (McDermott et al., 2009).

Biochemical Influences Our genes engineer our individual nervous systems, which operate electrochemically. The hormone testosterone, for example, circulates in the bloodstream and influences the neural systems that control aggression. A raging bull becomes a gentle Ferdinand when castration reduces its testosterone level. The same is true of mice. When injected with testosterone, gentle, castrated mice once again become aggressive.

Humans are less sensitive to hormonal changes. But as men age, their testosterone levels—and their aggressiveness—diminish. Hormonally charged, aggressive 17-year-olds mature into hormonally quieter and gentler 70-year-olds. Also, violent criminals tend to be muscular young males with higher-than-average testosterone levels, lower-than-average intelligence scores, and low levels of the neurotransmitter serotonin (Dabbs et al., 2001a; Pendick, 1994).

High testosterone correlates with irritability, assertiveness, impulsiveness, and low tolerance for frustration—qualities that predispose somewhat more aggressive responses to provocation or competition for status (Dabbs et al., 2001b; Harris, 1999; McAndrew, 2009). Among both teenage boys and adult men, high testosterone levels correlate with delinquency, hard drug use, and aggressive-bullying responses to frustration (Berman et al., 1993; Dabbs & Morris, 1990; Olweus et al., 1988). Drugs that sharply reduce testosterone levels subdue men's aggressive tendencies.

Another drug that sometimes circulates in the bloodstream—alcohol—*unleashes* aggressive responses to frustration. Across police data, prison surveys, and experiments, aggression-prone people are more likely to drink, and to become violent when intoxicated (White et al., 1993). National crime data indicate that 73 percent of Russian homicides and 57 percent of U.S. homicides were influenced by alcohol (Landberg & Norström, 2011). Alcohol affects aggression both biologically and psychologically (Bushman, 1993; Ito et al., 1996; Taylor & Chermack, 1993). Just *thinking* you've imbibed alcohol can increase aggression (Bègue et al., 2009). But so, too, does unknowingly ingesting alcohol slipped into a drink. Unless people are distracted, alcohol tends to focus their attention on a provocation rather than on inhibitory cues (Giancola & Corman, 2007). Alcohol also inclines people to interpret ambiguous acts (such as a bump in a crowd) as provocations (Bègue et al., 2010).

Neural Influences There is no one spot in the brain that controls aggression. Aggression is a complex behavior, and it occurs in particular contexts. But animal and human brains have neural systems that, given provocation, will either inhibit or facilitate aggression (Denson, 2011; Moyer, 1983; Wilkowski et al., 2011). Consider:

- Researchers implanted a radio-controlled electrode in the brain of the domineering leader of a caged monkey colony. The electrode was in an area that, when stimulated, inhibits aggression. When researchers placed the control button for the electrode in the colony's cage, one small monkey learned to push it every time the boss became threatening.

- A neurosurgeon, seeking to diagnose a disorder, implanted an electrode in the amygdala of a mild-mannered woman. Because the brain has no sensory receptors, she was unable to feel the stimulation. But at the flick of a switch she snarled, "Take my blood pressure. Take it now," then stood up and began to strike the doctor.

"It's a guy thing."

● Studies of violent criminals have revealed diminished activity in the frontal lobes, which play an important role in controlling impulses. If the frontal lobes are damaged, inactive, disconnected, or not yet fully mature, aggression may be more likely (Amen et al., 1996; Davidson et al., 2000; Raine, 1999, 2005).

frustration-aggression principle the principle that frustration—the blocking of an attempt to achieve some goal—creates anger, which can generate aggression.

Psychological and Social-Cultural Factors in Aggression

13-11: What psychological and social-cultural factors may trigger aggressive behavior?

Biological factors influence how easily aggression is triggered. But what psychological and social-cultural factors pull the trigger?

Aversive Events Suffering sometimes builds character. In laboratory experiments, however, those made miserable have often made others miserable (Berkowitz, 1983, 1989). This phenomenon is called the **frustration-aggression principle:** Frustration creates anger, which can spark aggression. One analysis of 27,667 hit-by-pitch Major League Baseball incidents between 1960 and 2004 revealed this link (Timmerman, 2007). Pitchers were most likely to hit batters when

● they had been frustrated by the previous batter hitting a home run.

● the current batter had hit a home run the last time at bat.

● a teammate had been hit by a pitch in the previous half inning.

Other aversive stimuli—hot temperatures, physical pain, personal insults, foul odors, cigarette smoke, crowding, and a host of others—can also evoke hostility. In laboratory experiments, when people get overheated, they think, feel, and act more aggressively. Simply thinking about words related to hot temperatures is enough to increase hostile thoughts (DeWall & Bushman, 2009). In baseball games, the number of hit batters rises with the temperature (Reifman et al., 1991; see **FIGURE 13.10**). And in the wider world, violent crime and spousal abuse rates have been higher during hotter years, seasons, months, and days (Anderson et al., 1997). From the available data, Craig Anderson and his colleagues (2000, 2011) have projected that, other things being equal, global warming of 4 degrees Fahrenheit (about 2 degrees Celsius) could induce tens of thousands of additional assaults and murders—and that's before the added violence inducement from climate change-related drought, poverty, food insecurity, and migration.

Reinforcement, Modeling, and Self-Control Aggression may naturally follow aversive events, but learning can alter natural reactions. As Chapter 7 explained, we learn when our behavior is reinforced, and we learn by watching others.

In situations where experience has taught us that aggression pays, we are likely to act aggressively again. Children whose aggression has successfully intimidated other children may become bullies. Animals that have successfully fought to get food or mates become increasingly ferocious. To foster a kinder, gentler world we had best model and reward sensitivity and cooperation from an early age, perhaps by training parents to discipline without modeling violence.

Parents of delinquent youngsters frequently cave in to (reward) their children's tears and temper tantrums. Then, exasperated, they discipline them with beatings (Patterson et al., 1982, 1992).

Parent-training programs often advise parents to avoid modeling violence by screaming and hitting. Instead, parents should reinforce desirable behaviors and frame statements positively. ("When you finish loading the dishwasher you can go play," rather than "If you don't load the dishwasher, there'll be no playing.").

AP Photo/Brita Meng Outzen

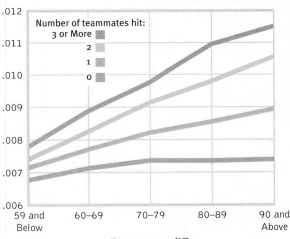

Probability of hit batter

Temperature (°F)

FIGURE 13.10

Temperature and retaliation Richard Larrick and his colleagues (2011) looked for occurrences of batters hit by pitchers during 4,566,468 pitcher-batter matchups across 57,293 Major League Baseball games since 1952. The probability of a hit batter increased if one or more of the pitcher's teammates had been hit, and also with temperature.

Tony Freeman/Photo Edit

Aggression-replacement program
Part of the rehabilitation of these juvenile offenders at the Missouri Division of Youth Services' Rosa Parks Center involves learning anger management and peaceful ways to resolve disputes. Here they "circle up" to resolve a problem peacefully.

Self-control curbs aggressive and criminal behavior. Alas, mental exhaustion, food deprivation, and other bodily challenges often deplete our self-control (Vohs et al., 2011). Picture yourself after a long challenging day at school or work, or after missing a meal or when sleep-deprived. Might you, without realizing what's happening, begin to snap at your friends or partner? Available research indicates that poor self-control is also "one of the strongest known correlates of crime" (Pratt & Cullen, 2000, p. 952).

One *aggression-replacement program* worked with juvenile offenders and gang members and their parents. It taught both generations new ways to control anger, and more thoughtful approaches to moral reasoning (Goldstein et al., 1998). The result? The youths' re-arrest rates dropped.

Different cultures model, reinforce, and evoke different tendencies toward violence. For example, U.S. men are less approving of male-to-female violence between romantic partners than are men from India, Japan, and Kuwait (Nayak et al., 2003). Crime rates have also been higher and average happiness has been lower in times and places marked by a great disparity between rich and poor (Messias et al., 2011; Oishi et al., 2011; Wilkinson & Pickett, 2009). In the United States, cultures and families that experience minimal father care also have had high violence rates (Triandis, 1994). Even after controlling for parental education, race, income, and teen motherhood, American male youths from father-absent homes have double their peers' incarceration rate (Harper & McLanahan, 2004).

Violence can also vary by culture within a country. Richard Nisbett and Dov Cohen (1996) analyzed violence among White Americans in southern towns settled by Scots-Irish herders whose tradition emphasized "manly honor," the use of arms to protect one's flock, and a history of coercive slavery. Compared with their White counterparts in New England towns settled by the more traditionally peaceful Puritan, Quaker, and Dutch farmer-artisans, the cultural descendants of those herders have had triple the homicide rates and were more supportive of physically punishing children, of warfare initiatives, and of uncontrolled gun ownership. "Culture-of-honor" states also have higher rates of students bringing weapons to school and of school shootings (Brown et al., 2009). Greater acceptance of violence in these states also seeps into the names of towns (for example, Gunpoint, Florida; Guntown, Mississippi; and War, West Virginia) (Kelly, 1999).

Media Models for Violence Parents are hardly the only aggression models. In the United States and elsewhere, TV, films, and video games offer supersized portions of violence. Repeatedly viewing on-screen violence teaches us **social scripts**—culturally provided mental files for how to act. When we find ourselves in new situations, uncertain how to behave, we rely on social scripts. After watching so many action films, adolescent boys may acquire a script that plays in their head when they face real-life conflicts. Challenged, they may "act like a man" by intimidating or eliminating the threat.

Music lyrics also write social scripts. In one set of experiments, German university men administered hotter chili sauce to a woman and recalled more negative feelings and beliefs about women after listening to woman-hating song lyrics. Man-hating song lyrics likewise increase aggression in women (Fischer & Greitemeyer, 2006).

Sexual aggression is sometimes modeled in X-rated films and pornography. Content analyses have revealed that X-rated films have sometimes included scenes of rape and sexual exploitation of women by men (Cowan et al., 1988; NCTV, 1987; Yang & Linz, 1990). These scenes have often included enactments of the *rape myth*—the idea that some women invite or enjoy rape and get "swept away" while being "taken." (In actuality, rape is traumatic, and it frequently harms women's reproductive and psychological health [Golding, 1996].) Most rapists accept this myth (Brinson, 1992). So do many men and women who watch a great deal of TV: Compared with those who watch little television, heavy viewers are more accepting of the rape myth (Kahlor & Morrison, 2007).

Surveys of American and Australian teens, university students, and young adults reveal a huge gender difference in viewing habits: Viewing X-rated films and Internet pornography is several times higher among males than among females (Carroll et al., 2008; Flood, 2007; Wolak et al., 2007). What effects might the social scripts from the $97 billion global pornography business have on the sexually aggressive behaviors of their

social script culturally modeled guide for how to act in various situations.

viewers (D'Orlando, 2011)? Most consumers of child and adult pornography commit no known sexual crimes (Seto, 2009). But they are more likely to accept the rape myth as reality (Kingston et al., 2009). And to people who are heavily exposed to pornography, sexual aggression seems less serious (Harris, 1994; Zillmann, 1989).

In one experiment, undergraduates viewed six brief, sexually explicit films each week for six weeks (Zillmann & Bryant, 1984). A control group viewed nonerotic films during the same six-week period. Three weeks later, both groups read a newspaper report about a man convicted but not yet sentenced for raping a hitchhiker. When asked to suggest an appropriate prison term, viewers of the sexually explicit films recommended sentences half as long as those recommended by the control group.

Experiments cannot elicit actual sexual violence, but they can assess a man's willingness to hurt a woman. Often the research gauges the effect of violent versus nonviolent erotic films on men's willingness to deliver supposed electric shocks to women who had earlier provoked them. These experiments suggest that it's less the eroticism than the depictions of sexual *violence* (whether in R-rated slasher films or X-rated films) that most directly affect men's acceptance and performance of aggression against women. A statement by 21 social scientists, including many of the researchers who conducted these experiments, noted, "Pornography that portrays sexual aggression as pleasurable for the victim increases the acceptance of the use of coercion in sexual relations" (Surgeon General, 1986). Contrary to much popular opinion, viewing such depictions does not provide an outlet for bottled-up impulses. Rather, "in laboratory studies measuring short-term effects, exposure to violent pornography increases punitive behavior toward women."

To a lesser extent, nonviolent pornography can also influence aggression. In a series of studies, Nathaniel Lambert and his colleagues (2011) used various methods to explore pornography's effects on aggression against relationship partners. They found that pornography consumption predicted both self-reported aggression and laboratory noise blasts to their partner, and that abstaining from customary pornography consumption decreased aggression (while abstaining from their favorite food did not).

Neil Malamuth (1996) has shown that sexually coercive men typically are sexually promiscuous and hostile in their relationships with women (**FIGURE 13.11**). Several factors can affect a man's tendencies toward sexual aggression, including media influences, dominance motives, disinhibition by alcohol, and a history of child abuse (Malamuth et al., 1991, 1995).

Do Violent Video Games Teach Social Scripts for Violence? Experiments in North America, Western Europe, Singapore, and Japan indicate that playing positive games produces positive effects (Gentile et al., 2009; Greitemeyer & Osswald, 2010). For example, playing Lemmings, where a goal is to help others, increases real-life helping. So, might a parallel effect occur after playing games that enact violence? Violent video games became an issue for public debate after teenagers in more than a dozen places seemed to mimic the carnage in the shooter games they had so often played (Anderson, 2004a). In 2002, two Grand Rapids, Michigan, teens and a man in his early twenties spent part of a night drinking beer and playing Grand Theft Auto III. Using simulated cars, they ran down pedestrians, then beat them with fists, leaving a bloody body behind (Kolker, 2002). The same teens and man then went out for a real drive. Spotting a 38-year-old man on a bicycle, they ran him down with their car, got out, stomped and punched him, and returned home to play the game some more. (The victim, a father of three, died six days later.)

When combining data from 400 studies with 130,296 participants, Craig Anderson and his colleagues (2010) found that playing violent video games did indeed increase aggression. The finding held for youth and for young adults; in North America, Japan, and Western Europe; and with each of three major research designs (correlational, experimental, and longitudinal). In a 2010 statement submitted for a U.S. Supreme Court case, Anderson was joined by more than 100 social scientists in explaining that "the psychological processes underlying such effects are well understood and include: imitation, observational learning, priming of cognitive, emotional, and behavioral scripts, physiological arousal, and emotional desensitization" (Sacks et al., 2011).

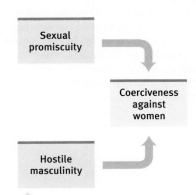

FIGURE 13.11

Men who sexually coerce women The recipe for coercion against women combines an impersonal approach to sex with a hostile masculinity. (Adapted from Malamuth, 1996.)

Coincidence or contributing factor? In 2011, Norwegian Anders Behring Breivik bombed government buildings in Oslo, and then went to a youth camp where he shot and killed 69 people, mostly teens. As a player of first-person shooter games, Breivik stirred debate when he commented that "I see MW2 [Modern Warfare 2] more as a part of my training-simulation than anything else." Did his violent game playing contribute to his violence, or was it a mere coincidental association? To explore such questions, psychologists experiment.

REUTERS/Andrew Berwick via www.freak.no/Handout

"What sense does it make to forbid selling to a 13-year-old a magazine with an image of a nude woman, while protecting the sale to that 13-year-old of an interactive video game in which he actively, but virtually, binds and gags the woman, then tortures and kills her?"

U.S. Supreme Court Justice Stephen Breyer, dissenting opinion, 2011

Consider some evidence:

- University men who spent the most hours playing violent video games tended to be the most physically aggressive (for example, to acknowledge having hit or attacked someone else) (Anderson & Dill, 2000).

- People with extensive experience in violent video gaming display desensitization to violence, as shown by blunted brain responses; they also are less likely to help an injured victim (Bartholow et al., 2006; Bushman & Anderson, 2009).

- After playing a violent rather than a neutral or prosocial video game, people become more likely to perceive immigrant outgroups as less than human (Greitemeyer & McLatchie, 2011).

Young adolescents who play a lot of violent video games see the world as more hostile. Compared with nongaming kids, they get into more arguments and fights and get worse grades (Gentile, 2009). Ah, but is this merely because naturally hostile kids are drawn to such games? Apparently not. Comparisons of gamers and nongamers who scored low in hostility revealed a difference in the number of reported fights: 38 percent of the violent-game players had been in fights, versus only 4 percent of the nongamers. Over time, the nongamers became more likely to have fights only if they started playing the violent games (Anderson, 2004a). Among German adolescents, today's violent game playing also predicts future aggression, but today's aggression does not predict future game playing (Möller & Krahé, 2008).

Some researchers believe that, due partly to the more active participation and rewarded violence of game play, violent video games have even greater effects on aggressive behavior and cognition than do violent television and movies (Anderson & Warburton, 2012). Some of these researchers suggest that the effects of violent gaming are comparable to the toxic effects of asbestos or second-hand smoke exposure (Bushman et al., 2010). "Playing violent video games probably will not turn your child into a psychopathic killer," acknowledged researcher Brad Bushman (2011), "but I would want to know how the child treats his or her parents, how they treat their siblings, how much compassion they have."

©Microsoft Corporation. All Rights Reserved.

Others are unimpressed by violent-game-effect findings (Ferguson & Kilburn, 2010). They note that from 1996 to 2006, youth violence was declining while video game sales were increasing. Moreover, some point out that avid game players are quick and sharp: They develop speedy reaction times and enhanced visual skills (Dye et al., 2009; Green et al., 2010). The focused fun of game playing can satisfy basic needs for a sense of competence, control, and social connection (Przbylski et al., 2010). And in fact, a 2011 Supreme Court decision overturned a California state law that banned violent video game sales to children (modeled after the bans on sales of sexually explicit materials to children). The First Amendment's free speech guarantee protects even offensive games, said the court's majority, which was unpersuaded by the evidence of harm. So, the debate continues.

★ ★ ★

To sum up, significant behaviors, such as aggression, usually have many determinants, making any single explanation an oversimplification. Asking what causes aggression is therefore like asking what causes cancer. Asbestos exposure, for example, is indeed a cancer cause, albeit only one among many. Research reveals many different biological, psychological, and social-cultural influences on aggressive behavior. Like so much else, aggression is a biopsychosocial phenomenon (**FIGURE 13.12**).

It is also important to note that many people are leading gentle, even heroic lives amid personal and social stresses, reminding us again that individuals differ. Indeed, historical trends suggest that the world is increasingly nonviolent (Pinker, 2011). The person matters. That people vary over time and place reminds us that environments also differ. Yesterday's plundering Vikings have become today's peace-promoting Scandinavians. Like all behavior, aggression arises from the interaction of persons and situations.

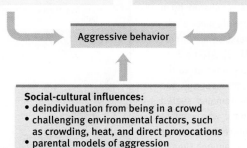

Biological influences:
• genetic influences
• biochemical influences, such as testosterone and alcohol
• neural influences, such as a severe head injury

Psychological influences:
• believing you've drunk alcohol (whether you actually have or not)
• frustration
• aggressive role models
• rewards for aggressive behavior
• low self-control

Aggressive behavior

Social-cultural influences:
• deindividuation from being in a crowd
• challenging environmental factors, such as crowding, heat, and direct provocations
• parental models of aggression
• minimal father involvement
• exposure to violent media

FIGURE 13.12

Biopsychosocial understanding of aggression Because many factors contribute to aggressive behavior, there are many ways to change such behavior, including learning anger management and communication skills, and avoiding violent media and video games.

RETRIEVE IT

• What psychological, biological, and social-cultural influences interact to produce aggressive behaviors?

ANSWER: Our biology (our genes, neural systems, and biochemistry—including testosterone and alcohol levels) influences our tendencies to be aggressive. Psychological factors (such as frustration, previous rewards for aggressive acts, and observation of others' aggression) can trigger any aggressive tendencies we may have. Social influences, such as exposure to violent media, and cultural influences, such as whether we've grown up in a "culture of honor" or had a father-absent home, can also affect our aggressive responses.

Attraction

Pause a moment and think about your relationships with two people—a close friend and someone who has stirred your feelings of romantic love. What psychological chemistry binds us together in these special sorts of attachments that help us cope with all other relationships? Social psychology suggests some answers.

The Psychology of Attraction

13-12: Why do we befriend or fall in love with some people but not others?

We endlessly wonder how we can win others' affection and what makes our own affections flourish or fade. Does familiarity breed contempt, or does it intensify affection? Do birds of a feather flock together, or do opposites attract? Is beauty only skin deep, or does attractiveness matter greatly? To explore these questions, let's consider three ingredients of our liking for one another: proximity, attractiveness, and similarity.

Proximity Before friendships become close, they must begin. *Proximity*—geographic nearness—is friendship's most powerful predictor. Proximity provides opportunities for aggression, but much more often it breeds liking. Study after study reveals that people are most inclined to like, and even to marry, those who live in the same neighborhood, who sit nearby in class, who work in the same office, who share the same parking lot, who eat in the same dining hall. Look around. Mating starts with meeting. (For a twenty-first-century technology that connects people not in physical proximity, see Close-Up: Online Matchmaking and Speed Dating on the next page.)

Online Matchmaking and Speed Dating

If you have not found a romantic partner in your immediate proximity, why not cast a wider net by joining the estimated 30 million people who each year try one of the 1500 online dating services (Ellin, 2009)?

Published research on the effectiveness of Internet matchmaking services is sparse. Nevertheless, Katelyn McKenna and John Bargh and their colleagues have offered a surprising finding: Compared with relationships formed in person, Internet-formed friendships and romantic relationships are, on average, more likely to last beyond two years (Bargh et al., 2002, 2004; McKenna & Bargh, 1998, 2000; McKenna et al., 2002). In one of their studies, people disclosed more, with less posturing, to those whom they met online. When conversing online with someone for 20 minutes, they felt more liking for that person than they did for someone they had met and talked with face to face. This was true even when (unknown to them) it was the same person! Internet friendships often feel as real and important to people as in-person relationships. Small wonder that Harris Interactive (2010) found one leading online matchmaker enabling more than 500 U.S. marriages a day.

Speed dating pushes the search for romance into high gear. In a process pioneered by a matchmaking Jewish rabbi, people meet a succession of prospective partners, either in person or via webcam (Bower, 2009). After a 3- to 8-minute conversation, people move on to the next person. (In an in-person meeting, one partner—usually the woman—remains seated and the other circulates.) Those who want to meet again can arrange for future contacts. For many participants, 4 minutes is enough time to form a feeling about a conversational partner and to register whether the partner likes them (Eastwick & Finkel, 2008a,b).

Researchers have quickly realized that speed dating offers a unique opportunity for studying influences on our first impressions of potential romantic partners. Among recent findings are these:

- Men are more transparent. Observers (male or female) watching videos of speed-dating encounters can read a man's level of romantic interest more accurately than a woman's (Place et al., 2009).
- Given more options, people's choices become more superficial. Meeting lots of potential partners leads people to focus

THEY MET ONLINE.

AND DO YOU, FUNNYGRL@BIZONE.NET, TAKE HARLEY99@COMCO.COM...

on more easily assessed characteristics, such as height and weight (Lenton & Francesconi, 2010). This was true even when researchers controlled for time spent with each partner.

- Men wish for future contact with more of their speed dates; women tend to be more choosy. But this gender difference disappears if the conventional roles are reversed, so that men stay seated while women circulate (Finkel & Eastwick, 2009).

---

mere exposure effect the phenomenon that repeated exposure to novel stimuli increases liking of them.

Proximity breeds liking partly because of the **mere exposure effect.** Repeated exposure to novel stimuli increases our liking for them. This applies to nonsense syllables, musical selections, geometric figures, Chinese characters, human faces, and the letters of our own name (Moreland & Zajonc, 1982; Nuttin, 1987; Zajonc, 2001). We are even somewhat more likely to marry someone whose first or last name resembles our own (Jones et al., 2004).

So, within certain limits, familiarity breeds fondness (Bornstein, 1989, 1999). Researchers demonstrated this by having four equally attractive women silently attend a 200-student class for zero, 5, 10, or 15 class sessions (Moreland & Beach, 1992). At the end of the course, students were shown slides of each woman and asked to rate her attractiveness. The most attractive? The ones they'd seen most often. The phenomenon would come as no surprise to the young Taiwanese man who wrote more than 700 letters to his girlfriend, urging her to marry him. She did marry—the mail carrier (Steinberg, 1993).

The mere exposure effect The mere exposure effect applies even to ourselves. Because the human face is not perfectly symmetrical, the face we see in the mirror is not the same face our friends see. Most of us prefer the familiar mirror image, while our friends like the reverse (Mita et al., 1977). The real British Prime Minister David Cameron is at left. The person he sees in the mirror each morning is shown at right, and that's the photo he would probably prefer.

Voter   George Bush   60:40 Blend

© Jeremy Bailenson and Nick Yee

FIGURE 13.13

I like the candidate who looks a bit like dear old me Jeremy Bailenson and his colleagues (2005) incorporated morphed features of voters' faces into the faces of 2004 U.S. presidential candidates George Bush (shown here) and John Kerry. Without conscious awareness of their own incorporated features, the participants became more likely to favor the candidate whose face incorporated some of their own features.

No face is more familiar than your own. And that helps explain an interesting finding by Lisa DeBruine (2004): We like other people when their faces incorporate some morphed features of our own. When DeBruine (2002) had McMaster University students (both men and women) play a game with a supposed other player, they were more trusting and cooperative when the other person's image had some of their own facial features morphed into it. In me I trust. (See also **FIGURE 13.13**.)

Physical Attractiveness Once proximity affords us contact, what most affects our first impressions? The person's sincerity? Intelligence? Personality? Hundreds of experiments reveal that it is something far more superficial: Physical appearance. This finding is unnerving for most of us who were taught that "beauty is only skin deep" and that "appearances can be deceiving."

In one early study, researchers randomly matched new University of Minnesota students for a Welcome Week dance (Walster et al., 1966). Before the dance, the researchers gave each student a battery of personality and aptitude tests, and they rated each student's level of physical attractiveness. On the night of the blind date, the couples danced and talked for more than two hours and then took a brief intermission to rate their dates. What determined whether they liked each other? Only one thing seemed to matter: appearance. Both the men and the women liked good-looking dates best. Women are more likely than men to say that another's looks don't affect them (Lippa, 2007). But studies show that a man's looks do affect women's behavior (Feingold, 1990; Sprecher, 1989; Woll, 1986). Speed-dating experiments confirm that attractiveness influences first impressions for both sexes (Belot & Francesconi, 2006; Finkel & Eastwick, 2008).

Physical attractiveness also predicts how often people date and how popular they feel. It affects initial impressions of people's personalities. We don't assume that attractive people are more compassionate, but research participants have perceived them as healthier, happier, more sensitive, more successful, and more socially skilled (Eagly et al., 1991; Feingold, 1992; Hatfield & Sprecher, 1986). Attractive, well-dressed people have been more likely to make a favorable impression on potential employers, and they have tended to be more successful in their jobs (Cash & Janda, 1984; Langlois et al., 2000; Solomon, 1987). Income analyses show a penalty for plainness or obesity and a premium for beauty (Engemann & Owyang, 2005).

An analysis of 100 top-grossing films from 1940 into the 1990s found that attractive characters were portrayed as morally superior to unattractive characters (Smith et al., 1999). But Hollywood modeling doesn't explain why, to judge from their gazing times, even babies have preferred attractive over unattractive faces (Langlois et al., 1987). Some blind people feel similarly, as University of Birmingham professor John Hull (1990, p. 23) discovered after going blind. A colleague's remarks on a woman's beauty would strangely affect his feelings. He found this "deplorable. . . . What can it matter to me what sighted men think of women . . . yet I do care what sighted men think, and I do not seem able to throw off this prejudice."

When Neanderthals fall in love.

© 1999 by Leigh Robin, Creators Syndicate, Inc.

"Personal beauty is a greater recommendation than any letter of introduction."

Aristotle, Apothegems, *330* B.C.E.

Percentage of Men and Women Who "Constantly Think About Their Looks"

	Men	Women
Canada	18%	20%
United States	17	27
Mexico	40	45
Venezuela	47	65

From Roper Starch survey, reported by McCool (1999).

Women have 91 percent of cosmetic procedures (ASPS, 2010). Women also recall others' appearance better than do men (Mast & Hall, 2006).

For those who find importance of looks unfair and unenlightened, two attractiveness findings may be reassuring. First, people's attractiveness has been surprisingly unrelated to their self-esteem and happiness (Diener et al., 1995; Major et al., 1984). Unless we have just compared ourselves with superattractive people, few of us (thanks, perhaps, to the mere exposure effect) view ourselves as unattractive (Thornton & Moore, 1993). Second, strikingly attractive people are sometimes suspicious that praise for their work may simply be a reaction to their looks. Less attractive people have been more likely to accept praise as sincere (Berscheid, 1981).

Beauty is in the eye of the culture. Hoping to look attractive, people across the globe have pierced and tattooed various body parts, lengthened their necks, bound their feet, and dyed or painted their skin and hair. They have gorged themselves to achieve a full figure or liposuctioned fat to achieve a slim one, applied chemicals hoping to rid themselves of unwanted hair or to regrow wanted hair, strapped on leather garments to make their breasts seem smaller or surgically filled their breasts with silicone and worn Wonderbras to make them look bigger. Cultural ideals change over time. For women in North America, the ultra-thin ideal of the Roaring Twenties gave way to the soft, voluptuous Marilyn Monroe ideal of the 1950s, only to be replaced by today's lean yet busty ideal.

If we're not born attractive, we may try to buy beauty. Americans now spend more on beauty supplies than on education and social services combined. Still not satisfied, millions undergo plastic surgery, teeth capping and whitening, Botox skin smoothing, and laser hair removal (ASPS, 2010).

Some aspects of attractiveness, however, do cross place and time (Cunningham et al., 2005; Langlois et al., 2000). By providing reproductive clues, bodies influence sexual attraction. As evolutionary psychologists explain (see Chapter 5), men in many cultures, from Australia to Zambia, judge women as more attractive if they have a youthful, fertile appearance, suggested by a low waist-to-hip ratio (Karremans et al., 2010; Perilloux et al., 2010; Platek & Singh, 2010). Women feel attracted to healthy-looking men, but especially—and the more so when ovulating—to those who seem mature, dominant, masculine, and affluent (Gallup & Frederick, 2010; Gangestad et al., 2010). But faces matter, too. When people separately rate opposite-sex faces and bodies, the face tends to be the better predictor of overall physical attractiveness (Currie & Little, 2009; Peters et al., 2007).

Our feelings also influence our attractiveness judgments. Imagine two people. The first is honest, humorous, and polite. The second is rude, unfair, and abusive. Which one is more attractive? Most people perceive the person with the appealing traits as also more physically attractive (Lewandowski et al., 2007). Those we like we find attractive. In a Rodgers and Hammerstein musical, Prince Charming asks Cinderella, "Do I love you because you're beautiful, or are you beautiful because I love you?" Chances are it's both. As we see our loved ones again and again, their physical imperfections grow less noticeable and their attractiveness grows more apparent (Beaman & Klentz, 1983; Gross & Crofton, 1977). Shakespeare said it in *A Midsummer Night's Dream:* "Love looks not with the eyes, but with the mind." Come to love someone and watch beauty grow.

In the eye of the beholder Conceptions of attractiveness vary by culture. Yet some adult physical features, such as a healthy appearance, seem attractive everywhere.

Extreme makeover In affluent, beauty-conscious cultures, increasing numbers of people, such as this woman from the American TV show *Extreme Makeover,* have turned to cosmetic surgery to improve their looks. If money were no concern, might you ever do the same?

Similarity So proximity has brought you into contact with someone, and your appearance has made an acceptable first impression. What now influences whether you will become friends? As you get to know each other better, will the chemistry be better if you are opposites or if you are alike?

It makes a good story—extremely different types liking or loving each other: Frog and Toad in Arnold Lobel's books, Edward and Bella in the *Twilight* series. The stories delight us by expressing what we seldom experience, for in real life, opposites retract (Rosenbaum, 1986). Compared with randomly paired people, friends and couples have been far more likely to share common attitudes, beliefs, and interests (and, for that matter, age, religion, race, education, intelligence, smoking behavior, and economic status).

Moreover, the more alike people are, the more their liking has endured (Byrne, 1971). Journalist Walter Lippmann was right to suppose that love lasts "when the lovers love many things together, and not merely each other." Similarity breeds content. Dissimilarity often fosters disfavor, which helps explain many straight men's disapproval of gay men who are doubly dissimilar from themselves in sexual orientation and gender roles (Lehavot & Lambert, 2007).

Proximity, attractiveness, and similarity are not the only determinants of attraction. We also like those who like us. This is especially so when our self-image is low. When we believe someone likes us, we feel good and respond to them warmly, which leads them to like us even more (Curtis & Miller, 1986). To be liked is powerfully rewarding.

Indeed, all the findings we have considered so far can be explained by a simple *reward theory of attraction:* We will like those whose behavior is rewarding to us, and we will continue relationships that offer more rewards than costs. When people live or work in close proximity with us, it costs less time and effort to develop the friendship and enjoy its benefits. When people are attractive, they are aesthetically pleasing, and associating with them can be socially rewarding. When people share our views, they reward us by validating our own.

Beauty grows with mere exposure Herman Miller, Inc.'s famed Aeron chair initially received high comfort ratings but abysmal beauty ratings. To some it looked like "lawn furniture" or "a giant prehistoric insect" (Gladwell, 2005). But then, with design awards, media visibility, and imitators, the ugly duckling came to be the company's best-selling chair ever and to be seen as beautiful. With people, too, beauty lies partly in the beholder's eye and can grow with exposure.

Aeron work chair, courtesy of Herman Miller, Inc.

RETRIEVE IT

• People tend to marry someone who lives or works nearby. This is an example of the _____ _____ _____ in action.

ANSWER: mere exposure effect

• How does being physically attractive influence others' perceptions?

ANSWER: Being physically attractive tends to elicit positive first impressions. People tend to assume that attractive people are healthier, happier, and more socially skilled than others are.

Romantic Love

13-13: How does romantic love typically change as time passes?

Sometimes people move quickly from initial impressions, to friendship, to the more intense, complex, and mysterious state of romantic love. If love endures, temporary *passionate love* will mellow into a lingering *companionate love* (Hatfield, 1988).

Snapshots at jasonlove.com

© Jason Love

Bill looked at Susan, Susan at Bill. Suddenly death didn't seem like an option. This was love at first sight.

"When two people are under the influence of the most violent, most insane, most delusive, and most transient of passions, they are required to swear that they will remain in that excited, abnormal, and exhausting condition continuously until death do them part."

George Bernard Shaw, "Getting Married," 1908

passionate love an aroused state of intense positive absorption in another, usually present at the beginning of a love relationship.

companionate love the deep affectionate attachment we feel for those with whom our lives are intertwined.

equity a condition in which people receive from a relationship in proportion to what they give to it.

self-disclosure revealing intimate aspects of oneself to others.

Passionate Love A key ingredient of **passionate love** is arousal. The two-factor theory of emotion (Chapter 10) can help us understand this intense positive absorption in another (Hatfield, 1988). That theory assumes that:

- emotions have two ingredients—*physical arousal* plus *cognitive appraisal.*
- arousal from any source can enhance one emotion or another, depending on how we interpret and label the arousal.

In one famous experiment, researchers studied people crossing two bridges above British Columbia's rocky Capilano River (Dutton & Aron, 1974, 1989). One, a swaying footbridge, was 230 feet above the rocks; the other was low and solid. The researchers had an attractive young woman intercept men coming off each bridge, and ask their help in filling out a short questionnaire. She then offered her phone number in case they wanted to hear more about her project. Far more of those who had just crossed the high bridge—which left their hearts pounding—accepted the number and later called the woman. To be revved up and to associate some of that arousal with a desirable person is to feel the pull of passion. Adrenaline makes the heart grow fonder. And when sexual desire is supplemented by a growing attachment, the result is the passion of romantic love (Berscheid, 2010).

Companionate Love Although the desire and attachment of romantic love often endure, the intense absorption in the other, the thrill of the romance, the giddy "floating on a cloud" feelings typically fade. Does this mean the French are correct in saying that "love makes the time pass and time makes love pass"? Or can friendship and commitment keep a relationship going after the passion cools?

The evidence indicates that, as love matures, it becomes a steadier **companionate love**—a deep, affectionate attachment (Hatfield, 1988). The flood of passion-facilitating hormones (testosterone, dopamine, adrenaline) subsides and another hormone, oxytocin, supports feelings of trust, calmness, and bonding with the mate. In the most satisfying of marriages, attraction and sexual desire endure, minus the obsession of early stage romance (Acevedo & Aron, 2009).

There may be adaptive wisdom to the shift from passion to attachment (Reis & Aron, 2008). Passionate love often produces children, whose survival is aided by the parents' waning obsession with one another. Failure to appreciate passionate love's limited half-life can doom a relationship (Berscheid et al., 1984). Indeed, recognizing the short duration of obsessive passionate love, some societies deem such feelings to be an irrational reason for marrying. Better, they say, to choose (or have someone choose for you) a partner with a compatible background and interests. Non-Western cultures, where people rate love less important for marriage, do have lower divorce rates (Levine et al., 1995).

One key to a gratifying and enduring relationship is **equity.** When equity exists—when both partners receive in proportion to what they give—their chances for sustained and satisfying companionate love have been good (Gray-Little & Burks, 1983; Van Yperen & Buunk, 1990). In one national survey, "sharing household chores" ranked third, after "faithfulness" and a "happy sexual relationship," on a list of nine things people associated with successful marriages. "I like hugs. I like kisses. But what I really love is help with the dishes," summarized the Pew Research Center (2007).

Equity's importance extends beyond marriage. Mutually sharing self and possessions, making decisions together, giving and getting emotional support, promoting and caring about each other's welfare—all of these acts are at the core of every type of loving relationship (Sternberg & Grajek, 1984). It's true for lovers, for parent and child, and for close friends.

Another vital ingredient of loving relationships is **self-disclosure,** the revealing of intimate details about ourselves—our likes and dislikes, our dreams and worries, our proud and shameful moments. "When I am with my friend," noted the Roman statesman Seneca, "me thinks I am alone, and as much at liberty to speak anything as to think it." Self-disclosure breeds liking, and liking breeds self-disclosure (Collins & Miller,

HI & LOIS

Reprinted with special permission of King Features Syndicate.

1994). As one person reveals a little, the other reciprocates, the first then reveals more, and on and on, as friends or lovers move to deeper and deeper intimacy (Baumeister & Bratslavsky, 1999).

One experiment marched student pairs through 45 minutes of increasingly self-disclosing conversation—from "When did you last sing to yourself?" to "When did you last cry in front of another person? By yourself?" Others spent the time with small-talk questions, such as "What was your high school like?" (Aron et al., 1997). By the experiment's end, those experiencing the escalating intimacy felt much closer to their conversation partner than did the small-talkers.

In addition to equity and self-disclosure, a third key to enduring love is *positive support*. While relationship conflicts are inevitable, we can ask ourselves whether our communications more often express sarcasm or support, scorn or sympathy, sneers or smiles. For unhappy couples, disagreements, criticisms, and put-downs are routine. For happy couples in enduring relationships, positive interactions (compliments, touches, laughing) outnumber negative interactions (sarcasm, disapproval, insults) by at least 5 to 1 (Gottman, 2007; see also Sullivan et al., 2010).

In the mathematics of love, self-disclosing intimacy + mutually supportive equity = enduring companionate love.

AP Photo/Archaeological Society SAP, ho

Love is an ancient thing In 2007, a 5000 to 6000 year old "Romeo and Juliet" young couple was unearthed locked in embrace, near Rome.

RETRIEVE IT

• How does the two-factor theory of emotion help explain *passionate love?*

ANSWER: Emotions consist of (1) physical arousal and (2) our interpretation of that arousal. Researchers have found that any source of arousal will be interpreted as passion in the presence of a desirable person.

• Two vital components for maintaining companionate love are _____ and _____-_____.

ANSWERS: equity; self-disclosure

Altruism

13-14: When are people most—and least—likely to help?

Altruism is an unselfish concern for the welfare of others. In rescuing his jailer, Dirk Willems exemplified altruism. So also did Carl Wilkens and Paul Ruesabagina in Kigali, Rwanda. Wilkens, a Seventh Day Adventist missionary, was living there in 1994 with his family when Hutu militia began to slaughter the Tutsis. The U.S. government, church leaders, and friends all implored Wilkens to leave. He refused. After evacuating his family, and even after every other American had left Kigali, he alone stayed and contested the 800,000-person genocide. When the militia came to kill him and his Tutsi servants, Wilkens' Hutu neighbors deterred them. Despite repeated death threats, he spent his days running roadblocks to take food and water to orphanages and to negotiate, plead, and bully his way through the bloodshed, saving lives time and again. "It just seemed the right thing to do," he later explained (Kristof, 2004).

altruism unselfish regard for the welfare of others.

REUTERS/Finbarr O' Reilly

Why do genocides occur? An estimated 800,000 people died during the Rwandan Genocide of 1994, when Hutu groups carried out mass killings of Tutsis. Social psychology research helps us understand some of the factors motivating genocides. We tend to categorize our world into us and them, and, when threatened, to feel greater animosity toward outside groups.

Elsewhere in Kigali, Rusesabagina, a Hutu married to a Tutsi and the acting manager of a luxury hotel, was sheltering more than 1200 terrified Tutsis and moderate Hutus. When international peacemakers abandoned the city and hostile militia threatened his guests in the "Hotel Rwanda" (as it came to be called in a 2004 movie), the courageous Rusesabagina began cashing in past favors. He bribed the militia and telephoned influential people abroad to exert pressure on local authorities, thereby sparing the lives of the hotel's occupants despite the surrounding chaos. Both Wilkens and Rusesabagina were displaying altruism, an unselfish regard for the welfare of others.

Altruism became a major concern of social psychologists after an especially vile act of sexual violence. On March 13, 1964, a stalker repeatedly stabbed Kitty Genovese, then raped her as she lay dying outside her Queens, New York, apartment at 3:30 A.M. "Oh, my God, he stabbed me!" Genovese screamed into the early morning stillness. "Please help me!" Windows opened and lights went on as neighbors heard her screams. Her attacker fled and then returned to stab and rape her again. Not until he had fled for good did anyone so much as call the police, at 3:50 A.M.

Bystander Intervention

Reflecting on the Genovese murder and other such tragedies, most commentators were outraged by the bystanders' "apathy" and "indifference." Rather than blaming the onlookers, social psychologists John Darley and Bibb Latané (1968b) attributed their inaction to an important situational factor—the presence of others. Given certain circumstances, they suspected, most of us might behave similarly.

After staging emergencies under various conditions, Darley and Latané assembled their findings into a decision scheme: We will help only if the situation enables us first to *notice* the incident, then to *interpret* it as an emergency, and finally to *assume responsibility* for helping (**FIGURE 13.14**). At each step, the presence of others can turn us away from the path that leads to helping.

Darley and Latané reached their conclusions after interpreting the results of a series of experiments. For example, they simulated a physical emergency in their laboratory as students participated in a discussion over an intercom. Each student was in a separate cubicle, and only the person whose microphone was switched on could be heard. When his turn came, one student (an accomplice of the experimenters) made sounds as though he were having an epileptic seizure, and he called for help (Darley & Latané, 1968a).

How did the other students react? As **FIGURE 13.15** shows, those who believed only they could hear the victim—and therefore thought they alone were responsible for helping him—usually went to his aid. Students who thought others also could hear the victim's cries were more likely to react as Kitty Genovese's neighbors had. When more people shared responsibility for helping—when there was a *diffusion of responsibility*—any single listener was less likely to help.

Hundreds of additional experiments have confirmed this **bystander effect.** For example, researchers and their assistants took 1497 elevator rides in three cities and

FIGURE 13.14

The decision-making process for bystander intervention Before helping, one must first notice an emergency, then correctly interpret it, and then feel responsible. (From Darley & Latané, 1968b.)

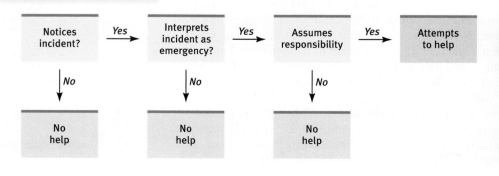

Viviane Moos/Corbis

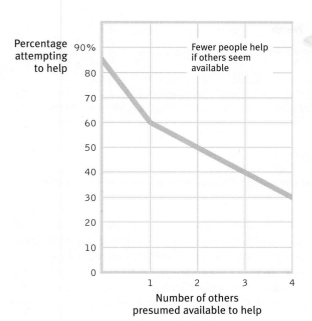

Percentage attempting to help

Fewer people help if others seem available

Number of others presumed available to help

FIGURE 13.15

Responses to a simulated physical emergency When people thought they alone heard the calls for help from a person they believed to be having an epileptic seizure, they usually helped. But when they thought four others were also hearing the calls, fewer than a third responded. (From Darley & Latané, 1968a.)

bystander effect the tendency for any given bystander to be less likely to give aid if other bystanders are present.

"accidentally" dropped coins or pencils in front of 4813 fellow passengers (Latané & Dabbs, 1975). When alone with the person in need, 40 percent helped; in the presence of 5 other bystanders, only 20 percent helped.

Observations of behavior in thousands of such situations—relaying an emergency phone call, aiding a stranded motorist, donating blood, picking up dropped books, contributing money, giving time—show that the *best* odds of our helping someone occur when

- the person appears to need and deserve help.
- the person is in some way similar to us.
- the person is a woman.
- we have just observed someone else being helpful.
- we are not in a hurry.
- we are in a small town or rural area.
- we are feeling guilty.
- we are focused on others and not preoccupied.
- we are in a good mood.

This last result, that happy people are helpful people, is one of the most consistent findings in all of psychology. As poet Robert Browning (1868) observed, "Oh, make us happy and you make us good!" It doesn't matter how we are cheered. Whether by being made to feel successful and intelligent, by thinking happy thoughts, by finding money, or even by receiving a posthypnotic suggestion, we become more generous and more eager to help (Carlson et al., 1988).

So happiness breeds helpfulness. But it's also true that helpfulness breeds happiness. Making charitable donations activates brain areas associated with reward (Harbaugh et al., 2007). That helps explain a curious finding: People who give money away are happier than those who spend it almost entirely on themselves. In one experiment, researchers gave people an envelope with cash and instructions either to spend it on themselves or to spend it on others (Dunn et al., 2008). Which group was happiest at the day's end? It was, indeed, those assigned to the spend-it-on-others condition.

RETRIEVE IT

• Why didn't anybody help Kitty Genovese? What social relations principle did this incident illustrate?

ANSWER: In the presence of others, an individual is less likely to notice a situation, correctly interpret it as an emergency, and then take responsibility for offering help. The Kitty Genovese case demonstrated this *bystander effect*, as each witness assumed many others were also aware of the event.

The Norms for Helping

13-15: How do social exchange theory and social norms explain helping behavior?

Why do we help? One widely held view is that self-interest underlies all human interactions, that our constant goal is to maximize rewards and minimize costs. Accountants call it *cost-benefit analysis.* Philosophers call it *utilitarianism.* Social psychologists call it **social exchange theory.** If you are pondering whether to donate blood, you may weigh the costs of doing so (time, discomfort, and anxiety) against the benefits (reduced guilt, social approval, and good feelings). If the rewards exceed the costs, you will help.

Others believe that we help because we have been socialized to do so, through norms that prescribe how we *ought* to behave. Through socialization, we learn the **reciprocity norm,** the expectation that we should return help, not harm, to those who have helped us. In our relations with others of similar status, the reciprocity norm compels us to give (in favors, gifts, or social invitations) about as much as we receive.

The reciprocity norm kicked in after Dave Tally, a Tempe, Arizona, homeless man, found $3300 in a backpack that had been lost by an Arizona State University student headed to buy a used car (Lacey, 2010). Instead of using the cash for much-needed bike repairs, food, and shelter, Tally turned the backpack in to the social service agency where he volunteered. To reciprocate Tally's help, the student thanked him with a monetary reward. Hearing about Tally's self-giving deeds, dozens of others also sent him money and job offers.

We also learn a **social-responsibility norm:** that we should help those who need our help, such as young children and others who cannot give as much as they receive, even if the costs outweigh the benefits. People who attend weekly religious services often are admonished to practice the social-responsibility norm, and sometimes they do. In American surveys, they have reported twice as many volunteer hours spent helping the poor and infirm, compared with those who rarely or never attend religious services (Hodgkinson & Weitzman, 1992; Independent Sector, 2002). Between 2006 and 2008, Gallup polls sampled more than 300,000 people across 140 countries, comparing those "highly religious" (who said religion was important to them and who had attended a religious service in the prior week) to those less religious. The highly religious, despite being poorer, were about 50 percent more likely to report having "donated money to a charity in the last month" and to have volunteered time to an organization (Pelham & Crabtree, 2008).

Although positive social norms encourage generosity and enable group living, conflicts often divide us.

Conflict and Peacemaking

With astonishing speed, recent democratic movements have swept away totalitarian rule in Eastern European and Arab countries. Yet *every day,* the world continues to spend more than $3 billion for arms and armies—money that could have been used for housing, nutrition, education, and health care. Knowing that wars begin in human minds, psychologists have wondered: What in the human mind causes destructive conflict? How might the perceived threats of social diversity be replaced by a spirit of cooperation?

social exchange theory the theory that our social behavior is an exchange process, the aim of which is to maximize benefits and minimize costs.

reciprocity norm an expectation that people will help, not hurt, those who have helped them.

social-responsibility norm an expectation that people will help those dependent upon them.

conflict a perceived incompatibility of actions, goals, or ideas.

social trap a situation in which the conflicting parties, by each rationally pursuing their self-interest, become caught in mutually destructive behavior.

Elements of Conflict

13-16: How do social traps and mirror-image perceptions fuel social conflict?

To a social psychologist, a **conflict** is a perceived incompatibility of actions, goals, or ideas. The elements of conflict are much the same, whether we are speaking of nations at war, cultural groups feuding within a society, or partners sparring in a relationship. In each situation, people become enmeshed in potentially destructive processes that can produce results no one wants. Among these processes are social traps and distorted perceptions.

Social Traps In some situations, we support our collective well-being by pursuing our personal interests. As capitalist Adam Smith wrote in *The Wealth of Nations* (1776), "It is not from the benevolence of the butcher, the brewer, or the baker that we expect our dinner, but from their regard to their own interest." In other situations, we harm our collective well-being by pursuing our personal interests. Such situations are **social traps.**

Consider the simple game matrix in **FIGURE 13.16**, which is similar to those used in experiments with countless thousands of people. Both sides can win or both can lose, depending on the players' individual choices. Pretend you are Person 1, and that you and Person 2 will each receive the amount shown after you separately choose either *A* or *B*. (You might invite someone to look at the matrix with you and take the role of Person 2.) Which do you choose—*A* or *B*?

You and Person 2 are caught in a dilemma. If you both choose *A*, you both benefit, making $5 each. Neither of you benefits if you both choose *B*, for neither of you makes anything. Nevertheless, on any single trial you serve your own interests if you choose *B*: You can't lose, and you might make $10. But the same is true for the other person. Hence, the social trap: As long as you both pursue your own immediate best interest and choose *B*, you will both end up with nothing—the typical result—when you could have made $5.

Many real-life situations similarly pit our individual interests against our communal well-being. Individual car owners reason, "Hybrid and electric cars are more expensive and not as cool as the model I'd like to buy. Besides, the fuel that I burn in my one car doesn't noticeably add to the greenhouse gases." When enough people reason similarly, the collective result threatens disaster—climate change with rising seas and more extreme weather.

Social traps challenge us to find ways of reconciling our right to pursue personal well-being with our responsibility for the well-being of all. Psychologists have therefore explored ways to convince people to cooperate for their mutual betterment—through

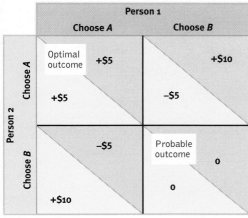

FIGURE 13.16
Social-trap game matrix By pursuing our self-interest and not trusting others, we can end up losers. To illustrate this, imagine playing the game above. The light-orange triangles show the outcomes for Person 1, which depend on the choices made by both players. If you were Person 1, would you choose *A* or *B*? (This game is called a *non-zero-sum* game because the outcomes need not add up to zero; both sides can win or both can lose.)

Not in my ocean! Many people support alternative energy sources, including wind turbines. But proposals to construct wind farms in real-world neighborhoods elicit less support. One such proposal, for locating wind turbines off the coast of Massachusetts' Nantucket Island, produced heated debate over the future benefits of clean energy versus the costs of altering treasured ocean views and, possibly, migratory bird routes.

mirror-image perceptions mutual views often held by conflicting people, as when each side sees itself as ethical and peaceful and views the other side as evil and aggressive.

agreed-upon *regulations,* through better *communication,* and through promoting *awareness* of our responsibilities toward community, nation, and the whole of humanity (Dawes, 1980; Linder, 1982; Sato, 1987). Given effective regulations, communication, and awareness, people more often cooperate, whether it be in playing a laboratory game or the real game of life.

Enemy Perceptions Psychologists have noted that those in conflict have a curious tendency to form diabolical images of one another. These distorted images are, ironically, so similar that we call them **mirror-image perceptions:** As we see "them"—as untrustworthy, with evil intentions—so "they" see us. Each demonizes the other.

Mirror-image perceptions can often feed a vicious cycle of hostility. If Juan believes Maria is annoyed with him, he may snub her, causing her to act in ways that justify his perception. As with individuals, so with countries. Perceptions become self-fulfilling prophecies.

We tend to see our own actions as responses to provocation, not as the causes of what happens next. Perceiving ourselves as returning tit for tat, we often hit back harder, as University College London volunteers did in one experiment (Shergill et al., 2003). After feeling pressure on their own finger, they were to use a mechanical device to press on another volunteer's finger. Although told to reciprocate with the same amount of pressure, they typically responded with about 40 percent more force than they had just experienced. Despite seeking only to respond in kind, their touches soon escalated to hard presses, much as when each child after a fight claims that "I just poked him, but he hit me harder."

The point is not that truth must lie midway between conflicting views (one may be more accurate). The point is that enemy perceptions often form mirror images. Moreover, as enemies change, so do perceptions. In American minds and media, the "bloodthirsty, cruel, treacherous" Japanese of World War II later became our "intelligent, hardworking, self-disciplined, resourceful allies" (Gallup, 1972).

RETRIEVE IT

- Why do sports fans tend to feel a sense of satisfaction when their archrival team loses? Why do such feelings, in other settings, make conflict resolution more challenging?

ANSWER: Sports fans may feel a part of an *ingroup* that sets itself apart from an *outgroup* (fans of the archrival team). Ingroup bias tends to develop, leading to prejudice and the view that the outgroup "deserves" misfortune. So, the archrival team's loss may seem justified. In conflicts, this kind of thinking is problematic, especially when each side in the conflict develops *mirror-image perceptions* of the other (distorted, negative images that are ironically similar).

Promoting Peace

13-17: How can we transform feelings of prejudice, aggression, and conflict into attitudes that promote peace?

How can we make peace? Can contact, cooperation, communication, and conciliation transform the ill will fed by prejudice and conflicts into peaceful attitudes? Research indicates that, in some cases, they can.

Contact Does it help to put two conflicting parties into close contact? It depends. When contact is noncompetitive and between parties of equal status, such as fellow store clerks, it typically helps. Initially prejudiced co-workers of different races have, in such circumstances, usually come to accept one another. This finding is confirmed by a statistical digest of more than 500 studies of face-to-face contact with outgroups (such as ethnic minorities, the elderly, and those with disabilities). Among the quarter-million people studied across 38 nations, contact has been correlated with, or in experimental studies has led to, more positive attitudes (Pettigrew & Tropp, 2011). Some examples:

- With interracial contact, South African Whites' and Blacks' "attitudes [have moved] into closer alignment" (Dixon et al., 2007; Finchilescu & Tredoux, 2010).

- Heterosexuals' attitudes toward gay people are influenced not only by what they know but also by whom they know (Smith et al., 2009). In one national survey, those who knowingly had a gay family member or close friend were twice as likely to support gay marriage as those who didn't—55 percent versus 25 percent (Neidorf & Morin, 2007).

- Even indirect contact with an outgroup member (via story reading or through a friend who has an outgroup friend) has reduced prejudice (Cameron & Rutland, 2006; Pettigrew et al., 2007).

However, contact is not always enough. In most desegregated schools, ethnic groups resegregate themselves in the lunchrooms and classrooms, and on the school grounds (Alexander & Tredoux, 2010; Clack et al., 2005; Schofield, 1986). People in each group often think that they would welcome more contact with the other group, but they assume the other group does not reciprocate the wish (Richeson & Shelton, 2007). "I don't reach out to them, because I don't want to be rebuffed; they don't reach out to me, because they're just not interested." When such mirror-image misperceptions are corrected, friendships may then form and prejudices melt.

Cooperation To see if enemies could overcome their differences, researcher Muzafer Sherif (1966) set a conflict in motion at a boys' summer camp. He separated 22 Oklahoma City boys into two separate camp areas. Then he had the two groups compete for prizes in a series of activities. Before long, each group became intensely proud of itself and hostile to the other group's "sneaky," "smart-alecky stinkers." Food wars broke out. Cabins were ransacked. Fistfights had to be broken up by camp counselors. Brought together, the two groups avoided each other, except to taunt and threaten. Little did they know that within a few days, they would be friends.

Sherif accomplished this by giving them **superordinate goals**—shared goals that could be achieved only through cooperation. When he arranged for the camp water supply to "fail," all 22 boys had to work together to restore water. To rent a movie in those pre-Netflix days, they all had to pool their resources. To move a stalled truck, the boys needed to combine their strength, pulling and pushing together. Having used isolation and competition to make strangers into enemies, Sherif used shared predicaments and goals to turn enemies into friends. What reduced conflict was not mere contact, but *cooperative* contact.

A shared predicament likewise had a powerfully unifying effect in the weeks after 9/11. Patriotism soared as Americans felt "we" were under attack. Gallup-surveyed approval of "our President" shot up from 51 percent the week before the attack to a highest-ever 90 percent level 10 days after (Newport, 2002). In chat groups and everyday speech, even the word *we* (relative to *I*) surged in the immediate aftermath (Pennebaker, 2002).

At such times, cooperation can lead people to define a new, inclusive group that dissolves their former subgroups (Dovidio & Gaertner, 1999). To accomplish this, you might seat members of two groups not on opposite sides, but alternately around a table. Give them a new, shared name. Have them work together. Then watch "us" and "them" become "we." After 9/11, one 18-year-old New Jersey man described this shift in his own social identity: "I just thought of myself as Black. But now I feel like I'm an American, more than ever" (Sengupta, 2001). In a real experiment, White Americans who read a newspaper article about a terrorist threat against all Americans subsequently expressed reduced prejudice against Black Americans (Dovidio et al., 2004).

If cooperative contact between rival group members encourages positive attitudes, might this principle bring people together in multicultural schools? Could interracial friendships replace competitive classroom situations with cooperative ones? Could cooperative learning maintain or even enhance student achievement? Experiments with adolescents from 11 countries confirm that, in each case, the answer is *Yes* (Roseth et al., 2008). In the classroom as in the sports arena, members of interracial groups who work together on projects typically come to feel friendly toward one another. Knowing this, thousands of teachers have made interracial cooperative learning part of their classroom experience.

superordinate goals shared goals that override differences among people and require their cooperation.

"You cannot shake hands with a clenched fist."

Indira Gandhi, 1971

Shawn Baldwin/Associated Press

Kofi Annan: "Most of us have overlapping identities which unite us with very different groups. We *can* love what we are, without hating what—and who—we are *not*. We can thrive in our own tradition, even as we learn from others" (Nobel lecture, 2001).

Syracuse Newspapers/ The Image Works

Superordinate goals override differences Cooperative efforts to achieve shared goals are an effective way to break down social barriers.

The power of cooperative activity to make friends of former enemies has led psychologists to urge increased international exchange and cooperation. As we engage in mutually beneficial trade, as we work to protect our common destiny on this fragile planet, and as we become more aware that our hopes and fears are shared, we can transform misperceptions that feed conflict into feelings of solidarity based on common interests.

Communication When real-life conflicts become intense, a third-party mediator—a marriage counselor, labor mediator, diplomat, community volunteer—may facilitate much-needed communication (Rubin et al., 1994). Mediators help each party to voice its viewpoint and to understand the other's needs and goals. If successful, mediators can replace a competitive *win-lose* orientation with a cooperative *win-win* orientation that leads to a mutually beneficial resolution. A classic example: Two friends, after quarreling over an orange, agreed to split it. One squeezed his half for juice. The other used the peel from her half to flavor a cake. If only the two had understood each other's motives, they could have hit on the win-win solution of one having all the juice, the other all the peel.

Conciliation Understanding and cooperative resolution are most needed, yet least likely, in times of anger or crisis (Bodenhausen et al., 1994; Tetlock, 1988). When conflicts intensify, images become more stereotyped, judgments more rigid, and communication more difficult, or even impossible. Each party is likely to threaten, coerce, or retaliate. In the weeks before the Persian Gulf war, the first President George Bush threatened, in the full glare of publicity, to "kick Saddam's ass." Saddam Hussein communicated in kind, threatening to make Americans "swim in their own blood."

Under such conditions, is there an alternative to war or surrender? Social psychologist Charles Osgood (1962, 1980) advocated a strategy of *Graduated and Reciprocated Initiatives in Tension-Reduction,* nicknamed **GRIT.** In applying GRIT, one side first announces its recognition of mutual interests and its intent to reduce tensions. It then initiates one or more small, conciliatory acts. Without weakening one's retaliatory capability, this modest beginning opens the door for reciprocity by the other party. Should the enemy respond with hostility, one reciprocates in kind. But so, too, with any conciliatory response.

In laboratory experiments, small conciliatory gestures—a smile, a touch, a word of apology—have allowed both parties to begin edging down the tension ladder to a safer rung where communication and mutual understanding can begin (Lindskold et al., 1978, 1988). In a real-world international conflict, U.S. President John F. Kennedy's gesture of stopping atmospheric nuclear tests began a series of reciprocated conciliatory acts that culminated in the 1963 atmospheric test-ban treaty.

As working toward shared goals reminds us, we are more alike than different. Civilization advances not by conflict and cultural isolation, but by tapping the knowledge, the skills, and the arts that are each culture's legacy to the whole human race. Thanks to cultural sharing, every modern society is enriched by a cultural mix (Sowell, 1991). We have China to thank for paper and printing and for the magnetic compass that opened the great explorations. We have Egypt to thank for trigonometry. We have the Islamic world and India's Hindus to thank for our Arabic numerals. While celebrating and claiming these diverse cultural legacies, we can also welcome the enrichment of today's social diversity. We can view ourselves as instruments in a human orchestra. And we—this book's worldwide readers—can therefore each affirm our own culture's heritage while building bridges of communication, understanding, and cooperation across our cultural traditions.

GRIT Graduated and Reciprocated Initiatives in Tension-Reduction—a strategy designed to decrease international tensions.

RETRIEVE IT

• What are some ways to reconcile conflicts and promote peace?

ANSWER: Peacemakers should encourage equal-status *contact,* cooperation to achieve *superordinate goals* (shared goals that override differences), understanding through communication, and reciprocated conciliatory gestures (each side gives a little).

CHAPTER REVIEW

Social Psychology

LEARNING OBJECTIVES

Test Yourself by taking a moment to answer each of these Learning Objective Questions (repeated here from within the chapter). Then turn to Appendix D, Complete Chapter Reviews, to check your answers. Research suggests that trying to answer these questions on your own will improve your long-term memory of the concepts (McDaniel et al., 2009).

Social Thinking

13-1: What do social psychologists study? How do we tend to explain others' behavior and our own?

13-2: How do attitudes and actions interact?

Social Influence

13-3: How do cultural norms affect our behavior?

13-4: What is automatic mimicry, and how do conformity experiments reveal the power of social influence?

13-5: What did Milgram's obedience experiments teach us about the power of social influence?

13-6: How is our behavior affected by the presence of others?

13-7: What are group polarization and groupthink, and how much power do we have as individuals?

Social Relations

13-8: What is prejudice? What are its social and emotional roots?

13-9: What are the cognitive roots of prejudice?

13-10: How does psychology's definition of *aggression* differ from everyday usage? What biological factors make us more prone to hurt one another?

13-11: What psychological and social-cultural factors may trigger aggressive behavior?

13-12: Why do we befriend or fall in love with some people but not with others?

13-13: How does romantic love typically change as time passes?

13-14: When are people most—and least—likely to help?

13-15: How do social exchange theory and social norms explain helping behavior?

13-16: How do social traps and mirror-image perceptions fuel social conflict?

13-17: How can we transform feelings of prejudice, aggression, and conflict into attitudes that promote peace?

TERMS AND CONCEPTS TO REMEMBER

Test yourself on these terms by trying to write down the definition in your own words before flipping back to the referenced page to check your answer.

social psychology, p. 458
attribution theory, p. 458
fundamental attribution error, p. 458
attitude, p. 460

peripheral route persuasion, p. 460
central route persuasion, p. 460
foot-in-the-door phenomenon, p. 461
role, p. 461
cognitive dissonance theory, p. 462
culture, p. 463
norm, p. 464
conformity, p. 466

normative social influence, p. 467
informational social influence, p. 467
social facilitation, p. 471
social loafing, p. 472
deindividuation, p. 472
group polarization, p. 473
groupthink, p. 474
prejudice, p. 476

EXPERIENCE THE TESTING EFFECT

Test yourself repeatedly throughout your studies. This will not only help you figure out what you know and don't know; the testing itself will help you learn and remember the information more effectively thanks to the *testing effect*.

1. If we encounter a person who appears to be high on drugs, and we make the fundamental attribution error, we will probably attribute the person's behavior to
   a. moral weakness or an addictive personality.
   b. peer pressure.
   c. the easy availability of drugs on city streets.
   d. society's acceptance of drug use.

2. Celebrity endorsements in advertising often lead consumers to purchase products through _____ (central/peripheral) route persuasion.

3. We tend to agree to a larger request more readily if we have already agreed to a small request. This tendency is called the _____ - _____ - _____ - _____ phenomenon.

4. Jamal's therapist has suggested that Jamal should "act as if" he is confident, even though he feels insecure and shy. Which social psychological theory would best support this suggestion, and what might the therapist be hoping to achieve?

5. Researchers have found that a person is most likely to conform to a group if
   a. the group members have diverse opinions.
   b. the person feels competent and secure.
   c. the person admires the group's status.
   d. no one else will observe the person's behavior.

6. In Milgram's experiments, the rate of compliance was highest when
   a. the "learner" was at a distance from the "teacher."
   b. the "learner" was close at hand.
   c. other "teachers" refused to go along with the experimenter.
   d. the "teacher" disliked the "learner."

7. Dr. Huang, a popular music professor, delivers fascinating lectures on music history but gets nervous and makes mistakes when describing exam statistics in front of the class. Why does his performance vary by task?

8. In a group situation that fosters arousal and anonymity, a person sometimes loses self-consciousness and self-control. This phenomenon is called _____.

9. Sharing our opinions with like-minded others tends to strengthen our views, a phenomenon referred to as _____ _____.

10. Prejudice toward a group involves negative feelings, a tendency to discriminate, and overly generalized beliefs referred to as _____.

11. If several well-publicized murders are committed by members of a particular group, we may tend to react with fear and suspicion toward all members of that group. In other words, we
    a. blame the victim.
    b. overgeneralize from vivid, memorable cases.
    c. view the world as just.
    d. rationalize inequality.

12. The other-race effect occurs when we assume that other groups are _____ (more/less) homogeneous than our own group.

13. Evidence of a biochemical influence on aggression is the finding that
    a. aggressive behavior varies widely from culture to culture.
    b. animals can be bred for aggressiveness.
    c. stimulation of an area of the brain's limbic system produces aggressive behavior.
    d. a higher-than-average level of the hormone testosterone is associated with violent behavior in males.

14. Studies show that parents of delinquent young people tend to use beatings to enforce discipline. This suggests that aggression can be
    a. learned through direct rewards.
    b. triggered by exposure to violent media.
    c. learned through observation of aggressive models.
    d. caused by hormone changes at puberty.

15. A conference of social scientists studying the effects of pornography unanimously agreed that violent pornography
    a. has little effect on most viewers.
    b. is the primary cause of reported and unreported rapes.
    c. leads viewers to be more accepting of coercion in sexual relations.
    d. has no effect, other than short-term arousal and entertainment.

16. The aspect of X-rated films that most directly influences men's aggression toward women seems to be the
    a. length of the film.
    b. eroticism portrayed.
    c. depictions of sexual violence.
    d. attractiveness of the actors.

17. The more familiar a stimulus becomes, the more we tend to like it. This exemplifies the _____ _____ effect.

18. A happy couple celebrating their 50th wedding anniversary is likely to experience deep _____ love, even though their _____ love has probably decreased over the years.

19. After vigorous exercise, you meet an attractive person, and you are suddenly seized by romantic feelings for that person. This response supports the two-factor theory of emotion, which assumes that emotions, such as passionate love, consist of physical arousal plus
    a. a reward.
    b. proximity.
    c. companionate love.
    d. our interpretation of that arousal.

20. The bystander effect states that a particular bystander is less likely to give aid if
    a. the victim is similar to the bystander in appearance.
    b. no one else is present.
    c. other people are present.
    d. the incident occurs in a deserted or rural area.

21. Our enemies often have many of the same negative impressions of us as we have of them. This exemplifies the concept of _____ - _____ perceptions.

22. One way of resolving conflicts and fostering cooperation is by giving rival groups shared goals that help them override their differences. These are called _____ goals.

Find answers to these questions in Appendix E, in the back of the book.

CHAPTER 14

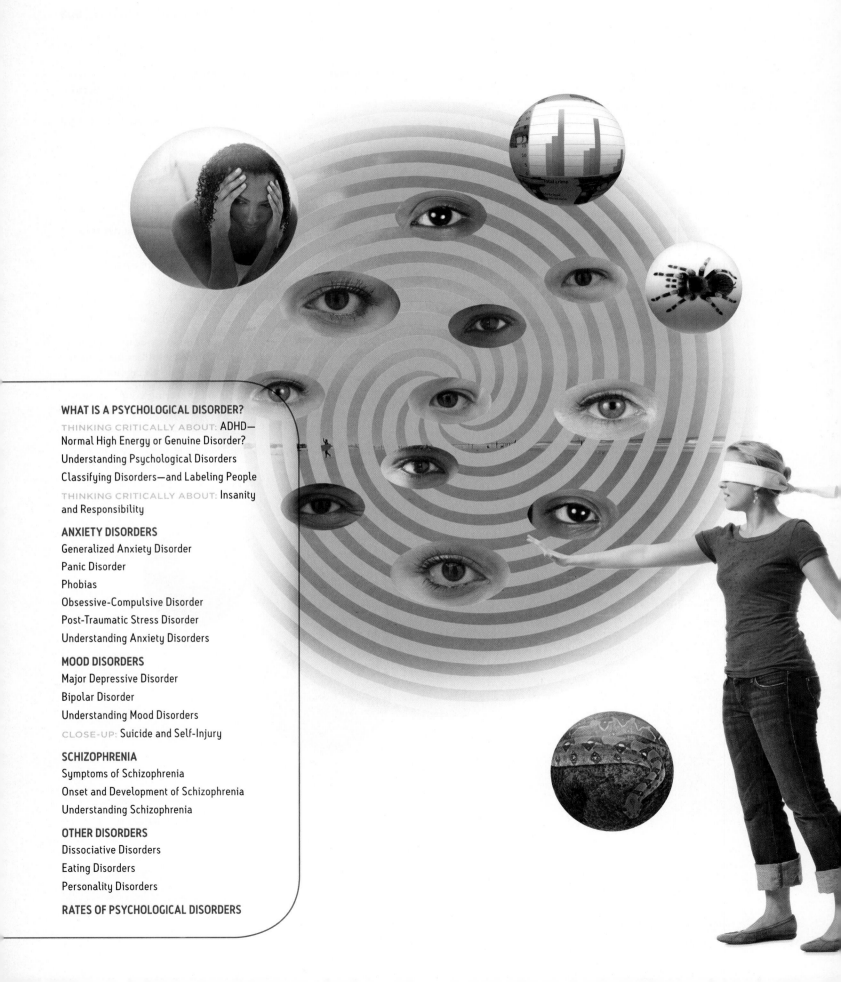

Psychological Disorders

I felt the need to clean my room . . . and would spend four to five hours at it. I would take every book out of the bookcase, dust and put it back . . . I couldn't stop.

Marc, diagnosed with obsessive-compulsive disorder (from Summers, 1996)

Whenever I get depressed it's because I've lost a sense of self. I can't find reasons to like myself. I think I'm ugly. I think no one likes me.

Greta, diagnosed with depression (from Thorne, 1993, p. 21)

Voices, like the roar of a crowd, came. I felt like Jesus; I was being crucified.

Stuart, diagnosed with schizophrenia (from Emmons et al., 1997)

Now and then, all of us feel, think, or act the way disturbed people do much of the time. We, too, get anxious, depressed, suspicious, deluded, or withdrawn, just less intensely and more briefly. So it's no wonder that we sometimes see ourselves in the psychological disorders we study.

Either personally or through friends or family, many of us will know the confusion and pain of unexplained physical symptoms, irrational fears, or a feeling that life is not worth living. Worldwide, some 450 million people suffer from mental or behavioral disorders (WHO, 2010). These disorders account for 15.4 percent of the years of life lost due to death or disability—scoring slightly below cardiovascular conditions and slightly above cancer (Murray & Lopez, 1996). Rates and symptoms vary by culture, but no known society is free of two terrible disorders: depression and schizophrenia (Baumeister & Härter, 2007; Draguns, 1990a,b, 1997). This chapter examines these and other disorders, and the next chapter considers their *treatment*. First, though, let's address some basic questions.

What Is a Psychological Disorder?

14-1: How should we draw the line between normal behavior and psychological disorder?

Most of us would agree that a family member who is depressed and refuses to get out of bed for three months has a psychological disorder. But what should we say about a grieving father who can't resume his usual social activities three months after his child has died? Where do we draw the line between clinical depression and understandable grief? Between bizarre irrationality and zany creativity? Between abnormality and normality?

In their search for answers, theorists and clinicians consider several perspectives:

- How should we *define* psychological disorders?
- How should we *understand* disorders—as sicknesses that need to be diagnosed and cured, or as natural responses to a troubling environment?
- How should we *classify* psychological disorders? And can we do so in a way that allows us to help people without stigmatizing them with *labels?*

A **psychological disorder** is a "significant dysfunction in an individual's cognitions, emotions, or behaviors." Such dysfunctions reflect "a disturbance in the psychological, biological, or developmental processes underlying mental functioning" (DSM-5 Task Force, 2012).

Dysfunctional behaviors are *maladaptive*—they interfere with normal day-to-day life. An intense fear of spiders may be abnormal, but if it doesn't interfere with your life, it is not a disorder. Marc's cleaning rituals (from this chapter's opening) did interfere with his work and leisure. If occasional sad moods persist and become disabling, they may signal a psychological disorder.

Distress often accompanies dysfunctional behaviors. Marc, Greta, and Stuart were all clearly distressed by their behaviors or emotions. In 1973, the American Psychiatric Association dropped homosexuality as a disorder as mental health workers came to consider same-sex attraction as not inherently dysfunctional or distressing. On the other hand, in the 1970s, high-energy children were typically viewed as normal youngsters running a bit wild. Today, more of them are seen as dysfunctional and diagnosed with *attention-deficit hyperactivity disorder (ADHD)*. (See Thinking Critically About: ADHD—Normal High Energy or Genuine Disorder?)

Understanding Psychological Disorders

14-3: How is our understanding of disorders affected by whether we use a medical model or a biopsychosocial approach?

The way we view a problem influences how we try to solve it. In earlier times, people often thought that strange behaviors were evidence that strange forces—the movements of the stars, god-like powers, or evil spirits—were at work. Had you lived during the Middle Ages, you might have said "The devil made him do it." To drive out demons, people considered "mad" were sometimes caged or given "therapies" such as genital mutilation, beatings, removal of teeth or lengths of intestines, or transfusions of animal blood (Farina, 1982).

Reformers, such as Philippe Pinel (1745–1826) in France, opposed such brutal treatments. Madness is not demon possession, he insisted, but a sickness of the mind caused by severe stress and inhumane conditions. Curing the sickness, he said, requires "moral treatment," including boosting patients' morale by unchaining them and talking with them. He and others worked to replace brutality with gentleness, isolation with activity, and filth with clean air and sunshine.

psychological disorder a significant dysfunction in a person's thoughts, feelings, or behaviors.

medical model the concept that diseases, in this case psychological disorders, have physical causes that can be *diagnosed, treated,* and, in most cases, *cured,* often through treatment in a *hospital.*

ADHD—Normal High Energy or Genuine Disorder?

14-2: Why is there controversy over attention-deficit hyperactivity disorder?

Eight-year-old Todd has always been energetic. At home, he chatters away and darts from one activity to the next, rarely settling down to read a book or focus on a game. At play, he is reckless and overreacts when playmates bump into him or take one of his toys. At school, his exasperated teacher complains that fidgety Todd doesn't listen, follow instructions, or stay in his seat and do his lessons. As he matures to adulthood, Todd's hyperactivity likely will subside, but his inattentiveness may persist (Kessler et al., 2010).

If taken for a psychological evaluation, Todd may be diagnosed with **attention-deficit hyperactivity disorder (ADHD),** as are some 5 percent of children and 3 percent of adolescents who display at least one of its key symptoms (extreme inattention, hyperactivity, and impulsivity) (Polanczyk et al., 2007). Studies also find 2.5 percent of adults—though a diminishing number with age—exhibiting ADHD symptoms (Simon et al., 2009).

To skeptics, being distractible, fidgety, and impulsive sounds like a "disorder" caused by a single genetic variation: a Y chromosome. And sure enough, ADHD is diagnosed three times more often in boys than in girls. Does energetic child + boring school = ADHD overdiagnosis? Is the label being applied to healthy schoolchildren who, in more natural outdoor environments, would seem perfectly normal?

Skeptics think so. In the decade after 1987, they note, the proportion of American children being treated for ADHD nearly quadrupled (Olfson et al., 2003). How commonplace the diagnosis is depends in part on teacher referrals. Some teachers refer lots of kids for ADHD assessment, others none. ADHD rates have varied by a factor of 10 in different counties of New York State (Carlson, 2000). Depending on where they live, children who are "a persistent pain in the neck in school" are often diagnosed with ADHD and given powerful prescription drugs, notes Peter Gray (2010). But the problem resides less in the child, he argues, than in today's abnormal environment that forces children to do what evolution has not prepared them to do—to sit for long hours in chairs.

On the other side of the debate are those who argue that the more frequent diagnoses of ADHD today reflect increased awareness of the disorder, especially in those areas where rates are highest. They acknowledge that diagnoses can be subjective and sometimes inconsistent—ADHD is not as objectively defined as is a broken arm. Nevertheless, declared the World Federation for Mental Health (2005), "there is strong agreement among the international scientific community that ADHD is a real neurobiological disorder whose existence should no longer be debated." In neuroimaging studies, ADHD has associations with abnormal brain activity patterns, noted a consensus statement by 75 researchers (Barkley et al., 2002).

What, then, is known about ADHD's causes? It is not caused by too much sugar or poor schools. ADHD often coexists with a learning disorder or with defiant and temper-prone behavior. ADHD is *heritable,* and research teams are sleuthing the culprit gene variations and abnormal neural pathways (Nikolas & Burt, 2010; Poelmans et al., 2011; Volkow et al., 2009; Williams et al., 2010). It is treatable with medications such as Ritalin and Adderall, which are considered stimulants but help calm hyperactivity and increase one's ability to sit and focus on a task—and to progress normally in school (Barbaresi et al., 2007). Psychological therapies, such as those focused on shaping behaviors in the classroom and at home, have also helped address the distress of ADHD (Fabiano et al., 2008).

The bottom line: Extreme inattention, hyperactivity, and impulsivity can derail social, academic, and vocational achievements, and these symptoms can be treated with medication and other treatment. But the debate continues over whether normal rambunctiousness is too often diagnosed as a psychiatric disorder, and whether there is a cost to the long-term use of stimulant drugs in treating ADHD.

. . . . . .

attention-deficit hyperactivity disorder (ADHD) a psychological disorder marked by the appearance by age 7 of one or more of three key symptoms: extreme inattention, hyperactivity, and impulsivity.

The Medical Model

By the 1800s, a medical breakthrough prompted further reform. Researchers discovered that syphilis, a sexually transmitted infection, invades the brain and distorts the mind. This discovery triggered an excited search for physical causes of mental disorders and for treatments that would cure them. Hospitals replaced asylums, and the **medical model** of mental disorders was born. This model is reflected in words we still use today. We speak of the mental *health* movement. A mental *illness* (also called a psycho*pathology*) needs to be *diagnosed* on the basis of its *symptoms*. It needs to be *treated* through *therapy*, which may include treatment in a psychiatric *hospital*. Recent discoveries that genetically influenced abnormalities in brain structure and biochemistry contribute to many disorders have energized the medical perspective.

"Moral treatment" Under Philippe Pinel's influence, hospitals sometimes sponsored patient dances, often called "lunatic balls," depicted in this painting by George Bellows (*Dance in a Madhouse*).

George Wesley Bellows, *Dance in a Madhouse*, 1907. © 1997 The Art Institute of Chicago

The Biopsychosocial Approach

To call psychological disorders "sicknesses" tilts research heavily toward the influence of biology and away from the influence of our personal histories and social and cultural surroundings. But as we have seen throughout this text, our behaviors, our thoughts, and our feelings are formed by the interaction of our biology, our psychology, and our social-cultural environment. As individuals, we differ in the amount of stress we experience and in the ways we cope with stressors. Cultures also differ in the sources of stress they produce and in the ways of coping they provide.

The environment's influence on disorders can be seen in culture-related symptoms (Beardsley, 1994; Castillo, 1997). Anxiety, for example, may be manifested in different ways in different cultures. In Malaysia, *amok*—a sudden outburst of violent behavior (thus the phrase "run amok")—may occur. In Latin American cultures, people may display symptoms of *susto,* a condition marked by severe anxiety, restlessness, and a fear of black magic. In Japanese culture, people may experience *taijin-kyofusho,* social anxiety about their appearance, combined with a readiness to blush and a fear of eye contact, or the extreme withdrawal of *hikikomori*. The eating disorders *anorexia nervosa* and *bulimia nervosa* occur mostly in North American and other Western cultures. Increasingly, however, such North American disorders are, along with McDonald's and MTV, spreading across the globe (Watters, 2010).

Other disorders, such as depression and schizophrenia, occur worldwide. From Asia to Africa and across the Americas, people with schizophrenia often act irrationally and speak in disorganized ways.

Disorders, it seems, reflect genetic predispositions and physiological states as well as psychological dynamics and social and cultural circumstances. The biopsychosocial approach recognizes that mind and body are inseparable (**FIGURE 14.1**). Negative emotions contribute to physical illness, and physical abnormalities contribute to negative emotions. We are physically embodied and socially embedded.

FIGURE 14.1
The biopsychosocial approach to psychological disorders Today's psychology studies how biological, psychological, and social-cultural factors interact to produce specific psychological disorders.

Biological influences:
- evolution
- individual genes
- brain structure and chemistry

Psychological influences:
- stress
- trauma
- learned helplessness
- mood-related perceptions and memories

Psychological disorder

Wavebreakmedia Ltd/ Jupiterimages

Social-cultural influences:
- roles
- expectations
- definitions of *normality* and *disorder*

- Are psychological disorders universal, or are they culture-specific? Explain with examples.

ANSWER: Some psychological disorders are culture-specific. For example, anorexia nervosa occurs mostly in Western cultures, and taijin-kyofusho appears largely in Japan. Other disorders, such as schizophrenia, occur in all cultures.

- What is the biopsychosocial perspective, and why is it important in our understanding of psychological disorders?

ANSWER: Biological, psychological, and social-cultural influences combine to produce psychological disorders. This broad perspective helps us understand that our well-being is affected by our genes, brain functioning, inner thoughts and feelings, and the influences of our social and cultural environment.

DSM-IV-TR the American Psychiatric Association's *Diagnostic and Statistical Manual of Mental Disorders,* Fourth Edition, with an updated "text revision"; a widely used system for classifying psychological disorders.

Classifying Disorders—and Labeling People

14-4: How and why do clinicians classify psychological disorders, and why do some psychologists criticize the use of diagnostic labels?

In biology, classification creates order and helps us communicate. To classify an animal as a "mammal" tells us a great deal—that it is warm-blooded, has hair or fur, and produces milk to feed its young. In psychiatry and psychology, classification serves the same ends. To classify a person's disorder as "schizophrenia" also tells us a great deal. It says that the person speaks in a disorganized way, has bizarre beliefs, shows either little emotion or inappropriate emotion, or is socially withdrawn. "Schizophrenia" is a quick way of describing a complex set of behaviors.

But diagnostic classification does more than give us a thumbnail sketch of a person's disordered behavior. In psychiatry and psychology, classification also attempts to predict the disorder's future course and to suggest appropriate treatment. It stimulates research into causes. Indeed, to study a disorder, we must first name and describe it.

Our current best scheme for describing disorders and estimating how often they occur has been the American Psychiatric Association's *Diagnostic and Statistical Manual of Mental Disorders,* Fourth Edition, now in its "text-revised" fourth edition **(DSM-IV-TR)**.

A new edition, DSM-5, is slated to appear in 2013. In 2010, the American Psychiatric Association released the first draft of that revision (Clay, 2011; www.DSM5.org; Miller & Holden, 2010). Some diagnostic labels are changing. "Mental retardation," for example, becomes "intellectual developmental disorder." Some new categories, such as "hypersexual disorder," "hoarding disorder," and "binge-eating disorder" have been added. The eleventh edition of the World Health Organization's *International Classification of Diseases* (ICD-11), covering both medical and psychological disorders, is expected in 2014 (Clay, 2010).

Despite its medical terminology *(diagnosing, symptoms, illness),* most practitioners find the DSM-IV-TR a helpful and practical tool. It is also financially necessary: North American health insurance companies usually require an ICD/DSM diagnosis before they pay for therapy.

The DSM-IV-TR categories and diagnostic guidelines (**TABLE 14.1** on the next page) have been fairly reliable. If one psychiatrist or psychologist diagnoses someone as having, say, schizophrenia, the chances are good that another mental health worker will independently give the same diagnosis. To reach a diagnosis, clinicians use a structured-interview procedure, consisting of a series of objective questions about observable behaviors, such as, "Is the person afraid to leave home?"

In one study, 16 psychologists used DSM guidelines in structured interviews with 75 patients with disorders. The psychologists' task was to diagnose each patient as having (1) depression, (2) generalized anxiety, or (3) some other disorder (Riskind et al., 1987). Another psychologist then viewed a videotape of each interview and offered a second, independent opinion. For 83 percent of the patients, the two opinions agreed.

Many examples in this chapter were drawn from case illustrations accompanying the DSM-IV-TR.

"I'm always like this, and my family was wondering if you could prescribe a mild depressant."

© 1992 by Sidney Harris.

Table 14.1
How Are Psychological Disorders Diagnosed?

Based on assessments, interviews, and observations, many clinicians diagnose by answering the following questions from the five levels, or *axes,* of the DSM-IV-TR. (Chapters in parentheses locate the topics in this text.)

<u>Axis I</u> Is a *Clinical Syndrome* present?
Using specifically defined criteria, clinicians may select none, one, or more syndromes from the following list:

- Disorders usually first diagnosed in infancy, childhood, and adolescence
- Delirium, dementia, amnesia, and other cognitive disorders (Chapter 5 and Chapter 8)
- Mental disorders due to a general medical condition
- Substance-related disorders (Chapter 3)
- Schizophrenia and other psychotic disorders (this chapter)
- Mood disorders (this chapter)
- Anxiety disorders (this chapter)
- Somatoform disorders
- Factitious disorders (intentionally faked)
- Dissociative disorders (this chapter)
- Eating disorders (this chapter)
- Sexual disorders and gender identity disorder (Chapter 5)
- Sleep disorders (Chapter 3)
- Impulse-control disorders not classified elsewhere
- Adjustment disorders
- Other conditions that may be a focus of clinical attention

<u>Axis II</u> Is a *Personality Disorder* or *Mental Retardation [Intellectual Developmental Disorder]* present?
Clinicians may or may not also select one of these two conditions.
<u>Axis III</u> Is a *General Medical Condition,* such as diabetes, hypertension, or arthritis, also present?
<u>Axis IV</u> Are *Psychosocial* or *Environmental Problems,* such as school or housing issues, also present?
<u>Axis V</u> What is the *Global Assessment* of this person's functioning?
Clinicians assign a code from 0–100.

Nevertheless, the DSM has its critics. Some have been concerned that it casts too wide a net and brings "almost any kind of behavior within the compass of psychiatry" (Eysenck et al., 1983). The number of DSM-IV disorder categories (nearly 300) is five times the number in the 1952 first edition. As that number has ballooned, so has the number of adults who meet the criteria for at least one of them. According to the U.S. National Institute of Mental Health (2008), 26 percent of all adults meet those criteria in any year, and 46 percent have met them at some time in their lives (Kessler et al., 2005).

Other critics register a more basic complaint—that these labels are at best arbitrary and at worst value judgments masquerading as science. Once we label a person, we view that person differently (Bathje & Pryor, 2011; Sadler et al., 2012). Labels can change reality by putting us on alert for evidence that confirms our view. When teachers were told certain students are "gifted," they acted in ways that brought out the creative behaviors they expected (Snyder, 1984). If we hear that a new co-worker is a difficult person, we may treat him suspiciously. He may in turn react to us as a difficult person would. Labels can be self-fulfilling.

The biasing power of labels was clear in a classic study. David Rosenhan (1973) and seven others went to hospital admissions offices, complaining of "hearing voices" saying *empty, hollow,* and *thud.* Apart from this complaint and giving false names and occupations, they answered questions truthfully. All eight of these normal people were misdiagnosed with disorders.

Should we be surprised? Surely not. As one psychiatrist noted, if someone swallowed blood, went to an emergency room, and spat it up, would we blame a doctor for diagnosing a bleeding ulcer? But what followed the Rosenhan study diagnoses was startling. Until being released an average of 19 days later, these eight "patients" showed no other symptoms. Yet after analyzing their (quite normal) life histories, clinicians were able to "discover" the causes of their disorders, such as having mixed emotions about a parent. Even the patients' routine note-taking behavior was misinterpreted as a symptom.

In another study, people watched videotaped interviews. If told the interviewees were job applicants, the viewers perceived them as normal (Langer & Abelson, 1974, 1980). Other viewers who were told they were watching psychiatric or cancer patients perceived the same interviewees as "different from most people." Labels matter. Therapists who thought they were watching an interview of a psychiatric patient perceived him as "frightened of his own aggressive impulses," a "passive, dependent type," and so forth. As Rosenhan discovered, a label can have "a life and an influence of its own."

Labels also have power outside the laboratory. Getting a job or finding a place to rent can be a challenge for people recently released from a mental hospital. The shame seems to be lifting as people better understand that many psychological disorders involve diseases of the brain, not failures of character (Solomon, 1996). Public figures have helped foster this understanding by speaking openly about their own struggles with disorders such as depression. The more contact we have with people with disorders, the more accepting our attitudes are (Kolodziej & Johnson, 1996).

The increased understanding of psychological disorders is reflected in some media portrayals that are reasonably accurate and sympathetic. But people with disorders have too often been portrayed as objects of humor or ridicule *(As Good as It Gets),* as homicidal maniacs (Hannibal Lecter in *Silence of the Lambs),* or as freaks (Nairn, 2007). In real life, mental disorders seldom lead to violence. The few who do commit violent acts tend to be those experiencing threatening delusions and hallucinated voices commanding them to act, or those whose dysfunctionality includes substance abuse (Douglas et al., 2009; Elbogen & Johnson, 2009; Fazel et al., 2009, 2010). In real life, people with disorders also are more likely to be the *victims* of violence than the perpetrators (Marley & Bulia, 2001). Indeed, reported the U.S. Surgeon General's Office (1999, p. 7), "There is very little risk of violence or harm to a stranger from casual contact with an individual who has a mental disorder." (Although most people with psychological disorders are not violent, those who are create a moral dilemma for society. For more on this topic, see Thinking Critically About: Insanity and Responsibility on the next page.)

Despite their risks, diagnostic labels have *benefits.* Mental health professionals have good reasons for using labels. Diagnostic labels help them communicate about their cases, pinpoint underlying causes, and share information about effective treatments. Diagnostic definitions are also useful in research exploring causes and treatments of disorder.

"What's the use of their having names," the Gnat said, "if they won't answer to them?"
"No use to *them*," said Alice; "but it's useful to the people that name them, I suppose."

Lewis Carroll, Through the Looking-Glass, *1871*

Accurate portrayal Recent films have offered some realistic depictions of psychological disorders. *Black Swan* (2010), shown here, portrayed a main character suffering a delusional disorder. *Temple Grandin* (2010) dramatized a lead character who successfully copes with autism. *A Single Man* (2009) depicted depression.

THINKING CRITICALLY ABOUT:

Insanity and Responsibility

The legal insanity defense was created in 1843, after deluded Scotsman Daniel M'Naughten tried to shoot England's prime minister (who he thought was persecuting him) but killed an assistant by mistake. Like U.S. President Ronald Reagan's near-assassin, John Hinckley, M'Naughten was sent to a mental hospital rather than to prison.

In both cases, the public was outraged. "Hinckley Insane, Public Mad," declared one headline. They were mad again when a deranged Jeffrey Dahmer in 1991 admitted murdering 15 young men and eating parts of their bodies. They were mad in 1998 when 15-year-old Kip Kinkel, driven by "those voices in my head," killed his parents and two fellow Springfield, Oregon, students and wounded 25 others. They were mad in 2002 when Andrea Yates, after being taken off her antipsychotic medication, was tried in Texas for drowning her five children. And they were mad in 2011, when an irrational Jared Loughner gunned down a crowd of people, including survivor Congresswoman Gabrielle Giffords, in an Arizona supermarket parking lot. Following their arrests, all of these people were sent to jails, not hospitals (though later, after another trial, Yates was instead hospitalized). As Yates' fate illustrates, 99 percent of those whose insanity defense is accepted are nonetheless institutionalized,

often for as long as those convicted of crimes (Lilienfeld & Arkowitz, 2011). Moreover, use of the insanity defense is actually rare—in only 8 uncontested instances in one analysis of 60,432 indictments (Council of State Governments, 2002).

Most people with psychological disorders are not violent. But what should society do with those who are? Many people who have been executed or are now on death row have been limited by intellectual disability or motivated by delusional voices. The State of Arkansas forced one murderer with schizophrenia,

Charles Singleton, to take two antipsychotic drugs—to make him mentally competent, so that he could then be put to death.

Which of Yates' two juries made the right decision? The first, which decided that people who commit such rare but terrible crimes should be held responsible? Or the second, which decided to blame the "madness" that clouds their vision? As we come to better understand the biological and environmental bases for all human behavior, from generosity to vandalism, when should we—and should we not—hold people accountable for their actions?

AP/Arizona Daily Star, Mamta Popat

Jail or hospital? Jared Lee Loughner was charged with the 2011 Tucson, Arizona, shooting that killed six people and left over a dozen others injured, including former U.S. Representative Gabrielle Giffords. Loughner had a history of mental health issues, including paranoid beliefs, and was diagnosed with schizophrenia. His behavior is not typical of people with schizophrenia. That disorder is usually associated with violence only when accompanied by substance abuse (Fazel et al., 2009).

RETRIEVE IT

• What is the value, and what are the dangers, of labeling individuals with disorders?

ANSWER: Therapists and others use disorder labels to communicate with one another in a common language, and to share concepts during research. Insurance companies require a diagnosis (a label) before they will pay for therapy. The danger of labeling people is that they will begin to act as they have been labeled, and also that labels can create expectations that will change our behavior toward the people we label.

Anxiety Disorders

14-5: What are the main anxiety disorders, and how do they differ from the ordinary worries and fears we all experience?

Anxiety is part of life. Speaking in front of a class, peering down from a ladder, or waiting to play in a big game might make any one of us feel nervous. At times we may feel anxious enough to avoid making eye contact or talking with someone—"shyness," we call it. Fortunately for most of us, our uneasiness is not intense and persistent.

Some of us, however, are more prone to notice and remember threats (Mitte, 2008). This tendency may place us at risk for one of the **anxiety disorders,** which occurs when the brain's danger detection system becomes hyperactive—producing distressing, persistent anxiety when no threat exists. Let's consider these five:

- *Generalized anxiety disorder,* in which a person is constantly tense, worried, and uneasy for no apparent reason
- *Panic disorder,* in which a person experiences sudden episodes of intense dread
- *Phobias,* in which a person is intensely and irrationally afraid of a specific object, activity, or situation
- *Obsessive-compulsive disorder,* in which a person is troubled by unwanted, repetitive thoughts or actions
- *Post-traumatic stress disorder,* in which a person has lingering memories, nightmares, and possibly other symptoms for weeks after a severely threatening, uncontrollable event

Generalized Anxiety Disorder

Tom is a 27-year-old electrician. For the past two years, he has been bothered by dizziness, sweating palms, and irregular heartbeat. He feels edgy and sometimes finds himself shaking. Tom has been reasonably successful in hiding his symptoms from his family and co-workers, but occasionally he has to leave work. He allows himself few other social contacts. Neither his family doctor nor a neurologist has been able to find any physical problem.

Tom's unfocused, out-of-control, negative feelings suggest a **generalized anxiety disorder.** The symptoms of this disorder are commonplace; their persistence, for six months or more, is not. People with this condition (two-thirds women) worry continually, and they are often jittery, on edge, and sleep deprived (McLean & Anderson, 2009). Concentration is difficult as attention switches from worry to worry. Their tension and apprehension may leak out through furrowed brows, twitching eyelids, trembling, perspiration, or fidgeting.

People may not be able to identify the cause of their anxiety, and therefore cannot relieve or avoid it. To use Sigmund Freud's term, the anxiety is *free-floating.* Generalized anxiety disorder and depression often go hand in hand, but even without depression this disorder tends to be disabling (Hunt et al., 2004; Moffitt et al., 2007b). Moreover, it may lead to physical problems, such as high blood pressure.

Panic Disorder

Panic disorder is an anxiety tornado. It strikes suddenly, wreaks havoc, and disappears. For the 1 person in 75 with this disorder, anxiety suddenly escalates into a terrifying *panic attack*—a minutes-long episode of intense fear that something horrible is about to happen. Irregular heartbeat, chest pains, shortness of breath, choking, trembling, or dizziness may accompany the panic.

One woman recalled suddenly feeling "hot and as though I couldn't breathe. My heart was racing and I started to sweat and tremble and I was sure I was going to faint. Then my fingers started to feel numb and tingly and things seemed unreal. It was so bad I wondered if I was dying and asked my husband to take me to the emergency room. By the time we got there (about 10 minutes) the worst of the attack was over and I just felt washed out" (Greist et al., 1986).

Panic attack symptoms are often misread as a heart attack or other serious physical ailment. Smokers have at least a doubled risk of panic disorder (Zvolensky & Bernstein, 2005). Because nicotine is a stimulant, lighting up doesn't help us to lighten up.

Phobias

We all live with some fears. People with **phobias** are consumed by a persistent, irrational fear and avoidance of some object, activity, or situation. Marilyn, an otherwise healthy and happy 28-year-old, so fears thunderstorms that she feels anxious as soon as a weather

anxiety disorders psychological disorders characterized by distressing, persistent anxiety or maladaptive behaviors that reduce anxiety.

generalized anxiety disorder an anxiety disorder in which a person is continually tense, apprehensive, and in a state of autonomic nervous system arousal.

panic disorder an anxiety disorder marked by unpredictable, minutes-long episodes of intense dread in which a person experiences terror and accompanying chest pain, choking, or other frightening sensations.

phobia an anxiety disorder marked by a persistent, irrational fear and avoidance of a specific object, activity, or situation.

Martin Harvey/Jupiterimages

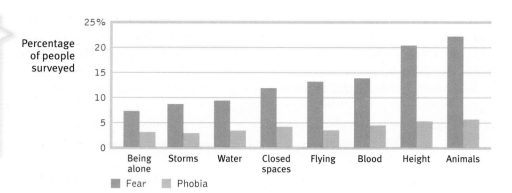

FIGURE 14.2

Some common and uncommon specific fears This national interview study identified the commonality of various specific fears. A strong fear becomes a phobia if it provokes a compelling but irrational desire to avoid the dreaded object or situation. (From Curtis et al., 1998.)

forecaster mentions possible storms later in the week. If her husband is away and a storm is forecast, she may stay with a close relative. During a storm, she hides from windows and buries her head to avoid seeing the lightning. *Specific phobias* such as Marilyn's typically focus on particular animals, insects, heights, blood, or closed spaces (**FIGURE 14.2**). People avoid the stimulus, such as high places, that arouses the fear.

Not all phobias are so specific. *Social phobia* is shyness taken to an extreme. Those with a social phobia have an intense fear of being judged by others. They avoid threatening social situations, such as speaking up in a group, eating out, or going to parties. Finding themselves in such a situation, they will sweat or tremble.

Much as fretting over insomnia may, ironically, cause insomnia, so worrying about anxiety—perhaps fearing another panic attack, or fearing anxiety-caused sweating in public—can amplify anxiety symptoms (Olatunji & Wolitzky-Taylor, 2009). After several panic attacks, people may come to fear the fear itself. This may trigger *agoraphobia,* fear or avoidance of situations in which panic may strike, escape might be difficult, and help unavailable. People with agoraphobia may avoid being outside the home, in a crowd, on a bus, or on an elevator.

After spending five years sailing the world, Charles Darwin began suffering panic disorder at age 28. Because of the attacks, he moved to the country, avoided social gatherings, and traveled only in his wife's company. But the relative seclusion did free him to focus on developing his evolutionary theory. "Even ill health," he reflected, "has saved me from the distraction of society and its amusements" (quoted in Ma, 1997).

Obsessive-Compulsive Disorder

Making everything perfect Soccer star David Beckham has openly discussed his obsessive-compulsive tendencies, which have driven him to line up objects in pairs or to spend hours straightening furniture (Adams, 2011).

Stephen Dunn/Getty Images

As with generalized anxiety and phobias, we can see aspects of our own behavior in **obsessive-compulsive disorder (OCD)**. *Obsessive thoughts* (recall Marc's focus on cleaning his room) are unwanted and so repetitive it may seem they will never end. *Compulsive behaviors* are responses to those thoughts (cleaning and cleaning and cleaning).

We all are at times obsessed with senseless or offensive thoughts that will not go away. Have you ever caught yourself behaving compulsively, perhaps rigidly checking, ordering, and cleaning before guests arrive, or lining up books and pencils "just so" before studying? On a small scale, obsessive thoughts and compulsive behaviors are a part of everyday life. They cross the fine line between normality and disorder when they *interfere* with everyday life and cause us distress. Checking to see that you locked the door is normal; checking 10 times is not. Washing your hands is normal; washing so often that your skin becomes raw is not. (**TABLE 14.2**

Table 14.2

Common Obsessions and Compulsions Among Children and Adolescents With Obsessive-Compulsive Disorder

Thought or Behavior	Percentage Reporting Symptom
Obsessions (repetitive *thoughts*)	
Concern with dirt, germs, or toxins	40
Something terrible happening (fire, death, illness)	24
Symmetry, order, or exactness	17
Compulsions (repetitive *behaviors*)	
Excessive hand washing, bathing, toothbrushing, or grooming	85
Repeating rituals (in/out of a door, up/down from a chair)	51
Checking doors, locks, appliances, car brakes, homework	46

Source: Adapted from Rapoport, 1989.

obsessive-compulsive disorder (OCD) an anxiety disorder characterized by unwanted repetitive thoughts (obsessions), actions (compulsions), or both.

post-traumatic stress disorder (PTSD) an anxiety disorder characterized by haunting memories, nightmares, social withdrawal, jumpy anxiety, and/or insomnia that lingers for four weeks or more after a traumatic experience.

offers more examples.) At some time during their lives, often during their late teens or twenties, 2 to 3 percent of people cross that line from normal rehearsals and fussy behaviors to debilitating disorder (Karno et al., 1988). Although the person knows them to be irrational, the anxiety-fueled obsessive thoughts become so haunting, the compulsive rituals so senselessly time consuming, that effective functioning becomes impossible.

OCD is more common among teens and young adults than among older people (Samuels & Nestadt, 1997). A 40-year follow-up study of 144 Swedish people diagnosed with the disorder found that, for most, the obsessions and compulsions had gradually lessened, though only 1 in 5 had completely recovered (Skoog & Skoog, 1999).

Post-Traumatic Stress Disorder

As an Iraq war soldier, Jesse "saw the murder of children, women. It was just horrible for anyone to experience." After calling in a helicopter strike on one house where he had seen ammunition crates carried in, he heard the screams of children from within. "I didn't know there were kids there," he recalls. Back home in Texas, he suffered "real bad flashbacks" (Welch, 2005).

Jesse is not alone. In one study of 103,788 veterans returning from Iraq and Afghanistan, 25 percent were diagnosed with a psychological disorder (Seal et al., 2007). The most frequent diagnosis was **post-traumatic stress disorder (PTSD).** Typical symptoms include recurring haunting memories and nightmares, a numb feeling of social withdrawal, jumpy anxiety, and trouble sleeping (Hoge et al., 2004, 2006, 2007; Kessler, 2000). Many battle-scarred veterans have been diagnosed with PTSD. Survivors of accidents, disasters, and violent and sexual assaults (including an estimated two-thirds of prostitutes) have also experienced these symptoms (Brewin et al., 1999; Farley et al., 1998; Taylor et al., 1998).

The greater one's emotional distress during a trauma, the higher the risk for post-traumatic symptoms (Ozer et al., 2003). One in 3 Vietnam veterans who had experienced heavy combat were diagnosed with PTSD (Centers for Disease Control Vietnam Experience Study, 1988; Dohrenwend et al., 2006). One in 10 veterans who had never seen combat received that diagnosis. Similar rates were found among New Yorkers who witnessed the 9/11 terrorist attacks. PTSD diagnoses among survivors who had been inside the World Trade Center during the attack were double the rates found among those who were outside (Bonanno et al., 2006). The more frequent and severe the trauma, the worse the long-term outcomes tend to be (Golding, 1999). In the 30 years after the Vietnam war, veterans who came home with a PTSD diagnosis had twice the normal likelihood of dying (Crawford et al., 2009).

About half of us will experience at least one traumatic event in our lifetime. Why do some people develop PTSD after a traumatic event, but others don't? Some people

Bringing the war home During his three deployments to Iraq, this Marine Staff Sergeant suffered traumatic brain injury. After his return home, he was diagnosed with post-traumatic stress disorder. He regularly travels two hours each way with his wife to Bethesda Naval Hospital for psychiatric and medical appointments.

Whitney Shefte/The Washington Post via Getty Images

may have more sensitive emotion-processing limbic systems that flood their bodies with stress hormones (Kosslyn, 2005; Ozer & Weiss, 2004). The odds of getting this disorder after a traumatic event are higher for women (about 1 in 10) than for men (1 in 20) (Olff et al., 2007; Ozer & Weiss, 2004).

Some psychologists believe that PTSD has been overdiagnosed, due partly to a broadening definition of *trauma* (Dobbs, 2009; McNally, 2003). Too often, say some critics, PTSD gets stretched to include normal bad memories and dreams after a bad experience. In such cases, well-intentioned attempts to have people relive the trauma may exacerbate their emotions and pathologize normal stress reactions (Wakefield & Spitzer, 2002). For example, survivors may be "debriefed" right after a trauma and asked to revisit the experience and vent emotions. This tactic has been generally ineffective and sometimes harmful (Bonanno et al., 2010).

Most people, male and female, display an impressive *survivor resiliency,* or ability to recover after severe stress (Bonanno et al., 2010). For more on human resilience and on the *post-traumatic growth* that some experience, see Chapter 15.

RETRIEVE IT

- Unfocused tension, apprehension, and arousal is called _____ _____ disorder. If a person is focusing anxiety on specific feared objects or situations, that person may have a(n) _____. Those who express anxiety through unwanted repetitive thoughts or actions may have a(n) _____-_____ disorder. Anxiety accompanied by recurring memories and nightmares, social withdrawal, and insomnia for weeks after a traumatic event may be diagnosed with _____-_____ _____ disorder. Those who experience unpredictable periods of terror and intense dread, accompanied by frightening physical sensations, may be diagnosed with a(n) _____ disorder.

ANSWERS: generalized anxiety; phobia; obsessive-compulsive; post-traumatic stress; panic

---

Understanding Anxiety Disorders

14-6: How do conditioning, cognition, and biology contribute to the feelings and thoughts that mark anxiety disorders?

Anxiety is both a feeling and a cognition—a doubt-laden appraisal of one's safety or social skill. How do these anxious feelings and cognitions arise? Sigmund Freud's psychoanalytic theory (Chapter 12) proposed that, beginning in childhood, people *repress* intolerable impulses, ideas, and feelings. This submerged mental energy sometimes, he thought, leaks out in odd symptoms, such as anxious hand washing. Few of today's psychologists interpret anxiety disorders this way. Most believe that three modern perspectives are more helpful:

Conditioning

When bad events happen unpredictably and uncontrollably, anxiety often develops (Field, 2006; Mineka & Oehlberg, 2008). In experiments, researchers have shown how classical conditioning can produce fear and anxiety. You may recall from Chapter 7 that infants have learned to fear furry objects that were paired with frightening noises. And by giving rats unpredictable electric shocks, researchers have created anxious animals (Schwartz, 1984). The rats, like assault victims who report feeling anxious when returning to the scene of the crime, become uneasy in their lab environment. That environment has become a cue for fear.

Such research helps explain how panic-prone people come to associate anxiety with certain cues, and why anxious people are hyperattentive to possible threats (Bar-Haim et al., 2007; Bouton et al., 2001). In one survey, 58 percent of those with social phobia said their disorder began after a traumatic event (Ost & Hugdahl, 1981).

How might conditioning magnify a single painful and frightening event into a full-blown phobia? The answer lies in part in stimulus generalization and reinforcement.

Stimulus generalization occurs when a person experiences a fearful event and later develops a fear of similar events. My car was once struck by another whose driver missed a stop sign. For months afterward, I felt a twinge of unease when any car approached from a side street. My fear eventually disappeared, but for others, fear may linger and grow. Marilyn's phobia (also shared by recording artist Madonna) may have similarly generalized after a terrifying or painful experience during a thunderstorm.

Once phobias and compulsions arise, *reinforcement* helps maintain them. Anything that helps us avoid or escape the feared situation reduces anxiety. This feeling of relief can reinforce phobic behaviors. Fearing a panic attack, a person may decide not to leave the house. Reinforced by feeling calmer, the person is likely to repeat that maladaptive behavior in the future (Antony et al., 1992). So, too, with compulsive behaviors. If washing your hands relieves your feelings of anxiety, you may wash your hands again when those feelings return.

Cognition

We learn some fears by observing others. Susan Mineka (1985, 2002) sought to explain why nearly all monkeys reared in the wild fear snakes, yet lab-reared monkeys do not. Surely, most wild monkeys do not actually suffer snake bites. Do they learn their fear through observation? To find out, Mineka experimented with six monkeys reared in the wild (all strongly fearful of snakes) and their lab-reared offspring (virtually none of which feared snakes). After repeatedly observing their parents or peers refusing to reach for food in the presence of a snake, the younger monkeys developed a similar strong fear of snakes. When retested three months later, their learned fear persisted. Humans likewise learn fears by observing others (Olsson et al., 2007).

Hemera Technologies/ Jupiterimages

Observational learning is not the only cognitive influence on anxiety. As the next chapter's discussion of cognitive-behavioral therapy illustrates, our interpretations and expectations, whether rational or irrational, shape our reactions. Whether we interpret the creaky sound in the old house simply as the wind or as a possible knife-wielding intruder determines whether we panic. People with anxiety disorders tend to be *hyper-vigilant*. For them, a pounding heart signals a heart attack. A lone spider near the bed is the frontrunner in an infestation. An everyday disagreement with a mate or a boss spells doom for the relationship. Anxiety is especially common when people cannot switch off such intrusive thoughts and perceive a loss of control and a sense of helplessness (Franklin & Foa, 2011).

Biology

Some aspects of anxiety disorders are not easily understandable in terms of conditioning and cognitive processes alone. Why do some of us develop lasting phobias after suffering traumas but others do not? Why do we learn some fears more readily than others? Why are some individuals more vulnerable to anxiety disorders? Our biology also plays a role.

Genes Among monkeys, fearfulness runs in families. A monkey reacts more strongly to stress if its close biological relatives have sensitive, high-strung temperaments (Suomi, 1986). So, too, with people. Some of us are predisposed to anxiety. If one identical twin has an anxiety disorder, the other is also likely to have it (Hettema et al., 2001; Kendler et al., 1992, 1999, 2002a,b). Even when raised separately, identical twins may develop similar phobias (Carey, 1990; Eckert et al., 1981). One pair of separated identical twins independently became so afraid of water that, at age 35, they would wade into the ocean backward and only up to their knees.

Given the genetic contribution to anxiety disorders, researchers are now sleuthing the culprit gene combinations. Among their findings are 17 gene variations that appear to be expressed with typical anxiety disorder symptoms (Hovatta et al., 2005), and others that are associated specifically with OCD (Dodman et al., 2010; Hu et al., 2006).

Some genes influence anxiety disorders by regulating brain levels of neurotransmitters, such as *serotonin,* which influences sleep and mood (Canli, 2008), and *glutamate,* which influences activity in the brain's alarm centers (Lafleur et al., 2006; Welch et al., 2007).

Genes matter. Some of us have genes that make us like orchids—fragile, yet capable of beauty under favorable circumstances. Others of us are like dandelions—hardy, and able to thrive in varied circumstances (Ellis & Boyce, 2008).

The Brain Our experiences alter our brain, paving new pathways. Traumatic fear-learning experiences can leave tracks in the brain creating fear circuits within the amygdala (Etkin & Wager, 2007; Kolassa & Elbert, 2007; Maren, 2007). These fear pathways create easy inroads for more fear experiences (Armony et al., 1998). Some antidepressant drugs dampen this fear-circuit activity and associated obsessive-compulsive behaviors.

Generalized anxiety, panic attacks, PTSD, and even obsessions and compulsions are manifested biologically. When the disordered brain detects that something is amiss, it generates a mental hiccup of repeating thoughts or actions (Gehring et al., 2000). Brain scans of people with anxiety disorders show higher-than-normal activity in areas involved in impulse control and habitual behaviors. Brain scans of people with OCD, for example, reveal elevated activity in specific brain areas during behaviors such as compulsive hand washing, checking, ordering, or hoarding (Insel, 2010; Mataix-Cols et al., 2004, 2005). As **FIGURE 14.3** shows, the *anterior cingulate cortex,* a brain region that monitors our actions and checks for errors, seems especially likely to be hyperactive in those with OCD (Maltby et al., 2005).

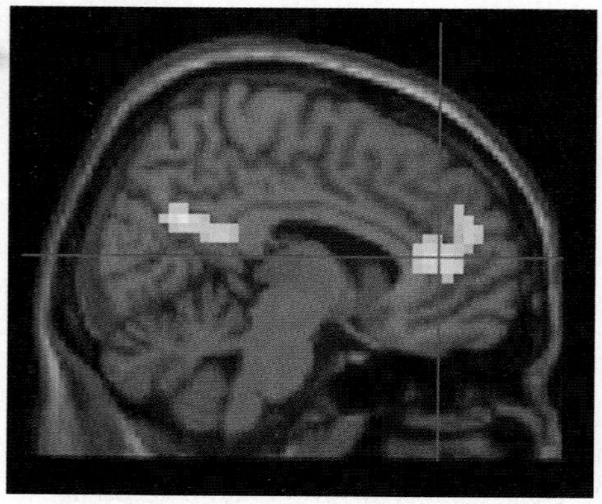

FIGURE 14.3

An obsessive-compulsive brain

Neuroscientists Nicholas Maltby, David Tolin, and their colleagues (2005) used functional MRI scans to compare the brains of those with and without OCD as they engaged in a challenging cognitive task. The scans of those with OCD showed elevated activity in the anterior cingulate cortex in the brain's frontal area (indicated by the yellow area on the far right).

Reprinted from *Neuroimage, 24,* Maltby, N., Tolin, D.F., Worhunsky, P., O'Keefe, T. M., & Kiehl, K. A., Dysfunctional action monitoring hyperactivates frontal-striatal circuits in obsessive-compulsive disorder: An event-related fMRI study, 495–503, 2005, with permission from Elsevier.

Natural Selection No matter how fearful or fearless we are, we humans seem biologically prepared to fear the threats our ancestors faced—spiders and snakes, closed spaces and heights, storms and darkness. (In the distant past, those who did not fear these threats were less likely to survive and leave descendants.) Thus, even in Britain, which has only one poisonous snake species, people often fear snakes. And we have fears at very young ages. Preschool children detect snakes in a scene faster than they spot flowers, caterpillars, or frogs (LoBue & DeLoache, 2008). Our Stone Age fears are easy to condition and hard to extinguish (Coelho & Purkis, 2009; Davey, 1995; Öhman, 2009).

Our modern fears may also have an evolutionary explanation. A modern fear of flying may have grown from a fear of confinement and heights, which can be traced to our biological past.

Moreover, consider what people tend *not* to learn to fear. World War II air raids produced remarkably few lasting phobias. As the air strikes continued, the British, Japanese, and German populations did not become more and more panicked. Rather, they grew more indifferent to planes outside their immediate neighborhoods (Mineka & Zinbarg, 1996). Evolution has not prepared us to fear bombs dropping from the sky.

Our phobias focus on dangers our ancestors faced. Our compulsive acts typically exaggerate behaviors that helped them survive. Grooming had survival value; it detected insects and infections. Gone wild, it becomes compulsive hair pulling. Washing up helped people stay healthy. Out of control, it becomes ritual hand washing. Checking territorial boundaries helped ward off enemies. In OCD, it becomes checking and rechecking an already locked door (Rapoport, 1989).

★ ★ ★

The biological perspective cannot explain all aspects of anxiety disorders, but it is clearly an important component.

Fearless The biological perspective helps us understand why most people would be too afraid to try U.S. Olympic snowboarder Shaun White's tricks. White is less vulnerable to a fear of heights than most of us!

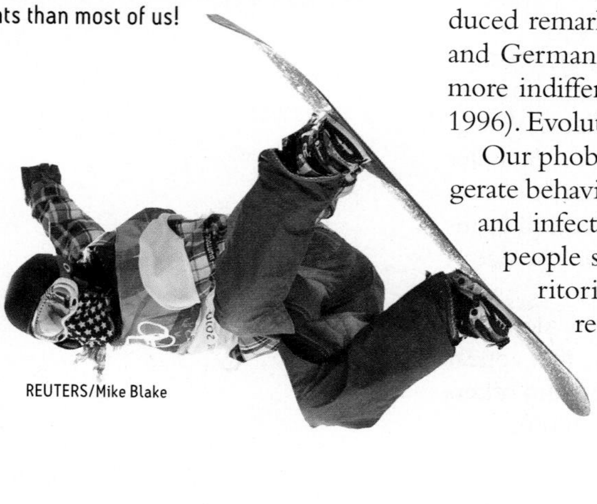

REUTERS/Mike Blake

- Researchers believe that anxiety disorders are influenced by conditioning, observational learning, and cognition. What biological factors contribute to these disorders?

ANSWER: Biological factors include inherited temperament differences; trauma-altered fear pathways in the brain; and outdated, inherited responses that had survival value for our distant ancestors.

mood disorders psychological disorders characterized by emotional extremes. See *major depressive disorder, mania,* and *bipolar disorder.*

Mood Disorders

14-7: What are mood disorders? How does major depressive disorder differ from bipolar disorder?

Most of us will indirectly or directly have some experience with **mood disorders.** These disorders, which are characterized by emotional extremes, appear in two principal forms. *Major depressive disorder* is a prolonged state of hopeless depression. *Bipolar disorder* (formerly called *manic-depressive disorder*) alternates between depression and overexcited hyperactivity.

Anxiety is a response to the threat of future loss. Depressed mood is often a response to past and current loss. To feel bad in reaction to profoundly sad events (such as the death of a loved one) is to be in touch with reality. In such times, depression is like a car's oil-pressure light—a signal that warns us to stop and take appropriate measures.

In the past year, have you at some time "felt so depressed that it was difficult to function"? If so, you may have more company than you know (Jordan et al., 2011). In one national survey, 31 percent of American collegians answered *Yes* to that question (ACHA, 2009). The college years are exciting, but also stressful. Perhaps you're weary from juggling school, work, and family responsibilities. Perhaps social stresses, such as a relationship gone sour or a feeling of being excluded have made you feel isolated or plunged you into despair. Dwelling on these thoughts may leave you feeling deeply discouraged about your life or your future. You may lack the energy to get things done or even to force yourself out of bed. You may be unable to concentrate, eat, or sleep normally. Occasionally you may even wonder if you would be better off dead.

These feelings are more likely to strike during the dark months of winter than the bright days of summer. For some people, winter darkness means more blue moods. When asked "Have you cried today?" Americans answered *Yes* doubly often in the winter (**TABLE 14.3**). For others, recurring depression during winter's dark months constitutes a *seasonal affective disorder.*

From an evolutionary perspective, depression makes sense. As social psychologist Daniel Gilbert (2006) warned, "If someone offered you a pill that would make you permanently happy, you would be well advised to run fast and run far. Emotion is a compass that tells us what to do, and a compass that is perpetually stuck on NORTH is worthless." Depression helps us face and solve problems.

Biologically speaking, life's purpose is survival and reproduction, not happiness. Coughing, vomiting, and various sorts of pain protect our body from dangerous toxins. Depression similarly protects us from dangerous thoughts and feelings, sending us into a sort of psychic hibernation. It slows us down, defuses aggression, helps us let go of unattainable goals, and restrains risk taking (Andrews & Thomson, 2009a,b; Wrosch & Miller, 2009). Grinding temporarily to a halt, as we do when feeling threatened, or when finding our goals are beyond our reach, gives us time to think hard and reconsider our options (Wrosch & Miller, 2009). After reassessing our life, we may redirect our energy in more promising ways (Watkins, 2008). Even mild sadness can improve people's recall, make them more discerning, and help them make complex decisions (Forgas, 2009). There is sense to suffering. But sometimes depression becomes seriously maladaptive. How do we recognize the fine line between a normal blue mood and abnormal depression?

Image Source/Getty Images

Table 14.3
Percentage Answering *Yes* When Asked "Have You Cried Today?"

	Men	Women
In August	4%	7%
In December	8%	21%

Source: Time/CNN survey, 1994

Major Depressive Disorder

Joy, contentment, sadness, and despair are different points on a continuum, points at which any of us may be found at any given moment. The difference between a blue mood after bad news and **major depressive disorder** is like the difference between gasping for breath after a hard run and having chronic asthma. Major depressive disorder occurs when at least five signs of depression last two or more weeks (**TABLE 14.4**). To sense what major depression feels like, suggest some clinicians, imagine combining the anguish of grief with the exhaustion you feel after pulling an all-nighter.

Table 14.4
Classifying Major Depressive Disorder

The DSM-IV-TR classifies major depressive disorder as the presence over a two-week period of at least five of the following symptoms (including depressed mood or loss of interest or pleasure). The symptoms must cause distress or impairment and not be attributable to substance abuse, bereavement, or another medical illness.

- Depressed mood most of the day
- Markedly diminished interest or pleasure in activities
- Significant weight loss or gain when not dieting, or significant decrease or increase in appetite
- Insomnia or sleeping too much
- Physical agitation or lethargy
- Fatigue or loss of energy nearly every day
- Feeling worthless, or excessive or inappropriate guilt
- Daily problems in thinking, concentrating, or making decisions
- Recurrent thoughts of death and suicide

Although phobias are more common, depression is the number-one reason people seek mental health services. At some point during their lifetime, 12 percent of Canadian adults and 17 percent of U.S. adults will experience depression (Holden, 2010; Patten et al., 2006). Worldwide, it is the leading cause of disability. In any given year, 5.8 percent of men and 9.5 percent of women will have a depressive episode (WHO, 2002).

Bipolar Disorder

In **bipolar disorder,** people bounce from one emotional extreme to the other. When a depressive episode ends, an intensely happy, hyperactive, wildly optimistic state called **mania** follows. But before long, the elated mood either returns to normal or plunges again into depression.

If depression is living in slow motion, mania is fast forward. During this phase, people are typically overtalkative, overactive, and elated. They have little need for sleep. They show fewer sexual inhibitions. Their speech is loud, flighty, and hard to interrupt, and they are easily irritated if crossed. Feeling extreme optimism and self-esteem, they find advice irritating. Yet they need protection from their poor judgment, which may lead to reckless spending or unsafe sex.

In milder forms, mania's energy and free-flowing thinking can fuel creativity. George Frideric Handel (1685–1759), who many believe suffered from a mild form of bipolar disorder, composed his three-hour-long *Messiah* during three weeks of intense, creative energy in 1742 (Keynes, 1980). Bipolar disorder strikes more often among those who rely on emotional expression and vivid imagery, such as poets and artists, and less often among those who rely on precision and logic, such as architects, designers, and journalists (Jamison, 1993, 1995; Kaufman & Baer, 2002; Ludwig, 1995).

"My life had come to a sudden stop. I was able to breathe, to eat, to drink, to sleep. I could not, indeed, help doing so; but there was no real life in me."

Leo Tolstoy, My Confession, 1887

major depressive disorder a mood disorder in which a person experiences, in the absence of drugs or another medical condition, two or more weeks of significantly depressed moods or diminished interest or pleasure in most activities, along with at least four other symptoms.

bipolar disorder a mood disorder in which a person alternates between the hopelessness and lethargy of depression and the overexcited state of mania. (Formerly called *manic-depressive disorder.*)

mania a hyperactive, wildly optimistic state in which dangerously poor judgment is common.

Actress Catherine Zeta-Jones
Kevin Mazur/WireImage

Writer Virginia Woolf
George C. Beresford/Hulton Getty
Pictures Library

Humorist Samuel Clemens (Mark Twain)
The Granger Collection

Producer Tim Burton
Jemal Countess/Getty Images

Creativity and bipolar disorder There are many creative artists, composers, writers, and musical performers with bipolar disorder. Madeleine L'Engle wrote in *A Circle of Quiet* (1972): "All the people in history, literature, art, whom I most admire: Mozart, Shakespeare, Homer, El Greco, St. John, Chekhov, Gregory of Nyssa, Dostoevsky, Emily Brontë: not one of them would qualify for a mental-health certificate."

Bipolar disorder is much less common than major depressive disorder, but it is often more dysfunctional. It afflicts as many men as women. The diagnosis is on the rise among adolescents, whose mood swings, sometimes prolonged, range from rage to bubbly. The trend was clear in U.S. National Center for Health Statistics annual physician surveys. Between 1994 and 2003, bipolar diagnoses in under-20 people showed an astonishing 40-fold increase—from an estimated 20,000 to 800,000 (Carey, 2007; Flora & Bobby, 2008; Moreno et al., 2007). The new popularity of the diagnosis, given in two-thirds of the cases to boys, has been a boon to companies whose drugs are prescribed to lessen mood swings.

Understanding Mood Disorders

14-8: How do the biological and social-cognitive perspectives explain mood disorders?

From thousands of studies of the causes, treatment, and prevention of mood disorders, researchers have pulled out some common threads. Any theory of depression must explain at least the following (Lewinsohn et al., 1985, 1998, 2003):

Behaviors and thoughts change with depression People trapped in a depressed mood are inactive and feel unmotivated. They are sensitive to negative happenings (Peckham et al., 2010). They recall negative information. And they expect negative outcomes (my team will lose, my grades will fall, my love will fail). When the mood lifts, these behaviors and thoughts disappear. Nearly half the time, people with depression also have symptoms of another disorder, such as anxiety or substance abuse.

Depression is widespread Depression is one of two disorders found worldwide. This suggests that depression's causes must also be common.

Women's risk of major depression is nearly double men's In 2009, when Gallup asked more than a quarter-million Americans if they had ever been diagnosed with depression, 13 percent of men and 22 percent of women said *Yes* (Pelham, 2009). This gender gap has been found worldwide (**FIGURE 14.4** on the next page). The trend begins in adolescence; preadolescent girls are not more depression prone than boys are (Hyde et al., 2008). With adolescence, girls often ruminate more and fret more about their bodies.

The depression gender gap fits a bigger pattern: Women are generally more vulnerable to disorders involving internalized states, such as depression, anxiety, and inhibited sexual desire. Men's disorders tend to be more external—alcohol dependence, antisocial conduct, lack of impulse control. When women get sad, they often get sadder than men do. When men get mad, they often get madder than women do.

Life after depression Writer J. K. Rowling reports suffering acute depression—a "dark time," with suicidal thoughts—between ages 25 and 28. It was, she said, a "terrible place" that did, however, form a foundation that allowed her "to come back stronger" (McLaughlin, 2010).

AP Photo/Jennifer Graylock

FIGURE 14.4

Gender and major depression Interviews with 89,037 adults in 18 countries (10 of which are shown here) confirm what many smaller studies have found: Women's risk of major depression is nearly double that of men's (Bromet et al., 2011). Data shown here are from "developed countries." "Developing countries," from Brazil to Ukraine, show the same pattern, with an overall female to male depression ratio of 1.97 to 1.

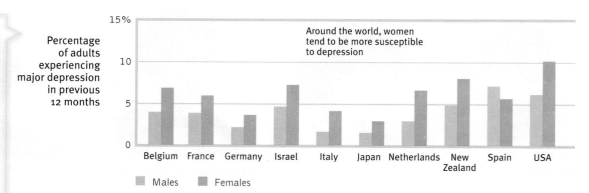

Percentage of adults experiencing major depression in previous 12 months

Around the world, women tend to be more susceptible to depression

Belgium France Germany Israel Italy Japan Netherlands New Zealand Spain USA

■ Males   ■ Females

Most major depressive episodes end on their own Although therapy often helps and tends to speed recovery, most people with major depression eventually return to normal even without professional help. The black cloud of depression comes and, a few weeks or months later, it often goes. For about half of those people, their depression will eventually recur (Burcusa & Iacono, 2007; Curry et al., 2011; Hardeveld et al., 2010). The condition will be chronic for about 20 percent (Klein, 2010).

On average, people with major depression today will spend about three-fourths of the next decade in a normal, nondepressed state (Furukawa et al., 2009). Recovery is more likely to endure (Belsher & Costello, 1988; Fergusson & Woodward, 2002; Kendler et al., 2001) when

- the first episode strikes later in life.
- there were few previous episodes.
- the person experiences minimal stress.
- there is ample social support.

Stressful events often precede depression A family member's death, a job loss, a marital crisis, or a physical assault increase one's risk of depression (Kendler et al., 2008; Monroe & Reid, 2009; Orth et al., 2009). One long-term study tracked rates of depression in 2000 people (Kendler, 1998). Among those who had experienced no stressful life event in the preceding month, the risk of depression was less than 1 percent. Among those who had experienced three such events in that month, the risk was 24 percent.

"I see depression as the plague of the modern era."

Lewis Judd, former chief, National Institute of Mental Health, 2000

With each new generation, depression is striking earlier (now often in the late teens) and affecting more people, with the highest rates in developed countries among young adults This has been true in Canada, England, France, Germany, Italy, Lebanon, New Zealand, Puerto Rico, Taiwan, and the United States (Collishaw et al., 2007; Cross-National Collaborative Group, 1992; Kessler et al., 2010; Twenge et al., 2008). In one study of Australian adolescents, 12 percent reported symptoms of depression (Sawyer et al., 2000). Most hid it from their parents; almost 90 percent of those parents perceived their depressed teen as *not* suffering depression. In North America, today's young adults are three times more likely than their grandparents to report having recently—or ever—suffered depression. This is true even though their grandparents have been at risk for many more years.

The increased risk among young adults appears partly real, but it may also reflect cultural differences between generations. Today's young people are more willing to talk openly about their depression. Psychological processes may also be at work. We tend to forget many negative experiences over time, so older generations may overlook depressed feelings they had in earlier years.

The emotional lives of men and women?

Paula Niedenthal

The Biological Perspective

Depression is a whole-body disorder. It involves genetic predispositions and biochemical imbalances as well as negative thoughts and a gloomy mood.

Genes and Depression We have long known that mood disorders run in families. The risk of major depression and bipolar disorder increases if you have a parent or sibling with the disorder (Sullivan et al., 2000). If one identical twin is diagnosed with major depressive disorder, the chances are about 1 in 2 that at some time the other twin will be, too. If one identical twin has bipolar disorder, the chances are 7 in 10 that the other twin will at some point be diagnosed similarly. Among fraternal twins, the corresponding odds are just under 2 in 10 (Tsuang & Faraone, 1990). The greater similarity among identical twins holds even among twins reared apart (DiLalla et al., 1996). Summarizing the major twin studies (see **FIGURE 14.5**), one research team estimated the heritability of major depression (the extent to which individual differences are attributable to genes) at 37 percent.

Moreover, adopted people with mood disorders often have close biological relatives who have mood disorders, become dependent on alcohol, or commit suicide (Wender et al., 1986). (Close-Up: Suicide and Self-Injury reports other research findings on the next page.)

Emotions are "postcards from our genes" (Plotkin, 1994). To tease out the genes that put people at risk for depression, researchers may use *linkage analysis*. After finding families in which the disorder appears across several generations, geneticists look for differences in DNA from affected and unaffected family members. Linkage analysis points them to a chromosome neighborhood. "A house-to-house search is then needed to find the culprit gene," note behavior genetics researchers Robert Plomin and Peter McGuffin (2003). Such studies reinforce the view that depression is a complex condition. Many genes work together, producing a mosaic of small effects that interact with other factors to put some people at greater risk. If the culprit gene variations can be identified, they may open the door to more effective drug therapy.

The Depressed Brain Scanning devices open a window on the brain's activity during depressed and manic states. During depression, brain activity slows; during mania, it increases (**FIGURE 14.6**). The left frontal lobe and an adjacent brain reward center, which are active during positive emotions, are less active during depressed states (Davidson et al., 2002; Heller et al., 2009). In one study of people with severe depression, MRI scans also found their frontal lobes were 7 percent smaller than normal (Coffey et al., 1993). Other studies show that the *hippocampus,* the memory-processing center linked with the brain's emotional circuitry, is vulnerable to stress-related damage.

At least two neurotransmitter systems are at work during the periods of brain activity and inactivity that accompany mood disorders. *Norepinephrine,* which increases arousal and boosts mood, is scarce during depression. Many people with a history of depression also have

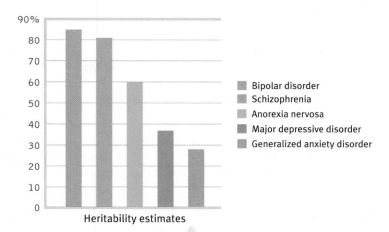

Legend:
- Bipolar disorder
- Schizophrenia
- Anorexia nervosa
- Major depressive disorder
- Generalized anxiety disorder

Heritability estimates

FIGURE 14.5
The heritability of various psychological disorders Researchers Joseph Bienvenu, Dimitry Davydow, and Kenneth Kendler (2011) aggregated data from studies of identical and fraternal twins to estimate the heritability of bipolar disorder, schizophrenia, anorexia nervosa, major depressive disorder, and generalized anxiety disorder.

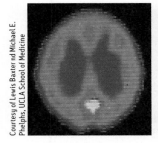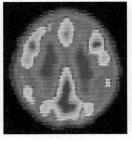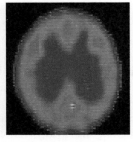

Courtesy of Lewis Baxter nd Michael E. Phelps, UCLA School of Medicine

Depressed state (May 17) **Manic state** (May 18) **Depressed state** (May 27)

FIGURE 14.6
The ups and downs of bipolar disorder These top-facing PET scans show that brain energy consumption rises and falls with the patient's emotional switches. Areas where the brain rapidly consumes glucose are shown in red in these images.

Suicide and Self-Injury

14-9: What factors affect suicide and self-injuring, and what are some of the important warning signs to watch for in suicide prevention efforts?

"But life, being weary of these worldly bars,
Never lacks power to dismiss itself."

William Shakespeare, *Julius Caesar,* 1599

Each year nearly 1 million despairing people worldwide will elect a permanent solution to what might have been a temporary problem. Comparing the suicide rates of different groups, researchers have found

- *national differences:* Britain's, Italy's, and Spain's suicide rates are little more than half those of Canada, Australia, and the United States. Austria's and Finland's are about double (WHO, 2011). Within Europe, people in the most suicide-prone country (Belarus) have been 16 times more likely to kill themselves than those in the least (Georgia).

- *racial differences:* Within the United States, Whites and Native Americans kill themselves twice as often as Blacks, Hispanics, and Asians (CDC, 2012).

- *gender differences:* Women are much more likely than men to attempt suicide (WHO, 2011). But men are two to four times more likely (depending on the country) to actually end their lives. Men use more lethal methods, such as firing a bullet into the head, the method of choice in 6 of 10 U.S. suicides.

- *age differences and trends:* In late adulthood, rates increase, peaking in middle age and beyond. In the last half of the twentieth century, the global rate of annual suicide deaths nearly doubled (WHO, 2008).

- *other group differences:* Suicide rates are much higher among those who are rich, not religious; single, widowed, or divorced (Hoyer & Lund, 1993; Stack, 1992; Stengel, 1981). When facing an unsupportive environment, including family or peer rejection, gay and lesbian youth are at increased risk of attempting suicide (Goldfried, 2001; Haas et al., 2011; Hatzenbuehler, 2011).

- *day of the week:* 25 percent of suicides occur on Wednesdays (Kposowa & D'Auria, 2009).

The risk of suicide is at least 5 times greater for those who have been depressed than for the general population (Bostwick & Pankratz, 2000). People seldom commit suicide while in the depths of depression, when energy and initiative are lacking. The risk increases when they begin to rebound and become capable of following through. Compared with people who do not have a disorder, those with alcohol dependence are roughly 100 times more likely to commit suicide; some 3 percent of them do (Murphy & Wetzel, 1990; Sher, 2006).

Because suicide is so often an impulsive act, environmental barriers (such as jump barriers on high bridges and the unavailability of loaded guns) can reduce suicides (Anderson, 2008). Although common sense might suggest that a determined person would simply find another way to complete the act, such restrictions give time for self-destructive impulses to subside.

Social suggestion may trigger suicide. Following highly publicized suicides and TV programs featuring suicide, known suicides increase. So do fatal auto and private airplane "accidents." One six-year study tracked suicide cases among all 1.2 million people who lived in metropolitan Stockholm at any time during the 1990s (Hedström et al., 2008). Men exposed to a family suicide were 8 times more likely to commit suicide than were nonexposed men. Although that phenomenon may be partly attributable to family genes, shared genetic predispositions do not explain why men exposed to a co-worker's suicide were 3.5 times more likely to commit suicide, compared with nonexposed men.

Suicide is not necessarily an act of hostility or revenge. The elderly sometimes choose death as an alternative to current or future suffering. In people of all ages, suicide may be a way of switching off unendurable pain and relieving a perceived burden on family members. "People desire death when two fundamental needs are frustrated to the point of extinction," noted Thomas Joiner (2006, p. 47): "The need to belong with or connect to others, and the need to feel effective with or to influence others." Suicidal urges typically arise when people feel disconnected from others, and a burden to them (Joiner, 2010), or when they feel defeated and trapped by an inescapable situation (Taylor et al., 2011). Thus, suicide rates increase a bit during economic recessions (Luo et al., 2011). Suicidal thoughts also may increase when people are driven to reach a goal or standard—to become thin or straight or rich—and find it unattainable (Chatard & Selimbegović, 2011).

In hindsight, families and friends may recall signs they believe should have forewarned them—verbal hints, giving away possessions, or withdrawal and preoccupation with death. To judge from surveys of 84,850 people across 17 nations, about 9 percent of people at some

a history of habitual smoking. This may indicate an attempt to self-medicate with inhaled nicotine, which can temporarily increase norepinephrine and boost mood (HMHL, 2002). But smoking also increases one's risk for future depression (Pasco et al., 2008).

Norepinephrine is overabundant during mania. Drugs that alleviate mania reduce norepinephrine. *Serotonin* is also scarce or inactive during depression (Carver et al., 2008). Drugs that relieve depression tend to increase serotonin or norepinephrine supplies by blocking either their reuptake (as Prozac, Zoloft, and Paxil do with serotonin) or their chemical breakdown. Repetitive physical exercise, such as jogging, reduces depression as it increases serotonin (Ilardi et al., 2009; Jacobs, 1994). Boosting serotonin may

point in their lives have thought seriously of suicide. About 30 percent of them (3 percent of the people in those nations) actually attempt it (Nock et al., 2008). For only about 1 in 25 does the attempt become their final act (AAS, 2009). Of those who die, one-third had tried to kill themselves previously, and most had discussed it beforehand. So, if a friend talks suicide to you, it's important to listen and to direct the person to professional help. Anyone who threatens suicide is at least sending a signal of feeling desperate or despondent.

Non-Suicidal Self-Injury

Suicide is not the only way to send a message or deal with distress. Some people, especially adolescents and young adults, may engage in *non-suicidal self-injury (NSSI)* (**FIGURE 14.7**). Such behavior includes cutting or burning the skin, hitting oneself, pulling out hair, inserting objects under the nails or skin, and self-administered tattooing (Fikke et al., 2011).

Why do people hurt themselves? Those who do so tend to be less able to tolerate emotional distress. They are often extremely self-critical, with poor communication and problem-solving skills (Nock, 2010). They may engage in NSSI to

- gain relief from intense negative thoughts through the distraction of pain.

- ask for help and gain attention.

- relieve guilt by self-punishment.

- get others to change their negative behavior (bullying, criticism).

- to fit in with a peer group.

Does NSSI lead to suicide? Usually not. Those who engage in NSSI are typically *suicide gesturers,* not *suicide attempters* (Nock & Kessler, 2006). Suicide gesturers engage in NSSI as a desperate but non-life-threatening form of communication or when they are feeling overwhelmed. But NSSI is a risk factor for *future* suicide attempts (Wilkinson & Goodyer, 2011). If people do not find help, their non-suicidal behavior may escalate to suicidal thoughts and, finally, to suicide attempts.

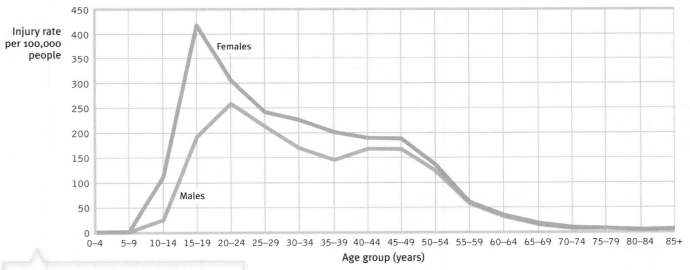

FIGURE 14.7
Rates of nonfatal self-injury in the U.S. Self-injury rates peak higher for females than for males (CDC, 2009).

promote recovery from depression by stimulating hippocampus neuron growth (Airan et al., 2007; Jacobs et al., 2000).

What's good for the heart is also good for the brain and mind. People who eat a heart-healthy "Mediterranean diet" (heavy on vegetables, fish, and olive oil) have a comparatively low risk of developing heart disease, late-life cognitive decline, and depression—all of which are associated with chronic inflammation (Dowlati et al., 2010; Sánchez-Villegas et al., 2009; Tangney et al., 2011). Excessive alcohol use also correlates with depression partly because depression can increase alcohol use but mostly because alcohol misuse *leads to* depression (Fergusson et al., 2009).

Susan Nolen-Hoeksema "This epidemic of morbid meditation is a disease that women suffer much more than men. Women can ruminate about anything and everything—our appearance, our families, our career, our health." (*Women Who Think Too Much: How to Break Free of Overthinking and Reclaim Your Life*, 2003)

The Social-Cognitive Perspective

Biological influences contribute to depression, but in the nature–nurture dance, thinking and acting also play a part. The *social-cognitive perspective* explores how people's assumptions and expectations influence what they perceive.

Depressed people see life through the dark glasses of low self-esteem (Orth et al., 2009). They have intensely negative views of themselves, their situation, and their future. Listen to Norman, a Canadian college professor, recalling his depression:

> I [despaired] of ever being human again. I honestly felt subhuman, lower than the lowest vermin. Furthermore, I . . . could not understand why anyone would want to associate with me, let alone love me. . . . I was positive that I was a fraud and a phony and that I didn't deserve my Ph.D. I didn't deserve to have tenure; I didn't deserve to be a Full Professor. . . . I didn't deserve the research grants I had been awarded; I couldn't understand how I had written books and journal articles. . . . I must have conned a lot of people. (Endler, 1982, pp. 45–49)

Expecting the worst, depressed people magnify bad experiences and minimize good ones, as Norman does here. Their *self-defeating beliefs* and *negative explanatory style* feed depression's vicious cycle.

Negative Thoughts and Negative Moods Interact Self-defeating beliefs may arise from *learned helplessness*. As we saw in Chapter 11, both dogs and humans act depressed, passive, and withdrawn after experiencing uncontrollable painful events. Learned helplessness is more common in women, who may respond more strongly to stress (Hankin & Abramson, 2001; Mazure et al., 2002; Nolen-Hoeksema, 2001, 2003). Do you agree or disagree that "I at least occasionally feel overwhelmed by all I have to do"? In a survey of women and men, 38 percent of women, but only 17 percent of men, agreed (Pryor et al., 2006). (Did your answer fit that pattern?) Men report spending more of their time in "light anxiety" activities such as sports, TV watching, and partying, possibly avoiding activities that might make them feel overwhelmed.

Why are women nearly twice as vulnerable to depression? Susan Nolen-Hoeksema (2003) believes this higher risk may relate to women's tendency to *overthink,* to brood or ruminate. Rumination can be adaptive when it helps us focus intently on a problem, thanks to the continuous firing of an attention-sustaining frontal lobe area (Altamirano et al., 2010; Andrews & Thomson, 2009a,b). When it becomes relentless, self-focused rumination is not adaptive. It diverts us from thinking about other life tasks and leaves us mired in negative emotions (Kuppens et al., 2010).

FIGURE 14.8
Explanatory style and depression
After a negative experience, a depression-prone person may respond with a negative explanatory style.

Breakup with a romantic partner

Stable "I'll never get over this."	Temporary "This is hard to take, but I will get through this."
Global "Without my partner, I can't seem to do anything right."	Specific "I miss my partner, but thankfully I have family and other friends."
Internal "Our breakup was all my fault."	External "It takes two to make a relationship work and it wasn't meant to be."
Depression	Successful coping

Even so, why do life's unavoidable failures lead only some people—women and men—and not others to become depressed? The answer lies partly in their *explanatory style*—who or what they blame for their failures. Think of how you might feel if you failed a test. If you can blame someone else ("What an unfair test!"), you are more likely to feel angry. If you blame yourself, you probably will feel stupid and depressed.

When bad events happen, depression-prone people tend to blame themselves (Mor & Winquist, 2002; Pyszczynski et al., 1991; Wood et al., 1990a,b). As **FIGURE 14.8** illustrates, they explain bad events in terms that are *stable* ("I'll never get over this"), *global* ("I can't do anything right"), and *internal* ("It's all my fault"). Their explanations are pessimistic, overgeneralized, self-focused, and self-blaming. The result may be a depressing sense of hopelessness (Abramson et al., 1989; Panzarella et al., 2006). As Martin Seligman has noted, "A recipe for severe depression is preexisting pessimism encountering failure" (1991, p. 78).

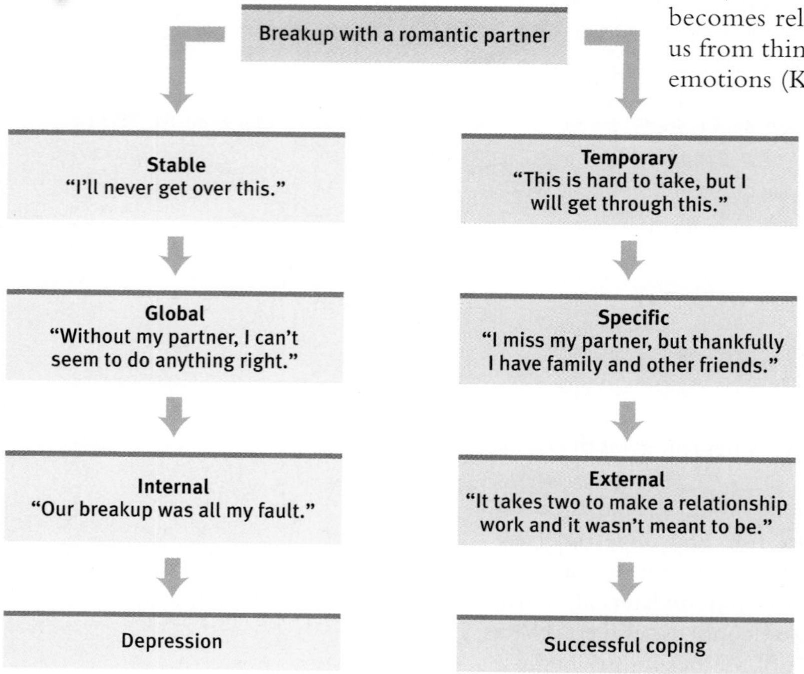

What then might we expect of new college students who are not depressed but do exhibit a pessimistic explanatory style? Lauren Alloy and her collaborators (1999) monitored Temple University and University of Wisconsin students every 6 weeks for 2.5 years. Among those identified as having a pessimistic thinking style, 17 percent had a first episode of major depression, as did only 1 percent of those who began college with an optimistic thinking style.

Critics note a chicken-and-egg problem nesting in the social-cognitive explanation of depression. Which comes first? The pessimistic explanatory style, or the depressed mood? Certainly, the negative explanations *coincide* with a depressed mood, and they are *indicators* of depression. But do they *cause* depression, any more than a speedometer's reading 70 mph *causes* a car's speed? Before or after being depressed, people's thoughts are less negative. Perhaps a depressed mood triggers negative thoughts. If you temporarily put people in a bad or sad mood, their memories, judgments, and expectations suddenly become more pessimistic. (See *state-dependent memory* in Chapter 8.)

Cultural forces may also nudge people toward or away from depression. Seligman (1991, 1995) has argued that in the West the rise of individualism and the decline of commitment to religion and family have forced young people to take personal responsibility for failure or rejection. In non-Western cultures, where close-knit relationships and cooperation are the norm, major depression is less common and less tied to self-blame over personal failure (WHO, 2004). In Japan, for example, depressed people instead tend to report feeling shame over letting others down (Draguns, 1990a).

Depression's Vicious Cycle No matter which comes first, rejection and depression feed each other. Depression, as we have seen, is often brought on by events that disrupt our sense of who we are and why we are worthy. The stressful experience may be losing a job, getting divorced or rejected, or suffering physical trauma. Such disruptions in turn lead to brooding, which is rich soil for growing negative feelings. And that negativity—being withdrawn, self-focused, and complaining—can by itself cause others to reject us (Furr & Funder, 1998; Gotlib & Hammen, 1992). Indeed, people deep in depression are at high risk for divorce, job loss, and other stressful life events. Weary of the person's fatigue, hopeless attitude, and lethargy, a spouse may threaten to leave, or a boss may begin to question the person's competence. New losses and stress then plunge the already-depressed person into even deeper misery. Misery may love another's company, but company does not love another's misery.

We can now assemble pieces of the depression puzzle (**FIGURE 14.9**): (1) Stressful events interpreted through (2) a brooding, negative explanatory style create (3) a hopeless, depressed state that (4) hampers the way the person thinks and acts. These thoughts and actions, in turn, fuel (1) negative experiences such as rejection. Depression is a snake that bites its own tail.

It is a cycle we can all recognize. When we *feel* down, we *think* negatively and remember bad experiences. On the brighter side, if we can recognize the cycle, we can break out of it. Each of the four points offers an exit. We could reverse our self-blame and negative outlook. We could turn our attention outward. We could engage in more pleasant activities and more competent behavior.

Britain's Prime Minister Winston Churchill called depression a "black dog" that periodically hounded him. Abraham Lincoln was so withdrawn and brooding as a young man that his friends feared he might take his own life (Kline, 1974). As their lives remind us, people can and do struggle through depression. Most regain their capacity to love, to work, and even to succeed at the highest levels.

"Some cause happiness wherever they go; others, whenever they go."

Irish writer Oscar Wilde (1854-1900)

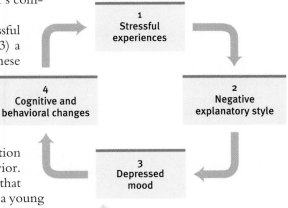

FIGURE 14.9

The vicious cycle of depressed thinking Cognitive therapists attempt to break this cycle, as we will see in Chapter 15, by changing the way depressed people process events. Psychiatrists prescribe medications to try to alter the biological roots of persistently depressed moods.

RETRIEVE IT

• What does it mean to say that "depression is a whole-body disorder"?

ANSWER: Many factors contribute to depression, including the biological influences of genetics and brain function. Social-cognitive factors also matter, including the interaction of explanatory style, mood, our responses to stressful experiences, and changes in our patterns of thinking and behaving. The whole body is involved.

schizophrenia   a group of severe disorders characterized by disorganized and delusional thinking, disturbed perceptions, and inappropriate emotions and behaviors.

psychosis   a psychological disorder in which a person loses contact with reality, experiencing irrational ideas and distorted perceptions.

delusions   false beliefs, often of persecution or grandeur, that may accompany psychotic disorders.

Schizophrenia

During their most severe periods, people with **schizophrenia** live in a private inner world, preoccupied with the strange ideas and images that haunt them. The word itself means "split" *(schizo)* "mind" *(phrenia)*. It refers *not* to a multiple-personality split but rather that the mind has suffered a split from reality that may show itself in disorganized thinking, disturbed perceptions, and inappropriate emotions and actions. Schizophrenia is the chief example of a **psychosis,** a disorder marked by irrationality, distorted perceptions, and lost contact with reality.

As you can imagine, these characteristics profoundly disrupt relationships and work. Given a supportive environment and medication, over 40 percent of people with schizophrenia will have periods of a year or more of normal life experience (Jobe & Harrow, 2010). Many others remain socially withdrawn and isolated or rejected for much of their lives (Hooley, 2010).

Symptoms of Schizophrenia

> **14-10:** What are the schizophrenia subtypes, and what patterns of thinking, perceiving, feeling, and behaving characterize schizophrenia?

Schizophrenia comes in varied forms. Schizophrenia patients with *positive symptoms* may experience hallucinations, talk in disorganized and deluded ways, and exhibit inappropriate laughter, tears, or rage. Those with *negative symptoms* have toneless voices, expressionless faces, or mute and rigid bodies. Thus, positive symptoms are the *presence* of inappropriate behaviors, and negative symptoms are the *absence* of appropriate behaviors. Because schizophrenia is a cluster of disorders, these varied symptoms may have more than one cause. **TABLE 14.5** lists the subtypes of schizophrenia.

Disorganized Thinking   Imagine trying to communicate with Maxine, a young woman whose thoughts spill out in no logical order. Her biographer, Susan Sheehan (1982, p. 25), observed her saying aloud to no one in particular, "This morning, when I was at Hillside [Hospital], I was making a movie. I was surrounded by movie stars. . . . I'm Mary Poppins. Is this room painted blue to get me upset? My grandmother died four weeks after my eighteenth birthday."

As this strange monologue illustrates, the thinking of a person with schizophrenia is fragmented and often distorted by false beliefs called **delusions.** Maxine believed she was Mary Poppins. People with paranoid tendencies often believe they are being threatened or pursued.

Table 14.5
Subtypes of Schizophrenia

Subtype	Symptoms
Paranoid	Preoccupation with delusions or hallucinations, often with themes of persecution or grandiosity
Disorganized	Disorganized speech or behavior, or flat or inappropriate emotion
Catatonic	Immobility (or excessive, purposeless movement), extreme negativism, and/or parrot-like repeating of another's speech or movements
Undifferentiated	Many and varied symptoms
Residual	Withdrawal, after hallucinations and delusions have disappeared

Disorganized thinking may appear as *word salad,* jumbled ideas that make no sense to others. One young man begged for "a little more allegro in the treatment," and suggested that "liberationary movement with a view to the widening of the horizon" will "ergo extort some wit in lectures."

Disorganized thoughts may result from a breakdown in *selective attention.* We normally have a remarkable capacity for giving our undivided attention to one set of sensory stimuli while filtering out others (Chapter 3). People with schizophrenia cannot do this. Thus, tiny, irrelevant stimuli, such as the grooves on a brick or the inflections of a voice, may distract their attention from a bigger event or a speaker's meaning. As one former patient recalled, "What had happened to me . . . was a breakdown in the filter, and a hodge-podge of unrelated stimuli were distracting me from things which should have had my undivided attention" (MacDonald, 1960, p. 218). This selective-attention difficulty is but one of dozens of cognitive differences associated with schizophrenia (Reichenberg & Harvey, 2007).

Disturbed Perceptions Delusions are false *beliefs. Hallucinations* are false perceptions—sensory experiences without sensory stimulation. People with schizophrenia may see, feel, taste, or smell things that are not there. Most often, however, the hallucinations are sounds, often voices making insulting remarks or giving orders. The voices may tell the person that she is bad or that she must burn herself with a cigarette lighter. Imagine your own reaction if a dream broke into your waking consciousness. Stuart Emmons described his experience:

> When someone asks me to explain schizophrenia I tell them, you know how sometimes in your dreams you are in them yourself and some of them feel like real nightmares? My schizophrenia was like I was walking through a dream. But everything around me was real. At times, today's world seems so boring and I wonder if I would like to step back into the schizophrenic dream, but then I remember all the scary and horrifying experiences (Emmons et al., 1997).

When the unreal seems real, the resulting perceptions are at best bizarre, at worst terrifying.

Inappropriate Emotions and Actions The expressed emotions of schizophrenia are often utterly inappropriate, split off from reality (Kring & Caponigro, 2010). Maxine laughed after recalling her grandmother's death. On other occasions, she cried when others laughed, or became angry for no apparent reason. Others with schizophrenia lapse into an emotionless *flat affect* state of no apparent feeling. Many people with schizophrenia have difficulty reading other peoples' facial emotions and states of mind (Green & Horan, 2010; Kohler et al., 2010).

Inappropriate motor behavior takes many forms. Some perform senseless, compulsive acts, such as continually rocking, or rubbing an arm. Others may remain motionless for hours (a condition called *catatonia*) and then become agitated.

Onset and Development of Schizophrenia

14-11: How do chronic and acute schizophrenia differ?

Nearly 1 in 100 people (about 60 percent of them men) will develop schizophrenia, joining the estimated 24 million people worldwide who have this dreaded disorder (Abel et al., 2010; WHO, 2011). It typically strikes as young people are maturing into adulthood. It knows no national boundaries. Men tend to be struck earlier, more severely, and slightly more often (Aleman et al., 2003; Picchioni & Murray, 2007). In studies of Swedish and Danish men, the risk was highest for those who were thin and young, and for those who had not been breast-fed (Sørensen et al., 2005, 2006; Zammit et al., 2007).

CRAIG
2006

Craig Geiser

Art by someone diagnosed with schizophrenia Commenting on the kind of artwork shown here (from Craig Geiser's 2010 art exhibit in Michigan), poet and art critic John Ashbery wrote: "The lure of the work is strong, but so is the terror of the unanswerable riddles it proposes."

Most schizophrenia patients smoke, often heavily. Nicotine apparently stimulates certain brain receptors, which helps focus attention (Diaz et al., 2008; Javitt & Coyle, 2004).

For some, schizophrenia appears suddenly, seemingly as a reaction to stress. For others, as was the case with Maxine, schizophrenia develops gradually, emerging from a long history of social inadequacy and poor school performance (MacCabe et al., 2008). This may help explain why people predisposed to schizophrenia often are found in the lower socioeconomic levels, or even homeless.

One rule holds true around the world (WHO, 1979): When schizophrenia is a slow-developing process (called *chronic,* or *process, schizophrenia*), recovery is doubtful. Social withdrawal, a negative symptom, is common among those with chronic schizophrenia (Kirkpatrick et al., 2006). Men, whose schizophrenia develops on average four years earlier than women's, more often exhibit negative symptoms and chronic schizophrenia (Räsänen et al., 2000).

Recovery is much more likely when a previously well-adjusted person develops schizophrenia rapidly (called *acute,* or *reactive, schizophrenia*) following some sort of life stress. People with reactive schizophrenia more often have the positive symptoms that respond to drug therapy (Fenton & McGlashan, 1991, 1994; Fowles, 1992).

Understanding Schizophrenia

Schizophrenia is the most dreaded psychological disorder. It is also one of the most heavily researched. Most research studies now link it with abnormal brain tissue and activity, and with genetic predispositions. Schizophrenia is a disease of the brain manifested in symptoms of the mind.

Brain Abnormalities

14-12: What brain abnormalities are associated with schizophrenia?

Might chemical imbalances in the brain explain schizophrenia? Scientists have long known that strange behavior can have strange chemical causes. Have you ever heard the saying "mad as a hatter"? That phrase dates back to the behavior of British hatmakers whose brains were slowly poisoned as they used their tongue and lips to moisten the brims of mercury-laden felt hats (Smith, 1983). Could schizophrenia symptoms have a similar biochemical key? Scientists are tracking the mechanisms by which chemicals produce hallucinations and other symptoms.

Dopamine Overactivity   One possible answer emerged when researchers examined schizophrenia patients' brains after death. They found an excess number of *dopamine* receptors, including a sixfold excess for the dopamine receptor D4 (Seeman et al., 1993; Wong et al., 1986). The resulting hyper-responsive dopamine system could intensify brain signals, creating positive symptoms such as hallucinations and paranoia (Grace, 2010). Other evidence reinforces this idea: Drugs that block dopamine receptors often lessen these symptoms; drugs that increase dopamine levels, such as amphetamines and cocaine, sometimes intensify them (Seeman, 2007; Swerdlow & Koob, 1987).

Abnormal Brain Activity and Anatomy   People with chronic schizophrenia often display abnormal activity in multiple brain areas. Some have abnormally low brain activity in the brain's frontal lobes, which are critical for reasoning, planning, and problem solving (Morey et al., 2005; Pettegrew et al., 1993; Resnick, 1992). The brain waves that reflect synchronized neural firing in the frontal lobes decline noticeably (Spencer et al., 2004; Symond et al., 2005). These out-of-sync neurons may disrupt neural network functioning.

One study took PET scans of brain activity while people were hallucinating (Silbersweig et al., 1995). When participants heard a voice or saw something, their brain became vigorously active in several core regions. One was the thalamus, the structure that filters incoming sensory signals and transmits them to the brain's cortex. Another PET scan study of people with paranoia found increased activity in the amygdala, a fear-processing center (Epstein et al., 1998).

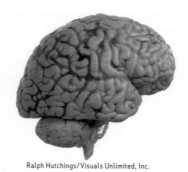

Ralph Hutchings/Visuals Unlimited, Inc.

Studying the neurophysiology of schizophrenia Psychiatrist E. Fuller Torrey is collecting the brains of hundreds of those who died as young adults and suffered disorders such as schizophrenia and bipolar disorder. Torrey is making tissue samples available to researchers worldwide.

Chris Usher

Many studies of people with schizophrenia have found enlarged, fluid-filled areas and a corresponding shrinkage and thinning of cerebral tissue (Goldman et al., 2009; Wright et al., 2000). Such brain abnormalities have even appeared in studies of people who would *later* develop this disorder, and in their close relatives (Karlsgodt et al., 2010). The greater the brain shrinkage, the more severe the thought disorder (Collinson et al., 2003; Nelson et al., 1998; Shenton, 1992).

One smaller-than-normal area is the cortex. Another is the corpus callosum connecting the two hemispheres (Arnone et al., 2008). The thalamus shrinks as well, which may explain why filtering sensory input and focusing attention can be difficult for people with schizophrenia (Andreasen et al., 1994; Ellison-Wright et al., 2008). The bottom line is that schizophrenia involves not one isolated brain abnormality but problems with several brain regions and their interconnections (Andreasen, 1997, 2001).

Prenatal Environment and Risk

14-13: What prenatal events are associated with increased risk of developing schizophrenia?

What causes brain abnormalities in people with schizophrenia? Some researchers point to mishaps during prenatal development or delivery (Fatemi & Folsom, 2009; Walker et al., 2010). Risk factors for schizophrenia include low birth weight, maternal diabetes, older paternal age, and oxygen deprivation during delivery (King et al., 2010). Famine may also increase risks. People conceived during the peak of World War II's Dutch famine developed schizophrenia at twice the normal rate. Those conceived during the famine of 1959 to 1961 in eastern China also displayed this doubled rate (St. Clair et al., 2005; Susser et al., 1996).

Let's consider another possible culprit. Might a midpregnancy viral infection impair fetal brain development (Patterson, 2007)? To test this fetal-virus idea, scientists have asked these questions:

- *Are people at increased risk of schizophrenia if, during the middle of their fetal development, their country experienced a flu epidemic?* The repeated answer has been *Yes* (Mednick et al., 1994; Murray et al., 1992; Wright et al., 1995).

- *Are people born in densely populated areas, where viral diseases spread more readily, at greater risk for schizophrenia?* The answer, confirmed in a study of 1.75 million Danes, has again been *Yes* (Jablensky, 1999; Mortensen, 1999).

- *Are people born during the winter and spring months—after the fall-winter flu season—also at increased risk?* The answer is again *Yes,* and the risk increases from 5 to 8 percent (Fox, 2010; Torrey et al., 1997, 2002).

- *In the Southern Hemisphere, where the seasons are the reverse of the Northern Hemisphere, are the months of above-average schizophrenia births similarly reversed?* Again, the answer has been *Yes*. In Australia, people born between August and October are at greater risk. But there is an exception: For people born in the Northern Hemisphere, who later moved to Australia, the risk is greater if they were born between January and March (McGrath et al., 1995, 1999).

- *Are mothers who report being sick with influenza during pregnancy more likely to bear children who develop schizophrenia?* In one study of nearly 8000 women, the answer was *Yes*. The schizophrenia risk increased from the customary 1 percent to about 2 percent—but only when infections occurred during the second trimester (Brown et al., 2000). Maternal influenza infection during pregnancy also affects brain development in monkeys (Short et al., 2010).

- *Does blood drawn from pregnant women whose offspring develop schizophrenia show higher-than-normal levels of antibodies that suggest a viral infection?* In one study of 27 women whose children later developed schizophrenia, the answer was *Yes* (Buka et al., 2001). In a huge California study, which collected blood samples from some 20,000 pregnant women during the 1950s and 1960s, the answer was again *Yes* (Brown et al., 2004). Another study found traces of a specific retrovirus (HERV) in nearly half of people with schizophrenia and virtually none in healthy people (Perron et al., 2008).

These converging lines of evidence suggest that fetal-virus infections contribute to the development of schizophrenia. This finding strengthens the U.S. government recommendation that "women who expect to be more than three months pregnant during the flu season" should have a flu shot (CDC, 2011).

Why might a second-trimester maternal flu bout put fetuses at risk? Is it the virus itself? The mother's immune response to it? Medications taken? (Wyatt et al., 2001). Does the infection weaken the brain's supportive glial cells, leading to reduced synaptic connections (Moises et al., 2002)? In time, answers may become available.

Genetic Influences

14-14: How do genes influence schizophrenia?

Fetal-virus infections may increase the odds that a child will develop schizophrenia. But many women get the flu during their second trimester of pregnancy, and only 2 percent of them bear children who develop schizophrenia. Why does prenatal exposure to the flu virus put some children at risk but not others? Could the answer be that some people are more vulnerable because of an inherited predisposition? The evidence is clear: The answer is *Yes*. For most people, the odds of being diagnosed with schizophrenia are nearly 1 in 100. For those who have a sibling or parent with the disorder, the odds increase to about 1 in 10. And if the affected sibling is an identical twin, the odds are close to 1 in 2 (**FIGURE 14.10**). Those odds are unchanged even when the twins are reared apart (Plomin et al., 1997). (Only about a dozen such cases are on record.)

Remember, though, that identical twins share more than their genes. They also share a prenatal environment. About two-thirds share a placenta and the blood it supplies; the other one-third have separate placentas. Shared placentas matter. If the co-twin of an identical twin with schizophrenia shared the placenta, the chances of developing the disorder are 6 in 10. If they had separate placentas (as do fraternal twins), the chances are only 1 in 10 (Davis et al., 1995a,b; Phelps et al., 1997). Twins who share a placenta are more likely to experience the same prenatal viruses. So perhaps shared germs as well as shared genes produce identical twin similarities.

Adoption studies help untangle genetic and environmental influences. Children adopted by someone who develops schizophrenia seldom "catch" the disorder. Rather, adopted children have a higher risk if a *biological* parent has schizophrenia (Gottesman, 1991). Genes matter.

The search is on for specific genes that, in some combination, might lead to schizophrenia-inducing brain abnormalities (Levinson et al., 2011; Mitchell & Porteous, 2011; Vacic et al., 2011; Wang et al., 2010). (It is not our genes but our brains that directly control our behavior.) Some of these genes influence the activity of dopamine and other brain neurotransmitters. Others affect the production of *myelin*, a fatty substance that coats the axons of nerve cells and lets impulses travel at high speed through neural networks.

Although genes matter, the genetic formula is not as straightforward as the inheritance of eye color. Genome studies of thousands of individuals with and without schizophrenia indicate that schizophrenia is influenced by many genes, each with very small effects (International Schizophrenia Consortium, 2009; Pogue-Geile & Yokley, 2010). Recall from Chapter 2 that *epigenetic* (literally "in addition to genetic") factors influence gene expression.

FIGURE 14.10

Risk of developing schizophrenia The lifetime risk of developing schizophrenia varies with one's genetic relatedness to someone having this disorder. Across countries, barely more than 1 in 10 fraternal twins, but some 5 in 10 identical twins, share a schizophrenia diagnosis. (Adapted from Gottesman, 2001.)

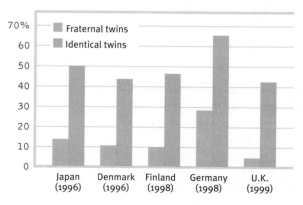

Schizophrenia risk for twins of those diagnosed with schizophrenia

- Fraternal twins
- Identical twins

Japan (1996) · Denmark (1996) · Finland (1998) · Germany (1998) · U.K. (1999)

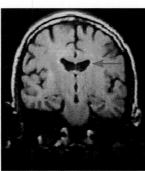

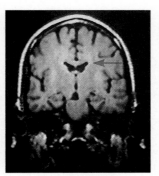

Both photos: Courtesy of Daniel R. Weinberger, M.D., NIH-NIMH/NSC

Schizophrenia   **No schizophrenia**

Schizophrenia in identical twins When twins differ, only the one afflicted with schizophrenia typically has enlarged, fluid-filled cranial cavities (right) (Suddath et al., 1990). The difference between the twins implies some nongenetic factor, such as a virus, is also at work.

Like hot water activating a tea bag, environmental factors such as viral infections, nutritional deprivation, and maternal stress can "turn on" the genes that put some of us at higher risk for this disorder. Identical twins' differing histories in the womb and beyond explain why only one may show differing gene expressions (Walker et al., 2010). As we have seen in so many different contexts, nature and nurture interact. Neither hand claps alone.

Thanks to our expanding understanding of genetic and brain influences on maladies such as schizophrenia, the general public increasingly attributes psychiatric disorders to biological factors (Pescosolido et al., 2010).

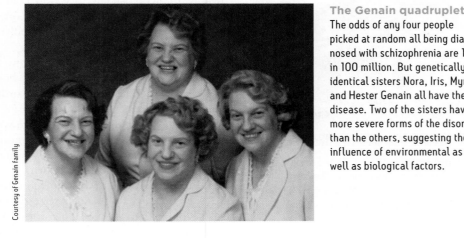

Courtesy of Genain family

The Genain quadruplets The odds of any four people picked at random all being diagnosed with schizophrenia are 1 in 100 million. But genetically identical sisters Nora, Iris, Myra, and Hester Genain all have the disease. Two of the sisters have more severe forms of the disorder than the others, suggesting the influence of environmental as well as biological factors.

★ ★ ★

Most of us can relate more easily to the ups and downs of mood disorders than to the strange thoughts, perceptions, and behaviors of schizophrenia. Sometimes our thoughts do jump around, but we rarely talk nonsensically. Occasionally we feel unjustly suspicious of someone, but we do not believe the world is plotting against us. Often our perceptions err, but rarely do we see or hear things that are not there. We have felt regret after laughing at someone's misfortune, but we rarely giggle in response to bad news. At times we just want to be alone, but we do not live in social isolation. However, millions of people around the world do talk strangely, suffer delusions, hear nonexistent voices, see things that are not there, laugh or cry at inappropriate times, or withdraw into private imaginary worlds. The quest to solve the cruel puzzle of schizophrenia therefore continues, more vigorously than ever.

RETRIEVE IT

- A person with schizophrenia who has _____ (positive/negative) symptoms may have an expressionless face and toneless voice. These symptoms are most common with _____ (chronic/acute) schizophrenia and are not likely to respond to drug therapy. Those with _____ (positive/negative) symptoms are likely to experience delusions and to be diagnosed with _____ (chronic/acute) schizophrenia, which is much more likely to respond to drug therapy.

ANSWERS: negative; chronic; positive; acute

- What factors contribute to the onset and development of schizophrenia?

ANSWER: Biological factors include abnormalities in brain structure and function, prenatal exposure to a maternal virus, and genetic factors. However, schizophrenia is more likely to develop given a high-risk environment.

Other Disorders

Dissociative Disorders

14-15: What are dissociative disorders, and why are they controversial?

Among the most bewildering disorders are the rare **dissociative disorders.** The person's conscious awareness is said to *dissociate* (become separated) from painful memories, thoughts, and feelings. The result may be a "fugue state," a sudden loss of memory or change in identity, often in response to an overwhelmingly stressful situation. Such was the case for one Vietnam veteran who was haunted by his comrades' deaths, and who had left his World Trade Center office shortly before the 9/11 attack. He disappeared on the way to work one day and was discovered six months later in a Chicago homeless shelter, reportedly with no memory of his identity or family (Stone, 2006).

Multiple personalities Chris Sizemore's story, told in the book and movie, *The Three Faces of Eve,* gave early visibility to what is now called *dissociative identity disorder.*

Dissociation itself is not so rare. Any one of us may have a fleeting sense of being unreal, of being separated from our body, of watching ourselves as if in a movie. A massive dissociation of self from ordinary consciousness occurs in **dissociative identity disorder (DID).** At different times, two or more distinct identities seem to control the person's behavior, each with its own voice and mannerisms. Thus, the person may be prim and proper one moment, loud and flirtatious the next. Typically, the original personality denies any awareness of the other(s).

People diagnosed with DID (formerly called *multiple personality disorder*) are rarely violent, but cases have been reported of dissociations into a "good" and a "bad" (or aggressive) personality—a modest version of the Dr. Jekyll–Mr. Hyde split immortalized in Robert Louis Stevenson's story. One unusual case involved Kenneth Bianchi, accused in the "Hillside Strangler" rapes and murders of 10 California women. During a hypnosis session with Bianchi, psychologist John Watkins (1984) "called forth" a hidden personality: "I've talked a bit to Ken, but I think that perhaps there might be another part of Ken that . . . maybe feels somewhat differently from the part that I've talked to. . . . Would you talk with me, Part, by saying, 'I'm here'?" Bianchi answered "Yes" and then claimed to be "Steve."

Speaking as Steve, Bianchi stated that he hated Ken because Ken was nice and that he (Steve), aided by a cousin, had murdered women. He also claimed Ken knew nothing about Steve's existence and was innocent of the murders. Was Bianchi's second personality a ruse, simply a way of disavowing responsibility for his actions? Indeed, Bianchi—a practiced liar who had read about multiple personality in psychology books—was later convicted.

The "Hillside Strangler" Kenneth Bianchi is shown here at his trial.

Understanding Dissociative Identity Disorder Skeptics have raised some serious questions about DID. First, they find it suspicious that the disorder has such a short history. Between 1930 and 1960, the number of North American DID diagnoses was 2 per decade. By the 1980s, when the DSM contained the first formal code for this disorder, the number exploded to more than 20,000 (McHugh, 1995a). The average number of displayed personalities also mushroomed—from 3 to 12 per patient (Goff & Simms, 1993).

Second, note the skeptics, DID is much less prevalent outside North America, although in other cultures some people are said to be "possessed" by an alien spirit (Aldridge-Morris, 1989; Kluft, 1991). In Britain, DID—which some have considered "a wacky American fad" (Cohen, 1995)—is rare. In India and Japan, it is essentially nonexistent (or at least unreported). Such findings, skeptics say, point to a cultural explanation—a disorder created by therapists in a particular social context (Merskey, 1992). Rather than being provoked by trauma, dissociative symptoms tend to be exhibited by suggestible, fantasy-prone people (Giesbrecht et al., 2008, 2010).

Third, instead of being a real disorder, skeptics have asked, could DID be an extension of our normal capacity for personality shifts? Nicholas Spanos (1986, 1994, 1996) asked college students to pretend they were accused murderers being examined by a psychiatrist. Given the same hypnotic treatment Bianchi received, most spontaneously expressed a second personality. This discovery made Spanos wonder: Are dissociative identities simply a more extreme version of the varied "selves" we normally present, as when we display a goofy, loud self while hanging out with friends, and a subdued, respectful self around grandparents? If so, say the critics, clinicians who discover multiple personalities may merely have triggered role-playing by fantasy-prone people. After all, clients do not enter therapy saying "Allow me to introduce myselves." Rather, note these skeptics, some therapists go fishing for multiple personalities: "Have you ever felt like another part of you does things you can't control? Does this part of you have a name? Can I talk to the angry part of you?" Once patients permit a therapist to talk, by name, "to the part of you that says those angry things," they begin acting out the fantasy. Like actors who lose themselves in their roles, vulnerable patients may "become" the parts they are acting out. The result may be the experience of another self.

Other researchers and clinicians believe DID is a real disorder. They have found support for this view in the distinct brain and body states associated with differing personalities (Putnam, 1991). Brain scans of people with DID have revealed activity in areas linked with traumatic memories (Elzinga et al., 2007). Handedness sometimes switches with personality (Henninger, 1992). Shifts in visual acuity and eye-muscle balance have been recorded as DID patients switched personalities, but not as control group members tried to simulate DID behavior (Miller et al., 1991).

Both the psychodynamic and learning perspectives have interpreted DID symptoms as ways of dealing with anxiety. Some psychodynamic theorists see them as defenses against the anxiety caused by unacceptable impulses. In this view, an immoral second personality could allow the discharge of forbidden impulses. (This explanation presumes the existence of repressed memories, which has been questioned by memory researchers; see Chapters 8 and 12.) Learning theorists see dissociative disorders as behaviors reinforced by anxiety reduction.

Some clinicians suggest including dissociative disorders under the umbrella of post-traumatic stress disorders. In this view, DID would be a natural, protective response to traumatic experiences during childhood (Putnam, 1995; Spiegel, 2008). Many DID patients recall being physically, sexually, or emotionally abused as children (Gleaves, 1996; Lilienfeld et al., 1999). In one study of 12 murderers diagnosed with DID, 11 had suffered severe abuse, even torture, in childhood (Lewis et al., 1997). One had been set afire by his parents. Another had been used in child pornography and was scarred from being made to sit on a stove burner. Some critics wonder, however, whether vivid imagination or therapist suggestion contributed to such recollections (Kihlstrom, 2005).

So the debate continues. On one side are those who believe multiple personalities are the desperate efforts of people trying to detach from a horrific existence. On the other are the skeptics who think DID is a condition constructed out of the therapist-patient interaction and acted out by fantasy-prone, emotionally vulnerable people. If the skeptics' view wins, predicted psychiatrist Paul McHugh (1995b), "this epidemic will end in the way that the witch craze ended in Salem. The [multiple personality phenomenon] will be seen as manufactured."

"Pretense may become reality."

Chinese proverb

"Would it be possible to speak with the personality that pays the bills?"

RETRIEVE IT

- The psychodynamic and learning perspectives agree that dissociative identity disorder symptoms are ways of dealing with anxiety. How do their explanations differ?

ANSWER: The psychodynamic explanation of DID symptoms is that they are defenses against anxiety generated by unacceptable urges. The learning perspective attempts to explain these symptoms as behaviors that have been reinforced by relieving anxiety in the past.

dissociative disorders disorders in which conscious awareness becomes separated (dissociated) from previous memories, thoughts, and feelings.

dissociative identity disorder (DID) a rare dissociative disorder in which a person exhibits two or more distinct and alternating personalities. Formerly called *multiple personality disorder*.

Reprinted by permission of *The New England Journal of Medicine*, 207, (Oct. 5, 1932), 613–617.

Dying to be thin Anorexia was identified and named in the 1870s, when it appeared among affluent adolescent girls (Brumberg, 2000). This 1930s photo illustrates the physical condition.

"Why do women have such low self-esteem? There are many complex psychological and societal reasons, by which I mean Barbie."

Dave Barry, 1999

© Julie Ridge/iStockphoto

A too-fat body image underlies anorexia.

Eating Disorders

14-16: What are the three main eating disorders, and how do biological, psychological, and social-cultural influences make people more vulnerable to these disorders?

Our bodies are naturally disposed to maintain a normal weight, including stored energy reserves for times when food becomes unavailable. Yet sometimes psychological influences overwhelm biological wisdom. This becomes painfully clear in three eating disorders:

- **Anorexia nervosa** typically begins as a weight-loss diet. People with anorexia—usually adolescents and 9 out of 10 times females—drop significantly below normal weight, typically by 15 percent or more. Yet they feel fat, fear gaining weight, remain obsessed with losing weight, and sometimes exercise excessively. About half of those with anorexia display a binge-purge-depression cycle.

- **Bulimia nervosa** may also be triggered by a weight-loss diet, broken by gorging on forbidden foods. In a cycle of repeating episodes, people with this disorder—mostly women in their late teens or early twenties—alternate binge eating and purging (through vomiting or laxative use) (Wonderlich et al., 2007). Fasting or excessive exercise may follow. Preoccupied with food (craving sweets and high-fat foods), and fearful of becoming overweight, binge-purge eaters experience bouts of depression and anxiety during and following binges (Hinz & Williamson, 1987; Johnson et al., 2002). Unlike anorexia, bulimia is marked by weight fluctuations within or above normal ranges, making the condition easy to hide.

- Those with **binge-eating disorder** engage in significant binge eating, followed by remorse, but they do not purge, fast, or exercise excessively, and thus may be overweight.

A U.S. National Institute of Mental Health-funded study reported that, at some point during their lifetime, 0.6 percent of people meet the criteria for anorexia, 1 percent for bulimia, and 2.8 percent for binge-eating disorder (Hudson et al., 2007). So, how can we explain these disorders?

Understanding Eating Disorders

Eating disorders do *not* provide (as some have speculated) a telltale sign of childhood sexual abuse (Smolak & Murnen, 2002; Stice, 2002). The family environment may provide a fertile ground for the growth of eating disorders in other ways, however.

- Mothers of girls with eating disorders tend to focus on their own weight and on their daughters' weight and appearance (Pike & Rodin, 1991).

- Bulimia patients' families have a higher-than-usual incidence of childhood obesity and negative self-evaluation (Jacobi et al., 2004).

- Anorexia patients' families tend to be competitive, high achieving, and protective (Pate et al., 1992; Yates, 1989, 1990).

Those with eating disorders often have low self-evaluations, set perfectionist standards, fret about falling short of expectations, and are intensely concerned with how others perceive them (Pieters et al., 2007; Polivy & Herman, 2002; Sherry & Hall, 2009). Some of these factors also predict teen boys' pursuit of unrealistic muscularity (Ricciardelli & McCabe, 2004).

Genetics also influence susceptibility to eating disorders. Twins are more likely to share the disorder if they are identical rather than fraternal (Culbert et al., 2009; Klump et al., 2009; Root et al., 2010). Scientists are now searching for culprit genes, which may influence the body's available serotonin and estrogen (Klump & Culbert, 2007).

But these disorders also have cultural and gender components. Ideal shapes vary across culture and time. In impoverished countries, including much of Africa—where plumpness means prosperity and thinness can signal poverty or illness—bigger seems better (Knickmeyer, 2001; Swami et al., 2010). Bigger does not seem better in Western cultures, where, according to 222 studies of 141,000 people, the rise in eating disorders in the last half of the twentieth century coincided with a dramatic increase in women having a poor body image (Feingold & Mazzella, 1998).

Those most vulnerable to eating disorders are also those (usually women or gay men) who most idealize thinness and have the greatest body dissatisfaction (Feldman & Meyer, 2010; Kane, 2010; Stice et al., 2010). Should it surprise us, then, that when women view real and doctored images of unnaturally thin models and celebrities, they often feel ashamed, depressed, and dissatisfied with their own bodies—the very attitudes that predispose eating disorders (Grabe et al., 2008; Myers & Crowther, 2009; Tiggeman & Miller, 2010)? Eric Stice and his colleagues (2001) tested this modeling idea by giving some adolescent girls (but not others) a 15-month subscription to an American teen-fashion magazine. Compared with their counterparts who had not received the magazine, vulnerable girls—defined as those who were already dissatisfied, idealizing thinness, and lacking social support—exhibited increased body dissatisfaction and eating disorder tendencies. But even ultra-thin models do not reflect the impossible standard of the classic Barbie doll, who had, when adjusted to a height of 5 feet 7 inches, a 32–16–29 figure (in centimeters, 82–41–73) (Norton et al., 1996).

It seems clear that the sickness of today's eating disorders lies in part within our weight-obsessed culture—a culture that says, in countless ways, "Fat is bad," that motivates millions of women to be "always dieting," and that encourages eating binges by pressuring women to live in a constant state of semistarvation. If cultural learning contributes to eating behavior, then might prevention programs increase acceptance of one's body? Reviews of prevention studies answer *Yes,* and especially if the programs are interactive and focused on girls over age 15 (Stice et al., 2007; Vocks et al., 2010).

"Thanks, but we don't eat."

"Skeletons on Parade" A newspaper article used this headline in criticizing the display of superthin models. Do such models make self-starvation fashionable?

RETRIEVE IT

- People with _____ (anorexia nervosa/bulimia nervosa) continue to want to lose weight even when they are underweight. Those with _____ (anorexia nervosa/bulimia nervosa) tend to have weight that fluctuates within or above normal ranges.

ANSWERS: anorexia nervosa; bulimia nervosa

Personality Disorders

14-17: What are the three clusters of personality disorders? What behaviors and brain activity characterize the antisocial personality?

The disruptive, inflexible, and enduring behavior patterns of **personality disorders** interfere with social functioning. These disorders tend to form three clusters, characterized by

- anxiety, such as a fearful sensitivity to rejection that predisposes the withdrawn *avoidant personality disorder.*

- eccentric or odd behaviors, such as the emotionless disengagement of the *schizoid personality disorder.*

anorexia nervosa an eating disorder in which a person (usually an adolescent female) maintains a starvation diet despite being significantly (15 percent or more) underweight.

bulimia nervosa an eating disorder in which a person alternates binge eating (usually of high-calorie foods) with purging (by vomiting or laxative use) or fasting.

binge-eating disorder significant binge-eating episodes, followed by distress, disgust, or guilt, but without the compensatory purging or fasting that marks bulimia nervosa.

personality disorders psychological disorders characterized by inflexible and enduring behavior patterns that impair social functioning.

No remorse Dennis Rader, known as the "BTK killer" in Kansas, was convicted in 2005 of killing 10 people over a 30-year span. Rader exhibited the extreme lack of conscience that marks antisocial personality disorder.

dramatic or impulsive behaviors, such as the attention-getting *histrionic personality disorder,* the self-focused and self-inflating *narcissistic personality disorder,* and the *antisocial personality disorder.*

These categories are not sharply distinguished, however, and some are slated to be revised or eliminated in the next DSM revision (Holden, 2010).

Antisocial Personality Disorder

The most troubling and heavily researched personality disorder is the **antisocial personality disorder.** You may have heard the older terms *sociopath* or *psychopath.* A person with this disorder is typically a male who shows no conscience, even toward friends and family. When an antisocial personality combines a keen intelligence with no conscience, the result may be a charming and clever con artist, a ruthless corporate executive (*Snakes in Suits* is a book on antisocial behavior in business)—or worse.

The disorder usually appears before age 15, as the person begins to lie, steal, fight, or display unrestrained sexual behavior (Cale & Lilienfeld, 2002). Not all such children become antisocial adults. Those who do (about half of them) will generally be unable to keep a job, irresponsible as a spouse and parent, and violent or otherwise criminal (Farrington, 1991). Despite their remorseless and sometimes criminal behavior, criminality is not an essential component of antisocial behavior (Skeem & Cooke, 2010). Moreover, many criminals do not fit the description of antisocial personality disorder. Why? Because they show responsible concern for their friends and family members.

"Thursday is out. I have jury duty."

Many criminals, like this one, exhibit a sense of conscience and responsibility in other areas of their life, and thus do not exhibit antisocial personality disorder.

Antisocial personalities behave impulsively, and then feel and fear little (Fowles & Dindo, 2009). The results can be horrifying, as they were in the case of Henry Lee Lucas. He killed his first victim when he was 13. He felt little regret then or later. He confessed that, during his 32 years of crime, he had brutally beaten, suffocated, stabbed, shot, or mutilated some 360 women, men, and children. For the last 6 years of his reign of terror, Lucas teamed with Ottis Elwood Toole, who reportedly slaughtered about 50 people he "didn't think was worth living anyhow" (Darrach & Norris, 1984).

Understanding Antisocial Personality Disorder Antisocial personality disorder is woven of both biological and psychological strands. No single gene codes for a complex behavior such as crime. Molecular geneticists have, however, identified some specific genes that are more common in those with antisocial personality disorder (Gunter et al., 2010). There may be a genetic predisposition toward a fearless and uninhibited life. Twin and adoption studies have revealed that biological relatives of people with antisocial and unemotional tendencies are at increased risk for antisocial behavior (Larsson et al., 2007; Livesley & Jang, 2008). The genes that put people at risk for antisocial behavior also increase the risk for dependence on alcohol and other drugs, which helps explain why these disorders often appear in combination (Dick, 2007).

Genetic influences, often in combination with childhood abuse, help wire the brain (Dodge, 2009). The genetic vulnerability of those with antisocial and unemotional

antisocial personality disorder a personality disorder in which a person (usually a man) exhibits a lack of conscience for wrongdoing, even toward friends and family members. May be aggressive and ruthless or a clever con artist.

tendencies appears as low arousal. Awaiting events that most people would find unnerving, such as electric shocks or loud noises, they show little autonomic nervous system arousal (Hare, 1975; van Goozen et al., 2007). Long-term studies show that their stress hormone levels are lower than average in their early teens, before they have committed any crime (**FIGURE 14.11**). And children who are slow to develop conditioned fears at age 3 are in later years more likely to commit a crime (Gao et al., 2010).

Other studies have found that preschool boys who later became aggressive or antisocial adolescents tended to be impulsive, uninhibited, unconcerned with social rewards, and low in anxiety (Caspi et al., 1996; Tremblay et al., 1994). These traits, if channeled in more productive directions, may lead to courageous heroism, adventurism, or star-level athleticism (Poulton & Milne, 2002). Lacking a sense of social responsibility, the same disposition may produce a cool con artist or killer (Lykken, 1995).

With antisocial behavior, as with so much else, nature and nurture interact and leave their marks on the brain. To explore the neural basis of antisocial personality disorder, scientists are identifying brain activity differences in antisocial criminals. Shown emotionally evocative photographs, such as a man holding a knife to a woman's throat, they display blunted heart rate and perspiration responses, and less activity in brain areas that typically respond to emotional stimuli (Harenski et al., 2010; Kiehl & Buckholtz, 2010). They also display a hyper-reactive dopamine reward system that predisposes their impulsive drive to do something rewarding, despite the consequences (Buckholtz et al., 2010). One study compared PET scans of 41 murderers' brains with those from people of similar age and sex. The murderers' frontal lobes, an area that helps control impulses, displayed reduced activity (Raine, 1999, 2005; **FIGURE 14.12**). This reduction was especially apparent in those who murdered impulsively. In a follow-up study, researchers found that violent repeat offenders had 11 percent less frontal lobe tissue than normal (Raine et al., 2000). This helps explain another finding: People with antisocial personality disorder fall far below normal in aspects of thinking such as planning, organization, and inhibition, which are all frontal lobe functions (Morgan & Lilienfeld, 2000). Such data remind us: Everything psychological is also biological.

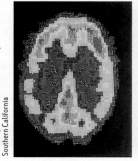

Courtesy of Adrian Raine, University of Southern California

Normal   Murderer

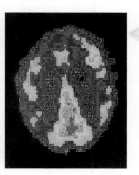

Adrenaline excretion (ng/min.)

Males with criminal convictions as adults had lower levels of arousal as 13-year-olds.

No criminal conviction
Criminal conviction

Nonstressful situation   Stressful situation

FIGURE 14.11

Cold-blooded arousability and risk of crime Levels of the stress hormone adrenaline were measured in two groups of 13-year-old Swedish boys. In both stressful and nonstressful situations, those who would later be convicted of a crime as 18- to 26-year-olds showed relatively low arousal. (From Magnusson, 1990.)

Does a full Moon trigger "madness" in some people? James Rotton and I. W. Kelly (1985) examined data from 37 studies that related lunar phase to crime, homicides, crisis calls, and mental hospital admissions. Their conclusion: There is virtually no evidence of "Moon madness." Nor does lunar phase correlate with suicides, assaults, emergency room visits, or traffic disasters (Martin et al., 1992; Raison et al., 1999).

FIGURE 14.12

Murderous minds These top-facing PET scans illustrate reduced activation (less red and yellow) in a murderer's frontal cortex—a brain area that helps brake impulsive, aggressive behavior. (From Raine, 1999.)

RETRIEVE IT

• How do biological and psychological factors contribute to antisocial personality disorder?

ANSWER: Twin and adoption studies show that biological relatives of people with this disorder are at increased risk for antisocial behavior. Negative environmental factors, such as poverty or childhood abuse, may channel genetic traits such as fearlessness in more dangerous directions—toward aggression and away from social responsibility.

Table 14.6
Percentage of Americans Reporting Selected Psychological Disorders in the Past Year

Psychological Disorder	Percentage
Generalized anxiety	3.1
Social phobia	6.8
Phobia of specific object or situation	8.7
Mood disorder	9.5
Obsessive-compulsive disorder (OCD)	1.0
Schizophrenia	1.1
Post-traumatic stress disorder (PTSD)	3.5
Attention-deficit hyperactivity disorder (ADHD)	4.1
Any mental disorder	26.2

Source: National Institute of Mental Health, 2008.

Rates of Psychological Disorders

14-18: How many people currently have, or have had, a psychological disorder? Is poverty a risk factor?

Who is most vulnerable to psychological disorders? At what times of life? To answer such questions, various countries have conducted lengthy, structured interviews with representative samples of thousands of their citizens. After asking hundreds of questions that probe for symptoms—"Has there ever been a period of two weeks or more when you felt like you wanted to die?"—the researchers have estimated the current, prior-year, and lifetime prevalence of various disorders.

How many people have, or have had, a psychological disorder? More than most of us suppose:

• The U.S. National Institute of Mental Health (2008, based on Kessler et al., 2005) estimates that 26 percent of adult Americans "suffer from a diagnosable mental disorder in a given year" (**TABLE 14.6**).

• A twenty-first-century World Health Organization (2004) study—based on 90-minute interviews of 60,463 people—estimated the number of prior-year mental disorders in 20 countries. As **FIGURE 14.13** displays, the lowest rate of reported mental disorders was in Shanghai, the highest rate in the United States. Moreover, people immigrating to the United States from Mexico, Africa, and Asia average better mental health than their U.S. counterparts with the same ethnic heritage (Breslau et al., 2007; Maldonado-Molina et al., 2011). For example, compared with people who have recently immigrated from Mexico, Mexican-Americans born in the United States are at greater risk of mental disorder—a phenomenon known as the *immigrant paradox* (Schwartz et al., 2010).

Who is most vulnerable to mental disorders? As we have seen, the answer varies with the disorder. One predictor of mental disorders—poverty—crosses ethnic and gender lines. The incidence of serious psychological disorders has been doubly high among those below the poverty line (Centers for Disease Control, 1992). This correlation, like so many others, raises further questions: Does poverty cause disorders? Or do disorders cause poverty? It is both, though the answer varies with the disorder. Schizophrenia understandably leads to poverty. Yet the stresses and demoralization of poverty can also precipitate disorders, especially depression in women and substance abuse in men (Dohrenwend et al., 1992). In one natural experiment on the poverty-pathology link, researchers tracked rates of behavior problems in North Carolina Native American children as economic development enabled a dramatic reduction in their community's poverty rate. As the study began, children of poverty exhibited more deviant and aggressive behaviors. After four years, children whose families had moved above the poverty line exhibited a 40 percent decrease in the behavior problems; those who continued in their previous positions below or above the poverty line exhibited no change (Costello et al., 2003).

FIGURE 14.13
Prior-year prevalence of disorders in selected areas
From World Health Organization (2004) interviews in 20 countries.

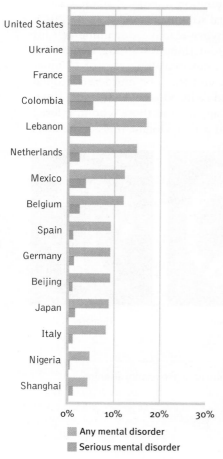

United States
Ukraine
France
Colombia
Lebanon
Netherlands
Mexico
Belgium
Spain
Germany
Beijing
Japan
Italy
Nigeria
Shanghai

0%   10%   20%   30%

■ Any mental disorder
■ Serious mental disorder

At what times of life do disorders strike? Usually by early adulthood. "Over 75 percent of our sample with any disorder had experienced [their] first symptoms by age 24," reported Lee Robins and Darrel Regier (1991, p. 331). Among the earliest to appear are symptoms of antisocial personality disorder (median age 8) and of phobias (median age 10). Alcohol dependence, obsessive-compulsive disorder, bipolar disorder, and schizophrenia symptoms appear at a median age near 20. Major depression often hits somewhat later, at a median age of 25. Such findings make clear the need for research and treatment to help the growing number of people, especially teenagers and young adults, with psychological disorders.

Although mindful of the pain, we can be encouraged by the many ordinary and exceptional people who pursue successful careers and enjoy fulfilling lives while enduring psychological difficulties. The bewilderment, fear, and sorrow caused by psychological disorders are real. But, as Chapter 15 shows, hope, too, is real.

RETRIEVE IT

• What is the relationship between poverty and psychological disorders?

ANSWER: Poverty-related stresses can help trigger disorders, but disabling disorders can also contribute to poverty. Thus, poverty and disorder are often a chicken-and-egg situation, and it's hard to know which came first.

CHAPTER REVIEW

Psychological Disorders

LEARNING OBJECTIVES

Test Yourself by taking a moment to answer each of these Learning Objective Questions (repeated here from within the chapter). Then turn to Appendix D, Complete Chapter Reviews, to check your answers. Research suggests that trying to answer these questions on your own will improve your long-term memory of the concepts (McDaniel et al., 2009).

What Is a Psychological Disorder?

14-1: How should we draw the line between normal behavior and psychological disorder?

14-2: Why is there controversy over attention-deficit hyperactivity disorder?

14-3: How is our understanding of disorders affected by whether we use a medical model or a biopsychosocial approach?

14-4: How and why do clinicians classify psychological disorders, and why do some psychologists criticize the use of diagnostic labels?

Anxiety Disorders

14-5: What are the main anxiety disorders, and how do they differ from the ordinary worries and fears we all experience?

14-6: How do conditioning, cognition, and biology contribute to the feelings and thoughts that mark anxiety disorders?

Mood Disorders

14-7: What are mood disorders? How does major depressive disorder differ from bipolar disorder?

14-8: How do the biological and social-cognitive perspectives explain mood disorders?

14-9: What factors affect suicide and self-injuring, and what are some of the important warning signs to watch for in suicide prevention efforts?

Schizophrenia

14-10: What are the schizophrenia subtypes, and what patterns of thinking, perceiving, feeling, and behaving characterize schizophrenia?

14-11: How do chronic and acute schizophrenia differ?

14-12: What brain abnormalities are associated with schizophrenia?

14-13: What prenatal events are associated with increased risk of developing schizophrenia?

14-14: How do genes influence schizophrenia?

Other Disorders

14-15: What are dissociative disorders, and why are they controversial?

14-16: What are the three main eating disorders, and how do biological, psychological, and social-cultural influences make people more vulnerable to these disorders?

14-17: What are the three clusters of personality disorders? What behaviors and brain activity characterize the antisocial personality?

Rates of Psychological Disorders

14-18: How many people currently have, or have had, a psychological disorder? Is poverty a risk factor?

TERMS AND CONCEPTS TO REMEMBER

Test yourself on these terms by trying to write down the definition in your own words before flipping back to the referenced page to check your answer.

psychological disorder, p. 506

attention-deficit hyperactivity disorder (ADHD), p. 507

medical model, p. 507

DSM-IV-TR, p. 509

anxiety disorders, p. 513

generalized anxiety disorder, p. 513

panic disorder, p. 513

phobia, p. 513

obsessive-compulsive disorder (OCD), p. 514

post-traumatic stress disorder (PTSD), p. 515

mood disorders, p. 519

major depressive disorder, p. 520

bipolar disorder, p. 520

mania, p. 520

schizophrenia, p. 528

psychosis, p. 528

delusions, p. 528

dissociative disorders, p. 534

dissociative identity disorder (DID), p. 534

anorexia nervosa, p. 536

bulimia nervosa, p. 536

binge-eating disorder, p. 536

personality disorders, p. 537

antisocial personality disorder, p. 538

EXPERIENCE THE TESTING EFFECT

Test yourself repeatedly throughout your studies. This will not only help you figure out what you know and don't know; the testing itself will help you learn and remember the information more effectively thanks to the *testing effect.*

1. Anna is embarrassed that it takes her several minutes to parallel-park her car. She usually gets out of the car once or twice to inspect her distance both from the curb and from the nearby cars. Should she worry about having a psychological disorder?

2. Although some psychological disorders are culture-bound, others are universal. For example, in every known culture some people have
   a. bulimia nervosa.   c. schizophrenia.
   b. anorexia nervosa.   d. *susto.*

3. A therapist says that psychological disorders are sicknesses and people with these disorders should be treated as patients in a hospital. This therapist believes in the _____ model.

4. Many psychologists reject the "disorders-as-illness" view and instead contend that other factors may also be involved—for example, the person's bad habits and poor social skills. This view represents the _____ approach.
   a. medical   c. biopsychosocial
   b. evil spirits   d. diagnostic labels

5. Most psychologists and psychiatrists have used _____ to classify psychological disorders.
   a. the DSM-IV-TR
   b. in-depth patient histories
   c. input from patients' family and friends
   d. the theories of Pinel, Rosenhan, and others

6. One study found that psychologists using DSM-IV agreed on a diagnosis for more than 80 percent of patients. The DSM-IV's reliability stems in part from its reliance on
   a. structured-interview procedures.
   b. in-depth patient histories.

c. input from patients' family and friends.

d. the theories of Pinel, Freud, and others.

7. Anxiety that takes the form of an irrational and maladaptive fear of a specific object, activity, or situation is called a _____.

8. An episode of intense dread, accompanied by trembling, dizziness, chest pains, or choking sensations and by feelings of terror, is called

   a. a specific phobia.
   b. compulsion.
   c. a panic attack.
   d. an obsessive fear.

9. Marina became consumed with the need to clean the entire house and refused to participate in any other activities. Her family consulted a therapist, who diagnosed her as having _____ – _____ disorder.

10. The learning perspective proposes that phobias are

    a. the result of individual genetic makeup.
    b. a way of repressing unacceptable impulses.
    c. conditioned fears.
    d. a symptom of having been abused as a child.

11. Two disorders are found worldwide. One is schizophrenia, and the other is _____.

12. Although bipolar disorder is as maladaptive as depression, it is much less common and it affects

    a. more women than men.
    b. more men than women.
    c. women and men equally.
    d. primarily scientists and doctors.

13. The rate of depression is _____ (increasing/decreasing) among young people.

14. Depression can often be alleviated by drugs that increase supplies of the neurotransmitters _____ and _____.

15. Psychologists who emphasize the importance of negative perceptions, beliefs, and thoughts in depression are working within the _____ – _____ perspective.

16. A person with positive symptoms of schizophrenia is most likely to experience

    a. catatonia.
    b. delusions.
    c. withdrawal.
    d. flat emotion.

17. People with schizophrenia may hear voices urging self-destruction, an example of a(n) _____.

18. Victor exclaimed, "The weather has been so schizophrenic lately: It's hot one day and freezing the next!" Is this an accurate comparison? Why or why not?

19. Chances for recovery from schizophrenia are best when

    a. onset is sudden, in response to stress.
    b. deterioration occurs gradually, during childhood.
    c. no environmental causes can be identified.
    d. there is a detectable brain abnormality.

20. Dissociative identity disorder is controversial because

    a. dissociation is actually quite rare.
    b. it was reported frequently in the 1920s but rarely today.
    c. it is almost never reported outside North America.
    d. its symptoms are nearly identical to those of obsessive-compulsive disorder.

21. Which of the following statements is true of bulimia nervosa?

    a. People with bulimia continue to want to lose weight even when they are underweight.
    b. Bulimia is marked by weight fluctuations within or above normal ranges.
    c. Bulimia patients often come from middle-class families that are competitive, high achieving, and protective.
    d. If one twin is diagnosed with bulimia, the chances of the other twin's sharing the disorder are greater if they are fraternal rather than identical twins.

22. A personality disorder, such as antisocial personality, is characterized by

    a. depression.
    b. hallucinations.
    c. enduring and inflexible behavior patterns that impair social functioning.
    d. an elevated level of autonomic nervous system arousal.

23. PET scans of murderers' brains have revealed

    a. higher-than-normal activation in the frontal lobes.
    b. lower-than-normal activation in the frontal lobes.
    c. more frontal lobe tissue than normal.
    d. no differences in brain structures or activity.

24. One predictor of psychiatric disorders that crosses ethnic and gender lines is _____.

25. The symptoms of _____ appear around age 10; _____ tends to appear later, around age 25.

    a. schizophrenia; bipolar disorder
    b. bipolar disorder; schizophrenia
    c. major depression; phobias
    d. phobias; major depression

Find answers to these questions in Appendix E, in the back of the book.

CHAPTER 15

Therapy

Kay Redfield Jamison, an award-winning clinical psychologist and world expert on the emotional extremes of bipolar disorder, knows her subject first-hand. "For as long as I can remember," she recalled in *An Unquiet Mind,* "I was frighteningly, although often wonderfully, beholden to moods. Intensely emotional as a child, mercurial as a young girl, first severely depressed as an adolescent, and then unrelentingly caught up in the cycles of manic-depressive illness by the time I began my professional life, I became, both by necessity and intellectual inclination, a student of moods" (1995, pp. 4–5). Her life was blessed with times of intense sensitivity and passionate energy. But like her father's, it was also at times plagued by reckless spending, racing conversation, and sleeplessness, alternating with swings into "the blackest caves of the mind."

Then, "in the midst of utter confusion," she made a sane and profoundly helpful decision. Risking professional embarrassment she made an appointment with a therapist, a psychiatrist she would visit weekly for years to come:

> He kept me alive a thousand times over. He saw me through madness, despair, wonderful and terrible love affairs, disillusionments and triumphs, recurrences of illness, an almost fatal suicide attempt, the death of a man I greatly loved, and the enormous pleasures and aggravations of my professional life. . . . He was very tough, as well as very kind, and even though he understood more than anyone how much I felt I was losing—in energy, vivacity, and originality—by taking medication, he never was seduced into losing sight of the overall perspective of how costly, damaging, and life threatening my illness was. . . . Although I went to him to be treated for an illness, he taught me . . . the total beholdenness of brain to mind and mind to brain (pp. 87–88).

"Psychotherapy heals," Jamison reports. "It makes some sense of the confusion, reins in the terrifying thoughts and feelings, returns some control and hope and possibility from it all."

In this chapter, we consider some of the healing options available to therapists and the people who seek their help.

psychotherapy treatment involving psychological techniques; consists of interactions between a trained therapist and someone seeking to overcome psychological difficulties or achieve personal growth.

biomedical therapy prescribed medications or procedures that act directly on the person's physiology.

eclectic approach an approach to psychotherapy that, depending on the client's problems, uses techniques from various forms of therapy.

Treating Psychological Disorders

15-1: How do psychotherapy, biomedical therapy, and an eclectic approach to therapy differ?

The long history of efforts to treat psychological disorders has included a bewildering mix of harsh and gentle methods. Well-meaning individuals have cut holes in people's heads and restrained, bled, or "beat the devil" out of them. They have administered drugs and electric shocks. But they also have given warm baths and massages and placed people in sunny, serene environments. And they have talked with their patients about childhood experiences, current feelings, and maladaptive thoughts and behaviors.

Reformers Philippe Pinel, Dorothea Dix, and others pushed for gentler, more humane treatments and for constructing mental hospitals. Since the 1950s, the introduction of effective drug therapies and community-based treatment programs have emptied most of those hospitals.

Today's therapies can be classified into two main categories. The therapist's training and expertise, as well as the disorder itself, influence the choice of treatment. In **psychotherapy,** a trained therapist uses psychological techniques to assist someone seeking to overcome difficulties or achieve personal growth. **Biomedical therapy** offers medication or other biological treatments.

Some therapists combine techniques. Jamison received psychotherapy in her meetings with her psychiatrist, and she took medications to control her wild mood swings. Indeed, half of all psychotherapists describe themselves as taking an integrative, **eclectic approach,** using a blend of therapies. Many patients receive psychotherapy combined with medication.

Let's look first at the psychotherapy options for those treated with "talk therapies."

Dorothea Dix (1802–1887)
"I . . . call your attention to the state of the Insane Persons confined within this Commonwealth, in cages."
Culver Pictures

The history of treatment Visitors to eighteenth-century mental hospitals paid to gawk at patients, as though they were viewing zoo animals. William Hogarth's (1697–1764) painting (left) captured one of these visits to London's St. Mary of Bethlehem hospital (commonly called Bedlam). Benjamin Rush (1746–1813), a founder of the movement for more humane treatment of the mentally ill, designed the chair on the right "for the benefit of maniacal patients." He believed the restraints would help them regain their sanity.

The Psychological Therapies

Among the dozens of types of psychotherapy, we will look at the most influential. Each is built on one or more of psychology's major theories: psychodynamic, humanistic, behavioral, and cognitive. Most of these techniques can be used one-on-one or in groups.

Psychoanalysis and Psychodynamic Therapy

15-2: What are the goals and techniques of psychoanalysis, and how have they been adapted in psychodynamic therapy?

Sigmund Freud's **psychoanalysis** was the first of the psychological therapies. Few clinicians today practice therapy as Freud did, but his work deserves discussion as part of the foundation for treating psychological disorders.

The Goals of Psychoanalysis

Psychoanalytic theory presumes that healthier, less anxious living becomes possible when people release the energy they had previously devoted to id-ego-superego conflicts (see Chapter 12). Freud assumed that we do not fully know ourselves. There are threatening things that we seem to want not to know—that we disavow or deny.

Freud's therapy aimed to bring patients' repressed or disowned feelings into conscious awareness. By helping them reclaim their unconscious thoughts and feelings and giving them *insight* into the origins of their disorders, he aimed to help them reduce growth-impeding inner conflicts.

The Techniques of Psychoanalysis

Psychoanalysis is historical reconstruction. Psychoanalytic theory emphasizes the formative power of childhood experiences and their ability to mold the adult. Thus, it aims to excavate the past in hope of loosening its bonds on the present. After discarding hypnosis as an unreliable excavator, Freud turned to *free association*.

Imagine yourself as a patient using free association. First, you relax, perhaps by lying on a couch. As the psychoanalyst sits out of your line of vision, you say aloud whatever comes to mind. At one moment, you're relating a childhood memory. At another, you're describing a dream or recent experience. It sounds easy, but soon you notice how often you edit your thoughts as you speak. You pause for a second before uttering an embarrassing thought. You omit what seems trivial, irrelevant, or shameful. Sometimes your mind goes blank or you clutch up, unable to remember important details. You may joke or change the subject to something less threatening.

To the analyst, these mental blocks indicate **resistance.** They hint that anxiety lurks and you are defending against sensitive material. The analyst will note your resistances and then provide insight into their meaning. If offered at the right moment, this **interpretation**—of, say, your not wanting to talk about your mother—may illuminate the underlying wishes, feelings, and conflicts you are avoiding. The analyst may also offer an explanation of how this resistance fits with other pieces of your psychological puzzle, including those based on analysis of your dream content.

Over many such sessions, your relationship patterns surface in your interactions, which may include strong positive or negative feelings for your analyst. The analyst may suggest you are **transferring** feelings, such as dependency or mingled love and anger, that you experienced in earlier relationships with family members or other important people. By exposing such feelings, you may gain insight into your current relationships.

Relatively few U.S. therapists now offer traditional psychoanalysis. Much of its underlying theory is not supported by scientific research (Chapter 12). Analysts' interpretations cannot be proven or disproven. And psychoanalysis takes considerable time and money, often years of several expensive sessions each week. Some of these problems have been addressed in the modern *psychodynamic perspective* that has evolved from psychoanalysis.

psychoanalysis Sigmund Freud's therapeutic technique. Freud believed the patient's free associations, resistances, dreams, and transferences—and the therapist's interpretations of them—released previously repressed feelings, allowing the patient to gain self-insight.

resistance in psychoanalysis, the blocking from consciousness of anxiety-laden material.

interpretation in psychoanalysis, the analyst's noting supposed dream meanings, resistances, and other significant behaviors and events in order to promote insight.

transference in psychoanalysis, the patient's transfer to the analyst of emotions linked with other relationships (such as love or hatred for a parent).

"I'm more interested in hearing about the eggs you're hiding from yourself."

"I haven't seen my analyst in 200 years. He was a strict Freudian. If I'd been going all this time, I'd probably almost be cured by now."

Woody Allen, after awakening from suspended animation in the movie Sleeper

psychodynamic therapy therapy deriving from the psychoanalytic tradition; views individuals as responding to unconscious forces and childhood experiences, and seeks to enhance self-insight.

insight therapies a variety of therapies that aim to improve psychological functioning by increasing a person's awareness of underlying motives and defenses.

Psychodynamic Therapy

Psychodynamic therapists don't talk much about id, ego, and superego. Instead they try to help people understand their current symptoms by focusing on themes across important relationships, including childhood experiences and the therapist relationship. "We can have loving feelings and hateful feelings toward the same person," and "we can desire something and also fear it," notes psychodynamic therapist Jonathan Shedler (2009). Client-therapist meetings take place once or twice a week (rather than several times per week), and often for only a few weeks or months (rather than several years). Rather than lying on a couch, out of the therapist's line of vision, patients meet with their therapist face to face as they explore and gain perspective into their defended-against thoughts and feelings.

Therapist David Shapiro (1999, p. 8) illustrates with the case of a young man who had told women that he loved them, when he knew full well that he didn't. They expected it, so he said it. But then with his wife, who wished he would say that he loved her, he found he *couldn't* do that—"I don't know why, but I can't."

THERAPIST: *Do you mean, then, that if you could, you would like to?*

PATIENT: *Well, I don't know. . . . Maybe I can't say it because I'm not sure it's true. Maybe I don't love her.*

Further interactions revealed that he could not express real love because it would feel "mushy" and "soft" and therefore unmanly. Shapiro noted that this young man was "in conflict with himself, and he [was] cut off from the nature of that conflict." With such patients, who are estranged from themselves, psychodynamic therapists "are in a position to introduce them to themselves," Shapiro added. "We can restore their awareness of their own wishes and feelings, and their awareness, as well, of their reactions against those wishes and feelings."

Exploring past relationship troubles may help clients understand the origin of their current difficulties. Shedler (2010a) recalled "Jeffrey's" complaints of difficulty getting along with his colleagues and wife, who saw him as hypercritical. Jeffrey then "began responding to me as if I were an unpredictable, angry adversary." Shedler seized this opportunity to help Jeffrey recognize the relationship pattern, and its roots in the attacks and humiliation he experienced from his alcohol-dependent father. He was then able to work through and let go of this defensive style of responding to people. Without embracing all aspects of Freud's theory, psychodynamic therapists aim to help people gain insight into their childhood experiences and unconscious dynamics.

Humanistic Therapies

15-3: What are the basic themes of humanistic therapy, and what are the specific goals and techniques of Rogers' client-centered approach?

The humanistic perspective (Chapter 12) has emphasized people's inherent potential for self-fulfillment. Not surprisingly, humanistic therapies attempt to reduce the inner conflicts that interfere with natural development and growth. To achieve this goal, humanistic therapists try to give clients new insights. Indeed, because they share this goal, the psychodynamic and humanistic therapies are often referred to as **insight therapies.**

Face-to-face therapy In contemporary psychodynamic therapy, the couch has disappeared. But the influence of psychoanalytic theory continues in some areas, as the therapist seeks information from the client's childhood and helps the person bring unconscious feelings into conscious awareness.

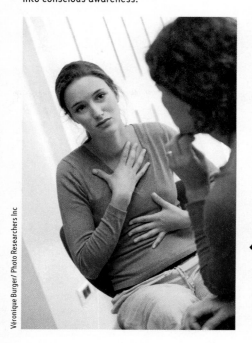

Véronique Burger / Photo Researchers Inc

But humanistic therapists differ from psychodynamic therapists in many other ways:

- *Humanistic therapists aim to boost people's self-fulfillment by helping them grow in self-awareness and self-acceptance.*

- *Promoting this growth, not curing illness, is the focus of therapy.* Thus, those in therapy became "clients" or just "persons" rather than "patients" (a change many other therapists have adopted).

- *The path to growth is taking immediate responsibility for one's feelings and actions, rather than uncovering hidden causes.*

- *Conscious thoughts are more important than the unconscious.*

- *The present and future are more important than the past.* Therapy thus focuses on exploring feelings as they occur, rather than achieving insights into the childhood origins of the feelings.

All these themes are present in the widely used humanistic technique that Carl Rogers (1902–1987) developed and called **client-centered therapy.** This therapy, now often called *person-centered therapy,* focuses on the person's conscious self-perceptions. It is *nondirective*—the therapist listens, without judging or interpreting, and refrains from directing the client toward certain insights.

Rogers (1961, 1980) believed that most people already possess the resources for growth. He encouraged therapists to foster that growth by exhibiting *genuineness, acceptance,* and *empathy.* By being *genuine,* therapists will express their true feelings. By being *accepting,* therapists may help clients feel freer and more open to change. By showing *empathy,* by sensing and reflecting their clients' feelings, therapists can help clients experience a deeper self-understanding and self-acceptance (Hill & Nakayama, 2000). As Rogers (1980, p. 10) explained:

> Hearing has consequences. When I truly hear a person and the meanings that are important to him at that moment, hearing not simply his words, but him, and when I let him know that I have heard his own private personal meanings, many things happen. There is first of all a grateful look. He feels released. He wants to tell me more about his world. He surges forth in a new sense of freedom. He becomes more open to the process of change.
>
> I have often noticed that the more deeply I hear the meanings of the person, the more there is that happens. Almost always, when a person realizes he has been deeply heard, his eyes moisten. I think in some real sense he is weeping for joy. It is as though he were saying, "Thank God, somebody heard me. Someone knows what it's like to be me."

To Rogers, "hearing" was **active listening.** The therapist echoes, restates, and clarifies what the client expresses (verbally or nonverbally). The therapist also acknowledges those expressed feelings. Active listening is now an accepted part of counseling practices in many schools, colleges, and clinics. Counselors listen attentively. They interrupt only to restate and confirm feelings, to accept what was said, or to check their understanding of something. In the following brief excerpt, note how Rogers tried to provide a psychological mirror that would help the client see himself more clearly:

ROGERS: *Feeling that now, hm? That you're just no good to yourself, no good to anybody. Never will be any good to anybody. Just that you're completely worthless, huh?—Those really are lousy feelings. Just feel that you're no good at all, hm?*

CLIENT: Yeah. (Muttering in low, discouraged voice) *That's what this guy I went to town with just the other day told me.*

ROGERS: *This guy that you went to town with really told you that you were no good? Is that what you're saying? Did I get that right?*

CLIENT: *M-hm.*

ROGERS: *I guess the meaning of that if I get it right is that here's somebody that meant something to you and what does he think of you? Why, he's told you that he thinks you're no good at all. And that just really knocks the props out from under you.* (Client weeps quietly.) *It just brings the tears.* (Silence of 20 seconds)

client-centered therapy a humanistic therapy, developed by Carl Rogers, in which the therapist uses techniques such as active listening within a genuine, accepting, empathic environment to facilitate clients' growth. (Also called *person-centered therapy.*)

active listening empathic listening in which the listener echoes, restates, and clarifies. A feature of Rogers' client-centered therapy.

"We have two ears and one mouth that we may listen the more and talk the less."

Zeno, 335–263 B.C.E.,
Diogenes Laertius

unconditional positive regard a caring, accepting, nonjudgmental attitude, which Carl Rogers believed would help clients develop self-awareness and self-acceptance.

behavior therapy therapy that applies learning principles to the elimination of unwanted behaviors.

CLIENT: *(Rather defiantly) I don't care though.*

ROGERS: *You tell yourself you don't care at all, but somehow I guess some part of you cares because some part of you weeps over it.*

(Meador & Rogers, 1984, p. 167)

Can a therapist be a perfect mirror, critics have asked, without selecting and interpreting what is reflected? Rogers conceded that no one can be *totally* nondirective. Nevertheless, he said, the therapist's most important contribution is to accept and understand the client. Given a nonjudgmental, grace-filled environment that provides **unconditional positive regard,** people may accept even their worst traits and feel valued and whole.

How can we develop our own communication strengths by listening more actively in our own relationships? Three Rogerian hints may help:

1. *Paraphrase.* Rather than saying "I know how you feel," check your understandings by summarizing the person's words in your own words.

2. *Invite clarification.* "What might be an example of that?" may encourage the person to say more.

3. *Reflect feelings.* "It sounds frustrating" might mirror what you're sensing from the person's body language and intensity.

Active listening Carl Rogers (right) empathized with a client during this group therapy session.

Behavior Therapies

15-4: How does the basic assumption of behavior therapy differ from the assumptions of psychodynamic and humanistic therapies? What techniques are used in exposure therapies and aversive conditioning?

The insight therapies assume that self-awareness and psychological well-being go hand in hand. Psychodynamic therapists expect people's problems to diminish as they gain insight into their unresolved and unconscious tensions. Humanistic therapists expect people's problems to diminish as they get in touch with their feelings. **Behavior therapists,** however, doubt the healing power of self-awareness. (You can become aware of why you are highly anxious during exams and still be anxious.) Rather than delving deeply below the surface looking for inner causes, they assume that problem behaviors *are* the problems. They view learning principles as useful tools for eliminating unwanted behaviors. They see phobias or sexual disorders, for example, as learned behaviors. If so, why not replace them with new, constructive behaviors learned through classical or operant conditioning?

Classical Conditioning Techniques

One cluster of behavior therapies derives from principles developed in Ivan Pavlov's conditioning experiments (Chapter 7). As Pavlov and others showed, we learn various behaviors and emotions through classical conditioning. If we're attacked by a dog, we may thereafter have a conditioned fear response when other dogs approach. (Our fear generalizes, and all dogs become conditioned stimuli.)

Could maladaptive symptoms be examples of conditioned responses? If so, might reconditioning be a solution? Learning theorist O. H. Mowrer thought so. He developed a successful conditioning therapy for chronic bed-wetters, using a liquid-sensitive pad connected to an alarm. If the sleeping child wets the bed pad, moisture triggers the alarm, waking the child. With sufficient repetition, this association of bladder relaxation with waking stops the bed-wetting. The treatment has been effective in three out of four cases and the success provides a boost to the child's self-image (Christophersen & Edwards, 1992; Houts et al., 1994).

Can we unlearn fear responses through new conditioning? Many people have. One example: The fear of riding in an elevator is often a learned fear response to the stimulus of being in a confined space. **Counterconditioning** pairs the trigger stimulus (the enclosed space of the elevator) with a new response (relaxation) that cannot coexist with fear. Behavior therapists have successfully counterconditioned many people with a fear of confined spaces. *Exposure therapies* and *aversive conditioning* illustrate counterconditioning. The goal of both techniques is replacing unwanted responses with new responses.

Exposure Therapies Picture this scene: Behavioral psychologist Mary Cover Jones is working with 3-year-old Peter, who is petrified of rabbits and other furry objects. To rid Peter of his fear, Jones plans to associate the fear-evoking rabbit with the pleasurable, relaxed response associated with eating. As Peter begins his midafternoon snack, she introduces a caged rabbit on the other side of the huge room. Peter, eagerly munching away on his crackers and drinking his milk, hardly notices. On succeeding days, she gradually moves the rabbit closer and closer. Within two months, Peter is holding the rabbit in his lap, even stroking it while he eats. Moreover, his fear of other furry objects has also gone away, having been *countered,* or replaced, by a relaxed state that cannot coexist with fear (Fisher, 1984; Jones, 1924).

Kim Reinick/
Shutterstock

Unfortunately for many who might have been helped by Jones' procedures, her story of Peter and the rabbit did not enter psychology's lore when it was reported in 1924. It was more than 30 years before psychiatrist Joseph Wolpe (1958; Wolpe & Plaud, 1997) refined Jones' counterconditioning technique into the **exposure therapies** used today. These therapies, in a variety of ways, try to change people's reactions by repeatedly exposing them to stimuli that trigger unwanted reactions. With repeated exposure to what they normally avoid or escape (behaviors that get reinforced by reduced anxiety), people adapt. We all experience this process in everyday life. A person moving to a new apartment may be annoyed by nearby loud traffic noise, but only for a while. With repeated exposure, the person adapts. So, too, with people who have fear reactions to specific events. Exposed repeatedly to the situation that once petrified them, they can learn to react less anxiously (Rosa-Alcázar et al., 2008; Wolitzky-Taylor et al., 2008).

One form of exposure therapy widely used to treat phobias is **systematic desensitization.** You cannot simultaneously be anxious and relaxed. Therefore, if you can repeatedly relax when facing anxiety-provoking stimuli, you can gradually eliminate your anxiety. The trick is to proceed gradually. If you feared public speaking, a behavior therapist might first ask you to make a list of anxiety-triggering speaking situations. Your list would range from situations that cause you to feel mildly anxious (perhaps speaking up in a small group of friends) to those that provoke panic (having to address a large audience).

counterconditioning behavior therapy procedures that use classical conditioning to evoke new responses to stimuli that are triggering unwanted behaviors; include *exposure therapies* and *aversive conditioning.*

exposure therapies behavioral techniques, such as *systematic desensitization* and *virtual reality exposure therapy,* that treat anxieties by exposing people (in imagination or actual situations) to the things they fear and avoid.

systematic desensitization a type of exposure therapy that associates a pleasant relaxed state with gradually increasing anxiety-triggering stimuli. Commonly used to treat phobias.

virtual reality exposure therapy an anxiety treatment that progressively exposes people to electronic simulations of their greatest fears, such as airplane flying, spiders, or public speaking.

aversive conditioning a type of counterconditioning that associates an unpleasant state (such as nausea) with an unwanted behavior (such as drinking alcohol).

In the next step, the therapist would train you in *progressive relaxation*. You would learn to relax one muscle group after another, until you achieved a comfortable, complete relaxation. Then the therapist might ask you to imagine, with your eyes closed, a mildly anxiety-arousing situation: You are having coffee with a group of friends and are trying to decide whether to speak up. If you feel any anxiety while imagining the scene, you will signal by raising your finger. Seeing the signal, the therapist will instruct you to switch off the mental image and go back to deep relaxation. This imagined scene is repeatedly paired with relaxation until you feel no trace of anxiety.

The therapist will then move to the next item on your list, again using relaxation techniques to desensitize you to each imagined situation. After several sessions, you will move to actual situations and practice what you had only imagined before. You will begin with relatively easy tasks and gradually move to more anxiety-filled ones. Conquering your anxiety in an actual situation, not just in your imagination, will raise your self-confidence (Foa & Kozak, 1986; Williams, 1987). Eventually, you may even become a confident public speaker.

If an anxiety-arousing situation is too expensive, difficult, or embarrassing to re-create, the therapist may recommend **virtual reality exposure therapy.** You would don a head-mounted display unit that projects a three-dimensional virtual world in front of your eyes. The lifelike scenes, which shift as your head turns, would be tailored to your particular fear. Experimentally treated fears include flying, heights, particular animals, and public speaking (Parsons & Rizzo, 2008). If you fear flying, you could peer out a virtual window of a simulated plane. You would feel the engine's vibrations and hear it roar as the plane taxis down the runway and takes off. In controlled studies, people participating in virtual reality exposure therapy have experienced significant relief from real-life fear (Hoffman, 2004; Meyerbroëker & Emmelkamp, 2010).

Aversive Conditioning Exposure therapies substitute a relaxed, positive response for a negative response to a *harmless* stimulus. **Aversive conditioning** substitutes a negative (aversive) response for a positive response to a *harmful* stimulus (such as alcohol). Exposure therapies help you accept what you *should* do. Aversive conditioning helps you to learn what you *should not* do.

The aversive conditioning procedure is simple: It associates the unwanted behavior with unpleasant feelings. To treat nail biting, one can paint the fingernails with a nasty-tasting nail polish (Baskind, 1997). To treat alcohol dependence, an aversion therapist offers the client appealing drinks laced with a drug that produces severe nausea. By linking alcohol with violent nausea (recall the taste-aversion experiments with rats and coyotes in Chapter 7), the therapist seeks to transform the person's reaction to alcohol from positive to negative (**FIGURE 15.1**).

Does aversive conditioning work? In the short run it may. In one classic study, 685 patients with alcohol dependence completed an aversion therapy program at a hospital (Wiens & Menustik, 1983). Over the next year, they returned for several booster

Virtual reality exposure therapy
Within the confines of a room, virtual reality technology exposes people to vivid simulations of feared stimuli, such as a plane's takeoff.

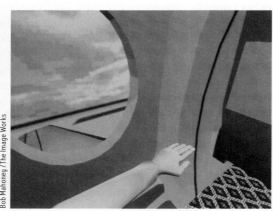

Bob Mahoney / The Image Works
Bob Mahoney / The Image Works

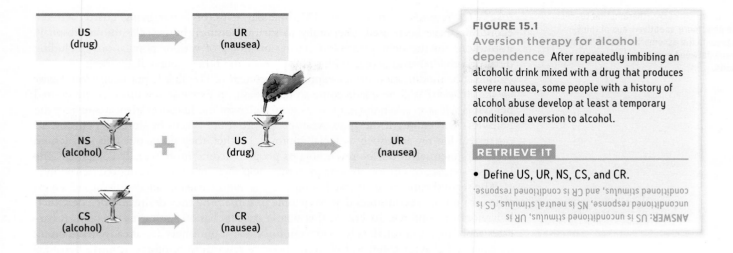

FIGURE 15.1
Aversion therapy for alcohol dependence After repeatedly imbibing an alcoholic drink mixed with a drug that produces severe nausea, some people with a history of alcohol abuse develop at least a temporary conditioned aversion to alcohol.

RETRIEVE IT

• Define US, UR, NS, CS, and CR.

ANSWER: US is unconditioned stimulus, UR is unconditioned response, NS is neutral stimulus, CS is conditioned stimulus, and CR is conditioned response.

treatments in which alcohol was paired with sickness. At the end of that year, 63 percent were still successfully abstaining. But after three years, only 33 percent had remained abstinent.

The problem, as we saw in Chapter 7, is that cognition influences conditioning. People know that outside the therapist's office they can drink without fear of nausea. Their ability to discriminate between the aversive conditioning situation and all other situations can limit the treatment's effectiveness. Thus, therapists often use aversive conditioning in combination with other treatments.

Operant Conditioning

15-5: What is the basic idea of operant conditioning therapy, and what arguments have been used for and against it?

A basic concept in operant conditioning (Chapter 7) is that our voluntary behaviors are strongly influenced by their consequences. Knowing this, behavior therapists can practice *behavior modification*. They reinforce behaviors they consider desirable. And they fail to reinforce—or sometimes punish—behaviors they consider undesirable.

Using operant conditioning to solve specific behavior problems has raised hopes for some seemingly hopeless cases. Children with intellectual disabilities have been taught to care for themselves. Socially withdrawn children with autism have learned to interact. People with schizophrenia have been helped to behave more rationally in their hospital ward. In such cases, therapists used positive reinforcers to *shape* behavior. In a step-by-step manner, they rewarded behaviors that came closer and closer to the desired behavior.

In extreme cases, treatment must be intensive. One study worked with 19 withdrawn, uncommunicative 3-year-olds with autism. For two years, 40 hours each week, the children's parents attempted to shape their behavior (Lovaas, 1987). They positively reinforced desired behaviors and ignored or punished aggressive and self-abusive behaviors. The combination worked wonders for some children. By first grade, 9 of the 19 were functioning successfully in school and exhibiting normal intelligence. In a group of 40 comparable children not undergoing this treatment, only 1 showed similar improvement. (Later studies focused on the effective aspect—positive reinforcement.)

The rewards used to modify behavior vary because people differ in what they find reinforcing. For some, the reinforcing power of attention or praise is enough. Others require concrete rewards, such as food. In institutional settings, therapists may create a **token economy.** When people display desired behavior, such as getting out of bed, washing, dressing, eating, talking meaningfully, cleaning their rooms, or playing cooperatively, they receive a token or plastic coin. Later, they can exchange a number of these

token economy an operant conditioning procedure in which people earn a token of some sort for exhibiting a desired behavior and can later exchange the tokens for various privileges or treats.

cognitive therapy therapy that teaches people new, more adaptive ways of thinking; based on the assumption that thoughts intervene between events and our emotional reactions.

tokens for rewards, such as candy, TV time, day trips, or better living quarters. Token economies have been used successfully in various settings (homes, classrooms, hospitals, institutions for the delinquent) and among members of various populations (including disturbed children and people with schizophrenia and other mental disabilities).

Behavior modification critics express two concerns. The first is practical: *How durable are the behaviors?* Will people become so dependent on extrinsic rewards that the desired behaviors will stop when the reinforcers stop? Behavior modification advocates believe the behaviors will endure if therapists wean people from the tokens by shifting them toward other, real-life rewards, such as social approval. Further, they point out that the desired behaviors themselves can be rewarding. As people become more socially competent, the intrinsic satisfactions of social interaction may help them maintain the desired behaviors.

The second concern is ethical: *Is it right for one human to control another's behavior?* Those who set up token economies deprive people of something they desire and decide which behaviors to reinforce. To critics, this whole process has an authoritarian taint. Advocates reply that control already exists; reinforcers and punishers are already maintaining destructive behavior patterns. Isn't using positive rewards to reinforce adaptive behavior more humane than institutionalizing or punishing people? Advocates also argue that the right to effective treatment and an improved life justifies temporary deprivation.

RETRIEVE IT

• How do the *insight therapies* differ from behavior therapies?

ANSWER: The *insight therapies*—psychodynamic and humanistic therapies—seek to relieve problems by providing an understanding of their origins. Behavior therapies assume the problem behavior *is* the problem and treat it directly.

• Some maladaptive behaviors are learned. What hope does this fact provide?

ANSWER: If a behavior can be learned, it can be *unlearned*, and replaced by other more adaptive responses.

• Exposure therapies and aversive conditioning are applications of _____ conditioning. Token economies are an application of _____ conditioning.

ANSWERS: classical; operant

Cognitive Therapies

Cognitive therapy for eating disorders aided by journaling Cognitive therapists guide people toward new ways of explaining their good and bad experiences. By recording positive events and how she has enabled them, this woman may become more mindful of her self-control and more optimistic.

15-6: What are the goals and techniques of the cognitive therapies and of cognitive-behavioral therapy?

People with specific fears and problem behaviors respond to behavior therapy. But how would you modify the wide assortment of behaviors that accompany major depression? And how would you treat generalized anxiety disorders, where unfocused anxiety doesn't lend itself to a neat list of anxiety-triggering situations? The *cognitive revolution* that has influenced other areas of psychology during the last half-century influenced therapy as well.

The **cognitive therapies** assume that our thinking colors our feelings (**FIGURE 15.2**). Between the event and our response lies the mind. Self-blaming and overgeneralized explanations of bad events are often an important part of the vicious cycle of depression (see Chapter 14). If depressed, we may interpret a suggestion as criticism, disagreement as dislike, praise as flattery, friendliness as pity. Dwelling on such thoughts sustains negative thinking. Cognitive therapists aim to help people change their minds with new, more constructive ways of thinking.

Lara Jo Regan/Gamma Liaison

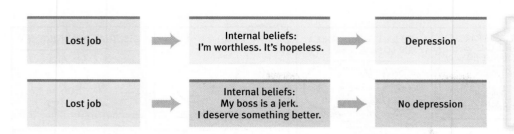

FIGURE 15.2
A cognitive perspective on psychological disorders The person's emotional reactions are produced not directly by the event but by the person's thoughts in response to the event.

Beck's Therapy for Depression

Cognitive therapist Aaron Beck's original training was in Freudian techniques, including dream analysis. Depressed people, he found, often reported dreams with negative themes of loss, rejection, and abandonment. These thoughts extended into their waking thoughts, even into therapy, as clients recalled and rehearsed their failings and worst impulses (Kelly, 2000). Beck and his colleagues (1979) wondered: How could they reverse their clients' negativity about themselves, their situations, and their futures? Beck's answer was the approach we now call cognitive therapy. Gentle questioning seeks to reveal irrational thinking and then to persuade people to remove the dark glasses through which they view life (Beck et al., 1979, pp. 145–146):

CLIENT: *I agree with the descriptions of me but I guess I don't agree that the way I think makes me depressed.*

BECK: *How do you understand it?*

CLIENT: *I get depressed when things go wrong. Like when I fail a test.*

BECK: *How can failing a test make you depressed?*

CLIENT: *Well, if I fail I'll never get into law school.*

BECK: *So failing the test means a lot to you. But if failing a test could drive people into clinical depression, wouldn't you expect everyone who failed the test to have a depression? . . . Did everyone who failed get depressed enough to require treatment?*

CLIENT: *No, but it depends on how important the test was to the person.*

BECK: *Right, and who decides the importance?*

CLIENT: *I do.*

BECK: *And so, what we have to examine is your way of viewing the test (or the way that you think about the test) and how it affects your chances of getting into law school. Do you agree?*

CLIENT: *Right.*

BECK: *Do you agree that the way you interpret the results of the test will affect you? You might feel depressed, you might have trouble sleeping, not feel like eating, and you might even wonder if you should drop out of the course.*

CLIENT: *I have been thinking that I wasn't going to make it. Yes, I agree.*

BECK: *Now what did failing mean?*

CLIENT: (tearful) *That I couldn't get into law school.*

BECK: *And what does that mean to you?*

CLIENT: *That I'm just not smart enough.*

BECK: *Anything else?*

CLIENT: *That I can never be happy.*

BECK: *And how do these thoughts make you feel?*

CLIENT: *Very unhappy.*

BECK: *So it is the meaning of failing a test that makes you very unhappy. In fact, believing that you can never be happy is a powerful factor in producing unhappiness. So, you get yourself into a trap—by definition, failure to get into law school equals "I can never be happy."*

"Life does not consist mainly, or even largely, of facts and happenings. It consists mainly of the storm of thoughts that are forever blowing through one's mind."

Mark Twain, 1835–1910

PEANUTS

Drawing by Charles Schulz; ©1956
Reprinted by permission of United
Feature Syndicate, Inc.

LIFE IS RARELY ALL ONE WAY, CHARLIE BROWN

YOU WIN A FEW, AND YOU LOSE A FEW!

REALLY?

GEE, THAT'D BE NEAT !!

We often think in words. Therefore, getting people to change what they say to themselves is an effective way to change their thinking. Perhaps you can identify with the anxious students who, before an exam, make matters worse with self-defeating thoughts: "This exam's probably going to be impossible. All these other students seem so relaxed and confident. I wish I were better prepared. Anyhow, I'm so nervous I'll forget everything." Psychologists call this sort of relentless, overgeneralized, self-blaming behavior *catastrophizing*.

To change such negative self-talk, therapists teach people to restructure their thinking in stressful situations (Meichenbaum, 1977, 1985). Sometimes it may be enough simply to say more positive things to yourself: "Relax. The exam may be hard, but it will be hard for everyone else, too. I studied harder than most people. Besides, I don't need a perfect score to get a good grade." Training people to "talk back" to negative thoughts can be effective. With such training, depression-prone children and college students have shown a halved rate of future depression (Brunwasser et al., 2009; Seligman, 2002; Stice et al., 2009). To a great extent, it is the thought that counts. **TABLE 15.1** provides a sampling of techniques commonly used in cognitive therapy.

Table 15.1
Selected Cognitive Therapy Techniques

Aim of Technique	Technique	Therapists' Directives
Reveal beliefs	Question your interpretations	Explore your beliefs, revealing faulty assumptions such as "I must be liked by everyone."
	Rank thoughts and emotions	Gain perspective by ranking your thoughts and emotions from mildly to extremely upsetting.
Test beliefs	Examine consequences	Explore difficult situations, assessing possible consequences and challenging faulty reasoning.
	Decatastrophize thinking	Work through the actual worst-case consequences of the situation you face (it is often not as bad as imagined). Then determine how to cope with the real situation you face.
Change beliefs	Take appropriate responsibility	Challenge total self-blame and negative thinking, noting aspects for which you may be truly responsible, as well as aspects that aren't your responsibility.
	Resist extremes	Develop new ways of thinking and feeling to replace maladaptive habits. For example, change from thinking "I am a total failure" to "I got a failing grade on that paper, and I can make these changes to succeed next time."

Cognitive-Behavioral Therapy

"The trouble with most therapy," said therapist Albert Ellis (1913–2007), "is that it helps you to feel better. But you don't get better. You have to back it up with action, action, action." **Cognitive-behavioral therapy** takes a double-barreled approach to depression and other disorders. This widely practiced integrative approach aims not only to alter the way people *think* but also to alter the way they *act*. Like other cognitive therapies, it seeks to make people aware of their irrational negative thinking and to replace it with new ways of thinking. Like other behavior therapies, it trains people to practice the more positive approach in everyday settings.

Cognitive-behavioral therapy has helped people with the disruptive emotions of anxiety and mood disorders (Aldao & Nolen-Hoeksema, 2010). In therapy, people learn

cognitive-behavioral therapy a popular integrative therapy that combines cognitive therapy (changing self-defeating thinking) with behavior therapy (changing behavior).

to replace catastrophizing with more realistic appraisals and, as homework, to practice behaviors that counter their problem (Kazantzis et al., 2010a,b; Moses & Barlow, 2006). A person with depression might keep a log of daily situations associated with negative and positive emotions and attempt to engage more in activities that lead to feeling good. Those who fear social situations might practice approaching people.

In one study, people with obsessive-compulsive behaviors learned to relabel their compulsive thoughts (Schwartz et al., 1996). Feeling the urge to wash their hands again, they would tell themselves, "I'm having a compulsive urge." They would explain to themselves that the hand-washing urge was a result of their brain's abnormal activity, which they had previously viewed in PET scans. Then, instead of giving in, they would spend 15 minutes in an enjoyable, alternative behavior, such as practicing an instrument, taking a walk, or gardening. This helped "unstick" the brain by shifting attention and engaging other brain areas. For two or three months, the weekly therapy sessions continued, with relabeling and refocusing practice at home. By the study's end, most participants' symptoms had diminished, and their PET scans revealed normalized brain activity. Many other studies confirm cognitive-behavioral therapy's effectiveness for those with anxiety, depression, or anorexia nervosa (Covin et al., 2008; Mitte, 2005; Norton & Price, 2007). Studies have also found that cognitive-behavioral skills can be effectively taught and therapy conducted over the Internet (Barak et al., 2008; Kessler et al., 2009; Marks & Cavanaugh, 2009; Stross, 2011).

RETRIEVE IT

• How do the humanistic and cognitive therapies differ?

ANSWER: By reflecting clients' feelings in a nondirective setting, the *humanistic therapies* attempt to foster personal growth by helping clients become more self-aware and self-accepting. By making clients aware of self-defeating patterns of thinking, *cognitive therapies* guide people toward more adaptive ways of thinking about themselves and their world.

• What is cognitive-behavioral therapy, and what sorts of problems does this therapy address?

ANSWER: This popular integrative therapy helps people change self-defeating thinking *and behavior*. It has been shown to be effective for those with obsessive-compulsive disorder, anxiety, mood disorders, and anorexia nervosa.

Group and Family Therapies

15-7: What are the aims and benefits of group and family therapy?

Group Therapy

Except for traditional psychoanalysis, most therapies may also occur in small groups. **Group therapy** does not provide the same degree of therapist involvement with each client. However, it offers benefits:

• *It saves therapists' time and clients' money,* often with no less effectiveness than individual therapy (Fuhriman & Burlingame, 1994).

• *It offers a social laboratory for exploring social behaviors and developing social skills.* Therapists frequently suggest group therapy for people experiencing frequent conflicts or for those whose behavior distresses others. For up to 90 minutes weekly, the therapist guides people's interactions as they discuss issues and try out new behaviors.

• *It enables people to see that others share their problems.* It can be a relief to discover that you are not alone—to learn that others, despite their composure, experience some of the same troublesome feelings and behaviors.

• *It provides feedback as clients try out new ways of behaving.* Hearing that you look poised, even though you feel anxious and self-conscious, can be reassuring.

group therapy therapy conducted with groups rather than individuals, permitting therapeutic benefits from group interaction.

family therapy therapy that treats the family as a system. Views an individual's unwanted behaviors as influenced by, or directed at, other family members.

Family Therapy

One special type of group interaction, **family therapy,** assumes that no person is an island. We live and grow in relation to others, especially our families, yet we also work to find an identity outside of our family. These two opposing tendencies can create stress for the individual and the family.

Unlike most psychotherapy, which focuses on what happens inside the person's own skin, family therapists work with multiple family members to heal relationships and to mobilize family resources. They tend to view the family as a system in which each person's actions trigger reactions from others, and they help family members discover their role within their family's social system. A child's rebellion, for example, affects and is affected by other family tensions. Therapists also attempt—usually with some success, research suggests—to open up communication within the family or to help family members discover new ways of preventing or resolving conflicts (Hazelrigg et al., 1987; Shadish et al., 1993).

Family therapy This type of therapy often acts as a preventive mental health strategy. The therapist helps family members understand how their ways of relating to one another create problems. The emphasis is not on changing the individuals but on changing their relationships and interactions.

Michael Newman/PhotoEdit

Self-Help Groups

More than 100 million Americans belong to small religious, interest, or self-help groups that meet regularly—and 9 in 10 report that group members "support each other emotionally" (Gallup, 1994). One analysis of online support groups and more than 14,000 self-help groups reported that most support groups focus on stigmatized or hard-to-discuss illnesses (Davison et al., 2000). AIDS patients were 250 times more likely than hypertension patients to be in support groups. People with anorexia and alcohol dependence often join groups; those with migraines and ulcers usually do not.

The grandparent of support groups, Alcoholics Anonymous (AA), reports having more than 2 million members in 114,000 groups worldwide. Its famous 12-step program, emulated by many other self-help groups, asks members to admit their powerlessness, to seek help from a higher power and from one another, and (the twelfth step) to take the message to others in need of it. Studies of 12-step programs such as AA have found that they help reduce alcohol dependence at rates comparable to other treatment interventions (Ferri et al., 2006; Moos & Moos, 2005). In one eight-year, $27 million investigation, AA participants reduced their drinking sharply, as did those assigned to cognitive-behavioral therapy or to "motivational therapy" (Project Match, 1997). In one study of 2300 veterans who sought treatment for alcohol dependence, a high level of AA involvement was followed by diminished alcohol problems (McKellar

With more than 2 million members worldwide, AA is said to be "the largest organization on Earth that nobody wanted to join" (Finlay, 2000).

et al., 2003). The more meetings members attend, the greater their alcohol abstinence (Moos & Moos, 2006).

In an individualist age, with more and more people living alone or feeling isolated, the popularity of support groups—for the addicted, the bereaved, the divorced, or simply those seeking fellowship and growth—may reflect a longing for community and connectedness.

★ ★ ★

For a synopsis of these modern psychotherapies, see **TABLE 15.2**.

Table 15.2
Comparing Modern Psychotherapies

Therapy	Presumed Problem	Therapy Aim	Therapy Technique
Psychodynamic	Unconscious conflicts from childhood experiences	Reduce anxiety through self-insight.	Interpret patients' memories and feelings.
Client-centered	Barriers to self-understanding and self-acceptance	Enable growth via unconditional positive regard, genuineness, and empathy.	Listen actively and reflect client's feelings.
Behavior	Dysfunctional behaviors	Relearn adaptive behaviors; extinguish problem ones.	Use classical conditioning (via exposure or aversion therapy) or operant conditioning (as in token economies).
Cognitive	Negative, self-defeating thinking	Promote healthier thinking and self-talk.	Train people to dispute negative thoughts and attributions.
Cognitive-behavioral	Self-harmful thoughts and behaviors	Promote healthier thinking and adaptive behaviors.	Train people to counter self-harmful thoughts and to act out their new ways of thinking.
Group and family	Stressful relationships	Heal relationships.	Develop an understanding of family and other social systems, explore roles, and improve communication.

RETRIEVE IT

- Which therapeutic technique focuses more on the present and future than the past, and involves unconditional positive regard and active listening?

ANSWER: humanistic therapy—specifically Carl Rogers' client-centered therapy

- Which of the following is NOT a benefit of group therapy?

  a. more focused attention from the therapist   c. social feedback

  b. less expensive   d. reassurance that others share troubles

ANSWER: a

Evaluating Psychotherapies

Many Americans have great confidence in psychotherapy's effectiveness. "Seek counseling" or "Ask your mate to find a therapist," advice columnists often advise. Before 1950, psychiatrists were the primary providers of mental health care. Today, psychotherapy is mostly offered by clinical and counseling psychologists; clinical social workers; pastoral, marital, abuse, and school counselors; and psychiatric nurses.

Is the faith that millions of people worldwide place in these therapists justified? The question, though simply put, is not simple to answer.

Is Psychotherapy Effective?

15-8: Does psychotherapy work? Who decides?

Measuring therapy's effectiveness is not like taking your body's temperature to see if your fever has gone away. If you and I were to undergo psychotherapy, how would we assess its effectiveness? By how we feel about our progress? By how our therapist feels about it? By how our friends and family feel about it? By how our behavior has changed?

Clients' Perceptions

If clients' testimonials were the only measuring stick, we could strongly assert that psychotherapy is effective. Consider the 2900 *Consumer Reports* readers who reported on their experiences with mental health professionals (1995; Kotkin et al., 1996; Seligman, 1995). How many were at least "fairly well satisfied"? Almost 90 percent (as was Kay Redfield Jamison, as we saw at this chapter's beginning). Among those who recalled feeling *fair* or *very poor* when beginning therapy, 9 in 10 now were feeling *very good, good,* or at least *so-so.* We have their word for it—and who should know better?

But client testimonials don't persuade everyone. Critics note reasons for skepticism:

- *Clients may need to justify their investment of effort and time.*

- *Clients generally speak kindly of their therapists.* Even if the problems remain, clients "work hard to find something positive to say. The therapist had been very understanding, the client had gained a new perspective, he learned to communicate better, his mind was eased, anything at all so as not to have to say treatment was a failure" (Zilbergeld, 1983, p. 117).

- *People often enter therapy in crisis.* When, with the normal ebb and flow of events, the crisis passes, people may assume their improvement was a result of the therapy.

Clinicians' Perceptions

If clinicians' perceptions were proof of therapy's effectiveness, we would have even more reason to celebrate. Case studies of successful treatment abound. Furthermore, therapists are like the rest of us. They treasure compliments from clients saying good-bye or later expressing their gratitude. The problem is that clients justify entering psychotherapy by emphasizing their unhappiness. They justify leaving by emphasizing their well-being. And they stay in touch only if they are satisfied. Thus, therapists are most aware of the failures of *other* therapists—those whose clients, having experienced only temporary relief, are now seeking a new therapist for their recurring problems. The same person, with the same recurring anxieties, depression, or marital difficulty, may be a "success" story in several therapists' files.

Outcome Research

How, then, can we objectively assess psychotherapy's effectiveness? What *outcomes* can we expect—what types of people and problems are best helped, and by what type of psychotherapy?

In search of answers, psychologists have turned to controlled research. This is a well-traveled path. In the 1800s, skeptical medical doctors began to realize that many patients got better on their own and that many fashionable treatments (bleeding, purging) might be doing no good. Sorting fact from superstition required following patients and recording outcomes with and without a particular treatment. Typhoid fever patients, for example, often improved after being bled, convincing most physicians that the treatment worked. Then came the shock. A control group was given mere bed rest, and after five weeks of fever, 70 percent improved, showing that the bleeding was worthless (Thomas, 1992).

In the twentieth century, psychology, with its many different therapy options, faced a similar challenge. British psychologist Hans Eysenck (1952) launched a spirited debate when he summarized 24 studies of psychotherapy outcomes. He found that two-thirds of those receiving psychotherapy for disorders not involving hallucinations or delusions improved markedly. To this day, no one disputes that optimistic estimate.

Why, then, are we still debating psychotherapy's effectiveness? Because Eysenck also reported similar improvement among *untreated* persons, such as those who were on waiting lists for treatment. With or without psychotherapy, he said, roughly two-thirds improved noticeably. Time was a great healer.

An avalanche of criticism greeted Eysenck's conclusions. Some pointed out errors in his analyses. Others noted that he based his ideas on only 24 studies. Now, more than a half-century later, there are hundreds of studies. The best of these are *randomized clinical trials:* Researchers randomly assign people on a waiting list to therapy or to no therapy. Later, they evaluate everyone and compare the outcomes, with assessments by others who don't know whether therapy was given. Simply said, *meta-analyses* (statistical digests of the results of many studies) give us the bottom-line results.

Psychotherapists welcomed the first meta-analysis of some 475 psychotherapy outcome studies (Smith et al., 1980). It showed that the average therapy client ends up better off than 80 percent of the untreated individuals on waiting lists (**FIGURE 15.3**). The claim is modest—by definition, about 50 percent of untreated people also are better off than the average untreated person. Dozens of subsequent summaries have now examined this question. Their verdict echoes the results of the earlier outcome studies: *Those not undergoing therapy often improve, but those undergoing therapy are more likely to improve and with less risk of relapse.*

Is psychotherapy also cost-effective? Again, the answer is *Yes.* Studies show that when people seek psychological treatment, their search for other medical treatment drops—by 16 percent in one digest of 91 studies (Chiles et al., 1999). Given the staggering annual cost of psychological disorders and substance abuse—including crime, accidents, lost work, and treatment—psychotherapy is a good investment, much like money spent on prenatal and well-baby care. Both reduce long-term costs. Boosting employees' psychological well-being can lower medical costs, improve work efficiency, and diminish absenteeism.

But note that the claim—that psychotherapy, *on average,* is somewhat effective—refers to no one therapy in particular. It is like reassuring lung-cancer patients that medical treatment of health problems is, "on average," somewhat effective. What people want to know is whether a *particular* treatment is effective for their specific problem.

Trauma These women are mourning the tragic loss of lives and homes in the 2010 earthquake in China. Those who suffer through such trauma may benefit from counseling, though many people recover on their own, or with the help of supportive relationships with family and friends. "Life itself still remains a very effective therapist," noted psychodynamic therapist Karen Horney (*Our Inner Conflicts,* 1945).

Feng Li/Getty Images

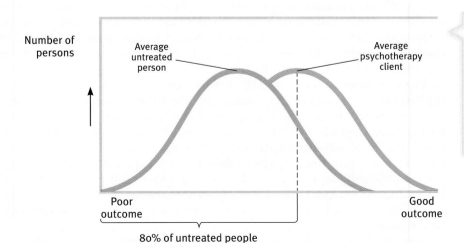

FIGURE 15.3
Treatment versus no treatment These two normal distribution curves based on data from 475 studies show the improvement of untreated people and psychotherapy clients. The outcome for the average therapy client surpassed that for 80 percent of the untreated people. (Adapted from Smith et al., 1980.)

Which Psychotherapies Work Best?

15-9: Are some psychotherapies more effective than others for specific disorders?

The early statistical summaries and surveys did not find that any one type of psychotherapy is generally better than others (Smith et al., 1977, 1980). Newer studies have similarly found little connection between clients' outcomes and their clinicians' experience, training, supervision, and licensing (Luborsky et al., 2002; Wampold, 2007). A *Consumer Reports'* survey illustrates: Were clients treated by a psychiatrist, psychologist, or social worker? Were they seen in a group or individual context? Did the therapist have extensive or relatively limited training and experience? It didn't matter. Clients seemed equally satisfied (Seligman, 1995).

So, was the dodo bird in *Alice in Wonderland* right: "Everyone has won and all must have prizes"? Not quite. Some forms of therapy get prizes for effectively treating *particular* problems. Behavioral conditioning therapies have had especially good results with specific behavior problems, such as bed-wetting, phobias, compulsions, marital problems, and sexual disorders (Baker et al., 2008; Hunsley & DiGiulio, 2002; Shadish & Baldwin, 2005). Psychodynamic therapy has had success with depression and anxiety (Driessen et al., 2010; Leichsenring & Rabung, 2008; Shedler, 2010b). And many studies confirm cognitive and cognitive-behavioral therapy's effectiveness (some say superiority) in coping with anxiety, post-traumatic stress disorder, and depression (Baker et al., 2008; De Los Reyes & Kazdin, 2009; Stewart & Chambliss, 2009; Tolin, 2010).

Moreover, we can say that therapy is most effective when the problem is clear-cut (Singer, 1981; Westen & Morrison, 2001). Those who experience phobias or panic, who are unassertive, or who are frustrated by sexual performance problems can hope for improvement. Those with less-focused problems, such as depression and anxiety, usually benefit in the short term but often relapse later. And those with the negative symptoms of chronic schizophrenia or a desire to change their entire personality are unlikely to benefit from psychotherapy alone (Pfammatter et al., 2006; Zilbergeld, 1983). The more specific the problem, the greater the hope.

But no prizes—and little or no scientific support—go to certain other therapies (Arkowitz & Lilienfeld, 2006). We would all therefore be wise to avoid energy therapies that propose to manipulate people's invisible energy fields, recovered-memory therapies that aim to unearth "repressed memories" of early child abuse (Chapter 8), and rebirthing therapies that engage people in reenacting the supposed trauma of their birth.

As with some medical treatments, it's possible for psychological treatments not only to be ineffective but harmful—by making people worse or preventing their getting better (Barlow, 2010; Castonguay et al., 2010; Dimidjian & Hollon, 2010). The National Science and Technology Council cites the Scared Straight program (seeking to deter children and youth from crime) as an example of well-intentioned programs that have proved ineffective or even harmful.

The evaluation question—which therapies get prizes and which do not?—lies at the heart of what some call psychology's civil war. To what extent should science guide both clinical practice and the willingness of health care providers and insurers to pay for psychotherapy? On one side are research psychologists using scientific methods to extend the list of well-defined and validated therapies for various disorders. They decry clinicians who "give more weight to their personal experiences" (Baker et al., 2008). On the other side are nonscientist therapists who view their practice as more art than science, something that cannot be described in a manual or tested in an experiment. People are too complex and psychotherapy is too intuitive for such an approach, many therapists say.

Between these two factions stand the science-oriented clinicians calling for **evidence-based practice,** which has been endorsed by the American Psychological Association, the Institute of Medicine, and others (2006; Baker et al., 2008; Levant &

"Whatever differences in treatment efficacy exist, they appear to be extremely small, at best."

Bruce Wampold et al. (1997)

"Different sores have different salves."

English proverb

evidence-based practice clinical decision making that integrates the best available research with clinical expertise and patient characteristics and preferences.

Hasan, 2008). Therapists using this approach integrate the best available research with clinical expertise and with patient preferences and characteristics (**FIGURE 15.4**). After rigorous evaluation, available therapies would be applied by clinicians who are mindful of their skills and of each patient's unique situation. Increasingly, insurer and government support for mental health services requires evidence-based practice.

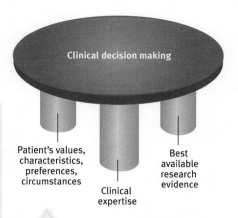

FIGURE 15.4
Evidence-based practice The ideal clinical decision making is a three-legged stool, upheld by research evidence, clinical expertise, and knowledge of the patient.

RETRIEVE IT

- Therapy is more likely to be helpful in those with the _____ (most/least) clearly defined problems.

ANSWER: most

- What is evidence-based practice?

ANSWER: Using this approach, therapists make decisions about treatment based on research evidence, clinical expertise, and knowledge of the client.

Evaluating Alternative Therapies

15-10: How do alternative therapies fare under scientific scrutiny?

Two tendencies create fertile soil for pseudotherapies:

- Many abnormal states of mind return to normal without treatment.

- Just *thinking* you are receiving an effective treatment can boost your spirits, relax your body, and offer relief. This *placebo effect* is well documented in reducing pain, depression, and anxiety (Kirsch & Sapirstein, 1998).

Alternative therapies are newer, nontraditional therapies, which often claim healing powers for varied ailments. Bolstered by anecdotes, heralded by the media, and broadcast on the Internet, alternative therapies have spread like wildfire. In one national survey, 57 percent of those with a history of anxiety attacks and 54 percent of those with a history of depression had used alternative treatments, such as herbal medicine, massage, and spiritual healing (Kessler et al., 2001).

Proponents of alternative therapies often feel that their personal testimonials are evidence enough. But how well do these therapies stand up to scientific scrutiny? There is little evidence for or against most of them. Some, however, have been the subject of controlled research. Let's consider two of them. As we do, remember that sifting sense from nonsense requires the scientific attitude: being skeptical but not cynical, open to surprises but not gullible.

Eye Movement Desensitization and Reprocessing (EMDR)

EMDR (eye movement desensitization and reprocessing) is a therapy adored by thousands and dismissed by thousands more as a sham—"an excellent vehicle for illustrating the differences between scientific and pseudoscientific therapy techniques," suggested James Herbert and seven others (2000).

Francine Shapiro (1989, 2007) developed EMDR while walking in a park and observing that anxious thoughts vanished as her eyes spontaneously darted about. Offering her novel anxiety treatment to others, she had people imagine traumatic scenes while she triggered eye movements by waving her finger in front of their eyes, supposedly enabling them to unlock and reprocess previously frozen memories. Tens of thousands of mental health professionals from more than 75 countries have since undergone training (EMDR, 2011). No new therapy has attracted so many devotees so quickly since Franz Anton Mesmer introduced hypnosis (then called *animal magnetism*) more than two centuries ago (also after feeling inspired by an outdoor experience).

Does EMDR work? Shapiro believes it does, and she cites four studies in which it worked for 84 to 100 percent of single-trauma victims (Shapiro, 1999, 2002). Moreover, the treatment need take no more than three 90-minute sessions. The Society of Clinical Psychology task force on empirically validated treatments has acknowledged that EMDR is "probably efficacious" for the treatment of nonmilitary post-traumatic stress disorder (Chambless et al., 1997; see also Bisson & Andrew, 2007; Rodenburg et al., 2009; Seidler & Wagner, 2006).

Why, wonder the skeptics, would rapidly moving one's eyes while recalling traumas be therapeutic? Some argue that the eye movements relax or distract patients, thus allowing memory-associated emotions to extinguish (Gunter & Bodner, 2008). Others believe the eye movements in themselves are *not* the therapeutic ingredient. Trials in which people imagined traumatic scenes and tapped a finger, or just stared straight ahead while the therapist's finger wagged, have also produced therapeutic results (Devilly, 2003). EMDR does work better than doing nothing, acknowledge the skeptics (Lilienfeld & Arkowitz, 2007), but many suspect that what is therapeutic is the combination of exposure therapy—repeatedly associating traumatic memories with a safe and reassuring context that provides some emotional distance from the experience—and a robust placebo effect. Had Mesmer's pseudotherapy been compared with no treatment at all, it, too (thanks to the healing power of positive belief), might have been found "probably efficacious," observed Richard McNally (1999).

> "Studies indicate that EMDR is just as effective with fixed eyes. If that conclusion is right, what's useful in the therapy (chiefly behavioral desensitization) is not new, and what's new is superfluous."
>
> Harvard Mental Health Letter, *2002*

Light Exposure Therapy

Have you ever found yourself oversleeping, gaining weight, and feeling lethargic during the dark mornings and overcast days of winter? Slowing down and conserving energy during the dark days of winter likely gave our distant ancestors a survival advantage. For people today, however, especially for women and those living far from the equator, the wintertime blahs can constitute *seasonal affective disorder,* a form of depression with the appropriate acronym *SAD.* To counteract these dark spirits, National Institute of Mental Health researchers in the early 1980s had an idea: Give SAD people a timed daily dose of intense light. Sure enough, people reported they felt better.

Was this a bright idea, or another dim-witted example of the placebo effect? Recent studies shed some light. One exposed some people with SAD to 90 minutes of bright light and others to a sham placebo treatment—a hissing "negative ion generator" about which the staff expressed similar enthusiasm (but which was generating nothing). After four weeks, 61 percent of those exposed to morning light had greatly improved, as had 50 percent of those exposed to evening light and 32 percent of those exposed to the placebo (Eastman et al., 1998). Other studies have found that 30 minutes of exposure to 10,000-lux white fluorescent light produced relief for more than half the people receiving morning light therapy (Flory et al., 2010; Terman et al., 1998, 2001). From 20 carefully controlled trials we have a verdict (Golden et al., 2005; Wirz-Justice, 2009): Morning bright light *does* dim SAD symptoms for many people. Moreover, it does so as effectively as taking antidepressant drugs or undergoing cognitive-behavioral therapy (Lam et al., 2006; Rohan et al., 2007). The effects are clear in brain scans; light therapy sparks activity in a brain region that influences the body's arousal and hormones (Ishida et al., 2005).

Light therapy To counteract winter depression, some people spend time each morning exposed to intense light that mimics natural outdoor light. These Norwegian high school students receive regular light therapy at school during the winter months. In the United States, light boxes to counteract SAD are available from health supply and lighting stores.

© Bryan & Cherry Alexander Photography/Alamy

RETRIEVE IT

- What are EMDR and light exposure therapy, and what have we learned from controlled research about the value of these therapies?

ANSWER: Some therapists use *eye movement desensitization and reprocessing* to treat anxiety sufferers—triggering eye movements in their clients as the client envisions traumatic memories in an effort to reprocess the negative events. Light exposure therapy treats those suffering from depression with prescribed time in front of very bright artificial light in the mornings. Research suggests that light therapy is as effective as drugs or cognitive-behavioral therapy for depression. EMDR has shown some effectiveness—not from the eye movement but rather from the exposure therapy nature of the treatments (and the placebo effect).

- What two tendencies can bias appraisals of the effectiveness of alternative therapies?

ANSWER: (a) There is a natural tendency for extraordinary happenings to return to a normal state. Clients may attribute their improvement to successful treatment. (b) The *placebo effect* is the healing power of *belief* in a treatment. Clients who expect a treatment to be effective may believe it was.

How Do Psychotherapies Help People?

15-11: What three elements are shared by all forms of psychotherapy?

How can it be that therapists' training and experience do not seem to influence clients' outcomes? The answer seems to be that all psychotherapies offer three basic benefits (Frank, 1982; Goldfried & Padawer, 1982; Strupp, 1986; Wampold 2001, 2007). These benefits are *hope for demoralized people; a new perspective on oneself and the world;* and *an empathic, trusting, caring relationship.*

Hope for Demoralized People People seeking therapy typically feel anxious, depressed, self-disapproving, and incapable of turning things around. What any psychotherapy offers is the expectation that, with commitment from the therapy seeker, things can and will get better. This belief, apart from any therapy technique, may improve morale, create feelings of self-efficacy, and reduce symptoms (Prioleau et al., 1983).

A New Perspective Every psychotherapy also offers people an explanation of their symptoms. Therapy is a new experience that can help people change their behaviors and their views of themselves. Armed with a believable fresh perspective, they may approach life with new energy.

An Empathic, Trusting, Caring Relationship No matter what technique they use, effective psychotherapists are empathic. They seek to understand people's experience. They communicate care and concern. And they earn trust through respectful listening, reassurance, and advice. These qualities were clear in recorded therapy sessions from 36 recognized master therapists (Goldfried et al., 1998). Some were cognitive-behavioral therapists. Others were psychodynamic therapists. Regardless, they were trikingly similar during the most significant parts of their sessions. At key moments, the empathic therapists of both types would help clients evaluate themselves, link one aspect of their life with another, and gain insight into their interactions with others. The emotional bond between psychotherapist and client—the *therapeutic alliance*—is a key aspect of effective psychotherapy (Klein et al., 2003; Wampold, 2001). One U.S. National Institute of Mental Health depression-treatment study confirmed that the most effective therapists were those who were perceived as most empathic and caring and who established the closest therapeutic bonds with their clients (Blatt et al., 1996).

A caring relationship Effective therapists form a bond of trust with their clients.

That all psychotherapies offer hope through a fresh perspective offered by a caring person is what also enables paraprofessionals (briefly trained caregivers) to assist so many troubled people so effectively (Christensen & Jacobson, 1994). These three common elements are also part of what the growing numbers of self-help and support groups offer their members. And they are part of what traditional healers have offered (Jackson, 1992). Healers everywhere—special people to whom others disclose their suffering, whether psychiatrists, witch doctors, or shamans—have listened in order to understand and to empathize, reassure, advise, console, interpret, or explain (Torrey, 1986). Such qualities may also explain why people who feel supported by close relationships—who enjoy the fellowship and friendship of caring people—have been less likely to need or seek therapy (Frank, 1982; O'Connor & Brown, 1984).

★ ★ ★

To recap, people who seek help usually improve. So do many of those who do not undergo psychotherapy, and that is a tribute to our human resourcefulness and our capacity to care for one another. Nevertheless, though the therapist's orientation and experience appear not to matter much, people who receive some psychotherapy usually improve more than those who do not. People with clear-cut, specific problems tend to improve the most.

RETRIEVE IT

- Those who undergo psychotherapy are _____ (more/less) likely to show improvement than those who do not undergo psychotherapy.

ANSWER: more

Culture and Values in Psychotherapy

15-12: How do culture and values influence the therapist-client relationship?

All psychotherapies offer hope. Nearly all psychotherapists attempt to enhance their clients' sensitivity, openness, personal responsibility, and sense of purpose (Jensen & Bergin, 1988). But in matters of diversity, therapists differ from one another and may differ from their clients (Delaney et al., 2007; Kelly, 1990).

These differences can create a mismatch when a therapist from one culture interacts with a client from another. In North America, Europe, and Australia, for example, many therapists reflect the majority culture's *individualism,* which often gives priority to personal desires and identity. Clients with a *collectivist* perspective, as with many from Asian cultures, may assume people will be more mindful of others' expectations. These clients may have trouble relating to therapies that require them to think only of their own well-being.

Such differences help explain minority populations' reluctance to use mental health services and tendency to prematurely terminate therapy (Chen et al., 2009; Sue, 2006). In one experiment, Asian-American clients matched with counselors who shared their cultural values (rather than mismatched with those who did not) perceived more counselor empathy and felt a stronger alliance with the counselor (Kim et al., 2005). Recognizing that therapists and clients may differ in their values, communication styles, and language, American Psychological Association–accredited therapy-training programs provide training in cultural sensitivity and recruit members of underrepresented cultural groups.

Therapist and client may also have differing religious perspectives. Highly religious people may prefer and benefit from religiously similar therapists (Masters, 2010; Smith et al., 2007; Wade et al., 2006). They may have trouble establishing an emotional bond with a therapist who does not share their values.

Albert Ellis, who advocated *rational-emotive behavior therapy (REBT),* and Allen Bergin, who was co-editor of the *Handbook of Psychotherapy and Behavior Change,* illustrated how sharply psychotherapists can differ, and how those differences can affect their view of a healthy person. Ellis (1980) assumed that "no one and nothing is supreme," that "self-gratification" should be encouraged, and that "unequivocal love, commitment, service, and . . . fidelity to any interpersonal commitment, especially marriage, leads to harmful consequences." Bergin (1980) assumed the opposite—that "because God is supreme, humility and the acceptance of divine authority are virtues," that "self-control and committed love and self-sacrifice are to be encouraged," and that "infidelity to any interpersonal commitment, especially marriage, leads to harmful consequences."

Bergin's and Ellis' values differed radically. However, they agreed that *psychotherapists' personal beliefs and values influence their practice.* Clients tend to adopt their therapists' values (Worthington et al., 1996). For that reason, some psychologists believe therapists should express those values more openly. (For therapy options, see Close-Up: A Consumer's Guide to Mental Health Professionals.)

CLOSE UP:

A Consumer's Guide to Mental Health Professionals

15-13: What should a person look for when selecting a therapist?

Life for everyone is marked by a mix of serenity and stress, blessing and bereavement, good moods and bad. So, when should we seek a mental health professional's help? The American Psychological Association offers these common trouble signals:

- Feelings of hopelessness
- Deep and lasting depression
- Self-destructive behavior, such as alcohol and drug abuse

- Disruptive fears
- Sudden mood shifts
- Thoughts of suicide
- Compulsive rituals, such as hand washing
- Sexual difficulties
- Hearing voices or seeing things that others don't experience

In looking for a psychotherapist, you may want to have a preliminary consultation with two or three. College health centers are generally good starting points, and they may offer some free services. In your consultations, you can describe your problem and learn each therapist's treatment approach. You can ask questions about the therapist's values, credentials (**TABLE 15.3**), state license, and fees. And you can assess your own feelings about each of them. The emotional bond between therapist and client is perhaps the most important factor in effective therapy.

Table 15.3
Therapists and Their Training

Type	Description
Clinical psychologists	Most are psychologists with a Ph.D. (includes research training) or Psy.D. (focuses on therapy) supplemented by a supervised internship and, often, postdoctoral training. About half work in agencies and institutions, half in private practice.
Psychiatrists	Psychiatrists are physicians who specialize in the treatment of psychological disorders. Not all psychiatrists have had extensive training in psychotherapy, but as M.D.s or D.O.s they can prescribe medications. Thus, they tend to see those with the most serious problems. Many have their own private practice.
Clinical or psychiatric social workers	A two-year master of social work graduate program plus postgraduate supervision prepares some social workers to offer psychotherapy, mostly to people with everyday personal and family problems. About half have earned the National Association of Social Workers' designation of clinical social worker.
Counselors	Marriage and family counselors specialize in family relations problems. Clergy provide counseling to countless people. Abuse counselors work with substance abusers and with spouse and child abusers and their victims. Mental health and other counselors may be required to have a two-year master's degree.

The Biomedical Therapies

Psychotherapy is one way to treat psychological disorders. The other, often used with serious disorders, is *biomedical therapy.* This changes the brain's functioning by altering its chemistry with drugs, or affecting its circuitry with electrical stimulation, magnetic impulses, or psychosurgery.

Drug Therapies

15-14: What are the drug therapies? How do double-blind studies help researchers evaluate a drug's effectiveness?

Drug or placebo effect? For many people, depression lifts while taking an antidepressant drug. But people given a placebo may experience the same effect. Double-blind clinical trials suggest that, especially for those with severe depression, antidepressant drugs do have at least a modest clinical effect.

By far the most widely used biomedical treatments today are the drug therapies. Since the 1950s, discoveries in **psychopharmacology** (the study of drug effects on mind and behavior) have revolutionized the treatment of people with severe disorders. Thanks to drug therapies and support from community mental health programs, the resident population of U.S. state and county mental hospitals has dropped to a small fraction of what it was a half-century ago. Efforts to minimize involuntary hospitalization have liberated hundreds of thousands of people from hospital confinement. For some unable to care for themselves, however, release from hospitals has meant homelessness.

Many new treatments, including drug therapy, are greeted by an initial wave of enthusiasm as many people apparently improve. But that enthusiasm often diminishes on closer examination. To judge the effectiveness of a new treatment, we also need to know the rates of

- normal recovery among untreated persons.
- recovery due to the *placebo effect,* which arises from the positive expectations of patients and mental health workers alike.

"Our psychopharmacologist is a genius."

To control for these influences when testing a new drug, researchers give half the patients the drug, and the other half a similar-appearing placebo. Because neither the staff nor the patients know who gets which, this is called a *double-blind procedure.* The good news: In double-blind studies, several types of drugs have proven useful in treating psychological disorders.

Antipsychotic Drugs

An accidental discovery launched a treatment revolution for people with *psychosis.* The discovery was that some drugs used for other medical purposes calmed the hallucinations or delusions that are part of the split from reality for these patients. **Antipsychotic drugs,** such as chlorpromazine (sold as Thorazine), reduce patients' overreactions to irrelevant stimuli. Thus, they provide the most help to people experiencing positive symptoms of schizophrenia, such as auditory hallucinations and paranoia (Lehman et al., 1998; Lenzenweger et al., 1989).

The molecules of most conventional antipsychotic drugs are similar enough to molecules of the neurotransmitter dopamine to occupy its receptor sites and block its activity. This finding reinforces the idea that an overactive dopamine system contributes to schizophrenia.

Perhaps you can guess an occasional side effect of L-dopa, a drug that raises dopamine levels for Parkinson's patients: hallucinations.

Antipsychotics also have powerful side effects. Some produce sluggishness, tremors, and twitches similar to those of Parkinson's disease (Kaplan & Saddock, 1989). Long-term use of antipsychotics can produce *tardive dyskinesia,* with involuntary movements of the facial muscles (such as grimacing), tongue, and limbs. Although not more effective in controlling schizophrenia symptoms, many of the newer-generation antipsychotics, such as risperidone (Risperdal) and olanzapine (Zyprexa), have fewer of these effects. These drugs may, however, increase the risk of obesity and diabetes (Buchanan et al., 2010; Tiihonen et al., 2009).

Despite their drawbacks, antipsychotics, combined with life-skills programs and family support, have given new hope to many people with schizophrenia (Guo, 2010). Hundreds of thousands of patients have left the wards of mental hospitals and returned to work and to near-normal lives (Leucht et al., 2003).

Antianxiety Drugs

Like alcohol, **antianxiety drugs,** such as Xanax or Ativan, depress central nervous system activity (and so should not be used in combination with alcohol). Antianxiety drugs are often used in combination with psychological therapy. One antianxiety drug, the antibiotic D-cycloserine, acts upon a receptor that, in combination with behavioral treatments, facilitates the extinction of learned fears. Experiments indicate that the drug enhances the benefits of exposure therapy and helps relieve the symptoms of post-traumatic stress disorder and obsessive-compulsive disorder (Davis, 2005; Kushner et al., 2007).

One criticism made of antianxiety drugs is that they may reduce symptoms without resolving underlying problems, especially if used as an ongoing treatment. "Popping a Xanax" at the first sign of tension can produce psychological dependence; the immediate relief reinforces a person's tendency to take drugs when anxious. Heavy use can also lead to physical dependence. Regular users who stop taking antianxiety drugs may experience increased anxiety, insomnia, and other withdrawal symptoms.

Over the dozen years at the end of the twentieth century, the rate of outpatient treatment for anxiety disorders nearly doubled. The proportion of psychiatric patients receiving medication during that time increased from 52 to 70 percent (Olfson et al., 2004). And the new standard drug treatment for anxiety disorders? Antidepressants.

Antidepressant Drugs

The **antidepressant drugs** were named for their ability to lift people up from a state of depression. Until recently, this was their main use. These drugs are now increasingly used to treat anxiety disorders, such as obsessive-compulsive disorder. They work by increasing the availability of norepinephrine or serotonin. These neurotransmitters elevate arousal and mood and are scarce during depression.

Fluoxetine, which tens of millions of users worldwide have known as Prozac, partially blocks the normal reuptake of excess serotonin from synapses (**FIGURE 15.5**). Prozac and its cousins Zoloft and Paxil are called *selective serotonin reuptake inhibitors (SSRIs)* because they slow (inhibit) the synaptic vacuuming up (reuptake) of serotonin. (Given their use

psychopharmacology the study of the effects of drugs on mind and behavior.

antipsychotic drugs drugs used to treat schizophrenia and other forms of severe thought disorder.

antianxiety drugs drugs used to control anxiety and agitation.

antidepressant drugs drugs used to treat depression and some anxiety disorders. Different types work by altering the availability of various neurotransmitters.

© John Greim/Agerotostock

FIGURE 15.5

Biology of antidepressants Shown here is the action of Prozac, which partially blocks the reuptake of serotonin.

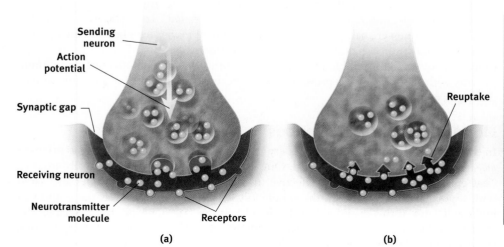

Message is sent across synaptic gap.

Message is received; excess neurotransmitter molecules are reabsorbed by sending neuron.

Sending neuron

Action potential

Synaptic gap

Receiving neuron

Neurotransmitter molecule

Receptors

Reuptake

(a)

(b)

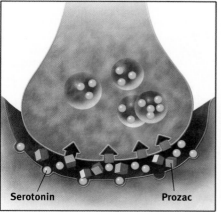

Prozac partially blocks normal reuptake of the neurotransmitter serotonin; excess serotonin in synapse enhances its mood-lifting effect.

Serotonin

Prozac

(c)

in treating other disorders, from anxiety to strokes, some professionals refer to *SSRI drugs* rather than *antidepressants* [Kramer, 2011].)

Other antidepressant drugs work by blocking the reabsorption or breakdown of both norepinephrine and serotonin. Though effective, these dual-action drugs have more potential side effects, such as dry mouth, weight gain, hypertension, or dizzy spells (Anderson, 2000; Mulrow, 1999). Administering them by means of a patch, bypassing the intestines and liver, helps reduce such side effects (Bodkin & Amsterdam, 2002).

After the introduction of SSRI drugs, the percentage of patients receiving medication for depression jumped dramatically, from 70 percent in 1987, the year before SSRIs were introduced, to 89 percent in 2001 (Olfson et al., 2003; Stafford et al., 2001). From 1996 to 2005, the number of Americans prescribed antidepressant drugs doubled, from 13 to 27 million (Olfson & Marcus, 2009). In Australia, antidepressant drug use increased 41 percent between 2002 and 2007 (Hollingworth et al., 2010).

Be advised: Patients with depression who begin taking antidepressants do not wake up the next day singing "Oh, what a beautiful morning!" Although the drugs begin to influence neurotransmission within hours, their full psychological effect often requires four weeks (and may involve a side effect of diminished sexual desire). One possible reason for the delay is that increased serotonin promotes *neurogenesis*—the birth of new brain cells, perhaps reversing stress-induced loss of neurons (Becker & Wojtowicz, 2007; Jacobs, 2004).

Antidepressant drugs are not the only way to give the body a lift. Aerobic exercise, which calms people who feel anxious and energizes those who feel depressed, does about as much good for most people with mild to moderate depression, and has additional positive side effects (more on this topic later in this chapter). Cognitive therapy, which helps people reverse their habits of thinking negatively, can boost the drug-aided relief from depression and reduce post-treatment relapses (Hollon et al., 2002; Keller et al., 2000; Vittengl et al., 2007). Antidepressant drugs work from the bottom up to affect the emotion-forming limbic system. Cognitive-behavioral therapy works from the top down to alter frontal lobe activity and change thought processes. Together, they can attack depression (and anxiety) from both below and above (Cuijpers et al., 2010; Walkup et al., 2008).

Everyone agrees that people with depression often improve after a month on antidepressant drugs. But after allowing for natural recovery and the placebo effect, how big is the drug effect? Not big, report some researchers (Kirsch et al., 1998, 2002, 2010). In double-blind clinical trials, placebos produced improvement comparable to about 75 percent of the active drug's effect. In a follow-up review that included unpublished clinical trials, the antidepressant drug effect was again modest (Kirsch et al., 2008). The placebo effect was less for those with severe depression, which made the added benefit of the drug somewhat greater for them. "Given these results, there seems little reason to prescribe antidepressant medication to any but the most severely depressed patients, unless alternative treatments have failed," Irving Kirsch concluded (BBC, 2008). A newer analysis confirms that the antidepressant benefit compared to placebos is "minimal or nonexistent, on average, in patients with mild or moderate symptoms." For those folks, aerobic exercise or psychotherapy is often effective. But among patients with "very severe" depression, the medication advantage becomes "substantial" (Fournier et al., 2010).

Mood-Stabilizing Medications

In addition to antipsychotic, antianxiety, and antidepressant drugs, psychiatrists have *mood-stabilizing drugs* in their arsenal. One of them, Depakote, was originally used to treat epilepsy. It was also found effective in controlling the manic episodes associated with bipolar disorder. Another, the simple salt *lithium,* effectively levels the emotional highs and lows of this disorder. Kay Redfield Jamison (1995, pp. 88–89) described the effect: "Lithium prevents my seductive but disastrous highs, diminishes my depressions, clears out the wool and webbing from my disordered thinking, slows me down, gentles

"If this doesn't help you don't worry, it's a placebo."

"No twisted thought without a twisted molecule."

Attributed to psychologist Ralph Gerard

me out, keeps me from ruining my career and relationships, keeps me out of a hospital, alive, and makes psychotherapy possible."

Australian physician John Cade discovered the benefits of lithium in the 1940s when he administered it to a patient with severe mania and the patient became perfectly well in less than a week (Snyder, 1986). Although we do not understand why, lithium works. About 7 in 10 people with bipolar disorder benefit from a long-term daily dose of this cheap salt (Solomon et al., 1995).

Their risk of suicide is but one-sixth that of people with bipolar disorder not taking lithium (Tondo et al., 1997). Lithium amounts in drinking water have correlated with lower suicide rates (across 18 Japanese cities and towns) and lower crime rates (across 27 Texas counties) (Ohgami et al., 2009; Schrauzer & Shrestha, 1990, 2010; Terao et al., 2010). Lithium also protects neural health, thus reducing bipolar patients' vulnerability to future dementia (Kessing et al., 2010).

"First of all I think you should know that last quarter's sales figures are interfering with my mood-stabilizing drugs."

RETRIEVE IT

- How do researchers evaluate the effectiveness of particular drug therapies?

  ANSWER: Researchers assign people to treatment and no-treatment conditions to see if those who receive the drug therapy improve more than those who don't. Double-blind controlled studies are most effective. If neither the therapist nor the client knows which participants have received the drug treatment, then any difference between the treated and untreated groups will reflect the drug treatment's actual effect.

- The drugs given most often to treat depression are called _____. The drugs that are now most commonly given to treat anxiety disorders are called _____. Schizophrenia is often treated with _____ drugs.

  ANSWERS: antidepressants; antidepressants (The antidepressants have been shown to be effective at treating both depression and anxiety.); antipsychotic

---

Brain Stimulation

15-15: How are brain stimulation and psychosurgery used in treating specific disorders?

Electroconvulsive Therapy

Another biomedical treatment, **electroconvulsive therapy (ECT),** manipulates the brain by shocking it. When ECT was first introduced in 1938, the wide-awake patient was strapped to a table and jolted with roughly 100 volts of electricity to the brain. The procedure, which produced racking convulsions and brief unconsciousness, gained a barbaric image. Although that image lingers, ECT has changed. Today, the patient receives a general anesthetic and a muscle relaxant to prevent convulsions. A psychiatrist then delivers to the patient's brain 30 to 60 seconds of electric current in briefer pulses, sometimes only to the brain's right side (**FIGURE 15.6** on the next page). Within 30 minutes, the patient awakens and remembers nothing of the treatment or of the preceding hours.

Study after study confirms that ECT can effectively treat severe depression in "treatment-resistant" patients who have not responded to drug therapy (Bailine et al., 2010; Fink, 2009; UK ECT Review Group, 2003). After three such sessions each week for two to four weeks, 80 percent or more of those receiving ECT improve markedly. They show some memory loss for the treatment period but no apparent brain damage. Modern ECT causes less memory disruption than earlier versions did (HMHL, 2007).

A *Journal of the American Medical Association* editorial concluded that "the results of ECT in treating severe depression are among the most positive treatment effects in all of medicine" (Glass, 2001). ECT reduces suicidal thoughts and has been credited with saving many from suicide (Kellner et al., 2005).

The medical use of electricity is an ancient practice. Physicians treated the Roman Emperor Claudius (10 B.C.E.–54 C.E.) for headaches by pressing electric eels to his temples.

electroconvulsive therapy (ECT) a biomedical therapy for severely depressed patients in which a brief electric current is sent through the brain of an anesthetized patient.

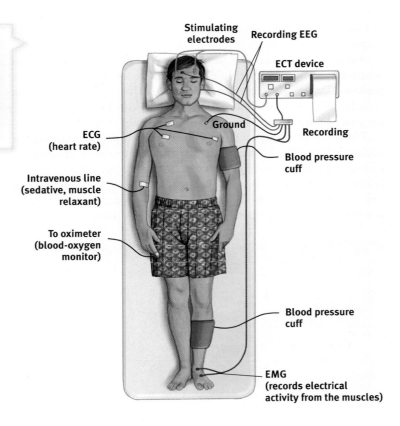

FIGURE 15.6
Electroconvulsive therapy Although controversial, ECT is often an effective treatment for depression that does not respond to drug therapy. "Electroconvulsive" is no longer accurate because patients are now given a drug that prevents convulsions.

How does ECT relieve severe depression? After more than 70 years, no one knows for sure. One patient likened ECT to the smallpox vaccine, which was saving lives before we knew how it worked. Perhaps the brief electric current calms neural centers where overactivity produces depression. ECT, like antidepressant drugs and exercise, also appears to boost the production of new brain cells (Bolwig & Madsen, 2007).

Skeptics have offered another possible explanation: ECT may trigger a placebo effect. Most ECT studies have failed to include a control group of patients who were randomly assigned to receive the same general anesthesia and to undergo simulated ECT, but without the shock. When patients are given this placebo treatment, their expectation of positive results is therapeutic without the shock (Read & Bentall, 2010). Nevertheless, a U.S. Food and Drug Administration (2011) research review concluded that ECT is more effective than a placebo, especially in the short run.

No matter how impressive the results, the idea of electrically shocking people still strikes many as barbaric, especially given our ignorance about why ECT works. Moreover, about 4 in 10 people treated with ECT relapse into depression within six months (Kellner et al., 2006). Nevertheless, in the minds of many psychiatrists and patients, ECT is a lesser evil than severe depression's misery, anguish, and risk of suicide. As research psychologist Norman Endler (1982) reported after ECT alleviated his deep depression, "A miracle had happened in two weeks."

Alternative Neurostimulation Therapies

Hopes are now rising for alternatives that jump-start neural circuits in the depressed brain. *Vagus nerve stimulation* stimulates a nerve deep in the neck, via an electrical device implanted in the chest. The device periodically sends signals to the brain's mood-related limbic system (Daskalakis et al., 2008).

Another new experimental procedure, *deep-brain stimulation,* is administered by a pacemaker that controls implanted electrodes (Lozano et al., 2008; Mayberg et al., 2005).

repetitive transcranial magnetic stimulation (rTMS) the application of repeated pulses of magnetic energy to the brain; used to stimulate or suppress brain activity.

The stimulation inhibits activity in a brain area that feeds negative emotions and thinking. With deep stimulation, some patients whose depression did not respond to drugs or ECT have found their depression lifting. To experimentally excite neurons that inhibit the brain area's negative emotion-feeding activity, neuroscientist Helen Mayberg and her colleagues (2005, 2006, 2007, 2009) drew upon the deep-brain stimulation technology sometimes used to treat Parkinson's tremors. Among an initial 20 patients receiving implanted electrodes and a pacemaker stimulator, 12 experienced relief, which was sustained over three to six years of follow-up (Kennedy et al., 2011). Some felt suddenly more aware and became more talkative and engaged; others improved only slightly if at all. Future research will explore whether Mayberg has discovered a switch that can lift depression. Other researchers are following up on reports that deep-brain stimulation can offer relief to people with obsessive-compulsive disorder (Rabins et al., 2009).

Depressed moods also seem to improve when repeated pulses of magnetic energy are applied to a person's brain. In a painless procedure called **repetitive transcranial magnetic stimulation (rTMS)**, a coiled wire sends a magnetic field through the skull to the brain (**FIGURE 15.7**). Unlike deep-brain stimulation, the magnetic energy penetrates only to the brain's surface. Unlike ECT, the rTMS procedure produces no memory loss or other serious side effects. (Headaches can result.) Wide-awake patients receive this treatment daily for several weeks.

Initial studies have found "modest" positive benefits of rTMS (Daskalakis et al., 2008; George et al., 2010; López-Ibor et al., 2008). How it works is unclear. One possible explanation is that the stimulation energizes the brain's left frontal lobe, which is relatively inactive during depression (Helmuth, 2001). Repeated stimulation may cause nerve cells to form new functioning circuits through the process of long-term potentiation. (See Chapter 8 for more details on LTP.)

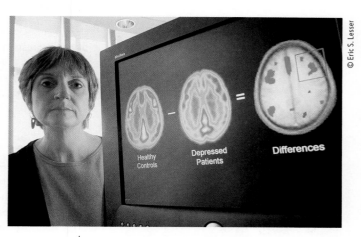

© Eric S. Lesser

A depression switch? By comparing the brains of patients with and without depression, researcher Helen Mayberg identified a brain area that appears active in people who are depressed or sad, and whose activity may be calmed by deep-brain stimulation.

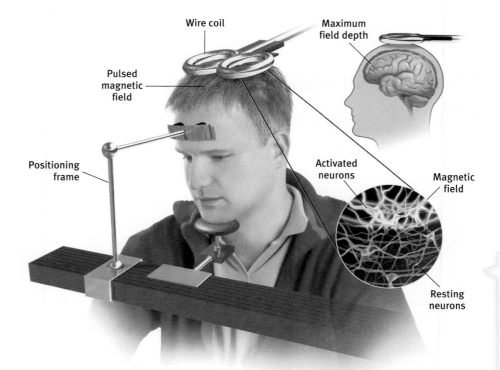

FIGURE 15.7
Magnets for the mind Repetitive transcranial magnetic stimulation (rTMS) sends a painless magnetic field through the skull to the surface of the cortex. Pulses can stimulate or dampen activity in various cortical areas. (From George, 2003.)

New York Times Co./Getty Images

Failed lobotomy This 1940 photo shows Rosemary Kennedy (center) at age 22 with brother (and future U.S. president) John and sister Jean. A year later her father, on medical advice, approved a lobotomy that was promised to control her reportedly violent mood swings. The procedure left her confined to a hospital with an infantile mentality until her death in 2005 at age 86.

psychosurgery surgery that removes or destroys brain tissue in an effort to change behavior.

lobotomy a psychosurgical procedure once used to calm uncontrollably emotional or violent patients. The procedure cut the nerves connecting the frontal lobes to the emotion-controlling centers of the inner brain.

Psychosurgery

Because its effects are irreversible, **psychosurgery**—surgery that removes or destroys brain tissue—is the most drastic and the least-used biomedical intervention for changing thoughts and behavior. In the 1930s, Portuguese physician Egas Moniz developed what would become the best-known psychosurgical operation: the **lobotomy.** Moniz cut nerves connecting the frontal lobes with the emotion-controlling centers of the inner brain. His crude but easy and inexpensive procedure took only about 10 minutes. After shocking the patient into a coma, he (and later other neurosurgeons) would hammer an instrument shaped like an ice pick through each eye socket, driving it into the brain. He then wiggled the instrument to sever connections running up to the frontal lobes. Tens of thousands of severely disturbed people were given lobotomies between 1936 and 1954 (Valenstein, 1986).

Although the intention was simply to disconnect emotion from thought, the effect was often more drastic. A lobotomy usually decreased the person's misery or tension. But it also produced a permanently listless, immature, uncreative personality. During the 1950s, after some 35,000 people had been lobotomized in the United States alone, calming drugs became available and psychosurgery was largely abandoned. Today, lobotomies are history. More precise, microscale psychosurgery is sometimes used in extreme cases. For example, if a patient has uncontrollable seizures, surgeons can destroy the specific nerve clusters that cause or transmit the convulsions. MRI-guided precision surgery is also occasionally done to cut the circuits involved in severe obsessive-compulsive disorder (Carey, 2009, 2011; Sachdev & Sachdev, 1997). Because these procedures are irreversible, neurosurgeons perform them only as a last resort.

Therapeutic Lifestyle Change

15-16: How, by adopting a healthier lifestyle, might people find some relief from depression, and how does this reflect our being biopsychosocial systems?

The effectiveness of the biomedical therapies reminds us of a fundamental lesson: *We find it convenient to talk of separate psychological and biological influences, but everything psychological is also biological.* Every thought and feeling depends on the functioning brain. Every creative idea, every moment of joy or anger, every period of depression emerges from the electrochemical activity of the living brain. The influence is two-way: When psychotherapy relieves obsessive-compulsive behavior, PET scans reveal a calmer brain (Schwartz et al., 1996).

For years, we have trusted our bodies to physicians and our minds to psychiatrists and psychologists. That neat separation no longer seems valid. Stress affects body chemistry and health. And chemical imbalances, whatever their cause, can produce psychological disorders. Anxiety disorders, major depression, bipolar disorder, and schizophrenia are all biological events. As we have seen over and again, *a human being is an integrated biopsychosocial system.*

That lesson has been applied by Stephen Ilardi (2009) and his colleagues in training seminars promoting *therapeutic lifestyle change.* Human brains and bodies were designed for physical activity and social engagement, they note. Our ancestors hunted, gathered, and built in groups, with little evidence of disabling depression. Indeed, those whose way of life entails strenuous physical activity, strong community ties, sunlight exposure, and plenty of sleep (think of foraging bands in Papua New Guinea, or Amish farming communities in North America) rarely experience depression. For both children and adults, outdoor activity in natural environments—perhaps a walk in the woods—reduces stress and promotes health (NEEF, 2011; Phillips, 2011). "Humans were never designed for the poorly nourished, sedentary, sleep-deprived, socially isolated, frenzied pace of twenty-first-century indoor life," says Ilardi (2009, p. viii).

©Randy Faris/Corbis

"Forest bathing" In several small studies, Japanese researchers have found that walks in the woods help lower stress hormone and blood pressure levels (Phillips, 2011).

The Ilardi team was also impressed by research showing that regular aerobic exercise rivals the healing power of antidepressant drugs, and that a complete night's sleep boosts mood and energy. So they invited small groups of people with depression to undergo a 12-week training program with the following goals:

- *Aerobic exercise,* 30 minutes a day, at least three times weekly (increases fitness and vitality, stimulates endorphins)
- *Adequate sleep,* with a goal of 7 to 8 hours a night (increases energy and alertness, boosts immunity)
- *Light exposure,* at least 30 minutes each morning with a light box (amplifies arousal, influences hormones)
- *Social connection,* with less alone time and at least two meaningful social engagements weekly (helps satisfy the human need to belong)
- *Anti-rumination,* by identifying and redirecting negative thoughts (enhances positive thinking)
- *Nutritional supplements,* including a daily fish oil supplement with omega-3 fatty acids (supports healthy brain functioning)

In one study of 74 people, 77 percent of those who completed the program experienced relief from depressive symptoms, compared with 19 percent in those assigned to a treatment-as-usual control condition. Future research will seek to replicate this striking result of lifestyle change. Researchers will also try to identify which parts of the treatment produce the therapeutic effect. For most people, the Latin adage has wisdom: *Mens sana in corpore sano:* "A healthy mind in a healthy body." (**FIGURE 15.8**)

TABLE 15.4 on the next page summarizes the biomedical therapies.

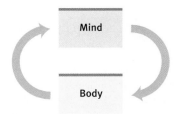

© Rubberball/Nicole Hill/Jupiterimages

FIGURE 15.8
Mind-body interaction The biomedical therapies assume that mind and body are a unit: Affect one and you will affect the other.

Table 15.4
Comparing Biomedical Therapies

Therapy	Presumed Problem	Therapy Aim	Therapy Technique
Drug therapies	Neurotransmitter malfunction	Control symptoms of psychological disorders.	Alter brain chemistry through drugs.
Brain stimulation	Severe, "treatment-resistant" depression	Alleviate depression that is unresponsive to drug therapy.	Stimulate brain through electroconvulsive shock, vagus nerve stimulation, deep-brain stimulation, or magnetic impulses.
Psychosurgery	Brain malfunction	Relieve severe disorders.	Remove or destroy brain tissue.
Therapeutic life-style change	Stress and unhealthy lifestyle	Restore healthy biological state.	Alter lifestyle through adequate exercise, sleep, and other changes.

RETRIEVE IT

- What are some examples of lifestyle changes we can make to enhance our mental health?

ANSWER: Exercise regularly, get enough sleep, get more exposure to light, nurture important relationships, redirect negative thinking, and eat a diet rich in omega-3 fatty acids.

Preventing Psychological Disorders

15-17: What is the rationale for preventive mental health programs?

We have seen that lifestyle change can help *reverse* some of the symptoms of psychological disorders. Might such change also *prevent* some disorders by building individuals' **resilience**—an ability to cope with stress and recover from adversity?

Resilience

Faced with unforeseen trauma, most adults exhibit resilience. This was true of New Yorkers in the aftermath of 9/11, especially those who enjoyed supportive close relationships and who had not recently experienced other stressful events (Bonanno et al., 2007). More than 9 in 10 New Yorkers, although stunned and grief-stricken by 9/11, did not have a dysfunctional stress reaction. By the following January, the stress symptoms of those who did were mostly gone (Person et al., 2006). Even in groups of combat-stressed veterans and political rebels who have survived dozens of episodes of torture, most do not later exhibit PTSD (Mineka & Zinbarg, 1996).

Psychologist Peter Suedfeld (1998, 2000) documented this resilience among Holocaust survivors, most of whom went on to live productive lives. "It is not always true that 'What doesn't kill you makes you stronger,' but it is often true," Suedfeld reported. "What doesn't kill you may reveal to you just how strong you really are." He speaks from experience. As a boy, Suedfeld survived the Holocaust, though his mother did not. Fellow survivor Ervin Staub has described "altruism born of suffering" (Staub & Vollhardt, 2008). Although nothing justifies terror and victimization, those who have suffered, he reports, often develop a greater-than-usual sensitivity to suffering. They have a greater empathy for others who suffer, an increased sense of responsibility, and an enlarged capacity for caring. Staub is a living example of his own work. He was spared from being sent to the Auschwitz death camps, thanks to a heroic intervention. Since that time, his lifelong mission has been to understand why some people perpetrate evil, some stand by, and some help.

Struggling with challenging crises can also lead to *post-traumatic growth* (Tedeschi & Calhoun, 2004). Many cancer survivors have reported a greater appreciation for life,

resilience the personal strength that helps most people cope with stress and recover from adversity and even trauma.

more meaningful relationships, increased personal strength, changed priorities, and a richer spiritual life. Out of even our worst experiences some good can come. Suffering can lead to new sensitivity and strength.

Creating Healthy Environments

We have seen that psychotherapies and biomedical therapies tend to locate the cause of psychological disorders within the person with the disorder. These therapies try to treat people by giving them insight into their problems, by changing their thinking, by helping them gain control with drugs. Yet according to the preventive view, it is not just the person who needs treatment, but also the person's social context.

Many psychological disorders are understandable responses to a disturbing and stressful society. Better to prevent a problem by reforming a sick situation and by developing people's coping competencies than to wait for a problem to arise and then treat it.

A story about the rescue of a drowning person from a rushing river illustrates the importance of prevention: Having successfully administered first aid to the first victim, the rescuer spots another struggling person and pulls her out, too. After a half-dozen repetitions, the rescuer suddenly turns and starts running away while the river sweeps yet another floundering person into view. "Aren't you going to rescue that fellow?" asks a bystander. "Heck no," the rescuer replies. "I'm going upstream to find out what's pushing all these people in."

Preventive mental health is upstream work. It seeks to prevent psychological casualties by identifying and wiping out the conditions that cause them. Poverty, meaningless work, constant criticism, unemployment, racism, sexism, and heterosexism can undermine people's sense of competence, personal control, and self-esteem. Such stresses increase their risk of depression, alcohol dependence, and suicide.

To prevent psychological casualties, said George Albee (1986), caring people should therefore support programs that control or eliminate these stressful situations. We eliminated smallpox not by treating the afflicted but by vaccinating the healthy. We conquered yellow fever by controlling mosquitoes. Preventing psychological problems means empowering those who have learned an attitude of helplessness, changing environments that breed loneliness, renewing the disintegrating family, promoting communication training for couples, and bolstering parents' and teachers' skills. "Everything aimed at improving the human condition, at making life more fulfilling and meaningful, may be considered part of primary prevention of mental or emotional disturbance" (Kessler & Albee, 1975, p. 557).

Prevention includes the cognitive training that promotes positive thinking in children at risk for depression (Brunwasser et al., 2009; Gillham et al., 2006; Stice et al., 2009). A 2009 National Research Council and Institute of Medicine report—*Preventing Mental, Emotional, and Behavioral Disorders Among Young People*—offers encouragement. It documents that intervention efforts often based on cognitive-behavioral therapy principles significantly boost child and adolescent flourishing. Through such preventive efforts and healthy lifestyles, fewer of us will fall into the rushing river of psychological disorders.

Among the upstream prevention workers mindful of how people interact with their environments are the *community psychologists*. Through their focus on creating environments that support psychological health, their research, and their social action, community psychologists aim to empower people and to enhance their competence, health, and well-being.

> "It is better to prevent than to cure."
> *Peruvian folk wisdom*

RETRIEVE IT

• What is the difference between preventive mental health and psychological or biomedical therapy?

ANSWER: Psychological and biomedical therapies attempt to relieve people's suffering from psychological disorders. Preventive mental health attempts to prevent suffering by identifying and eliminating the conditions that cause disorders.

★ ★ ★

If you just finished reading this book, your introduction to psychological science is completed. Our tour of psychological science has taught me much—and you, too?—about our moods and memories, about the reach of our unconscious, about how we flourish and struggle, about how we perceive our physical and social worlds, and about how our biology and culture in turn shape us. My hope, as your guide on this tour, is that you have shared some of my fascination, grown in your understanding and compassion, and sharpened your critical thinking. I also hope you enjoyed the ride.

With every good wish in your future endeavors,

David G. Myers
www.davidmyers.org

CHAPTER REVIEW

Therapy

LEARNING OBJECTIVES

Test Yourself by taking a moment to answer each of these Learning Objective Questions (repeated here from within the chapter). Then turn to Appendix D, Complete Chapter Reviews, to check your answers. Research suggests that trying to answer these questions on your own will improve your long-term memory of the concepts (McDaniel et al., 2009).

Treating Psychological Disorders

15-1: How do psychotherapy, biomedical therapy, and an eclectic approach to therapy differ?

The Psychological Therapies

15-2: What are the goals and techniques of psychoanalysis, and how have they been adapted in psychodynamic therapy?

15-3: What are the basic themes of humanistic therapy, and what are the specific goals and techniques of Rogers' client-centered approach?

15-4: How does the basic assumption of behavior therapy differ from the assumptions of psychodynamic and humanistic therapies? What techniques are used in exposure therapies and aversive conditioning?

15-5: What is the basic idea of operant conditioning therapy, and what arguments have been used for and against it?

15-6: What are the goals and techniques of the cognitive therapies and of cognitive-behavioral therapy?

15-7: What are the aims and benefits of group and family therapy?

Evaluating Psychotherapies

15-8: Does psychotherapy work? Who decides?

15-9: Are some psychotherapies more effective than others for specific disorders?

15-10: How do alternative therapies fare under scientific scrutiny?

15-11: What three elements are shared by all forms of psychotherapy?

15-12: How do culture and values influence the therapist-client relationship?

15-13: What should a person look for when selecting a therapist?

The Biomedical Therapies

15-14: What are the drug therapies? How do double-blind studies help researchers evaluate a drug's effectiveness?

15-15: How are brain stimulation and psychosurgery used in treating specific disorders?

15-16: How, by adopting a healthier lifestyle, might people find some relief from depression, and how does this reflect our being biopsychosocial systems?

Preventing Psychological Disorders

15-17: What is the rationale for preventive mental health programs?

TERMS AND CONCEPTS TO REMEMBER

Test yourself on these terms by trying to write down the definition in your own words before flipping back to the referenced page to check your answer.

psychotherapy, p. 546

biomedical therapy, p. 546

eclectic approach, p. 546

psychoanalysis, p. 547

resistance, p. 547

interpretation, p. 547

transference, p. 547

psychodynamic therapy, p. 548

insight therapies, p. 548

client-centered therapy, p. 549

active listening, p. 549

unconditional positive regard, p. 550

behavior therapy, p. 550

counterconditioning, p. 551

exposure therapies, p. 551

systematic desensitization, p. 551

virtual reality exposure therapy, p. 552

aversive conditioning, p. 552

token economy, p. 553

cognitive therapy, p. 554

cognitive-behavioral therapy, p. 556

group therapy, p. 557

family therapy, p. 558

evidence-based practice, p. 562

psychopharmacology, p. 568

antipsychotic drugs, p. 568

antianxiety drugs, p. 569

antidepressant drugs, p. 569

electroconvulsive therapy (ECT), p. 571

repetitive transcranial magnetic stimulation (rTMS), p. 573

psychosurgery, p. 574

lobotomy, p. 574

resilience, p. 576

EXPERIENCE THE TESTING EFFECT

Test yourself repeatedly throughout your studies. This will not only help you figure out what you know and don't know; the testing itself will help you learn and remember the information more effectively thanks to the *testing effect*.

1. A therapist who helps patients search for the unconscious roots of their problem and offers interpretations of their behaviors, feelings, and dreams, is drawing from
   a. psychoanalysis.
   b. humanistic therapies.
   c. client-centered therapy.
   d. behavior therapy.

2. _____ therapies are designed to help individuals discover the thoughts and feelings that guide their motivation and behavior.

3. Compared with psychoanalysts, humanistic therapists are more likely to emphasize
   a. hidden or repressed feelings.
   b. childhood experiences.
   c. psychological disorders.
   d. self-fulfillment and growth.

4. A therapist who restates and clarifies the client's statements is practicing _____ _____.

5. The goal of behavior therapy is to
   a. identify and treat the underlying causes of the problem.
   b. improve learning and insight.
   c. eliminate the unwanted behavior.
   d. improve communication and social sensitivity.

6. Behavior therapists often use _____ techniques such as systematic desensitization and aversive conditioning to encourage clients to produce new responses to old stimuli.

7. The technique of _____ _____ teaches people to relax in the presence of progressively more anxiety-provoking stimuli.

8. After a near-fatal car accident, Rico developed such an intense fear of driving on the freeway that he takes lengthy alternative routes to work each day. Which psychological therapy might best help Rico overcome his phobia, and why?

9. At a treatment center, people who display a desired behavior receive coins that they can later exchange for other rewards. This is an example of a(n) _____ _____.

10. Cognitive therapy has been especially effective in treating
    a. nail biting.
    b. phobias.
    c. alcohol dependence.
    d. depression.

11. _____ – _____ therapists help people to change their self-defeating ways of thinking and to act out those changes in their daily behavior.

12. In family therapy, the therapist assumes that
    a. only one family member needs to change.
    b. each person's actions trigger reactions from other family members.
    c. dysfunctional families must improve their interactions or give up their children.
    d. All of the above.

13. The most enthusiastic or optimistic view of the effectiveness of psychotherapy comes from
    a. outcome research.
    b. randomized clinical trials.
    c. reports of clinicians and clients.
    d. a government study of treatment for depression.

14. Studies show that _____ therapy is the most effective treatment for most psychological disorders.
    a. behavior
    b. humanistic
    c. psychodynamic
    d. no one type of

15. What are the three components of evidence-based practice?

16. How does the placebo effect bias patients' attitudes about the effectiveness of drug therapies?

17. Some antipsychotic drugs, used to calm people with schizophrenia, can have unpleasant side effects, most notably
    a. hyperactivity.
    b. convulsions and momentary memory loss.
    c. sluggishness, tremors, and twitches.
    d. paranoia.

18. Drugs like Xanax and Ativan, which depress central nervous system activity, can lead to psychological and physical dependency when used as ongoing treatment. These drugs are referred to as _____ drugs.

19. A simple salt that often brings relief to patients suffering the highs and lows of bipolar disorder is _____.

20. When drug therapies have not been effective, electroconvulsive therapy (ECT) may be used as treatment, largely for people with
    a. severe obsessive-compulsive disorder.
    b. severe depression.
    c. schizophrenia.
    d. anxiety disorders.

21. An approach that seeks to identify and alleviate conditions that put people at high risk for developing psychological disorders is called
    a. deep-brain stimulation.
    b. the mood-stabilizing perspective.
    c. spontaneous recovery.
    d. biomedical therapy.

Find answers to these questions in Appendix E, in the back of the book.

Experience more of the
TESTING EFFECT

Multiple-format self-tests and more may be found at www.worthpublishers.com/myers.

Statistical Reasoning in Everyday Life

In descriptive, correlational, and experimental research, statistics are tools that help us see and interpret what the unaided eye might miss. Sometimes the unaided eye misses badly, as it did when researchers asked 5522 Americans to estimate (as a percentage) the portion of the country's wealth possessed by the richest 20 percent of the population (Norton & Ariely, 2011). The average person's guess—58 percent—"dramatically underestimated" the actual figure. (The wealthiest 20 percent possess 84 percent of the wealth.)

Accurate statistical understanding benefits everyone. To be an educated person today is to be able to apply simple statistical principles to everyday reasoning. We needn't memorize complicated formulas to think more clearly and critically about data.

Off-the-top-of-the-head estimates often misread reality and then mislead the public. Someone throws out a big, round number. Others echo it, and before long the big, round number becomes public misinformation. A few examples:

- *Ten percent of people are lesbians or gay men.* Or is it 2 to 3 percent, as suggested by various national surveys (Chapter 5)?

- *We ordinarily use but 10 percent of our brain.* Or is it closer to 100 percent (Chapter 2)?

- *The human brain has 100 billion nerve cells.* Or is it more like 40 billion, as suggested by one extrapolation from sample counts (Chapter 2)?

The point to remember: Doubt big, round, undocumented numbers.

Statistical illiteracy also feeds needless health scares (Gigerenzer et al., 2008, 2009, 2010). In the 1990s, the British press reported a study showing that women taking a particular contraceptive pill had a 100 percent increased risk of blood clots that could produce strokes. This caused thousands of women to stop taking the pill, leading to a wave of unwanted pregnancies and an estimated 13,000 additional abortions (which also are associated with increased blood clot risk). And what did the study find? A 100 percent increased risk, indeed—but only from 1 in 7000 to 2 in 7000. Such false alarms underscore the need to teach statistical reasoning and to present statistical information more transparently.

Asked about the *ideal* wealth distribution in America, Democrats and Republicans were surprisingly similar. In the Democrats' ideal world, the richest 20 percent would possess 30 percent of the wealth. Republicans preferred a similar 35 percent (Norton & Ariely, 2011).

Describing Data

A-1: How can we describe data with measures of central tendency and variation?

Once researchers have gathered their data, they must organize them in some meaningful way. One way to do this is to convert the data into a simple *bar graph,* as in **FIGURE A.1** on the next page, which displays a distribution of different brands of trucks still on the road after a decade. When reading statistical graphs such as this, take care. It's easy to design a graph to make a difference look big (Figure A.1a) or small (Figure A.1b). The secret lies in how you label the vertical scale (the *y-axis*).

"Figures can be misleading—so I've written a song which I think expresses the real story of the firm's performance this quarter."

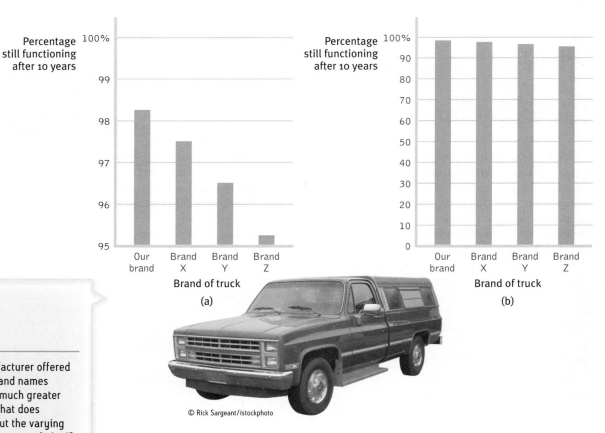

© Rick Sargeant/istockphoto

The average person has one ovary and one testicle.

mode the most frequently occurring score(s) in a distribution.

mean the arithmetic average of a distribution, obtained by adding the scores and then dividing by the number of scores.

median the middle score in a distribution; half the scores are above it and half are below it.

range the difference between the highest and lowest scores in a distribution.

standard deviation a computed measure of how much scores vary around the mean score.

The point to remember: Think smart. When viewing figures in magazines, on TV, or online, read the scale labels and note their range.

Measures of Central Tendency

The next step is to summarize the data using some *measure of central tendency,* a single score that represents a whole set of scores. The simplest measure is the **mode,** the most frequently occurring score or scores. The most familiar is the **mean,** or arithmetic average—the total sum of all the scores divided by the number of scores. The midpoint—the 50th percentile—is the **median**. On a divided highway, the median is the middle. So, too, with data: If you arrange all the scores in order from the highest to the lowest, half will be above the median and half will be below it.

Measures of central tendency neatly summarize data. But consider what happens to the mean when a distribution is lopsided, or *skewed* by a few way-out scores. With income data, for example, the mode, median, and mean often tell very different stories (**FIGURE A.2**). This happens because the mean is biased by a few extreme scores. When Microsoft co-founder Bill Gates sits down in an intimate café, its average (mean) customer instantly becomes a billionaire. But the median customers' wealth remains unchanged. Understanding this, you can see how a British newspaper could accurately run the headline "Income for 62% Is Below Average" (Waterhouse, 1993). Because the bottom *half* of British income earners received only a *quarter* of the national income cake, most British people, like most people everywhere, made less than the mean. Mean and median tell different true stories.

The point to remember: Always note which measure of central tendency is reported. If it is a mean, consider whether a few atypical scores could be distorting it.

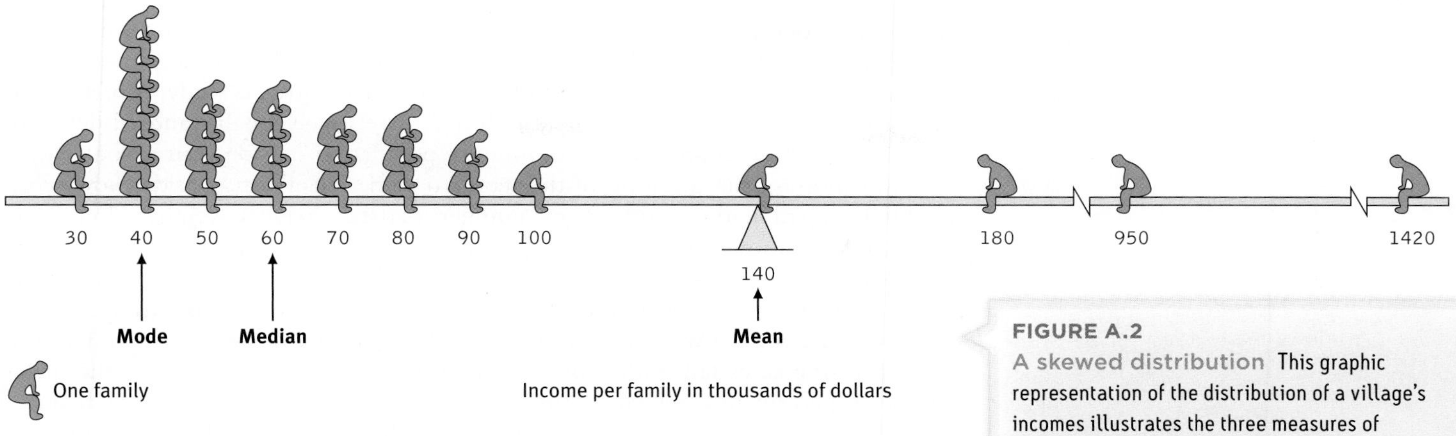

30 40 50 60 70 80 90 100   140   180   950   1420

↑ Mode   ↑ Median   Mean

One family   Income per family in thousands of dollars

FIGURE A.2
A skewed distribution This graphic representation of the distribution of a village's incomes illustrates the three measures of central tendency—mode, median, and mean. Note how just a few high incomes make the mean—the fulcrum point that balances the incomes above and below—deceptively high.

Measures of Variation

Knowing the value of an appropriate measure of central tendency can tell us a great deal. But the single number omits other information. It helps to know something about the amount of *variation* in the data—how similar or diverse the scores are. Averages derived from scores with low variability are more reliable than averages based on scores with high variability. Consider a basketball player who scored between 13 and 17 points in each of the season's first 10 games. Knowing this, we would be more confident that she would score near 15 points in her next game than if her scores had varied from 5 to 25 points.

The **range** of scores—the gap between the lowest and highest—provides only a crude estimate of variation. A couple of extreme scores in an otherwise uniform group, such as the $950,000 and $1,420,000 incomes in Figure A.2, will create a deceptively large range.

The more useful standard for measuring how much scores deviate from one another is the **standard deviation.** It better gauges whether scores are packed together or dispersed, because it uses information from each score. The computation (see **TABLE A.1**) assembles information about how much individual scores differ from

Table A.1
Standard Deviation is Much More Informative Than Mean Alone

	Test Scores in Class A			Test Scores in Class B	
Score	Deviation from the Mean	Squared Deviation	Score	Deviation from the Mean	Squared Deviation
72	−8	64	60	−20	400
74	−6	36	60	−20	400
77	−3	9	70	−10	100
79	−1	1	70	−10	100
82	+2	4	90	+10	100
84	+4	16	90	+10	100
85	+5	25	100	+20	400
87	+7	49	100	+20	400

Total = 640   Sum of (deviations)^2 = 204   Total = 640   Sum of (deviations)^2 = 2000

Mean = 640 ÷ 8 = 80   Mean = 640 ÷ 8 = 80

Standard deviation =

$$\sqrt{\frac{\text{Sum of (deviations)}^2}{\text{Number of scores}}} = \sqrt{\frac{204}{8}} = 5.0$$

Standard deviation =

$$\sqrt{\frac{\text{Sum of (deviations)}^2}{\text{Number of scores}}} = \sqrt{\frac{2000}{8}} = 15.8$$

the mean. Note that the test scores in Class A and Class B have the same mean (80), but very different standard deviations, which tell us more about how the students in each class are really faring. If your college or university attracts students of a certain ability level, their intelligence scores will have a relatively small standard deviation compared with the more diverse community population outside your school.

You can grasp the meaning of the standard deviation if you consider how scores tend to be distributed in nature. Large numbers of data—heights, weights, intelligence scores, grades (though not incomes)—often form a symmetrical, *bell-shaped* distribution. Most cases fall near the mean, and fewer cases fall near either extreme. This bell-shaped distribution is so typical that we call the curve it forms the **normal curve.**

As **FIGURE A.3** shows, a useful property of the normal curve is that roughly 68 percent of the cases fall within one standard deviation on either side of the mean. About 95 percent of cases fall within two standard deviations. Thus, as Chapter 9 notes, about 68 percent of people taking an intelligence test will score within ±15 points of 100. About 95 percent will score within ±30 points.

FIGURE A.3

The normal curve Scores on aptitude tests tend to form a normal, or bell-shaped, curve. For example, the Wechsler Adult Intelligence Scale calls the average score 100.

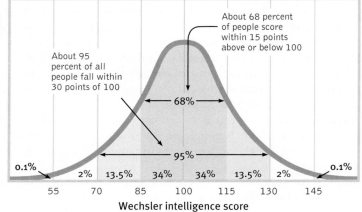

Number of scores

About 95 percent of all people fall within 30 points of 100

About 68 percent of people score within 15 points above or below 100

68%

95%

0.1%   2%   13.5%   34%   34%   13.5%   2%   0.1%

55   70   85   100   115   130   145

Wechsler intelligence score

normal curve *(normal distribution)* a symmetrical, bell-shaped curve that describes the distribution of many types of data; most scores fall near the mean (about 68 percent fall within one standard deviation of it) and fewer and fewer near the extremes.

correlation coefficient a statistical index of the relationship between two things (from −1 to +1).

scatterplot a graphed cluster of dots, each of which represents the values of two variables. The slope of the points suggests the direction of the relationship between the two variables. The amount of scatter suggests the strength of the correlation (little scatter indicates high correlation).

Correlation: A Measure of Relationships

A-2: What does it mean when we say two things are correlated?

Throughout this book we often ask how strongly two things are related: For example, how closely related are the personality scores of identical twins? How well do intelligence test scores predict vocational achievement? How closely is stress related to disease?

As we saw in Chapter 1, describing behavior is a first step toward predicting it. When naturalistic observation and surveys reveal that one trait or behavior accompanies another, we say the two *correlate*. A **correlation coefficient** is a statistical measure of relationship. In such cases, **scatterplots** can be very revealing.

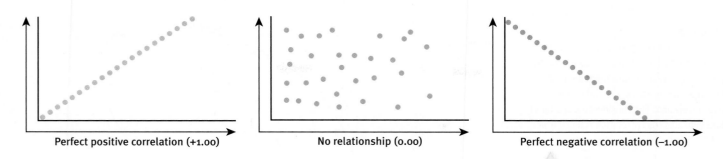

Perfect positive correlation (+1.00)   No relationship (0.00)   Perfect negative correlation (−1.00)

FIGURE A.4
Scatterplots, showing patterns of correlation Correlations can range from +1.00 (scores on one measure increase in direct proportion to scores on another) to –1.00 (scores on one measure decrease precisely as scores rise on the other).

Each dot in a scatterplot represents the values of two variables. The three scatterplots in **FIGURE A.4** illustrate the range of possible correlations from a perfect positive to a perfect negative. (Perfect correlations rarely occur in the "real world.") A correlation is positive if two sets of scores, such as height and weight, tend to rise or fall together.

Saying that a correlation is "negative" says nothing about its strength or weakness. A correlation is negative if two sets of scores relate inversely, one set going up as the other goes down.

Statistics can help us see what the naked eye sometimes misses. To demonstrate this for yourself, try an imaginary project. Wondering if tall men are more or less easygoing, you collect two sets of scores: men's heights and men's temperaments. You measure the heights of 20 men, and you have someone else independently assess their temperaments (from zero for extremely calm to 100 for highly reactive).

With all the relevant data right in front of you (**TABLE A.2**), can you tell whether the correlation between height and reactive temperament is positive, negative, or close to zero?

Comparing the columns in Table A.2, most people detect very little relationship between height and temperament. In fact, the correlation in this imaginary example is positive, +0.63, as we can see if we display the data as a scatterplot. In **FIGURE A.5** (on the next page) moving from left to right, the upward, oval-shaped slope of the cluster of points shows that our two imaginary sets of scores (height and temperament) tend to rise together.

If we fail to see a relationship when data are presented as systematically as in Table A.2, how much less likely are we to notice them in everyday life? To see what is right in front of us, we sometimes need statistical illumination. We can easily see evidence of gender discrimination when given statistically summarized information about job level, seniority, performance, gender, and salary. But we often see no discrimination when the same information dribbles in, case by case (Twiss et al., 1989).

The point to remember: Correlation coefficients tell us nothing about cause and effect, but they can help us see the world more clearly by revealing the extent to which two things relate.

Regression Toward the Mean

A-3: What is regression toward the mean?

Correlations not only make visible the relationships we might otherwise miss, they also restrain our "seeing" nonexistent relationships. When we believe there is a relationship between two things, we are likely to notice and recall instances that confirm our belief. If we believe that dreams are forecasts of actual events, we may notice and recall confirming instances more than disconfirming instances. The result is an *illusory correlation.*

Table A.2
Height and Temperamental Reactivity of 20 Men

Person	Height in Inches	Temperament
1	80	75
2	63	66
3	61	60
4	79	90
5	74	60
6	69	42
7	62	42
8	75	60
9	77	81
10	60	39
11	64	48
12	76	69
13	71	72
14	66	57
15	73	63
16	70	75
17	63	30
18	71	57
19	68	84
20	70	39

FIGURE A.5

Scatterplot for height and reactive temperament This display of data from 20 imagined people (each represented by a data point) reveals an upward slope, indicating a positive correlation. The considerable scatter of the data indicates the correlation is much lower than +1.0.

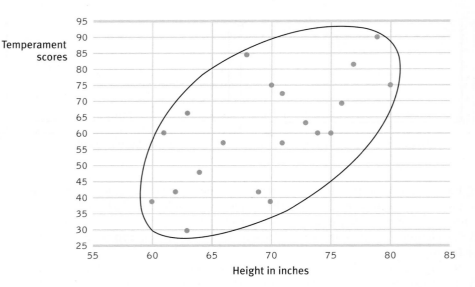

Illusory correlations feed an illusion of control—that chance events are subject to our personal control. Gamblers, remembering their lucky rolls, may come to believe they can influence the roll of the dice by again throwing gently for low numbers and hard for high numbers. The illusion that uncontrollable events correlate with our actions is also fed by a statistical phenomenon called **regression toward the mean.** Average results are more typical than extreme results. Thus, after an unusual event, things tend to return toward their average level; extraordinary happenings tend to be followed by more ordinary ones.

The point may seem obvious, yet we regularly miss it: We sometimes attribute what may be a normal regression (the expected return to normal) to something we have done. Consider two examples:

- Students who score much lower or higher on an exam than they usually do are likely, when retested, to return to their average.

- Unusual ESP subjects who defy chance when first tested nearly always lose their "psychic powers" when retested (a phenomenon parapsychologists have called the *decline effect*).

Failure to recognize regression is the source of many superstitions and of some ineffective practices as well. When day-to-day behavior has a large element of chance fluctuation, we may notice that others' behavior improves (regresses toward average) after we criticize them for very bad performance, and that it worsens (regresses toward average) after we warmly praise them for an exceptionally fine performance. Ironically, then, regression toward the average can mislead us into feeling rewarded for having criticized others and into feeling punished for having praised them (Tversky & Kahneman, 1974).

The point to remember: When a fluctuating behavior returns to normal, there is no need to invent fancy explanations for why it does so. Regression toward the mean is probably at work.

"Once you become sensitized to it, you see regression everywhere."
Psychologist Daniel Kahneman (1985)

RETRIEVE IT

- You hear the school basketball coach telling her friend that she rescued her team's winning streak by yelling at them after they played unusually badly in the first half of the game. What is another explanation of why the team's performance improved?

ANSWER: The team's poor performance was not their typical behavior. Their return to their normal—their winning streak—may just have been a case of regression toward the mean.

regression toward the mean the tendency for extreme or unusual scores or events to fall back (regress) toward the average.

Significant Differences

A-4: How do we know whether an observed difference can be generalized to other populations?

Data are "noisy." The average score in one group could conceivably differ from the average score in another group not because of any real difference but merely because of chance fluctuations in the people sampled. How confidently, then, can we infer that an observed difference is not just a fluke—a chance result from the research sample? For guidance, we can ask whether the observed difference between the two groups is reliable and significant.

When Is an Observed Difference Reliable?

In deciding when it is safe to generalize from a sample, we should keep three principles in mind:

1. **Representative samples are better than biased (unrepresentative) samples.** The best basis for generalizing is from a representative sample of cases, not from the exceptional and memorable cases one finds at the extremes. Research never randomly samples the whole human population. Thus, it pays to keep in mind what population a study has sampled. (To see how an unrepresentative sample can lead you astray, see Close-Up: Cross-Sectional and Longitudinal Studies.)

CLOSE UP:

Cross-Sectional and Longitudinal Studies

A-5: What are cross-sectional studies and longitudinal studies, and why is it important to know which method was used?

When interpreting research results, smart thinkers consider how researchers arrived at their conclusions. One way studies vary is in the time period for gathering data.

In **cross-sectional studies,** researchers compare different groups at the same time. When researchers compare intelligence test scores among people in differing age groups, older adults, on average, give fewer correct answers than do younger adults. This could suggest that mental ability declines with age, and indeed, that was the conclusion drawn from many early cross-sectional studies of intelligence.

In **longitudinal studies,** researchers study and restudy the same group at different times in their life span. Around 1920, colleges began giving intelligence tests to entering students, and several psychologists saw their chance to study intelligence

longitudinally. What they expected to find was a decrease in intelligence after about age 30 (Schaie & Geiwitz, 1982). What they actually found was a surprise: Until late in life, intelligence remained stable. On some tests, it even increased.

Why did these new results differ from the earlier cross-sectional findings? In retrospect, researchers realized that cross-sectional studies that compared 70-year-olds and 30-year-olds were comparing people not only of two different ages but also of two different eras. They were comparing

• generally less-educated people (born, say, in the early 1900s) with better-educated people (born after 1950).

• people raised in large families with people raised in smaller families.

• people from less-affluent families with people from more-affluent families.

Others have since pointed out that longitudinal studies have their own pitfalls. Participants who survive to the end of longitudinal studies may be the healthiest (and brightest) people. When researchers adjust for the loss of participants, as did one study following more than 2000 people over age 75 in Cambridge, England, they find a steeper intelligence decline, especially as people age after 85 (Brayne et al., 1999).

The point to remember: When interpreting research results, pay attention to the methodology used, such as whether it was a longitudinal or cross-sectional study.

. . . . . .

cross-sectional study research in which people of different ages are compared with one another.

longitudinal study research in which the same people are restudied and retested over a long period of time.

statistical significance a statistical statement of how likely it is that an obtained result occurred by chance.

2. **Less-variable observations are more reliable than those that are more variable.** As we noted earlier, in the example of the basketball player whose game-to-game points were consistent, an average is more reliable when it comes from scores with low variability.

3. **More cases are better than fewer cases.** An eager prospective student visits two university campuses, each for a day. At the first, the student randomly attends two classes and discovers both instructors to be witty and engaging. At the next campus, the two sampled instructors seem dull and uninspiring. Returning home, the student (discounting the small sample size of only two teachers at each institution) tells friends about the "great teachers" at the first school, and the "bores" at the second. Again, we know it but we ignore it: *Averages based on many cases are more reliable* (less variable) than averages based on only a few cases.

The point to remember: Smart thinkers are not overly impressed by a few anecdotes. Generalizations based on a few unrepresentative cases are unreliable.

When Is an Observed Difference "Significant"?

Perhaps you've compared men's and women's scores on a laboratory test of aggression, and you've found a gender difference. But individuals differ. How likely is it that the difference you observed was just a fluke? Statistical testing can estimate the probability of the result occurring by chance.

Here is the underlying logic: When averages from two samples are each reliable measures of their respective populations (as when each is based on many observations that have small variability), then their *difference* is likely to be reliable as well. (Example: The less the variability in women's and in men's aggression scores, the more confidence we would have that any observed gender difference is reliable.) And when the difference between the sample averages is *large,* we have even more confidence that the difference between them reflects a real difference in their populations.

In short, when sample averages are reliable, and when the difference between them is relatively large, we say the difference has **statistical significance.** This means that the observed difference is probably not due to chance variation between the samples.

In judging statistical significance, psychologists are conservative. They are like juries who must presume innocence until guilt is proven. For most psychologists, proof beyond a reasonable doubt means not making much of a finding unless the odds of its occurring by chance, if no real effect exists, are less than 5 percent.

When reading about research, you should remember that, given large enough or homogeneous enough samples, a difference between them may be "statistically significant" yet have little practical significance. For example, comparisons of intelligence test scores among hundreds of thousands of first-born and later-born individuals indicate a highly significant tendency for first-born individuals to have higher average scores than their later-born siblings (Kristensen & Bjerkedal, 2007; Zajonc & Markus, 1975). But because the scores differ by only one to three points, the difference has little practical importance.

PEANUTS

The point to remember: Statistical significance indicates the *likelihood* that a result will happen by chance. But this does not say anything about the *importance* of the result.

RETRIEVE IT

Can you solve this puzzle?

The registrar's office at the University of Michigan has found that usually about 100 students in Arts and Sciences have perfect marks at the end of their first term at the university. However, only about 10 to 15 students graduate with perfect marks. What do you think is the most likely explanation for the fact that there are more perfect marks after one term than at graduation (Jepson et al., 1983)?

ANSWER: Averages based on fewer courses are more variable, which guarantees a greater number of extremely low and high marks at the end of the first term.

APPENDIX REVIEW

Statistical Reasoning in Everyday Life

LEARNING OBJECTIVES

Test Yourself by taking a moment to answer each of these Learning Objective Questions (repeated here from within the Appendix). Then turn to Appendix D, Complete Chapter Reviews, to check your answers. Research suggests that trying to answer these questions on your own will improve your long-term memory of the concepts (McDaniel et al., 2009).

Describing Data

A-1: How can we describe data with measures of central tendency and variation?

A-2: What does it mean when we say two things are correlated?

A-3: What is regression toward the mean?

Significant Differences

A-4: How do we know whether an observed difference can be generalized to other populations?

A-5: What are cross-sectional studies and longitudinal studies, and why is it important to know which method was used?

TERMS AND CONCEPTS TO REMEMBER

Test yourself on these terms by trying to write down the definition before flipping back to the referenced page to check your answer.

mode, p. A-2

mean, p. A-2

median, p. A-2

range, p. A-3

standard deviation, p. A-3

normal curve, p. A-4

correlation coefficient, p. A-4

scatterplot, p. A-4

regression toward the mean, p. A-6

cross-sectional study, p. A-7

longitudinal study, p. A-7

statistical significance, p. A-8

EXPERIENCE THE TESTING EFFECT

Test yourself repeatedly throughout your studies. This will not only help you figure out what you know and don't know; the testing itself will help you learn and remember the information more effectively thanks to the *testing effect.*

1. Which of the three measures of central tendency is most easily distorted by a few very large or very small scores?

   a. The mode

   b. The mean

   c. The median

   d. They are all equally vulnerable to distortion from atypical scores.

2. The standard deviation is the most useful measure of variation in a set of data because it tells us

   a. the difference between the highest and lowest scores in the set.

   b. the extent to which the sample being used deviates from the bigger population it represents.

   c. how much individual scores differ from the mode.

   d. how much individual scores differ from the mean.

3. Another name for a bell-shaped distribution, in which most scores fall near the middle and fewer scores fall at each extreme, is a _____ _____.

4. In a _____ correlation, the scores rise and fall together; in a(n) _____ correlation, one score falls as the other rises.

   a. positive; negative

   b. positive; illusory

   c. negative; inverse

   d. strong; weak

5. If a study revealed that tall people were less intelligent than short people, this would suggest that the correlation between height and intelligence is _____ (positive/negative).

6. A _____ provides a visual representation of the direction and the strength of a relationship between two variables.

7. What is regression toward the mean, and how can it influence our interpretation of events?

8. In _____-_____ studies, a characteristic is assessed across different age groups at the same time.

9. When sample averages are _____ and the difference between them is _____, we can say the difference has statistical significance.

   a. reliable; large

   b. reliable; small

   c. due to chance; large

   d. due to chance; small

Find answers to these questions in Appendix E, in the back of the book.

Experience more of the **TESTING** EFFECT

Multiple-format self-tests and more may be found at www.worthpublishers.com/myers.

Psychology at Work

B-1: What is "flow," and what are the three subfields of industrial-organizational psychology?

For most of us, work is life's biggest single waking activity. To live is to work. Work helps satisfy several levels of need identified in Abraham Maslow's (1970) hierarchy of needs (see Chapter 10). Work supports us. Work connects us. Work defines us. Meeting someone for the first time and wondering "Who are you?" we may ask, "So, what do you do?"

Individuals across various occupations vary in their attitudes toward their work. Some view their work as a *job*, an unfulfilling but necessary way to make money. Others view their work as a *career*, an opportunity to advance from one position to a better position. The rest—those who view their work as a *calling*, a fulfilling and socially useful activity—report the highest satisfaction with their work and with their lives (Wrzesniewski et al., 1997, 2001).

This finding would not surprise Mihaly Csikszentmihalyi [chick-SENT-me-hi] (1990, 1999). He has observed that people's quality of life increases when they are purposefully engaged. Between the anxiety of being overwhelmed and stressed, and the apathy of being underwhelmed and bored, lies a zone in which people experience **flow.** Can you recall being in a zoned-out flow state while texting or playing a video game? If so, then perhaps you can sympathize with the two Northwest Airlines pilots who in 2009 were so focused on their laptops that they missed Earth-to-pilot messages from their control tower. The pilots flew 150 miles past their Minneapolis destination—and lost their jobs.

Csikszentmihalyi formulated the flow concept after studying artists who spent hour after hour painting or sculpting with enormous concentration. Immersed in a project, they worked as if nothing else mattered, and then, when finished, they promptly forgot about it. The artists seemed driven less by the external rewards of producing art—money, praise, promotion—than by the intrinsic rewards of creating the work.

Csikszentmihalyi's later observations—of dancers, chess players, surgeons, writers, parents, mountain climbers, sailors, and farmers; of Australians, North Americans, Koreans, Japanese, and Italians; of people from their teens to their golden years—confirmed an overriding principle: It's exhilarating to flow with

Sometimes, Gene Weingarten noted (2002), a humor writer knows "when to just get out of the way." Here are some sample job titles from the U.S. Department of Labor *Dictionary of Occupational Titles:* animal impersonator, human projectile, banana ripening-room supervisor, impregnator, impregnator helper, dope sprayer, finger waver, rug scratcher, egg smeller, bottom buffer, cookie breaker, brain picker, hand pouncer, bosom presser, and mother repairer.

Have you ever noticed that when you are immersed in an activity, time flies? And that when you are watching the clock, it seems to move more slowly? French researchers confirmed that the more people attend to an event's duration, the longer it seems to last (Couli et al., 2004).

Hill Street Studios/Matthew Palmer/Jupiterimages

Disrupted flow Internet-related distractions can disrupt flow. It takes time to refocus mental concentration after the distraction of an e-mail or a text.

flow a completely involved, focused state of consciousness, with diminished awareness of self and time, resulting from optimal engagement of one's skills.

an activity that fully engages our skills. Flow experiences boost our sense of self-esteem, competence, and well-being. Idleness may sound like bliss, but purposeful work enriches our lives. Busy people are happier (Hsee et al., 2010; Robinson & Martin, 2008). One research team interrupted people on about a quarter-million occasions (using an iPhone application), and found people's minds wandering 47 percent of the time. They were, on average, happier when *not* mind-wandering (Killingsworth & Gilbert, 2010).

The modern workforce
The editorial team that supports the creation of this book and its teaching package works both in-house and from far-flung places. Clockwise from top left are Nancy Fleming in Massachusetts, Kevin Feyen in New York, Betty Probert and Don Probert in Florida, Christine Brune in Alaska, Trish Morgan in Alberta, Tracey Kuehn in New York, and Kathryn Brownson in Michigan.

In many nations, work has been changing, from farming to manufacturing to *knowledge work*. More and more work is outsourced to temporary employees and consultants or done by telecommuters communicating electronically from remote virtual workplaces. As work changes, will our attitudes toward our work also change? Will our satisfaction with work increase or decrease? Will the *psychological contract*—the sense of mutual obligations between workers and employers—become more or less trusting and secure? These are among the questions that fascinate psychologists who study work-related behavior.

Industrial-organizational (I/O) psychology applies psychology's principles to the workplace (see Close-Up: I/O Psychology at Work). Here we consider three of I/O psychology's subfields:

- **Personnel psychology** applies psychology's methods and principles to selecting and evaluating workers. Personnel psychologists match people with jobs, by identifying and placing well-suited candidates.

- **Organizational psychology** considers how work environments and management styles influence worker motivation, satisfaction, and productivity. Organizational psychologists modify jobs and supervision in ways that boost morale and productivity.

CLOSE UP:

I/O Psychology at Work

As scientists, consultants, and management professionals, industrial-organizational (I/O) psychologists are found working in varied areas:

Personnel Psychology

Selecting and placing employees

- Developing and validating assessment tools for selecting, placing, and promoting workers
- Analyzing job content
- Optimizing worker placement

Training and developing employees

- Identifying needs

- Designing training programs
- Evaluating training programs

Appraising performance

- Developing criteria
- Measuring individual performance
- Measuring organizational performance

Organizational Psychology

Developing organizations

- Analyzing organizational structures
- Maximizing worker satisfaction and productivity
- Facilitating organizational change

Enhancing quality of work life

- Expanding individual productivity
- Identifying elements of satisfaction
- Redesigning jobs

Human Factors (Engineering) Psychology

- Designing optimum work environments
- Optimizing person-machine interactions
- Developing systems technologies

Source: Adapted from the Society of Industrial and Organizational Psychology (www.siop.org).

- **Human factors psychology** explores how machines and environments can be optimally designed to fit human abilities. Human factors psychologists study people's natural perceptions and inclinations to create user-friendly machines and work settings.

RETRIEVE IT

- What is the value of finding flow in our work?

ANSWER: We become more likely to view our work as fulfilling and socially useful.

Personnel Psychology

B-2: How do personnel psychologists help organizations with employee selection, work placement, and performance appraisal?

Psychologists can assist organizations at various stages of selecting and assessing employees. They may help identify needed job skills, decide upon selection methods, recruit and evaluate applicants, introduce and train new employees, and appraise their performance.

Harnessing Strengths

As a new AT&T human resources executive, psychologist Mary Tenopyr (1997) was assigned to solve a problem: Customer-service representatives were failing at a high rate. After concluding that many of the hires were ill-matched to the demands of their new job, Tenopyr developed a new selection instrument:

1. She asked new applicants to respond to various test questions (without as yet making any use of their responses).

2. She followed up later to assess which applicants excelled on the job.

3. She identified the earlier test questions that best predicted success.

The happy result of her data-driven work was a new test that enabled AT&T to identify likely-to-succeed customer-service representatives. Personnel selection techniques such as this one aim to match people's strengths with work that enables them and their organization to flourish. Marry the strengths of people with the tasks of organizations and the result is often prosperity and profit.

Your strengths are any enduring qualities that can be productively applied. Are you naturally curious? Persuasive? Charming? Persistent? Competitive? Analytical? Empathic? Organized? Articulate? Neat? Mechanical? Any such trait, if matched with suitable work, can function as a strength (Buckingham, 2007). (See Close-Up: Discovering Your Strengths.)

Gallup researchers Marcus Buckingham and Donald Clifton (2001) have argued that the first step to a stronger organization is instituting a *strengths-based selection system*. Thus, as a manager, you would first identify a group of the most effective people in any role—the ones you would want to hire more of—and compare their strengths with those of a group of the least effective people in that role. In defining these groups, you would try to measure performance as objectively as possible. In one Gallup study of more than 5000 telecommunications customer-service representatives, those evaluated most favorably by their managers were strong in "harmony" and "responsibility," while those actually rated most effective by customers were strong in energy, assertiveness, and eagerness to learn.

An example: If you needed to hire new people in software development, and you had discovered that your best software developers are analytical, disciplined,

Artistic strengths At age 21, Henri Matisse was a sickly and often depressed lawyer's clerk. When his mother gave him a box of paints to cheer him up one day, he felt the darkness lift and his energy surge. He began to fill his days with painting and drawing and went on to art school and a life as one of the world's great painters. For Matisse, doing art felt like "a comfortable armchair." That is how exercising our strengths often feels.

Discovering Your Strengths

You can use some of the techniques personnel psychologists have developed to identify your own strengths and pinpoint types of work that will likely prove satisfying and successful. Buckingham and Clifton (2001) have suggested asking yourself these questions:

- What activities give me pleasure? (Bringing order out of chaos? Playing host? Helping others? Challenging sloppy thinking?)

- What activities leave me wondering, "When can I do this again?" (Rather than, "When will this be over?")

- What sorts of challenges do I relish? (And which do I dread?)

- What sorts of tasks do I learn easily? (And which do I struggle with?)

Some people find themselves in flow—their skills engaged and time flying—when teaching or selling or writing or cleaning or consoling or creating or repairing. If an activity feels good, if it comes easily, if you look forward to it, then look deeper and see your strengths at work.

Satisfied and successful people devote far less time to correcting their deficiencies than to accentuating their strengths. Top performers are "rarely well rounded," Buckingham and Clifton found (p. 26). Instead, they have sharpened their existing skills. Given the persistence of our traits and temperaments, we should focus not on our deficiencies, but rather on identifying and employing our talents. There may be limits to the benefits of assertiveness training if you are extremely shy, of public speaking courses if you tend to be nervous and soft spoken, or of drawing classes if you express your artistic side in stick figures.

Identifying your talents can help you recognize the activities you learn quickly and find absorbing. Knowing your strengths, you can develop them further.

and eager to learn, you would focus employment ads less on experience than on the identified strengths. Thus "Do you take a logical and systematic approach to problem solving *[analytical]*? Are you a perfectionist who strives for timely completion of your projects *[disciplined]*? Do you want to master Python, Java, and C# *[eager to learn]*? If you can say *yes* to these questions, then please call . . ."

Identifying people's strengths and matching those strengths to work is a first step toward workplace effectiveness. To assess applicants' strengths and decide who is best suited to the job, personnel managers use various tools (Sackett & Lievens, 2008), including ability tests (see Chapter 9), personality tests (Chapter 12), and behavioral observations in "assessment centers" that simulate job tasks (Chapter 12). Here we focus on job interviews.

Do Interviews Predict Performance?

Interviewers tend to feel confident in their ability to predict long-term job performance from a traditional, get-acquainted interview. What's therefore shocking is how error prone interviewers' predictions are, whether of future job success or graduate school success. From their review of 85 years of personnel-selection research, I/O psychologists Frank Schmidt and John Hunter (1998; Schmidt, 2002) determined that for all but less-skilled jobs, general mental ability best predicts on-the-job performance. Subjective overall evaluations from informal interviews are more useful than handwriting analysis (which is worthless). But informal interviews are less informative than aptitude tests, work samples, job knowledge tests, and past job performance. If there's a contest between what our gut tells us about someone and what test scores, work samples, and past performance tell us, we should distrust our gut.

> "Interviews are a terrible predictor of performance."
>
> *Laszlo Bock, Google's Vice President, People Operations, 2007*

Unstructured Interviews and the Interviewer Illusion

Traditional *unstructured interviews* can provide a sense of someone's personality—their expressiveness, warmth, and verbal ability, for example. But these informal interviews also give interviewees considerable power to control the impression they are making in the interview situation (Barrick et al., 2009). Why, then, do many interviewers have such faith in their ability to discern interviewees' fitness for a job? "I have excellent interviewing skills, so I don't need reference checking as much as someone who doesn't have my ability to read people," is a comment too often heard by I/O consultants. This tendency to overrate their ability to predict people's futures has been labeled the *interviewer illusion* (Nisbett, 1987). Four factors explain the gap between interviewers' overconfidence and the resulting reality:

- *Interviewers presume that people are what they seem to be in the interview situation.* An unstructured interview may create a false impression of a person's behavior toward others in different situations. As Chapter 13 explained, when meeting others, we discount the enormous influence of varying situations and mistakenly presume that what we see is what we will get. But mountains of research on everything from chattiness to conscientiousness reveal that how we behave reflects not only our enduring traits but also the details of the particular situation (such as wanting to impress in a job interview).

- *Interviewers' preconceptions and moods color how they perceive interviewees' responses* (Cable & Gilovich, 1998; Macan & Dipboye, 1994). If interviewers instantly like a person who perhaps is similar to themselves, they may interpret the person's assertiveness as indicating "confidence" rather than "arrogance." If told certain applicants have been prescreened, interviewers are disposed to judge them more favorably.

- *Interviewers more often follow the successful careers of those they have hired than the successful careers of those they have rejected and lost track of.* This missing feedback prevents interviewers from getting a reality check on their hiring ability.

- *Interviews disclose the interviewee's good intentions, which are less revealing than habitual behaviors* (Ouellette & Wood, 1998). Intentions matter. People change. But the best predictor of the person we will be is the person we have been. Compared with work-avoiding university students, those who engage in their tasks are more likely, a decade and more later, to be engaged workers (Salmela-Aro et al., 2009). Educational attainments predict job performance partly because people who have shown up for school each day and done their tasks also tend to show up for work and do their tasks (Ng & Feldman, 2009). Wherever we go, we take ourselves along.

Hoping to improve prediction and selection, personnel psychologists have put people in simulated work situations, scoured sources for information on past performance, aggregated evaluations from multiple interviews, administered tests, and developed job-specific interviews.

"Between the idea and reality . . . falls the shadow."

T. S. Eliot, The Hollow Men, 1925

Structured Interviews

Unlike casual conversation aimed at getting a feel for someone, **structured interviews** offer a disciplined method of collecting information. A personnel psychologist may analyze a job, script questions, and train interviewers. The interviewers then put the same questions, in the same order, to all applicants, and rate each applicant on established scales.

In an unstructured interview, someone might ask, "How organized are you?" "How well do you get along with people?" or "How do you handle stress?" Street-smart applicants know how to score high: "Although I sometimes drive myself too hard, I handle stress by prioritizing and delegating, and by making sure I leave time for sleep and exercise."

By contrast, structured interviews pinpoint strengths (attitudes, behaviors, knowledge, and skills) that distinguish high performers in a particular line of work. The process includes outlining job-specific situations and asking candidates to explain how they would handle them, and how they handled similar situations in their prior employment: "Tell me about a time when you were caught between conflicting demands, without time to accomplish both. How did you handle that?"

To reduce memory distortions and bias, the interviewer takes notes and makes ratings as the interview proceeds and avoids irrelevant and follow-up questions.

structured interview interview process that asks the same job-relevant questions of all applicants, each of whom is rated on established scales.

The structured interview therefore feels less warm, but that can be explained to the applicant: "This conversation won't typify how we relate to each other in this organization."

A review of 150 findings revealed that structured interviews had double the predictive accuracy of unstructured seat-of-the-pants interviews (Schmidt & Hunter, 1998; Wiesner & Cronshaw, 1988). Structured interviews also reduce bias, such as against overweight applicants (Kutcher & Bragger, 2004). Thanks partly to its greater reliability and partly to its job-analysis focus, the predictive power of one structured interview is roughly equal to that of the average judgment from three or four unstructured interviews (Huffcutt et al., 2001; Schmidt & Zimmerman, 2004).

If, instead, we let our intuitions bias the hiring process, Malcolm Gladwell noted (2000, p. 86), then "all we will have done is replace the old-boy network, where you hired your nephew, with the new-boy network, where you hire whoever impressed you most when you shook his hand. Social progress, unless we're careful, can merely be the means by which we replace the obviously arbitrary with the not so obviously arbitrary."

To recap, personnel psychologists assist organizations in analyzing jobs, recruiting well-suited applicants, selecting and placing employees, and appraising employees' performance (**FIGURE B.1**)—the topic we turn to next.

FIGURE B.1
Personnel psychologists' tasks
Personnel psychologists consult in human resources activities, from job definition to employee appraisal.

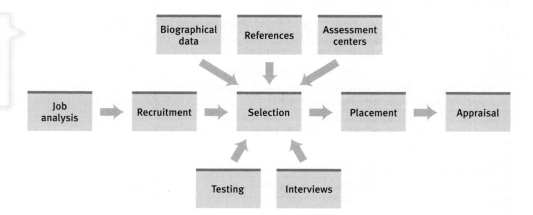

Appraising Performance

Performance appraisal serves organizational purposes: It helps decide who to retain, how to appropriately reward and pay people, and how to better harness employee strengths, sometimes with job shifts or promotions. Performance appraisal also serves individual purposes: Feedback affirms workers' strengths and helps motivate needed improvements.

Performance appraisal methods include

- *checklists* on which supervisors simply check specific behaviors that describe the worker ("always attends to customers' needs," "takes long breaks").

- *graphic rating scales* on which a supervisor checks, perhaps on a five-point scale, how often a worker is dependable, productive, and so forth.

- *behavior rating scales* on which a supervisor checks scaled behaviors that describe a worker's performance. If rating the extent to which a worker "follows procedures," the supervisor might mark the employee somewhere between "often takes shortcuts" and "always follows established procedures" (Levy, 2003).

In some organizations, performance feedback comes not only from supervisors but also from all organizational levels. If you join an organization that practices *360-degree feedback* (**FIGURE B.2**), you will rate yourself, your manager, and your other colleagues. And you will be rated by your manager, other colleagues, and customers (Green, 2002). The net result is often more open communication and more complete appraisal.

Performance appraisal, like other social judgments, is vulnerable to bias (Murphy & Cleveland, 1995). *Halo errors* occur when one's overall evaluation of an employee, or of a personal trait such as their friendliness, biases ratings of their specific work-related behaviors, such as their reliability. *Leniency* and *severity errors* reflect evaluators' tendencies to be either too easy or too harsh on everyone. *Recency errors* occur when raters focus only on easily remembered recent behavior. By using multiple raters and developing objective, job-relevant performance measures, personnel psychologists seek to support their organizations while also helping employees perceive the appraisal process as fair.

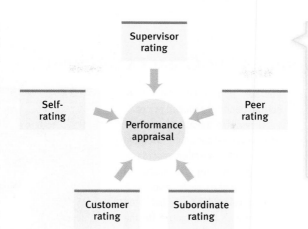

RETRIEVE IT

- A human resources director explains to you that "I don't bother with tests or references. It's all about the interview." Based on I/O research, what concerns does this raise?

ANSWER: (1) Interviewers may presume people are what they seem to be in interviews. (2) Interviewers' preconceptions and moods color how they perceive interviewees' responses. (3) Interviewers tend to track the successful careers of those they hire, not the successful careers of those they reject. (4) Interviews tend to disclose prospective workers' good intentions, not their habitual behaviors.

Organizational Psychology

B-3: What is the role of organizational psychologists?

The appraisal of work and the matching of talents to work matter, but so does overall motivation. Organizational psychologists assist with efforts to motivate employees and keep them engaged.

Satisfaction and Engagement

Partly because work is such a big part of life, I/O psychologists study employee satisfaction. Satisfaction with work feeds satisfaction with life (Bowling et al., 2010; and see Close-Up: Doing Well While Doing Good on the next page). Moreover, as we saw in Chapter 11, decreased job stress feeds improved health.

Satisfied employees also contribute to successful organizations. Positive moods at work enhance creativity, persistence, and helpfulness (Brief & Weiss, 2002; Kaplan et al., 2009). Are engaged, happy workers also less often absent? Less likely to quit? Less prone to theft? More punctual? More productive? Conclusive evidence of satisfaction's benefits is, some have said, the Holy Grail of I/O psychology. Statistical digests of prior research have found a modest positive correlation between individual job satisfaction and performance (Judge et al., 2001; Ng et al., 2009; Parker et al., 2003). In one analysis of 4500 employees at 42 British manufacturing companies, the most productive workers tended to be those in satisfying work environments

"The only place success comes before work is in the dictionary."

Former Green Bay Packers football coach Vince Lombardi

Doing Well While Doing Good—"The Great Experiment"

At the end of the 1700s, the New Lanark, Scotland, cotton mill had more than 1000 workers. Many were children drawn from Glasgow's poorhouses. They worked 13-hour days and lived in grim conditions. Their education and sanitation were neglected. Theft and drunkenness were commonplace. Most families occupied just one room.

On a visit to Glasgow, Welsh-born Robert Owen—an idealistic young cotton-mill manager—chanced to meet and fall in love with the mill owner's daughter. After their marriage, Owen, with several partners, purchased the mill and on the first day of the 1800s took control as its manager. Before long, he began what he said was "the most important experiment for the happiness of the human race that had yet been instituted at any time in any part of the world" (Owen, 1814). The exploitation of child and adult labor was, he observed, producing unhappy and inefficient workers. Believing that better working and living conditions could pay economic dividends, he undertook numerous innovations: a nursery for preschool children, education for older children (with encouragement rather than corporal punishment), Sundays off, health care, paid sick days, unemployment pay for days when the mill could not

operate, and a company store selling goods at reduced prices.

Owen also innovated a goals- and worker-assessment program that included detailed records of daily productivity and costs. By each employee's workstation, one of four colored boards indicated that person's performance for the previous day. Owen could walk through the mill and at a glance see how individuals were performing. There was, he said, "no beating, no abusive language. . . . I merely looked at the person and then at the [color]. . . . I could at once see by the expression [which color] was shown."

The commercial success that followed was essential to sustaining what became a movement toward humanitarian reforms. By 1816, with decades of profitability still ahead, Owen believed he had demonstrated "that society may be formed so as to exist without crime, without poverty, with health greatly improved, with little if any misery, and with intelligence and

The great experiment New Lanark Mills, which today is preserved as a World Heritage Site (www.newlanark.org), provided an influential demonstration of how industries could do well while doing good. In its heyday, New Lanark was visited by many European royals and reformers who came to observe its vibrant workforce and prosperous business.

happiness increased a hundredfold." Although his Utopian vision has not been fulfilled, Owen's great experiment did lay the groundwork for employment practices that have today become accepted in much of the world.

Courtesy of New Lanark World Heritage Site

(Patterson et al., 2004). But does satisfaction *produce* better job performance? The debate continues.

Nevertheless, some organizations do have a knack for cultivating more engaged and productive employees. In the United States, the *Fortune* "100 Best Companies to Work For" have also produced markedly higher-than-average returns for their investors (Fulmer et al., 2003). Other positive data come from the biggest-ever I/O study, an analysis of Gallup data from more than 198,000 employees (**TABLE B.1**) in nearly 8000 business units of 36 large companies (including some 1100 bank branches, 1200 stores, and 4200 teams or departments). James Harter, Frank Schmidt, and Theodore Hayes (2002) explored correlations between various measures of organizational success and *employee engagement*—the extent of workers' involvement, enthusiasm, and identification with their organizations (**TABLE B.2**). They found that engaged workers (compared with disengaged workers who were just putting in

An engaged employee Mohamed Mamow, left, was joined by his employer in saying the Pledge of Allegiance as he became a U.S. citizen. Mamow and his wife met in a Somali refugee camp and now are parents of five children, whom he supports by working as a machine operator. Mindful of his responsibility— "I don't like to lose my job. I have a responsibility for my children and my family"—he arrives for work a half hour early and tends to every detail on his shift. "He is an extremely hardworking employee," noted his employer, and "a reminder to all of us that we are really blessed" (Roelofs, 2010).

Darren Breen, Grand Rapids Press, 9/22/2010

Table B.1
The Gallup Workplace Audit

Overall satisfaction—On a 5-point scale, where 5 is extremely satisfied and 1 is extremely dissatisfied, how satisfied are you with *(name of company)* as a place to work? _____ On a scale of 1 to 5, where 1 is strongly disagree and 5 is strongly agree, please indicate your agreement with the following items.

1. I know what is expected from me at work.

2. I have the materials and equipment I need to do my work right.

3. At work, I have the opportunity to do what I do best every day.

4. In the last seven days, I have received recognition or praise for doing good work.

5. My supervisor, or someone at work, seems to care about me as a person.

6. There is someone at work who encourages my development.

7. At work, my opinions seem to count.

8. The mission/purpose of my company makes me feel my job is important.

9. My associates (fellow employees) are committed to doing quality work.

10. I have a best friend at work.

11. In the last six months, someone at work has talked to me about my progress.

12. This last year, I have had opportunities at work to learn and grow.

Note: These statements are proprietary and copyrighted by The Gallup Organization. They may not be printed or reproduced in any manner without the written consent of The Gallup Organization. Reprinted here by permission.

time) knew what was expected of them, had what they needed to do their work, felt fulfilled in their work, had regular opportunities to do what they did best, perceived that they were part of something significant, and had opportunities to learn and develop. They also found that business units with engaged employees had more loyal customers, lower turnover rates, higher productivity, and greater profits.

But what causal arrows explain this correlation between business success and employee morale and engagement? Does success boost morale, or does high morale boost success? In a follow-up longitudinal study of 142,000 workers, Harter and his colleagues (2010) found that, over time, employee attitudes predicted future business success (more than the other way around). Another analysis compared companies with top-quartile versus below-average employee engagement levels. Over a three-year period, earnings grew 2.6 times faster for the companies with highly engaged workers (Ott, 2007).

Table B.2
Three Types of Employees

Engaged: working with passion and feeling a profound connection to their company or organization.

Not engaged: putting in the time but investing little passion or energy into their work.

Actively disengaged: unhappy workers undermining what their colleagues accomplish.

(*Source:* Adapted from Gallup via Crabtree, 2005.)

Managing Well

B-4: What are some effective leadership techniques?

Every leader dreams of managing in ways that enhance people's satisfaction, engagement, and productivity and their organization's success. Effective leaders harness job-relevant strengths, set goals, and choose an appropriate leadership style.

Harnessing Job-Relevant Strengths

"The major challenge for CEOs over the next 20 years will be the effective deployment of human assets," observed Marcus Buckingham (2001). That challenge is "about psychology. It's about getting [individuals] to be more productive, more

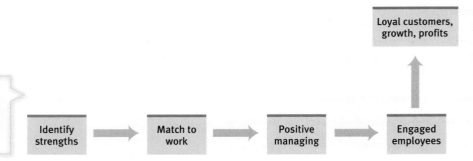

FIGURE B.3
On the right path The Gallup Organization offers this path to organizational success. (Adapted from Fleming, 2001.)

Identify strengths → Match to work → Positive managing → Engaged employees → Loyal customers, growth, profits

Positive coaching Larry Brown has been an adviser to the youth sports organization The Positive Coaching Alliance. He was observed during practices offering his players 4 to 5 positive comments for every negative comment (Insana, 2005). In 2004, he coached his underdog Detroit Pistons to the National Basketball Association championship.

focused, more fulfilled than [they were] yesterday." The first step, he and others have maintained, is selecting the right people, followed by discerning employees' natural talents, adjusting work roles to suit those talents, and developing talents into great strengths (**FIGURE B.3**). Consider the faculty at a given college or university. Should everyone be expected to teach the same course load, advise the same number of students, serve on the same number of committees, and engage in the same amount of research? Or should each job description be tailored to harness a specific person's unique strengths?

Given that our temperament and our traits tend to follow us throughout our lives, managers would be wise to spend less time trying to instill talents that are not there and more time developing and drawing out those that are there (Tucker, 2002). Managers who excel

- start by helping people identify and measure their talents.
- match tasks to talents and then give people freedom to do what they do best.
- care how their people feel about their work.
- reinforce positive behaviors through recognition and reward.

Thus, rather than focusing on weaknesses and packing people off to training seminars to fix those problems, effective managers focus training time on educating people about their strengths and building upon them (which means not promoting people into roles ill-suited to their strengths). In Gallup surveys, 77 percent of engaged workers, and only 23 percent of not-engaged workers, strongly agreed that "my supervisor focuses on my strengths or positive characteristics" (Krueger & Killham, 2005).

Celebrating engaged and productive employees in every organizational role builds upon a basic principle of operant conditioning (Chapter 7): To teach a behavior, catch a person doing something right and reinforce it. It sounds simple, but many managers are like parents who, when a child brings home near-perfect scores, focus on the one low score in a troublesome biology class and ignore the rest. "Sixty-five percent of Americans received NO praise or recognition in the workplace last year," reported the Gallup Organization (2004).

Setting Specific, Challenging Goals

In everyday life, our achievement goals sometimes involve approaching high levels of mastery or performance (such as mastering the material for this class and getting a high grade) and sometimes involve avoiding failure (Elliot & McGregor, 2001). In many situations, specific, challenging goals motivate achievement, especially when combined with progress reports (Johnson et al., 2006; Latham & Locke, 2007). Specific, measurable objectives, such as "finish gathering the history paper information by Friday," serve to direct attention, promote effort, motivate persistence, and stimulate creative strategies.

When people state goals together with *subgoals* and *implementation intentions*—action plans that specify when, where, and how they will march toward achieving those goals—they become more focused in their work, and on-time completion becomes more likely (Burgess et al., 2004; Fishbach et al., 2006; Koestner et al., 2002). Through a task's ups and downs, people best sustain their mood and motivation when they focus on immediate goals (such as daily study) rather than distant goals (such as a course grade). Better to have one's nose to the grindstone than one's eye on the ultimate prize (Houser-Marko & Sheldon, 2008). Thus, before beginning each new edition of this book, my editor, my associates, and I *manage by objectives*—we agree on target dates for the completion and editing of each chapter draft. If we focus on achieving each of these short-term goals, the prize—an on-time book—takes care of itself. So, to motivate high productivity, effective leaders work with people to define explicit goals, subgoals, and implementation plans, and then they provide feedback on progress.

Choosing an Appropriate Leadership Style

Leadership varies from a boss-focused directive style to an empowered-worker democratic style in which people cooperate in setting goals and developing strategies. Which works best may depend on the situation and the leader. The best leadership style for leading a discussion may not be the best style for leading troops on a charge (Fiedler, 1981). Moreover, different leaders are suited to different styles. Some excel at **task leadership**—setting standards, organizing work, and focusing attention on goals. Being goal-oriented, task leaders are good at keeping a group centered on its mission. Typically, they have a directive style, which can work well if the leader is bright enough to give good orders (Fiedler, 1987).

Other managers excel at **social leadership**—explaining decisions, mediating conflicts, and building high-achieving teams (Evans & Dion, 1991). Social leaders often have a democratic style: They delegate authority and welcome the participation of team members. Many experiments have demonstrated that social leadership is good for morale. Subordinates usually felt more satisfied and motivated, and performed better, when they participated in decision making (Cawley et al., 1998; Pereira & Osburn, 2007). Moreover, when members are sensitive to one another and participate equally, groups solve problems with greater "collective intelligence" (Woolley et al., 2010).

Because effective leadership styles vary with the situation and the person, the once-popular *great person theory of leadership*—that all great leaders share certain traits—now seems overstated (Vroom & Jago, 2007; Wielkiewicz & Stelzner, 2005). The same coach may seem great or inferior depending on the strength of the team and its competition. But a leader's personality does matter (Zaccaro, 2007). Effective leaders tend to be neither extremely assertive (impairing social relationships) or unassertive (limiting task leadership) (Ames, 2008). Effective leaders of laboratory

task leadership goal-oriented leadership that sets standards, organizes work, and focuses attention on goals.

social leadership group-oriented leadership that builds teamwork, mediates conflict, and offers support.

"Good leaders don't ask more than their constituents can give, but they often ask—and get—more than their constituents intended to give or thought it was possible to give."

John W. Gardner, Excellence, 1984

groups, work teams, and large corporations have also been found to exude a *charisma* that blends a goal-based vision, clear communication, and optimism that inspires others to follow (House & Singh, 1987; Shamir et al., 1993).

In one study of 50 Dutch companies, the firms with highest morale had chief executives who most inspired their colleagues "to transcend their own self-interests for the sake of the collective" (de Hoogh et al., 2004). *Transformational leadership* of this kind motivates others to identify with and commit themselves to the group's mission. Transformational leaders, many of whom are natural extraverts, articulate high standards, inspire people to share their vision, and offer personal attention (Bono & Judge, 2004). The frequent result is more engaged, trusting, and effective workers (Turner et al., 2002). As leaders, women more than men tend to exhibit transformational leadership qualities. Alice Eagly (2007) believes this helps explain why companies with female top managers have recently tended to enjoy superior financial results, even after controlling for such variables as company size.

Data compiled from studies in India, Taiwan, and Iran indicate that effective managers—whether in coal mines, banks, or government offices—often exhibit a high degree of *both* task and social leadership (Smith & Tayeb, 1989). As achievement-minded people, effective managers certainly care about how well work is done, yet at the same time they are sensitive to their subordinates' needs. In one national survey of American workers, those in family-friendly organizations offering flexible-time hours reported feeling greater loyalty to their employers (Roehling et al., 2001). A work environment that satisfies one's need to belong also energizes employees. Employees who enjoy high-quality colleague relationships also engage their work with more vigor (Carmeli et al., 2009). Gallup researchers have asked more than 15 million employees worldwide if they have a "best friend at work." The 30 percent who do "are *seven times* as likely to be engaged in their jobs" as those who don't, report Tom Rath and James Harter (2010). And, as we noted earlier, positive, engaged employees are a mark of thriving organizations.

Increased employee participation in decision making is part of a management style that has spread from Sweden and Japan to many other locations (Naylor, 1990; Sundstrom et al., 1990). Although managers often think better of work they have directly supervised, studies reveal a *voice effect*: Given a chance to voice their opinion during a decision-making process, people have responded more positively to the decision (van den Bos & Spruijt, 2002). They also feel more empowered and are likely, therefore, to be more creative (Hennessey & Amabile, 2010; Huang et al., 2010).

The ultimate in employee participation is the employee-owned company. One such company in my town, the Fleetwood Group, is a 165-employee manufacturer of educational furniture and wireless electronic clickers. When its founder gave 45 percent of the company to his employees, who later bought out other family stockholders, Fleetwood became one of America's first companies with an employee stock ownership plan (ESOP). Today, every employee owns part of the company, and as a group they own 100 percent. The more years employees work, the more they own, yet no one owns more than 5 percent. Like every corporate president, Doug Ruch works for his stockholders, who also just happen to be his employees.

As a company that endorses faith-inspired "servant leadership" and "respect and care for each team member-owner," Fleetwood is free to place people above profits. Thus, when orders lagged during the recent recession, the employee-owners decided that job security meant more to them than profits. So the company paid otherwise idle workers to do community service—answering phones at nonprofit agencies, building Habitat for Humanity houses, and the like.

Fleetwood employees "act like they own the place"; Ruch contends that employee ownership attracts and retains talented people, "drives dedication," and gives Fleetwood "a sustainable competitive advantage." With stock growth averaging 17 percent a year, Fleetwood was named the 2006 National ESOP of the year.

★ ★ ★

We have considered *personnel psychology* (the I/O subfield that focuses on employee selection, placement, appraisal, and development). And we have considered *organizational psychology* (the I/O subfield that focuses on worker satisfaction and productivity, and on organizational change). Finally, we turn to *human factors psychology,* which explores the human-machine interface.

RETRIEVE IT

- What characteristics are important for transformational leaders?

ANSWER: Transformational leaders are able to inspire others to share a vision and commit themselves to a group's mission. They tend to be naturally extraverted and set high standards.

The Human Factor

B-5: How do human factors psychologists work to create user-friendly machines and work settings?

Designs sometimes neglect the human factor. Psychologist Donald Norman, an MIT alumnus with a Ph.D., bemoaned the complexity of assembling his new HDTV, related components, and seven remotes into a usable home theater system: "I was VP of Advanced Technology at Apple. I can program dozens of computers in dozens of languages. I understand television, really, I do. . . . It doesn't matter: I am overwhelmed."

How much easier life might be if engineers would routinely test their designs and instructions on real people. *Human factors psychologists* work with designers and engineers to tailor appliances, machines, and work settings to our natural perceptions and inclinations. Bank ATM machines are internally more complex than remote controls ever were, yet, thanks to human factors engineering, ATMs are easier to operate. Digital recorders have solved the TV recording problem with a simple select-and-click menu system ("record that one"). Apple has similarly engineered easy usability with the iPhone and iPad.

Norman (2001) hosts a website (www.jnd.org) that illustrates good designs that fit people (see **FIGURE B.4**). Human factors psychologists also help design efficient environments. An ideal kitchen layout, researchers have found, puts needed items close to their usage point and near eye level. It locates work areas to enable doing tasks in order, such as placing the refrigerator, stove, and sink in a triangle.

The Ride On Carry On foldable chair attachment, "designed by a flight attendant mom," enables a small suitcase to double as a stroller.
Courtesy www.rideoncarryon.com

The Oxo measuring cup allows the user to see the quantity from above.
Courtesy OXO Good Grips

The Chatsford Teapot comes with a built-in strainer.
Courtesy The London Teapot Company Ltd.

FIGURE B.4
Designing products that fit people
Human factors psychologist Donald Norman offers these and other examples of effectively designed products.

It creates counters that enable hands to work at or slightly below elbow height (Boehm-Davis, 2005).

Understanding human factors can help prevent accidents. By studying the human factor in driving accidents, psychologists seek to devise ways to reduce the distractions, fatigue, and inattention that contribute to 1.3 million annual worldwide traffic fatalities (Lee, 2008). Two-thirds of commercial air accidents have been caused by human error (Nickerson, 1998). After beginning commercial flights in the 1960s, the Boeing 727 was involved in several landing accidents caused by pilot error. Psychologist Conrad Kraft (1978) noted a common setting for these accidents: All took place at night, and all involved landing short of the runway after crossing a dark stretch of water or unilluminated ground. Kraft reasoned that, on rising terrain, city lights beyond the runway would project a larger retinal image, making the ground seem farther away than it was. By re-creating these conditions in flight simulations, Kraft discovered that pilots were deceived into thinking they were flying higher than their actual altitudes (**FIGURE B.5**). Aided by Kraft's finding, the airlines began requiring the co-pilot to monitor the altimeter—calling out altitudes during the descent—and the accidents diminished.

Later Boeing psychologists worked on other human factors problems (Murray, 1998): How should airlines best train and manage mechanics to reduce the maintenance errors that underlie about 50 percent of flight delays and 15 percent of accidents? What illumination and typeface would make on-screen flight data easiest to read? How could warning messages be most effectively worded—as an action statement ("Pull Up") rather than a problem statement ("Ground Proximity")?

Consider, finally, the available *assistive listening* technologies for people with hearing loss in various theaters, auditoriums, and places of worship. One technology, commonly available in the United States, requires a headset attached to a pocket-sized receiver that detects infrared or FM signals from the room's sound system. The well-meaning people who design, purchase, and install these systems correctly understand that the technology puts sound directly into the user's ears. Alas, few people with hearing loss undergo the hassle and embarrassment of locating, requesting, wearing, and returning a conspicuous headset. Most such units therefore sit in closets. Britain, the Scandinavian countries, Australia, and now parts of the United States, have instead installed *loop systems* (see www.hearingloop.org) that broadcast customized sound directly through a person's own hearing aid. When suitably equipped, a hearing aid can be transformed by a discrete touch of a switch into an in-the-ear loudspeaker. Offered convenient, inconspicuous, personalized sound, many more people elect to use assistive listening.

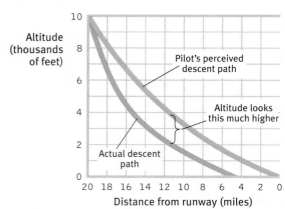

FIGURE B.5
The human factor in accidents
Lacking distance cues when approaching a runway from over a dark surface, pilots simulating a night landing tended to fly too low. (From Kraft, 1978.)

The human factor in safe landings
Advanced cockpit design and rehearsed emergency procedures aided pilot Chesley "Sully" Sullenberger, a U.S. Air Force Academy graduate who studied psychology and human factors. In January 2009, Sullenberger's instantaneous decisions safely guided his disabled airplane onto New York City's Hudson River, where all 155 of the passengers and crew were safely evacuated.

Designs that enable safe, easy, and effective interactions between people and technology often seem obvious after the fact. Why, then, aren't they more common? Technology developers sometimes mistakenly assume that others share their expertise—that what's clear to them will similarly be clear to others (Camerer et al., 1989; Nickerson, 1999). When people rap their knuckles on a table to convey a familiar tune (try this with a friend), they often expect their listener to recognize it. But for the listener, this is a near-impossible task (Newton, 1991). When you know a thing, it's hard to mentally simulate what it's like not to know, and that is called the *curse of knowledge*.

The point to remember: Everyone benefits when designers and engineers tailor machines and environments to fit human abilities and behaviors, when they user-test their inventions before production and distribution, and when they remain mindful of the curse of knowledge.

RETRIEVE IT

• What are the three main divisions within industrial-organizational psychology?

ANSWER: personnel, organizational, human factors

APPENDIX REVIEW

Psychology at Work

LEARNING OBJECTIVES

Test Yourself by taking a moment to answer each of these Learning Objective Questions (repeated here from within the Appendix). Then turn to Appendix D, Complete Chapter Reviews, to check your answers. Research suggests that trying to answer these questions on your own will improve your long-term memory of the concepts (McDaniel et al., 2009).

B-1: **What is "flow," and what are the three subfields of industrial-organizational psychology?**

Personnel Psychology

B-2: **How do personnel psychologists help organizations with employee selection, work placement, and performance appraisal?**

Organizational Psychology

B-3: **What is the role of organizational psychologists?**

B-4: **What are some effective leadership techniques?**

The Human Factor

B-5: **How do human factors psychologists work to create user-friendly machines and work settings?**

TERMS AND CONCEPTS TO REMEMBER

Test yourself on these terms by trying to write down the definition before flipping back to the referenced page to check your answer.

flow, p. B-1

industrial-organizational (I/O) psychology, p. B-2

personnel psychology, p. B-2

organizational psychology, p. B-2

human factors psychology, p. B-3

structured interview, p. B-5

task leadership, p. B-11

social leadership, p. B-11

EXPERIENCE THE TESTING EFFECT

Test yourself repeatedly throughout your studies. This will not only help you figure out what you know and don't know; the testing itself will help you learn and remember the information more effectively thanks to the *testing effect*.

1. People who view their work as a calling often experience _____, a focused state of consciousness, with diminished awareness of themselves and of time.
   a. stress
   b apathy
   c. flow
   d. facilitation

2. _____ psychologists study the recruitment, selection, placement, training, appraisal, and development of employees; _____ _____ psychologists focus on how people and machines interact, and on optimizing devices and work environments.

3. A personnel psychologist scripted a set of questions to ask all applicants for a job opening. She then trained the firm's interviewers to ask only these questions, to take notes, and to rate applicants' responses. This technique is known as a(n)
   a. structured interview.
   b. unstructured interview.
   d. performance appraisal checklist.
   c. behavior rating scale.

4. In your job, you rate your own performance, your manager's, and your peers'. Your manager, your peers, and your customers also rate your performance. Your organization is using a form of performance appraisal called
   a. flow procedure.
   b. graphic feedback.
   c. structured interviews.
   d. 360-degree feedback.

5. What type of goals will best help you stay focused and motivated to do your best work in this class?

6. Research indicates that women are more likely than men to have a _____ leadership style.

7. Effective managers exhibit
   a. only task leadership.
   b. only social leadership.
   c. both task and social leadership, depending on the situation and the person.
   d. task leadership for building teams and social leadership for setting standards.

8. To reduce users' frustration and to avoid accidents, human factors psychologists help organizations avoid the curse of knowledge, which is the tendency for
   a. a little bit of knowledge to be dangerous for the user.
   b. users to override machines and resort to familiar habits.
   c. engineers and designers to assume that users are idiots and need overly detailed instructions.
   d. engineers and designers to assume that others will share their knowledge.

Find answers to these questions in Appendix E in the back of the book.

Experience more of the
TESTING EFFECT

Multiple-format self-tests and more may be found at www.worthpublishers.com/myers.

Subfields of Psychology

Jennifer Zwolinski, University of San Diego

What can you do with a degree in psychology? Lots!

As a psychology major, you will graduate with a scientific mind-set and an awareness of basic principles of human behavior (biological mechanisms, development, cognition, psychological disorders, social interaction). This background will prepare you for success in many areas, including business, the helping professions, health services, marketing, law, sales, and teaching. You may even go on to graduate school for specialized training to become a psychology professional. This appendix describes psychology's specialized subfields.[1] I also provide updated information about CAREERS IN PSYCHOLOGY at www.yourpsychportal.com, where you can learn more about the many interesting options available to those with bachelor's, master's, and doctoral degrees in psychology.

If you are like most psychology students, you may be unaware of the wide variety of specialties and work settings available in psychology (Terre & Stoddart, 2000). To date, the American Psychological Association (APA) has formed 56 divisions (**TABLE C.1** on the next page). The following paragraphs (arranged alphabetically) describe some careers in the main specialty areas of psychology, most of which require a graduate degree in psychology.

Clinical psychologists promote psychological health in individuals, groups, and organizations. Some clinical psychologists specialize in specific psychological disorders. Others treat a range of disorders, from adjustment difficulties to severe psychopathology. Clinical psychologists might engage in research, teaching, assessment, and consultation. Some hold workshops and lectures on psychological issues for other professionals or for the public. Clinical psychologists work in a variety of settings, including private practice, industry, mental health service organizations, schools, universities, legal systems, medical systems, counseling centers, government agencies, and military services.

To become a clinical psychologist, you will need to earn a doctorate from a clinical psychology program. The APA sets the standards for clinical psychology graduate programs, offering accreditation (official recognition) to those who meet their standards. In all U.S. states, clinical psychologists working in independent practice must obtain a license to offer services such as therapy and testing.

Cognitive psychologists study thought processes and focus on such topics as perception, language, attention, problem solving, memory, judgment and decision making, forgetting, and intelligence. Research interests include designing computer-based models of thought processes and identifying biological correlates of cognition. As a cognitive psychologist, you might work as a professor, industrial consultant, or human factors specialist in an educational or business setting.

Community psychologists move beyond focusing on specific individuals or families and deal with broad problems of mental health in community settings. These psychologists believe that human behavior is powerfully influenced by the interaction between people and their physical, social, political, and economic

---

[1]Although this text covers the world of psychology for students in many countries, this appendix draws primarily from available U.S. data. Its descriptions of psychology's subfields are, however, also applicable in many other countries.

Table C.1

APA Divisions by Number and Name

1. Society for General Psychology	29. Psychotherapy
2. Society for the Teaching of Psychology	30. Society of Psychological Hypnosis
3. Experimental Psychology	31. State, Provincial, and Territorial Psychological Association Affairs
4. *There is currently no Division 4.*	32. Society for Humanistic Psychology
5. Evaluation, Measurement, and Statistics	33. Intellectual and Developmental Disabilities
6. Behavioral Neuroscience and Comparative Psychology	34. Society for Environmental, Population, and Conservation Psychology
7. Developmental Psychology	35. Society for the Psychology of Women
8. Society for Personality and Social Psychology	36. Society for the Psychology of Religion and Spirituality
9. Society for the Psychological Study of Social Issues (SPSSI)	37. Society for Child and Family Policy and Practice
10. Society for the Psychology of Aesthetics, Creativity, and the Arts	38. Health Psychology
11. *There is currently no Division 11.*	39. Psychoanalysis
12. Society of Clinical Psychology	40. Clinical Neuropsychology
13. Society of Consulting Psychology	41. American Psychology-Law Society
14. Society for Industrial and Organizational Psychology	42. Psychologists in Independent Practice
15. Educational Psychology	43. Society for Family Psychology
16. School Psychology	44. Society for the Psychological Study of Lesbian, Gay, Bisexual, and Transgender Issues
17. Society of Counseling Psychology	45. Society for the Psychological Study of Ethnic Minority Issues
18. Psychologists in Public Service	46. Media Psychology
19. Society for Military Psychology	47. Exercise and Sport Psychology
20. Adult Development and Aging	48. Society for the Study of Peace, Conflict, and Violence: Peace Psychology Division
21. Applied Experimental and Engineering Psychology	49. Society of Group Psychology and Group Psychotherapy
22. Rehabilitation Psychology	50. Society of Addiction Psychology
23. Society for Consumer Psychology	51. Society for the Psychological Study of Men and Masculinity
24. Theoretical and Philosophical Psychology	52. International Psychology
25. Behavior Analysis	53. Society of Clinical Child and Adolescent Psychology
26. Society for the History of Psychology	54. Society of Pediatric Psychology
27. Society for Community Research and Action: Division of Community Psychology	55. American Society for the Advancement of Pharmacotherapy
28. Psychopharmacology and Substance Abuse	56. Trauma Psychology

Source: American Psychological Association.

environments. They seek to promote psychological health by enhancing environmental settings, focusing on preventive measures and crisis intervention, with special attention to the problems of underserved groups and ethnic minorities. Given the shared emphasis on prevention, some community psychologists collaborate with professionals in other areas, such as public health. As a community psychologist, your work settings could include federal, state, and local departments of mental health, corrections, and welfare. You might conduct research or help

Cognitive consulting Cognitive psychologists may advise businesses on how to operate more effectively by understanding the human factors involved.

Karen Moskowitz/Getty Images

evaluate research in health service settings, serve as an independent consultant for a private or government agency, or teach and consult as a college or university faculty member.

Counseling psychologists help people adjust to life transitions or make lifestyle changes. Although similar to clinical psychologists, counseling psychologists typically help people with adjustment problems rather than severe psychopathology. Like clinical psychologists, counseling psychologists conduct therapy and provide assessments to individuals and groups. As a counseling psychologist, you would emphasize your clients' strengths, helping them to use their own skills, interests, and abilities to cope during transitions. You might find yourself working in an academic setting as a faculty member or administrator or in a university counseling center, community mental health center, business, or private practice. As with clinical psychology, if you plan to work in independent practice you will need to obtain a state license to provide counseling services to the public.

Eitan Abromovich/AFP/Getty Images

Coping with disaster After Peru's deadly August 2007 earthquake, this community psychologist working with Médecins Sans Frontières (Doctors Without Borders) helped survivors cope with the loss of their homes and, for many, the death of family members and friends.

Developmental psychologists conduct research in age-related behavioral changes and apply their scientific knowledge to educational, child-care, policy, and related settings. As a developmental psychologist, you would investigate change across a broad range of topics, including the biological, psychological, cognitive, and social aspects of development. Developmental psychology informs a number of applied fields, including educational psychology, school psychology, child psychopathology, and gerontology. The field also informs public policy in areas such as education and child-care reform, maternal and child health, and attachment and adoption. You would probably specialize in a specific stage of the life span, such as infancy, childhood, adolescence, or middle or late adulthood. Your work setting could be an educational institution, day-care center, youth group program, or senior center.

Educational psychologists are interested in the psychological processes involved in learning. They study the relationship between learning and the physical and social environments, and they develop strategies for enhancing the learning process. As an educational psychologist, working in a university psychology department or school of education, you might conduct basic research on topics related to learning or develop innovative methods of teaching to enhance the learning process. You might design effective tests, including measures of aptitude and achievement. You might be employed by a school or government agency or charged with designing and implementing effective employee-training programs in a business setting.

Experimental psychologists are a diverse group of scientists who investigate a variety of basic behavioral processes in humans and other animals. Prominent areas of experimental research include comparative methods of science, motivation, learning, thought, attention, memory, perception, and language. Most experimental psychologists identify with a particular subfield, such as cognitive psychology, depending on their interests and training. It is important to note that experimental research methods are not limited to the field of experimental psychology; many other subfields rely on experimental methodology to conduct studies. As an experimental psychologist, you would most likely work in an academic setting, teaching courses and supervising students' research in addition to conducting your own research. Or you might be employed by a research institution, zoo, business, or government agency.

Forensic psychologists apply psychological principles to legal issues. They conduct research on the interface of law and psychology, help to create public policies related to mental health, help law-enforcement agencies in criminal investigations, or consult on jury selection and deliberation processes. They also provide assessment to assist the legal community. Although most forensic psychologists are clinical psychologists, they might have expertise in other areas of psychology, such as social or cognitive psychology. Some also hold law degrees. As a forensic psychologist, you might work in a university psychology department, law school, research organization, community mental health agency, law-enforcement agency, court, or correctional setting.

Health psychologists are researchers and practitioners concerned with psychology's contribution to promoting health and preventing disease. As applied psychologists or clinicians, they may help individuals lead healthier lives by designing, conducting, and evaluating programs to stop smoking, lose weight, improve sleep, manage pain, prevent the spread of sexually transmitted infections, or treat psychosocial problems associated with chronic and terminal illnesses. As researchers and clinicians, they identify conditions and practices associated with health and illness to help create effective interventions. In public service, health psychologists study and work to improve government policies and health care systems. As a health psychologist, you could be employed in a hospital, medical school, rehabilitation center, public health agency, college or university, or, if you are also a clinical psychologist, in private practice.

Industrial-organizational (I/O) psychologists study the relationship between people and their working environments. They may develop new ways to increase productivity, improve personnel selection, or promote job satisfaction in an organizational setting. Their interests include organizational structure and change, consumer behavior, and personnel selection and training. As an I/O psychologist, you might conduct workplace training or provide organizational analysis and development. You may find yourself working in business, industry, the government, or a college or university. Or you may be self-employed as a consultant or work for a management consulting firm.

Neuropsychologists investigate the relationship between neurological processes (structure and function of the brain) and behavior. As a neuropsychologist you might assess, diagnose, or treat central nervous system disorders, such as Alzheimer's disease or stroke. You might also evaluate individuals for evidence of head injuries; learning and developmental disabilities, such as autism; and other psychiatric disorders, such as attention-deficit hyperactivity disorder (ADHD). If you are a *clinical neuropsychologist,* you might work in a hospital's neurology, neurosurgery, or psychiatric unit. Neuropsychologists also work in academic settings, where they conduct research and teach.

Psychometric and quantitative psychologists study the methods and techniques used to acquire psychological knowledge. A psychometrician may update existing neurocognitive or personality tests or devise new tests for use in clinical and

AP Photo/Jennifer Graylock

Criminal profiling On the popular U.S. TV show *Law and Order: Special Victims Unit,* Dr. George Huang (played by B. D. Wong) was an FBI agent and psychiatrist who used his background in forensic psychology to conduct criminal investigations.

school settings or in business and industry. These psychologists also administer, score, and interpret such tests. Quantitative psychologists collaborate with researchers to design, analyze, and interpret the results of research programs. As a psychometric or quantitative psychologist, you would need to be well trained in research methods, statistics, and computer technology. You would most likely be employed by a university or college, testing company, private research firm, or government agency.

Rehabilitation psychologists are researchers and practitioners who work with people who have lost optimal functioning after an accident, illness, or other event. As a rehabilitation psychologist, you would probably work in a medical rehabilitation institution or hospital. You might also work in a medical school, university, state or federal vocational rehabilitation agency, or in private practice serving people with physical disabilities.

School psychologists are involved in the assessment of and intervention for children in educational settings. They diagnose and treat cognitive, social, and emotional problems that may negatively influence children's learning or overall functioning at school. As a school psychologist, you would collaborate with teachers, parents, and administrators, making recommendations to improve student learning. You would work in an academic setting, a federal or state government agency, a child guidance center, or a behavioral research laboratory.

Social psychologists are interested in our interactions with others. Social psychologists study how our beliefs, feelings, and behaviors are affected by and influence other people. They study topics such as attitudes, aggression, prejudice, interpersonal attraction, group behavior, and leadership. As a social psychologist, you would probably be a college or university faculty member. You might also work in organizational consultation, market research, or other applied psychology fields. Some social psychologists work for hospitals, federal agencies, or businesses performing applied research.

Sport psychologists study the psychological factors that influence, and are influenced by, participation in sports and other physical activities. Their professional activities include coach education and athlete preparation, as well as research and teaching. Sport psychologists who also have a clinical or counseling degree can apply those skills to working with individuals with psychological problems, such as anxiety or substance abuse, that might interfere with optimal performance. As a sport psychologist, if you were not working in an academic or research setting, you would most likely work as part of a team or an organization or in a private capacity.

★ ★ ★

So, the next time someone asks you what you will do with your psychology degree, tell them you have a lot of options. You might use your acquired skills and understanding to get a job and succeed in any number of fields, or you might pursue graduate school and then career opportunities in associated professions. In any case, what you have learned about behavior and mental processes will surely enrich your life (Hammer, 2003).

Class counselor School psychologists, who have their master's degree in psychology, may find themselves working with students individually or in groups, as well as in a consultative role for their school's administrators.

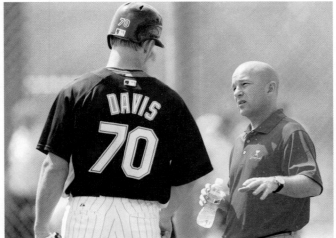

Curing catchers Sport psychologists often work directly with athletes to help them improve their performance. Here the Florida Marlins team psychologist consults with catching prospect Brad Davis during spring training.

Complete Chapter Reviews

CHAPTER 1 Thinking Critically With Psychological Science

WHAT IS PSYCHOLOGY?

1-1: What are some important milestones in psychology's development?

Wilhelm Wundt established the first psychological laboratory in 1879 in Germany. Two early schools were *structuralism* and *functionalism*. Early researchers defined *psychology* as a "science of mental life." In the 1920s, under the influence of John B. Watson and the *behaviorists,* the field's focus changed to the "scientific study of observable behavior." In the 1960s, the *humanistic psychologists* and the *cognitive psychologists* revived interest in the study of mental processes. *Psychology* is now defined as the science of behavior and mental processes.

CONTEMPORARY PSYCHOLOGY

1-2: What is psychology's historic big issue?

Psychology's biggest and most enduring issue has been the *nature-nurture issue,* which focuses on the relative contributions of genes and experience. Today's science emphasizes the interaction of genes and experiences in specific environments. Charles Darwin's view that *natural selection* shapes behaviors as well as bodies is an important principle in contemporary psychology.

1-3: What are psychology's levels of analysis and related perspectives?

The *biopsychosocial approach* integrates information from three differing but complementary *levels of analysis:* the biological, psychological, and social-cultural. This approach offers a more complete understanding than could usually be reached by relying on only one of psychology's current perspectives (neuroscience, evolutionary, behavior genetics, psychodynamic, behavioral, cognitive, and social-cultural).

1-4: What are psychology's main subfields?

Within the science of psychology, researchers may conduct *basic research* to increase the field's knowledge base (often in biological, developmental, cognitive, personality, and social psychology) or *applied research* to solve practical problems (in industrial-organizational psychology and other areas). Those who engage in psychology as a helping profession may assist people as *counseling psychologists* (helping people with problems in living or achieving greater well-being) or as *clinical psychologists,* studying and assessing people with psychological disorders and treating them with psychotherapy. (*Psychiatrists* also study, assess, and treat people with disorders, but as medical doctors, they may prescribe drugs in addition to psychotherapy.) *Positive psychology* attempts to discover and promote traits that help people to thrive.

THE NEED FOR PSYCHOLOGICAL SCIENCE

1-5: How do hindsight bias, overconfidence, and the tendency to perceive order in random events illustrate why science-based answers are more valid than those based on intuition and common sense?

Hindsight bias (also called the "I-knew-it-all-along phenomenon") is the tendency to believe, after learning an outcome, that we would have foreseen it. Overconfidence in our judgments results partly from our bias to seek information that confirms them. These tendencies, plus our eagerness to perceive patterns in random events, lead us to overestimate our intuition. Although limited by the testable questions it can address, scientific inquiry can help us overcome our intuition's biases and shortcomings.

1-6: How do the scientific attitude's three main components relate to critical thinking?

The scientific attitude equips us to be curious, skeptical, and humble in scrutinizing competing ideas or our own observations. This attitude carries into everyday life as *critical thinking,* which puts ideas to the test by examining assumptions, discerning hidden values, evaluating evidence, and assessing conclusions.

HOW DO PSYCHOLOGISTS ASK AND ANSWER QUESTIONS?

1-7: How do theories advance psychological science?

Psychological *theories* are explanations that apply an integrated set of principles to organize observations and generate *hypotheses*—predictions that can be used to check the theory or produce practical applications of it. By testing their hypotheses, researchers can confirm, reject, or revise their theories. To enable other researchers to *replicate* the studies, researchers report them using precise *operational definitions* of their procedures and concepts. If others achieve similar results, confidence in the conclusion will be greater.

1-8: How do psychologists use case studies, naturalistic observations, and surveys to observe and describe behavior, and why is random sampling important?

Descriptive methods, which include *case studies, naturalistic observations,* and *surveys,* show us what can happen, and they may offer ideas for further study. The best basis for generalizing about a *population* is a representative sample; in a *random sample,* every person in the entire population being studied has an equal chance of participating. Descriptive methods cannot show cause and effect because researchers cannot control variables.

1-9: What are positive and negative correlations, and why do they enable prediction but not cause-effect explanation?

In a positive *correlation,* two factors increase or decrease together. In a negative correlation, one item increases as the other decreases. A *correlation coefficient* can describe the strength and direction of a relationship between two variables, from +1.00 (a perfect positive correlation) through zero (no correlation at all) to −1.00 (a perfect negative correlation). A correlation can indicate the possibility of a cause-effect relationship, but it does not prove the direction of the influence, or whether an underlying third factor may explain the correlation.

1-10: What are the characteristics of experimentation that make it possible to isolate cause and effect?

To discover cause-effect relationships, psychologists conduct *experiments,* manipulating one or more factors of interest and controlling other factors. Using *random assignment,* they can minimize *confounding variables,* such as preexisting differences between the *experimental group* (exposed to the treatment) and the *control group* (given a placebo or different version of the treatment). The *independent variable* is the factor the experimenter manipulates to study its effect; the *dependent variable* is the factor the experimenter measures to discover any changes occurring in response to the manipulations. Studies may use a *double-blind procedure* to avoid the *placebo effect.*

FREQUENTLY ASKED QUESTIONS ABOUT PSYCHOLOGY

1-11: Can laboratory experiments illuminate everyday life?

Researchers intentionally create a controlled, artificial environment in the laboratory in order to test general theoretical principles. These general principles help explain everyday behaviors.

1-12: Does behavior depend on one's culture and gender?

Attitudes and behaviors may vary somewhat by gender or across *cultures,* but because of our shared human kinship, the underlying processes and principles are more similar than different.

1-13: Why do psychologists study animals, and what ethical guidelines safeguard human and animal research participants?

Some psychologists are primarily interested in animal behavior; others want to better understand the physiological and psychological processes shared by humans and other species. Government agencies have established standards for animal care and housing. Professional associations and funding agencies also establish guidelines for protecting animals' well-being. The APA ethics code outlines standards for safeguarding human participants' well-being, including obtaining their *informed consent* and *debriefing* them later.

1-14: Is psychology free of value judgments?

Psychologists' values influence their choice of research topics, their theories and observations, their labels for behavior, and their professional advice. Applications of psychology's principles have been used mainly in the service of humanity.

IMPROVE YOUR RETENTION—AND YOUR GRADES

1-15: How can psychological principles help you learn and remember?

The *testing effect* shows that learning and memory are enhanced by actively retrieving, rather than simply rereading, previously studied material. The *SQ3R* study method— survey, question, read, retrieve, and review—applies principles derived from memory research. Four additional tips are (1) distribute your study time; (2) learn to think critically; (3) process class information actively; and (4) overlearn.

CHAPTER 2 > The Biology of Behavior

BIOLOGY AND BEHAVIOR

2-1: Why are psychologists concerned with human biology?

Psychologists working from a *biological* perspective study the links between biology and behavior. We are biopsychosocial systems, in which biological, psychological, and social-cultural factors interact to influence behavior.

NEURAL COMMUNICATION

2-2: What are neurons, and how do they transmit information?

Neurons are the elementary components of the nervous system, the body's speedy electrochemical information system. A neuron receives signals through its branching *dendrites,* and sends signals through its *axons.* Some axons are encased in a *myelin sheath,* which enables faster transmission. *Glial cells* provide myelin, and they support, nourish, and protect neurons; they may also play a role in learning and thinking. If the combined signals received by a neuron exceed a minimum *threshold,* the neuron fires, transmitting an electrical impulse (the *action potential*) down its axon by means of a chemistry-to-electricity process. The neuron's reaction is an all-or-none process.

2-3: How do nerve cells communicate with other nerve cells?

When action potentials reach the end of an axon (the axon terminals), they stimulate the release of *neurotransmitters.* These chemical messengers carry a message from the sending neuron across a *synapse* to receptor sites on a receiving neuron. The sending neuron, in a process called reuptake, then normally reabsorbs the excess neurotransmitter molecules in the synaptic gap. If incoming signals are strong enough, the receiving neuron generates its own action potential and relays the message to other cells.

2-4: How do neurotransmitters influence behavior?

Neurotransmitters travel designated pathways in the brain and may influence specific behaviors and emotions. Acetylcholine affects muscle action, learning, and memory. *Endorphins* are natural opiates released in response to pain and exercise. Drugs and other chemicals affect brain chemistry at synapses.

THE NERVOUS SYSTEM

2-5: What are the functions of the nervous system's main divisions, and what are the three main types of neurons?

The *central nervous system (CNS)*—the brain and the spinal cord—is the *nervous system's* decision maker. The *peripheral nervous system (PNS),* which connects the CNS to the rest of the body by means of *nerves,* gathers information and transmits CNS decisions to the rest of the body. The two main PNS divisions are the *somatic nervous system* (which enables voluntary control of the skeletal muscles) and the *autonomic nervous system* (which controls involuntary muscles and glands by means of its *sympathetic* and *parasympathetic* divisions). Neurons cluster into working networks. There are three types of neurons: (1) *Sensory (afferent) neurons* carry incoming information from sensory receptors to the brain and spinal cord. (2) *Motor (efferent) neurons* carry information from the brain and spinal cord out to the muscles and glands. (3) *Interneurons* communicate within the brain and spinal cord and between sensory and motor neurons.

THE ENDOCRINE SYSTEM

2-6: How does the endocrine system transmit information and interact with the nervous system?

The *endocrine system* is a set of glands that secrete *hormones* into the bloodstream, where they travel through the body and affect other tissues, including the brain. The endocrine system's master gland, the *pituitary,* influences hormone release by other glands, including the *adrenal glands*. In an intricate feedback system, the brain's hypothalamus influences the pituitary gland, which influences other glands, which release hormones, which in turn influence the brain.

THE BRAIN

2-7: How do neuroscientists study the brain's connections to behavior and mind?

Clinical observations and *lesioning* reveal the general effects of brain damage. Electrical, chemical, or magnetic stimulation can also reveal aspects of information processing in the brain. *MRI* scans show anatomy. *EEG, PET,* and *fMRI (functional MRI)* recordings reveal brain function.

2-8: What structures make up the brainstem, and what are the functions of the brainstem, thalamus, and cerebellum?

The *brainstem,* the oldest part of the brain, is responsible for automatic survival functions. Its components are the *medulla* (which controls heartbeat and breathing), the pons (which helps coordinate movements), and the *reticular formation* (which affects arousal). The *thalamus,* sitting above the brainstem, acts as the brain's sensory switchboard. The *cerebellum,* attached to the rear of the brainstem, coordinates muscle movement and balance and also helps process sensory information.

2-9: What are the limbic system's structures and functions?

The *limbic system* is linked to emotions, memory, and drives. Its neural centers include the hippocampus (which processes conscious memories); the *amygdala* (involved in responses of aggression and fear); and the *hypothalamus* (involved in various bodily maintenance functions, pleasurable rewards, and the control of the endocrine system). The hypothalamus controls the pituitary (the "master gland") by stimulating it to trigger the release of hormones.

2-10: What are the functions of the various cerebral cortex regions?

The *cerebral cortex* has two hemispheres, and each hemisphere has four lobes: the *frontal, parietal, occipital,* and *temporal.* Each lobe performs many functions and interacts with other areas of the cortex. The *motor cortex,* at the rear of the frontal lobes, controls voluntary movements. The *sensory cortex,* at the front of the parietal lobes, registers and processes body touch and movement sensations. Body parts requiring precise control (in the motor cortex) or those that are especially sensitive (in the sensory cortex) occupy the greatest amount of space. Most of the brain's cortex—the major portion of each of the four lobes—is devoted to uncommitted *association areas,* which integrate information involved in learning, remembering, thinking, and other higher-level functions. Our mental experiences arise from coordinated brain activity.

2-11: To what extent can a damaged brain reorganize itself, and what is neurogenesis?

If one hemisphere is damaged early in life, the other will pick up many of its functions by reorganizing or building new pathways. This *plasticity* diminishes later in life. The brain sometimes mends itself by forming new neurons, a process known as *neurogenesis.*

2-12: What do split brains reveal about the functions of our two brain hemispheres?

Split-brain research (experiments on people with a severed *corpus callosum*) has confirmed that in most people, the left hemisphere is the more verbal, and that the right hemisphere excels in visual perception and the recognition of emotion. Studies of healthy people with intact brains confirm that each hemisphere makes unique contributions to the integrated functioning of the brain.

BEHAVIOR GENETICS: PREDICTING INDIVIDUAL DIFFERENCES

2-13: What are genes, and how do behavior geneticists explain our individual differences?

Genes are the biochemical units of heredity that make up *chromosomes,* the threadlike coils of *DNA.* When genes are "turned on" (expressed), they provide the code for creating the proteins that form our body's building blocks. Most human traits are influenced by many genes acting together. *Behavior geneticists* seek to quantify genetic and *environmental* influences on our traits, in part through studies of *identical* (monozygotic) *twins, fraternal* (dizygotic) *twins,* and adoptive families. Heritable individual differences (in traits such as height and weight) do not necessarily explain gender or ethnic group differences. Shared family environments have little effect on personality.

2-14: How do heredity and environment work together?

Our genetic predispositions and our specific environments *interact.* Environments can trigger gene activity, and genetically influenced traits can evoke responses from others. The field of *epigenetics* studies the influences on gene expression that occur without changes in DNA.

EVOLUTIONARY PSYCHOLOGY: UNDERSTANDING HUMAN NATURE

2-15: How do evolutionary psychologists use natural selection to explain behavior tendencies?

Evolutionary psychologists seek to understand how our traits and behavior tendencies are shaped by *natural selection,* as genetic variations increasing the odds of reproducing and surviving in their particular environment are most likely to be passed on to future generations. Some variations arise from *mutations* (random errors in gene replication), others from new gene combinations at conception. Humans share a genetic legacy and are predisposed to behave in ways that promoted our ancestors' surviving and reproducing. Charles Darwin's theory of evolution is an organizing principle in biology. He anticipated today's application of evolutionary principles in psychology.

CHAPTER 3 ▷ Consciousness and the Two-Track Mind

THE BRAIN AND CONSCIOUSNESS

3-1: What is the place of consciousness in psychology's history?

Since 1960, under the influence of cognitive psychology, neuroscience, and *cognitive neuroscience,* our awareness of ourselves and our environment—our *consciousness*—has reclaimed its place as an important area of research. After initially claiming consciousness as its area of study in the nineteenth century, psychologists had abandoned it in the first half of the twentieth century, turning instead to the study of observable behavior because they believed consciousness was too difficult to study scientifically.

3-2: What is the "dual processing" being revealed by today's cognitive neuroscience?

Scientists studying the brain mechanisms underlying consciousness and cognition have discovered that the mind processes information on two separate tracks, one operating at an explicit, conscious level (conscious sequential processing) and the other at an implicit, unconscious level (unconscious parallel processing). This *dual processing* affects our perception, memory, attitudes, and other cognitions.

3-3: How much information do we consciously attend to at once?

We *selectively attend* to, and process, a very limited portion of incoming information, blocking out much and often shifting the spotlight of our attention from one thing to another. Focused intently on one task, we often display *inattentional blindness* to other events and *change blindness* to changes around us.

SLEEP AND DREAMS

3-4: How do our biological rhythms influence our daily functioning?

Our bodies have an internal biological clock, roughly synchronized with the 24-hour cycle of night and day. This *circadian rhythm* appears in our daily patterns of body temperature, arousal, sleeping, and waking. Age and experiences can alter these patterns, resetting our biological clock.

3-5: What is the biological rhythm of our sleeping and dreaming stages?

Younger adults cycle through four distinct *sleep* stages about every 90 minutes. (The sleep cycle repeats more frequently for older adults.) Leaving the *alpha waves* of the awake, relaxed stage, we descend into the irregular brain waves of non-REM stage 1 (NREM-1) sleep, often with *hallucinations*, such as the sensation of falling or floating. NREM-2 sleep (in which we spend the most time) follows, lasting about 20 minutes, with its characteristic sleep spindles. We then enter NREM-3 sleep, lasting about 30 minutes, with large, slow *delta waves*. About an hour after falling asleep, we begin periods of *REM* (rapid eye movement) *sleep*. Most dreaming occurs in this stage (also known as paradoxical sleep) of internal arousal but outward paralysis. During a normal night's sleep, NREM-3 sleep shortens and REM and NREM-2 sleep lengthens.

3-6: How do biology and environment interact in our sleep patterns?

Our biology—our circadian rhythm as well as our age and our body's production of melatonin (influenced by the brain's *suprachiasmatic nucleus*)—interacts with cultural expectations and individual behaviors to determine our sleeping and waking patterns.

3-7: What are sleep's functions?

Sleep may have played a protective role in human evolution by keeping people safe during potentially dangerous periods. Sleep also helps restore and repair damaged neurons. REM and NREM-2 sleep help strengthen neural connections that build enduring memories. Sleep promotes creative problem solving the next day, and, finally, during deep sleep, the pituitary gland secretes a growth hormone necessary for muscle development.

3-8: How does sleep loss affect us, and what are the major sleep disorders?

Sleep deprivation causes fatigue and irritability, and it impairs concentration, productivity, and memory consolidation. It can also lead to depression, obesity, joint pain, a suppressed immune system, and slowed performance (with greater vulnerability to accidents). Sleep disorders include *insomnia* (recurring wakefulness); *narcolepsy* (sudden uncontrollable sleepiness or lapsing into REM sleep); *sleep apnea* (the stopping of breathing while asleep; associated with obesity, especially in men); *night terrors* (high arousal and the appearance of being terrified; NREM-3 disorder found mainly in children); sleepwalking (NREM-3 disorder also found mainly in children); and sleeptalking.

3-9: What do we dream?

We usually *dream* of ordinary events and everyday experiences, most involving some anxiety or misfortune. Fewer than 10 percent (and less among women) of dreams have any sexual content. Most dreams occur during REM sleep.

3-10: What are the functions of dreams?

There are five major views of the function of dreams. (1) Freud's wish-fulfillment: Dreams provide a psychic "safety valve," with *manifest content* (story line) acting as a censored version of *latent content* (underlying meaning that gratifies our unconscious wishes). (2) Information-processing: Dreams help us sort out the day's events and consolidate them in memory. (3) Physiological function: Regular brain stimulation may help develop and preserve neural pathways in the brain. (4) Neural activation: The brain attempts to make sense of neural static by weaving it into a story line. (5) Cognitive development: Dreams reflect the dreamer's level of development. Most sleep theorists agree that REM sleep and its associated dreams serve an important function, as shown by the *REM rebound* that occurs following REM deprivation in humans and other species.

HYPNOSIS

3-11: What is hypnosis, and what powers does a hypnotist have over a hypnotized subject?

Hypnosis is a social interaction in which one person suggests to another that certain perceptions, feelings, thoughts, or behaviors will occur spontaneously. Highly hypnotizable people are able to focus attention totally on a task. Hypnosis does not enhance recall of forgotten events (it may even evoke false memories). It cannot force people to act against their will, though hypnotized people, like unhypnotized people, may perform unlikely acts. *Posthypnotic suggestions* have helped people harness their own healing powers but have not been very effective in treating addiction. Hypnosis can help relieve pain.

3-12: Is hypnosis an extension of normal consciousness or an altered state?

Many psychologists believe that hypnosis is a form of normal social influence and that hypnotized people act out the role of "good subject" by following directions given by an authoritative person. Other psychologists view hypnosis as a *dissociation*—a split between normal sensations and conscious awareness. Selective attention may also contribute by blocking attention to certain stimuli.

DRUGS AND CONSCIOUSNESS

3-13: What are tolerance, dependence, and addiction, and what are some common misconceptions about addiction?

Psychoactive drugs alter perceptions and moods. They may produce *tolerance:* With repeated use, achieving the desired effect requires larger doses. Continued use may lead to *physical* or *psychological dependence. Addiction* is compulsive drug craving and use. Three common misconceptions are that addictive drugs quickly corrupt; therapy is always required to overcome addiction; and the concept of addiction can meaningfully be extended beyond chemical dependence to a wide range of other behaviors.

3-14: What are depressants, and what are their effects?

Depressants, such as alcohol, *barbiturates,* and the *opiates,* dampen neural activity and slow body functions. Alcohol tends to disinhibit, increasing the likelihood that we will act on our impulses, whether harmful or helpful. It also impairs judgment, disrupts memory processes by suppressing REM sleep, and reduces self-awareness and self-control. User expectations strongly influence alcohol's behavioral effects.

3-15: What are stimulants, and what are their effects?

Stimulants—including caffeine, *nicotine,* cocaine, the *amphetamines, methamphetamine,* and *Ecstasy*—excite neural activity and speed up body functions, triggering energy and mood changes. All are highly addictive. Nicotine's effects make smoking a difficult habit to kick, yet the percentage of Americans who smoke has been dramatically decreasing. Cocaine gives users a fast high, followed within an hour by a crash. Its risks include cardiovascular stress and suspiciousness. Use of methamphetamines may permanently reduce dopamine production. Ecstasy (MDMA) is a combined stimulant and mild hallucinogen that produces euphoria and feelings of intimacy. Its users risk immune system suppression, permanent damage to mood and memory, and (if taken during physical activity) dehydration and escalating body temperatures.

3-16: What are hallucinogens, and what are their effects?

Hallucinogens—such as *LSD* and marijuana—distort perceptions and evoke hallucinations—sensory images in the absence of sensory input. The user's mood and expectations influence the effects of LSD, but common experiences are hallucinations and emotions varying from euphoria to panic. Marijuana's main ingredient, *THC,* may trigger feelings of disinhibition, euphoria, relaxation, relief from pain, and intense sensitivity to sensory stimuli. It may also increase feelings of depression or anxiety, impair motor coordination and reaction time, disrupt memory formation, and damage lung tissue (because of the inhaled smoke).

3-17: Why do some people become regular users of consciousness-altering drugs?

Some people may be biologically vulnerable to particular drugs, such as alcohol. Psychological factors (such as stress, depression, and hopelessness) and social factors (such as peer pressure) combine to lead many people to experiment with—and sometimes become dependent on—drugs. Cultural and ethnic groups have differing rates of drug use. Each type of influence—biological, psychological, and social-cultural—offers a possible path for drug prevention and treatment programs.

CHAPTER 4 > Developing Through the Life Span

DEVELOPMENTAL PSYCHOLOGY'S MAJOR ISSUES

4-1: What three issues have engaged developmental psychologists?

Developmental psychologists study physical, mental, and social changes throughout the life span. They focus on three issues: nature and nurture (the interaction between our genetic inheritance and our experiences); continuity and stages (whether development is gradual and continuous or a series of relatively abrupt changes); and stability and change (whether our traits endure or change as we age).

PRENATAL DEVELOPMENT AND THE NEWBORN

4-2: What is the course of prenatal development, and how do teratogens affect that development?

The life cycle begins at conception, when one sperm cell unites with an egg to form a *zygote.* The zygote's inner cells become the *embryo,* and the outer cells become the placenta. In the next 6 weeks, body organs begin to form and function, and by 9 weeks, the *fetus* is recognizably human. *Teratogens* are potentially harmful agents that can pass through the placental screen and harm the developing embryo or fetus, as happens with *fetal alcohol syndrome.*

4-3: What are some newborn abilities, and how do researchers explore infants' mental abilities?

Babies are born with sensory equipment and reflexes that facilitate their survival and their social interactions with adults. For example, they quickly learn to discriminate

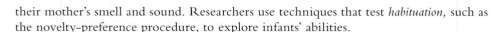

their mother's smell and sound. Researchers use techniques that test *habituation,* such as the novelty-preference procedure, to explore infants' abilities.

INFANCY AND CHILDHOOD

4-4: During infancy and childhood, how do the brain and motor skills develop?

The brain's nerve cells are sculpted by heredity and experience. As a child's brain develops, neural connections grow more numerous and complex. Experiences then trigger a pruning process, in which unused connections weaken and heavily used ones strengthen. This process continues until puberty. Early childhood is an important period for shaping the brain, but our brain modifies itself in response to our learning throughout life. In childhood, complex motor skills—sitting, standing, walking—develop in a predictable sequence, though the timing of that sequence is a function of individual *maturation* and culture. We have no conscious memories of events occurring before about age 3½. This infantile amnesia occurs in part because major brain areas have not yet matured.

4-5: From the perspectives of Piaget, Vygotsky, and today's researchers, how does a child's mind develop?

In his theory of *cognitive* development, Jean Piaget proposed that children actively construct and modify their understanding of the world through the processes of *assimilation* and *accommodation.* They form *schemas* that help them organize their experiences. Progressing from the simplicity of the *sensorimotor stage* of the first two years, in which they develop *object permanence,* children move to more complex ways of thinking. In the *preoperational stage* (about age 2 to about 6 or 7), they develop a *theory of mind.* (Children with *autism* have trouble understanding others' states of mind.) In the preoperational stage, children are *egocentric* and unable to perform simple logical operations. At about age 7, they enter the *concrete operational stage* and are able to comprehend the principle of *conservation.* By about age 12, children enter the *formal operational stage* and can reason systematically. Research supports the sequence Piaget proposed, but it also shows that young children are more capable, and their development more continuous, than he believed. Lev Vygotsky's studies of child development focused on the ways a child's mind grows by interacting with the social environment. In his view, parents and caretakers provide temporary scaffolds enabling children to step to higher levels of learning.

4-6: How do parent-infant attachment bonds form?

At about 8 months, soon after object permanence develops, children separated from their caregivers display *stranger anxiety.* Infants form *attachments* not simply because parents gratify biological needs but, more important, because they are comfortable, familiar, and responsive. Ducks and other animals have a more rigid attachment process, called *imprinting,* that occurs during a *critical period.*

4-7: How have psychologists studied attachment differences, and what have they learned?

Attachment has been studied in strange situation experiments, which show that some children are securely attached and others are insecurely attached. Infants' differing attachment styles reflect both their individual *temperament* and the responsiveness of their parents and child-care providers. Adult relationships seem to reflect the attachment styles of early childhood, lending support to Erik Erikson's idea that *basic trust* is formed in infancy by our experiences with responsive caregivers.

4-8: How does childhood neglect or abuse affect children's attachments?

Children are very resilient, but those who are severely neglected by their parents, or otherwise prevented from forming attachments at an early age, may be at risk for attachment problems.

4-9: How does day care affect children?

Quality day care, with responsive adults interacting with children in a safe and stimulating environment, does not appear to harm children's thinking and language skills. Some studies have linked extensive time in day care with increased aggressiveness and defiance, but other factors—the child's temperament, the parents' sensitivity, and the family's economic and educational levels and culture—also matter.

4-10: What are three parenting styles, and how do children's traits relate to them?

Parenting styles—authoritarian, permissive, and authoritative—reflect varying degrees of control. Children with high self-esteem tend to have authoritative parents and to be self-reliant and socially competent, but the direction of cause and effect in this relationship is not clear. Child-rearing practices reflect both individual and cultural values.

ADOLESCENCE

4-11: How is *adolescence* defined, and how do physical changes affect developing teens?

Adolescence is the transition period from childhood to adulthood, extending from *puberty* to social independence. Boys seem to benefit from "early" maturation, girls from "late" maturation. The brain's frontal lobes mature and myelin growth increases during adolescence and the early twenties, enabling improved judgment, impulse control, and long-term planning.

4-12: How did Piaget, Kohlberg, and later researchers describe adolescent cognitive and moral development?

Piaget theorized that adolescents develop a capacity for formal operations and that this development is the foundation for moral judgment. Lawrence Kohlberg proposed a stage theory of moral reasoning, from a preconventional morality of self-interest, to a conventional morality concerned with upholding laws and social rules, to (in some people) a postconventional morality of universal ethical principles. Other researchers believe that morality lies in moral intuition and moral action as well as thinking. Some critics argue that Kohlberg's postconventional level represents morality from the perspective of individualist, middle-class people.

4-13: What are the social tasks and challenges of adolescence?

Erikson theorized that each life stage has its own psychosocial task, and that a chief task of adolescence is solidifying one's sense of self—one's *identity*. This often means "trying on" a number of different roles. *Social identity* is the part of the self-concept that comes from a person's group memberships.

4-14: How do parents and peers influence adolescents?

During adolescence, parental influence diminishes and peer influence increases, in part because of the selection effect—the tendency to choose similar others. But adolescents also do adopt their peers' ways of dressing, acting, and communicating. Parents have more influence in religion, politics, and college and career choices.

4-15: What is emerging adulthood?

The transition from adolescence to adulthood is now taking longer. *Emerging adulthood* is the period from age 18 to the mid-twenties, when many young people are not yet fully independent. But critics note that this stage is found mostly in today's Western cultures.

ADULTHOOD

4-16: What physical changes occur during middle and late adulthood?

Muscular strength, reaction time, sensory abilities, and cardiac output begin to decline in the late twenties and continue to decline throughout middle adulthood (roughly age 40 to 65) and late adulthood (the years after 65). Women's period of fertility ends with *menopause* around age 50; men have no similar age-related sharp drop in hormone levels or fertility. In late adulthood, the immune system weakens, increasing susceptibility to life-threatening illnesses. Chromosome tips (telomeres) wear down, reducing the chances of normal genetic replication. But for some, longevity-supporting genes, low stress, and good health habits enable better health in later life.

4-17: How does memory change with age?

As the years pass, recall begins to decline, especially for meaningless information, but recognition memory remains strong. Developmental researchers study age-related changes (such as memory) with *cross-sectional studies* (comparing people of different ages) and *longitudinal studies* (retesting the same people over a period of years). "Terminal decline" describes the cognitive decline in the final few years of life.

4-18: What themes and influences mark our social journey from early adulthood to death?

Adults do not progress through an orderly sequence of age-related social stages. Chance events can determine life choices. The *social clock* is a culture's preferred timing for social events, such as marriage, parenthood, and retirement. Adulthood's dominant themes are love and work, which Erikson called *intimacy* and generativity.

4-19: Do self-confidence and life satisfaction vary with life stages?

Self-confidence tends to strengthen across the life span. Surveys show that life satisfaction is unrelated to age. Positive emotions increase after midlife and negative ones decrease.

4-20: A loved one's death triggers what range of reactions?

People do not grieve in predictable stages, as was once supposed. Strong expressions of emotion do not purge grief, and bereavement therapy is not significantly more effective than grieving without such aid. Erikson viewed the late-adulthood psychosocial task as developing a sense of integrity (versus despair).

CHAPTER 5 > Gender and Sexuality

GENDER DEVELOPMENT

5-1: What are some gender similarities and differences in aggression, social power, and social connectedness?

Gender refers to the socially constructed roles and characteristics by which a culture defines "male" and "female." We are more alike than different, thanks to our similar genetic makeup—we see, hear, learn, and remember similarly. Males and females do differ in body fat, muscle, height, age of onset of puberty, life expectancy, and vulnerability to certain disorders. Men admit to more *aggression* than women do, and they are more likely to be physically aggressive. Women's aggression is more likely to be relational. In most societies, men have more social power, and their leadership style tends to be directive, whereas women's is more democratic. Women focus more on social connectedness, and they "tend and befriend."

5-2: How is our biological sex determined, and how do sex hormones influence prenatal and adolescent development?

Both sex chromosomes and sex hormones influence development. Biological sex is determined by the father's contribution to the twenty-third pair of chromosomes. The mother always contributes an *X chromosome*. The father may also contribute an X chromosome, producing a female, or a *Y chromosome,* producing a male by triggering additional *testosterone* release and the development of male sex organs. Intersex individuals are born with intermediate or unusual combinations of male and female characteristics. During *puberty*, both *primary* and *secondary sex characteristics* develop. Sex-related genes and physiology influence behavioral and cognitive gender differences between males and females.

5-3: How do gender roles and gender typing influence gender development?

Gender roles, the behaviors a culture expects from its males and females, vary across place and time. *Social learning theory* proposes that we learn *gender identity*—our sense of being male or female—as we learn other things: through reinforcement, punishment, and observation. Critics argue that cognition also plays a role because modeling and rewards cannot explain *gender typing*. *Transgender* people's gender identity or expression differs from their birth sex. Their sexual orientation may be heterosexual, homosexual, bisexual, or asexual.

HUMAN SEXUALITY

5-4: How do hormones influence human sexual motivation?

The female *estrogen* and male *testosterone* hormones influence human sexual behavior less directly than they influence sexual behavior in other species. Women's sexuality is more responsive to testosterone level than to estrogen level. Short-term shifts in testosterone level are normal in men, partly in response to stimulation.

5-5: What is the human sexual response cycle, and how do sexual dysfunctions and paraphilias differ?

William Masters and Virginia Johnson described four stages in the human *sexual response cycle:* excitement, plateau, orgasm (which seems to involve similar feelings and brain activity in males and females), and resolution. During the resolution phase, males experience a *refractory period,* during which renewed arousal and orgasm are impossible. *Sexual dysfunctions* are problems that consistently impair sexual arousal or functioning. They can often be successfully treated by behaviorally oriented therapy or drug therapy. Sexual paraphilias are conditions, which may be classified as disorders, in which sexual arousal is related to socially undesirable behavior.

5-6: How can sexually transmitted infections be prevented?

Safe-sex practices help prevent sexually transmitted infections (STIs). Condoms are especially effective in preventing transmission of HIV, the virus that causes *AIDS*. A vaccination administered before sexual contact can prevent most human papilloma virus infections.

5-7: How do external and imagined stimuli contribute to sexual arousal?

External stimuli can trigger sexual arousal in both men and women. In experiments, depictions of sexual coercion have increased acceptance of rape. Sexually explicit material may lead people to perceive their partners as comparatively less appealing and to devalue their relationships. Imagined stimuli (dreams and fantasies) also influence sexual arousal.

5-8: What factors influence teenagers' sexual behaviors and use of contraceptives?

Rates of teen intercourse vary from culture to culture and era to era. Factors contributing to teen pregnancy include minimal communication about birth control with parents, partners, and peers; guilt related to sexual activity; alcohol use; and mass media norms of unprotected and impulsive sexuality. High intelligence, religious engagement, father presence, and participation in service learning programs have been predictors of teen sexual restraint.

SEXUAL ORIENTATION

5-9: What has research taught us about sexual orientation?

Sexual orientation is an enduring sexual attraction toward members of one's own sex (homosexual orientation), the other sex (heterosexual orientation), or both sexes (bisexual orientation). Sexual orientation is not an indicator of mental health. There is no evidence that environmental influences determine sexual orientation. Evidence for biological influences includes the presence of same-sex attraction in many animal species; straight-gay differences in body and brain characteristics; higher rates in certain families and in identical twins; exposure to certain hormones during critical periods of prenatal development; and the fraternal birth-order effect.

AN EVOLUTIONARY EXPLANATION OF HUMAN SEXUALITY

5-10: How might an evolutionary psychologist explain gender differences in sexuality and mating preferences?

Evolutionary psychologists use natural selection to explain why men tend to have a recreational view of sexual activity and women tend to have a relational view. They reason that men's attraction to multiple healthy, fertile appearing partners increases their chances of spreading their genes widely. Because women incubate and nurse babies, they increase their own and their children's chances of survival by searching for mates with the potential for long-term investment in their joint offspring.

5-11: What are the key criticisms of evolutionary explanations of human sexuality, and how do evolutionary psychologists respond?

Critics argue that evolutionary psychologists (1) start with an effect and work backward to an explanation, (2) absolve people from taking responsibility for their sexual behavior, and (3) do not recognize social and cultural influences. Evolutionary psychologists respond that understanding our predispositions can help us overcome them. They recognize the importance of social and cultural influences, but they also cite the value of testable predictions based on evolutionary principles.

CHAPTER 6 > Sensation and Perception

BASIC PRINCIPLES OF SENSATION AND PERCEPTION

6-1: What are *sensation* and *perception?* What do we mean by *bottom-up processing* and *top-down processing?*

Sensation is the process by which our sensory receptors and nervous system receive and represent stimulus energies from our environment. *Perception* is the process of organizing and interpreting this information, enabling recognition of meaningful events. Sensation and perception are actually parts of one continuous process. *Bottom-up processing* is sensory analysis that begins at the entry level, with information flowing from the sensory receptors to the brain. *Top-down processing* is information processing guided by high-level mental processes, as when we construct perceptions by filtering information through our experience and expectations.

6-2: What three steps are basic to all our sensory systems?

Our senses (1) receive sensory stimulation (often using specialized receptor cells); (2) transform that stimulation into neural impulses; and (3) deliver the neural information to the brain. *Transduction* is the process of converting one form of energy into another.

6-3: What are the absolute and difference thresholds, and do stimuli below the absolute threshold have any influence on us?

Our *absolute threshold* for any stimulus is the minimum stimulation necessary for us to be consciously aware of it 50 percent of the time. (Stimuli below that threshold are *subliminal.*) *Signal detection theory* predicts how and when we will detect a faint stimulus amid background noise. Individual absolute thresholds vary, depending on the strength of the signal and also on our experience, expectations, motivation, and alertness. Our *difference threshold* (also called *just noticeable difference,* or *jnd*) is the difference we can discern between two stimuli 50 percent of the time. *Weber's law* states that two stimuli must differ by a constant proportion (not a constant amount) to be perceived as different. *Priming* shows that we process some information from stimuli below our absolute threshold for conscious awareness, but the effect is too fleeting to enable exploitation with subliminal messages.

6-4: What is the function of sensory adaptation?

Sensory adaptation (our diminished sensitivity to constant or routine odors, sounds, and touches) focuses our attention on informative changes in our environment.

6-5: How do our expectations, contexts, emotions, and motivation influence our perceptions?

Perceptual set is a mental predisposition that functions as a lens through which we perceive the world. Our learned concepts (schemas) prime us to organize and interpret ambiguous stimuli in certain ways. Our physical and emotional context, as well as our motivation, can create expectations and color our interpretation of events and behaviors.

VISION

6-6: What is the energy that we see as visible light?

What we see as light is only a thin slice of the broad spectrum of electromagnetic energy. The portion visible to humans extends from the blue-violet to the red light wavelengths.

6-7: How does the eye transform light energy into neural messages, and how do the eye and brain process that information?

After entering the eye and being focused by a lens, light energy particles strike the eye's inner surface, the *retina,* where light-sensitive *rods* and color-sensitive *cones* convert the light energy into neural impulses. The *hue* we perceive in a light depends on its *wavelength,* and its brightness depends on its *intensity.* After processing by bipolar and ganglion cells in the eyes' retina, neural impulses travel through the *optic nerve,* to the thalamus, and on to the visual cortex. In the visual cortex, *feature detectors* respond to specific features of the visual stimulus. Supercell clusters in other critical areas respond to more complex patterns. Through *parallel processing,* the brain handles many aspects of vision (color, movement, form, and depth) simultaneously. Other neural teams integrate the results, comparing them with stored information and enabling perceptions.

6-8: What theories help us understand color vision?

The *Young-Helmholtz trichromatic (three-color) theory* proposed that the retina contains three types of color receptors. Contemporary research has found three types of cones, each most sensitive to the wavelengths of one of the three primary colors of light (red, green, or blue). Hering's *opponent-process theory* proposed three additional color processes (red-versus-green, blue-versus-yellow, black-versus-white). Contemporary research has confirmed that, en route to the brain, neurons in the retina and the thalamus code the color-related information from the cones into pairs of opponent colors. These two theories, and the research supporting them, show that color processing occurs in two stages.

6-9: How did the Gestalt psychologists understand perceptual organization, and how do figure-ground and grouping principles contribute to our perceptions?

Gestalt psychologists searched for rules by which the brain organizes fragments of sensory data into *gestalts* (from the German word for "whole"), or meaningful forms. In pointing out that the whole may exceed the sum of its parts, they noted that we filter sensory information and construct our perceptions. To recognize an object, we must first perceive it (see it as a *figure*) as distinct from its surroundings (the *ground*). We bring order and form to stimuli by organizing them into meaningful *groups,* following such rules as proximity, continuity, and closure.

6-10: How do we use binocular and monocular cues to perceive the world in three dimensions?

Depth perception is our ability to see objects in three dimensions and judge distance. The *visual cliff* and other research demonstrate that many species perceive the world in three dimensions at, or very soon after, birth. *Binocular cues,* such as *retinal disparity,* are depth cues that rely on information from both eyes. *Monocular cues* (such as relative size, interposition, relative height, relative motion, linear perspective, and light and shadow) let us judge depth using information transmitted by only one eye.

6-11: How do perceptual constancies help us organize our sensations into meaningful perceptions?

Perceptual constancy enables us to perceive objects as stable despite the changing image they cast on our retinas. *Color constancy* is our ability to perceive consistent color in objects, even though the lighting and wavelengths shift. Brightness (or lightness) constancy is our ability to perceive an object as having a constant lightness even when its illumination—the light cast upon it—changes. Our brain constructs our experience of an object's color or brightness through comparisons with other surrounding objects. Shape constancy is our ability to perceive familiar objects (such as an opening door) as unchanging in shape. Size constancy is perceiving objects as unchanging in size despite their changing retinal images. Knowing an object's size gives us clues to its distance; knowing its distance gives clues about its size, but we sometimes misread monocular distance cues and reach the wrong conclusions, as in the Moon illusion.

6-12: What does research on restored vision, sensory restriction, and perceptual adaptation reveal about the effects of experience on perception?

Experience guides our perceptual interpretations. People blind from birth who gained sight after surgery lack the experience to visually recognize shapes, forms, and complete faces. Sensory restriction research indicates that there is a critical period for some aspects of sensory and perceptual development. Without early stimulation, the brain's neural organization does not develop normally. People given glasses that shift the world slightly to the left or right, or even upside down, experience *perceptual adaptation*. They are initially disoriented, but they manage to adapt to their new context.

HEARING

6-13: What are the characteristics of air pressure waves that we hear as sound, and how does the ear transform sound energy into neural messages?

Sound waves are bands of compressed and expanded air. Our ears detect these changes in air pressure and transform them into neural impulses, which the brain decodes as sound. Sound waves vary in amplitude, which we perceive as differing loudness, and in *frequency,* which we experience as differing *pitch.* The outer ear is the visible portion of the ear. The *middle ear* is the chamber between the eardrum and *cochlea.* The *inner ear* consists of the cochlea, semicircular canals, and vestibular sacs. Through a mechanical chain of events, sound waves traveling through the auditory canal cause tiny vibrations in the eardrum. The bones of the middle ear amplify the vibrations and relay them to the fluid-filled cochlea. Rippling of the basilar membrane, caused by pressure changes in the cochlear fluid, causes movement of the tiny hair cells, triggering neural messages to be sent (via the thalamus) to the auditory cortex in the brain. *Sensorineural hearing loss* (or nerve deafness) results from damage to the cochlea's hair cells or their associated nerves. *Conduction hearing loss* results from damage to the mechanical system that transmits sound waves to the cochlea. *Cochlear implants* can restore hearing for some people.

6-14: What theories help us understand pitch perception?

Place theory explains how we hear high-pitched sounds, and *frequency theory* explains how we hear low-pitched sounds. (A combination of the two theories explains how we hear pitches in the middle range.) Place theory proposes that our brain interprets a particular pitch by decoding the place where a sound wave stimulates the cochlea's basilar membrane. Frequency theory proposes that the brain deciphers the frequency of the neural impulses traveling up the auditory nerve to the brain.

6-15: How do we locate sounds?

Sound waves strike one ear sooner and more intensely than the other. The brain analyzes the minute differences in the sounds received by the two ears and computes the sound's source.

THE OTHER SENSES

6-16: How do we sense touch?

Our sense of touch is actually several senses—pressure, warmth, cold, and pain—that combine to produce other sensations, such as "hot."

6-17: How can we best understand and control pain?

Pain reflects bottom-up sensations (such as input from nociceptors, the sensory receptors that detect hurtful temperatures, pressure, or chemicals) and top-down processes (such as experience, attention, and culture). One theory of pain is that a *"gate"* in the spinal cord either opens to permit pain signals traveling up small nerve fibers to reach the brain, or closes to prevent their passage. The biopsychosocial perspective views our perception of pain as the sum of biological, psychological, and social-cultural influences. Pain treatments often combine physical and psychological elements, including placebos and distractions.

6-18: How do we experience taste and smell?

Taste and smell are chemical senses. Taste is a composite of five basic sensations—sweet, sour, salty, bitter, and umami—and of the aromas that interact with information from the taste receptor cells of the taste buds. There are no basic sensations for smell. We have some 5 million olfactory receptor cells, with about 350 different receptor proteins. Odor molecules trigger combinations of receptors, in patterns that the olfactory cortex interprets. The receptor cells send messages to the brain's olfactory bulb, then to the temporal lobe, and to parts of the limbic system.

6-19: How do we sense our body's position and movement?

Through *kinesthesis,* we sense the position and movement of our body parts. We monitor our head's (and thus our body's) position and movement, and maintain our balance with our *vestibular sense.*

SENSORY INTERACTION

6-20: How do our senses interact?

Our senses can influence one another. This *sensory interaction* occurs, for example, when the smell of a favorite food amplifies its taste. *Embodied cognition* is the influence of bodily sensations, gestures, and other states on cognitive preferences and judgments.

6-21: What are the claims of ESP, and what have most research psychologists concluded after putting these claims to the test?

Parapsychology is the study of paranormal phenomena, including *extrasensory perception (ESP)* and psychokinesis. The three most testable forms of ESP are telepathy (mind-to-mind communication), clairvoyance (perceiving remote events), and precognition (perceiving future events). Skeptics argue that (1) to believe in ESP, you must believe the brain is capable of perceiving without sensory input; (2) researchers have been unable to replicate ESP phenomena under controlled conditions.

CHAPTER 7 > Learning

HOW DO WE LEARN?

7-1: What is learning, and what are some basic forms of learning?

Learning is the process of acquiring new and relatively enduring information or behaviors. In *associative learning,* we learn that certain events occur together. In classical conditioning, we learn to associate two or more stimuli (a *stimulus* is any event or situation that evokes a response). In operant conditioning, we learn to associate a response and its consequences. Through *cognitive learning,* we acquire mental information that guides our behavior. For example, in observational learning, we learn new behaviors by observing events and watching others.

CLASSICAL CONDITIONING

7-2: What are the basic components of classical conditioning, and what was behaviorism's view of learning?

Classical conditioning is a type of learning in which an organism comes to associate stimuli. In classical conditioning, an *NS* is a stimulus that elicits no response before conditioning. A *UR* is an event that occurs naturally (such as salivation), in response to some stimulus. A *US* is something that naturally and automatically (without learning) triggers the unlearned response (as food in the mouth triggers salivation). A *CS* is a previously neutral stimulus (such as a tone) that, after association with a US (such as food) comes to trigger a CR. A *CR* is the learned response (salivating) to the originally neutral (but now conditioned) stimulus. Ivan Pavlov's work on classical conditioning laid the foundation for *behaviorism,* the view that psychology should be an objective science that studies behavior without reference to mental processes. The behaviorists believed that the basic laws of learning are the same for all species, including humans.

7-3: In classical conditioning, what are the processes of acquisition, extinction, spontaneous recovery, generalization, and discrimination?

In classical conditioning, *acquisition* is associating an NS with the US so that the NS begins triggering the CR. Acquisition occurs most readily when the NS is presented just before (ideally, about a half-second before) a US, preparing the organism for the upcoming event. This finding supports the view that classical conditioning is biologically adaptive. *Extinction* is diminished responding when the CS no longer signals an impending US. *Spontaneous recovery* is the appearance of a formerly extinguished response, following a rest period. *Generalization* is the tendency to respond to stimuli that are similar to a CS. *Discrimination* is the learned ability to distinguish between a CS and other irrelevant stimuli.

7-4: Why does Pavlov's work remain so important, and what have been some applications of his work to human health and well-being?

Pavlov taught us that significant psychological phenomena can be studied objectively, and that classical conditioning is a basic form of learning that applies to all species. Classical conditioning techniques are used to improve human health and well-being in many areas, including behavioral therapy for some types of psychological disorders. The body's immune system may also respond to classical conditioning.

OPERANT CONDITIONING

7-5: What is operant conditioning, and how is operant behavior reinforced and shaped?

In *operant conditioning,* behaviors followed by reinforcers increase; those followed by punishers often decrease. Expanding on Edward Thorndike's *law of effect,* B. F. Skinner and others found that the behavior of rats or pigeons placed in an *operant chamber* (Skinner box) can be *shaped* by using reinforcers to guide closer and closer approximations of the desired behavior.

7-6: How do positive and negative reinforcement differ, and what are the basic types of reinforcers?

Reinforcement is any consequence that strengthens behavior. *Positive reinforcement* adds a desirable stimulus to increase the frequency of a behavior. *Negative reinforcement* removes an aversive stimulus to increase the frequency of a behavior. *Primary reinforcers* (such as receiving food when hungry or having nausea end during an illness) are innately satisfying—no learning is required. *Conditioned* (or secondary) *reinforcers* (such as cash) are satisfying because we have learned to associate them with more basic rewards (such as the food or medicine we buy with them). Immediate reinforcers (such as a purchased treat) offer immediate payback; delayed reinforcers (such as a weekly paycheck) require the ability to delay gratification.

7-7: How do different reinforcement schedules affect behavior?

A *reinforcement schedule* defines how often a response will be reinforced. In *continuous reinforcement* (reinforcing desired responses every time they occur), learning is rapid, but so is extinction if rewards cease. In *partial (intermittent) reinforcement* (reinforcing responses only sometimes), initial learning is slower, but the behavior is much more resistant to extinction. *Fixed-ratio schedules* reinforce behaviors after a set number of responses; *variable-ratio schedules,* after an unpredictable number. *Fixed-interval schedules* reinforce behaviors after set time periods; *variable-interval schedules,* after unpredictable time periods.

7-8: How does punishment differ from negative reinforcement, and how does punishment affect behavior?

Punishment administers an undesirable consequence (such as spanking) or withdraws something desirable (such as taking away a favorite toy) in an attempt to decrease the frequency of a behavior (a child's disobedience). Negative reinforcement (taking an aspirin) removes an aversive stimulus (a headache). This desired consequence (freedom from pain) increases the likelihood that the behavior (taking aspirin to end pain) will be repeated. Punishment can have undesirable side effects, such as suppressing rather than changing unwanted behaviors; teaching aggression; creating fear; encouraging discrimination (so that the undesirable behavior appears when the punisher is not present); and fostering depression and feelings of helplessness.

7-9: **Why did Skinner's ideas provoke controversy, and how might his operant conditioning principles be applied at school, in sports, at work, and at home?**

Critics of Skinner's principles believed the approach dehumanized people by neglecting their personal freedom and seeking to control their actions. Skinner replied that people's actions are already controlled by external consequences, and that reinforcement is more humane than punishment as a means for controlling behavior. In school, teachers can use shaping techniques to guide students' behaviors, and they can use interactive software and websites to provide immediate feedback. In sports, coaches can build players' skills and self-confidence by rewarding small improvements. At work, managers can boost productivity and morale by rewarding well-defined and achievable behaviors. At home, parents can reward desired behaviors but not undesirable ones. We can shape our own behaviors by stating our goals, monitoring the frequency of desired behaviors, reinforcing desired behaviors, and gradually reducing rewards as behaviors become habitual. Operant conditioning techniques are also used in behavior modification therapies.

7-10: **How does operant conditioning differ from classical conditioning?**

In operant conditioning, an organism learns associations between its own behavior and resulting events; this form of conditioning involves *operant behavior* (behavior that operates on the environment, producing rewarding or punishing consequences). In classical conditioning, the organism forms associations between stimuli-events it does not control; this form of conditioning involves *respondent behavior* (automatic responses to some stimulus).

BIOLOGY, COGNITION, AND LEARNING

7-11: **How do biological constraints affect classical and operant conditioning?**

Classical conditioning principles, we now know, are constrained by biological predispositions, so that learning some associations is easier than learning others. Learning is adaptive: Each species learns behaviors that aid its survival. Biological constraints also place limits on operant conditioning. Training that attempts to override biological constraints will probably not endure because animals will revert to predisposed patterns.

7-12: **How do cognitive processes affect classical and operant conditioning?**

In classical conditioning, animals may learn when to expect a US and may be aware of the link between stimuli and responses. In operant conditioning, *cognitive mapping* and *latent learning* research demonstrate the importance of cognitive processes in learning. Other research shows that excessive rewards (driving *extrinsic motivation*) can undermine *intrinsic motivation*.

LEARNING BY OBSERVATION

7-13: **What is observational learning, and how do some scientists believe it is enabled by mirror neurons?**

In *observational learning,* as we observe and imitate others we learn to anticipate a behavior's consequences because we experience vicarious reinforcement or vicarious punishment. Our brain's frontal lobes have a demonstrated ability to mirror the activity of another's brain. (Some psychologists believe *mirror* neurons enable this process.) The same areas fire when we perform certain actions (such as responding to pain or moving our mouth to form words) as when we observe someone else performing those actions.

7-14: What is the impact of prosocial modeling and of antisocial modeling?

Children tend to imitate what a model does and says, whether the behavior being *modeled* is *prosocial* (positive, constructive, and helpful) or antisocial. If a model's actions and words are inconsistent, children may imitate the hypocrisy they observe.

CHAPTER 8 Memory

STUDYING MEMORY

8-1: What is memory, and how is it measured?

Memory is learning that has persisted over time, through the storage and retrieval of information. Evidence of memory may be *recalling* information, *recognizing* it, or *relearning* it more easily on a later attempt.

8-2: How do psychologists describe the human memory system?

Psychologists use memory models to think and communicate about memory. Information-processing models involve three processes: *encoding, storage,* and *retrieval.* The connectionism information-processing model views memories as products of interconnected neural networks. The three processing stages in the Atkinson-Shiffrin model are *sensory memory, short-term memory,* and *long-term memory.* More recent research has updated this model to include two important concepts: (1) *working memory,* to stress the active processing occurring in the second memory stage; and (2) automatic processing, to address the processing of information outside of conscious awareness.

BUILDING MEMORIES: ENCODING

8-3: How do explicit and implicit memories differ?

Through parallel processing, the human brain processes many things simultaneously, on dual tracks. *Explicit* (declarative) *memories*—our conscious memories of facts and experiences—form through *effortful processing,* which requires conscious effort and attention. *Implicit* (nondeclarative) *memories*—of skills and classically conditioned associations—happen without our awareness, through *automatic processing.*

8-4: What information do we automatically process?

In addition to skills and classically conditioned associations, we automatically process incidental information about space, time, and frequency.

8-5: How does sensory memory work?

Sensory memory feeds some information into working memory for active processing there. An *iconic memory* is a very brief (a few tenths of a second) sensory memory of visual stimuli; an *echoic memory* is a three- or four-second sensory memory of auditory stimuli.

8-6: What is the capacity of our short-term and working memory?

Short-term memory capacity is about seven items, plus or minus two, but this information disappears from memory quickly without rehearsal. Working memory capacity varies, depending on age, intelligence level, and other factors.

8-7: What are some effortful processing strategies that can help us remember new information?

Effective effortful processing strategies include *chunking, mnemonics,* hierarchies, and distributed practice sessions. The *testing effect* is the finding that consciously retrieving, rather than simply rereading, information enhances memory.

8-8: What are the levels of processing, and how do they affect encoding?

Depth of processing affects long-term retention. In *shallow processing,* we encode words based on their structure or appearance. Retention is best when we use *deep processing,* encoding words based on their meaning. We also more easily remember material that is personally meaningful—the self-reference effect.

MEMORY STORAGE

8-9: What are the capacity and location of our long-term memories?

Our long-term memory capacity is essentially unlimited. Memories are not stored intact in the brain in single spots. Many parts of the brain interact as we form and retrieve memories.

8-10: What roles do the frontal lobes and hippocampus play in memory storage?

The frontal lobes and *hippocampus* are parts of the brain network dedicated to explicit memory formation. Many brain regions send information to the frontal lobes for processing. The hippocampus, with the help of surrounding areas of cortex, registers and temporarily holds elements of explicit memories before moving them to other brain regions for long-term storage.

8-11: What roles do the cerebellum and basal ganglia play in our memory processing?

The cerebellum and basal ganglia are parts of the brain network dedicated to implicit memory formation. The cerebellum is important for storing classically conditioned memories. The basal ganglia are involved in motor movement and help form procedural memories for skills. Many reactions and skills learned during our first three years continue into our adult lives, but we cannot consciously remember learning these associations and skills, a phenomenon psychologists call "infantile amnesia."

8-12: How do emotions affect our memory processing?

Emotional arousal causes an outpouring of stress hormones, which lead to activity in the brain's memory-forming areas. Significantly stressful events can trigger very clear *flashbulb memories*.

8-13: How do changes at the synapse level affect our memory processing?

Long-term potentiation (LTP) appears to be the neural basis of learning. In LTP, neurons become more efficient at releasing and sensing the presence of neurotransmitters, and more connections develop between neurons.

RETRIEVAL: GETTING INFORMATION OUT

8-14: How do external cues, internal emotions, and order of appearance influence memory retrieval?

Three measures of retention are recalling information, recognizing it, or relearning it more easily on a later attempt. External cues activate associations that help us retrieve memories; this process may occur without our awareness, as it does in *priming*. Returning to the same physical context or emotional state *(mood congruency)* in which we formed a memory can help us retrieve it. The *serial position effect* accounts for our tendency to recall best the last items (which may still be in working memory) and the first items (which we've spent more time rehearsing) in a list.

FORGETTING

8-15: Why do we forget?

Anterograde amnesia is an inability to form new memories. *Retrograde amnesia* is an inability to retrieve old memories. Normal forgetting can happen because we have never encoded information; because the physical trace has decayed; or because we cannot retrieve what we have encoded and stored. Retrieval problems may result from *proactive* (forward-acting) *interference,* as prior learning interferes with recall of new information, or from *retroactive* (backward-acting) *interference,* as new learning disrupts recall of old information. Some believe that motivated forgetting occurs, but researchers have found little evidence of *repression*.

MEMORY CONSTRUCTION ERRORS

8-16: How do misinformation, imagination, and source amnesia influence our memory construction? How do we decide whether a memory is real or false?

In experiments demonstrating the *misinformation effect,* people have formed false memories, incorporating misleading details, after receiving wrong information after an event, or after repeatedly imagining and rehearsing something that never happened. When we reassemble a memory during retrieval, we may attribute it to the wrong source *(source amnesia)*. Source amnesia may help explain *déjà vu*. False memories feel like real memories and can be persistent but are usually limited to the gist of the event.

8-17: How reliable are young children's eyewitness descriptions, and why are reports of repressed and recovered memories so hotly debated?

Children are susceptible to the misinformation effect, but if questioned in neutral words they understand, they can accurately recall events and people involved in them. The debate (between memory researchers and some well-meaning therapists) focuses on whether most memories of early childhood abuse are repressed and can be recovered during therapy using "memory work" techniques using leading questions or hypnosis. Psychologists now agree that (1) sexual abuse happens; (2) injustice happens; (3) forgetting happens; (4) recovered memories are commonplace; (5) memories of things that happened before age 3 are unreliable; (6) memories "recovered" under hypnosis or the influence of drugs are especially unreliable; and (7) memories, whether real or false, can be emotionally upsetting.

IMPROVING MEMORY

8-18: How can you use memory research findings to do better in this and other courses?

Memory research findings suggest the following strategies for improving memory: Study repeatedly, make material meaningful, activate retrieval cues, use mnemonic devices, minimize interference, sleep more, and test yourself to be sure you can retrieve, as well as recognize, material.

CHAPTER 9 > Thinking, Language, and Intelligence

THINKING

9-1: What is cognition, and what are the functions of concepts?

Cognition refers to all the mental activities associated with thinking, knowing, remembering, and communicating. We use *concepts,* mental groupings of similar objects, events, ideas, or people, to simplify and order the world around us. We form most concepts around *prototypes,* or best examples of a category.

9-2: What cognitive strategies assist our problem solving, and what obstacles hinder it?

An *algorithm* is a methodical, logical rule or procedure (such as a step-by-step description for evacuating a building during a fire) that guarantees a solution to a problem. A *heuristic* is a simpler strategy (such as running for an exit if you smell smoke) that is usually speedier than an algorithm but is also more error-prone. *Insight* is not a strategy-based solution, but rather a sudden flash of inspiration that solves a problem. Obstacles to problem solving include *confirmation bias,* which predisposes us to verify rather than challenge our hypotheses, and fixation, such as *mental set,* which may prevent us from taking the fresh perspective that would lead to a solution.

9-3: What is intuition, and how can the availability heuristic, overconfidence, belief perseverance, and framing influence our decisions and judgments?

Intuition is the effortless, immediate, automatic feeling or thoughts we often use instead of systematic reasoning. Heuristics enable snap judgments. Using the *availability heuristic,* we judge the likelihood of things based on how readily they come to mind, which often leads us to fear the wrong things. *Overconfidence* can lead us to overestimate the accuracy of our beliefs. When a belief we have formed and explained has been discredited, *belief perseverance* may cause us to cling to that belief. A remedy for belief perseverance is to consider how we might have explained an opposite result. *Framing* is the way a question or statement is worded. Subtle wording differences can dramatically alter our responses.

9-4: How do smart thinkers use intuition?

As people gain expertise, they grow adept at making quick, shrewd judgments. Smart thinkers welcome their intuitions (which are usually adaptive), but when making complex decisions they gather as much information as possible and then take time to let their two-track mind process all available information.

9-5: What is creativity, and what fosters it?

Creativity, the ability to produce novel and valuable ideas, correlates somewhat with aptitude, but is more than school smarts. Aptitude tests require *convergent thinking,* but creativity requires *divergent thinking.* Robert Sternberg has proposed that creativity has five components: expertise; imaginative thinking skills; a venturesome personality; intrinsic motivation; and a creative environment that sparks, supports, and refines creative ideas.

9-6: What do we know about animal thinking?

Researchers make inferences about other species' consciousness and intelligence based on behavior. Evidence from studies of various species shows that other animals use concepts, numbers, and tools and that they transmit learning from one generation to the next (cultural transmission). And, like humans, other species also show insight, self-awareness, altruism, cooperation, and grief.

LANGUAGE

9-7: What are the structural components of a language?

Phonemes are a *language's* basic units of sound. *Morphemes* are the elementary units of meaning. *Grammar*—the system of rules that enables us to communicate—includes semantics (rules for deriving meaning) and syntax (rules for ordering words into sentences).

9-8: What are the milestones in language development, and how do we acquire language?

Language development's timing varies, but all children follow the same sequence. Receptive language (the ability to understand what is said to or about you) develops before productive language (the ability to produce words). At about 4 months of age, infants *babble,* making sounds found in languages from all over the world. By about 10 months, their babbling contains only the sounds found in their household language. Around 12 months of age, children begin to speak in single words. This *one-word stage* evolves into *two-word (telegraphic)* utterances before their second birthday, after which they begin speaking in full sentences. Linguist Noam Chomsky has proposed that all human languages share a universal grammar—the basic building blocks of language—and that humans are born with a predisposition to learn language. B.F. Skinner believed we learn language as we learn other things—by association, imitation, and reinforcement. We acquire a specific language through learning as our biology and experience interact. Childhood is a critical period for learning to speak and/or sign fluently.

9-9: What brain areas are involved in language processing and speech?

Aphasia is an impairment of language, usually caused by left-hemisphere damage. Two important language- and speech-processing areas are *Broca's area,* a region of the frontal lobe that controls language expression, and *Wernicke's area,* a region in the left temporal lobe that controls language reception. Language processing is spread across other brain areas as well, where different neural networks handle specific linguistic subtasks.

9-10: Do other animals share our capacity for language?

A number of chimpanzees and bonobos have (1) learned to communicate with humans by signing or by pushing buttons wired to a computer, (2) developed vocabularies of nearly 400 words, (3) communicated by stringing these words together, (4) taught their skills to younger animals, and (5) demonstrated some understanding of syntax. But only humans communicate in complex sentences. Nevertheless, other animals' impressive abilities to think and communicate challenge humans to consider what this means about the moral rights of other species.

THINKING AND LANGUAGE

9-11: **What is the relationship between thinking and language, and what is the value of thinking in images?**

Although Benjamin Lee Whorf's *linguistic determinism* hypothesis suggested that language determines thought, it is more accurate to say that language influences thought. Different languages embody different ways of thinking, and immersion in bilingual education can enhance thinking. We often think in images when we use implicit (nondeclarative, procedural) memory—our automatic memory system for motor and cognitive skills and classically conditioned associations. Thinking in images can increase our skills when we mentally practice upcoming events.

INTELLIGENCE

9-12: **How do psychologists define *intelligence,* and what are the arguments for *g*?**

Intelligence is a mental quality consisting of the ability to learn from experience, solve problems, and use knowledge to adapt to new situations. Charles Spearman proposed that we have one *general intelligence (g)* underlying all other specific mental abilities. He helped develop factor analysis, a statistical procedure that identifies clusters of related abilities.

9-13: **How do Gardner's and Sternberg's theories of multiple intelligences differ?**

Savant syndrome seems to support Howard Gardner's view that we have multiple intelligences. He proposed eight independent intelligences: linguistic, logical-mathematical, musical, spatial, bodily-kinesthetic, intrapersonal, interpersonal, and naturalist. Robert Sternberg's triarchic theory proposes three intelligence areas that predict real-world skills: analytical (academic problem-solving), creative, and practical.

9-14: **What are the four components of emotional intelligence?**

Emotional intelligence, which is an aspect of social intelligence, is the ability to perceive, understand, manage, and use emotions. Emotionally intelligent people achieve greater personal and professional success. Some critics question whether calling these abilities "intelligence" stretches that concept too far.

9-15: **When and why were intelligence tests created, and how do today's tests differ from early intelligence tests?**

Alfred Binet started the modern intelligence-testing movement in France in 1904 when he developed questions to help predict children's future progress in the Paris school system. During the early twentieth century, Lewis Terman of Stanford University revised Binet's work for use in the United States (which resulted in the *Stanford-Binet* intelligence test). William Stern contributed the concept of the *IQ* (intelligence quotient). The most widely used intelligence tests today are the *Wechsler Adult Intelligence Scale (WAIS)* and Wechsler's tests for children. These tests differ from their predecessors in the way they offer an overall intelligence score as well as scores for various verbal and performance areas.

9-16: **What is a normal curve, and what does it mean to say that a test has been standardized and is reliable and valid?**

The distribution of test scores often forms a *normal* (bell-shaped) *curve* around the central average score, with fewer and fewer scores at the extremes. *Standardization* establishes a basis for meaningful score comparisons by giving a test to a representative sample of future test-takers. *Reliability* is the extent to which a test yields consistent results (on two halves of the test, or when people are retested). *Validity* is the extent to which a test measures or predicts what it is supposed to. A test has *content validity* if it samples the pertinent behavior (as a driving test measures driving ability). It has *predictive validity* if it predicts a behavior it was designed to predict. (Aptitude tests have predictive ability if they can predict future achievements.)

9-17: **What are the traits of those at the low and high intelligence extremes?**

At the low extreme are those with unusually low scores. An intelligence test score of or below 70 is one diagnostic criterion for the diagnosis of *intellectual disability;* other criteria are limited conceptual, social, and practical skills. One condition included in this category is *Down syndrome,* a developmental disorder caused by an extra copy of chromosome 21. People at the high-intelligence extreme tend to be healthy and well-adjusted, as well as unusually successful academically.

9-18: How does aging affect crystallized and fluid intelligence?

Cross-sectional studies (comparing people of different ages) and longitudinal studies (retesting the same group over a period of years) have shown that *fluid intelligence* declines in older adults, in part because neural processing slows. *Crystallized intelligence* tends to increase. The stability of intelligence test scores increases with age.

9-19: What evidence points to a genetic influence on intelligence, and what is heritability?

Studies of twins, family members, and adoptees indicate a significant hereditary contribution to intelligence scores. Intelligence seems to be polygenetic, and researchers are searching for genes that exert an influence. *Heritability* is the proportion of variation among individuals that can be attributed to genes.

9-20: What does evidence reveal about environmental influences on intelligence?

Studies of twins, family members, and adoptees also provide evidence of environmental influences. Test scores of identical twins raised apart are slightly less similar (though still very highly correlated) than the scores of identical twins raised together. Studies of children reared in extremely impoverished environments with minimal social interaction indicate that life experiences can significantly influence intelligence test performance. No evidence supports the idea that normal, healthy children can be molded into geniuses by growing up in an exceptionally enriched environment.

9-21: How and why do the genders differ in mental ability scores?

Males and females tend to have the same average intelligence test scores, but they differ in some specific abilities. Girls are better spellers, more verbally fluent, better at locating objects, better at detecting emotions, and more sensitive to touch, taste, and color. Boys outperform girls at spatial ability and related mathematics, though girls outperform boys in math computation. Boys also outnumber girls at the low and high extremes of mental abilities. Evolutionary and cultural explanations have been proposed for these gender differences.

9-22: How and why do racial and ethnic groups differ in mental ability scores?

Racial and ethnic groups differ in their average intelligence test scores. The evidence suggests that environmental differences are largely, perhaps entirely, responsible for these group differences.

9-23: Are intelligence tests inappropriately biased?

Aptitude tests aim to predict how well a test-taker will perform in a given situation. So they are necessarily "biased" in the sense that they are sensitive to performance differences caused by cultural experience. By "inappropriately biased," psychologists mean that a test predicts less accurately for one group than for another. In this sense, most experts consider the major aptitude tests unbiased. *Stereotype threat,* a self-confirming concern that one will be evaluated based on a negative stereotype, affects performance on all kinds of tests.

CHAPTER 10 Motivation and Emotion

MOTIVATIONAL CONCEPTS

10-1: How do psychologists define *motivation*? From what perspectives do they view motivated behavior?

Motivation is a need or desire that energizes and directs behavior. The *instinct/evolutionary* perspective explores genetic influences on complex behaviors.

Drive-reduction theory explores how physiological needs create aroused tension states (drives) that direct us to satisfy those needs. Environmental *incentives* can intensify drives. Drive-reduction's goal is *homeostasis,* maintaining a steady internal state. Arousal theory proposes that some behaviors (such as those driven by curiosity) do not reduce physiological needs but rather are prompted by a search for an optimum level of arousal. The *Yerkes-Dodson law* states that performance increases with arousal, but only to a certain point, after which it decreases. Performance peaks at lower levels of arousal for difficult tasks, and at higher levels for easy or well-learned tasks. Abraham Maslow's *hierarchy of needs* proposes a pyramid of human needs, from basic needs such as hunger and thirst up to higher-level needs such as self-actualization and self-transcendence.

HUNGER

10-2: What physiological factors produce hunger?

Hunger's pangs correspond to the stomach's contractions, but hunger also has other causes. Neural areas in the brain, some within the hypothalamus, monitor blood chemistry (including level of *glucose*) and incoming information about the body's state. Appetite hormones include insulin (controls blood glucose); ghrelin (secreted by an empty stomach); orexin (secreted by the hypothalamus); leptin (secreted by fat cells); and PYY (secreted by the digestive tract). *Basal metabolic rate* is the body's resting rate of energy expenditure. The body may have a *set point* (a biologically fixed tendency to maintain an optimum weight) or a looser settling point (also influenced by the environment).

10-3: What cultural and situational factors influence hunger?

Hunger also reflects our memory of when we last ate and our expectation of when we should eat again. Humans as a species prefer certain tastes (such as sweet and salty), but our individual preferences are also influenced by conditioning, culture, and situation. Some taste preferences, such as the avoidance of new foods, or of foods that have made us ill, have survival value.

10-4: What factors predispose some people to become and remain obese?

Genes and environment interact to produce obesity. Obesity correlates with depression, especially among women. Twin and adoption studies indicate that body weight is also genetically influenced. Environmental influences include lack of exercise, an abundance of high-calorie food, and social influence. Those wishing to lose weight are advised to make a lifelong change in habits: Get enough sleep; boost energy expenditure through exercise; limit variety and minimize exposure to tempting food cues; eat healthy foods and reduce portion sizes; space meals throughout the day; beware of the binge; monitor eating during social events; forgive the occasional lapse; and connect to a support group.

THE NEED TO BELONG

10-5: What evidence points to our human need to belong?

Our need to affiliate or belong—to feel connected and identified with others—had survival value for our ancestors, which may explain why humans in every society live in groups. Because of their need to belong, people suffer when socially excluded, and they may engage in self-defeating behaviors (performing below their ability) or in antisocial behaviors. Feeling loved activates brain regions associated with reward and safety systems. Social isolation can put us at risk mentally and physically.

10-6: How does social networking influence us?

We connect with others through social networking, strengthening our relationships with those we already know. When networking, people tend toward increased self-disclosure. Working out strategies for self-control and disciplined usage can help people maintain a healthy balance between social connections and school and work performance.

ACHIEVEMENT MOTIVATION

10-7: What is achievement motivation?

Achievement motivation is a desire for significant accomplishment, for mastery of skills or ideas, for control, and for rapidly attaining a high standard. Achievements are more closely related to grit (passionate dedication to a long-term goal) than to raw ability.

EMOTION: AROUSAL, BEHAVIOR, AND COGNITION

10-8: How do arousal, cognition, and expressive behavior interact in emotion?

Emotions are psychological responses of the whole organism involving an interplay among physiological arousal, expressive behaviors, and conscious experience. Theories of emotion generally address two major questions: (1) Does physiological arousal come before or after emotional feelings, and (2) how do cognition and feeling interact? The *James-Lange theory* maintains that emotional feelings follow our body's response to emotion-inducing stimuli. The *Cannon-Bard theory* proposes that our physiological response to an emotion-inducing stimulus occurs at the same time as our subjective feeling of the emotion (one does not cause the other). The Schachter-Singer *two-factor theory* holds that our emotions have two ingredients, physical arousal and a cognitive label, and the cognitive labels we put on our states of arousal are an essential ingredient of emotion. Lazarus agreed that many important emotions arise from our interpretations or inferences. Zajonc and LeDoux, however, believe that some simple emotional responses occur instantly, not only outside our conscious awareness, but before any cognitive processing occurs. This interplay between emotion and cognition illustrates our dual-track mind.

EMBODIED EMOTION

10-9: What are some of the basic emotions?

Izard's 10 basic emotions are joy, interest-excitement, surprise, sadness, anger, disgust, contempt, fear, shame, and guilt.

10-10: What is the link between emotional arousal and the autonomic nervous system?

The arousal component of emotion is regulated by the autonomic nervous system's sympathetic (arousing) and parasympathetic (calming) divisions. In a crisis, the fight-or-flight response automatically mobilized your body for action.

10-11: Do different emotions activate different physiological and brain-pattern responses?

Emotions may be similarly arousing, but some subtle physiological responses, such as facial muscle movements, distinguish them. Meaningful differences have also been found in activity in some brain pathways and cortical areas.

10-12: How effective are polygraphs in using body states to detect lies?

Polygraphs, which measure several physiological indicators of emotion, are not accurate enough to justify widespread use in business and law enforcement. The use of guilty knowledge questions and new forms of technology may produce better indications of lying.

EXPRESSED AND EXPERIENCED EMOTION

10-13: How do we communicate nonverbally?

Much of our communication is through body movements, facial expressions, and voice tones. Even seconds-long filmed slices of behavior can reveal feelings.

10-14: How do women and men differ in their emotional expressions and experiences?

Women tend to read emotional cues more easily and to be more empathic. Their faces also express more emotion.

10-15: Do gestures and facial expressions mean the same thing in all cultures?

The meaning of gestures varies with culture, but facial expressions, such as those of happiness and fear, are common the world over. Cultures also differ in the amount of emotion they express.

10-16: How do our facial expressions influence our feelings?

Research on the *facial feedback effect* shows that our facial expressions can trigger emotional feelings and signal our body to respond accordingly. We also mimic others' expressions, which helps us empathize.

CHAPTER 11 > Stress, Health, and Human Flourishing

STRESS AND HEALTH

11-1: What events provoke stress responses, and how do we respond and adapt to stress?

Stress is the process by which we appraise and respond to stressors (catastrophic events, significant live changes, and daily hassles) that challenge or threaten us. Walter Cannon viewed the stress response as a "fight-or-flight" system. Hans Selye proposed a general three-stage (alarm-resistance-exhaustion) *general adaptation syndrome (GAS)*. Facing stress, women may have a *tend-and-befriend* response; men may withdraw socially, turn to alcohol, or become aggressive.

11-2: How does stress make us more vulnerable to disease?

Psychoneuroimmunologists study mind-body interactions, including stress-related physical illnesses, such as hypertension and some headaches. Stress diverts energy from the immune system, inhibiting the activities of its B and T lymphocytes, macrophages, and NK cells. Stress does not cause diseases such as AIDS and cancer, but by altering our immune functioning it may make us more vulnerable to them and influence their progression.

11-3: Why are some of us more prone than others to coronary heart disease?

Coronary heart disease, North America's number one cause of death, has been linked with the reactive, anger-prone *Type A* personality. Compared with relaxed, easygoing *Type B* personalities, Type A people secrete more of the hormones that accelerate the buildup of plaque on the heart's artery walls. Chronic stress also contributes to persistent inflammation, which heightens the risk of clogged arteries and depression.

11-4: What are some healthful ways to cope with feelings of anger?

Chronic hostility is one of the negative emotions linked to heart disease. Emotional *catharsis* may be temporarily calming, but in the long run it does not reduce anger. Rehearsing anger can make us more angry. Controlled assertions of feelings may resolve conflicts, and forgiveness may rid us of angry feelings.

COPING WITH STRESS

11-5: In what two ways do people try to alleviate stress?

We use *problem-focused coping* to change the stressor or the way we interact with it. We use *emotion-focused coping* to avoid or ignore stressors and attend to emotional needs related to stress reactions.

11-6: How does a perceived lack of control affect health?

Being unable to avoid repeated aversive events can lead to *learned helplessness*. People who perceive an *internal locus of control* achieve more, enjoy better health, and are happier than those who perceive an *external locus of control*. *Self-control* requires attention and energy, but it predicts good adjustment, better grades, and social success. A perceived lack of control provokes an outpouring of hormones that put people's health at risk.

11-7: What are the links among basic outlook on life, social support, stress, and health?

Studies of people with an optimistic outlook show that their immune system is stronger, their blood pressure does not increase as sharply in response to stress, their recovery from heart bypass surgery is faster, and their life expectancy is longer, compared with their pessimistic counterparts. Social support promotes health by calming us, reducing blood pressure and stress hormones, and by fostering stronger immune functioning.

REDUCING STRESS

11-8: How effective is aerobic exercise as a way to manage stress and improve well-being?

Aerobic exercise is sustained, oxygen-consuming activity that increases heart and lung fitness. It increases arousal, leads to muscle relaxation and sounder sleep, triggers production of neurotransmitters, and enhances self-image. It can relieve depression and, in later life, is associated with better cognitive functioning and longer life.

11-9: In what ways might relaxation and meditation influence stress and health?

Relaxation and meditation have been shown to reduce stress by relaxing muscles, lowering blood pressure, improving immune functioning, and lessening anxiety and depression. Massage therapy also relaxes muscles and reduces depression.

11-10: What is the faith factor, and what are some possible explanations for the link between faith and health?

The faith factor is the finding that religiously active people tend to live longer than those who are not religiously active. Possible explanations may include the effect of intervening variables, such as the healthy behaviors, social support, or positive emotions often found among people who regularly attend religious services.

HAPPINESS

11-11: What are the main effects of being happy?

A good mood brightens people's perceptions of the world. Happy people tend to be healthy, energized, and satisfied with life. They also are more willing to help others (the *feel-good, do-good phenomenon*).

11-12: What is subjective well-being, and what topics do positive psychology researchers explore? What are the three "pillars" of the movement?

Subjective well-being is your perception of being happy or satisfied with life. *Positive psychologists* study use scientific methods to study human flourishing, including topics such as positive emotions, positive health, positive neuroscience, and positive education. The three pillars of positive psychology are positive well-being; positive character; and positive groups, communities, and cultures.

11-13: How do time, wealth, adaptation, and comparison affect our happiness levels?

The moods triggered by good or bad events seldom last beyond that day. Even significant good events, such as sudden wealth, seldom increase happiness for long. Happiness is relative to our own experiences (the *adaptation-level phenomenon*) and to others' success (the *relative deprivation* principle).

11-14: What are some predictors of happiness, and how can we be happier?

Some individuals, because of their genetic predispositions and personal histories, are happier than others. Cultures, which vary in the traits they value and the behaviors they expect and reward, also influence personal levels of happiness. Those who want to be happier can (1) realize that financial success may not lead to enduring happiness; (2) take control of their time; (3) act happy to trigger facial and behavioral feedback; (4) seek skill-engaging work and leisure to foster "flow"; (5) exercise; (6) get adequate sleep; (7) nurture close relationships; (8) focus beyond themselves; (9) record and express their gratitude; (10) nurture their spiritual self.

CHAPTER 12 > Personality

Personality is an individual's characteristic pattern of thinking, feeling, and acting.

PSYCHODYNAMIC THEORIES

Psychodynamic theories view personality from the perspective that behavior is a dynamic interaction between the conscious and unconscious mind. The theories trace their origin to Sigmund Freud's theory of *psychoanalysis*.

12-1: How did Sigmund Freud's treatment of psychological disorders lead to his view of the unconscious mind?

In treating patients whose disorders had no clear physical explanation, Freud concluded that these problems reflected unacceptable thoughts and feelings, hidden away in the *unconscious* mind. To explore this hidden part of a patient's mind, Freud used *free association* and dream analysis.

12-2: What was Freud's view of personality?

Freud believed that personality results from conflict arising from the interaction among the mind's three systems: the *id* (pleasure-seeking impulses), *ego* (reality-oriented executive), and *superego* (internalized set of ideals, or conscience).

12-3: What developmental stages did Freud propose?

He believed children pass through five *psychosexual stages* (oral, anal, phallic, latency, and genital). Unresolved conflicts at any stage can leave a person's pleasure-seeking impulses *fixated* (stalled) at that stage.

12-4: How did Freud think people defended themselves against anxiety?

For Freud, anxiety was the product of tensions between the demands of the id and superego. The ego copes by using unconscious *defense mechanisms,* such as *repression,* which he viewed as the basic mechanism underlying and enabling all the others.

12-5: Which of Freud's ideas did his followers accept or reject?

Freud's early followers, the neo-Freudians, accepted many of his ideas. They differed in placing more emphasis on the conscious mind and in stressing social motives more than sex or aggression. Contemporary psychodynamic theorists and therapists reject Freud's emphasis on sexual motivation. They stress, with support from modern research findings, the view that much of our mental life is unconscious, and they believe that our childhood experiences influence our adult personality and attachment patterns. Many also believe that our species' shared evolutionary history shaped some universal predispositions.

12-6: What are projective tests, how are they used, and what are some criticisms of them?

Projective tests attempt to assess personality by showing people ambiguous stimuli (open to many possible interpretations) and treating their answers as revelations of unconscious motives. One such test, the *Rorschach inkblot test,* has low reliability and validity, except in a few areas, such as hostility and anxiety.

12-7: How do contemporary psychologists view Freud's psychoanalysis?

They give Freud credit for drawing attention to the vast unconscious, to the struggle to cope with our sexuality, to the conflict between biological impulses and social restraints, and for some forms of defense mechanisms (false consensus effect/projection; reaction formation). But his concept of repression, and his view of the unconscious as a collection of repressed and unacceptable thoughts, wishes, feelings, and memories, cannot survive scientific scrutiny. Freud offered after-the-fact explanations, which are hard to test scientifically. Research does not support many of Freud's specific ideas, such as the view that development is fixed in childhood. (We now know it is lifelong.)

12-8: How has modern research developed our understanding of the unconscious?

Current research confirms that we do not have full access to all that goes on in our mind, but the current view of the unconscious is that it is a separate and parallel track of information processing which occurs outside our awareness. This processing includes schemas that control our perceptions; priming; implicit memories of learned skills; instantly activated emotions; and stereotypes that our information processing of others' traits and characteristics.

HUMANISTIC THEORIES

12-9: How did humanistic psychologists view personality, and what was their goal in studying personality?

The *humanistic psychologists'* view of personality focused on the potential for healthy personal growth and people's striving for self-determination and self-realization. Abraham Maslow proposed that human motivations form a hierarchy of needs; if basic needs are fulfilled, people will strive toward *self-actualization* and self-transcendence. Carl Rogers believed that the ingredients of a growth-promoting environment are genuineness, acceptance (including *unconditional positive regard),* and empathy. *Self-concept* was a central feature of personality for both Maslow and Rogers.

12-10: How did humanistic psychologists assess a person's sense of self?

Some rejected any standardized assessments and relied on interviews and conversations. Rogers sometimes used questionnaires in which people described their ideal and actual selves, which he later used to judge progress during therapy.

12-11: How have humanistic theories influenced psychology? What criticisms have they faced?

Humanistic psychology helped renew interest in the concept of self. Critics have said that humanistic psychology's concepts were vague and subjective, its values self-centered, and its assumptions naively optimistic.

TRAIT THEORIES

12-12: How do psychologists use traits to describe personality?

Trait theorists see personality as a stable and enduring pattern of behavior. They describe our differences rather than trying to explain them. Using factor analysis, they identify clusters of behavior tendencies that occur together. Genetic predispositions influence many traits.

12-13: What are personality inventories, and what are their strengths and weaknesses as trait-assessment tools?

Personality inventories (such as the *MMPI*) are questionnaires on which people respond to items designed to gauge a wide range of feelings and behaviors. Test items are *empirically derived,* and the tests are objectively scored. But people can fake their answers to create a good impression, and the ease of computerized testing may lead to misuse of the tests.

12-14: Which traits seem to provide the most useful information about personality variation?

The Big Five personality factors—conscientiousness, agreeableness, neuroticism, openness, and extraversion (CANOE)—currently offer the clearest picture of personality. These factors are stable and appear to be found in all cultures.

12-15: Does research support the consistency of personality traits over time and across situations?

A person's average traits persist over time and are predictable over many different situations. But traits cannot predict behavior in any one particular situation.

SOCIAL-COGNITIVE THEORIES

12-16: How do the social-cognitive theorists view personality development, and how do they explore behavior?

Albert Bandura first proposed the *social-cognitive perspective,* which views personality as the product of the interaction between a person's traits (including thinking) and the situation—the social context. Social-cognitive researchers apply principles of learning, cognition, and social behavior to personality. *Reciprocal determinism* is a term describing the interaction and mutual influence of behavior, internal personal factors, and environmental factors.

12-17: What criticisms have social-cognitive researchers faced?

Social-cognitive researchers build on well-established concepts of learning and cognition. They tend to believe that the best way to predict someone's behavior in a given situation is to observe that person's behavior in similar situations. They have been faulted for underemphasizing the importance of unconscious motives, emotions, and biologically influenced traits.

EXPLORING THE SELF

12-18: Why has psychology generated so much research on the self? How important is self-esteem to psychology and to our well-being?

The *self* is the center of personality, organizing our thoughts, feelings, and actions. Considering possible selves helps motivate us toward positive development, but focusing too intensely on ourselves can lead to the *spotlight effect*. *Self-esteem* is our feeling of self-worth; *self-efficacy* is our sense of competence on a task. High self-esteem correlates with less pressure to conform, persistence at difficult tasks, and social skills. But the direction of the correlation is not clear. Psychologists are now more pessimistic about the value of unrealistically promoting children's feelings of self-worth, rather than rewarding their achievements, which lead to feelings of competence.

12-19: What evidence reveals self-serving bias, and how do defensive and secure self-esteem differ?

Self-serving bias is our tendency to perceive ourselves favorably, as when viewing ourselves as better than average or when accepting credit for our successes but not blame for our failures. *Narcissism* is excessive self-love and self-absorption. Defensive (unrealistically high) self-esteem is fragile, focuses on sustaining itself, and views failure or criticism as a threat. Secure self-esteem enables us to feel accepted for who we are.

12-20: How do individualist and collectivist cultures influence people?

Within any culture, the degree of individualism or collectivism varies from person to person. Cultures based on self-reliant *individualism,* like those found in North America and Western Europe, tend to value personal independence and individual achievement. They define identity in terms of self-esteem, personal goals and attributes, and personal rights and liberties. Cultures based on socially connected *collectivism,* like those in many parts of Asia and Africa, tend to value interdependence, tradition, and harmony, and they define identity in terms of group goals, commitments, and belonging to one's group.

CHAPTER 13 | Social Psychology

SOCIAL THINKING

13-1: What do social psychologists study? How do we tend to explain others' behavior and our own?

Social psychologists use scientific methods to study how people think about, influence, and relate to one another. They study the social influences that explain why the same person will act differently in different situations. When explaining others' behavior, we may—especially if we come from an individualistic Western culture—commit the *fundamental attribution error,* by underestimating the influence of the situation and overestimating the effects of stable, enduring traits. When explaining our own behavior, we more readily attribute it to the influence of the situation.

13-2: How do attitudes and actions interact?

Attitudes are feelings, often influenced by our beliefs, that predispose us to respond in certain ways. *Peripheral route persuasion* uses incidental cues (such as celebrity endorsement) to try to produce fast but relatively thoughtless changes in attitudes. *Central route persuasion* offers evidence and arguments to trigger thoughtful responses. When other influences are minimal, attitudes that are stable, specific, and easily recalled can affect our actions. Actions can modify attitudes, as in the *foot-in-the-door phenomenon* (complying with a large request after having agreed to a small request) and *role* playing (acting a social part by following guidelines for expected behavior). When our attitudes don't fit with our actions, *cognitive dissonance theory* suggests that we will reduce tension by changing our attitudes to match our actions.

SOCIAL INFLUENCE

13-3: How do cultural norms affect our behavior?

A *culture* is an enduring set of behaviors, ideas, attitudes, values, and traditions shared by a group and transmitted from one generation to the next. Cultural *norms* are understood rules that inform members of a culture about accepted and expected behaviors. Cultures differ across time and space, and cultures change.

13-4: What is automatic mimicry, and how do conformity experiments reveal the power of social influence?

Automatic mimicry (the chameleon effect)—our tendency to unconsciously imitate others' expressions, postures, and voice tones—is a form of *conformity*. Solomon Asch and others have found that we are most likely to adjust our behavior or thinking to coincide with a group standard when (a) we feel incompetent or insecure, (b) our group has at least three people, (c) everyone else agrees, (d) we admire the group's status and attractiveness, (e) we have not already committed to another response, (f) we know we are being observed, and (g) our culture encourages respect for social standards. We may conform to gain approval *(normative social influence)* or because we are willing to accept others' opinions as new information *(informational social influence)*.

13-5: What did Milgram's obedience experiments teach us about the power of social influence?

Stanley Milgram's experiments—in which people obeyed orders even when they thought they were harming another person—demonstrated that strong social influences can make ordinary people conform to falsehoods or give in to cruelty. Obedience was highest when (a) the person giving orders was nearby and was perceived as a legitimate authority figure; (b) the research was supported by a prestigious institution; (c) the victim was depersonalized or at a distance; and (d) there were no role models for defiance.

13-6: How is our behavior affected by the presence of others?

In *social facilitation,* the mere presence of others arouses us, improving our performance on easy or well-learned tasks but decreasing it on difficult ones. In *social loafing,* participating in a group project makes us feel less responsible, and we may free-ride on others' efforts. When the presence of others both arouses us and makes us feel anonymous, we may experience *deindividuation*—loss of self-awareness and self-restraint.

13-7: What are group polarization and groupthink, and how much power do we have as individuals?

In *group polarization,* group discussions with like-minded others strengthen members' prevailing beliefs and attitudes. Internet communication magnifies this effect, for better and for worse. *Groupthink* is driven by a desire for harmony within a decision-making group, overriding realistic appraisal of alternatives. The power of the individual and the power of the situation interact. A small minority that consistently expresses its views may sway the majority.

SOCIAL RELATIONS

13-8: What is prejudice? What are its social and emotional roots?

Prejudice is an unjustifiable, usually negative, attitude toward a group and its members. Prejudice's three components are beliefs (often *stereotypes*), emotions, and predispositions to action *(discrimination)*. Overt prejudice in North America has decreased over time, but implicit prejudice—an automatic, unthinking attitude—continues. The social roots of prejudice include social inequalities and divisions. Higher-status groups often justify their privileged position with the *just-world phenomenon*. We tend to favor our own group *(ingroup bias)* as we divide ourselves into "us" (the *ingroup*) and "them" (the *outgroup*). Prejudice can also be a tool for protecting our emotional well-being, as when we focus our anger by blaming events on a *scapegoat*.

13-9: What are the cognitive roots of prejudice?

The cognitive roots of prejudice grow from our natural ways of processing information: forming categories, remembering vivid cases, and believing that the world is just and our own and our culture's ways of doing things are the right ways.

13-10: How does psychology's definition of *aggression* differ from everyday usage? What biological factors make us more prone to hurt one another?

In psychology, *aggression* is any physical or verbal behavior intended to hurt or destroy. Biology influences our threshold for aggressive behaviors at three levels: genetic (inherited traits), neural (activity in key brain areas), and biochemical (such as alcohol or excess testosterone in the bloodstream). Aggression is a complex behavior resulting from the interaction of biology and experience.

13-11: What psychological and social-cultural factors may trigger aggressive behavior?

Frustration *(frustration-aggression principle),* previous reinforcement for aggressive behavior, and observing an aggressive role model, and poor self-control can all contribute to aggression. Media portrayals of violence provide *social scripts* that children learn to follow. Viewing sexual violence contributes to greater aggression toward women. Playing violent video games increases aggressive thoughts, emotions, and behaviors.

13-12: Why do we befriend or fall in love with some people but not others?

Proximity (geographical nearness) increases liking, in part because of the *mere exposure effect*—exposure to novel stimuli increases liking of those stimuli. Physical attractiveness increases social opportunities and improves the way we are perceived. Similarity of attitudes and interests greatly increases liking, especially as relationships develop. We also like those who like us.

13-13: How does romantic love typically change as time passes?

Intimate love relationships start with *passionate love*—an intensely aroused state. Over time, the strong affection of *companionate love* may develop, especially if enhanced by an *equitable* relationship and by intimate *self-disclosure*.

13-14: When are people most—and least—likely to help?

Altruism is unselfish regard for the well-being of others. We are most likely to help when we (a) notice an incident, (b) interpret it as an emergency, and (c) assume responsibility for helping. Other factors, including our mood and our similarity to the victim, also affect our willingness to help. We are least likely to help if other bystanders are present (the *bystander effect*).

13-15: How do social exchange theory and social norms explain helping behavior?

Social exchange theory is the view that we help others because it is in our own self-interest; in this view, the goal of social behavior is maximizing personal benefits and minimizing costs. Others believe that helping results from socialization, in which we are taught guidelines for expected behaviors in social situations, such as the *reciprocity norm* and the *social-responsibility norm*.

13-16: How do social traps and mirror-image perceptions fuel social conflict?

A *conflict* is a perceived incompatibility of actions, goals, or ideas. *Social traps* are situations in which people in conflict pursue their own individual self-interest, harming the collective well-being. Individuals and cultures in conflict also tend to form *mirror-image perceptions:* Each party views the opponent as untrustworthy and evil-intentioned, and itself as an ethical, peaceful victim.

13-17: How can we transform feelings of prejudice, aggression, and conflict into attitudes that promote peace?

Peace can result when individuals or groups work together to achieve *superordinate* (shared) *goals*. Research indicates that four processes—contact, cooperation, communication, and conciliation—help promote peace.

CHAPTER 14 > Psychological Disorders

WHAT IS A PSYCHOLOGICAL DISORDER?

14-1: How should we draw the line between normal behavior and psychological disorder?

The DSM-5 Task Force defined a *psychological disorder* as a "significant dysfunction in an individual's cognitions, emotions, or behaviors," reflecting "a disturbance in the psychological, biological, or developmental processes underlying mental functioning." Dysfunctional behaviors are maladaptive and often distress the person with the disorder.

14-2: Why is there controversy over attention-deficit hyperactivity disorder?

A child who by age 7 displays extreme inattention, hyperactivity, and impulsivity may be diagnosed with *attention-deficit hyperactivity disorder (ADHD)* and treated with medication and other therapy. The controversy centers on whether the growing number of ADHD cases reflects overdiagnosis or increased awareness of the disorder. Long-term effects of stimulant-drug treatment for ADHD are not yet known.

14-3: How is our understanding of disorders affected by whether we use a medical model or a biopsychosocial approach?

The *medical model* assumes that psychological disorders are mental illnesses with physical causes that can be diagnosed, treated, and, in most cases, cured through therapy, sometimes in a hospital. The biopsychosocial perspective assumes that three sets of influences—biological (evolution, genetics, brain structure and chemistry), psychological (stress, trauma, learned helplessness, mood-related perceptions and memories), and social and cultural circumstances (roles, expectations, definitions of "normality" and "disorder")—interact to produce specific psychological disorders.

14-4: How and why do clinicians classify psychological disorders, and why do some psychologists criticize the use of diagnostic labels?

The American Psychiatric Association's *DSM-IV-TR (Diagnostic and Statistical Manual of Mental Disorders)* contains diagnostic labels and descriptions that provide a common language and shared concepts for communications and research. (*DSM-5* will soon replace and update *DSM-IV-TR.*) Some critics believe the DSM editions have become too detailed and extensive. Most U.S. health insurance organizations require an ICD/DSM diagnosis before paying for therapy. Other critics view DSM diagnoses as arbitrary labels that create preconceptions which bias perceptions of the labeled person's past and present behavior. One such label, "insanity," raises moral and ethical questions about whether society should hold people with disorders responsible for their violent actions. Most people with disorders are nonviolent and are more likely to be victims than attackers.

ANXIETY DISORDERS

14-5: What are the main anxiety disorders, and how do they differ from the ordinary worries and fears we all experience?

Anxious feelings and behaviors are classified as an *anxiety disorder* only when they form a pattern of distressing, persistent anxiety or maladaptive behaviors that reduce anxiety. People with *generalized anxiety disorder* feel persistently and uncontrollably tense and apprehensive, for no apparent reason. In the more extreme *panic disorder,* anxiety escalates into periodic episodes of intense dread. Those with a *phobia* may be irrationally afraid of a specific object or situation. Persistent and repetitive thoughts (obsessions) and actions (compulsions) characterize *obsessive-compulsive disorder.* Symptoms of *post-traumatic stress disorder* include four or more weeks of haunting memories, nightmares, social withdrawal, jumpy anxiety, and sleep problems following some traumatic experience.

14-6: How do conditioning, cognition, and biology contribute to the feelings that mark anxiety disorders?

The learning perspective views anxiety disorders as a product of fear conditioning, stimulus generalization, fearful-behavior reinforcement, and observational learning of others' fears and cognitions (interpretations, irrational beliefs, and hypervigilance). The biological perspective considers the role that fears of life-threatening animals, objects or situations played in natural selection and evolution; genetic predispositions for high levels of emotional reactivity and neurotransmitter production; and abnormal responses in the brain's fear circuits.

MOOD DISORDERS

14-7: What are mood disorders? How does major depressive disorder differ from bipolar disorder?

Mood disorders are characterized by emotional extremes. A person with *major depressive disorder* experiences two or more weeks of seriously depressed moods and feelings of worthlessness, and takes little interest in, and derives little pleasure from, most activities. A person with the less common condition of *bipolar disorder* experiences not only depression but also *mania*—episodes of hyperactive and wildly optimistic, impulsive behavior.

14-8: How do the biological and social-cognitive perspectives explain mood disorders?

The biological perspective on depression focuses on genetic predispositions and on abnormalities in brain structures and function (including those found in neurotransmitter systems). The social-cognitive perspective views depression as an ongoing cycle of stressful experiences (interpreted through negative beliefs, attributions, and memories) leading to negative moods and actions and fueling new stressful experiences.

14-9: What factors affect suicide and self-injuring, and what are some of the important warning signs to watch for in suicide prevention efforts?

Suicide rates differ by nation, race, gender, age group, income, religious involvement, marital status, and (for gay and lesbian youth) social support structure. Those with depression are more at risk for suicide than others are, but social suggestion, health status, and economic and social frustration are also contributing factors. Non-suicidal self-injury (NSSI) does not usually lead to suicide but may escalate to suicidal thoughts and acts if untreated. People who engage in NSSI do not tolerate stress well and tend to be self-critical, with poor communication and problem-solving skills. Environmental barriers (such as jump barriers) are effective in preventing suicides. Forewarnings of suicide may include verbal hints, giving away possessions, withdrawal, preoccupation with death, and discussing one's own suicide.

SCHIZOPHRENIA

14-10: What the schizophrenia subtypes, and what patterns of thinking, perceiving, feeling, and behaving characterize schizophrenia?

Schizophrenia is a group of disorders that typically strike during late adolescence, affect men very slightly more than women, and seem to occur in all cultures. Schizophrenia's subtypes are paranoid, disorganized, catatonic, undifferentiated, and residual. Symptoms are disorganized and delusional thinking, disturbed perceptions, and inappropriate emotions and actions. *Delusions* are false beliefs; hallucinations are sensory experiences without sensory stimulation. Schizophrenia symptoms may be positive (the presence of inappropriate behaviors) or negative (the absence of appropriate behaviors).

14-11: How do chronic and acute schizophrenia differ?

In chronic (or process) schizophrenia, the disorder develops gradually and recovery is doubtful. In acute (or reactive) schizophrenia, the onset is sudden, in reaction to stress, and the prospects for recovery are brighter.

14-12: What brain abnormalities are associated with schizophrenia?

People with schizophrenia have increased dopamine receptors, which may intensify brain signals, creating positive symptoms such as hallucinations and paranoia. Brain abnormalities associated with schizophrenia include enlarged, fluid-filled cerebral cavities and corresponding decreases in the cortex. Brain scans reveal abnormal activity in the frontal lobes, thalamus, and amygdala. Interacting malfunctions in multiple brain regions and their connections may produce schizophrenia's symptoms.

14-13: What prenatal events are associated with an increased risk of developing schizophrenia?

Possible contributing factors include viral infections or famine conditions during the mother's pregnancy; low weight or oxygen deprivation at birth; and maternal diabetes or older paternal age.

14-14: How do genes influence schizophrenia?

Twin and adoption studies indicate that the predisposition to schizophrenia is inherited. Multiple genes probably interact to produce schizophrenia. No environmental causes invariably produce schizophrenia, but environmental events (such as prenatal viruses or maternal stress) may "turn on" genes for this disorder in those who are predisposed to it.

OTHER DISORDERS

14-15: What are dissociative disorders, and why are they controversial?

Dissociative disorders are conditions in which conscious awareness seems to become separated from previous memories, thoughts, and feelings. Skeptics note that *dissociative identity disorder,* formerly known as multiple personality disorder, increased dramatically in the late twentieth century, that it is rarely found outside North America, and that it may reflect role-playing by people who are vulnerable to therapists' suggestions. Others view this disorder as a manifestation of feelings of anxiety, or as a response learned when behaviors are reinforced by anxiety-reduction.

14-16: What are the three main eating disorders, and how do biological, psychological, and social-cultural influences make people more vulnerable to these disorders?

In those with eating disorders (most often women or gay men), psychological factors can overwhelm the body's tendency to maintain a normal weight. Despite being significantly underweight, people with *anorexia nervosa* (usually adolescent females) continue to diet and exercise excessively because they view themselves as fat. Those with *bulimia nervosa* (usually females in their teens and twenties) secretly binge and then compensate by purging, fasting, or excessive exercise. Those with *binge-eating disorder* binge but do not follow with purging, fasting, and exercise. Cultural pressures, low self-esteem, and negative emotions interact with stressful life experiences and genetics to produce eating disorders.

14-17: What are the three clusters of personality disorders? What behaviors and brain activity characterize the antisocial personality?

Personality disorders are disruptive, inflexible, and enduring behavior patterns that impair social functioning. This disorder forms three clusters, based on main characteristics: (1) anxiety; (2) eccentric or odd behaviors; and (3) dramatic or impulsive behaviors. *Antisocial personality disorder* (one of those in the third cluster) is characterized by a lack of conscience and, sometimes, aggressive and fearless behavior. Genetic predispositions may interact with the environment to produce the altered brain activity associated with antisocial personality disorder.

RATES OF PSYCHOLOGICAL DISORDERS

14-18: How many people currently have, or have had, a psychological disorder? Is poverty a risk factor?

Psychological disorder rates vary, depending on the time and place of the survey. In one multinational survey, rates for any disorder ranged from less than 5 percent (Shanghai) to more than 25 percent (the United States). Poverty is a risk factor: Conditions and experiences associated with poverty contribute to the development of psychological disorders. But some disorders, such as schizophrenia, can drive people into poverty.

CHAPTER 15 > Therapy

TREATING PSYCHOLOGICAL DISORDERS

15-1: How do *psychotherapy, biomedical therapy,* and an *eclectic approach* to therapy differ?

Psychotherapy is treatment involving psychological techniques; it consists of interactions between a trained therapist and someone seeking to overcome psychological difficulties or achieve personal growth. The major psychotherapies derive from psychology's psychodynamic, humanistic, behavioral, and cognitive perspectives. *Biomedical therapy* treats psychological disorders with medications or procedures that act directly on a patient's physiology. An *eclectic approach* combines techniques from various forms of therapy.

THE PSYCHOLOGICAL THERAPIES

15-2: What are the goals and techniques of psychoanalysis, and how have they been adapted in psychodynamic therapy?

Through *psychoanalysis,* Sigmund Freud tried to give people self-insight and relief from their disorders by bringing anxiety-laden feelings and thoughts into conscious awareness. Psychoanalytic techniques included using free association and *interpretation* of instances of *resistance* and *transference. Psychodynamic therapy* has been influenced by traditional psychoanalysis but differs from it in many ways, including the lack of belief in id, ego, and superego. This contemporary therapy is briefer, less expensive, and more focused on helping the client find relief from current symptoms. Psychodynamic therapists help clients understand how past relationships create themes that may be acted out in present relationships.

15-3: What are the basic themes of humanistic therapy, and what are the specific goals and techniques of Rogers' client-centered approach?

Both psychoanalytic and humanistic therapists are *insight therapies*—they attempt to improve functioning by increasing clients' awareness of motives and defenses. Humanistic therapy's goals have included helping clients grow in self-awareness and self-acceptance; promoting personal growth rather than curing illness; helping clients take responsibility for their own growth; focusing on conscious thoughts rather than unconscious motivations; and seeing the present and future as more important than the past. Carl Rogers' *client-centered therapy* proposed that therapists' most important contributions are to function as a psychological mirror through *active listening* and to provide a growth-fostering environment of *unconditional positive regard,* characterized by genuineness, acceptance, and empathy.

15-4: How does the basic assumption of behavior therapy differ from the assumptions of psychodynamic and humanistic therapies? What techniques are used in exposure therapies and aversive conditioning?

Behavior therapies are not insight therapies. Their goal is to apply learning principles to modify problem behaviors. Classical conditioning techniques, including *exposure therapies* (such as *systematic desensitization* or *virtual reality exposure therapy)* and *aversive conditioning,* attempt to change behaviors through *counterconditioning*—evoking new responses to old stimuli that trigger unwanted behaviors.

15-5: What is the basic idea of operant conditioning therapy, and what arguments have been used for and against it?

Therapy based on operant conditioning principles uses behavior modification techniques to change unwanted behaviors through positively reinforcing desired behaviors and ignoring or punishing undesirable behaviors. Critics maintain that (1) techniques such as those used in *token economies* may produce behavior changes that disappear when rewards end, and (2) deciding which behaviors should change is authoritarian and unethical. Proponents argue that treatment with positive rewards is more humane than punishing people or institutionalizing them for undesired behaviors.

15-6: What are the goals and techniques of the cognitive therapies and of cognitive-behavioral therapy?

The *cognitive therapies,* such as Aaron Beck's cognitive therapy for depression, assume that our thinking influences our feelings, and that the therapist's role is to change clients' self-defeating thinking by training them to view themselves in more positive ways. Rational-emotive behavior therapy is a confrontational cognitive therapy that actively challenges irrational beliefs. The widely researched and practiced *cognitive-behavioral therapy* combines cognitive therapy and behavior therapy by helping clients regularly act out their new ways of thinking and talking in their everyday life.

15-7: What are the aims and benefits of group and family therapy?

Group therapy sessions can help more people and costs less per person than individual therapy would. Clients may benefit from exploring feelings and developing social skills in a group situation, from learning that others have similar problems, and from getting feedback on new ways of behaving. *Family therapy* views a family as an interactive system and attempts to help members discover the roles they play and to learn to communicate more openly and directly.

EVALUATING PSYCHOTHERAPIES

15-8: Does psychotherapy work? Who decides?

Clients' and therapists' positive testimonials cannot prove that psychotherapy is actually effective, and the placebo effect makes it difficult to judge whether improvement occurred because of the treatment. Using meta-analyses to statistically combine the results of hundreds of randomized psychotherapy outcome studies, researchers have found that those not undergoing treatment often improve, but those undergoing psychotherapy are more likely to improve more quickly, and with less chance of relapse.

15-9: Are some psychotherapies more effective than others for specific disorders?

No one type of psychotherapy is generally superior to all others. Therapy is most effective for those with clear-cut, specific problems. Some therapies—such as behavior conditioning for treating phobias and compulsions—are more effective for specific disorders. Psychodynamic therapy has been effective for depression and anxiety, and cognitive and cognitive-behavioral therapies have been effective in coping with anxiety, PTSD, and depression. *Evidence-based practice* integrates the best available research with clinicians' expertise and patients' characteristics, preferences, and circumstances.

15-10: How do alternative therapies fare under scientific scrutiny?

Abnormal states tend to return to normal on their own, and the placebo effect can create the impression that a treatment has been effective. These two tendencies complicate assessments of alternative therapies (nontraditional therapies that claim to cure certain ailments). EMDR has shown some effectiveness—not from the eye movement but rather from the exposure therapy nature of the treatments. Light exposure therapy does seem to relieve the symptoms of seasonal affective disorder (SAD) by activating a brain region that influences arousal and hormones.

15-11: What three elements are shared by all forms of psychotherapy?

All psychotherapies offer new hope for demoralized people; a fresh perspective; and (if the therapist is effective) an empathic, trusting, and caring relationship. The emotional bond of trust and understanding between therapist and client—the therapeutic alliance—is an important element in effective therapy.

15-12: How do culture and values influence the therapist-client relationship?

Therapists differ in the values that influence their goals in therapy and their views of progress. These differences may create problems if therapists and clients differ in their cultural or religious perspectives.

15-13: What should a person look for when selecting a therapist?

A person seeking therapy may want to ask about the therapist's treatment approach, values, credentials, and fees. An important consideration is whether the therapy seeker feels comfortable and able to establish a bond with the therapist.

THE BIOMEDICAL THERAPIES

15-14: What are the drug therapies? How do double-blind studies help researchers evaluate a drug's effectiveness?

Psychopharmacology, the study of drug effects on mind and behavior, has helped make drug therapy the most widely used biomedical therapy. *Antipsychotic drugs,* used in treating schizophrenia, block dopamine activity. Side effects may include tardive dyskinesia (with involuntary movements of facial muscles, tongue, and limbs) or increased risk of obesity and diabetes. *Antianxiety drugs,* which depress central nervous system activity, are used to treat anxiety disorders. These drugs can be physically and psychologically addictive. *Antidepressant drugs,* which increase the availability of serotonin and norepinephrine, are used for depression, with modest effectiveness beyond that of placebo drugs. The antidepressants known as selective serotonin reuptake inhibitors (often called SSRI drugs) are now used to treat other disorders, including strokes and anxiety disorders. Lithium and Depakote are mood stabilizers prescribed for those with bipolar disorder. Studies may use a double-blind procedure to avoid the placebo effect and researcher's bias.

15-15: How are brain stimulation and psychosurgery used in treating specific disorders?

Electroconvulsive therapy (ECT), in which a brief electric current is sent through the brain of an anesthetized patient, is an effective, last-resort treatment for severely depressed people who have not responded to other therapy. Newer alternative treatments for depression include vagus nerve stimulation, *repetitive transcranial magnetic stimulation (rTMS)* and, in preliminary clinical experiments, deep-brain stimulation that calms an overactive brain region linked with negative emotions. *Psychosurgery* removes or destroys brain tissue in hopes of modifying behavior. Radical psychosurgical procedures such as *lobotomy* were once popular, but neurosurgeons now rarely perform brain surgery to change behavior or moods. Brain surgery is a last-resort treatment because its effects are irreversible.

15-16: How, by adopting a healthier lifestyle, might people find some relief from depression, and how does this reflect our being biopsychosocial systems?

Depressed people who undergo a program of aerobic exercise, adequate sleep, light exposure, social engagement, negative-thought reduction, and better nutrition often gain some relief. In our integrated biopsychosocial system, stress affects our body chemistry and health; chemical imbalances can produce depression; and social support and other lifestyle changes can lead to relief of symptoms.

PREVENTING PSYCHOLOGICAL DISORDERS

15-17: What is the rationale for preventive mental health programs?

Preventive mental health programs are based on the idea that many psychological disorders could be prevented by changing oppressive, esteem-destroying environments into more benevolent, nurturing environments that foster growth, self-confidence, and *resilience.* Struggling with challenges can lead to post-traumatic growth. Community psychologists are often active in preventive mental health programs.

APPENDIX A Statistical Reasoning in Everyday Life

DESCRIBING DATA

A-1: How can we describe data with measures of central tendency and variation?

A measure of central tendency is a single score that represents a whole set of scores. Three such measures are the *mode* (the most frequently occurring score), the *mean* (the arithmetic average), and the *median* (the middle score in a group of data). Measures of variation tell us how diverse data are. Two measures of variation are the *range* (which describes the gap between the highest and lowest scores) and the *standard deviation* (which states how much scores vary around the mean, or average, score). Scores often form a *normal* (or bell-shaped) *curve.*

A-2: What does it mean when we say two things are correlated?

When we say two things are correlated, we are saying that they accompany each other in their movements. The strength of their relationship is expressed as a *correlation coefficient,* which ranges from +1.00 (a perfect positive correlation) through 0 (no correlation) to −1.00 (a perfect negative correlation). Their relationship may be displayed in a *scatterplot,* in which each dot represents a value for the two variables. Correlations predict but cannot explain.

A-3: What is regression toward the mean?

Regression toward the mean is the tendency for extreme or unusual scores to fall back toward their average.

SIGNIFICANT DIFFERENCES

A-4: How do we know whether an observed difference can be generalized to other populations?

To feel confident about generalizing an observed difference to other populations, we would want to know that the sample studied was representative of the larger population being studied; that the observations, on average, had low variability; that the sample consisted of more than a few cases; and that the observed difference was *statistically significant.*

A-5: What are cross-sectional studies and longitudinal studies, and why is it important to know which method was used?

In a *cross-sectional study,* people of different ages are compared. In a *longitudinal study,* a group of people is studied periodically over a long period of time. To draw meaningful conclusions about a study's results, we need to know whether the study used a representative sample to draw its conclusions. Studies of intelligence and aging, for example, have drawn different conclusions depending on whether a cross-sectional or longitudinal study was used.

APPENDIX B > Psychology at Work

B-1: What is "flow," and what are the three subfields of industrial-organizational psychology?

Flow is a completely involved, focused state of consciousness with diminished awareness of self and time. It results from fully engaging one's skills. *Industrial-organizational (I/O) psychology's* three subfields are *personnel, organizational,* and *human factors psychology.*

PERSONNEL PSYCHOLOGY

B-2: How do personnel psychologists help organizations with employee selection, work placement, and performance appraisal?

Personnel psychologists work with organizations to devise selection methods for new employees; recruit and evaluate applicants; design and evaluate training programs; identify people's strengths; analyze job content; and appraise individual and organizational performance. Unstructured, subjective interviews foster the interviewer illusion; *structured interviews* pinpoint job-relevant strengths and are better predictors of performance. Checklists, graphic rating scales, and behavior rating scales are useful performance appraisal methods.

ORGANIZATIONAL PSYCHOLOGY

B-3: What is the role of organizational psychologists?

Organizational psychologists examine influences on worker satisfaction and productivity and facilitate organizational change. Employee satisfaction and engagement tend to correlate with organizational success.

B-4: What are some effective leadership techniques?

Effective leaders harness job-relevant strengths; set specific challenging goals; and choose an appropriate leadership style. Leadership style may be goal-oriented *(task leadership)*, group-oriented *(social leadership)*, or some combination of the two.

THE HUMAN FACTOR

B-5: How do human factors psychologists work to create user-friendly machines and work settings?

Human factors psychologists contribute to human safety and improved design by encouraging developers and designers to consider human perceptual abilities, to avoid the curse of knowledge, and to test users to reveal perception-based problems.

Answers for *Experience the Testing Effect* Questions

CHAPTER 1 Thinking Critically With Psychological Science

1. Wilhelm Wundt

2. a

3. a

4. b

5. The environment (nurture) has an influence on us, but that influence is constrained by our biology (nature). Nature and nurture interact. People predisposed to be very tall (nature), for example, are unlikely to become Olympic gymnasts, no matter how hard they work (nurture).

6. d

7. psychiatrist

8. c

9. Hindsight bias

10. d

11. The scientific attitude teaches us to look for evidence instead of relying on our often fallible intuition. In evaluating a claim in the media, look for any signs of empirical evidence, preferably from several studies. Ask the following questions in your analysis: Are claims based on scientific findings? Have several studies replicated the findings and confirmed them? Are any experts cited? If so, research their background. Are they affiliated with a credible university, college, or institution? Have they conducted or written about scientific research?

12. hypotheses

13. c

14. representative

15. negative

16. a

17. *(a) Alcohol use is associated with violence. (One interpretation: Drinking triggers or unleashes aggressive behavior.)* Perhaps anger triggers drinking, or perhaps the same genes or child-rearing practices are predisposing both drinking and aggression. (Here researchers have learned that drinking does indeed trigger aggressive behavior.) *(b) Educated people live longer, on average, than less-educated people. (One interpretation: Education lengthens life and enhances health.)* Perhaps richer people can afford more education and better health care. (Research supports this conclusion.)

(c) Teens engaged in team sports are less likely to use drugs, smoke, have sex, carry weapons, and eat junk food than are teens who do not engage in team sports. (One interpretation: Team sports encourage healthy living.) Perhaps some third factor explains this correlation—teens who use drugs, smoke, have sex, carry weapons, and eat junk food may be "loners" who do not enjoy playing on any team. *(d) Adolescents who frequently see smoking in movies are more likely to smoke. (One interpretation: Movie stars' behavior influences impressionable teens.)* Perhaps adolescents who smoke and attend movies frequently have less parental supervision and more access to spending money than other adolescents.

18. experiments

19. placebo

20. c

21. independent variable

22. b

23. b

24. d

CHAPTER 2 The Biology of Behavior

1. axon

2. c

3. a

4. neurotransmitters

5. b

6. c

7. autonomic

8. central

9. a

10. adrenal glands

11. b

12. d

13. c

14. cerebellum

15. b

16. amygdala

17. b

18. hypothalamus

19. d

20. The visual cortex is a neural network of sensory neurons connected via interneurons to other neural networks, including auditory networks. This allows you to integrate visual and auditory information to respond when a friend you recognize greets you at a party.

21. c

22. association areas

23. frontal

24. You would hear sounds, but without the temporal lobe association areas you would be unable to make sense of what you were hearing.

25. c

26. ON; HER

27. a

28. b

29. Behavior geneticists study the relative power and limits of genetic and environmental influences on behavior.

30. chromosomes

31. gene

32. b

33. c

34. identical

35. b

CHAPTER 3 Consciousness and the Two-Track Mind

1. inattentional blindness

2. unconscious; conscious

3. circadian rhythm

4. b

5. NREM-3

6. It increases in duration.

7. c

8. With narcolepsy, the person periodically falls directly into REM sleep, with no warning; with sleep apnea, the person repeatedly awakens during the night.

9. d

10. The neural activation theory suggests that dreams are the brain's attempt to make sense of random neural activity.

11. The information-processing explanation of dreaming proposes that brain activity during REM sleep enables us to sift through *what one has dwelt on by day*.

12. REM rebound

13. a

14. c

15. dissociation

16. tolerance

17. a

18. Alcohol is a disinhibitor—it makes us more likely to do what we would have done when sober, whether that is being helpful or being aggressive.

19. d

20. LSD

21. a

22. b

CHAPTER 4 Developing Through the Life Span

1. continuity/stages

2. c

3. teratogens

4. a

5. frontal

6. b

7. We have no conscious memories of events occurring before about age 3½, in part because major brain areas have not yet matured.

8. Infants in Piaget's *sensorimotor stage* tend to be focused only on their own perceptions of the world and may, for example, be unaware that objects continue to exist when unseen. A child in the *preoperational stage* is still egocentric and incapable of appreciating simple logic, such as the reversibility of operations. A preteen in the *concrete operational stage* is beginning to think logically about concrete events but not about abstract concepts.

9. a

10. stranger anxiety

11. Before these studies, many psychologists believed that infants became attached to those who nourished them.

12. temperament

13. b

14. formal operations

15. b

16. emerging adulthood

17. b

18. a

19. Cross-sectional studies compare people of different ages. Longitudinal studies restudy and retest the same people over a long period of time.

20. generativity

21. c

22. b

CHAPTER 5 Gender and Sexuality

1. c

2. Y

3. d

4. 11; 13

5. intersex

6. b

7. gender identity

8. b

9. b

10. Sexual dysfunctions are problems that men and women may have related to sexual arousal and sexual function. Paraphilias are conditions, which may be classified as psychological disorders, where sexual arousal is associated with socially unacceptable target partners and/or suffering of self or others.

11. Does; doesn't

12. c

13. d

14. c

15. Researchers have found no evidence that any environmental factor (parental relationships, childhood experiences, peer relationships, or dating experiences) influences the development of our sexual orientation.

CHAPTER 6 Sensation and Perception

1. b

2. perception

3. d

4. just noticeable difference

5. b

6. d

7. a

8. wavelength

9. a

10. c

11. c

12. feature detectors

13. parallel processing

14. d

15. Your brain constructs this perception of color in two stages. In the first stage, the lemon reflects light energy into your eyes, where it is transformed into neural messages. Three sets of cones, each sensitive to a different light frequency (red, blue, and green) process color. In this case, the light energy stimulates both red-sensitive and green-sensitive cones. In the second stage, opponent-process cells sensitive to paired opposites of color (red/green, yellow/blue, and black/white) evaluate the incoming neural messages as they pass through your optic nerve to the thalamus and visual cortex. When the yellow-sensitive opponent-process cells are stimulated, you identify the lemon as yellow.

16. d

17. a

18. b

19. c

20. monocular

21. b

22. b

23. perceptual adaptation

24. cochlea

25. The *outer ear* collects sound waves, which are translated into mechanical waves by the *middle ear* and turned into fluid waves in the *inner ear*. The *auditory nerve* then translates the energy into electrical waves and sends them to the brain, which perceives and interprets the sound.

26. Place; frequency

27. c

28. Our experience of pain is influenced by biological factors (such as sensory receptors that detect pressure), psychological factors (such as our focused attention), and social-cultural factors (such as social expectations about tolerance and expression of pain).

29. We feel pain in our brain, so we may diminish the experience of pain by changing the messages sent to the brain. Gate-control theory proposes that our pain sensory receptors send signals to the spinal cord, which relays messages to the brain. Small fibers in the spinal cord open the gate to pain; large fibers close the gate, blocking those signals. Meditation triggers large-fiber activity by shifting our attention elsewhere (toward the breath or repeated word); exercise triggers large-fiber activity by generating competing stimulation and endorphin release.

30. Kinesthesis; vestibular sense

31. Your vestibular sense regulates balance and body positioning through kinesthetic receptors triggered by fluid in your inner ear. Wobbly legs and a spinning world are signs that these receptors are still responding to the ride's turbulence. As your vestibular sense adjusts to solid ground, your balance will be restored.

32. We have specialized receptors for detecting sweet, salty, sour, bitter, and umami tastes. Being able to detect pleasurable tastes enabled our ancestors to seek out energy- and protein-rich foods. Detecting aversive tastes deterred them from eating toxic substances, increasing their chances of survival.

33. d

34. d

CHAPTER 7 Learning

1. information; behaviors

2. c

3. conditioned

4. discrimination

5. b

6. A sexual image is a US that triggers a UR of interest or arousal. Before the advertisement pairs a product with a sexual image, the product is an NS. Over time the product can become a CS that triggers the CR of interest or arousal.

7. Skinner's

8. shaping

9. b

10. Your instructor could reinforce your attentive behavior by taking away something you dislike. For example, your instructor could offer to shorten the length of an assigned paper or replace lecture time with an in-class activity. In both cases, the instructor would remove something aversive in order to negatively reinforce your focused attention.

11. partial

12. a

13. variable-interval

14. c

15. d

16. b

17. b

18. latent learning

19. observational learning

20. vicarious; vicarious

21. a

22. mirror

23. c

CHAPTER 8 Memory

1. recall

2. encoding; storage; retrieval

3. a

4. iconic; echoic

5. seven

6. mnemonics

7. a

8. implicit

9. c

10. d

11. Memories are stored within a web of many associations, one of which is mood. When you recall happy moments from your past, you deliberately activate these positive links. You may then experience mood-congruent memory and recall other happy moments, which could improve your mood and brighten your interpretation of current events.

12. a

13. d

14. d

15. retroactive

16. repression

17. b

18. Eliza's immature hippocampus and lack of verbal skills would have prevented her from encoding an explicit memory of the wedding reception at the age of two. It's more likely that Eliza learned information (from hearing the story repeatedly) that she eventually constructed into a memory that feels very real.

19. source amnesia

20. déjà vu

21. b

22. b

CHAPTER 9 Thinking, Language, and Intelligence

1. concept

2. algorithm

3. Oscar will need to guard against *confirmation bias* (searching for support for his own views and ignoring contradictory evidence) as he seeks out opposing viewpoints. Even if Oscar encounters new information that disproves his beliefs, *belief perseverance* may lead him to cling to these views anyway. It will take more compelling evidence to change his beliefs than it took to create them.

4. c

5. availability

6. framing

7. b

8. c

9. phonemes; morphemes; grammar

10. telegraphic speech

11. universal grammar

12. a

13. general intelligence *(g)*

14. c

15. academic; practical; creative

16. d

17. d

18. c

19. reliability

20. a

21. c

22. c

23. The heritability (difference due to genes) of body weight will be greater in country X, where environmental differences in available nutrition are minimal.

24. Stereotype threat

CHAPTER 10 Motivation and Emotion

1. b

2. a

3. incentive

4. Arousal

5. b

6. a

7. Maslow's hierarchy of needs best supports this statement because it addresses the primacy of some motives over others. Once our basic physiological needs are met, safety concerns are addressed next, followed by belongingness and love needs (such as the desire to kiss).

8. homeostasis

9. c

10. glucose; low

11. basal metabolic

12. d

13. Sanjay's plan is problematic. After he gains weight, the extra fat will require less energy to maintain than it did to gain in the first place. Sanjay may have a hard time getting rid of it later, when his metabolism slows down in an effort to retain his body weight.

14. c

15. Monitor the time spent on cell phones and Facebook, as well as our feelings about that time. Hide distracting online friends. Turn off or put away distracting devices. Consider a Facebook fast, and get outside and away from technology regularly.

16. James-Lange

17. b

18. c

19. A polygraph measures physiological changes, such as heart rate and perspiration, that are associated with emotions. Its use as a lie detector is controversial because the measure cannot distinguish between emotions with similar physiology (such as anxiety and guilt).

20. facial feedback

CHAPTER 11 Stress, Health, and Human Flourishing

1. resistance; exhaustion

2. tend; befriend

3. b

4. d

5. lymphocytes

6. c

7. Type A individuals frequently experience negative emotions (anger, depression), during which the sympathetic nervous system diverts blood away from the liver. This leaves fat and cholesterol circulating in the bloodstream for deposit near the heart and other organs, increasing the risk of heart disease and other health problems. Thus, Type A individuals actually harm themselves by directing anger at others.

8. negative

9. emotion

10. b

11. internal

12. d

13. aerobic

14. c

15. d

16. Positive

17. b

18. relative deprivation

CHAPTER 12 Personality

1. repression

2. c

3. superego

4. b

5. anxiety

6. Projective

7. d

8. a

9. a

10. d

11. Freud might argue that the criminal may have lacked the proper guidance as a child for developing a strong superego, allowing the id free rein. Rogers might assert that the criminal was raised in an environment lacking genuineness, acceptance (unconditional positive regard), and empathy, which inhibited psychological growth and led to a negative self-concept.

12. unconditional positive regard

13. trait

14. c

15. b

16. b

17. a

18. social-cognitive

19. b

20. Yes, if that self-love is of the *secure* type. Secure self-esteem promotes a focus beyond the self and a higher quality of life. Excessive self-love may promote artificially high or defensive self-esteem, which may lead to unhappiness if negative external feedback triggers anger or aggression.

21. b.

CHAPTER 13 Social Psychology

1. a

2. peripheral

3. foot-in-the-door

4. Cognitive dissonance theory best supports this suggestion. If Jamal acts confident, his behavior will contradict his negative self-thoughts, creating cognitive dissonance. To relieve the tension, Jamal may realign his attitudes with his actions by viewing himself as more outgoing and confident.

5. c

6. a

7. The presence of a large audience generates arousal and strengthens Dr. Huang's most likely response: enhanced performance on a task he has mastered (teaching music history) and impaired performance on a task he finds difficult (statistics).

8. deindividuation

9. group polarization

10. stereotypes

11. b

12. more

13. d

14. c

15. c

16. c

17. mere exposure

18. companionate; passionate

19. d

20. c

21. mirror-image

22. superordinate

CHAPTER 14 Psychological Disorders

1. No. Anna's behavior is unusual, causes her distress, and may make her a few minutes late on occasion, but it does not appear to significantly disrupt her ability to function. Like most of us, Anna demonstrates some unusual behaviors that are not disabling or dysfunctional, and, thus, do not suggest a psychological disorder.

2. c

3. medical

4. c

5. a

6. a

7. phobia

8. c

9. obsessive-compulsive

10. c

11. depression

12. c

13. increasing

14. norepinephrine; serotonin

15. social-cognitive

16. b

17. hallucination

18. No. Schizophrenia involves the altered perceptions, emotions, and behaviors of a mind split from reality. It does not involve rapid changes in mood or identity, as suggested by this comparison.

19. a

20. c

21. b

22. c

23. b

24. poverty

25. d

CHAPTER 15 Therapy

1. a

2. Insight

3. d

4. active listening

5. c

6. counterconditioning

7. systematic desensitization

8. Behavior therapies are often the best choice for treating phobias. Viewing Rico's fear of the freeway as a learned response, a behavior therapist might help Rico learn to replace his anxious response to freeway driving with a relaxation response.

9. token economy

10. d

11. Cognitive-behavioral

12. b

13. c

14. d

15. research evidence, clinical expertise, and knowledge of the patient

16. The placebo effect is the healing power of belief in a treatment. When patients expect a treatment to be effective, they may believe it was.

17. c

18. antianxiety

19. lithium

20. b

21. d

APPENDIX A Statistical Reasoning in Everyday Life

1. b

2. d

3. normal curve

4. a

5. negative

6. scatterplot

7. Regression toward the mean is a statistical phenomenon describing the tendency of extreme scores or outcomes to return to normal after an unusual event. Without knowing this, we may inaccurately decide the return to normal was a result of our own behavior.

8. cross-sectional

9. a

APPENDIX B Psychology at Work

1. c

2. Personnel; human factors

3. a

4. d

5. Focusing on specific, short-term goals, such as maintaining a regular study schedule, will be more helpful than focusing on more distant general goals, such as earning a good grade in this class.

6. transformational

7. c

8. d

A

absolute threshold   the minimum stimulation needed to detect a particular stimulus 50 percent of the time. (p. 193)

accommodation   (1) in developmental psychology, adapting our current understandings (schemas) to incorporate new information. (2) in sensation and perception, the process by which the eye's lens changes shape to focus near or far objects on the retina. (pp. 125, 201)

achievement motivation   a desire for significant accomplishment, for mastery of skills or ideas, for control, and for rapidly attaining a high standard. (p. 370)

achievement test   a test designed to assess what a person has learned. (p. 334)

acquisition   in classical conditioning, the initial stage, when one links a neutral stimulus and an unconditioned stimulus so that the neutral stimulus begins triggering the conditioned response. In operant conditioning, the strengthening of a reinforced response. (p. 241)

action potential   a neural impulse; a brief electrical charge that travels down an axon. (p. 37)

active listening   empathic listening in which the listener echoes, restates, and clarifies. A feature of Rogers' client-centered therapy. (p. 549)

adaptation-level phenomenon   our tendency to form judgments (of sounds, of lights, of income) relative to a neutral level defined by our prior experience. (p. 416)

addiction   compulsive drug craving and use, despite adverse consequences. (p. 101)

adolescence   the transition period from childhood to adulthood, extending from puberty to independence. (p. 140)

adrenal [ah-DREEN-el] **glands**   a pair of endocrine glands that sit just above the kidneys and secrete hormones (epinephrine and norepinephrine) that help arouse the body in times of stress. (p. 45)

aerobic exercise   sustained exercise that increases heart and lung fitness; may also alleviate depression and anxiety. (p. 407)

aggression   any physical or verbal behavior intended to hurt or destroy. (pp. 164, 481)

AIDS (acquired immune deficiency syndrome)   a life-threatening, sexually transmitted infection caused by the *human immunodeficiency virus* (HIV). AIDS depletes the immune system, leaving the person vulnerable to infections. (p. 174)

alcohol dependence   (popularly known as alcoholism). Alcohol use marked by tolerance, withdrawal if suspended, and a drive to continue use. (p. 102)

algorithm   a methodical, logical rule or procedure that guarantees solving a par-

ticular problem. Contrasts with the usually speedier—but also more error-prone—use of *heuristics*. (p. 307)

alpha waves   the relatively slow brain waves of a relaxed, awake state. (p. 85)

altruism   unselfish regard for the welfare of others. (p. 493)

amphetamines   drugs that stimulate neural activity, causing speeded-up body functions and associated energy and mood changes. (p. 104)

amygdala [uh-MIG-duh-la]   two lima-bean-sized neural clusters in the limbic system; linked to emotion. (p. 50)

anorexia nervosa   an eating disorder in which a person (usually an adolescent female) maintains a starvation diet despite being significantly (15 percent or more) underweight. (p. 536)

anterograde amnesia   an inability to form new memories. (p. 290)

antianxiety drugs   drugs used to control anxiety and agitation. (p. 569)

antidepressant drugs   drugs used to treat depression and some anxiety disorders. Different types work by altering the availability of various neurotransmitters. (p. 569)

antipsychotic drugs   drugs used to treat schizophrenia and other forms of severe thought disorder. (p. 568)

antisocial personality disorder   a personality disorder in which a person (usually a man) exhibits a lack of conscience for wrongdoing, even toward friends and family members. May be aggressive and ruthless or a clever con artist. (p. 538)

anxiety disorders   psychological disorders characterized by distressing, persistent anxiety or maladaptive behaviors that reduce anxiety. (p. 513)

aphasia   impairment of language, usually caused by left-hemisphere damage either to Broca's area (impairing speaking) or to Wernicke's area (impairing understanding). (p. 322)

applied research   scientific study that aims to solve practical problems. (p. 9)

aptitude test   a test designed to predict a person's future performance; *aptitude* is the capacity to learn. (p. 334)

assimilation   interpreting our new experiences in terms of our existing schemas. (p. 125)

association areas   areas of the cerebral cortex that are not involved in primary motor or sensory functions; rather, they are involved in higher mental functions such as learning, remembering, thinking, and speaking. (p. 56)

associative learning   learning that certain events occur together. The events may be two stimuli (as in classical conditioning) or a

response and its consequences (as in operant conditioning). (p. 238)

attachment   an emotional tie with another person; shown in young children by their seeking closeness to the caregiver and showing distress on separation. (p. 132)

attention-deficit hyperactivity disorder (ADHD)   a psychological disorder marked by the appearance by age 7 of one or more of three key symptoms: extreme inattention, hyperactivity, and impulsivity. (p. 507)

attitude   feelings, often influenced by our beliefs, that predispose us to respond in a particular way to objects, people, and events. (p. 460)

attribution theory   the theory that we explain someone's behavior by crediting either the situation or the person's disposition. (p. 458)

audition   the sense or act of hearing. (p. 216)

autism   a disorder that appears in childhood and is marked by deficient communication, social interaction, and understanding of others' states of mind. (p. 130)

automatic processing   unconscious encoding of incidental information, such as space, time, and frequency, and of well-learned information, such as word meanings. (p. 274)

autonomic [aw-tuh-NAHM-ik] **nervous system (ANS)**   the part of the peripheral nervous system that controls the glands and the muscles of the internal organs (such as the heart). Its sympathetic division arouses; its parasympathetic division calms. (p. 42)

availability heuristic   estimating the likelihood of events based on their availability in memory; if instances come readily to mind (perhaps because of their vividness), we presume such events are common. (p. 309)

aversive conditioning   a type of counterconditioning that associates an unpleasant state (such as nausea) with an unwanted behavior (such as drinking alcohol). (p. 552)

axon   the neuron extension that passes messages through its branches to other neurons or to muscles or glands. (p. 36)

B

babbling stage   beginning at about 4 months, the stage of speech development in which the infant spontaneously utters various sounds at first unrelated to the household language. (p. 320)

barbiturates drugs that depress central nervous system activity, reducing anxiety but impairing memory and judgment. (p. 103)

basal metabolic rate the body's resting rate of energy expenditure. (p. 358)

basic research pure science that aims to increase the scientific knowledge base. (p. 9)

basic trust according to Erik Erikson, a sense that the world is predictable and trustworthy; said to be formed during infancy by appropriate experiences with responsive caregivers. (p. 135)

behavior genetics the study of the relative power and limits of genetic and environmental influences on behavior. (p. 62)

behavior therapy therapy that applies learning principles to the elimination of unwanted behaviors. (p. 550)

behaviorism the view that psychology (1) should be an objective science that (2) studies behavior without reference to mental processes. Most research psychologists today agree with (1) but not with (2). (pp. 4, 240)

belief perseverance clinging to one's initial conceptions after the basis on which they were formed has been discredited. (p. 312)

binge-eating disorder significant binge-eating episodes, followed by distress, disgust, or guilt, but without the compensatory purging or fasting that marks bulimia nervosa. (p. 536)

binocular cues depth cues, such as retinal disparity, that depend on the use of two eyes. (p. 210)

biological psychology the scientific study of the links between biological (genetic, neural, hormonal) and psychological processes. (Some biological psychologists call themselves *behavioral neuroscientists, neuropsychologists, behavior geneticists, physiological psychologists,* or *biopsychologists.*) (p. 36)

biomedical therapy prescribed medications or procedures that act directly on the person's physiology. (p. 546)

biopsychosocial approach an integrated approach that incorporates biological, psychological, and social-cultural levels of analysis. (p. 6)

bipolar disorder a mood disorder in which a person alternates between the hopelessness and lethargy of depression and the overexcited state of mania. (Formerly called manic-depressive disorder.) (p. 520)

blind spot the point at which the optic nerve leaves the eye, creating a "blind" spot because no receptor cells are located there. (p. 202)

blindsight a condition in which a person can respond to a visual stimulus without consciously experiencing it. (p. 79)

bottom-up processing analysis that begins with the sensory receptors and works up to the brain's integration of sensory information. (p. 192)

brainstem the oldest part and central core of the brain, beginning where the spinal cord swells as it enters the skull; the brainstem is responsible for automatic survival functions. (p. 47)

Broca's area controls language expression—an area of the frontal lobe, usually in the left hemisphere, that directs the muscle movements involved in speech. (p. 323)

bulimia nervosa an eating disorder in which a person alternates binge eating (usually of high-calorie foods) with purging (by vomiting or laxative use) or fasting. (p. 536)

bystander effect the tendency for any given bystander to be less likely to give aid if other bystanders are present. (p. 494)

C

Cannon-Bard theory the theory that an emotion-arousing stimulus simultaneously triggers (1) physiological responses and (2) the subjective experience of emotion. (p. 372)

case study an observation technique in which one person is studied in depth in the hope of revealing universal principles. (p. 17)

catharsis in psychology, the idea that "releasing" aggressive energy (through action or fantasy) relieves aggressive urges. (p. 398)

central nervous system (CNS) the brain and spinal cord. (p. 41)

central route persuasion occurs when interested people focus on the arguments and respond with favorable thoughts. (p. 460)

cerebellum [sehr-uh-BELL-um] the "little brain" at the rear of the brainstem; functions include processing sensory input, coordinating movement output and balance, and enabling nonverbal learning and memory. (p. 50)

cerebral [seh-REE-bruhl] **cortex** the intricate fabric of interconnected neural cells covering the cerebral hemispheres; the body's ultimate control and information-processing center. (p. 53)

change blindness failing to notice changes in the environment. (p. 82)

chromosomes threadlike structures made of DNA molecules that contain the genes. (p. 62)

chunking organizing items into familiar, manageable units; often occurs automatically. (p. 276)

circadian [ser-KAY-dee-an] **rhythm** the biological clock; regular bodily rhythms (for example, of temperature and wakefulness) that occur on a 24-hour cycle. (p. 83)

classical conditioning a type of learning in which one learns to link two or more stimuli and anticipate events. (p. 239)

client-centered therapy a humanistic therapy, developed by Carl Rogers, in which the therapist uses techniques such as active listening within a genuine, accepting, empathic environment to facilitate clients' growth. (Also called *person-centered therapy.*) (p. 549)

clinical psychology a branch of psychology that studies, assesses, and treats people with psychological disorders. (p. 9)

cochlea [KOHK-lee-uh] a coiled, bony, fluid-filled tube in the inner ear; sound waves traveling through the cochlear fluid trigger nerve impulses. (p. 216)

cochlear implant a device for converting sounds into electrical signals and stimulating the auditory nerve through electrodes threaded into the cochlea. (p. 218)

cognition all the mental activities associated with thinking, knowing, remembering, and communicating. (pp. 124, 306)

cognitive dissonance theory the theory that we act to reduce the discomfort (dissonance) we feel when two of our thoughts (cognitions) are inconsistent. For example, when we become aware that our attitudes and our actions clash, we can reduce the resulting dissonance by changing our attitudes. (p. 462)

cognitive learning the acquisition of mental information, whether by observing events, by watching others, or through language. (p. 239)

cognitive map a mental representation of the layout of one's environment. For example, after exploring a maze, rats act as if they have learned a cognitive map of it. (p. 259)

cognitive neuroscience the interdisciplinary study of the brain activity linked with cognition (including perception, thinking, memory, and language). (pp. 4, 78)

cognitive therapy therapy that teaches people new, more adaptive ways of thinking; based on the assumption that thoughts intervene between events and our emotional reactions. (p. 554)

cognitive-behavioral therapy a popular integrative therapy that combines cognitive therapy (changing self-defeating thinking) with behavior therapy (changing behavior). (p. 556)

collective unconscious Carl Jung's concept of a shared, inherited reservoir of memory traces from our species' history. (p. 428)

collectivism giving priority to the goals of one's group (often one's extended family or work group) and defining one's identity accordingly. (p. 451)

color constancy   perceiving familiar objects as having consistent color, even if changing illumination alters the wavelengths reflected by the object. (p. 212)

companionate love   the deep affectionate attachment we feel for those with whom our lives are intertwined. (p. 492)

concept   a mental grouping of similar objects, events, ideas, and people. (p. 306)

concrete operational stage   in Piaget's theory, the stage of cognitive development (from about 6 or 7 to 11 years of age) during which children gain the mental operations that enable them to think logically about concrete events. (p. 128)

conditioned reinforcer   a stimulus that gains its reinforcing power through its association with a primary reinforcer; also known as a *secondary reinforcer*. (p. 248)

conditioned response (CR)   in classical conditioning, a learned response to a previously neutral (but now conditioned) stimulus (CS). (p. 240)

conditioned stimulus (CS)   in classical conditioning, an originally irrelevant stimulus that, after association with an unconditioned stimulus (US), comes to trigger a conditioned response (CR). (p. 240)

conduction hearing loss   hearing loss caused by damage to the mechanical system that conducts sound waves to the cochlea. (p. 217)

cones   retinal receptor cells that are concentrated near the center of the retina and that function in daylight or in well-lit conditions. The cones detect fine detail and give rise to color sensations. (p. 202)

confirmation bias   a tendency to search for information that supports our preconceptions and to ignore or distort contradictory evidence. (p. 307)

conflict   a perceived incompatibility of actions, goals, or ideas. (p. 497)

conformity   adjusting our behavior or thinking to coincide with a group standard. (p. 466)

confounding variable   a factor other than the independent variable that might produce an effect in an experiment. (p. 24)

consciousness   our awareness of ourselves and our environment. (p. 78)

conservation   the principle (which Piaget believed to be a part of concrete operational reasoning) that properties such as mass, volume, and number remain the same despite changes in the forms of objects. (p. 127)

content validity   the extent to which a test samples the behavior that is of interest. (p. 337)

continuous reinforcement   reinforcing the desired response every time it occurs. (p. 249)

control group   in an experiment, the group *not* exposed to the treatment; contrasts with the experimental group and serves as a comparison for evaluating the effect of the treatment. (p. 22)

convergent thinking   narrows the available problem solutions to determine the single best solution. (p. 314)

coping   alleviating stress using emotional, cognitive, or behavioral methods. (p. 401)

coronary heart disease   the clogging of the vessels that nourish the heart muscle; the leading cause of death in many developed countries. (p. 397)

corpus callosum   [KOR-pus kah-LOW-sum]   the large band of neural fibers connecting the two brain hemispheres and carrying messages between them. (p. 59)

correlation   a measure of the extent to which two factors vary together, and thus of how well either factor predicts the other. (p. 20)

correlation coefficient   a statistical index of the relationship between two things (from 1 to +1). (pp. 20, A-4)

counseling psychology   a branch of psychology that assists people with problems in living (often related to school, work, or relationships) and in achieving greater well-being. (p. 9)

counterconditioning   behavior therapy procedures that use classical conditioning to evoke new responses to stimuli that are triggering unwanted behaviors; include *exposure therapies* and *aversive conditioning*. (p. 551)

creativity   the ability to produce novel and valuable ideas. (p. 314)

critical period   an optimal period early in the life of an organism when exposure to certain stimuli or experiences produces normal development. (p. 123)

critical thinking   thinking that does not blindly accept arguments and conclusions. Rather, it examines assumptions, discerns hidden values, evaluates evidence, and assesses conclusions. (p. 15)

cross-sectional study   a study in which people of different ages are compared with one another. (pp. 153, A-7)

crystallized intelligence   our accumulated knowledge and verbal skills; tends to increase with age. (p. 337)

culture   the enduring behaviors, ideas, attitudes, values, and traditions shared by a group of people and transmitted from one generation to the next. (pp. 26, 463)

D

debriefing   the postexperimental explanation of a study, including its purpose and any deceptions, to its participants. (p. 28)

deep processing   encoding semantically, based on the meaning of the words; tends to yield the best retention. (p. 278)

defense mechanisms   in psychoanalytic theory, the ego's protective methods of reducing anxiety by unconsciously distorting reality. (p. 427)

deindividuation   the loss of self-awareness and self-restraint occurring in group situations that foster arousal and anonymity. (p. 472)

déjà vu   that eerie sense that "I've experienced this before." Cues from the current situation may subconsciously trigger retrieval of an earlier experience. (p. 296)

delta waves   the large, slow brain waves associated with deep sleep. (p. 85)

delusions   false beliefs, often of persecution or grandeur, that may accompany psychotic disorders. (p. 528)

dendrites   a neuron's bushy, branching extensions that receive messages and conduct impulses toward the cell body. (p. 36)

dependent variable   the outcome factor; the variable that may change in response to manipulations of the independent variable. (p. 24)

depressants   drugs (such as alcohol, barbiturates, and opiates) that reduce neural activity and slow body functions. (p. 102)

depth perception   the ability to see objects in three dimensions although the images that strike the retina are two-dimensional; allows us to judge distance. (p. 210)

developmental psychology   a branch of psychology that studies physical, cognitive, and social change throughout the life span. (p. 118)

difference threshold   the minimum difference between two stimuli required for detection 50 percent of the time. We experience the difference threshold as a *just noticeable difference* (or *jnd*). (p. 194)

discrimination   (1) in classical conditioning, the learned ability to distinguish between a conditioned stimulus and stimuli that do not signal an unconditioned stimulus. (2) in social psychology, unjustifiable negative behavior toward a group and its members. (pp. 244, 476)

dissociation   a split in consciousness, which allows some thoughts and behaviors to occur simultaneously with others. (p. 99)

dissociative disorders   disorders in which conscious awareness becomes separated (dissociated) from previous memories, thoughts, and feelings. (p. 534)

dissociative identity disorder (DID)   a rare dissociative disorder in which a person exhibits two or more distinct and alternating personalities. Formerly called multiple personality disorder. (p. 534)

divergent thinking expands the number of possible problem solutions (creative thinking that diverges in different directions). (p. 314)

DNA (*deoxyribonucleic acid*) a complex molecule containing the genetic information that makes up the chromosomes. (p. 62)

double-blind procedure an experimental procedure in which both the research participants and the research staff are ignorant (blind) about whether the research participants have received the treatment or a placebo. Commonly used in drug-evaluation studies. (p. 23)

Down syndrome a condition of mild to severe intellectual disability and associated physical disorders caused by an extra copy of chromosome 21. (p. 338)

dream a sequence of images, emotions, and thoughts passing through a sleeping person's mind. Dreams are notable for their hallucinatory imagery, discontinuities, and incongruities, and for the dreamer's delusional acceptance of the content and later difficulties remembering it. (p. 93)

drive-reduction theory the idea that a physiological need creates an aroused tension state (a drive) that motivates an organism to satisfy the need. (p. 353)

DSM-IV-TR the American Psychiatric Association's Diagnostic and Statistical Manual of Mental Disorders, Fourth Edition, with an updated "text revision"; a widely used system for classifying psychological disorders. (p. 509)

dual processing the principle that information is often simultaneously processed on separate conscious and unconscious tracks. (p. 79)

E

echoic memory a momentary sensory memory of auditory stimuli; if attention is elsewhere, sounds and words can still be recalled within 3 or 4 seconds. (p. 276)

eclectic approach an approach to psychotherapy that, depending on the client's problems, uses techniques from various forms of therapy. (p. 546)

Ecstasy (MDMA) a synthetic stimulant and mild hallucinogen. Produces euphoria and social intimacy, but with short-term health risks and longer-term harm to serotonin-producing neurons and to mood and cognition. (p. 107)

effortful processing encoding that requires attention and conscious effort. (p. 274)

ego the largely conscious, "executive" part of personality that, according to Freud, mediates among the demands of the id, superego, and reality. The ego operates on the *reality principle,* satisfying the id's desires in ways that will realistically bring pleasure rather than pain. (p. 425)

egocentrism in Piaget's theory, the preoperational child's difficulty taking another's point of view. (p. 128)

electroconvulsive therapy (ECT) a biomedical therapy for severely depressed patients in which a brief electric current is sent through the brain of an anesthetized patient. (p. 571)

electroencephalogram (EEG) an amplified recording of the waves of electrical activity sweeping across the brain's surface. These waves are measured by electrodes placed on the scalp. (p. 48)

embodied cognition the influence of bodily sensations, gestures, and other states on cognitive preferences and judgments. (p. 229)

embryo the developing human organism from about 2 weeks after fertilization through the second month. (p. 119)

emerging adulthood for some people in modern cultures, a period from the late teens to mid-twenties, bridging the gap between adolescent dependence and full independence and responsible adulthood. (p. 149)

emotion a response of the whole organism, involving (1) physiological arousal, (2) expressive behaviors, and (3) conscious experience. (p. 372)

emotional intelligence the ability to perceive, understand, manage, and use emotions. (p. 333)

emotion-focused coping attempting to alleviate stress by avoiding or ignoring a stressor and attending to emotional needs related to one's stress reaction. (p. 401)

empirically derived test a test (such as the MMPI) developed by testing a pool of items and then selecting those that discriminate between groups. (p. 437)

encoding the processing of information into the memory system-for example, by extracting meaning. (p. 273)

endocrine [EN-duh-krin] **system** the body's "slow" chemical communication system; a set of glands that secrete hormones into the bloodstream. (p. 45)

endorphins [en-DOR-fins] "morphine within"—natural, opiate-like neurotransmitters linked to pain control and to pleasure. (p. 40)

environment every nongenetic influence, from prenatal nutrition to the people and things around us. (p. 62)

epigenetics the study of environmental influences on gene expression that occur without a DNA change. (p. 67)

equity a condition in which people receive from a relationship in proportion to what they give to it. (p. 492)

estrogens sex hormones, such as estradiol, secreted in greater amounts by females than by males and contributing to female sex characteristics. In nonhuman female mammals, estrogen levels peak during ovulation, promoting sexual receptivity. (p. 171)

evidence-based practice clinical decision making that integrates the best available research with clinical expertise and patient characteristics and preferences. (p. 562)

evolutionary psychology the study of the evolution of behavior and the mind, using principles of natural selection. (p. 68)

experiment a research method in which an investigator manipulates one or more factors (independent variables) to observe the effect on some behavior or mental process (the dependent variable). By *random assignment* of participants, the experimenter aims to control other relevant factors. (p. 22)

experimental group in an experiment, the group exposed to the treatment, that is, to one version of the independent variable. (p. 22)

explicit memory memory of facts and experiences that one can consciously know and "declare." (Also called *declarative memory.*) (p. 274)

exposure therapies behavioral techniques, such as *systematic desensitization* and *virtual reality exposure therapy,* that treat anxieties by exposing people (in imagination or actual situations) to the things they fear and avoid. (p. 551)

external locus of control the perception that chance or outside forces beyond our personal control determine our fate. (p. 403)

extinction the diminishing of a conditioned response; occurs in classical conditioning when an unconditioned stimulus does not follow a conditioned stimulus; occurs in operant conditioning when a response is no longer reinforced. (p. 242)

extrasensory perception (ESP) the controversial claim that perception can occur apart from sensory input; includes telepathy, clairvoyance, and precognition. (p. 230)

extrinsic motivation a desire to perform a behavior to receive promised rewards or avoid threatened punishment. (p. 260)

F

facial feedback effect the tendency of facial muscle states to trigger corresponding feelings, such as fear, anger, or happiness. (p. 384)

family therapy therapy that treats the family as a system. Views an individual's unwanted behaviors as influenced by, or directed at, other family members. (p. 558)

feature detectors nerve cells in the brain that respond to specific features of the stimulus, such as shape, angle, or movement. (p. 204)

feel-good, do-good phenomenon people's tendency to be helpful when already in a good mood. (p. 413)

fetal alcohol syndrome (FAS) physical and cognitive abnormalities in children caused by a pregnant woman's heavy drinking. In severe cases, symptoms include noticeable facial misproportions. (p. 120)

fetus the developing human organism from 9 weeks after conception to birth. (p. 119)

figure-ground the organization of the visual field into objects (the *figures*) that stand out from their surroundings (the *ground*). (p. 209)

fixation according to Freud, a lingering focus of pleasure-seeking energies at an earlier psychosexual stage, in which conflicts were unresolved. (p. 426)

fixed-interval schedule in operant conditioning, a reinforcement schedule that reinforces a response only after a specified time has elapsed. (p. 250)

fixed-ratio schedule in operant conditioning, a reinforcement schedule that reinforces a response only after a specified number of responses. (p. 249)

flashbulb memory a clear memory of an emotionally significant moment or event. (p. 283)

flow a completely involved, focused state of consciousness, with diminished awareness of self and time, resulting from optimal engagement of one's skills. (p. B-1)

fluid intelligence our ability to reason speedily and abstractly; tends to decrease during late adulthood. (p. 337)

fMRI (functional MRI) a technique for revealing bloodflow and, therefore, brain activity by comparing successive MRI scans. fMRI scans show brain function. (p. 48)

foot-in-the-door phenomenon the tendency for people who have first agreed to a small request to comply later with a larger request. (p. 461)

formal operational stage in Piaget's theory, the stage of cognitive development (normally beginning about age 12) during which people begin to think logically about abstract concepts. (p. 129)

fovea the central focal point in the retina, around which the eye's cones cluster. (p. 203)

framing the way an issue is posed; how an issue is framed can significantly affect decisions and judgments. (p. 312)

fraternal twins twins who develop from separate (dizygotic) fertilized eggs. They are genetically no closer than ordinary brothers and sisters, but they share a fetal environment. (p. 63)

free association in psychoanalysis, a method of exploring the unconscious in which the person relaxes and says whatever comes to mind, no matter how trivial or embarrassing. (p. 424)

frequency the number of complete wavelengths that pass a point in a given time (for example, per second). (p. 216)

frequency theory in hearing, the theory that the rate of nerve impulses traveling up the auditory nerve matches the frequency of a tone, thus enabling us to sense its pitch. (p. 219)

frontal lobes portion of the cerebral cortex lying just behind the forehead; involved in speaking and muscle movements and in making plans and judgments. (p. 53)

frustration-aggression principle the principle that frustration—the blocking of an attempt to achieve some goal—creates anger, which can generate aggression. (p. 483)

functionalism early school of thought promoted by James and influenced by Darwin; explored how mental and behavioral processes function—how they enable the organism to adapt, survive, and flourish. (p. 3)

fundamental attribution error the tendency for observers, when analyzing another's behavior, to underestimate the impact of the situation and to overestimate the impact of personal disposition. (p. 458)

G

gate-control theory the theory that the spinal cord contains a neurological "gate" that blocks pain signals or allows them to pass on to the brain. The "gate" is opened by the activity of pain signals traveling up small nerve fibers and is closed by activity in larger fibers or by information coming from the brain. (p. 221)

gender the socially constructed roles and characteristics by which a culture defines *male* and *female*. (p. 164)

gender identity our sense of being male or female. (p. 170)

gender role a set of expected behaviors for males or for females. (p. 169)

gender-typing the acquisition of a traditional masculine or feminine role. (p. 170)

general adaptation syndrome (GAS) Selye's concept of the body's adaptive response to stress in three phases—alarm, resistance, exhaustion. (p. 393)

general intelligence (g) a general intelligence factor that, according to Spearman and others, underlies specific mental abilities and is therefore measured by every task on an intelligence test. (p. 330)

generalization the tendency, once a response has been conditioned, for stimuli similar to the conditioned stimulus to elicit similar responses. (p. 243)

generalized anxiety disorder an anxiety disorder in which a person is continually tense, apprehensive, and in a state of autonomic nervous system arousal. (p. 513)

genes the biochemical units of heredity that make up the chromosomes; segments of DNA capable of synthesizing proteins. (p. 62)

gestalt an organized whole. Gestalt psychologists emphasized our tendency to integrate pieces of information into meaningful wholes. (p. 208)

glial cells (glia) cells in the nervous system that support, nourish, and protect neurons; they may also play a role in learning and thinking. (p. 37)

glucose the form of sugar that circulates in the blood and provides the major source of energy for body tissues. When its level is low, we feel hunger. (p. 357)

grammar in a language, a system of rules that enables us to communicate with and understand others. In a given language, *semantics* is the set of rules for deriving meaning from sounds, and *syntax* is the set of rules for combining words into grammatically sensible sentences. (p. 319)

GRIT Graduated and Reciprocated Initiatives in Tension-Reduction—a strategy designed to decrease international tensions. (p. 500)

group polarization the enhancement of a group's prevailing inclinations through discussion within the group. (p. 473)

group therapy therapy conducted with groups rather than individuals, permitting therapeutic benefits from group interaction. (p. 557)

grouping the perceptual tendency to organize stimuli into coherent groups. (p. 209)

groupthink the mode of thinking that occurs when the desire for harmony in a decision-making group overrides a realistic appraisal of alternatives. (p. 474)

H

habituation decreasing responsiveness with repeated stimulation. As infants gain familiarity with repeated exposure to a visual stimulus, their interest wanes and they look away sooner. (p. 121)

hallucinations false sensory experiences, such as seeing something in the absence of an external visual stimulus. (p. 85)

hallucinogens psychedelic ("mind-manifesting") drugs, such as LSD, that distort perceptions and evoke sensory images in the absence of sensory input. (p. 107)

health psychology a subfield of psychology that provides psychology's contribution to behavioral medicine. (p. 394)

heritability the proportion of variation among individuals that we can attribute to genes. The heritability of a trait may vary, depending on the range of populations and environments studied. (p. 340)

heuristic a simple thinking strategy that often allows us to make judgments and solve problems efficiently; usually speedier but also more error prone than *algorithms*. (p. 307)

hierarchy of needs Maslow's pyramid of human needs, beginning at the base with physiological needs that must first be satisfied before higher-level safety needs and then psychological needs become active. (p. 355)

hindsight bias the tendency to believe, after learning an outcome, that one would have foreseen it. (Also known as the *I-knew-it-all-along phenomenon*.) (p. 11)

hippocampus a neural center located in the limbic system; helps process explicit memories for storage. (p. 281)

homeostasis a tendency to maintain a balanced or constant internal state; the regulation of any aspect of body chemistry, such as blood glucose, around a particular level. (p. 353)

hormones chemical messengers that are manufactured by the endocrine glands, travel through the bloodstream, and affect other tissues. (p. 45)

hue the dimension of color that is determined by the wavelength of light; what we know as the color names *blue, green*, and so forth. (p. 200)

human factors psychology an I/O psychology subfield that explores how people and machines interact and how machines and physical environments can be made safe and easy to use. (p. B-3)

humanistic psychology historically significant perspective that emphasized the growth potential of healthy people. (p. 4)

humanistic theories view personality with a focus on the potential for healthy personal growth. (p. 432)

hypnosis a social interaction in which one person (the hypnotist) suggests to another (the subject) that certain perceptions, feelings, thoughts, or behaviors will spontaneously occur. (p. 97)

hypothalamus [hi-po-THAL-uh-muss] a neural structure lying below *(hypo)* the thalamus; it directs several maintenance activities (eating, drinking, body temperature), helps govern the endocrine system via the pituitary gland, and is linked to emotion and reward. (p. 51)

hypothesis a testable prediction, often implied by a theory. (p. 16)

I

iconic memory a momentary sensory memory of visual stimuli; a photographic or picture-image memory lasting no more than a few tenths of a second. (p. 276)

id a reservoir of unconscious psychic energy that, according to Freud, strives to satisfy basic sexual and aggressive drives. The id operates on the *pleasure principle,* demanding immediate gratification. (p. 425)

identical twins twins who develop from a single (monozygotic) fertilized egg that splits in two, creating two genetically identical organisms. (p. 63)

identification the process by which, according to Freud, children incorporate their parents' values into their developing superegos. (p. 426)

identity our sense of self; according to Erikson, the adolescent's task is to solidify a sense of self by testing and integrating various roles. (p. 144)

implicit memory retention independent of conscious recollection. (Also called *nondeclarative memory*.) (p. 274)

imprinting the process by which certain animals form attachments during a critical period very early in life. (p. 133)

inattentional blindness failing to see visible objects when our attention is directed elsewhere. (p. 81)

incentive a positive or negative environmental stimulus that motivates behavior. (p. 353)

independent variable the experimental factor that is manipulated; the variable whose effect is being studied. (p. 24)

individualism giving priority to one's own goals over group goals and defining one's identity in terms of personal attributes rather than group identifications. (p. 451)

industrial-organizational (I/O) psychology the application of psychological concepts and methods to optimizing human behavior in workplaces. (p. B-2)

informational social influence influence resulting from one's willingness to accept others' opinions about reality. (p. 467)

informed consent giving potential participants enough information about a study to enable them to decide whether they wish to participate. (p. 28)

ingroup "Us"—people with whom we share a common identity. (p. 478)

ingroup bias the tendency to favor our own group. (p. 478)

inner ear the innermost part of the ear, containing the cochlea, semicircular canals, and vestibular sacs. (p. 216)

insight a sudden realization of a problem's solution; contrasts with strategy-based solutions. (p. 307)

insight therapies a variety of therapies that aim to improve psychological functioning by increasing a person's awareness of underlying motives and defenses. (p. 548)

insomnia recurring problems in falling or staying asleep. (p. 91)

instinct a complex behavior that is rigidly patterned throughout a species and is unlearned. (p. 352)

intellectual disability a condition of limited mental ability, indicated by an intelligence test score of 70 or below and difficulty in adapting to the demands of life. (Formerly referred to as *mental retardation*.) (p. 338)

intelligence mental quality consisting of the ability to learn from experience, solve problems, and use knowledge to adapt to new situations. (p. 329)

intelligence quotient (IQ) defined originally as the ratio of mental age *(ma)* to chronological age *(ca)* multiplied by 100 (thus, $IQ = ma/ca \times 100$). On contemporary intelligence tests, the average performance for a given age is assigned a score of 100. (p. 334)

intelligence test a method for assessing an individual's mental aptitudes and comparing them with those of others, using numerical scores. (p. 333)

intensity the amount of energy in a light or sound wave, which we perceive as brightness or loudness, as determined by the wave's amplitude. (p. 200)

interaction the interplay that occurs when the effect of one factor (such as environment) depends on another factor (such as heredity). (p. 67)

internal locus of control the perception that you control your own fate. (p. 403)

interneurons neurons within the brain and spinal cord that communicate internally and intervene between the sensory inputs and motor outputs. (p. 41)

interpretation in psychoanalysis, the analyst's noting supposed dream meanings, resistances, and other significant behaviors and events in order to promote insight. (p. 547)

intimacy in Erikson's theory, the ability to form close, loving relationships; a primary developmental task in late adolescence and early adulthood. (p. 145)

intrinsic motivation a desire to perform a behavior effectively for its own sake. (p. 260)

intuition an effortless, immediate, automatic feeling or thought, as contrasted with explicit, conscious reasoning. (p. 308)

J

James-Lange theory the theory that our experience of emotion is our awareness of our physiological responses to emotion-arousing stimuli. (p. 372)

just-world phenomenon the tendency for people to believe the world is just and that people therefore get what they deserve and deserve what they get. (p. 478)

K

kinesthesis [kin-ehs-THEE-sehs] the system for sensing the position and movement of individual body parts. (p. 227)

L

language our spoken, written, or signed words and the ways we combine them to communicate meaning. (p. 318)

latent content according to Freud, the underlying meaning of a dream (as distinct from its manifest content). (p. 95)

latent learning learning that occurs but is not apparent until there is an incentive to demonstrate it. (p. 260)

law of effect Thorndike's principle that behaviors followed by favorable consequences become more likely, and that behaviors followed by unfavorable consequences become less likely. (p. 246)

learned helplessness the hopelessness and passive resignation an animal or human learns when unable to avoid repeated aversive events. (p. 402)

learning the process of acquiring through experience new and relatively enduring information or behaviors. (p. 238)

lesion [LEE-zhuhn] tissue destruction. A brain lesion is a naturally or experimentally caused destruction of brain tissue. (p. 46)

levels of analysis the differing complementary views, from biological to psychological to social-cultural, for analyzing any given phenomenon. (p. 6)

limbic system neural system (including the *hippocampus, amygdala,* and *hypothalamus*) located below the cerebral hemispheres; associated with emotions and drives. (p. 50)

linguistic determinism Whorf's hypothesis that language determines the way we think. (p. 326)

lobotomy a psychosurgical procedure once used to calm uncontrollably emotional or violent patients. The procedure cut the nerves connecting the frontal lobes to the emotion-controlling centers of the inner brain. (p. 574)

longitudinal study research in which the same people are restudied and retested over a long period of time. (pp. 153, A-7)

long-term memory the relatively permanent and limitless storehouse of the memory system. Includes knowledge, skills, and experiences. (p. 273)

long-term potentiation (LTP) an increase in a cell's firing potential after brief, rapid stimulation. Believed to be a neural basis for learning and memory. (p. 284)

LSD a powerful hallucinogenic drug; also known as acid *(lysergic acid diethylamide).* (p. 107)

M

major depressive disorder a mood disorder in which a person experiences, in the absence of drugs or another medical condition, two or more weeks of significantly depressed moods or diminished interest or pleasure in most activities, along with at least four other symptoms. (p. 520)

mania a hyperactive, wildly optimistic state in which dangerously poor judgment is common. (p. 520)

manifest content according to Freud, the remembered story line of a dream (as distinct from its latent, or hidden, content). (p. 94)

maturation biological growth processes that enable orderly changes in behavior, relatively uninfluenced by experience. (p. 121)

mean the arithmetic average of a distribution, obtained by adding the scores and then dividing by the number of scores. (p. A-2)

median the middle score in a distribution; half the scores are above it and half are below it. (p. A-2)

medical model the concept that diseases, in this case psychological disorders, have physical causes that can be diagnosed, treated, and, in most cases, cured, often through treatment in a hospital. (p. 507)

medulla [muh-DUL-uh] the base of the brainstem; controls heartbeat and breathing. (p. 47)

memory the persistence of learning over time through the storage and retrieval of information. (p. 272)

menarche [meh-NAR-key] the first menstrual period. (p. 167)

menopause the time of natural cessation of menstruation; also refers to the biological changes a woman experiences as her ability to reproduce declines. (p. 151)

mental age a measure of intelligence test performance devised by Binet; the chronological age that most typically corresponds to a given level of performance. Thus, a child who does as well as an average 8-year-old is said to have a mental age of 8. (p. 334)

mental set a tendency to approach a problem in one particular way, often a way that has been successful in the past. (p. 308)

mere exposure effect the phenomenon that repeated exposure to novel stimuli increases liking of them. (p. 488)

methamphetamine a powerfully addictive drug that stimulates the central nervous system, with speeded-up body functions and associated energy and mood changes; over time, appears to reduce baseline dopamine levels. (p. 106)

middle ear the chamber between the eardrum and cochlea containing three tiny bones (hammer, anvil, and stirrup) that concentrate the vibrations of the eardrum on the cochlea's oval window. (p. 216)

Minnesota Multiphasic Personality Inventory (MMPI) the most widely researched and clinically used of all personality tests. Originally developed to identify emotional disorders (still considered its most appropriate use), this test is now used for many other screening purposes. (p. 437)

mirror neurons frontal lobe neurons that some scientists believe fire when performing certain actions or when observing another doing so. The brain's mirroring of another's action may enable imitation and empathy. (p. 262)

mirror-image perceptions mutual views often held by conflicting people, as when each side sees itself as ethical and peaceful and views the other side as evil and aggressive. (p. 498)

misinformation effect incorporating misleading information into one's memory of an event. (p. 295)

mnemonics [nih-MON-iks] memory aids, especially those techniques that use vivid imagery and organizational devices. (p. 277)

mode the most frequently occurring score(s) in a distribution. (p. A-2)

modeling the process of observing and imitating a specific behavior. (p. 261)

monocular cues depth cues, such as interposition and linear perspective, available to either eye alone. (p. 211)

mood disorders psychological disorders characterized by emotional extremes. See major depressive disorder, mania, and bipolar disorder. (p. 519)

mood-congruent memory the tendency to recall experiences that are consistent with one's current good or bad mood. (p. 288)

morpheme in a language, the smallest unit that carries meaning; may be a word or a part of a word (such as a prefix). (p. 319)

motivation   a need or desire that energizes and directs behavior. (p. 352)

motor cortex   an area at the rear of the frontal lobes that controls voluntary movements. (p. 54)

motor (efferent) neurons   neurons that carry outgoing information from the brain and spinal cord to the muscles and glands. (p. 41)

MRI (magnetic resonance imaging) a technique that uses magnetic fields and radio waves to produce computer-generated images of soft tissue. MRI scans show brain anatomy. (p. 48)

mutation   a random error in gene replication that leads to a change. (p. 69)

myelin [MY-uh-lin] **sheath**   a fatty tissue layer segmentally encasing the axons of some neurons; enables vastly greater transmission speed as neural impulses hop from one node to the next. (p. 37)

N

narcissism   excessive self-love and self-absorption. (p. 449)

narcolepsy   a sleep disorder characterized by uncontrollable sleep attacks. The sufferer may lapse directly into REM sleep, often at inopportune times. (p. 92)

natural selection   the principle that, among the range of inherited trait variations, those contributing to reproduction and survival will most likely be passed on to succeeding generations. (pp. 6, 68)

naturalistic observation   observing and recording behavior in naturally occurring situations without trying to manipulate and control the situation. (p. 18)

nature–nurture issue   the longstanding controversy over the relative contributions that genes and experience make to the development of psychological traits and behaviors. Today's psychological science sees traits and behaviors arising from the interaction of nature and nurture. (p. 5)

near–death experience   an altered state of consciousness reported after a close brush with death (such as through cardiac arrest); often similar to drug-induced hallucinations. (p. 107)

negative reinforcement   increasing behaviors by stopping or reducing negative stimuli. A negative reinforcer is any stimulus that, when *removed* after a response, strengthens the response. (*Note:* Negative reinforcement is not punishment.) (p. 248)

nerves   bundled axons that form neural "cables" connecting the central nervous system with muscles, glands, and sense organs. (p. 41)

nervous system   the body's speedy, electrochemical communication network, consisting of all the nerve cells of the peripheral and central nervous systems. (p. 41)

neurogenesis   the formation of new neurons. (p. 58)

neuron   a nerve cell; the basic building block of the nervous system. (p. 36)

neurotransmitters   chemical messengers that cross the synaptic gaps between neurons. When released by the sending neuron, neurotransmitters travel across the synapse and bind to receptor sites on the receiving neuron, thereby influencing whether that neuron will generate a neural impulse. (p. 39)

neutral stimulus (NS)   in classical conditioning, a stimulus that elicits no response before conditioning. (p. 240)

nicotine   a stimulating and highly addictive psychoactive drug in tobacco. (p. 104)

night terrors   a sleep disorder characterized by high arousal and an appearance of being terrified; unlike nightmares, night terrors occur during NREM-3 sleep, within two or three hours of falling asleep, and are seldom remembered. (p. 93)

norm   an understood rule for accepted and expected behavior. Norms prescribe "proper" behavior. (p. 464)

normal curve   *(normal distribution)* a symmetrical, bell-shaped curve that describes the distribution of many types of data; most scores fall near the mean (about 68 percent fall within one standard deviation of it) and fewer and fewer near the extremes. (pp. 336, A-4)

normative social influence   influence resulting from a person's desire to gain approval or avoid disapproval. (p. 467)

O

object permanence   the awareness that things continue to exist even when not perceived. (p. 126)

observational learning   learning by observing others. (p. 261)

obsessive-compulsive disorder (OCD) an anxiety disorder characterized by unwanted repetitive thoughts (obsessions), actions (compulsions), or both. (p. 514)

occipital [ahk-SIP-uh-tuhl] **lobes**   portion of the cerebral cortex lying at the back of the head; includes areas that receive information from the visual fields. (p. 53)

Oedipus [ED-uh-puss] **complex**   according to Freud, a boy's sexual desires toward his mother and feelings of jealousy and hatred for the rival father. (p. 426)

one–word stage   the stage in speech development, from about age 1 to 2, during which a child speaks mostly in single words. (p. 320)

operant behavior   behavior that operates on the environment, producing consequences. (p. 256)

operant chamber   in operant conditioning research, a chamber (also known as a *Skinner box*) containing a bar or key that an animal can manipulate to obtain a food or water reinforcer; attached devices record the animal's rate of bar pressing or key pecking. (p. 246)

operant conditioning   a type of learning in which behavior is strengthened if followed by a reinforcer or diminished if followed by a punisher. (p. 246)

operational definition   a statement of the procedures (operations) used to define research variables. For example, *human intelligence* may be operationally defined as "what an intelligence test measures." (p. 16)

opiates   opium and its derivatives, such as morphine and heroin; they depress neural activity, temporarily lessening pain and anxiety. (p. 103)

opponent-process theory   the theory that opposing retinal processes (red-green, yellow-blue, white-black) enable color vision. For example, some cells are stimulated by green and inhibited by red; others are stimulated by red and inhibited by green. (p. 207)

optic nerve   the nerve that carries neural impulses from the eye to the brain. (p. 202)

organizational psychology   an I/O psychology subfield that examines organizational influences on worker satisfaction and productivity and facilitates organizational change. (p. B-2)

other-race effect   the tendency to recall faces of one's own race more accurately than faces of other races. Also called the *cross-race effect* and the *own-race bias*. (p. 480)

outgroup   "Them"—those perceived as different or apart from our ingroup. (p. 478)

overconfidence   the tendency to be more confident than correct—to overestimate the accuracy of our beliefs and judgments. (p. 311)

P

panic disorder   an anxiety disorder marked by unpredictable, minutes-long episodes of intense dread in which a person experiences terror and accompanying chest pain, choking, or other frightening sensations. (p. 513)

parallel processing   the processing of many aspects of a problem simultaneously; the brain's natural mode of information processing for many functions, including vision. Contrasts with the step-by-step (serial) processing of most computers and of conscious problem solving. (p. 205)

parapsychology   the study of paranormal phenomena, including ESP and psychokinesis. (p. 230)

parasympathetic nervous system   the division of the autonomic nervous system that calms the body, conserving its energy. (p. 42)

parietal [puh-RYE-uh-tuhl] **lobes**   portion of the cerebral cortex lying at the top of the head and toward the rear; receives sensory input for touch and body position. (p. 53)

partial (intermittent) reinforcement   reinforcing a response only part of the time; results in slower acquisition of a response but much greater resistance to extinction than does continuous reinforcement. (p. 249)

passionate love   an aroused state of intense positive absorption in another, usually present at the beginning of a love relationship. (p. 492)

perception   the process of organizing and interpreting sensory information, enabling us to recognize meaningful objects and events. (p. 192)

perceptual adaptation   in vision, the ability to adjust to an artificially displaced or even inverted visual field. (p. 215)

perceptual constancy   perceiving objects as unchanging (having consistent color, brightness, shape, and size) even as illumination and retinal images change. (p. 212)

perceptual set   a mental predisposition to perceive one thing and not another. (p. 197)

peripheral nervous system (PNS)   the sensory and motor neurons that connect the central nervous system (CNS) to the rest of the body. (p. 41)

peripheral route persuasion   occurs when people are influenced by incidental cues, such as a speaker's attractiveness. (p. 460)

personality   an individual's characteristic pattern of thinking, feeling, and acting. (p. 423)

personality disorders   psychological disorders characterized by inflexible and enduring behavior patterns that impair social functioning. (p. 537)

personality inventory   a questionnaire (often with *true-false* or *agree-disagree* items) on which people respond to items designed to gauge a wide range of feelings and behaviors; used to assess selected personality traits. (p. 437)

personnel psychology   an I/O psychology subfield that focuses on employee recruitment, selection, placement, training, appraisal, and development. (p. B-2)

PET (positron emission tomography) scan   a visual display of brain activity that detects where a radioactive form of glucose goes while the brain performs a given task. (p. 48)

phobia   an anxiety disorder marked by a persistent, irrational fear and avoidance of a specific object, activity, or situation. (p. 513)

phoneme   in a language, the smallest distinctive sound unit. (p. 319)

physical dependence   a physiological need for a drug, marked by unpleasant withdrawal symptoms when the drug is discontinued. (p. 102)

pitch   a tone's experienced highness or lowness; depends on frequency. (p. 216)

pituitary gland   the endocrine system's most influential gland. Under the influence of the hypothalamus, the pituitary regulates growth and controls other endocrine glands. (p. 45)

place theory   in hearing, the theory that links the pitch we hear with the place where the cochlea's membrane is stimulated. (p. 219)

placebo [pluh-SEE-bo; Latin for "I shall please"] **effect**   experimental results caused by expectations alone; any effect on behavior caused by the administration of an inert substance or condition, which the recipient assumes is an active agent. (p. 23)

plasticity   the brain's ability to change, especially during childhood, by reorganizing after damage or by building new pathways based on experience. (p. 57)

polygraph   a machine, commonly used in attempts to detect lies, that measures several of the physiological responses (such as perspiration and cardiovascular and breathing changes) accompanying emotion. (p. 379)

population   all those in a group being studied, from which samples may be drawn. (*Note:* Except for national studies, this does *not* refer to a country's whole population.) (p. 20)

positive psychology   the scientific study of human functioning, with the goals of discovering and promoting strengths and virtues that help individuals and communities to thrive. (pp. 9, 413)

positive reinforcement   increasing behaviors by presenting positive reinforcers. A positive reinforcer is any stimulus that, when *presented* after a response, strengthens the response. (p. 248)

posthypnotic suggestion   a suggestion, made during a hypnosis session, to be carried out after the subject is no longer hypnotized; used by some clinicians to help control undesired symptoms and behaviors. (p. 98)

post-traumatic stress disorder (PTSD) an anxiety disorder characterized by haunting memories, nightmares, social withdrawal, jumpy anxiety, and/or insomnia that lingers for four weeks or more after a traumatic experience. (p. 515)

predictive validity   the success with which a test predicts the behavior it is designed to predict; it is assessed by computing the correlation between test scores and the criterion behavior. (Also called *criterion-related validity.*) (p. 337)

prejudice   an unjustifiable and usually negative attitude toward a group and its members. Prejudice generally involves stereotyped beliefs, negative feelings, and a predisposition to discriminatory action. (p. 476)

preoperational stage   in Piaget's theory, the stage (from about 2 to about 6 or 7 years of age) during which a child learns to use language but does not yet comprehend the mental operations of concrete logic. (p. 127)

primary reinforcer   an innately reinforcing stimulus, such as one that satisfies a biological need. (p. 248)

primary sex characteristics   the body structures (ovaries, testes, and external genitalia) that make sexual reproduction possible. (p. 167)

priming   the activation, often unconsciously, of certain associations, thus predisposing one's perception, memory, or response. (pp. 194, 287)

proactive interference   the disruptive effect of prior learning on the recall of new information. (p. 292)

problem-focused coping   attempting to alleviate stress directly—by changing the stressor or the way we interact with that stressor. (p. 401)

projective test   a personality test, such as the Rorschach, that provides ambiguous stimuli designed to trigger projection of one's inner dynamics. (p. 429)

prosocial behavior   positive, constructive, helpful behavior. The opposite of antisocial behavior. (p. 263)

prototype   a mental image or best example of a category. Matching new items to a prototype provides a quick and easy method for sorting items into categories (as when comparing feathered creatures to a prototypical bird, such as a robin). (p. 306)

psychiatry   a branch of medicine dealing with psychological disorders; practiced by physicians who sometimes provide medical (for example, drug) treatments as well as psychological therapy. (p. 9)

psychoactive drug   a chemical substance that alters perceptions and moods. (p. 100)

psychoanalysis   (1) Sigmund Freud's theory of personality that attributes thoughts and actions to unconscious motives and conflicts. (2) Freud's therapeutic technique used in treating psychological disorders. Freud believed that the patient's free associations, resistances, dreams, and transferences—and the therapist's interpretations of them—released previously repressed feelings, allowing the patient to gain self-insight. (pp. 424, 547)

psychodynamic theories view personality with a focus on the unconscious and the importance of childhood experiences. (p. 424)

psychodynamic therapy therapy deriving from the psychoanalytic tradition; views individuals as responding to unconscious forces and childhood experiences, and seeks to enhance self-insight. (p. 548)

psychological dependence a psychological need to use a drug, such as to relieve negative emotions. (p. 102)

psychological disorder a significant dysfunction in a person's thoughts, feelings, or behaviors. (p. 506)

psychology the science of behavior and mental processes. (p. 4)

psychoneuroimmunology the study of how psychological, neural, and endocrine processes together affect the immune system and resulting health. (p. 394)

psychopharmacology the study of the effects of drugs on mind and behavior. (p. 568)

psychosexual stages the childhood stages of development (oral, anal, phallic, latency, genital) during which, according to Freud, the id's pleasure-seeking energies focus on distinct erogenous zones. (p. 426)

psychosis a psychological disorder in which a person loses contact with reality, experiencing irrational ideas and distorted perceptions. (p. 528)

psychosurgery surgery that removes or destroys brain tissue in an effort to change behavior. (p. 574)

psychotherapy treatment involving psychological techniques; consists of interactions between a trained therapist and someone seeking to overcome psychological difficulties or achieve personal growth. (p. 546)

puberty the period of sexual maturation, during which a person becomes capable of reproducing. (pp. 140, 167)

punishment an event that tends to *decrease* the behavior it follows. (p. 251)

R

random assignment assigning participants to experimental and control groups by chance, thus minimizing preexisting differences between the different groups. (p. 22)

random sample a sample that fairly represents a population because each member has an equal chance of inclusion. (p. 20)

range the difference between the highest and lowest scores in a distribution. (p. A-3)

recall a measure of memory in which the person must retrieve information learned earlier, as on a fill-in-the-blank test. (p. 272)

reciprocal determinism the interacting influences of behavior, internal cognition, and environment. (p. 443)

reciprocity norm an expectation that people will help, not hurt, those who have helped them. (p. 496)

recognition a measure of memory in which the person need only identify items previously learned, as on a multiple-choice test. (p. 272)

reflex a simple, automatic response to a sensory stimulus, such as the knee-jerk response. (p. 44)

refractory period a resting period after orgasm, during which a man cannot achieve another orgasm. (p. 173)

regression toward the mean the tendency for extreme or unusual scores or events to fall back (regress) toward the average. (p. A-6)

reinforcement in operant conditioning, any event that *strengthens* the behavior it follows. (p. 247)

reinforcement schedule a pattern that defines how often a desired response will be reinforced. (p. 249)

relative deprivation the perception that one is worse off relative to those with whom one compares oneself. (p. 417)

relearning a measure of memory that assesses the amount of time saved when learning material again. (p. 272)

reliability the extent to which a test yields consistent results, as assessed by the consistency of scores on two halves of the test, or on retesting. (p. 336)

REM rebound the tendency for REM sleep to increase following REM sleep deprivation (created by repeated awakenings during REM sleep). (p. 96)

REM sleep rapid eye movement sleep; a recurring sleep stage during which vivid dreams commonly occur. Also known as *paradoxical sleep,* because the muscles are relaxed (except for minor twitches) but other body systems are active. (p. 84)

repetitive transcranial magnetic stimulation (rTMS) the application of repeated pulses of magnetic energy to the brain; used to stimulate or suppress brain activity. (p. 573)

replication repeating the essence of a research study, usually with different participants in different situations, to see whether the basic finding extends to other participants and circumstances. (p. 16)

repression in psychoanalytic theory, the basic defense mechanism that banishes from consciousness anxiety-arousing thoughts, feelings, and memories. (pp. 294, 427)

resilience the personal strength that helps most people cope with stress and recover from adversity and even trauma. (p. 576)

resistance in psychoanalysis, the blocking from consciousness of anxiety-laden material. (p. 547)

respondent behavior behavior that occurs as an automatic response to some stimulus. (p. 254)

reticular formation a nerve network that travels through the brainstem and plays an important role in controlling arousal. (p. 49)

retina the light-sensitive inner surface of the eye, containing the receptor rods and cones plus layers of neurons that begin the processing of visual information. (p. 201)

retinal disparity a binocular cue for perceiving depth: By comparing images from the retinas in the two eyes, the brain computes distance—the greater the disparity (difference) between the two images, the closer the object. (p. 210)

retrieval the process of getting information out of memory storage. (p. 273)

retroactive interference the disruptive effect of new learning on the recall of old information. (p. 293)

retrograde amnesia an inability to retrieve information from one's past. (p. 290)

rods retinal receptors that detect black, white, and gray; necessary for peripheral and twilight vision, when cones don't respond. (p. 202)

role a set of expectations (norms) about a social position, defining how those in the position ought to behave. (pp. 169, 461)

Rorschach inkblot test the most widely used projective test, a set of 10 inkblots, designed by Hermann Rorschach; seeks to identify people's inner feelings by analyzing their interpretations of the blots. (p. 429)

S

savant syndrome a condition in which a person otherwise limited in mental ability has an exceptional specific skill, such as in computation or drawing. (p. 330)

scapegoat theory the theory that prejudice offers an outlet for anger by providing someone to blame. (p. 479)

scatterplot a graphed cluster of dots, each of which represents the values of two variables. The slope of the points suggests the direction of the relationship between the two variables. The amount of scatter suggests the strength of the correlation (little scatter indicates high correlation). (p. A-4)

schema a concept or framework that organizes and interprets information. (p. 125)

schizophrenia a group of severe disorders characterized by disorganized and delusional thinking, disturbed perceptions, and inappropriate emotions and behaviors. (p. 528)

secondary sex characteristics nonreproductive sexual traits, such as female breasts and hips, male voice quality, and body hair. (p. 167)

selective attention the focusing of conscious awareness on a particular stimulus. (p. 80)

self in contemporary psychology, assumed to be the center of personality, the organizer of our thoughts, feelings, and actions. (p. 447)

self-actualization according to Maslow, one of the ultimate psychological needs that arises after basic physical and psychological needs are met and self-esteem is achieved; the motivation to fulfill one's potential. (p. 433)

self-concept all our thoughts and feelings about ourselves, in answer to the question, "Who am I?" (p. 434)

self-control the ability to control impulses and delay short-term gratification for greater long-term rewards. (p. 403)

self-disclosure revealing intimate aspects of oneself to others. (p. 492)

self-efficacy one's sense of competence and effectiveness. (p. 447)

self-esteem one's feelings of high or low self-worth. (p. 447)

self-serving bias a readiness to perceive oneself favorably. (p. 448)

sensation the process by which our sensory receptors and nervous system receive and represent stimulus energies from our environment. (p. 192)

sensorimotor stage in Piaget's theory, the stage (from birth to about 2 years of age) during which infants know the world mostly in terms of their sensory impressions and motor activities. (p. 126)

sensorineural hearing loss hearing loss caused by damage to the cochlea's receptor cells or to the auditory nerves; also called *nerve deafness*. (p. 217)

sensory (afferent) neurons neurons that carry incoming information from the sensory receptors to the brain and spinal cord. (p. 41)

sensory adaptation diminished sensitivity as a consequence of constant stimulation. (p. 196)

sensory cortex area at the front of the parietal lobes that registers and processes body touch and movement sensations. (p. 55)

sensory interaction the principle that one sense may influence another, as when the smell of food influences its taste. (p. 228)

sensory memory the immediate, very brief recording of sensory information in the memory system. (p. 273)

serial position effect our tendency to recall best the last (a *recency effect*) and first items (a *primacy effect*) in a list. (p. 288)

set point the point at which your "weight thermostat" is supposedly set. When your body falls below this weight, increased hunger and a lowered metabolic rate may combine to restore the lost weight. (p. 358)

sexual dysfunction a problem that consistently impairs sexual arousal or functioning. (p. 173)

sexual orientation an enduring sexual attraction toward members of either one's own sex (homosexual orientation), the other sex (heterosexual orientation), or both sexes (bisexual orientation). (p. 178)

sexual response cycle the four stages of sexual responding described by Masters and Johnson—excitement, plateau, orgasm, and resolution. (p. 173)

shallow processing encoding on a basic level based on the structure or appearance of words. (p. 278)

shaping an operant conditioning procedure in which reinforcers guide behavior toward closer and closer approximations of the desired behavior. (p. 247)

short-term memory activated memory that holds a few items briefly, such as seven digits of a phone number while dialing, before the information is stored or forgotten. (p. 273)

signal detection theory a theory predicting how and when we detect the presence of a faint stimulus *(signal)* amid background stimulation *(noise)*. Assumes there is no single absolute threshold and that detection depends partly on a person's experience, expectations, motivation, and alertness. (p. 193)

sleep periodic, natural loss of consciousness—as distinct from unconsciousness resulting from a coma, general anesthesia, or hibernation. (Adapted from Dement, 1999.) (p. 85)

sleep apnea a sleep disorder characterized by temporary cessations of breathing during sleep and repeated momentary awakenings. (p. 92)

social clock the culturally preferred timing of social events such as marriage, parenthood, and retirement. (p. 154)

social exchange theory the theory that our social behavior is an exchange process, the aim of which is to maximize benefits and minimize costs. (p. 496)

social facilitation improved performance on simple or well-learned tasks in the presence of others. (p. 471)

social identity the "we" aspect of our self-concept; the part of our answer to "Who am I?" that comes from our group memberships. (p. 144)

social leadership group-oriented leadership that builds teamwork, mediates conflict, and offers support. (p. B-11)

social learning theory the theory that we learn social behavior by observing and imitating and by being rewarded or punished. (p. 170)

social loafing the tendency for people in a group to exert less effort when pooling their efforts toward attaining a common goal than when individually accountable. (p. 472)

social psychology the scientific study of how we think about, influence, and relate to one another. (p. 458)

social script culturally modeled guide for how to act in various situations. (p. 484)

social trap a situation in which the conflicting parties, by each rationally pursuing their self-interest, become caught in mutually destructive behavior. (p. 497)

social-cognitive perspective views behavior as influenced by the interaction between people's traits (including their thinking) and their social context. (p. 443)

social-responsibility norm an expectation that people will help those dependent upon them. (p. 496)

somatic nervous system the division of the peripheral nervous system that controls the body's skeletal muscles. Also called the *skeletal nervous system*. (p. 42)

source amnesia attributing to the wrong source an event we have experienced, heard about, read about, or imagined. (Also called *source misattribution*.) Source amnesia, along with the misinformation effect, is at the heart of many false memories. (p. 296)

spacing effect the tendency for distributed study or practice to yield better long-term retention than is achieved through massed study or practice. (p. 278)

split brain a condition resulting from surgery that isolates the brain's two hemispheres by cutting the fibers (mainly those of the corpus callosum) connecting them. (p. 59)

spontaneous recovery the reappearance, after a pause, of an extinguished conditioned response. (p. 242)

spotlight effect overestimating others' noticing and evaluating our appearance, performance, and blunders (as if we presume a spotlight shines on us). (p. 447)

SQ3R a study method incorporating five steps: *S*urvey, *Q*uestion, *R*ead, *R*etrieve, *R*eview. (p. 29)

standard deviation a computed measure of how much scores vary around the mean score. (p. A-3)

standardization defining uniform testing procedures and meaningful scores by comparison with the performance of a pretested group. (p. 336)

Stanford–Binet the widely used American revision (by Terman at Stanford University) of Binet's original intelligence test. (p. 334)

statistical significance a statistical statement of how likely it is that an obtained result occurred by chance. (p. A-8)

stereotype a generalized (sometimes accurate but often overgeneralized) belief about a group of people. (p. 476)

stereotype threat a self-confirming concern that one will be evaluated based on a negative stereotype. (p. 346)

stimulants drugs (such as caffeine, nicotine, and the more powerful amphetamines, cocaine, Ecstasy, and methamphetamine) that excite neural activity and speed up body functions. (p. 104)

stimulus any event or situation that evokes a response. (p. 238)

storage the retention of encoded information over time. (p. 273)

stranger anxiety the fear of strangers that infants commonly display, beginning by about 8 months of age. (p. 132)

stress the process by which we perceive and respond to certain events, called *stressors,* that we appraise as threatening or challenging. (p. 390)

structuralism early school of thought promoted by Wundt and Titchener; used introspection to reveal the structure of the human mind. (p. 3)

structured interview interview process that asks the same job-relevant questions of all applicants, each of whom is rated on established scales. (p. B-5)

subjective well-being self-perceived happiness or satisfaction with life. Used along with measures of objective well-being (for example, physical and economic indicators) to evaluate people's quality of life. (p. 413)

subliminal below one's absolute threshold for conscious awareness. (p. 194)

superego the part of personality that, according to Freud, represents internalized ideals and provides standards for judgment (the conscience) and for future aspirations. (p. 425)

superordinate goals shared goals that override differences among people and require their cooperation. (p. 499)

suprachiasmatic nucleus (SCN) a pair of cell clusters in the hypothalamus that responds to light-sensitive retinal proteins; causes pineal gland to increase or decrease production of melatonin, thus modifying our feelings of sleepiness. (p. 87)

survey a technique for ascertaining the self-reported attitudes or behaviors of a particular group, usually by questioning a representative, random sample of the group. (p. 19)

sympathetic nervous system the division of the autonomic nervous system that arouses the body, mobilizing its energy in stressful situations. (p. 42)

synapse [SIN-aps] the junction between the axon tip of the sending neuron and the dendrite or cell body of the receiving neuron. The tiny gap at this junction is called the *synaptic gap* or *synaptic cleft*. (p. 39)

systematic desensitization a type of exposure therapy that associates a pleasant relaxed state with gradually increasing anxiety-triggering stimuli. Commonly used to treat phobias. (p. 551)

T

task leadership goal-oriented leadership that sets standards, organizes work, and focuses attention on goals. (p. B-11)

telegraphic speech early speech stage in which a child speaks like a telegram—"go car"—using mostly nouns and verbs. (p. 320)

temperament a person's characteristic emotional reactivity and intensity. (p. 134)

temporal lobes portion of the cerebral cortex lying roughly above the ears; includes the auditory areas, each receiving information primarily from the opposite ear. (p. 53)

tend and befriend under stress, people (especially women) often provide support to others (tend) and bond with and seek support from others (befriend). (p. 393)

teratogens (literally, "monster maker") agents, such as toxins, chemicals, and viruses, that can reach the embryo or fetus during prenatal development and cause harm. (p. 120)

testing effect enhanced memory after retrieving, rather than simply rereading, information. Also sometimes referred to as a *retrieval practice effect* or *test-enhanced learning*. (pp. 29, 278)

testosterone the most important of the male sex hormones. Both males and females have it, but the additional testosterone in males stimulates the growth of the male sex organs in the fetus and the development of the male sex characteristics during puberty. (p. 167)

thalamus [THAL-uh-muss] the brain's sensory router, located on top of the brainstem; it directs messages to the sensory receiving areas in the cortex and transmits replies to the cerebellum and medulla. (p. 48)

THC the major active ingredient in marijuana; triggers a variety of effects, including mild hallucinations. (p. 108)

theory an explanation using an integrated set of principles that organizes observations and predicts behaviors or events. (p. 15)

theory of mind people's ideas about their own and others' mental states—about their feelings, perceptions, and thoughts, and the behaviors these might predict. (p. 128)

threshold the level of stimulation required to trigger a neural impulse. (p. 37)

token economy an operant conditioning procedure in which people earn a token of some sort for exhibiting a desired behavior and can later exchange the tokens for various privileges or treats. (p. 553)

tolerance with repeated use, achieving the desired effect requires larger doses. (p. 100)

top-down processing information processing guided by higher-level mental processes, as when we construct perceptions drawing on our experience and expectations. (p. 192)

trait a characteristic pattern of behavior or a disposition to feel and act, as assessed by self-report inventories and peer reports. (p. 435)

transduction conversion of one form of energy into another. In sensation, the transforming of stimulus energies, such as sights, sounds, and smells, into neural impulses our brain can interpret. (p. 192)

transference in psychoanalysis, the patient's transfer to the analyst of emotions linked with other relationships (such as love or hatred for a parent). (p. 547)

transgender an umbrella term describing people whose gender identity or expression differs from that associated with their birth sex. (p. 170)

two-factor theory the Schachter-Singer theory that to experience emotion one must (1) be physically aroused and (2) cognitively label the arousal. (p. 373)

two-word stage beginning about age 2, the stage in speech development during which a child speaks mostly in two-word statements. (p. 320)

Type A Friedman and Rosenman's term for competitive, hard-driving, impatient, verbally aggressive, and anger-prone people. (p. 398)

Type B Friedman and Rosenman's term for easygoing, relaxed people. (p. 398)

U

unconditional positive regard a caring, accepting, nonjudgmental attitude, which Carl Rogers believed would help clients develop self-awareness and self-acceptance. (pp. 433, 550)

unconditioned response (UR) in classical conditioning, an unlearned, naturally occurring response (such as salivation) to an unconditioned stimulus (US) (such as food in the mouth). (p. 240)

unconditioned stimulus (US) in classical conditioning, a stimulus that unconditionally—naturally and automatically—triggers a response (UR). (p. 240)

unconscious   according to Freud, a reservoir of mostly unacceptable thoughts, wishes, feelings, and memories. According to contemporary psychologists, information processing of which we are unaware. (p. 424)

V

validity   the extent to which a test measures or predicts what it is supposed to. (See also *content validity* and *predictive validity*.) (p. 337)

variable-interval schedule   in operant conditioning, a reinforcement schedule that reinforces a response at unpredictable time intervals. (p. 250)

variable-ratio schedule   in operant conditioning, a reinforcement schedule that reinforces a response after an unpredictable number of responses. (p. 249)

vestibular sense   the sense of body movement and position, including the sense of balance. (p. 227)

virtual reality exposure therapy   an anxiety treatment that progressively exposes people to electronic simulations of their greatest fears, such as airplane flying, spiders, or public speaking. (p. 552)

visual cliff   a laboratory device for testing depth perception in infants and young animals. (p. 210)

W

wavelength   the distance from the peak of one light or sound wave to the peak of the next. Electromagnetic wavelengths vary from the short blips of cosmic rays to the long pulses of radio transmission. (p. 200)

Weber's law   the principle that, to be perceived as different, two stimuli must differ by a constant minimum percentage (rather than a constant amount). (p. 195)

Wechsler Adult Intelligence Scale (WAIS)   the WAIS is the most widely used intelligence test; contains verbal and performance (nonverbal) subtests. (p. 334)

Wernicke's area   controls language reception—a brain area involved in language comprehension and expression; usually in the left temporal lobe. (p. 323)

withdrawal   the discomfort and distress that follow discontinuing the use of an addictive drug. (p. 102)

working memory   a newer understanding of short-term memory that focuses on conscious, active processing of incoming auditory and visual-spatial information, and of information retrieved from long-term memory. (p. 273)

X

X chromosome   the sex chromosome found in both men and women. Females have two X chromosomes; males have one. An X chromosome from each parent produces a female child. (p. 167)

Y

Y chromosome   the sex chromosome found only in males. When paired with an X chromosome from the mother, it produces a male child. (p. 167)

Yerkes–Dodson law   the principle that performance increases with arousal only up to a point, beyond which performance decreases. (p. 354)

Young–Helmholtz trichromatic (three-color) theory   the theory that the retina contains three different color receptors—one most sensitive to red, one to green, one to blue—which, when stimulated in combination, can produce the perception of any color. (p. 207)

Z

zygote   the fertilized egg; it enters a 2-week period of rapid cell division and develops into an embryo. (p. 119)

A

AAS. (2009, April 25). *USA suicide: 2006 final data.* Prepared for the American Association of Suicidology by J. L. McIntosh (www.suicidology.org). (p. 525)

Abel, E. L., & Kruger, M. L. (2010). Smile intensity in photographs predicts longevity. *Psychological Science, 21,* 542–544. (p. 400)

Abel, K. M., Drake, R., & Goldstein, J. M. (2010). Sex differences in schizophrenia. *International Review of Psychiatry, 22,* 417–428. (p. 529)

Abrams, D. B., & Wilson, G. T. (1983). Alcohol, sexual arousal, and self-control. *Journal of Personality and Social Psychology, 45,* 188–198. (p. 103)

Abrams, L. (2008). Tip-of-the-tongue states yield language insights. *American Scientist, 96,* 234–239. (p. 292)

Abrams, M. (2002, June). Sight unseen—Restoring a blind man's vision is now a real possibility through stem-cell surgery. But even perfect eyes cannot see unless the brain has been taught to use them. *Discover, 23,* 54–60. (p. 215)

Abramson, L. Y., Metalsky, G. I., & Alloy, L. B. (1989). Hopelessness depression: A theory-based subtype. *Psychological Review, 96,* 358–372. (p. 526)

Abrevaya, J. (2009). Are there missing girls in the United States? Evidence from birth data. *American Economic Journal: Applied Economics, 1*(2), 1–34. (p. 476)

Acevedo, B. P., & Aron, A. (2009). Does a long-term relationship kill romantic love? *Review of General Psychology, 13,* 59–65. (p. 492)

ACHA. (2009). *American College Health Association-National College Health Assessment II: Reference group executive summary Fall 2008.* Baltimore: American College Health Association. (p. 519)

Ackerman, D. (2004). *An alchemy of mind: The marvel and mystery of the brain.* New York: Scribner. (p. 39)

Ackerman, J. M., Nocera, C. C., & Bargh, J. A. (2010). Incidental haptic sensations influence social judgments and decisions. *Science, 328,* 1712–1715. (p. 229)

ACMD. (2009). *MDMA ('ecstasy'): A review of its harms and classification under the misuse of drugs act 1971.* London: Home Office; Advisory Council on the Misuse of Drugs. (pp. 106, 107)

Adams, S. (2011, February 6). OCD: David Beckham has it—as do over a million other Britons. *The Telegraph* (www.telegraph.co.uk). (p. 514)

Adelmann, P. K., Antonucci, T. C., Crohan, S. F., & Coleman, L. M. (1989). Empty nest, cohort, and employment in the well-being of midlife women. *Sex Roles, 20,* 173–189. (p. 156)

Ader, R., & Cohen, N. (1985). CNS-immune system interactions: Conditioning phenomena. *Behavioral and Brain Sciences, 8,* 379–394. (p. 245)

Affleck, G., Tennen, H., Urrows, S., & Higgins, P. (1994). Person and contextual features of daily stress reactivity: Individual differences in relations of undesirable daily events with mood disturbance and chronic pain intensity. *Journal of Personality and Social Psychology, 66,* 329–340. (p. 414)

Agrillo, C. (2011). Near-death experience: Out-of-body and out-of-brain? *Review of General Psychology, 15,* 1–10. (p. 107)

Ai, A. L., Park, C. L., Huang, B., Rodgers, W., & Tice, T. N. (2007). Psychosocial mediation of religious coping styles: A study of short-term psychological distress following cardiac surgery. *Personality and Social Psychology Bulletin, 33,* 867–882. (p. 412)

Aiello, J. R., Thompson, D. D., & Brodzinsky, D. M. (1983). How funny is crowding anyway? Effects of room size, group size, and the introduction of humor. *Basic and Applied Social Psychology, 4,* 193–207. (p. 471)

Aimone, J. B., Jessberger, S., & Gage, F. H. (2010, last modified February 5). Adult neurogenesis. *Scholarpedia* (www.scholarpedia.org). (p. 58)

Ainsworth, M. D. S. (1973). The development of infant-mother attachment. In B. Caldwell & H. Ricciuti (Eds.), *Review of child development research* (Vol. 3). Chicago: University of Chicago Press. (p. 134)

Ainsworth, M. D. S. (1979). Infant-mother attachment. *American Psychologist, 34,* 932–937. (p. 134)

Ainsworth, M. D. S. (1989). Attachments beyond infancy. *American Psychologist, 44,* 709–716. (p. 134)

Airan, R. D., Meltzer, L. A., Roy, M., Gong, Y., Chen, H., & Deisseroth, K. (2007). High-speed imaging reveals neurophysiological links to behavior in an animal model of depression. *Science, 317,* 819–823. (p. 525)

Åkerstedt, T., Kecklund, G., & Axelsson, J. (2007). Impaired sleep after bedtime stress and worries. *Biological Psychology, 76,* 170–173. (p. 92)

Alanko, K., Santtila, P., Harlaar, N., Witting, K., Varjonen, M., Jern, P., Johansson, A., von der Pahlen, B., & Sandnabba, N. K. (2010). Common genetic effects of gender atypical behavior in childhood and sexual orientation in adulthood: A study of Finnish twins. *Archives of Sexual Behavior, 39,* 81–92. (p. 181)

Albee, G. W. (1986). Toward a just society: Lessons from observations on the primary prevention of psychopathology. *American Psychologist, 41,* 891–898. (p. 577)

Alcock, J. (2011, March/April). Back from the future: Parapsychology and the Bem affair. *Skeptical Inquirer,* pp. 31–39. (p. 232)

Aldao, A., & Nolen-Hoeksema, S. (2010). Emotion-regulation strategies across psychopathology: A meta-analytic review. *Clinical Psychology Review, 30,* 217–237. (p. 556)

Aldrich, M. S. (1989). Automobile accidents in patients with sleep disorders. *Sleep, 12,* 487–494. (p. 92)

Aldridge-Morris, R. (1989). *Multiple personality: An exercise in deception.* Hillsdale, NJ: Erlbaum. (p. 534)

Aleman, A., Kahn, R. S., & Selten, J-P. (2003). Sex differences in the risk of schizophrenia: Evidence from meta-analysis. *Archives of General Psychiatry, 60,* 565–571. (p. 529)

Alexander, L., & Tredoux, C. (2010). The spaces between us: A spatial analysis of informal segregation. *Journal of Social Issues, 66,* 367–386. (p. 499)

Allard, F., & Burnett, N. (1985). Skill in sport. *Canadian Journal of Psychology, 39,* 294–312. (p. 277)

Allen, J. R., & Setlow, V. P. (1991). Heterosexual transmission of HIV: A view of the future. *Journal of the American Medical Association, 266,* 1695–1696. (p. 174)

Allen, K. (2003). Are pets a healthy pleasure? The influence of pets on blood pressure. *Current Directions in Psychological Science, 12,* 236–239. (p. 406)

Allen, M. W., Gupta, R., & Monnier, A. (2008). The interactive effect of cultural symbols and human values on taste evaluation. *Journal of Consumer Research, 35,* 294–308. (p. 225)

Allesøe, K., Hundrup, V. A., Thomsen, J. F., & Osler, M. (2010). Psychosocial work environment and risk of ischaemic heart disease in women: The Danish Nurse Cohort Study. *Occupational and Environmental Medicine, 67,* 318–322. (p. 400)

Alloy, L. B., Abramson, L. Y., Whitehouse, W. G., Hogan, M. E., Tashman, N. A., Steinberg, D. L., Rose, D. T., & Donovan, P. (1999). Depressogenic cognitive styles: Predictive validity, information processing and personality characteristics, and developmental origins. *Behaviour Research and Therapy, 37,* 503–531. (p. 527)

Allport, G. W. (1954). *The nature of prejudice.* New York: Addison-Wesley. (p. 17, 478)

Allport, G. W., & Odbert, H. S. (1936). Trait-names: A psycho-lexical study. *Psychological Monographs, 47*(1). (p. 436)

Almas, I., Cappelen, A. W., Sørensen, E. Ø., & Tungodden, B. (2010). Fairness and the development of inequality acceptance. *Science, 328,* 1176–1178. (p. 141)

Altamirano, L. J., Miyake, A., & Whitmer, A. J. (2010). When mental inflexibility facilitates executive control: Beneficial side effects of ruminative tendencies on goal maintenance. *Psychological Science, 21,* 1377–1382. (p. 526)

Altman, L. K. (2004, November 24). Female cases of HIV found rising worldwide. *New York Times* (www.nytimes.com). (p. 396)

Alwin, D. F. (1990). Historical changes in parental orientations to children. In N. Mandell (Ed.), *Sociological studies of child development* (Vol. 3). Greenwich, CT: JAI Press. (p. 138)

AMA. (2010, accessed 13 January). Women medical school applicants (Table 2 of Statistics History). ama-assn.org. (p. 186)

Amabile, T. M. (1983). *The social psychology of creativity*. New York: Springer-Verlag. (p. 448)

Amabile, T. M., & Hennessey, B. A. (1992). The motivation for creativity in children. In A. K. Boggiano & T. S. Pittman (Eds.), *Achievement and motivation: A social-developmental perspective*. New York: Cambridge University Press. (p. 315)

Amato, P. R., Booth, A., Johnson, D. R., & Rogers, S. J. (2007). *Alone together: How marriage in America is changing.* Cambridge, MA: Harvard University Press. (p. 169)

Ambady, N., Hallahan, M., & Rosenthal, R. (1995). On judging and being judged accurately in zero-acquaintance situations. *Journal of Personality and Social Psychology, 69,* 518–529. (p. 381)

Ambady, N., & Rosenthal, R. (1992). Thin slices of expressive behavior as predictors of interpersonal consequences: A meta-analysis. *Psychological Bulletin, 111,* 256–274. (p. 443)

Ambady, N., & Rosenthal, R. (1993). Half a minute: Predicting teacher evaluations from thin slices of nonverbal behavior and physical attractiveness. *Journal of Personality and Social Psychology, 64,* 431–441. (p. 443)

Ambrose, C. T. (2010). The widening gyrus. *American Scientist, 98,* 270–274. (p. 123)

Amedi, A., Floel, A., Knect, S., Zohary, E., & Cohen, L. (2004). Transcranial magnetic stimulation of the occipital pole interferes with verbal processing in blind subjects. *Nature Neuroscience, 7,* 1266–1270. (p. 58)

Amedi, A., Merabet, L. B., Bermpohl, F., & Pascual-Leone, A. (2005). The occipital cortex in the blind: Lessons about plasticity and vision. *Current Directions in Psychological Science, 14,* 306–311. (p. 58)

Amen, D. G., Stubblefield, M., Carmichael, B., & Thisted, R. (1996). Brain SPECT findings and aggressiveness. *Annals of Clinical Psychiatry, 8,* 129–137. (p. 483)

American Academy of Pediatrics. (2009). Policy statement—media violence. *Pediatrics, 124,* 1495–1503. (p. 265)

American Enterprise. (1992, January/February). Women, men, marriages & ministers. p. 106. (p. 452)

American Psychological Association. (2006). Evidence-based practice in psychology (from APA Presidential Task Force on Evidence-Based Practice). *American Psychologist, 61,* 271–285. (p. 562)

American Psychological Association. (2007). Answers to your questions about sexual ori- entation and homosexuality. (www.apa.org. Accessed December 6, 2007). (p. 179)

Ames, D. R. (2008). In search of the right touch: Interpersonal assertiveness in organi- zational life. *Current Directions in Psychological Science, 17,* 381–385. (p. B-11)

Andersen, R. A., Hwang, E. J., & Mulliken, G. H. (2010). Cognitive neural prosthet- ics. *Annual Review of Psychology, 61,* 169–190. (pp. 54, 317)

Andersen, S. M. (1998). *Service learning: A national strategy for youth development.* A posi- tion paper issued by the Task Force on Education Policy. Washington, DC: Institute for Communitarian Policy Studies, George Washington University. (p. 143)

Anderson, A. K., & Phelps, E. A. (2000). Expression without recognition: Contributions of the human amygdala to emotional com- munication. *Psychological Science, 11,* 106–111. (p. 51)

Anderson, B. L. (2002). Biobehavioral outcomes following psychological interventions for can- cer patients. *Journal of Consulting and Clinical Psychology, 70,* 590–610. (p. 397)

Anderson, C. A. (2004a). An update on the effects of playing violent video games. *Journal of Adolescence, 27,* 113–122. (pp. 485, 486)

Anderson, C. A., Anderson, K. B., Dorr, N., DeNeve, K. M., & Flanagan, M. (2000). Temperature and aggression. In M. P. Zanna (Ed.), *Advances in Experimental Social Psychology.* San Diego: Academic Press. (p. 483)

Anderson, C. A., Bushman, B. J., & Groom, R. W. (1997). Hot years and serious and deadly assault: Empirical tests of the heat hypothesis. *Journal of Personality and Social Psychology, 73,* 1213–1223. (p. 483)

Anderson, C. A., & Delisi, M. (2011). Implications of global climate change for vio- lence in developed and developing countries. In J. Forgas, A. Kruglanski., & K. Williams (eds.), *The psychology of social conflict and aggression.* New York: Psychology Press. (p. 483)

Anderson, C. A., & Dill, K. E. (2000). Video games and aggressive thoughts, feelings, and behavior in the laboratory and in life. *Journal of Personality and Social Psychology, 78,* 772–790. (p. 486)

Anderson, C. A., & Gentile, D. A. (2008). Media violence, aggression, and public policy. In E. Borgida & S. Fiske (Eds.), *Beyond com- mon sense: Psychological science in the courtroom.* Malden, MA: Blackwell. (p. 265)

Anderson, C. A., Gentile, D. A., & Buckley, K. E. (2007). *Violent video game effects on children and adolescents: Theory, research, and public policy.* New York: Oxford University Press. (p. 281)

Anderson, C. A., Lindsay, J. J., & Bushman, B. J. (1999). Research in the psychological laboratory: Truth or triviality? *Current Directions in Psychological Science, 8,* 3–9. (p. 26)

Anderson, C. A., Shibuya, A., Ihori, N., Swing, E. L., Bushman, B. J., Sakamoto, A., Rothstein, H. R., & Saleem, M. (2010). Violent video game effects on aggression, empathy, and prosocial behavior in Eastern and Western countries: A meta-analytic review. *Psychological Bulletin, 136,* 151–173. (p. 485)

Anderson, C. A., & Warburton, W. A. (2012). The impact of violent video games: An overview. In W. Warburton & D. Braunstein (Eds.), *Growing up fast and furious.* Annandale, NSW, Australia: The Federation Press. (p. 486)

Anderson, I. M. (2000). Selective serotonin reuptake inhibitors versus tricyclic antidepres- sants: A meta-analysis of efficacy and toler- ability. *Journal of Affective Disorders, 58,* 19–36. (p. 570)

Anderson, J. R., Myowa-Yamakoshi, M., & Matsuzawa, T. (2004). Contagious yawning in chimpanzees. *Biology Letters, 271,* S468–S470. (p. 465)

Anderson, R. C., Pichert, J. W., Goetz, E. T., Schallert, D. L., Stevens, K. V., & Trollip, S. R. (1976). Instantiation of gen- eral terms. *Journal of Verbal Learning and Verbal Behavior, 15,* 667–679. (p. 292)

Anderson, S. (2008, July 6). The urge to end it all. *New York Times* (www.nytimes.com). (p. 524)

Anderson, S. E., Dallal, G. E., & Must, A. (2003). Relative weight and race influence average age at menarche: Results from two nationally representative surveys of U.S. girls studied 25 years apart. *Pediatrics, 111,* 844–850. (p. 167)

Anderson, S. R. (2004). *Doctor Dolittle's delusion: Animals and the uniqueness of human language.* New Haven: Yale University Press. (p. 324)

Andreasen, N. C. (1997). Linking mind and brain in the study of mental illnesses: A project for a scientific psychopathology. *Science, 275,* 1586–1593. (p. 531)

Andreasen, N. C. (2001). *Brave new brain: Conquering mental illness in the era of the genome.* New York: Oxford University Press. (p. 531)

Andreasen, N. C., Arndt, S., Swayze, V., II, Cizadlo, T., & Flaum, M. (1994). Thalamic abnormalities in schizophrenia visualized through magnetic resonance image averaging. *Science, 266,* 294–298. (p. 531)

Andrews, P. W., & Thomson, J. A., Jr. (2009a). The bright side of being blue: Depression as an adaptation for analyzing complex problems. *Psychological Review, 116,* 620–654. (pp. 519, 526)

Andrews, P. W., & Thomson, J. A., Jr. (2009b, January/February). Depression's evolutionary roots. *Scientific American Mind,* pp. 57–61. (pp. 519, 526)

Angelsen, N. K., Vik, T., Jacobsen, G., & Bakketeig, L. S. (2001). Breast feeding and cognitive development at age 1 and 5 years. *Archives of Disease in Childhood, 85,* 183–188. (p. 22)

Antoni, M. H., & Lutgendorf, S. K. (2007). Psychosocial factors and disease progression in cancer. *Current Directions in Psychological Science, 16,* 42–46. (p. 397)

Antony, M. M., Brown, T. A., & Barlow, D. H. (1992). Current perspectives on panic and panic disorder. *Current Directions in Psychological Science, 1,* 79–82. (p. 517)

Antrobus, J. (1991). Dreaming: Cognitive processes during cortical activation and high afferent thresholds. *Psychological Review, 98,* 96–121. (p. 95)

AP. (2007). AP-Ipsos poll of 1,013 U.S. adults taken October 16–18, 2007 and distributed via Associated Press. (p. 230)

AP. (2009, May 9). AP-mtvU poll: Financial worries, stress and depression on college campus. www.hosted.ap.org. (p. 89, 390)

APA. (2002). *Ethical principles of psychologists and code of conduct.* Washington, DC: American Psychological Association. (p. 27)

APA. (2007). Answers to your questions about sexual orientation and homosexuality (www.apa.org. Accessed December 6, 2007). (p. 177)

APA. (2010a, accessed July 31). *Answers to your questions about transgender individuals and gender identity.* Washington, DC: American Psychological Association. (p. 171)

APA. (2010b, November 9). *Stress in America findings.* Washington, DC: American Psychological Association. (p. 392)

Archer, J. (2004). Sex differences in aggression in real-world settings: A meta-analytic review. Review of *General Psychology, 8,* 291–322. (p. 164)

Archer, J. (2006). Cross-cultural differences in physical aggression between partners: A social-role analysis. *Personality and Social Psychology Review, 10,* 133–153. (p. 164)

Archer, J. (2009). Does sexual selection explain human sex differences in aggression? *Behavioral and Brain Sciences, 32,* 249–311. (p. 164)

Arendt, H. (1963). *Eichmann in Jerusalem: A report on the banality of evil.* New York: Viking Press. (p. 143)

Ariely, D. (2009). *Predictably irrational: The hidden forces that shape our decisions.* HarperCollins. (p. 287)

Aries, E. (1987). Gender and communication. In P. Shaver & C. Henrick (Eds.), *Review of Personality and Social Psychology, 7,* 149–176. (p. 165)

Arjamaa, O., & Vuorisalo, T. (2010). Gene-culture coevolution and human diet. *American Scientist, 98,* 140–147. (p. 359)

Arkowitz, H., & Lilienfeld, S. O. (2006, April/May). Psychotherapy on trial. *Scientific American: Mind,* pp. 42–49. (p. 562)

Armony, J. L., Quirk, G. J., & LeDoux, J. E. (1998). Differential effects of amygdala lesions on early and late plastic components of auditory cortex spike trains during fear conditioning. *Journal of Neuroscience, 18,* 2592–2601. (p. 518)

Arnett, J. J. (1999). Adolescent storm and stress, reconsidered. *American Psychologist, 54,* 317–326. (p. 140)

Arnett, J. J. (2006). Emerging adulthood: Understanding the new way of coming of age. In J. J. Arnett & J. L. Tanner (Eds.), *Emerging adults in America: Coming of age in the 21st cen-*

tury. Washington, DC: American Psychological Association. (p. 149)

Arnett, J. J. (2007). Socialization in emerging adulthood: From the family to the wider world, from socialization to self-socialization. In J. E. Grusec & P. D. Hastings (Eds.), *Handbook of socialization: Theory and research.* New York: Guilford Press. (p. 149)

Arnone, D., McIntosh, A. M., Tan, G. M. Y., & Ebmeier, K. P. (2008). Meta-analysis of magnetic resonance imaging studies of the corpus callosum in schizophrenia. *Schizophrenia Research, 101,* 124–132. (p. 531)

Aron, A. P., Melinat, E., Aron, E. N., Vallone, R. D., & Bator, R. J. (1997). The experimental generation of interpersonal closeness: A procedure and some preliminary findings. *Personality and Social Psychology Bulletin, 23,* 363–377. (p. 493)

Aronson, E. (2001, April 13). Newsworthy violence. E-mail to SPSP discussion list, drawing from *Nobody Left to Hate.* New York: Freeman. (p. 146)

Artiga, A. I., Viana, J. B., Maldonado, C. R., Chandler-Laney, P. C., Oswald, K. D., & Boggiano, M. M. (2007). Body composition and endocrine status of long-term stress-induced binge-eating rats. *Physiology and Behavior, 91,* 424–431. (p. 359)

Asch, S. E. (1955). Opinions and social pressure. *Scientific American, 193,* 31–35. (p. 466)

Aserinsky, E. (1988, January 17). Personal communication. (p. 84)

Askay, S. W., & Patterson, D. R. (2007). Hypnotic analgesia. *Expert Review of Neurotherapeutics, 7,* 1675–1683. (p. 98)

Aspinwall, L. G., & Tedeschi, R. G. (2010). The value of positive psychology for health psychology: Progress and pitfalls in examining the relation of positive phenomena to health. *Annals of Behavioral Medicine, 39,* 4–15. (p. 404)

ASPS. (2010). *2010 report of the 2009 statistics: National Clearinghouse of Plastic Surgery Statistics.* American Society of Plastic Surgeons (www.plasticsurgery.org). (p. 490)

Aspy, C. B., Vesely, S. K., Oman, R. F., Rodine, S., Marshall, L., & McLeroy, K. (2007). Parental communication and youth sexual behaviour. *Journal of Adolescence, 30,* 449–466. (p. 176)

Assanand, S., Pinel, J. P. J., & Lehman, D. R. (1998). Personal theories of hunger and eating. *Journal of Applied Social Psychology, 28,* 998–1015. (p. 359)

Astin, A. W., Astin, H. S., & Lindholm, J. A. (2004). *Spirituality in higher education: A national study of college students' search for meaning and purpose.* Los Angeles: Higher Education Research Institute, UCLA. (pp. 144, 145)

Atkinson, R. C., & Shiffrin, R. M. (1968). Human memory: A control system and its control processes. In K. Spence (Ed.), *The psychology of learning and motivation* (Vol. 2). New York: Academic Press. (p. 273)

Austin, E. J., Deary, I. J., Whiteman, M. C., Fowkes, F. G. R., Pedersen, N. L.,

Rabbitt, P., Bent, N., & McInnes, L. (2002). Relationships between ability and personality: Does intelligence contribute positively to personal and social adjustment? *Personality and Individual Differences, 32,* 1391–1411. (p. 339)

Australian Unity. (2008). *What makes us happy? The Australian Unity Wellbeing Index.* South Melbourne: Australian Unity. (p. 415)

Auyeung, B., Baron-Cohen, S., Ashwin, E., Knickmeyer, R., Taylor, K., Hackett, G., & Hines, M. (2009). Fetal testosterone predicts sexually differentiated childhood behavior in girls and in boys. *Psychological Science, 20,* 144–148. (p. 130)

Averill, J. R. (1993). William James's other theory of emotion. In M. E. Donnelly (Ed.), *Reinterpreting the legacy of William James.* Washington, DC: American Psychological Association. (p. 372)

Aviezer, H., Hassin, R. R., Ryan, J., Grady, C., Susskind, J., Anderson, A., Moscovitch, M., & Bentin, S. (2008). Angry, disgusted, or afraid? Studies on the malleability of emotion perception. *Psychological Science, 19,* 724–732. (p. 384)

Ax, A. F. (1953). The physiological differentiation of fear and anger in humans. *Psychosomatic Medicine, 15,* 433–442. (p. 378)

Ayan, S. (2009, April/May). Laughing matters. *Scientific American Mind,* pp. 24–31. (p. 405)

Aydin, N., Fischer, P., & Frey, D. (2010). Turning to God in the face of estracism: Effects of social exclusion on religiousness. *Personality and Social Psychology Bulletin, 36,* 742–753. (p. 366)

Azar, B. (1998, June). Why can't this man feel whether or not he's standing up? *APA Monitor* (www.apa.org/monitor/jun98/touch.html). (p. 227)

Azevedo, F. A., Carvalho, L. R., Grinberg, L. T., Farfel, J. M., Ferretti, R. E., Leite, R. E., Jacob Filho, W., Lent, R., & Herculano-Houzel, S. (2009). Equal numbers of neuronal and nonneuronal cells make the human brain an isometrically scaled-up primate brain. *Journal of Comparative Neurology, 513,* 532–541. (p. 44)

B

Baas, M., De Dreu, C. K. W., & Nijstad, B. A. (2008). A meta-analysis of 25 years of mood-creativity research: Hedonic tone, activation, or regulatory focus? *Psychological Bulletin, 134,* 779–806. (p. 412)

Babad, E., Bernieri, F., & Rosenthal, R. (1991). Students as judges of teachers' verbal and nonverbal behavior. *American Educational Research Journal, 28,* 211–234. (p. 380)

Babyak, M., Blumenthal, J. A., Herman, S., Khatri, P., Doraiswamy, M., Moore, K., Craighead, W. W., Baldewics, T. T., & Krishnan, K. R. (2000). Exercise treatment for major depression: Maintenance of therapeutic benefit at ten months. *Psychosomatic Medicine, 62,* 633–638. (p. 408)

Bachman, J., O'Malley, P. M., Schulenberg, J. E., Johnston, L. D., Freedman-Doan, P., & Messersmith, E. E. (2007). *The education-drug use connection: How successes and failures in school relate to adolescent smoking, drinking, drug use, and delinquency.* Mahwah, NJ: Earlbaum. (p. 111)

Back, M. D., Stopfer, J. M., Vazire, S., Gaddis, S., Schmukle, S. C., Egloff, B., & Gosling, S. D. (2010). Facebook profiles reflect actual personality not self-idealization. *Psychological Science, 21,* 372–374. (pp. 368, 442)

Backman, L., & MacDonald, S. W. S. (2006). Death and cognition: Synthesis and outlook. *European Psychologist, 11,* 224–235. (p. 153)

Baddeley, A. D. (1982). *Your memory: A user's guide.* New York: Macmillan. (p. 286)

Baddeley, A. D. (2001). Is working memory still working? *American Psychologist, 56,* 849–864. (p. 273)

Baddeley, A. D. (2002, June). Is working memory still working? *European Psychologist, 7,* 85–97. (pp. 273, 274)

Baddeley, A. D., Thomson, N., & Buchanan, M. (1975). Word length and the structure of short-term memory. *Journal of Verbal Learning and Verbal Behavior, 14,* 575–589. (p. 276)

Baddeley, J. L., & Singer J. A. (2009). A social interactional model of bereavement narrative disclosure. *Review of General Psychology, 13,* 202–218. (p. 158)

Bagemihl, B. (1999). *Biological exuberance: Animal homosexuality and natural diversity.* New York: St. Martins. (p. 180)

Bahrick, H. P. (1984). Semantic memory content in permastore: 50 years of memory for Spanish learned in school. *Journal of Experimental Psychology: General, 111,* 1–29. (pp. 291, 292)

Bahrick, H. P., Bahrick, L. E., Bahrick, A. S., & Bahrick, P. E. (1993). Maintenance of foreign language vocabulary and the spacing effect. *Psychological Science, 4,* 316–321. (p. 278)

Bahrick, H. P., Bahrick, P. O., & Wittlinger, R. P. (1975). Fifty years of memory for names and faces: A cross-sectional approach. *Journal of Experimental Psychology: General, 104,* 54–75. (p. 285)

Bailenson, J. N., Iyengar, S., & Yee, N. (2005). Facial identity capture and presidential candidate preference. Paper presented at the Annual Conference of the International Communication Association. (p. 489)

Bailey, J. M., Gaulin, S., Agyei, Y., & Gladue, B. A. (1994). Effects of gender and sexual orientation on evolutionary relevant aspects of human mating psychology. *Journal of Personality and Social Psychology, 66,* 1081–1093. (p. 184)

Bailey, J. M., Kirk, K. M., Zhu, G., Dunne, M. P., & Martin, N. G. (2000). Do individual differences in sociosexuality represent genetic or environmentally contingent strategies? Evidence from the Australian twin registry. *Journal of Personality and Social Psychology, 78,* 537–545. (p. 184)

Bailey, R. E., & Gillaspy, J. A., Jr. (2005). Operant psychology goes to the fair: Marian and Keller Breland in the popular press, 1947–1966. *The Behavior Analyst, 28,* 143–159. (p. 258)

Bailine, S., & 10 others. (2010). Electroconvulsive therapy is equally effective in unipolar and bipolar depression. *Acta Psychiatrica Scandinavica, 121,* 431–436. (p. 571)

Baillargeon, R. (1995). A model of physical reasoning in infancy. In C. Rovee-Collier & L. P. Lipsitt (Eds.), *Advances in infancy research* (Vol. 9). Stamford, CT: Ablex. (p. 127)

Baillargeon, R. (2008). Innate ideas revisited: For a principle of persistence in infants' physical reasoning. *Perspectives in Psychological Science, 3,* 2–13. (p. 127)

Baker, E. L. (1987). The state of the art of clinical hypnosis. *International Journal of Clinical and Experimental Hypnosis, 35,* 203–214. (p. 98)

Baker, T. B., McFall, R. M., & Shoham, V. (2008). Current status and future prospects of clinical psychology: Toward a scientifically principles approach to mental and behavioral health care. *Psychological Science in the Public Interest, 9,* 67–103. (p. 562)

Baker, T. B., Piper, M. E., McCarthy, D. E., Majeskie, M. R., & Fiore, M. C. (2004). Addiction motivation reformulated: An affective processing model of negative reinforcement. *Psychological Review, 111,* 33–51. (p. 248)

Bakermans-Kranenburg, M. J., van IJzendoorn, M. H., & Juffer, F. (2003). Less is more: Meta-analyses of sensitivity and attachment interventions in early childhood. *Psychological Bulletin, 129,* 195–215. (p. 135)

Balcetis, E., & Dunning, D. (2006). See what you want to see: Motivational influences on visual perception. *Journal of Personality and Social Psychology, 91,* 612–625. (p. 199)

Balcetis, E., & Dunning, D. (2010). Wishful seeing: More desire objects are seen as closer. *Psychological Science, 21,* 147–152. (p. 199)

Balsam, K. F., Beauchaine, T. P., Rothblum, E. S., & Solomon, S. E. (2008). Three-year follow-up of same-sex couples who had civil unions in Vermont, same-sex couples not in civil unions, and heterosexual married couples. *Developmental Psychology, 44,* 102–116. (p. 155)

Balter, M. (2010). Animal communication helps reveal roots of language. *Science, 328,* 969–970. (p. 324)

Balter, M. (2011, April 25). What does IQ really measure? *ScienceNOW.* (p. 342)

Bambico, F. R., Nguyen N-T., Katz, N., & Gobbi, G. (2010). Chronic exposure to cannabinoids during adolescence but not during adulthood impairs emotional behaviour and monoaminergic neurotransmission. *Neurobiology of Disease, 37,* 641–655. (p. 108)

Bancroft, J., Loftus, J., & Long, J. S. (2003). Distress about sex: A national survey of women in heterosexual relationships. *Archives of Sexual Behavior, 32,* 193–208. (p. 174)

Bandura, A. (1982). The psychology of chance encounters and life paths. *American Psychologist, 37,* 747–755. (p. 154)

Bandura, A. (1986). *Social foundations of thought and action: A social-cognitive theory.* Englewood Cliffs, NJ: Prentice-Hall. (p. 443)

Bandura, A. (2005). The evolution of social cognitive theory. In K. G. Smith & M. A. Hitt (Eds.), *Great minds in management: The process of theory development.* Oxford: Oxford University Press. (pp. 154, 261)

Bandura, A. (2006). Toward a psychology of human agency. *Perspectives on Psychological Science, 1,* 164–180. (p. 443)

Bandura, A. (2008). An agentic perspective on positive psychology. In S. J. Lopez (Ed.), *The science of human flourishing.* Westport, CT: Praeger. (p. 443)

Bandura, A., Ross, D., & Ross, S. A. (1961). Transmission of aggression through imitation of aggressive models. *Journal of Abnormal and Social Psychology, 63,* 575–582. (p. 261)

Bar-Haim, Y., Lamy, D., Pergamin, L., Bakermans-Kranenburg, M. J., & van IJzendoorn, M. H. (2007). Threat-related attentional bias in anxious and nonanxious individuals: A meta-analytic study. *Psychological Bulletin, 133,* 1–24. (p. 516)

Barak, A., Hen, L., Boniel-Nissim, M., & Shapira, N. (2008). A comprehensive review and a meta-analysis of the effectiveness of Internet-based psychotherapeutic interventions. *Journal of Technology in Human Services, 26,* 108–160. (p. 557)

Barash, D. P. (2006, July 14). I am, therefore I think. *Chronicle of Higher Education,* pp. B9, B10. (p. 78)

Barbaresi, W. J., Katusic, S. KI., Colligan, R. C., Weaver, A. L., & Jacobsen, S. J. (2007). Modifiers of long-term school outcomes for children with attention-deficit/hyperactivity disorder: Does treatment with stimulant medication make a difference? Results from a population-based study. *Journal of Developmental and Behavioral Pediatrics, 28,* 274–287. (p. 507)

Barber, T. X. (2000). A deeper understanding of hypnosis: Its secrets, its nature, its essence. *American Journal of Clinical Hypnosis, 42,* 208–272. (p. 99)

Bargh, J. A., & Chartrand, T. L. (1999). The unbearable automaticity of being. *American Psychologist, 54,* 462–479. (p. 80)

Bargh, J. A., & McKenna, K. Y. A. (2004). The Internet and social life. *Annual Review of Psychology, 55,* 573–590. (p. 488)

Bargh, J. A., McKenna, K. Y. A., & Fitzsimons, G. M. (2002). Can you see the real me? Activation and expression of the "true self" on the Internet. *Journal of Social Issues, 58,* 33–48. (p. 488)

Bargh, J. A., & Morsella, E. (2008). The unconscious mind. *Perspectives on Psychological Science, 3,* 73–79. (p. 432)

Barinaga, M. B. (1992). The brain remaps its own contours. *Science, 258,* 216–218. (p. 58)

Barinaga, M. B. (1997). How exercise works its magic. *Science, 276,* 1325. (p. 407)

Barkley, R. A., & 74 others. (2002). International consensus statement (January 2002). *Clinical Child and Family Psychology Review, 5,* 2. (p. 507)

Barlow, D. H. (2010). Negative effects from psychological treatments: A perspective. *American Psychologist, 65,* 13–20. (p. 562)

Barnes, M. L., & Sternberg, R. J. (1989). Social intelligence and decoding of nonverbal cues. *Intelligence, 13,* 263–287. (p. 381)

Barnier, A. J., & McConkey, K. M. (2004). Defining and identifying the highly hypnotizable person. In M. Heap, R. J. Brown, & D. A. Oakley (Eds.), *High hypnotisability: Theoretical, experimental and clinical issues.* London: Brunner-Routledge. (p. 97)

Baron-Cohen, S. (2008). Autism, hypersystemizing, and truth. *Quarterly Journal of Experimental Psychology, 61,* 64–75. (p. 130)

Baron-Cohen, S. (2009). Autism: The empathizing-systemizing (E-S) theory. *The Year in Cognitive Neuroscience, 1156,* 68–80. (p. 130)

Baron-Cohen, S., Golan, O., Chapman, E., & Granader, Y. (2007). Transported to a world of emotion. *The Psychologist, 20,* 76–77. (p. 131)

Barrett, L. F. (2006). Are emotions natural kinds? *Perspectives on Psychological Science, 1,* 28–58. (pp. 372, 377)

Barrett, L. F., & Bliss-Moreau, E. (2009). She's emotional. He's having a bad day: Attributional explanations for emotion stereotypes. *Emotion, 9,* 649–658. (p. 381)

Barrett, L. F., Lane, R. D., Sechrest, L., & Schwartz, G. E. (2000). Sex differences in emotional awareness. *Personality and Social Psychology Bulletin, 26,* 1027–1035. (p. 381)

Barrick, M. R., Shaffer, J. A., & DeGrassi, S. W. (2009). What you see may not be what you get: Relationships among self-presentation tactics and ratings of interview and job performance. *Journal of Applied Psychology, 94,* 1304–1411. (p. B-4)

Barry, D. (1995, September 17). Teen smokers, too, get cool, toxic, waste-blackened lungs. *Asbury Park Press,* p. D3. (p. 104)

Barry, D. (2002, April 26). *The Dave Barry 2002 Calendar.* Kansas City: Andrews McMeel. (p. 27)

Bartels, M., & Boomsma, D. I. (2009). Born to be happy? The etiology of subjective well-being. *Behavior Genetics, 39,* 605–615. (p. 418)

Bartholow, B. C., Bushman, B. J., & Sestir, M. A. (2006). Chronic violent video game exposure and desensitization to violence: Behavioral and event-related brain potential data. *Journal of Experimental Social Psychology, 42,* 532–539. (p. 486)

Bashore, T. R., Ridderinkhof, K. R., & van der Molen, M. W. (1997). The decline of cognitive processing speed in old age. *Current Directions in Psychological Science, 6,* 163–169. (p. 152)

Baskind, D. E. (1997, December 14). Personal communication, from Delta College. (p. 552)

Bates, L. A., & Byrne, R. W. (2010, September/October). Imitation: What animal imitation tells us about animal cognition. *Wiley Interdisciplinary Reviews: Cognitive Science, 1,* 685–695. (p. 262)

Bathje, G. J., & Pryor, J. B. (2011). The relationships of public and self-stigma to seeking mental health services. *Journal of Mental Health Counseling, 33,* 161–177. (p. 510)

Bauer, P. J. (2002). Long-term recall memory: Behavioral and neurodevelopmental changes in the first 2 years of life. *Current Directions in Psychology, 11,* 137–141. (p. 124)

Bauer, P. J. (2007). Recall in infancy: A neurodevelopmental account. *Current Directions in Psychological Science, 16,* 142–146. (p. 124)

Bauer, P. J., Burch, M. M., Scholin, S. E., & Güler, O. E. (2007). Using cue words to investigate the distribution of autobiographical memories in childhood. *Psychological Science, 18,* 910–916. (p. 282)

Baum, A., & Posluszny, D. M. (1999). Health psychology: Mapping biobehavioral contributions to health and illness. *Annual Review of Psychology, 50,* 137–163. (p. 396)

Baumann, J., & DeSteno, D. (2010). Emotion guided threat detection: Expecting guns where there are none. *Journal of Personality and Social Psychology, 99,* 595–610. (p. 199)

Baumeister, H., & Härter, M. (2007). Prevalence of mental disorders based on general population surveys. *Social Psychiatry and Psychiatric Epidemiology, 42,* 537–546. (p. 505)

Baumeister, R. F. (1989). The optimal margin of illusion. *Journal of Social and Clinical Psychology, 8,* 176–189. (p. 312)

Baumeister, R. F. (1996). Should schools try to boost self-esteem? Beware the dark side. *American Educator, 20,* 43. (p. 449)

Baumeister, R. F. (2000). Gender differences in erotic plasticity: The female sex drive as socially flexible and responsive. *Psychological Bulletin, 126,* 347–374. (p. 179)

Baumeister, R. F. (2001, April). Violent pride: Do people turn violent because of self-hate, or self-love? *Scientific American,* pp. 96–101. (p. 449)

Baumeister, R. F. (2005). *The cultural animal: Human nature, meaning, and social life.* New York: Oxford University Press. (p. 463)

Baumeister, R. F. (2006, August/September). Violent pride. *Scientific American Mind,* pp. 54–59. (p. 447)

Baumeister, R. F., & Bratslavsky, E. (1999). Passion, intimacy, and time: Passionate love as a function of change in intimacy. *Personality and Social Psychology Review, 3,* 49–67. (p. 493)

Baumeister, R. F., Catanese, K. R., & Vohs, K. D. (2001). Is there a gender difference in strength of sex drive? Theoretical views, conceptual distinctions, and a review of relevant evidence. *Personality and Social Psychology Review, 5,* 242–273. (p. 183)

Baumeister, R. F., Dale, K., & Sommer, K. L. (1998). Freudian defense mechanisms and empirical findings in modern personality and social psychology: Reaction formation, projection, displacement, undoing, isolation, sublimation, and denial. *Journal of Personality, 66,* 1081–1125. (p. 432)

Baumeister, R. F., & Exline, J. J. (2000). Self-control, morality, and human strength. *Journal of Social and Clinical Psychology, 19,* 29–42. (p. 403)

Baumeister, R. F., & Leary, M. R. (1995). The need to belong: Desire for interpersonal attachments as a fundamental human motivation. *Psychological Bulletin, 117,* 497–529. (p. 364)

Baumeister, R. F., & Tice, D. M. (1986). How adolescence became the struggle for self: A historical transformation of psychological development. In J. Suls & A. G. Greenwald (Eds.), *Psychological perspectives on the self* (Vol. 3). Hillsdale, NJ: Erlbaum. (p. 148)

Baumeister, R. F., Twenge, J. M., & Nuss, C. K. (2002). Effects of social exclusion on cognitive processes: Anticipated aloneness reduces intelligent thought. *Journal of Personality and Social Psychology, 83,* 817–827. (p. 366)

Baumgardner, A. H., Kaufman, C. M., & Levy, P. E. (1989). Regulating affect interpersonally: When low esteem leads to greater enhancement. *Journal of Personality and Social Psychology, 56,* 907–921. (p. 448)

Baumrind, D. (1996). The discipline controversy revisited. *Family Relations, 45,* 405–414. (p. 138)

Baumrind, D., Larzelere, R. E., & Cowan, P. A. (2002). Ordinary physical punishment: Is it harmful? Comment on Gershoff (2002). *Psychological Bulletin, 128,* 602–611. (p. 252)

Bavelier, D., Newport, E. L., & Supalla, T. (2003). Children need natural languages, signed or spoken. *Cerebrum, 5*(1), 19–32. (p. 321)

BBC. (2008, February 26). Anti-depressants 'of little use.' *BBC News* (www.news.bbc.co.uk). (p. 570)

Beaman, A. L., & Klentz, B. (1983). The supposed physical attractiveness bias against supporters of the women's movement: A meta-analysis. *Personality and Social Psychology Bulletin, 9,* 544–550. (p. 490)

Beardsley, L. M. (1994). Medical diagnosis and treatment across cultures. In W. J. Lonner & R. Malpass (Eds.), *Psychology and culture.* Boston: Allyn & Bacon. (p. 508)

Bearzi, M., & Stanford, C. (2010). A bigger, better brain. *American Scientist, 98,* 402–409. (p. 318)

Beauchamp, G. K. (1987). The human preference for excess salt. *American Scientist, 75,* 27–33. (p. 359)

Beck, A. T., Rush, A. J., Shaw, B. F., & Emery, G. (1979). *Cognitive therapy of depression.* New York: Guilford Press. (p. 555)

Beck, H. P., Levinson, S., & Irons, G. (2009). Finding Little Albert: A journey to John B. Watson's infant laboratory. *American Psychologist, 64,* 605–614. (p. 245)

Beck, H. P., Levinson, S., & Irons, G. (2010). The evidence supports Douglas Merritte as Little Albert. *American Psychologist, 65,* 301–303. (p. 245)

Becker, D. V., Kenrick, D. T., Neuberg, S. L., Blackwell, K. C., & Smith, D. M. (2007). The confounded nature of angry men and happy women. *Journal of Personality and Social Psychology, 92,* 179–190. (pp. 381, 382)

Becker, S., & Wojtowicz, J. M. (2007). A model of hippocampal neurogenesis in memory and mood disorders. *Trends in Cognitive Sciences, 11,* 70–76. (p. 570)

Becklen, R., & Cervone, D. (1983). Selective looking and the noticing of unexpected events. *Memory and Cognition, 11,* 601–608. (p. 81)

Beckman, M. (2004). Crime, culpability, and the adolescent brain. *Science, 305,* 596–599. (p. 141)

Bègue, L., Bushman, B. J., Giancola, P. R., Subra, B., & Rosset, E. (2010). "There is no such thing as an accident," especially when people are drunk. *Personality and Social Psychology Bulletin, 36,* 1301–1304. (p. 482)

Bègue, L., Subra, B., Arvers, P., Muller, D., Bricout, V., & Zorman, M. (2009). A message in a bottle: Extrapharmacological effects of alcohol on aggression. *Journal of Experimental Social Psychology, 45,* 137–142. (p. 482)

Beilin, H. (1992). Piaget's enduring contribution to developmental psychology. *Developmental Psychology, 28,* 191–204. (p. 129)

Bell, A. P., Weinberg, M. S., & Hammersmith, S. K. (1981). *Sexual preference: Its development in men and women.* Bloomington: Indiana University Press. (p. 179)

Belluck, P. (2010, February 16). Wanted: Volunteers, all pregnant. *New York Times* (www.nytimes.com). (p. 130)

Belot, M., & Francesconi, M. (2006, November). *Can anyone be 'the one'? Evidence on mate selection from speed dating.* London: Centre for Economic Policy Research (www.cepr.org). (p. 489)

Belsher, G., & Costello, C. G. (1988). Relapse after recovery from unipolar depression: A critical review. *Psychological Bulletin, 104,* 84–96. (p. 522)

Belsky, J., Houts, R. M., & Fearon, R. M. P. (2010). Infant attachment security and the timing of puberty: Testing an evolutionary hypothesis. *Psychological Science, 21,* 1195–1201. (p. 167)

Bem, D. J. (1984). Quoted in *The Skeptical Inquirer, 8,* 194. (p. 231)

Bem, D. J. (2011). Feeling the future: Experimental evidence for anomalous retroactive influences on cognition and affect. *Journal of Personality and Social Psychology, 100,* 407–425. (p. 231)

Bem, S. L. (1987). Masculinity and femininity exist only in the mind of the perceiver. In J. M. Reinisch, L. A. Rosenblum, & S. A. Sanders (Eds.), *Masculinity/femininity: Basic perspectives.* New York: Oxford University Press. (p. 170)

Bem, S. L. (1993). *The lenses of gender.* New Haven, CT: Yale University Press. (p. 170)

Ben-Shakhar, G., & Elaad, E. (2003). The validity of psychophysiological detection of information with the guilt knowledge test: A meta-analytic review. *Journal of Applied Psychology, 88,* 131–151. (p. 379)

Benjamin, L. T., Jr., & Simpson, J. A. (2009). The power of the situation: The impact of Milgram's obedience studies on personality and social psychology. *American Psychologist, 64,* 12–19. (p. 467)

Benjamins, M. R., Ellison, C. G., & Rogers, R. G. (2010). Religious involvement and mortality risk among pre-retirement aged U.S. adults. In C. E. Ellison & R. A. Hummer (Eds.), *Religion, families, and health: Population-based research in the United States.* New Brunswick, NJ: Rutgers University Press. (p. 411)

Bennett, W. I. (1995). Beyond overeating. *New England Journal of Medicine, 332,* 673–674. (p. 363)

Benson, H. (1996). *Timeless healing: The power and biology of belief.* New York: Scribner. (p. 410)

Berghuis, P., & 16 others. (2007). Hardwiring the brain: Endocannabinoids shape neuronal connectivity. *Science, 316,* 1212–1216. (p. 108)

Bergin, A. E. (1980). Psychotherapy and religious values. *Journal of Consulting and Clinical Psychology, 48,* 95–105. (p. 567)

Berk, L. E. (1994, November). Why children talk to themselves. *Scientific American,* pp. 78–83. (p. 129)

Berk, L. S., Felten, D. L., Tan, S. A., Bittman, B. B., & Westengard, J. (2001). Modulation of neuroimmune parameters during the eustress of humor-associated mirthful laughter. *Alternative Therapies, 7,* 62–76. (p. 405)

Berkowitz, L. (1983). Aversively stimulated aggression: Some parallels and differences in research with animals and humans. *American Psychologist, 38,* 1135–1144. (p. 483)

Berkowitz, L. (1989). Frustration-aggression hypothesis: Examination and reformulation. *Psychological Bulletin, 106,* 59–73. (p. 483)

Berman, M., Gladue, B., & Taylor, S. (1993). The effects of hormones, Type A behavior pattern, and provocation on aggression in men. *Motivation and Emotion, 17,* 125–138. (p. 482)

Berman, M. G., Jonides, J., & Kaplan, S. (2008). The cognitive benefits of interacting with nature. *Psychological Science, 19,* 1207–1212. (p. 369)

Bernal, S., Dehaene-Lambertz, G. Millotte, S., & Christophe, A. (2010). Two-year-olds compute syntactic structure on-line. *Developmental Science, 13,* 69–76. (p. 321)

Bernieri, F., Davis, J., Rosenthal, R., & Knee, C. (1994). Interactional synchrony and rapport: Measuring synchrony in displays devoid of sound and facial affect. *Personality and Social Psychology Bulletin, 20,* 303–311. (p. 263)

Bernstein, D. M., & Loftus, E. F. (2009). How to tell if a particular memory is true or false. *Perspectives on Psychological Science, 4,* 370–374. (p. 294)

Bernstein, D. M., & Loftus, E. F. (2009). The consequences of false memories for food preferences and choices. *Perspectives on Psychological Science, 4,* 135–139. (p. 295)

Bernstein, M. J., Young, S. G., & Claypool, H. M. (2010). Is Obama's win a gain for Blacks? Changes in implicit racial prejudice following the 2008 election. *Social Psychology, 41,* 147–151. (p. 477)

Berridge, K. C., & Winkielman, P. (2003). What is an unconscious emotion? (The case of unconscious "liking"). *Cognition and Emotion, 17,* 181–211. (p. 374)

Berscheid, E. (1981). An overview of the psychological effects of physical attractiveness and some comments upon the psychological effects of knowledge of the effects of physical attractiveness. In G. W. Lucker, K. Ribbens, & J. A. McNamara (Eds.), *Psychological aspects of facial form* (Craniofacial growth series). Ann Arbor: Center for Human Growth and Development, University of Michigan. (p. 490)

Berscheid, E. (1985). Interpersonal attraction. In G. Lindzey & E. Aronson (Eds.), *The handbook of social psychology.* New York: Random House. (p. 364)

Berscheid, E. (2010). Love in the fourth dimension. *Annual Review of Psychology, 61,* 1–25. (p. 492)

Berscheid, E., Gangestad, S. W., & Kulakowski, D. (1984). Emotion in close relationships: Implications for relationship counseling. In S. D. Brown & R. W. Lent (Eds.), *Handbook of counseling psychology.* New York: Wiley. (p. 492)

Berti, A., Cottini, G., Gandola, M., Pia, L., Smania, N., Stracciari, A., Castiglioni, I., Vallar, G., & Paulesu, E. (2005). Shared cortical anatomy for motor awareness and motor control. *Science, 309,* 488–491. (p. 61)

Beyerstein, B., & Beyerstein, D. (Eds.). (1992). *The write stuff: Evaluations of graphology.* Buffalo, NY: Prometheus Books. (p. 438)

Bhatt, R. S., Wasserman, E. A., Reynolds, W. F., Jr., & Knauss, K. S. (1988). Conceptual behavior in pigeons: Categorization of both familiar and novel examples from four classes of natural and artificial stimuli. *Journal of Experimental Psychology: Animal Behavior Processes, 14,* 219–234. (p. 247)

Bialystok, E., & Craik, F. I. M. (2010). Cognitive and linguistic processing in the bilingual mind. *Current Directions in Psychological Science, 19,* 19–23. (p. 327)

Bianchi, S. M., Milkie, M. A., Sayer, L. C., & Robinson, J. P. (2000). Is anyone doing the housework? Trends in the gender division of household labor. *Social Forces, 79,* 191–228. (p. 186)

Bianchi, S. M., Robinson, J. P., & Milkie, M. A. (2006). *Changing rhythms of American family life.* New York: Russell Sage. (p. 186)

Biederman, I., & Vessel, E. A. (2006). Perceptual pleasure and the brain. *American Scientist, 94,* 247–253. (p. 354)

Bienvenu, O. J., Davydow, D. S., & Kendler, K. S. (2011). Psychiatric 'diseases' *versus* behavioral disorders and degree of genetic influence. *Psychological Medicine, 41,* 33–40. (p. 523)

Bilefsky, D. (2009, March 11). Europeans debate castration of sex offenders. *New York Times* (www.nytimes.com). (p. 172)

Binet, A. (1909). *Les idées mordermes sur les enfants.* Paris: Flammarion (quoted by A. Clarke & A. Clarke, Born to be bright. *The Psychologist, 19,* 409. (p. 334)

Bird, C. D., & Emery, N. J. (2009). Rooks use stones to raise the water level to reach a floating worm. *Current Biology, 19,* 1410–1414. (p. 318)

Birnbaum, G. E., Reis, H. T., Mikulincer, M., Gillath, O., & Orpaz, A. (2006). When sex is more than just sex: Attachment orientations, sexual experience, and relationship quality. *Journal of Personality and Social Psychology, 91,* 929–943. (p. 135)

Birnbaum, S. G., Yuan, P. X., Wang, M., Vijayraghavan, S., Bloom, A. K., Davis, D. J., Gobeski, K. T., Sweatt, J. D., Manhi, H. K., & Arnsten, A. F. T. (2004). Protein kinase C overactivity impairs prefrontal cortical regulation of working memory. *Science, 306,* 882–884. (p. 283)

Biro, D., Humle, T., Koops, K., Sousa, C., Hayashi, M., & Matsuzawa, T. (2010). Chimpanzee mothers at Bossou, Guinea carry the mummified remains of their dead infants. *Current Biology, 20,* R351–R352. (p. 317)

Biro, F. M., & 9 others. (2010). Pubertal assessment method and baseline characteristics in a mixed longitudinal study of girls. *Pediatrics, 126,* e583–e590. (p. 167)

Bishop, D. I., Weisgram, E. S., Holleque, K. M., Lund, K. E., & Wheeler, J. R. (2005). Identity development and alcohol consumption: current and retrospective self-reports by college students. *Journal of Adolescence, 28,* 523–533. (p. 110, 145)

Bishop, G. D. (1991). Understanding the understanding of illness: Lay disease representations. In J. A. Skelton & R. T. Croyle (Eds.), *Mental representation in health and illness.* New York: Springer-Verlag. (p. 306)

Bisson, J., & Andrew, M. (2007). Psychological treatment of post-traumatic stress disorder (PTSD). *Cochrane Database of Systematic Reviews 2007,* Issue 3. Art. No: CD003388. (p. 564)

Bjork, E. L., & Bjork, R. A. (2011). Making things hard on yourself, but in a good way: Creating desirable difficulties to enhance learning. In M. A. Gernsbacher, M. A. Pew, L. M. Hough, & J. R. Pomerantz (eds.), *Psychology and the real world.* New York: Worth Publishers. (p. 30)

Bjorklund, D. F., & Green, B. L. (1992). The adaptive nature of cognitive immaturity. *American Psychologist, 47,* 46–54. (p. 131)

Blackhart, G. C., Nelson, B. C., Knowles, M. L., & Baumeister, R. F. (2009). Rejectioneleicits emotional reactions but neither causes immediate distress nor lowers self-esteem: A meta-analytic review of 192 studies on social exclusion. *Personality and Social Psychology Bulletin, 13,* 269–309. (p. 365)

Blakemore, S-J. (2008). Development of the social brain during adolescence. *Quarterly Journal of Experimental Psychology, 61,* 40–49. (p. 140)

Blakemore, S-J., Wolpert, D. M., & Frith, C. D. (1998). Central cancellation of self-produced tickle sensation. *Nature Neuroscience, 1,* 635–640. (p. 220)

Blakeslee, S. (2006, January 10). Cells that read minds. *New York Times* (www.nytimes.com). (p. 262)

Blanchard, R. (1997). Birth order and sibling sex ratio in homosexual versus heterosexual males and females. *Annual Review of Sex Research, 8,* 27–67. (p. 182)

Blanchard, R. (2008a). Review and theory of handedness, birth order, and homosexuality in men. *Laterality, 13,* 51–70. (p. 182)

Blanchard, R. (2008b). Sex ratio of older siblings in heterosexual and homosexual, right-handed and non-right-handed men. *Archives of Sexual Behavior, 37,* 977–981. (p. 182)

Blanchard-Fields, F. (2007). Everyday problem solving and emotion: An adult developmental perspective. *Current Directions in Psychological Science, 16,* 26–31. (p. 338)

Blankenburg, F., Taskin, B., Ruben, J., Moosmann, M., Ritter, P., Curio, G., & Villringer, A. (2003). Imperceptive stimuli and sensory processing impediment. *Science, 299,* 1864. (p. 194)

Blanton, H., Jaccard, J., Christie, C., & Gonzales, P. M. (2007). Plausible assumptions, questionable assumptions and post hoc rationalizations: Will the real IAT please stand up? *Journal of Experimental Social Psychology, 43,* 399–409. (p. 477)

Blanton, H., Jaccard, J., Gonzales, P. M., & Christie, C. (2006). Decoding the implicit association test: Implications for criterion prediction. *Journal of Experimental Social Psychology, 42,* 192–212. (p. 477)

Blanton, H., Jaccard, J., Klick, J., Mellers, B., Mitchell, G., & Tetlock, P. E. (2009). Strong claims and weak evidence: Reassessing the predictive validity of the IAT. *Journal of Applied Psychology, 94,* 567–582. (p. 477)

Blascovich, J., Seery, M. D., Mugridge, C. A., Norris, R. K., & Weisbuch, M. (2004). Predicting athletic performance from cardiovascular indexes of challenge and threat. *Journal of Experimental Social Psychology, 40,* 683–688. (p. 391)

Blass, T. (1996). Stanley Milgram: A life of inventiveness and controversy. In G. A. Kimble, C. A. Boneau, & M. Wertheimer (Eds.), *Portraits of pioneers in psychology* (Vol. II). Washington, DC and Mahwah, NJ: American Psychological Association and Lawrence Erlbaum Publishers. (p. 469)

Blass, T. (1999). The Milgram paradigm after 35 years: Some things we now know about obedience to authority. *Journal of Applied Social Psychology, 29,* 955–978. (p. 468)

Blatt, S. J., Sanislow, C. A., III, Zuroff, D. C., & Pilkonis, P. (1996). Characteristics of effective therapists: Further analyses of data from the National Institute of Mental Health Treatment of Depression Collaborative Research Program. *Journal of Consulting and Clinical Psychology, 64,* 1276–1284. (p. 565)

Block, J. (2010). The five-factor framing of personality and beyond: Some ruminations. *Psychological Inquiry, 21,* 2–25. (p. 440)

Bloom, B. C. (Ed.). (1985). *Developing talent in young people.* New York: Ballantine. (p. 371)

Bloom, F. E. (1993, January/February). What's new in neurotransmitters. *BrainWork,* pp. 7–9. (p. 40)

Bloom, P. (2000). *How children learn the meanings of words.* Cambridge, MA: MIT Press. (p. 319)

BLS. (2011, June 22). American time use survey summary. Bureau of Labor Statistics (www.bls.gov). (p. 464)

Blum, K., Cull, J. G., Braverman, E. R., & Comings, D. E. (1996). Reward deficiency syndrome. *American Scientist, 84,* 132–145. (p. 52)

Boag, S. (2006). Freudian repression, the common view, and pathological science. *Review of General Psychology, 10,* 74–86. (p. 431)

Bocklandt, S., Horvath, S., Vilain, E., & Hamer, D. H. (2006). Extreme skewing of X chromosome inactivation in mothers of homosexual men. *Human Genetics, 118,* 691–694. (p. 181)

Bodenhausen, G. V., Sheppard, L. A., & Kramer, G. P. (1994). Negative affect and social judgment: The differential impact of anger and sadness. *European Journal of Social Psychology, 24,* 45–62. (p. 500)

Bodkin, J. A., & Amsterdam, J. D. (2002). Transdermal selegiline in major depression: A double-blind, placebo-controlled, parallel-group study in outpatients. *American Journal of Psychiatry, 159,* 1869–1875. (p. 570)

Boehm, K. E., Schondel, C. K., Marlowe, A. L., & Manke-Mitchell, L. (1999). Teens' concerns: A national evaluation. *Adolescence, 34,* 523–528. (p. 146)

Boehm-Davis, D. A. (2005). Improving product safety and effectiveness in the home. In R. S. Nickerson (Ed.), *Reviews of human factors and ergonomics.* Volume 1 (pp. 219–253). Santa Monica, CA: Human Factors and Ergonomics Society, 219–253. (p. B-14)

Boesch-Achermann, H., & Boesch, C. (1993). Tool use in wild chimpanzees: New light from dark forests. *Current Directions in Psychological Science, 2,* 18–21. (p. 317)

Bogaert, A. F. (2003). Number of older brothers and sexual orientation: New texts and the attraction/behavior distinction in two national probability samples. *Journal of Personality and Social Psychology, 84,* 644–652. (p. 182)

Bogaert, A. F. (2004). Asexuality: Prevalence and associated factors in a national probability sample. *Journal of Sex Research, 41,* 279–287. (p. 171)

Bogaert, A. F. (2006a). Toward a conceptual understanding of asexuality. *Review of General Psychology, 10,* 241–250. (p. 182)

Bogaert, A. F. (2006b). Biological versus non-biological older brothers and men's sexual orientation. *Proceedings of the National Academy of Sciences, 103,* 10771–10774. (p. 171)

Bogaert, A. F. (2010). Physical development and sexual orientation in men and women: An analysis of NATSAL-2000. *Archives of Sexual Behavior, 39,* 110–116. (p. 182)

Boggiano, A. K., Harackiewicz, J. M., Bessette, M. M., & Main, D. S. (1985). Increasing children's interest through performance-contingent reward. *Social Cognition, 3,* 400–411. (p. 260)

Boggiano, M. M., Chandler, P. C., Viana, J. B., Oswald, K. D., Maldonado, C. R., & Wauford, P. K. (2005). Combined dieting and stress evoke exaggerated responses to opioids in binge-eating rats. *Behavioral Neuroscience, 119,* 1207–1214. (p. 359)

Bohman, M., & Sigvardsson, S. (1990). Outcome in adoption: Lessons from longitudinal studies. In D. Brodzinsky & M. Schechter (Eds.), *The psychology of adoption.* New York: Oxford University Press. (p. 66)

Bolger, N., DeLongis, A., Kessler, R. C., & Schilling, E. A. (1989). Effects of daily stress on negative mood. *Journal of Personality and Social Psychology, 57,* 808–818. (p. 414)

Bolwig, T. G., & Madsen, T. M. (2007). Electroconvulsive therapy in melancholia: The role of hippocampal neurogenesis. *Acta Psychiatrica Scandinavica, 115,* 130–135. (p. 572)

Bonanno, G. A. (2004). Loss, trauma, and human resilience: Have we underestimated the human capacity to thrive after extremely aversive events? *American Psychologist, 59,* 20–28. (p. 158)

Bonanno, G. A., Brewin, C. R., Kaniasty, K., & La Greca, A. M. (2010). Weighing the costs of disaster: Consequences, risks, and resilience in individuals, families, and communities. *Psychological Science in the Public Interest, 11,* 1–49. (p. 516)

Bonanno, G. A., Galea, S., Bucciarelli, A., & Vlahov, D. (2006). Psychological resilience after disaster. *Psychological Science, 17,* 181–186. (p. 515)

Bonanno, G. A., Galea, S., Bucciarelli, A., & Vlahov, D. (2007). What predicts psychological resilience after disaster? The role of demographics, resources, and life stress. *Journal of Consulting and Clinical Psychology, 75*(5), 671–682. (p. 576)

Bonanno, G. A., & Kaltman, S. (1999). Toward an integrative perspective on bereavement. *Psychological Bulletin, 125,* 760–777. (p. 158)

Bond, C. F., Jr., & DePaulo, B. M. (2006). Accuracy of deception judgments. *Personality and Social Psychology Review, 10,* 214–234. (p. 380)

Bond, C. F., Jr., & DePaulo, B. M. (2008). Individual differences in detecting deception:

Accuracy and bias. *Psychological Bulletin, 134,* 477–492. (p. 380)

Bond, M. H. (1988). Finding universal dimensions of individual variation in multi-cultural studies of values: The Rokeach and Chinese values surveys. *Journal of Personality and Social Psychology, 55,* 1009–1015. (p. 451)

Bond, R., & Smith, P. B. (1996). Culture and conformity: A meta-analysis of studies using Asch's (1952b, 1956) line judgment task. *Psychological Bulletin, 119,* 111–137. (p. 467)

Bonetti, L., Campbell, M. A., & Gilmore, L. (2010). The relationship of loneliness and social anxiety with children's and adolescents' online communication. *Cyberpsychology, Behavior, and Social Networking, 13,* 279–285. (p. 368)

Bonezzi, A., Brendl, C. M., & DeAngelis, M. (2011). Stuck in the middle: The psychophysics of goal pursuit. *Psychological Science, 22,* 607–612. (p. 370)

Bono, J. E., & Judge, T. A. (2004). Personality and transformational and transactional leadership: A meta-analysis. *Journal of Applied Psychology, 89,* 901–910. (p. B-12)

Bor, D. (2010, July/August). The mechanics of mind reading. *Scientific American,* pp. 52–57. (p. 78)

Boring, E. G. (1930). A new ambiguous figure. *American Journal of Psychology, 42,* 444–445. (p. 197)

Bornstein, M. H., Cote, L. R., Maital, S., Painter, K., Park, S-Y., Pascual, L., Pecheux, M-G., Ruel, J., Venute, P., & Vyt, A. (2004). Cross-linguistic analysis of vocabulary in young children: Spanish, Dutch, French, Hebrew, Italian, Korean, and American English. *Child Development, 75,* 1115–1139. (p. 321)

Bornstein, M. H., Tal, J., Rahn, C., Galperin, C. Z., Pecheux, M-G., Lamour, M., Toda, S., Azuma, H., Ogino, M., & Tamis-LeMonda, C. S. (1992a). Functional analysis of the contents of maternal speech to infants of 5 and 13 months in four cultures: Argentina, France, Japan, and the United States. *Developmental Psychology, 28,* 593–603. (p. 139)

Bornstein, M. H., Tamis-LeMonda, C. S., Tal, J., Ludemann, P., Toda, S., Rahn, C. W., Pecheux, M-G., Azuma, H., & Vardi, D. (1992b). Maternal responsiveness to infants in three societies: The United States, France, and Japan. *Child Development, 63,* 808–821. (p. 139)

Bornstein, R. F. (1989). Exposure and affect: Overview and meta-analysis of research, 1968–1987. *Psychological Bulletin, 106,* 265–289. (p. 133, 488)

Bornstein, R. F. (1999). Source amnesia, misattribution, and the power of unconscious perceptions and memories. *Psychoanalytic Psychology, 16,* 155–178. (p. 488)

Bornstein, R. F., Galley, D. J., Leone, D. R., & Kale, A. R. (1991). The temporal stability of ratings of parents: Test-retest reliability and

influence of parental contact. *Journal of Social Behavior and Personality, 6,* 641–649. (p. 288)

Boroditsky, L. (2009, June 12). How does our language shape the way we think? www.edge.org. (pp. 318, 326)

Boroditsky, L. (2011, February). How language shapes thought. *Scientific American,* pp. 63–65. (p. 326)

Boscarino, J. A. (1997). Diseases among men 20 years after exposure to severe stress: Implications for clinical research and medical care. *Psychosomatic Medicine, 59,* 605–614. (p. 391)

Bosma, H., Marmot, M. G., Hemingway, H., Nicolson, A. C., Brunner, E., & Stansfeld, S. A. (1997). Low job control and risk of coronary heart disease in Whitehall II (prospective cohort) study. *British Medical Journal, 314,* 558–565. (p. 402)

Bosma, H., Peter, R., Siegrist, J., & Marmot, M. (1998). Two alternative job stress models and the risk of coronary heart disease. *American Journal of Public Health, 88,* 68–74. (p. 402)

Bostwick, J. M., & Pankratz, V. S. (2000). Affective disorders and suicide risk: A re-examination. *American Journal of Psychiatry, 157,* 1925–1932. (p. 524)

Bosworth, R. G., & Dobkins, K. R. (1999). Left-hemisphere dominance for motion processing in deaf signers. *Psychological Science, 10,* 256–262. (p. 58)

Bothwell, R. K., Brigham, J. C., & Malpass, R. S. (1989). Cross-racial identification. *Personality and Social Psychology Bulletin, 15,* 19–25. (p. 480)

Bouchard, T. J., Jr. (1981, December 6). Interview on Nova: Twins [program broadcast by the Public Broadcasting Service]. (p. 65)

Bouchard, T. J., Jr. (2009). Genetic influences on human intelligence (Spearman's *g*): How much? *Annals of Human Biology, 36,* 527–544. (p. 65)

Bouton, M. E., Mineka, S., & Barlow, D. H. (2001). A modern learning theory perspective on the etiology of panic disorder. *Psychological Review, 108,* 4–32. (p. 516)

Bower, B. (2009, February 14). The dating go round. *Science News,* pp. 22–25. (p. 488)

Bower, G. H. (1986). Prime time in cognitive psychology. In P. Eelen (Ed.), *Cognitive research and behavior therapy: Beyond the conditioning paradigm.* Amsterdam: North Holland Publishers. (p. 287)

Bower, G. H., Clark, M. C., Lesgold, A. M., & Winzenz, D. (1969). Hierarchical retrieval schemes in recall of categorized word lists. *Journal of Verbal Learning and Verbal Behavior, 8,* 323–343. (p. 278)

Bower, G. H., & Morrow, D. G. (1990). Mental models in narrative comprehension. *Science, 247,* 44–48. (p. 279)

Bower, J. E., Kemeny, M. E., Taylor, S. E., & Fahey, J. L. (1998). Cognitive processing, discovery of meaning, CD4 decline, and AIDS-related mortality among bereaved

HIV-seropositive men. *Journal of Consulting and Clinical Psychology, 66,* 979–986. (p. 396)

Bower, J. M., & Parsons, L. M. (2003, August). Rethinking the "lesser brain." *Scientific American,* pp. 50–57. (p. 50)

Bowers, J. S. (2009). On the biological plausibility of grandmother cells: Implications for neural network theories in psychology and neuroscience. *Psychological Review, 116,* 220–251. (p. 205)

Bowers, J. S., Mattys, S. L., & Gage, S. H. (2009). Preserved implicit knowledge of a forgotten childhood language. *Psychological Science, 20,* 1064–1069. (p. 124)

Bowers, K. S. (1984). Hypnosis. In N. Endler & J. M. Hunt (Eds.), *Personality and behavioral disorders* (2nd ed.). New York: Wiley. (p. 97)

Bowers, K. S. (1987, July). Personal communication. (p. 97)

Bowler, M. C., & Woehr, D. J. (2006). A meta-analytic evaluation of the impact of dimension and exercise factors on assessment center ratings. *Journal of Applied Psychology, 91,* 1114–1124. (p. 445)

Bowling, N., A., Eschleman, K. J., & Wang, Q. (2010). A meta-analytic examination of the relationship between job satisfaction and subjective well-being. *Journal of Occupational and Organizational Psychology, 83,* 915–934. (p. B-7)

Boxer, P., Huesmann, L. R., Bushman, B. J., O'Brien, M., & Moceri, D. (2009). The role of violent media preference in cumulative developmental risk for violence and general aggression. *Journal of Youth and Adolescence, 38,*417–428. (p. 265)

Boyatzis, C. J., Matillo, G. M., & Nesbitt, K. M. (1995). Effects of the "Mighty Morphin Power Rangers" on children's aggression with peers. *Child Study Journal, 25,* 45–55. (p. 265)

Braden, J. P. (1994). *Deafness, deprivation, and IQ.* New York: Plenum. (p. 343)

Bradley, D. R., Dumais, S. T., & Petry, H. M. (1976). Reply to Cavonius. *Nature, 261,* 78. (p. 208)

Bradley, R. B., & 15 others. (2008). Influence of child abuse on adult depression: Moderation by the corticotropin-releasing hormone receptor gene. *Archives of General Psychiatry, 65,* 190–200. (p. 137)

Bradshaw, C., Kahn, A. S., & Saville, B. K. (2010). To hook up or date: Which gender benefits? *Sex Roles, 62,* 661–669. (p. 184)

Braiker, B. (2005, October 18). A quiet revolt against the rules on SIDS. *New York Times* (www.nytimes.com). (p. 123)

Brainerd, C. J. (1996). Piaget: A centennial celebration. *Psychological Science, 7,* 191–195. (p. 125)

Branas, C. C., Richmond, T. S., Culhane, D. P., Ten Have, Thomas, R., & Wiebe, D. J. (2009). Investigating the link between gun possession and gun assault. *American Journal of Public Health, 99,* 2034–2040. (p. 481)

Brandon, S., Boakes, J., Glaser, & Green, R. (1998). Recovered memories of childhood sexual abuse: Implications for clinical prac-tice. *British Journal of Psychiatry, 172,* 294–307. (p. 299)

Brang, D., Edwards, L., Ramachandran, V. S., & Coulson, S. (2008). Is the sky 2? Contextual priming in grapheme-color synaesthesia. *Psychological Science, 19,* 421–428. (p. 229)

Brannon, L. A., & Brock, T. C. (1993). Comment on report of HIV infection in rural Florida: Failure of instructions to correct for gross underestimation of phantom sex partners in perception of AIDS risk. *New England Journal of Medicine, 328,* 1351–1352. (p. 174)

Bransford, J. D., & Johnson, M. K. (1972). Contextual prerequisites for understanding: Some investigations of comprehension and recall. *Journal of Verbal Learning and Verbal Behavior, 11,* 717–726. (p. 279)

Braun, S. (1996). New experiments underscore warnings on maternal drinking. *Science, 273,* 738–739. (p. 120)

Braun, S. (2001, Spring). Seeking insight by prescription. *Cerebrum,* pp. 10–21. (p. 107)

Braunstein, G. D., Sundwall, D. A., Katz, M., Shifren, J. L., Buster, J. E., Simon, J. A., Bachman, G., Aguirre, O. A., Lucas, J. D., Rodenberg, C., Buch, A., & Watts, N. B. (2005). Safety and efficacy of a testosterone patch for the treatment of hypoactive sexual desire disorder in surgically menopausal women: A randomized, placebo-controlled trial. *Archives of Internal Medicine, 165,* 1582–1589. (p. 172)

Bray, D. W., & Byham, W. C. (1991, Winter). Assessment centers and their derivatives. *Journal of Continuing Higher Education,* pp. 8–11. (p. 445)

Bray, D. W., & Byham, W. C., interviewed by Mayes, B. T. (1997). Insights into the history and future of assessment centers: An interview with Dr. Douglas W. Bray and Dr. William Byham. *Journal of Social Behavior and Personality, 12,* 3–12. (p. 445)

Brayne, C., Spiegelhalter, D. J., Dufouil, C., Chi, L-Y., Dening, T. R., Paykel, E. S., O'Connor, D.W., Ahmed, A., McGee, M. A., & Huppert, F.A. (1999). Estimating the true extent of cognitive decline in the old old. *Journal of the American Geriatrics Society, 47,* 1283–1288. (p. A-7)

Breedlove, S. M. (1997). Sex on the brain. *Nature, 389,* 801. (p. 180)

Brehm, S., & Brehm, J. W. (1981). *Psychological reactance: A theory of freedom and control.* New York: Academic Press. (p. 474)

Breslau, J., Aguilar-Gaxiola, S., Borges, G., Kendler, K. S., Su, M., & Kessler, R. C. (2007). Risk for psychiatric disorder among immigrants and their US-born descendants. *Journal of Nervous and Mental Disease, 195,* 189–195. (p. 540)

Brewer, C. L. (1990). Personal correspondence. (p. 67)

Brewer, C. L. (1996). Personal communication. (p. 6)

Brewer, M. B., & Chen, Y-R. (2007). Where (who) are collectives in collectivism? Toward conceptual clarification of individualism and collectivism. *Psychological Review, 114,* 133–151. (p. 451)

Brewer, W. F. (1977). Memory for the pragmatic implications of sentences. *Memory & Cognition, 5,* 673–678. (p. 279)

Brewin, C. R., Andrews, B., Rose, S., & Kirk, M. (1999). Acute stress disorder and posttraumatic stress disorder in victims of violent crime. *American Journal of Psychiatry, 156,* 360–366. (p. 515)

Brewin, C. R., Kleiner, J. S., Vasterling J. J., & Field, A. P. (2007). Memory for emotionally neutral information in posttraumatic stress disorder: A meta-analytic investigation. *Journal of Abnormal Psychology, 116,* 448–463. (p. 283)

Brief, A. P., & Weiss, H. M. (2002). Organizational behavior: Affect in the workplace. *Annual Review of Psychology, 53,* 279–307. (p. B-7)

Briñol, P., Petty, R. E., & Barden, J. (2007). Happiness versus sadness as a determinant of thought confidence in persuasion: A self-validation analysis. *Journal of Personality and Social Psychology, 93,* 711–727. (p. 412)

Briscoe, D. (1997, February 16). Women lawmakers still not in charge. *Grand Rapids Press,* p. A23. (p. 170)

Brislin, R. W. (1988). Increasing awareness of class, ethnicity, culture, and race by expanding on students' own experiences. In I. Cohen (Ed.), *The G. Stanley Hall Lecture Series.* Washington, DC: American Psychological Association. (p. 463)

Brissette, I., & Cohen, S. (2002). The contribution of individual differences in hostility to the associations between daily interpersonal conflict, affect, and sleep. *Personality and Social Psychology Bulletin, 28,* 1265–1274. (p. 92)

British Psychological Society. (1993). Ethical principles for conducting research with human participants. *The Psychologist: Bulletin of the British Psychological Society, 6,* 33–36. (p. 438)

Brockmann, H., Delhey, J., Welzel, C., & Yuan, H. (2009). The China puzzle: Falling happiness in a rising economy. *Journal of Happiness Studies, 10,* 387–405. (p. 415)

Brody, J. E. (2002, November 26). When the eyelids snap shut at 65 miles an hour. *New York Times* (www.nytimes.com). (p. 90)

Brody, J. E. (2003, September). Addiction: A brain ailment, not a moral lapse. *New York Times* (www.nytimes.com). (p. 101)

Brody, S., & Tillmann, H. C. (2006). The post-orgasmic prolactin increase following intercourse is greater than following masturbation and suggests greater satiety. *Biological Psychology, 71,* 312–315. (p. 178)

Bromet, E., & 21 others. (2011). Cross-national epidemiology of DSM-IV major depressive episode. *BMC Medicine, 9,* 90. (p. 522)

Brown, A. S. (2003). A review of the déjà vu experience. *Psychological Bulletin, 129,* 394–413. (p. 296)

Brown, A. S. (2004). Getting to grips with déja vu. *The Psychologist, 17,* 694–696. (p. 296)

Brown, A. S., Begg, M. D., Gravenstein, S., Schaefer, C. A., Wyatt, R. J., Bresnahan, M., Babulas, V. P., & Susser, E. S. (2004). Serologic evidence of prenatal influenza in the etiology of schizophrenia. *Archives of General Psychiatry, 61*, 774–780. (p. 532)

Brown, A. S., Schaefer, C. A., Wyatt, R. J., Goetz, R., Begg, M. D., Gorman, J. M., & Susser, E. S. (2000). Maternal exposure to respiratory infections and adult schizophrenia spectrum disorders: A prospective birth cohort study. *Schizophrenia Bulletin, 26*, 287–295. (p. 531)

Brown, E. L., & Deffenbacher, K. (1979). *Perception and the senses.* New York: Oxford University Press. (p. 219)

Brown, J. A. (1958). Some tests of the decay theory of immediate memory. *Quarterly Journal of Experimental Psychology, 10*, 12–21. (p. 276)

Brown, J. D., Steele, J. R., & Walsh-Childers, K. (2002). *Sexual teens, sexual media: Investigating media's influence on adolescent sexuality.* Mahwah, NJ: Erlbaum. (p. 176)

Brown, R. (1986). Linguistic relativity. In S. H. Hulse & B. F. Green, Jr. (Eds.), *One hundred years of psychological research in America.* Baltimore: Johns Hopkins University Press. (p. 326)

Brown, R. P., Osterman, L. L., & Barnes, C. D. (2009). School violence and the culture of honor. *Psychological Science, 20*, 1400–1405. (p. 484)

Brown, S. L., Brown, R. M., House, J. S., & Smith, D. M. (2008). Coping with spousal loss: Potential buffering effects of self-reported helping behavior. *Personality and Social Psychology Bulletin, 34*, 849–861. (p. 158)

Brown, S. W., Garry, M., Loftus, E., Silver, B., DuBois, K., & DuBreuil, S. (1996). People's beliefs about memory: Why don't we have better memories? Paper presented at the American Psychological Society convention. (p. 294)

Browning, C. (1992). *Ordinary men: Reserve police battalion 101 and the final solution in Poland.* New York: HarperCollins. (p. 469)

Bruce, D., Dolan, A., & Phillips-Grant, K. (2000). On the transition from childhood amnesia to the recall of personal memories. *Psychological Science, 11*, 360–364. (p. 124)

Bruce-Keller, A. J., Keller, J. N., & Morrison, C. D. (2009). Obesity and vulnerability of the CNS. *Biochemica et Biophysica Acta, 1792*, 395–400. (p. 361)

Bruck, M., & Ceci, S. J. (1999). The suggestibility of children's memory. *Annual Review of Psychology, 50*, 419–439. (p. 297)

Bruck, M., & Ceci, S. J. (2004). Forensic developmental psychology: Unveiling four common misconceptions. *Current Directions in Psychological Science, 15*, 229–232. (p. 297)

Bruer, J. T. (1999). *The myth of the first three years: A new understanding of early brain development and lifelong learning.* New York: Free Press. (p. 341)

Brumberg, J. J. (2000). *Fasting girls: The history of anorexia nervosa.* New York: Vintage. (p. 536)

Bruno, M-A., Bernheim, J. L., Ledoux, D., Pellas, F., Demertzi, A., & Laureys, S. (2011). A survey on self-assessed well-being in a cohort of chronic locked-in syndrome patients: Happy majority, miserable minority. *BMJ Open.* bmjopen.bmj.com/content/early/2011/02/16/bmjopen-2010-000039.short?rss=1.1. (p. 415)

Bruno, M-A., Pellas, F., & Laureys, S. (2008). Quality of life in locked-in syndrome survivors. In J. L. Vincent (ed.), *2008 yearbook of intensive care and emergency medicine.* New York: Springer. (p. 415)

Brunwasser, S. M., Gillham, J. E., & Kim, E. S. (2009). A meta-analytic review of the Penn Resiliency Program's effect on depressive symptoms. *Journal of Consulting and Clinical Psychology, 77*, 1042–1054. (pp. 556, 577)

Bryant, A. N., & Astin, H. A. (2008). The correlates of spiritual struggle during the college years. *Journal of Higher Education, 79*, 1–27. (p. 145)

Bryant, G. A., & Haselton, M. G. (2009). Vocal cues of ovulation in human females. *Biology Letters, 5*(1), 12–15. (p. 172)

Bryant, R. A. (2001). Posttraumatic stress disorder and traumatic brain injury: Can they coexist? *Clinical Psychology Review, 21*, 931–948. (p. 299)

Buchanan, R. W., & 10 others. (2010). The 2009 schizophrenia PORT psychopharmacological treatment recommendations and summary statements. *Schizophrenia Bulletin, 36*, 71–93. (p. 568)

Buchanan, T. W. (2007). Retrieval of emotional memories. *Psychological Bulletin, 133*, 761–779. (p. 283)

Buck, L. B., & Axel, R. (1991). A novel multigene family may encode odorant receptors: A molecular basis for odor recognition. *Cell, 65*, 175–187. (p. 226)

Buckholtz, J. W., & 13 others. (2010). Mesolimbic dopamine reward system hypersensitivity in individuals with psychopathic traits. *Nature Neuroscience, 13*, 419–421. (p. 539)

Buckingham, M. (2001, August). Quoted by P. LaBarre, "Marcus Buckingham thinks your boss has an attitude problem." *The Magazine* (fastcompany.com/online/49/buckingham.html). (p. B-9)

Buckingham, M. (2007). *Go put your strengths to work: 6 powerful steps to achieve outstanding performance.* New York: Free Press. (p. B-3)

Buckingham, M., & Clifton, D. O. (2001). *Now, discover your strengths.* New York: Free Press. (pp. B-3, B-4)

Buckley, K. E., & Leary, M. R. (2001). Perceived acceptance as a predictor of social, emotional, and academic outcomes. Paper presented at the Society of Personality and Social Psychology annual convention. (p. 365)

Buehler, R., Griffin, D., & Ross, M. (1994). Exploring the "planning fallacy": Why people underestimate their task completion times. *Journal of Personality and Social Psychology, 67*, 366–381. (p. 312)

Buffardi, L. E., & Campbell, W. K. (2008). Narcissism and social networking web sites. *Personality and Social Psychology Bulletin, 34*, 1303–1314. (p. 370)

Bugelski, B. R., Kidd, E., & Segmen, J. (1968). Image as a mediator in one-trial paired-associate learning. *Journal of Experimental Psychology, 76*, 69–73. (p. 277)

Bugental, D. B. (1986). Unmasking the "polite smile": Situational and personal determinants of managed affect in adult-child interaction. *Personality and Social Psychology Bulletin, 12*, 7–16. (p. 380)

Buka, S. L., Tsuang, M. T., Torrey, E. F., Klebanoff, M. A., Wagner, R. L., & Yolken, R. H. (2001). Maternal infections and subsequent psychosis among offspring. *Archives of General Psychiatry, 58*, 1032–1037. (p. 531)

Buller, D. J. (2005). *Adapting minds: Evolutionary psychology and the persistent quest for human nature.* Cambridge, MA: MIT Press/Bradford Books. (p. 185)

Buller, D. J. (2009, January). Four fallacies of pop evolutionary psychology. *Scientific American*, pp. 74–81. (p. 185)

Bullough, V. (1990). The Kinsey scale in historical perspective. In D. P. McWhirter, S. A. Sanders, & J. M. Reinisch (Eds.), *Homosexuality/heterosexuality: Concepts of sexual orientation.* New York: Oxford University Press. (p. 178)

Bunde, M., & Suls, J. (2006). A quantitative analysis of the relationship between the Cook-Medley Hostility Scale and traditional coronary artery disease risk factors. *Health Psychology, 25*, 493–500. (p. 399)

Buquet, R. (1988). Le reve et les deficients visuels [Dreams and the visually-impaired]. *Psychanalyse-a-l'Universite, 13*, 319–327. (p. 93)

Burcusa, S. L., & Iacono, W. G. (2007). Risk for recurrence in depression. *Clinical Psychology Review, 27*, 959–985. (p. 522)

Bureau of Labor Statistics. (2004, September 14). *American time-user survey summary.* Washington, DC: United States Department of Labor (www.bls.gov). (p. 169)

Burger, J. M. (2009). Replicating Milgram: Would people still obey today? *American Psychologist, 64*, 1–11. (p. 468)

Burgess, M., Enzle, M. E., & Schmaltz, R. (2004). Defeating the potentially deleterious effects of externally imposed deadlines: Practitioners' rules-of-thumb. *Personality and Social Psychology Bulletin, 30*, 868–877. (p. B-11)

Buri, J. R., Louiselle, P. A., Misukanis, T. M., & Mueller, R. A. (1988). Effects of parental authoritarianism and authoritativeness on self-esteem. *Personality and Social Psychology Bulletin, 14*, 271–282. (p. 138)

Burish, T. G., & Carey, M. P. (1986). Conditioned aversive responses in cancer chemotherapy patients: Theoretical and developmental analysis. *Journal of Counseling and Clinical Psychology, 54*, 593–600. (p. 258)

Burk, W. J., Denissen, J., Van Doorn, M. D., Branje, S. J. T., & Laursen, B. (2009). The vicissitudes of conflict measurement: Stability and reliability in the frequency of disagreements. *European Psychologist, 14*, 153–159. (p. 146)

Burke, D. M., & Shafto, M. A. (2004). Aging and language production. *Current Directions in Psychological Science, 13*, 21–24. (p. 153)

Burns, B. C. (2004). The effects of speed on skilled chess performance. *Psychological Science, 15*, 442–447. (p. 313)

Burns, J. M., & Swerdlow, R. H. (2003). Right orbitofrontal tumor with pedophilia symptom and constructional apraxia sign. *Archives of Neurology, 60*, 437–440. (p. 35)

Burris, C. T., & Branscombe, N. R. (2005). Distorted distance estimation induced by a self-relevant national boundary. *Journal of Experimental Social Psychology, 41*, 305–312. (p. 327)

Burton, C. M., & King, L. A. (2008). Effects of (very) brief writing on health: The two-minute miracle. *British Journal of Health Psychology, 13*, 9–14. (p. 407)

Busby, D. M., Carroll, J. S., & Willoughby, B. J. (2010). Compatibility or restraint? The effects of sexual timing on marriage relationships. *Journal of Family Psychology, 24*, 766–774. (p. 178)

Bushman, B. J. (1993). Human aggression while under the influence of alcohol and other drugs: An integrative research review. *Current Directions in Psychological Science, 2*, 148–152. (p. 482)

Bushman, B. J. (2002). Does venting anger feed or extinguish the flame? Catharsis, rumination, distraction, anger, and aggressive responding. *Personality and Social Psychology Bulletin, 28*, 724–731. (pp. 398, 399)

Bushman, B. J. (2011, July 7). Quoted in S. Vendantam, "It's a duel: How do violent video games affect kids? www.npr.org. (p. 486)

Bushman, B. J., & Anderson, C. A. (2009). Comfortably numb: Desensitizing effects of violent media on helping others. *Psychological Science, 20*, 273–277. (pp. 265, 486)

Bushman, B. J., & Baumeister, R. F. (1998). Threatened egotism, narcissism, self-esteem, and direct and displaced aggression: Does self-love or self-hate lead to violence? *Journal of Personality and Social Psychology, 75*, 219–229. (p. 449)

Bushman, B. J., Baumeister, R. F., Thomaes, S., Ryu, E., Begeer, S., & West, S. G. (2009). Looking again, and harder, for a link between low self-esteem and aggression. *Journal of Personality, 77*, 427–446. (p. 449)

Bushman, B. J., Moeller, S. J., & Crocker, J. (2011). Sweets, sex, or self-esteem? Comparing the value of self-esteem boosts with other pleasant rewards. *Journal of Personality*, in press. (onlinelibrary.wiley.com/doi/10.1111/j.1467-6494.2010.00712.x/abstract). (p. 434)

Bushman, B. J., Rothstein, H. R., & Anderson, C. A. (2010). Much ado about something: Violent video game effects and a school of red herring: Reply to Ferguson and Kilburn (2010). *Psychological Bulletin, 136*, 182–187. (p. 486)

Busnel, M. C., Granier-Deferre, C., & Lecanuet, J. P. (1992, October). Fetal audition. *New York Academy of Sciences, 662*, 118–134. (p. 119)

Buss, A. H. (1989). Personality as traits. *American Psychologist, 44*, 1378–1388. (p. 443)

Buss, D. M. (1994). The strategies of human mating: People worldwide are attracted to the same qualities in the opposite sex. *American Scientist, 82*, 238–249. (p. 184)

Buss, D. M. (1995). Evolutionary psychology: A new paradigm for psychological science. *Psychological Inquiry, 6*, 1–30. (p. 184)

Buss, D. M. (1996). Sexual conflict: Evolutionary insights into feminism and the "battle of the sexes." In D. M. Buss & N. M. Malamuth (Eds.), *Sex, power, conflict: Evolutionary and feminist perspectives*. New York: Oxford University Press. (p. 184)

Buss, D. M. (2008). Female sexual psychology. World Question Center 2008 (edge.org). (p. 175)

Buss, D. M. (2009). The great struggles of life: Darwin and the emergence of evolutionary psychology. *American Psychologist, 64*, 140–148. (p. 184)

Buster, J. E., Kingsberg, S. A., Aguirre, O., Brown, C., Breaux, J. G., Buch, A., Rodenberg, C. A., Wekselman, K., & Casson, P. (2005). Testosterone patch for low sexual desire in surgically menopausal women: A randomized trial. *Obstetrics and Gynecology, 105*(5), 944–952. (p. 172)

Butcher, L. M., Davis, O. S. P., Craig, I. W., & Plomin, R. (2008). Genome-wide quantitative trait locus association scan of general cognitive ability using pooled DNA and 500K single nucleotide polymorphism microarrays. *Genes, Brain and Behavior, 7*, 435–446. (p. 340)

Butler, R. A. (1954, February). Curiosity in monkeys. *Scientific American*, pp. 70–75. (p. 353)

Byers-Heinlein, K., Burns, T. C., & Werker, J. F. (2010). The roots of bilingualism in newborns. *Psychological Science, 21*, 343–348. (p. 119)

Bynum, R. (2004, November 1). Associated Press article. (p. 221)

Byrne, D. (1971). *The attraction paradigm*. New York: Academic Press. (p. 491)

Byrne, D. (1982). Predicting human sexual behavior. In A. G. Kraut (Ed.), *The G. Stanley Hall Lecture Series* (Vol. 2). Washington, DC: American Psychological Association. (p. 172, 242)

Byrne, R. W. (1991, May/June). Brute intellect. *The Sciences*, pp. 42–47. (p. 323)

Byrne, R. W., Bates, L. A., & Moss, C. J. (2009). Elephant cognition in primate perspective. *Comparative Cognition & Behavior Reviews, 4*, 1–15. (p. 317)

Byrne, R. W., & Corp, N. (2004). Neocortex size predicts deception in primates. *Proceedings of the Royal Society B, 271*, 1693–1699. (p. 18)

C

Cable, D. M., & Gilovich, T. (1998). Looked over or overlooked? Prescreening decisions and post-interview evaluations. *Journal of Personality and Social Psychology, 83*, 501–508. (p. B-5)

Cacioppo, J. T., & Hawkley, L. C. (2009). Perceived social isolation and cognition. *Trends in Cognitive Sciences, 13*, 447–454. (pp. 365, 366)

Cahill, L. (1994). (Beta)-adrenergic activation and memory for emotional events. *Nature, 371*, 702–704. (p. 283)

Cahn, B. R., & Polich, J. (2006). Meditation states and traits: EEG, ERP, and neuroimaging studies. *Psychological Bulletin, 132*, 180–211. (p. 410)

Cale, E. M., & Lilienfeld, S. O. (2002). Sex differences in psychopathy and antisocial personality disorder: A review and integration. *Clinical Psychology Review, 22*, 1179–1207. (p. 538)

Call, K. T., Riedel, A. A., Hein, K., McLoyd, V., Petersen, A., & Kipke, M. (2002). Adolescent health and well-being in the twenty-first century: A global perspective. *Journal of Research on Adolescence, 12*, 69–98. (p. 176)

Callaghan, T., Rochat, P., Lillard, A., Claux, M. L., Odden, H., Itakura, S., Tapanya, S., & Singh, S. (2005). Synchrony in the onset of mental-state reasoning. *Psychological Science, 16*, 378–384. (p. 128)

Calvo-Merino, B., Glaser, D. E., Grèzes, J., Passingham, R. E., & Haggard, P. (2004). Action observation and acquired motor skills: An fMRI study with expert dancers. *Cerebral Cortex, 15*, 1243–1249. (p. 328)

Camerer, C. F., Loewenstein, G., & Weber, M. (1989). The curse of knowledge in economic settings: An experimental analysis. *Journal of Political Economy, 97*, 1232–1254. (p. B-15)

Cameron, L., & Rutland, A. (2006). Extended contact through story reading in school: Reducing children's prejudice toward the disabled. *Journal of Social Issues, 62*, 469–488. (p. 499)

Campbell, A. (2010). Oxytocin and human social behavior. *Personality and Social Psychology Review, 14*, 281–205. (p. 393)

Campbell, D. T. (1975). On the conflicts between biological and social evolution and between psychology and moral tradition. *American Psychologist, 30*, 1103–1126. (p. 416)

Campbell, D. T., & Specht, J. C. (1985). Altruism: Biology, culture, and religion. *Journal of Social and Clinical Psychology, 3*(1), 33–42. (p. 435)

Campbell, M. W., & de Waal, F. B. M. (2011). Ingroup-outgroup bias in contagious yawning by chimpanzees supports link to empathy. *PLoS One, 6*, e18283. (p. 479)

Campbell, S. (1986). *The Loch Ness Monster: The evidence*. Willingborough, Northamptonshire, U.K.: Acquarian Press. (p. 197)

Camperio-Ciani, A., Corna, F., & Capiluppi, C. (2004). Evidence for maternally inherited factors favouring male homosexuality and promoting female fecundity. *Proceedings of the Royal Society of London B, 271*, 2217–2221. (p. 181)

Camperio-Ciani, A., Lemmola, F., & Blecher, S. R. (2009). Genetic factors increase fecundity in female maternal relatives of bisexual men as in homosexuals. *Journal of Sexual Medicine, 6,* 449–455. (p. 181)

Campos, J. J., Bertenthal, B. I., & Kermoian, R. (1992). Early experience and emotional development: The emergence of wariness and heights. *Psychological Science, 3,* 61–64. (p. 210)

Canli, T. (2008, February/March). The character code. *Scientific American Mind,* pp. 53–57. (p. 518)

Canli, T., Desmond, J. E., Zhao, Z., & Gabrieli, J. D. E. (2002). Sex differences in the neural basis of emotional memories. *Proceedings of the National Academy of Sciences, 99,* 10789–10794. (p. 382)

Cannon, W. B. (1929). *Bodily changes in pain, hunger, fear, and rage.* New York: Branford. (pp. 357, 392)

Cannon, W. B., & Washburn, A. L. (1912). An explanation of hunger. *American Journal of Physiology, 29,* 441–454. (p. 357)

Cantor, N., & Kihlstrom, J. F. (1987). *Personality and social intelligence.* Englewood Cliffs, NJ: Prentice-Hall. (p. 333)

Cantril, H., & Bumstead, C. H. (1960). *Reflections on the human venture.* New York: New York University Press. (p. 475)

Caplan, N., Choy, M. H., & Whitmore, J. K. (1992, February). Indochinese refugee families and academic achievement. *Scientific American,* pp. 36–42. (pp. 147, 345)

Card, N. A., Stucky, B. C., Sawalani, G. M., & Little, T. D. (2008). Direct and indirect aggression during childhood and adolescence: A meta-analytic review of gender differences, intercorrelations, and relations to maladjustment. *Child Development, 79,* 1185–1229. (p. 164)

Carey, B. (2007, September 4). Bipolar illness soars as a diagnosis for the young. *New York Times* (www.nytimes.com). (p. 521)

Carey, B. (2009, November 27). Surgery for mental ills offers both hope and risk. *New York Times* (www.nytimes.com). (p. 574)

Carey, B. (2010). Seeking emotional clues without facial cues. *New York Times* (www.nytimes.com). (p. 385)

Carey, B. (2011, February 14). Wariness on surgery of the mind. *New York Times* (www.nytimes.com). (p. 574)

Carey, G. (1990). Genes, fears, phobias, and phobic disorders. *Journal of Counseling and Development, 68,* 628–632. (p. 517)

Carli, L. L., & Leonard, J. B. (1989). The effect of hindsight on victim derogation. *Journal of Social and Clinical Psychology, 8,* 331–343. (p. 481)

Carlson, C. L. (2000). ADHD is overdiagnosed. In R. L. Atkinson, R. C. Atkinson, E. E. Smith, D. J. Bem, & S. Nolen-Hoeksema (Eds.), *Hilgard's introduction to psychology* (13th ed.). Fort Worth: Harcourt. (p. 507)

Carlson, M., Charlin, V., & Miller, N. (1988). Positive mood and helping behavior: A test of six hypotheses. *Journal of Personality and Social Psychology, 55,* 211–229. (p. 495)

Carlson, S. (1985). A double-blind test of astrology. *Nature, 318,* 419–425. (p. 438)

Carmeli, A., Ben-Hador, B., Waldman, D. A., & Rupp, D. E. (2009). How leaders cultivate social capital and nurture employee vigor: Implications for job performance. *Journal of Applied Psychology, 94,* 1553–1561. (p. B-12)

Carnahan, T., & McFarland, S. (2007). Revisiting the Stanford Prison Experiment: Could participant self-selection have led to the cruelty? *Personality and Social Psychology Bulletin, 33,* 603–614. (p. 462)

Carpusor, A., & Loges, W. E. (2006). Rental discrimination and ethnicity in names. *Journal of Applied Social Psychology, 36,* 934–952. (p. 24)

Carroll, D., Davey Smith, G., & Bennett, P. (1994, March). Health and socio-economic status. *The Psychologist,* pp. 122–125. (p. 402)

Carroll, J. M., & Russell, J. A. (1996). Do facial expressions signal specific emotions? Judging emotion from the face in context. *Journal of Personality and Social Psychology, 70,* 205–218. (p. 383)

Carroll, J. S., Padilla-Walker, L. M., Nelson, L. J., Olson, C. D., Barry, C. M., & Madsen, S. D. (2008). Generation XXX: Pornography acceptance and use among emerging adults. *Journal of Adolescent Research, 23,* 6–30. (p. 484)

Carskadon, M. A. (2002). *Adolescent sleep patterns: Biological, social, and psychological influences.* New York: Cambridge University Press. (p. 90)

Carstensen, L. L., & Mikels, J. A. (2005). At the intersection of emotion and cognition: Aging and the positivity effect. *Current Directions in Psychological Science, 14,* 117–121. (pp. 156, 338)

Carter, R. (1998). *Mapping the mind.* Berkeley: University of California Press. (p. 41)

Carter, T. J., & Gilovich, T. (2010). The relative relativity of material and experiential purchases. *Journal of Personality and Social Psychology, 98,* 146–159. (p. 418)

Carver, C. S., Johnson, S. L., & Joormann, J. (2008). Serotonergic function, two-mode models of self-regulation, and vulnerability to depression: What depression has in common with impulsive aggression. *Psychological Bulletin, 134,* 912–943. (p. 524)

Carver, C. S., Scheier, M. F., & Segerstrom, S. C. (2010). Optimism. *Clinical Psychology Review, 30,* 879–889. (p. 404)

CASA. (2003). *The formative years: Pathways to substance abuse among girls and young women ages 8–22.* New York: National Center on Addiction and Substance Use, Columbia University. (pp. 103, 110)

CASA. (2004). *CASA 2004 teen survey.* National Center on Addiction and Substance Abuse, Columbia University (www.casacolumbia.org). (p. 174)

Casey, B. J., Getz, S., & Galvan, A. (2008). The adolescent brain. *Developmental Review, 28,* 62–77. (p. 140)

Cash, T., & Janda, L. H. (1984, December). The eye of the beholder. *Psychology Today,* pp. 46–52. (p. 489)

Caspi, A. (2000). The child is father of the man: Personality continuities from childhood to adulthood. *Journal of Personality and Social Psychology, 78,* 158–172. (p. 134)

Caspi, A., Moffitt, T. E., Newman, D. L., & Silva, P. A. (1996). Behavioral observations at age 3 years predict adult psychiatric disorders: Longitudinal evidence from a birth cohort. *Archives of General Psychiatry, 53,* 1033–1039. (p. 539)

Cassidy, J., & Shaver, P. R. (1999). *Handbook of attachment.* New York: Guilford. (p. 133)

Castillo, R. J. (1997). *Culture and mental illness: A client-centered approach.* Pacific Grove, CA: Brooks/Cole. (p. 508)

Castonguay, L. G., Boswell, J. F., Constantino, M. J., Goldfried, M. R., & Hill, C. E. (2010). Training implications of harmful effects of psychological treatments. *American Psychologist, 65,* 34–49. (p. 562)

Cattell, R. B. (1963). Theory of fluid and crystallized intelligence: A critical experiment. *Journal of Educational Psychology, 54,* 1–22. (p. 337)

Cavalli-Sforza, L., Menozzi, P., & Piazza, A. (1994). *The history and geography of human genes.* Princeton, NJ: Princeton University Press. (p. 344)

Cavigelli, S. A., & McClintock, M. K. (2003). Fear of novelty in infant rats predicts adult corticosterone dynamics and an early death. *Proceedings of the National Academy of Sciences, 100,* 16131–16136. (p. 393)

Cawley, B. D., Keeping, L. M., & Levy, P. E. (1998). Participation in the performance appraisal process and employee reactions: A meta-analytic review of field investigations. *Journal of Applied Psychology, 83,* 615–633. (p. B-11)

CDC. (2009a). *Self-harm, all injury causes, nonfatal injuries and rates per 100,000.* National Center for Injury Prevention and Control. http://webappa.cdc.gov/cgi-bin/broker.exe. (p. 525)

CDC. (2009b, December 18). Prevalence of autism spectrum disorders—Autism and developments disabilities monitoring network, United States, 2006 (corresponding author: Catherine Rice). *MMWR, 58*(SS10), 1–20. (www.cdc.gov). (p. 130)

CDC. (2011a). Resources for Entertainment Education Content Developers. Centers for Disease Control and Prevention (www.cdc.gov/healthcommunication/ToolsTemplates/EntertainmentEd/Tips/Influenza.html). (p. 532)

CDC. (2011b, February). *HIV surveillance report, 2009,* vol. 21. Centers for Disease Control and Prevention (www.cdc.gov/hiv/topics/surveillance/basic.htm:hivaidsage). (p. 174)

CDC. (2011c, accessed April 20). *Who's at risk? Tobacco use—smoking.* Centers for Disease Control and Prevention (cdc.gov/vitalsigns/TobaccoUse/Smoking/Risk.html). (p. 112)

CDC. (2012, May 11). Suicide rates among persons ages 10 years and older, by race/ethnicity and sex, United States, 2005–2009. National Suicide Statistics at a Glance, Centers for disease Control and Prevention (www.cdc.gov). (p. 524)

Ceci, S. J. (1993). Cognitive and social factors in children's testimony. Master lecture, American Psychological Association convention. (pp. 297, 298)

Ceci, S. J., & Bruck, M. (1993). Child witnesses: Translating research into policy. *Social Policy Report* (Society for Research in Child Development), 7(3), 1–30. (p. 297)

Ceci, S. J., & Bruck, M. (1995). *Jeopardy in the courtroom: A scientific analysis of children's testimony.* Washington, DC: American Psychological Association. (p. 297)

Ceci, S. J., Huffman, M. L. C., Smith, E., & Loftus, E. F. (1994). Repeatedly thinking about a non-event: Source misattributions among preschoolers. *Consciousness and Cognition, 3,* 388–407. (p. 297)

Ceci, S. J., & Williams, W. M. (1997). Schooling, intelligence, and income. *American Psychologist, 52,* 1051–1058. (p. 342)

Ceci, S. J., & Williams, W. M. (2009). *The mathematics of sex: How biology and society conspire to limit talented women and girls.* New York: Oxford University Press. (p. 342)

Centers for Disease Control. (1992, September 16). Serious mental illness and disability in the adult household population: United States, 1989. *Advance Data* No. 218 from *Vital and Health Statistics,* National Center for Health Statistics. (p. 540)

Centers for Disease Control Vietnam Experience Study. (1988). Health status of Vietnam veterans. *Journal of the American Medical Association, 259,* 2701–2709. (p. 515)

Centerwall, B. S. (1989). Exposure to television as a risk factor for violence. *American Journal of Epidemiology, 129,* 643–652. (p. 265)

Cepeda, N. J., Pashler, H., Vul, E., Wixted, J. T., & Rohrer, D. (2006). Distributed practice in verbal recall tasks: A review and quantitative synthesis. *Psychological Bulletin, 132,* 354–380. (p. 278)

Cepeda, N. J., Vul, E., Rohrer, D., Wixed, J. T., & Pashler, H. (2008). Spacing effects in learning: A temporal ridgeline of optimal retention. *Psychological Science, 19,* 1095–1102. (p. 278)

Cerella, J. (1985). Information processing rates in the elderly. *Psychological Bulletin, 98,* 67–83. (p. 152)

CFI. (2003, July). *International developments. Report.* Amherst, NY: Center for Inquiry International. (p. 232)

Chabris, C. F., & Simons, D. (2010). *The invisible gorilla: And other ways our intuitions deceive us.* New York: Crown. (p. 82)

Chambless, D. L., Baker, M. J., Baucom, D. H., Beutler, L. E., Calhoun, K. S., Crits-Christoph, P., Daiuto, A., DeRubeis, R., Detweiler, J., Haaga, D. A. F., Johnson, S. B., McCurry, S., Mueser, K. T., Pope, K. S., Sanderson, W. C., Shoham, V., Stickle, T., Williams, D. A., & Woody, S. R. (1997). Update on empirically validated therapies, II. *The Clinical Psychologist, 51*(1), 3–16. (p. 564)

Chamove, A. S. (1980). Nongenetic induction of acquired levels of aggression. *Journal of Abnormal Psychology, 89,* 469–488. (p. 264)

Champagne, F. A. (2010). Early adversity and developmental outcomes: Interaction between genetics, epigenetics, and social experiences across the life span. *Perspectives on Psychological Science, 5,* 564–574. (p. 67)

Champagne, F. A., Francis, D. D., Mar, A, & Meaney, M. J. (2003). Naturally-occurring variations in maternal care in the rat as a mediating influence for the effects of environment on the development of individual differences in stress reactivity. *Physiology & Behavior, 79,* 359–371. (p. 68)

Champagne, F. A., & Mashoodh, R. (2009). Genes in context: Gene-environment interplay and the origins of individual differences in behavior. *Current Directions in Psychological Science, 18,* 127–131. (p. 68)

Chance News. (1997, 25 November). More on the frequency of letters in texts. Dart.Chance@Dartmouth.edu. (p. 20)

Chandler, J., & Schwarz, N. (2009). How extending your middle finger affects your perception of others: learned movements influence concept accessibility. *Journal of Experimental Social Psychology, 45,* 123–128. (p. 385)

Chandra, A., Mosher, W. D., & Copen, C. (2011, March). Sexual behavior, sexual attraction, and sexual identity in the United States: Data from the 2006–2008 National Survey of Family Growth. *National Health Statistics Reports,* Number 36 (Centers for Disease Control and Prevention). (p. 178)

Chaplin, W. F., Phillips, J. B., Brown, J. D., Clanton, N. R., & Stein, J. L. (2000). Handshaking, gender, personality, and first impressions. *Journal of Personality and Social Psychology, 79,* 110–117. (p. 379)

Charness, N., & Boot, W. R. (2009). Aging and information technology use. *Current Directions in Psychological Science, 18,* 253–258. (p. 338)

Charpak, G., & Broch, H. (2004). *Debunked! ESP, telekinesis, and other pseudoscience.* Baltimore, MD: Johns Hopkins University Press. (p. 231)

Chartrand, T. L., & Bargh, J. A. (1999). The chameleon effect: The perception-behavior link and social interaction. *Journal of Personality and Social Psychology, 76,* 893–910. (p. 465)

Chatard, A., & Selimbegović, L. (2011). When self-destructive thoughts flash through the mind: Failure to meet standards affects the accessibility of suicide-related thoughts. *Journal of Personality and Social Psychology, 100,* 587–605. (p. 524)

Chater, N., Reali, F., & Christiansen, M. H. (2009). Restrictions on biological adaptation in language evolution. *PNAS, 106,* 1015–1020. (p. 321)

Cheek, J. M., & Melchior, L. A. (1990). Shyness, self-esteem, and self-consciousness. In H. Leitenberg (Ed.), *Handbook of social and evaluation anxiety.* New York: Plenum. (p. 451)

Cheit, R. E. (1998). Consider this, skeptics of recovered memory. *Ethics & Behavior, 8,* 141–160. (p. 431)

Chen, A. W., Kazanjian, A., & Wong, H. (2009). Why do Chinese Canadians not consult mental health services: Health status, language or culture? *Transcultural Psychiatry, 46,* 623–640. (p. 566)

Chen, E. (2004). Why socioeconomic status affects the health of children: A psychosocial perspective. *Current Directions in Psychological Science, 13,* 112–115. (p. 402)

Chen, S-Y., & Fu, Y-C. (2008). Internet use and academic achievement: Gender differences in early adolescence. *Adolescence, 44,* 797–812. (p. 369)

Chen, X., Beydoun, M. A., & Wang, Y. (2008). Is sleep duration associated with childhood obesity? A systematic review and meta-analysis. *Obesity, 16,* 265–274. (p. 90)

Cherkas, L. F., Hunkin, J. L., Kato, B. S., Richards, J. B., Gardner, J. P., Surdulescu, G. L., Kimura, M., Lu, X., Spector, T. D., & Aviv, A. (2008). The association between physical activity in leisure time and leukocyte telomere length. *Archives of Internal Medicine, 168,* 154–158. (p. 152)

Cherniss, C. (2010a). Emotional intelligence: Toward clarification of a concept. *Industrial and Organizational Psychology, 3,* 110–126. (p. 333)

Cherniss, C. (2010b). Emotional intelligence: New insights and further clarifications. *Industrial and Organizational Psycvhology, 3,* 183–191. (p. 333)

Chess, S., & Thomas, A. (1987). *Know your child: An authoritative guide for today's parents.* New York: Basic Books. (p. 134)

Cheung, B. Y., Chudek, M., & Heine, S. J. (2011). Evidence for a sensitive period for acculturation: Younger immigrants report acculturating at a faster rate. *Psychological Science, 22,* 147–152. (p. 321)

Chida, Y., & Hamer, M. (2008). Chronic psychosocial factors and acute physiological responses to laboratory-induced stress in healthy populations: A quantitative review of 30 years of investigations. *Psychological Bulletin, 134,* 829–885. (p. 398)

Chida, Y., Hamer, M., Wardle, J., & Steptoe, A. (2008). Do stress-related psychosocial factors contribute to cancer incidence and survival? *Nature Reviews: Clinical Oncology, 5,* 466–475. (p. 397)

Chida, Y., & Steptoe, A. (2009). The association of anger and hostility with future coronary heart disease: A meta-analytic review of prospective evidence. *Journal of the American College of Cardiology, 17,* 936–946. (p. 398)

Chida, Y., Steptoe, A., & Powell, L. H. (2009). Religiosity/spirituality and mortality. *Psychotherapy and Psychosomatics, 78,* 81–90. (p. 412)

Chiles, J. A., Lambert, M. J., & Hatch, A. L. (1999). The impact of psychological interventions on medical cost offset: A meta-analytic review. *Clinical Psychology; Science and Practice, 6,* 204–220. (p. 561)

Chivers, M. L. (2005). A brief review and discussion of sex differences in the specificity of sexual arousal. *Sexual and Relationship Therapy, 20,* 377–390. (p. 179)

Chivers, M. L., Seto, M. C., Lalumière, M. L., Laan, E., & Grimbos, T. (2010). Agreement of self-reported and genital measures of sexual arousal in men and women: A meta-analysis. *Archives of Sexual Behavior, 39,* 5–56. (p. 175)

Choi, C. Q. (2008, March). Do you need only half your brain? *Scientific American,* p. 104. (p. 58)

Choi, I., & Choi, Y. (2002). Culture and self-concept flexibility. *Personality and Social Psychology Bulletin, 28,* 1508–1517. (p. 451)

Chomsky, N. (1972). *Language and mind.* New York: Harcourt Brace. (p. 323)

Christakis, N. A., & Fowler, J. H. (2007). The spread of obesity in a large social network over 32 years. *New England Journal of Medicine, 357,* 370–379. (p. 362)

Christakis, N. A., & Fowler, J. H. (2008, May). The collective dynamics of smoking in a large social network. *New England Journal of Medicine, 358*(21), 2249–2258. (p. 112)

Christakis, N. A., & Fowler, J. H. (2009). *Connected: The surprising power of social networks and how they shape our lives.* New York: Little, Brown. (p. 407)

Christensen, A., & Jacobson, N. S. (1994). Who (or what) can do psychotherapy: The status and challenge of nonprofessional therapies. *Psychological Science, 5,* 8–14. (p. 566)

Christophersen, E. R., & Edwards, K. J. (1992). Treatment of elimination disorders: State of the art 1991. *Applied & Preventive Psychology, 1,* 15–22. (p. 551)

Chua, H. F., Boland, J. E., & Nisbett, R. E. (2005). Cultural variation in eye movements during scene perception. *Proceedings of the National Academy of Sciences, 102,* 12629–12633. (p. 458)

Chugani, H. T., & Phelps, M. E. (1986). Maturational changes in cerebral function in infants determined by 18FDG positron emission tomography. *Science, 231,* 840–843. (p. 122)

Church, T. S., Thomas, D. M., Tudor-Locke, C., Katzmarzyk, P. T., Earnest, C. P., Rodarte, R. Q., Martin, C. K., Blair, S. N., & Bouchard, C. (2011). Trends over 5 decades in U.S. occupation-related physical activity and their associations with obesity. *PLoS ONE, 6(5),* e19657. (p. 362)

CIA. (2010). *The World Fact Book:* Literacy. Washington, D.C.: CIA (https://www.cia.gov/library/publications/the-world-factbook/fields/2103.html). (p. 476)

Cialdini, R. B. (1993). *Influence: Science and practice* (3rd ed.). New York: HarperCollins. (p. 461)

Cialdini, R. B., & Richardson, K. D. (1980). Two indirect tactics of image management: Basking and blasting. *Journal of Personality and Social Psychology, 39,* 406–415. (p. 479)

Ciarrochi, J., Forgas, J. P., & Mayer, J. D. (2006). *Emotional intelligence in everyday life* (2nd ed.). New York: Psychology Press. (p. 333)

Cin, S. D., Gibson, B., Zanna, M. P., Shumate, R., & Fong, G. T. (2007). Smoking in movies, implicit associations of smoking with the self, and intentions to smoke. *Psychological Science, 18,* 559–563. (p. 111)

Circle of Prevention. (2002). Economic independence for women leaving or living in abusive relationships. Government of Newfoundland and Labrador (www.gov.nl.ca/VPI/publications/economicindependence.pdf). (p. 464)

Clack, B., Dixon, J., & Tredoux, C. (2005). Eating together apart: Patterns of segregation in a multi-ethnic cafeteria. *Journal of Community and Applied Social Psychology, 15,* 1–16. (p. 499)

Clancy, S. A. (2005). *Abducted: How people come to believe they were kidnapped by aliens.* Cambridge, MA: Harvard University Press. (p. 85)

Clancy, S. A. (2010). *The trauma myth: The truth about the sexual abuse of children—and its aftermath.* New York: Basic Books. (p. 136)

Clark, A., Seidler, A., & Miller, M. (2001). Inverse association between sense of humor and coronary heart disease. *International Journal of Cardiology, 80,* 87–88. (p. 405)

Clark, K. B., & Clark, M. P. (1947). Racial identification and preference in Negro children. In T. M. Newcomb & E. L. Hartley (Eds.), *Readings in social psychology.* New York: Holt. (p. 29)

Clay, R. A. (2010, July/August). Defining disease worldwide. *Monitor on Psychology,* pp. 54–57. (p. 509)

Clay, R. A. (2011, January). Revising the DSM. *Monitor on Psychology,* pp. 54–55. (p. 509)

Cleary, A. M. (2008). Recognition memory, familiarity, and déjà vu experiences. *Current Directions in Psychological Science, 17,* 353–357. (p. 296)

Coan, J. A., Schaefer, H. S., & Davidson, R. J. (2006). Lending a hand: Social regulation of the neural response to threat. *Psychological Science, 17,* 1032–1039. (p. 405)

Coelho, C. M., & Purkis, H. (2009). The origins of specific phobias: Influential theories and current perspectives. *Review of General Psychology, 13,* 335–348. (p. 518)

Coffey, C. E., Wilkinson, W. E., Weiner, R. D., Parashos, I. A., Djang, W. T., Webb, M. C., Figiel, G. S., & Spritzer, C. E. (1993). Quantitative cerebral anatomy in depression: A controlled magnetic resonance imaging study. *Archives of General Psychiatry, 50,* 7–16. (p. 523)

Cohen, A. B. (2009). Many forms of culture. *American Psychologist, 64,* 194–204. (pp. 452, 463)

Cohen, D. (1995, June 17). Now we are one, or two, or three. *New Scientist,* pp. 14–15. (p. 534)

Cohen, N. (2011, January 30). Define gender gap? Look up Wikipedia's contributor list. *New York Times* (www.nytimes.com). (p. 166)

Cohen, P. (2007, November 15). Freud is widely taught at universities, except in the psychology department. *New York Times* (www.nytimes.com). (p. 424)

Cohen, P. (2010, June 11). Long road to adulthood is growing even longer. *New York Times* (www.nytimes.com). (p. 149)

Cohen, R. (2011, March 12). The happynomics of life. *New York Times* (www.nytimes.com). (p. 419)

Cohen, S. (2004). Social relationships and health. *American Psychologist, 59,* 676–684. (p. 406)

Cohen, S., Doyle, W. J., Alper, C. M., Janicki-Deverts, D., & Turner, R. B. (2009). Sleep habits and susceptibility to the common cold. *Archives of Internal Medicine, 169,* 62–67. (p. 90)

Cohen, S., Doyle, W. J., Skoner, D. P., Rabin, B. S., & Gwaltney, J. M., Jr. (1997). Social ties and susceptibility to the common cold. *Journal of the American Medical Association, 277,* 1940–1944. (pp. 402, 406)

Cohen, S., Doyle, W. J., Turner, R., Alper, C. M., & Skoner, D. P. (2003). Sociability and susceptibility to the common cold. *Psychological Science, 14,* 389–395. (p. 395)

Cohen, S., Kaplan, J. R., Cunnick, J. E., Manuck, S. B., & Rabin, B. S. (1992). Chronic social stress, affiliation, and cellular immune response in nonhuman primates. *Psychological Science, 3,* 301–304. (p. 394)

Cohen, S., & Pressman, S. D. (2006). Positive affect and health. *Current Directions in Psychological Science, 15,* 122–125. (p. 395)

Cohen, S., Tyrrell, D. A. J., & Smith, A. P. (1991). Psychological stress and susceptibility to the common cold. *New England Journal of Medicine, 325,* 606–612. (p. 395)

Colapinto, J. (2000). *As nature made him: The boy who was raised as a girl.* New York: HarperCollins. (p. 169)

Colarelli, S. M., & Dettman, J. R. (2003). Intuitive evolutionary perspectives in marketing. *Psychology and Marketing, 20,* 837–865. (p. 70)

Colarelli, S. M., Spranger, J. L., & Hechanova, M. R. (2006). Women, power, and sex composition in small groups: An evolutionary perspective. *Journal of Organizational Behavior, 27,* 163–184. (p. 165)

Colcombe, S. J., Kramer, A. F., Erickson, K. I., Scalf, P., McAuley, E., Cohen, N. J., Webb, A., Jerome, G. J., Marquex, D. X., & Elavsky, S. (2004). Cardiovascular fitness, cortical plasticity, and aging. *Proceedings of the National Academy of Sciences, 101,* 3316–3321. (p. 152)

Cole, K. C. (1998). *The universe and the teacup: The mathematics of truth and beauty.* New York: Harcourt Brace. (p. 104)

Coley, R. L., Medeiros, B. L., & Schindler, H. (2008). Using sibling differences to estimate effects of parenting on adolescent sexual risk behaviors. *Journal of Adolescent Health, 43,* 133–140. (p. 177)

Collins, D. W., & Kimura, D. (1997). A large sex difference on a two-dimensional mental rotation task. *Behavioral Neuroscience, 111,* 845–849. (p. 342)

Collins, F. (2006). *The language of God.* New York: Free Press. (p. 70)

Collins, G. (2009, March 9). The rant list. *New York Times* (nytimes.com). (p. 28)

Collins, N. L., & Miller, L. C. (1994). Self-disclosure and liking: A meta-analytic review. *Psychological Bulletin, 116,* 457–475. (pp. 492, 493)

Collins, R. L., Elliott, M. N., Berry, S. H., Danouse, D. E., Kunkel, D., Hunter, S. B., & Miu, A. (2004). Watching sex on television predicts adolescent initiation of sexual behavior. *Pediatrics, 114,* 280–289. (p. 21)

Collins, W. A., Welsh, D. P., & Furman, W. (2009). Adolescent romantic relationships. *Annual Review of Psychology, 60,* 631–652. (p. 145)

Collinson, S. L., MacKay, C. E., James, A. C., Quested, D. J., Phillips, T., Roberts, N., & Crow, T. J. (2003). Brain volume, asymmetry and intellectual impairment in relation to sex in early-onset schizophrenia. *British Journal of Psychiatry, 183,* 114–120. (p. 531)

Collishaw, S., Pickles, A., Natarajan, L., & Maughan, B. (2007, June). 20-year trends in depression and anxiety in England. Paper presented at the Thirteenth Scientific Meeting on The Brain and the Developing Child, London. (p. 522)

Colombo, J. (1982). The critical period concept: Research, methodology, and theoretical issues. *Psychological Bulletin, 91,* 260–275. (p. 133)

Comfort, A. (1992). *The new joy of sex.* New York: Pocket. (p. 151)

Comstock, G. (2008). A sociological perspective on television violence and aggression. *American Behavioral Scientist, 51,* 1184–1211. (p. 265)

Confer, J. C., Easton, J. A., Fleischman, D. S., Goetz, C. D., Lewis, D. M. G., Perilloux, C., & Buss, D. M. (2010). Evolutionary psychology: Controversies, questions, prospects, and limitations. *American Psychologist, 65,* 110–126. (pp. 185, 186)

Conley, C. S., & Rudolph, K. D. (2009). The emerging sex difference in adolescent depression: Interacting contributions of puberty and peer stress. *Development and Psychopathology, 21,* 593–620. (p. 140)

Conn, V. S. (2010). Depressive symptom outcomes of physical activity interventions: Meta-analysis findings. *Annals of Behavioral Medicine, 39,* 128–138. (p. 408)

Connor, C. E. (2010). A new viewpoint on faces. *Science, 330,* 764–765. (p. 204)

Connor-Smith, J. K., & Flachsbart, C. (2007). Relations between personality and coping: A meta-analysis. *Journal of Personality and Social Psychology, 93,* 1080–1107. (p. 401)

Consumer Reports. (1995, November). Does therapy help? Pp. 734–739. (p. 560)

Conway, A. R. A., Skitka, L. J., Hemmerich, J. A., & Kershaw, T. C. (2009). Flashbulb memory for 11 September 2001. *Applied Cognitive Psychology, 23,* 605–623. (p. 283)

Conway, M. A., Wang, Q., Hanyu, K., & Haque, S. (2005). A cross-cultural investigation of autobiographical memory. On the universality and cultural variation of the reminiscence bump. *Journal of Cross-Cultural Psychology, 36,* 739–749. (p. 153)

Cooke, L. J., Wardle, J., & Gibson, E. L. (2003). Relationship between parental report of food neophobia and everyday food consumption in 2–6-year-old children. *Appetite, 41,* 205–206. (p. 224)

Cooper, K. J. (1999, May 1). This time, copycat wave is broader. *Washington Post* (www.washingtonpost.com). (p. 465)

Cooper, M. (2010, October 18). From Obama, the tax cut nobody heard of. *New York Times* (www.nytimes.com). (p. 479)

Cooper, M. L. (2006). Does drinking promote risky sexual behavior? A complex answer to a simple question. *Current Directions in Psychological Science, 15,* 19–23. (p. 102)

Cooper, W. H., & Withey, M. J. (2009). The strong situation hypothesis. *Personality and Social Psychology Review, 13,* 62–72. (p. 443)

Coopersmith, S. (1967). *The antecedents of self-esteem.* San Francisco: Freeman. (p. 138)

Copeland, W., Shanahan, L., Miller, S., Costello, E. J., Angold, A., & Maughan, B. (2010). Outcomes of early pubertal timing in young women: A prospective population-based study. *American Journal of Psychiatry, 167,* 1218–1225. (p. 140)

Corballis, M. C. (2002). *From hand to mouth: The origins of language.* Princeton, NJ: Princeton University Press. (p. 324)

Corballis, M. C. (2003). From mouth to hand: Gesture, speech, and the evolution of right-handedness. *Behavioral and Brain Sciences, 26,* 199–260. (p. 324)

Coren, S. (1996). *Sleep thieves: An eye-opening exploration into the science and mysteries of sleep.* New York: Free Press. (pp. 89, 91)

Corey, D. P., & 15 others. (2004). TRPA1 is a candidate for the mechanosensitive transduction channel of vertebrate hair cells. *Nature, 432,* 723–730. (p. 217)

Corina, D. P. (1998). The processing of sign language: Evidence from aphasia. In B. Stemmer & H. A. Whittaker (Eds.), *Handbook of neurolinguistics.* San Diego: Academic Press. (p. 61)

Corina, D. P., Vaid, J., & Bellugi, U. (1992). The linguistic basis of left hemisphere specialization. *Science, 255,* 1258–1260. (p. 61)

Corkin, S., quoted by R. Adelson (2005, September). Lessons from H. M. *Monitor on Psychology,* p. 59. (p. 290)

Corneille, O., Huart, J., Becquart, E., & Brédart, S. (2004). When memory shifts toward more typical category exemplars: Accentuation effects in the recollection of ethnically ambiguous faces. *Journal of Personality and Social Psychology, 86,* 236–250. (p. 306)

Correll, J., Park, B., Judd, C. M., & Wittenbrink, B. (2002). The police officer's dilemma: Using ethnicity to disambiguate potentially threatening individuals. *Journal of Personality and Social Psychology, 83,* 1314–1329. (p. 477)

Correll, J., Park, B., Judd, C. M., Wittenbrink, B., Sadler, M. S., & Keesee, T. (2007). Across the thin blue line: Police officers and racial bias in the decision to shoot. *Journal of Personality and Social Psychology, 92,* 1006–1023. (p. 477)

Costa, P. T., Jr., & McCrae, R. R. (2009). The five-factor model and the NEO inventories. In J. N. Butcher (ed.), *Oxford handbook of personality assessment.* New York: Oxford University Press. (p. 439)

Costa, P. T., Jr., Terracciano, A., & McCrae, R. R. (2001). Gender differences in personality traits across cultures: Robust and surprising findings. *Journal of Personality and Social Psychology, 81,* 322–331. (p. 381)

Costello, E. J., Compton, S. N., Keeler, G., & Angold, A. (2003). Relationships between poverty and psychopathology: A natural experiment. *Journal of the American Medical Association, 290,* 2023–2029. (pp. 21, 540)

Coughlin, J. F., Mohyde, M., D'Ambrosio, L. A., & Gilbert, J. (2004). *Who drives older driver decisions?* Cambridge, MA: MIT Age Lab. (p. 152)

Couli, J. T., Vidal, F., Nazarian, B., & Macar, F. (2004). Functional anatomy of the attentional modulation of time estimation. *Science, 303,* 1506–1508. (p. B-1)

Council of State Governments. (2002). *Criminal justice/mental health consensus project.* Lexington, KY: Author. (p. 512)

Courtney, J. G., Longnecker, M. P., Theorell, T., & de Verdier, M. G. (1993). Stressful life events and the risk of colorectal cancer. *Epidemiology, 4,* 407–414. (p. 397)

Covin, R., Ouimet, A. J., Seeds, P. M., & Dozois, D. J. A. (2008). A meta-analysis of CBT for pathological worry among clients with GAD. *Journal of Anxiety Disorders, 22,* 108–116. (p. 557)

Cowan, G., Lee, C., Levy, D., & Snyder, D. (1988). Dominance and inequality in X-rated videocassettes. *Psychology of Women Quarterly, 12,* 299–311. (p. 484)

Cowan, N. (1988). Evolving conceptions of memory storage, selective attention, and their mutual constraints within the human information-processing system. *Psychological Bulletin, 104,* 163–191. (p. 276)

Cowan, N. (2010). The magical mystery four: How is working memory capacity limited, and why? *Current Directions in Psychological Science, 19,* 51–57. (p. 273)

Cowart, B. J. (1981). Development of taste perception in humans: Sensitivity and preference throughout the life span. *Psychological Bulletin, 90,* 43–73. (p. 224)

Cowart, B. J. (2005). Taste, our body's gustatory gatekeeper. *Cerebrum, 7*(2), 7–22. (pp. 224, 225)

Cox, J. J., & 18 others. (2006). An *SCN9A* channelopathy causes congenital inability to experience pain. *Nature, 444,* 894–898. (p. 222)

Coyne, J. C., Ranchor, A. V., & Palmer, S. C. (2010). Meta-analysis of stress-related factors in cancer. *Nature Reviews: Clinical Oncology, 7,* doi:10.1038/ncponc1134-c1. (p. 397)

Coyne, J. C., Stefanek, M., & Palmer, S. C. (2007). Psychotherapy and survival in cancer: The conflict between hope and evidence. *Psychological Bulletin, 133,* 367–394. (p. 397)

Coyne, J. C., & Tennen, H. (2010). Positive psychology in cancer care: Bad science, exaggerated claims, and unproven medicine. *Annals of Behavioral Medicine, 39,* 16–26. (p. 397)

Coyne, J. C., Thombs, B. C., Stefanek, M., & Palmer, S. C. (2009). Time to let go of the illusion that psychotherapy extends the survival of cancer patients: Reply to Kraemer, Kuchler, and Spiegel (2009). *Psychological Bulletin, 135,* 179–182. (p. 397)

Crabbe, J. C. (2002). Genetic contributions to addiction. *Annual Review of Psychology, 53,* 435–462. (p. 110)

Crabtree, S. (2005, January 13). Engagement keeps the doctor away. *Gallup Management Journal* (gmj.gallup.com). (p. B-9)

Crabtree, S. (2010, July 14). Personal correspondence (Gallup Organization). (p. 156)

Craik, F. I. M., & Tulving, E. (1975). Depth of processing and the retention of words in episodic memory. *Journal of Experimental Psychology: General, 104,* 268–294. (p. 279)

Crandall, J. E. (1984). Social interest as a moderator of life stress. *Journal of Personality and Social Psychology, 47,* 164–174. (p. 435)

Crawford, E. F., Drescher, K. D., & Rosen, C. S. (2009). Predicting mortality in veterans with posttraumatic stress disorder thirty years after Vietnam. *Journal of Nervous and Mental Disease, 197,* 260–265. (p. 515)

Crawley, J. N. (2007). Testing hypotheses about autism. *Science, 318,* 56–57. (p. 131)

Credé, M., & Kuncel, N. R. (2008). Study habits, skills, and attitudes: The third pillar supporting collegiate academic performance. *Perspectives on Psychological Science, 3,* 425–453. (p. 342)

Crews, F. T., He, J., & Hodge, C. (2007). Adolescent cortical development: A critical period of vulnerability for addiction. *Pharmacology, Biochemistry and Behavior, 86,* 189–199. (pp. 102, 141)

Crews, F. T., Mdzinarishvili, A., Kim, D., He, J., & Nixon, K. (2006). Neurogenesis in adolescent brain is potently inhibited by ethanol. *Neuroscience, 137,* 437–445. (p. 102)

Crocker, J., & Park, L. E. (2004). The costly pursuit of self-esteem. *Psychological Bulletin, 130,* 392–414. (p. 450)

Crocker, J., Thompson, L. L., McGraw, K. M., & Ingerman, C. (1987). Downward comparison, prejudice, and evaluation of others: Effects of self-esteem and threat. *Journal of Personality and Social Psychology, 52,* 907–916. (p. 479)

Croft, R. J., Klugman, A., Baldeweg, T., & Gruzelier, J. H. (2001). Electrophysiological evidence of serotonergic impairment in long-term MDMA ("Ecstasy") users. *American Journal of Psychiatry, 158,* 1687–1692. (p. 107)

Crook, T. H., & West, R. L. (1990). Name recall performance across the adult life-span. *British Journal of Psychology, 81,* 335–340. (p. 153)

Cross, S., & Markus, H. (1991). Possible selves across the life span. *Human Development, 34,* 230–255. (p. 447)

Cross-National Collaborative Group. (1992). The changing rate of major depression. *Journal of the American Medical Association, 268,* 3098–3105. (p. 522)

Crowell, J. A., & Waters, E. (1994). Bowlby's theory grown up: The role of attachment in adult love relationships. *Psychological Inquiry, 5,* 1–22. (p. 133)

Csikszentmihalyi, M. (1990). *Flow: The psychology of optimal experience.* New York: Harper & Row. (p. B-1)

Csikszentmihalyi, M. (1999). If we are so rich, why aren't we happy? *American Psychologist, 54,* 821–827. (p. B-1)

Csikszentmihalyi, M., & Hunter, J. (2003). Happiness in everyday life: The uses of experience sampling. *Journal of Happiness Studies, 4,* 185–199. (p. 146)

Cuijpers, P., van Straten, A., Schuurmans, J., van Oppen, P., Hollon, S. D., & Andersson, G. (2010). Psychotherapy for chronic major depression and dysthymia: A meta-analysis. *Clinical Psychology Review, 30,* 51–62. (p. 570)

Culbert, K. M., Burt, S. A., McGue, M., Iacono, W. G., & Klump, K. L. (2009). Puberty and the genetic diathesis of disordered eating attitudes and behaviors. *Journal of Abnormal Psychology, 118,* 788–796. (p. 536)

Cullum, J., & Harton, H. C. (2007). Cultural evolution: Interpersonal influence, issue importance, and the development of shared attitudes in college residence halls. *Personality and Social Psychology Bulletin, 33,* 1327–1339. (p. 467)

Cummings, R. A. (2006, April 4). *Australian Unity Wellbeing Index: Survey 14.1.* Australian Centre on Quality of Life, Deakin University, Melbourne: Report 14.1. (p. 415)

Cunningham, M. R., & others. (2005). "Their ideas of beauty are, on the whole, the same as ours": Consistency and variability in the cross-cultural perception of female physical attractiveness. *Journal of Personality and Social Psychology, 68,* 261–279. (p. 490)

Cunningham, W. A., Johnson, M. K., Raye, C. L., Gatenby, J. C., Gore, J. C., & Banaji, M. R. (2004). Separable neural components in the processing of Black and White faces. *Psychological Science, 15,* 806–813. (p. 477)

Currie, T. E., & Little, A. C. (2009). The relative importance of the face and body in judgments of human physical attractiveness. *Evolution and Human Behavior, 30,* 409–416. (p. 490)

Curry, J., & 22 others. (2011). Recovery and recurrence following treatment for adolescent major depression. *Archives of General Psychiatry, 68,* 263–269. (p. 522)

Curtis, G. C., Magee, W. J., Eaton, W. W., Wittchen, H-U., & Kessler, R. C. (1998). Specific fears and phobias: Epidemiology and classification. *British Journal of Psychiatry, 173,* 212–217. (p. 514)

Curtis, R. C., & Miller, K. (1986). Believing another likes or dislikes you: Behaviors making the beliefs come true. *Journal of Personality and Social Psychology, 51,* 284–290. (p. 491)

Custers, R., & Aarts, H. (2010). The unconscious will: How the pursuit of goals operates outside of conscious awareness. *Science, 329,* 47–50. (p. 313)

Cyders, M. A., & Smith, G. T. (2008). Emotion-based dispositions to rash action: Positive and negative urgency. *Psychological Bulletin, 134,* 807–828. (p. 371)

Czeisler, C. A., Allan, J. S., Strogatz, S. H., Ronda, J. M., Sanchez, R., Rios, C. D., Freitag, W. O., Richardson, G. S., & Kronauer, R. E. (1986). Bright light resets the human circadian pacemaker independent of the timing of the sleep-wake cycle. *Science, 233,* 667–671. (p. 88)

Czeisler, C. A., Duffy, J. F., Shanahan, T. L., Brown, E. N., Mitchell, J. F., Rimmer, D. W., Ronda, J. M., Silva, E. J., Allan, J. S., Emens, J. S., Dijk, D-J., & Kronauer, R. E. (1999). Stability, precision, and near-24-hour period of the human circadian pacemaker. *Science, 284,* 2177–2181. (p. 87)

Czeisler, C. A., Kronauer, R. E., Allan, J. S., & Duffy, J. F. (1989). Bright light induction of strong (type O) resetting of the human circadian pacemaker. *Science, 244,* 1328–1333. (p. 88)

D

Dabbs, J. M., Jr., Bernieri, F. J., Strong, R. K., Campo, R., & Milun, R. (2001b). Going on stage: Testosterone in greetings and meetings. *Journal of Research in Personality, 35,* 27–40. (p. 482)

Dabbs, J. M., Jr., & Morris, R. (1990). Testosterone, social class, and antisocial behavior in a sample of 4,462 men. *Psychological Science, 1,* 209–211. (p. 482)

Dabbs, J. M., Jr., Riad, J. K., & Chance, S. E. (2001a). Testosterone and ruthless homicide. *Personality and Individual Differences, 31,* 599–603. (p. 482)

Damasio, A. R. (2003). *Looking for Spinoza: Joy, sorrow, and the feeling brain.* New York: Harcourt. (p. 372)

Damasio, A. R. (2010). *Self comes to mind: Constructing the conscious brain.* New York: Pantheon. (p. 447)

Damasio, H., Grabowski, T., Frank, R., Galaburda, A. M., & Damasio, A. R. (1994). The return of Phineas Gage: Clues about the brain from the skull of a famous patient. *Science, 264,* 1102–1105. (p. 57)

Damon, W., Menon, J., & Bronk, K. (2003). The development of purpose during adolescence. *Applied Developmental Science, 7,* 119–128. (p. 145)

Danner, D. D., Snowdon, D. A., & Friesen, W. V. (2001). Positive emotions in early life and longevity: Findings from the Nun Study. *Journal of Personality and Social Psychology, 80,* 804–813. (p. 405)

Danso, H., & Esses, V. (2001). Black experimenters and the intellectual test performance of white participants: The tables are turned. *Journal of Experimental Social Psychology, 37,* 158–165. (p. 346)

Danziger, S., & Ward, R. (2010). Language changes implicit associations between ethnic groups and evaluation in bilinguals. *Psychological Science, 21,* 799–800. (p. 326)

Dapretto, M., Davies, M. S., Pfeifer, J. H., Scott, A. A., Sigman, M., Bookheimer, S. Y., & Iacoboni, M. (2006). Understanding emotions in others: Mirror neuron dysfunction in children with autism spectrum disorders. *Nature Neuroscience, 9,* 28–30. (p. 131)

Darley, J. M. (2009). Morality in the law: The psychological foundations of citizens' desires to punish transgressions. *Annual Review of Law and Social Science, 5,* 1–23. (p. 143)

Darley, J. M., & Alter, A. (2011). Behavioral issues of punishment and deterrence. In E. Shafir (Ed.), *The behavioral foundations of policy.* Princeton, NJ: Princeton University Press and the Russell Sage Foundation. (p. 251)

Darley, J. M., & Latané, B. (1968a). Bystander intervention in emergencies: Diffusion of responsibility. *Journal of Personality and Social Psychology, 8,* 377–383. (pp. 494, 495)

Darley, J. M., & Latané, B. (1968b, December). When will people help in a crisis? *Psychology Today,* pp. 54–57, 70–71. (p. 494)

Darrach, B., & Norris, J. (1984, August). An American tragedy. *Life,* pp. 58–74. (p. 538)

Darwin, C. (1859). *On the origin of species by means of natural selection.* London: John Murray. (p. 70)

Darwin, C. (1872). *The expression of the emotions in man and animals.* London: John Murray, Albemarle Street. (pp. 223, 384)

Daskalakis, Z. J., Levinson, A. J., & Fitzgerald, P. B. (2008). Repetitive transcranial magnetic stimulation for major depressive disorder: A review. *Canadian Journal of Psychiatry, 53,* 555–564. (p. 572, 573)

Daum, I., & Schugens, M. M. (1996). On the cerebellum and classical conditioning. *Psychological Science, 5,* 58–61. (p. 282)

Davey, G. C. L. (1992). Classical conditioning and the acquisition of human fears and phobias: A review and synthesis of the literature. *Advances in Behavior Research and Therapy, 14,* 29–66. (p. 258)

Davey, G. C. L. (1995). Preparedness and phobias: Specific evolved associations or a generalized expectancy bias? *Behavioral and Brain Sciences, 18,* 289–297. (p. 518)

Davidoff, J. (2004). Coloured thinking. *The Psychologist, 17,* 570–572. (p. 326)

Davidson, R. J. (2000). Affective style, psychopathology, and resilience: Brain mechanisms and plasticity. *American Psychologist, 55,* 1196–1209. (p. 378)

Davidson, R. J. (2003). Affective neuroscience and psychophysiology: Toward a synthesis. *Psychophysiology, 40,* 655–665. (p. 378)

Davidson, R. J., Kabat-Zinn, J., Schumacher, J., Rosenkranz, M., Muller, D., Santorelli, S. F., Urbanowski, F., Harrington, A., Bonus, K., & Sheridan, J. F. (2003). Alterations in brain and immune function produced by mindfulness meditation. *Psychosomatic Medicine, 65,* 564–570. (p. 410)

Davidson, R. J., Pizzagalli, D., Nitschke, J. B., & Putnam, K. (2002). Depression: Perspectives from affective neuroscience. *Annual Review of Psychology, 53,* 545–574. (p. 523)

Davidson, R. J., Putnam, K. M., & Larson, C. L. (2000). Dysfunction in the neural circuitry of emotion regulation—a possible prelude to violence. *Science, 289,* 591–594. (p. 483)

Davies, M. F. (1997). Positive test strategies and confirmatory retrieval processes in the evaluation of personality feedback. *Journal of Personality and Social Psychology, 73,* 574–583. (p. 439)

Davies, P. (2007). *Cosmic jackpot: Why our universe is just right for life.* Boston: Houghton Mifflin. (p. 72)

Davis, B. E., Moon, R. Y., Sachs, H. C., & Ottolini, M. C. (1998). Effects of sleep position on infant motor development. *Pediatrics, 102,* 1135–1140. (p. 123)

Davis, J. O., & Phelps, J. A. (1995). Twins with schizophrenia: Genes or germs? *Schizophrenia Bulletin, 21,* 13–18. (p. 532)

Davis, J. O., Phelps, J. A., & Bracha, H. S. (1995). Prenatal development of monozygotic twins and concordance for schizophrenia. *Schizophrenia Bulletin, 21,* 357–366. (p. 532)

Davis, M. (2005). Searching for a drug to extinguish fear. *Cerebrum, 7*(3), 47–58. (p. 569)

Davison, K. P., Pennebaker, J. W., & Dickerson, S. S. (2000). Who talks? The social psychology of illness support groups. *American Psychologist, 55,* 205–217. (p. 558)

Dawes, R. M. (1980). Social dilemmas. *Annual Review of Psychology, 31,* 169–193. (p. 498)

Dawes, R. M. (1994). *House of cards: Psychology and psychotherapy built on myth.* New York: Free Press. (p. 447)

Dawkins, R. (1998). *Unweaving the rainbow.* Boston: Houghton Mifflin. (p. 71)

Dawkins, R. (2007, July 1). Inferior design. *New York Times* (www.nytimes.com). (p. 69)

Dean, G. A., Kelly, I. W., Saklofske, D. H., & Furnham, A. (1992). Graphology and human judgment. In B. Beyerstein & D. Beyerstein (Eds.), *The write stuff: Evaluations of graphology.* Buffalo, NY: Prometheus Books. (p. 438)

Deary, I. J., Johnson, W., & Houlihan, L. M. (2009). Genetic foundations of human intelligence. *Human Genetics, 126,* 215–232. (p. 340)

Deary, I. J., & Matthews, G. (1993). Personality traits are alive and well. *The Psychologist: Bulletin of the British Psychological Society, 6,* 299–311. (p. 442)

Deary, I. J., Penke, L., & Johnson, W. (2009). The neuroscience of human intelligence differences. *Nature Reviews: Neuroscience, 11,* 201–211. (p. 340)

Deary, I. J., Thorpe, G., Wilson, V., Starr, J. M., & Whalley, L. J. (2003). Population sex differences in IQ at age 11: The Scottish mental survey 1932. *Intelligence, 31,* 533–541. (p. 342)

de Boysson-Bardies, B., Halle, P., Sagart, L., & Durand, C. (1989). A cross linguistic investigation of vowel formats in babbling. *Journal of Child Language, 16,* 1–17. (p. 320)

DeBruine, L. M. (2002). Facial resemblance enhances trust. *Proceedings of the Royal Society of London, 269,* 1307–1312. (p. 489)

DeBruine, L. M. (2004). Facial resemblance increases the attractiveness of same-sex faces more than other-sex faces. *Proceedings of the Royal Society of London B, 271,* 2085–2090. (p. 489)

DeCasper, A. J., Lecanuet, J-P., Busnel, M-C., & others. (1994). Fetal reactions to recurrent maternal speech. *Infant Behavior and Development, 17,* 159–164. (p. 119)

DeCasper, A. J., & Prescott, P. A. (1984). Human newborns' perception of male voices: Preference, discrimination and reinforcing value. *Developmental Psychobiology, 17,* 481–491. (p. 119)

DeCasper, A. J., & Spence, M. J. (1986). Prenatal maternal speech influences newborns' perception of speech sounds. *Infant Behavior and Development, 9,* 133–150. (p. 119)

Deci, E. L., Koestner, R., & Ryan, R. M. (1999, November). A meta-analytic review of experiments examining the effects of extrinsic rewards on intrinsic motivation. *Psychological Bulletin, 125*(6), 627–668. (p. 260)

Deci, E. L., & Ryan, R. M. (1985). *Intrinsic motivation and self-determination in human behavior.* New York: Plenum Press. (p. 260)

Deci, E. L., & Ryan, R. M. (Eds.). (2002). *Handbook of self-determination research.* Rochester, NY: University of Rochester Press. (p. 364)

Deci, E. L., & Ryan, R. M. (2009). Self-determination theory: A consideration of human motivational universals. In P. J. Corr & G. Matthews (eds.), *The Cambridge Handbook of Personality Psychology.* New York: Cambridge University Press. (pp. 260, 364)

de Courten-Myers, G. M. (2005, February 4). Personal correspondence (estimating total brain neurons, extrapolating from her carefully estimated 20 to 23 billion cortical neurons). (pp. 44, 53)

De Dreu, C. K. W., Greer, L. L., Handgraaf, M. J. J., Shalvi, S., Van Kleef, G. A., Baas, M., Ten Velden, F. S., Van Dijk, E., & Feith, S. W. W. (2010). The neuropeptide oxytocin regulated parochial altruism in intergroup conflict among humans. *Science, 328,* 1409–1411. (p. 45)

De Gelder, B. (2010, May). Uncanny sight in the blind. *Scientific American,* pp. 61–65. (p. 80)

de Gonzales, A. B., & 33 others. (2010). Body-mass index and mortality among 1.46 million white adults. *New England Journal of Medicine, 363,* 2211–2219. (p. 361)

Dehaene, S. (2009, November 24). Signatures of consciousness. *Edge is Paris.* www.Edge.org. (p. 194)

Dehne, K. L., & Riedner, G. (2005). *Sexually transmitted infections among adolescents: The need for adequate health services.* Geneva: World Health Organization. (p. 174)

de Hoogh, A. H. B., den Hartog, D. N., Koopman, P. L., Thierry, H., van den Berg, P. T., van der Weide, J. G., & Wilderom, C. P. M. (2004). Charismatic leadership, environmental dynamism, and performance. *European Journal of Work and Organisational Psychology, 13,* 447–471. (p. B-12)

De Koninck, J. (2000). Waking experiences and dreaming. In M. Kryger, T. Roth, & W. Dement (Eds.), *Principles and practice of sleep medicine* (3rd ed.). Philadelphia: Saunders. (p. 93)

DeLamater, J. D., & Sill, M. (2005). Sexual desire in later life. *Journal of Sex Research, 42,* 138–149. (p. 151)

Delaney, H. D., Miller, W. R., & Bisonó, A. M. (2007). Religiosity and spirituality among psychologists: A survey of clinician members of the American Psychological Association. *Professional Psychology; Research and Practice, 38,* 538–546. (p. 566)

Delaunay-El Allam, M., Soussignan, R., Patris, B., Marlier, L., & Schaal, B. (2010). Long-lasting memory for an odor acquired at the mother's breast. *Developmental Science, 13,* 849–863. (p. 121)

Delgado, J. M. R. (1969). *Physical control of the mind: Toward a psychocivilized society.* New York: Harper & Row. (p. 54)

DeLoache, J. S. (1987). Rapid change in the symbolic functioning of very young children. *Science, 238,* 1556–1557. (p. 128)

DeLoache, J. S., Chiong, C., Sherman, K., Islam, N., Vanderborght, M., Troseth, G. L., Strouse, G. A., & O'Doherty, K. (2010). Do babies learn from baby media? *Psychological Science, 21,* 1570–1574. (p. 341)

DeLoache, J. S., Uttal, D. H., & Rosengren, K. S. (2004). Scale errors offer evidence for a perception-action dissociation early in life. *Science, 304,* 1027–1029. (p. 125)

De Los Reyes, A., & Kazdin, A. E. (2009). Identifying evidence-based interventions for children and adolescents using the range of possible changes model: A meta-analytic illustration. *Behavior Modification, 33,* 583–617. (p. 562)

Dement, W. C. (1978). *Some must watch while some must sleep.* New York: Norton. (pp. 84, 92)

Dement, W. C. (1999). *The promise of sleep.* New York: Delacorte Press. (pp. 84, 85, 87, 89, 90, 92)

Dement, W. C., & Wolpert, E. A. (1958). The relation of eye movements, body mobility, and external stimuli to dream content. *Journal of Experimental Psychology, 55,* 543–553. (p. 94)

Demir, E., & Dickson, B. J. (2005). Fruitless splicing specifies male courtship behavior in Drosophila. *Cell, 121,* 785–794. (p. 181)

de Moraes, L. (2010, March 18). Reality show contestants willing to kill in French experiment. *Washington Post* (www.washingtonpost.com). (p. 468)

DeNeve, K. M., & Cooper, H. (1998). The happy personality: A meta-analysis of 137 personality traits and subjective well-being. *Psychological Bulletin, 124,* 197–229. (p. 417)

Dennett, D. C. (1991). *Consciousness explained.* Boston: Little, Brown. (p. 259)

Denson, T. F. (2011). A social neuroscience perspective on the neurobiological bases of aggression. In P. R. Shaver, & M. Mikulincer (Eds.), *Human aggression and violence: Causes, manifestations, and consequences.* Washington, DC: U. S. American Psychological Association. (p. 482)

Denton, K., & Krebs, D. L. (1990). From the scene to the crime: The effect of alcohol and social context on moral judgment. *Journal of Personality and Social Psychology, 59,* 242–248. (p. 102)

Der, G., Batty, G. D., & Deary, I. J. (2006). Effect of breast feeding on intelligence in children: Prospective study, sibling pairs analysis, and meta-analysis. *British Medical Journal, 333,* 945. (p. 22)

De Raad, B., Barelds, D. P. H., Levert, E., Ostendorf, F., Mlačić, B., Di Blas, L., Hřebíčková, M., Szirmák, Z., Szarota, P., Perugini, M., Church, A. T., & Katigbak, M. S. (2010). Only three factors of personality description are fully replicable across languages: A comparison of 14 trait taxonomies. *Journal of Personality and Social Psychology, 98,* 160–173. (p. 440)

Dermer, M., Cohen, S. J., Jacobsen, E., & Anderson, E. A. (1979). Evaluative judgments of aspects of life as a function of vicarious exposure to hedonic extremes. *Journal of Personality and Social Psychology, 37,* 247–260. (p. 417)

DeSteno, D., Petty, R. E., Wegener, D. T., & Rucker, D. D. (2000). Beyond valence in the perception of likelihood: The role of emotion specificity. *Journal of Personality and Social Psychology, 78,* 397–416. (p. 288)

Dettman, S. J., Pinder, D., Briggs, R. J. S., Dowell, R. C., & Leigh, J. R. (2007). Communication development in children who receive the cochlear implant younger than 12 months: Risk versus benefits. *Ear and Hearing, 28*(2), Supplement 11S–18S. (p. 218)

Deutsch, J. A. (1972, July). Brain reward: ESP and ecstasy. *Psychology Today,* 46–48. (p. 52)

DeValois, R. L., & DeValois, K. K. (1975). Neural coding of color. In E. C. Carterette & M. P. Friedman (Eds.), *Handbook of perception: Vol. V. Seeing.* New York: Academic Press. (p. 207)

Devilly, G. J. (2003). Eye movement desensitization and reprocessing: A chronology of its development and scientific standing. *Scientific Review of Mental Health Practice, 1,* 113–118. (p. 564)

De Vogli, R., Chandola, T., & Marmot, M. G. (2007). Negative aspects of close relationships and heart disease. *Archives of Internal Medicine, 167,* 1951–1957. (p. 405)

Dew, M. A., Hoch, C. C., Buysse, D. J., Monk, T. H., Begley, A. E., Houck, P. R., Hall, M., Kupfer, D. J., Reynolds, C. F., III (2003). Healthy older adults' sleep predicts all-cause mortality at 4 to 19 years of follow-up. *Psychosomatic Medicine, 65,* 63–73. (p. 90)

de Waal, F. B. M. (2005, September 23). We're all Machiavellians. *Chronicle of Higher Education.* (p. 18)

de Waal, F. B. M. (2009, October). The empathy instinct. *Discover,* pp. 54–57. (p. 465)

DeWall, C. N., Baumeister, R. F., Stillman, T. F., & Gailliot, M. T. (2007). Violence restrained: Effects of self-regulation and its depletion on aggression. *Journal of Experimental Social Psychology, 43,* 62–76. (p. 403)

DeWall, C. N., & Bushman, B. J. (2009). Hot under the collar in a lukewarm environment: Words associated with hot temperature increase aggressive thoughts and hostile perceptions. *Journal of Experimental Social Psychology, 45,* 1045–1047. (p. 483)

DeWall, C. N., MacDonald, G., Webster, G. D., Masten, C. L., Baumeister, R. F., Powell, C., Combs, D., Schurtz, D. R., Stillman, T. F., Tice, D. M., & Eisenberger, N. I. (2010). Acetaminophen reduces social pain: Behavioral and neural evidence. *Psychological Science, 21,* 931–937. (p. 366)

DeWall, C. N., Pond, R. S., Jr., Campbell, W. K., & Twenge, J. M. (2011). Tuning in to psychological change: Linguistic markers of psychological traits and emotions over time in popular U.S. song lyrics. *Psychology of Aesthetics, Creativity, and the Arts,* 5(3), 200–207. (doi: 10.1037/a0023195). (p. 449)

de Wit, L., Luppino, F., van Straten, A., Penninx, B., Zitman, F., & Cuijpers, P. (2010). Depression and obesity: A meta-analysis of community-based studies. *Psychiatry Research, 178,* 230–235. (p. 361)

De Wolff, M. S., & van IJzendoorn, M. H. (1997). Sensitivity and attachment: A meta-analysis on parental antecedents of infant attachment. *Child Development, 68,* 571–591. (p. 134)

DeYoung, C. G., Hirsch, J. B., Shane, M. S., Papademetris, X., Rajeevan, N., & Gray, J. R. (2010). Testing predictions from personality neuroscience: Brain structure and the Big Five. *Psychological Science, 21,* 820–828. (p. 440)

Diaconis, P. (2002, August 11). Quoted by L. Belkin, The odds of that. *New York Times* (www.nytimes.com). (p. 13)

Diaconis, P., & Mosteller, F. (1989). Methods for studying coincidences. *Journal of the American Statistical Association, 84,* 853–861. (p. 13)

Diamond, J. (2001, February). A tale of two reputations: Why we revere Darwin and give Freud a hard time. *Natural History,* pp. 20–24. (p. 70)

Diamond, L. (2008). *Sexual fluidity: Understanding women's love and desire.* Cambridge, MA: Harvard University Press. (p. 179)

Diaz, F. J., Velásquex, D. M., Susce, M. T., & de Leon, J. (2008). The association between schizophrenia and smoking: Unexplained by either the illness or the prodromal period. *Schizophrenia Research, 104,* 214–219. (p. 529)

Dick, D. M. (2007). Identification of genes influencing a spectrum of externalizing psychopathology. *Current Directions in Psychological Science, 16,* 331–335. (p. 538)

Dickens, W. T., & Flynn, J. R. (2006). Black Americans reduce the racial IQ gap: Evidence from standardization samples. *Psychological Science, 17,* 913–920. (p. 343)

Dickerson, S. S., & Kemeny, M. E. (2004). Acute stressors and cortisol responses: A theoretical integration and synthesis of laboratory research. *Psychological Bulletin, 130,* 355–391. (p. 401)

Dickinson, H. O., Parkinson, K. M., Ravens-Sieberer, U., Schirripa, G., Thyen, U., Arnaud, C., Beckung, E., Fauconnier, J., McManus, V., Michelsen, S. I., Parkes, J., & Colver, A. F. (2007). Self-reported quality of life of 8–12-year-old children with cerebral palsy: A cross-sectional European study. *Lancet, 369,* 2171–2178. (p. 414)

Dickson, B. J. (2005, June 3). Quoted in E. Rosenthal, For fruit flies, gene shift tilts sex orientation. *New York Times* (www.nytimes.com). (p. 181)

Diekelmann, S., & Born, J. (2010). The memory function of sleep. *Nature Neuroscience, 11,* 114–126. (p. 293)

Diener, E. (2006). Guidelines of national indicators of subjective well-being and ill-being. *Journal of Happiness Studies, 7,* 397–404. (p. 419)

Diener, E., & Biswas-Diener, R. (2002). Will money increase subjective well-being? A literature review and guide to needed research. *Social Indicators Research, 57,* 119–169. (p. 415)

Diener, E., & Biswas-Diener, R. (2009). *Rethinking happiness: The science of psychological wealth.* Malden, MA: Wiley Blackwell. (pp. 415, 419)

Diener, E., & Chan, M. (2011). Happy people live longer: Subjective well-being contributes to health and longevity. *Applied Psychology: Health and Well-Being, 3,* 1–43. (p. 399)

Diener, E., Lucas, R. E., & Scollon, C. N. (2006). Beyond the hedonic treadmill: Revising the adaptation theory of well-being. *American Psychologist, 61,* 305–314. (p. 414)

Diener, E., Nickerson, C., Lucas, R. E., & Sandvik, E. (2002). Dispositional affect and job outcomes. *Social Indicators Research, 59,* 229–259. (p. 413)

Diener, E., & Oishi, S. (2000). Money and happiness: Income and subjective well-being across nations. In E. Diener & E. M. Suh (Eds.), *Subjective well-being across cultures.* Cambridge, MA: MIT Press. (p. 416)

Diener, E., Oishi, S., & Lucas, R. E. (2003). Personality, culture, and subjective well-being: Emotional and cognitive evaluations of life. *Annual Review of Psychology, 54,* 403–425. (pp. 417, 418)

Diener, E., & Seligman, M. E. P. (2002). Very happy people. *Psychological Science, 13,* 81–84. (p. 364)

Diener, E., Tay, L., & Myers, D. G. (2011). The religion paradox: If religion makes people happy, why are so many dropping out? *Journal of Personality and Social Psychology, 101,* 1278–1290. (p. 19)

Diener, E., Wolsic, B., & Fujita, F. (1995). Physical attractiveness and subjective well-being. *Journal of Personality and Social Psychology, 69,* 120–129. (p. 490)

DiFranza, J. R. (2008, May). Hooked from the first cigarette. *Scientific American,* pp. 82–87. (p. 104)

Dijksterhuis, A., & Aarts, H. (2003). On wildebeests and humans: The preferential detection of negative stimuli. *Psychological Science, 14,* 14–18. (p. 380)

DiLalla, D. L., Carey, G., Gottesman, I. I., & Bouchard, T. J., Jr. (1996). Heritability of MMPI personality indicators of psychopathology in twins reared apart. *Journal of Abnormal Psychology, 105,* 491–499. (p. 523)

Dimberg, U., Thunberg, M., & Elmehed, K. (2000). Unconscious facial reactions to emotional facial expressions. *Psychological Science, 11,* 86–89. (pp. 375, 385)

Dimidjian, S., & Hollon, S. D. (2010). How would we know if psychotherapy were harmful? *American Psychologist, 65,* 21–33. (p. 562)

Dinges, N. G., & Hull, P. (1992). Personality, culture, and international studies. In D. Lieberman (Ed.), *Revealing the world: An interdisciplinary reader for international studies.* Dubuque, IA: Kendall-Hunt. (p. 326)

Dingfelder, S. F. (2010, November). A second chance for the Mexican wolf. *Monitor on Psychology,* pp. 20–21. (p. 257)

Dion, K. K., & Dion, K. L. (1993). Individualistic and collectivistic perspectives on gender and the cultural context of love and intimacy. *Journal of Social Issues, 49,* 53–69. (p. 452)

Dirix, C. E. H., Nijhuis, J. G., Jongsma, H. W., & Hornstra, G. (2009). Aspects of fetal learning and memory. *Child Development, 80,* 1251–1258. (p. 120)

DiSalvo, D. (2010, January/February). Are social networks messing with your head? *Scientific American Mind,* pp. 48–55. (p. 368)

Discover. (1996, May). A fistful of risks. pp. 82–83. (p. 104)

Di Tella, R., & MacCulloch, R. (2010). Happiness adaptation to income beyond "basic needs." In E. Diener, J. Helliwell, & D. Kahneman (eds.), *International Differences in Well-Being,* pp. 217–247. New York: Oxford University Press. (pp. 415, 416)

Dittrich, L. (2010, October 25). The brain that changed everything. *Esquire* (www.esquire.com). (p. 290)

Dixon, J., Durrheim, K., & Tredoux, C. (2007). Intergroup contact and attitudes toward the principle and practice of racial equality. *Psychological Science, 18,* 867–872. (p. 498)

Dobbs, D. (2009, April). The post-traumatic stress trap. *Scientific American,* pp. 64–69. (p. 516)

Dodge, K. A. (2009). Mechanisms of gene-environment interaction effects in the development of conduct disorder. *Perspectives on Psychological Science, 4,* 408–414. (p. 538)

Dodman, N. H., Karlsson, E. K., Moon-Fanelli, A., Galdzicka, M., Perloski, M., Shuster, L., Lindblad-Toh, K., & Ginns, E. I. (2010). A canine chromosome 7 locus confers compulsive disorder susceptibility. *Molecular Psychiatry 15,* 8–10. (p. 517)

Doherty, E. W., & Doherty, W. J. (1998). Smoke gets in your eyes: Cigarette smoking and divorce in a national sample of American adults. *Families, Systems, and Health, 16,* 393–400. (p. 105)

Dohrenwend, B. P., Levav, I., Shrout, P. E., Schwartz, S., Naveh, G., Link, B. G., Skodol, A. E., & Stueve, A. (1992). Socioeconomic status and psychiatric disorders: The causation-selection issue. *Science, 255,* 946–952. (p. 540)

Dohrenwend, B. P., Pearlin, L., Clayton, P., Hamburg, B., Dohrenwend, B. P., Riley, M., & Rose, R. (1982). Report on stress and life events. In G. R. Elliott & C. Eisdorfer (Eds.), *Stress and human health: Analysis and implications of research* (A study by the Institute of Medicine/National Academy of Sciences). New York: Springer. (p. 392)

Dohrenwend, B. P., Turner, J. B., Turse, N. A., Adams, B. G., Koenen, K. C., & Marshall, R. (2006). The psychological risks of Vietnam for U.S. veterans: A revisit with new data and methods. *Science, 313,* 979–982. (p. 515)

Dolezal, H. (1982). *Living in a world transformed.* New York: Academic Press. (p. 215)

Domhoff, G. W. (1996). *Finding meaning in dreams: A quantitative approach.* New York: Plenum. (p. 93)

Domhoff, G. W. (2003). *The scientific study of dreams: Neural networks, cognitive development, and content analysis.* Washington, DC: APA Books. (p. 95)

Domhoff, G. W. (2007). Realistic simulations and bizarreness in dream content: Past findings and suggestions for future research. In D. Barrett & P. McNamara (Eds.), *The new science of dreaming: Content, recall, and personality characteristics.* Westport, CT: Praeger. (p. 93)

Domhoff, G. W. (2010). The case for a cognitive theory of dreams. Unpublished manuscript: University of California at Santa Cruz (dreamresearch.net/Library/domhoff_2010.html). (p. 96)

Domhoff, G. W. (2011). The neural substrate for dreaming: Is it a subsystem of the default network? *Consciousness and Cognition, 20,* 1163–1174. (p. 96)

Domjan, M. (1992). Adult learning and mate choice: Possibilities and experimental evidence. *American Zoologist, 32,* 48–61. (p. 242)

Domjan, M. (1994). Formulation of a behavior system for sexual conditioning. *Psychonomic Bulletin & Review, 1,* 421–428. (p. 242)

Domjan, M. (2005). Pavlovian conditioning: A functional perspective. *Annual Review of Psychology, 56.* (p. 242)

Donlea, J. M., Ramanan, N., & Shaw, P. J. (2009). Use-dependent plasticity in clock neurons regulates sleep need in *Drosophila. Science, 324,* 105–108. (p. 87)

Donnellan, M. B., Trzesniewski, K. H., Robins, R. W., Moffitt, T. E., & Caspi, A. (2005). Low self-esteem is related to aggression, antisocial behavior, and delinquency. *Psychological Science, 16,* 328–335. (p. 444)

Donnerstein, E. (1998). Why do we have those new ratings on television. Invited address to the National Institute on the Teaching of Psychology. (pp. 264, 265)

Donnerstein, E. (2011). The media and aggression: From TV to the Internet. In J. Forgas, A. Kruglanski, & K. Williams (eds.), *The psychology of social conflict and aggression.* New York: Psychology Press. (pp. 264, 265)

Donnerstein, E., Linz, D., & Penrod, S. (1987). *The question of pornography.* New York: Free Press. (p. 265)

Donvan, J., & Zucker, C. (2010, October). Autism's first child. *The Atlantic* (www.theatlantic.com). (p. 130)

D'Orlando, F. (2011). The demand for pornography. *Journal of Happiness Studies, 12,* 51–75. (p. 485)

Doss, B. D., Rhoades, G. K., Stanley, S. M., & Markman, H. J. (2009). The effect of the transition to parenthood on relationship quality: An 8-year prospective study. *Journal of Personality and Social Psychology, 96,* 601–619. (p. 155)

Dotan-Eliaz, O., Sommer, K. L., & Rubin, S. (2009). Multilingual groups: Effects of linguistic ostracism on felt rejection and anger, coworker attraction, perceived team potency, and creative performance. *Basic and Applied Social Psychology, 31,* 363–375. (pp. 365, 366)

Douglas, K. S., Guy, L. S., & Hart, S. D. (2009). Psychosis as a risk factor for violence to others: A meta-analysis. *Psychological Bulletin, 135,* 679–706. (p. 511)

Douthat, R. (2010, November 28). The partisan mind. *New York Times* (www.nytimes.com). (p. 479)

Dovidio, J. F., & Gaertner, S. L. (1999). Reducing prejudice: Combating intergroup biases. *Current Directions in Psychological Science, 8,* 101–105. (p. 499)

Dovidio, J. F., ten Vergert, M., Stewart, T. L., Gaertner, S. L., Johnson, J. D., Esses, V. M., Riek, B. M., & Pearson, A. R. (2004). Perspective and prejudice: Antecedents and mediating mechanisms. *Personality and Social Psychology Bulletin, 30,* 1537–1549. (p. 499)

Dowlati, Y., Herrmann, N., Swardfager, W., Liu, H., Sham, L., Reim, E. K., & Lanctôt, K. (2010). A meta-analysis of cytokines in major depression. *Biological Psychiatry, 67,* 466–457. (p. 525)

Downing, P. E., Jiang, Y., & Shuman, M. (2001). A cortical area selective for visual processing of the human body. *Science, 293,* 2470–2473. (p. 204)

Downs, E., & Smith, S. L. (2010). Keepin abreast of hypersexuality: A video game character content analysis. *Sex Roles, 62,* 721–733. (p. 177)

Doyle, R. (2005, March). Gay and lesbian census. *Scientific American,* p. 28. (p. 184)

Draguns, J. G. (1990a). Normal and abnormal behavior in cross-cultural perspective: Specifying the nature of their relationship. *Nebraska Symposium on Motivation 1989, 37,* 235–277. (pp. 505, 527)

Draguns, J. G. (1990b). Applications of cross-cultural psychology in the field of mental health. In R. W. Brislin (Ed.), *Applied cross-cultural psychology.* Newbury Park, CA: Sage. (p. 505)

Draguns, J. G. (1997). Abnormal behavior patterns across cultures: Implications for counseling and psychotherapy. *International Journal of Intercultural Relations, 21,* 213–248. (p. 505)

Driessen, E., Cuijpers, P., de Maat, S. C. M., Abbas, A. A., de Jonghe, F., & Dekker, J. J. M. (2010). The efficacy of short-term psychodynamic psychotherapy for depression: A meta-analysis. *Clinical Psychology Review, 30,* 25–36. (p. 562)

Druckman, D., & Bjork, R. A. (Eds.). (1994). *Learning, remembering, believing: Enhancing human performance.* Washington, DC: National Academy Press. (pp. 97, 98)

DSM-5 Task Force. (2012). Definition of a mental disorder. Washington, D.C.: American Psychiatric Association (www.dsm5.org). (p. 506)

Duckworth, A. L., Quinn, P. D., Lynam, D. R., Loeber, R., & Stouthamer-Loeber, M. (2011). Role of test motivation in intelligence testing. *PNAS, 108,* 7716–7720. (p. 342)

Duckworth, A. L., Quinn, P. D., & Seligman, M. E. P. (2009). Positive predictors of teacher effectiveness. *Journal of Positive Psychology, 4,* 540–547. (p. 370)

Duckworth, A. L., & Seligman, M. E. P. (2005). Discipline outdoes talent: Self-discipline predicts academic performance in adolescents. *Psychological Science, 12,* 939–944. (p. 370)

Duckworth, A. L., & Seligman, M. E. P. (2006). Self-discipline gives girls the edge: Gender in self-discipline, grades, and achievement tests. *Journal of Educational Psychology, 98,* 198–208. (p. 370)

Duclos, S. E., Laird, J. D., Sexter, M., Stern, L., & Van Lighten, O. (1989). Emotion-specific effects of facial expressions and postures on emotional experience. *Journal of Personality and Social Psychology, 57,* 100–108. (p. 384)

Duffy, M. (2003, June 9). Weapons of mass disappearance. *Time,* pp. 28–33. (p. 462)

Duggan, J. P., & Booth, D. A. (1986). Obesity, overeating, and rapid gastric emptying in rats with ventromedial hypothalamic lesions. *Science, 231,* 609–611. (p. 357)

Dumont, K. A., Widom, C. S., & Czaja, S. J. (2007). Predictors of resilience in abused and neglected children grown-up: The role of individual and neighborhood characteristics. *Child Abuse & Neglect, 31,* 255–274. (p. 136)

Dunbar, R. I. M. (1992, June). Neocortex size as a constraint on group size in primates. *Journal of Human Evolution, 22,* 469–493. (p. 369)

Dunbar, R. I. M. (2010, December 25). You've got to have (150) friends. *New York Times* (www.nytimes.com). (p. 369)

Dunn, E. W., Aknin, L. B., & Norton, M. I. (2008). Spending money on others promotes happiness. *Science, 319,* 1687–1688. (p. 495)

Dunn, M., & Searle, R. (2010). Effect of manipulated prestige-car ownership on both sex attractiveness ratings. *British Journal of Psychology, 101,* 69–80. (p. 184)

Dunson, D. B., Colombo, B., & Baird, D. D. (2002). Changes with age in the level and duration of fertility in the menstrual cycle. *Human Reproduction, 17,* 1399–1403. (p. 151)

Dutton, D. G., & Aron, A. P. (1974). Some evidence for heightened sexual attraction under conditions of high anxiety. *Journal of Personality and Social Psychology, 30,* 510–517. (p. 492)

Dutton, D. G., & Aron, A. P. (1989). Romantic attraction and generalized liking for others who are sources of conflict-based arousal. *Canadian Journal of Behavioural Sciences, 21,* 246–257. (p. 492)

Dweck, C. S. (2006). *Mindset: The new psychology of success.* New York: Random House. (p. 346)

Dweck, C. S. (2007, November 28). The secret to raising smart kids. *Scientific American Mind*, pp. 36–43 (http://www.sciam.com). (p. 346)

Dweck, C. S. (2008). Can personality be changed? The role of beliefs in personality and change. *Current Directions in Psychological Science, 17*, 391–394. (p. 346)

Dye, M. W. G., Green, C. S., & Bavelier, D. (2009). Increasing speed of processing with action video games. *Current Directions in Psychological Science, 18*, 321–326. (p. 486)

Dyrdal, G. M., & Lucas, R. E. (2011). Reaction and adaptation to the birth of a child: A couple level analysis. Unpublished manuscript, Michigan State University. (p. 154)

E

Eagleman, D. (2011, September). Secret life of the mind. *Discover*, pp. 50–53. (p. 79)

Eagly, A. H. (2007). Female leadership advantage and disadvantage: Resolving the contradictions. *Psychology of Women Quarterly, 31*, 1–12. (p. B-12)

Eagly, A. H. (2009). The his and hers of prosocial behavior: An examination of the social psychology of gender. *American Psychologist, 64*, 644–658. (pp. 166, 185)

Eagly, A. H., Ashmore, R. D., Makhijani, M. G., & Kennedy, L. C. (1991). What is beautiful is good, but . . .: A meta-analytic review of research on the physical attractiveness stereotype. *Psychological Bulletin, 110*, 109–128. (p. 489)

Eagly, A. H., & Carli, L. L. (2007). *Through the labyrinth: The truth about how women become leaders.* Cambridge, MA: Harvard University Press. (p. 165)

Eagly, A. H., & Wood, W. (1999). The origins of sex differences in human behavior: Evolved dispositions versus social roles. *American Psychologist, 54*, 408–423. (p. 185)

Eastman, C. L., Boulos, Z., Terman, M., Campbell, S. S., Dijk, D-J., & Lewy, A. J. (1995). Light treatment for sleep disorders: Consensus report. VI. Shift work. *Journal of Biological Rhythms, 10*, 157–164. (p. 88)

Eastman, C. L., Young, M. A., Fogg, L. F., Liu, L., & Meaden, P. M. (1998). Bright light treatment of winter depression: A placebo-controlled trial. *Archives of General Psychiatry, 55*, 883–889. (p. 564)

Eastwick, P. W., & Finkel, E. J. (2008a). Sex differences in mate preferences revisited: Do people know what they initially desire in a romantic partner? *Journal of Personality and Social Psychology, 94*, 245–264. (p. 488)

Eastwick, P. W., & Finkel, E. J. (2008b). Speed-dating as a methodological innovation. *The Psychologist, 21*, 402–403. (p. 488)

Ebbinghaus, H. (1885/1964). *Memory: A contribution to experimental psychology* (H. A. Ruger & C. E. Bussenius, Trans.). New York: Dover. (pp. 278, 291)

Ebel-Lam, A. P., MacDonald, T. K., Zanna, M. P., & Fong, G. T. (2009). An experimental investigation of the interactive effects of alcohol and sexual arousal on intentions to have unprotected sex. *Basic and Applied Social psychology, 31*, 226–233. (p. 102)

Eberhardt, J. L. (2005). Imaging race. *American Psychologist, 60*, 181–190. (p. 477)

Eckensberger, L. H. (1994). Moral development and its measurement across cultures. In W. J. Lonner & R. Malpass (Eds.), *Psychology and culture.* Boston: Allyn & Bacon. (p. 142)

Ecker, C., & 10 others. (2010). Describing the brain in autism in five dimensions—Magnetic Resonance Imaging-assisted diagnosis of autism spectrum disorder using a multiparameter classification approach. *Journal of Neuroscience, 30*, 10612–10623. (p. 131)

Eckert, E. D., Heston, L. L., & Bouchard, T. J., Jr. (1981). MZ twins reared apart: Preliminary findings of psychiatric disturbances and traits. In L. Gedda, P. Paris, & W. D. Nance (Eds.), *Twin research: Vol. 3. Pt. B. Intelligence, personality, and development.* New York: Alan Liss. (p. 517)

Eckholm, E. (2010, September 21). Woman on death row runs out of appeals. *New York Times* (www.nytimes.com). (p. 338)

Ecklund-Flores, L. (1992). The infant as a model for the teaching of introductory psychology. Paper presented to the American Psychological Association annual convention. (p. 119)

Economist. (2001, December 20). An anthropology of happiness. *The Economist* (www.economist.com/world/asia). (p. 365)

Edwards, R. R., Campbell, C., Jamison, R. N., & Wiech, K. (2009). The neurobiological underpinnings of coping with pain. *Current Directions in Psychological Science, 18*, 237–241. (p. 223)

Eibl-Eibesfeldt, I. (1971). *Love and hate: The natural history of behavior patterns.* New York: Holt, Rinehart & Winston. (p. 383)

Eich, E. (1990). Learning during sleep. In R. B. Bootzin, J. F. Kihlstrom, & D. L. Schacter (Eds.), *Sleep and cognition.* Washington, DC: American Psychological Association. (p. 94)

Ein-Dor, T., Mikulincer, M., Doron, G., & Shaver, P. R. (2010). The attachment paradox: How can so many of us (the insecure ones) have no adaptive advantages? *Perspectives on Psychological Science, 5*, 123–141. (p. 135)

Eippert, F., Finsterbush, J., Bingel, U., & Büchel, C. (2009). Direct evidence for spinal cord involvement in placebo analgesia. *Science, 326*, 404. (p. 223)

Eisenberg, N., & Lennon, R. (1983). Sex differences in empathy and related capacities. *Psychological Bulletin, 94*, 100–131. (p. 382)

Eisenberger, N. I., Master, S. L., Inagaki, T. K., Taylor, S. E., Shirinyan, D., Lieberman, M. D., & Nalifoff, B. D. (2011). Attachment figures activate a safety signal-related neural region and reduce pain experience. *Proceedings of the National Academy of Sciences, 108*, 11721–11726. (p. 365)

Eisenberger, R., & Aselage, J. (2009). Incremental effects of reward on experienced performance pressure: Positive outcomes for intrinsic interest and creativity. *Journal of Organizational Behavior, 30*, 95–117. (p. 260)

Ekman, P. (1994). Strong evidence for universals in facial expressions: A reply to Russell's mistaken critique. *Psychological Bulletin, 115*, 268–287. (p. 383)

Ekman, P., & Friesen, W. V. (1975). *Unmasking the face.* Englewood Cliffs, NJ: Prentice-Hall. (p. 383)

Ekman, P., Friesen, W. V., O'Sullivan, M., Chan, A., Diacoyanni-Tarlatzis, I., Heider, K., Krause, R., LeCompte, W. A., Pitcairn, T., Ricci-Bitti, P. E., Scherer, K., Tomita, M., & Tzavaras, A. (1987). Universals and cultural differences in the judgments of facial expressions of emotion. *Journal of Personality and Social Psychology, 53*, 712–717. (p. 383)

Elbert, T., Pantev, C., Wienbruch, C., Rockstroh, B., & Taub, E. (1995). Increased cortical representation of the fingers of the left hand in string players. *Science, 270*, 305–307. (p. 122)

Elbogen, E. B., & Johnson, S. C. (2009). The intricate link between violence and mental disorder: Results from the National Epidemiologic Survey on Alcohol and Related Conditions. *Archives of General Psychiatry, 66*, 152–161. (p. 511)

Elfenbein, H. A., & Ambady, N. (1999). *Does it take one to know one? A meta-analysis of the universality and cultural specificity of emotion recognition.* Unpublished manuscript, Harvard University. (p. 383)

Elfenbein, H. A., & Ambady, N. (2002). On the universality and cultural specificity of emotion recognition: A meta-analysis. *Psychological Bulletin, 128*, 203–235. (p. 383)

Elfenbein, H. A., & Ambady, N. (2003a). Universals and cultural differences in recognizing emotions. *Current Directions in Psychological Science, 12*, 159–164. (p. 383)

Elfenbein, H. A., & Ambady, N. (2003b). When familiarity breeds accuracy: Cultural exposure and facial emotion recognition. *Journal of Personality and Social Psychology, 85*, 276–290. (p. 383)

Elkind, D. (1970). The origins of religion in the child. *Review of Religious Research, 12*, 35–42. (p. 141)

Elkind, D. (1978). *The child's reality: Three developmental themes.* Hillsdale, NJ: Erlbaum. (p. 141)

Ellenbogen, J. M., Hu, P. T., Payne, J. D., Titone, D., & Walker, M. P. (2007). Human relational memory requires time and sleep. *Proceedings of the National Academy of Sciences, 104*, 7723–7728. (p. 89)

Ellin, A. (2009, February 12). The recession. Isn't it romantic? *New York Times* (www.nytimes.com). (p. 488)

Elliot, A. J., & McGregor, H. A. (2001). A 2x2 achievement goal framework. *Journal of Personality and Social Psychology, 80*, 501–519. (p. B-10)

Elliot, A. J., & Niesta, D. (2008). Romantic red: Red enhances men's attraction to women. *Journal of Personality and Social Psychology, 95*, 1150–1164. (p. 257)

Ellis, A. (1980). Psychotherapy and atheistic values: A response to A. E. Bergin's "Psychotherapy and religious values." *Journal of Consulting and Clinical Psychology, 48,* 635–639. (p. 567)

Ellis, A., & Becker, I. M. (1982). *A guide to personal happiness.* North Hollywood, CA: Wilshire Book Co. (p. 245)

Ellis, B. J., Bates, J. E., Dodge, K. A., Fergusson, D. M., John, H. L., Pettit, G. S., & Woodward, L. (2003). Does father absence place daughters at special risk for early sexual activity and teenage pregnancy? *Child Development, 74,* 801–821. (p. 177)

Ellis, B. J., & Boyce, W. T. (2008). Biological sensitivity to context. *Current Directions in Psychological Science, 17,* 183–187. (p. 518)

Ellis, L., & Ames, M. A. (1987). Neurohormonal functioning and sexual orientation: A theory of homosexuality-heterosexuality. *Psychological Bulletin, 101,* 233–258. (p. 181)

Ellis, L., Hershberger, S., Field, E., Wersinger, S., Pellis, S., Geary, D., Palmer, C., Hovenga, K., Hetsroni, A., & Karadi, K. (2008). *Sex differences: Summarizing more than a century of scientific research.* New York: Psychology Press. (p. 164)

Ellison-Wright, I., Glahn, D. C., Laird, A. R., Thelen, S. M., & Bullmore, E. (2008). The anatomy of first-episode and chronic schizophrenia: An anatomical likelihood estimation meta-analysis. *American Journal of Psychiatry, 165,* 1015–1023. (p. 531)

Else-Quest, N. M., Hyde, J. S., & Linn, M. C. (2010). Cross-national patterns of gender differences in mathematics: A meta-analysis. *Psychological Bulletin, 136,* 103–127. (p. 342)

Elzinga, B. M., Ardon, A. M., Heijnis, M. K., De Ruiter, M. B., Van Dyck, R., & Veltman, D. J. (2007). Neural correlates of enhanced working-memory performance in dissociative disorder: A functional MRI study. *Psychological Medicine, 37,* 235–245. (p. 535)

EMDR. (2011, February 18). E-mail correspondence from Robbie Dunton, EMDR Institute (www.emdr.org). (p. 563)

Emerging Trends. (1997, September). *Teens turn more to parents than friends on whether to attend church.* Princeton, NJ: Princeton Religion Research Center. (p. 146)

Emery, G., Jr. (2004). *Psychic predictions 2004.* Committee for the Scientific Investigation of Claims of the Paranormal (www.csicop.org). (p. 230)

Emery, G., Jr. (2006, January 17). Psychic predictions 2005. *Skeptical Inquirer* (www.csicop.org). (p. 230)

Emmons, R. A. (2007). *Thanks! How the new science of gratitude can make you happier.* Boston: Houghton Mifflin. (p. 418)

Emmons, S., Geisler, C., Kaplan, K. J., & Harrow, M. (1997). *Living with schizophrenia.* Muncie, IN: Taylor and Francis (Accelerated Development). (pp. 505, 529)

Empson, J. A. C., & Clarke, P. R. F. (1970). Rapid eye movements and remembering. *Nature, 227,* 287–288. (p. 95)

Endler, N. S. (1982). *Holiday of darkness: A psychologist's personal journey out of his depression.* New York: Wiley. (pp. 526, 572)

Engemann, K. M., & Owyang, M. T. (2005, April). So much for that merit raise: The link between wages and appearance. *Regional Economist* (www.stlouisfed.org). (p. 489)

Engen, T. (1987). Remembering odors and their names. *American Scientist, 75,* 497–503. (p. 226)

Engle, R. W. (2002). Working memory capacity as executive attention. *Current Directions in Psychological Science, 11,* 19–23. (p. 273)

Epel, E. S. (2009). Telomeres in a life-span perspective: A new "psychobiomarker"? *Current Directions in Psychological Science, 18,* 6–9. (p. 152)

Epley, N., & Dunning, D. (2000). Feeling "holier than thou": Are self-serving assessments produced by errors in self- or social prediction? *Journal of Personality and Social Psychology, 79,* 861–875. (p. 449)

Epley, N., Keysar, B., Van Boven, L., & Gilovich, T. (2004). Perspective taking as egocentric anchoring and adjustment. *Journal of Personality and Social Psychology, 87,* 327–339. (p. 128)

Epstein, J., Stern, E., & Silbersweig, D. (1998). Mesolimbic activity associated with psychosis in schizophrenia: Symptom-specific PET studies. In J. F. McGinty (Ed.), *Advancing from the ventral striatum to the extended amygdala: Implications for neuropsychiatry and drug use: In honor of Lennart Heimer. Annals of the New York Academy of Sciences, 877,* 562–574. (p. 530)

Epstein, S. (1983a). Aggregation and beyond: Some basic issues on the prediction of behavior. *Journal of Personality, 51,* 360–392. (p. 442)

Epstein, S. (1983b). The stability of behavior across time and situations. In R. Zucker, J. Aronoff, & A. I. Rabin (Eds.), *Personality and the prediction of behavior.* San Diego: Academic Press. (p. 442)

Erdberg, P. (1990). Rorschach assessment. In G. Goldstein & M. Hersen (Eds.), *Handbook of psychological assessment, 2nd ed.* New York: Pergamon. (p. 430)

Erdelyi, M. H. (1985). *Psychoanalysis: Freud's cognitive psychology.* New York: Freeman. (p. 431)

Erdelyi, M. H. (1988). Repression, reconstruction, and defense: History and integration of the psychoanalytic and experimental frameworks. In J. Singer (Ed.), *Repression: Defense mechanism and cognitive style.* Chicago: University of Chicago Press. (p. 431)

Erdelyi, M. H. (2006). The unified theory of repression. *Behavioral and Brain Sciences, 29,* 499–551. (p. 431)

Erel, O., & Burman, B. (1995). Interrelatedness of marital relations and parent-child relations: A meta-analytic review. *Psychological Bulletin, 118,* 108–132. (p. 155)

Erickson, K. I. (2009). Aerobic fitness is associated with hippocampal volume in elderly humans. *Hippocampus, 19,* 1030–1039. (p. 152)

Erickson, K. I., & 9 others. (2010). Physical activity predicts gray matter volume in late adulthood: The Cardiovascular Health Study. *Neurology, 75,* 1415–1422. (p. 151)

Erickson, M. F., & Aird, E. G. (2005). *The motherhood study: Fresh insights on mothers' attitudes and concerns.* New York: The Motherhood Project, Institute for American Values. (p. 155)

Ericsson, K. A. (2001). Attaining excellence through deliberate practice: Insights from the study of expert performance. In M. Ferrari (Ed.), *The pursuit of excellence in education.* Hillsdale, NJ: Erlbaum. (p. 371)

Ericsson, K. A. (2002). Attaining excellence through deliberate practice: Insights from the study of expert performance. In C. Desforges & R. Fox (Eds.), *Teaching and learning: The essential readings.* Malden, MA: Blackwell Publishers. (p. 332)

Ericsson, K. A. (2006). The influence of experience and deliberate practice on the development of superior expert performance. In K. A. Ericsson, N. Charness, P. J. Feltovich, & R. R. Hoffman (Eds.), *The Cambridge handbook of expertise and expert performance.* Cambridge: Cambridge University Press. (p. 371)

Ericsson, K. A. (2007). Deliberate practice and the modifiability of body and mind: Toward a science of the structure and acquisition of expert and elite performance. *International Journal of Sport Psychology, 38,* 4–34. (pp. 332, 371)

Ericsson, K. A., Roring, R. W., & Nandagopal, K. (2007). Giftedness and evidence for reproducibly superior performance: An account based on the expert performance framework. *High Ability Studies, 18,* 3–56. (p. 346)

Erikson, E. H. (1963). *Childhood and society.* New York: Norton. (p. 143)

Erikson, E. H. (1983, June). A conversation with Erikson (by E. Hall). *Psychology Today,* pp. 22–30. (p. 135)

Erol, R. Y., & Orth, U. (2011). Self-esteem development from age 14 to 30 years: A longitudinal study. *Journal of Personality and Social Psychology, 101,* 607–619. (p. 145)

Ertmer, D. J., Young, N. M., & Nathani, S. (2007). Profiles of focal development in young cochlear implant recipients. *Journal of Speech, Language, and Hearing Research, 50,* 393–407. (p. 321)

Escobar-Chaves, S. L., Tortolero, S. R., Markham, C. M., Low, B. J., Eitel, P., & Thickstun, P. (2005). Impact of the media on adolescent sexual attitudes and behaviors. *Pediatrics, 116,* 303–326. (p. 177)

Escobedo, J. R., & Adolphs, R. (2010). Becoming a better person: Temporal remoteness biases autobiographical memories for moral events. *Emotion, 10,* 511–518. (p. 450)

Eskine, K. J., Kacinik, N. A., & Prinz, J. J. (2011). A bad taste in the mouth: Gustatory disgust influences moral judgment. *Psychological Science, 22,* 295–299. (p. 142)

ESPAD. (2003). *Summary of the 2003 findings.* European School Survey Project on Alcohol and Other Drugs. (www.espad.org). (p. 111)

Esser, J. K., & Lindoerfer, J. S. (1989). Groupthink and the space shuttle Challenger accident: Toward a quantitative case analysis. *Journal of Behavioral Decision Making, 2,* 167–177. (p. 474)

Esterson, A. (2001). The mythologizing of psychoanalytic history: Deception and self-deception in Freud's accounts of the seduction theory episode. *History of Psychiatry, 12,* 329–352. (p. 430)

Etkin, A., & Wager, T. D. (2007). Functional neuroimaging of anxiety: A meta-analysis of emotional processing in PTSD, social anxiety disorder, and specific phobia. *American Journal of Psychiatry, 164,* 1476–1488. (p. 518)

Eurich, T. L., Krause, D. E., Cigularov, K., & Thornton, G. C., III. (2009). Assessment centers: Current practices in the United States. *Journal of Business Psychology, 24,* 387–407. (p. 445)

Euston, D. R., Tatsuno, M., & McNaughton, B. L. (2007). Fast-forward playback of recent memory sequences in prefrontal cortex during sleep. *Science, 318,* 1147–1150. (p. 282)

Evans, C. R., & Dion, K. L. (1991). Group cohesion and performance: A meta-analysis. *Small Group Research, 22,* 175–186. (p. B-11)

Evans, G. W., Palsane, M. N., & Carrere, S. (1987). Type A behavior and occupational stress: A cross-cultural study of blue-collar workers. *Journal of Personality and Social Psychology, 52,* 1002–1007. (p. 398)

Evans, N., & Levinson, S. C. (2009). The myth of language universals: Language diversity and its importance for cognitive science. *Behavioral and Brain Sciences, 32,* 429–492. (p. 321)

Everson, S. A., Goldberg, D. E., Kaplan, G. A., Cohen, R. D., Pukkala, E., Tuomilehto, J., & Salonen, J. T. (1996). Hopelessness and risk of mortality and incidence of myocardial infarction and cancer. *Psychosomatic Medicine, 58,* 113–121. (p. 405)

Exner, J. E. (2003). *The Rorschach: A comprehensive system, 4th edition.* Hoboken, NJ: Wiley. (p. 430)

Eysenck, H. J. (1952). The effects of psychotherapy: An evaluation. *Journal of Consulting Psychology, 16,* 319–324. (p. 561)

Eysenck, H. J. (1990, April 30). An improvement on personality inventory. *Current Contents: Social and Behavioral Sciences, 22*(18), 20. (p. 436)

Eysenck, H. J. (1992). Four ways five factors are *not* basic. *Personality and Individual Differences, 13,* 667–673. (p. 436)

Eysenck, H. J., & Grossarth-Maticek, R. (1991). Creative novation behaviour therapy as a prophylactic treatment for cancer and coronary heart disease: Part II—Effects of treatment. *Behaviour Research and Therapy, 29,* 17–31. (p. 410)

Eysenck, H. J., Wakefield, J. A., Jr., & Friedman, A. F. (1983). Diagnosis and clinical assessment: The DSM-III. *Annual Review of Psychology, 34,* 167–193. (p. 510)

Eysenck, M. W., MacLeod, C., & Mathews, A. (1987). Cognitive functioning and anxiety. *Psychological Research, 49,* 189–195. (p. 444)

Eysenck, S. B. G., & Eysenck, H. J. (1963). The validity of questionnaire and rating assessments of extraversion and neuroticism, and their factorial stability. *British Journal of Psychology, 54,* 51–62. (p. 436)

F

Fabiano, G. A., Pelham, Jr., W. E., Coles, E. K., Gnagy, E. M., Chronis-Tuscano, A., & O'Connor, B. C. (2008). A meta-analysis of behavioral treatments for attention-deficit/hyperactivity disorder. *Clinical Psychology Review, 29,* 129–140. (p. 507)

Fagan, J. F., & Holland, C. R. (2007). Equal opportunity and racial differences in IQ. *Intelligence, 30,* 361–387. (pp. 344, 345)

Fagan, J. F., & Holland, C. R. (2009). Culture-fair prediction of academic achievement. *Intelligence, 37,* 62–67. (p. 345)

Falk, C. F., Heine, S. J., Yuki, M., & Takemura, K. (2009). Why do Westerners self-enhance more than East Asians? *European Journal of Personality, 23,* 183–203. (p. 449)

Falk, R., Falk, R., & Ayton, P. (2009). Subjective patterns of randomness and choice: Some consequences of collective responses. *Journal of Experimental Psychology: Human Perception and Performance, 35,* 203–224. (p. 12)

Fanti, K. A., Vanman, E., Henrich, C. C., & Avraamides, M. N. (2009). Desensitization to media violence over a short period of time. *Aggressive Behavior, 35,* 179–187. (p. 265)

Farah, M. J., Rabinowitz, C., Quinn, G. E., & Liu, G. T. (2000). Early commitment of neural substrates for face recognition. *Cognitive Neuropsychology, 17,* 117–124. (p. 58)

Farina, A. (1982). The stigma of mental disorders. In A. G. Miller (Ed.), *In the eye of the beholder.* New York: Praeger. (p. 506)

Farley, M., Baral, I., Kiremire, M., & Sezgin, U. (1998). Prostitution in five countries: Violence and post-traumatic stress disorder. *Feminism and Psychology, 8,* 405–426. (p. 515)

Farrington, D. P. (1991). Antisocial personality from childhood to adulthood. *The Psychologist: Bulletin of the British Psychological Society, 4,* 389–394. (p. 538)

Fatemi, S. H., & Folsom, T. D. (2009). The neurodevelopmental hypothesis of schizophrenia, revisted. *Schizophrenia Bulletin, 35,* 528–548. (p. 531)

Fazel, S., Langstrom, N., Hjern, A., Grann, M., & Lichtenstein, P. (2009). Schizophrenia, substance abuse, and violent crime. *JAMA, 301,* 2016–2023. (pp. 511, 512)

Fazel, S., Lichtenstein, P, Grann, M, Goodwin, G. M., & Långström, N. (2010). Bipolar disorder and violent crime: new evidence from population-based longitudinal studies and systematic review. *Archives of General Psychiatry, 67,* 931–938. (p. 511)

FBI. (2009). *Uniform Crime Reports.* Table 3. Washington, DC: Federal Bureau of Investigation. (p. 165)

Feder, H. H. (1984). Hormones and sexual behavior. *Annual Review of Psychology, 35,* 165–200. (p. 171)

Feeney, D. M. (1987). Human rights and animal welfare. *American Psychologist, 42,* 593–599. (p. 27)

Feeney, J. A., & Noller, P. (1990). Attachment style as a predictor of adult romantic relationships. *Journal of Personality and Social Psychology, 58,* 281–291. (p. 135)

Feigenson, L., Carey, S., & Spelke, E. (2002). Infants' discrimination of number vs. continuous extent. *Cognitive Psychology, 44,* 33–66. (p. 127)

Feingold, A. (1990). Gender differences in effects of physical attractiveness on romantic attraction: A comparison across five research paradigms. *Journal of Personality and Social Psychology, 59,* 981–993. (p. 489)

Feingold, A. (1992). Good-looking people are not what we think. *Psychological Bulletin, 111,* 304–341. (p. 489)

Feingold, A., & Mazzella, R. (1998). Gender differences in body image are increasing. *Psychological Science, 9,* 190–195. (p. 537)

Feinstein, J. S., Duff, M. C., & Tranel, D. (2010, April 27). Sustained experiences of emotion after loss of memory in patients with amnesia. *Proceedings of the National Academy of Sciences, 107,* 7674–7679. (p. 283)

Feldman, M. B., & Meyer, I. H. (2010). Comorbidity and age of onset of eating disorders in gay men, lesbians, and bisexuals. *Psychiatry research, 180,* 126–131. (p. 537)

Feng, J., Spence, I., & Pratt, J. (2007). Playing an action video game reduces gender differences in spatial cognition. *Psychological Science, 18,* 850–855. (p. 342)

Fenton, W. S., & McGlashan, T. H. (1991). Natural history of schizophrenia subtypes: II. Positive and negative symptoms and long-term course. *Archives of General Psychiatry, 48,* 978–986. (p. 530)

Fenton, W. S., & McGlashan, T. H. (1994). Antecedents, symptom progression, and long-term outcome of the deficit syndrome in schizophrenia. *American Journal of Psychiatry, 151,* 351–356. (p. 530)

Ferguson, C. (2009, June 14). Not every child is secretly a genius. *The Chronicle Review* (http://chronicle.com/article/Not-Every-Child-Is-Secretly/48001). (pp. 265, 332)

Ferguson, C. J. (2010). A meta-analysis of normal and disordered personality across the life span. *Journal of Personality and Social Psychology, 98,* 659–667. (p. 158)

Ferguson, C. J., & Kilburn, J. (2010). Much ado about nothing: The misestimation and overinterpretation of violent video game effects in Eastern and Western nations: Common on Anderson et al. (2010). *Psychological Bulletin, 136,* 174–178. (p. 486)

Ferguson, E. D. (1989). Adler's motivational theory: An historical perspective on belonging and the fundamental human striving. *Individual Psychology, 45,* 354–361. (p. 364)

Ferguson, E. D. (2001). Adler and Dreikurs: Cognitive-social dynamic innovators. *Journal of Individual Psychology, 57,* 324–341. (p. 364)

Ferguson, E. D. (2003). Social processes, personal goals, and their intertwining: Their importance in Adlerian theory and practice. *Journal of Individual Psychology, 59,* 136–144. (p. 428)

Ferguson, E. D. (2010). Editor's notes: Adler's innovative contributions regarding the need to belong. *Journal of Individual Psychology, 66*(1), 1–7. (p. 364)

Ferguson, M. J., & Zayas, V. (2009). Automatic evaluation. *Current Directions in Psychological Science, 18,* 362–366. (p. 194)

Fergusson, D. M., Boden, J. M., & Horwood, L. J. (2009). Tests of causal links between alcohol abuse or dependence and major depression. *Archives of General Psychiatry, 66,* 260–266. (p. 525)

Fergusson, D. M., & Woodward, L. G. (2002). Mental health, educational, and social role outcomes of adolescents with depression. *Archives of General Psychiatry, 59,* 225–231. (p. 522)

Fernandez-Dols, J-M., & Ruiz-Belda, M-A. (1995). Are smiles a sign of happiness? Gold medal winners at the Olympic Games. *Journal of Personality and Social Psychology, 69,* 1113–1119. (p. 383)

Fernyhough, C. (2008). Getting Vygotskian about theory of mind: Mediation, dialogue, and the development of social understanding. *Developmental Review, 28,* 225–262. (p. 129)

Ferri, M., Amato, L., & Davoli, M. (2006). Alcoholics Anonymous and other 12-step programmes for alcohol dependence. *Cochrane Database of Systematic Reviews,* Issue 3. Art. No.: CD005032. (p. 558)

Ferriman, K., Lubinski, D., & Benbow, C. P. (2009). Work preferences, life values, and personal views of top math/science graduate students and the profoundly gifted: Developmental changes and gender differences during emerging adulthood and parenthood. *Journal of Personality and Social Psychology, 97,* 517–522. (p. 166)

Ferris, C. F. (1996, March). The rage of innocents. *The Sciences,* pp. 22–26. (p. 136)

Festinger, L. (1957). *A theory of cognitive dissonance.* Stanford: Stanford University Press. (p. 462)

Fiedler, F. E. (1981). Leadership effectiveness. *American Behavioral Scientist, 24,* 619–632. (p. B-11)

Fiedler, F. E. (1987, September). When to lead, when to stand back. *Psychology Today,* pp. 26–27. (p. B-11)

Fiedler, K., Nickel, S., Muehlfriedel, T., & Unkelbach, C. (2001). Is mood congruency an effect of genuine memory or response bias? *Journal of Experimental Social Psychology, 37,* 201–214. (p. 288)

Field, A. P. (2006). Is conditioning a useful framework for understanding the development and treatment of phobias? *Clinical Psychology Review, 26,* 857–875. (p. 516)

Field, T. (1996). Attachment and separation in young children. *Annual Review of Psychology, 47,* 541–561. (p. 137)

Field, T., Diego, M., & Hernandez-Reif, M. (2007). Massage therapy research. *Developmental Review, 27,* 75–89. (p. 122)

Field, T., Hernandez-Reif, M., Feijo, L., & Freedman, J. (2006). Prenatal, perinatal and neonatal stimulation: A survey of neonatal nurseries. *Infant Behavior & Development, 29,* 24–31. (p. 122)

Fields, R. D. (2004, April). The other half of the brain. *Scientific American,* pp. 54–61. (p. 37)

Fields, R. D. (2008, March). White matter. *Scientific American,* pp. 54–61. (p. 37)

Fields, R. D. (2009). *The other brain: From dementia to schizophrenia, how new discoveries about the brain are revolutionizing medicine and science.* New York: Simon & Schuster. (p. 37)

Fikke, L. T., Melinder, A., & Landrø, N. I. (2011). Executive functions are impaired in adolescents engaging in non-suicidal self-injury. *Psychological Medicine, 41,* 601–610. (p. 525)

Fincham, F. D., & Bradbury, T. N. (1993). Marital satisfaction, depression, and attributions: A longitudinal analysis. *Journal of Personality and Social Psychology, 64,* 442–452. (p. 459)

Finchilescu, G., & Tredoux, C. (eds.) (2010). Intergroup relations in post apartheid South Africa: Change, and obstacles to change. *Journal of Social Issues, 66,* 223–236. (p. 498)

Fingelkurts, A. A., & Fingelkurts, A. A. (2009). Is our brain hardwired to produce God, or is our brain hardwire to perceive God? A systematic review on the role of the brain in mediating religious experience. *Cognitive Processes, 10,* 293–326. (p. 57)

Fingerman, K. L., & Charles, S. T. (2010). It takes two to tango: Why older people have the best relationships. *Current Directions in Psychological Science, 19,* 172–176. (p. 156)

Fink, G. R., Markowitsch, H. J., Reinkemeier, M., Bruckbauer, T., Kessler, J., & Heiss, W-D. (1996). Cerebral representation of one's own past: Neural networks involved in autobiographical memory. *Journal of Neuroscience, 16,* 4275–4282. (p. 281)

Fink, M. (2009). *Electroconvulsive therapy: A guide for professionals and their patients.* New York; Oxford University Press. (p. 571)

Finkel, E. J., & Eastwick, P. W. (2008). Speed-dating. *Current Directions in Psychological Science, 17,* 193–197. (p. 489)

Finkel, E. J., & Eastwick, P. W. (2009). Arbitrary social norms influence sex differences in romantic selectivity. *Psychological Science 20,* 1290–1295. (p. 488)

Finlay, S. W. (2000). Influence of Carl Jung and William James on the origin of alcoholics anonymous. *Review of General Psychology, 4,* 3–12. (pp. 558, 559)

Finzi, E., & Wasserman, E. (2006). Treatment of depression with botulinum toxin A: A case series. *Dermatological Surgery, 32,* 645–650. (p. 385)

Fiore, M. C., & 23 others. (2008). *Treating tobacco use and dependence: 2008 update. Clinical practice guideline.* Rockville, MD: U.S. Department of Health and Human Services, Public Health Service. (p. 105)

Fischer, P., & Greitemeyer, T. (2006). Music and aggression: The impact of sexual-aggressive song lyrics on aggression-related thoughts, emotions, and behavior toward the same and the opposite sex. *Personality and Social Psychology Bulletin, 32,* 1165–1176. (p. 484)

Fischhoff, B. (1982). Debiasing. In D. Kahneman, P. Slovic, & A. Tversky (Eds.), *Judgment under uncertainty: Heuristics and biases.* New York: Cambridge University Press. (p. 312)

Fischhoff, B., Slovic, P., & Lichtenstein, S. (1977). Knowing with certainty: The appropriateness of extreme confidence. *Journal of Experimental Psychology: Human Perception and Performance, 3,* 552–564. (p. 311)

Fischtein, D. S., Herold, E. S., & Desmarais, S. (2007). How much does gender explain in sexual attitudes and behaviors? A survey of Canadian adults. *Archives of Sexual Behavior, 36,* 451–461. (p. 184)

Fishbach, A., Dhar, R., & Zhang, Y. (2006). Subgoals as substitutes or complements: The role of goal accessibility. *Journal of Personality and Social Psychology, 91,* 232–242. (p. B-11)

Fisher, H. E. (1993, March/April). After all, maybe it's biology. *Psychology Today,* pp. 40–45. (p. 154)

Fisher, H. E., Aron, A., Mashek, D., Li, H., & Brown, L. L. (2002). Defining the brain systems of lust, romantic attraction, and attachment. *Archives of Sexual Behavior, 31,* 413–419. (p. 173)

Fisher, H. T. (1984). Little Albert and Little Peter. *Bulletin of the British Psychological Society, 37,* 269. (p. 551)

Fisher, K., Egerton, M., Gershuny, J. I., & Robinson, J. P. (2006). Gender convergence in the American Heritage Time Use Study (AHTUS). *Social Indicators Research, 82,* 1–33. (p. 169)

Flack, W. F. (2006). Peripheral feedback effects of facial expressions, bodily postures, and vocal expressions on emotional feelings. *Cognition and Emotion, 20,* 177–195. (p. 385)

Flegal, K. M., Carroll, M. D., Ogden, C. L., & Curtin, L. R. (2010). Prevalence and trends in obesity among US adults, 1999–2008. *JAMA, 303,* 235–241. (p. 361)

Fleming, I., Baum, A., & Weiss, L. (1987). Social density and perceived control as mediator of crowding stress in high-density residential neighborhoods. *Journal of Personality and Social Psychology, 52,* 899–906. (p. 403)

Fleming, J. H. (2001, Winter/Spring). Introduction to the special issue on linkage analysis. *The Gallup Research Journal*, pp. i–vi. (p. B-10)

Fleming, J. H., & Scott, B. A. (1991). The costs of confession: The Persian Gulf War POW tapes in historical and theoretical perspective. *Contemporary Social Psychology, 15,* 127–138. (p. 382)

Fletcher, G. J. O., Fitness, J., & Blampied, N. M. (1990). The link between attributions and happiness in close relationships: The roles of depression and explanatory style. *Journal of Social and Clinical Psychology, 9,* 243–255. (p. 459)

Flood, M. (2007). Exposure to pornography among youth in Australia. *Journal of Sociology, 43,* 45–60. (p. 484)

Flora, S. R. (2004). *The power of reinforcement.* Albany, NJ: SUNY Press. (p. 253)

Flora, S. R., & Bobby, S. E. (2008, September/October). The bipolar bamboozle. *Skeptical Inquirer*, pp. 41–45. (p. 521)

Flory, R., Ametepe, J., & Bowers, B. (2010). A randomized, place-controlled trial of bright light and high-density negative air ions for treatment of Season Affective Disorder. *Psychiatry Research, 177,* 101–108. (p. 564)

Flouri, E., & Buchanan, A. (2004). Early father's and mother's involvement and child's later educational outcomes. *British Journal of Educational Psychology, 74,* 141–153. (p. 135)

Foa, E. B., & Kozak, M. J. (1986). Emotional processing of fear: Exposure to corrective information. *Psychological Bulletin, 99,* 20–35. (p. 552)

Food and Drug Administration (2011). FDA Executive Summary. Prepared for the January 27–28, 2011 meeting of the Neurological Devices Panel (www.fda.gov). (p. 572)

Ford, E. S. (2002). Does exercise reduce inflammation? Physical activity and B-reactive protein among U.S. adults. *Epidemiology, 13,* 561–569. (p. 407)

Foree, D. D., & LoLordo, V. M. (1973). Attention in the pigeon: Differential effects of food-getting versus shock-avoidance procedures. *Journal of Comparative and Physiological Psychology, 85,* 551–558. (p. 258)

Forer, B. R. (1949). The fallacy of personal validation: A classroom demonstration of gullibility. *Journal of Abnormal and Social Psychology, 44,* 118–123. (p. 439)

Forgas, J. P. (2008). Affect and cognition. *Perspectives on Psychological Science, 3,* 94–101. (p. 412)

Forgas, J. P. (2009, November/December). Think negative! *Australian Science*, pp. 14–17. (p. 519)

Forgas, J. P., Bower, G. H., & Krantz, S. E. (1984). The influence of mood on perceptions of social interactions. *Journal of Experimental Social Psychology, 20,* 497–513. (p. 288)

Forhan, S. E., Gottlieb, S. L., Sternberg, M. R., Xu, F., Datta, D., Berman, S., & Markowitz, L. (2008). Prevalence of sexually transmitted infections and bacterial vaginosis among female adolescents in the United States: Data from the National Health and Nutrition Examination Survey (NHANES) 2003–2004. Paper presented to the 2008 National STD Prevention Conference, Chicago, Illinois. (p. 174)

Forman, D. R., Aksan, N., & Kochanska, G. (2004). Toddlers' responsive imitation predicts preschool-age conscience. *Psychological Science, 15,* 699–704. (p. 264)

Foss, D. J., & Hakes, D. T. (1978). *Psycholinguistics: An introduction to the psychology of language.* Englewood Cliffs, NJ: Prentice-Hall. (p. 430)

Foulkes, D. (1999). *Children's dreaming and the development of consciousness.* Cambridge, MA: Harvard University Press. (p. 96)

Fournier, J. C., DeRubeis, R. J., Hollon, S. D., Dimidjian, S., Amsterdam, J. D., Shelton, R. C., & Fawcett, J. (2010). Antidepressant drug effects and depression severity: A patient-level meta-analysis. *Journal of the American Medical Association, 303,* 47–53. (p. 570)

Fouts, R. S. (1992). Transmission of a human gestural language in a chimpanzee mother-infant relationship. *Friends of Washoe, 12/13,* pp. 2–8. (p. 324)

Fouts, R. S. (1997). *Next of kin: What chimpanzees have taught me about who we are.* New York: Morrow. (p. 324)

Fowles, D. C. (1992). Schizophrenia: Diathesis-stress revisited. *Annual Review of Psychology, 43,* 303–336. (p. 530)

Fowles, D. C., & Dindo, L. (2009). Temperament and psychopathy: A dual-pathway model. *Current Directions in Psychological Science, 18,* 179–183. (p. 538)

Fox, D. (2010, June). The insanity virus. *Discover,* pp. 58–64. (p. 531)

Fox, J. L. (1984). The brain's dynamic way of keeping in touch. *Science, 225,* 820–821. (p. 58)

Fox, N. A., Hane, A. E., & Pine, D. S. (2007). Plasticity for affective neurocircuitry. *Current Directions in Psychological Science, 16,* 1–5. (p. 134)

Fozard, J. L., & Popkin, S. J. (1978). Optimizing adult development: Ends and means of an applied psychology of aging. *American Psychologist, 33,* 975–989. (p. 151)

Fracassini, C. (2000, August 27). Holidaymakers led by the nose in sales quest. *Scotland on Sunday.* (p. 226)

Fraley, R. C. (2002). Attachment stability from infancy to adulthood: Meta-analysis and dynamic modeling of developmental mechanisms. *Personality and Social Psychology Review, 6,* 123–151. (p. 135)

Fraley, R. C., Vicary, A. M., Brumbaugh, C. C., & Roisman, G. I. (2011). Patterns of stability in adult attachment: An empirical test of two models of continuity and change. *Journal of Personality and Social Psychology, 101,* 974–992. (pp. 135, 365)

Frank, J. D. (1982). Therapeutic components shared by all psychotherapies. In J. H. Harvey & M. M. Parks (Eds.), *The Master Lecture Series: Vol. 1. Psychotherapy research and behavior change.* Washington, DC; American Psychological Association. (pp. 565, 566)

Frankel, A., Strange, D. R., & Schoonover, R. (1983). CRAP: Consumer rated assessment procedure. In G. H. Scherr & R. Liebmann-Smith (Eds.), *The best of The Journal of Irreproducible Results.* New York: Workman Publishing. (p. 438)

Frankenburg, W., Dodds, J., Archer, P., Shapiro, H., & Bresnick, B. (1992). The Denver II: A major revision and restandardization of the Denver Developmental Screening Test. *Pediatrics, 89,* 91–97. (p. 123)

Franklin, M., & Foa, E. B. (2011). Treatment of obsessive-compulsive disorder. *Annual Review of Clinical Psychology, 7,* 229–243. (p. 517)

Franz, E. A., Waldie, K. E., & Smith, M. J. (2000). The effect of callosotomy on novel versus familiar bimanual actions: A neural dissociation between controlled and automatic processes? *Psychological Science, 11,* 82–85. (p. 61)

Frasure-Smith, N., & Lesperance, F. (2005). Depression and coronary heart disease: Complex synergism of mind, body, and environment. *Current Directions in Psychological Science, 14,* 39–43. (p. 400)

Frattaroli, J. (2006). Experimental disclosure and its moderators: A meta-analysis. *Psychological Bulletin, 132,* 823–865. (p. 406)

Fredrickson, B. L. (2006). The broaden-and-build theory of positive emotions. In M. Csikszentmihalyi & I. S. Csikszentmihalyi (Eds.), *A life worth living: Contributions to positive psychology.* New York: Oxford University Press. (p. 412)

Freedman, D. H. (2011, February). How to fix the obesity crisis. *Scientific American,* pp. 40–47. (p. 363)

Freedman, D. J., Riesenhuber, M., Poggio, T., & Miller, E. K. (2001). Categorical representation of visual stimuli in the primate prefrontal cortex. *Science, 291,* 312–316. (p. 317)

Freedman, J. L. (1988). Television violence and aggression: What the evidence shows. In S. Oskamp (Ed.), *Television as a social issue.* Newbury Park, CA: Sage. (p. 265)

Freedman, J. L., & Fraser, S. C. (1966). Compliance without pressure: The foot-in-the-door technique. *Journal of Personality and Social Psychology, 4,* 195–202. (p. 461)

Freedman, J. L., & Perlick, D. (1979). Crowding, contagion, and laughter. *Journal of Experimental Social Psychology, 15,* 295–303. (p. 471)

Freeman, E. C., & Twenge, J. M. (2010, January). Using MySpace increases the endorsement of narcissistic personality traits. Poster presented at the annual conference of the Society for Personality and Social Psychology, Las Vegas, NV. (p. 370)

Freeman, W. J. (1991, February). The physiology of perception. *Scientific American,* pp. 78–85. (p. 216)

Freud, S. (1931; reprinted 1961). Female sexuality. In J. Strachey (Trans.), *The standard edition of the complete psychological works of Sigmund Freud.* London: Hogarth Press. (p. 424)

Freud, S. (1935; reprinted 1960). *A general introduction to psychoanalysis.* New York: Washington Square Press. (p. 154)

Freyd, J. J., DePrince, A. P., & Gleaves, D. H. (2007). The state of betrayal trauma theory: Reply to McNally—Conceptual issues and future directions. *Memory, 15,* 295–311. (p. 298)

Freyd, J. J., Putnam, F. W., Lyon, T. D., Becker-Blease, K. A., Cheit, R. E., Siegel, N. B., & Pezdek, K. (2005). The science of child sexual abuse. *Science, 308,* 501. (p. 137)

Fridlund, A. J., Beck, H. P., Goldie, W. D., & Irons, G. (2012). Little Albert: A neurologically impaired child. *History of Psychology,* in press. (p. 245)

Friedman, M., & Ulmer, D. (1984). *Treating Type A behavior—and your heart.* New York: Knopf. (pp. 397, 409)

Friedman, R., & James, J. W. (2008). The myth of the sages of dying, death and grief. *Skeptic, 14*(2), 37–41. (p. 158)

Friedman, S. L., & Boyle, D. E. (2008). Attachment in US children experiencing non-maternal care in the early 1990s. *Attachment & Human Development, 10,* 225–261. (p. 137)

Frijda, N. H. (1988). The laws of emotion. *American Psychologist, 43,* 349–358. (p. 416)

Frisch, M., & Zdravkovic, S. (2010). Body size at birth and same-sex marriage in young adulthood. *Archives of Sexual Behavior, 39,* 117–123. (p. 182)

Frith, U., & Frith, C. (2001). The biological basis of social interaction. *Current Directions in Psychological Science, 10,* 151–155. (p. 130)

Fritz, T., Jentschke, S., Gosselin, N., Sammler, D., Peretz, I., Turner, R., Friederici, A., & Koelsch, S. (2009). Universal recognition of three basic emotions in music. *Current Biology, 19,* 573–576. (p. 383)

Fromkin, V., & Rodman, R. (1983). *An introduction to language* (3rd ed.). New York: Holt, Rinehart & Winston. (p. 321)

Fry, A. F., & Hale, S. (1996). Processing speed, working memory, and fluid intelligence: Evidence for a developmental cascade. *Psychological Science, 7,* 237–241. (p. 152)

Fry, R., & Cohn, D. (2010, January 19). Women, men and the new economics of marriage. Pew Research Center (pewresearch.org). (p. 170)

Fuhriman, A., & Burlingame, G. M. (1994). Group psychotherapy: Research and practice. In A. Fuhriman & G. M. Burlingame (Eds.), *Handbook of group psychotherapy.* New York; Wiley. (p. 557)

Fuller, M. J., & Downs, A. C. (1990). Spermarche is a salient biological marker in men's development. Poster presented at the American Psychological Society convention. (p. 168)

Fulmer, C. A., Gelfand, M. J., Kruglanski, A. W., Kim-Prieto, C., Diener, E., Pierro, A., & Higgins, E. T. (2010). On "feeling right" in cultural contexts: How person-culture match affects self-esteem and subjective well-being. *Psychological Science, 21,* 1563–1569. (p. 444)

Fulmer, I. S., Gerhart, B., & Scott, K. S. (2003). Are the 100 best better? An empirical investigation of the relationship between being a "great place to work" and firm performance. *Personnel Psychology, 56,* 965–993. (p. B-8)

Funder, D. C. (2001). Personality. *Annual Review of Psychology, 52,* 197–221. (p. 440)

Funder, D. C. (2009). Persons, behaviors and situations: An agenda for personality psychology in the postwar era. *Journal of Research in Personality, 43,* 155–162. (p. 444)

Funder, D. C., & Block, J. (1989). The role of ego-control, ego-resiliency, and IQ in delay of gratification in adolescence. *Journal of Personality and Social Psychology, 57,* 1041–1050. (p. 143)

Furlow, F. B., & Thornhill, R. (1996, January/ February). The orgasm wars. *Psychology Today,* pp. 42–46. (p. 173)

Furnham, A. (1982). Explanations for unemployment in Britain. *European Journal of Social Psychology, 12,* 335–352. (p. 459)

Furnham, A., & Baguma, P. (1994). Cross-cultural differences in the evaluation of male and female body shapes. *International Journal of Eating Disorders, 15,* 81–89. (p. 361)

Furnham, A., & Wu, J. (2008). Gender differences in estimates of one's own and parental intelligence in China. *Individual Differences Research, 6,* 1–12. (p. 476)

Furr, R. M., & Funder, D. C. (1998). A multi-modal analysis of personal negativity. *Journal of Personality and Social Psychology, 74,* 1580–1591. (p. 527)

Furukawa, T. A., Yoshimura, R., Harai, H., Imaizumi, T., Takeuchi, H., Kitamua, T., & Takahashi, K. (2009). How many well vs. unwell days can you expect over 10 years, once you become depressed? *Acta Psychiatrica Scandinavica, 119,* 290–297. (p. 522)

G

Gable, S. L., Gonzaga, G. C., & Strachman, A. (2006). Will you be there for me when things go right? Supportive responses to positive event disclosures. *Journal of Personality and Social Psychology, 91,* 904–917. (p. 156)

Gabrieli, J. D. E., Desmond, J. E., Demb, J. E., Wagner, A. D., Stone, M. V., Vaidya, C. J., & Glover, G. H. (1996). Functional magnetic resonance imaging of semantic memory processes in the frontal lobes. *Psychological Science, 7,* 278–283. (p. 281)

Gailliot, M. T., Baumeister, R. F., DeWall, C. N., Maner, J. K., & Plant, E. A. (2007). Self-control relies on glucose as a limited energy source: Willpower is more than a metaphor. *Journal of Personality and Social Psychology, 92,* 325–336. (p. 403)

Galambos, N. L. (1992). Parent-adolescent relations. *Current Directions in Psychological Science, 1,* 146–149. (p. 146)

Galanter, E. (1962). Contemporary psychophysics. In R. Brown, E. Galanter, E. H. Hess, & G. Mandler (Eds.), *New directions in psychology.* New York: Holt Rinehart & Winston. (p. 193)

Galati, D., Scherer, K. R., & Ricci-Bitti, P. E. (1997). Voluntary facial expression of emotion: Comparing congenitally blind with normally sighted encoders. *Journal of Personality and Social Psychology, 73,* 1363–1379. (p. 383)

Gale, C. R., Batty, G. D., & Deary, I. J. (2008). Locus of control at age 10 years and health outcomes and behaviors at age 30 years: The 1970 British Cohort Study. *Psychosomatic Medicine, 70,* 397–403. (p. 403)

Galinsky, E., Aumann, K., & Bond, J. T. (2008). *Times are changing: Gender and generation at work and at home.* Work and Families Institute (www.familiesandwork.org). (p. 448)

Gallese, V., Gernsbacher, M. A., Heyes, C., Hickok, G., & Iacoboni, M. (2011). Mirror neuron forum. *Perspectives on Psychological Science, 6,* 369–407. (pp. 131, 262)

Gallo, W. T., Teng, H. M., Falba, T. A., Kasl, S. V., Krumholz, H. M., & Bradley, E. H. (2006). The impact of late career job loss on myocardial infarction and stroke: A 10 year follow up using the health and retirement survey. *Occupational and Environmental Medicine, 63,* 683–687. (pp. 391, 400)

Gallup. (2010, accessed June 28). Gallup daily: U.S. mood. Based on the Gallup-Healthways well-being index. www.gallup.com. (p. 19)

Gallup Brain. (2008, accessed February 20). Woman for president: Question qn2f, March, 2007 wave. Brain.Gallup.com. (p. 476)

Gallup, G. G., Jr., & Frederick, D. A. (2010). The science of sex appeal: An evolutionary perspective. *Review of General Psychology, 14,* 240–250. (p. 490)

Gallup, G. H. (1972). *The Gallup poll: Public opinion 1935–1971* (Vol. 3). New York: Random House. (p. 498)

Gallup, G. H., Jr. (1994, October). Millions finding care and support in small groups. *Emerging Trends,* pp. 2–5. (p. 558)

Gallup, G. H., Jr. (2002, April 30). Education and youth. *Gallup Tuesday Briefing* (www.gallup.com/poll/tb/educaYouth/20020430.asp). (p. 264)

Gallup Organization. (2003, July 8). American public opinion about Iraq. *Gallup Poll News Service* (www.gallup.com). (p. 462)

Gallup Organization. (2004, August 16). 65% of Americans receive NO praise or recognition in the workplace. E-mail from Tom Rath: bucketbook@gallup.com. (p. B-10)

Gangestad, S. W., & Simpson, J. A. (2000). The evolution of human mating: Trade-offs and strategic pluralism. *Behavioral and Brain Sciences, 23,* 573–587. (p. 184)

Gangestad, S. W., Thornhill, R., & Garver-Apgar, C. E. (2010). Men's facial masculinity predicts changes in their female partners' sexual interests across the ovulatory cycle, whereas men's intelligence does not. *Evolution and Human Behavior, 31,* 412–424. (p. 490)

Gangwisch, J. E., Babiss, L. A., Malaspina, D., Turner, J. B., Zammit, G. K., & Posner, K. (2010). Earlier parental set bedtimes as a protective factor against depression and suicidal ideation. *Sleep, 33*, 97–106. (p. 89)

Gao, Y., Raine, A., Venables, P. H., Dawson, M. E., & Mednick, S. A. (2010). Association of poor child fear conditioning and adult crime. *American Journal of Psychiatry, 167*, 56–60. (p. 539)

Garber, K. (2007). Autism's cause may reside in abnormalities at the synapse. *Science, 317*, 190–191. (p. 131)

Garcia, J., & Gustavson, A. R. (1997, January). Carl R. Gustavson (1946–1996): Pioneering wildlife psychologist. *APS Observer*, pp. 34–35. (p. 257)

Garcia, J., & Koelling, R. A. (1966). Relation of cue to consequence in avoidance learning. *Psychonomic Science, 4*, 123–124. (p. 256)

Gardner, H. (1983). *Frames of mind: The theory of multiple intelligences.* New York: Basic Books. (p. 330)

Gardner, H. (1998a, March 19). An intelligent way to progress. *The Independent* (London), p. E4. (p. 331)

Gardner, H. (1998b, November 5). Do parents count? *New York Review of Books* (www.nybooks.com). (p. 147)

Gardner, H. (1999). *Multiple views of multiple intelligence.* New York: Basic Books. (p. 333)

Gardner, H. (2006). *The development and education of the mind: The selected works of Howard Gardner.* New York: Routledge/Taylor & Francis. (p. 330)

Gardner, J., & Oswald, A. J. (2007). Money and mental well-being: A longitudinal study of medium–sized lottery wins. *Journal of Health Economics, 6*, 49–60. (p. 416)

Gardner, M. (2006, January/February). The memory wars, part one. *Skeptical Inquirer, 30*, 28–31. (p. 298)

Gardner, R. A., & Gardner, B. I. (1969). Teaching sign language to a chimpanzee. *Science, 165*, 664–672. (p. 324)

Garfield, C. (1986). *Peak Performers: The new heroes of American Business.* New York: Morrow. (p. 328)

Garon, N., Bryson, S. E., & Smith, I. M. (2008). Executive function in preschoolers: A review using an integrative framework. *Psychological Bulletin, 134*, 31–60. (p. 122)

Garrett, B. L. (2008). Judging innocence. *Columbia Law Review, 108*, 55–142. (p. 297)

Garry, M., Loftus, E. F., & Brown, S. W. (1994). Memory: A river runs through it. *Consciousness and Cognition, 3*, 438–451. (p. 431)

Garry, M., Manning, C. G., Loftus, E. F., & Sherman, S. J. (1996). Imagination inflation: Imagining a childhood event inflates confidence that it occurred. *Psychonomic Bulletin & Review, 3*, 208–214. (p. 295)

Gartrell, N., & Bos, H. (2010). U.S. national longitudinal lesbian family study: Psychological adjustment of 17-year-old adolescents. *Pediatrics, 126*, 28–36. (p. 180)

Gatchel, R. J., Peng, Y. B., Peters, M. L., Fuchs, P. N., & Turk, D. C. (2007). The biopsychosocial approach to chronic pain: Scientific advances and future directions. *Psychological Bulletin, 133*, 581–624. (p. 221)

Gawande, A. (1998, September 21). The pain perplex. *The New Yorker*, pp. 86–94. (p. 222)

Gawin, F. H. (1991). Cocaine addiction: Psychology and neurophysiology. *Science, 251*, 1580–1586. (p. 106)

Gazzaniga, M. S. (1967, August). The split brain in man. *Scientific American*, pp. 24–29. (pp. 59, 60)

Gazzaniga, M. S. (1983). Right hemisphere language following brain bisection: A 20–year perspective. *American Psychologist, 38*, 525–537. (p. 60)

Gazzaniga, M. S. (1988). Organization of the human brain. *Science, 245*, 947–952. (pp. 61, 101)

Ge, X., & Natsuaki, M. N. (2009). In search of explanations for early pubertal timing effects on developmental psychopathology. *Current Directions in Psychological Science, 18*, 327–441. (p. 140)

Geary, D. C. (1995). Sexual selection and sex differences in spatial cognition. *Learning and Individual Differences, 7*, 289–301. (p. 342)

Geary, D. C. (1996). Sexual selection and sex differences in mathematical abilities. *Behavioral and Brain Sciences, 19*, 229–247. (p. 342)

Geary, D. C. (1998). *Male, female: The evolution of human sex differences.* Washington, DC: American Psychological Association. (p. 184)

Geary, D. C. (2010). *Male, female: The evolution of human sex differences* (second edition). Washington, DC: American Psychological Association. (p. 167)

Geary, D. C., Salthouse, T. A., Chen, G-P., & Fan, L. (1996). Are East Asian versus American differences in arithmetical ability a recent phenomenon? *Developmental Psychology, 32*, 254–262. (p. 344)

Geen, R. G., & Quanty, M. B. (1977). The catharsis of aggression: An evaluation of a hypothesis. In L. Berkowitz (Ed.), *Advances in experimental social psychology* (Vol. 10). New York: Academic Press. (p. 398)

Geen, R. G., & Thomas, S. L. (1986). The immediate effects of media violence on behavior. *Journal of Social Issues, 42*(3), 7–28. (p. 265)

Gehring, W. J., Wimke, J., & Nisenson, L. G. (2000). Action monitoring dysfunction in obsessive-compulsive disorder. *Psychological Science, 11*(1), 1–6. (p. 518)

Geier, A. B., Rozin, P., & Doros, G. (2006). Unit bias: A new heuristic that helps explain the effects of portion size on food intake. *Psychological Science, 17*, 521–525. (p. 360)

Gelman, D. (1989, May 15). Voyages to the unknown. *Newsweek*, pp. 66–69. (p. 383)

Genesee, F., & Gándara, P. (1999). Bilingual education programs: A cross-national perspective. *Journal of Social Issues, 55*, 665–685. (p. 327)

Gentile, B., Twenge, J. M., & Campbell, W. K. (2010). Birth cohort differences in self-esteem, 1988–2008: A cross-temporal meta-analysis. *Review of General Psychology, 14*, 261–268. (p. 449)

Gentile, D. (2009). Pathological video-game use among youth ages 8 to 18: A national study. *Psychological Science, 20*, 594–602. (p. 101)

Gentile, D. A., Anderson, C. A., Yukawa., S., Ihori, N., Saleem, M., Ming, L. K., Shibuya, A., Liau, A. K., Khoo, A., & Sakamoto, A. (2009). The effects of prosocial video games on prosocial behaviors: International evidence from correlational, experimental, and longitudinal studies. *Personality and Social Psychology Bulletin, 35*, 752–763. (pp. 485, 486)

Gentile, D. A., Lynch, P. J., Linder, J. R., & Walsh, D. A. (2004). The effects of violent video game habits on adolescent hostility, aggressive behaviors, and school performance. *Journal of Adolescence, 27*, 5–22. (p. 265)

George, L. K., Ellison, C. G., & Larson, D. B. (2002). Explaining the relationships between religious involvement and health. *Psychological Inquiry, 13*, 190–200. (p. 412)

George, M. S. (2003, September). Stimulating the brain. *Scientific American*, pp. 67–73. (p. 573)

George, M. S., & 12 others. (2010). Daily left prefrontal transcranial magnetic stimulation therapy for major depressive disorder: A sham-controlled randomized trial. *Archives of General Psychiatry, 67*, 507–516. (p. 573)

Geraerts, E., Bernstein, D. M., Merckelbach, H., Linders, C., Raymaekers, L., & Loftus, E. F. (2008). Lasting false beliefs and their behavioral consequences. *Psychological Science, 19*, 749–753. (p. 295)

Geraerts, E., Schooler, J. W., Merckelbach, H., Jelicic, M., Hauer, B. J. A., & Ambadar, Z. (2007). The reality of recovered memories: Corroborating continuous and discontinuous memories of childhood sexual abuse. *Psychological Science, 18*, 564–568. (p. 299)

Gerhart, K. A., Koziol-McLain, J., Lowenstein, S. R., & Whiteneck, G. G. (1994). Quality of life following spinal cord injury: Knowledge and attitudes of emergency care providers. *Annals of Emergency Medicine, 23*, 807–812. (p. 414)

Gernsbacher, M. A., Dawson, M., & Goldsmith, H. H. (2005). Three reasons not to believe in an autism epidemic. *Current Directions in Psychological Science, 14*, 55–58. (p. 130)

Gerrard, M., & Luus, C. A. E. (1995). Judgments of vulnerability to pregnancy: The role of risk factors and individual differences. *Personality and Social Psychology Bulletin, 21*, 160–171. (p. 176)

Gershoff, E. T. (2002). Parental corporal punishment and associated child behaviors and experiences: A meta-analytic and theoretical review. *Psychological Bulletin, 128*, 539–579. (p. 251)

Gershoff, E. T., Grogan-Kaylor, A., Lansford, J. E., Chang, L., Zelli, A., Deater-Deckard, K., & Dodge, K. A. (2010). Parent discipline practices in an international sample: Associations with child behaviors and moderation by perceived normativeness. *Child Development, 81,* 487–502. (p. 252)

Gerstorf, D., Ram, N., Röcke, C., Lindenberger, U., & Smith, J. (2008). Decline in life satisfaction in old age: Longitudinal evidence for links to distance-to-death. *Psychology and Aging, 23,* 154–168. (p. 156)

Gertner, J. (2010, May 10). The rise and fall of the G.D.P. *New York Times* (www.nytimes.com). (p. 419)

Geschwind, N. (1979, September). Specializations of the human brain. *Scientific American, 241,* 180–199. (p. 323)

Gfeller, J. D., Lynn, S. J., & Pribble, W. E. (1987). Enhancing hypnotic susceptibility: Interpersonal and rapport factors. *Journal of Personality and Social Psychology, 52,* 586–595. (p. 99)

Giancola, P. R., & Corman, M. D. (2007). Alcohol and aggression: A test of the attention-allocation model. *Psychological Science, 18,* 649–655. (p. 482)

Giancola, P. R., Josephs, R. A., Parrott, D. J., & Duke, A. A. (2010). Alcohol myopia revisited: Clarifying aggression and other acts of disinhibition through a distorted lens. *Perspectives on Psychological Science, 5,* 265–278. (p. 103)

Gibbons, F. X. (1986). Social comparison and depression: Company's effect on misery. *Journal of Personality and Social Psychology, 51,* 140–148. (p. 417)

Gibbs, W. W. (1996, June). Mind readings. *Scientific American,* pp. 34–36. (p. 54)

Gibson, E. J., & Walk, R. D. (1960, April). The "visual cliff." *Scientific American,* pp. 64–71. (p. 210)

Gibson, H. B. (1995, April). Recovered memories. *The Psychologist,* pp. 153–154. (p. 97)

Gick, B., & Derrick, D. (2009). Aero-tactile integration in speech perception. *Nature, 462,* 502–504. (p. 228)

Giesbrecht, T., Lynn, S. J., Lilienfeld, S. O., & Merckelbach, H. (2008). Cognitive processes in dissociation: An analysis of core theoretical assumptions. *Psychological Bulletin, 134,* 617–647. (p. 534)

Giesbrecht, T., Lynn, S. J., Lilienfeld, S. O., & Merckelbach, H. (2010). Cognitive processes, trauma, and dissociation—Misconceptions and misrepresentations: Reply to Bremner (2010). *Psychological Bulletin, 136,* 7–11. (p. 534)

Gigerenzer, G. (2004). Dread risk, September 11, and fatal traffic accidents. *Psychological Science, 15,* 286–287. (p. 310)

Gigerenzer, G. (2006). Out of the frying pan into the fire: Behavioral reactions to terrorist attacks. *Risk Analysis, 26,* 347–351. (p. 310)

Gigerenzer, G. (2010). *Rationality for mortals: How people cope with uncertainty.* New York: Oxford University Press. (p. A-1)

Gigerenzer, G., Gaissmaier, W., Kurz-Milcke, E., Schwartz, L. M., & Woloshin, S. (2008). Helping doctors and patients make sense of health statistics. *Psychological Science in the Public Interest, 8,* 53–96. (p. A-1)

Gigerenzer, G., Gaissmaier, W., Kurz-Milcke, E., Schwartz, L. M., & Woloshin, S. (2009, April/May). Knowing your chances. *Scientific American Mind,* pp. 44–51. (p. A-1)

Gilbert, D. T. (2006). *Stumbling on happiness.* New York: Knopf. (pp. 156, 294, 373, 449, 519)

Gilbert, D. T., Pelham, B. W., & Krull, D. S. (2003). The psychology of good ideas. *Psychological Inquiry, 14,* 258–260. (p. 11)

Gilbert, D. T., Pinel, E. C., Wilson, T. D., Blumberg, S. J., & Wheatley, T. P. (1998). Immune neglect: A source of durability bias in affective forecasting. *Journal of Personality and Social Psychology, 75,* 617–638. (p. 414)

Giles, D. E., Dahl, R. E., & Coble, P. A. (1994). Childbearing, developmental, and familial aspects of sleep. In J. M. Oldham & M. B. Riba (Eds.), *Review of psychiatry* (Vol. 13). Washington, DC: American Psychiatric Press. (p. 93)

Gilestro, G. F., Tononi, G., & Cirelli, C. (2009). Widespread changes in synaptic markers as a function of sleep and wakefulness in *Drosophila. Science, 324,* 109–112. (p. 88)

Gill, A. J., Oberlander, J., & Austin, E. (2006). Rating e-mail personality at zero acquaintance. *Personality and Individual Differences, 40,* 497–507. (p. 443)

Gillham, J. E., Hamilton, J., Freres, D. R., Patton, K., & Gallop, R. (2006). Preventing depression among early adolescents in the primary care setting: A randomized controlled study of the Penn Resiliency Program. *Journal of Abnormal Child Psychology, 34,* 195–211. (p. 577)

Gillison, M. L., Broutian, T., Pickard, R. K. L., Tong, Z-Y., Xiao, W., Kahle, L., Graubard, B. I., & Chaturvedi, A. K. (2012). Prevalence of oral HPV infection in the United States, 2009–2010. *JAMA, 307*(7), 693–703. (p. 174)

Gilovich, T. (1996). The spotlight effect: Exaggerated impressions of the self as a social stimulus. Unpublished manuscript, Cornell University. (p. 447)

Gilovich, T., Kruger, J., & Medvec, V. H. (2002). The spotlight effect revisited: Overestimating the manifest variability of our actions and appearance. *Journal of Experimental Social Psychology, 38,* 93–99. (p. 447)

Gilovich, T., & Medvec, V. H. (1995). The experience of regret: What, when, and why. *Psychological Review, 102,* 379–395. (p. 156)

Gilovich, T., & Savitsky, K. (1999). The spotlight effect and the illusion of transparency: Egocentric assessments of how we are seen by others. *Current Directions in Psychological Science, 8,* 165–168. (p. 447)

Gilovich, T., Vallone, R., & Tversky, A. (1985). The hot hand in basketball: On the misperception of random sequences. *Cognitive Psychology, 17,* 295–314. (p. 13)

Giltay, E. J., Geleijnse, J. M., Zitman, F. G., Buijsse, B., & Kromhout, D. (2007). Lifestyle and dietary correlates of dispositional optimism in men: The Zutphen Elderly Study. *Journal of Psychosomatic Research, 63,* 483–490. (p. 404)

Giltay, E. J., Geleijnse, J. M., Zitman, F. G., Hoekstra, T., & Schouten, E. G. (2004). Dispositional optimism and all-cause and cardiovascular mortality in a prospective cohort of elderly Dutch men and women. *Archives of General Psychiatry, 61,* 1126–1135. (p. 404)

Gingerich, O. (1999, February 6). Is there a role for natural theology today? *The Real Issue* (www.origins.org/real/n9501/natural.html). (p. 71)

Gladue, B. A. (1990). Hormones and neuroendocrine factors in atypical human sexual behavior. In J. R. Feierman (Ed.), *Pedophilia: Biosocial dimensions.* New York: Springer-Verlag. (p. 181)

Gladwell, M. (2000, May 9). The new-boy network: What do job interviews really tell us? *New Yorker,* pp. 68–86. (p. B-6)

Gladwell, M. (2005). *Blink: The power of thinking without thinking.* New York: Little, Brown. (p. 491)

Glasman, L. R., & Albarracin, D. (2006). Forming attitudes that predict future behavior: A meta-analysis of the attitude-behavior relation. *Psychological Bulletin, 132,* 778–822. (p. 460)

Glass, R. I. (2004). Perceived threats and real killers. *Science, 304,* 927. (p. 311)

Glass, R. M. (2001). Electroconvulsive therapy: Time to bring it out of the shadows. *Journal of the American Medical Association, 285,* 1346–1348. (p. 571)

Gleaves, D. H. (1996). The sociocognitive model of dissociative identity disorder: A reexamination of the evidence. *Psychological Bulletin, 120,* 42–59. (p. 535)

Glick, P., Gottesman, D., & Jolton, J. (1989). The fault is not in the stars: Susceptibility of skeptics and believers in astrology to the Barnum effect. *Personality and Social Psychology Bulletin, 15,* 572–583. (p. 439)

Gluszek, A., & Dovidio, J. F. (2010). The way *they* speak: A social psychological perspective on the stigma of nonnative accents in communication. *Personality and Social Psychology Review, 14,* 214–237. (p. 478)

Godden, D. R., & Baddeley, A. D. (1975). Context-dependent memory in two natural environments: On land and underwater. *British Journal of Psychology, 66,* 325–331. (p. 287)

Goff, D. C., & Simms, C. A. (1993). Has multiple personality disorder remained consistent over time? *Journal of Nervous and Mental Disease, 181,* 595–600. (p. 534)

Golan, O., Ashwin, E., Granader, Y., McClintock, S., Day, K., Leggett, V., & Baron-Cohen, S. (2010). Enhancing emotion recognition in children with autism spectrum conditions: An intervention using animated vehicles with real emotional faces. *Journal of Autism Development and Disorders, 40,* 269–279. (p. 131)

Gold, M., & Yanof, D. S. (1985). Mothers, daughters, and girlfriends. *Journal of Personality and Social Psychology, 49,* 654–659. (p. 146)

Goldberg, J. (2007, accessed May 31). *Quivering bundles that let us hear.* Howard Hughes Medical Institute (www.hhmi.org/senses/c120.html). (p. 217)

Goldberg, W. A., Prause, J., Lucas-Thompson, R., & Himsel, A. (2008). Maternal employment and children's achievement in context: A meta-analysis of four decades of research. *Psychological Bulletin, 134,* 77–108. (p. 137)

Golden, R. N., Gaynes, B. N., Ekstrom, R. D., Hamer, R. M., Jacobsen, F. M., Suppes, T., Wisner, K. L., & Nemeroff, C. B. (2005). The efficacy of light therapy in the treatment of mood disorders: A review and meta-analysis of the evidence. *American Journal of Psychiatry, 162,* 656–662. (p. 564)

Golder, S. A., & Macy, M. W. (2011). Diurnal and seasonal mood vary with work, sleep, and day-length across diverse cultures. *Science, 333,* 1878–1881. (p. 414)

Goldfried, M. R. (2001). Integrating gay, lesbian, and bisexual issues into mainstream psychology. *American Psychologist, 56,* 977–988. (p. 524)

Goldfried, M. R., & Padawer, W. (1982). Current status and future directions in psychotherapy. In M. R. Goldfried (Ed.), *Converging themes in psychotherapy: Trends in psychodynamic, humanistic, and behavioral practice.* New York; Springer. (p. 565)

Goldfried, M. R., Raue, P. J., & Castonguay, L. G. (1998). The therapeutic focus in significant sessions of master therapists: A comparison of cognitive-behavioral and psychodynamic-interpersonal interventions. *Journal of Consulting and Clinical Psychology, 66,* 803–810. (p. 565)

Goldin-Meadow, S., & Beilock, S. L. (2010). Action's influence on thought: The case of gesture. *Perspectives on Psychological Science, 5,* 664–674. (p. 385)

Golding, J. M. (1996). Sexual assault history and women's reproductive and sexual health. *Psychology of Women Quarterly, 20,* 101–121. (p. 484)

Golding, J. M. (1999). Sexual-assault history and the long-term physical health problems: Evidence from clinical and population epidemiology. *Current Directions in Psychological Science, 8,* 191–194. (p. 515)

Goldman, A. L., Pezawas, L., Mattay, V. S., Fischl, B., Verchinski, B. A., Chen, Q., Weinberger, D. R., & Meyer-Lindenberg, A. (2009). Widespread reductions of cortical thickness in schizophrenia and spectrum disorders and evidence of heritability. *Archives of General Psychiatry, 66,* 467–477. (p. 531)

Goldstein, A. P., Glick, B., & Gibbs, J. C. (1998). *Aggression replacement training: A compre-hensive intervention for aggressive youth* (rev. ed.). Champaign, IL: Research Press. (p. 484)

Goldstein, I. (2000, August). Male sexual circuitry. *Scientific American,* pp. 70–75. (p. 45)

Goldstein, I., Lue, T. F., Padma-Nathan, H., Rosen, R. C., Steers, W. D., & Wicker, P. A. (1998). Oral sildenafil in the treatment of erectile dysfunction. *New England Journal of Medicine, 338,* 1397–1404. (p. 23)

Goleman, D. (1980, February). 1,528 little geniuses and how they grew. *Psychology Today,* pp. 28–53. (p. 370)

Goleman, D. (2006). *Social intelligence.* New York: Bantam Books. (p. 333)

Gonsalkorale, K., & Williams, K. D. (2006). The KKK would not let me play: Ostracism even by a despised outgroup hurts. *European Journal of Social Psychology, 36,* 1–11. (p. 366)

González-Vallejo, C., Lassiter, G. D., Bellezza, F. S., & Lindberg, M. J. (2008). "Save angels perhaps": A critical examination of unconscious thought theory and the deliberation-without-attention effect. *Review of General Psychology, 12,* 282–296. (p. 313)

Goodall, J. (1968). The behaviour of free-living chimpanzees in the Gombe Stream Reserve. *Animal Behaviour Monographs, 1,* 161–311. (p. 147)

Goodall, J. (1986). *The chimpanzees of Gombe: Patterns of behavior.* Cambridge, MA: Harvard University Press. (p. 479)

Goodall, J. (1998). Learning from the chimpanzees: A message humans can understand. *Science, 282,* 2184–2185. (p. 18)

Goode, E. (1999, April 13). If things taste bad, 'phantoms' may be at work. *New York Times* (www.nytimes.com). (p. 222)

Goodman, G. S. (2006). Children's eyewitness memory: A modern history and contemporary commentary. *Journal of Social Issues, 62,* 811–832. (p. 298)

Goodman, G. S., Ghetti, S., Quas, J. A., Edelstein, R. S., Alexander, K. W., Redlich, A. D., Cordon, I. M., & Jones, D. P. H. (2003). A prospective study of memory for child sexual abuse: New findings relevant to the repressed-memory controversy. *Psychological Science, 14,* 113–118. (p. 299)

Goodstein, L., & Glaberson, W. (2000, April 9). The well-marked roads to homicidal rage. *New York Times* (www.nytimes.com). (p. 445)

Goodwin, P. Y., Mosher, W. D., & Chandra, A. (2010). Marriage and cohabitation in the United States: A statistical portrait based on Cycle 6 (2002) of the National Survey of Family Growth. National Center for Health Statistics. *Vital Health Statistics, 23*(28). (p. 155)

Gopnik, A., & Meltzoff, A. N. (1986). Relations between semantic and cognitive development in the one-word stage: The specificity hypothesis. *Child Development, 57,* 1040–1053. (p. 327)

Goranson, R. E. (1978). *The hindsight effect in problem solving.* Unpublished manuscript, cited by G. Wood (1984), Research methodology: A decision-making perspective. In A. M. Rogers & C. J. Scheirer (Eds.), *The G. Stanley Hall Lecture Series* (Vol. 4). Washington, DC. (p. 12)

Gorchoff, S. M., John, O. P., & Helson, R. (2008). Contextualizing change in marital satisfaction during middle age. *Psychological Science, 19,* 1194–1200. (p. 156)

Gordon, P. (2004). Numerical cognition without words: Evidence from Amazonia. *Science, 306,* 496–499. (p. 326)

Gore-Felton, C., Koopman, C., Thoresen, C., Arnow, B., Bridges, E., & Spiegel, D. (2000). Psychologists' beliefs and clinical characteristics: Judging the veracity of childhood sexual abuse memories. *Professional Psychology: Research and Practice, 31,* 372–377. (p. 299)

Gosling, S. D. (2008). *Snoop: what your stuff says about you.* New York: Basic Books. (p. 442)

Gosling, S. D., Gladdis, S., & Vazire, S. (2007). Personality impressions based on Facebook profiles. Paper presented at the Society for Personality and Social Psychology meeting. (p. 442)

Gosling, S. D., Ko, S. J., Mannarelli, T., & Morris, M. E. (2002). A room with a cue: Personality judgments based on offices and bedrooms. *Journal of Personality and Social Psychology, 82,* 379–398. (p. 442)

Gosling, S. D., Kwan, V. S. Y., & John, O. P. (2003). A dog's got personality: A cross-species comparative approach to personality judgments in dogs and humans. *Journal of Personality and Social Psychology, 85,* 1161–1169. (p. 437)

Gotlib, I. H., & Hammen, C. L. (1992). *Psychological aspects of depression: Toward a cognitive-interpersonal integration.* New York: Wiley. (p. 527)

Gottesman, I. I. (1991). *Schizophrenia genesis: The origins of madness.* New York: Freeman. (p. 532)

Gottesman, I. I. (2001). Psychopathology through a life span—genetic prism. *American Psychologist, 56,* 867–881. (p. 532)

Gottfredson, L. S. (2002a). Where and why g matters: Not a mystery. *Human Performance, 15,* 25–46. (p. 332)

Gottfredson, L. S. (2002b). g: Highly general and highly practical. In R. J. Sternberg & E. L. Grigorenko (Eds.), *The general factor of intelligence: How general is it?* Mahwah, NJ: Erlbaum. (p. 332)

Gottfredson, L. S. (2003a). Dissecting practical intelligence theory: Its claims and evidence. *Intelligence, 31,* 343–397. (p. 332)

Gottfredson, L. S. (2003b). On Sternberg's "Reply to Gottfredson." *Intelligence, 31,* 415–424. (p. 332)

Gottfried, J. A., O'Doherty, J., & Dolan, R. J. (2003). Encoding predictive reward value in human amygdala and orbitofrontal cortex. *Science, 301,* 1104–1108. (p. 240)

Gottman, J. (2007). *Why marriages succeed or fail—2007 publication.* London: Bloomsbury. (p. 493)

Gottman, J., with Silver, N. (1994). *Why marriages succeed or fail.* New York: Simon & Schuster. (p. 155)

Gould, E. (2007). How widespread is adult neurogenesis in mammals? *Nature Neuroscience, 8,* 481–488. (p. 58)

Gould, S. J. (1981). *The mismeasure of man.* New York: Norton. (p. 334)

Gould, S. J. (1997, June 12). Darwinian fundamentalism. *The New York Review of Books, XLIV*(10), 34–37. (p. 185)

Grabe, S., Ward, L. M., & Hyde, J. S. (2008). The role of the media in body image concerns among women: A meta-analysis of experimental and correlational studies. *Psychological Bulletin, 134,* 460–476. (p. 537)

Grace, A. A. (2010). Ventral hippocampus, interneurons, and schizophrenia: A new understanding of the pathophysiology of schizophrenia and its implications for treatment and prevention. *Current Directions in Psychological Science, 19,* 232–237. (p. 530)

Grady, C. L., McIntosh, A. R., Horwitz, B., Maisog, J. M., Ungeleider, L. G., Mentis, M. J., Pietrini, P., Schapiro, M. B., & Haxby, J. V. (1995). Age-related reductions in human recognition memory due to impaired encoding. *Science, 269,* 218–221. (p. 291)

Graf, P. (1990). Life-span changes in implicit and explicit memory. *Bulletin of the Psychonomic Society, 28,* 353–358. (p. 153)

Graham, J. E., Christian, L. M., & Kiecolt-Glaser, J. K. (2006). Marriage, health, and immune function. In S. R. H. Beach & others (Eds.), *Relational processes and DSM-5: Neuroscience, assessment, prevention, and treatment.* Washington, DC: American Psychiatric Association. (p. 405)

Grant, N., Wardle, J., & Steptoe, A. (2009). The relationship between life satisfaction and health behavior: A cross-cultural analysis of young adults. *International Journal of Behavioral Medicine, 16,* 259–268. (p. 408)

Gray, P. B. (2010, July 7). ADHD and school: The problem of assessing normaly in an abnormal environment. *Psychology Today Blog* (www.psychologytoday.com). (p. 507)

Gray, P. B., & Anderson, K. G. (2010). *Fatherhood: Evolution and human paternal behavior.* Cambridge, MA: Harvard University Press. (p. 185)

Gray, P. B., Yang, C-F. J., & Pope, Jr., H. G. (2006). Fathers have lower salivary testosterone levels than unmarried men and married non-fathers in Beijing, China. *Proceedings of the Royal Society, 273,* 333–339. (p. 172)

Gray-Little, B., & Burks, N. (1983). Power and satisfaction in marriage: A review and critique. *Psychological Bulletin, 93,* 513–538. (p. 492)

Green, B. (2002). Listening to leaders: Feedback on 360-degree feedback one year later. *Organizational Development Journal, 20,* 8–16. (p. B-7)

Green, C. S., Pouget, A., & Bavelier, D. (2010). Improved probabilistic inference, as a general learning mechanism with action video games. *Current Biology, 20,* 1573–1579. (p. 486)

Green, J. D., Sedikides, C., & Gregg, A. P. (2008). Forgotten but not gone: The recall and recognition of self-threatening memories. *Journal of Experimental Social Psychology, 44,* 547–561. (p. 431)

Green, J. T., & Woodruff-Pak, D. S. (2000). Eyeblink classical conditioning: Hippocampal formation is for neutral stimulus associations as cerebellum is for association-response. *Psychological Bulletin, 126,* 138–158. (p. 282)

Green, M. F., & Horan, W. P. (2010). Social cognition in schizophrenia. *Current Directions in Psychological Science, 19,* 243–248. (p. 529)

Greenberg, J. (2008). Understanding the vital human quest for self-esteem. *Perspectives on Psychological Science, 3,* 48–55. (p. 447)

Greene, J. (2010). *Remarks to An Edge conference: The new science of morality.* www.edge.org. (p. 143)

Greene, J., Sommerville, R. B., Nystrom, L. E., Darley, J. M., & Cohen, J. D. (2001). An fMRI investigation of emotional engagement in moral judgment. *Science, 293,* 2105. (p. 143)

Greenwald, A. G. (1992). Subliminal semantic activation and subliminal snake oil. Paper presented to the American Psychological Association Convention, Washington, DC. (p. 195)

Greenwald, A. G., McGhee, D. E., & Schwartz, J. L. K. (1998). Measuring individual differences in implicit cognition: The implicit association test. *Journal of Personality and Social Psychology, 74,* 1464–1480. (p. 477)

Greenwald, A. G., Oakes, M. A., & Hoffman, H. (2003). Targets of discrimination: Effects of race on responses to weapons holders. *Journal of Experimental Social Psychology, 39,* 399. (p. 477)

Greenwald, A. G., Poehlman, T. A., Uhlmann, E. L., & Banaji, M. R. (2009). Understanding and using the implicit association test: III. Meta-analysis of the predictive validity. *Journal of Personality and Social Psychology, 97,* 17–41. (p. 477)

Greenwald, A. G., Spangenberg, E. R., Pratkanis, A. R., & Eskenazi, J. (1991). Double-blind tests of subliminal self-help audiotapes. *Psychological Science, 2,* 119–122. (p. 195)

Gregory, A. M., Rijksdijk, F. V., Lau, J. Y., Dahl, R. E., & Eley, T. C. (2009). The direction of longitudinal associations between sleep problems and depression symptoms: A study of twins aged 8 and 10 years. *Sleep, 32,* 189–199. (p. 90)

Gregory, R. L. (1978). *Eye and brain: The psychology of seeing* (3rd ed.). New York: McGraw-Hill. (p. 215)

Gregory, R. L., & Gombrich, E. H. (Eds.). (1973). *Illusion in nature and art.* New York: Charles Scribner's Sons. (p. 198)

Greif, E. B., & Ulman, K. J. (1982). The psychological impact of menarche on early adolescent females: A review of the literature. *Child Development, 53,* 1413–1430. (p. 168)

Greist, J. H., Jefferson, J. W., & Marks, I. M. (1986). *Anxiety and its treatment: Help is available.* Washington, DC: American Psychiatric Press. (p. 513)

Greitemeyer, T., & McLatchie, N. (2011). Denying humanness to others: A newly discovered mechanism by which violent video games increase aggressive behavior. *Psychological Science, 22,* 655–659. (p. 486)

Greitemeyer, T., & Osswald, S. (2010). Effects of prosocial video games on prosocial behavior. *Journal of Personality and Social Psychology, 98,* 211–221. (p. 485)

Greyson, B. (2010). Implications of near-death experiences for a postmaterialist psychology. *Review of Religion and Spirituality, 2,* 37–45. (p. 107)

Grèzes, J., & Decety, J. (2001). Function anatomy of execution, mental simulation, observation, and verb generation of actions: A meta-analysis. *Human Brain Mapping, 12,* 1–19. (p. 328)

Griffiths, M. (2001). Sex on the Internet: Observations and implications for Internet sex addiction. *Journal of Sex Research, 38,* 333–342. (p. 101)

Grilo, C. M., & Pogue-Geile, M. F. (1991). The nature of environmental influences on weight and obesity: A behavior genetic analysis. *Psychological Bulletin, 110,* 520–537. (p. 361)

Grinker, R. R. (2007). *Unstrange minds: Remapping the world of autism.* New York: Basic Books. (p. 130)

Grobstein, C. (1979, June). External human fertilization. *Scientific American,* pp. 57–67. (p. 119)

Grogan-Kaylor, A. (2004). The effect of corporal punishment on antisocial behavior in children. *Social Work Research, 28,* 153–162. (p. 252)

Groothuis, T. G. G., & Carere, C. (2005). Avian personalities: Characterization and epigenesis. *Neuroscience and Biobehavioral Reviews, 29,* 137–150. (p. 437)

Gross, A. E., & Crofton, C. (1977). What is good is beautiful. *Sociometry, 40,* 85–90. (p. 490)

Gross, T. F. (2009). Own-ethnicity bias in the recognition of Black, East Asian, Hispanic, and White faces. *Basic and Applied Social Psychology, 31,* 128–135. (p. 480)

Grossberg, S. (1995). The attentive brain. *American Scientist, 83,* 438–449. (p. 199)

Grossmann, I., Na, J., Varnum, M. E. W., Park, D. C., Kitayama, S., & Nisbett, R. E. (2010). Reasoning about social conflicts improves into old age. *PNAS, 107,* 7246–7250. (p. 338)

Gruder, C. L. (1977). Choice of comparison persons in evaluating oneself. In J. M. Suls & R. L. Miller (Eds.), *Social comparison processes.* New York: Hemisphere. (p. 417)

Guerin, B. (1986). Mere presence effects in humans: A review. *Journal of Personality and Social Psychology, 22,* 38–77. (p. 471)

Guerin, B. (2003). Language use as social strategy: A review and an analytic framework for the social sciences. *Review of General Psychology, 7,* 251–298. (p. 318)

Guiso, L., Monte, F., Sapienza, P., & Zingales, L. (2008). Culture, gender, and math. *Science, 320,* 1164–1165. (p. 343)

Gunstad, J., Strain, G., Devlin, M. J., Wing, R., Cohen, R. A., Paul, R. H., Crosby, R. D., & Mitchell, J. E. (2011). Improved memory function 12 weeks after bariatric surgery. *Surgery for Obesity and Related Diseases, 7,* 465–472. (p. 361)

Gunter, R. W., & Bodner, G. E. (2008). How eye movements affect unpleasant memories: Support for a working-memory account. *Behaviour Research and Therapy, 46,* 913–931. (p. 564)

Gunter, T. D., Vaughn, M. G., & Philibert, R. A. (2010). Behavioral genetics in antisocial spectrum disorders and psychopathy: A review of the recent literature. *Behavioral Sciences and the Law, 28,* 148–173. (p. 538)

Guo, X., & 19 others. (2010). Effect of antipsychotic medication alone vs combined with psychosocial intervention on outcomes of early-stage schizophrenia. *Archives of General Psychiatry, 67,* 895–904. (p. 569)

Gustavson, C. R., Garcia, J., Hankins, W. G., & Rusiniak, K. W. (1974). Coyote predation control by aversive conditioning. *Science, 184,* 581–583. (p. 257)

Gustavson, C. R., Kelly, D. J., & Sweeney, M. (1976). Prey-lithium aversions I: Coyotes and wolves. *Behavioral Biology, 17,* 61–72. (p. 257)

Guttmacher Institute. (1994). *Sex and America's teenagers.* New York: Alan Guttmacher Institute. (pp. 148, 174)

Guttmacher Institute. (2000). *Fulfilling the promise: Public policy and U.S. family planning clinics.* New York: Alan Guttmacher Institute. (p. 148)

H

H., Sally. (1979, August). Videotape recording number T–3, Fortunoff Video Archive of Holocaust Testimonies. New Haven, CT: Yale University Library. (p. 431)

Haas, A. P., & 25 others. (2011). Suicide and suicide risk in lesbian, gay, bisexual, and transgender populations: Review and recommendations. *Journal of Homosexuality, 58,* 10–51. (p. 524)

Haase, C. M., Tomasik, M. JH., & Silbereisen, R. K. (2008). Premature behavioral autonomy: Correlates in late adolescence and young adulthood. *European Psychologist, 13,* 255–266. (p. 138)

Haber, R. N. (1970, May). How we remember what we see. *Scientific American,* pp. 104–112. (p. 272)

Hagger, M. S., Wood, C., Stiff, C., & Chatzisarantis, N. L. D. (2010). Ego depletion and the strength model of self-control: A meta-analysis. *Psychological Bulletin, 136,* 495–525. (p. 403)

Haidt, J. (2000). The positive emotion of elevation. *Prevention and Treatment, 3,* article 3 (journals.apa.org/prevention/volume3). (p. 142)

Haidt, J. (2002). The moral emotions. In R. J. Davidson, K. Scherer, & H. H. Goldsmith (Eds.), *Handbook of affective sciences.* New York: Oxford University Press. (p. 142)

Haidt, J. (2006). *The happiness hypothesis: Finding modern truth in ancient wisdom.* New York: Basic Books. (p. 142)

Haidt, J. (2010). Moral psychology must not be based on faith and hope: Commentary on Narvaez. *Perspectives on Psychological Science, 5,* 182–184. (p. 142)

Hakuta, K., Bialystok, E., & Wiley, E. (2003). Critical evidence: A test of the critical-period hypothesis for second-language acquisition. *Psychological Science, 14,* 31–38. (p. 321)

Halberstadt, J., Sherman, S. J., & Sherman, J. W. (2011). Why Barack Obama is black. *Psychological Science, 22,* 29–33. (p. 480)

Haldeman, D. C. (1994). The practice and ethics of sexual orientation conversion therapy. *Journal of Consulting and Clinical Psychology, 62,* 221–227. (p. 179)

Haldeman, D. C. (2002). Gay rights, patient rights: The implications of sexual orientation conversion therapy. *Professional Psychology: Research and Practice, 33,* 260–264. (p. 179)

Hall, C. S., Dornhoff, W., Blick, K. A., & Weesner, K. E. (1982). The dreams of college men and women in 1950 and 1980: A comparison of dream contents and sex differences. *Sleep, 5,* 188–194. (p. 93)

Hall, C. S., & Lindzey, G. (1978). *Theories of personality* (2nd ed.). New York: Wiley. (p. 431)

Hall, G. (1997). Context aversion, Pavlovian conditioning, and the psychological side effects of chemotherapy. *European Psychologist, 2,* 118–124. (p. 258)

Hall, G. S. (1904). *Adolescence: Its psychology and its relations to physiology, anthropology, sex, crime, religion and education (Vol. I).* New York: Appleton-Century-Crofts. (p. 140)

Hall, J. A. (1984). *Nonverbal sex differences: Communication accuracy and expressive style.* Baltimore: Johns Hopkins University Press. (p. 381)

Hall, J. A. (1987). On explaining gender differences: The case of nonverbal communication. In P. Shaver & C. Hendrick (Eds.), *Review of Personality and Social Psychology, 7,* 177–200. (p. 381)

Hall, J. G. (2003). Twinning. *Lancet, 362,* 735–743. (p. 64)

Hall, S. S. (2004, May). The good egg. *Discover,* pp. 30–39. (p. 119)

Hall, W. (2006). The mental health risks of adolescent cannabis use. *PloS Medicine, 3*(2), e39. (p. 108)

Halpern, C. T., Joyner, K., Udry, J. R., & Suchindran, C. (2000). Smart teens don't have sex (or kiss much either). *Journal of Adolescent Health, 26*(3), 213–215. (p. 177)

Halpern, D. F. (2000). *Sex-related ability differences: Changing perspectives, changing minds.* Mahwah, NJ: Erlbaum. (p. 342)

Halpern, D. F., Benbow, C. P., Geary, D. C., Gur, R. C., Hyde, J. S., & Gernsbacher, M. A. (2007). The science of sex differences in science and mathematics. *Psychological Science in the Public Interest, 8,* 1–51. (p. 342)

Halsey, A., III. (2010, January 26). U.S. bans truckers, bus drivers from texting while driving. *Washington Post* (www.washingtonpost.com). (p. 81)

Hammer, E. (2003). How lucky you are to be a psychology major. *Eye on Psi Chi,* 4–5. (p. C-5)

Hammersmith, S. K. (1982, August). Sexual preference: An empirical study from the Alfred C. Kinsey Institute for Sex Research. Paper presented at the meeting of the American Psychological Association, Washington, DC. (p. 179)

Hammond, D. C. (2008). Hypnosis as sole anesthesia for major surgeries: Historical and contemporary perspectives. *American Journal of Clinical Hypnosis, 51,* 101–121. (p. 98)

Hampson, R. (2000, April 10). In the end, people just need more room. *USA Today,* p. 19A. (p. 362)

Hancock, K. J., & Rhodes, G. (2008). Contact, configural coding and the other-race effect in face recognition. *British Journal of Psychology, 99,* 45–56. (p. 480)

Hankin, B. L., & Abramson, L. Y. (2001). Development of gender differences in depression: An elaborated cognitive vulnerability-transactional stress theory. *Psychological Bulletin, 127,* 773–796. (p. 526)

Hansen, C. H., & Hansen, R. D. (1988). Finding the face-in-the-crowd: An anger superiority effect. *Journal of Personality and Social Psychology, 54,* 917–924. (p. 380)

Harbaugh, W. T., Mayr, U., & Burghart, D. R. (2007). Neural responses to taxation and voluntary giving reveal motives for charitable donations. *Science, 316,* 1622–1625. (p. 495)

Harber, K. D. (1998), Feedback to minorities: Evidence of a positive bias. *Journal of Personality and Social Psychology, 74,* 622–628. (p. 477)

Hardeveld, H. S., De Graaf, R., Nolen, W. A., & Beckman, A. T. F. (2010). Prevalence and predictors of recurrence of major depressive disorder in the adult population. *Acta Psychiatrica Scandinavia, 122,* 184–191. (p. 522)

Hardt, O., Einarsson, E. O., & Nader, K. (2010). A bridge over troubled water: Reconsolidation as a link between cognitive and neuroscientific memory research traditions. *Annual Review of Psychology, 61,* 141–167. (p. 294)

Hare, R. D. (1975). Psychophysiological studies of psychopathy. In D. C. Fowles (Ed.), *Clinical applications of psychophysiology.* New York: Columbia University Press. (p. 539)

Harenski, C. L., Harenski, K. A., Shane, M. W., & Kiehl, K. A. (2010). Aberrant neural processing of moral violations in criminal psychopaths. *Journal of Abnormal Psychology, 119,* 863–874. (p. 539)

Harkins, S. G., & Szymanski, K. (1989). Social loafing and group evaluation. *Journal of Personality and Social Psychology, 56,* 934–941. (p. 472)

Harlow, H. F., Harlow, M. K., & Suomi, S. J. (1971). From thought to therapy: Lessons from a primate laboratory. *American Scientist, 59,* 538–549. (p. 132)

Harmon-Jones, E., Abramson, L. Y., Sigelman, J., Bohlig, A., Hogan, M. E., & Harmon-Jones, C. (2002). Proneness to hypomania/mania symptoms or depression symptoms and asymmetrical frontal cortical responses to an anger-evoking event. *Journal of Personality and Social Psychology, 82,* 610–618. (p. 378)

Harper, C., & McLanahan, S. (2004). Father absence and youth incarceration. *Journal of Research on Adolescence, 14,* 369–397. (p. 484)

Harper's Index. (2010, September). India mobile phones, p. 11. (p. 367)

Harris, B. (1979). Whatever happened to Little Albert? *American Psychologist, 34,* 151–160. (p. 245)

Harris Interactive. (2010). 2009 eHarmony® marriage metrics study: Methodological notes. www.eharmony.com/harrisinteractivepoll. (p. 488)

Harris, J. A. (1999). Review and methodological considerations in research on testosterone and aggression. *Aggression and Violent Behavior, 4,* 273–291. (p. 482)

Harris, J. R. (1998). *The nurture assumption.* New York: Free Press. (pp. 135, 146)

Harris, J. R. (2000). Beyond the nurture assumption: Testing hypotheses about the child's environment. In J. G. Borkowski & S. L. Ramey (Eds.), *Parenting and the child's world: Influences on academic, intellectual, and social-emotional development.* Washington, DC: APA Books. (p. 146)

Harris, J. R. (2006). *No two are alike: Human nature and human individuality.* New York: Norton. (p. 65)

Harris, J. R. (2007, August 8). Do pals matter more than parents? *The Times* (www.timesonline.co.uk). (p. 146)

Harris, R. J. (1994). The impact of sexually explicit media. In J. Brant & D. Zillmann (Eds.), *Media effects: Advances in theory and research.* Hillsdale, NJ: Erlbaum. (p. 485)

Harriston, K. A. (1993, December 24). 1 shakes, 1 snoozes: Both win $45 million. *Washington Post* release (in *Tacoma News Tribune,* pp. A1, A2). (p. 445)

Harter, J. K., Schmidt, F. L., Asplund, J. W., Killham, E. A., & Agrawal, S. (2010). Causal impact of employee work perceptions on the bottom line of organizations. *Perspectives on Psychological Science, 5,* 378–389. (p. B-9)

Harter, J. K., Schmidt, F. L., & Hayes, T. L. (2002). Business-unit-level relationship between employee satisfaction, employee engagement, and business outcomes: A meta-analysis. *Journal of Applied Psychology, 87,* 268–279. (p. B-8)

Hartmann, E. (1981, April). The strangest sleep disorder. *Psychology Today,* pp. 14, 16, 18. (p. 93)

Hartwig, M., & Bond, C. F., Jr. (2011). Why do lie-catchers fail? A lens model meta-analysis of human lie judgments. *Psychological Bulletin, 137,* 643–659. (p. 380)

Harvard Mental Health Letter. (2002, February). EMDR (Eye movement and reprocessing). *Harvard Mental Health Letter, 18,* 4–5. (p. 564)

Haslam, S. A., & Reicher, S. (2007). Beyond the banality of evil: Three dynamics of an interactionist social psychology of tyranny. *Personality and Social Psychology Bulletin, 33,* 615–622. (p. 462)

Hassan, B., & Rahman, Q. (2007). Selective sexual orientation-related differences in object location memory. *Behavioral Neuroscience, 121,* 625–633. (p. 183)

Hatfield, E. (1988). Passionate and companionate love. In R. J. Sternberg & M. L. Barnes (Eds.), *The psychology of love.* New Haven, CT: Yale University Press. (pp. 491, 492)

Hatfield, E., & Sprecher, S. (1986). *Mirror, mirror . . . The importance of looks in everyday life.* Albany: State University of New York Press. (p. 489)

Hathaway, S. R. (1960). *An MMPI Handbook* (Vol. 1, Foreword). Minneapolis: University of Minnesota Press rev. ed. (p. 1972). (p. 437)

Hatzenbuehler, M. L. (2011). The social environment and suicide attempts in lesbian, gay, and bisexual youth. *Pediatrics, 127,* 896–903. (p. 524)

Havas, D. A., Glenberg, A. M., Gutowski, K. A., Lucarelli, M. J., & Davidson, R. J. (2010). Cosmetic use of Botulinum Toxin-A affects processing of emotional language. *Psychological Science, 21,* 895–900. (p. 385)

Havas, D. A., Glenberg, A. M., & Rink, M. (2007). Emotion simulation during language comprehension. *Psychonomic Bulletin & Review, 14,* 436–441. (p. 385)

Haworth, C. M. A., & 17 others. (2009). A twin study of the genetics of high cognitive ability selected from 11,000 twin pairs in sex studies from four countries. *Behavior Genetics, 39,* 359–370. (p. 339)

Haworth, C. M. A., & 23 others. (2010). The heritability of general cognitive ability increases linearly from childhood to young adulthood. *Molecular Psychiatry, 15,* 1112–1120. (p. 340)

Haxby, J. V. (2001, July 7). Quoted by B. Bower, Faces of perception. *Science News,* pp. 10–12. See also J. V. Haxby, M. I. Gobbini, M. L. Furey, A. Ishai, J. L. Schouten & P. Pietrini, Distributed and overlapping representations of faces and objects in ventral temporal cortex. *Science, 293,* 2425–2430. (p. 204)

Haynes, J-D., & Rees, G. (2005). Predicting the orientation of invisible stimuli from activity in human primary visual cortex. *Nature Neuroscience, 8,* 686–691. (p. 194)

Haynes, J-D., & Rees, G. (2006). Decoding mental states from brain activity in humans. *Nature Reviews Neuroscience, 7,* 523–534. (p. 194)

Hazan, C., & Shaver, P. R. (1994). Attachment as an organizational framework for research on close relationships. *Psychological Inquiry, 5,* 1–22. (p. 137)

Hazelrigg, M. D., Cooper, H. M., & Borduin, C. M. (1987). Evaluating the effectiveness of family therapies: An integrative review and analysis. *Psychological Bulletin, 101,* 428–442. (p. 558)

He, Y., Jones, C. R., Fujiki, N., Xu, Y., Guo, B., Holder, J. L., Jr., Rossner, M. J., Nishino, S., & Fu, Y-H. (2009). The transcriptional repressor DEC2 regulates sleep length in mammals. *Science, 325,* 866–870. (p. 87)

Headey, B., Muffels, R., & Wagner, G. G. (2010). Long-running German panel survey shows that personal and economic choices, not just genes, matter for happiness. *PNAS, 107,* 17922–17926. (p. 417)

Health Canada. (2012). Major findings from the Canadian Alcohol and Drug Use Monitoring Survey (CADUMS) 2011. Health Canada (www.hc-sc.gc.ca/hc-ps/drugs-drogues/stat/index-eng.php). (p. 109)

Heavey, C. L., & Hurlburt, R. T. (2008). The phenomena of inner experience. *Consciousness and Cognition, 17,* 798–810. (p. 326)

Hedström, P., Liu, K-Y., & Nordvik, M. K. (2008). Interaction domains and suicides: A population-based panel study of suicides in the Stockholm metropolitan area, 1991–1999. *Social Forces, 2,* 713–740. (p. 524)

Heider, F. (1958). *The psychology of interpersonal relations.* New York: Wiley. (p. 458)

Heiman, J. R. (1975, April). The physiology of erotica: Women's sexual arousal. *Psychology Today,* pp. 90–94. (p. 175)

Heine, S. J., & Buchtel, E. E. (2009). Personality: The universal and the culturally specific. *Annual Review of Psychology, 60,* 369–394. (p. 440)

Heine, S. J., & Hamamura, T. (2007). In search of East Asian self-enhancement. *Personality and Social Psychology Review, 11,* 4–27. (p. 449)

Heine, S. J., & Ruby, M. B. (2010). Cultural psychology. *Wiley Interdisciplinary Reviews: Cognitive Science, 1,* 254–266. (p. 458)

Hejmadi, A., Davidson, R. J., & Rozin, P. (2000). Exploring Hindu Indian emotion expressions: Evidence for accurate recognition by Americans and Indians. *Psychological Science, 11,* 183–187. (p. 380)

Helfand, D. (2011, January 7). An assault on rationality. *New York Times* (www.nytimes.com). (p. 232)

Heller, A. S., Johnstone, T., Schackman, A. J., Light, S. N., Peterson, M. J., Kolden, G. G., Kalin, N. H., & Davidson, R. J. (2009). Reduced capacity to sustain positive emotion in major depression reflects diminished maintenance of fronto-striatal brain activation. *PNAS, 106,* 22445–22450. (p. 523)

Heller, W. (1990, May/June). Of one mind: Second thoughts about the brain's dual nature. *The Sciences*, pp. 38–44. (p. 61)

Helmreich, W. B. (1992). *Against all odds: Holocaust survivors and the successful lives they made in America.* New York: Simon & Schuster. (pp. 136, 431)

Helmreich, W. B. (1994). Personal correspondence. Department of Sociology, City University of New York. (p. 431)

Helms, J. E., Jernigan, M., & Mascher, J. (2005). The meaning of race in psychology and how to change it: A methodological perspective. *American Psychologist, 60,* 27–36. (p. 344)

Helmuth, L. (2001). Boosting brain activity from the outside in. *Science, 292,* 1284–1286. (p. 573)

Helton, W. S. (2008). Expertise acquisition as sustained learning in humans and other animals: Commonalities across species. *Animal Cognition, 11,* 99–107. (p. 332)

Hembree, R. (1988). Correlates, causes, effects, and treatment of test anxiety. *Review of Educational Research, 58,* 47–77. (p. 354)

Hemenover, S. H. (2003). The good, the bad, and the healthy: Impacts of emotional disclosure of trauma on resilient self-concept and psychological distress. *Personality and Social Psychology Bulletin, 29,* 1236–1244. (p. 407)

Henderlong, J., & Lepper, M. R. (2002). The effects of praise on children's intrinsic motivation: A review and synthesis. *Psychological Bulletin, 128,* 774–795. (p. 260)

Henderson, J. M. (2007). Regarding scenes. *Current Directions in Psychological Science, 16,* 219–222. (p. 196)

Henig, R. M. (2010, August 18). What is it about 20-somethings? *New York Times* (www.nytimes.com). (p. 148)

Henkel, L. A., Franklin, N., & Johnson, M. K. (2000, March). Cross-modal source monitoring confusions between perceived and imagined events. *Journal of Experimental Psychology: Learning, Memory, & Cognition, 26,* 321–335. (p. 296)

Henley, N. M. (1989). Molehill or mountain? What we know and don't know about sex bias in language. In M. Crawford & M. Gentry (Eds.), *Gender and thought: Psychological perspectives.* New York: Springer-Verlag. (p. 327)

Hennenlotter, A., Dresel, C., Castrop, F., Ceballos Baumann, A., Wohschlager, A., & Haslinger, B. (2008). The link between facial feedback and neural activity within central circuitries of emotion: New insights from Botulinum Toxin-induced denervation of frown muscles. *Cerebral Cortex, 19,* 537–542. (p. 385)

Hennessey, B. A., & Amabile, T. M. (2010). Creativity. *Annual Review of Psychology, 61,* 569–598. (pp. 314, B-12)

Henninger, P. (1992). Conditional handedness: Handedness changes in multiple personality disordered subject reflect shift in hemispheric dominance. *Consciousness and Cognition, 1,* 265–287. (p. 535)

Henrich, J., Heine, S. J., & Norenzayan, A. (2010). The weirdest people in the world? *Behavioral and Brain Sciences, 33,* 61–135. (p. 26)

Hepper, P. (2005). Unravelling our beginnings. *The Psychologist, 18,* 474–477. (p. 119)

Herbenick, D., Reece, M., Schick, V., Sanders, S. A., Dodge, B., & Fortenberry, J. D. (2010a). Sexual behavior in the United States: Results from a national probability sample of men and women ages 14–94. *Journal of Sexual Medicine,* 7(suppl. 5): 255–265. (p. 178)

Herbert, J. D., Lilienfeld, S. O., Lohr, J. M., Montgomery, R. W., O'Donohue, W. T., Rosen, G. M., & Tolin, D. F. (2000). Science and pseudoscience in the development of eye movement desensitization and reprocessing: Implications for clinical psychology. *Clinical Psychology Review, 20,* 945–971. (p. 563)

Herman, C. P., & Polivy, J. (1980). Restrained eating. In A. J. Stunkard (Ed.), *Obesity.* Philadelphia: Saunders. (p. 363)

Herman, C. P., Roth, D. A., & Polivy, J. (2003). Effects of the presence of others on food intake: A normative interpretation. *Psychological Bulletin, 129,* 873–886. (p. 360)

Herman-Giddens, M. E., Wang, L., & Koch, G. (2001). Secondary sexual characteristics in boys: Estimates from the National Health and Nutrition Examination Survey III, 1988–1994. *Archives of Pediatrics and Adolescent Medicine, 155,* 1022–1028. (p. 168)

Hernandez, A. E., & Li, P. (2007). Age of acquisition: Its neural and computational mechanisms. *Psychological Bulletin, 133,* 638–650. (p. 321)

Herrmann, E., Call, J., Hernández-Lloreda, M. V., Hare, B., & Tomasello, M. (2007). Humans have evolved specialized skills of social cognition: The cultural intelligence hypothesis. *Science, 317,* 1360–1365. (p. 262)

Herrmann, E., Hernández-Lloreda, V., Call, J., Hare, B., & Tomasello, M. (2010). The structure of individual differences in the cognitive abilities of children and chimpanzees. *Psychological Science, 21,* 102–110. (p. 325)

Herrnstein, R. J., & Loveland, D. H. (1964). Complex visual concept in the pigeon. *Science, 146,* 549–551. (p. 247)

Hershenson, M. (1989). *The moon illusion.* Hillsdale, NJ: Erlbaum. (p. 213)

Hertenstein, M. J., Hansel, C., Butts, S., Hile, S. (2009). Smile intensity in photographs predicts divorce later in life. *Motivation & Emotion, 33,* 99–105. (pp. 158, 159)

Hertenstein, M. J., Keltner, D., App, B. Bulleit, B., & Jaskolka, A. (2006). Touch communicates distinct emotions. *Emotion, 6,* 528–533. (pp. 133, 220)

Herz, R. S. (2001). Ah sweet skunk! Why we like or dislike what we smell. *Cerebrum, 3*(4), 31–47. (p. 226)

Herz, R. S., Beland, S. L., & Hellerstein, M. (2004). Changing odor hedonic perception through emotional associations in humans. *International Journal of Comparative Psychology, 17,* 315–339. (p. 226)

Herzog, H. (2010). *Some we love, some we hate, some we eat: Why it's so hard to think straight about animals.* New York: Harper. (p. 406)

Hess, E. H. (1956, July). Space perception in the chick. *Scientific American,* pp. 71–80. (p. 215)

Hess, U., & Thibault, P. (2009). Darwin and emotion expression. *American Psychologist, 64,* 120–128. (p. 383)

Hetherington, M. M., Anderson, A. S., Norton, G. N. M., & Newson, L. (2006). Situational effects on meal intake: A comparison of eating alone and eating with others. *Physiology and Behavior, 88,* 498–505. (p. 360)

Hettema, J. M., Neale, M. C., & Kendler, K. S. (2001). A review and meta-analysis of the genetic epidemiology of anxiety disorders. *American Journal of Psychiatry, 158,* 1568–1578. (p. 517)

Hickok, G., Bellugi, U., & Klima, E. S. (2001, June). Sign language in the brain. *Scientific American,* pp. 58–65. (p. 61)

Hilgard, E. R. (1986). *Divided consciousness: Multiple controls in human thought and action.* New York: Wiley. (p. 99)

Hilgard, E. R. (1992). Dissociation and theories of hypnosis. In E. Fromm & M. R. Nash (Eds.), *Contemporary hypnosis research.* New York: Guilford. (p. 99)

Hill, C. E., & Nakayama, E. Y. (2000). Client-centered therapy: Where has it been and where is it going? A comment on Hathaway. *Journal of Clinical Psychology, 56,* 961–875. (p. 549)

Hines, M. (2004). *Brain gender.* New York: Oxford University Press. (p. 167)

Hingson, R. W., Heeren, T., & Winter, M. R. (2006). Age at drinking onset and alcohol dependence. *Archives of Pediatrics & Adolescent Medicine, 160,* 739–746. (p. 111)

Hintzman, D. L. (1978). *The psychology of learning and memory.* San Francisco: Freeman. (p. 277)

Hinz, L. D., & Williamson, D. A. (1987). Bulimia and depression: A review of the affective variant hypothesis. *Psychological Bulletin, 102,* 150–158. (p. 536)

Hjelmborg, J. v. B., Fagnani, C., Silventoinen, K., McGue, M., Korkeila, M., Christensen, K., Rissanen, A., & Kaprio, J. (2008). Genetic influences on growth traits of BMI: A longitudinal study of adult twins. *Obesity, 16,* 847–852. (p. 362)

HMHL. (2002a, January). Disaster and trauma. *Harvard Mental Health Letter,* pp. 1–5. (p. 391)

HMHL. (2002b, August). Smoking and depression. *Harvard Mental Health Letter,* pp. 6–7. (p. 524)

HMHL. (2007, February). Electroconvulsive therapy. *Harvard Mental Health Letter,* Harvard Medical School, pp. 1–4. (p. 571)

Hobaiter, C., & Byrne, R. W. (2011). The gestural repertoire of the wild chimpanzee. *Animal Cognition,* DOI: 10.1007/s10071-011-0409-2. (p. 324)

Hobson, J. A. (1995, September). Quoted by C. H. Colt, The power of dreams. *Life,* pp. 36–49. (p. 95)

Hobson, J. A. (2003). *Dreaming: An introduction to the science of sleep.* New York: Oxford. (p. 95)

Hobson, J. A. (2004). *13 dreams Freud never had: The new mind science.* New York: Pi Press. (p. 95)

Hobson, J. A. (2009). REM sleep and dreaming: Towards a theory of protoconsciousness. *Nature Reviews, 10,* 803–814. (p. 95)

Hochberg, L. R., Serruya, M. D., Friehs, G. M., Mukand, J. A., Saleh, M., Caplan, A. H., Branner, A., Chen, D., Penn, R. D., & Donoghue, J. P. (2006). Neuronal ensemble control of prosthetic devices by a human with tetraplegia. *Nature, 442,* 164–171. (p. 54)

Hodgkinson, V. A., & Weitzman, M. S. (1992). *Giving and volunteering in the United States.* Washington, DC: Independent Sector. (p. 496)

Hoebel, B. G., & Teitelbaum, P. (1966). Effects of forcefeeding and starvation on food intake and body weight in a rat with ventromedial hypothalamic lesions. *Journal of Comparative and Physiological Psychology, 61,* 189–193. (p. 357)

Hoeft, F., Watson, C. L., Kesler, S. R., Bettinger, K. E., & Reiss, A. L. (2008). Gender differences in the mesocorticolimbic system during computer game-play. *Journal of Psychiatric Research, 42,* 253–258. (p. 101)

Hoffman, C., & Hurst, N. (1990). Gender stereotypes: Perception or rationalization? *Journal of Personality and Social Psychology, 58,* 197–208. (p. 478)

Hoffman, D. D. (1998). *Visual intelligence: How we create what we see.* New York: Norton. (p. 205)

Hoffman, H. G. (2004, August). Virtual-reality therapy. *Scientific American,* pp. 58–65. (pp. 223, 552)

Hofmann, S. G., Sawyer, A. T., Witt, A. A., & Oh, D. (2010). The effect of mindfulness-based therapy on anxiety and depression: A meta-analytic review. *Journal of Consulting and Clinical Psychology, 78,* 169–183. (p. 410)

Hogan, R. (1998). Reinventing personality. *Journal of Social and Clinical Psychology, 17,* 1–10. (p. 442)

Hoge, C. W., & Castro, C. A. (2006). Post-traumatic stress disorder in UK and U.S. forces deployed to Iraq. *Lancet, 368,* 837. (p. 515)

Hoge, C. W., Castro, C. A., Messer, S. C., McGurk, D., Cotting, D. I., & Koffman, R. L. (2004). Combat duty in Iraq and Afghanistan, mental health problems, and barriers to care. *New England Journal of Medicine, 351,* 13–22. (p. 515)

Hoge, C. W., Terhakopian, A., Castro, C. A., Messer, S. C., & Engel, C. C. (2007). Association of posttraumatic stress disorder with somatic symptoms, health care visits, and absenteeism among Iraq War veterans. *American Journal of Psychiatry, 164,* 150–153. (p. 515)

Hogg, M. A. (1996). Intragroup processes, group structure and social identity. In W. P. Robinson (Ed.), *Social groups and identities: Developing the legacy of Henri Tajfel.* Oxford: Butterworth Heinemann. (p. 478)

Hogg, M. A. (2006). Social identity theory. In P. J. Burke (Ed.), *Contemporary social psychological theories.* Stanford, CA: Stanford University Press. (p. 478)

Hohmann, G. W. (1966). Some effects of spinal cord lesions on experienced emotional feelings. *Psychophysiology, 3,* 143–156. (p. 372)

Hokanson, J. E., & Edelman, R. (1966). Effects of three social responses on vascular processes. *Journal of Personality and Social Psychology, 3,* 442–447. (p. 398)

Holahan, C. K., & Sears, R. R. (1995). *The gifted group in later maturity.* Stanford, CA: Stanford University Press. (p. 339)

Holden, C. (1980a). Identical twins reared apart. *Science, 207,* 1323–1325. (p. 65)

Holden, C. (1980b, November). Twins reunited. *Science, 80,* 55–59. (p. 65)

Holden, C. (2010a). Behavioral addictions debut in proposed DSM-5. *Science, 327,* 935. (p. 538)

Holden, C. (2010b). Experts map the terrain of mood disorders. *Science, 327,* p. 1068. (p. 520)

Holliday, R. E., & Albon, A. J. (2004). Minimizing misinformation effects in young children with cognitive interview mnemonics. *Applied Cognitive Psychology, 18,* 263–281. (p. 298)

Hollingworth, S. A., Burgess, P. M., & Whiteford, H. A. (2010). Affective and anxiety disorders: Prevalence, treatment and antidepressant medication use. *Australian and New Zealand Journal of Psychiatry, 44,* 513–519. (p. 570)

Hollis, K. L. (1997). Contemporary research on Pavlovian conditioning: A "new" functional analysis. *American Psychologist, 52,* 956–965. (p. 242)

Hollon, S. D., Thase, M. E., & Markowitz, J. C. (2002). Treatment and prevention of depression. *Psychological Science in the Public Interest, 3,* 39–77. (p. 570)

Holstege, G., Georgiadis, J. R., Paans, A. M. J., Meiners, L. C., van der Graaf, F. H. C. E., & Reinders, A. A. T. S. (2003a). Brain activation during male ejaculation. *Journal of Neuroscience, 23,* 9185–9193. (p. 173)

Holstege, G., Reinders, A. A. T., Paans, A. M. J., Meiners, L. C., Pruim, J., & Georgiadis, J. R. (2003b). *Brain activation during female sexual orgasm.* Program No. 727.7. Washington, DC: Society for Neuroscience. (p. 173)

Holt, L. (2002, August). Reported in "Sounds of speech," p. 26, and in personal correspondence, July 18, 2002. (p. 319)

Holtgraves, T. (2011). Text messaging, personality, and the social context. *Journal of Research in Personality, 45,* 92–99. (p. 440)

Holt-Lunstad, J., Smith, T. B., & Layton, J. B. (2010). Social relationships and mortality risk: A meta-analytic review. *PLoS Medicine, 7* (www.plosmedicine.org: e1000316). (p. 405)

Homer, B. D., Solomon, T. M., Moeller, R. W., Mascia, A., DeRaleau, L., & Halkitis, P. N. (2008). Methamphetamine abuse and impairment of social functioning: A review of the underlying neurophysiological causes and behavioral implications. *Psychological Bulletin, 134,* 301–310. (p. 106)

Hooley, J. M. (2010). Social factors in schizophrenia. *Current Directions in Psychological Science, 19,* 238–242. (p. 528)

Hooper, J., & Teresi, D. (1986). *The three-pound universe.* New York: Macmillan. (p. 52)

Hopkins, E. D., & Cantalupo, C. (2008). Theoretical speculations on the evolutionary origins of hemispheric specialization. *Current Directions in Psychological Science, 17,* 233–237. (p. 61)

Hopwood, C. J., Donnellan, M. B., Blonigen, D. M., Krueger, R. F., McGue, M., Iacono, W. G., & Burt, S. A. (2011). Genetic and environmental influences on personality trait stability and growth during the transition to adulthood: A three-wave longitudinal study. *Journal of Personality and Social Psychology, 100,* 545–556. (p. 158)

Hor, H., & Tafti, M. (2009). How much sleep do we need? *Science, 325,* 825–826. (p. 87)

Horn, J. L. (1982). The aging of human abilities. In J. Wolman (Ed.), *Handbook of developmental psychology.* Englewood Cliffs, NJ: Prentice-Hall. (p. 337)

Horwood, L. J., & Fergusson, D. M. (1998). Breastfeeding and later cognitive and academic outcomes. *Pediatrics, 101*(1). (p. 21)

Hostetter, A. B. (2011). When do gestures communicate? A meta-analysis. *Psychological Bulletin, 137,* 297–315. (p. 324)

Hou, W-H., Chiang, P-T, Hsu, T-Y, Chiu, S-Y, & Yen, Y-C. (2010). Treatment effects of massage therapy in depressed people: A meta-analysis. *Journal of Clinical Psychiatry, 71,* 894–901. (p. 410)

House, R. J., & Singh, J. V. (1987). Organizational behavior: Some new directions for I/O psychology. *Annual Review of Psychology, 38,* 669–718. (p. B-12)

Houser-Marko, L., & Sheldon, K. M. (2008). Eyes on the prize or nose to the grindstone? The effects of level of goal evaluation on mood and motivation. *Personality and Social Psychology Bulletin, 34,* 1556–1569. (p. B-11)

Houts, A. C., Berman, J. S., & Abramson, H. (1994). Effectiveness of psychological and pharmacological treatments for nocturnal enuresis. *Journal of Consulting and Clinical Psychology, 62,* 737–745. (p. 551)

Hovatta, I., Tennant, R. S., Helton, R., Marr, R. A., Singer, O., Redwine, J. M., Ellison, J. A., Schadt, E. E., Verma, I. M., Lockhart, D. J., & Barlow, C. (2005). Glyoxalase 1 and glutathione reductase 1 regulate anxiety in mice. *Nature, 438,* 662–666. (p. 517)

Howe, M. L. (1997). Children's memory for traumatic experiences. *Learning and Individual Differences, 9*, 153–174. (p. 298)

Howell, A. J. (2009). Flourishing: Achievement-related correlates of students' well-being. *Journal of Positive Psychology, 4*, 1–13. (p. 346)

Howell, R. T., & Howell, C. J. (2008). The relation of economic status to subjective well-being in developing countries: A meta-analysis. *Psychological Bulletin, 134*, 536–560. (p. 415)

Hoyer, G., & Lund, E. (1993). Suicide among women related to number of children in marriage. *Archives of General Psychiatry, 50*, 134–137. (p. 524)

Hsee, C. K., Yang, A. X., & Wang, L. (2010). Idleness aversion and the need for justifiable busyness. *Psychological Science, 21*, 926–930. (p. B-2)

Hu, X-Z., Lipsky, R. H., Zhu, G., Akhtar, L. A., Taubman, J., Greenberg, B. D., Xu, K., Arnold, P. D., Richter, M. A., Kennedy, J. L., Murphy, D. L., & Goldman, D. (2006). Serotonin transporter promoter gain-of-function genotypes are linked to obsessive-compulsive disorder. *American Journal of Human Genetics, 78*, 815–826. (p. 517)

Huang, C. (2010). Mean-level change in self-esteem from childhood through adulthood meta-analysis of longitudinal studies. *Review of General Psychology, 14*, 251–260. (p. 156)

Huang, X., Iun, J., Liu, A., & Gong, Y. (2010). Does participative leadership enhance work performance by inducing empowerment or trust? The differential effects on managerial and non-managerial subordinates. *Journal of Organizational Behavior, 31*, 122–143. (p. B-12)

Huart, J., Corneille, O., & Becquart, E. (2005). Face-based categorization, context-based categorization, and distortions in the recollection of gender ambiguous faces. *Journal of Experimental Social Psychology, 41*, 598–608. (p. 306)

Hubbard, E. M., Arman, A. C., Ramachandran, V. S., & Boynton, G. M. (2005). Individual differences among grapheme-color synesthetes: Brain-behavior correlations. *Neuron, 45*, 975–985. (p. 229)

Hubel, D. H. (1979, September). The brain. *Scientific American*, pp. 45–53. (p. 196)

Hubel, D. H., & Wiesel, T. N. (1979, September). Brian mechanisms of vision. *Scientific American*, pp. 150–162. (p. 204)

Hublin, C., Kaprio, J., Partinen, M., Heikkila, K., & Koskenvuo, M. (1997). Prevalence and genetics of sleepwalking—A population-based twin study. *Neurology, 48*, 177–181. (p. 93)

Hublin, C., Kaprio, J., Partinen, M., & Koskenvuo, M. (1998). Sleeptalking in twins: Epidemiology and psychiatric comorbidity. *Behavior Genetics, 28*, 289–298. (p. 93)

Hucker, S. J., & Bain, J. (1990). Androgenic hormones and sexual assault. In W. Marshall, R. Law, & H. Barbaree (Eds.), *The handbook on sexual assault*. New York: Plenum. (p. 172)

Hudson, J. I., Hiripi, E., Pope, H. G., & Kessler, R. C. (2007). The prevalence and correlates of eating disorders in the National Comorbidity Survey Replication. *Biological Psychiatry, 61*, 348–358. (p. 536)

Huey, E. D., Krueger, F., & Grafman, J. (2006). Representations in the human prefrontal cortex. *Current Directions in Psychological Science, 15*, 167–171. (p. 56)

Huffcutt, A. I., Conway, J. M., Roth, P. L., & Stone, N. J. (2001). Identification and meta-analytic assessment of psychological constructs measured in employment interviews. *Journal of Applied Psychology, 86*, 897–913. (p. B-6)

Hugenberg, K., & Bodenhausen, G. V. (2003). Facing prejudice: Implicit prejudice and the perception of facial threat. *Psychological Science, 14*, 640–643. (p. 477)

Hugenberg, K., Young, S. G., Bernstein, M. J., & Sacco, D. F. (2010). The categorization-individuation model: An integrative account of the other-race recognition deficit. *Psychological Review, 117*, 1168–1187. (p. 480)

Hughes, J. R. (2010). Craving among long-abstinent smokers: An Internet survey. *Nicotine & Tobacco Research, 12*, 459–462. (p. 105)

Hugick, L. (1989, July). Women play the leading role in keeping modern families close. *Gallup Report, No. 286*, p. 27–34. (p. 166)

Huizink, A. C., & Mulder, E. J. (2006). Maternal smoking, drinking or cannabis use during pregnancy and neurobehavioral and cognitive functioning in human offspring. *Neuroscience and Biobehavioral Reviews, 30*, 24–41. (p. 108)

Hulbert, A. (2005, November 20). The prodigy puzzle. *New York Times Magazine* (www.nytimes.com). (p. 339)

Hull, H. R., Morrow, M. L., Dinger, M. K., Han, J. L., & Fields, D. A. (2007, November 20). Characterization of body weight and composition changes during the sophomore year of college. *BMC Women's Health, 7*, 21 (biomed-central.com). (p. 90)

Hull, J. G., & Bond, C. F., Jr. (1986). Social and behavioral consequences of alcohol consumption and expectancy: A meta-analysis. *Psychological Bulletin, 99*, 347–360. (p. 103)

Hull, J. M. (1990). *Touching the rock: An experience of blindness*. New York: Vintage Books. (pp. 287, 489)

Hülsheger, U. R., Anderson, N., & Salgado, J. F. (2009). Team-level predictors of innovation at work: A comprehensive meta-analysis spanning three decades of research. *Journal of Applied Psychology, 94*, 1128–1145. (p. 315)

Hummer, R. A., Rogers, R. G., Nam, C. B., & Ellison, C. G. (1999). Religious involvement and U.S. adult mortality. *Demography, 36*, 273–285. (p. 411)

Humphrey, S. E., Nahrgang, J. D., & Morgeson, F. P. (2007). Integrating motivational, social, and contextual work design features: A meta-analytic summary and theoretical extension of the work design literature. *Journal of Applied Psychology, 92*, 1332–1356. (p. 402)

Hunsberger, J. G., Newton, S. S., Bennett, A. H., Duman, C. H., Russell, D. S., Salton, S. R., & Duman, R. S. (2007). Antidepressant actions of the exercise-regulated gene VGF. *Nature Medicine, 13*, 1476–1482. (p. 408)

Hunsley, J., & Di Giulio, G. (2002). Dodo bird, phoenix, or urban legend? The question of psychotherapy equivalence. *Scientific Review of Mental Health Practice, 1*, 11–22. (p. 562)

Hunt, C., Slade, T., & Andrews, G. (2004). Generalized anxiety disorder and major depressive disorder comorbidity in the National Survey of Mental Health and Well-Being. *Depression and Anxiety, 20*, 23–31. (p. 513)

Hunt, E., & Carlson, J. (2007). Considerations relating to the study of group differences in intelligence. *Perspectives on Psychological Science, 2*, 194–213. (p. 345)

Hunt, J. M. (1982). Toward equalizing the developmental opportunities of infants and preschool children. *Journal of Social Issues, 38*(4), 163–191. (p. 341)

Hunt, M. (1990). *The compassionate beast: What science is discovering about the humane side of humankind*. New York: William Morrow. (p. 28)

Hunt, M. (1993). *The story of psychology*. New York: Doubleday. (pp. 2, 5, 245, 339)

Hunt, M. (2007). *The story of psychology*. New York: Anchor. (p. 427)

Hunter, S., & Sundel, M. (Eds.). (1989). *Midlife myths: Issues, findings, and practice implications*. Newbury Park, CA: Sage. (p. 154)

Hurlburt, R. T., & Akhter, S. A. (2008). Unsymbolized thinking. *Consciousness and Cognition, 17*, 1364–1374. (p. 326)

Hurst, M. (2008, April 22). Who gets any sleep these days? Sleep patterns of Canadians. *Canadian Social Trends*. Statistics Canada Catalogue No. 11–008. (p. 87)

Huston, A. C., Donnerstein, E., Fairchild, H., Feshbach, N. D., Katz, P. A., & Murray, J. P. (1992). *Big world, small screen: The role of television in American society*. Lincoln: University of Nebraska Press. (p. 264)

Hutchinson, R. (2006). *Calum's road*. Edinburgh: Burlinn Limited. (p. 370)

Hvistendahl, M. (2009). Making every baby girl count. *Science, 323*, 1164–1166. (p. 477)

Hvistendahl, M. (2010). Has China outgrown the one-child policy? *Science, 329*, 1458–1461. (pp. 476, 477)

Hvistendahl, M. (2011). China's population growing slowly, changing fast. *Science, 332*, 650–651. (pp. 476, 477)

Hyde, J. S. (2005). The gender similarities hypothesis. *American Psychologist, 60*, 581–592. (pp. 164, 184)

Hyde, J. S., & Mertz, J. E. (2009). Gender, culture, and mathematics performance. *Proceedings of the National Academy of Sciences, 106*, 8801–8807. (p. 342)

Hyde, J. S., Mezulis, A. H., & Abramson, L. Y. (2008). The ABCs of depression: Integrating affective, biological, and cognitive models to explain the emergence of the gender difference in depression. *Psychological Review, 115,* 291–313. (p. 521)

Hyman, I. E., Jr., Boss, S. M., Wise, B. M., McKenzie, K. E., & Caggiano, J. M. (2010). Did you see the unicycling clown? Inattentional blindness while walking and talking on a cell phone. *Applied Cognitive Psychology, 24,* 597–607. (p. 82)

Hyman, R. (1981). Cold reading: How to convince strangers that you know all about them. In K. Frazier (Ed.), *Paranormal borderlands of science.* Buffalo, NY: Prometheus. (p. 438)

I

Iacoboni, M. (2008). *Mirroring people: The new science of how we connect with others.* New York: Farrar, Straus & Giroux. (p. 262)

Iacoboni, M. (2009). Imitation, empathy, and mirror neurons. *Annual Review of psychology, 60,* 653–670. (p. 262)

IAP. (2006, June 21). IAP statement on the teaching of evolution. *The Interacademy Panel on International Issues* (www.interacademies.net/iap). (p. 70)

Ickes, W., Snyder, M., & Garcia, S. (1997). Personality influences on the choice of situations. In R. Hogan, J. Johnson, & S. Briggs (Eds.). *Handbook of personality psychology.* San Diego, CA: Academic Press. (p. 444)

Idson, L. C., & Mischel, W. (2001). The personality of familiar and significant people: The lay perceiver as a social-cognitive theorist. *Journal of Personality and Social Psychology, 80,* 585–596. (p. 459)

IJzerman, H., & Semin, G. R. (2009). The thermometer of social relations: Mapping social proximity on temperature. *Psychological Science, 20,* 1214–1220. (p. 228)

Ikonomidou, C., Bittigau, P., Ishimaru, M. J., Wozniak, D. F., Koch, C., Genz, K., Price, M. T., Stefovska, V., Hoerster, F., Tenkova, T., Dikranian, K., & Olney, J. W. (2000). Ethanol-induced apoptotic neurodegeneration and fetal alcohol syndrome. *Science, 287,* 1056–1060. (p. 120)

Ilardi, S. S. (2009). *The depression cure: The six-step program to beat depression without drugs.* Cambridge, MA: De Capo Lifelong Books. (pp. 524, 575)

Inbar, Y., Cone, J., & Gilovich, T. (2010). People's intuitions about intuitive insight and intuitive choice. *Journal of Personality and Social Psychology, 99,* 232–247. (p. 313)

Inbar, Y., Pizarro, D., & Bloom, P. (2011). Disgusting smells cause decreased liking of gay men. Unpublished manuscript, Tilburg University. (p. 226)

Independent Sector. (2002). *Faith and philanthropy: The connection between charitable giving behavior and giving to religion.* Washington, DC: Author. (p. 496)

Ingham, A. G., Levinger, G., Graves, J., & Peckham, V. (1974). The Ringelmann effect: Studies of group size and group performance. *Journal of Experimental Social Psychology, 10,* 371–384. (p. 472)

Inglehart, R. (1990). *Culture shift in advanced industrial society.* Princeton, NJ: Princeton University Press. (p. 365)

Inman, M. L., & Baron, R. S. (1996). Influence of prototypes on perceptions of prejudice. *Journal of Personality and Social Psychology, 70,* 727–739. (p. 306)

Insana, R. (2005, February 21). Coach says honey gets better results than vinegar (interview with Larry Brown). *USA Today,* p. 4B. (p. B-10)

Insel, T. R. (2010, April). Faulty circuits. *Scientific American,* pp. 44–51. (p. 518)

International Schizophrenia Consortium. (2009). Common polygenic variation contributes to risk of schizophrenia and bipolar disorder. *Nature, 460,* 748–752. (p. 532)

Inzlicht, M., & Ben-Zeev, T. (2000). A threatening intellectual environment: Why females are susceptible to experiencing problem-solving deficits in the presence of males. *Psychological Science, 11,* 365–371. (p. 346)

Inzlicht, M., & Gutsell, J. N. (2007). Running on empty: Neural signals for self-control failure. *Psychological Science, 18,* 933–937. (p. 404)

Inzlicht, M., & Kang, S. K. (2010). Stereotype threat spillover: How coping with threats to social identity affects aggression, eating, decision making, and attention. *Journal of Personality and Social Psychology, 99,* 467–481. (p. 346)

IPPA. (2009, January 22). Membership letter. International Positive Psychology Association. (p. 414)

IPPA. (2010, August). International conference on positive psychology and education in China, by S. Choong. *The IPPA Newsletter,* International Positive Psychology Association. (p. 414)

Ipsos. (2010a, June 29). Online Canadians report a large 35% decline in the amount of email received. www.ipsos-na.com. (p. 367)

Ipsos. (2010b, April 8). One in five (20%) global citizens believe that alien being have come down to earth and walk amongst us in our communities disguised as humans. www.ipsos-na.com. (p. 19)

IPU. (2011). Women in national parliaments: Situation as of 31 November 2011. International Parliamentary Union (www.ipu.org). (p. 165)

Ireland, M. E., & Pennebaker, J. W. (2010). Language style matching in writing: Synchrony in essays, correspondence, and poetry. *Journal of Personality and Social Psychology, 99,* 549–571. (p. 263)

Ironson, G., Solomon, G. F., Balbin, E. G., O'Cleirigh, C., George, A., Kumar, M., Larson, D., & Woods, T. E. (2002). The Ironson-Woods spiritual/religiousness index is associated with long survival, health behaviors, less distress, and low cortisol in people with HIV/AIDS. *Annals of Behavioral Medicine, 24,* 34–48. (p. 412)

Irwin, M. R., Cole, J. C., & Nicassio, P. M. (2006). Comparative meta-analysis of behavioral interventions for insomnia and their efficacy in middle-aged adults and in older adults 55+ years of age. *Health Psychology, 25,* 3–14. (p. 91)

Isaacson, W. (2009, Spring). *Einstein's final quest.* In Character. http://incharacter.org/features/einsteins-final-quest. (p. 346)

Ishida, A., Mutoh, T., Ueyama, T., Brando, H., Masubuchi, S., Nakahara, D., Tsujimoto, G., & Okamura, H. (2005). Light activates the adrenal gland: Timing of gene expression and glucocorticoid release. *Cell Metabolism, 2,* 297–307. (p. 564)

Iso, H., Simoda, S., & Matsuyama, T. (2007). Environmental change during postnatal development alters behaviour. *Behavioural Brain Research, 179,* 90–98. (p. 58)

Ito, T. A., Miller, N., & Pollock, V. E. (1996). Alcohol and aggression: A meta-analysis on the moderating effects of inhibitory cues, triggering events, and self-focused attention. *Psychological Bulletin, 120,* 60–82. (p. 482)

ITU. (2010). The world in 2010: ICT facts and figures. International Telecommunication Union (www.itu.int/ict). (p. 367)

Izard, C. E. (1977). *Human emotions.* New York: Plenum Press. (pp. 376, 383)

Izard, C. E. (1994). Innate and universal facial expressions: Evidence from developmental and cross-cultural research. *Psychological Bulletin, 114,* 288–299. (p. 383)

J

Jablensky, A. (1999). Schizophrenia: Epidemiology. *Current Opinion in Psychiatry, 12,* 19–28. (p. 531)

Jackson, G. (2009). Sexual response in cardiovascular disease. *Journal of Sex Research, 46,* 233–236. (p. 173)

Jackson, J. M., & Williams, K. D. (1988). *Social loafing: A review and theoretical analysis.* Unpublished manuscript, Fordham University. (p. 472)

Jackson, J. S., Brown, K. T., Brown, T. N., & Marks, B. (2001). Contemporary immigration policy orientations among dominant-group members in western Europe. *Journal of Social Issues, 57,* 431–456. (p. 476)

Jackson, S. W. (1992). The listening healer in the history of psychological healing. *American Journal Psychiatry, 149,* 1623–1632. (p. 566)

Jacobi, C., Hayward, C., deZwaan, M., Kraemer, H. C., & Agras, W. S. (2004). Coming to terms with risk factors for eating disorders: Application of risk terminology and suggestions for a general taxonomy. *Psychological Bulletin, 130,* 19–65. (p. 536)

Jacobs, B. L. (1994). Serotonin, motor activity, and depression-related disorders. *American Scientist, 82,* 456–463. (pp. 408, 524)

Jacobs, B. L. (2004). Depression: The brain finally gets into the act. *Current Directions in Psychological Science, 13,* 103–106. (p. 570)

Jacobs, B. L., van Praag, H., & Gage, F. H. (2000). Adult brain neurogenesis and psychiatry: A novel theory of depression. *Molecular Psychiatry, 5,* 262–269. (p. 525)

Jacques, C., & Rossion, B. (2006). The speed of individual face categorization. *Psychological Science, 17,* 485–492. (p. 191)

Jacques-Tiura, A. J., Abbey, A., Parkhill, M. R., & Zawacki, T. (2007). Why do some men misperceive women's sexual intentions more frequently than others do? An application of the confluence model. *Personality and Social Psychology Bulletin, 33,* 1467–1480. (p. 459)

James, K. (1986). Priming and social categorizational factors: Impact on awareness of emergency situations. *Personality and Social Psychology Bulletin, 12,* 462–467. (p. 287)

James, W. (1890). *The principles of psychology* (Vol. 2). New York: Holt. (pp. 45, 99, 220, 289, 300, 372, 384, 446, 463)

Jameson, D. (1985). Opponent-colors theory in light of physiological findings. In D. Ottoson & S. Zeki (Eds.), *Central and peripheral mechanisms of color vision.* New York: Macmillan. (p. 212)

Jamieson, J. P. (2010). The home field advantage in athletics: A meta-analysis. *Journal of Applied Social Psychology, 40,* 1819–1848. (p. 471)

Jamison, K. R. (1993). *Touched with fire: Manic-depressive illness and the artistic temperament.* New York: Free Press. (p. 520)

Jamison, K. R. (1995). *An unquiet mind.* New York: Knopf. (pp. 520, 545, 570)

Janis, I. L. (1982). *Groupthink: Psychological studies of policy decisions and fiascoes.* Boston: Houghton Mifflin. (p. 474)

Janis, I. L. (1986). Problems of international crisis management in the nuclear age. *Journal of Social Issues, 42*(2), 201–220. (p. 308)

Janoff-Bulman, R., Timko, C., & Carli, L. L. (1985). Cognitive biases in blaming the victim. *Journal of Experimental Social Psychology, 21,* 161–177. (p. 481)

Jaremka, L. M., Gabriel, S., & Carvallo, M. (2011). What makes us feel the best also makes us feel the worst: The emotional impact of independent and interdependent experiences. *Self and Identity, 10,* 44–63. (p. 365)

Jarrett, B., Bloch, G. J., Bennett, D., Bleazard, B., & Hedges, D. (2010). The influence of body mass index, age and gender on current illness: A cross-sectional study. *International Journal of Obesity, 34,* 429–436. (p. 361)

Javitt, D. C., & Coyle, J. T. (2004, January). Decoding schizophrenia. *Scientific American,* pp. 48–55. (p. 529)

Jenkins, J. G., & Dallenbach, K. M. (1924). Obliviscence during sleep and waking. *American Journal of Psychology, 35,* 605–612. (p. 293)

Jenkins, J. M., & Astington, J. W. (1996). Cognitive factors and family structure associated with theory of mind development in young children. *Developmental Psychology, 32,* 70–78. (p. 128)

Jensen, J. P., & Bergin, A. E. (1988). Mental health values of professional therapists: A national interdisciplinary survey. *Professional Psychology; Research and Practice, 19,* 290–297. (p. 566)

Jensen, M. P. (2008). The neurophysiology of pain perception and hypnotic analgesia: Implications for clinical practice. *American Journal of Clinical Hypnosis, 51,* 123–147. (p. 98)

Jepson, C., Krantz, D. H., & Nisbett, R. E. (1983). Inductive reasoning: Competence or skill. *The Behavioral and Brain Sciences, 3,* 494–501. (p. A-9)

Jessberger, S., Aimone, J. B., & Gage, F. H. (2008). *Neurogenesis. In learning and memory: A comprehensive reference.* Oxford: Elsevier. (p. 58)

Jiang, Y., Costello, P., Fang, F., Huang, M., He, S. (2006). A gender- and sexual orientation-dependent spatial attentional effect of invisible things. *Proceedings of the National Academy of Sciences, 103,* 17048–17052. (p. 194)

Job, V., Dweck, C.S., & Walton, G.M. (2010). Ego depletion–Is it all in your head?: Implicit theories about willpower affect self-regulation. *Psychological Science, 21.* Published online at: http://pss.sagepub.com/content/early/2010/09/28/0956797610384745. (p. 403)

Jobe, T. H., & Harrow, M. (2010). Schizophrenia course, long-term outcome, recovery, and prognosis. *Current Directions in Psychological Science, 19,* 220–225. (p. 528)

Johnson, D. L., Wiebe, J. S., Gold, S. M., Andreasen, N. C., Hichwa, R. D., Watkins, G. L., & Ponto, L. L. B. (1999). Cerebral blood flow and personality: A positron emission tomography study. *American Journal of Psychiatry, 156,* 252–257. (p. 437)

Johnson, E. J., & Goldstein, D. (2003). Do defaults save lives? *Science, 302,* 1338–1339. (p. 313)

Johnson, J. A. (2007, June 26). Not so situational. Commentary on the SPSP listserv (spsp-discuss@stolaf.edu). (p. 462)

Johnson, J. G., Cohen, P., Kotler, L., Kasen, S., & Brook, J. S. (2002). Psychiatric disorders associated with risk for the development of eating disorders during adolescence and early adulthood. *Journal of Consulting and Clinical Psychology, 70,* 1119–1128. (p. 536)

Johnson, J. S., & Newport, E. L. (1991). Critical period affects on universal properties of language: The status of subjacency in the acquisition of a second language. *Cognition, 39,* 215–258. (pp. 321, 322)

Johnson, M. H. (1992). Imprinting and the development of face recognition: From chick to man. *Current Directions in Psychological Science, 1,* 52–55. (p. 133)

Johnson, M. H., & Morton, J. (1991). *Biology and cognitive development: The case of face recognition.* Oxford: Blackwell Publishing. (p. 121)

Johnson, R. E., Chang, C-H., & Lord, R. G. (2006). Moving from cognition to behavior: What the research says. *Psychological Bulletin, 132,* 381–415. (p. B-10)

Johnson, W. (2010). Understanding the genetics of intelligence: Can height help? Can corn oil? *Current Directions in Psychological Science, 19,* 177–182. (p. 340)

Johnson, W., Carothers, A., & Deary, I. J. (2008). Sex differences in variability in general intelligence: A new look at the old question. *Perspectives on Psychological Science, 3,* 518–531. (pp. 332, 342)

Johnson, W., Carothers, A., & Deary, I. J. (2009). A role for the X chromosome in sex differences in variability in general intelligence? *Perspectives on Psychological Science, 4,* 598–611. (p. 340)

Johnson, W., Turkheimer, E., Gottesman, I. I., & Bouchard, Jr., T. J. (2009). Beyond heritability: Twin studies in behavioral research. *Current Directions in Psychological Science, 18,* 217–220. (p. 64)

Johnston, L. D., O'Malley, P. M., Bachman, J. G., & Schulenberg, J. E. (2007). *Monitoring the Future national results on adolescent drug use: Overview of key findings, 2006.* Bethesda, MD: National Institute on Drug Abuse. (p. 111)

Johnston, L. D., O'Malley, P. M., Bachman, J. G., & Schulenberg, J. E. (2011). *Monitoring the future national results on adolescent drug use: Overview of key findings, 2010.* Ann Arbor, MI: Institute for Social Research, University of Michigan. (pp. 106, 109)

Johnston, L. D., O'Malley, P. M., Bachman, J. G., & Schulenberg, J. E. (2012). *Monitoring the Future national results on adolescent drug use: Overview of key findings, 2011.* Ann Arbor: Institute for Social Research, The University of Michigan. (p. 110)

Joiner, T. E., Jr. (2006). *Why people die by suicide.* Cambridge, MA: Harvard University Press. (p. 524)

Joiner, T. E., Jr. (2010). *Myths about suicide.* Cambridge, MA: Harvard University Press. (p. 524)

Jokela, M., Elovainio, M., Archana, S-M., & Kivimäki, M. (2009). IQ, socioeconomic status, and early death: The US National Longitudinal Survey of Youth. *Psychosomatic Medicine, 71,* 322–328. (p. 402)

Jones, A. C., & Gosling, S. D. (2005). Temperament and personality in dogs (*Canis familiaris*): A review and evaluation of past research. *Applied Animal Behaviour Science, 95,* 1–53. (p. 437)

Jones, J. M. (2007, July 25). Latest Gallup update shows cigarette smoking near historical lows. *Gallup Poll News Service* (poll.gallup.com). (p. 105)

Jones, J. M., & Moore, D. W. (2003, June 17). Generational differences in support for a woman president. The Gallup Organization (www.gallup.com). (p. 476)

Jones, J. T., Pelham, B. W., Carvallo, M., & Mirenberg, M. C. (2004). How do I love thee? Let me count the Js: Implicit egotism and interpersonal attraction. *Journal of Personality and Social Psychology, 87,* 665–683. (p. 488)

Jones, L. (2000, December). Skeptics New Year quiz. *Skeptical Briefs*, p. 11. (p. 439)

Jones, M. C. (1924). A laboratory study of fear: The case of Peter. *Journal of Genetic Psychology*, *31*, 308–315. (p. 551)

Jones, M. V., Paull, G. C., & Erskine, J. (2002). The impact of a team's aggressive reputation on the decisions of association football referees. *Journal of Sports Sciences*, *20*, 991–1000. (p. 200)

Jones, S. S. (2007). Imitation in infancy: The development of mimicry. *Psychological Science*, *18*, 593–599. (p. 262)

Jones, S. S., Collins, K., & Hong, H-W. (1991). An audience effect on smile production in 10–month-old infants. *Psychological Science*, *2*, 45–49. (p. 383)

Jones, W. H., Carpenter, B. N., & Quintana, D. (1985). Personality and interpersonal predictors of loneliness in two cultures. *Journal of Personality and Social Psychology*, *48*, 1503–1511. (p. 26)

Jordan, A. H., Monin, B., Dweck, C. S., Lovett, B. J., John, O. P., & Gross, J. J. (2011). Misery has more company than people think: Underestimating the prevalence of others' negative emotions. *Personality and Social Psychology Bulletin*, *37*, 120–135. (p. 519)

Jose, A., O'Leary, D., & Moyer, A. (2010). Does premarital cohabitation predict subsequent marital stability and marital quality? A meta-analysis. *Journal of Marriage and Family*, *72*, 105–116. (p. 155)

Joseph, D. L., & Newman, D. A. (2010). Emotional intelligence: An integrative meta-analysis and cascading model. *Journal of Applied Psychology*, *95*, 54–78. (p. 333)

Joseph, J. (2001). Separated twins and the genetics of personality differences: A critique. *American Journal of Psychology*, *114*, 1–30. (p. 65)

Jost, J. T., Kay, A. C., & Thorisdottir, H. (eds.) (2009). *Social and psychological bases of ideology and system justification*. New York: Oxford University Press. (p. 481)

Jovanovic, T., Blanding, N. Q., Norrholm, S. D., Duncan, E., Bradley, B., & Ressler, K. J. (2009). Childhood abuse is associated with increased startle reactivity in adulthood. *Depression and Anxiety*, *26*, 1018–1026. (p. 136)

Judge, T. A., Thoresen, C. J., Bono, J. E., & Patton, G. K. (2001). The job satisfaction/job performance relationship: A qualitative and quantitative review. *Psychological Bulletin*, *127*, 376–407. (p. B-7)

Jung-Beeman, M., Bowden, E. M., Haberman, J., Frymiare, J. L., Arambel-Liu, S., Greenblatt, R., Reber, P. J., & Kounios, J. (2004). Neural activity when people solve verbal problems with insight. *PloS Biology 2*(4), e111. (p. 308)

Just, M. A., Keller, T. A., & Cynkar, J. (2008). A decrease in brain activation associated with driving when listening to someone speak. *Brain Research*, *1205*, 70–80. (p. 81)

K

Kagan, J. (1976). Emergent themes in human development. *American Scientist*, *64*, 186–196. (p. 135)

Kagan, J. (1984). *The nature of the child*. New York: Basic Books. (p. 132)

Kagan, J. (1995). On attachment. *Harvard Review of Psychiatry*, *3*, 104–106. (p. 134)

Kagan, J. (1998). *Three seductive ideas*. Cambridge, MA: Harvard University Press. (p. 158)

Kagan, J. (2010). *The temperamental thread: How genes, culture, time, and luck make us who we are*. Washington, DC: Dana Press. (p. 437)

Kagan, J., Arcus, D., Snidman, N., Feng, W. Y., Hendler, J., & Greene, S. (1994). Reactivity in infants: A cross-national comparison. *Developmental Psychology*, *30*, 342–345. (p. 134)

Kagan, J., Lapidus, D. R., & Moore, M. (1978, December). Infant antecedents of cognitive functioning: A longitudinal study. *Child Development*, *49*(4), 1005–1023. (p. 158)

Kagan, J., & Snidman, N. (2004). *The long shadow of temperament*. Cambridge, MA: Belknap Press. (p. 134)

Kagan, J., Snidman, N., & Arcus, D. M. (1992). Initial reactions to unfamiliarity. *Current Directions in Psychological Science*, *1*, 171–174. (p. 134)

Kahlor, L., & Morrison, D. (2007). Television viewing and rape myth acceptance among college women. *Sex Roles*, *56*, 729–739. (p. 484)

Kahneman, D. (1985, June). Quoted by K. McKean, Decisions, decisions. *Discover*, pp. 22–31. (p. A-6)

Kahneman, D. (1999). Assessments of objective happiness: A bottom-up approach. In D. Kahneman, E. Diener, & N. Schwartz (Eds.), *Understanding well-being: Scientific perspectives on enjoyment and suffering*. New York: Russell Sage Foundation. (p. 222)

Kahneman, D. (2005a, January 13). What were they thinking? Q&A with Daniel Kahneman. *Gallup Management Journal* (gmj.gallup.com). (pp. 309, 416)

Kahneman, D. (2005b, February 10). Are you happy now? *Gallup Management Journal* interview (www.gmj.gallup.com). (p. 415)

Kahneman, D., Fredrickson, B. L., Schreiber, C. A., & Redelmeier, D. A. (1993). When more pain is preferred to less: Adding a better end. *Psychological Science*, *4*, 401–405. (p. 222)

Kahneman, D., Krueger, A. B., Schkade, D. A., Schwarz, N., & Stone, A. A. (2004). A survey method for characterizing daily life experience: The day reconstruction method. *Science*, *306*, 1776–1780. (p. 414)

Kahneman, D., & Renshon, J. (2007, January/February). Why hawks win. *Foreign Policy* (www.foreignpolicy.com). (p. 449)

Kail, R. (1991). Developmental change in speed of processing during childhood and adolescence. *Psychological Bulletin*, *109*, 490–501. (p. 152)

Kail, R., & Hall, L. K. (2001). Distinguishing short-term memory from working memory. *Memory & Cognition*, *29*, 1–9. (p. 273)

Kaiser. (2010, January). Generation M^2: Media in the lives of 8- to 18-year-olds (by V. J. Rideout, U. G. Foeher, & D. F. Roberts). Menlo Park, CA: Henry J. Kaiser Family Foundation. (pp. 21, 367, 369)

Kamarck, T., & Jennings, J. R. (1991). Biobehavioral factors in sudden cardiac death. *Psychological Bulletin*, *109*, 42–75. (p. 399)

Kamel, N. S., & Gammack, J. K. (2006). Insomnia in the elderly: Cause, approach, and treatment. *American Journal of Medicine*, *119*, 463–469. (p. 86)

Kamil, A. C., & Cheng, K. (2001). Way-finding and landmarks: The multiple-bearings hypothesis. *Journal of Experimental Biology*, *204*, 103–113. (p. 281)

Kaminski, J., Cali, J., & Fischer, J. (2004). Word learning in a domestic dog: Evidence for "fast mapping." *Science*, *304*, 1682–1683. (p. 325)

Kanaya, T., Scullin, M. H., & Ceci, S. J. (2003). The Flynn effect and U.S. policies: The impact of rising IQ scores on American society via mental retardation diagnoses. *American Psychologist*, *58*, 778–790. (p. 338)

Kandel, D. B., & Raveis, V. H. (1989). Cessation of illicit drug use in young adulthood. *Archives of General Psychiatry*, *46*, 109–116. (p. 112)

Kandel, E. R., & Schwartz, J. H. (1982). Molecular biology of learning: Modulation of transmitter release. *Science*, *218*, 433–443. (p. 283)

Kandler, C., Bleidorn, W., Riemann, R., Spinath, F. M., Thiel, W., & Angleitner, A. (2010). Sources of cumulative continuity in personality: A longitudinal multiple-rater twin study. *Journal of Personality and Social Psychology*, *98*, 995–1008. (p. 158)

Kane, G. D. (2010). Revisiting gay men's body image issues: Exposing the fault lines. *Review of General Psychology*, *14*, 311–317. (p. 537)

Kaplan, H. I., & Saddock, B. J. (Eds.). (1989). *Comprehensive textbook of psychiatry, V*. Baltimore, MD: Williams and Wilkins. (p. 568)

Kaplan, R. M., & Kronick, R. G. (2006). Marital status and longevity in the United States population. *Journal of Epidemiology and Community Health*, *60*, 760–765. (p. 405)

Kaplan, S., Bradley, J. C., Luchman, J. N., & Haynes, D. (2009). On the role of positive and negative affectivity in job performance: A meta-analytic investigation. *Journal of Applied Psychology*, *94*, 162–176. (p. B-7)

Kaprio, J., Koskenvuo, M., & Rita, H. (1987). Mortality after bereavement: A prospective study of 95,647 widowed persons. *American Journal of Public Health*, *77*, 283–287. (p. 392)

Karacan, I., Aslan, C., & Hirshkowitz, M. (1983). Erectile mechanisms in man. *Science*, *220*, 1080–1082. (p. 86)

Karacan, I., Goodenough, D. R., Shapiro, A., & Starker, S. (1966). Erection cycle during sleep in relation to dream anxiety. *Archives of General Psychiatry, 15,* 183–189. (p. 86)

Karau, S. J., & Williams, K. D. (1993). Social loafing: A meta-analytic review and theoretical integration. *Journal of Personality and Social Psychology, 65,* 681–706. (p. 472)

Kark, J. D., Shemi, G., Friedlander, Y., Martin, O., Manor, O., & Blondheim, S. H. (1996). Does religious observance promote health? Mortality in secular vs. religious kibbutzim in Israel. *American Journal of Public Health, 86,* 341–346. (p. 410)

Karlsgodt, K. H., Sun, D., & Cannon, T. D. (2010). Structural and functional brain abnormalities in schizophrenia. *Current Directions in Psychological Science, 19,* 226–231. (p. 531)

Karni, A., Meyer, G., Rey-Hipolito, C., Jezzard, P., Adams, M. M., Turner, R., & Ungerleider, L. G. (1998). The acquisition of skilled motor performance: Fast and slow experience-driven changes in primary motor cortex. *Proceedings of the National Academy of Sciences, 95,* 861–868. (p. 123)

Karni, A., & Sagi, D. (1994). Dependence on REM sleep for overnight improvement of perceptual skills. *Science, 265,* 679–682. (p. 95)

Karno, M., Golding, J. M., Sorenson, S. B., & Burnam, A. (1988). The epidemiology of obsessive-compulsive disorder in five US communities. *Archives of General Psychiatry, 45,* 1094–1099. (p. 515)

Karpicke, J. D., & Roediger, H. L., III. (2008). The critical importance of retrieval for learning. *Science, 319,* 966–968. (p. 29)

Karremans, J. C., Frankenhis, W. E., & Arons, S. (2010). Blind men prefer a low waist-to-hip ratio. *Evolution and Human Behavior, 31,* 182–186. (p. 490)

Karremans, J. C., Stroebe, W., & Claus, J. (2006). Beyond Vicary's fantasies: The impact of subliminal priming and brand choice. *Journal of Experimental Social Psychology, 42,* 792–798. (p. 195)

Kasen, S., Chen, H., Sneed, J., Crawford, T., & Cohen, P. (2006). Social role and birth cohort influences on gender-linked personality traits in women: A 20-year longitudinal analysis. *Journal of Personality and Social Psychology, 91,* 944–958. (p. 166)

Kashima, Y., Siegal, M., Tanaka, K., & Kashima, E. S. (1992). Do people believe behaviours are consistent with attitudes? Towards a cultural psychology of attribution processes. *British Journal of Social Psychology, 31,* 111–124. (p. 451)

Kasser, T. (2002). *The high price of materialism.* Cambridge, MA: MIT Press. (p. 415)

Kasser, T. (2011). Cultural values and the well-being of future generations: A cross-national study. *Journal of Cross-Cultural Psychology, 42, 42,* 206–215. (p. 415)

Katz-Wise, S. L., Priess, H. A., & Hyde, J. S. (2010). Gender-role attitudes and behavior across the transition to parenthood. *Developmental Psychology, 46,* 18–28. (p. 166)

Kaufman, J., & Zigler, E. (1987). Do abused children become abusive parents? *American Journal of Orthopsychiatry, 57,* 186–192. (p. 136)

Kaufman, J. C., & Baer, J. (2002). I bask in dreams of suicide: Mental illness, poetry, and women. *Review of General Psychology, 6,* 271–286. (p. 520)

Kaufman, L., & Kaufman, J. H. (2000). Explaining the moon illusion. *Proceedings of the National Academy of Sciences, 97,* 500–505. (p. 213)

Kawakami, K., Dunn, E., Karmali, F., & Dovidio, J. F. (2009). Mispredicting affective and behavioral responses to racism. *Science, 323,* 276–278. (p. 476)

Kay, A. C., Baucher, D., Peach, J. M., Laurin, K., Friesen, J., Zanna, M. P., & Spencer, S. J. (2009). Inequality, discrimination, and the power of the status quo: Direct evidence for a motivation to see the way things are as the way they should be. *Journal of Personality and social Psychology, 97,* 421–434. (p. 481)

Kayser, C. (2007, April/May). Listening with your eyes. *Scientific American Mind,* pp. 24–29. (p. 228)

Kazantzis, N., & Dattilio, F. M. (2010b). Definitions of homework, types of homework and ratings of the importance of homework among psychologists with cognitive behavior therapy and psychoanalytic theoretical orientations. *Journal of Clinical Psychology, 66,* 758–773. (p. 557)

Kazantzis, N., Whittington, C., & Dattilio, F. M. (2010a). Meta-analysis of homework effects in cognitive and behavioral therapy: A replication and extension. *Clinical Psychology; Science and Practice, 17,* 144–156. (p. 557)

Kazdin, A. E., & Benjet, C. (2003). Spanking children: Evidence and issues. *Current Directions in Psychological Science, 12,* 99–103. (p. 251)

Keesey, R. E., & Corbett, S. W. (1983). Metabolic defense of the body weight set-point. In A. J. Stunkard & E. Stellar (Eds.), *Eating and its disorders.* New York: Raven Press. (p. 358)

Keith, S. W., & 19 others. (2006). Putative contributors to the secular increase in obesity: Exploring the roads less traveled. *International Journal of Obesity, 30,* 1585–1594. (p. 362)

Keller, J. (2007, March 9). As football players get bigger, more of them risk a dangerous sleep disorder. *Chronicle of Higher Education,* pp. A43–A44. (p. 92)

Keller, M. B., McCullough, J. P., Klein, D. N., Arnow, B., Dunner, D. L., Gelenberg, A. J., Markowitz, J. C., Nemeroff, C. B., Russell, J. M., Thase, M. E., Trivedi, M. H., & Zajecka J. (2000), A comparison of nefazodone, the cognitive behavioral-analysis system of psychotherapy, and their combination for the treatment of chronic depression. *New England Journal of Medicine, 342,* 1462–1470. (p. 570)

Kellerman, J., Lewis, J., & Laird, J. D. (1989). Looking and loving: The effects of mutual gaze on feelings of romantic love. *Journal of Research in Personality, 23,* 145–161. (p. 379)

Kellermann, A. L. (1997). Comment: Gunsmoke—changing public attitudes toward smoking and firearms. *American Journal of Public Health, 87,* 910–913. (p. 481)

Kellermann, A. L., Rivara, F. P., Rushforth, N. B., Banton, H. G., Feay, D. T., Francisco, J. T., Locci, A. B., Prodzinski, J., Hackman, B. B., & Somes, G. (1993). Gun ownership as a risk factor for homicide in the home. *New England Journal of Medicine, 329,* 1084–1091. (p. 481)

Kellermann, A. L., Somes, G., Rivara, F. P., Lee, R. K., & Banton, J. G. (1998). Injuries and deaths due to firearms in the home. *Journal of Trauma, 45,* 263–267. (p. 481)

Kelling, S. T., & Halpern, B. P. (1983). Taste flashes: Reaction times, intensity, and quality. *Science, 219,* 412–414. (p. 224)

Kellner, C. H., & 15 others. (2005). Relief of expressed suicidal intent by ECT: A consortium for research in ECT study. *American Journal of Psychiatry, 162,* 977–982. (p. 571)

Kellner, C. H., & 16 others. (2006). Continuation electroconvulsive therapy vs. pharmacotherapy for relapse prevention in major depression: A multisite study from the Consortium for Research in Electroconvulsive Therapy (CORE). *Archives of General Psychiatry, 63,* 1337–1344. (p. 572)

Kelly, A. E. (2000). Helping construct desirable identities: A self-presentational view of psychotherapy. *Psychological Bulletin, 126,* 475–494. (p. 555)

Kelly, D. J., Quinn, P. C., Slater, A. M., Lee, K., Ge, L., & Pascalis, O. (2007). The other-race effect develops during infancy: Evidence of perceptual narrowing. *Psychological Science, 18,* 1084–1089. (p. 480)

Kelly, I. W. (1997). Modern astrology: A critique. *Psychological Reports, 81,* 1035–1066. (p. 438)

Kelly, I. W. (1998). Why astrology doesn't work. *Psychological Reports, 82,* 527–546. (p. 438)

Kelly, M. H. (1999). Regional naming patterns and the culture of honor. *Names, 47,* 3–20. (p. 484)

Kelly, S. D., Özyürek, A., & Maris, E. (2010). Two sides of the same coin: Speech and gesture mutually interact to enhance comprehension. *Psychological Science, 21,* 260–267. (p. 324)

Kelly, T. A. (1990). The role of values in psychotherapy: A critical review of process and outcome effects. *Clinical Psychology Review, 10,* 171–186. (p. 566)

Kempe, R. S., & Kempe, C. C. (1978). *Child abuse.* Cambridge, MA: Harvard University Press. (p. 136)

Kendall-Tackett, K. A. (Ed.). (2004). *Health consequences of abuse in the family: A clinical guide for evidence-based practice.* Washington, DC: American Psychological Association. (p. 137)

Kendall-Tackett, K. A., Williams, L. M., & Finkelhor, D. (1993). Impact of sexual abuse on children: A review and synthesis of recent empirical studies. *Psychological Bulletin, 113,* 164–180. (pp. 137, 298)

Kendler, K. S. (1997). Social support: A genetic-epidemiologic analysis. *American Journal of Psychiatry, 154,* 1398–1404. (p. 444)

Kendler, K. S. (1998, January). Major depression and the environment: A psychiatric genetic perspective. *Pharmacopsychiatry, 31*(1), 5–9. (p. 522)

Kendler, K. S., Jacobson, K. C., Myers, J., & Prescott, C. A. (2002a). Sex differences in genetic and environmental risk factors for irrational fears and phobias. *Psychological Medicine, 32,* 209–217. (p. 517)

Kendler, K. S., Karkowski, L. M., & Prescott, C. A. (1999). Fears and phobias: Reliability and heritability. *Psychological Medicine, 29,* 539–553. (p. 517)

Kendler, K. S., Myers, J., & Prescott, C. A. (2002b). The etiology of phobias: An evaluation of the stress-diathesis model. *Archives of General Psychiatry, 59,* 242–248. (p. 517)

Kendler, K. S., Myers, J., & Zisook, S. (2008). Does bereavement-related major depression differ from major depression associated with other stressful life events? *American Journal of Psychiatry, 165,* 1449–1455. (p. 522)

Kendler, K. S., Neale, M. C., Kessler, R. C., Heath, A. C., & Eaves, L. J. (1992). Generalized anxiety disorder in women: A population-based twin study. *Archives of General Psychiatry, 49,* 267–272. (p. 517)

Kendler, K. S., Neale, M. C., Thornton, L. M., Aggen, S. H., Gilman, S. E., & Kessler, R. C. (2002). Cannabis use in the last year in a U.S. national sample of twin and sibling pairs. *Psychological Medicine, 32,* 551–554. (p. 110)

Kendler, K. S., Thornton, L. M., & Gardner, C. O. (2001). Genetic risk, number of previous depressive episodes, and stressful life events in predicting onset of major depression. *American Journal of Psychiatry, 158,* 582–586. (p. 522)

Kennedy, S., & Over, R. (1990). Psychophysiological assessment of male sexual arousal following spinal cord injury. *Archives of Sexual Behavior, 19,* 15–27. (p. 45)

Kennedy, S. H., Giacobbe, P., Rizvi, S. J., Placenza, F. M., Nishikawa, Y., Mayberg, H. S., & Lozano, A. M. (2011). Deep brain stimulation for treatment-resistant depression: Follow-up after 3 to 6 years. *American Journal of Psychiatry, 168,* 502–510. (p. 573)

Kenrick, D. T., & Funder, D. C. (1988). Profiting from controversy: Lessons from the person-situation debate. *American Psychologist, 43,* 23–34. (p. 442)

Kenrick, D. T., Griskevicious, V., Neuberg, S. L., & Schaller, M. (2010). Renovating the pyramid of needs: Contemporary extensions build upon ancient foundations. *Perspectives on Psychological Science, 5,* 292–314. (p. 355)

Kenrick, D. T., & Gutierres, S. E. (1980). Contrast effects and judgments of physical attractiveness: When beauty becomes a social problem. *Journal of Personality and Social Psychology, 38,* 131–140. (p. 176)

Kenrick, D. T., Gutierres, S. E., & Goldberg, L. L. (1989). Influence of popular erotica on judgments of strangers and mates. *Journal of Experimental Social Psychology, 25,* 159–167. (p. 176)

Kenrick, D. T., Nieuweboer, S., & Buunk, A. P. (2009). Universal mechanisms and cultural diversity: Replacing the blank slate with a coloring book. In M. Schaller, A. Norenzayan, S. Heine, A. Norenzayan, T. Yamagishi, & T. Kameda (eds.), *Evolution, culture, and the human mind.* Mahwah, NJ: Lawrence Erlbaum. (pp. 122, 184)

Kensinger, E. A. (2007). Negative emotion enhances memory accuracy: Behavioral and neuroimaging evidence. *Current Directions in Psychological Science, 16,* 213–218. (p. 283)

Keough, K. A., Zimbardo, P. G., & Boyd, J. N. (1999). Who's smoking, drinking, and using drugs? Time perspective as a predictor of substance use. *Basic and Applied Social Psychology, 2,* 149–164. (p. 425)

Kernis, M. H. (2003). Toward a conceptualization of optimal self-esteem. *Psychological Inquiry, 14,* 1–26. (p. 450)

Kerr, N. L., & Bruun, S. E. (1983). Dispensability of member effort and group motivation losses: Free-rider effects. *Journal of Personality and Social Psychology, 44,* 78–94. (p. 472)

Kerr, R. A. (2009). Amid worrisome signs of warming, 'climate fatigue' sets in. *Science, 326,* 926–928. (p. 460)

Kessing, L. V., Forman, J. L., & Andersen, P. K. (2010). Does lithium protect against dementia? *Bipolar Disorders, 12,* 87–94. (p. 571)

Kessler, D., Lewis, G., Kaur, S., Wiles, N., King, M., Welch, S., Sharp, D. J., Araya, R., Hollinghurst, & Peters, T. J. (2009). Therapist-delivered Internet psychotherapy for depression primary care: A randomized controlled trial. *The Lancet, 374,* 628–634. (p. 557)

Kessler, M., & Albee, G. W. (1975). Primary prevention. *Annual Review of Psychology, 26,* 557–591. (p. 577)

Kessler, R. C. (2000). Posttraumatic stress disorder: The burden to the individual and to society. *Journal of Clinical Psychiatry, 61*(suppl. 5), 4–12. (p. 515)

Kessler, R. C., & 12 others. (2010a). Structure and diagnosis of adult attention-deficit/hyperactivity disorder: Analysis of expanded symptom criteria from the adult ADHD Clinical Diagnostic Scale. *Archives of General Psychiatry, 67,* 1168–1178. (p. 507)

Kessler, R. C., & 22 others. (2010b). Age differences in the prevalence and co-morbidity of DSM-IV major depressive episodes: Results from the WHO World Mental Health Survey Initiative. *Depression and Anxiety, 27,* 351–364. (p. 522)

Kessler, R. C., Berglund, P., Demler, O., Jin, R., Merikangos, K. R., & Walters, E. E. (2005). Lifetime prevalence and age-of-onset distributions of DSM-IV disorders in the National Comorbidity Survey Replication. *Archives of General Psychiatry, 62,* 593–602. (pp. 510, 540)

Kessler, R. C., Foster, C., Joseph, J., Ostrow, D., Wortman, C., Phair, J., & Chmiel, J. (1991). Stressful life events and symptom onset in HIV infection. *American Journal of Psychiatry, 148,* 733–738. (p. 397)

Kessler, R. C., Soukup, J., Davis, R. B., Foster, D. F., Wilkey, S. A., Van Rompay, M. I., & Eisenberg, D. M. (2001). The use of complementary and alternative therapies to treat anxiety and depression in the United States. *American Journal of Psychiatry, 158,* 289–294. (p. 563)

Keynes, M. (1980, December 20/27). Handel's illnesses. *Lancet,* pp. 1354–1355. (p. 520)

Keys, A., Brozek, J., Henschel, A., Mickelsen, O., & Taylor, H. L. (1950). *The biology of human starvation.* Minneapolis: University of Minnesota Press. (p. 356)

Kiecolt-Glaser, J. K. (2009). Psychoneuro-immunology: Psychology's gateway to the biomedical future. *Perspectives on Psychological Science, 4,* 367–369. (p. 394)

Kiecolt-Glaser, J. K., & Glaser, R. (1995). Psychoneuroimmunology and health consequences: Data and shared mechanisms. *Psychosomatic Medicine, 57,* 269–274. (p. 396)

Kiecolt-Glaser, J. K., Loving, T. J., Stowell, J. R., Malarkey, W. B., Lemeshow, S., Dickinson, S. L., & Glaser, R. (2005). Hostile marital interactions, proinflammatory cytokine production, and wound healing. *Archives of General Psychiatry, 62,* 1377–1384. (p. 395)

Kiecolt-Glaser, J. K., Page, G. G., Marucha, P. T., MacCallum, R. C., & Glaser, R. (1998). Psychological influences on surgical recovery: Perspectives from psychoneuroimmunology. *American Psychologist, 53,* 1209–1218. (p. 395)

Kiehl, K. A., & Buckholtz, J. W. (2010, September/October). Inside the mind of a psychopath. *Scientific American Mind,* pp. 22–29. (p. 539)

Kihlstrom, J. F. (2005). Dissociative disorders. *Annual Review of Clinical Psychology, 1,* 227–253. (p. 535)

Kihlstrom, J. F. (2006). Repression: A unified theory of a will-o'-the-wisp. *Behavioral and Brain Sciences, 29,* 523. (p. 431)

Killingsworth, M. A., & Gilbert, D. T. (2010). A wandering mind is an unhappy mind. *Science, 330,* 932. (pp. 368, B-2)

Kim, B. S. K., Ng, G. F., & Ahn, A. J. (2005). Effects of client expectation for counseling success, client-counselor worldview match, and client adherence to Asian and European American cultural values on counseling process with Asian Americans. *Journal of Counseling Psychology, 52,* 67–76. (p. 566)

Kim, G., & Tong, A. (2010, February 23). Airline passengers have grown, seats haven't. *Sacramento Bee* (reprinted by *Grand Rapids Press*, pp. B1, B3). (p. 362)

Kim, H., & Markus, H. R. (1999). Deviance or uniqueness, harmony or conformity? A cultural analysis. *Journal of Personality and Social Psychology, 77,* 785–800. (p. 451)

Kimata, H. (2001). Effect of humor on allergen-induced wheal reactions. *Journal of the American Medical Association, 285,* 737. (p. 405)

Kimble, G. A. (1981). *Biological and cognitive constraints on learning.* Washington, DC: American Psychological Association. (p. 256)

King, R. N., & Koehler, D. J. (2000). Illusory correlations in graphological interference. *Journal of Experimental Psychology: Applied, 6,* 336–348. (p. 438)

King, S., St-Hilaire, A., & Heidkamp, D. (2010). Prenatal factors in schizophrenia. *Current Directions in Psychological Science, 19,* 209–213. (p. 531)

Kingston, D. W., Malamuth, N. M., Fedoroff, N. M., & Marshall, W. L. (2009). The importance of individual differences in pornography use: Theoretical perspectives and implications for treating sexual offenders. *Journal of Sex Research, 46,* 216–232. (p. 485)

Kinnier, R. T., & Metha, A. T. (1989). Regrets and priorities at three stages of life. *Counseling and Values, 33,* 182–193. (p. 156)

Kinzler, K. D., Shutts, K., Dejesus, J., & Spelke, E. S. (2009). Accent trumps race in guiding children's social preferences. *Social Cognition, 27,* 623–634. (p. 478)

Kirby, D. (2002). Effective approaches to reducing adolescent unprotected sex, pregnancy, and childbearing. *Journal of Sex Research, 39,* 51–57. (p. 177)

Kirkpatrick, B., Fenton, W. S., Carpenter, W. T., Jr., & Marder, S. R. (2006). The NIMH-MATRICS consensus statement on negative symptoms. *Schizophrenia Bulletin, 32,* 214–219. (p. 530)

Kirsch, I. (1996). Hypnotic enhancement of cognitive-behavioral weight loss treatments: Another meta-reanalysis. *Journal of Consulting and Clinical Psychology, 64,* 517–519. (p. 98)

Kirsch, I. (2010). *The emperor's new drugs: Exploding the antidepressant myth.* New York: Basic Books. (pp. 23, 570)

Kirsch, I., & Braffman, W. (2001). Imaginative suggestibility and hypnotizability. *Current Directions in Psychological Science, 10,* 57–61. (p. 97)

Kirsch, I., Deacon, B. J., Huedo-Medina, T. B., Scoboria, A., Moore, T. J., & Johnson, B. T. (2008). Initial severity and antidepressant benefits: A meta-analysis of data submitted to the Food and Drug Administration. *Public Library of Science Medicine, 5,* e45. (p. 570)

Kirsch, I., & Lynn, S. J. (1995). The altered state of hypnosis. *American Psychologist, 50,* 846–858. (p. 98)

Kirsch, I., Moore, T. J., Scoboria, A., & Nicholls, S. S. (2002, July 15). New study finds little difference between effects of antidepressants and placebo. *Prevention and Treatment* (journals.apa.org/prevention). (p. 570)

Kirsch, I., & Sapirstein, G. (1998). Listening to Prozac but hearing placebo: A meta-analysis of antidepressant medication. *Prevention and Treatment, 1,* posted June 26 at (journals.apa.org/prevention/volume1). (pp. 563, 570)

Kisley, M. A., Wood, S., & Burrows, C. L. (2007). Looking at the sunny side of life: Age-related change in an event-related potential measure of the negativity bias. *Psychological Science, 18,* 838–843. (p. 157)

Kitayama, S., Ishii, K., Imada, T., Takemura, K., & Ramaswamy, J. (2006). Voluntary settlement and the spirit of independence: Evidence from Japan's "northern frontier." *Journal of Personality and Social Psychology, 91,* 369–384. (p. 452)

Kitayama, S., Park, H., Sevincer, A. T., Karasawa, M., & Uskul, A. K. (2009). A cultural task analysis of implicit independence: Comparing North America, Western Europe, and East Asia. *Journal of Personality and Social Psychology, 97,* 236–255. (p. 458)

Kivimaki, M., Leino-Arjas, P., Luukkonen, R., Rihimaki, H., & Kirjonen, J. (2002). Work stress and risk of cardiovascular mortality: Prospective cohort study of industrial employees. *British Medical Journal, 325,* 857. (p. 402)

Klayman, J., & Ha, Y-W. (1987). Confirmation, disconfirmation, and information in hypothesis testing. *Psychological Review, 94,* 211–228. (p. 307)

Klein, D. N. (2010). Chronic depression: Diagnosis and classification. *Current Directions in Psychological Science, 19,* 96–100. (p. 522)

Klein, D. N., & 16 others. (2003). Therapeutic alliance in depression treatment: Controlling for prior change and patient characteristics. *Journal of Consulting and Clinical Psychology, 71,* 997–1006. (p. 565)

Kleinke, C. L. (1986). Gaze and eye contact: A research review. *Psychological Bulletin, 1000,* 78–100. (p. 379)

Kleinmuntz, B., & Szucko, J. J. (1984). A field study of the fallibility of polygraph lie detection. *Nature, 308,* 449–450. (p. 379)

Kleitman, N. (1960, November). Patterns of dreaming. *Scientific American,* pp. 82–88. (p. 84)

Klemm, W. R. (1990). Historical and introductory perspectives on brainstem-mediated behaviors. In W. R. Klemm & R. P. Vertes (Eds.), *Brainstem mechanisms of behavior.* New York: Wiley. (p. 47)

Klimstra, T. A., Hale, III, W. W., Raaijmakers, Q. A. W., Branje, S. J. T., & Meeus, W. H. J. (2009). Maturation of personality in adolescence. *Journal of Personality and Social Psychology, 96,* 898–912. (p. 145)

Kline, D., & Schieber, F. (1985). Vision and aging. In J. E. Birren & K. W. Schaie (Eds.), *Handbook of the psychology of aging.* New York: Van Nostrand Reinhold. (p. 151)

Kline, N. S. (1974). *From sad to glad.* New York: Ballantine Books. (p. 527)

Klinke, R., Kral, A., Heid, S., Tillein, J., & Hartmann, R. (1999). Recruitment of the auditory cortex in congenitally deaf cats by long-term cochlear electrostimulation. *Science, 285,* 1729–1733. (p. 218)

Kluft, R. P. (1991). Multiple personality disorder. In A. Tasman & S. M. Goldfinger (Eds.), *Review of Psychiatry* (Vol. 10). Washington, DC: American Psychiatric Press. (p. 534)

Klump, K. L., & Culbert, K. M. (2007). Molecular genetic studies of eating disorders: Current status and future directions. *Current Directions in Psychological Science, 16,* 37–41. (p. 536)

Klump, K. L., Suisman, J. L., Burt, S. A., McGue, M., & Iacono, W. G. (2009). Genetic and environmental influences on disordered eating: An adoption study. *Journal of Abnormal Psychology, 118,* 797–805. (p. 536)

Knapp, S., & VandeCreek, L. (2000, August). Recovered memories of childhood abuse: Is there an underlying professional consensus? *Professional Psychology: Research and Practice, 31,* 365–371. (p. 299)

Knickmeyer, E. (2001, August 7). In Africa, big is definitely better. *Seattle Times,* p. A7. (p. 537)

Knight, R. T. (2007). Neural networks debunk phrenology. *Science, 316,* 1578–1579. (p. 57)

Knight, W. (2004, August 2). Animated face helps deaf with phone chat. NewScientist.com. (p. 228)

Knoblich, G., & Oellinger, M. (2006, October/November). The Eureka moment. *Scientific American Mind,* pp. 38–43. (p. 307)

Knutson, K. L., Spiegel, K., Penev, P., & Van Cauter, E. (2007). The metabolic consequences of sleep deprivation. *Sleep Medicine Reviews, 11,* 163–178. (p. 90)

Ko, C-K., Yen, J-Y., Chen, C-C., Chen, S-H., & Yen, C-F. (2005). Proposed diagnostic criteria of Internet addiction for adolescents. *Journal of Nervous and Mental Disease, 193,* 728–733. (p. 101)

Koenen, K. C., Moffitt, T. E., Roberts, A. L., Martin, L. T., Kubzansky, L., Harrington, H., Poulton, R., & Caspi, A. (2009). Childhood IQ and adult mental disorders: A test of the cognitive reserve hypothesis. *American Journal of Psychiatry, 166,* 50–57. (p. 339)

Koenig, H. G., King, D. E., & Carson, V. B. (2011). *Handbook of religion and health.* New York: Oxford University Press. (p. 410)

Koenig, H. G., & Larson, D. B. (1998). Use of hospital services, religious attendance, and religious affiliation. *Southern Medical Journal, 91,* 925–932. (p. 412)

Koenig, L. B., McGue, M., Krueger, R. F., & Bouchard, T. J., Jr. (2005). Genetic and environmental influences on religiousness: Findings for retrospective and current religiousness ratings. *Journal of Personality, 73,* 471–488. (p. 66)

Koenig, L. B., & Vaillant, G. E. (2009). A prospective study of church attendance and health over the lifespan. *Health Psychology, 28,* 117–124. (p. 411)

Koenigs, M., Young, L., Adolphs, R., Tranel, D., Cushman, F., Hauser, M., & Damasio, A. (2007). Damage to the prefrontal cortex increases utilitarian moral judgements. *Nature, 446,* 908–911. (p. 57)

Koestner, R., Lekes, N., Powers, T. A., & Chicoine, E. (2002). Attaining personal goals: Self-concordance plus implementation intentions equals success. *Journal of Personality and Social Psychology, 83,* 231–244. (p. B-11)

Kohlberg, L. (1981). *The philosophy of moral development: Essays on moral development* (Vol. I). San Francisco: Harper & Row. (p. 142)

Kohlberg, L. (1984). *The psychology of moral development: Essays on moral development* (Vol. II). San Francisco: Harper & Row. (p. 142)

Kohler, C. G., Walker, J. B., Martin, E. A., Healey, K. M., & Moberg, P. J. (2010). Facial emotion perception in schizophrenia: A meta-analytic review. *Schizophrenia Bulletin, 36,* 1009–1019. (p. 529)

Kohler, I. (1962, May). Experiments with goggles. *Scientific American,* pp. 62–72. (p. 215)

Köhler, W. (1925; reprinted 1957). *The mentality of apes.* London: Pelican. (p. 317)

Kohn, P. M., & Macdonald, J. E. (1992). The survey of recent life experiences: A decontaminated hassles scale for adults. *Journal of Behavioral Medicine, 15,* 221–236. (p. 392)

Kolassa, I-T., & Elbert, T. (2007). Structural and functional neuroplasticity in relation to traumatic stress. *Current Directions in Psychological Science, 16,* 321–325. (p. 518)

Kolata, G. (1987). Metabolic catch-22 of exercise regimens. *Science, 236,* 146–147. (p. 363)

Kolb, B. (1989). Brain development, plasticity, and behavior. *American Psychologist, 44,* 1203–1212. (p. 58)

Kolb, B., & Whishaw, I. Q. (1998). Brain plasticity and behavior. *Annual Review of Psychology, 49,* 43–64. (p. 122)

Kolker, K. (2002, December 8). Video violence disturbs some: Others scoff at influence. *Grand Rapids Press,* pp. A1, A12. (p. 485)

Kolodziej, M. E., & Johnson, B. T. (1996). Interpersonal contact and acceptance of persons with psychiatric disorders: A research synthesis. *Journal of Consulting and Clinical Psychology, 64,* 1387–1396. (p. 511)

Koltko-Rivera, M. E. (2006). Rediscovering the later version of Maslow's hierarchy of needs: Self-transcendence and opportunities for theory, research, and unification. *Review of General Psychology, 10,* 302–317. (p. 355)

Konkle, T., Brady, T. F., Alvarez, G. A., & Oliva, A. (2010). Conceptual distinctiveness supports detailed visual long-term memory for real-world objects. *Journal of Experimental Psychology: General, 139,* 558–578. (p. 272)

Kontula, O., & Haavio-Mannila, E. (2009). The impact of aging on human sexual activity and sexual desire. *Journal of Sex Research, 46,* 46–56. (p. 151)

Kornell, N., & Bjork, R. A. (2008). Learning concepts and categories: Is spacing the "enemy of induction?" *Psychological Science, 19,* 585–592. (p. 30)

Kosfeld, M., Heinrichs, M., Zak, P. J., Fischbacher, U., & Fehr, E. (2005). Oxytocin increases trust in humans. *Nature, 435,* 673–676. (p. 45)

Kosslyn, S. M. (2005). Reflective thinking and mental imagery: A perspective on the development of posttraumatic stress disorder. *Development and Psychopathology, 17,* 851–863. (p. 516)

Kosslyn, S. M., & Koenig, O. (1992). *Wet mind: The new cognitive neuroscience.* New York: Free Press. (p. 44)

Kosslyn, S. M., Thompson, W. L., Costantini-Ferrando, M. F., Alpert, N. M., & Spiegel, D. (2000). Hypnotic visual illusion alters color processing in the brain. *American Journal of Psychiatry, 157,* 1279–1284. (p. 99)

Kotchick, B. A., Shaffer, A., & Forehand, R. (2001). Adolescent sexual risk behavior: A multi-system perspective. *Clinical Psychology Review, 21,* 493–519. (p. 176)

Koten, J. W., Jr., Wood, G., Hagoort, P., Goebel, R., Propping, P., Willmes, K., & Boomsma, D. I. (2009). Genetic contribution to variation in cognitive function: An fMRI study in twins. *Science, 323,* 1737–1740. (p. 340)

Kotkin, M., Daviet, C., & Gurin, J. (1996). The *Consumer Reports* mental health survey. *American Psychologist, 51,* 1080–1082. (p. 560)

Kounios, J., & Beeman, M. (2009). The *Aha!* moment: The cognitive neuroscience of insight. *Current Directions in Psychological Science, 18,* 210–215. (p. 307)

Kposowa, A. J., & D'Auria, S. (2009). Association of temporal factors and suicides in the United States, 2000–2004. *Social Psychiatry and Psychiatric Epidemiology, 45,* 433–445. (p. 524)

Kraft, C. (1978). A psychophysical approach to air safety: Simulator studies of visual illusions in night approaches. In H. L. Pick, H. W. Leibowitz, J. E. Singer, A. Steinschneider, & H. W. Stevenson (Eds.), *Psychology: From research to practice.* New York: Plenum Press. (p. B-14)

Kraft, R. N. (2002). *Memory perceived: Recalling the Holocaust.* Westport, CT: Praeger. (p. 299)

Kramer, A. (2010). Personal corrspondence. (p. 414)

Kramer, A. F., & Erickson, K. I. (2007). Capitalizing on cortical plasticity: Influence of physical activity on cognition and brain function. *Trends in Cognitive Sciences, 11,* 342–348. (p. 408)

Kramer, M. S., & 17 others. (2008). Breastfeeding and child cognitive development: New evidence from a large randomized trial. *Archives of General Psychiatry, 65,* 578–584. (p. 23)

Kramer, P. D. (2011, July 9). In defense of antidepressants. *New York Times* (www.nytimes.com). (p. 570)

Kranz, F., & Ishai, A. (2006). Face perception is modulated by sexual preference. *Current Biology, 16,* 63–68. (p. 181)

Kraul, C. (2010, October 12). Chief engineer knew it would take a miracle. *Los Angeles Times* (www.latimes.com). (p. 230)

Kraut, R. E., & Johnston, R. E. (1979). Social and emotional messages of smiling: An ethological approach. *Journal of Personality and Social Psychology, 37,* 1539–1553. (p. 383)

Kraut, R. E., Patterson, M., Lundmark, V., Kiesler, S., Mukopadhyay, T., & Scherlis, W. (1998). Internet paradox: A social technology that reduces social involvement and psychological well being? *American Psychologist, 53,* 1017–1031. (p. 368)

KRC Research & Consulting. (2001, August 7). Memory isn't quite what it used to be (survey for General Nutrition Centers). *USA Today,* p. D1. (p. 153)

Krebs, D. L., & Van Hesteren, F. (1994). The development of altruism: Toward an integrative model. *Developmental Review, 14,* 103–158. (p. 143)

Kring, A. M., & Caponigro, J. M. (2010). Emotion in schizophrenia: Where feeling meets thinking. *Current Directions in Psychological Science, 19,* 255–259. (p. 529)

Kring, A. M., & Gordon, A. H. (1998). Sex differences in emotion: Expression, experience, and physiology. *Journal of Personality and Social Psychology, 74,* 686–703. (p. 382)

Kristensen, P., & Bjerkedal, T. (2007). Explaining the relation between birth order and intelligence. *Science, 316,* 1717. (p. A-8)

Kristof, N. D. (2004, July 21). Saying no to killers. *New York Times* (www.nytimes.com). (p. 493)

Kross, E., Berman, M. G., Mischel, W., Smith, E. E., & Wager, T. D. (2011). Social rejection shares somatosensory representations with physical pain. *PNAS, 108,* 6270–6275. (p. 366)

Krueger, J., & Killham, E. (2005, December 8). At work, feeling good matters. *Gallup Management Journal* (www.gmj.gallup.com). (p. B-10)

Kruger, J., Epley, N., Parker, J., & Ng, Z-W. (2005). Egocentrism over e-mail: Can we communicate as well as we think? *Journal of Personality and Social Psychology, 89,* 925–936. (pp. 128, 381)

Krupa, D. J., Thompson, J. K., & Thompson, R. F. (1993). Localization of a memory trace in the mammalian brain. *Science, 260,* 989–991. (p. 282)

Krützen, M., Mann, J., Heithaus, M. R., Connor, R. C., Bejder, L., & Sherwin, W. B. (2005). Cultural transmission of tool use in bottlenose dolphins. *Proceedings of the National Academy of Sciences, 102,* 8939–8943. (p. 318)

Kubey, R., & Csikszentmihalyi, M. (2002, February). Television addiction is no mere metaphor. *Scientific American,* pp. 74–80. (p. 264)

Kübler, A., Winter, S., Ludolph, A. C., Hautzinger, M., & Birbaumer, N. (2005).

Severity of depressive symptoms and quality of life in patients with amyotrophic lateral sclerosis. *Neurorehabilitation and Neural Repair, 19*(3), 182–193. (p. 414)

Kubzansky, L. D., Koenen, K. C., Jones, C., & Eaton, W. W. (2009). A prospective study of posttraumatic stress disorder symptoms and coronary heart disease in women. *Health Psychology, 28,* 125–130. (p. 400)

Kubzansky, L. D., Sparrow, D., Vokanas, P., & Kawachi, I. (2001). Is the glass half empty or half full? A prospective study of optimism and coronary heart disease in the normative aging study. *Psychosomatic Medicine, 63,* 910–916. (pp. 399, 400)

Kuhl, P. K., & Meltzoff, A. N. (1982). The bimodal perception of speech in infancy. *Science, 218,* 1138–1141. (p. 320)

Kuhn, D. (2006). Do cognitive changes accompany developments in the adolescent brain? *Perspectives on Psychological Science, 1,* 59–67. (p. 140)

Kujala, U. M., Kaprio, J., Sarna, S., & Koskenvuo, M. (1998). Relationship of leisure-time physical activity and mortality: The Finnish twin cohort. *Journal of the American Medical Association, 279,* 440–444. (p. 407)

Kuncel, N. R., & Hezlett, S. A. (2010). Fact and fiction in cognitive ability testing for admissions and hiring decisions. *Current Directions in Psychological Science, 19,* 339–345. (p. 332)

Kunkel, D. (2001, February 4). *Sex on TV.* Menlo Park, CA: Henry J. Kaiser Family Foundation (www.kff.org). (p. 176)

Kuntsche, E., Knibbe, R., Gmel, G., & Engels, R. (2005). Why do young people drink? A review of drinking motives. *Clinical Psychology Review, 25,* 841–861. (p. 111)

Kuppens, P., Allen, N. B., & Sheeber, L. B. (2010). Emotional inertia and psychological maladjustment. *Psychological Science, 21,* 984–991. (p. 526)

Kushner, M. G., Kim, S. W., Conahue, C., Thuras, P., Adson, D., Kotlyar, M., McCabe, J., Peterson, J., & Foa, E. B. (2007). D-cycloserine augmented exposure therapy for obsessive-compulsive disorder. *Biological Psychiatry, 62,* 835–838. (p. 569)

Kutas, M. (1990). Event-related brain potential (ERP) studies of cognition during sleep: Is it more than a dream? In R. R. Bootzin, J. F. Kihlstrom, & D. Schacter (Eds.), *Sleep and cognition.* Washington, DC: American Psychological Association. (p. 83)

Kutcher, E. J., & Bragger, J. D. (2004). Selection interviews of overweight job applicants: Can structure reduce the bias? *Journal of Applied Social Psychology, 34,* 1993–2022. (p. B-6)

L

Labouvie-Vief, G., & Schell, D. A. (1982). Learning and memory in later life. In B. B. Wolman (Ed.), *Handbook of developmental psychology.* Englewood Cliffs, NJ: Prentice-Hall. (p. 153)

Lac, A., & Crano, W. D. (2009). Monitoring matters: Meta-analytic review reveals the reliable linkage of parental monitoring with adolescent marijuana use. *Perspectives on Psychological Science, 4,* 578–586. (p. 111)

Lacey, H. P., Smith, D. M., & Ubel, P. A. (2006). Hope I die before I get old: Mispredicting happiness across the lifespan. *Journal of Happiness Studies, 7,* 167–182. (p. 156)

Lacey, M. (2010, December 11). He found bag of cash, but did the unexpected. *New York Times* (www.nytimes.com). (p. 496)

Lachman, M. E. (2004). Development in midlife. *Annual Review of Psychology, 55,* 305–331. (p. 154)

Ladd, G. T. (1887). *Elements of physiological psychology.* New York: Scribner's. (p. 78)

Lafleur, D. L., Pittenger, C., Kelmendi, B., Gardner, T., Wasylink, S., Malison, R. T., Sanacora, G., Krystal, J. H., & Coric, V. (2006). N-acetylcysteine augmentation in serotonin reuptake inhibitor refractory obsessive-compulsive disorder. *Psychopharmacology, 184,* 254–256. (p. 518)

Laird, J. D. (1974). Self-attribution of emotion: The effects of expressive behavior on the quality of emotional experience. *Journal of Personality and Social Psychology, 29,* 475–486. (p. 384)

Laird, J. D. (1984). The real role of facial response in the experience of emotion: A reply to Tourangeau and Ellsworth, and others. *Journal of Personality and Social Psychology, 47,* 909–917. (p. 384)

Laird, J. D., Cuniff, M., Sheehan, K., Shulman, D., & Strum, G. (1989). Emotion specific effects of facial expressions on memory for life events. *Journal of Social Behavior and Personality, 4,* 87–98. (p. 384)

Lally, P., Van Jaarsveld, C. H. M., Potts, H. W. W., & Wardle, J. (2010). How are habits formed? Modelling habit formation in the real world. *European Journal of Social Psychology, 40,* 998–1009. (p. 238)

Lalumière, M. L., Blanchard, R., & Zucker, K. J. (2000). Sexual orientation and handedness in men and women: A meta-analysis. *Psychological Bulletin, 126,* 575–592. (p. 182)

Lam, R. W., Levitt, A. J., Levitan, R. D., Enns, M. W., Morehouse, R., Michalak, E. E., & Tam, E. M. (2006). The Can-SAD study: A randomized controlled trial of the effectiveness of light therapy and fluoxetine in patients with winter seasonal affective disorder. *American Journal of Psychiatry, 163,* 805–Lehman, A. F. (p. 568)

Lambert, N. M., DeWall, C. N., Bushman, B. J., Tillman, T. F., Fincham, F. D., Pond, Jr., R. S., & Gwinn, A. M. (2011). Lashing out in lust: Effect of pornography on nonsexual, physical aggression against relationship partners. Paper presentation at the Society for Personality and Social Psychology convention. (p. 485)

Lambert, W. E. (1992). Challenging established views on social issues: The power and limitations of research. *American Psychologist, 47,* 533–542. (p. 327)

Lambert, W. E., Genesee, F., Holobow, N., & Chartrand, L. (1993). Bilingual education for majority English-speaking children. *European Journal of Psychology of Education, 8,* 3–22. (p. 327)

Lambird, K. H., & Mann, T. (2006). When do ego threats lead to self-regulation failure? Negative consequences of defensive high self-esteem. *Personality and Social Psychology Bulletin, 32,* 1177–1187. (p. 450)

Landauer, T. (2001, September). Quoted by R. Herbert, You must remember this. *APS Observer,* p. 11. (p. 300)

Landauer, T. K., & Whiting, J. W. M. (1979). Correlates and consequences of stress in infancy. In R. Munroe, B. Munroe, & B. Whiting (Eds.), *Handbook of cross-cultural human development.* New York: Garland. (p. 391)

Landberg, J., & Norström, T. (2011). Alcohol and homicide in Russia and the United States: A comparative analysis. *Journal of Studies on Alcohol and Drugs, 72,* 723–730. (p. 482)

Landry, M. J. (2002). MDMA: A review of epidemiologic data. *Journal of Psychoactive Drugs, 34,* 163–169. (p. 107)

Langer, E. J. (1983). *The psychology of control.* Beverly Hills, CA: Sage. (p. 402)

Langer, E. J., & Abelson, R. P. (1974). A patient by any other name . . .: Clinician group differences in labeling bias. *Journal of Consulting and Clinical Psychology, 42,* 4–9. (p. 511)

Langer, E. J., & Imber, L. (1980). The role of mindlessness in the perception of deviance. *Journal of Personality and Social Psychology, 39,* 360–367. (p. 511)

Langlois, J. H., Kalakanis, L., Rubenstein, A. J., Larson, A., Hallam, M., & Smoot, M. (2000). Maxims or myths of beauty? A meta-analytic and theoretical review. *Psychological Bulletin, 126,* 390–423. (pp. 489, 490)

Langlois, J. H., Roggman, L. A., Casey, R. J., Ritter, J. M., Rieser-Danner, L. A., & Jenkins, V. Y. (1987). Infant preferences for attractive faces: Rudiments of a stereotype? *Developmental Psychology, 23,* 363–369. (p. 489)

Lángström, N. H., Rahman, Q., Carlström, E., & Lichtenstein, P. (2008). Genetic and environmental effects on same-sex sexual behavior: A population study of twins in Sweden. *Archives of Sexual Behavior.* (p. 181)

Lángström, N. H., Rahman, Q., Carlström, E., & Lichtenstein, P. (2010). Genetic and environmental effects on same-sex sexual behavior: A population study of twins in Sweden. *Archives of Sexual Behavior, 39,* 75–80. (p. 181)

Lankford, A. (2009). Promoting aggression and violence at Abu Ghraib: The U.S. military's transformation of ordinary people into torturers. *Aggression and Violent Behavior, 14,* 388–395. (p. 470)

Larkin, K., Resko, J. A., Stormshak, F., Stellflug, J. N., & Roselli, C. E. (2002). Neuroanatomical correlates of sex and sexual partner preference in sheep. Paper presented at Society for Neuroscience convention. (p. 181)

Larrick, R. P., Timmerman, T. A., & Carton, A. M., & Abrevaya, J. (2011). Temper, temperature, and temptation: Heat-related retaliation in baseball. *Psychological Science, 22,* 423–428. (p. 483)

Larsen, R. J., & Diener, E. (1987). Affect intensity as an individual difference characteristic: A review. *Journal of Research in Personality, 21,* 1–39. (pp. 134, 375)

Larson, R. W., & Verma, S. (1999). How children and adolescents spend time across the world: Work, play, and developmental opportunities. *Psychological Bulletin, 125,* 701–736. (p. 344)

Larsson, H., Tuvblad, C., Rijsdijk, F. V., Andershed, H., Grann, M., & Lichetenstein, P. (2007). A common genetic factor explains the association between psychopathic personality and antisocial behavior. *Psychological Medicine, 37,* 15–26. (p. 538)

Larzelere, R. E. (2000). Child outcomes of non-abusive and customary physical punishment by parents: An updated literature review. *Clinical Child and Family Psychology Review, 3,* 199–221. (p. 252)

Larzelere, R. E., & Kuhn, B. R. (2005). Comparing child outcomes of physical punishment and alternative disciplinary tactics: A meta-analysis. *Clinical Child and Family Psychology Review, 8,* 1–37. (p. 252)

Larzelere, R. E., Kuhn, B. R., & Johnson, B. (2004). The intervention selection bias: An underrecognized confound in intervention research. *Psychological Bulletin, 130,* 289–303. (p. 252)

Lashley, K. S. (1950). In search of the engram. In *Symposium of the Society for Experimental Biology* (Vol. 4). New York: Cambridge University Press. (p. 281)

Lassiter, G. D., & Irvine, A. A. (1986). Videotaped confessions: The impact of camera point of view on judgments of coercion. *Journal of Personality and Social Psychology, 16,* 268–276. (p. 459)

Lassiter, G. D., Lindberg, M. JH., Gonzáles-Vallego, C., Bellezza, F. S., & Phillips, N. D. (2009). The deliberation-without-attention effect: Evidence for an artifactual interpretation. *Psychological Science, 20,* 671–675. (p. 313)

Latané, B. (1981). The psychology of social impact. *American Psychologist, 36,* 343–356. (p. 472)

Latané, B., & Dabbs, J. M., Jr. (1975). Sex, group size and helping in three cities. *Sociometry, 38,* 180–194. (p. 495)

Latané, B., & Nida, S. (1981). Ten years of research on group size and helping. *Psychological Bulletin, 89,* 308–324. (p. 472)

Latham, G. P., & Locke, E. A. (2007). New developments in and directions for goal-setting research. *European Psychologist, 12,* 290–300. (p. B-10)

Laudenslager, M. L., & Reite, M. L. (1984). Losses and separations: Immunological consequences and health implications. *Review of Personality and Social Psychology, 5,* 285–312. (p. 401)

Laumann, E. O., Gagnon, J. H., Michael, R. T., & Michaels, S. (1994). *The social organization of sexuality: Sexual practices in the United States.* Chicago: University of Chicago Press. (p. 184)

Laws, K. R., & Kokkalis, J. (2007). Ecstasy (MDMA) and memory function: A meta-analytic update. *Human Psychopharmacology: Clinical and Experimental, 22,* 381–388. (p. 107)

Lazaruk, W. (2007). Linguistic, academic, and cognitive benefits of French immersion. *Canadian Modern Language Review, 63,* 605–628. (p. 327)

Lazarus, R. S. (1991). Progress on a cognitive-motivational-relational theory of emotion. *American Psychologist, 46,* 352–367. (p. 375)

Lazarus. R. S. (1998). *Fifty years of the research and theory of R. S. Lazarus: An analysis of historical and perennial issues.* Mahwah, NJ: Erlbaum. (pp. 375, 390)

Lazer, D., & 14 others. (2009). Computational social science. *Science, 323,* 721–723. (p. 474)

Lea, S. E. G. (2000). Towards an ethical use of animals. *The Psychologist, 13,* 556–557. (p. 27)

Leaper, C., & Ayres, M. M. (2007). A meta-analytic review of gender variations in adults' language use: Talkativeness, affiliative speech, and assertive speech. *Personality and Social Psychology Review, 11,* 328–363. (p. 165)

Leary, M. R. (1999). The social and psychological importance of self-esteem. In R. M. Kowalski & M. R. Leary (Eds.), *The social psychology of emotional and behavioral problems.* Washington, DC: APA Books. (p. 447)

Leary, M. R., Haupt, A. L., Strausser, K. S., & Chokel, J. T. (1998). Calibrating the sociometer: The relationship between interpersonal appraisals and state self-esteem. *Journal of Personality and Social Psychology, 74,* 1290–1299. (p. 364)

LeDoux, J. E. (1996). *The emotional brain: The mysterious underpinnings of emotional life.* New York: Simon & Schuster. (p. 282)

LeDoux, J. E. (2002). *The synaptic self.* London: Macmillan. (pp. 123, 374)

LeDoux, J. E. (2009, July/August). Quoted by K. McGowan, Out of the past. *Discover,* pp. 28–37. (p. 294)

LeDoux, J. E., & Armony, J. L. (1999). Can neurobiology tell us anything about human feelings? In D. Kahneman, E. Diener, & N. Schwartz (Eds.), *Well-being: The foundations of hedonic psychology.* New York: Sage. (p. 375)

Lee, J. D. (2008). Fifty years of driving safety research. *Human Factors, 50,* 521–528. (p. B-14)

Lee, L., Frederick, S., & Ariely, D. (2006). Try it, you'll like it: The influence of expectation, consumption, and revelation on preferences for beer. *Psychological Science, 17,* 1054–1058. (p. 198)

Lee, P. S. N., Leung, L., Lo, V., Xiong, C., & Wu, T. (2011). Internet communication versus face-to-face interaction in quality of life. *Social Indicators Research, 100,* 375–389. (p. 368)

Lee, S. W. S., Schwarz, N., Taubman, D., & Hou, M. (2010). Sneezing in times of a flue pandemic: Public sneezing increases perception of unrelated risks and shifts preferences for federal spending. *Psychological Science, 21,* 375–377. (p. 310)

Lefcourt, H. M. (1982). *Locus of control: Current trends in theory and research.* Hillsdale, NJ: Erlbaum. (p. 403)

Legrand, L. N., Iacono, W. G., & McGue, M. (2005). Predicting addiction. *American Scientist, 93,* 140–147. (p. 111)

Lehavot, K., & Lambert, A. J. (2007). Toward a greater understanding of antigay prejudice: On the role of sexual orientation and gender role violation. *Basic and Applied Social Psychology, 29,* 279–292. (p. 491)

Lehman, A. F., Steinwachs, D. M., Dixon, L. B., Goldman, H. H., Osher, F., Postrado, L., Scott, J. E., Thompson, J. W., Fahey, M., Fischer, P., Kasper, J. A., Lyles, A., Skinner, E. A., Buchanan, R., Carpenter, W. T., Jr., Levine, J., McGlynn, E. A., Rosenheck, R., & Zito, J. (1998). Translating research into practice: The schizophrenic patient outcomes research team (PORT) treatment recommendations. *Schizophrenia Bulletin, 24,* 1–10. (p. 568)

Lehman, D. R., Wortman, C. B., & Williams, A. F. (1987). Long-term effects of losing a spouse or child in a motor vehicle crash. *Journal of Personality and Social Psychology, 52,* 218–231. (p. 157)

Leichsenring, F., & Rabung, S. (2008). Effectiveness of long-term psychodynamic psychotherapy: A meta-analysis. *JAMA, 300,* 1551–1565. (p. 562)

Leitenberg, H., & Henning, K. (1995). Sexual fantasy. *Psychological Bulletin, 117,* 469–496. (pp. 172, 176)

Lemonick, M. D. (2002, June 3). Lean and hungrier. *Time,* p. 54. (p. 358)

L'Engle, M. (1972). *A Circle of Quiet.* New York: HarperCollins. (pp. 346, 521)

L'Engle, M. (1973). *A Wind in the Door, 87.* New York: Farrar, Straus and Giroux. (p. 10)

Lenhart, A. (2010, April 20). Teens, cell phones and texting. Pew Internet and American Life Project. Pew Research Center (www.pewresearch.org). (pp. 165, 367)

Lennox, B. R., Bert, S., Park, G., Jones, P. B., & Morris, P. G. (1999). Spatial and temporal mapping of neural activity associated with auditory hallucinations. *Lancet, 353,* 644. (p. 56)

Lenton, A. P., & Francesconi, M. (2010). How humans cognitively manage an abundance of mate options. *Psychological Science, 21,* 528–533. (p. 488)

Lenzenweger, M. F., Dworkin, R. H., & Wethington, E. (1989). Models of positive and negative symptoms in schizophrenia: An empirical evaluation of latent structures. *Journal of Abnormal Psychology, 98,* 62–70. (p. 568)

Leonhard, C., & Randler, C. (2009). In sync with the family: Children and partners influence the sleep-wake circadian rhythm and social habits of women. *Chronobiology International, 26,* 510–525. (p. 84)

Leserman, J., Jackson, E. D., Petitto, J. M., Golden, R. N., Silva, S. G., Perkins, D. O., Cai, J., Folds, J. D., & Evans, D. L. (1999). Progression to AIDS: The effects of stress, depressive symptoms, and social support. *Psychosomatic Medicine, 61,* 397–406. (p. 396)

Lester, W. (2004, May 26). AP polls: Nations value immigrant workers. *Associated Press* release. (p. 476)

Leucht, S., Barnes, T. R. E., Kissling, W., Engel, R. R., Correll, C., & Kane, J. M. (2003). Relapse prevention in schizophrenia with new-generation antipsychotics: A systematic review and exploratory meta-analysis of randomized, controlled trials. *American Journal of Psychiatry, 160,* 1209–1222. (p. 569)

Leung, A. K-Y., Maddux, W. W., Galinsky, A. D., & Chiu, C-Y. (2008). Multicultural experience enhances creativity: The when and how. *American Psychologist, 63,* 169–181. (p. 315)

Levant, R. F., & Hasan, N. T. (2008). Evidence-based practice in psychology. *Professional Psychology: Research and Practice, 39,* 658–662. (pp. 562, 563)

LeVay, S. (1991). A difference in hypothalamic structure between heterosexual and homosexual men. *Science, 253,* 1034–1037. (p. 180)

LeVay, S. (1994, March). Quoted in D. Nimmons, Sex and the brain. *Discover,* p. 64–71. (p. 180)

LeVay, S. (2011). *Gay, straight, and the reason why: The science of sexual orientation.* New York: Oxford University Press. (pp. 181, 182, 183)

Levenson, R. W. (1992). Autonomic nervous system differences among emotions. *Psychological Science, 3,* 23–27. (p. 378)

Levin, R., & Nielsen, T. A. (2007). Disturbed dreaming, posttraumatic stress disorder, and affect distress: A review and neurocognitive model. *Psychological Bulletin, 133,* 482–528. (p. 94)

Levin, R., & Nielsen, T. A. (2009). Nightmares, bad dreams, and emotion dysregulation. *Current Directions in Psychological Science, 18,* 84–87. (p. 94)

Levine, J. A., Lanningham-Foster, L. M., McCrady, S. K., Krizan, A. C., Olson, L. R., Kane, P. H., Jensen, M. D., & Clark, M. M. (2005). Interindividual variation in posture allocation: Possible role in human obesity. *Science, 307,* 584–586. (p. 361)

Levine, R. V., & Norenzayan, A. (1999). The pace of life in 31 countries. *Journal of Cross-Cultural Psychology, 30,* 178–205. (p. 19)

Levine, R. V., Sato, S., Hashimoto, T., & Verma, J. (1995). Love and marriage in eleven cultures. *Journal of Cross-Cultural Psychology, 26,* 554–571. (p. 492)

Levinson, D. F., & 23 others. (2011). Copy number variants in schizophrenia: Confirmation of five previous findings and new evidence for 3q29 microdeletions and VIPR2

duplications. *American Journal of Psychiatry, 168,* 302–316. (p. 532)

Levy, P. E. (2003). Industrial/organizational psychology: Understanding the workplace. Boston: Houghton Mifflin. (p. B-6)

Lewandowski, G. W., Jr., Aron, A., & Gee, J. (2007). Personality goes a long way: The malleability of opposite-sex physical attractiveness. *Personality Relationships, 14,* 571–585. (p. 490)

Lewinsohn, P. M., Hoberman, H., Teri, L., & Hautziner, M. (1985). An integrative theory of depression. In S. Reiss & R. Bootzin (Eds.), *Theoretical issues in behavior therapy.* Orlando, FL: Academic Press. (p. 521)

Lewinsohn, P. M., Petit, J., Joiner, T. E., Jr., & Seeley, J. R. (2003). The symptomatic expression of major depressive disorder in adolescents and young adults. *Journal of Abnormal Psychology, 112,* 244–252. (p. 521)

Lewinsohn, P. M., Rohde, P., & Seeley, J. R. (1998). Major depressive disorder in older adolescents: Prevalence, risk factors, and clinical implications. *Clinical Psychology Review, 18,* 765–794. (p. 521)

Lewinsohn, P. M., & Rosenbaum, M. (1987). Recall of parental behavior by acute depressives, remitted depressives, and nondepressives. *Journal of Personality and Social Psychology, 52,* 611–619. (p. 288)

Lewis, C. S. (1960). *Mere Christianity.* New York: Macmillan. (p. 4)

Lewis, D. O., Pincus, J. H., Bard, B., Richardson, E., Prichep, L. S., Feldman, M., & Yeager, C. (1988). Neuropsychiatric, psychoeducational, and family characteristics of 14 juveniles condemned to death in the United States. *American Journal of Psychiatry, 145,* 584–589. (p. 136)

Lewis, D. O., Yeager, C. A., Swica, Y., Pincus, J. H., & Lewis, M. (1997). Objective documentation of child abuse and dissociation in 12 murderers with dissociative identity disorder. *American Journal of Psychiatry, 154,* 1703–1710. (p. 535)

Lewis, M. (1992). Commentary. *Human Development, 35,* 44–51. (p. 288)

Lewontin, R. (1976). Race and intelligence. In N. J. Block & G. Dworkin (Eds.), *The IQ controversy: Critical readings.* New York: Pantheon. (p. 343)

Li, J., Laursen, T. M., Precht, D. H., Olsen, J., & Mortensen, P. B. (2005). Hospitalization for mental illness among parents after the death of a child. *New England Journal of Medicine, 352,* 1190–1196. (p. 157)

Li, J. C., Dunning, D., & Malpass, R. L. (1996). Cross-racial identification among European-Americans basketball fandom and the contact hypothesis. Unpublished manuscript, Cornell University. (p. 480)

Li, N., & DiCarlo, J. J. (2008). Unsupervised natural experience rapidly alters invariant object representation in visual cortex. *Science, 321,* 1502–1506. (p. 213)

Li, Y., Johnson, E. J., & Zaval, L. (2011). Local warming: Daily temperature change influences belief in global warming. *Psychological Science, 22,* 454–459. (p. 310)

Li, Z. H., Jiang, D., Pepler, D., & Craig, W. (2010). Adolescent romantic relationships in China and Canada: A cross-national comparison. *Internal Journal of Behavioral Development, 34,* 113–120. (p. 145)

Liang, K. Y., Mintun, M. A., Fagan, A. M., Goate, A.M., Bugg, J.M., Holtzman, D. M., Morris, J. C., & Head, D. (2010). Exercise and Alzheimer's disease biomarkers in cognitively normal older adults. *Annals of Neurology, 68,* 311–318. (p. 152)

Liberman, V., Boehm, J. K., Lyubomirsky, S., & Ross, L. D. (2009). Happiness and memory: Affective significance of endowment and contrast. *Emotion, 9,* 666–680. (p. 412)

Libertus, M. E., & Brannon, E. M. (2009). Behavioral and neural basis of number sense in infancy. *Current Directions in Psychological Science, 18,* 346–351. (p. 127)

Licata, A., Taylor, S., Berman, M., & Cranston, J. (1993). Effects of cocaine on human aggression. *Pharmacology Biochemistry and Behavior, 45,* 549–552. (p. 106)

Lichtenstein, P., Calström, E., Råstam, M., Gillberg, C., & Anckarsäter, H. (2010). The genetics of autim spectrum disorders and related neuropsychiatric disorders in childhood. *American Journal of Psychiatry, 167,* 1357–1363. (pp. 105, 130)

Lieberman, M. D., & Eisenberger, N. I. (2009). Pains and pleasures of social life. *Science, 323,* 890–893. (p. 366)

Lieberman, M. D., Eisenberger, N. I., Crockett, M. J., Tom, S. M., Pfeifer, J. H., & Way, B. M. (2007). Putting feelings into words: Affect labeling disrupts amygdala activity in response to affective stimuli. *Psychological Science, 18,* 421–428. (p. 406)

Lievens, F., Dilchert, S., & Ones, D. S. (2009). The importance of exercise and dimension factors in assessment centers: Simultaneous examinations of construct-related and criterion-related validity. *Human Performance, 22,* 375–390. (p. 445)

Lilienfeld, S. O. (2009, Winter). Tips for spotting psychological pseudoscience: A student-friendly guide. *Eye of Psi Chi,* pp. 23–26. (p. 231)

Lilienfeld, S. O., & Arkowitz, H. (2007, April/May). Autism: An epidemic. *Scientific American Mind,* pp. 82–83. (p. 130)

Lilienfeld, S. O., & Arkowitz, H. (2007, December, 2006/January, 2007). Taking a closer look: Can moving your eyes back and forth help to ease anxiety? *Scientific American Mind,* pp. 80–81. (p. 564)

Lilienfeld, S. O., & Arkowitz, H. (2011, January/February). The insanity verdict on trial. *Scientific American,* pp. 64–65. (p. 512)

Lilienfeld, S. O., Lynn, S. J., Kirsch, I., Chaves, J. F., Sarbin, T. R., Ganaway, G. K., & Powell, R. A. (1999). Dissociative identity disorder and the sociocognitive model: Recalling the lessons of the past. *Psychological Bulletin, 125,* 507–523. (p. 535)

Lilienfeld, S. O., Wood, J. M., & Garb, H. N. (2001, May). What's wrong with this picture? *Scientific American*, pp. 81–87. (p. 430)

Lim, J., & Dinges, D. F. (2010). A meta-analysis of the impact of short-term sleep deprivation on cognitive variables. *Psychological Bulletin, 136*, 375–389. (p. 90)

Lindberg, S. M., Hyde, J. S., Linn, M. C., & Petersen, J. L. (2010). New trends in gender and mathematics performance: A meta-analysis. *Psychological Bulletin, 136*, 1125–1135. (p. 342)

Linder, D. (1982). Social trap analogs: The tragedy of the commons in the laboratory. In V. J. Derlega & J. Grzelak (Eds.), *Cooperative and helping behavior: Theories and research*. New York: Academic Press. (p. 498)

Lindner, I., Echterhoff, G., Davidson, P. S. R., & Brand, M. (2010). Observation inflation: Your actions become mine. *Psychological Science, 21*, 1291–1299. (p. 263)

Lindskold, S. (1978). Trust development, the GRIT proposal, and the effects of conciliatory acts on conflict and cooperation. *Psychological Bulletin, 85*, 772–793. (p. 500)

Lindskold, S., & Han, G. (1988). GRIT as a foundation for integrative bargaining. *Personality and Social Psychology Bulletin, 14*, 335–345. (p. 500)

Lindson, N., Aveyard, P., & Hughes, J. R. (2010). Reduction versus abrupt cessation in smokers who want to quit (review). *Cochrane Collaboration* (Cochrane Library, Issue 3; www.thecochranelibrary.com). (p. 105)

Lippa, R. A. (2005). *Gender, nature, and nurture* (2nd ed.). Mahwah, NJ: Erlbaum. (p. 166)

Lippa, R. A. (2006). The gender reality hypothesis. *American Psychologist, 61*, 639–640. (p. 166)

Lippa, R. A. (2007). The relation between sex drive and sexual attraction to men and women: A cross-national study of heterosexual, bisexual, and homosexual men and women. *Archives of Sexual Behavior, 36*, 209–222. (p. 489)

Lippa, R. A. (2008). Sex differences and sexual orientation differences in personality: Findings from the BBC Internet survey. *Archives of Sexual Behavior, Special Issue: Biological research on sex-dimorphic behavior and sexual orientation, 37*(1), 173–187. (pp. 166, 184)

Lipps, H. M. (1999). *A new psychology of women: Gender, culture, and ethnicity*. Mountain View, CA: Mayfield Publishing. (p. 476)

Lipsitt, L. P. (2003). Crib death: A biobehavioral phenomenon? *Current Directions in Psychological Science, 12*, 164–170. (p. 123)

Liu, H. (2009). Till Death Do Us Part: Marital Status and Mortality Trends, 1986–2000. *Journal of Marriage and Family, 71*, 1158–1173. (p. 405)

Liu, Y., Balaraman, Y., Wang, G., Nephew, K. P., & Zhou, F. C. (2009). Alcohol exposure alters DNA methylation profiles in mouse embryos at early neurulation. *Epigenetics, 4*, 500–511. (p. 120)

Livesley, W. J., & Jang, K. L. (2008). The behavioral genetics of personality disorder. *Annual Review of Clinical Psychology, 4*, 247–274. (p. 538)

Livingstone, M., & Hubel, D. H. (1988). Segregation of form, color, movement, and depth: Anatomy, physiology, and perception. *Science, 240*, 740–749. (p. 205)

LoBue, V., & DeLoache, J. S. (2008). Detecting the snake in the grass: Attention to fear-relevant stimuli by adults and young children. *Psychological Science, 19*, 284–289. (p. 518)

Loehlin, J. C., Horn, J. M., & Ernst, J. L. (2007). Genetic and environmental influences on adult life outcomes: Evidence from the Texas adoption project. *Behavior Genetics, 37*, 463–476. (p. 66)

Loehlin, J. C., McCrae, R. R., & Costa, P. T., Jr. (1998). Heritabilities of common and measure-specific components of the Big Five personality factors. *Journal of Research in Personality, 32*, 431–453. (p. 440)

Loehlin, J. C., & Nichols, R. C. (1976). *Heredity, environment, and personality*. Austin: University of Texas Press. (p. 64)

Loftus, E. F. (1980). *Memory: Surprising new insights into how we remember and why we forget*. Reading, MA: Addison-Wesley. (p. 97)

Loftus, E. F., & Ketcham, K. (1994). *The myth of repressed memory*. New York: St. Martin's Press. (pp. 93, 281)

Loftus, E. F., Levidow, B., & Duensing, S. (1992). Who remembers best? Individual differences in memory for events that occurred in a science museum. *Applied Cognitive Psychology, 6*, 93–107. (p. 295)

Loftus, E. F., & Loftus, G. R. (1980). On the permanence of stored information in the human brain. *American Psychologist, 35*, 409–420. (p. 281)

Loftus, E. F., & Palmer, J. C. (1974, October). Reconstruction of automobile destruction: An example of the interaction between language and memory. *Journal of Verbal Learning & Verbal Behavior, 13*(5), 585–589. (p. 295)

Logan, T. K., Walker, R., Cole, J., & Leukefeld, C. (2002). Victimization and substance abuse among women: Contributing factors, interventions, and implications. *Review of General Psychology, 6*, 325–397. (p. 110)

Logue, A. W. (1998a). Laboratory research on self-control: Applications to administration. *Review of General Psychology, 2*, 221–238. (p. 249)

Logue, A. W. (1998b). Self-control. In W. T. O'Donohue (Ed.), *Learning and behavior therapy*. Boston, MA: Allyn & Bacon. (p. 249)

London, P. (1970). The rescuers: Motivational hypotheses about Christians who saved Jews from the Nazis. In J. Macaulay & L. Berkowitz (Eds.), *Altruism and helping behavior*. New York: Academic Press. (p. 263)

Looy, H. (2001). Sex differences: Evolved, constructed, and designed. *Journal of Psychology and Theology, 29*, 301–313. (p. 185)

Lopes, P. N., Brackett, M. A., Nezlek, J. B., Schutz, A., Sellin, II, & Salovey, P. (2004). Emotional intelligence and social interaction. *Personality and Social Psychology Bulletin, 30*, 1018–1034. (p. 333)

López-Ibor, J. J., López-Ibor, M-I., & Pastrana, J. I. (2008). Transcranial magnetic stimulation. *Current Opinion in Psychiatry, 21*, 640–644. (p. 573)

Lord, C. G., Lepper, M. R., & Preston, E. (1984). Considering the opposite: A corrective strategy for social judgment. *Journal of Personality and Social Psychology, 47*, 1231–1247. (p. 312)

Lord, C. G., Ross, L., & Lepper, M. (1979). Biased assimilation and attitude polarization: The effects of prior theories on subsequently considered evidence. *Journal of Personality and Social Psychology, 37*, 2098–2109. (p. 312)

Lorenz, K. (1937). The companion in the bird's world. *Auk, 54*, 245–273. (p. 133)

Louie, K., & Wilson, M. A. (2001). Temporally structured replay of awake hippocampal ensemble activity during rapid eye movement sleep. *Neuron, 29*, 145–156. (p. 95)

Lourenco, O., & Machado, A. (1996). In defense of Piaget's theory: A reply to 10 common criticisms. *Psychological Review, 103*, 143–164. (p. 129)

Lovaas, O. I. (1987). Behavioral treatment and normal educational and intellectual functioning in young autistic children. *Journal of Consulting and Clinical Psychology, 55*, 3–9. (p. 553)

Lowry, P. E. (1997). The assessment center process: New directions. *Journal of Social Behavior and Personality, 12*, 53–62. (p. 445)

Lozano, A., Mayberg, H., Giacobbe, P., Hami, C., Craddock, R., & Kennedy, S. (2008). Subcallosal cingulated gyrus deep brain stimulation for treatment-resistant depression. *Biological Psychiatry, 64*, 461–467. (p. 572)

Lu, Z-L., Williamson, S. J., & Kaufman, L. (1992). Behavioral lifetime of human auditory sensory memory predicted by physiological measures. *Science, 258*, 1668–1670. (p. 276)

Lubinski, D. (2009a). Cognitive epidemiology: with emphasis on untangling cognitive ability and socioeconomic status. *Intelligence, 37*, 625–633. (p. 339)

Luborsky, L., Rosenthal, R., Diguer, L., Andrusyna, T. P., Berman, J. S., Levitt, J. T., Seligman, D. A., & Krause, E. D. (2002). The dodo bird verdict is alive and well—mostly. *Clinical Psychology: Science and Practice, 9*, 2–34. (p. 562)

Lucas, R. E. (2007a). Adaptation and the set-point model of subjective well-being. *Current Directions in Psychological Science, 16*, 75–79. (p. 414)

Lucas, R. E. (2007b). Long-term disability is associated with lasting changes in subjective well-being: Evidence from two nationally representative longitudinal studies. *Journal of Personality and Social Psychology, 92*, 717–730. (p. 414)

Lucas, R. E. (2008). Personality and subjective well-being. In M. Eid & R. Larsen (Eds.), *The science of subjective well-being*. New York: Guilford. (p. 418)

Lucas, R. E., Clark, A. E., Georgellis, Y., & Diener, E. (2004). Unemployment alters the set point for life satisfaction. *Psychological Science, 15,* 8–13. (p. 417)

Lucas, R. E., & Donnellan, M. B. (2007). How stable is happiness? Using the STARTS model to estimate the stability of life satisfaction. *Journal of Research in Personality, 41,* 1091–1098. (p. 418)

Lucas, R. E., & Donnellan, M. B. (2009). Age differences in personality: Evidence from a nationally representative Australian sample. *Developmental Psychology, 45,* 1353–1363. (p. 159)

Lucas, R. E., & Schimmack, U. (2009). Income and well-being: How big is the gap between the rich and the poor? *Journal of Research in Personality, 43,* 75–78. (p. 415)

Lucas-Thompson, R. G., Goldberg, W. A., & Prause, J. (2010). Maternal work early in the lives of children and its distal associations with achievement and behavior problems: A meta-analysis. *Psychological Bulletin, 136,* 915–942. (p. 137)

Lucero, S. M., Kusner, K. G., & Speace, E. A. (2008, May 24). Religiousness and adolescent sexual behavior: A meta-analytic review. Paper presented at Association for Psychological Science Convention. (p. 177)

Ludwig, A. M. (1995). *The price of greatness: Resolving the creativity and madness controversy.* New York: Guilford Press. (p. 520)

Lumeng, J. C., Forrest, P., Appugliese, D. P., Kaciroti, N., Corwyn, R. F., Bradley, R. H. (2010). Weight status as a predictor of being bullied in third through sixth grades. *Pediatrics, 125,* e1301–7. (p. 361)

Luo, F., Florence, C. S., Quispe-Agnoli, M., Ouyang, L., & Crosby, A. E. (2011). Impact of business cycles on US suicide rates, 1928–2007. *American Journal of Public Health, 101,* 1139–1146. (p. 524)

Luo, M. (2011, January 25). In firearms research, cause is often the missing element. *New York Times* (www.nytimes.com). (p. 21)

Luppino, F. S., de Wit, L. M., Bouvy, P. F., Stijnen, T., Cuijpers, P., Penninx, W. J. H., & Zitman, F. G. (2010). Overweight, obesity, and depression. *Archives of General Psychiatry, 67,* 220–229. (p. 361)

Luria, A. M. (1968). In L. Solotaroff (Trans.), *The mind of a mnemonist.* New York: Basic Books. (p. 272)

Lustig, C., & Buckner, R. L. (2004). Preserved neural correlates of priming in old age and dementia. *Neuron, 42,* 865–875. (p. 290)

Lutfey, K. E., Link, C. L., Rosen, R. C., Wiegel, M., & McKinlay, J. B. (2009). Prevalence and correlates of sexual activity and function in women: Results from the Boston Area Community Health (BACH) survey. *Archives of Sexual Behavior, 38,* 514–527. (p. 174)

Lutgendorf, S. K., Russell, D., Ullrich, P., Harris, T. B., & Wallace, R. (2004). Religious participation, interleukin-6, and mortality in older adults. *Health Psychology, 23,* 465–475. (p. 412)

Lyall, S. (2005, November 29). What's the buzz? Rowdy teenagers don't want to hear it. *New York Times* (www.nytimes.com). (p. 152)

Lykken, D. T. (1991). Science, lies, and controversy: An epitaph for the polygraph. Invited address upon receipt of the Senior Career Award for Distinguished Contribution to Psychology in the Public Interest, American Psychological Association convention. (p. 379)

Lykken, D. T. (1995). *The antisocial personalities.* Hillsdale, NJ: Erlbaum. (pp. 482, 539)

Lykken, D. T. (1999). *Happiness: The Nature and Nurture of Joy and Contentment.* New York: Golden Books. (p. 339)

Lynch, G. (2002). Memory enhancement: The search for mechanism-based drugs. *Nature Neuroscience, 5* (suppl.), 1035–1038. (p. 284)

Lynch, G., & Staubli, U. (1991). Possible contributions of long-term potentiation to the encoding and organization of memory. *Brain Research Reviews, 16,* 204–206. (p. 284)

Lynn, M. (1988). The effects of alcohol consumption on restaurant tipping. *Personality and Social Psychology Bulletin, 14,* 87–91. (p. 102)

Lynn, S. J., Rhue, J. W., & Weekes, J. R. (1990). Hypnotic involuntariness: A social cognitive analysis. *Psychological Review, 97,* 169–184. (p. 99)

Lynne, S. D., Graber, J. A., Nichols, T. R., Brooks-Gunn, J., & Botvin, G. J. (2007). Links between pubertal timing, peer influences, and externalizing behaviors among urban students followed through middle school. *Journal of Adolescent Health, 40,* 181.e7–181.e13. (p. 140)

Lyons, D. E., Young, A. G., Keil, F. C. (2007). The hidden structure of overimitation. *PNAS, 104,* 19751–10756. (p. 262)

Lyons, L. (2004, February 3). Growing up lonely: Examining teen alienation. *Gallup Poll Tuesday Briefing* (www.gallup.com). (p. 144)

Lyons, L. (2005, January 4). Teens stay true to parents' political perspectives. *Gallup Poll News Service* (www.gallup.com). (p. 146)

Lytton, H., & Romney, D. M. (1991). Parents' differential socialization of boys and girls: A meta-analysis. *Psychological Bulletin, 109,* 267–296. (p. 170)

Lyubomirsky, S. (2001). Why are some people happier than others? The role of cognitive and motivational processes in well-being. *American Psychologist, 56,* 239–249. (p. 417)

Lyubomirsky, S. (2008). *The How of happiness.* New York: Penguin. (p. 389)

Lyubomirsky, S., Sousa, L., & Dickerhoof, R. (2006). The costs and benefits of writing, talking, and thinking about life's triumphs and defeats. *Journal of Personality and Social Psychology, 90*(4), 690–708. (p. 407)

M

Ma, L. (1997, September). On the origin of Darwin's ills. *Discover,* p. 27. (p. 514)

Maas, J. B. (1999). *Power sleep. The revolutionary program that prepares your mind and body for peak performance.* New York: HarperCollins. (p. 90)

Maas, J. B., & Robbins, R. S. (2010). *Sleep for success: Everything you must know about sleep but are too tired to ask.* Bloomington, IN: Author House. (pp. 89, 90)

Maass, A., D'Ettole, C., & Cadinu, M. (2008). Checkmate? The role of gender stereotypes in the ultimate intellectual sport. *European Journal of Social Psychology, 38,* 231–245. (p. 346)

Maass, A., Karasawa, M., Politi, F., & Suga, S. (2006). Do verbs and adjectives play different roles in different cultures? A cross-linguistic analysis of person representation. *Journal of Personality and Social Psychology, 90,* 734–750. (p. 452)

Macaluso, E., Frith, C. D., & Driver, J. (2000). Modulation of human visual cortex by crossmodal spatial attention. *Science, 289,* 1206–1208. (p. 228)

Macan, T. H., & Dipboye, R. L. (1994). The effects of the application on processing of information from the employment interview. *Journal of Applied Social Psychology, 24,* 1291. (p. B-5)

MacCabe, J. H., Lambe, M. P., Cnattingius, S., Torrång, A., Björk, C., Sham, P. C., David, A. S., Murray, R. M., & Hultman, C. M. (2008). Scholastic achievement at age 16 and risk of schizophrenia and other psychoses: A national cohort study. *Psychological Medicine, 38,* 1133–1140. (p. 530)

Maccoby, E. E. (1990). Gender and relationships: A developmental account. *American Psychologist, 45,* 513–520. (p. 165)

Maccoby, E. E. (1995). Divorce and custody: The rights, needs, and obligations of mothers, fathers, and children. *Nebraska Symposium on Motivation, 42,* 135–172. (p. 169)

Maccoby, E. E. (1998). *The paradox of gender.* Cambridge, MA: Harvard University Press. (p. 166)

Maccoby, E. E. (2002). Gender and group process: A developmental perspective. *Current Directions in Psychological Science, 11,* 54–58. (p. 473)

MacDonald, G., & Leary, M. R. (2005). Why does social exclusion hurt? The relationship between social and physical pain. *Psychological Bulletin, 131,* 202–223. (p. 366)

MacDonald, N. (1960). Living with schizophrenia. *Canadian Medical Association Journal, 82,* 218–221. (p. 529)

MacDonald, T. K., & Hynie, M. (2008). Ambivalence and unprotected sex: Failure to predict sexual activity and decreased condom use. *Journal of Applied Social Psychology, 38,* 1092–1107. (p. 176)

MacDonald, T. K., Zanna, M. P., & Fong, G. T. (1995). Decision making in altered states: Effects of alcohol on attitudes toward drinking and driving. *Journal of Personality and Social Psychology, 68,* 973–985. (p. 102)

MacFarlane, A. (1978, February). What a baby knows. *Human Nature,* pp. 74–81. (p. 121)

Macfarlane, J. W. (1964). Perspectives on personality consistency and change from the guidance study. *Vita Humana, 7,* 115–126. (p. 140)

Machin, S., & Pekkarinen, T. (2008). Global sex differences in test score variability. *Science, 322,* 1331–1332. (p. 342)

Maciejewski, P. K., Zhang, B., Block, S. D., & Prigerson, H. G. (2007). An empirical examination of the stage theory of grief. *Journal of the American Medical Association, 297,* 722–723. (p. 158)

Mack, A., & Rock, I. (2000). *Inattentional blindness.* Cambridge, MA: MIT Press. (p. 81)

Macmillan, M., & Lena, M. L. (2010). Rehabilitating Phineas Gage. *Neuropsychological Rehabilitation, 17,* 1–18. (p. 56)

MacNeilage, P. F., & Davis, B. L. (2000). On the origin of internal structure of word forms. *Science, 288,* 527–531. (p. 320)

MacNeilage, P. F., Rogers, L. J., & Vallortigara, G. (2009, July). Origins of the left and right brain. *Scientific American,* pp. 60–67. (p. 61)

Maddi, S. R., Harvey, R. H., Khoshaba, D. M., Fazel, M., & Resurreccion, N. (2009). Hardiness training facilitates performance in college. *Journal of Positive Psychology, 4,* 566–577. (p. 371)

Maddieson, I. (1984). *Patterns of sounds.* Cambridge: Cambridge University Press. (p. 319)

Maddux, W. W., Adam, H., & Galinsky, A. D. (2010). When in Rome . . . learn why the Romand do what they do: How multicultural learning experiences facilitate creativity. *Personality and Social Psychology Bulletin, 36,* 731–741. (p. 315)

Maddux, W. W., & Galinsky, A. D. (2009). Cultural borders and mental barriers: The relationship between living abroad and creativity. *Journal of Personality and Social Psychology, 96,* 1047–1061. (p. 315)

Maes, H. H. M., Neale, M. C., & Eaves, L. J. (1997). Genetic and environmental factors in relative body weight and human adiposity. *Behavior Genetics, 27,* 325–351. (p. 362)

Maestripieri, D. (2003). Similarities in affiliation and aggression between cross-fostered rhesus macaque females and their biological mothers. *Developmental Psychobiology, 43,* 321–327. (p. 66)

Maestripieri, D. (2005). Early experience affects the intergenerational transmission of infant abuse in rhesus monkeys. *Proceedings of the National Academy of Sciences, 102,* 9726–9729. (p. 136)

Maglaty, J. (2011, April 8). When did girls start wearing pink? *Smithsonian.com.* (p. 164)

Magnusson, D. (1990). Personality research—challenges for the future. *European Journal of Personality, 4,* 1–17. (p. 539)

Maguire, E. A., Spiers, H. J., Good, C. D., Hartley, T., Frackowiak, R. S. J., & Burgess, N. (2003a). Navigation expertise and the human hippocampus: A structural brain imaging analysis. *Hippocampus, 13,* 250–259. (p. 281)

Maguire, E. A., Valentine, E. R., Wilding, J. M., & Kapur, N. (2003b). Routes to remembering: The brains behind superior memory. *Nature Neuroscience, 6,* 90–95. (pp. 277, 281)

Mahowald, M. W., & Ettinger, M. G. (1990). Things that go bump in the night: The parsomias revisted. *Journal of Clinical Neurophysiology, 7,* 119–143. (p. 93)

Maier, S. F., Watkins, L. R., & Fleshner, M. (1994). Psychoneuroimmunology: The interface between behavior, brain, and immunity. *American Psychologist, 49,* 1004–1017. (p. 394)

Major, B., Carrington, P. I., & Carnevale, P. J. D. (1984). Physical attractiveness and self-esteem: Attribution for praise from an other-sex evaluator. *Personality and Social Psychology Bulletin, 10,* 43–50. (p. 490)

Major, B., Schmidlin, A. M., & Williams, L. (1990). Gender patterns in social touch: The impact of setting and age. *Journal of Personality and Social Psychology, 58,* 634–643. (p. 165)

Malamuth, N. M. (1996). Sexually explicit media, gender differences, and evolutionary theory. *Journal of Communication, 46,* 8–31. (p. 485)

Malamuth, N. M., & Check, J. V. P. (1981). The effects of media exposure on acceptance of violence against women: A field experiment. *Journal of Research in Personality, 15,* 436–446. (p. 175)

Malamuth, N. M., Linz, D., Heavey, C. L., Barnes, G., & Acker, M. (1995). Using the confluence model of sexual aggression to predict men's conflict with women: A 10-year follow-up study. *Journal of Personality and Social Psychology, 69,* 353–369. (p. 485)

Malamuth, N. M., Sockloskie, R. J., Koss, M. P., & Tanaka, J. S. (1991). Characteristics of aggressors against women: Testing a model using a national sample of college students. *Journal of Consulting and Clinical Psychology, 59,* 670–681. (p. 485)

Maldonado-Molina, M. M., Reingle, J. M., Jennings, W. G., & Prado, G. (2011). Drinking and driving among immigrant and US-born Hispanic young adults: Results from a longitudinal and nationally representative study. *Addictive Behavior, 36,* 381–388. (p. 540)

Malkiel, B. (2004). *A random walk down Wall Street* (8th ed.). New York: Norton. (p. 311)

Malkiel, B. (2007). *A random walk down Wall Street: The time-tested strategy for successful investing (revised and updated).* New York: Norton. (p. 13)

Malle, B. F. (2006). The actor-observer asymmetry in attribution: A (surprising) meta-analysis. *Psychological Bulletin, 132,* 895–919. (p. 459)

Malle, B. F., Knobe, J. M., & Nelson, S. E. (2007). Actor-observe asymmetries in explanations of behavior: New answers to an old question. *Journal of Personality and Social Psychology, 93,* 491–514. (p. 459)

Malmquist, C. P. (1986). Children who witness parental murder: Post-traumatic aspects. *Journal of the American Academy of Child Psychiatry, 25,* 320–325. (p. 431)

Malnic, B., Hirono, J., Sato, T., & Buck, L. B. (1999). Combinatorial receptor codes for odors. *Cell, 96,* 713–723. (p. 226)

Maltby, N., Tolin, D.F., Worhunsky, P., O'Keefe, T. M., & Kiehl, K. A. (2005). Dysfunctional action monitoring hyperactivates frontal-striatal circuits in obsessive-compulsive disorder: An event-related fMRI study. *NeuroImage, 24,* 495-503. (p. 518)

Mampe, B., Friederici, A. D., Christophe, A., & Wermke, K. (2009). Newborns' cry melody is shaped by their native language. *Current Biology, 19,* 1–4. (p. 120)

Manson, J. E. (2002). Walking compared with vigorous exercise for the prevention of cardiovascular events in women. *New England Journal of Medicine, 347,* 716–725. (p. 407)

Maquet, P. (2001). The role of sleep in learning and memory. *Science, 294,* 1048–1052. (p. 95)

Maquet, P., Peters, J-M., Aerts, J., Delfiore, G., Degueldre, C., Luxen, A., & Franck, G. (1996). Functional neuroanatomy of human rapid-eye-movement sleep and dreaming. *Nature, 383,* 163–166. (p. 95)

Mar, R. A., & Oatley, K. (2008). The function of fiction is the abstraction and simulation of social experience. *Perspectives on Psychological Science, 3,* 173–192. (p. 263)

Marcus, B., Machilek, F., & Schütz, A. (2006). Personality in cyberspace: Personal web sites as media for personality expressions and impressions. *Journal of Personality and Social Psychology, 90,* 1014–1031. (p. 442)

Maren, S. (2007). The threatened brain. *Science, 317,* 1043–1044. (p. 518)

Margolis, M. L. (2000). Brahms' lullaby revisited: Did the composer have obstructive sleep apnea? *Chest, 118,* 210–213. (p. 92)

Marinak, B. A., & Gambrell, L. B. (2008). Intrinsic motivation and rewards: What sustains young children's engagement with text? *Literacy Research and Instruction, 47,* 9–26. (p. 260)

Markovizky, G., & Samid, Y. (2008). The process of immigrant adjustment: The role of time in determining psychological adjustment. *Journal of Cross-Cultural Psychology, 39,* 782–798. (p. 391)

Markowitsch, H. J. (1995). Which brain regions are critically involved in the retrieval of old episodic memory? *Brain Research Reviews, 21,* 117–127. (p. 281)

Marks, I., & Cavanagh, K. (2009). Computer-aided psychological treatments: Evolving issues. *Annual Review of Clinical Psychology, 5,* 121–141. (p. 557)

Markus, H. R., & Kitayama, S. (1991). Culture and the self: Implications for cognition, emotion, and motivation. *Psychological Review, 98,* 224–253. (pp. 326, 398, 451)

Markus, H. R., & Nurius, P. (1986). Possible selves. *American Psychologist, 41,* 954–969. (p. 447)

Markus, H. R., Uchida, Y., Omoregie, H., Townsend, S. S. M., & Kitayama, S. (2006). Going for the gold: Models of agency in Japanese and American contexts. *Psychological Science, 17,* 103–112. (p. 452)

Marley, J., & Bulia, S. (2001). Crimes against people with mental illness: Types, perpetrators and influencing factors. *Social Work, 46,* 115–124. (p. 511)

Marmot, M. G., Bosma, H., Hemingway, H., Brunner, E., & Stansfeld, S. (1997). Contribution to job control and other risk factors to social variations in coronary heart disease incidents. *Lancet, 350,* 235–239. (p. 402)

Marsh, A. A., Elfenbein, H. A., & Ambady, N. (2003). Nonverbal "accents": Cultural differences in facial expressions of emotion. *Psychological Science, 14,* 373–376. (p. 383)

Marsh, H. W., & Craven, R. G. (2006). Reciprocal effects of self-concept and performance from a multidimensional perspective: Beyond seductive pleasure and unidimensional perspectives. *Perspectives on Psychological Science, 1,* 133–163. (p. 447)

Marsh, H. W., & Parker, J. W. (1984). Determinants of student self-concept: Is it better to be a relatively large fish in a small pond even if you don't learn to swim as well? *Journal of Personality and Social Psychology, 47,* 213–231. (p. 417)

Marshall, M. J. (2002). *Why spanking doesn't work.* Springville, UT: Bonneville Books. (p. 251)

Marshall, R. D., Bryant, R. A., Amsel, L., Suh, E. J., Cook, J. M., & Neria, Y. (2007). The psychology of ongoing threat: Relative risk appraisal, the September 11 attacks, and terrorism-related fears. *American Psychologist, 62,* 304–316. (p. 309)

Marteau, T. M. (1989). Framing of information: Its influences upon decisions of doctors and patients. *British Journal of Social Psychology, 28,* 89–94. (p. 312)

Marti, M. W., Robier, D. M., & Baron, R. S. (2000). Right before our eyes: The failure to recognize non-prototypical forms of prejudice. *Group Processes and Intergroup Relations, 3,* 403–418. 409–416. (p. 306)

Martin, C. K., Anton, S. D., Walden, H., Arnett, C., Greenway, F. L., & Williamson, D. A. (2007). Slower eating rate reduces the food intake of men, but not women: Implications for behavioural weight control. *Behaviour Research and Therapy, 45,* 2349–2359. (p. 363)

Martin, C. L., & Ruble, D. (2004). Children's search for gender cues. *Current Directions in Psychological Science, 13,* 67–70. (p. 170)

Martin, C. L., Ruble, D. N., & Szkrybalo, J. (2002). Cognitive theories of early gender development. *Psychological Bulletin, 128,* 903–933. (p. 170)

Martin, R. J., White, B. D., & Hulsey, M. G. (1991). The regulation of body weight. *American Scientist, 79,* 528–541. (p. 358)

Martin, R. M., Goodall, S. H., Gunnell, D., & Smith, G. D. (2007). Breast feeding in infancy and social mobility: 60-year follow-up of the Boyd Orr cohort. *Archives of Disease in Childhood, 92,* 317–321. (p. 22)

Martin, S. J., Kelly, I. W., & Saklofske, D. H. (1992). Suicide and lunar cycles: A critical review over 28 years. *Psychological Reports, 71,* 787–795. (p. 539)

Martino, S. C., Collins, R. L., Kanouse, D. E., Elliott, M., & Berry, S. H. (2005). Social cognitive processes mediating the relationship between exposure to television's sexual content and adolescents' sexual behavior. *Journal of Personality and Social Psychology, 89,* 914–924. (p. 177)

Martins, Y., Preti, G., Crabtree, C. R., & Wysocki, C. J. (2005). Preference for human body odors is influenced by gender and sexual orientation. *Psychological Science, 16,* 694–701. (p. 181)

Marx, D. M., Ko, S. J., & Friedman, R. A. (2009). "Obama effect": How a salient role model reduces race-based performance differences. *Journal of Experimental Social Psychology, 45,* 953–956. (p. 346)

Masicampo, E. J., & Baumeister, R. F. (2008). Toward a physiology of dual-process reasoning and judgment: Lemonade, willpower, and the expensive rule-based analysis. *Psychological Science, 19,* 255–260. (p. 404)

Maslow, A. H. (1970). *Motivation and personality* (2nd ed.). New York: Harper & Row. (pp. 355, 433, B-1)

Maslow, A. H. (1971). *The farther reaches of human nature.* New York: Viking Press. (p. 355)

Mason, A. E., Sbarra, D. A., & Mehl, M. R. (2010). Thin-slicing divorce: Thirty seconds of information predict changes in psychological adjustment over 90 days. *Psychological Science, 21,* 1420–1422. (p. 381)

Mason, C., & Kandel, E. R. (1991). Central visual pathways. In E. R. Kandel, J. H. Schwartz, & T. M. Jessell (Eds.), *Principles of neural science* (3rd ed.). New York: Elsevier. (p. 41)

Mason, H. (2003, March 25). Wake up, sleepy teen. *Gallup Poll Tuesday Briefing* (www.gallup.com). (p. 90)

Mason, H. (2003, September 2). Americans, Britons at odds on animal testing. *Gallup Poll News Service* (www.gallup.com). (p. 27)

Mason, H. (2005, January 25). Who dreams, perchance to sleep? *Gallup Poll News Service* (www.gallup.com). (pp. 89, 90)

Masse, L. C., & Tremblay, R. E. (1997). Behavior of boys in kindergarten and the onset of substance use during adolescence. *Archives of General Psychiatry, 54,* 62–68. (p. 110)

Massimini, M., Ferrarelli, F., Huber, R., Esser, S. K., Singh, H., & Tononi, G. (2005). Breakdown of cortical effective connectivity during sleep. *Science, 309,* 2228–2232. (p. 84)

Mast, M. S., & Hall, J. A. (2006). Women's advantage at remembering others' appearance: A systematic look at the why and when of a gender difference. *Personality and Social Psychology Bulletin, 32,* 353–364. (p. 490)

Masten, A. S. (2001). Ordinary magic: Resilience processes in development. *American Psychologist, 56,* 227–238. (p. 136)

Masters, K. S. (2010). The role of religion in therapy: Time for psychologists to have a little faith? *Cognitive and Behavioral Practice, 17,* 393–400. (p. 566)

Masters, W. H., & Johnson, V. E. (1966). *Human sexual response.* Boston: Little, Brown. (p. 173)

Mastroianni, G. R. (2002). Milgram and the Holocaust: A reexamination. *Journal of Theoretical and Philosophical Psychology, 22,* 158–173. (p. 469)

Mastroianni, G. R., & Reed, G. (2006). Apples, barrels, and Abu Ghraib. *Sociological Focus, 39,* 239–250. (p. 462)

Masuda, T., Ellsworth, P. C., Mesquita, B., Leu, J., Tanida, S., & Van de Veerdonk, E. (2008). Placing the face in context: Cultural differences in the perception of facial emotion. *Journal of Personality and Social Psychology, 94,* 365–381. (p. 383)

Mataix-Cols, D., Rosario-Campos, M. C., & Leckman, J. F. (2005). A multidimensional model of obsessive-compulsive disorder. *American Journal of Psychiatry, 162,* 228–238. (p. 518)

Mataix-Cols, D., Wooderson, S., Lawrence, N., Brammer, M. J., Speckens, A., & Phillips, M. L. (2004). Distinct neural correlates of washing, checking, and hoarding symptom dimensions in obsessive-compulsive disorder. *Archives of General Psychiatry, 61,* 564–576. (p. 518)

Mather, M., Canli, T., English, T., Whitfield, S., Wais, P., Ochsner, K., Gabrieli, J. D. E., & Carstensen, L. L. (2004). Amygdala responses to emotionally valenced stimuli in older and younger adults. *Psychological Science, 15,* 259–263. (p. 157)

Matsumoto, D. (1994). *People: Psychology from a cultural perspective.* Pacific Grove, CA: Brooks/Cole. (p. 326)

Matsumoto, D., & Ekman, P. (1989). American-Japanese cultural differences in intensity ratings of facial expressions of emotion. *Motivation and Emotion, 13,* 143–157. (p. 383)

Matsumoto, D., Willingham, B., & Olide, A. (2009b). Sequential dynamics of culturally moderated facial expressions of emotion. *Psychological Science, 20,* 1269–1275. (p. 383)

Matthews, K. A. (2005). Psychological perspectives on the development of coronary heart disease. *American Psychologist, 60,* 783–796. (p. 400)

Matthews, R. N., Domjan, M., Ramsey, M., & Crews, D. (2007). Learning effects on sperm competition and reproductive fitness. *Psychological Science, 18,* 758–762. (p. 242)

Maurer, D., & Maurer, C. (1988). *The world of the newborn.* New York: Basic Books. (p. 121)

Mauss, I. B., Shallcross, A. J., Troy, A. S., John, O. P., Ferrer, E., Wilhelm, F. H., & Gross, J. J. (2011). Don't hide your happiness! Positive emotion dissociation, social connectedness, and psychological functioning. *Journal of Personality and Social Psychology, 100,* 738–748. (p. 412)

May, C., & Hasher, L. (1998). Synchrony effects in inhibitory control over thought and action. *Journal of Experimental Psychology: Human Perception and Performance, 24,* 363–380. (p. 83)

May, P. A., & Gossage, J. P. (2001). Estimating the prevalence of fetal alcohol syndrome: A summary. *Alcohol Research and Health, 25,* 159–167. (p. 120)

May, R. (1982). The problem of evil: An open letter to Carl Rogers. *Journal of Humanistic Psychology, 22,* 10–21. (p. 435)

Mayberg, H. S. (2006). Defining neurocircuits in depression: Strategies toward treatment selection based on neuroimaging phenotypes. *Psychiatric Annals, 36,* 259–268. (p. 573)

Mayberg, H. S. (2007). Defining the neural circuitry of depression: Toward a new nosology with therapeutic implications. *Biological Psychiatry, 61,* 729–730. (p. 573)

Mayberg, H. S. (2009). Targeted Modulation of Neural Circuits: A New Treatment Strategy for Depression. *Journal of Clinical Investigation, 119,* 717–25. (p. 573)

Mayberg, H. S., Lozano, A. M., Voon, V., McNeely, H. E., Seminowicz, D., Hamani, C., Schwalb, J. M., & Kennedy, S. H. (2005). Deep brain stimulation for treatment-resistant depression. *Neuron, 45,* 651–660. (pp. 572, 573)

Mayberry, R. I., Lock, E., & Kazmi, H. (2002). Linguistic ability and early language exposure. *Nature, 417,* 38. (p. 322)

Mayer, J. D., Salovey, P., & Caruso, D. (2002). *The Mayer-Salovey-Caruso emotional intelligence test (MSCEIT).* Toronto: Multi-Health Systems, Inc. (p. 333)

Mayer, J. D., Salovey, P., & Caruso, D. R. (2008). Emotional intelligence: New ability or eclectic traits? *American Psychologist, 63,* 503–517. (p. 333)

Mays, V. M., Cochran, S. D., & Barnes, N. W. (2007). Race, race-based discrimination, and health outcomes among African Americans. *Annual Review of Psychology, 58,* 201–225. (p. 392)

Mazure, C., Keita, G., & Blehar, M. (2002). *Summit on women and depression: Proceedings and recommendations.* Washington, DC: American Psychological Association (www.apa.org/pi/wpo/women&depression.pdf). (p. 526)

Mazzoni, G., & Memon, A. (2003). Imagination can create false autobiographical memories. *Psychological Science, 14,* 186–188. (p. 295)

Mazzoni, G., Scoboria, A., & Harvey, L. (2010). Nonbelieved memories. *Psychological Science, 21,* 1334–1340. (p. 295)

Mazzoni, G., & Vannucci, M. (2007). Hindsight bias, the misinformation effect, and false autobiographical memories. *Social Cognition, 25,* 203–220. (p. 297)

McAndrew, F. T. (2009). The interacting roles of testosterone and challenges to status in human male aggression. *Aggression and Violent Behavior, 14,* 330–335. (p. 482)

McAneny, L. (1996, September). Large majority think government conceals information about UFO's. *Gallup Poll Monthly,* pp. 23–26. (p. 296)

McBurney, D. H. (1996). *How to think like a psychologist: Critical thinking in psychology.* Upper Saddle River, NJ: Prentice-Hall. (p. 56)

McBurney, D. H., & Collings, V. B. (1984). *Introduction to sensation and perception* (2nd ed.). Englewood Cliffs, NJ: Prentice-Hall. (pp. 213, 214)

McBurney, D. H., & Gent, J. F. (1979). On the nature of taste qualities. *Psychological Bulletin, 86,* 151–167. (p. 224)

McCain, N. L., Gray, D. P., Elswick, R. K., Jr., Robins, J. W., Tuck, I., Walter, J. M., Rausch, S. M., & Ketchum, J. M. (2008). A randomized clinical trial of alternative stress management interventions in persons with HIV infection. *Journal of Consulting and Clinical Psychology, 76,* 431–441. (p. 396)

McCann, I. L., & Holmes, D. S. (1984). Influence of aerobic exercise on depression. *Journal of Personality and Social Psychology, 46,* 1142–1147. (p. 408)

McCann, U. D., Eligulashvili, V., & Ricaurte, G. A. (2001). (+−)3,4−Methylenedioxymethamphetamine ('Ecstasy')-induced serotonin neurotoxicity: Clinical studies. *Neuropsychobiology, 42,* 11–16. (p. 107)

McCarthy, P. (1986, July). Scent: The tie that binds? *Psychology Today,* pp. 6, 10. (p. 225)

McCauley, C. R. (2002). Psychological issues in understanding terrorism and the response to terrorism. In C. E. Stout (Ed.), *The psychology of terrorism* (Vol. 3). Westport, CT: Praeger/Greenwood. (p. 473)

McCauley, C. R., & Segal, M. E. (1987). Social psychology of terrorist groups. In C. Hendrick (Ed.), *Group processes and intergroup relations.* Beverly Hills, CA: Sage. (p. 473)

McClendon, B. T., & Prentice-Dunn, S. (2001). Reducing skin cancer risk: An intervention based on protection motivation theory. *Journal of Health Psychology, 6,* 321–328. (p. 460)

McClintock, M. K., & Herdt, G. (1996, December). Rethinking puberty: The development of sexual attraction. *Current Directions in Psychological Science, 5*(6), 178–183. (p. 167)

McClure, M. J., Lydon, J. E., Baccus, J. R., & Baldwin, M. W. (2010). A signal detection analysis of chronic attachment anxiety at speed dating: Being unpopular is only the first part of the problem. *Personality and Social Psychology Bulletin, 36,* 1024–1036. (p. 194)

McConkey, K. M. (1995). Hypnosis, memory, and the ethics of uncertainty. *Australian Psychologist, 30,* 1–10. (p. 97)

McConnell, A. R., Brown, C. M., Shoda, T. M., Stayton, L. E., & Martin, C. E. (2011). Friends with benefits: On the positive consequences of pet ownership. *Journal of Personality and Social Psychology, 101,* 1239–1252. (p. 406)

McConnell, R. A. (1991). National Academy of Sciences opinion on parapsychology. *Journal of the American Society for Psychical Research, 85,* 333–365. (p. 230)

McCool, G. (1999, October 26). Mirror-gazing Venezuelans top of vanity stakes. *Toronto Star* (via web.lexis-nexis.com). (p. 490)

McCrae, R. R. (2009). The five-factor model of personality traits: Consensus and controversy. In P. J. Corr & G. Matthews, Gerald (eds.). *The Cambridge handbook of personality psychology.* New York: Cambridge University Press. (p. 440)

McCrae, R. R. (2011). Personality theories for the 21st century. *Teaching of Psychology, 38,* 209–214. (p. 440)

McCrae, R. R., & Costa, P. T., Jr. (1990). *Personality in adulthood.* New York: Guilford. (p. 154)

McCrae, R. R., & Costa, P. T., Jr. (1994). The stability of personality: Observations and evaluations. *Current Directions in Psychological Science, 3,* 173–175. (p. 441)

McCrae, R. R., Costa, P. T., Jr., Ostendorf, F., Angleitner, A., Hrebickova, M., Avia, M. D., Sanz, J., Sanchez-Bernardos, M. L., Kusdil, M. E., Woodfield, R., Saunders, P. R., & Smith, P. B. (2000). Nature over nurture: Temperament, personality, and life span development. *Journal of Personality and Social Psychology, 78,* 173–186. (p. 134)

McCrae, R. R., Scally, M., Terraccioani, A., Abecasis, G. R., & Costa, Jr., P. T. (2010). An alternative to the search for single polymorphisms: Toward molecular personality scales for the Five-Factor Model. *Journal of Personality and Social Psychology, 99,* 1014–1024. (p. 440)

McCrae, R. R., Terracciano, A., & Khoury, B. (2007). *Dolce far niente:* The positive psychology of personality stability and invariance. In A. D. Ong & M. H. Van Dulmen (Eds.), *Oxford handbook of methods in positive psychology.* New York: Oxford University Press. (p. 134)

McCrink, K., & Wynn, K. (2004). Large-number addition and subtraction by 9-month-old infants. *Psychological Science, 15,* 776–781. (p. 127)

McCullough, M. E., Hoyt, W. T., Larson, D. B., Koenig, H. G., & Thoresen, C. (2000). Religious involvement and mortality: A meta-analytic review. *Health Psychology, 19,* 211–222. (p. 411)

McCullough, M. E., & Laurenceau, J-P. (2005). Religiousness and the trajectory of self-rated health across adulthood. *Personality and Social Psychology Bulletin, 31,* 560–573. (p. 411)

McCullough, M. E., & Willoughby, B. L. B. (2009). Religion, self-regulation, and self-control: Associations, explanations, and implications. *Psychological Bulletin, 135,* 69–93. (p. 411)

McDaniel, M. A., Howard, D. C., & Einstein, G. O. (2009). The read-recite-review study strategy: Effective and portable. *Psychological Science, 20,* 516–522. (p. 29, 31, 72, 113, 159, 187, 232, 267, 301, 347, 386, 419, 453, 501, 541, 578, A-9, B-15)

McDermott, R., Tingley, D., Cowden, J., Frazzetto, G., & Johnson, D. D. P. (2009). Monoamine oxidase A gene (MAOA) predicts behavioral aggression following provocation. *Proceedings of the National Academy of Sciences, 106,* 2118–2123. (p. 482)

McEvoy, S. P., Stevenson, M. R., McCartt, A. T., Woodward, M., Hawroth, C., Palamara, P., & Ceracelli, R. (2005). Role of mobile phones in motor vehicle crashes resulting in hospital attendance: A case-crossover study. *British Medical Journal, 33,* 428. (p. 81)

McEvoy, S. P., Stevenson, M. R., & Woodward, M. (2007). The contribution of passengers versus mobile phone use to motor vehicle crashes resulting in hospital attendance by the driver. *Accident Analysis and Prevention, 39,* 1170–1176. (p. 81)

McFarland, C., & Ross, M. (1987). The relation between current impressions and memories of self and dating partners. *Psychological Bulletin, 13,* 228–238. (p. 297)

McGaugh, J. L. (1994). Quoted by B. Bower, Stress hormones hike emotional memories. *Science News, 146,* 262. (p. 283)

McGaugh, J. L. (2003). *Memory and emotion: The making of lasting memories.* New York: Columbia University Press. (p. 283)

McGhee, P. E. (1976, June). Children's appreciation of humor: A test of the cognitive congruency principle. *Child Development, 47*(2), 420–426. (p. 129)

McGowan, P. O., Sasaki, A., D'Alessio, A. C., Dymov, S., Labonté, B., Szyl, M., Turecki, G., & Meaney, M. J. (2009). Epigenetic regulation of the glucocorticoid receptor in human brain associates with childhood abuse. *Nature Neuroscience, 12,* 342–348. (p. 68)

McGrath, J. J., & Welham, J. L. (1999). Season of birth and schizophrenia: A systematic review and meta-analysis of data from the Southern hemisphere. *Schizophrenia Research, 35,* 237–242. (p. 531)

McGrath, J. J., Welham, J., & Pemberton, M. (1995). Month of birth, hemisphere of birth and schizophrenia. *British Journal of Psychiatry, 167,* 783–785. (p. 531)

McGue, M. (2010). The end of behavioral genetics? *Behavioral Genetics, 40,* 284–296. (p. 68)

McGue, M., & Bouchard, T. J., Jr. (1998). Genetic and environmental influences on human behavioral differences. *Annual Review of Neuroscience, 21,* 1–24. (p. 66)

McGue, M., Bouchard, T. J., Jr., Iacono, W. G., & Lykken, D. T. (1993). Behavioral genetics of cognitive ability: A life-span perspective. In R. Plomin & G. E. McClearn (Eds.), *Nature, nurture and psychology.* Washington, DC: American Psychological Association. (p. 340)

McGuire, W. J. (1986). The myth of massive media impact: Savings and salvagings. In G. Comstock (Ed.), *Public communication and behavior.* Orlando, FL: Academic Press. (p. 265)

McGurk, H., & MacDonald, J. (1976). Hearing lips and seeing voices. *Nature, 264,* 746–748. (p. 228)

McHugh, P. R. (1995a). Witches, multiple personalities, and other psychiatric artifacts. *Nature Medicine, 1*(2), 110–114. (p. 534)

McHugh, P. R. (1995b). Resolved: Multiple personality disorder is an individually and socially created artifact. *Journal of the American Academy of Child and Adolescent Psychiatry, 34,* 957–959. (p. 535)

McKay, J. (2000). Building self-esteem in children. In M. McKay & P. Fanning (eds.), *Self-esteem.* New York: New Harbinger/St. Martins. (p. 447)

McKellar, J., Stewart, E., & Humphreys, K. (2003). Alcoholics Anonymous involvement and positive alcohol-related outcomes: Cause, consequence, or just a correlate? A prospective 2-year study of 2,319 alcohol-dependent men. *Journal of Consulting and Clinical Psychology, 71,* 302–308. (p. 558)

McKenna, K. Y. A., & Bargh, J. A. (1998). Coming out in the age of the Internet: Identity "demarginalization" through virtual group participation. *Journal of Personality and Social Psychology, 75,* 681–694. (p. 488)

McKenna, K. Y. A., & Bargh, J. A. (2000). Plan 9 from cyberspace: The implications of the Internet for personality and social psychology. *Personality and Social Psychology Review, 4,* 57–75. (p. 488)

McKenna, K. Y. A., Green, A. S., & Gleason, M. E. J. (2002). What's the big attraction? Relationship formation on the Internet. *Journal of Social Issues, 58,* 9–31. (p. 488)

McKone, E., Kanwisher, N., & Duchaine, B. C. (2007). Can generic expertise explain special processing for faces? *Trends in Cognitive Sciences, 11,* 8–15. (p. 204)

McLaughlin, M. (2010, October 2). JK Rowling: Depression, the 'terrible place that allowed me to come back stronger.' *The Scotsman* (www.scotsman.com). (p. 521)

McLean, C. P., & Anderson, E. R. (2009). Brave men and timid women? A review of the gender differences in fear and anxiety. *Clinical Psychology Review, 29,* 496–505. (p. 513)

McMurray, B. (2007). Defusing the childhood vocabulary explosion. *Science, 317,* 631. (p. 319)

McMurray, C. (2004, January 13). U.S., Canada, Britain: Who's getting in shape? *Gallup Poll Tuesday Briefing* (www.gallup.com). (p. 408)

McNally, R. J. (1999). EMDR and Mesmerism: A comparative historical analysis. *Journal of Anxiety Disorders, 13,* 225–236. (p. 564)

McNally, R. J. (2003). *Remembering trauma.* Cambridge, MA: Harvard University Press. (pp. 299, 516)

McNally, R. J. (2007). Betrayal trauma theory: A critical appraisal. *Memory, 15,* 280–294. (p. 299)

McNeil, B. J., Pauker, S. G., & Tversky, A. (1988). On the framing of medical decisions. In D. E. Bell, H. Raiffa, & A. Tversky (Eds.), *Decision making: Descriptive, normative, and prescriptive interactions.* New York: Cambridge University Press. (p. 312)

McWhorter, J. (2012, April 23). Talking with your fingers. *New York Times* (www.nytimes.com). (p. 367)

Mead, G. E., Morley, W., Campbell, P., Greig, C. A., McMurdo, M., & Lawlor, D. A. (2010). Exercise for depression. *Cochrance Database Systematic Reviews,* Issue 3. Art. No.: CD004366. (p. 408)

Meador, B. D., & Rogers, C. R. (1984). Person-centered therapy. In R. J. Corsini (Ed.), *Current psychotherapies* (3rd ed.). Itasca, IL: Peacock. (p. 550)

Medical Institute for Sexual Health. (1994, April). Condoms ineffective against human papilloma virus. *Sexual Health Update,* p. 2. (p. 174)

Mednick, S. A., Huttunen, M. O., & Machon, R. A. (1994). Prenatal influenza infections and adult schizophrenia. *Schizophrenia Bulletin, 20,* 263–267. (p. 531)

Mehl, M. R., Gosling, S. D., & Pennebaker, J. W. (2006). Personality in its natural habitat: Manifestations and implicit folk theories of personality in daily life. *Journal of Personality and Social Psychology, 90,* 862–877. (p. 442)

Mehl, M. R., & Pennebaker, J. W. (2003). The sounds of social life: A psychometric analysis of students' daily social environments and natural conversations. *Journal of Personality and Social Psychology, 84,* 857–870. (p. 19)

Mehl, M. R., Vazire, S., Holleran, S. E., & Clark, C. S. (2010). Eavesdropping on happiness: Well-being is related to having less small talk and more substantive conversations. *Psychological Science, 21,* 539–541. (p. 418)

Mehta, M. R. (2007). Cortico-hippocampal interaction during up-down states and memory consolidation. *Nature Neuroscience, 10,* 13–15. (p. 282)

Meichenbaum, D. (1977). *Cognitive-behavior modification: An integrative approach.* New York; Plenum Press. (p. 556)

Meichenbaum, D. (1985). *Stress inoculation training.* New York: Pergamon. (p. 556)

Meijer, E. H., & Verschuere, B. (2010). The polygraph and the detection of deception. *Journal of Forensic Psychology Practice, 10,* 525–538. (p. 379)

Meltzoff, A. N. (1988). Infant imitation after a 1-week delay: Long-term memory for novel acts and multiple stimuli. *Developmental Psychology, 24,* 470–476. (p. 262)

Meltzoff, A. N., Kuhl, P. K., Movellan, J., & Sejnowski, T. J. (2009). Foundations for a new science of learning. *Science, 325,* 284–288. (pp. 262, 320)

Meltzoff, A. N., & Moore, M. K. (1989). Imitation in newborn infants: Exploring the range of gestures imitated and the underlying mechanisms. *Developmental Psychology, 25,* 954–962. (pp. 262, 265)

Meltzoff, A. N., & Moore, M. K. (1997). Explaining facial imitation: A theoretical model. *Early Development and Parenting, 6,* 179–192. (pp. 262, 265)

Melzack, R. (1990, February). The tragedy of needless pain. *Scientific American*, pp. 27–33. (p. 101)

Melzack, R. (1992, April). Phantom limbs. *Scientific American*, pp. 120–126. (p. 222)

Melzack, R. (1998, February). Quoted in Phantom limbs. *Discover*, p. 20. (p. 222)

Melzack, R. (2005). Evolution of the neuromatrix theory of pain. *Pain Practice, 5*, 85–94. (p. 222)

Melzack, R., & Wall, P. D. (1965). Pain mechanisms: A new theory. *Science, 150*, 971–979. (p. 221)

Melzack, R., & Wall, P. D. (1983). *The challenge of pain*. New York: Basic Books. (p. 221)

Mendes, E. (2010a, February 9). Six in 10 overweight or obese in U.S., more in '09 than in '08. www.gallup.com. (p. 361)

Mendes, E. (2010b, June 2). U.S. exercise levels up, but demographic differences remain. www.gallup.com. (p. 409)

Mendle, J., Turkheimer, E., & Emery, R. E. (2007). Detrimental psychological outcomes associated with early pubertal timing in adolescent girls. *Developmental Review, 27*, 151–171. (p. 140)

Mendolia, M., & Kleck, R. E. (1993). Effects of talking about a stressful event on arousal: Does what we talk about make a difference? *Journal of Personality and Social Psychology, 64*, 283–292. (p. 406)

Merari, A. (2002). Explaining suicidal terrorism: Theories versus empirical evidence. Invited address to the American Psychological Association. (p. 473)

Meriac, J. P., Hoffman, B. J., Woehr, D. J., & Fleisher, M. S. (2008). Further evidence for the validity of assessment center dimensions: A meta-analysis of the incremental criterion-related validity of dimension ratings. *Journal of Applied Psychology, 93*, 1042–1052. (p. 445)

Merskey, H. (1992). The manufacture of personalities: The production of multiple personality disorder. *British Journal of Psychiatry, 160*, 327–340. (p. 534)

Mesch, G. (2001). Social relationships and Internet use among adolescents in Israel. *Social Science Quarterly, 82*, 329–340. (p. 368)

Mesoudi, A. (2009). How cultural evolutionary theory can inform social psychology and vice versa. *Psychological Review, 116*, 929–952. (p. 464)

Messias, E., Eaton, W. W., Grooms, A. N. (2011). Economic grand rounds: Income inequality and depression prevalence across the United States: An ecological study. *Psychiatric Services, 62*, 710–712. (p. 484)

Messinis, L., Kyprianidou, A., Malefaki, S., & Papathanasopoulos, P. (2006). Neuropsychological deficits in long-term frequent cannabis users. *Neurology, 66*, 737–739. (p. 108)

Mestel, R. (1997, April 26). Get real, Siggi. *New Scientist* (www.newscientist.com/ns/970426/siggi.html). (p. 94)

Meston, C. M., & Buss, D. M. (2007). Why humans have sex. *Archives of Sexual Behavior, 36*, 477–507. (p. 175)

Metcalfe, J. (1986). Premonitions of *insight* predict impending error. *Journal of Experimental Psychology: Learning, Memory, and Cognition, 12*, 623–634. (p. 307)

Metcalfe, J. (1998). Cognitive optimism: Self-deception or memory-based processing heuristics. *Personality and Social Psychology Review, 2*, 100–110. (p. 311)

Metzler, D. K., Jensvold, M. L., Fouts, D. H., & Fouts, R. S. (2010, Spring). Vocabulary growth in adult cross-fostered chimpanzees. *Friends of Washoe*, pp. 13–16. (p. 324)

Meyer-Bahlburg, H. F. L. (1995). Psychoneuroendocrinology and sexual pleasure: The aspect of sexual orientation. In P. R. Abramson & S. D. Pinkerton (Eds.), *Sexual nature/sexual culture*. Chicago: University of Chicago Press. (p. 181)

Meyerbroëker, K., & Emmelkamp, P. M. (2010). Virtual reality exposure therapy in anxiety disorders: A systematic review of process-and-outcome studies. *Depression and Anxiety, 27*, 933–944. (p. 552)

Mezulis, A. M., Abramson, L. Y., Hyde, J. S., & Hankin, B. L. (2004). Is there a universal positivity bias in attributions? A meta-analytic review of individual, developmental, and cultural differences in the self-serving attributional bias. *Psychological Bulletin, 130*, 711–747. (p. 448)

Michaels, J. W., Bloomel, J. M., Brocato, R. M., Linkous, R. A., & Rowe, J. S. (1982). Social facilitation and inhibition in a natural setting. *Replications in Social Psychology, 2*, 21–24. (p. 471)

Middlebrooks, J. C., & Green, D. M. (1991). Sound localization by human listeners. *Annual Review of Psychology, 42*, 135–159. (p. 219)

Miers, R. (2009, Spring). Calum's road. *Scottish Life*, pp. 36–39, 75. (p. 370)

Mikulincer, M., & Shaver, P. R. (2001). Attachment theory and intergroup bias: Evidence that priming the secure base schema attenuates negative reactions to out-groups. *Journal of Personality and Social Psychology, 81*, 97–115. (p. 479)

Milan, R. J., Jr., & Kilmann, P. R. (1987). Interpersonal factors in premarital contraception. *Journal of Sex Research, 23*, 289–321. (p. 176)

Miles, D. R., & Carey, G. (1997). Genetic and environmental architecture of human aggression. *Journal of Personality and Social Psychology, 72*, 207–217. (p. 481)

Milgram, S. (1963). Behavioral study of obedience. *Journal of Abnormal & Social Psychology, 67*(4), 371–378. (p. 467)

Milgram, S. (1974). *Obedience to authority*. New York: Harper & Row. (pp. 467, 468, 470)

Miller, G. (2004). Axel, Buck share award for deciphering how the nose knows. *Science, 306*, 207. (p. 226)

Miller, G. (2005). The dark side of glia. *Science, 308*, 778–781. (p. 37)

Miller, G. (2008). Tackling alcoholism with drugs. *Science, 320*, 168–170. (p. 110)

Miller, G. (2012). Drone wars. *Science, 336*, 842–843. (p. 469)

Miller, G., & Holden, C. (2010). Proposed revisions to psychiatry's canon unveiled. *Science, 327*, 770–771. (p. 509)

Miller, G., Tybur, J. M., & Jordan, B. D. (2007). Ovulatory cycle effects on tip earnings by lap dancers: Economic evidence for human estrus? *Evolution and Human Behavior, 28*, 375–381. (p. 172)

Miller, G. A. (1956). The magical number seven, plus or minus two: Some limits on our capacity for processing information. *Psychological Review, 63*, 81–97. (p. 276)

Miller, G. E., & Blackwell, E. (2006). Turning up the heat: Inflammation as a mechanism linking chronic stress, depression, and heart disease. *Current Directions in Psychological Science, 15*, 269–272. (p. 400)

Miller, H. C., Pattison, K. F., DeWall, C. N., Rayburn-Reeves, R., & Zentall, T. R. (2010). Self-control without a "self"? Common self-control processes in humans and dogs. *Psychological Science, 21*, 534–538. (p. 404)

Miller, J. G., & Bersoff, D. M. (1995). Development in the context of everyday family relationships: Culture, interpersonal morality and adaptation. In M. Killen & D. Hart (Eds.), *Morality in everyday life: A developmental perspective*. New York: Cambridge University Press. (p. 142)

Miller, K. I., & Monge, P. R. (1986). Participation, satisfaction, and productivity: A meta-analytic review. *Academy of Management Journal, 29*, 727–753. (p. 403)

Miller, L. K. (1999). The Savant Syndrome: Intellectual impairment and exceptional skill. *Psychological Bulletin, 125*, 31–46. (p. 330)

Miller, N. E. (1985, February). Rx: Biofeedback. *Psychology Today*, pp. 54–59. (p. 409)

Miller, P. A., Eisenberg, N., Fabes, R. A., & Shell, R. (1996). Relations of moral reasoning and vicarious emotion to young children's prosocial behavior toward peers and adults. *Developmental Psychology, 32*, 210–219. (p. 143)

Miller, P. J. O., Aoki, K., Rendell, L. E., & Amano, M. (2008). Stereotypical resting behavior of the sperm whale. *Current Biology, 18*, R21–R23. (p. 83)

Miller, S. D., Blackburn, T., Scholes, G., White, G. L., & Mamalis, N. (1991). Optical differences in multiple personality disorder: A second look. *Journal of Nervous and Mental Disease, 179*, 132–135. (p. 535)

Miller, S. L., & Maner, J. K. (2010). Scent of a woman: Men's testosterone responses to olfactory ovulation cues. *Psychological Science, 21*, 276–283. (p. 172)

Miller, S. L., & Maner, J. K. (2011). Ovulation as a male mating prime: Subtle signs of women's fertility influence men's mating cognition and behavior. *Journal of Personality and Social Psychology, 100,* 295–308. (p. 172)

Milner, A. D., & Goodale, M. A. (2008). Two visual systems re-viewed. *Neuropsychologia, 46,* 774–785. (p. 79)

Milyavskaya, M., Gingras, I., Mageau, G. A., Koestner, R., Gagnon, H., Fang, J., & Bolché, J. (2009). Balance across contexts: Importance of balanced need satisfaction across various life domains. *Personality and Social Psychology Bulletin, 35,* 1031–1045. (p. 364)

Mineka, S. (1985). The frightful complexity of the origins of fears. In F. R. Brush & J. B. Overmier (Eds.), *Affect, conditioning and cognition: Essays on the determinants of behavior.* Hillsdale, NJ: Erlbaum. (p. 517)

Mineka, S. (2002). Animal models of clinical psychology. In N. Smelser & P. Baltes (Eds.), *International encyclopedia of the social and behavioral sciences.* Oxford, England: Elsevier Science. (p. 517)

Mineka, S., & Oehlberg, K. (2008). The relevance of recent developments in classical conditioning to understanding the etiology and maintenance of anxiety disorders. *Acta Psychologica, 127,* 567–580. (p. 516)

Mineka, S., & Zinbarg, R. (1996). Conditioning and ethological models of anxiety disorders: Stress-in-dynamic-context anxiety models. In D. Hope (Ed.), *Perspectives on anxiety, panic, and fear* (Nebraska Symposium on Motivation). Lincoln: University of Nebraska Press. (pp. 518, 576)

Minsky, M. (1986). *The society of mind.* New York: Simon & Schuster. (pp. 46, 78)

Mischel, W. (1968). *Personality and assessment.* New York: Wiley. (p. 442)

Mischel, W. (1981). Current issues and challenges in personality. In L. T. Benjamin, Jr. (Ed.), *The G. Stanley Hall Lecture Series* (Vol. 1). Washington, DC: American Psychological Association. (p. 445)

Mischel, W. (2009). From *Personality and Assessment* (1968) to personality science. *Journal of Research in Personality, 43,* 282–290. (p. 442)

Mischel, W., Shoda, Y., & Peake, P. K. (1988). The nature of adolescent competencies predicted by preschool delay of gratification. *Journal of Personality and Social Psychology, 54,* 687–696. (p. 143)

Mischel, W., Shoda, Y., & Rodriguez, M. L. (1989). Delay of gratification in children. *Science, 244,* 933–938. (pp. 143, 249)

Miserandino, M. (1991). Memory and the seven dwarfs. *Teaching of Psychology, 18,* 169–171. (p. 285)

Mishkin, M. (1982). A memory system in the monkey. *Philosophical Transactions of the Royal Society of London: Biological Sciences, 298,* 83–95. (p. 282)

Mishkin, M., Suzuki, W. A., Gadian, D. G., & Vargha-Khadem, F. (1997). Hierarchical organization of cognitive memory. *Philosophical Transactions of the Royal Society of London: Biological Sciences, 352,* 1461–1467. (p. 282)

Mishra, A., & Mishra, H. (2010). Border bias: The belief that state borders can protect against disasters. *Psychological Science, 21,* 1582–1586. (p. 327)

Mita, T. H., Dermer, M., & Knight, J. (1977). Reversed facial images and the mere-exposure hypothesis. *Journal of Personality and Social Psychology, 35,* 597–601. (p. 488)

Mitani, J. C., Watts, D. P., & Amsler, S. J. (2010). Lethal intergroup aggression leads to territorial expansion in wild chimpanzees. *Current Biology, 20,* R507–R509. (p. 317)

Mitchell, D. B. (2006). Nonconscious priming after 17 years: Invulnerable implicit memory? *Psychological Science, 17,* 925–929. (p. 272)

Mitchell, J. P. (2009). Social psychology as a natural kind. *Cell, 13,* 246–251. (p. 447)

Mitchell, K. J., & Porteous, D. J. (2011). Rethinking the genetic architecture of schizophrenia. *Psychological Medicine, 41,* 19–32. (p. 532)

Mitte, K. (2005). Meta-analysis of cognitive-behavioral treatments for generalized anxiety disorder: A comparison with pharmacotherapy. *Psychological Bulletin, 131,* 785–795. (p. 557)

Mitte, K. (2008). Memory bias for threatening information in anxiety and anxiety disorders: A meta-analytic review. *Psychological Bulletin, 134,* 886–911. (p. 513)

Mobbs, D., Yu, R., Meyer, M., Passamonti, L., Seymour, B., Calder, A. J., Schweizer, S., Frith, C. D., & Dalgeish, T. (2009). A key role for similarity in vicarious reward. *Science, 324,* 900. (p. 261)

Moffitt, T. E., & 12 others. (2011). A gradient of childhood self-control predicts health, wealth, and public safety. *Proceedings of the National Academy of Sciences, 108,* 2693–2698. (p. 158)

Moffitt, T. E., Caspi, A., Harrington, H., & Milne, B. J. (2002). Males on the life-course-persistent and adolescence-limited antisocial pathways: Follow-up at age 26 years. *Development and Psychopathology, 14,* 179–207. (p. 159)

Moffitt, T. E., Harrington, H., Caspi, A., Kim-Cohen, J., Goldberg, D., Gregory, A. M., & Poulton, R. (2007b). Depression and generalized anxiety disorder: Cumulative and sequential comorbidity in a birth cohort followed prospectively to age 32 years. *Archives of General Psychiatry, 64,* 651–660. (p. 513)

Moghaddam, F. M. (2005). The staircase to terrorism: A psychological exploration. *American Psychologist, 60,* 161–169. (p. 473)

Mohr, H., Pritchard, J., & Lush, T. (2010, May 29). BP has been good at downplaying disaster. *Associated Press.* (p. 311)

Moises, H. W., Zoega, T., & Gottesman, I. I. (2002, July 3). The glial growth factors deficiency and synaptic destabilization hypothesis of schizophrenia. *BMC Psychiatry, 2*(8) (www.biomedcentral.com/1471–244X/2/8). (p. 532)

Möller, I., & Krahé, B. A. (2008). Exposure to violence video games and aggression in German adolescents: A longitudinal analysis. *Aggressive Behavior, 34,* 1–14. (p. 486)

Mondloch, C. J., Lewis, T. L., Budreau, D. R., Maurer, D., Dannemiller, J. L., Stephens, B. R., & Kleiner-Gathercoal, K. A. (1999). Face perception during early infancy. *Psychological Science, 10,* 419–422. (p. 121)

Money, J. (1987). Sin, sickness, or status? Homosexual gender identity and psychoneuroendocrinology. *American Psychologist, 42,* 384–399. (p. 181)

Money, J., Berlin, F. S., Falck, A., & Stein, M. (1983). *Antiandrogenic and counseling treatment of sex offenders.* Baltimore: Department of Psychiatry and Behavioral Sciences, The Johns Hopkins University School of Medicine. (p. 172)

Monroe, S. M., & Reid, M. W. (2009). Life stress and major depression. *Currents Directions in Psychological Science, 18,* 68–72. (p. 522)

Mooallem, J. (2009, February 19). Rescue flight. *New York Times Magazine* (www.nytimes.com). (p. 133)

Mook, D. G. (1983). In defense of external invalidity. *American Psychologist, 38,* 379–387. (p. 26)

Moorcroft, W. H. (2003). *Understanding sleep and dreaming.* New York: Kluwer/Plenum. (pp. 84, 95)

Moore, D. W. (2004, December 17). Sweet dreams go with a good night's sleep. *Gallup News Service* (www.gallup.com). (p. 87)

Moore, D. W. (2005, June 16). Three in four Americans believe in paranormal. *Gallup New Service* (www.gallup.com). (p. 230)

Moore, D. W. (2006, February 6). Britons outdrink Canadians, Americans. *Gallup News Service* (poll.gallup.com). (p. 111)

Moos, R. H., & Moos, B. S. (2005). Sixteen-year changes and stable remission among treated and untreated individuals with alcohol use disorders. *Drug and Alcohol Dependence, 80,* 337–347. (p. 558)

Moos, R. H., & Moos, B. S. (2006). Participation in treatment and Alcoholics Anonymous: A 16-year follow-up of initially untreated individuals. *Journal of Clinical Psychology, 62,* 735–750. (p. 559)

Mor, N., & Winquist, J. (2002). Self-focused attention and negative affect: A meta-analysis. *Psychological Bulletin, 128,* 638–662. (p. 526)

Morales, L. (2011, May 27). U.S. adults estimate that 25% of Americans are gay or lesbian. (www.gallup.com). (p. 178)

More, H. L., Hutchinson, J. R., Collins, D. F., Weber, D. J., Aung, S. K. H., & Donelan, J. M. (2010). Scaling of sensorimotor control in terrestrial mammals. *Proceedings of the Royal Society B, 277,* 3563–3568. (p. 37)

Moreira, M. T., Smith, L. A., & Foxcroft, D. (2009). Social norms interventions to reduce alcohol misuse in university or college students. *Cochrane Database of Systematic Reviews.* 2009, Issue 3., Art. No.: CD006748. (p. 112)

Moreland, R. L., & Beach, S. R. (1992). Exposure effects in the classroom: The development of affinity among students. *Journal of Experimental Social Psychology, 28,* 255–276. (p. 488)

Moreland, R. L., & Zajonc, R. B. (1982). Exposure effects in person perception: Familiarity, similarity, and attraction. *Journal of Experimental Social Psychology, 18,* 395–415. (p. 488)

Morell, V. (1995). Zeroing in on how hormones affect the immune system. *Science, 269,* 773–775. (p. 394)

Morelli, G. A., Rogoff, B., Oppenheim, D., & Goldsmith, D. (1992). Cultural variation in infants' sleeping arrangements: Questions of independence. *Developmental Psychology, 26,* 604–613. (p. 139)

Moreno, C., Laje, G., Blanco, C., Jiang, H., Schmidt, A. B., & Olfson, M. (2007). National trends in the outpatient diagnosis and treatment of bipolar disorder in youth. *Archives of General Psychiatry, 64,* 1032–1039. (p. 521)

Morewedge, C. K., & Norton, M. I. (2009). When dreaming is believing. The (motivated) interpretation of dreams. *Journal of Personality and Social Psychology, 96,* 249–264. (p. 230)

Morey, R. A., Inan, S., Mitchell, T. V., Perkins, D. O., Lieberman, J. A., & Belger, A. (2005). Imaging frontostriatal function in ultra-high-risk, early, and chronic schizophrenia during executive processing. *Archives of General Psychiatry, 62,* 254–262. (p. 530)

Morgan, A. B., & Lilienfeld, S. O. (2000). A meta-analytic review of the relation between antisocial behavior and neuropsychological measures of executive function. *Clinical Psychology Review, 20,* 113–136. (p. 539)

Mori, K., & Mori, H. (2009). Another test of the passive facial feedback hypothesis: When you face smiles, you feel happy. *Perceptual and Motor Skills, 109,* 1–3. (p. 385)

Morris, G., Baker-Ward, L., & Bauer, P. J. (2010). What remains of that day: The survival of children's autobiographical memories across time. *Applied Cognitive Psychology, 24,* 527–544. (p. 124)

Morrison, A. R. (2003). The brain on night shift. *Cerebrum, 5*(3), 23–36. (p. 86)

Morrison, C. (2007). *What does contagious yawning tell us about the mind?* Unpublished manuscript, University of Leeds. (p. 465)

Mortensen, E. L., Michaelsen, K. F., Sanders, S. A., & Reinisch, J. M. (2002). The association between duration of breastfeeding and adult intelligence. *Journal of the American Medical Association, 287,* 2365–2371. (p. 22)

Mortensen, P. B. (1999). Effects of family history and place and season of birth on the risk of schizophrenia. *New England Journal of Medicine, 340,* 603–608. (p. 531)

Moruzzi, G., & Magoun, H. W. (1949). Brain stem reticular formation and activation of the EEG. *Electroencephalography and Clinical Neurophysiology, 1,* 455–473. (p. 49)

Moscovici, S. (1985). Social influence and conformity. In G. Lindzey & E. Aronson (Eds.), *The handbook of social psychology* (3rd ed). Hillsdale, N.J.: Erlbaum. (p. 475)

Moses, E. B., & Barlow, D. H. (2006). A new unified treatment approach for emotional disorders based on emotion science. *Current Directions in Psychological Science, 15,* 146–150. (p. 557)

Mosher, W. D., Chandra, A., & Jones, J. (2005, September 15). Sexual behavior and selected health measures: Men and women 15–44 years of age, United States, 2002. *Advance Data from Vital and Health Statistics,* No. 362, National Center for Health Statistics, Centers for Disease Control and Prevention, U.S. Department of Health and Human Services. (p. 179)

Mosing, M. A., Zietsch, B. P., Shekar, S. N., Wright, M. J., & Martin, N. G. (2009). Genetic and environmental influences on optimism and its relationship to mental and self-rated health: A study of aging twins. *Behavior Genetics, 39,* 597–604. (p. 405)

Moss, A. C., & Albery, I. P. (2009). A dual-process model of the alcohol-behavior link for social drinking. *Psychological Bulletin, 135,* 516–530. (p. 103)

Moss, A. J., Allen, K. F., Giovino, G. A., & Mills, S. L. (1992, December 2). Recent trends in adolescent smoking, smoking-update correlates, and expectations about the future. *Advance Data No. 221* (from Vital and Health Statistics of the Centers for Disease Control and Prevention). (p. 111)

Moss, H. A., & Susman, E. J. (1980). Longitudinal study of personality development. In O. G. Brim, Jr., & J. Kagan (Eds.), *Constancy and change in human development.* Cambridge, MA: Harvard University Press. (p. 158)

Motivala, S. J., & Irwin, M. R. (2007). Sleep and immunity: Cytokine pathways linking sleep and health outcomes. *Current Directions in Psychological Science, 16,* 21–25. (p. 90)

Moyer, K. E. (1983). The physiology of motivation: Aggression as a model. In C. J. Scheier & A. M. Rogers (Eds.), *G. Stanley Hall Lecture Series* (Vol. 3). Washington, DC: American Psychological Association. (p. 482)

Mroczek, D. K., & Kolarz, D. M. (1998). The effect of age on positive and negative affect: A developmental perspective on happiness. *Journal of Personality and Social Psychology, 75,* 1333–1349. (p. 154)

Muhlnickel, W. (1998). Reorganization of auditory cortex in tinnitus. *Proceedings of the National Academy of Sciences, 95,* 10340–10343. (p. 56)

Mukamel, R., Ekstrom, A. D., Kaplan, J., Iacoboni, M., & Fried, I. (2010). Single-neuron responses in humans during execution and observation of actions. *Current Biology, 20,* 750–756. (p. 262)

Mulcahy, N. J., & Call, J. (2006). Apes save tools for future use. *Science, 312,* 1038–1040. (p. 317)

Muller, J. E., Mittleman, M. A., Maclure, M., Sherwood, J. B., & Tofler, G. H. (1996). Triggering myocardial infarction by sexual activity. *Journal of the American Medical Association, 275,* 1405–1409. (p. 173)

Muller, J. E., & Verier, R. L. (1996). Triggering of sudden death—Lessons from an earthquake. *New England Journal of Medicine, 334,* 461. (p. 391)

Mullin, C. R., & Linz, D. (1995). Desensitization and resensitization to violence against women: Effects of exposure to sexually violent films on judgments of domestic violence victims. *Journal of Personality and Social Psychology, 69,* 449–459. (p. 265)

Mulrow, C. D. (1999, March). Treatment of depression—newer pharmacotherapies, summary. *Evidence Report/Technology Assessment, 7.* Agency for Health Care Policy and Research, Rockville, MD. (http://www.ahrq.gov/clinic/deprsumm.htm). (p. 570)

Munsey, C. (2010, June). Medicine or menace? Psychologists' research can inform the growing debate over legalizing marijuana. *Monitor on Psychology,* pp. 50–55. (p. 108)

Murphy, G. E., & Wetzel, R. D. (1990). The lifetime risk of suicide in alcoholism. *Archives of General Psychiatry, 47,* 383–392. (p. 524)

Murphy, K. (2008, October 28). 21-year study of children set to begin. *New York Times* (www.nytimes.com). (p. 130)

Murphy, K. R., & Cleveland, J. N. (1995). *Understanding performance appraisal: Social, organizational, and goal-based perspectives.* Thousand Oaks, CA: Sage. (p. B-7)

Murphy, S. T., Monahan, J. L., & Zajonc, R. B. (1995). Additivity of nonconscious affect: Combined effects of priming and exposure. *Journal of Personality and Social Psychology, 69,* 589–602. (p. 374)

Murray, B. (1998, May). Psychology is key to airline safety at Boeing. *The APA Monitor,* p. 36. (p. B-14)

Murray, C. J., & Lopez, A. D. (Eds.). (1996). *The global burden of disease: A comprehensive assessment of mortality and disability from diseases, injuries, and risk factors in 1990 and projected to 2020.* Cambridge, MA: Harvard University Press. (p. 505)

Murray, H. (1938). *Explorations in personality.* New York: Oxford University Press. (p. 370)

Murray, H. A., & Wheeler, D. R. (1937). A note on the possible clairvoyance of dreams. *Journal of Psychology, 3,* 309–313. (pp. 17, 230)

Murray, J. P. (2008). Media violence: The effects are both real and strong. *American Behavioral Scientist, 51,* 1212–1230. (p. 265)

Murray, R., Jones, P., O'Callaghan, E., Takei, N., & Sham, P. (1992). Genes, viruses, and neurodevelopmental schizophrenia. *Journal of Psychiatric Research, 26,* 225–235. (p. 531)

Murray, R. M., Morrison, P. D., Henquet, C., & Di Forti, M. (2007). Cannabis, the mind and society: The hash realities. *Nature Reviews: Neuroscience, 8,* 885–895. (p. 108)

Murray, S. L., Bellavia, G. M., Rose, P., & Griffin, D. W. (2003). Once hurt, twice hurtful: How perceived regard regulates daily marital interactions. *Journal of Personality and Social Psychology, 84,* 126–147. (p. 200)

Musick, M. A., Herzog, A. R., & House, J. S. (1999). Volunteering and mortality among older adults: Findings from a national sample. *Journals of Gerontology, 54B,* 173–180. (p. 411)

Mustanski, B. S., & Bailey, J. M. (2003). A therapist's guide to the genetics of human sexual orientation, *Sexual and Relationship Therapy, 18,* 1468–1479. (p. 181)

Mydans, S. (2002, May 17). In Pakistan, rape victims are the 'criminals.' *New York Times* (www.nytimes.com). (p. 481)

Myers, D. G. (1993). *The pursuit of happiness.* New York: Harper. (p. 417)

Myers, D. G. (2000). *The American paradox: Spiritual hunger in an age of plenty.* New Haven, CT: Yale University Press. (p. 417)

Myers, D. G. (2001, December). Do we fear the right things? *American Psychological Society Observer,* p. 3. (p. 310)

Myers, D. G. (2002). *Intuition: Its powers and perils.* New Haven, CT: Yale University Press. (p. 13)

Myers, D. G. (2013). *Social psychology, 11th Edition.* New York: McGraw-Hill. (p. 448)

Myers, D. G., & Bishop, G. D. (1970). Discussion effects on racial attitudes. *Science, 169,* 78–779. (p. 473)

Myers, D. G., & Diener, E. (1995). Who is happy? *Psychological Science, 6,* 10–19. (p. 417)

Myers, D. G., & Diener, E. (1996, May). The pursuit of happiness. *Scientific American.* (p. 417)

Myers, D. G., & Scanzoni, L. D. (2005). *What God has joined together?* San Francisco: HarperSanFrancisco. (pp. 155, 179)

Myers, T. A., & Crowther, J. H. (2009). Social comparison as a predictor of body dissatisfaction: A meta-analytic review. *Journal of Abnormal Psychology, 118,* 683–698. (p. 537)

N

Nagourney, A. (2002, September 25). For remarks on Iraq, Gore gets praise and scorn. *New York Times* (www.nytimes.com). (p. 460)

Nairn, R. G. (2007). Media portrayals of mental illness, or is it madness? A review. *Australian Psychologist, 42,* 138–146. (p. 511)

Napolitan, D. A., & Goethals, G. R. (1979). The attribution of friendliness. *Journal of Experimental Social Psychology, 15,* 105–113. (p. 458)

Narvaez, D. (2010). Moral complexity: The fatal attraction of truthiness and the importance of mature moral functioning. *Perspectives on Psychological Science, 5,* 163–181. (p. 143)

Nash, M. R. (2001, July). The truth and the hype of hypnosis. *Scientific American,* pp. 47–55. (p. 98)

National Academy of Sciences. (2001). *Exploring the biological contributions to human health: Does sex matter?* Washington, DC: Institute of Medicine, National Academy Press. (p. 169)

National Autistic Society (NAS). (2011, accessed May 11). *Statistics: How many people have autistic spectrum disorders.* www.autism.org.uk. (p. 130)

National Center for Health Statistics. (1990). *Health, United States, 1989.* Washington,

DC: U.S. Department of Health and Human Services. (p. 152)

National Center for Health Statistics. (2004, December 15). Marital status and health: United States, 1999–2002 (by Charlotte A. Schoenborn). *Advance Data from Vital and Human Statistics, number 351.* Centers for Disease Control and Prevention. (p. 405)

National Institute of Mental Health. (2008). *The numbers count: Mental disorders in America.* (nimh.nih.gov). (pp. 510, 540)

National Research Council. (1990). *Human factors research needs for an aging population.* Washington, DC: National Academy Press. (p. 151)

National Safety Council. (2010a). Transportation mode comparison in *Injury facts 2010 edition.* www.nsc.org. (p. 310)

National Safety Council. (2010b, January 12). *NSC estimates 1.6 million crashes caused by cell phone use and texting.* www.nsc.org. (p. 81)

National Sleep Foundation (NSF). (2009). *2009 sleep in America poll: Summary of findings.* Washington, DC: National Sleep Foundation (www.sleepfoundation.org). (p. 92)

National Sleep Foundation (NSF). (2010, March 8). *2010 sleep in America poll.* www.sleepfoundation.org. (p. 87)

Nave, C. S., Sherman, R. A., Funder, D.C., Hampson, S. E., & Goldberg, L. R. (2010). On the contextual independence of personality: Teachers' assessments predict directly observed behavior after four decades. *Social Psychological and Personality Science, 3,* 1–9. (p. 158)

Nayak, M. B., Byrne, C. A., Martin, M. K., & Abraham, A. G. (2003). Attitudes toward violence against women: A cross-nation study. *Sex Roles, 9,* 333–342. (p. 484)

Naylor, T. H. (1990). Redefining corporate motivation, Swedish style. *Christian Century, 107,* 566–570. (p. B-12)

Nazimek, J. (2009). Active body, healthy mind. *The Psychologist, 22,* 206–208. (p. 152)

NCASA. (2007). *Wasting the best and the brightest: Substance abuse at America's colleges and universities.* New York: National Center on Addiction and Drug Abuse, Columbia University. (p. 112)

NCTV News. (1987, July-August). More research links harmful effects to non-violent porn, p. 12. (p. 484)

Nedeltcheva, A. V., Kilkus, J. M., Imperial, J., Schoeller, D. A., & Penev, P. D. (2010). Insufficient sleep undermines dietary efforts to reduce adiposity. *Annals of Internal Medicine, 153,* 435–441. (p. 362)

NEEF. (2011: *children's health and nature.* National Environmental Education Foundation (www.neefusa.org). (p. 575)

Neese, R. M. (1991, November/December). What good is feeling bad? The evolutionary benefits of psychic pain. *The Sciences,* pp. 30–37. (pp. 220, 257)

Neidorf, S., & Morin, R. (2007, May 23). Four-in-ten Americans have close friends or relatives who are gay. *Pew Research Center Publications* (pewresearch.org). (p. 499)

Neimeyer, R. A., & Currier, J. M. (2009). Grief therapy: Evidence of efficacy and emerging directions. *Current Directions in Psychological Science, 18,* 352–356. (p. 158)

Neisser, U. (1979). The control of information pickup in selective looking. In A. D. Pick (Ed.), *Perception and its development: A tribute to Eleanor J. Gibson.* Hillsdale, NJ: Erlbaum. (p. 81)

Neisser, U., Boodoo, G., Bouchard, T. J., Jr., Boykin, A. W., Brody, N., Ceci, S. J., Halpern, D. F., Loehlin, J. C., Perloff, R., Sternberg, R. J., & Urbina, S. (1996). Intelligence: Knowns and unknowns. *American Psychologist, 51,* 77–101. (pp. 340, 345)

Neisser, U., Winograd, E., & Weldon, M. S. (1991). Remembering the earthquake: "What I experienced" vs. "How I heard the news." Paper presented to the Psychonomic Society convention. (p. 283)

Neitz, J., Carroll, J., & Neitz, M. (2001). Color vision: Almost reason enough for having eyes. *Optics & Photonics News 12,* 26–33. (p. 206)

Neitz, J., Geist, T., & Jacobs, G. H. (1989). Color vision in the dog. *Visual Neuroscience, 3,* 119–125. (p. 207)

Nelson, C. A., III, Furtado, E. Z., Fox, N. A., & Zeanah, C. H., Jr. (2009). The deprived human brain. *American Scientist, 97,* 222–229. (pp. 136, 341)

Nelson, M. D., Saykin, A. J., Flashman, L. A., & Riordan, H. J. (1998). Hippocampal volume reduction in schizophrenia as assessed by magnetic resonance imaging. *Archives of General Psychiatry, 55,* 433–440. (p. 531)

Nemeth, C. J., & Ormiston, M. (2007). Creative idea generation: Harmony versus stimulation. *European Journal of Social Psychology, 37,* 524–535. (p. 474)

Nes, R. B., Czajkowski, N., & Tambs, K. (2010). Family matters: Happiness in nuclear families and twins. *Behavior Genetics, 40,* 577–590. (p. 418)

Nesca, M., & Koulack, D. (1994). Recognition memory, sleep and circadian rhythms. *Canadian Journal of Experimental Psychology, 48,* 359–379. (p. 293)

Nestoriuc, Y., Rief, W., & Martin, A. (2008). Meta-analysis of biofeedback for tension-type headache: Efficacy, specificity, and treatment moderators. *Journal of Consulting and Clinical Psychology, 76,* 379–396. (p. 409)

Neubauer, D. N. (1999). Sleep problems in the elderly. *American Family Physician, 59,* 2551–2558. (p. 86)

Neumann, R., & Strack, F. (2000). "Mood contagion": The automatic transfer of mood between persons. *Journal of Personality and Social Psychology, 79,* 211–223. (pp. 385, 465)

Newberg, A., & D'Aquili, E. (2001). *Why God won't go away: Brain science and the biology of belief.* New York: Simon & Schuster. (p. 410)

Newcomb, M. D., & Harlow, L. L. (1986). Life events and substance use among adolescents: Mediating effects of perceived loss of control and meaninglessness in life. *Journal of Personality and Social Psychology, 51,* 564–577. (p. 110)

Newell, B. R., Wong, K. Y., Cheung, J. C. H., & Rakow, T. (2008, August 23). Think, blink, or sleep on it? The impact of modes of thought on complex decision making. *Quarterly Journal of Experimental Psychology:* DOI: 10.1080/17470210802215202. (p. 313)

Newman, L. S., & Baumeister, R. F. (1996). Toward an explanation of the UFO abduction phenomenon: Hypnotic elaboration, extraterrestrial sadomasochism, and spurious memories. *Psychological Inquiry, 7,* 99–126. (p. 97)

Newport, E. L. (1990). Maturational constraints on language learning. *Cognitive Science, 14,* 11–28. (p. 322)

Newport, F. (2001, February). Americans see women as emotional and affectionate, men as more aggressive. *The Gallup Poll Monthly,* pp. 34–38. (p. 381)

Newport, F. (2002, July 29). Bush job approval update. *Gallup News Service* (www.gallup.com/poll/releases/pr020729.asp). (p. 499)

Newport, F. (2007, June 11). Majority of Republicans doubt theory of evolution. *Gallup Poll* (www.galluppoll.com). (p. 71)

Newport, F. (2010, March 11). Americans' global warming concerns continue to drop. *Gallup* (www.gallup.com). (p. 460)

Newport, F., Argrawal, S., & Witters, D. (2010, December 23). Very religious Americans lead healthier lives. *Gallup* (www.gallup.com). (p. 411)

Newport, F., Jones, J. M., Saad, L., & Carroll, J. (2007, April 27). Gallup poll review: 10 key points about public opinion on Iraq. *The Gallup Poll* (www.galluppoll.com). (p. 165)

Newport, F., Moore, D. W., Jones, J. M., & Saad, L. (2003, March 21). Special release: American opinion on the war. *Gallup Poll Tuesday Briefing* (www.gallup.com). (p. 462)

Newport, F., & Pelham, B. (2009, December 14). Don't worry, be 80: Worry and stress decline with age. *Gallup* (www.gallup.com). (p. 392)

Newton, E. L. (1991). The rocky road from actions to intentions. *Dissertation Abstracts International, 51*(8–B), 4105. (p. B-15)

Nezlek, J. B. (2001). Daily psychological adjustment and the planfulness of day-to-day behavior. *Journal of Social and Clinical Psychology, 20,* 452–475. (p. 403)

Ng, S. H. (1990). Androcentric coding of *man* and *his* in memory by language users. *Journal of Experimental Social Psychology, 26,* 455–464. (p. 327)

Ng, T. W. H., & Feldman, D. C. (2009). How broadly does education contribute to job performance. *Personnel Psychology, 62,* 89–134. (p. B-5)

Ng, T. W. H., Sorensen, K. L., & Eby, L. T. (2006). Locus of control at work: A meta-analysis. *Journal of Organizational Behavior, 27,* 1057–1087. (p. 403)

Ng, T. W. H., Sorensen, K. L., & Yim, F. H. K. (2009). Does the job satisfaction—job performance relationship vary across cultures? *Journal of Cross-Cultural Psychology, 40,* 761–796. (p. B-7)

Nguyen, H-H. D., & Ryan, A. M. (2008). Does stereotype threat affect test performance of minorities and women? A meta-analysis of experimental evidence. *Journal of Applied Psychology, 93,* 1314–1334. (p. 346)

NHTSA. (2000). *Traffic safety facts 1999: Older population.* Washington, DC: National Highway Traffic Safety Administration (National Transportation Library; www.ntl.bts.gov). (p. 152)

NICHD. (2006). Child-care effect sizes for the NICHD study of early child care and youth development. *American Psychologist, 61,* 99–116. (p. 137)

NICHD Early Child Care Research Network. (2002). Structure/process/outcome: Direct and indirect effects of caregiving quality on young children's development. *Psychological Science, 13,* 199–206. (p. 137)

NICHD Early Child Care Research Network. (2003). Does amount of time spent in child care predict socioemotional adjustment during the transition to kindergarten? *Child Development, 74,* 976–1005. (p. 137)

Nickell, J. (Ed.). (1994). *Psychic sleuths: ESP and sensational cases.* Buffalo, NY: Prometheus Books. (p. 230)

Nickell, J. (1996, May/June). A study of fantasy proneness in the thirteen cases of alleged encounters in John Mack's abduction. *Skeptical Inquirer,* pp. 18–20, 54. (p. 97)

Nickell, J. (2005, July/August). The case of the psychic detectives. *Skeptical Inquirer* (skeptically.org/skepticism/id10.html). (p. 230)

Nickerson, R. S. (1998). Applied experimental psychology. *Applied Psychology: An International Review, 47,* 155–173. (p. B-14)

Nickerson, R. S. (1999). How we know—and sometimes misjudge—what others know: Imputing one's own knowledge to others. *Psychological Bulletin, 125,* 737–759. (p. B-15)

Nickerson, R. S. (2002). The production and perception of randomness. *Psychological Review, 109,* 330–357. (p. 12)

Nickerson, R. S. (2005). Bertrand's chord, Buffon's needles, and the concept of randomness. *Thinking & Reasoning, 11,* 67–96. (p. 12)

Nicolaus, L. K., Cassel, J. F., Carlson, R. B., & Gustavson, C. R. (1983). Taste-aversion conditioning of crows to control predation on eggs. *Science, 220,* 212–214. (p. 257)

NIDA. (2002). Methamphetamine abuse and addiction. *Research Report Series.* National Institute on Drug Abuse, NIH Publication Number 02–4210. (p. 106)

NIDA. (2005, May). Methamphetamine. *NIDA Info Facts.* National Institute on Drug Abuse. (p. 106)

NIDCD. (2011). Quick statistics. National Institute on Deafness and Other Communication Disorders (www.nidcd.nih.gov). (p. 218)

Nie, N. H. (2001). Sociability, interpersonal relations and the Internet: Reconciling conflicting findings. *American Behavioral Scientist, 45,* 420–435. (p. 368)

Nielsen, K. M., Faergeman, O., Larsen, M. L., & Foldspang, A. (2006). Danish singles have a twofold risk of acute coronary syndrome: Data from a cohort of 138,290 persons. *Journal of Epidemiology and Community Health, 60,* 721–728. (p. 405)

Nielsen, M., & Tomaseli, K. (2010). Overimitation in Kalahari Bushman children and the origins of human cultural cognition. *Psychological Science, 21,* 729–736. (p. 262)

Niemiec, C. P., Ryan, R. M., & Deci, E. L. (2009). The path taken: Consequences of attaining intrinsic and extrinsic aspirations in post-college life. *Journal of Research in Personality, 43,* 291–306. (p. 415)

Nier, J. A. (2004). Why does the "above average effect" exist? Demonstrating idiosyncratic trait definition. *Teaching of Psychology, 31,* 53–54. (p. 449)

Nightingale, F. (1860/1969). *Notes on nursing.* Mineola, NY: Dover. (p. 406)

NIH. (2001, July 20). *Workshop summary: Scientific evidence on condom effectiveness for sexually transmitted disease (STD) prevention.* Bethesda: National Institute of Allergy and Infectious Diseases, National Institutes of Health. (p. 174)

NIH. (2006, December 4). NIDA researchers complete unprecedented scan of human genome that may help unlock the genetic contribution to tobacco addiction. *NIH News,* National Institutes of Health (www.nih.gov). (p. 110)

NIH. (2010). *Teacher's guide: Information about sleep.* National Institutes of Health (www.science.education.nih.gov). (p. 88)

Nikolas, M. A., & Burt, A. (2010). Genetic and environmental influences on ADHD symptom dimensions of inattention and hyperactivity: A meta-analysis. *Journal of Abnormal Psychology, 119,* 1–17. (p. 507)

Nir, Y., & Tononi, G. (2010). Dreaming and the brain: From phenomenology to neurophysiology. *Trends in Cognitive Sciences, 14,* 88–100. (p. 96)

Nisbett, R. E. (1987). Lay personality theory: Its nature, origin, and utility. In N. E. Grunberg, R. E. Nisbett, & others, *A distinctive approach to psychological research: The influence of Stanley Schachter.* Hillsdale, NJ: Erlbaum. (p. B-5)

Nisbett, R. E. (2003). *The geography of thought: How Asians and Westerners think differently . . . and why.* New York: Free Press. (p. 458)

Nisbett, R. E. (2009). *Intelligence and how to get it: Why schools and culture count.* New York: Norton, 344; *Why schools and culture count.* New York: Norton. (p. 343)

Nisbett, R. E., & Cohen, D. (1996). *Culture of honor: The psychology of violence in the South.* Boulder, CO: Westview Press. (p. 484)

Nixon, G. M., Thompson, J. M. D., Han, D. Y., Becroft, D. M., Clark, P. M., Robinson, E., Waldie, K E., Wild, C. J., Black, P. N., & Mitchell, E. A. (2008). Short sleep duration in middle childhood: Risk factors and consequences. *Sleep, 31*, 71–78. (p. 90)

Nock, M. K. (2010). Self-injury. *Annual Review of Clinical Psychology, 6*, 339–363. (p. 525)

Nock, M. K., Borges, G., Bromet, E. J., Alonso, J., Angermeyer, M., Beautrais, A., Bruffaerts, R., Chiu, W. T., de Girolamo, G., Gluzman, S., de Graaf, R., Gureje, O., Haro, J. M., Huang, Y., Karam, E., Kessler, R. C., Lepine, J. P., Levinson, D., Medina-Mora, M. E., Ono, Y., Posada-Villa, J., Williams, D. (2008). Cross-national prevalence and risk factors for suicidal ideation, plans, and attempts. *British Journal of Psychiatry, 192*, 98–105. (p. 525)

Nock, M. K., & Kessler, R. C. (2006). Prevalence of and risk factors for suicide attempts versus suicide gestures: Analysis of the National Comorbidity Survey. *Journal of Abnormal Psychology, 115*, 616–623. (p. 525)

Noel, J. G., Forsyth, D. R., & Kelley, K. N. (1987). Improving the performance of failing students by overcoming their self-serving attributional biases. *Basic and Applied Social Psychology, 8*, 151–162. (p. 404)

Noice, H., & Noice, T. (2006). What studies of actors and acting can tell us about memory and cognitive functioning. *Current Directions in Psychological Science, 15*, 14–18. (p. 280)

Nolen-Hoeksema, S. (2001). Gender differences in depression. *Current Directions in Psychological Science, 10*, 173–176. (p. 526)

Nolen-Hoeksema, S. (2003). *Women who think too much: How to break free of overthinking and reclaim your life.* New York: Holt. (p. 526)

Nolen-Hoeksema, S., & Larson, J. (1999). *Coping with loss.* Mahwah, NJ: Erlbaum. (p. 158)

NORC. (2010). National Opinion Research Center (University of Chicago) General Social Survey data, 1972 through 2008, accessed via sda.berkeley.edu. (p. 365)

Nordgren, L. F., van der Pligt, J., & van Harreveld, F. (2006). Visceral drives in retrospect: Explanations about the inaccessible past. *Psychological Science, 17*, 635–640. (p. 356)

Nordgren, L. F., van der Pligt, J., & van Harreveld, F. (2007). Evaluating Eve: Visceral states influence the evaluation of impulsive behavior. *Journal of Personality and Social Psychology, 93*, 75–84. (p. 356)

Norman, D. A. (2001). The perils of home theater (www.jnd.org/dn.mss/ProblemsOfHomeTheater.html). (p. B-13)

Norman, E. (2010). "The unconscious" in current psychology. *European Psychologist, 15*, 193–201. (p. 431)

Norton, K. L., Olds, T. S., Olive, S., & Dank, S. (1996). Ken and Barbie at life size. *Sex Roles, 34*, 287–294. (p. 537)

Norton, M. I., & Ariely, D. (2011). Building a better America—One wealth quintile at a time. *Perspectives on Psychological Science, 6*, 9–12. (p. A-1)

Norton, P. J., & Price, E. C. (2007). A meta-analytic review of adult cognitive-behavioral treatment outcome across the anxiety disorders. *Journal of Nervous and Mental Disease, 195*, 521–531. (p. 557)

Nowak, R. (1994). Nicotine scrutinized as FDA seeks to regulate cigarettes. *Science, 263*, 1555–1556. (p. 104)

Nurmikko, A. V., Donoghue, J. P., Hochberg, L. R., Patterson, W. R., Song, Y-K., Bull, C. W., Borton, D. A., Laiwalla, F., Park, S., Ming, Y., & Aceros, J. (2010). *Listening to brain microcircuits for interfacing with external world—Progress in wireless implantable microelectronic neuroengineering devices.* Proceedings of the IEEE, 98, 375–388. (p. 54)

Nurnberger, J. I., Jr., & Bierut, L. J. (2007, April). Seeking the connections: Alcoholism and our genes. *Scientific American*, pp. 46–53. (p. 110)

Nuttin, J. M., Jr. (1987). Affective consequences of mere ownership: The name letter effect in twelve European languages. *European Journal of Social Psychology, 17*, 381–402. (p. 488)

O

Oakley, D. A., & Halligan, P. W. (2009). Hypnotic suggestion and cognitive neuroscience. *Trends in Cognitive Science, 13*, 264–270. (p. 99)

Oaten, M., & Cheng, K. (2006a). Longitudinal gains in self-regulation from regular physical exercise. *British Journal of Health Psychology, 11*, 717–733. (p. 404)

Oaten, M., & Cheng, K. (2006b). Improved self-control: The benefits of a regular program of academic study. *Basic and Applied Social Psychology, 28*, 1–16. (p. 404)

Oberlander, J., & Gill, A. J. (2006). Language with character: A stratified corpus comparison of individual differences in e-mail communication. *Discourse Processes, 42*, 239–270. (p. 443)

Oberman, L. M., & Ramachandran, V. S. (2007). The simulating social mind: The role of the mirror neuron system and simulation in the social and communicative deficits of autism spectrum disorders. *Psychological Bulletin, 133*, 310–327. (p. 131)

Ochsner, K. N., Ray, R. R., Hughes, B., McRae, K., Cooper, J. C., Weber, J., Gabrieli, J. D. E., & Gross, J. J. (2009). Bottom-up and top-down processes in emotion generation: Common and distinct neural mechanisms. *Psychological Science, 20*, 1322–1331. (p. 374)

O'Connor, P., & Brown, G. W. (1984). Supportive relationships: Fact or fancy? *Journal of Social and Personal Relationships, 1*, 159–175. (p. 566)

Odgers, C. L., Caspi, A., Nagin, D. S., Piquero, A. R., Slutske, W. S., Milne, B. J., Dickson, N., Poulton, R., & Moffitt, T. E. (2008). Is it important to prevent early exposure to drugs and alcohol among adolescents? *Psychological Science, 19*, 1037–1044. (p. 111)

O'Donnell, L., Stueve, A., O'Donnell, C., Duran, R., San Doval, A., Wilson, R. F., Haber, D., Perry, E., & Pleck, J. H. (2002). Long-term reduction in sexual initiation and sexual activity among urban middle schoolers in the reach for health service learning program. *Journal of Adolescent Health, 31*, 93–100. (p. 177)

Oettingen, G., & Mayer, D. (2002). The motivating function of thinking about the future: Expectations versus fantasies. *Journal of Personality and Social Psychology, 83*, 1198–1212. (p. 404)

Offer, D., Ostrov, E., Howard, K. I., & Atkinson, R. (1988). *The teenage world: Adolescents' self-image in ten countries.* New York: Plenum. (p. 146)

Ohgami, H., Terao, T., Shiotsuki, I., Ishii, N., & Iwata, N. (2009). Lithium levels in drinking water and risk of suicide. *British Journal of Psychiatry, 194*, 464–465. (p. 571)

Öhman, A. (2009). Of snakes and fears: An evolutionary perspective on the psychology of fear. *Scandinavian Journal of Psychology, 50*, 543–552. (p. 518)

Oishi, S., Diener, E. F., Lucas, R. E., & Suh, E. M. (1999). Cross-cultural variations in predictors of life satisfaction: Perspectives from needs and values. *Personality and Social Psychology Bulletin, 25*, 980–990. (p. 355)

Oishi, S., Kesebir, S., & Diener, E. (2011). Income inequality and happiness. *Psychological Science, 22*, 1095–1100. (p. 484)

Oishi, S., & Schimmack, U. (2010). Culture and well-being: A new inquiry into the psychological wealth of nations. *Perspectives in Psychological Science, 5*, 463–471. (p. 419)

Oishi, S., & Schimmack, U. (2010). Residential mobility, well-being, and mortality. *Journal of Personality and Social Psychology, 98*, 980–994. (p. 365)

Okimoto, T. G., & Brescoll, V. L. (2010). The price of power: Power seeking and backlash against female politicians. *Personality and social Psychology Bulletin, 36*, 923–936. (p. 165)

Olatunji, B. O., & Wolitzky-Taylor, K. B. (2009). Anxiety sensitivity and the anxiety disorders: A meta-analytic review and synthesis. *Psychological Bulletin, 135*, 974–999. (p. 514)

Olds, J. (1958). Self-stimulation of the brain. *Science, 127*, 315–324. (p. 51)

Olds, J. (1975). Mapping the mind onto the brain. In F. G. Worden, J. P. Swazey, & G. Adelman (Eds.), *The neurosciences: Paths of discovery.* Cambridge, MA: MIT Press. (p. 51)

Olds, J., & Milner, P. (1954). Positive reinforcement produced by electrical stimulation of the septal area and other regions of rat brain. *Journal of Comparative and Physiological Psychology, 47*, 419–427. (p. 51)

Olff, M., Langeland, W., Draijer, N., & Gersons, B. P. R. (2007). Gender differences in posttraumatic stress disorder. *Psychological Bulletin, 135*, 183–204. (p. 516)

Olfson, M., Gameroff, M. J., Marcus, S. C., & Jensen, P. S. (2003). National trends in the treatment of attention deficit hyperactivity disorder. *American Journal of Psychiatry, 160*, 1071–1077. (p. 507)

Olfson, M., & Marcus, S. C. (2009). National patterns in antidepressant medication treatment. *Archives of General Psychiatry, 66,* 848–856. (p. 570)

Olfson, M., Marcus, S. C., Wan, G. J., & Geissler, E. C. (2004). National trends in the outpatient treatment of anxiety disorders. *Journal of Clinical Psychiatry, 65,* 1166–1173. (p. 569)

Olfson, M., Shaffer, D., Marcus, S. C., & Greenberg, T. (2003). Relationship between antidepressant medication treatment and suicide in adolescents. *Archives of General Psychiatry, 60,* 978–982. (p. 570)

Oliner, S. P., & Oliner, P. M. (1988). *The altruistic personality: Rescuers of Jews in Nazi Europe.* New York: Free Press. (p. 263)

Olivola, C. Y., & Todorov, A. (2010). Elected in 100 milliseconds: Appearance-based trait inferences and voting. *Journal of Nonverbal Behavior, 54,* 83–110. (p. 380)

Olsson, A., Nearing, K. I., & Phelps, E. A. (2007). Learning fears by observing others: The neural systems of social fear transmission. *Social Cognitive and Affective Neuroscience, 2,* 3–11. (p. 517)

Olweus, D., Mattsson, A., Schalling, D., & Low, H. (1988). Circulating testosterone levels and aggression in adolescent males: A causal analysis. *Psychosomatic Medicine, 50,* 261–272. (p. 482)

Oman, D., Kurata, J. H., Strawbridge, W. J., & Cohen, R. D. (2002). Religious attendance and cause of death over 31 years. *International Journal of Psychiatry in Medicine, 32,* 69–89. (p. 411)

O'Neil, J. (2002, September 3). Vital signs: Behavior: Parent smoking and teenage sex. *New York Times.* (p. 22)

O'Neill, M. J. (1993). The relationship between privacy, control, and stress responses in office workers. Paper presented to the Human Factors and Ergonomics Society convention. (p. 402)

Ong, A. D., Fuller-Rowell, T., & Burrow, A. L. (2009). Racial discrimination and the stress process. *Journal of Personality and Social Psychology, 96,* 1259–1271. (p. 392)

Oppenheimer, D. M., & Trail, T. E. (2010). Why leaning to the left makes you lean to the left: Effects of spatial orientation on political attitudes. *Social Cognition, 28,* 651–661. (p. 229)

Oren, D. A., & Terman, M. (1998). Tweaking the human circadian clock with light. *Science, 279,* 333–334. (p. 88)

Orne, M. T., & Evans, F. J. (1965). Social control in the psychological experiment: Antisocial behavior and hypnosis. *Journal of Personality and Social Psychology, 1,* 189–200. (p. 98)

Orth, U., Robins, R. W., & Meier, L. L. (2009). Disentangling the effects of low self-esteem and stressful events on depression: Findings from three longitudinal studies. *Personality Processes and Individual Differences, 97,* 307–321. (p. 447)

Orth, U., Robins, R. W., & Roberts, B. W. (2008). Low self-esteem prospectively predicts depression in adolescence and young adulthood. *Journal of Personality and Social Psychology, 95,* 695–708. (p. 447)

Orth, U., Robins, R. W., Trzesniewski, K. H., Maes, J., & Schmitt, M. (2009). Low self-esteem is a risk factor for depressive symptoms from young adulthood to old age. *Journal of Abnormal Psychology, 118,* 472–478. (pp. 522, 526)

Osborne, C., Manning, W. D., & Smock, P. J. (2007). Married and cohabiting parents' relationship stability: A focus on race and ethnicity. *Journal of Marriage and Family, 69,* 1345–1366. (p. 155)

Osborne, L. (1999, October 27). A linguistic big bang. *New York Times Magazine* (www.nytimes.com). (p. 321)

Osgood, C. E. (1962). *An alternative to war or surrender.* Urbana: University of Illinois Press. (p. 500)

Osgood, C. E. (1980). GRIT: A strategy for survival in mankind's nuclear age? Paper presented at the Pugwash Conference on New Directions in Disarmament. (p. 500)

Oskarsson, A. T., Van Voven, L., McClelland, G. H., & Hastie, R. (2009). What's next? Judging sequences of binary events. *Psychological Bulletin, 135,* 262–285. (p. 12)

OSS Assessment Staff. (1948). *The assessment of men.* New York: Rinehart. (p. 445)

Ost, L. G., & Hugdahl, K. (1981). Acquisition of phobias and anxiety response patterns in clinical patients. *Behaviour Research and Therapy, 16,* 439–447. (p. 516)

Ostfeld, A. M., Kasl, S. V., D'Atri, D. A., & Fitzgerald, E. F. (1987). *Stress, crowding, and blood pressure in prison.* Hillsdale, NJ: Erlbaum. (p. 403)

O'Sullivan, M., Frank, M. G., Hurley, C. M., & Tiwana, J. (2009). Police lie detection accuracy: The effect of lie scenario. *Law and Human Behavior, 33,* 530–538. (p. 380)

Osvath, M. (2009). Spontaneous planning for future stone throwing by a male chimpanzee. *Current Biology, 19,* R190–R191. (p. 318)

Oswald, A. J., & Powdthavee, N. (2006). *Does happiness adapt? A longitudinal study of disability with implications for economists and judges* (Discussion Paper No. 2208). Bonn: Institute for the Study of Labor. (p. 414)

Ott, B. (2007, June 14). Investors, take note: Engagement boosts earnings. *Gallup Management Journal* (gmj.gallup.com). (p. B-9)

Ott, C. H., Lueger, R. J., Kelber, S. T., & Prigerson, H. G. (2007). Spousal bereavement in older adults: Common, resilient, and chronic grief with defining characteristics. *Journal of Nervous and Mental Disease, 195,* 332–341. (p. 158)

Ouellette, J. A., & Wood, W. (1998). Habit and intention in everyday life: The multiple processes by which past behavior predicts future behavior. *Psychological Bulletin, 124,* 54–74. (p. 445, B-5)

Owen, R. (1814). First essay in *New view of society or the formation of character.* Quoted in *The story of New Lamark.* New Lamark Mills, Lamark, Scotland: New Lamark Conservation Trust, 1993. (p. B-8)

Owens, J. A., Belon, K., & Moss, P. (2010). Impact of delaying school start time on adolescent sleep, mood, and behavior. *Archives of Pediatric Adolescent Medicine, 164,* 608–614. (p. 90)

Oxfam. (2005, March 26). *Three months on: New figures show tsunami may have killed up to four times as many women as men.* Oxfam Press Release (www.oxfam.org.uk). (p. 170)

Ozer, E. J., Best, S. R., Lipsey, T. L., & Weiss, D. S. (2003). Predictors of posttraumatic stress disorder and symptoms in adults: A meta-analysis. *Psychological Bulletin, 129,* 52–73. (p. 515)

Ozer, E. J., & Weiss, D. S. (2004). Who develops posttraumatic stress disorder. *Current Directions in Psychological Science, 13,* 169–172. (p. 516)

Özgen, E. (2004). Language, learning, and color perception. *Current Directions in Psychological Science, 13,* 95–98. (p. 327)

P

Pacifici, R., Zuccaro, P., Farre, M., Pichini, S., Di Carlo, S., Roset, P. N., Ortuno, J., Pujadus, M., Bacosi, A., Menoyo, E., Segura, J., & de la Torre, R. (2001). Effects of repeated doses of MDMA ("Ecstasy") on cell-mediated immune response in humans. *Life Sciences, 69,* 2931–2941. (p. 107)

Padgett, V. R. (1989). Predicting organizational violence: An application of 11 powerful principles of obedience. Paper presented to the American Psychological Association convention. (p. 469)

Pagani, L. S., Fitzpatrick, C., Barnett, T. A., & Dubow, E. (2010). Prospective associations between early childhood television exposure and academic, psychosocial, and physical well-being by middle childhood. *Archivers of Pediatric and Adolescent Medicine, 164,* 425–431. (p. 363)

Page, S. E. (2007). *The difference: How the power of diversity creates better groups, firms, schools, and societies.* Princeton, NJ: Princeton University Press. (p. 474)

Palladino, J. J., & Carducci, B. J. (1983). "Things that go bump in the night": Students' knowledge of sleep and dreams. Paper presented at the meeting of the Southeastern Psychological Association. (p. 83)

Pallier, C., Colomé, A., & Sebastián-Gallés, N. (2001). The influence of native-language phonology on lexical access: Exemplar-based versus abstract lexical entries. *Psychological Science, 12,* 445–448. (p. 320)

Palmer, S., Schreiber, C., & Box, C. (1991). Remembering the earthquake: "Flashbulb" memory for experienced vs. reported events. Paper presented to the Psychonomic Society convention. (p. 283)

Pandey, J., Sinha, Y., Prakash, A., & Tripathi, R. C. (1982). Right-left political ideologies and attribution of the causes of poverty. *European Journal of Social Psychology, 12,* 327–331. (p. 459)

Panksepp, J. (2007). Neurologizing the psychology of affects: How appraisal-based constructivism and basic emotion theory can coexist. *Perspectives on Psychological Science, 2,* 281–295. (p. 378)

Panzarella, C., Alloy, L. B., & Whitehouse, W. G. (2006). Expanded hopelessness theory of depression: On the mechanisms by which social support protects against depression. *Cognitive Theory and Research, 30,* 307–333. (p. 526)

Park, C. L. (2007). Religiousness/spirituality and health: A meaning systems perspective. *Journal of Behavioral Medicine, 30,* 319–328. (p. 411)

Park, G., Lubinski, D., & Benbow, C. P. (2007). Contrasting intellectual patterns predict creativity in the arts and sciences. *Psychological Science, 18,* 948–952. (p. 339)

Park, G., Lubinski, D., & Benbow, C. P. (2008). Ability differences among people who have commensurate degrees matter for scientific creativity. *Psychological Science, 19,* 957–961. (p. 314)

Park, R. L. (1999, July 12). Liars never break a sweat. *New York Times* (www.nytimes.com). (p. 379)

Parker, C. P., Baltes, B. B., Young, S. A., Huff, J. W., Altmann, R. A., LaCost, H. A., & Roberts, J. E. (2003). Relationships between psychological climate perceptions and work outcomes: A meta-analytic review. *Journal of Organizational Behavior, 24,* 389–416. (p. B-7)

Parker, E. S., Cahill, L., & McGaugh, J. L. (2006). A case of unusual autobiographical remembering. *Neurocase, 12,* 35–49. (p. 289)

Parsons, T. D., & Rizzo, A. A. (2008). Affective outcomes of virtual reality exposure therapy for anxiety and specific phobias: A meta-analysis. *Journal of Behavior Therapy and Experimental Psychiatry, 39,* 250–261. (p. 552)

Pasco, J. A., Williams, L. A., Jacks, F. N., Ng, F., Henry, M. J., Nicholson, G. C., Kotowicz, M. A., & Berk, M. (2008). Tobacco smoking as a risk factor for major depressive disorder: Population-based study. *British Journal of Psychiatry, 193,* 322–326. (p. 524)

Pascoe, E. A., & Richman, L. S. (2009). Perceived discrimination and health: A meta-analytic review. *Psychological Bulletin, 135,* 531–554. (p. 392)

Passell, P. (1993, March 9). Like a new drug, social programs are put to the test. *New York Times,* pp. C1, C10. (p. 24)

Pastalkova, E., Serrano, P., Pinkhasova, D., Wallace, E., Fenton, A. A., & Sacktor, T. C. (2006). Storage of spatial information by the maintenance mechanism of LTP. *Science, 313,* 1141–1144. (p. 284)

Patall, E. A., Cooper, H., & Robinson, J. C. (2008). The effects of choice on intrinsic motivation and related outcomes: A meta-analysis of research findings. *Psychological Bulletin, 134,* 270–300. (p. 260)

Pate, J. E., Pumariega, A. J., Hester, C., & Garner, D. M. (1992). Cross-cultural patterns in eating disorders: A review. *Journal of the American Academy of Child and Adolescent Psychiatry, 31,* 802–809. (p. 536)

Patel, S. R., Malhotra, A., White, D. P., Gottlieb, D. J., & Hu, F. B. (2006). Association between reduced sleep and weight gain in women. *American Journal of Epidemiology, 164,* 947–954. (p. 90)

Patten, S. B., Wang, J. L., Williams, J. V. A., Currie, S., Beck, C. A., Maxwell, C. J., & el–Guebaly, N. (2006). Descriptive epidemiology of major depression in Canada. *Canadian Journal of Psychiatry, 51,* 84–90. (p. 520)

Patterson, F. (1978, October). Conversations with a gorilla. *National Geographic,* pp. 438–465. (p. 324)

Patterson, G. R., Chamberlain, P., & Reid, J. B. (1982). A comparative evaluation of parent training procedures. *Behavior Therapy, 13,* 638–650. (pp. 252, 483)

Patterson, G. R., Reid, J. B., & Dishion, T. J. (1992). *Antisocial boys.* Eugene, OR: Castalia. (p. 483)

Patterson, M., Warr, P., & West, M. (2004). Organizational climate and company productivity: The role of employee affect and employee level. *Journal of Occupational and Organizational Psychology, 77,* 193–216. (p. B-8)

Patterson, P. H. (2007). Maternal effects on schizophrenia risk. *Science, 318,* 576–577. (p. 531)

Pauker, K., Weisbuch, M., Ambady, N., Sommers, S. R., Adams, Jr., R. B., & Ivcevic, Z. (2009). Not so Black and White: Memory for ambiguous group members. *Journal of Personality and Social Psychology, 96,* 795–810. (p. 344)

Paulesu, E., Demonet, J-F., Fazio, F., McCrory, E., Chanoine, V., Brunswick, N., Cappa, S. F., Cossu, G., Habib, M., Frith, C. D., & Frith, U. (2001). Dyslexia: Cultural diversity and biological unity. *Science, 291,* 2165–2167. (p. 26)

Paus, T., Zijdenbos, A., Worsley, K., Collins, D. L., Blumenthal, J., Giedd, J. N., Rapoport, J. L., & Evans, A. C. (1999). Structural maturation of neural pathways in children and adolescents: In vivo study. *Science, 283,* 1908–1911. (p. 122)

Pavlov, I. (1927). *Conditioned reflexes: An investigation of the physiological activity of the cerebral cortex.* Oxford: Oxford University Press. (pp. 239, 243)

Payne, B. K. (2006). Weapon bias: Split-second decisions and unintended stereotyping. *Current Directions in Psychological Science, 15,* 287–291. (p. 477)

Payne, B. K., & Corrigan, E. (2007). Emotional constraints on intentional forgetting. *Journal of Experimental Social Psychology, 43,* 780–786. (p. 294)

Payne, B. K., Krosnick, J. A., Pasek, J., Lelkes, Y., Akhtar, O., & Tompson, T. (2010). Implicit and explicit prejudice in the 2008 American presidential election. *Journal of Experimental Social Psychology, 46,* 367–374. (p. 477)

Payne, J. W., Samper, A., Bettman, J. R., & Luce, M. F. (2008). Boundary conditions on unconscious thought in complex decision making. *Psychological Science, 19,* 1118–1123. (p. 313)

Peckham, A. D., McHugh, R. K., & Otto, M. W. (2010). A meta-analysis of the magnitude of biased attention in depression. *Depression and Anxiety, 27,* 1135–1142. (p. 521)

Pedersen, A., Zachariae, R., & Bovbjerg, D. H. (2010). Influence of psychological stress on upper respiratory infection—A meta-analysis of prospective studies. *Psychosomatic Medicine, 72,* 823–832. (p. 395)

Pedersen, N. L., Plomin, R., McClearn, G. E., & Friberg, L. (1988). Neuroticism, extraversion, and related traits in adult twins reared apart and reared together. *Journal of Personality and Social Psychology, 55,* 950–957. (p. 65)

Peigneux, P., Laureys, S., Fuchs, S., Collette, F., Perrin, F., Reggers, J., Phillips, C., Degueldre, C., Del Fiore, G., Aerts, J., Luxen, A., & Maquet, P. (2004). Are spatial memories strengthened in the human hippocampus during slow wave sleep? *Neuron, 44,* 535–545. (pp. 88, 282)

Pekkanen, J. (1982, June). Why do we sleep? *Science, 82,* p. 86. (p. 89)

Pelham, B. W. (1993). On the highly positive thoughts of the highly depressed. In R. F. Baumeister (Ed.), *Self-esteem: The puzzle of low self-regard.* New York: Plenum. (p. 448)

Pelham, B. W. (2009, October 22). About one in six Americans report history of depression. *Gallup* (www.gallup.com). (p. 521)

Pelham, B. W., & Crabtree, S. (2008, October 8). Worldwide, highly religious more likely to help others. Gallup Poll (www.gallup.com). (p. 496)

Pendick, D. (1994, January/February). The mind of violence. *Brain Work: The Neuroscience Newsletter,* pp. 1–3, 5. (p. 482)

Pennebaker, J. W. (1985). Traumatic experience and psychosomatic disease: Exploring the roles of behavioral inhibition, obsession, and confiding. *Canadian Psychology, 26,* 82–95. (p. 407)

Pennebaker, J. W. (1990). *Opening up: The healing power of confiding in others.* New York: William Morrow. (pp. 407, 431)

Pennebaker, J. W. (2002, January 28). Personal communication. (p. 499)

Pennebaker, J. W., Barger, S. D., & Tiebout, J. (1989). Disclosure of traumas and health among Holocaust survivors. *Psychosomatic Medicine, 51,* 577–589. (p. 406)

Pennebaker, J. W., & O'Heeron, R. C. (1984). Confiding in others and illness rate among spouses of suicide and accidental death victims. *Journal of Abnormal Psychology, 93,* 473–476. (p. 406)

Pennebaker, J. W., & Stone, L. D. (2003). Words of wisdom: Language use over the life span. *Journal of Personality and Social Psychology, 85,* 291–301. (p. 156)

Peplau, L. A., & Fingerhut, A. W. (2007). The close relationships of lesbians and gay men. *Annual Review of Psychology, 58,* 405–424. (p. 155)

Peplau, L. A., & Garnets, L. D. (2000). A new paradigm for understanding women's sexuality and sexual orientation. *Journal of Social Issues, 56,* 329–350. (p. 179)

Peppard, P. E., Szklo-Coxe, M., Hia, K. M., & Young, T. (2006). Longitudinal association of sleep-related breathing disorder and depression. *Archives of Internal Medicine, 166,* 1709–1715. (p. 92)

Pepperberg, I. M. (2006). Grey parrot numerical competence: A review. *Animal Cognition, 9,* 377–391. (p. 317)

Pepperberg, I. M. (2009). *Alex & me: How a scientist and a parrot discovered a hidden world of animal intelligence—and formed a deep bond in the process.* New York: Harper. (p. 317)

Perani, D., & Abutalebi, J. (2005). The neural basis of first and second language processing. *Current Opinion in Neurobiology, 15,* 202–206. (p. 323)

Pereira, A. C., Huddleston, D. E., Brickman, A. M., Sosunov, A. A., Hen, R., McKhann, G. M., Sloan, R., Gage, F. H., Brown, T. R., & Small, S. A. (2007). An *in vivo* correlate of exercise-induced neurogenesis in the adult dentate gyrus. *Proceedings of the National Academic of Sciences, 104,* 5638–5643. (pp. 58, 151)

Pereira, G. M., & Osburn, H. G. (2007). Effects of participation in decision making on performance and employee attitudes: A quality circles meta-analysis. *Journal of Business Psychology, 22,* 145–153. (pp. 152, B-11)

Perilloux, H. K., Webster, G. D., & Gaulin, S. J. (2010). Signals of genetic quality and maternal investment capacity: The dynamic effects of fluctuating asymmetry and waist-to-hip ratio on men's ratings of women's attractiveness *Social Pcholoy and Personalty Science, 1,* 34–42. (pp. 184, 490)

Perkins, A., & Fitzgerald, J. A. (1997). Sexual orientation in domestic rams: Some biological and social correlates. In L. Ellis & L. Ebertz (Eds.), *Sexual orientation: Toward biological understanding.* Westport, CT: Praeger Publishers. (p. 180)

Perlmutter, M. (1983). Learning and memory through adulthood. In M. W. Riley, B. B. Hess, & K. Bond (Eds.), *Aging in society: Selected reviews of recent research.* Hillsdale, NJ: Erlbaum. (p. 153)

Perra, O., Williams, J. H. G., Whiten, A., Fraser, L., Benzie, H., & Perrett, D. I. (2008). Imitation and 'theory of mind' competencies in discrimination of autism from other neurodevelopmental disorders. *Research in Autism Disorders, 2,* 456–468. (p. 131)

Perrett, D. I., Harries, M., Misflin, A. J., & Chitty, A. J. (1988). Three stages in the classification of body movements by visual neurons. In H. B. Barlow, C. Blakemore, & M. Weston Smith (Eds.), *Images and understanding.* Cambridge: Cambridge University Press. (p. 204)

Perrett, D. I., Hietanen, J. K., Oram, M. W., & Benson, P. J. (1992). Organization and functions of cells responsive to faces in the temporal cortex. *Philosophical Transactions of the Royal Society of London: Series B, 335,* 23–30. (p. 204)

Perrett, D. I., May, K. A., & Yoshikawa, S. (1994). Facial shape and judgments of female attractiveness. *Nature, 368,* 239–242. (p. 204)

Perron, H., Mekaoui, L., Bernard, C., Veas, F., Stefas, I., & Leboyer, M. (2008). Endogenous retrovirus type W GAG and envelope protein antigenemia in serum of schizophrenic patients. *Biological Psychiatry, 64,* 1019–1023. (p. 532)

Person, C., Tracy, M., & Galea, S. (2006). Risk factors for depression after a disaster. *Journal of Nervous and Mental Disease, 194,* 659–666. (p. 576)

Pert, C. B. (1986). Quoted in J. Hooper & D. Teresi, *The three-pound universe.* New York: Macmillan. (p. 52)

Pert, C. B., & Snyder, S. H. (1973). Opiate receptor: Demonstration in nervous tissue. *Science, 179,* 1011–1014. (p. 40)

Perugini, E. M., Kirsch, I., Allen, S. T., Coldwell, E., Meredith, J., Montgomery, G. H., & Sheehan, J. (1998). Surreptitious observation of responses to hypnotically suggested hallucinations: A test of the compliance hypothesis. *International Journal of Clinical and Experimental Hypnosis, 46,* 191–203. (p. 99)

Peschel, E. R., & Peschel, R. E. (1987). Medical insights into the castrati in opera. *American Scientist, 75,* 578–583. (p. 172)

Pescosolido, B. A., Martin, J. K., Long, J. S., Medina, T. R., Phelan, J. C., & Link, B. G. (2010). (p. 533)

Peters, M., Rhodes, G., & Simmons, L. W. (2007). Contributions of the face and body to overall attractiveness. *Animal Behaviour, 73,* 937–942. (p. 490)

Peters, T. J., & Waterman, R. H., Jr. (1982). *In search of excellence: Lessons from America's best-run companies.* New York: Harper & Row. (p. 254)

Petersen, J. L., & Hyde, J. S. (2010). A meta-analytic review of research on gender differences in sexuality, 1993–2007. *Psychological Bulletin, 136,* 21–38. (p. 184)

Petersen, J. L., & Hyde, J. S. (2011). Gender differences in sexual attitudes and behaviors: A review of meta-analytic results and large datasets. *Journal of Sex Research, 48,* 149–165. (p. 172)

Peterson, C., & Barrett, L. C. (1987). Explanatory style and academic performance among university freshmen. *Journal of Personality and Social Psychology, 53,* 603–607. (p. 404)

Peterson, C., Peterson, J., & Skevington, S. (1986). Heated argument and adolescent development. *Journal of Social and Personal Relationships, 3,* 229–240. (p. 141)

Peterson, L. R., & Peterson, M. J. (1959). Short-term retention of individual verbal items. *Journal of Experimental Psychology, 58,* 193–198. (p. 276)

Petitto, L. A., & Marentette, P. F. (1991). Babbling in the manual mode: Evidence for the ontogeny of language. *Science, 251,* 1493–1496. (p. 320)

Pettegrew, J. W., Keshavan, M. S., & Minshew, N. J. (1993). 31P nuclear magnetic resonance spectroscopy: Neurodevelopment and schizophrenia. *Schizophrenia Bulletin, 19,* 35–53. (p. 530)

Petticrew, M., Bell, R., & Hunter, D. (2002). Influence of psychological coping on survival and recurrence in people with cancer: Systematic review. *British Medical Journal, 325,* 1066. (p. 397)

Petticrew, M., Fraser, J. M., & Regan, M. F. (1999). Adverse life events and risk of breast cancer: A meta-analysis. *British Journal of Health Psychology, 4,* 1–17. (p. 397)

Pettigrew, T. F. (1998). Reactions toward the new minorities of western Europe. *Annual Review of Sociology, 24,* 77–103. (p. 476)

Pettigrew, T. F. (2006). A two-level approach to anti-immigrant prejudice and discrimination. In R. Mahalingam (Ed.), *Cultural psychology of immigrants.* Mahwah, NJ: Erlbaum. (p. 476)

Pettigrew, T. F., Christ, O., Wagner, U., & Stellmacher, J. (2007). Direct and indirect intergroup contact effects on prejudice: A normative interpretation. *International Journal of Intercultural Relations, 31,* 411–425. (p. 499)

Pettigrew, T. F., & Tropp, L. R. (2011). *When groups meet: The dynamics of intergroup contact.* New York: Psychology Press. (p. 498)

Pew Research Center. (2006, November 14). Attitudes toward homosexuality in African countries (pewresearch.org). (p. 178)

Pew Research Center. (2007, July 18). Modern marriage: "I like hugs. I like kisses. But what I really love is help with the dishes." Pew Research Center (www.pewresearch.org). (p. 492)

Pew Research Center. (2010, February 1). Almost all millennials accept interracial dating and marriage. Pew Research Center. (www.pewresearch.org). (p. 476)

Pew. (2007, January 24). *Global warming: A divide on causes and solutions.* Pew Research Center for the People and the Press. (p. 310)

Pew. (2009a, November 4). Social isolation and new technology: How the Internet and mobile phones impact Americans' social networks. Pew Research Center (www.pewresearch.org). (p. 368)

Pew. (2009b, November 16). Teens and distracted driving. Internet & American Life Project, Pew Research Center (www.pewinternet.org). (p. 81)

Pew. (2010a). Home broadband 2010. Pew Internet & American Life Project, Pew Research Center (www.pewinternet.org). (p. 338)

Pew. (2010b, July 1). Gender equality universally embraced, but inequalities acknowledged. Pew Research Center Publications (pewresearch. org). (p. 169)

Pfammatter, M., Junghan, U. M., Brenner, H. D. (2006). Efficacy of psychological therapy in schizophrenia: Conclusions from meta-analyses. *Schizophrenia Bulletin, 32,* S64–S80. (p. 562)

Phelps, J. A., Davis J. O., & Schartz, K. M. (1997). Nature, nurture, and twin research strategies. *Current Directions in Psychological Science, 6,* 117–120. (p. 532)

Philip Morris. (2003). Philip Morris USA youth smoking prevention. Teenage attitudes and behavior study, 2002. In "Raising kids who don't smoke," vol. 1(2). (p. 111)

Phillips, A. C., Batty, G. D., Gale, C. R., Deary, I. J., Osborn, D., MacIntyre, K., & Carroll, D. (2009). Generalized anxiety disorder, major depressive disorder, and their comorbidity as predictors of all-cause and cardiovascular mortality: The Vietnam Experience Study. *Psychosomatic Medicine, 71,* 395–403. (p. 405)

Phillips, A. L. (2011). A walk in the woods. *American Scientist, 69,* 301–302. (p. 575)

Phillips, D. P. (1985). Natural experiments on the effects of mass media violence on fatal aggression: Strengths and weaknesses of a new approach. In L. Berkowitz (Ed.), *Advances in experimental social psychology* (Vol. 19). Orlando, FL: Academic Press. (p. 465)

Phillips, D. P., Carstensen, L. L., & Paight, D. J. (1989). Effects of mass media news stories on suicide, with new evidence on the role of story content. In D. R. Pfeffer (Ed.), *Suicide among youth: Perspectives on risk and prevention.* Washington, DC: American Psychiatric Press. (p. 465)

Phillips, J. L. (1969). *Origins of intellect: Piaget's theory.* San Francisco: Freeman. (p. 128)

Piaget, J. (1930). *The child's conception of physical causality.* London: Routledge & Kegan Paul. (p. 125)

Piaget, J. (1932). *The moral judgment of the child.* New York: Harcourt, Brace & World. (p. 142)

Picchioni, M. M., & Murray, R. M. (2007). Schizophrenia. *British Medical Journal, 335,* 91–95. (p. 529)

Pido-Lopez, J., Imami, N., & Aspinall, R. (2001). Both age and gender affect thymic output: More recent thymic migrants in females than males as they age. *Clinical and Experimental Immunology, 125,* 409–413. (p. 394)

Pieters, G. L. M., de Bruijn, E. R. A., Maas, Y., Hultijn, W., Vandereycken, W., Peuskens, J., & Sabbe, B. G. (2007). Action

monitoring and perfectionism in anorexia nervosa. *Brain and Cognition, 63,* 42–50. (p. 536)

Pike, K. M., & Rodin, J. (1991). Mothers, daughters, and disordered eating. *Journal of Abnormal Psychology, 100,* 198–204. (p. 536)

Piliavin, J. A. (2003). Doing well by doing good: Benefits for the benefactor. In C. L. M. Keyes & J. Haidt (Eds.), *Flourishing: Positive psychology and the life well-lived.* Washington, DC: American Psychological Association. (p. 143)

Pillemer, D. B. (1995). What is remembered about early childhood events? Invited paper presentation to the American Psychological Society convention. (p. 124)

Pillemer, D. B. (1998). *Momentous events, vivid memories.* Cambridge, MA: Harvard University Press. (p. 153)

Pillemer, D. B., Ivcevic, Z., Gooze, R. A., & Collins, K. A. (2007). Self-esteem memories: Feeling good about achievement success, feeling bad about relationship distress. *Personality and Social Psychology Bulletin, 33,* 1292–1305. (p. 366)

Pilley, J. W., & Reid, A. K. (2011). Border collie comprehends object names as verbal referents. *Behavioural Processes, 86,* 184–195. (p. 325)

Pillsworth, E. G., & Haselton, M. G. (2006). Male sexual attractiveness predicts differential ovulatory shifts in female extra-pair attraction and male mate retention. *Evolution and Human Behavior, 27,* 247–258. (p. 172)

Pillsworth, M. G., Haselton, M. G., & Buss, D. M. (2004). Ovulatory shifts in female desire. *Journal of Sex Research, 41,* 55–65. (p. 172)

Pinker, S. (1995). The language instinct. *The General Psychologist, 31,* 63–65. (p. 324)

Pinker, S. (1998). Words and rules. *Lingua, 106,* 219–242. (p. 318)

Pinker, S. (2008). *The sexual paradox: Men, women, and the real gender gap.* New York: Scribner. (p. 166)

Pinker, S. (2011, September 27). A history of violence. *Edge* (www.edge.org). (p. 486)

Pinkham, A. E., Griffin, M., Baron, R., Sasson, N. J., & Gur, R. C. (2010). The face in the crowd effect: Anger superiority when using real faces and multiple identities. *Emotion, 10,* 141–146. (p. 380)

Pipe, M-E. (1996). Children's eyewitness memory. *New Zealand Journal of Psychology, 25,* 36–43. (p. 298)

Pipe, M-E., Lamb, M. E., Orbach, Y., & Esplin, P. W. (2004). Recent research on children's testimony about experienced and witnessed events. *Developmental Review, 24,* 440–468. (p. 298)

Pipher, M. (2002). *The middle of everywhere: The world's refugees come to our town.* New York: Harcourt Brace. (pp. 365, 391)

Pitcher, D., Walsh, V., Yovel, G., & Duchaine, B. (2007). TMS evidence for the involvement of the right occipital face area in early face processing. *Current Biology, 17,* 1568–1573. (p. 204)

Place, S. S., Todd, P. M., Penke, L., & Asendorph, J. B. (2009). The ability to judge the romantic interest of others. *Psychological Science, 20,* 22–26. (pp. 380, 488)

Plassmann, H., O'Doherty, J., Shiv, B., & Rangel, A. (2008). Marketing actions can modulate neural representations of experienced pleasantness. *Proceedings of the National Academy of Sciences, 105,* 1050–1054. (p. 225).

Platek, S. M., & Singh, D. (2010) Optimal waist-to-hip ratios in women activate neural reward centers in men. PLoS ONE 5(2): e9042. doi:10.1371/journal.pone.0009042. (p. 490)

Pleck, J. H., Sonenstein, F. L., & Ku, L. C. (1993). Masculinity ideology: Its impact on adolescent males' heterosexual relationships. *Journal of Social Issues, 49,* 11–29. (p. 184)

Pliner, P. (1982). The effects of mere exposure on liking for edible substances. *Appetite: Journal for Intake Research, 3,* 283–290. (p. 360)

Pliner, P., Pelchat, M., & Grabski, M. (1993). Reduction of neophobia in humans by exposure to novel foods. *Appetite, 20,* 111–123. (p. 360)

Plomin, R. (1999). Genetics and general cognitive ability. *Nature, 402*(Suppl), C25–C29. (p. 330)

Plomin, R. (2003). General cognitive ability. In R. Plomin, J. C. DeFries, I. W. Craig, & P. McGuffin (Eds.), *Behavioral genetics in a postgenomic world.* Washington, DC: APA Books. (p. 340)

Plomin, R. (2011). Why are children in the same family so different? Nonshared environment three decades later. *International Journal of Epidemiology, 40,* 582–592. (pp. 66, 147)

Plomin, R., & Bergeman, C. S. (1991). The nature of nurture: Genetic influence on "environmental" measures. *Behavioral and Brain Sciences, 14,* 373–427. (p. 67)

Plomin, R., & Daniels, D. (1987). Why are children in the same family so different from one another? *Behavioral and Brain Sciences, 10,* 1–60. (p. 147)

Plomin, R., & DeFries, J. C. (1998, May). The genetics of cognitive abilities and disabilities. *Scientific American,* pp. 62–69. (p. 341)

Plomin, R., DeFries, J. C., McClearn, G. E., & Rutter, M. (1997). *Behavioral genetics.* New York: Freeman. (pp. 63, 69, 181, 362, 532)

Plomin, R., McClearn, G. E., Pedersen, N. L., Nesselroade, J. R., & Bergeman, C. S. (1988). Genetic influence on childhood family environment perceived retrospectively from the last half of the life span. *Developmental Psychology, 24,* 37–45. (p. 67)

Plomin, R., & McGuffin, P. (2003). Psychopathology in the postgenomic era. *Annual Review of Psychology, 54,* 205–228. (p. 523)

Plomin, R., Reiss, D., Hetherington, E. M., & Howe, G. W. (1994, January). Nature and nurture: Genetic contributions to measures of the family environment. *Developmental Psychology, 30*(1), 32–43. (p. 67)

Plotkin, H. (1994). *Darwin machines and the nature of knowledge.* Cambridge, MA: Harvard University Press. (p. 523)

Plous, S., & Herzog, H. A. (2000). Poll shows researchers favor lab animal protection. *Science, 290,* 711. (p. 27)

Poelmans, G., Pauls, D. L., Buitelaar, J. K., & Franke, B. (2011). Integrated genome-wide association study findings: Identification of a neurodevelopmental network for attention deficit hyperactivity disorder. *American Journal of Psychiatry, 168,* 365–377. (p. 507)

Pogue-Geile, M. F., & Yokley, J. L. (2010). Current research on the genetic contributors to schizophrenia. *Current Directions in Psychological Science, 19,* 214–219. (p. 532)

Polanczyk, G., De Lima, M. S., Horta, B. L., Biederman, J., & Rohde, L. A. (2007). The worldwide prevalence of ADHD: A systematic review and metaregression analysis. *American Journal of Psychiatry, 164,* 942–948. (p. 507)

Poldrack, R. A., Halchenko, Y. O., & Hanson, S. J. (2009). Decoding the large-scale structure of brain function by classifying mental states across individuals. *Psychological Science, 20,* 1364–1372. (p. 49)

Polivy, J., & Herman, C. P. (2002). Causes of eating disorders. *Annual Review of Psychology, 53,* 187–213. (p. 536)

Polivy, J., Herman, C. P., & Coelho, J. S. (2008). Caloric restriction in the presence of attractive food cues: External cues, eating, and weight. *Physiology and Behavior, 94,* 729–733. (p. 360)

Pollak, S. D. (2008). Mechanisms linking early experience and the emergence of emotions. *Current Directions in Psychological Science, 17,* 370–375. (p. 136)

Pollak, S. D., Cicchetti, D., & Klorman, R. (1998). Stress, memory, and emotion: Developmental considerations from the study of child maltreatment. *Developmental Psychopathology, 10,* 811–828. (p. 243)

Pollak, S. D., & Kistler, D. J. (2002). Early experience is associated with the development of categorical representations for facial expressions of emotion. *Proceedings of the National Academy of Sciences, 99,* 9072–9076. (p. 380)

Pollak, S. D., & Tolley-Schell, S. A. (2003). Selective attention to facial emotion in physically abused children. *Journal of Abnormal Psychology, 112,* 323–328. (p. 380)

Pollard, R. (1992). 100 years in psychology and deafness: A centennial retrospective. Invited address to the American Psychological Association convention, Washington, DC. (p. 324)

Pollick, A. S., & de Waal, F. B. M. (2007). Ape gestures and language evolution. *Proceedings of the National Academic of Sciences, 104,* 8184–8189. (p. 324)

Poole, D. A., & Lindsay, D. S. (1995). Interviewing preschoolers: Effects of nonsuggestive techniques, parental coaching and leading questions on reports of nonexperienced events. *Journal of Experimental Child Psychology, 60,* 129–154. (p. 296)

Poole, D. A., & Lindsay, D. S. (2001). Children's eyewitness reports after exposure to misinformation from parents. *Journal of Experimental Psychology: Applied, 7,* 27–50. (p. 296)

Poole, D. A., & Lindsay, D. S. (2002). Reducing child witnesses' false reports of misinformation from parents. *Journal of Experimental Child Psychology, 81,* 117–140. (p. 296)

Poon, L. W. (1987). Myths and truisms: Beyond extant analyses of speed of behavior and age. Address to the Eastern Psychological Association convention. (p. 152)

Popenoe, D. (1993). The evolution of marriage and the problem of stepfamilies: A biosocial perspective. Paper presented at the National Symposium on Stepfamilies, Pennsylvania State University. (p. 452)

Poremba, A., & Gabriel, M. (2001). Amygdalar efferents initiate auditory thalamic discriminative training-induced neuronal activity. *Journal of Neuroscience, 21,* 270–278. (p. 51)

Porter, D., & Neuringer, A. (1984). Music discriminations by pigeons. *Journal of Experimental Psychology: Animal Behavior Processes, 10,* 138–148. (p. 247)

Porter, S., & Peace, K. A. (2007). The scars of memory: A prospective, longitudinal investigation of the consistency of traumatic and positive emotional memories in adulthood. *Psychological Science, 18,* 435–441. (p. 299)

Porter, S., & ten Brinke, L. (2008). Reading between the lies: Identifying concealed and falsified emotions in universal facial expressions. *Psychological Science, 19,* 508–514. (p. 380)

Posner, M. I., & Carr, T. H. (1992). Lexical access and the brain: Anatomical constraints on cognitive models of word recognition. *American Journal of Psychology, 105,* 1–26. (p. 323)

Poulton, R., & Milne, B. J. (2002). Low fear in childhood is associated with sporting prowess in adolescence and young adulthood. *Behaviour Research and Therapy, 40,* 1191–1197. (p. 539)

Powell, K. E., Thompson, P. D., Caspersen, C. J., & Kendrick, J. S. (1987). Physical activity and the incidence of coronary heart disease. *Annual Review of Public Health, 8,* 253–287. (p. 407)

Powell, R. A., & Boer, D. P. (1994). Did Freud mislead patients to confabulate memories of abuse? *Psychological Reports, 74,* 1283–1298. (p. 430)

Pratt, T. C., & & Cullen, F. T. (2000). The empirical status of Gottfredson and Hirschi's general theory of crime: A meta-analysis. *Criminology, 38,* 931–964. (p. 484)

Premack, D. G., & Woodruff, G. (1978). Does the chimpanzee have a theory of mind? *Behavioral and Brain Sciences, 1,* 515–526. (p. 128)

Prentice, D. A., & Miller, D. T. (1993). Pluralistic ignorance and alcohol use on campus: Some consequences of misperceiving the social norm. *Journal of Personality and Social Psychology, 64,* 243–256. (p. 112)

Principe, G. F., Kanaya, T., Ceci, S. J., & Singh, M. (2006). Believing is seeing: How rumors can engender false memories in preschoolers. *Psychological Science, 17,* 243–248. (p. 298)

Prioleau, L., Murdock, M., & Brody, N. (1983). An analysis of psychotherapy versus placebo studies. *The Behavioral and Brain Sciences, 6,* 275–310. (p. 565)

Project Match Research Group. (1997). Matching alcoholism treatments to client heterogeneity: Project MATCH posttreatment drinking outcomes. *Journal of Studies on Alcohol, 58,* 7–29. (p. 558)

Pronin, E. (2007). Perception and misperception of bias in human judgment. *Trends in Cognitive Sciences, 11,* 37–43. (p. 449)

Propper, R. E., Stickgold, R., Keeley, R., & Christman, S. D. (2007). Is television traumatic? Dreams, stress, and media exposure in the aftermath of September 11, 2001. *Psychological Science, 18,* 334–340. (p. 94)

Provine, R. R. (2001). *Laughter: A scientific investigation.* New York: Penguin. (p. 18)

Provine, R. R., Krosnowski, K. A., & Brocato, N. W. (2009). Tearing: Breakthrough in human emotional signaling. *Evolutionary Psychology, 7,* 52–56. (p. 384)

Pryor, J. H., Hurtado, S., DeAngelo, L., Blake, L. P., & Tran, S. (2010). *The American Freshman: National Norms Fall 2009; Expanded edition.* Higher Education Research Institute, UCLA. (p. 343)

Pryor, J. H., Hurtado, S., DeAngelo, L., Blake, L. P., & Tran, S. (2011). *The American Freshman: National Norms Fall 2010.* Higher Education Research Institute, UCLA. (p. 166, 367, 390)

Pryor, J. H., Hurtado, S., Saenz, V. B., Korn, J. S., Santos, J. L., & Korn, W. S. (2006). *The American freshman: National norms for fall 2006.* Los Angeles: UCLA Higher Education Research Institute. (p. 526)

Pryor, J. H., Hurtado, S., Saenz, V. B., Lindholm, J. A., Korn, W. S., & Mahoney, K. M. (2005). *The American freshman: National norms for fall 2005.* Los Angeles: Higher Education Research Institute, UCLA. (p. 184)

Przbylski, A. K., Rigby, C. S., & Ryan, R. M. (2010). A motivational model of video game engagement. *Review of General Psychology, 14,* 154–166. (p. 486)

Psychologist. (2003, April). Who's the greatest? *The Psychologist, 16,* p. 17. (p. 129)

PTC. (2007, January 10). *Dying to entertain: Violence on prime time broadcast TV, 1998 to 2006.* Parents Television Council (www.parentstv.org). (p. 264)

Puetz, T. W., O'Connor, P. J., & Dishman, R. K. (2006). Effects of chronic exercise on feelings of energy and fatigue: A quantitative synthesis. *Psychological Bulletin, 132,* 866–876. (p. 408)

Pulkkinen, L. (2004). A longitudinal study on social development as an impetus for school reform toward an integrated school day. *European Psychologist, 9,* 125–141. (p. 137)

Pulkkinen, L. (2006). The Jyväskylä longitudinal study of personality and social development (JYLS). In L. Pulkkinen, J. Kaprio, & R. J. Rose (Eds.), *Socioemotional development and health from adolescence to adulthood* (Cambridge studies on child and adolescent health). New York: Cambridge University Press. (p. 137)

Putnam, F. W. (1991). Recent research on multiple personality disorder. *Psychiatric Clinics of North America, 14,* 489–502. (p. 535)

Putnam, F. W. (1995). Rebuttal of Paul McHugh. *Journal of the American Academy of Child and Adolescent Psychiatry, 34,* 963. (p. 535)

Putnam, R. (2000). *Bowling alone.* New York: Simon and Schuster. (p. 464)

Pyszczynski, T. A., Hamilton, J. C., Greenberg, J., & Becker, S. E. (1991). Self-awareness and psychological dysfunction. In C. R. Snyder & D. O. Forsyth (Eds.), *Handbook of social and clinical psychology: The health perspective.* New York: Pergamon. (p. 526)

Pyszczynski, T. A., Rothschild, Z., & Abdollahi, A. (2008). Terrorism, violence, and hope for peace: A terror management perspective. *Current Directions in Psychological Science 17,* 318–322. (p. 479)

Pyszczynski, T. A., Solomon, S., & Greenberg, J. (2002). *In the wake of 9/11: The psychology of terror.* Washington, DC: American Psychological Association. (p. 479)

Q

Qin, H-F., & Piao, T-J. (2011). Dispositional optimism and life satisfaction of Chinese and Japanese college students: Examining the mediating effects of affects and coping efficacy. *Chinese Journal of Clinical Psychology, 19,* 259–261. (p. 404)

Qirko, H. N. (2004). "Fictive kin" and suicide terrorism. *Science, 304,* 49–50. (p. 473)

Quinn, P. C., Bhatt, R. S., Brush, D., Grimes, A., & Sharpnack, H. (2002). Development of form similarity as a Gestalt grouping principle in infancy. *Psychological Science, 13,* 320–328. (p. 209)

Quinn, P. J., Williams, G. M., Najman, J. M., Andersen, M. J., & Bor, W. (2001). The effect of breastfeeding on child development at 5 years: A cohort study. *Journal of Pediatrics & Child Health, 3,* 465–469. (p. 22)

Quoidbach, J., Dunn, E. W., Petrides, K. V., & Mikolajczak, M. (2010). Money giveth, money taketh away: The dual effect of wealth on happiness. *Psychological Science, 21,* 759–763. (p. 415)

R

Rabbitt, P. (2006). Tales of the unexpected: 25 years of cognitive gerontology. *The Psychologist, 19,* 674–676. (p. 153)

Rabins, P., & 18 others. (2009). Scientific and ethical issues related to deep brain stimulation for disorders of mood, behavior, and thought. *Archives of General Psychiatry, 66,* 931–937. (p. 573)

Racsmány, M., Conway, M. A., & Demeter, G. (2010). Consolidation of episodic memories during sleep: Long-term effects of retrieval practice. *Psychological Science, 21,* 80–85. (p. 88)

Radford, B. (2010, February 18). Tiger Woods and sex addiction: Real disease or easy excuse? LiveScience.com (accessed via news.yahoo.com). (pp. 101, 230)

Rahman, Q., & Koerting, J. (2008). Sexual orientation-related differences in allocentric spatial memory tasks. *Hippocampus, 18,* 55–63. (pp. 182, 183)

Rahman, Q., Wilson, G. D., & Abrahams, S. (2003). Biosocial factors, sexual orientation and neurocognitive functioning. *Psychoneuroendocrinology, 29,* 867–881. (pp. 181, 183)

Raine, A. (1999). Murderous minds: Can we see the mark of Cain? *Cerebrum: The Dana Forum on Brain Science 1*(1), 15–29. (pp. 483, 539)

Raine, A. (2005). The interaction of biological and social measures in the explanation of antisocial and violent behavior. In D. M. Stoff & E. J. Susman (Eds.) *Developmental psychobiology of aggression.* New York: Cambridge University Press. (pp. 483, 539)

Raine, A., Lencz, T., Bihrle, S., LaCasse, L., & Colletti, P. (2000). Reduced prefrontal gray matter volume and reduced autonomic activity in antisocial personality disorder. *Archives of General Psychiatry, 57,* 119–127. (p. 539)

Rainie, L., Purcell, K., Goulet, L. S., & Hampton, K. H. (2011, June 16). Social networking sites and our lives. *Pew Research Center* (pewresearch.org). (p. 368)

Rainville, P., Duncan, G. H., Price, D. D., Carrier, B., & Bushnell, M. C. (1997). Pain affect encoded in human anterior cingulate but not somatosensory cortex. *Science, 277,* 968–971. (p. 100)

Raison, C. L., Klein, H. M., & Steckler, M. (1999). The mood and madness reconsidered. *Journal of Affective Disorders, 53,* 99–106. (p. 539)

Rajendran, G., & Mitchell, P. (2007). Cognitive theories of autism. *Developmental Review, 27,* 224–260. (p. 130)

Ralston, A. (2004). Enough rope. Interview for ABC TV, Australia, by Andrew Denton. (www.abc.net.au/enoughrope/stories/s1227885.htm). (p. 351)

Ramachandran, V. S., & Blakeslee, S. (1998). *Phantoms in the brain: Probing the mysteries of the human mind.* New York: Morrow. (pp. 58, 222)

Ramírez-Esparza, N., Gosling, S. D., Benet-Martínez, V., Potter, J. P., & Pennebaker, J. W. (2006). Do bilinguals have two personalities? A special case of cultural frame switch-ing. *Journal of Research in Personality, 40,* 99–120. (p. 326)

Randi, J. (1999, February 4). 2000 club mailing list e-mail letter. (p. 232)

Randler, C. (2008). Morningness–eveningness and satisfaction with life. *Social Indicators Research, 86,* 297–302. (p. 84)

Randler, C. (2009). Proactive people are morning people. *Journal of Applied Social Psychology, 39,* 2787–2797. (p. 84)

Randler, C., & Bausback, V. (2010). Morningness-eveningness in women around the transition through menopause and its relationship with climacteric complaints. *Biological Rhythm Research, 41,* in press. (p. 84)

Randler, C., & Frech, D. (2009). Young people's time-of-day preferences affect their school performance. *Journal of Youth Studies, 12,* 653–667. (p. 84)

Rapoport, J. L. (1989, March). The biology of obsessions and compulsions. *Scientific American,* pp. 83–89. (pp. 515, 518)

Räsänen, S., Pakaslahti, A., Syvalahti, E., Jones, P. B., & Isohanni, M. (2000). Sex differences in schizophrenia: A review. *Nordic Journal of Psychiatry, 54,* 37–45. (p. 530)

Rasch, B., & Born, J. (2008). Reactivation and consolidation of memory during sleep. *Current Directions in Psychological Science, 17,* 188–192. (p. 88)

Rasmussen, H. N., Scheier, M. F., & Greenhouse, J. B. (2010). Optimism and physical health: A meta-analytic review. *Annals of Behavioral Medicine, 37,* 239–256. (p. 404)

Rath, T., & Harter, J. K. (2010, August 19). Your friends and your social wellbeing: Close friendships are vital to health, happiness, and even workplace productivity. *Gallup Management Journal* (ww.gmj.gallup.com). (p. B-12)

Ray, O., & Ksir, C. (1990). *Drugs, society, and human behavior* (5th ed.). St. Louis: Times Mirror/Mosby. (p. 106)

Raynor, H. A., & Epstein, L. H. (2001). Dietary variety, energy regulation, and obesity. *Psychological Bulletin, 127,* 325–341. (p. 359)

Read, J., & Bentall, R. (2010). The effectiveness of electroconvulsive therapy: A literature review. *Epidemiologica e Psichiatria Sociale, 19,* 333–347. (p. 572)

Reason, J. (1987). The Chernobyl errors. *Bulletin of the British Psychological Society, 40,* 201–206. (p. 474)

Reason, J., & Mycielska, K. (1982). *Absent-minded? The psychology of mental lapses and everyday errors.* Englewood Cliffs, NJ: Prentice-Hall. (p. 198)

Reed, P. (2000). Serial position effects in recognition memory for odors. *Journal of Experimental Psychology: Learning, Memory, and Cognition, 26,* 411–422. (p. 288)

Rees, M. (1999). *Just six numbers: The deep forces that shape the universe.* New York: Basic Books. (p. 71)

Regan, P. C., & Atkins, L. (2007). Sex differences and similarities in frequency and intensity of sexual desire. *Social Behavior and Personality, 34,* 95–102. (p. 184)

Reichardt, C. S. (2010). Testing astrological predictions about sex, marriage, and selfishness. *Skeptic Magazine, 15*(4), 40–45. (p. 438)

Reichenberg, A., Gross, R., Weiser, M., Bresnahan, M., Silverman, J., Harlap, S., Rabinoqitz, J., Shulman, C., Malaspina, D., Lubin, G., Knobler, H Y., Davidson, M., & Susser, E. (2007). Advancing paternal age and autism. *Archives of General Psychiatry, 63,* 1026–1032. (p. 130)

Reichenberg, A., & Harvey, P. D. (2007). Neuropsychological impairments in schizophrenia: Integration of performance-based and brain imaging findings. *Psychological Bulletin, 133,* 833–858. (p. 529)

Reichert, R. A., Robb, M. B., Fender, J. G., & Wartella, E. (2010). Word learning from baby videos. *Archives of Pediatrics & Adolescent Medicine, 164,* 432–437. (p. 341)

Reichle, E. D., Reineberg, A. E., & Schooler, J. W. (2010). Eye movements during mindless reading. *Psychological Science, 21,* 1300–1310. (p. 80)

Reifman, A., & Cleveland, H. H. (2007). Shared environment: A quantitative review. Paper presented to the Society for Research in Child Development, Boston, MA. (p. 66)

Reifman, A. S., Larrick, R. P., & Fein, S. (1991). Temper and temperature on the diamond: The heat-aggression relationship in major league baseball. *Personality and Social Psychology Bulletin, 17,* 580–585. (p. 483)

Reimann, F., & 24 others. (2010). Pain perception is altered by a nucleotide polymorphism in *SCN9A. PNAS, 107,* 5148–5153. (p. 221)

Reiner, W. G., & Gearhart, J. P. (2004). Discordant sexual identity in some genetic males with cloacal exstrophy assigned to female sex at birth. *New England Journal of Medicine, 350,* 333–341. (p. 169)

Reis, H. T., & Aron, A. (2008). Love: What is it, why does it matter, and how does it operate? *Perspectives on Psychological Science, 3,* 80–86. (p. 492)

Reis, H. T., Smith, S. M., Carmichael, C. L., Caprariello, P. A., Tsa, F-F., Rodrigues, A., & Maniaci, M. R. (2010). Are you happy for me? How sharing positive events with others provides personal and interpersonal benefits. *Journal of Personality and Social Psychology, 99,* 311–329. (p. 364)

Reis, S. M. (2001). Toward a theory of creativity in diverse creative women. In M. Bloom & T. Gullotta (Eds.), *Promoting creativity across the life span* (pp. 231–276). Washington, DC: CWLA. (p. 315)

Reisenzein, R. (1983). The Schachter theory of emotion: Two decades later. *Psychological Bulletin, 94,* 239–264. (p. 373)

Reiser, M. (1982). *Police psychology.* Los Angeles: LEHI. (p. 230)

Reitzle, M. (2006). The connections between adulthood transitions and the self-perception of being adult in the changing contexts of East and West Germany. *European Psychologist, 11,* 25–38. (p. 149)

Remick, A. K., Polivy, J., & Pliner, P. (2009). Internal and external moderators of the effect of variety on food intake. *Psychological Bulletin, 135,* 434–451. (p. 360)

Remington, A., Swettenham, J., Campbell, R., & Coleman, M. (2009). Selective attention and perceptual load in autism spectrum disorder. *Psychological Science, 20,* 1388–1393. (p. 130)

Remley, A. (1988, October). From obedience to independence. *Psychology Today,* pp. 56–59. (p. 138)

Renner, M. J., & Renner, C. H. (1993). Expert and novice intuitive judgments about animal behavior. *Bulletin of the Psychonomic Society, 31,* 551–552. (p. 122)

Renner, M. J., & Rosenzweig, M. R. (1987). *Enriched and impoverished environments: Effects on brain and behavior.* New York: Springer-Verlag. (p. 122)

Renninger, K. A., & Granott, N. (2005). The process of scaffolding in learning and development. *New Ideas in Psychology, 23*(3), 111–114. (p. 129)

Rentfrow, P. J., & Gosling, S. D. (2003). The Do Re Mi's of everyday life: The structure and personality correlates of music preferences. *Journal of Personality and Social Psychology, 84,* 1236–1256. (p. 442)

Rentfrow, P. J., & Gosling, S. D. (2006). Message in a ballad: The role of music preferences in interpersonal perception. *Psychological Science, 17,* 236–242. (p. 442)

Repetti, R. L., Taylor, S. E., & Seeman, T. E. (2002). Risky families: Family social environments and the mental and physical health of offspring. *Psychological Bulletin, 128,* 330–366. (p. 391)

Repetti, R. L., Wang, S-W., & Saxbe, D. (2009). Bringing it all back home: How outside stressors shape families' everyday lives. *Current Directions in Psychological Science, 18,* 106–111. (p. 392)

Rescorla, R. A., & Wagner, A. R. (1972). A theory of Pavlovian conditioning: Variations in the effectiveness of reinforcement and nonreinforcement. In A. H. Black & W. F. Perokasy (Eds.), *Classical conditioning II: Current theory.* New York: Appleton-Century-Crofts. (p. 259)

Resnick, M. D., Bearman, P. S., Blum, R. W., Bauman, K. E., Harris, K. M., Jones, J., Tabor, J., Beuhring, T., Sieving, R., Shew, M., Bearinger, L. H., & Udry, J. R. (1997). Protecting adolescents from harm: Findings from the National Longitudinal Study on Adolescent Health. *Journal of the American Medical Association, 278,* 823–832. (pp. 21, 82, 146)

Resnick, S. M. (1992). Positron emission tomography in psychiatric illness. *Current Directions in Psychological Science, 1,* 92–98. (p. 530)

Rethorst, C. D., Wipfli, B. M., & Landers, D. M. (2009). The antidepressive effects of exercise: A meta-analysis of randomized trials. *Sports Medicine, 39,* 491–511. (p. 408)

Reuters. (2000, July 5). Many teens regret decision to have sex (National Campaign to Prevent Teen Pregnancy survey). www.washingtonpost.com. (p. 176)

Reyna, V. F., & Farley, F. (2006). Risk and rationality in adolescent decision making: Implications for theory, practice, and public policy. *Psychological Science in the Public Interest, 7*(1), 1–44. (p. 141)

Reynolds, C. R., Niland, J., Wright, J. E., & Rosenn, M. (2010). Failure to apply the Flynn correction in death penalty litigation: Standard practice of today maybe, but certainly malpractice of tomorrow. *Journal of Psychoeducational Assessment, 28,* 477–481. (p. 338)

Reynolds, G. (2009, November 18). Phys ed: Why exercise makes you less anxious. *New York Times blog* (well.blogs.nytimes.com). (p. 408)

Rhoades, G. K., Stanley, S. M., & Markman, H. J. (2009). The pre-engagement cohabitation effect: A replication and extension of previous findings. *Journal of Family Psychology, 23,* 107–111. (p. 155)

Rholes, W. S., & Simpson, J. A. (Eds.). (2004). *Adult attachment: Theory, research, and clinical implications.* New York: Guilford. (p. 135)

Rholes, W. S., Simpson, J. A., & Friedman, M. (2006). Avoidant attachment and the experience of parenting. *Personality and Social Psychology Bulletin, 32,* 275–285. (p. 135)

Ribeiro, R., Gervasoni, D., Soares, E. S., Zhou, Y., Lin, S-C., Pantoja, J., Lavine, M., & Nicolelis, M. A. L. (2004). Long-lasting novelty-induced neuronal reverberation during slow-wave sleep in multiple forebrain areas. *PloS Biology, 2*(1), e37 (www.plosbiology.org). (p. 88)

Ricciardelli, L. A., & McCabe, M. P. (2004). A biopsychosocial model of disordered eating and the pursuit of muscularity in adolescent boys. *Psychological Bulletin, 130,* 179–205. (p. 536)

Rice, M. E., & Grusec, J. E. (1975). Saying and doing: Effects on observer performance. *Journal of Personality and Social Psychology, 32,* 584–593. (p. 264)

Richeson, J. A., & Shelton, J. N. (2007). Negotiating interracial interactions. *Current Directions in Psychological Science, 16,* 316–320. (p. 499)

Rieff, P. (1979). *Freud: The mind of a moralist* (3rd ed.). Chicago: University of Chicago Press. (p. 431)

Riis, J., Loewenstein, G., Baron, J., Jepson, C., Fagerlin, A., & Ubel, P. A. (2005). Ignorance of hedonic adaptation to hemodialysis: A study using ecological momentary assessment. *Journal of Experimental Psychology: General, 134,* 3–9. (p. 414)

Riley, L. D., & Bowen, C. (2005). The sandwich generation: Challenges and coping strategies of multigenerational families. *The Family Journal, 13,* 52–58. (p. 154)

Rindermann, H., & Ceci, S. J. (2009). Educational policy and country outcomes in international cognitive competence studies.

Perspectives on Psychological Science, 4, 551–577. (p. 344)

Riskind, J. H., Beck, A. T., Berchick, R. J., Brown, G., & Steer, R. A. (1987). Reliability of DSM-III diagnoses for major depression and generalized anxiety disorder using the structured clinical interview for DSM-III. *Archives of General Psychiatry, 44,* 817–820. (p. 509)

Rizzolatti, G., Fadiga, L., Fogassi, L., & Gallese, V. (2002). From mirror neurons to imitation: Facts and speculations. In A. N. Meltzoff & W. Prinz (Eds.), *The imitative mind: Development, evolution, and brain bases.* Cambridge: Cambridge University Press. (p. 262)

Rizzolatti, G., Fogassi, L., & Gallese, V. (2006, November). Mirrors in the mind. *Scientific American,* pp. 54–61. (p. 262)

Roberson, D., Davidoff, J., Davies, I. R. L., & Shapiro, L. R. (2004). The development of color categories in two languages: A longitudinal study. *Journal of Experimental Psychology: General, 133,* 554–571. (p. 326)

Roberson, D., Davies, I. R. L., Corbett, G. G., & Vandervyver, M. (2005). Free-sorting of colors across cultures: Are there universal grounds for grouping? *Journal of Cognition and Culture, 5,* 349–386. (p. 326)

Roberts, B. W., Caspi, A., & Moffitt, T. E. (2001). The kids are alright: Growth and stability in personality development from adolescence to adulthood. *Journal of Personality and Social Psychology, 81,* 670–683. (p. 159)

Roberts, B. W., Caspi, A., & Moffitt, T. E. (2003). Work experiences and personality development in young adulthood. *Journal of Personality and Social Psychology, 84,* 582–593. (p. 159)

Roberts, B. W., & DelVecchio, W. F. (2000). The rank-order consistency of personality traits from childhood to old age: A quantitative review of longitudinal studies. *Psychological Bulletin, 126,* 3–25. (p. 441)

Roberts, B. W., Kuncel, N. R., Shiner, R., Caspi, A., & Goldberg, L. R. (2007). The power of personality: The comparative validity of personality traits, socioeconomic status, and cognitive ability for predicting important life outcomes. *Perspectives on Psychological Science, 2,* 313–345. (p. 442)

Roberts, B. W., & Mroczek, D. (2008). Personality trait change in adulthood. *Current Directions in Psychological Science, 17,* 31–35. (p. 159)

Roberts, B. W., Walton, K. E., & Viechtbauer, W. (2006). Patterns of mean-level change in personality traits across the life course: A meta-analysis of longitudinal studies. *Psychological Bulletin, 132,* 1–25. (p. 159)

Roberts, L. (1988). Beyond Noah's ark: What do we need to know? *Science, 242,* 1247. (p. 403)

Roberts, T-A. (1991). Determinants of gender differences in responsiveness to others' evaluations. *Dissertation Abstracts International, 51*(8–B). (p. 165)

Robertson, K. F., Smeets, S., Lubinski, D., & Benbow, C. P. (2010). Beyond the threshold hypothesis: Even among the gifted and top math/science graduate students, cognitive abilitieis, vocational interests, and lifestyle preferences matter for career choice, performance, and persistence. *Current Directions in Psychological Science, 19,* 346–351. (p. 314)

Robins, L. N., Davis, D. H., & Goodwin, D. W. (1974). Drug use by U.S. Army enlisted men in Vietnam: A follow-up on their return home. *American Journal of Epidemiology, 99,* 235–249. (p. 112)

Robins, L. N., & Regier, D. A. (Eds.). (1991). *Psychiatric disorders in America.* New York: Free Press. (p. 541)

Robins, R. W., & Trzesniewski, K. H. (2005). Self-esteem development across the lifespan. *Current Directions in Psychological Science, 14*(3), 158–162. (p. 156)

Robins, R. W., Trzesniewski, K. H., Tracy, J. L., Gosling, S. D., & Potter, J. (2002). Global self-esteem across the lifespan. *Psychology and Aging, 17,* 423–434. (p. 145)

Robinson, F. P. (1970). *Effective study.* New York: Harper & Row. (p. 29)

Robinson, J. P., & Martin, S. (2008). What Do Happy People Do? *Social Indicators Research, 89,* 565–571. (p. B-2)

Robinson, J. P., & Martin, S. (2009). Changes in American daily life: 1965–2005. *Social Indicators Research, 93,* 47–56. (pp. 87, 264)

Robinson, T. E., & Berridge, K. C. (2003). Addiction. *Annual Review of Psychology, 54,* 25–53. (p. 101)

Robinson, T. N. (1999). Reducing children's television viewing to prevent obesity. *Journal of the American Medical Association, 282,* 1561–1567. (p. 363)

Robinson, T. N., Borzekowski, D. L. G., Matheson, D. M., & Kraemer, H. C. (2007). Effects of fast food branding on young children's taste preferences. *Archives of Pediatric and Adolescent Medicine, 161,* 792–797. (p. 198)

Robinson, V. M. (1983). Humor and health. In P. E. McGhee & J. H. Goldstein (Eds.), *Handbook of humor research: Vol. II. Applied studies.* New York: Springer-Verlag. (p. 405)

Rochat, F. (1993). How did they resist authority? Protecting refugees in Le Chambon during World War II. Paper presented at the American Psychological Association convention. (p. 470)

Rock, I., & Palmer, S. (1990, December). The legacy of Gestalt psychology. *Scientific American,* pp. 84–90. (p. 209)

Rodenburg, R., Benjamin, A., de Roos, C., Meijer, A. M., & Stams, G. J. (2009). Efficacy of EMDR in children: A meta-analysis. *Clinical Psychology Review, 29,* 599–606. (p. 564)

Rodin, J. (1986). Aging and health: Effects of the sense of control. *Science, 233,* 1271–1276. (p. 402)

Roediger, H. L., III, & Finn, B. (2010, March/April). The pluses of getting it wrong. *Scientific American Mind,* pp. 39–41. (p. 30)

Roediger, H. L., III, & Karpicke, J. D. (2006). Test-enhanced learning: Taking memory tests improves long-term retention. *Psychological Science, 17,* 249–255. (pp. 29, 278)

Roediger, H. L., III, & McDermott, K. B. (1995). Creating false memories: Remembering words not presented in lists. *Journal of Experimental Psychology: Learning, Memory, and Cognition, 21,* 803–814. (p. 297)

Roediger, H. L., III, Wheeler, M. A., & Rajaram, S. (1993). Remembering, knowing, and reconstructing the past. In D. L. Medin (Ed.), *The psychology of learning and motivation: Advances in research and theory* (Vol. 30). Orlando, FL: Academic Press. (p. 297)

Roehling, P. V., Roehling, M. V., & Moen, P. (2001). The relationship between work-life policies and practices and employee loyalty: A life course perspective. *Journal of Family and Economic Issues, 22,* 141–170. (p. B-12)

Roelofs, T. (2010, September 22). Somali refugee takes oath of U.S. citizenship year after his brother. *Grand Rapids Press* (www.mlive.com). (p. B-8)

Roenneberg, T., Kuehnle, T., Pramstaller, P. P., Ricken, J., Havel, M., Guth, A., Merrow, M. (2004). A marker for the end of adolescence. *Current Biology, 14,* R1038–R1039. (p. 84)

Roese, N. J., & Summerville, A. (2005). What we regret most . . . and why. *Personality and Social Psychology Bulletin, 31,* 1273–1285. (p. 156)

Roesser, R. (1998). What you should know about hearing conservation. *Better Hearing Institute* (www.betterhearing.org). (p. 217)

Rogers, C. R. (1958). Reinhold Niebuhr's *The self and the dramas of history:* A criticism. *Pastoral Psychology, 9,* 15–17. (p. 448)

Rogers, C. R. (1961). *On becoming a person: A therapist's view of psychotherapy.* Boston; Houghton Mifflin. (p. 549)

Rogers, C. R. (1980). *A way of being.* Boston: Houghton Mifflin. (pp. 433, 549)

Rohan, K. J., Roecklein, K. A., Lindsey, K. T., Johnson, L. G., Lippy, R. D., Lacy, T. J., & Barton, F. B. (2007). A randomized controlled trial of cognitive-behavioral therapy, light therapy, and their combination for seasonal affective disorder. *Journal of Consulting and Clinical Psychology, 75,* 489–500. (p. 564)

Rohner, R. P. (1986). *The warmth dimension: Foundations of parental acceptance-rejection theory.* Newbury Park, CA: Sage. (p. 139)

Rohner, R. P., & Veneziano, R. A. (2001). The importance of father love: History and contemporary evidence. *Review of General Psychology, 5,* 382–405. (pp. 135, 138)

Rohrer, D., & Pashler, H. (2007). Increasing retention without increasing study time. *Current Directions in Psychological Science, 16,* 183–186. (p. 278)

Roiser, J. P., Cook, L. J., Cooper, J. D., Rubinsztein, D. C., & Sahakian, B. J. (2005). Association of a functional polymorphism in the serotonin transporter gene with abnormal emotional processing in Ecstasy users. *American Journal of Psychiatry, 162,* 609–612. (p. 107)

Rokach, A., Orzeck, T., Moya, M., & Exposito, F. (2002). Causes of loneliness in North America and Spain. *European Psychologist, 7*, 70–79. (p. 26)

Ronay, R., & von Hippel, W. (2010). The presence of an attractive woman elevates testosterone and physical risk taking in young men. *Social Psychology and Personality Science, 1*, 57–64. (p. 172)

Root, T. L., Thornton, L. M., Lindroos, A. K., Stunkard, A. J., Lichtenstein, P., Pedersen, N. L., Rasmussen, F., & Bulik, C. M. (2010). Shared and unique genetic and environmental influences on binge eating and night eating: A Swedish twin study. *Eating Behaviors, 11*, 92–98. (p. 536)

Rosa-Alcázar, A. I., Sáncez-Meca, J., Gómez-Conesa, A., & Marín-Martínez, F. (2008). Psychological treatment of obsessive-compulsive disorder: A meta-analysis. *Clinical Psychology Review, 28*, 1310–1325. (p. 551)

Rosch, E. (1978). Principles of categorization. In E. Rosch & B. L. Lloyd (Eds.), *Cognition and categorization.* Hillsdale, NJ: Erlbaum. (p. 306)

Rose, A. J., & Rudolph, K. D. (2006). A review of sex differences in peer relationship processes: Potential trade-offs for the emotional and behavioral development of girls and boys. *Psychological Bulletin, 132*, 98–131. (p. 165)

Rose, J. S., Chassin, L., Presson, C. C., & Sherman, S. J. (1999). Peer influences on adolescent cigarette smoking: A prospective sibling analysis. *Merrill-Palmer Quarterly, 45*, 62–84. (pp. 111, 146)

Rose, R. J. (2004). Developmental research as impetus for school reform. *European Psychologist, 9*, 142–144. (p. 137)

Rose, R. J., Viken, R. J., Dick, D. M., Bates, J. E., Pulkkinen, L., & Kaprio, J. (2003). It *does* take a village: Nonfamiliar environments and children's behavior. *Psychological Science, 14*, 273–277. (p. 146)

Rose, S. (1999). Precis of lifelines: Biology, freedom, determinism. *Behavioral and Brain Sciences, 22*, 871–921. (p. 185)

Roselli, C. E., Larkin, K., Schrunk, J. M., & Stormshak, F. (2004). Sexual partner preference, hypothalamic morphology and aromatase in rams. *Physiology and Behavior, 83*, 233–245. (p. 181)

Roselli, C. E., Resko, J. A., & Stormshak, F. (2002). Hormonal influences on sexual partner preference in rams. *Archives of Sexual Behavior, 31*, 43–49. (p. 181)

Rosenbaum, M. (1986). The repulsion hypothesis: On the nondevelopment of relationships. *Journal of Personality and Social Psychology, 51*, 1156–1166. (p. 491)

Rosenberg, N. A., Pritchard, J. K., Weber, J. L., Cann, H. M., Kidd, K. K., Zhivotosky, L. A., & Feldman, M. W. (2002). Genetic structure of human populations. *Science, 298*, 2381–2385. (p. 344)

Rosenberg, T. (2010, November 1). The opt-out solution. *New York Times* (www.nytimes.com). (p. 313)

Rosenhan, D. L. (1973). On being sane in insane places. *Science, 179*, 250–258. (p. 510)

Rosenthal, R., Hall, J. A., Archer, D., DiMatteo, M. R., & Rogers, P. L. (1979). The PONS test: Measuring sensitivity to nonverbal cues. In S. Weitz (Ed.), *Nonverbal communication* (2nd ed.). New York: Oxford University Press. (p. 381)

Rosenzweig, M. R. (1984). Experience, memory, and the brain. *American Psychologist, 39*, 365–376. (p. 122)

Roseth, C. J., Johnson, D. W., & Johnson, R. T. (2008). Promoting early adolescents' achievement and peer relationships: The effects of cooperative, competitive, and individualistic goal structures. *Psychological Bulletin, 134*, 223–246. (p. 499)

Rosin, H. (2010, July, August). The end of men. *The Atlantic* (www.theatlantic.com). (p. 170)

Ross, J. (2006, December). Sleep on a problem . . . it works like a dream. *The Psychologist, 19*, 738–740. (p. 88)

Ross, L. (1977). The intuitive psychologist and his shortcomings: Distortions in the attribution process. In L. Berkowitz (Ed.) *Advances in experimental social psychology* (Vol. 10). New York: Academic Press. (p. 458)

Ross, M., McFarland, C., & Fletcher, G. J. O. (1981). The effect of attitude on the recall of personal histories. *Journal of Personality and Social Psychology, 40*, 627–634. (p. 293)

Ross, M., Xun, W. Q. E., & Wilson, A. E. (2002). Language and the bicultural self. *Personality and Social Psychology Bulletin, 28*, 1040–1050. (p. 326)

Rossi, P. J. (1968). Adaptation and negative aftereffect to lateral optical displacement in newly hatched chicks. *Science, 160*, 430–432. (p. 215)

Rostosky, S. S., Riggle, E. D. G., Horne, S. G., Denton, F. N., & Huellemeier, J. D. (2010). Lesbian, gay, and bisexual individuals' psychological reactions to amendments denying access to civil marriage. *American Journal of Orthopsychiatry, 80*, 302–310. (p. 392)

Roth, T., Roehrs, T., Zwyghuizen-Doorenbos, A., Stpeanski, E., & Witting, R. (1988). Sleep and memory. In I. Hindmarch & H. Ott (Eds.), *Benzodiazepine receptor ligans, memory and information processing.* New York: Springer-Verlag. (p. 94)

Rothbart, M., Fulero, S., Jensen, C., Howard, J., & Birrell, P. (1978). From individual to group impressions: Availability heuristics in stereotype formation. *Journal of Experimental Social Psychology, 14*, 237–255. (p. 480)

Rothbart, M. K., Ahadi, S. A., & Evans, D. E. (2000). Temperament and personality: Origins and outcomes. *Journal of Personality and Social Psychology, 78*, 122–135. (p. 134)

Rothbaum, F., & Tsang, B. Y-P. (1998). Lovesongs in the United States and China: On the nature of romantic love. *Journal of Cross-Cultural Psychology, 29*, 306–319. (p. 452)

Rothman, A. J., & Salovey, P. (1997). Shaping perceptions to motivate healthy behavior: The role of message framing. *Psychological Bulletin, 121*, 3–19. (p. 312)

Rotton, J., & Kelly, I. W. (1985). Much ado about the full moon: A metaanalysis of lunar-lunacy research. *Psychological Bulletin, 97*, 286–306. (p. 539)

Rovee-Collier, C. (1989). The joy of kicking: Memories, motives, and mobiles. In P. R. Solomon, G. R. Goethals, C. M. Kelley, & B. R. Stephens (Eds.), *Memory: Interdisciplinary approaches.* New York: Springer-Verlag. (p. 124)

Rovee-Collier, C. (1993). The capacity for long-term memory in infancy. *Current Directions in Psychological Science, 2*, 130–135. (p. 287)

Rovee-Collier, C. (1997). Dissociations in infant memory: Rethinking the development of implicit and explicit memory. *Psychological Review, 104*, 467–498. (p. 124)

Rovee-Collier, C. (1999). The development of infant memory. *Current Directions in Psychological Science, 8*, 80–85. (p. 124)

Rowe, D. C. (1990). As the twig is bent? The myth of child-rearing influences on personality development. *Journal of Counseling and Development, 68*, 606–611. (p. 66)

Rowe, D. C., Almeida, D. M., & Jacobson, K. C. (1999). School context and genetic influences on aggression in adolescence. *Psychological Science, 10*, 277–280. (p. 481)

Rowe, D. C., Jacobson, K. C., & Van den Oord, E. J. C. G. (1999). Genetic and environmental influences on vocabulary IQ: Parental education level as moderator. *Child Development, 70*(5), 1151–1162. (p. 340)

Royal College of Psychiatrists. (2009.) *Good psychiatric practice* (3rd ed.). London: Royal College of Psychiatrists. (p. 183)

Rozin, P., Dow, S., Mosovitch, M., & Rajaram, S. (1998). What causes humans to begin and end a meal? A role for memory for what has been eaten, as evidenced by a study of multiple meal eating in amnesic patients. *Psychological Science, 9*, 392–396. (p. 359)

Rozin, P., Millman, L., & Nemeroff, C. (1986). Operation of the laws of sympathetic magic in disgust and other domains. *Journal of Personality and Social Psychology, 50*, 703–712. (p. 244)

Rubenstein, J. S., Meyer, D. E., & Evans, J. E. (2001). Executive control of cognitive processes in task switching. *Journal of Experimental Psychology: Human Perception and Performance, 27*, 763–797. (p. 81)

Rubin, D. C., Rahhal, T. A., & Poon, L. W. (1998). Things learned in early adulthood are remembered best. *Memory and Cognition, 26*, 3–19. (p. 153)

Rubin, J. Z., Pruitt, D. G., & Kim, S. H. (1994). *Social conflict: Escalation, stalemate, and settlement.* New York: McGraw-Hill. (p. 500)

Rubin, L. B. (1985). *Just friends: The role of friendship in our lives.* New York: Harper & Row. (p. 166)

Rubin, Z. (1970). Measurement of romantic love. *Journal of Personality and Social Psychology, 16*, 265–273. (p. 379)

Ruchlis, H. (1990). *Clear thinking: A practical introduction.* Buffalo, NY: Prometheus Books. (p. 307)

Rueckert, L., Doan, T., & Branch, B. (2010). Emotion and relationship effects on gender differences in empathy. Presented at the annual meeting of the Association for Psychological Science, Boston, MA, May, 2010. (p. 382)

Ruffin, C. L. (1993). Stress and health—little hassles vs. major life events. *Australian Psychologist, 28,* 201–208. (p. 392)

Rule, B. G., & Ferguson, T. J. (1986). The effects of media violence on attitudes, emotions, and cognitions. *Journal of Social Issues, 42*(3), 29–50. (p. 265)

Rumbaugh, D. M. (1977). *Language learning by a chimpanzee: The Lana project.* New York: Academic Press. (p. 324)

Rushton, J. P. (1975). Generosity in children: Immediate and long-term effects of modeling, preaching, and moral judgment. *Journal of Personality and Social Psychology, 31,* 459–466. (p. 264)

Russell, B. (1930/1985). *The conquest of happiness.* London: Unwin Paperbacks. (p. 417)

Rusting, C. L., & Nolen-Hoeksema, S. (1998). Regulating responses to anger: Effects of rumination and distraction on angry mood. *Journal of Personality and Social Psychology, 74,* 790–803. (p. 398)

Ryan, R. M. (1999, February 2). Quoted by Alfie Kohn, In pursuit of affluence, at a high price. *New York Times* (www.nytimes.com). (pp. 415, 416)

Ryan, R. M., & Deci, E. L. (2004). Avoiding death or engaging life as accounts of meaning and culture: Comment on Pyszczynski et al. (2004). *Psychological Bulletin, 130,* 473–477. (p. 450)

Rydell, R. J., Rydell, M. T., & Boucher, K. L. (2010). The effect of negative performance stereotypes on learning. *Journal of Personality and Social Psychology, 99,* 883–896. (p. 346)

Ryugo, D. K., Baker, C. A., Montey K. L., Chang, L.Y., Coco, A., Fallon, J. B., Shepherd, R. K. (2010). Synaptic plasticity after chemical deafening and electrical stimulation of the auditory nerve in cats. *Journal of Comparative Neurology, 518,* 1046–1063. (p. 218)

S

Saad, L. (2002, November 21). Most smokers wish they could quit. *Gallup News Service* (www.gallup.com). (p. 105)

Sabbagh, M. A., Xu, F., Carlson, S. M., Moses, L. J., & Lee, K. (2006). The development of executive functioning and theory of mind: A comparison of Chinese and U.S. preschoolers. *Psychological Science, 17,* 74–81. (p. 128)

Sabini, J. (1986). Stanley Milgram (1933–1984). *American Psychologist, 41,* 1378–1379. (p. 467)

Sachdev, P., & Sachdev, J. (1997). Sixty years of psychosurgery: Its present status and its future. *Australian and New Zealand Journal of Psychiatry, 31,* 457–464. (p. 574)

Sackett, P. R., Borneman, M. J., & Connelly, B. S. (2008). High-stakes testing in higher education and employment: Appraising the evidence for validity and fairness. *American Psychologist, 63,* 215–227. (p. 346)

Sackett, P. R., Hardison, C. M., & Cullen, M. J. (2004). On interpreting stereotype threat as accounting for African American-White differences on cognitive tests. *American Psychologist, 59,* 7–13. (p. 346)

Sackett, P. R., & Lievens, F. (2008). Personnel selection. *Annual Review of Psychology, 59,* 419–450. (p. B-4)

Sacks, D. P., Bushman, B. J., & Anderson, C. A. (2011). Do violent video games harm children? Comparing the scientific amicus curiae "experts" in Brown v. Entertainment Merchants Association. *Northwestern University Law Review Colloquy, 106,* 1–12. (p. 485)

Sacks, O. (1985). *The man who mistook his wife for a hat.* New York: Summit Books. (pp. 227, 290)

Sadato, N., Pascual-Leone, A., Grafman, J., Ibanez, V., Deiber, M-P., Dold, G., & Hallett, M. (1996). Activation of the primary visual cortex by Braille reading in blind subjects. *Nature, 380,* 526–528. (p. 58)

Sadler, M. S., Meagor, E. L., & Kaye, M. E. (2012). Stereotypes of mental disorders differ in competence and warmth. *Social Science and Medicine, 74,* 915–922. (p. 510)

Sagan, C. (1979). *Broca's brain.* New York: Random House. (p. 14)

Sagan, C. (1987, February 1). The fine art of baloney detection. *Parade.* (p. 231)

Salmela-Aro, K., Tolvanen, A., & Nurmi, J. (2009). Achievement strategies during university studies predict early career burnout and engagement. *Journal of Vocational Behavior, 75,* 162–172. (p. B-5)

Salmon, P. (2001). Effects of physical exercise on anxiety, depression, and sensitivity to stress: A unifying theory. *Clinical Psychology Review, 21,* 33–61. (p. 408)

Salovey, P. (1990, January/February). Interview. *American Scientist,* pp. 25–29. (p. 413)

Salthouse, T. A. (2009). When does age-related cognitive decline begin? *Neurobiology of Aging, 30,* 507–514. (p. 337)

Salthouse, T. A. (2010b). Selective review of cognitive aging. *Journal of the International Neuropsychological Society, 16,* 754–760. (p. 337)

Sampson, E. E. (2000). Reinterpreting individualism and collectivism: Their religious roots and monologic versus dialogic person–other relationship. *American Psychologist, 55,* 1425–1432. (p. 451)

Samuels, J., & Nestadt, G. (1997). Epidemiology and genetics of obsessive-compulsive disorder. *International Review of Psychiatry, 9,* 61–71. (p. 515)

Samuels, S., & McCabe, G. (1989). Quoted by P. Diaconis & F. Mosteller, Methods for studying coincidences. *Journal of the American Statistical Association, 84,* 853–861. (p. 13)

Sánchez-Villegas, A., Delgado-Rodríguez, M., Alonson, A., Schlatter, J., Lahortiga, F., Majem, L. S., & Martínez-González, M. A. (2009). Association of the Mediterranean dietary pattern with the incidence of depression. *Archives of General Psychiatry, 66,* 1090–1098. (p. 525)

Sandfort, T. G. M., de Graaf, R., Bijl, R., & Schnabel, P. (2001). Same-sex sexual behavior and psychiatric disorders. *Archives of General Psychiatry, 58,* 85–91. (pp. 178, 179)

Sandkühler, S., & Bhattacharya, J. (2008). Deconstructing insight: EEG correlates of insightful problem solving. *PloS ONE, 3,* e1459 (www.plosone.org). (p. 307)

Sandler, W., Meir, I., Padden, C., & Aronoff, M. (2005). The emergence of grammar: Systematic structure in a new language. *Proceedings of the National Academy of Sciences, 102,* 2261–2265. (p. 321)

Santos, A., Meyer-Lindenberg, A., & Deruelle, C. (2010). Absence of racial, but not gender, stereotyping in Williams syndrome children. *Current Biology, 20,* R307–R308. (p. 479)

Sanz, C., Blicher, A., Dalke, K., Gratton-Fabri, L., McClure-Richards, T., & Fouts, R. (1998, Winter-Spring). Enrichment object use: Five chimpanzees' use of temporary and semi-permanent enrichment objects. *Friends of Washoe, 19*(1,2), 9–14. (p. 324)

Sanz, C., Morgan, D., & Gulick, S. (2004). New insights into chimpanzees, tools, and termites from the Congo Basin. *American Naturalist, 164,* 567–581. (p. 317)

Sapadin, L. A. (1988). Friendship and gender: Perspectives of professional men and women. *Journal of Social and Personal Relationships, 5,* 387–403. (p. 166)

Saphire-Bernstein, S., Way, B. M., Kim, H. S, Sherman, D. K., & Taylor, S. E. (2011). Oxytocin receptor gene (*OXTR*) is related to psychological resources. *Proceedings of the National Academy of Sciences, 108,* 15118–15122. (p. 405)

Sapolsky, B. S., & Tabarlet, J. O. (1991). Sex in primetime television: 1979 versus 1989. *Journal of Broadcasting and Electronic Media, 35,* 505–516. (p. 176)

Sapolsky, R. (2005). The influence of social hierarchy on primate health. *Science, 308,* 648–652. (p. 402)

Sapolsky, R. (2010, November 14). This is your brain on metaphors. *New York Times* (www.nytimes.com). (p. 378)

Sato, K. (1987). Distribution of the cost of maintaining common resources. *Journal of Experimental Social Psychology, 23,* 19–31. (p. 498)

Saulny, S. (2006, June 21). A legacy of the storm: Depression and suicide. *New York Times* (www.nytimes.com). (p. 391)

Savage-Rumbaugh, E. S., Murphy, J., Sevcik, R. A., Brakke, K. E., Williams, S. L., & Rumbaugh, D. M., with commentary by Bates, E. (1993). Language comprehension in ape and child. *Monographs of the Society for Research in Child Development, 58* (233), 1–254. (p. 325)

Savage-Rumbaugh, E. S., Rumbaugh, D., & Fields, W. M. (2009). Empirical Kanzi: The ape language controversy revisited. *Skeptic, 15,* 25–33. (p. 325)

Savic, I., Berglund, H., & Lindstrom, P. (2005). Brain response to putative pheromones in homosexual men. *Proceedings of the National Academy of Sciences, 102,* 7356–7361. (p. 181)

Savitsky, K., Epley, N., & Gilovich, T. (2001). Do others judge us as harshly as we think? Overestimating the impact of our failures, shortcomings, and mishaps. *Journal of Personality and Social Psychology, 81,* 44–56. (p. 447)

Savitsky, K., & Gilovich, T. (2003). The illusion of transparency and the alleviation of speech anxiety. Journal *of Experimental Social Psychology, 39,* 618–625. (p. 447)

Savoy, C., & Beitel, P. (1996). Mental imagery for basketball. *International Journal of Sport Psychology, 27,* 454–462. (p. 328)

Sawyer, M. G., Arney, F. M., Baghurst, P. A., Clark, J. J., Graetz, B. W., Kosky, R. J., Nurcombe, B., Patton, G. C., Prior, M. R., Raphael, B., Rey, J., Whaites, L. C., & Zubrick, S. R. (2000). *The mental health of young people in Australia.* Canberra: Mental Health and Special Programs Branch, Commonwealth Department of Health and Aged Care. (p. 522)

Sayal, K., Heron, J., Golding, J., Alati, R., Smith, G. D., Gray, R., & Emond, A. (2009). Binge pattern of alcohol consumption during pregnancy and childhood mental health outcomes: Longitudinal population-based study. *Pediatrics, 123,* e289. (p. 120)

Sayette, M. A., Loewenstein, G., Griffin, K. M., & Black, J. J. (2008). Exploring the cold-to-hot empathy gap in smokers. *Psychological Science, 19,* 926–932. (p. 104)

Sayette, M. A., Reichle, E. D., & Schooler, J. W. (2009). Lost in the sauce: The effects of alcohol on mind wandering. *Psychological Science, 20,* 747–752. (p. 103)

Sayette, M. A., Schooler, J. W., & Reichle, E. D. (2010). Out for a smoke: The impact of cigarette craving on zoning out during reading. *Psychological Science, 21,* 26–30. (p. 104)

Sbarra, D. A. (2009). Marriage protects men from clinically meaningful elevations in C-reactive protein: Results from the National Social Life, Health, and Aging Project (NSHAP). *Psychosomatic Medicine, 71,* 828–835. (p. 405)

Scarborough, E., & Furumoto, L. (1987). *Untold lives: The first generation of American women psychologists.* New York: Columbia University Press. (p. 3)

Scarr, S. (1984, May). What's a parent to do? A conversation with E. Hall. *Psychology Today,* pp. 58–63. (p. 342)

Scarr, S. (1989). Protecting general intelligence: Constructs and consequences for interventions. In R. J. Linn (Ed.), *Intelligence: Measurement, theory, and public policy.* Champaign: University of Illinois Press. (p. 332)

Scarr, S. (1990). Back cover comments on J. Dunn & R. Plomin (1990), *Separate lives: Why siblings are so different.* New York: Basic Books. (p. 67)

Scarr, S. (1993, May/June). Quoted by *Psychology Today,* Nature's thumbprint: So long, superparents, p. 16. (p. 147)

Scarr, S. (1997). Why child care has little impact on most children's development. *Current Directions in Psychological Science, 6,* 143–148. (p. 137)

Schab, F. R. (1991). Odor memory: Taking stock. *Psychological Bulletin, 109,* 242–251. (p. 226)

Schachter, S., & Singer, J. E. (1962). Cognitive, social and physiological determinants of emotional state. *Psychological Review, 69,* 379–399. (p. 373)

Schacter, D. L. (1992). Understanding implicit memory: A cognitive neuroscience approach. *American Psychologist, 47,* 559–569. (p. 290)

Schacter, D. L. (1996). *Searching for memory: The brain, the mind, and the past.* New York: Basic Books. (pp. 152, 281, 290, 431)

Schafer, G. (2005). Infants can learn decontextualized words before their first birthday. *Child Development, 76,* 87–96. (p. 320)

Schafer, J., Caetano, R., & Clark, C. L. (1998). Rates of intimate partner violence among U.S. couples. *American Journal of Public Health, 88,* 1702–1704. (p. 481)

Schaie, K. W., & Geiwitz, J. (1982). *Adult development and aging.* Boston: Little, Brown. (p. A-7)

Schalock, R. L., Borthwick-Duffy, S., Bradley, V. J., Buntinx, W. H. E., Coulter, D. L., Craig, E. M. (2010). *Intellectual disability: Definition, classification, and systems of supports* (11th edition). Washington, DC: American Association on Intellectual and Developmental Disabilities. (p. 338)

Scheibe, S., & Carstensen, L. L. (2010). Emotional aging: Recent findings and future trends. *Journal of Gerontology: Psychological Sciences, 65B,* 135–144. (p. 156)

Schein, E. H. (1956). The Chinese indoctrination program for prisoners of war: A study of attempted brainwashing. *Psychiatry, 19,* 149–172. (p. 461)

Scherer, K. R., Banse, R., & Wallbott, H. G. (2001). Emotion inferences from vocal expression correlate across languages and cultures. *Journal of Cross-Cultural Psychology, 32,* 76–92. (p. 380)

Schiavi, R. C., & Schreiner-Engel, P. (1988). Nocturnal penile tumescence in healthy aging men. *Journal of Gerontology: Medical Sciences, 43,* M146–M150. (p. 86)

Schick, V., Herbenick, D., Reece, M., Sanders, S. A., Dodge, B., Middlestadt, S. E., & Fortenberry, J. D. (2010). Sexual behaviors, condom use, and sexual health of Americans over 50: Implications for sexual health promotion for older adults. *Journal of Sexual Medicine, 7*(suppl 5), 315–329. (p. 151)

Schiffenbauer, A., & Schiavo, R. S. (1976). Physical distance and attraction: An intensification effect. *Journal of Experimental Social Psychology, 12,* 274–282. (p. 471)

Schilt, T., de Win, M. M. L, Koeter, M., Jager, G., Korf, D. J., van den Brink, W., & Schmand, B. (2007). Cognition in novice Ecstasy users with minimal exposure to other drugs. *Archives of General Psychiatry, 64,* 728–736. (p. 107)

Schimel, J., Arndt, J., Pyszczynski, T., & Greenberg, J. (2001). Being accepted for who we are: Evidence that social validation of the intrinsic self reduces general defensiveness. *Journal of Personality and Social Psychology, 80,* 35–52. (p. 435)

Schimmack, U., & Lucas, R. (2007). Marriage matters: Spousal similarity in life satisfaction. *Schmollers Jahrbuch, 127,* 1–7. (p. 418)

Schimmack, U., Oishi, S., & Diener, E. (2005). Individualism: A valid and important dimension of cultural differences between nations. *Personality and Social Psychology Review, 9,* 17–31. (p. 451)

Schlaug, G., Jancke, L., Huang, Y., & Steinmetz, H. (1995). In vivo evidence of structural brain asymmetry in musicians. *Science, 267,* 699–701. (p. 48)

Schmader, T. (2010). Stereotype threat deconstructed. *Current Directions in Psychological Science, 19,* 14–18. (p. 345)

Schmidt, F. L. (2002). The role of general cognitive ability and job performance: Why there cannot be a debate. *Human Performance, 15,* 187–210. (p. B-4)

Schmidt, F. L., & Hunter, J. E. (1998). The validity and utility of selection methods in personnel psychology: Practical and theoretical implications of 85 years of research findings. *Psychological Bulletin, 124,* 262–274. (pp. 445, B-4, B-6)

Schmidt, F. L., & Zimmerman, R. D. (2004). A counterintuitive hypothesis about employment interview validity and some supporting evidence. *Journal of Applied Psychology, 89,* 553–561. (p. B-6)

Schmitt, D. P. (2005). Sociosexuality from Argentina to Zimbabwe: A 48-nation study of sex, culture, and strategies of human mating. *Behavioral and Brain Sciences, 28,* 247–311. (p. 184)

Schmitt, D. P. (2007). Sexual strategies across sexual orientations: How personality traits and culture relate to sociosexuality among gays, lesbians, bisexuals, and heterosexuals. *Journal of Psychology and Human Sexuality, 18,* 183–214. (p. 184)

Schmitt, D. P., & Allik, J. (2005). Simultaneous administration of the Rosenberg Self-esteem Scale in 53 nations: Exploring the universal and culture-specific features of global self-esteem. *Journal of Personality and Social Psychology, 89,* 623–642. (p. 449)

Schmitt, D. P., Allik, J., McCrae, R. R., & Benet-Martínez, V., with many others. (2007). The geographic distribution of Big

Five personality traits: Patterns and profiles of human self-description across 56 nations. *Journal of Cross-Cultural Psychology, 38*, 173–212. (p. 440)

Schmitt, D. P., & Pilcher, J. J. (2004). Evaluating evidence of psychological adaptation: How do we know one when we see one? *Psychological Science, 15*, 643–649. (p. 70)

Schnall, E., Wassertheil-Smoller, S., Swencionis, C., Zemon, V., Tinker, L., O'Sullivan. M. J., Van Horn, K., & Goodwin, M. (2010). The relationship between religion and cardiovascular outcomes and all-cause mortality in the women's health initiative observational study. *Psychology and Health, 25*, 249–263. (p. 411)

Schnall, S., Haidt, J., Clore, G. L., & Jordan, A. (2008). Disgust as embodied moral judgment. *Personality and Social Psychology Bulletin, 34*, 1096–1109. (p. 226)

Schneider, R. H., Alexander, C. N., Staggers, F., Rainforth, M., Salerno, J. W., Hartz, A., Arndt, S., Barnes, V. A., & Nidich, S. (2005). Long-term effects of stress reduction on mortality in persons > or = 55 years of age with systemic hypertension. *American Journal of Cardiology, 95*, 1060–1064. (p. 410)

Schneiderman, N. (1999). Behavioral medicine and the management of HIV/AIDS. *International Journal of Behavioral Medicine, 6*, 3–12. (p. 396)

Schneier, B. (2007, May 17). Virginia Tech lesson: Rare risks breed irrational responses. *Wired* (www.wired.com). (p. 311)

Schoenborn, C. A., & Adams, P. F. (2008). *Sleep duration as a correlate of smoking, alcohol use, leisure-time physical inactivity, and obesity among adults: United States, 2004–2006.* Centers for Disease Control and Prevention (www.cdc.gov/nchs). (p. 90)

Schoeneman, T. J. (1994). Individualism. In V. S. Ramachandran (Ed.), *Encyclopedia of human behavior.* San Diego: Academic Press. (p. 452)

Schofield, J. W. (1986). Black-White contact in desegregated schools. In M. Hewstone & R. Brown (Eds.), *Contact and conflict in intergroup encounters.* Oxford: Basil Blackwell. (p. 499)

Schonfield, D., & Robertson, B. A. (1966). Memory storage and aging. *Canadian Journal of Psychology, 20*, 228–236. (p. 153)

Schooler, J. W., Gerhard, D., & Loftus, E. F. (1986). Qualities of the unreal. *Journal of Experimental Psychology: Learning, Memory, and Cognition, 12*, 171–181. (p. 297)

Schorr, E. A., Fox, N.A., van Wassenhove, V., & Knudsen, E.I. (2005). Auditory-visual fusion in speech perception in children with cochlear implants. *Proceedings of the National Academy of Sciences, 102*, 18748–18750. (p. 218)

Schrauzer, G. N., & Shrestha, K. P. (1990). Lithium in drinking water and the incidences of crimes, suicides, and arrests related to drug addictions. *Biological Trace Element Research, 25*(2), 105–113. (p. 571)

Schrauzer, G. N., & Shrestha, K. P. (2010). Lithium in drinking water. *British Journal of Psychiatry, 196*, 159. (p. 571)

Schueller, S. M. (2010). Preferences for positive psychology exercises. *Journal of Positive Psychology, 5*, 192–203. (p. 413)

Schuman, H., & Scott, J. (1989, June). Generations and collective memories. *American Sociological Review, 54*(3), 359–381. (p. 153)

Schumann, K., & Ross, M. (2010). Why women apologize more than men: gender differences in thresholds for perceiving offensive behavior. *Psychological Science, 21*, 1649–1655. (p. 165)

Schwartz, B. (1984). *Psychology of learning and behavior* (2nd ed.). New York: Norton. (pp. 244, 516)

Schwartz, J., & Estrin, J. (2004, November 7). Living for today, locked in a paralyzed body. *New York Times* (www.nytimes.com). (p. 414)

Schwartz, J. M., Stoessel, P. W., Baxter, L. R., Jr., Martin, K. M., & Phelps, M. E. (1996). Systematic changes in cerebral glucose metabolic rate after successful behavior modification treatment of obsessive-compulsive disorder. *Archives of General Psychiatry, 53*, 109–113. (pp. 557, 574)

Schwartz, S. H., & Rubel-Lifschitz, T. (2009). Cross-national variation in the size of sex differences in values: Effects of gender equality. *Journal of Personality and Social Psychology, 97*, 171–185. (p. 165)

Schwartz, S. J., Unger, J. B., Zamboanga, B. L., & Szapocznik, J. (2010). Rethinking the concept of acculturation: Implications for theory and research. *American Psychologist, 65*, 237–251. (p. 540)

Schwarz, N., Strack, F., Kommer, D., & Wagner, D. (1987). Soccer, rooms, and the quality of your life: Mood effects on judgments of satisfaction with life in general and with specific domains. *European Journal of Social Psychology, 17*, 69–79. (p. 288)

Sclafani, A. (1995). How food preferences are learned: Laboratory animal models. *Proceedings of the Nutrition Society, 54*, 419–427. (p. 360)

Scott, D. J., & others. (2004, November 9). U-M team reports evidence that smoking affects human brain's natural "feel good" chemical system (press release by Kara Gavin). University of Michigan Medical School (www.med.umich.edu). (p. 104)

Scott, D. J., Stohler, C. S., Egnatuk, C. M., Wang, H., Koeppe, R. A., & Zubieta, J-K. (2007). Individual differences in reward responding explain placebo-induced expectations and effects. *Neuron, 55*, 325–336. (p. 223)

Scott, K. M., & 18 others. (2010). Gender and the relationship between marital status and first onset of mood, anxiety and substance use disorders. *Psychological Medicine, 40*, 1495–1505. (p. 155)

Scott, W. A., Scott, R., & McCabe, M. (1991). Family relationships and children's personality: A cross-cultural, cross-source comparison. *British Journal of Social Psychology, 30*, 1–20. (p. 139)

Scottish Parliament. (2010, April). External research on sexualised goods aimed at children. SP Paper 374. scottish.parliament.uk/s3/committees/equal/reports-10/eor10-02.htm. (p. 177)

Scullin, M. K., & McDaniel, M. A. (2010). Remembering to execute a goal: Sleep on it! *Psychological Science, 21*, 1028–1035. (p. 293)

Sdorow, L. M. (2005). The people behind psychology. In B. Perlman, L. McCann, & W. Buskist (Eds.), *Voices of experience: Memorable talks from the National Institute on the Teaching of Psychology.* Washington, DC: American Psychological Society. (p. 429)

Seal, K. H., Bertenthal, D., Miner, C. R., Sen, S., & Marmar, C. (2007). Bringing the war back home: Mental health disorders among 103,788 U.S. veterans returning from Iraq and Afghanistan seen at Department of Veterans Affairs facilities. *Archives of Internal Medicine, 167*, 467–482. (p. 515)

Sebat, J., & 31 others. (2007). Strong association of de novo copy number mutations with autism. *Science, 316*, 445–449. (p. 130)

Sechrest, L., Stickle, T. R., & Stewart, M. (1998). The role of assessment in clinical psychology. In A. Bellack, M. Hersen (Series eds.) & C. R. Reynolds (Vol. ed.), *Comprehensive clinical psychology: Vol 4: Assessment.* New York: Pergamon. (p. 430)

Seeman, P. (2007). Dopamine and schizophrenia. *Scholarpedia, 2*(10), 3634 (www.scholarpedia.org). (p. 530)

Seeman, P., Guan, H-C., & Van Tol, H. H. M. (1993). Dopamine D4 receptors elevated in schizophrenia. *Nature, 365*, 441–445. (p. 530)

Segall, M. H., Dasen, P. R., Berry, J. W., & Poortinga, Y. H. (1990). *Human behavior in global perspective: An introduction to cross-cultural psychology.* New York: Pergamon. (pp. 129, 169)

Segerstrom, S. C. (2007). Stress, energy, and immunity. *Current Directions in Psychological Science, 16*, 326–330. (p. 391)

Segerstrom, S. C., Taylor, S. E., Kemeny, M. E., & Fahey, J. L. (1998). Optimism is associated with mood, coping, and immune change in response to stress. *Journal of Personality and Social Psychology, 74*, 1646–1655. (p. 404)

Seidler, G. H., & Wagner, F. E. (2006). Comparing the efficacy of EMDR and trauma-focused cognitive-behavioral therapy in the treatment of PTSD: A meta-analytic study. *Psychological Medicine, 36*, 1515–1522. (p. 564)

Self, C. E. (1994). *Moral culture and victimization in residence halls.* Unpublished master's thesis. Bowling Green University. (p. 112)

Seligman, M. E. P. (1975). *Helplessness: On depression, development and death.* San Francisco: Freeman. (p. 402)

Seligman, M. E. P. (1991). *Learned optimism.* New York: Knopf. (pp. 78, 402, 526, 527)

Seligman, M. E. P. (1994). *What you can change and what you can't.* New York: Knopf. (pp. 147, 407, 447)

Seligman, M. E. P. (1995). The effectiveness of psychotherapy: The Consumer Reports study. *American Psychologist, 50,* 965–974. (pp. 527, 560, 562)

Seligman, M. E. P. (2002). *Authentic happiness: Using the new positive psychology to realize your potential for lasting fulfillment.* New York: Free Press. (pp. 9, 414, 447, 556)

Seligman, M. E. P. (2004). Eudaemonia, the good life. A talk with Martin Seligman. www.edge.org. (p. 414)

Seligman, M. E. P. (2008). Positive health. *Applied Psychology, 17,* 3–18. (p. 413)

Seligman, M. E. P. (2011). *Flourish: A visionary new understanding of happiness and well-being.* New York: Free Press. (pp. 9, 414)

Seligman, M. E. P., Ernst, R. M., Gillham, J., Reivich, K., & Linkins, M. (2009). Positive education: Positive psychology and classroom interventions. *Oxford Review of Education, 35,* 293–311. (p. 413)

Seligman, M. E. P., Peterson, C., Barsky, A. J., Boehm, J. K., Kubzansky, L. D., & Park, N. (2011). Positive health and health assets: Reanalysis of longitudinal data-sets. Unpublished manuscript, University of Pennsylvania. (p. 413)

Seligman, M. E. P., Steen, T. A., Park, N., & Peterson, C. (2005). Positive psychology progress: Empirical validation of interventions. *American Psychologist, 60,* 410–421. (pp. 9, 413, 418)

Seligman, M. E. P., & Yellen, A. (1987). What is a dream? *Behavior Research and Therapy, 25,* 1–24. (p. 84)

Sellers, H. (2010). *You don't look like anyone I know.* New York: Riverhead Books. (p. 191)

Selye, H. (1936). A syndrome produced by diverse nocuous agents. *Nature, 138,* 32. (p. 393)

Selye, H. (1976). *The stress of life.* New York: McGraw-Hill. (p. 393)

Senate Intelligence Committee. (2004, July 9). *Report of the Select Committee on Intelligence on the U.S. intelligence community's prewar intelligence assessments on Iraq.* Washington, DC: Author. (pp. 308, 474)

Senghas, A., & Coppola, M. (2001). Children creating language: How Nicaraguan Sign Language acquired a spatial grammar. *Psychological Science, 12,* 323–328. (p. 321)

Sengupta, S. (2001, October 10). Sept. 11 attack narrows the racial divide. *New York Times* (www.nytimes.com). (p. 499)

Senju, A., Maeda, M., Kikuchi, Y., Hasegawa, T., Tojo, Y., & Osanai, H. (2007). Absence of contagious yawning in children with autism spectrum disorder. *Biology Letters, 3,* 706–708. (p. 131)

Senju, A., Southgate, V., White, S., & Frith, U. (2009). Mindblind eyes: An absence of spontaneous theory of mind in Asperger syndrome. *Science, 325,* 883–885. (p. 130)

Service, R. F. (1994). Will a new type of drug make memory-making easier? *Science, 266,* 218–219. (p. 284)

Seto, M. C. (2009, April 6–7). Assessing the risk posed by child pornography offenders. Paper prepared for the G8 Global Symposium, University of North Carolina. (p. 485)

Shadish, W. R., & Baldwin, S. A. (2005). Effects of behavioral marital therapy: A meta-analysis of randomized controlled trials. *Journal of Consulting and Clinical Psychology, 73,* 6–14. (p. 562)

Shadish, W. R., Montgomery, L. M., Wilson, P., Wilson, M. R., Bright, I., & Okwumabua, T. (1993). Effects of family and marital psychotherapies: A meta-analysis. *Journal of Consulting and Clinical Psychology, 61,* 992–1002. (p. 558)

Shafir, E., & LeBoeuf, R. A. (2002). Rationality. *Annual Review of Psychology, 53,* 491–517. Times, p. B1. (p. 313)

Shamir, B., House, R. J., & Arthur, M. B. (1993). The motivational effects of charismatic leadership: A self-concept based theory. *Organizational Science, 4*(4), 577–594. (p. B-12)

Shanahan, L., McHale, S. M., Osgood, D. W., & Crouter, A. C. (2007). Conflict frequency with mothers and fathers from middle childhood to late adolescence: Within- and between-families comparisons. *Developmental Psychology, 43,* 539–550. (pp. 145, 146)

Shapiro, D. (1999). *Psychotherapy of neurotic character.* New York: Basic Books. (p. 548)

Shapiro, F. (1989). Efficacy of the eye movement desensitization procedure in the treatment of traumatic memories. *Journal of Traumatic Stress, 2,* 199–223. (p. 563)

Shapiro, F. (1999). Eye movement desensitization and reprocessing (EMDR) and the anxiety disorders: Clinical and research implications of an integrated psychotherapy treatment. *Journal of Anxiety Disorders, 13,* 35–67. (p. 564)

Shapiro, F. (Ed.). (2002). *EMDR as an integrative psychotherapy approach: Experts of diverse orientations explore the paradigm prism.* Washington, DC; APA Books. (p. 564)

Shapiro, F. (2007). EMDR and case conceptualization from an adaptive information processing perspective. In F. Shapiro, F. W. Kaslow, & L. Maxfield (Eds.), *Handbook of EMDR and family therapy processes.* Hoboken, NJ: Wiley. (p. 563)

Shapiro, K. A., Moo, L. R., & Caramazza, A. (2006). Cortical signatures of noun and verb production. *Proceedings of the National Academic of Sciences, 103,* 1644–1649. (p. 323)

Shargorodsky, J., Curhan, S. G., Curhan, G. C., & Eavey, R. (2010). Changes of prevalence of hearing loss in US adolescents. *JAMA, 304,* 772–778. (p. 217)

Sharma, A. R., McGue, M. K., & Benson, P. L. (1998). The psychological adjustment of United States adopted adolescents and their nonadopted siblings. *Child Development, 69,* 791–802. (p. 66)

Shattuck, P. T. (2006). The contribution of diagnostic substitution to the growing administrative prevalence of autism in US special education. *Pediatrics, 117,* 1028–1037. (p. 130)

Shaver, P. R., & Mikulincer, M. (2007). Adult attachment strategies and the regulation of emotion. In J. J. Gross (Ed.), *Handbook of emotion regulation.* New York: Guilford Press. (p. 135)

Shaver, P. R., Morgan, H. J., & Wu, S. (1996). Is love a basic emotion? *Personal Relationships, 3,* 81–96. (p. 376)

Shaw, B. A., Liang, J., & Krause, N. (2010). Age and race differences in the trajectories of self-esteem. *Psychology and Aging, 25,* 84–94. (p. 159)

Shedler, J. (2009, March 23). That was then, this is now: Psychoanalytic psychotherapy for the rest of us. Unpublished manuscript, Department of Psychiatry, University of Colorado Health Sciences Center. (p. 548)

Shedler, J. (2010a, November/December). Getting to know me. *Scientific American Mind,* pp. 53–57. (p. 548)

Shedler, J. (2010b). The efficacy of psychodynamic psychotherapy. *American Psychologist, 65,* 98–109. (pp. 427, 562)

Sheehan, S. (1982). *Is there no place on earth for me?* Boston: Houghton Mifflin. (p. 528)

Sheldon, K. M., Abad, N., & Hinsch, C. (2011). A two-process view of Facebook use and relatedness need-satisfaction: Disconnection drives use, and connection rewards it. *Journal of Personality and Social Psychology, 100,* 766–775. (pp. 364, 368)

Sheldon, K. M., Elliot, A. J., Kim, Y., & Kasser, T. (2001). What is satisfying about satisfying events? Testing 10 candidate psychological needs. *Journal of Personality and Social Psychology, 80,* 325–339. (p. 364)

Sheldon, K. M., & Niemiec, C. P. (2006). It's not just the amount that counts: Balanced need satisfaction also affects well-being. *Journal of Personality and Social Psychology, 91,* 331–341. (p. 364)

Sheldon, M. S., Cooper, M. L., Geary, D. C., Hoard, M., & DeSoto, M. C. (2006). Fertility cycle patterns in motives for sexual behavior. *Personality and Social Psychology Bulletin, 32,* 1659–1673. (p. 172)

Shenton, M. E. (1992). Abnormalities of the left temporal lobe and thought disorder in schizophrenia: A quantitative magnetic resonance imaging study. *New England Journal of Medicine, 327,* 604–612. (p. 531)

Shepard, R. N. (1990). *Mind sights.* New York: Freeman. (pp. 28, 199)

Shepherd, C. (1997, April). News of the weird. *Funny Times,* p. 15. (p. 64)

Shepherd, C. (1999, June). News of the weird. *Funny Times,* p. 21. (p. 362)

Sher, L. (2006). Alcohol consumption and suicide. *QJM: An International Journal of Medicine, 99,* 57–61. (p. 524)

Shergill, S. S., Bays, P. M., Frith, C. D., & Wolpert, D. M. (2003). Two eyes for an eye: The neuroscience of force escalation. *Science, 301,* 187. (p. 498)

Sherif, M. (1966). *In common predicament: Social psychology of intergroup conflict and cooperation.* Boston: Houghton Mifflin. (p. 499)

Sherry, D., & Vaccarino, A. L. (1989). Hippocampus and memory for food caches in black-capped chickadees. *Behavioral Neuroscience, 103,* 308–318. (p. 281)

Sherry, S. B., & Hall, P. A. (2009). The perfectionism model of binge eating: Tests of an integrative model. *Journal of Personality and Social Psychology, 96,* 690–709. (p. 536)

Shettleworth, S. J. (1973). Food reinforcement and the organization of behavior in golden hamsters. In R. A. Hinde & J. Stevenson-Hinde (Eds.), *Constraints on learning.* London: Academic Press. (p. 258)

Shettleworth, S. J. (1993). Where is the comparison in comparative cognition? Alternative research programs. *Psychological Science, 4,* 179–184. (p. 282)

Shifren, J. L., Monz, B. U., Russo, P. A., Segreti, A., Johannes, C. B. (2008). Sexual problems and distress in United States women: Prevalence and correlates. *Obstetrics & Gynecology, 112,* 970–978. (p. 174)

Shinkareva, S. V., Mason, R. A., Malave, V. L., Wang, W., Mitchell, T. M., & Just, M. A. (2008, January 2). Using fMRI brain activation to identify cognitive states associated with perceptions of tools and dwellings. *PloS One 3*(1), 31394. (p. 78)

Short, S. J., Lubach, G. R., Karasin, A. I., Olsen, C. W., Styner, M., Knickmeyer, R. C., Gilmore, J. H., & Coe, C. L. (2010). Maternal influenza infection during pregnancy impacts postnatal brain development in the rhesus monkey. *Biological Psychiatry, 67,* 965–973. (p. 531)

Shute, N. (2010, October). Desperate for an autism cure. *Scientific American,* pp. 80–85. (p. 130)

Siahpush, M., Spittal, M., & Singh, G. K. (2008). Happiness and life satisfaction prospectively predict self-rated health, physical health and the presence of limiting long-term health conditions. *American Journal of Health Promotion, 23,* 18–26. (p. 399)

Siegel, J. M. (1990). Stressful life events and use of physician services among the elderly: The moderating role of pet ownership. *Journal of Personality and Social Psychology, 58,* 1081–1086. (pp. 405, 407)

Siegel, J. M. (2001). The REM sleep-memory consolidation hypothesis. *Science, 294,* 1058–1063. (p. 95)

Siegel, J. M. (2003, November). Why we sleep. *Scientific American,* pp. 92–97. (p. 88)

Siegel, J. M. (2009). Sleep viewed as a state of adaptive inactivity. *Nature Reviews Neuroscience, 10,* 747–753. (p. 88)

Siegel, R. K. (1977, October). Hallucinations. *Scientific American,* pp. 132–140. (p. 108)

Siegel, R. K. (1980). The psychology of life after death. *American Psychologist, 35,* 911–931. (p. 107)

Siegel, R. K. (1982, October). Quoted by J. Hooper, Mind tripping. *Omni,* pp. 72–82, 159–160. (p. 107)

Siegel, R. K. (1984, March 15). Personal communication. (p. 107)

Siegel, R. K. (1990). *Intoxication.* New York: Pocket Books. (pp. 101, 106, 108)

Siegel, S. (2005). Drug tolerance, drug addiction, and drug anticipation. *Current Directions in Psychological Science, 14,* 296–300. (p. 245)

Silber, M. H., & 11 others. (2008). The visual scoring of sleep in adults. *Journal of Clinical Sleep Medicine, 3,* 121–131. (p. 85)

Silbersweig, D. A., Stern, E., Frith, C., Cahill, C., Holmes, A., Grootoonk, S., Seaward, J., McKenna, P., Chua, S. E., Schnorr, L., Jones, T., & Frackowiak, R. S. J. (1995). A functional neuroanatomy of hallucinations in schizophrenia. *Nature, 378,* 176–179. (p. 530)

Silva, A. J., Stevens, C. F., Tonegawa, S., & Wang, Y. (1992). Deficient hippocampal long-term potentiation in alpha-calcium-calmodulin kinase II mutant mice. *Science, 257,* 201–206. (p. 284)

Silva, C. E., & Kirsch, I. (1992). Interpretive sets, expectancy, fantasy proneness, and dissociation as predictors of hypnotic response. *Journal of Personality and Social Psychology, 63,* 847–856. (p. 97)

Silver, M., & Geller, D. (1978). On the irrelevance of evil: The organization and individual action. *Journal of Social Issues, 34,* 125–136. (p. 470)

Silver, N. (2009, December 27). The odds of airborne terror. www.fivethirtyeight.com. (p. 311)

Silveri, M. M., Rohan, M. L., Pimental, P. J., Gruber, S. A., Rosso, I. M., & Yurgelun-Todd, D. A. (2006). Sex differences in the relationship between white matter microstructure and impulsivity in adolescents. *Magnetic Resonance Imaging, 24,* 833–841. (p. 140)

Silverman, K., Evans, S. M., Strain, E. C., & Griffiths, R. R. (1992). Withdrawal syndrome after the double-blind cessation of caffeine consumption. *New England Journal of Medicine, 327,* 1109–1114. (p. 104)

Simek, T. C., & O'Brien, R. M. (1981). *Total golf: A behavioral approach to lowering your score and getting more out of your game.* Huntington, NY: B-MOD Associates. (p. 254)

Simek, T. C., & O'Brien, R. M. (1988). A chaining-mastery, discrimination training program to teach Little Leaguers to hit a baseball. *Human Performance, 1,* 73–84. (p. 254)

Simon, H. (1998, November 16). Flash of genius (interview with P. E. Ross). *Forbes,* pp. 98–104. (p. 371)

Simon, H. (2001, February). Quoted by A. M. Hayashi, When to trust your gut. *Harvard Business Review,* pp. 59–65. (p. 313)

Simon, H. A., & Chase, W. G. (1973). Skill in chess. *American Scientist, 61,* 394–403. (p. 332)

Simon, V., Czobor, P., Bálint, S., Mésáros, A., & Bitter, I. (2009). Prevalence and correlates of adult attention-deficit hyperactivity disorder: Meta-analysis. *British Journal of Psychiatry, 194,* 204–211. (p. 507)

Simons, D. J., & Chabris, C. F. (1999). Gorillas in our midst: Sustained inattentional blindness for dynamic events. *Perception, 28,* 1059–1074. (p. 82)

Simons, D. J., & Levin, D. T. (1998). Failure to detect changes to people during a real-world interaction. *Psychonomic Bulletin & Review, 5,* 644–649. (p. 82)

Simonton, D. K. (1988). Age and outstanding achievement: What do we know after a century of research? *Psychological Bulletin, 104,* 251–267. (p. 338)

Simonton, D. K. (1990). Creativity in the later years: Optimistic prospects for achievement. *The Gerontologist, 30,* 626–631. (p. 338)

Simonton, D. K. (1992). The social context of career success and course for 2,026 scientists and inventors. *Personality and Social Psychology Bulletin, 18,* 452–463. (p. 315)

Simonton, D. K. (2000). Methodological and theoretical orientation and the long-term disciplinary impact of 54 eminent psychologists. *Review of General Psychology, 4,* 13–24. (p. 266)

Sin, N. L., & Lyubomirsky, S. (2009). Enhancing well-being and alleviating depressive symptoms with positive psychology interventions: A practice-friendly meta-analysis. *Journal of Clinical Psychology: In Session, 65,* 467–487. (pp. 413, 418)

Sinclair, R. C., Hoffman, C., Mark, M. M., Martin, L. L., & Pickering, T. L. (1994). Construct accessibility and the misattribution of arousal: Schachter and Singer revisited. *Psychological Science, 5,* 15–18. (p. 373)

Singelis, T. M., Bond, M. H., Sharkey, W. F., & Lai, C. S. Y. (1999). Unpacking culture's influence on self-esteem and embarrassability: The role of self-construals. *Journal of Cross-Cultural Psychology, 30,* 315–341. (p. 451)

Singelis, T. M., & Sharkey, W. F. (1995). Culture, self-construal, and embarrassability. *Cross-Cultural Psychology, 26,* 622–644. (p. 451)

Singer, J. L. (1981). Clinical intervention: New developments in methods and evaluation. In L. T. Benjamin, Jr. (Ed.), *The G. Stanley Hall Lecture Series* (Vol. 1). Washington, DC; American Psychological Association. (p. 562)

Singer, T., Seymour, B., O'Doherty, J., Kaube, H., Dolan, R. J., & Frith, C. (2004). Empathy for pain involves the affective but not sensory components of pain. *Science, 303,* 1157–1162. (p. 222, 263)

Singh, D. (1993). Adaptive significance of female physical attractiveness: Role of waist-to-hip ratio. *Journal of Personality and Social Psychology, 65,* 293–307. (p. 185)

Singh, D. (1995). Female health, attractiveness, and desirability for relationships: Role of breast asymmetry and waist-to-hip ratio. *Ethology and Sociobiology, 16,* 465–481. (p. 184)

Singh, D., & Randall, P. K. (2007). Beauty is in the eye of the plastic surgeon: Waist-hip ration (WHR) and women's attractiveness. *Personality and Individual Differences, 43,* 329–340. (p. 185)

Singh, S. (1997). *Fermat's enigma: The epic quest to solve the world's greatest mathematical problem.* New York: Bantam Books. (p. 314)

Singh, S., & Riber, K. A. (1997, November). Fermat's last stand. *Scientific American,* pp. 68–73. (p. 315)

Sio, U. N., & Ormerod, T. C. (2009). Does incubation enhance problem solving? A meta-analtic review. *Psychological Bulletin, 135,* 94–120. (p. 314)

Sipski, M. L., & Alexander, C. J. (1999). Sexual response in women with spinal cord injuries: Implications for our understanding of the able bodied. *Journal of Sex and Marital Therapy, 25,* 11–22. (p. 45)

Sireteanu, R. (1999). Switching on the infant brain. *Science, 286,* 59, 61. (p. 218)

Skeem, J. L., & Cooke, D. J. (2010). Is criminal behavior a central component of psychopathy? Conceptual directions for resolving the debate. *Psychological Assessment, 22,* 433–445. (p. 538)

Skinner, B. F. (1953). *Science and human behavior.* New York: Macmillan. (p. 249)

Skinner, B. F. (1956). A case history in scientific method. *American Psychologist, 11,* 221–233. (p. 250)

Skinner, B. F. (1957). *Verbal behavior.* Englewood Cliffs, NJ: Prentice-Hall. (p. 321)

Skinner, B. F. (1961, November). Teaching machines. *Scientific American,* pp. 91–102. (pp. 249, 258)

Skinner, B. F. (1983, September). Origins of a behaviorist. *Psychology Today,* pp. 22–33. (p. 253)

Skinner, B. F. (1986). What is wrong with daily life in the Western world? *American Psychologist, 41,* 568–574. (p. 253)

Skinner, B. F. (1988). The school of the future. Address to the American Psychological Association convention. (p. 253)

Skinner, B. F. (1989). Teaching machines. *Science, 243,* 1535. (p. 253)

Sklar, L. S., & Anisman, H. (1981). Stress and cancer. *Psychological Bulletin, 89,* 369–406. (p. 397)

Skoog, G., & Skoog, I. (1999). A 40-year follow-up of patients with obsessive-compulsive disorder. *Archives of General Psychiatry, 56,* 121–127. (p. 515)

Skov, R. B., & Sherman, S. J. (1986). Information-gathering processes: Diagnosticity, hypothesis-confirmatory strategies, and perceived hypothesis confirmation. *Journal of Experimental Social Psychology, 22,* 93–121. (p. 307)

Sleep Foundation. (2006). The ABC's of back-to-school sleep schedules: The consequences of insufficient sleep. National Sleep Foundation (press release) (www.sleepfoundation.org). (p. 89)

Sloan, R. P. (2005). Field analysis of the literature on religion, spirituality, and health. Columbia University (available at www.metanexus.net/tarp). (p. 411)

Sloan, R. P., & Bagiella, E. (2002). Claims about religious involvement and health outcomes. *Annals of Behavioral Medicine, 24,* 14–21. (p. 411)

Sloan, R. P., Bagiella, E., & Powell, T. (1999). Religion, spirituality, and medicine. *Lancet, 353,* 664–667. (p. 411)

Sloan, R. P., Bagiella, E., VandeCreek, L., & Poulos, P. (2000). Should physicians prescribe religious activities? *New England Journal of Medicine, 342,* 1913–1917. (p. 411)

Slopen, N., Glynn, R. J., Buring, J., & Albert, M. A. (2010, November 23). Job strain, job insecurity, and incident cardiovascular disease in the Women's Health Study (Abstract 18520). *Circulation,* A18520 (circ.ahajournals.org). (p. 400)

Slovic, P. (2007). "If I look at the mass I will never act": Psychic numbing and genocide. *Judgment and Decision Making, 2,* 79–95. (p. 310)

Slovic, P. (2010, Winter). The more who die, the less we care: Confronting psychic numbing. *Trauma Psychology* (APA Division 56 Newsletter), pp. 4–8. (p. 311)

Slovic, P., Finucane, M., Peters, E., & MacGregor, D. G. (2002). The affect heuristic. In T. Gilovich, D. Griffin, & D. Kahneman (Eds.), *Intuitive judgment: Heuristics and biases.* New York: Cambridge University Press. (p. 105)

Small, D. A., Loewenstein, G., & Slovic, P. (2007). Sympathy and callousness: The impact of deliberative thought on donations to identifiable and statistical victims. *Organizational Behavior and Human Decision Processes, 102,* 143–153. (p. 311)

Small, M. F. (1997). Making connections. *American Scientist, 85,* 502–504. (p. 139)

Smedley, A., & Smedley, B. D. (2005). Race as biology is fiction, racism as a social problem is real: Anthropological and historical perspectives on the social construction of race. *American Psychologist, 60,* 16–26. (p. 344)

Smelser, N. J., & Mitchell, F. (Eds.). (2002). *Terrorism: Perspectives from the behavioral and social sciences.* Washington, DC: National Research Council, National Academies Press. (p. 480)

Smilek, D., Carriere, J. S. A., & Cheyne, J. A. (2010). Out of mind, out of sight: Eye blinking as indicator and embodiment of mind wandering. *Psychological Science, 21,* 786–789. (p. 81)

Smith, A. (1983). Personal correspondence. (p. 530)

Smith, B. C. (2011, January 16). The senses and the multi-sensory. *World Question Center* (www.edge.org). (p. 228)

Smith, C. (2006, January 7). Nearly 100, LSD's father ponders his "problem child." *New York Times* (www.nytimes.com). (p. 107)

Smith, D. M., Loewenstein, G., Jankovic, A., & Ubel, P. A. (2009). Happily hopeless: Adaptation to a permanent, but not to a temporary, disability. *Health Psychology, 28,* 787–791. (p. 414)

Smith, E., & Delargy, M. (2005). Locked-in syndrome. *British Medical Journal, 330,* 406–409. (p. 415)

Smith, M. B. (1978). Psychology and values. *Journal of Social Issues, 34,* 181–199. (p. 435)

Smith, M. L., & Glass, G. V. (1977). Meta-analysis of psychotherapy outcome studies. *American Psychologist, 32,* 752–760. (p. 562)

Smith, M. L., Glass, G. V., & Miller, R. L. (1980). *The benefits of psychotherapy.* Baltimore: Johns Hopkins Press. (pp. 561, 562)

Smith, P. B., & Tayeb, M. (1989). Organizational structure and processes. In M. Bond (Ed.), *The cross-cultural challenge to social psychology.* Newbury Park, CA: Sage. (p. B-12)

Smith, S. J., Axelton, A. M., & Saucier, D. A. (2009). The effects of contact on sexual prejudice: A meta-analysis. *Sex Roles, 61,* 178–191. (pp. 414, 499)

Smith, S. M., McIntosh, W. D., & Bazzini, D. G. (1999). Are the beautiful good in Hollywood? An investigation of the beauty-and-goodness stereotype on film. *Basic and Applied Social Psychology, 21,* 69–80. (p. 489)

Smith, T. B., Bartz, J., & Richards, P. S. (2007). Outcomes of religious and spiritual adaptations to psychotherapy: A meta-analytic review. *Psychotherapy Research, 17,* 643–655. (p. 566)

Smith, T. W. (1998, December). *American sexual behavior: Trends, sociodemographic differences, and risk behavior* (National Opinion Research Center GSS Topical Report No. 25). (p. 179)

Smolak, L., & Murnen, S. K. (2002). A meta-analytic examination of the relationship between child sexual abuse and eating disorders. *International Journal of Eating Disorders, 31,* 136–150. (p. 536)

Smoreda, Z., & Licoppe, C. (2000). Gender-specific use of the domestic telephone. *Social Psychology Quarterly, 63,* 238–252. (p. 165)

Snedeker, J., Geren, J., & Shafto, C. L. (2007). Starting over: International adoption as a natural experiment in language development. *Psychological Science, 18,* 79–86. (p. 321)

Snodgrass, S. E., Higgins, J. G., & Todisco, L. (1986). The effects of walking behavior on mood. Paper presented at the American Psychological Association convention. (p. 385)

Snyder, S. H. (1984). Neurosciences: An integrative discipline. *Science, 225,* 1255–1257. (pp. 39, 510)

Snyder, S. H. (1986). *Drugs and the brain.* New York: Scientific American Library. (p. 571)

Social Watch. (2006, March 8). No country in the world treats its women as well as its men (www.socialwatch.org). (p. 169)

Society for Personality Assessment. (2005). The status of the Rorschach in clinical and forensic practice: An official statement by the Board of Trustees of the Society for Personality Assessment. *Journal of Personality Assessment, 85,* 219–237. (p. 430)

Solomon, D. A., Keitner, G. I., Miller, I. W., Shea, M. T., & Keller, M. B. (1995). Course of illness and maintenance treatments for patients with bipolar disorder. *Journal of Clinical Psychiatry, 56*, 5–13. (p. 571)

Solomon, J. (1996, May 20). Breaking the silence. *Newsweek*, pp. 20–22. (p. 511)

Solomon, M. (1987, December). Standard issue. *Psychology Today*, pp. 30–31. (p. 489)

Song, S. (2006, March 27). Mind over medicine. *Time*, p. 47. (p. 98)

Sontag, S. (1978). *Illness as metaphor.* New York: Farrar, Straus, & Giroux. (p. 397)

Sørensen, H. J., Mortensen, E. L., Reinisch, J. M., & Mednick, S. A. (2005). Breastfeeding and risk of schizophrenia in the Copenhagen Perinatal Cohort. *Acta Psychiatrica Scandinavica, 112*, 26–29. (p. 529)

Sørensen, H. J., Mortensen, E. L., Reinisch, J. M., & Mednick, S. A. (2006). Height, weight, and body mass index in early adulthood and risk of schizophrenia. *Acta Psychiatrica Scandinavica, 114*, 49–54. (p. 529)

Sorkhabi, N. (2005). Applicability of Baumrind's parent typology to collective cultures: Analysis of cultural explanations of parent socialization effects. *International Journal of Behavioral Development, 29*, 552–563. (p. 138)

Soussignan, R. (2001). Duchenne smile, emotional experience, and autonomic reactivity: A test of the facial feedback hypothesis. *Emotion, 2*, 52–74. (p. 385)

Sowell, T. (1991, May/June). Cultural diversity: A world view. *American Enterprise*, pp. 44–55. (p. 500)

Spanos, N. P. (1982). A social psychological approach to hypnotic behavior. In G. Weary & H. L. Mirels (Eds.), *Integrations of clinical and social psychology.* New York: Oxford. (p. 99)

Spanos, N. P. (1986). Hypnosis, nonvolitional responding, and multiple personality: A social psychological perspective. *Progress in Experimental Personality Research, 14*, 1–62. (p. 535)

Spanos, N. P. (1991). Hypnosis, hypnotizability, and hypnotherapy. In C. R. Snyder & D. R. Forsyth (Eds.), *Handbook of social and clinical psychology: The health perspective.* New York: Pergamon Press. (p. 98)

Spanos, N. P. (1994). Multiple identity enactments and multiple personality disorder: A sociocognitive perspective. *Psychological Bulletin, 116*, 143–165. (p. 535)

Spanos, N. P. (1996). *Multiple identities and false memories: A sociocognitive perspective.* Washington, DC: American Psychological Association Books. (pp. 98, 535)

Spanos, N. P., & Coe, W. C. (1992). A social-psychological approach to hypnosis. In E. Fromm & M. R. Nash (Eds.), *Contemporary hypnosis research.* New York: Guilford. (p. 99)

Sparrow, B., Liu, J., & Wegner, D. M. (2011). Google effects on memory: Cognitive consequences of having information at our fingertips. *Science, 333*, 776–778. (p. 274)

Speer, N. K., Reynolds, J. R., Swallow, K. M., & Zacks, J. M. (2009). Reading stories activates neural representations of visual and motor experiences. *Psychological Science, 20*, 989–999. (pp. 263, 323)

Spelke, E. S., & Kinzler, K. D. (2007). Core knowledge. *Developmental Science, 10*, 89–96. (p. 127)

Spence, I., & Feng, J. (2010). Video games and spatial cognition. *Review of General Psychology, 14*, 92–104. (p. 215)

Spencer, K. M., Nestor, P. G., Perlmutter, R., Niznikiewicz, M. A., Klump, M. C., Frumin, M., Shenton, M. E., & McCarley, R. W. (2004). Neural synchrony indexes disordered perception and cognition in schizophrenia. *Proceedings of the National Academy of Sciences, 101*, 17288–17293. (p. 530)

Spencer, S. J., Steele, C. M., & Quinn, D. M. (1997). Stereotype threat and women's math performance. Unpublished manuscript, Hope College. (p. 346)

Sperling, G. (1960). The information available in brief visual presentations. *Psychological Monographs, 74* (Whole No. 498). (p. 275)

Sperry, R. W. (1964). Problems outstanding in the evolution of brain function. James Arthur Lecture, American Museum of Natural History, New York. Cited by R. Ornstein (1977), *The psychology of consciousness* (2nd ed.). New York: Harcourt Brace Jovanovich. (p. 61)

Sperry, R. W. (1985). Changed concepts of brain and consciousness: Some value implications. *Zygon, 20*, 41–57. (p. 206)

Spiegel, D. (2007). The mind prepared: Hypnosis in surgery. *Journal of the National Cancer Institute, 99*, 1280–1281. (p. 98)

Spiegel, D. (2008, January 31). *Coming apart: Trauma and the fragmentation of the self.* Dana Foundation (www.dana.org). (p. 535)

Spiegel, K., Leproult, R., L'Hermite-Balériaux, M., Copinschi, G., Penev, P. D., & Van Cauter, E. (2004). Leptin levels are dependent on sleep duration: Relationships with sympathovagal balance, carbohydrate regulation, cortisol, and thyrotropin. *Journal of Clinical Endocrinology and Metabolism, 89*, 5762–5771. (p. 90)

Spielberger, C., & London, P. (1982). Rage boomerangs. *American Health, 1*, 52–56. (p. 399)

Sprecher, S. (1989). The importance to males and females of physical attractiveness, earning potential, and expressiveness in initial attraction. *Sex Roles, 21*, 591–607. (p. 489)

Spring, B., Pingitore, R., Bourgeois, M., Kessler, K. H., & Bruckner, E. (1992). The effects and non-effects of skipping breakfast: Results of three studies. Paper presented at the American Psychological Association convention. (p. 363)

Squire, L. R. (1992). Memory and the hippocampus: A synthesis from findings with rats, monkeys, and humans. *Psychological Review, 99*, 195–231. (p. 281)

Squire, L. R., & Zola-Morgan, S. (1991, September 20). The medial temporal lobe memory system. *Science, 253*, 1380–1386. (p. 282)

Srivastava, A., Locke, E. A., & Bartol, K. M. (2001). Money and subject well-being: It's not the money, it's the motives. *Journal of Personality and Social Psychology, 80*, 959–971. (p. 415)

Srivastava, S., John, O. P., Gosling, S. D., & Potter, J. (2003). Development of personality in early and middle adulthood: Set like plaster or persistent change? *Journal of Personality & Social Psychology, 84*, 1041–1053. (p. 440)

Srivastava, S., McGonigal, K. M., Richards, J. M., Butler, E. A., & Gross, J. J. (2006). Optimism in close relationships: How seeing things in a positive light makes them so. *Journal of Personality and Social Psychology, 91*, 143–153. (p. 404)

Stack, S. (1992). Marriage, family, religion, and suicide. In R. Maris, A. Berman, J. Maltsberger, & R. Yufit (Eds.), *Assessment and prediction of suicide.* New York: Guilford Press. (p. 524)

Stafford, R. S., MacDonald, E. A., & Finkelstein, S. N. (2001). National patterns of medication treatment for depression, 1987 to 2001. *Primary Care Companion Journal of Clinical Psychiatry, 3*, 232–235. (p. 570)

Stager, C. L., & Werker, J. F. (1997). Infants listen for more phonetic detail in speech perception than in word-learning tasks. *Nature, 388*, 381–382. (p. 320)

Stanford University Center for Narcolepsy. (2002). Narcolepsy is a serious medical disorder and a key to understanding other sleep disorders (www.med.stanford.edu/school/Psychiatry/narcolepsy). (p. 92)

Stanley, D., Phelps, E., & Banaji, M. (2008). The neural basis of implicit attitudes. *Current Directions in Psychological Science, 17*, 164–170. (p. 477)

Stanley, J. C. (1997). Varieties of intellectual talent. *Journal of Creative Behavior, 31*, 93–119. (p. 339)

Stanovich, K. (1996). *How to think straight about psychology.* New York: HarperCollins. (p. 424)

Stark, R. (2003a). *For the glory of God: How monotheism led to reformations, science, witch-hunts, and the end of slavery.* Princeton, NJ: Princeton University Press. (p. 14)

Stark, R. (2003b, October-November). False conflict: Christianity is not only compatible with science—it created it. *American Enterprise*, pp. 27–33. (p. 14)

Statistics Canada. (1999). *Statistical report on the health of Canadians.* Prepared by the Federal, Provincial and Territorial Advisory Committee on Population Health for the Meeting of Ministers of Health, Charlottetown, PEI, September 16–17, 1999. (p. 145)

Statistics Canada. (2010). Languages. Canada year book. 11-402-X. (p. 327)

Statistics Canada. (2010). *Victims and persons accused of homicide, by age and sex.* Table 253-0003. (p. 165)

Staub, E. (1989). *The roots of evil: The psychological and cultural sources of genocide.* New York: Cambridge University Press. (p. 461)

Staub, E., & Vollhardt, J. (2008). Altruism born of suffering: The roots of caring and helping after experiences of personal and political victimization. *American Journal of Orthopsychiatry, 78,* 267–280. (p. 576)

St. Clair, D., Xu, M., Wang, P., Yu, Y., Fang, Y., Zhang, F., Zheng, X., Gu, N., Feng, G., Sham, P., & He, L. (2005). Rates of adult schizophrenia following prenatal exposure to the Chinese famine of 1959–1961. *Journal of the American Medical Association, 294,* 557–562. (p. 531)

Steel, P., Schmidt, J., & Schultz, J. (2008). Refining the relationship between personality and subject well-being. *Psychological Bulletin, 134,* 138–161. (p. 417)

Steele, C. M. (1990, May). A conversation with Claude Steele. *APS Observer,* pp. 11–17. (p. 343)

Steele, C. M. (1995, August 31). Black students live down to expectations. *New York Times.* (p. 346)

Steele, C. M. (2010). *Whistling Vivaldi: And other clues to how stereotypes affect us.* New York: Norton. (p. 346)

Steele, C. M., & Josephs, R. A. (1990). Alcohol myopia: Its prized and dangerous effects. *American Psychologist, 45,* 921–933. (p. 103)

Steele, C. M., Spencer, S. J., & Aronson, J. (2002). Contending with group image: The psychology of stereotype and social identity threat. *Advances in Experimental Social Psychology, 34,* 379–440. (p. 346)

Stein, S. (2009, August 20). New poll: 77 percent support "choice" of public option. *Huffington Post* (huffingtonpost.com). (p. 19)

Steinberg, L. (1987, September). Bound to bicker. *Psychology Today,* pp. 36–39. (p. 146)

Steinberg, L. (2007). Risk taking in adolescence: New perspectives from brain and behavioral science. *Current Directions in Psychological Science, 16,* 55–59. (p. 141)

Steinberg, L. (2010, March). Analyzing adolescence. Interview with Sara Martin. *Monitor on Psychology,* pp. 26–29. (p. 141)

Steinberg, L., Cauffman, E., Woolard, J., Graham, S., & Banich, M. (2009). Are adolescents less mature than adults? Minors' access to abortion, the juvenile death penalty, and the alleged APA "flip-flop." *American Psychologist, 64,* 583–594. (p 141)

Steinberg, L., & Morris, A. S. (2001). Adolescent development. *Annual Review of Psychology, 52,* 83–110. (pp. 138, 146)

Steinberg, L., & Scott, E. S. (2003). Less guilty by reason of adolescence: Developmental immaturity, diminished responsibility, and the juvenile death penalty. *American Psychologist, 58,* 1009–1018. (p. 141)

Steinberg, N. (1993, February). Astonishing love stories (from an earlier United Press International report). *Games,* p. 47. (p. 488)

Steinhauer, J. (1999, November 29). Number of twins rises: So does parental stress. *New York Times* (www.nytimes.com). (p. 64)

Steinhauer, J., & Holson, L. M. (2008, September 20). As text messages fly, danger lurks. *New York Times* (www.nytimes.com). (p. 146)

Steinmetz, J. E. (1999). The localization of a simple type of learning and memory: The cerebellum and classical eyeblink conditioning. *Contemporary Psychology, 7,* 72–77. (p. 282)

Stengel, E. (1981). Suicide. In *The new Encyclopaedia Britannica, macropaedia* (Vol. 17, pp. 777–782). Chicago: Encyclopaedia Britannica. (p. 524)

Stepanikova, I., Nie, N. H., & He, X. (2010). Time on the Internet at home, loneliness, and life satisfaction: Evidence from panel time-diary data. *Computers in Human Behavior, 26,* 329–338. (p. 368)

Steptoe, A., Chida, Y., Hamer, M., & Wardle, J. (2010). Author reply: Meta-analysis of stress-related factors in cancer. *Nature Reviews: Clinical Oncology, 7,* doi:10.1038/ncponc1134-c2. (p. 397)

Stern, M., & Karraker, K. H. (1989). Sex stereotyping of infants: A review of gender labeling studies. *Sex Roles, 20,* 501–522. (p. 198)

Sternberg, E. M. (2006). A compassionate universe? *Science, 311,* 611–612. (p. 315)

Sternberg, E. M. (2009). *Healing spaces: The science of place and well-being.* Cambridge, MA: Harvard University Press. (p. 394)

Sternberg, R. J. (1985). *Beyond IQ: A triarchic theory of human intelligence.* New York: Cambridge University Press. (p. 331)

Sternberg, R. J. (1988). Applying cognitive theory to the testing and teaching of intelligence. *Applied Cognitive Psychology, 2,* 231–255. (p. 314)

Sternberg, R. J. (1999). The theory of successful intelligence. *Review of General Psychology, 3,* 292–316. (p. 331)

Sternberg, R. J. (2003). Our research program validating the triarchic theory of successful intelligence: Reply to Gottfredson. *Intelligence, 31,* 399–413. (pp. 314, 331)

Sternberg, R. J. (2006). The Rainbow Project: Enhance the SAT through assessments of analytical, practical, and creative skills. *Intelligence, 34,* 321–350. (p. 332)

Sternberg, R. J. (2007, July 6). Finding students who are wise, practical, and creative. *The Chronicle Review* (www.chronicle.com). (p. 332)

Sternberg, R. J. (2010). Assessment of gifted students for identification purposes: new techniques for a new millennium. *Learning and Individual Differences, 20,* 327–336. (p. 332)

Sternberg, R. J., & Grajek, S. (1984). The nature of love. *Journal of Personality and Social Psychology, 47,* 312–329. (p. 492)

Sternberg, R. J., & Kaufman, J. C. (1998). Human abilities. *Annual Review of Psychology, 49,* 479–502. (p. 329)

Sternberg, R. J., & Lubart, T. I. (1991). An investment theory of creativity and its development. *Human Development,* 1–31. (p. 314)

Sternberg, R. J., & Lubart, T. I. (1992). Buy low and sell high: An investment approach to creativity. *Psychological Science, 1,* 1–5. (p. 314)

Stetter, F., & Kupper, S. (2002). Autogenic training: A meta-analysis of clinical outcome studies. *Applied Psychophysiology and Biofeedback, 27,* 45–98. (p. 409)

Stevenson, H. W. (1992, December). Learning from Asian schools. *Scientific American,* pp. 70–76. (p. 344)

Stevenson, R. J., & Tomiczek, C. (2007). Olfactory-induced synesthesias: A review and model. *Psychological Bulletin, 133,* 294–309. (p. 229)

Stewart, R. E., & Chambless, D. L. (2009). Cognitive-behavioral therapy for adult anxiety disorders in clinical practice: A meta-analysis of effectiveness studies. *Journal of Consulting and Clinical Psychology, 77,* 595–606. (p. 562)

Stice, E. (2002). Risk and maintenance factors for eating pathology: A meta-analytic review. *Psychological Bulletin, 128,* 825–848. (p. 536)

Stice, E., Ng, J., & Shaw, H. (2010). Risk factors and prodromal eating pathology. *Journal of Child Psychology and Psychiatry, 51,* 518–525. (p. 537)

Stice, E., Shaw, H., Bohon, C., Marti, C. N., & Rohde, P. (2009). A meta-analytic review of depression prevention programs for children and adolescents: Factors that predict magnitude of intervention effects. *Journal of Consulting and Clinical Psychology, 77,* 486–503. (pp. 556, 577)

Stice, E., Shaw, H., & Marti, C. N. (2007). A meta-analytic review of eating disorder prevention programs: Encouraging findings. *Annual Review of Clinical Psychology, 3,* 233–257. (p. 537)

Stice, E., Spangler, D., & Agras, W. S. (2001). Exposure to media-portrayed thin-ideal images adversely affects vulnerable girls: A longitudinal experiment. *Journal of Social and Clinical Psychology, 20,* 270–288. (p. 537)

Stickgold, R. (2000, March 7). Quoted by S. Blakeslee, For better learning, researchers endorse "sleep on it" adage. *New York Times,* p. F2. (pp. 94, 95)

Stickgold, R., & Ellenbogen, J. M. (2008, August/September). Quiet! Sleeping brain at work. *Scientific American Mind,* pp. 23–29. (p. 88)

Stickgold, R., Hobson, J. A., Fosse, R., & Fosse, M. (2001). Sleep, learning, and dreams: Off-line memory processing. *Science, 294,* 1052–1057. (p. 95)

Stickgold, R., Malia, A., Maquire, D., Roddenberry, D., & O'Connor, M. (2000, October 13). Replaying the game: Hypnagogic images in normals and amnesics. *Science, 290,* 350–353. (p. 95)

Stiglitz, J. (2009, September 13). Towards a better measure of well-being. *Financial Times* (www.ft.com). (p. 419)

Stillman, T. F., Baumeister, R. F., Vohs, K. D., Lambert, N. M., Fincham, F. D., & Brewer, L. E. (2010). Personal philosophy and personnel achievement: Belief in free will predicts better job performance. *Social Psychological and Personality Science, 1,* 43–50. (p. 403)

Stinson, D. A., Logel, C., Zanna, M. P., Holmes, J. G., Cameron, J. J., Wood, J. V., & Spencer, S. J. (2008). The cost of lower self-esteem: Testing a self- and social-bonds model of health. *Journal of Personality and Social Psychology, 94,* 412–428. (p. 407)

Stith, S. M., Rosen, K. H., Middleton, K. A., Busch, A. L., Lunderberg, K., & Carlton, R. P. (2000). The intergenerational transmission of spouse abuse: A meta-analysis. *Journal of Marriage and the Family, 62,* 640–654. (p. 264)

St. Jacques, P. L., Dolcos, F., & Cabeza, R. (2009). Effects of aging on functional connectivity of the amygdala for subsequent memory of negative pictures: A network analysis of fMRI data. *Psychological Science, 20,* 74–84. (p. 157)

Stockton, M. C., & Murnen, S. K. (1992). Gender and sexual arousal in response to sexual stimuli: A meta-analytic review. Paper presented at the American Psychological Society convention. (p. 175)

Stone, A. A., & Neale, J. M. (1984). Effects of severe daily events on mood. *Journal of Personality and Social Psychology, 46,* 137–144. (p. 414)

Stone, A. A., Schwartz, J. E., Broderick, J. E., & Deaton, A. (2010). A snapshot of the age distribution of psychological well-being in the United States. *PNAS, 107,* 9985–9990. (p. 156)

Stone, A. A., Schwartz, J. E., Broderick, J. E., & Shiffman, S. S. (2005). Variability of momentary pain predicts recall of weekly pain: A consequences of the peak (or salience) memory heuristic. *Personality and Social Psychology Bulletin, 31,* 1340–1346. (p. 222)

Stone, G. (2006, February 17). Homeless man discovered to be lawyer with amnesia. *ABC News* (abcnews.go.com). (p. 534)

Stoolmiller, M. (1999). Implications of the restricted range of family environments for estimates of heritability and nonshared environment in behavior-genetic adoption studies. *Psychological Bulletin, 125,* 392–409. (p. 66)

Storbeck, J., Robinson, M. D., & McCourt, M. E. (2006). Semantic processing precedes affect retrieval: The neurological case for cognitive primary in visual processing. *Review of General Psychology, 10,* 41–55. (p. 375)

Storm, L., Tressoldi, P. E., & Di Risio, L. (2010a). A meta-analysis with nothing to hide: Reply to Hyman (2010). *Psychological Bulletin, 136,* 491–494. (p. 230)

Storm, L., Tressoldi, P. E., & Di Risio, L. (2010b). Meta-analysis of free-response studies, 1992–2008: Assessing the noise reduction model in parapsychology *Psychological Bulletin, 136,* 471–485. (p. 230)

Storms, M. D. (1973). Videotape and the attribution process: Reversing actors' and observers' points of view. *Journal of Personality and Social Psychology, 27,* 165–175. (p. 459)

Storms, M. D. (1983). *Development of sexual orientation.* Washington, DC: Office of Social and Ethical Responsibility, American Psychological Association. (p. 179)

Storms, M. D., & Thomas, G. C. (1977). Reactions to physical closeness. *Journal of Personality and Social Psychology, 35,* 412–418. (p. 471)

Stout, J. A., & Dasgupta, N. (2011). When *he* doesn't mean *you*: Gender-exclusive language as ostracism. *Personality and Social Psychology Bulletin, 37,* 75–769. (p. 366)

Stowell, J. R., Oldham, T., & Bennett, D. (2010). Using student response systems ("clickers") to combat conformity and shyness. *Teaching of Psychology, 37,* 135–140. (p. 467)

Strack, F., Martin, L., & Stepper, S. (1988). Inhibiting and facilitating conditions of the human smile: A nonobtrusive test of the facial feedback hypothesis. *Journal of Personality and Social Psychology, 54,* 768–777. (p. 384)

Strahan, E. J., Spencer, S. J., & Zanna, M. P. (2002). Subliminal priming and persuasion: Striking while the iron is hot. *Journal of Experimental Social Psychology, 38,* 556–568. (p. 195)

Stranahan, A. M., Khalil, D., & Gould, E. (2006). Social isolation delays the positive effects of running on adult neurogenesis. *Nature Neuroscience, 9,* 526–533. (p. 58)

Strand, S., Deary, I. J., & Smith, P. (2006). Sex differences in cognitive abilities test scores: A UK national picture. *British Journal of Educational Psychology, 76,* 463–480. (p. 342)

Strange, D., Hayne, H., & Garry, M. (2008). A photo, a suggestion, a false memory. *Applied Cognitive Psychology, 22,* 587–603. (p. 295)

Strasburger, V. C., Jordan, A. B., & Donnerstein, E. (2010). Health effects of media on children and adolescents. *Pediatrics, 125,* 756–767. (p. 264)

Stratton, G. M. (1896). Some preliminary experiments on vision without inversion of the retinal image. *Psychological Review, 3,* 611–617. (p. 215)

Straub, R. O., Seidenberg, M. S., Bever, T. G., & Terrace, H. S. (1979). Serial learning in the pigeon. *Journal of the Experimental Analysis of Behavior, 32,* 137–148. (p. 324)

Straus, M. A., & Gelles, R. J. (1980). *Behind closed doors: Violence in the American family.* New York: Anchor/Doubleday. (p. 252)

Straus, M. A., Sugarman, D. B., & Giles-Sims, J. (1997). Spanking by parents and subsequent antisocial behavior of children. *Archives of Pediatric Adolescent Medicine, 151,* 761–767. (p. 252)

Strawbridge, W. J. (1999). Mortality and religious involvement: A review and critique of the results, the methods, and the measures. Paper presented at a Harvard University conference on religion and health, sponsored by the National Institute for Health Research and the John Templeton Foundation. (p. 411)

Strawbridge, W. J., Cohen, R. D., & Shema, S. J. (1997). Frequent attendance at religious services and mortality over 28 years. *American Journal of Public Health, 87,* 957–961. (p. 411)

Strawbridge, W. J., Shema, S. J., Cohen, R. D., & Kaplan, G. A. (2001). Religious attendance increases survival by improving and maintaining good health behaviors, mental health, and social relationships. *Annals of Behavioral Medicine, 23,* 68–74. (p. 411)

Strayer, D. L., & Drews, F A. (2007). Cell-phone-induced driver distraction. *Current Directions in Psychological Science, 16,* 128–131. (p. 81)

Strick, M., Dijksterhuis, A., & van Baaren, R. B. (2010). Unconscious-thought effects take place off-line, not on-line. *Psychological Science, 21,* 484–488. (p. 313)

Stroebe, W. (2012). The truth about Triplett (1898), but nobody seems to care. *Perspectives on Psychological Science, 7,* 54–57. (p. 471)

Stroebe, W., Schut, H., & Stroebe, M. S. (2005). Grief work, disclosure and counseling: Do they help the bereaved? *Clinical Psychology Review, 25,* 395–414. (p. 158)

Stross, R. (2011, July 9). The therapist will see you now, via the web. *New York Times* (www.nytimes.com). (p. 557)

Strully, K. W. (2009). Job loss and health in the U.S. labor market. *Demography, 46,* 221–246. (p. 392)

Strupp, H. H. (1986). Psychotherapy: Research, practice, and public policy (How to avoid dead ends). *American Psychologist, 41,* 120–130. (p. 565)

Su, R., Rounds, J., & Armstrong, P. I. (2009). Men and things, women and people: A meta-analysis of sex differences in interests. *Psychological Bulletin, 135,* 859–884. (p. 166)

Subiaul, F., Cantlon, J. F., Holloway, R. L., & Terrace, H. S. (2004). Cognitive imitation in rhesus macaques. *Science, 305,* 407–410. (p. 263)

Subrahmanyam, K., & Greenfield, P. (2008). Online communication and adolescent relationships. *The Future of Children, 18,* 119–146. (p. 146)

Suddath, R. L., Christison, G. W., Torrey, E. F., Casanova, M. F., & Weinberger, D. R. (1990). Anatomical abnormalities in the brains of monozygotic twins discordant for schizophrenia. *New England Journal of Medicine, 322,* 789–794. (p. 533)

Sue, S. (2006). Research to address racial and ethnic disparities in mental health: Some lessons learned. In S. I. Donaldson, D. E. Berger, & K. Pezdek (Eds.), *Applied psychology; New frontiers and rewarding careers.* Mahwah, NJ; Erlbaum. (p. 566)

Suedfeld, P. (1998). Homo invictus: The indomitable species. *Canadian Psychology, 38,* 164–173. (p. 576)

Suedfeld, P. (2000). Reverberations of the Holocaust fifty years later: Psychology's contributions to understanding persecution and genocide. *Canadian Psychology, 41,* 1–9. (p. 576)

Suedfeld, P., & Mocellin, J. S. P. (1987). The "sensed presence" in unusual environments. *Environment and Behavior, 19,* 33–52. (p. 107)

Suinn, R. M. (1997). Mental practice in sports psychology: Where have we been, Where do we go? *Clinical Psychology: Science and Practice, 4,* 189–207. (p. 328)

Sullivan, D., & von Wachter, T. (2009). Job displacement and mortality: An analysis using administrative data. *Quarterly Journal of Economics, 124,* 1265–1306. (p. 391)

Sullivan, K. T., Pasch, L. A., Johnson, M. D., & Bradbury, T. N. (2010). Social support, problem solving, and the longitudinal course of newlywed marriage. *Journal of Personality and Social Psychology, 98,* 631–644. (p. 493)

Sullivan, P. F., Neale, M. C., & Kendler, K. S. (2000). Genetic epidemiology of major depression: Review and meta-analysis. *American Journal of Psychiatry, 157,* 1552–1562. (p. 523)

Sullivan/Anderson, A. (2009, March 30). How to end the war over sex ed. *Time,* pp. 40–43. (p. 176)

Suls, J. M., & Tesch, F. (1978). Students' preferences for information about their test performance: A social comparison study. *Journal of Experimental Social Psychology, 8,* 189–197. (p. 417)

Summers, M. (1996, December 9). Mister clean. *People Weekly,* pp. 139–142. (p. 505)

Sun, Q. I., Townsend, M. K., Okereke, O., Franco, O. H., Hu, F. B., & Grodstein, F. (2009). Adiposity and weight change in mid-life in relation to healthy survival after age 70 in women: Prospective cohort study. *British Medical Journal, 339,* b3796. (p. 361)

Sundstrom, E., De Meuse, K. P., & Futrell, D. (1990). Work teams: Applications and effectiveness. *American Psychologist, 45,* 120–133. (p. B-12)

Sunstein, C. R. (2007). On the divergent American reactions to terrorism and climate change. *Columbia Law Review, 107,* 503–557. (p. 309)

Suomi, S. J. (1986). Anxiety-like disorders in young nonhuman primates. In R. Gettleman (Ed.), *Anxiety disorders of childhood.* New York: Guilford Press. (p. 517)

Suppes, P. (1982). Quoted by R. H. Ennis, Children's ability to handle Piaget's propositional logic: A conceptual critique. In S. Modgil & C. Modgil (Eds.), *Jean Piaget: Consensus and controversy.* New York: Praeger. (p. 129)

Surgeon General. (1986). *The surgeon general's workshop on pornography and public health,* June 22–24. Report prepared by E. P. Mulvey & J. L. Haugaard and released by Office of the Surgeon General on August 4, 1986. (p. 485)

Surgeon General. (1999). *Mental health: A report of the surgeon general.* Rockville, MD: U.S. Department of Health and Human Services. (p. 511)

Susser, E. S., Neugenbauer, R., Hoek, H. W., Brown, A. S., Lin, S., Labovitz, D., & Gorman, J. M. (1996). Schizophrenia after prenatal famine. *Archives of General Psychiatry, 53(1),* 25–31. (p. 531)

Sutcliffe, J. S. (2008). Insights into the pathogenesis of autism. *Science, 321,* 208–209. (p. 130)

Sutherland, A. (2006, June 25). What Shamu taught me about a happy marriage, *New York Times.* (p. 255)

Swami, V., & 60 others. (2010). The attractive female body weight and female body dissatisfaction in 26 countries across 10 world regions: Results of the international body project I. *Personality and Social Psychology Bulletin, 36,* 309–325. (p. 537)

Swami, V., Henderson, G., Custance, D., & Tovée, M. J. (2011). A cross-cultural investigation of men's judgments of female body weight in Britain and Indonesia. *Journal of Cross-Cultural Psychology, 42,* 140–145. (p. 361)

Swann, W. B., Jr., Chang-Schneider, C., & McClarty, K. L. (2007). Do people's self-views matter: Self-concept and self-esteem in everyday life. *American Psychologist, 62,* 84–94. (p. 447)

Sweat, J. A., & Durm, M. W. (1993). Psychics: Do police departments really use them? *Skeptical Inquirer, 17,* 148–158. (p. 230)

Swerdlow, N. R., & Koob, G. F. (1987). Dopamine, schizophrenia, mania, and depression: Toward a unified hypothesis of cortico-stiato-pallido-thalamic function (with commentary). *Behavioral and Brain Sciences, 10,* 197–246. (p. 530)

Swim, J. K., Johnston, K., & Pearson, N. B. (2009). Daily experiences with heterosexism: Relations between heterosexist hassles and psychological well-being. *Journal of Social and Clinical Psychology, 28,* 597–629. (p. 392)

Symbaluk, D. G., Heth, C. D., Cameron, J., & Pierce, W. D. (1997). Social modeling, monetary incentives, and pain endurance: The role of self-efficacy and pain perception. *Personality and Social Psychology Bulletin, 23,* 258–269. (p. 222)

Symond, M. B., Harris, A. W. F., Gordon, E., & Williams, L. M. (2005). (p. 530)

Symons, C. S., & Johnson, B. T. (1997). The self-reference effect in memory: A meta-analysis. *Psychological Bulletin, 121(3),* 371–394. (p. 280)

T

Taha, F. A. (1972). A comparative study of how sighted and blind perceive the manifest content of dreams. *National Review of Social Sciences, 9(3),* 28. (p. 93)

Taheri, S. (2004a, 20 December). Does the lack of sleep make you fat? *University of Bristol Research News* (www.bristol.ac.uk). (p. 362)

Taheri, S., Lin, L., Austin, D., Young, T., & Mignot, E. (2004b). Short sleep duration is associated with reduced leptin, elevated ghrelin, and increased body mass index. *PLoS Medicine, 1(3),* e62. (p. 362)

Tajfel, H. (Ed.). (1982). *Social identity and intergroup relations.* New York: Cambridge University Press. (p. 478)

Talal, N. (1995). Quoted by V. Morell, Zeroing in on how hormones affect the immune system. *Science, 269,* 773–775. (p. 394)

Talarico, J. M., & Rubin, D. C. (2003). Confidence, not consistency, characterizes flashbulb memories. *Psychological Science, 14,* 455–461. (p. 283)

Talarico, J. M., & Rubin, D. C. (2007). Flashbulb memories are special after all; in phenomenology, not accuracy. *Applied Cognitive Psychology, 21,* 557–578. (p. 283)

Tamres, L. K., Janicki, D., & Helgeson, V. S. (2002). Sex differences in coping behavior: A meta-analytic review and an examination of relative coping. *Personality and Social Psychology Review, 6,* 2–30. (p. 166)

Tang, S-H., & Hall, V. C. (1995). The overjustification effect: A meta-analysis. *Applied Cognitive Psychology, 9,* 365–404. (p. 260)

Tangney, C. C., Kwasny, M. J., Li, H., Wilson, R. S., Evans, D. A., & Morris, M. C. (2011). Adherence to a Mediterranean-type dietary pattern and cognitive decline in a community population. *American Journal of Clinical Nutrition, 93,* 601–607. (p. 525)

Tangney, J. P., Baumeister, R. F., & Boone, A. L. (2004). High self-control predicts good adjustment, less pathology, better grades, and interpersonal success. *Journal of Personality, 72,* 271–324. (p. 403)

Tannen, D. (1990). *You just don't understand: Women and men in conversation.* New York: Morrow. (p. 165)

Tannen, D. (2001). *You just don't understand: Women and men in conversation.* New York: Harper. (p. 27)

Tannenbaum, P. (2002, February). Quoted in R. Kubey & M. Csikszentmihalyi, Television addiction is no mere metaphor. *Scientific American,* pp. 74–80. (p. 196)

Tanner, J. M. (1978). *Fetus into man: Physical growth from conception to maturity.* Cambridge, MA: Harvard University Press. (p. 168)

Tardif, T., Fletcher, P., Liang, W., Zhang, Z., Kaciroti, N., & Marchman, V. A. (2008). Baby's first 10 words. *Developmental Psychology, 44,* 929–938. (p. 320)

Taubes, G. (2001). The soft science of dietary fat. *Science, 291,* 2536–2545. (p. 363)

Taubes, G. (2002, July 7). What if it's all been a big fat lie? *New York Times* (www.nytimes.com). (p. 363)

Tavris, C. (1982, November). Anger defused. *Psychology Today,* pp. 25–35. (p. 398)

Tavris, C., & Aronson, E. (2007). *Mistakes were made (but not by me).* Orlando, FL: Harcourt. (p. 293)

Tay, L., & Diener, E. (2011). Needs and subjective well-being around the world. *Journal of Personality and Social Psychology, 101,* 354–365. (p. 355)

Taylor, C. A., Manganello, J. A., Lee, S. J., & Rice, J. C. (2010). Mothers' spanking of 3-year-old children and subsequent risk of children's aggressive behavior. *Pediatrics, 125,* 1057–1065. (p. 252)

Taylor, K., & Rohrer, D. (2010). The effects of interleaved practice. *Applied Cognitive Psychology, 24,* 837–848. (p. 30)

Taylor, P. J., Gooding, P., Wood, A. M., & Tarrier, N. (2011). The role of defeat and entrapment in depression, anxiety, and suicide. *Psychological Bulletin, 137,* 391–420. (p. 524)

Taylor, P. J., Russ-Eft, D. F., & Chan, D. W. L. (2005). A meta-analytic review of behavior modeling training. *Journal of Applied Psychology, 90,* 692–709. (p. 263)

Taylor, S., Kuch, K., Koch, W. J., Crockett, D. J., & Passey, G. (1998). The structure of posttraumatic stress symptoms. *Journal of Abnormal Psychology, 107,* 154–160. (p. 515)

Taylor, S. E. (1989). *Positive illusions.* New York: Basic Books. (p. 312)

Taylor, S. E. (2002). *The tending instinct: How nurturing is essential to who we are and how we live.* New York: Times Books. (p. 166)

Taylor, S. E. (2006). Tend and befriend: Biobehavioral bases of affiliation under stress. *Current Directions in Psychological Science, 15,* 273–277. (p. 393)

Taylor, S. E., Cousino, L. K., Lewis, B. P., Gruenewald, T. L., Gurung, R. A. R., & Updegraff, J. A. (2000). Biobehavioral responses to stress in females: Tend-and-befriend, not fight-or-flight. *Psychological Review, 107,* 411–430. (p. 393)

Taylor, S. E., Pham, L. B., Rivkin, I. D., & Armor, D. A. (1998). Harnessing the imagination: Mental simulation, self-regulation, and coping. *American Psychologist, 53,* 429–439. (p. 328)

Taylor, S. P., & Chermack, S. T. (1993). Alcohol, drugs and human physical aggression. *Journal of Studies on Alcohol,* Supplement No. 11, 78–88. (p. 482)

Tedeschi, R. G., & Calhoun, L. G. (2004). Posttraumatic growth: Conceptual foundations and empirical evidence. *Psychological Inquiry, 15,* 1–18. (p. 576)

Teghtsoonian, R. (1971). On the exponents in Stevens' law and the constant in Ekinan's law. *Psychological Review, 78,* 71–80. (p. 195)

Teicher, M. H. (2002, March). The neurobiology of child abuse. *Scientific American,* pp. 68–75. (p. 137)

Teller. (2009, April 20). Quoted by J. Lehrer, Magic and the brain: Teller reveals the neuroscience of illusion. *Wired Magazine* (www.wired.com). (p. 82)

Tenopyr, M. L. (1997). Improving the workplace: Industrial/organizational psychology as a career. In R. J. Sternberg (Ed.), *Career paths in psychology: Where your degree can take you.* Washington, DC: American Psychological Association. (p. B-3)

Terao, T., Ohgami, H., Shlotsuki, I., Ishil, N., & Iwata, N. (2010). Author's reply. *British Journal of Psychiatry, 196,* 160. (p. 571)

Terman, J. S., Terman, M., Lo, E-S., & Cooper, T. B. (2001). Circadian time of morning light administration and therapeutic response in winter depression. *Archives of General Psychiatry, 58,* 69–73. (p. 564)

Terman, M., Terman, J. S., & Ross, D. C. (1998). A controlled trial of timed bright light and negative air ionization for treatment of winter depression. *Archives of General Psychiatry, 55,* 875–882. (p. 564)

Terrace, H. S. (1979, November). How Nim Chimpsky changed my mind. *Psychology Today,* pp. 65–76. (p. 324)

Terre, L., & Stoddart, R. (2000). Cutting edge specialties for graduate study in psychology. *Eye on Psi Chi,* 23–26. (p. C-1)

Tesser, A., Forehand, R., Brody, G., & Long, N. (1989). Conflict: The role of calm and angry parent-child discussion in adolescent development. *Journal of Social and Clinical Psychology, 8,* 317–330. (p. 146)

Tetlock, P. E. (1988). Monitoring the integrative complexity of American and Soviet policy rhetoric: What can be learned? *Journal of Social Issues, 44,* 101–131. (p. 500)

Tetlock, P. E. (1998). Close-call counterfactuals and belief-system defenses: I was not almost wrong but I was almost right. *Journal of Personality and Social Psychology, 75,* 639–652. (p. 12)

Tetlock, P. E. (2005). *Expert political judgement: How good is it? How can we know?* Princeton, NJ: Princeton University Press. (p. 12)

Thaler, R. H., & Sunstein, C. R. (2008). *Nudge: Improving decisions about health, wealth, and happiness.* New Haven, CT: Yale University Press. (p. 312)

Thatcher, R. W., Walker, R. A., & Giudice, S. (1987). Human cerebral hemispheres develop at different rates and ages. *Science, 236,* 1110–1113. (pp. 122, 149)

Thayer, R. E. (1987). Energy, tiredness, and tension effects of a sugar snack versus moderate exercise. *Journal of Personality and Social Psychology, 52,* 119–125. (p. 408)

Thayer, R. E. (1993). Mood and behavior (smoking and sugar snacking) following moderate exercise: A partial test of self-regulation theory. *Personality and Individual Differences, 14,* 97–104. (p. 408)

Théoret, H., Halligan, H., Kobayashi, M., Fregni, F., Tager-Flusberg, H., & Pascual-Leone, A. (2005). Impaired motor facilitation during action observation in individuals with autism spectrum disorder. *Current Biology, 15,* R84–R85. (p. 131)

Thernstrom, M. (2006, May 14). My pain, my brain. *New York Times* (www.nytimes.com). (p. 223)

Thiel, A., Hadedank, B., Herholz, K., Kessler, J., Winhuisen, L., Haupt, W. F., & Heiss, W-D. (2006). From the left to the right: How the brain compensates progressive loss of language function. *Brain and Language, 98,* 57–65. (p. 58)

Thomas, A., & Chess, S. (1986). The New York Longitudinal Study: From infancy to early adult life. In R. Plomin & J. Dunn (Eds.), *The study of temperament: Changes, continuities, and challenges.* Hillsdale, NJ: Erlbaum. (p. 159)

Thomas, L. (1983). *The youngest science: Notes of a medicine watcher.* New York: Viking Press. (p. 40)

Thomas, L. (1992). *The fragile species.* New York: Scribner's. (pp. 71, 321, 560)

Thompson, G. (2010). The $1 million dollar challenge. *Skeptic Magazine, 15,* 8–9. (p. 232)

Thompson, J. K., Jarvie, G. J., Lahey, B. B., & Cureton, K. J. (1982). Exercise and obesity: Etiology, physiology, and intervention. *Psychological Bulletin, 91,* 55–79. (p. 363)

Thompson, P. M., Cannon, T. D., Narr, K. L., van Erp, T., Poutanen, V-P., Huttunen, M., Lönnqvist, J., Standerskjöld-Nordenstam, C-G., Kaprio, J., Khaledy, M., Dail, R., Zoumalan, C. I., & Toga, A. W. (2001). Genetic influences on brain structure. *Nature Neuroscience, 4,* 1253–1258. (p. 340)

Thompson, P. M., Giedd, J. N., Woods, R. P., MacDonald, D., Evans, A. C., & Toga, A. W. (2000). Growth patterns in the developing brain detected by using continuum mechanical tensor maps. *Nature, 404,* 190–193. (p. 122)

Thompson, R., Emmorey, K., & Gollan, T. H. (2005). "Tip of the fingers" experiences by Deaf signers. *Psychological Science, 16,* 856–860. (p. 292)

Thompson-Schill, S. L., Ramscar, M., & Chrysikou, E. G. (2009). Cognition without control: When a little frontal lobe goes a long way. *Current Directions in Psychological Science, 18,* 259–263. (p. 122)

Thomson, R., & Murachver, T. (2001). Predicting gender from electronic discourse. *British Journal of Social Psychology, 40,* 193–208 (and personal correspondence from T. Murachver, May 23, 2002). (p. 165)

Thorndike, E. L. (1898). Animal intelligence: An experimental study of the associative processes in animals. *Psychological Review Monograph Supplement 2,* 4–160. (p. 246)

Thorne, J., with Rothstein, L. (1993). *You are not alone: Words of experience and hope for the journey through depression.* New York: HarperPerennial. (p. 505)

Thornton, B., & Moore, S. (1993). Physical attractiveness contrast effect: Implications for self-esteem and evaluations of the social self. *Personality and Social Psychology Bulletin, 19,* 474–480. (p. 490)

Thorpe, W. H. (1974). *Animal nature and human nature.* London: Methuen. (p. 325)

Tickle, J. J., Hull, J. G., Sargent, J. D., Dalton, M. A., & Heatherton, T. F. (2006). A structural equation model of social influences and exposure to media smoking on adolescent smoking. *Basic and Applied Social Psychology, 28,* 117–129. (p. 111)

Tiedens, L. Z. (2001). Anger and advancement versus sadness and subjugation: The effect of negative emotion expressions on social status conferral. *Journal of Personality and Social Psychology, 80,* 86–94. (p. 398)

Tiggemann, M., & Miller, J. (2010). The Internet and adolescent girls' weight satisfaction and drive for thinness. *Sex Roles, 63*, 79–90. (p. 537)

Tiihonen, J., Lönnqvist, J., Wahlbeck, K., Klaukka, T., Niskanen, L., Tanskanen, A., Haukka, J. (2009). 11-year follow-up of mortality in patients with schizophrenia: a population-based cohort study (FIN11 study). *Lancet, 374*, 260–267. (p. 568)

Time. (1997, December 22). Greeting card association data, p. 19. (p. 166)

Time. (2009, Oct. 14). The state of the American woman. pp. 32–33. (p. 166)

Time/CNN Survey. (1994, December 19). Vox pop: Happy holidays, *Time.* (p. 519)

Timmerman, T. A. (2007). "It was a thought pitch": Personal, situational, and target influences on hit-by-pitch events across time. *Journal of Applied Psychology, 92*, 876–884. (p. 483)

Tinbergen, N. (1951). *The study of instinct.* Oxford: Clarendon. (p. 352)

Tirrell, M. E. (1990). Personal communication. (p. 242)

Toews, P. (2004, December 30). *Dirk Willems: A heart undivided.* Mennonite Brethren Historical Commission (www.mbhistory.org/profiles/dirk.en.html). (p. 457)

Tolin, D. F. (2010). Is cognitive-behavioral therapy more effective than other therapies? A meta-analytic review. *Clinical psychology Review, 30*, 710–720. (p. 562)

Tolman, E. C., & Honzik, C. H. (1930). Introduction and removal of reward, and maze performance in rats. *University of California Publications in Psychology, 4*, 257–275. (p. 260)

Tolstoy, L. (1904). *My confessions.* Boston: Dana Estes. (p. 28)

Tondo, L., Jamison, K. R., & Baldessarini, R. J. (1997). Effect of lithium maintenance on suicidal behavior in major mood disorders. In D. M. Stoff & J. J. Mann (Eds.), *The neurobiology of suicide: From the bench to the clinic.* New York; New York Academy of Sciences. (p. 571)

Toni, N., Buchs, P-A., Nikonenko, I., Bron, C. R., & Muller, D. (1999). LTP promotes formation of multiple spine synapses between a single axon terminal and a dendrite. *Nature, 402*, 421–442. (p. 284)

Topolinski, S., & Reber, R. (2010). Gaining insight into the "aha" experience. *Current Directions in Psychological Science, 19*, 401–405. (p. 307)

Torrey, E. F. (1986). *Witchdoctors and psychiatrists.* New York: Harper & Row. (p. 566)

Torrey, E. F., & Miller, J. (2002). *The invisible plague: The rise of mental illness from 1750 to the present.* New Brunswick, NJ: Rutgers University Press. (p. 531)

Torrey, E. F., Miller, J., Rawlings, R., & Yolken, R. H. (1997). Seasonality of births in schizophrenia and bipolar disorder: A review of the literature. *Schizophrenia Research, 28*, 1–38. (p. 531)

Totterdell, P., Kellett, S., Briner, R. B., & Teuchmann, K. (1998). Evidence of mood linkage in work groups. *Journal of Personality and Social Psychology, 74*, 1504–1515. (p. 465)

Tracy, J. L., Cheng, J. T., Robins, R. W., & Trzesniewski, K. H. (2009). Authentic and hubristic pride: The affective core of self-esteem and narcissism. *Self and Identity, 8*, 196–213. (p. 450)

Tracy, J. L., & Robins, R. W. (2004). Show your pride: Evidence for a discrete emotion expression. *Psychological Science, 15*, 194–197. (p. 376)

Trautwein, U., Lüdtke, O., Köller, O., & Baumert, J. (2006). Self-esteem, academic self-concept, and achievement: How the learning environment moderates the dynamics of self-concept. *Journal of Personality and Social Psychology, 90*, 334–349. (p. 447)

Treffert, D. A., & Christensen, D. D. (2005, December). Inside the mind of a savant. *Scientific American*, pp. 108–113. (p. 331)

Treffert, D. A., & Wallace, G. L. (2002). Island of genius—The artistic brilliance and dazzling memory that sometimes accompany autism and other disorders hint at how all brains work. *Scientific American, 286*, 76–86. (p. 330)

Treisman, A. (1987). Properties, parts, and objects. In K. R. Boff, L. Kaufman, & J. P. Thomas (Eds.), *Handbook of perception and human performance.* New York: Wiley. (p. 209)

Tremblay, R. E., Pihl, R. O., Vitaro, F., & Dobkin, P. L. (1994). Predicting early onset of male antisocial behavior from preschool behavior. *Archives of General Psychiatry, 51*, 732–739. (p. 539)

Trewin, D. (2001). *Australian social trends 2001.* Canberra: Australian Bureau of Statistics. (p. 169)

Triandis, H. C. (1994). *Culture and social behavior.* New York: McGraw-Hill. (pp. 451, 452, 484)

Triandis, H. C., Bontempo, R., Villareal, M. J., Asai, M., & Lucca, N. (1988). Individualism and collectivism: Cross-cultural perspectives on self-ingroup relationships. *Journal of Personality and Social Psychology, 54*, 323–338. (p. 452)

Trillin, C. (2006, March 27). Alice off the page. *The New Yorker*, p. 44. (p. 434)

Trimble, J. E. (1994). Cultural variations in the use of alcohol and drugs. In W. J. Lonner & R. Malpass (Eds.), *Psychology and culture.* Boston: Allyn & Bacon. (p. 111)

Triplett, N. (1898). The dynamogenic factors in pacemaking and competition. *American Journal of Psychology, 9*, 507–533. (p. 471)

Trut, L. N. (1999). Early canid domestication: The farm-fox experiment. *American Scientist, 87*, 160–169. (p. 69)

Tsai, J. L., & Chentsova-Dutton, Y. (2003). Variation among European Americans in emotional facial expression. *Journal of Cross-Cultural Psychology, 34*, 650–657. (p. 384)

Tsai, J. L., Miao, F. F., Seppala, E., Fung, H. H., & Yeung, D. Y. (2007). Influence and adjustment goals: Sources of cultural differences in ideal affect. *Journal of Personality and Social Psychology, 92*, 1102–1117. (p. 383)

Tsang, Y. C. (1938). Hunger motivation in gastrectomized rats. *Journal of Comparative Psychology, 26*, 1–17. (p. 357)

Tsuang, M. T., & Faraone, S. V. (1990). *The genetics of mood disorders.* Baltimore, MD: Johns Hopkins University Press. (p. 523)

Tuber, D. S., Miller, D. D., Caris, K. A., Halter, R., Linden, F., & Hennessy, M. B. (1999). Dogs in animal shelters: Problems, suggestions, and needed expertise. *Psychological Science, 10*, 379–386. (p. 27)

Tucker, K. A. (2002). I believe you can fly. *Gallup Management Journal* (www.gallupjournal.com/CA/st/20020520.asp). (p. B-10)

Tucker-Drob, E. M., Rhemtulla, M., Harden, K. P., Turkheimer, E., & Fask, D. (2011). Emergence of a gene x socioeconomic status interaction on infant mental ability between 10 months and 2 years. *Psychological Science, 22*, 125–133. (p. 340)

Tully, T. (2003). Reply: The myth of a myth. *Current Biology, 13*, R426. (p. 240)

Turkheimer, E., Haley, A., Waldron, M., D'Onofrio, B., & Gottesman, I. I. (2003). Socioeconomic status modifies heritability of IQ in young children. *Psychological Science, 14*, 623–628. (p. 340)

Turner, J. C. (1987). *Rediscovering the social group: A self-categorization theory.* New York: Basil Blackwell. (p. 478)

Turner, J. C. (2007). Self-categorization theory. In R. Baumeister & K. Vohs (Eds.), *Encyclopedia of social psychology.* Thousand Oaks, CA: Sage. (p. 478)

Turner, N., Barling, J., & Zacharatos, A. (2002). Positive psychology at work. In C. R. Snyder & S. J. Lopez (Eds.), *The handbook of positive psychology.* New York: Oxford University Press. (p. B-12)

Turpin, A. (2005, April 3). The science of psi. *FT Weekend*, pp. W1, W2. (p. 230)

Tversky, A. (1985, June). Quoted in K. McKean, Decisions, decisions. *Discover*, pp. 22–31. (p. 309)

Tversky, A., & Kahneman, D. (1974). Judgment under uncertainty: Heuristics and biases. *Science, 185*, 1124–1131. (p. 308, A-6)

Twenge, J. M. (1997). Changes in masculine and feminine traits over time: A meta-analysis. *Sex Roles 36*(5–6), 305–325. (p. 163)

Twenge, J. M. (2006). *Generation me.* New York: Free Press. (p. 449)

Twenge, J. M., Abebe, E. M., & Campbell, W. K. (2010). Fitting in or standing out: Trends in American parents' choices for children's names, 1880–2007. *Social Psychology and Personality Science, 1*, 19–25. (p. 452)

Twenge, J. M., Baumeister, R. F., DeWall, C. N., Ciarocco, N. J., & Bartels, J. M. (2007). Social exclusion decreases prosocial behavior. *Journal of Personality and Social Psychology, 92*, 56–66. (p. 366)

Twenge, J. M., Baumeister, R. F., Tice, D. M., & Stucke, T. S. (2001). If you can't join them, beat them: Effects of social exclusion on aggressive behavior. *Journal of Personality and Social Psychology, 81,* 1058–1069. (p. 366)

Twenge, J. M., Catanese, K. R., & Baumeister, R. F. (2002). Social exclusion causes self-defeating behavior. *Journal of Personality and Social Psychology, 83,* 606–615. (p. 366)

Twenge, J. M., & Foster, J. D. (2010). Birth cohort increases in narcissistic personality traits among American college students, 1982–2009. *Social Psychological and Personality Science, 1,* 99–106. (p. 449)

Twenge, J. M., Gentile, B., DeWall, C. D., Ma, D., & Lacefield, K. (2008). *A growing disturbance: Increasing psychopathology in young people 1938–2007 in a meta-analysis of the MMPI.* Unpublished manuscript, San Diego State University. (p. 522)

Twenge, J. M., Gentile, B., DeWall, C. N., Ma, D. S., Lacefield, K., & Schurtz, D. R. (2010). Birth cohort increases in psychopathology among young Americans, 1938–2007: A cross-temporal meta-analysis of the MMPI. *Clinical Psychology Review, 30,* 145–154. (p. 403)

Twenge, J. M., & Nolen-Hoeksema, S. (2002). Age, gender, race, socioeconomic status, and birth cohort differences on the children's depression inventory: A meta-analysis. *Journal of Abnormal Psychology, 111,* 578–588. (p. 145)

Twenge, J. M., Zhang, L., & Im, C. (2004). It's beyond my control: A cross-temporal meta-analysis of increasing externality in locus of control, 1960-2002. *Personality and Social Psychology Review, 8,* 308-319. (p. 403)

Twiss, C., Tabb, S., & Crosby, F. (1989). Affirmative action and aggregate data: The importance of patterns in the perception of discrimination. In F. Blanchard & F. Crosby (Eds.), *Affirmative action: Social psychological perspectives.* New York: Springer-Verlag. (p. A-5)

U

Uchida, Y., & Kitayama, S. (2009). Happiness and unhappiness in East and West: Themes and variations. *Emotion, 9,* 441–456. (p. 418)

Uchino, B. N. (2009). Understanding the links between social support and physical health. *Perspectives on Psychological Science, 4,* 236–255. (p. 405)

Uchino, B. N., Cacioppo, J. T., & Kiecolt-Glaser, J. K. (1996). The relationship between social support and physiological processes: A review with emphasis on underlying mechanisms and implications for health. *Psychological Bulletin, 119,* 488–531. (p. 405)

Uchino, B. N., Uno, D., & Holt-Lunstad, J. (1999). Social support, physiological processes, and health. *Current Directions in Psychological Science, 8,* 145–148. (p. 405)

Udry, J. R. (2000). Biological limits of gender construction. *American Sociological Review, 65,* 443–457. (p. 167)

Uga, V., Lemut, M. C., Zampi, C., Zilli, I., & Salzarulo, P. (2006). Music in dreams. *Consciousness and Cognition, 15,* 351–357. (p. 94)

UK ECT Review Group. (2003). Efficacy and safety of electroconvulsive therapy in depressive disorders: A systematic review and meta-analysis. *Lancet, 361,* 799–808. (p. 571)

UNAIDS. (2005). *AIDS epidemic update, December 2005.* United Nations (www.unaids.org). (p. 396)

UNAIDS. (2010). *UNAIDS report on the global AIDS epidemic 2010.* www.unaids.org. (pp. 174, 396)

UNAIDS. (2011). UNAIDS World Aids Day Report 2011. www.unaids.org. (p. 396)

Urbina, I. (2010, May 29). Documents show early worries about safety of rig. *New York Times* (www.nytimes.com). (p. 311)

Urry, H. L., & Gross, J. J. (2010). Emotion regulation in older age. *Current Directions in Psychological Science, 19,* 352–357. (p. 156)

Urry, H. L., Nitschke, J. B., Dolski, I., Jackson, D. C., Dalton, K. M., Mueller, C. J., Rosenkranz, M. A., Ryff, C. D., Singer, B. H., & Davidson, R. J. (2004). Making a life worth living: Neural correlates of well-being. *Psychological Science, 15,* 367–372. (p. 378)

Ursu, S., Stenger, V. A., Shear, M. K., Jones, M. R., & Carter, C. S. (2003). Overactive action monitoring in obsessive-compulsive disorder: Evidence from functional magnetic resonance imaging. *Psychological Science, 14,* 347–353. (p. 518)

V

Vacic, V., & 29 others. (2011). Duplications of the neuropeptide receptor gene *VIPR2* confer significant risk for schizophrenia. *Nature, 471,* 499–503. (p. 532)

Vaidya, J. G., Gray, E. K., Haig, J., & Watson, D. (2002). On the temporal stability of personality: Evidence for differential stability and the role of life experiences. *Journal of Personality and Social Psychology, 83,* 1469–1484. (p. 440)

Vaillant, G. E. (1977). *Adaptation to life.* New York: Little, Brown. (p. 297)

Vaillant, G. E. (2002). *Aging well: Surprising guideposts to a happier life from the landmark Harvard study of adult development.* Boston: Little, Brown. (p. 405)

Vaillant, G. E. (2009). Quoted by J. W. Shenk, What makes us happy? *The Atlantic* (www.theatlantic.com). (p. 367)

Valenstein, E. S. (1986). *Great and desperate cures: The rise and decline of psychosurgery.* New York; Basic Books. (p. 574)

Valkenburg, P. M., & Peter, J. (2009). Social consequences of the Internet for adolescents: A decade of research. *Current Directions in Psychological Science, 18,* 1–5. (pp. 146, 368)

van Anders, S. M., & Dunn, E. J. (2009). Are gonadal steroids linked with orgasm perceptions and sexual assertiveness in women and men? *Journal of Sexual Medicine, 6,* 739–751. (p. 172)

Van Baaren, R. B., Holland, R. W., Kawakami, K., & van Knippenberg, A. (2004). Mimicry and pro-social behavior. *Psychological Science, 15,* 71–74. (p. 465)

Van Baaren, R. B., Holland, R. W., Steenaert, B., & van Knippenberg, A. (2003). Mimicry for money: Behavioral consequences of imitation. *Journal of Experimental Social Psychology, 39,* 393–398. (p. 465)

van Boxtel, H. W., Orobio de Castro, B., & Goossens, F. A. (2004). High self-perceived social competence in rejected children is related to frequent fighting. *European Journal of Developmental Psychology, 1,* 205–214. (p. 449)

Van Cauter, E., Holmback, U., Knutson, K., Leproult, R., Miller, A., Nedeltcheva, A., Pannain, S., Penev, P., Tasali, E., & Spiegel, K. (2007). Impact of sleep and sleep loss on neuroendocrine and metabolic function. *Hormone Research, 67*(1), Supp. 1: 2–9. (p. 90)

Vance, E. B., & Wagner, N. N. (1976). Written descriptions of orgasm: A study of sex differences. *Archives of Sexual Behavior, 5,* 87–98. (p. 173)

Vandell, D. L., Belsky, J., Burchinal, M., Steinberg, L., Vandergrift, N., & NICHD Early Child Care Research Network (2010). Do effects of early child care extend to age 15 years? Results from the NICHD study of early child care and youth development. *Child Development, 81,* 737–756. (p. 137)

Vandenberg, S. G., & Kuse, A. R. (1978). Mental rotations: A group test of three-dimensional spatial visualization. *Perceptual and Motor Skills, 47,* 599–604. (p. 343)

van den Bos, K., & Spruijt, N. (2002). Appropriateness of decisions as a moderator of the psychology of voice. *European Journal of Social Psychology, 32,* 57–72. (p. B-12)

Van den Bussche, E., Van Den Noortgate, W., & Reynvoet, B. (2009). Mechanisms of masked priming: A meta-analysis. *Psychological Bulletin, 135,* 452–477. (p. 194)

Van Dyke, C., & Byck, R. (1982, March). Cocaine. *Scientific American,* pp. 128–141. (p. 106)

van Engen, M. L., & Willemsen, T. M. (2004). Sex and leadership styles: A meta-analysis of research published in the 1990s. *Psychological Reports, 94,* 3–18. (p. 165)

van Goozen, S. H. M., Fairchild, G., Snoek, H., & Harold, G. T. (2007). The evidence for a neurobiological model of childhood antisocial behavior. *Psychological Bulletin, 133,* 149–182. (p. 539)

van Hemert, D. A., Poortinga, Y. H., & van de Vijver, F. J. R. (2007). Emotion and culture: A meta-analysis. *Cognition and Emotion, 21,* 913–943. (p. 383)

van Honk, J., Schutter, D. J., Bos, P. A., Kruijt, A-W., Lentje, E. G., & Baron-Cohen, S. (2011). Testosterone administration impairs cognitive empathy in women depending on second-to-fourth digit ratio. *Proceedings of the National Academy of Sciences, 108,* 3448–3452. (p. 130)

Van IJzendoorn, M. H., & Juffer, F. (2005). Adoption is a successful natural intervention enhancing adopted children's IQ and school performance. *Current Directions in Psychological Science, 14,* 326–330. (p. 340)

Van IJzendoorn, M. H., & Juffer, F. (2006). The Emanual Miller Memorial Lecture 2006: Adoption as intervention. Meta-analytic evidence for massive catch-up and plasticity in physical, socio-emotional, and cognitive development. *Journal of Child Psychology and Psychiatry, 47,* 1228–1245. (pp. 66, 340)

van IJzendoorn, M. H., & Kroonenberg, P. M. (1988). Cross-cultural patterns of attachment: A meta-analysis of the strange situation. *Child Development, 59,* 147–156. (p. 134)

Van IJzendoorn, M. H., Luijk, M. P. C. M., & Juffer, F. (2008). IQ of children growing up in children's homes: A meta-analysis on IQ delays in ophanages. *Merrill-Palmer Quarterly, 54,* 341–366. (pp. 136, 341)

Van Leeuwen, M. S. (1978). A cross-cultural examination of psychological differentiation in males and females. *International Journal of Psychology, 13,* 87–122. (p. 169)

van Praag, H. (2009). Exercise and the brain: Something to chew on. *Trends in Neuroscience, 32,* 283–290. (p. 408)

Van Rooy, D. L., & Viswesvaran, C. (2004). Emotional intelligence: A meta-analytic investigation of predictive validity and nomological net. *Journal of Vocational Behavior, 65,* 71–95. (p. 333)

Van Yperen, N. W., & Buunk, B. P. (1990). A longitudinal study of equity and satisfaction in intimate relationships. *European Journal of Social Psychology, 20,* 287–309. (p. 492)

Van Zeijl, J., Mesman, J., Van IJzendoorn, M. H., Bakermans-Kranenburg, M. J., Juffer, F., Stolk, M. N., Koot, H. M., & Alink, L. R. A. (2006). Attachment-based intervention for enhancing sensitive discipline in mothers of 1- to 3-year-old children at risk for externalizing behavior problems: A randomized controlled trial. *Journal of Consulting and Clinical Psychology, 74,* 994–1005. (p. 135)

Vasey, P. L., & VanderLaan, D. P. (2010). An adaptive cognitive dissociation between willingness to help kin and nonkin in Samoan *Fa'afafine. Psychological Science, 21,* 292–297. (p. 181)

Vaughn, K. B., & Lanzetta, J. T. (1981). The effect of modification of expressive displays on vicarious emotional arousal. *Journal of Experimental Social Psychology, 17,* 16–30. (p. 385)

Vecera, S. P., Vogel, E. K., & Woodman, G. F. (2002). Lower region: A new cue for figure-ground assignment. *Journal of Experimental Psychology: General, 13,* 194–205. (p. 211)

Veenhoven, R. (2009). World data base of happiness: Tool for dealing with the 'data-deluge.' *Psychological Topics, 18,* 221–246. (p. 417)

Vekassy, L. (1977). Dreams of the blind. *Magyar Pszichologiai Szemle, 34,* 478–491. (p. 93)

Veltkamp, M., Custers, R., & Aarts, H. (2011). Motivating consumer behavior by subliminal conditioning in the absence of basic needs: Striking even while the iron is cold. *Journal of Consumer Psychology, 21,* 49–56. (p. 195)

Verbeek, M. E. M., Drent, P. J., & Wiepkema, P. R. (1994). Consistent individual differences in early exploratory behaviour of male great tits. *Animal Behaviour, 48,* 1113–1121. (p. 437)

Verhaeghen, P., & Salthouse, T. A. (1997). Meta-analyses of age-cognition relations in adulthood: Estimates of linear and nonlinear age effects and structural models. *Psychological Bulletin, 122,* 231–249. (p. 152)

Verosky, S. C., & Todorov, A. (2010). Generalization of affective learning about faces to perceptually similar faces. *Psychological Science, 21,* 779–785. (p. 244)

Vertes, R. P., & Siegel, J. M. (2005). Time for the sleep community to take a critical look at the purported role of sleep in memory processing. *Sleep, 28,* 1228–1229. (p. 95)

Verwijmeren, T., Karremans, J. C., Stroebe, W., & Wigboldus, D. H. J. (2011a). The workings and limits of subliminal advertising: The role of habits. *Journal of Consumer Psychology, 21,* 206–213. (p. 195)

Verwijmeren, T., Karremans, J. C., Stroebe, W., Wigboldus, D. H. J., & Ooigen, I. (2011b). Vicary's victory: Subliminal ads in movies work! Poster presented at the Society for Personality and Social Psychology meeting, San Antonio, TX. (p. 195)

Vigil, J. M. (2009). A socio-relational framework of sex differences in the expression of emotion. *Behavioral and Brain Sciences, 32,* 375–428. (p. 381)

Vigil, J. M., Geary, D. C., & Byrd-Craven, J. (2005). A life history assessment of early childhood sexual abuse in women. *Developmental Psychology, 41,* 553–561. (p. 167)

Vigliocco, G., & Hartsuiker, R. J. (2002). The interplay of meaning, sound, and syntax in sentence production. *Psychological Bulletin, 128,* 442–472. (p. 319)

Vining, E. P. G., Freeman, J. M., Pillas, D. J., Uematsu, S., Carson, B. S., Brandt, J., Boatman, D., Pulsifer, M. B., & Zukerberg, A. (1997). Why would you remove half a brain? The outcome of 58 children after hemispherectomy—The Johns Hopkins Experience: 1968 to 1996. *Pediatrics, 100,* 163–171. (p. 58)

Vinkhuyzen, A. A. E., van der Sluis, S., Posthuma, D., & Boomsma, D. I. (2009). The heritability of aptitude and exceptional talent across different domains in adolescents and young adults. *Behavior Genetics, 39,* 380–392. (p. 340)

Visalberghi, E. Addessi, E., Truppa, V., Spagnoletti, N., Ottoni, E., Izar, P., & Fragaszy, D. (2009). Selection of effective stone tools by wild bearded capuchin monkeys. *Current Biology, 19,* 213–217. (p. 318)

Visich, P. S., & Fletcher, E. (2009). Myocardial infarction. In J. K. Ehrman, P. M., Gordon, P. S. Visich, & S. J. Keleyian (Eds.). *Clinical exercise physiology, 2nd Edition.* Champaign, IL: Human Kinetics. (p. 407)

Visser, B. A., Ashton, M. C., & Vernon, P. A. (2006). Beyond *g:* Putting multiple intelligences theory to the test. *Intelligence, 34*(5), 487–502. (p. 333)

Vita, A. J., Terry, R. B., Hubert, H. B., & Fries, J. F. (1998). Aging, health risks, and cumulative disability. *New England Journal of Medicine, 338,* 1035–1041. (p. 105)

Vitello, P. (2006, June 12). A ring tone meant to fall on deaf ears. *New York Times* (www. nytimes.com). (p. 152)

Vitiello, M. V. (2009). Recent advances in understanding sleep and sleep disturbances in older adults: Growing older does not mean sleeping poorly. *Current Directions in Psychological Science, 18,* 316–320. (p. 92)

Vitória, P. D., Salgueiro, M. F., Silva, S. A., & De Vries, H. (2009). The impact of social influence on adolescent intention to smoke: Combining types and referents of influence. *British Journal of Health Psychology, 14,* 681–699. (p. 111)

Vittengl, J. R., Clark, L. A., Dunn, T. W., & Jarrett, R. B. (2007). Reducing relapse and recurrence in unipolar depression: A comparative meta-analysis of cognitive-behavioral therapy's effects. *Journal of Consulting and Clinical Psychology, 75,* 475–488. (p. 570)

Voas, D. (2008, March/April). Ten million marriages: An astrological detective story. *Skeptical Inquirer,* pp. 52–55. (p. 438)

Vocks, S., Tuschen-Caffier, B., Pietrowsky, R., Rustenbach, S. J., Kersting, A., & Herpertz, S. (2010). Meta-analysis of the effectiveness of psychological and pharmacological treatments for binge eating disorder. *International Journal of Eating Disorders, 43,* 205–217. (p. 537)

Vogel, G. (2010). Long-fought compromise reached on European animal rules. *Science, 329,* 1588–1589. (p. 27)

Vohs, K. D., Glass, B. D., Maddox, W. T., & Markman, A. B. (2011). Ego depletion is not just fatigue: Evidence from a total sleep deprivation experiment. *Social Psychological and Personality Science, 2,* 166–173. (p. 484)

Vohs, K. D., Mead, N. L., & Goode, M. R. (2006). The psychological consequences of money. *Science, 314,* 1154–1156. (p. 287)

Volkow, N. D., & 12 others. (2009). Evaluating dopamine reward pathway in ADHD: Clinical implications. *JAMA, 302,* 1084–1091. (p. 507)

von Békésy, G. (1957, August). The ear. *Scientific American,* pp. 66–78. (p. 219)

von Hippel, W. (2007). Aging, executive functioning, and social control. *Current Directions in Psychological Science, 16,* 240–244. (p. 152)

von Senden, M. (1932). *The perception of space and shape in the congenitally blind before and after operation.* Glencoe, IL: Free Press. (p. 215)

Vroom, V. H., & Jago, A. G. (2007). The role of the situation in leadership. *American Psychologist, 62,* 17–24. (p. B-11)

VTTI. (2009, September). *Driver distraction in commercial vehicle operations.* Virginia Tech Transportation Institute and U.S. Department of Transportation. (p. 81)

Vyazovskiy, V. V., Cirelli, C., Pfister-Genskow, M., Faraguna, U., & Tononi, G. (2008). Molecular and electrophysiological evidence for net synaptic potentiation in wake and depression in sleep. *Nature Neuroscience, 11,* 200–208. (p. 88)

W

Waber, R. L., Shiv, B., Carmon, & Ariely, D. (2008). Commercial features of placebo and therapeutic efficacy. *Journal of the American Medical Association, 299,* 1016–1017. (p. 23)

Wacker, J., Chavanon, M.-L., & Stemmler, G. (2006). Investigating the dopaminergic basis of extraversion in humans: A multilevel approach. *Journal of Personality and Social Psychology, 91,* 177–187. (p. 437)

Wade, K. A., Garry, M., Read, J. D., & Lindsay, D. S. (2002). A picture is worth a thousand lies: Using false photographs to create false childhood memories. *Psychonomic Bulletin & Review, 9,* 597–603. (p. 295)

Wade, N. G., Worthington, E. L., Jr., & Vogel, D. L. (2006). Effectiveness of religiously tailored interventions in Christian therapy. *Psychotherapy Research, 17,* 91–105. (p. 566)

Wagar, B. M., & Cohen, D. (2003). Culture, memory, and the self: An analysis of the personal and collective self in long-term memory. *Journal of Experimental Social Psychology, 39,* 458–475. (p. 280)

Wagenmakers, E-J., Wetzels, R., Borsboom, D., & van der Maas, H. (2011). Why psychologists must change the way they analyze their data: The case of psi. *Journal of Personality and Social Psychology, 100,* 1–12. (p. 232)

Wager, T. D. (2005). The neural bases of placebo effects in pain. *Current Directions in Psychological Science, 14,* 175–179. (p. 223)

Wagner, D. D., Cin, S. D., Sargent, J. C., Kelley, W. M., & Heatherton, T. F. (2011). Spontaneous action representation in smokers when watching movie characters smoke. *Journal of Neuroscience, 31,* 894–898. (p. 263)

Wagner, U., Gais, S., Haider, H., Verleger, R., & Born, J. (2004). Sleep inspires insight. *Nature, 427,* 352–355. (p. 89)

Wagstaff, G. (1982). Attitudes to rape: The "just world" strikes again? *Bulletin of the British Psychological Society, 13,* 275–283. (p. 459)

Wahlberg, D. (2001, October 11). We're more depressed, patriotic, poll finds. *Grand Rapids Press,* p. A15. (p. 391)

Wai, J., Cacchio, M., Putallaz, M., & Makel, M. C. (2010). Sex differences in the right tail of cognitive abilities: A 30 year examination. *Intelligence, 38,* 412–423. (p. 342)

Wai, J., Lubinski, D., & Benbow, C. P. (2005). Creativity and occupational accomplishments among intellectually precocious youths: An age 13 to age 33 longitudinal study. *Journal of Educational Psychology, 97,* 484–492. (p. 339)

Wakefield, J. C., & Spitzer, R. L. (2002). Lowered estimates—but of what? *Archives of General Psychiatry, 59,* 129–130. (p. 516)

Walker, E., Shapiro, D., Esterberg, M., & Trotman, H. (2010). Neurodevelopment and schizophrenia: Broadening the focus. *Current Directions in Psychological Science, 19,* 204–208. (pp. 531, 533)

Walker, M. P., & van der Helm, E. (2009). Overnight therapy? The role of sleep in emotional brain processing. *Psychological Bulletin, 135,* 731–748. (p. 90)

Walker, W. R., Skowronski, J. J., & Thompson, C. P. (2003). Life is pleasant—and memory helps to keep it that way! *Review of General Psychology, 7,* 203–210. (p. 157)

Walkup, J. T., & 12 others. (2008). Cognitive behavioral therapy, sertraline, or a combination in childhood anxiety. *New England Journal of Medicine, 359,* 2753–2766. (p. 570)

Wall, P. D. (2000). *Pain: The science of suffering.* New York: Columbia University Press. (p. 221)

Wallace, D. S., Paulson, R. M., Lord, C. G., & Bond, C. F., Jr. (2005). Which behaviors do attitudes predict? Meta-analyzing the effects of social pressure and perceived difficulty. *Review of General Psychology, 9(3),* 214–227. (p. 460)

Wallach, M. A., & Wallach, L. (1983). *Psychology's sanction for selfishness: The error of egoism in theory and therapy.* New York: Freeman. (p. 435)

Wallach, M. A., & Wallach, L. (1985, February). How psychology sanctions the cult of the self. *Washington Monthly,* pp. 46–56. (p. 435)

Walster (Hatfield), E., Aronson, V., Abrahams, D., & Rottman, L. (1966). Importance of physical attractiveness in dating behavior. *Journal of Personality and Social Psychology, 4,* 508–516. (p. 489)

Walton, G. M., & Spencer S. J. (2009). Latent ability: Grades and test scores systematically underestimate the intellectual ability of negatively stereotyped students. *Psychological Science, 20,* 1132–1139. (p. 346)

Wampold, B. E. (2001). *The great psychotherapy debate: Models, methods, and findings.* Mahwah, NJ; Erlbaum. (p. 565)

Wampold, B. E. (2007). Psychotherapy: The humanistic (and effective) treatment. *American Psychologist, 62,* 857–873. (pp. 562, 565)

Wampold, B. E., Mondin, G. W., Moody, M., & Ahn, H. (1997). The flat earth as a metaphor for the evidence for uniform efficacy of bona fide psychotherapies: Reply to Crits-Christoph (1997) and Howard et al. (1997). *Psychological Bulletin, 122,* 226–230. (p. 562)

Wang, K-S., Liu, X-F., & Aragam, N. (2010). A genome-wide meta-analysis identified novel loci associated with schizophrenia and bipolar disorder. *Schizophrenia Research, 124,* 192–199. (p. 532)

Wang, Q., Bowling, N. A., & Eschleman, K. J. (2010). A meta-analytic examination of work and general locus of control. *Journal of Applied Psychology, 95,* 761–768. (p. 402)

Wang, S-H., Baillargeon, R., & Brueckner, L. (2004). Young infants' reasoning about hidden objects: Evidence from violation-of-expectation tasks with test trials only. *Cognition, 93,* 167–198. (p. 127)

Wang, X. T., & Dvorak, R. D. (2010). Sweet future: Fluctuating blood glucose levels affect future discounting. *Psychological Science, 21,* 183–188. (p. 404)

Wansink, B. (2007). *Mindless eating: Why we eat more than we think.* New York: Bantam Dell. (p. 360)

Wansink, B., van Ittersum, K., & Painter, J. E. (2006). Ice cream illusions: Bowls, spoons, and self-served portion sizes. *American Journal of Preventive Medicine, 31,* 240–243. (p. 360)

Ward, A., & Mann, T. (2000). Don't mind if I do: Disinhibited eating under cognitive load. *Journal of Personality and Social Psychology, 78,* 753–763. (p. 363)

Ward, C. (1994). Culture and altered states of consciousness. In W. J. Lonner & R. Malpass (Eds.), *Psychology and culture.* Boston: Allyn & Bacon. (p. 100)

Ward, J. (2003). State of the art synaesthesia. *The Psychologist, 16,* 196–199. (p. 229)

Ward, K. D., Klesges, R. C., & Halpern, M. T. (1997). Predictors of smoking cessation and state-of-the-art smoking interventions. *Journal of Socies Issues, 53,* 129–145. (p. 105)

Ward, L. M., & Friedman, K. (2006). Using TV as a guide: Associations between television viewing and adolescents' sexual attitudes and behavior. *Journal of Research on Adolescence, 16,* 133–156. (p. 177)

Wardle, J., Cooke, L. J., Gibson, L., Sapochnik, M., Sheiham, A., & Lawson, M. (2003). Increasing children's acceptance of vegetables: A randomized trial of parent-led exposure. *Appetite, 40,* 155–162. (p. 224)

Wargo, E. (2007, December). Understanding the have-knots. *APS Observer,* pp. 18–21. (p. 410)

Warner, J., McKeown, E., Johnson, K., Ramsay, A., Cort, C., & King, M. (2004). Rates and predictors of mental illness in gay men, lesbians and bisexual men and women. *British Journal of Psychiatry, 185,* 479–485. (p. 179)

Wason, P. C. (1960). On the failure to eliminate hypotheses in a conceptual task. *Quarterly Journal of Experimental Psychology, 12,* 129–140. (p. 307)

Wason, P. C. (1981). The importance of cognitive illusions. *The Behavioral and Brain Sciences, 4,* 356. (p. 307)

Wasserman, E. A. (1993). Comparative cognition: Toward a general understanding of cognition in behavior. *Psychological Science, 4,* 156–161. (p. 247)

Wasserman, E. A. (1995). The conceptual abilities of pigeons. *American Scientist, 83,* 246–255. (p. 317)

Wastell, C. A. (2002). Exposure to trauma: The long-term effects of suppressing emotional reactions. *Journal of Nervous and Mental Disorders, 190,* 839–845. (p. 407)

Waterhouse, R. (1993, July 19). Income for 62 percent is below average pay. *The Independent,* p. 4. (p. A-2)

Waterman, A. S. (1988). Identity status theory and Erikson's theory: Commonalities and differences. *Developmental Review, 8,* 185–208. (p. 145)

Watkins, E. R. (2008). Constructive and unconstructive repetitive thought. *Psychological Bulletin, 134,* 163–206. (p. 519)

Watkins, J. G. (1984). The Bianchi (L. A. Hillside Strangler) case: Sociopath or multiple personality? *International Journal of Clinical and Experimental Hypnosis, 32,* 67–101. (p. 534)

Watson, D. (2000). *Mood and temperament.* New York: Guilford Press. (pp. 408, 414)

Watson, J. B. (1913). Psychology as the behaviorist views it. *Psychological Review, 20,* 158–177. (pp. 78, 239, 245)

Watson, J. B. (1924). The unverbalized in human behavior. *Psychological Review, 31,* 339–347. (p. 245)

Watson, J. B., & Rayner, R. (1920). Conditioned emotional reactions. *Journal of Experimental Psychology, 3,* 1–14. (p. 245)

Watson, R. I., Jr. (1973). Investigation into deindividuation using a cross-cultural survey technique. *Journal of Personality and Social Psychology, 25,* 342–345. (p. 472)

Watson, S. J., Benson, J. A., Jr., & Joy, J. E. (2000). NEWS AND VIEWS—Marijuana and medicine: Assessing the science base: A summary of the 1999 Institute of Medicine report. *Archives of General Psychiatry, 57,* 547–553. (p. 108)

Watters, E. (2010). *Crazy like us: The globalization of the American psyche.* New York: Free Press. (p. 508)

Wayment, H. A., & Peplau, L. A. (1995). Social support and well-being among lesbian and heterosexual women: A structural modeling approach. *Personality and Social Psychology Bulletin, 21,* 1189–1199. (p. 155)

Weaver, J. B., Masland, J. L., & Zillmann, D. (1984). Effect of erotica on young men's aesthetic perception of their female sexual partners. *Perceptual and Motor Skills, 58,* 929–930. (p. 176)

Webb, W. B. (1992). *Sleep: The gentle tyrant.* Bolton, MA: Anker. (p. 92)

Webb, W. B., & Campbell, S. S. (1983). Relationships in sleep characteristics of identical and fraternal twins. *Archives of General Psychiatry, 40,* 1093–1095. (p. 87)

Webley, K. (2009, June 15). Behind the drop in Chinese adoptions. *Time,* p. 55. (p. 477)

Wegman, H. L., & Stetler, C. (2009). A meta-analytic review of the effects of childhood abuse on medical outcomes in adulthood. *Psychosomatic Medicine, 71,* 805–812. (p. 137)

Weinberger, D. R. (2001, March 10). A brain too young for good judgment. *New York Times* (www.nytimes.com). (p. 141)

Weingarten, G. (2002, March 10). Below the beltway. *Washington Post,* p. WO3. (p. B-1)

Weisbuch, M., Ivcevic, Z., & Ambady, N. (2009). On being liked on the web and in the "real world": Consistency in first impressions across personal webpages and spontaneous behavior. *Journal of Experimental Social Psychology, 45,* 573–576. (p. 368)

Weiskrantz, L. (2009). *Blindsight.* Oxford: Oxford University Press. (p. 79)

Weiskrantz, L. (2010). Blindsight in hindsight. *The Psychologist, 23,* 356–358. (p. 79)

Weiss, A., King, J. E., & Figueredo, A. J. (2000). The heritability of personality factors in chimpanzees (Pan troglodytes). *Behavior Genetics, 30,* 213–221. (p. 418)

Weiss, A., King, J. E., & Perkins, L. (2006). Personality and subjective well-being in orangutans (*Pongo pygmaeus* and *Pongo abelii*). *Journal of Personality and Social Psychology, 90,* 501–511. (pp. 418, 437)

Welch, J. M., Lu, J., Rodriquiz, R. M., Trotta, N. C., Peca, J., Ding, J.-D., Feliciano, C., Chen, M., Adams, J. P., Luo, J., Dudek, S. M., Weinberg, R. J., Calakos, N., Wetsel, W. C., & Feng, G. (2007). Cortico-striatal synaptic defects and OCD-like behaviours in *Sapap3*-mutant mice. *Nature, 448,* 894–900. (p. 518)

Welch, W. W. (2005, February 28). Trauma of Iraq war haunting thousands returning home. *USA Today* (www.usatoday.com). (p. 515)

Weller, S., & Davis-Beaty, K. (2002). The effectiveness of male condoms in prevention of sexually transmitted diseases (protocol). *Cochrane Database of Systematic Reviews,* Issue 4, Art. No. CD004090. (p. 174)

Wellman, H. M., & Gelman, S. A. (1992). Cognitive development: Foundational theories of core domains. *Annual Review of Psychology, 43,* 337–375. (p. 127)

Wells, D. L. (2009). The effects of animals on human health and well-being. *Journal of Social Issues, 65,* 523–543. (p. 406)

Wells, G. L. (1981). Lay analyses of causal forces on behavior. In J. Harvey (Ed.), *Cognition, social behavior and the environment.* Hillsdale, NJ: Erlbaum. (p. 238)

Wender, P. H., Kety, S. S., Rosenthal, D., Schulsinger, F., Ortmann, J., & Lunde, I. (1986). Psychiatric disorders in the biological and adoptive families of adopted individuals with affective disorders. *Archives of General Psychiatry, 43,* 923–929. (p. 523)

Westen, D. (1996). Is Freud really dead? Teaching psychodynamic theory to introductory psychology. Presentation to the Annual Institute on the Teaching of Psychology, St. Petersburg Beach, Florida. (p. 428)

Westen, D. (1998). The scientific legacy of Sigmund Freud: Toward a psychodynamically informed psychological science. *Psychological Bulletin, 124,* 333–371. (p. 430)

Westen, D. (2007). *The political brain: The role of emotion in deciding the fate of the nation.* New York: PublicAffairs. (p. 375)

Westen, D., & Morrison, K. (2001). A multidimensional meta-analysis of treatments for depression, panic, and generalized anxiety disorder: An empirical examination of the status of empirically supported therapies. *Journal of Consulting and Clinical Psychology, 69,* 875–899, 562)

Whalen, P. J., Shin, L. M., McInerney, S. C., Fisher, H., Wright, C. I., & Rauch, S. L. (2001). A functional MRI study of human amygdala responses to facial expressions of fear versus anger. *Emotion, 1,* 70–83. (p. 378)

Whaley, S. E., Sigman, M., Beckwith, L., Cohen, S. E., & Espinosa, M. P. (2002). Infant-caregiver interaction in Kenya and the United States: The importance of multiple caregivers and adequate comparison samples. *Journal of Cross-Cultural Psychology, 33,* 236–247. (p. 137)

Whang, W., Kubzansky, L, D., Kawachi, I., Rexrode, K. M., Kroenke, C. H., Glynn, R. J., Garan, H., & Albert, C. M. (2009). Depression and risk of sudden cardiac death and coronary heart disease in women. *Journal of the American College of Cardiology, 53,* 950–958. (p. 400)

Wheelwright, J. (2004, August). Study the clones first. *Discover,* pp. 44–50. (p. 64)

Whetten, K., Ostermann J., Whetten R.A., Pence B.W., O'Donnell K., Messer L.C., Thielman N.M., & The Positive Outcomes for Orphans (POFO) Research Team. (2009, December 18). A comparison of the wellbeing of orphans and abandoned children ages 6–12 in institutional and community-based care settings in 5 less wealthy nations. (p. 137)

White, H. R., Brick, J., & Hansell, S. (1993). A longitudinal investigation of alcohol use and aggression in adolescence. *Journal of Studies on Alcohol,* Supplement No. 11, 62–77. (p. 482)

White, L., & Edwards, J. (1990). Emptying the nest and parental well-being: An analysis of national panel data. *American Sociological Review, 55,* 235–242. (p. 156)

White, R. A. (1998). Intuition, heart knowledge, and parapsychology. *Journal of the American Society for Psychical Research, 92,* 158–171. (p. 231)

Whitehead, B. D., & Popenoe, D. (2001). *The state of our unions 2001: The social health of marriage in America.* Rutgers University: The National Marriage Project. (p. 155)

Whiten, A., & Boesch, C. (2001, January). Cultures of chimpanzees. *Scientific American,* pp. 60–67. (p. 317)

Whiten, A., & Byrne, R. W. (1988). Tactical deception in primates. *Behavioral and Brain Sciences, 11,* 233–244, 267–273. (p. 18)

Whiting, B. B., & Edwards, C. P. (1988). *Children of different worlds: The formation of social* *behavior.* Cambridge, MA: Harvard University Press. (p. 139)

Whitley, B. E., Jr. (1999). Right-wing authoritarianism, social dominance orientation, and prejudice. *Journal of Personality and Social Psychology, 77,* 126–134. (p. 479)

Whitlock, J. R., Heynen, A. L., Shuler, M. G., & Bear, M. F. (2006). Learning induces long-term potentiation in the hippocampus. *Science, 313,* 1093–1097. (p. 284)

Whitmer, R. A., Gustafson, D. R., Barrett-Connor, E. B., Haan, M. N., Gunderson, E. P., & Yaffe, K. (2008). Central obesity and increased risk of dementia more than three decades later. *Neurology, 71,* 1057–1064. (p. 361)

WHO. (1979). *Schizophrenia: An international followup study.* Chicester, England: Wiley. (p. 530)

WHO. (2000). *Effectiveness of male latex condoms in protecting against pregnancy and sexually transmitted infections.* World Health Organization (www.who.int). (p. 174)

WHO. (2002). *The global burden of disease.* Geneva: World Health Organization (www.who.int/msa/mnh/ems/dalys/intro.htm). (p. 520)

WHO. (2003). *The male latex condom: Specification and guidelines for condom procurement.* Department of Reproductive Health and Research, Family and Community Health, World Health Organization. (p. 174)

WHO. (2004a). Prevalence, severity, and unmet need for treatment of mental disorders in the World Health Organization World Mental Health Surveys. *Journal of the American Medical Association, 291,* 2581–2590. (pp. 527, 540)

WHO. (2004b). *Women, girls, HIV, and AIDS.* World Health Organization, Western Pacific Regional Office. (p. 174)

WHO. (2007). Obesity and overweight. (www.who.int/dietphysicalactivity/publications/facts/obesity/en/). (p. 361)

WHO. (2008a). *Mental health (nearly 1 million annual suicide deaths).* Geneva: World Health Organization (www.who.int/mental_health/en). (p. 524)

WHO. (2008b). The numbers count: Mental disorders in America (www.nimh.nih.gov). (p. 101)

WHO. (2008c). *WHO report on the global tobacco epidemic, 2008.* Geneva: World Health Organization (www.who.int). (p. 104)

WHO. (2010, September). Mental health: Strengthening our response. Fact sheet N°220. Retrieved online at www.who.int/mediacentre/factsheets/fs220/en/. (p. 505)

WHO. (2011a). Country reports and charts available. Geneva: World Health Organization (int/mental_health/prevention/suicide/country_reports/en/index.html). (p. 524)

WHO. (2011b). Schizophrenia. Geneva: World Health Organization (www.who.int). (p. 529)

Whooley, M. A., & 11 others. (2008). Depressive symptoms, health behaviors, and risk of cardiovascular events in patients with coronary heart disease. *JAMA, 300,* 2379–2388. (p. 400)

Whorf, B. L. (1956). Science and linguistics. In J. B. Carroll (Ed.), *Language, thought, and reality: Selected writings of Benjamin Lee Whorf.* Cambridge, MA: MIT Press. (p. 326)

Wicherts, J. M., Dolan, C. V., Carlson, J. S., & van der Maas, H. L. J. (2010). Raven's test performance of sub-Saharan Africans: Mean level, psychometric properties, and the Flynn Effect. *Learning and Individual Differences, 20,* 135–151. (p. 344)

Wickelgren, I. (2009, September/October). I do not feel your pain. *Scientific American Mind,* pp. 51–57. (p. 221)

Wickelgren, W. A. (1977). *Learning and memory.* Englewood Cliffs, NJ: Prentice-Hall. (p. 280)

Wielkiewicz, R. M., & Stelzner, S. P. (2005). An ecological perspective on leadership theory, research, and practice. *Review of General Psychology, 9,* 326–341. (p. B-11)

Wiens, A. N., & Menustik, C. E. (1983). Treatment outcome and patient characteristics in an aversion therapy program for alcoholism. *American Psychologist, 38,* 1089–1096. (p. 552)

Wierson, M., & Forehand, R. (1994). Parent behavioral training for child noncompliance: Rationale, concepts, and effectiveness. *Current Directions in Psychological Science, 3,* 146–149. (p. 254)

Wierzbicki, M. (1993). Psychological adjustment of adoptees: A meta-analysis. *Journal of Clinical Child Psychology, 22,* 447–454. (p. 66)

Wiesel, T. N. (1982). Postnatal development of the visual cortex and the influence of environment. *Nature, 299,* 583–591. (p. 215)

Wiesner, W. H., & Cronshow, S. P. (1988). A meta-analytic investigation of the impact of interview format and degree of structure on the validity of the employment interview. *Journal of Occupational Psychology, 61,* 275–290. (p. B-6)

Wigdor, A. K., & Garner, W. R. (1982). *Ability testing: Uses, consequences, and controversies.* Washington, DC: National Academy Press. (p. 345)

Wilcox, A. J., Baird, D. D., Dunson, D. B., McConnaughey, D. R., Kesner, J. S., & Weinberg, C. R. (2004). On the frequency of intercourse around ovulation: Evidence for biological influences. *Human Reproduction, 19,* 1539–1543. (p. 172)

Wilder, D. A. (1981). Perceiving persons as a group: Categorization and intergroup relations. In D. L. Hamilton (Ed.), *Cognitive processes in stereotyping and intergroup behavior.* Hillsdale, NJ: Erlbaum. (p. 478)

Wilford, J. N. (1999, February 9). New findings help balance the cosmological books. *New York Times* (www.nytimes.com). (p. 71)

Wilkinson, P., & Goodyer, I. (2011). Non-suicidal self-injury. *European Child & Adolescent Psychiatry, 20,* 103–108. (p. 525)

Wilkinson, R., & Pickett, K. (2009). *The spirit level: Why greater equality makes societies stronger.* London: Bloomsbury Press. (p. 484)

Wilkowski, B. M., Robinson, M. D., & Troop-Gordon, W. (2011). How does cognitive control reduce anger and aggression? The role of conflict monitoring and forgiveness processes. *Journal of Personality and Social Psychology, 98,* 830–840. (p. 482)

Williams, C. L., & Berry, J. W. (1991). Primary prevention of acculturative stress among refugees. *American Psychologist, 46,* 632–641. (p. 391)

Williams, J. E., & Best, D. L. (1990). *Measuring sex stereotypes: A multination study.* Newbury Park, CA: Sage. (p. 165)

Williams, J. H. G., Waister, G. D., Gilchrist, A., Perrett, D. I., Murray, A. D., & Whiten, A. (2006). Neural mechanisms of imitation and 'mirror neuron' functioning in autistic spectrum disorder. *Neuropsychogia, 44,* 610–621. (p. 157)

Williams, K. D. (2007). Ostracism. *Annual Review of Psychology, 58,* 425–452. (pp. 366, 367)

Williams, K. D. (2009). Ostracism: A temporal need-threat model. *Advances in Experimental Social Psychology, 41,* 275–313. (p. 366)

Williams, K. D., & Zadro, L. (2001). Ostracism: On being ignored, excluded and rejected. In M. Leary (Ed.), *Rejection.* New York: Oxford University Press. (p. 366)

Williams, L. A., & DeSteno, D. (2009). Adaptive social emotion or seventh sin? *Psychological Science, 20,* 284–288. (p. 450)

Williams, L. E., & Bargh, J. A. (2008). Experiencing physical warmth promotes interpersonal warmth. *Science, 322,* 606–607. (p. 228)

Williams, N. M., & 13 others. (2010). Rare chromosomal deletions and duplications in attention-deficit hyperactivity disorder: A genome-wide analysis. *Lancet, 376,* 1401–1408. (p. 507)

Williams, S. L. (1987). Self-efficacy and mastery-oriented treatment for severe phobias. Paper presented to the American Psychological Association convention. (p. 552)

Willingham, D. T. (2010, Summer). Have technology and multitasking rewired how students learn? *American Educator,* pp. 23–28, 42. (pp. 276, 369)

Willis, J., & Todorov, A. (2006). First impressions: Making up your mind after a 100-ms. exposure to a face. *Psychological Science, 17,* 592–598. (p. 380)

Willmuth, M. E. (1987). Sexuality after spinal cord injury: A critical review. *Clinical Psychology Review, 7,* 389–412. (p. 176)

Wilson, A. E., & Ross, M. (2001). From chump to champ: People's appraisals of their earlier and present selves. *Journal of Personality and Social Psychology, 80,* 572–584. (p. 450)

Wilson, D. (2011, June 22). U.S. releases graphic images to deter smokers. *New York Times* (www.nytimes.com). (p. 310)

Wilson, G. D., & Rahman, Q. (2005). *Born Gay: The biology of sex orientation.* London: Peter Owen Publishers. (p. 181)

Wilson, R. S. (1979). Analysis of longitudinal twin data: Basic model and applications to physical growth measures. *Acta Geneticae medicae et Gemellologiae, 28,* 93–105. (p. 123)

Wilson, R. S., Beck, T. L., Bienias, J. L., & Bennett, D. A. (2007). Terminal cognitive decline: Accelerated loss of cognition in the last years of life. *Psychosomatic Medicine, 69,* 131–137. (p. 153)

Wilson, R. S., & Matheny, A. P., Jr. (1986). Behavior-genetics research in infant temperament: The Louisville twin study. In R. Plomin & J. Dunn (Eds.), *The study of temperament: Changes, continuities, and challenges.* Hillsdale, NJ: Erlbaum. (p. 134)

Wilson, T. D. (2002). *Strangers to ourselves: Discovering the adaptive unconscious.* Cambridge, MA: Harvard University Press. (p. 80)

Wilson, T. D. (2006). The power of social psychological interventions. *Science, 313,* 1251–1252. (p. 346)

Wilson, W. A., & Kuhn, C. M. (2005). How addiction hijacks our reward system. *Cerebrum, 7*(2), 53–66. (p. 110)

Windholz, G. (1989, April-June). The discovery of the principles of reinforcement, extinction, generalization, and differentiation of conditional reflexes in Pavlov's laboratories. *Pavlovian Journal of Biological Science, 26,* 64–74. (p. 243)

Windholz, G. (1997). Ivan P. Pavlov: An overview of his life and psychological work. *American Psychologist, 52,* 941–946. (p. 241)

Windle, G., Hughes, D., Linck, P., Russell, I., & Woods, B. (2010). Is exercise effective in promoting mental well-being in older age? A systematic review. *Aging and Mental Health, 14,* 652–669. (p. 408)

Winner, E. (2000). The origins and ends of giftedness. *American Psychologist, 55,* 159–169. (p. 339)

Winter, W. C., Hammond, W. R., Green, N. H., Zhang, Z., & Bilwise, D. L. (2009). Measuring circadian advantage in major league baseball: A 10-year retrospective study. *Internal Journal of Sports Physiology and Performance, 4,* 394–401. (p. 88)

Wirz-Justice, A. (2009). From the basic neuroscience of circadian clock function to light therapy for depression: On the emergence of chronotherapeutics. *Journal of Affective Disorders, 116,* 159–160. (p. 564)

Witelson, S. F., Kigar, D. L., & Harvey, T. (1999). The exceptional brain of Albert Einstein. *Lancet, 353,* 2149–2153. (p. 57)

Witt, J. K., & Proffitt, D. R. (2005). See the ball, hit the ball: Apparent ball size is correlated with batting average. *Psychological Science, 16,* 937–938. (p. 200)

Witvliet, C. V. O., Ludwig, T., & Vander Laan, K. (2001). Granting forgiveness or harboring grudges: Implications for emotions, physiology, and health. *Psychological Science, 12,* 117–123. (p. 399)

Witvliet, C. V. O., & Vrana, S. R. (1995). Psychophysiological responses as indices of affective dimensions. *Psychophysiology, 32,* 436–443. (p. 378)

Wixted, J. T., & Ebbesen, E. B. (1991). On the form of forgetting. *Psychological Science, 2,* 409–415. (p. 291)

Wolak, J., Mitchell, K., & Finkelhor, D. (2007). Unwanted and wanted exposure to online pornography in a national sample of youth Internet users. *Pediatrics, 119,* 247–257. (p. 484)

Wolfson, A. R., & Carskadon, M. A. (1998). Sleep schedules and daytime functioning in adolescents. *Child Development, 69,* 875–887. (p. 95)

Wolitzky-Taylor, K. B., Horowitz, J. D., Powers, M. B., & Telch, M. J. (2008). Psychological approaches in the treatment of specific phobias: A meta-analysis. *Clinical Psychology Review, 28,* 1021–1037. (p. 551)

Woll, S. (1986). So many to choose from: Decision strategies in videodating. *Journal of Social and Personal Relationships, 3,* 43–52. (p. 489)

Wolpe, J. (1958). *Psychotherapy by reciprocal inhibition.* Stanford, CA: Stanford University Press. (p. 551)

Wolpe, J., & Plaud, J. J. (1997). Pavlov's contributions to behavior therapy: The obvious and the not so obvious. *American Psychologist, 52,* 966–972. (p. 551)

Wonderlich, S. A., Joiner, T. E., Jr., Keel, P. K., Williamson, D. A., & Crosby, R. D. (2007). Eating disorder diagnoses: Empirical approaches to classification. *American Psychologist, 62,* 167–180. (p. 536)

Wong, D. F., Wagner, H. N., Tune, L. E., Dannals, R. F., et al. (1986). Positron emission tomography reveals elevated D_2 dopamine receptors in drug-naive schizophrenics. *Science, 234,* 1588–1593. (p. 530)

Wood, D., Harms, P., & Vazire, S. (2010). Perceiver effects as projective tests: What your perceptions of others say about you. *Journal of Personality and Social Psychology, 99,* 174–190. (p. 432)

Wood, J. M. (2003, May 19). Quoted by R. Mestel, Rorschach tested: Blot out the famous method? Some experts say it has no place in psychiatry. *Los Angeles Times* (www.latimes.com). (p. 430)

Wood, J. M. (2006, Spring). The controversy over Exner's Comprehensive System for the Rorschach: The critics speak. *Independent Practitioner* (works.bepress.com/james_wood/7). (p. 430)

Wood, J. M., Bootzin, R. R., Kihlstrom, J. F., & Schacter, D. L. (1992). Implicit and explicit memory for verbal information presented during sleep. *Psychological Science, 3,* 236–239. (p. 293)

Wood, J. M., Lilienfeld, S. O., Nezworski, M. T., Garb, H. N., Allen, K. H., & Wildermuth, J. L. (2010). Validity of Rorschach inkblot scores for discriminating psychopaths from nonpsychopaths in forensic populations: A meta-analysis. *Psychological Assessment, 22,* 336–349. (p. 430)

Wood, J. V., Heimpel, S. A., Manwell, L. A., & Whittington, E. J. (2009). This mood is familiar and I don't deserve to feel better anyway: Mechanisms underlying self-esteem differences in motivation to repair sad moods. *Journal of Personality and Social Psychology, 96,* 363–380. (p. 447)

Wood, J. V., Saltzberg, J. A., & Goldsamt, L. A. (1990a). Does affect induce self-focused attention? *Journal of Personality and Social Psychology, 58,* 899–908. (p. 526)

Wood, J. V., Saltzberg, J. A., Neale, J. M., Stone, A. A., & Rachmiel, T. B. (1990b). Self-focused attention, coping responses, and distressed mood in everyday life. *Journal of Personality and Social Psychology, 58,* 1027–1036. (p. 526)

Wood, W. (1987). Meta-analytic review of sex differences in group performance. *Psychological Bulletin, 102,* 53–71. (p. 165)

Wood, W., & Eagly, A. H. (2002). A cross-cultural analysis of the behavior of women and men: Implications for the origins of sex differences. *Psychological Bulletin, 128,* 699–727. (pp. 163, 165)

Wood, W., & Eagly, A. H. (2007). Social structural origins of sex differences in human mating. In S. W. Gagestad & J. A. Simpson (Eds.), *The evolution of mind: Fundamental questions and controversies.* New York: Guilford Press.). (p. 165)

Wood, W., & Neal, D. T. (2007, October). A new look at habits and the habit-goal interface. *Psychological Review, 114,* 843–863. (p. 238)

Wood, W., Lundgren, S., Ouellette, J. A., Busceme, S., & Blackstone, T. (1994). Minority influence: A meta-analytic review of social influence processes. *Psychological Bulletin, 115,* 323–345. (p. 475)

Woods, N. F., Dery, G. K., & Most, A. (1983). Recollections of menarche, current menstrual attitudes, and premenstrual symptoms. In S. Golub (Ed.), *Menarche: The transition from girl to woman.* Lexington, MA: Lexington Books. (p. 168)

Woodward, B. (2002). *Bush at war.* New York: Simon & Schuster. (p. 10)

Woolcock, N. (2004, September 3). Driver thought everyone else was on wrong side. *The Times,* p. 22. (p. 467)

Woolley, A. W., Chabris, C. F., Pentland, A., Hasmi, N., & Malone, T. W. (2010). Evidence for a collective intelligence factor in the performance of human groups. *Science, 330,* 686–688. (p. B-11)

World Federation for Mental Health. (2005). ADHD: The hope behind the hype (www.wfmh.org). (p. 507)

Worobey, J., & Blajda, V. M. (1989). Temperament ratings at 2 weeks, 2 months, and 1 year: Differential stability of activity and emotionality. *Developmental Psychology, 25,* 257–263. (p. 134)

Wortham, J. (2010, May 13). Cellphones now used more for data than for calls. *New York Times* (www.nytimes.com). (p. 367)

Worthington, E. L., Jr. (1989). Religious faith across the life span: Implications for counseling and research. *The Counseling Psychologist, 17,* 555–612. (p. 141)

Worthington, E. L., Jr., Kurusu, T. A., McCullogh, M. E., & Sandage, S. J. (1996). Empirical research on religion and psychotherapeutic processes and outcomes: A 10-year review and research prospectus. *Psychological Bulletin, 119,* 448–487. (p. 567)

Wortman, C. B., & Silver, R. C. (1989). The myths of coping with loss. *Journal of Consulting and Clinical Psychology, 57,* 349–357. (p. 158)

Wren, C. S. (1999, April 8). Drug survey of children finds middle school a pivotal time. *New York Times* (www.nytimes.com). (p. 112)

Wright, I. C., Rabe-Hesketh, S., Woodruff, P. W. R., David, A. S., Murray, R. M., & Bullmore, E. T. (2000). Meta-analysis of regional brain volumes in schizophrenia. *American Journal of Psychiatry, 157,* 16–25. (p. 531)

Wright, J. (2006, March 16). Boomers in the bedroom: Sexual attitudes and behaviours in the boomer generation. Ipsos Reid survey (www.ipsos-na.com). (p. 151)

Wright, P., Takei, N., Rifkin, L., & Murray, R. M. (1995). Maternal influenza, obstetric complications, and schizophrenia. *American Journal of Psychiatry, 152,* 1714–1720. (p. 531)

Wright, P. H. (1989). Gender differences in adults' same- and cross-gender friendships. In R. G. Adams & R. Blieszner (Eds.), *Older adult friendships: Structure and process.* Newbury Park, CA: Sage. (p. 165)

Wright, W. (1998). *Born that way: Genes, behavior, personality.* New York: Knopf. (p. 65)

Wrosch, C., & Miller, G. E. (2009). Depressive symptoms can be useful: Self-regulatory and emotional benefits of dysphoric mood in adolescence. *Journal of Personality and Social Psychology, 96,* 1181–1190. (p. 519)

Wrzesniewski, A., & Dutton, J. E. (2001). Crafting a job: Revisioning employees as active crafters of their work. *Academy of Management Review, 26,* 179–201. (p. B-1)

Wrzesniewski, A., McCauley, C. R., Rozin, P., & Schwartz, B. (1997). Jobs, careers, and callings: People's relations to their work. *Journal of Research in Personality, 31,* 21–33. (p. B-1)

Wuethrich, B. (2001, March). Features—GETTING STUPID—Surprising new neurological behavioral research reveals that teenagers who drink too much may permanently damage their brains and seriously compromise their ability to learn. *Discover, 56,* 56–64. (p. 103)

Wulsin, L. R., Vaillant, G. E., & Wells, V. E. (1999). A systematic review of the mortality of depression. *Psychosomatic Medicine, 61,* 6–17. (p. 400)

Wyatt, J. K., & Bootzin, R. R. (1994). Cognitive processing and sleep: Implications for enhancing job performance. *Human Performance, 7,* 119–139. (pp. 94, 293)

Wyatt, R. J., Henter, I., & Sherman-Elvy, E. (2001). Tantalizing clues to preventing schizophrenia. *Cerebrum: The Dana Forum on Brain Science, 3,* pp. 15–30. (p. 532)

Wynn, K. (1992). Addition and subtraction by human infants. *Nature, 358,* 749–759. (p. 127)

Wynn, K. (2000). Findings of addition and subtraction in infants are robust and consistent: Reply to Wakeley, Rivera, and Langer. *Child Development, 71,* 1535–1536. (p. 127)

Wynne, C. D. L. (2004). *Do animals think?* Princeton, NJ: Princeton University Press. (p. 324)

Wynne, C. D. L. (2008). Aping language: A skeptical analysis of the evidence for nonhuman primate language. *Skeptic, 13*(4), 10–13. (p. 324)

X

Xu, Y., & Corkin, S. (2001). H.M. revisits the Tower of Hanoi puzzle. *Neuropsychology, 15,* 69–79. (p. 290)

Y

Yamagata, S., & 11 others. (2006). Is the genetic structure of human personality universal? A cross-cultural twin study from North America, Europe, and Asia. *Journal of Personality and Social Psychology, 90,* 987–998. (p. 440)

Yang, N., & Linz, D. (1990). Movie ratings and the content of adult videos: The sex-violence ratio. *Journal of Communication, 40*(2), 28–42. (p. 484)

Yankelovich Partners. (1995, May/June). Growing old. *American Enterprise,* p. 108. (p. 152)

Yarkoni, T. (2010). Personality in 100,000 words: A large-scale analysis of personality and word use among bloggers. *Journal of Research in Personality, 44,* 363–373. (p. 443)

Yarnell, P. R., & Lynch, S. (1970, April 25). Retrograde memory immediately after concussion. *Lancet,* pp. 863–865. (p. 284)

Yates, A. (1989). Current perspectives on the eating disorders: I. History, psychological and biological aspects. *Journal of the American Academy of Child and Adolescent Psychiatry, 28,* 813–828. (p. 536)

Yates, A. (1990). Current perspectives on the eating disorders: II. Treatment, outcome, and research directions. *Journal of the American Academy of Child and Adolescent Psychiatry, 29,* 1–9. (p. 536)

Yates, W. R. (2000). Testosterone in psychiatry. *Archives of General Psychiatry, 57,* 155–156. (p. 172)

Ybarra, O. (1999). Misanthropic person memory when the need to self-enhance is absent. *Personality and Social Psychology Bulletin, 25,* 261–269. (p. 448)

Yerkes, R. M., & Dodson, J. D. (1908). The relation of strength of stimulus to rapidity of habit-formation. *Journal of comparative Neurology and Psychology, 18,* 459–482. (p. 354)

Yeung, J. W. K., Chan, Y, & Lee, B. L. K. (2009). Youth religiosity and substance use: A meta-analysis from 1995 to 2007. *Psychological Reports, 105,* 255–266. (p. 111)

Youngentob, S. L., & Glendinning, J. I. (2009). Fetal ethanol exposure increases ethanol intake by making it smell and taste better. *PNAS, 106,* 5359. (p. 120)

Youngentob, S. L., Kent, P. F., Scheehe, P. R., Molina, J. C., Spear, N. E., &

Youngentob, L. M. (2007). Experience-induced fetal plasticity: The effect of gestational ethanol exposure on the behavioral and neurophysiologic olfactory response to ethanol odor in early postnatal and adult rats. *Behavioral Neuroscience, 121,* 1293–1305. (p. 120)

Younger, J., Aron, A., Parke, S., Chatterjee, N., & Mackey, S. (2010). Viewing pictures of a romantic partner reduces experimental pain: Involvement of neural reward systems. *PLoS ONE 5*(10): e13309. doi:10.1371/journal.pone.0013309. (p. 365)

Yücel, M., Solowij, N., Respondek, C., Whittle, S., Fornito, A., Pantelis, C., & Lubman, D. I. (2008). Regional brain abnormalities associated with long-term cannabis use. *Archives of General Psychiatry, 65,* 694–701. (p. 108)

Yuki, M., Maddux, W. W., & Masuda. T. (2007). Are the windows to the soul the same in the East and West? Cultural differences in using the eyes and mouth as cues to recognize emotions in Japan and the United States. *Journal of Experimental Social Psychology, 43,* 303–311. (p. 383)

Z

Zabin, L. S., Emerson, M. R., & Rowland, D. L. (2005). Child sexual abuse and early menarche: The direction of their relationship and its implications. *Journal of Adolescent Health, 36,* 393–400. (p. 167)

Zaccaro, S. J. (2007). Triat-based perspectives of leadership. *American Psychologist, 62,* 6–16. (p. B-11)

Zadra, A., Pilon, M., & Montplaisir, J. (2008). Polysomnographic diagnosis of sleepwalking: Effects of sleep deprivation. *Annals of Neurology, 63,* 513–519. (p. 93)

Zagorsky, J. L. (2007). Do you have to be smart to be rich? The impact of IQ on wealth, income and financial distress. *Intelligence, 35,* 489–501. (p. 332)

Zajonc, R. B. (1965). Social facilitation. *Science, 149,* 269–274. (p. 471)

Zajonc, R. B. (1980). Feeling and thinking: Preferences need no inferences. *American Psychologist, 35,* 151–175. (p. 374)

Zajonc, R. B. (1984a). On the primacy of affect. *American Psychologist, 39,* 117–123. (p. 374)

Zajonc, R. B. (1984b, July 22). Quoted by D. Goleman, Rethinking IQ tests and their value. *The New York Times,* p. D22. (p. 334)

Zajonc, R. B. (2001). Mere exposure: A gateway to the subliminal. *Current Directions in Psychological Science, 10,* 224–228. (p. 488)

Zajonc, R. B., & Markus, G. B. (1975). Birth order and intellectual development. *Psychological Review, 82,* 74–88. (p. A-8)

Zammit, S., Rasmussen, F., Farahmand, B., Gunnell, D., Lewis, G., Tynelius, P., & Brobert, G. P. (2007). Height and body mass index in young adulthood and risk of schizophrenia: A longitudinal study of 1,347,520 Swedish men. *Acta Psychiatrica Scandinavica, 116,* 378–385. (p. 529)

Zauberman, G., & Lynch, J. G., Jr. (2005). Resource slack and propensity to discount delayed investments of time versus money. *Journal of Experimental Psychology: General, 134,* 23–37. (p. 312)

Zeelenberg, R., Wagenmakers, E-J., & Rotteveel, M. (2006). The impact of emotion on perception. *Psychological Science, 17,* 287–291. (p. 374)

Zeidner, M. (1990). Perceptions of ethnic group modal intelligence: Reflections of cultural stereotypes or intelligence test scores? *Journal of Cross-Cultural Psychology, 21,* 214–231. (p. 343)

Zeidner, M., Roberts, R. D., & Matthews, G. (2008). The science of emotional intelligence: Current consensus and controversies. *European Psychologist, 13,* 64–78. (p. 333)

Zeineh, M. M., Engel, S. A., Thompson, P. M., & Bookheimer, S. Y. (2003). Dynamics of the hippocampus during encoding and retrieval of face-name pairs. *Science, 299,* 577–580. (p. 281)

Zell, E., & Alicke, M. D. (2010). The local dominance effect in self-evaluation: Evidence and explanations. *Personality and Social Psychology Review, 14,* 368–384. (p. 417)

Zhang, S., & Kline, S. L. (2009). Can I make my own decision? A cross-cultural study of perceived social network influence in mate selection. *Journal of Cross Cultural Psychology, 40,* 3–23. (p. 451)

Zhong, C-B., Dijksterhuis, A., & Galinsky, A. D. (2008). The merits of unconscious thought in creativity. *Psychological Science, 19,* 912–918. (p. 315)

Zhong, C-B., & Leonardelli, G. J. (2008). Cold and lonely: Does social exclusion literally feel cold? *Psychological Science, 19,* 838–842. (p. 228)

Zhu, W. X., Lu, L., & Hesketh, T. (2009). China's excess males, sex selective abortion, and one child policy: Analysis of data from 2005 national intercensus survey. *British Medical Journal (BMJ), 338,* b1211. (p. 477)

Zietsch, B. P., Morley, K. I., Shekar, S. N., Verweij, K. J. H., Keller, M. C., Macgregor, S., Wright, M. J., Bailey, J. M., & Martin, N. G. (2008). Genetic factors predisposing to homosexuality may increase mating success in heterosexuals. *Evolution and Human Behavior, 29,* 424–433. (p. 181)

Zilbergeld, B. (1983). *The shrinking of America: Myths of psychological change.* Boston; Little, Brown. (pp. 560, 562)

Zillmann, D. (1986). Effects of prolonged consumption of pornography. Background paper for *The surgeon general's workshop on pornography and public health,* June 22–24. Report prepared by E. P. Mulvey & J. L. Haugaard and released by Office of the Surgeon General on August 4, 1986. (p. 373)

Zillmann, D. (1989). Effects of prolonged consumption of pornography. In D. Zillmann & J. Bryant (Eds.), *Pornography: Research advances and policy considerations.* Hillsdale, NJ: Erlbaum. (pp. 175, 176, 485)

Zillmann, D., & Bryant, J. (1984). Effects of massive exposure to pornography. In N. Malamuth & E. Donnerstein (Eds.), *Pornography and sexual aggression.* Orlando, FL: Academic Press. (p. 485)

Zimbardo, P. G. (1970). The human choice: Individuation, reason, and order versus deindividuation, impulse, and chaos. In W. J. Arnold & D. Levine (Eds.), *Nebraska Symposium on Motivation, 1969.* Lincoln, NE: University of Nebraska Press. (p. 472)

Zimbardo, P. G. (1972, April). Pathology of imprisonment. *Transaction/Society,* pp. 4–8. (p. 461)

Zimbardo, P. G. (2001, September 16). Fighting terrorism by understanding man's capacity for evil. Op-ed essay distributed by spsp-discuss@stolaf.edu. (p. 479)

Zimbardo, P. G. (2004, May 25). *Journalist interview re: Abu Ghraib prison abuses: Eleven answers to eleven questions.* Unpublished manuscript, Stanford University. (p. 462)

Zimbardo, P. G. (2007, September). Person x situation x system dynamics. *The Observer* (Association for Psychological Science), p. 43. (p. 462)

Zimmer-Gembeck, M. J., & Helfand, M. (2008). Ten years of longitudinal research on U.S. adolescent sexual behavior: Developmental correlates of sexual intercourse, and the importance of age, gender and ethnic background. *Developmental Review, 28,* 153–224. (p. 176)

Zogby, J. (2006, March). Survey of teens and adults about the use of personal electronic devices and head phones. *Zogby International.* (p. 217)

Zou, Z., Li, F., & Buck, L. B. (2005). From the cover: Odor maps in the olfactory cortex. *Proceedings of the National Academy of Sciences, 102,* 7724–7729. (p. 226)

Zubieta, J-K., Bueller, J. A., Jackson, L. R., Scott, D. J., Xu, Y., Koeppe, R. A., Nichols, T. E., & Stohler, C. S. (2005). Placebo effects mediated by endogenous opioid activity on μ-opioid receptors. *Journal of Neuroscience, 25,* 7754–7762. (p. 223)

Zubieta, J-K., Heitzeg, M. M., Smith, Y. R., Bueller, J. A., Xu, K., Xu, Y., Koeppe, R. A., Stohler, C. S., & Goldman, D. (2003). COMT val158met genotype affects μ-opioid neurotransmitter responses to a pain stressor. *Science, 299,* 1240–1243. (p. 222)

Zucker, G. S., & Weiner, B. (1993). Conservatism and perceptions of poverty: An attributional analysis. *Journal of Applied Social Psychology, 23,* 925–943. (p. 459)

Zuckerman, M. (1979). *Sensation seeking: Beyond the optimal level of arousal.* Hillsdale, NJ: Erlbaum. (p. 353)

Zuckerman, M. (2009). Sensation seeking. In M. Zuckerman (Ed.), *Handbook of individual differences in social behavior.* New York: Guilford Press. (p. 353)

Zvolensky, M. J., & Bernstein, A. (2005). Cigarette smoking and panic psychopathology. *Current Directions in Psychological Science, 14,* 301–305. (p. 513)